Contemporary
Literary Criticism

Guide to Gale Literary Criticism Series

When you need to review criticism of literary works, these are the Gale series to use:

If the author's death date is:	You should turn to:

If the author's death date is: | **You should turn to:**

After Dec. 31, 1959 (or author is still living)

CONTEMPORARY LITERARY CRITICISM

for example: Jorge Luis Borges, Anthony Burgess,
William Faulkner, Mary Gordon,
Ernest Hemingway, Iris Murdoch

1900 through 1959

TWENTIETH-CENTURY LITERARY CRITICISM

for example: Willa Cather, F. Scott Fitzgerald,
Henry James, Mark Twain, Virginia Woolf

1800 through 1899

NINETEENTH-CENTURY LITERATURE CRITICISM

for example: Fedor Dostoevski, George Sand,
Gerard Manley Hopkins, Emily Dickinson

1400 through 1799

LITERATURE CRITICISM FROM 1400 TO 1800 (excluding Shakespeare)

for example: Anne Bradstreet, Pierre Corneille,
Daniel Defoe, Alexander Pope,
Jonathan Swift, Phillis Wheatley

SHAKESPEAREAN CRITICISM

Shakespeare's plays and poetry

Gale also publishes related criticism series:

CONTEMPORARY ISSUES CRITICISM

Presents criticism on contemporary authors writing
on current issues. Topics covered include the social
sciences, philosophy, economics, natural science, law,
and related areas.

CHILDREN'S LITERATURE REVIEW

Covers authors of all eras. Presents criticism on
authors and author/illustrators who write for the
preschool to junior-high audience.

ISSN 0091-3421

Volume 32

Contemporary Literary Criticism

Excerpts from Criticism of the
Works of Today's Novelists, Poets,
Playwrights, Short Story Writers, Scriptwriters,
and Other Creative Writers

Jean C. Stine
Daniel G. Marowski
EDITORS

Gale Research Company
Book Tower
Detroit, Michigan 48226

STAFF

Jean C. Stine, Daniel G. Marowski, *Editors*

Roger Matuz, Jane E. Neidhardt, Marjorie Wachtel,
Robyn V. Young, *Senior Assistant Editors*

Melissa Reiff Hug, John G. Kuhnlein, Molly L. Norris, Sean R. Pollock,
Jeffrey T. Rogg, Lisa M. Rost, Jane C. Thacker, Debra A. Wells, *Assistant Editors*

Sharon R. Gunton, Thomas Ligotti,
Phyllis Carmel Mendelson, *Contributing Editors*

Lizbeth A. Purdy, *Production Supervisor*
Denise Michlewicz Broderick, *Production Coordinator*
Eric Berger, *Assistant Production Coordinator*
Robin L. Du Blanc, Kelly King Howes, *Editorial Assistants*

Linda M. Pugliese, *Manuscript Coordinator*
Donna Craft, *Assistant Manuscript Coordinator*
Colleen M. Crane, Maureen A. Puhl, Rosetta Irene Simms, *Manuscript Assistants*

Victoria B. Cariappa, *Research Coordinator*
Jeannine Schiffman Davidson, *Assistant Research Coordinator*
Kevin John Campbell, Rebecca Nicholaides,
Kyle Schell, Valerie Webster, *Research Assistants*

Janice M. Mach, *Permissions Coordinator*
Patricia A. Seefelt, *Assistant Permissions Coordinator, Illustrations*
Margaret A. Chamberlain, Mary M. Matuz, Susan D. Nobles, *Senior Permissions Assistants*
Sandra C. Davis, Kathy Grell, Josephine M. Keene, *Permissions Assistants*
H. Diane Cooper, Dorothy J. Fowler, Yolanda Parker,
Mabel E. Schoening, *Permissions Clerks*

Frederick G. Ruffner, *Publisher*
James M. Ethridge, *Executive Vice-President/Editorial*
Dedria Bryfonski, *Editorial Director*
Christine Nasso, *Director, Literature Division*
Laurie Lanzen Harris, *Senior Editor, Literary Criticism Series*

Copyright © 1985 by Gale Research Company

Library of Congress Catalog Card Number 76-38938
ISBN 0-8103-4406-8
ISSN 0091-3421

Printed in the United States

Contents

Preface

Literary criticism is, by definition, "the art of evaluating or analyzing with knowledge and propriety works of literature." The complexity and variety of the themes and forms of contemporary literature make the function of the critic especially important to today's reader. It is the critic who assists the reader in identifying significant new writers, recognizing trends in critical methods, mastering new terminology, and monitoring scholarly and popular sources of critical opinion.

Until the publication of the first volume of *Contemporary Literary Criticism (CLC)* in 1973, there existed no ongoing digest of current literary opinion. *CLC,* therefore, has fulfilled an essential need.

Scope of the Work

CLC presents significant passages from published criticism of works by today's creative writers. Each volume of *CLC* includes excerpted criticism on about 60 authors who are now living or who died after December 31, 1959. Since the series began publication, more than 1,700 authors have been included. The majority of authors covered by *CLC* are living writers who continue to publish; therefore, an author frequently appears in more than one volume. There is, of course, no duplication of reprinted criticism.

Authors are selected for inclusion for a variety of reasons, among them: the publication of a critically acclaimed new work, the reception of a major literary award, or the dramatization of a literary work as a movie or television screenplay. For example, the present volume includes Elizabeth Bishop, whose *The Complete Poems: 1927-1979* and *The Collected Prose* were recently published; Milan Kundera, whose international fame grew with the publication of his novel *The Unbearable Lightness of Being;* and Joan Didion, whose latest books, *Salvador* and *Democracy,* received much attention from the literary world. Perhaps most importantly, authors who appear frequently on the syllabuses of high school and college literature classes are heavily represented in *CLC.* Albert Camus and Tom Robbins are examples of writers of this stature in the present volume. Attention is also given to several other groups of writers—authors of considerable public interest—about whose work criticism is often difficult to locate. These are the contributors to the well-loved but nonscholarly genres of mystery and science fiction, as well as writers who appeal specifically to young adults and writers for the nonprint media, including scriptwriters, lyricists, and cartoonists. Foreign writers and authors who represent particular ethnic groups in the United States are also featured in each volume.

Format of the Book

Altogether there are about 750 individual excerpts in each volume—with an average of about 11 excerpts per author—taken from hundreds of literary reviews, general magazines, scholarly journals, and monographs. Contemporary criticism is loosely defined as that which is relevant to the evaluation of the author under discussion; this includes criticism written at the beginning of an author's career as well as current commentary. Emphasis has been placed on expanding the sources for criticism by including an increasing number of scholarly and specialized periodicals. Students, teachers, librarians, and researchers frequently find that the generous excerpts and supplementary material provided by the editors supply them with all the information that they need to write a term paper, analyze a poem, or lead a book discussion group. However, complete bibliographical citations facilitate the location of the original source as well as provide all of the information necessary for a term paper footnote or bibliography.

A *CLC* author entry consists of the following elements:

● The **author heading** cites the author's full name, followed by birth date, and death date when applicable. The portion of the name outside the parentheses denotes the form under which the author has most commonly published. If an author has written consistently under a pseudonym, the pseudonym will be listed in the author heading and the real name given on the first line of the biographical and critical introduction. Also located at the beginning of the introduction to the author entry are any important name variations under which an author has written. Uncertainty as to a birth or death date is indicated by a question mark.

- A **portrait** of the author is included when available.

- A brief **biographical and critical introduction** to the author and his or her work precedes the excerpted criticism. However, *CLC* is not intended to be a definitive biographical source. Therefore, *cross-references* have been included to direct the reader to other useful sources published by the Gale Research Company: *Contemporary Authors* now includes detailed biographical and bibliographical sketches on more than 80,000 authors; *Children's Literature Review* presents excerpted criticism on the works of authors of children's books; *Something about the Author* contains heavily illustrated biographical sketches on writers and illustrators who create books for children and young adults; *Contemporary Issues Criticism* presents excerpted commentary on the nonfiction works of authors who influence contemporary thought; *Dictionary of Literary Biography* provides original evaluations of authors important to literary history; and the new *Contemporary Authors Autobiography Series* offers autobiographical essays by prominent writers. Previous volumes of *CLC* in which the author has been featured are also listed in the introduction.

- The **excerpted criticism** represents various kinds of critical writing—a particular essay may be normative, descriptive, interpretive, textual, appreciative, comparative, or generic. It may range in form from the brief review to the scholarly monograph. Essays are selected by the editors to reflect the spectrum of opinion about a specific work or about an author's writing in general. The excerpts are presented chronologically, adding a useful perspective to the entry. All titles by the author featured in the entry are printed in boldface type, which enables the reader to easily identify the works being discussed.

- A complete **bibliographical citation** designed to help the user find the original essay or book follows each excerpt. An asterisk (*) at the end of a citation indicates the essay is on more than one author.

Other Features

- A list of **Authors Forthcoming in *CLC*** previews the authors to be researched for future volumes.

- An **Appendix** lists the sources from which material in the volume has been reprinted. Many other sources have also been consulted during the preparation of the volume.

- A **Cumulative Index to Authors** lists all the authors who have appeared in *Contemporary Literary Criticism, Twentieth-Century Literary Criticism, Nineteenth-Century Literature Criticism,* and *Literature Criticism from 1400 to 1800,* along with cross-references to other Gale series: *Children's Literature Review, Authors in the News, Contemporary Authors, Contemporary Authors Autobiography Series, Dictionary of Literary Biography, Something about the Author,* and *Yesterday's Authors of Books for Children.* Users will welcome this cumulated author index as a useful tool for locating an author within the various series. The index, which lists birth and death dates when available, will be particularly valuable for those authors who are identified with a certain period but whose death date causes them to be placed in another, or for those authors whose careers span two periods. For example, F. Scott Fitzgerald is found in *Twentieth-Century Literary Criticism,* yet a writer often associated with him, Ernest Hemingway, is found in *Contemporary Literary Criticism.*

- A **Cumulative Index to Critics** lists the critics and the author entries in which the critics' essays appear.

Acknowledgments

The editors wish to thank the copyright holders of the excerpted articles included in this volume for permission to use the material and the photographers and individuals who provided photographs for us. We are grateful to the staffs of the following libraries for making their resources available to us: Detroit Public Library and the libraries of Wayne State University, the University of Michigan, and the University of Detroit. We also wish to thank Jeri Yaryan for her assistance with copyright research.

Suggestions Are Welcome

The editors welcome the comments and suggestions of readers to expand the coverage and enhance the usefulness of the series.

Authors Forthcoming in *CLC*

Contemporary Literary Criticism, Volume 33 will contain criticism on a number of authors not previously listed and will also feature criticism on newer works by authors included in earlier volumes. Volume 34 will be a yearbook devoted to an examination of the outstanding achievements and the trends in literature during 1984. Material in Volume 35 will be selected to be of special interest to young adult readers.

To Be Included in Volume 33

Ayi Kwei Armah (Ghanaian novelist, short story writer, and poet)—Armah's early novels, including *The Beautyful Ones Are Not Yet Born,* indirectly indict colonialism in their description of the cultural and political corruption of postindependence Africa; his later historical novels, *Two Thousand Seasons* and *The Healers,* turn to the past as a model for Africa's future.

Alan Ayckbourn (English dramatist)—A popular and prolific playwright, Ayckbourn is best known for farces that examine middle-class marriage and society, including *Absurd Person Singular, The Norman Conquests,* and *Bedroom Farce.*

Saul Bellow (American novelist and short story writer)—Nobel laureate Bellow's recent volume of short stories, *Him with His Foot in His Mouth,* received an enthusiastic critical response, confirming Bellow's reputation as a thoughtful purveyor of the worth of life.

Art Buchwald (American humorist and journalist)—*While Reagan Slept,* a volume of political humor, is the latest of over thirty collections of Buchwald's syndicated newspaper columns.

Harvey Fierstein (American dramatist)—In his Tony Award-winning plays, *Torch Song Trilogy* and *La Cage aux folles,* Fierstein blurs the distinction between homosexual and heterosexual concepts of love, attacking stereotypes through humor and satire.

John Fowles (English novelist)—*Mantissa,* the most recent work by the author of *The French Lieutenant's Woman,* is a dialogue between the writer and his muse about creativity, literary theory, and sex.

Jim Harrison (American poet, novelist, scriptwriter, and critic)—A native of rural northern Michigan, Harrison imbues his prose and poetry with a strong sense of the outdoors. His latest works include *New & Selected Poems 1961-1981* and the novels *Warlock* and *Sundog.*

Stratis Haviaras (Greek-born American novelist and poet)—Haviaras's two highly regarded novels, *When the Tree Sings* and *The Heroic Age,* examine the turbulent events of recent Greek history through the eyes of children.

C.L.R. James (West Indian nonfiction writer, novelist, dramatist, and short story writer)—James is widely recognized in England for his writings on Third World politics. His study of sports and society, *Beyond a Boundary,* has received substantial critical attention in the United States.

Arthur Kopit (American dramatist and scriptwriter)—A prominent figure in contemporary American theater, Kopit has added *Nine* and *End of the World* to his already impressive body of work.

Joyce Carol Oates (American novelist, short story writer, poet, dramatist, and critic)—Recent additions to the canon of this versatile and prolific author include *A Bloodsmoor Romance, The Profane Art, Mysteries of Winterthurn, Angel of Light,* and *Solstice.*

Pier Paolo Pasolini (Italian poet, dramatist, novelist, and filmmaker)—Regarded by some critics as the most notable poet of post-World War II Italy, Pasolini was a social reformer whose criticism of the Italian government and the Roman Catholic church incensed most factions of Italian society.

Thomas Pynchon (American novelist and short story writer)—Pynchon's early writing style and initial thematic concerns are evident in *Slow Learner,* a recently published collection of short stories written prior to his three celebrated novels.

Maya Angelou (American novelist, poet, dramatist, and scriptwriter)—Best known for her series of autobiographical novels that began with *I Know Why the Caged Bird Sings,* Angelou has continued this acclaimed series with her recent book, *The Heart of a Woman.*

Bruce Catton (American historian, essayist, journalist, and editor)—One of the foremost authorities on the Civil War, Catton is widely praised for the literary skills he brings to his historical works.

Peter Dickinson (Zambian-born English novelist, short story writer, scriptwriter, and editor)—Highly regarded for his ability to create intriguing storylines, Dickinson has recently written several works for both adults and young adults that will be covered in his entry, including *Hindsight* and *Giant Cold.*

Frank Herbert (American novelist, short story writer, nonfiction writer, and editor)—The best-selling author of the *Dune* series has added a fifth novel to this acclaimed science fiction saga with the publication of *Heretics of Dune.*

Langston Hughes (American novelist, poet, dramatist, short story writer, biographer, and essayist)—A leading member of the Harlem Renaissance, Hughes has earned a place of prominence among twentieth-century American authors for his endearing humor and his insightful examinations of racial injustice.

Aldous Huxley (English novelist, short story writer, dramatist, poet, essayist, and scriptwriter)—Criticism will focus on Huxley's utopian and dystopian fiction and nonfiction, with an emphasis on his classic novel *Brave New World.*

M.E. Kerr (American novelist)—A prolific author of fiction for young adults, Kerr has recently published the novels *What I Really Think of You* and *Him She Loves?* and her autobiography, *Me, Me, Me, Me, Me: Not a Novel.*

John Lennon (English songwriter and fiction writer)—One of contemporary music's most important figures, Lennon has influenced the lives of young people for over twenty years through his music and lyrics.

Paul McCartney (English songwriter)—McCartney has sustained much of the popular appeal he enjoyed as a member of the Beatles through solo projects and recordings with his band, Wings.

Marshall McLuhan (Canadian nonfiction writer and critic)—Both acclaimed and denounced for his theories of mass culture and communication, McLuhan examined the role of the media and its implications for future societies.

Margaret Mead (American anthropologist and nonfiction writer)—Mead is credited with having revolutionized the field of anthropology by broadening its scope to include such areas of scholarship as sociology, psychology, and economics.

Prince (American songwriter and scriptwriter)—The enormous popular success of his first film, *Purple Rain,* has contributed to this sometimes controversial performer's rise to stardom.

Carl Sandburg (American poet, short story writer, novelist, editor, biographer, and essayist)—A recipient of two Pulitzer Prizes, Sandburg was one of America's most revered literary figures. He is often said to have captured the essence of the nation through the eloquence of his colloquial verse.

Thornton Wilder (American dramatist, novelist, and scriptwriter)—Criticism will focus on *Our Town,* a play about life in a small American town for which Wilder earned one of his three Pulitzer Prizes.

Pat Barker

1943-

English novelist.

Barker has gained prominence for her two novels of industrial England, *Union Street* (1982) and *Blow Your House Down* (1984). The first portrays the lives of seven working-class women in England's economically depressed northeast, an area not unlike that in which Barker herself was raised. Abandoning the traditional structure of the novel, Barker used a technique which she referred to as the "compound-eye approach" because each of the women narrates her own story yet all the stories are interconnected. Her second novel also focuses on a working-class community in which a group of prostitutes are victimized by a series of Jack-the-Ripper-type murders. Katha Pollitt says of both books: "Mrs. Barker is able to see her characters from within, as they see themselves, and thereby reveals [their] full individuality and humanity."

EILEEN FAIRWEATHER

Being hailed as "Lawrentian" might thrill some new writers, but not Pat Barker. . . . [Her novel may be] the latest, long over-due working-class masterpiece, but its story and sympathies are firmly based on the lives of working-class women, not men. And for that, as Barker ruefully says, there is next to no literary tradition.

It was Angela Carter who recognised the talent and singularity of Barker's writing, and helped nurse *Union Street* into life. Prejudice about working-class and feminist writing being what it is, however, it is perhaps necessary to say immediately what Barker's book isn't: two-dimensional, self-indulgent, propagandistic, or blood-soaked eeh-bah-gum realism. Summed up as the story of seven women living on the same street in the North East during the 1973 miners' strike, it may sound drab. But *Union Street* is beautifully written and not worthy of attention only as a didn't-she-do-well adjunct to the male, bourgeois body of 'real' literature. Through language which is both authentically working class and poetic, Pat Barker deals with universals.

Here, however, love and marital conflict, loneliness and fear of death, are shown in far sharper relief than in more polite novels. For the experience and emotions of Barker's characters are over-laid with the desperation of poverty and the constrictions of being female. They are 'the working class within the working class': the unsupported mother, the old, the family living on female wages, the long-term unemployed. They endure the kind of penny-pinching, slum existence which, says the author, Tories, southerners and 'even some trade unionists' would prefer to believe ended 50 years ago. From experience, Pat Barker knows otherwise. . . .

That *Union Street* is written from the 'inside' should, however, be obvious from the very first page.

Where well-meaning slummers like Orwell or Nell Dunn might have us gawp at a delinquent child, or sluttish mother, Barker forces us to become them. Each character is unequivocally evoked from within their own point of view. Achieving this

intimate, dignified focus was not easy. Sensitivity to Bernstein's theories about the working class's 'restricted code' meant, says Pat, 'that without meaning to, I kept undermining my characters by slipping into middle-class style language and distanced observation.'

With the encouragement of Angela Carter, she recovered from this failure of nerve, and ditched all her 'genteel qualifications' in favour of unimpeded, vivid dialogue, imagery and inner narration. Carter also gave Pat Barker the confidence to return *Union Street* to its first, highly original form—less that of a conventional novel than of a cycle of interwoven stories. The characters in each one are, 'autonomous, but inter-connected, being alternately seen through their own then others' eyes.' Barker calls this illuminating switching of focus 'the compound eye approach. For just as insects' eyes have many different lenses so must a writer.'

In not having one central character who insistently dwarfs all the others, *Union Street* is a refreshing departure from the semi-autobiographical, self-pitying novels of many working-class men and middle-class feminists. Barker also consciously avoided making her male characters 'cardboard cut-out baddies, as in so much feminist fiction'. Thus, when a man who feels humiliated by retirement and unloved by his family goes off with an ageing, drunken prostitute, we empathise with his loneliness—even if, in the next story, we learn how much it is of his own making. D. H. Lawrence, Pat Barker notes, alternately understands then rages against the 'male-excluding' bonds between working-class women and their children. In *Union Street,* she unambivalently portrays these as 'a survival mechanism: not a matriarchal plot, but an inevitability in the face of male indifference, selfishness and often brutality'.

In literature, Pat Barker could find almost no record of 'this tradition of courage and endurance among ordinary working-class women.' (p. 21)

Pat Barker is not so much proud as sad to be among the first to record such lives. (p. 22)

Having a tradition matters, she says, because the absence of one implies that your subject matter is itself insignificant. How much more difficult then to muster the mad dashes of confidence which every writer needs in order to believe in their right to say, 'Hey, world—listen to me!' How many working-class women's voices have been silenced not just by poverty and over-work, but by the patriarchal censorship which parades as 'impartial' art criticism?

While she was writing *Union Street,* she felt continually inhibited by the fear that her raw portrayal of sexual and economic oppression would result in her being 'dismissed, politely, as a liar'. Certainly, one fairly typical rejection letter from a male publisher told her to 'Cheer up—life really isn't so depressing'.

What one man finds depressing, another (woman?) may find moving and liberating when expressed. (pp. 22-3)

The story is not 'merely' or gratuitously gynaecological, but is actually about a kind of love and heroism which male writers have rarely recognised.

[A] lack of bitterness characterises *Union Street.* . . . Pat Barker does 'look back in anger', but her vision is such that she also illuminates what should be recognised as universals of the human condition—'even' if her characters are of a class and sex normally deemed irrelevant to art. *Union Street* is a painful read, but for that there should be no apologies. (p. 23)

> Eileen Fairweather, "The Voices of Women," in New Statesman, *Vol. 103, No. 2669, May 14, 1982, pp. 21-3.*

HERMIONE LEE

The seven narratives of Pat Barker's *Union Street* are . . . solidly linked. Each deals with a woman living in an English working-class city street in the North East, during the winter of the miner's strike. . . .

No grim detail is avoided . . . , and no idiom goes unnoted. . . . An authorial voice, which speaks of 'stoicism' and 'horror,' makes sure we are moved. The result is a serious, well-meant, gripping set of case-histories, but not a novel.

> Hermione Lee, "At Spaghetti Junction," in The Observer, *May 30, 1982, p. 31.**

KATE FULLBROOK

[*Union Street*] is lost in that sometimes interesting but always dangerous area that looms invitingly between literature and the social worker's casebook. Although direct echoes of Lawrence's *Sons and Lovers* and Dickens's *Our Mutual Friend* find their way into the composition, and a vision of plain women

as heroic stoics reminiscent of Gertrude Stein in *Three Lives* dominates the thought behind the novel, the reader is left with the uneasy feeling that the author is not quite comfortable with fiction as the appropriate milieu for her enterprise. The result is a heavily 'committed' version of the seven ages of women embedded in a portrait of a working-class street in a North of England industrial city in the 1970s.

Each of the seven representative women is allotted a section of her own, but the separate stories interlock and all contribute to the overall themes of inevitable suffering and unremarked endurance as the hallmarks of female and proletarian experience. The book is drenched in (mostly women's) blood and grounded in the paradox of fecundity that both degrades the characters and makes their lives worth living. The stories themselves are hard-hitting and painful. . . . The narrative moves in a full circle emphasized by the supportive contact made between the youngest woman and the oldest. *Union Street,* a moving celebration of 'union' indeed, is compulsive reading despite its flaws.

> Kate Fullbrook, in a review of "Union Street," in British Book News, *October, 1982, p. 640.*

ELIZABETH WARD

Pat Barker achieves immediate distinction with *Union Street.* Into the jaded, overcrowded, imitative world of first novels she has introduced a book that is at once mature, faultlessly constructed, and daring enough to take as its subject life itself in the most elemental sense: poverty, sexuality, rape, pregnancy, abortion, marriage, birth, sickness, prostitution, decrepitude and death, all interlocking. Where a less gifted writer might have fallen headlong here into the double trap of stridency and mawkishness, Pat Barker keeps her story so free of abstract moralizing that its final effect is close to visionary. (p. 3)

The book's vision, if it is a vision, is of a life brutal and scabrous in the extreme. Lives such as these, it seems to say, would be falsified by the modesty of literary circumlocution. So the material is almost unremittingly sensational. Certainly, if you are not shocked by the marvelously frank speech, the frequent exposure of genitalia (with varying degrees of distaste), or the spattering of excrement and sperm and phlegm, you will be shocked by the abuse of children, old people, simple girls and deformed men—that is, the systematic creation of *victims*—which, the book suggests, this depressed life will breed. A great part of *Union Street*'s strength lies in its completely unsentimental characterization of the English working classes.

And yet, miraculously, Pat Barker also sees in each of these seven lives a flicker of affirmation or, in a theological sense which she does not at all press, salvation. There are two ways in which this spirit of hope is sustained throughout the book. One is the irrepressible humor which keeps bobbing to the surface of each grim life. (pp. 3-4)

Pat Barker's *Union Street* is a singularly powerful achievement. On the evidence of this one book, her most promising quality is, perhaps, the unusual combination of a strictly naturalistic style with a genuinely poetic sensibility. (p. 4)

> Elizabeth Ward, "On the Seamy Side of the Street," in Book World—The Washington Post, *September 18, 1983, pp. 3-4.*

JEFFREY SCHAIRE

[*Union Street*] is a product of the grim wasteland of England's industrial northeast. It is the hard winter of 1973; a miner's strike amplifies a landscape of gray drizzle, physical and spiritual impoverishment. Against this background seven women enact their individual rites of passage.... When it was published in Britain it was called feminist, proletarian, socialist-realist; Lawrencian, Osbornian, Sillitoe-esque.... There are those who've found it too grim and gritty, and those who've called it "the undiluted gospel of the distaff side."

But Pat Barker's work sits squarely in the tradition of Willa Cather.... Barker's working-class world of shabby, burnt-out buildings and daily work in the cake factory calls to mind the arid, provincial small towns of Willa Cather's shoreless plains, the "iron country" from which there is no escape....

Union Street reaches into human truths that are older than the sad historical milieu in which they are acted out; these women's lives are not wasted in history. They are, rather, gathered up in images of startling intimacy and concreteness....

Union Street, written in prose that is spare, transparent, exacting, redeems and salvages the lives of these women, who are simultaneously specific, real, and Everywoman. Pat Barker's creative vision is as in touch with the psychologically primordial as Melville's; she might have entitled her book *Moby-Jane.*

> *Jeffrey Schaire, in a review of "Union Street," in Harper's, Vol. 267, No. 1602, October, 1983, p. 76.*

IVAN GOLD

["**Union Street**"] is set in the early 1970's in an unnamed city in England's industrial Northeast. The impoverished, grimy town has two basic industries: the steelworks, from which the men are frequently furloughed or prematurely retired, and the cake factory, where many of the women work or have worked. Miss Barker skillfully employs the factory setting to touch on matters like automation, race prejudice, feeblemindedness and the sheer human hardship experienced by some of those trapped on the assembly line....

Her novel is divided into seven sections, each named for a particular female....

Together, the seven sections explore every permutation and nuance (both within and outside the desperate social milieu that is this author's artistic capital) of growing up, growing old, making do, making a living, having babies, raising children, absorbing grief, loving someone or hating where you are meant to love. Scores of characters, apart from the seven women named, spring vibrantly to life: their suitors, parents, siblings, husbands, children, their doctors and nurses and neighbors, as well as the denizens of the streets a cut above Union Street or a cut below. The seven women move easily and resonantly in and out of one another's lives and stories.

This is a hoary fictional technique. John Dos Passos' "U.S.A." comes quickly to mind, as does (for an American equivalent to the grinding, desperate poverty) the fiction of Harriette Arnow. Yet Miss Barker is equally capable of brilliantly bending the technical rules. Having situated us more or less comfortably in the head of Muriel Scaife, whose sickly young husband is about to die, she veers with great effect into the inner life of 12-year-old Richard Scaife, who will soon be dealing with the loss of the father he never really had. At the end of this story

there is a scene in which Miss Barker manages to convey, with stunning economy and skill, the ineffable communion between bereaved wife and bereaved son.

Her gifts are equally in evidence in "Lisa Goddard," in which the harried mother of two young sons miserably awaits the birth of her third child, unwanted and overdue.... Here Miss Barker's magic lies in showing us how Lisa Goddard falls in love with her newborn daughter before they ever leave the hospital; you have to read it to believe it. (p. 9)

Miss Barker's pungent, raunchy North Country dialogue and her exact use of obscure words and neologisms, like a man's cheeks *juddering* while he sleeps, or the *scrumpling* of a newspaper for a fire, or an old woman's *muculent* eyes, alternate with passages of fine understated wit.... All in all, Pat Barker gives the sense of a writer who has enormous power that she has scarcely had to tap to write a first-rate first novel. (p. 27)

> *Ivan Gold, "North Country Women," in The New York Times Book Review, October 2, 1983, pp. 9, 27.*

DIANE COLE

Barker's characters may sound less like material for serious drama than a shelfload of case histories, but Barker details the particularities of each life so richly and carefully that she cannot be mistaken for either a dry sociologist or a sentimental reporter. Some readers may object that Barker has made her characters laugh with such bitter humor, that one cannot help but yearn for some illusion of a possible escape.

But her vision is as unremitting as the world she describes, and her hard, spare prose is as chilling. Of Alice's final struggle she writes: "In the ruins of her mind, something so new and unused that it could only be spirit was struggling to stand up. Oh, but it was hard. She could not sustain the effort. She fell back, she dwindled, became again a heap of old garbage waiting for the pit. She preferred it like that. She turned to darkness and away from light."

Union Street provides no happy endings, no place of refuge. Out of grim reality, Pat Barker has crafted a splendid novel of the British working class.

> *Diane Cole, "Great Expectations," in Ms., Vol. XII, No. 7, January, 1984, pp. 12, 14-15.**

MICHAEL GORRA

Barker has the rare ability to communicate the physical, to make one feel her characters living, feel "the blood squeezing through [their] veins" in the way that Lawrence wanted for his own characters. Her first book [*Union Street*] is an almost hellish cycle of seven stories about the working-class women who live along the Union Street of the title, in an unnamed city in the North of England. But sex is more important than class here. Barker writes about a crucial stage in the life of a different woman in each story. But she uses the woman's experience to embody a segment of the collective experience of the sex as a whole, from childhood to old age, producing a feminine version of Marcel Marceau's pantomime in the process, whose effect is intensified by the fact that each of the women knows the other six, and appears in their stories as well as her own. Barker's characters are dominated by biology, by the sheer fact of being female. Their relations with men are essentially violent, for both men and women in *Union Street* lack an adequate emotional language and so despise one another, turning physical life into an indignity in the process. (p. 154)

Barker's sense of physical violence at the core of everyday life seems to me too strong, too obsessive to proceed from any political position. It is so honestly come by that for me the inextricability of sex and violence in *Union Street* is harrowing rather than morbid. *Union Street* is too relentless for one to be "happy" while reading it. But something in me both likes and admires Barker's ability to move and appall me.... (p. 155)

> *Michael Gorra, "Laughter and Bloodshed," in* The Hudson Review, *Vol. XXXVII, No. 1, Spring, 1984, pp. 151-64.*

ANGELA McROBBIE

Blow Your House Down lacks, I think, both spirit and direction. It is set in the industrial North where a series of murders similar to those by the Ripper are being carried out. The novel traces the responses of those women who feel most under threat. It's 'gritty', 'tough' and 'hard-hitting' in the tradition of much British Sixties realist writing. Barker certainly avoids patronising the women she describes. They are, without exception, poor, and prostitution is better paid than the only other work available—gutting chickens in a local factory.

There are two problems with the book. First that to attract the attention of the reader Barker, is forced to go along partially with the conventions of the thriller. Much of the writing orbits around the death of two women from within the community. This means that the same old atmospherics have to be conjured up, the darkened street and the vulnerable lonely figure tottering along in high heels. As though to counteract this Barker has one of her characters stab the main suspect. But I'm not sure this works. What more can be done with the image of the prostitute? From Walter Benjamin to Martin Scorsese she has been a figure who represents a challenge to the hypocrisies of conventional sexual morality, but *always* she is punished: possibly because in one sense she also challenges the men themselves. For women it's a different matter. Prostitution is simply a dangerous, demeaning way to earn a living, and this is what comes across most strongly in *Blow Your House Down*.

> *Angela McRobbie, "Cross Winds," in* New Statesman, *Vol. 107, No. 2777, June 8, 1984, pp. 24-5.**

CAROLA DIBBELL

An ocean away from the fights of early '80s British feminism, I found [*Union Street*] direct, subtle, and devastating. If the feminist overview was occasionally routine, the undertaking itself was far from it, and the tone far from obvious. Barker was sympathetic, but as she tallied the willingness of woman after woman to let fate make decisions, to play by the rules of class as well as society—never to complain, never to ask for help, never to leave—there were flashes of frustration, of impatience, even anger. She didn't patronize: she credited her subjects with the ability to reason, to choose, to change, and when they didn't, she sometimes lost her temper like a real sister. I thought that was honest.

In her second novel, *Blow Your House Down*, Barker is clearly asking for trouble again. This time, her protagonists are working-class women who did break the rules and, in a way, leave the world they were raised in. Like Barker herself, they're

professionals. The main characters—single mothers, battered wives, lesbians—are, as the narrative gradually reveals, prostitutes.

Barker has taken up one of the thorniest of feminist subjects—that peculiar "victimless crime" in which the criminal is the victim. The prostitute is where the buck stops in various cultural contradictions of sexism, like the one where a man can't respect the woman he desires, because a good woman is too pure for sex....

Barker doesn't explore the psychological factors that might have led her subjects into the business. These are neither rebels nor criminal types, nor even troubled victims of bad homes. Their motives are economic. They sell—actually rent out—their bodies as a last resort....

Barker's perception of the nature and purpose of the work is both shrewd and troubling....

Most of the customers are married and, just as conventional wisdom has it, they want to complain about their problems at home more than they want sex. But what they're really paying for is to not be criticized. The product that Brenda sells isn't so much a man's ejaculation as his ego, and her tools—under bridges, in deserted buildings, on rubble piles—aren't exotic wiles plus the thrill of sin, but rather patience and persistence. One woman complains that what she minds most about the work is that she can never laugh anymore, for fear her trick will think she's laughing at him. A laugh at the wrong time can set her back 10 minutes. It can even cost her life. Indeed, as we come to realize via the subtly suspenseful pacing of the first section, there is a real plot in this slice of life, and it concerns a jack-the-ripper type who specializes in whores. By the start of the book he's already killed one of Brenda's crowd, and he'll soon kill another before our eyes.

For all her matter-of-factness, Barker has a flair for the drama of the psycho-crime. The strongest story in *Union Street* was about the rape of an 11-year-old girl—the child's mesmerized collaboration, her complex, rather frightening defenses later. As *Blow Your House Down* clicks into gear, it looks as if this feminist chronicler of the working class has succeeded in constructing a conventional thriller on her own terms. She cannily exploits the creepiness inherent in her settings—the shadows, the little slip-ups, the suspicious behavior of any customer. One victim's photo, mounted on a billboard, peers eerily over scene after scene.

Somewhere in the last half of the book, the plot recedes and a theme takes over.... The theme seems to be the warning quoted from Nietzsche as the book's preface: "Whoever fights monsters should see to it that in the process he does not become a monster." ...

But another theme is hinted by the title, copped from the wicked wolf's threat to the three little pigs, and here things get confusing. Either the title choice is extremely casual, or it raises pretty specific expectations. Is the first victim's passivity straw, Jan's vengeance wood, and Maggie's marriage brick? And if that's the comparison, is there a hint of a warning that, given the dangers to which all women are prey, we'd survive better by keeping the good men on our side? I wouldn't want a simple moral bludgeoned on such a many-layered story, but as it stands now, so many ideas are raised with so few narrative connections that the uncertain denouement ... can't sustain them. *Union Street*'s looser structure left space for connections to be found or not, but *Blow Your House Down* is tighter and more novelistic, while not quite tight or novelistic enough. . . .

Barker has an original voice, blunt but tactful, deft but plainspoken, and both her books offer reads no less provocative for being fast. Her feminism and her class concerns—that's to say, her interest in those women who are in the wrong class to be feminist—stay connected down to the core of her vision, and in many ways that vision is more original and more daring in the newer work. Her feminism is open-minded, personal, not too clubbish or academic, and it serves her well with a difficult subject. The connections she draws betwen "bad" and "good" women are not the predictable ones. Only the conclusion, or lack of one, is unsatisfying. Maybe Barker was bending over backwards to end her story of prostitution and misogyny on a positive note when there just isn't one. Maybe she hesitated to air a position on men that she knew could provoke still more ideological controversy. Or maybe—and I say this like a real sister, the irritating kind—she could have done a tiny rewrite.

> Carola Dibbell, "Work Ethics," in VLS, *No. 28, September, 1984, p. 15.*

KATHA POLLITT

Pat Barker's extraordinary first novel, "Union Street," deserved every bit of the high praise heaped on it. . . . Set in England's grim and grimy Northeast, its seven loosely linked chapters offer a vision of working-class women's lives that is mordant, heartbreaking and—at least to my knowledge—unique. . . . Delicately and compassionately, Mrs. Barker caught the central contradiction of her heroines' lives, which is that they believe in female inferiority while being themselves far stronger than their menfolk, and derive their sense of worth from keeping up a front of brisk respectability that divides them from each other.

"Blow Your House Down" is set in the same part of England as "Union Street"—perhaps even the same neighborhood. . . . And when we meet Brenda, the first section's main character, she seems like just another Union Street matron, hurrying through the evening chores in order to meet a friend for a drink. And an ordinary Union Street matron is exactly what Brenda is, except that like Kath and Audrey and Jean and the other women who gather each night for lager-and-lime at the Palmerston pub, she is a prostitute. She is also a woman who is risking her life—a homicidal maniac is on the loose and prostitutes are his prey.

It's the plot of a thousand thrillers, told this time from the point of view not of the male detective but from that of the victims and potential victims. (p. 7)

"Blow Your House Down" is swift, spare and utterly absorbing—you'll probably read it, as I did, in one tense sitting. It's also a bit puzzling. I wish I understood the relevance of the title, with its reference to the story of the Three Little Pigs, and I wish I understood what Mrs. Barker wants us to make of the story of Maggie, told in Part Four. A middle-aged married woman who works in the chicken factory, Maggie is attacked, perhaps by the killer, while walking through the prostitutes' turf on her way to meet a friend for a drink. Only Brenda stops to help her—passers-by assume Maggie's just another prostitute getting hers, a view the police at first share. Mrs. Barker's feminist argument is clear enough—sexual violence puts all women at risk, there are no "good" women and "bad" women, the victim of a sex crime is herself treated as a criminal.

Beyond these points, though, Maggie's story seems to undermine Brenda's and Jean's. . . .

If the plot of "Blow Your House Down" could have used some rethinking, the novel nonetheless presents a remarkable portrait of the women themselves. Literature is full of prostitutes, of course, but most of them are male fantasies of one sort or another—hearts of gold, sex goddesses, calculating bitches, masochists. Brenda and her friends fit none of these stereotypes. None, for example, feels anything remotely approaching a sexual feeling for her customers—"if they were nasty you hated them; if they were nice you hated yourself," thinks Brenda—and indeed sex has rarely seemed as unappealing as it does in Mrs. Barker's bleakly matter-of-fact descriptions. Prostitution is here a matter of practical economics. For these uneducated women, most of whom have children and no husbands, the only jobs available are in the chicken factory or on the streets. And the streets pay better and offer more camaraderie, more autonomy and, ironically, hours more suitable for child rearing.

In Britain, Mrs. Barker is regarded as a regional writer, but this is surely a trivializing misnomer. What distinguishes her novels is not their regional qualities—an unusual setting, salty dialect, ways of life unfamiliar to the middle-class reader. It's that Mrs. Barker is able to make us see her characters from within, as they see themselves, and thereby reveals the full individuality and humanity of women who have got short shrift both in literature and in life. That makes Pat Barker a feminist. It also makes her a wonderful writer. (p. 9)

> *Katha Pollitt, "Bait for a Killer," in* The New York Times Book Review, *October 21, 1984, pp. 7, 9.*

Thomas Bernhard

1931-

Austrian novelist, dramatist, poet, autobiographer, and journalist.

Although not yet well known in the United States, Bernhard is renowned in Europe as a major author of fiction and drama. The most distinctive characteristic of his fiction is his relentlessly pessimistic view of the human condition; death, sickness, and madness are his obsessive concerns. Bernhard's dense and compulsively repetitive prose is dominated by monologues. Punctuation is minimal and few paragraph indentations interrupt the flow of the text. "It is a single stream of language," wrote George Steiner, who called Bernhard "the most original, concentrated novelist writing in German." Other critics view Bernhard's work with reservations, finding it strange and baffling but nevertheless effective in depicting the fragmentation of modern existence.

Bernhard's novels, called "black idylls" by one critic, share several characteristics: the settings are rural, decaying Austria stripped of all pastoral elements, the protagonists are hopelessly isolated aristocratic men, and the narratives focus without pathos on their self-imposed destruction. *Frost* (1963), Bernhard's first novel, concerns a reclusive old man whose psychological disintegration is recorded daily by a young medical student. In *Verstörung* (1967; *Gargoyles*) a son accompanies his father, a country doctor, on his rounds and is shocked by the depravity and hopelessness of the situations they confront. The major portion of the novel portrays a failing prince living in the remains of a castle. This novel has been interpreted as an allegory of Austria's decline. *Das Kalkwerk* (1970; *The Lime Works*) won the Georg Büchner prize and relates the story of a flawed genius who isolates himself from all but his crippled wife, whom he eventually murders. In *Korrektur* (1975; *Correction*) an aristocrat inherits a fortune but commits suicide. The hopelessness within Bernhard's fiction is relentless.

Bernhard's plays are equally depressing in their emphasis on death. Martin Esslin, commenting on the lack of conventional plot in Bernhard's drama, described it as "a theatre of images, static situations that are merely gradually elaborated and intensified." One of his better-known plays, *Ein fest für Boris* (1970), depicts a frenetic birthday party attended by grotesque cripples who fail to notice that the guest of honor, also a cripple, dies during the party.

Bernhard's several volumes of autobiography provide a connection between his life and his fiction. His illegitimate birth led to a disastrous relationship with his mother and he was raised by his grandfather, after whom many of his eccentric protagonists are modeled. His repressive schooling was interrupted by a serious lung ailment from which he nearly died. This probably accounts for his obsession with disease and dying. Upon recovering, Bernhard studied music and theater; some critics have noted techniques of musical composition in his prose. Although not directly addressed in his work, the cataclysmic events of the Second World War era overshadowed Bernhard's youth and probably contributed to his bleak world

© Isolde Ohlbaum

view. Despite his expressed disdain for Austria, Bernhard continues to live there.

(See also *CLC*, Vol. 3 and *Contemporary Authors*, Vols. 85-88.)

ROBERT MAURER

Thomas Bernhard is evidently a writer who prefers great risks, like a swimmer who chooses to enter the water with a quadruple flip from the highest board rather than feet first from poolside. His performance may not be flawless. It isn't in *Gargoyles*, ... [his first work] to appear in English. Nevertheless, his daring is remarkable, and the chances he takes pay off: for him, two literary prizes in his native Austria during 1968; for the reader, interest, suggestiveness, depth, and the realization that here is a novelist with uncommon talents of the sort possessed by Kafka, Musil, and Beckett, with whose visions of isolation and despair he has been associated by German critics.

Early one morning a doctor sets out on his daily rounds with his son. Even before their journey begins through a forbidding mountainous countryside, the father has visited a dying schoolmaster and a child who has fallen into a tub full of boiling water. "Everyone I have to visit and touch and treat proves to be sick and sad," the doctor warns the boy. (p. 34)

The doctor's forewarning should not be lost on Bernhard's readers, for the succession of grotesque portraits that follow seems almost to have been inspired by one of Kafka's aphorisms: "What is laid upon us is to accomplish the negative; the positive is already given." . . . [The last patient they visit is] Prince Saurau, whose "deadly monologue" consumes more than half the novel and whose voice most closely approaches that of Bernhard—brilliant, erudite, incoherent, aphoristic, possessed by belief that his son will one day destroy everything he has built. Unrewarding cases all, the doctor concludes.

Bernhard's vision is of a world out of joint, sick, perhaps incurable. *Verstörung,* his original title, translates as something like "deranged" or "disordered," and these words more exactly fit his central thrust than a title implying a parade of capricious monsters. Speaking through the Prince, he pinpoints his purpose: "Illnesses lead man by the shortest path to himself." The idea is not original in modern fiction; in fact, it is familiarly crucial enough to deserve systematic critical study one day soon, infusing as it does Mann's *The Magic Mountain,* Sartre's *Nausea,* Camus's *The Plague,* Kafka's *The Country Doctor,* and scores of other works, in all of which man is seen afflicted with mental and physical tumors, as he is in *Gargoyles,* and of which the resultant effects are disgust, isolation, imminent doubt, brutality, obsessions, perversion, hopelessness.

What Bernhard shares with the best of these writers is the ability to extract more than utter gloom from his landscape of inconceivable devastation. While the external surface of life is unquestionably grim, he somehow suggests more—the mystic element in experience that calls for symbolic interpretation; the inner significance of states that are akin to surrealistic dream-worlds; man's yearning for health, compassion, sanity. What he lacks, at least in this novel, is the necessary distance from the confused world he portrays. Episodic, repetitious, disorganized, overly dense at times with forthright philosophic precepts, ultimately inconclusive (for even the tale of doctor and son is never resolved), *Gargoyles* seems itself an exercise in derangement, a kind of imitative form that inevitably argues against total success. Far greater this, however, than the safer, duller way. (pp. 34, 39)

> Robert Maurer, in a review of "Gargoyles," in Saturday Review, Vol. LIII, No. 44, October 31, 1970, pp. 34, 39.

D. A. CRAIG

Few present day novelists writing in German make such compulsive reading as Thomas Bernhard. . . . Few evoke such powerful and haunting images of people and the landscape they live in, and in a language which is individual, direct and new without any attempt to be clever or to hide an insufficiency of content behind a smart playing about with words.

Thomas Bernhard writes of a predominantly rural Austria evidently still suffering from the traumatic experience of two world wars, of its reduction from a multinational empire imbued with fine traditions to a small, almost isolated, inward-looking state festering in the mountains and forests of Central Europe. No direct mention is made of the catastrophes, but they are implicit in the introspective sickness of many of his characters. The introspection exists too in his language which so often turns violently in on itself like a whirlpool. Few writers have managed to convey obsessive violence so directly. (p. 343)

Bernhard's Austria of the 1960s is a land which has withdrawn in on itself; it is a prison, mental home or hospital of hopeless cases. Austria is in the final state of decay and the people of that country are the victims of that decay. In his speech in 1968 before the Austrian Kultusminister he speaks of 'das Dämonische in uns' as being 'ein immerwährender vaterländischer Kerker, in dem die Elemente der Dummheit und der Rücksichtslosigkeit zur tagtäglichen Notdurft geworden sind'. He adds: 'Wir bevölkern ein Trauma, wir fürchten uns, wir haben ein Recht, uns zu fürchten, wir sehen schon, wenn auch undeutlich im Hintergrund: die Riesen der Angst (. . .) wir sind auch nichts und verdienen nichts als das Chaos'. Even abroad, whether in London or so far away as New York, says the Prince von Saurau in *Verstörung,* the sickness of their homeland still haunts them. The inevitable consequences are disease, insanity and death. . . . *Frost* is set . . . [in a] cold dark landscape: forests descending into a gorge, isolated from the outer world, claustrophobic, a place where one is alone with one's own fantasies and obsessions. Austria becomes as it were a microcosm of the decay and disintegration of Europe as a whole, lost in the rain and cold. . . . In *Das Kalkwerk,* also set in isolation, the cold and 'Finsternis' are still as strongly present. The disintegration of Austria is brought home in the recurrent theme of the breaking up or falling apart of houses and estates handed down by families through the generations. These estates in their peculiar isolation at times exert a seductive and destructive influence on their owners, as Hochgobernitz in *Verstörung* or *Ungenach* in the short story of the same name. It is hard, sometimes impossible to escape from them, just as it is impossible for most of Bernhard's characters who go abroad to escape from Austria, to stay away. They will come back expecting to fulfil their life's ambitions there, but find instead destruction. . . . In Austria the lower classes tend to be mentally deficient, criminal or physically ill while the higher echelons become insane. (pp. 344-45)

In contrast Bernhard often writes of the English-speaking world as a sort of refuge from the dangers of his own country: one of the half-brothers in *Ungenach* appears to find safety from his past in the USA. . . . (p. 345)

The Englishman in *Midland in Stilfs,* on a visit to this lonely Austrian village, remains untouched by the morbidity of the life there, where the half-wit Roth blows up chickens with a bicycle pump until they burst. The visit of the Englishman Midland makes them happy; he is described as an 'Enthusiast'; he is 'ausgestattet mit den Kennzeichen einer Welt, die wir seit vielen Jahren nicht einmal mehr vom Hörensagen kennen'. Bernhard treats Midland with a gentleness, warmth and light humour unapparent in his attitude to other characters.

Marcel Reich-Ranicki in his essay on *Verstörung,* 'Konfesionen eines Besessenen' (*Literatur der kleinen Schritte,* Munich 1967) attacks Bernhard's aggressive attitude to his fatherland as extraordinarily one-sided and finds that it goes beyond bounds to become monotonous, especially when accompanied by such general aggression in other directions. His later novel *Das Kalkwerk,* however, shows a considerable toning down of this aggression and thereby gains in verisimilitude. . . . Urs Jenny in a short article 'Österreichische Agonie' (*Süddeutsche Zeitung,* 7-8 Dec. 1968) rightly points out how Bernhard reflects the disintegration of the country in the disintegration of families: parents commit suicide and a son dies of epilepsy (*Amras*), or father and son after him slowly become insane in the confines of their inheritance (*Verstörung*).

But the parallel exists for Bernhard in the workings of nature itself: nature is obviously and fundamentally a destructive and self-destructive force whose end is death, total annihilation, 'Finsternis'.

His characters feel with more than one sense the dark forces: what they hear and smell haunts them. Strauch, the degenerating sometime painter in *Frost,* continually hears the barking of dogs, which without reason attack human beings in the streets and yards, while the rivers 'atmen den Geruch der Verwesung ihres ganzen Flußlaufes auf'. . . . For Saurau the identification between the decaying world outside him and that within is almost complete, a process, 'in dem alles vernichtet wird, um dann endgültig zu sein'. Later he remarks, 'dieser Vorgang ist immer ein von innen ausgehender, sich nach außen vollziehender'. A mind which sees the process going in this direction is introverted to the point of dangerous imbalance.

Because the 'normal' state of nature is 'Finsternis' and 'Chaos', it is natural that man too should move towards that state. Natural too therefore that disease, madness and crime are end-products of nature whereas health, sanity and temperate living are unnatural. People are violent, objects of fear rather than of love. Many of his main characters suffer therefore from paranoia. Sometimes this violence is expressed by insane laughter: one thinks of Höller and his nephew in *Das Kalkwerk* who disturb Konrad by their 'unheimliches Gelächter', or of the father in *Amras* who laughs as he poisons himself. There is a suppressed violence in this laughter, a laughter which often presages an act of violence or is suspected by those who hear it as portending such an act.

Jens Tismar ('Thomas Bernhards Erzählerfiguren', in *Über Thomas Bernhard* Edition Suhrkamp Nr. 401) points out that, because Bernhard's characters live in a relationship to nature rather than to a consumer society, they are thus the first to be struck by violence, which has its origin in nature. Those who live closest to nature are least protected against it. Man is stripped of the sophistication a city civilization allows him and is at the mercy of the power that ultimately governs him. The state is the first attempt of man to mitigate the destructive forces of nature, but soon the state becomes party to this decay and destruction.

It is common in Bernhard's prose work to encounter men engaged in study of some sort which will reach fruition through being written down, through a personal act of creation; an attempt, one would think, to assert oneself against the inevitable destruction of the personality. This attempt, particularly convincing and moving in the case of Konrad in *Das Kalkwerk,* is usually a failure, and it is not so much a case of artistic creation as the desire of an ordinary man to lend some point to his existence—a desire which is not fulfilled because of the conditions in which men live and because of the almost universal inability in the ordinary man to preserve 'Furchtlosigkeit vor Realisierung, vor Verwirklichung'. . . . Men usually fail and nature takes its course.

Bernhard's minor characters are generally the rural proletariat: Fleischhauer, Furhmänner, Holzhauer, Wasenmeister or Forst- and Gutsverwaler. These characters are so often described in a way which suggests they are capable of acts of violence and are manifestations of the violent natural world in which they live and work. Even their names, at times, have a ring of violence: Höller, Zehetmayer, Henzig, Krainer. One is often reminded of Samuel Beckett (and in other facets of Bernhard's writing too) whose choice of names is as peculiar. His women

characters contribute to the feeling of inevitable decay and destruction: the step-mother in *Ungenach,* the Wirtin in *Frost* and most of all Konrad's wife in *Das Kalkwerk,* whose persecution of her husband is partly responsible for his downfall.

Bernhard is a writer with obsessions, and nowhere are these obsessions more obvious than in the style itself. Words are repeated over and over again, and acquire thereby a certain violence as well as conveying the effect of reported gossip. Words such as 'total', 'verheerend', 'lächerlich', 'tatsächlich', 'tagtäglich', 'nurmehr' and the constant driving of the language into the superlative give a relentlessness to his narration. (pp. 345-48)

These obsessions are one of the main contributions to the violence and directness of his language, obsessions expressing an obsession: progress towards the absolute—death. Schmidt-Dengler writes of the 'Prozeß der Verabsolutierung' in Bernhard ('Der Tod als Naturwissenschaft neben dem Leben, Leben' in *Über Thomas Bernhard* Edition Suhrkamp Nr. 401); some like Jens Tismar are reminded of Kleist. The violence comes through with his frequent use of blunt unsophisticated words of a concrete character: *Kopf, Schädeldecke, Dummkopf, Hirn* and his use of powerfully evocative compounds: *Geschlechtergestank, Zeitungswahnsinn, Maschinenwahnsinn, Denkgebäude, Kopfmüll.* This directness recalls Nietzsche as well as Kleist, and there is evidence, in *Verstörung* at least, for a preoccupation with Nietzsche.

The primary attraction of Bernhard is no doubt his individual and compulsive style, the extraordinary gift he has, like Kleist, of capturing the reader in the first phrases and taking him through, almost breathless, to the end of the work. In no work is he more successful than in *Das Kalkwerk,* his most achieved work so far. The sentences are long and intertwined: separable prefixes are often left too long before they appear. His style is compulsive: it reads like a newspaper report of local gossip about a crime committed in the area. This means that much is in reported speech and therefore in the subjunctive—practically the entire *Das Kalkwerk* is so. One feels confronted by a long pent-up confession to which one feels the obligation to give complete attention.

His first novel *Frost* won the special attention of Carl Zuckmayer who in *Die Zeit* (21 June 1963) wrote a most favourable criticism (*Ein Simbild der großen Kälte*). He called it 'eines der aufwühlendsten und eindringlichsten Prosawerke . . . seit Peter Weiß''. It is a novel which describes the collapse of every relationship to the human world, a complete laying bare of the remains of a soul. It concerns 'die Verfrostung des Malers Strauch' and resembles a terrifying fairy story. The novel is, in its own words, 'Expeditionen in Urwälder des Alleinseins'. A medical student is sent by an Assistenzarzt to observe his brother, a painter, who has burnt all his paintings, and in the village of Weng is undergoing a process of mental disintegration. He is to make his report and send it to the brother. The brother himself does not go, a sign of the estrangement already in the Strauch family.

Apart from his striking style Bernhard's most impressive achievement in *Frost* is his evocation of this mountain village. Very soon one is immersed in the dark landscape—the cold, smells, rough labourers, slaughter-houses, a bird crushed to death, the barking of dogs, the uncouth inn where they lodge. A greater part of the text is made up of Strauch's monologues and the interpolations of the student seem at times detrimental to the flow of the text. At times the student is occupied with moral questions; this element has disappeared by his later novels. ('Aber eine Stimme, die einfach unüberhörbar ist, sagt mir, daß Selbstmord Sünde ist.') This makes *Frost* as a whole too long because it interrupts the single-mindedness which gives his later work its power.

Strauch extracts a perverse enjoyment from his mental disintegration: he relishes telling the young man of his decline and compares it to the decline of the state, thereby revealing his megalomania. . . . He seems worn-out physically, sees no point in striving, in exertion; once one has achieved one's aim the effort shows itself to have been worthless. He make himself the centre of interest, talks unremittingly of his hallucinations, sickness and festering in Weng. His last contact with the outer world is through newspapers, which Zuckmayer calls 'ein letzter, kindlicher Versuch der Kommunikation'.

His relationship with other people in the valley is paranoid. His suspicions of the Wirtin know few bounds, indeed they show a strange fascination with her. (pp. 348-49)

He lacks the 'Fiurchtlosigkeit vor Realisierung' that Konrad lacked. Instead he indulges his fantasy and this will lead him to his end. The main failures of *Frost* are its length and failure to work out thoroughly, as Bernhard does in *Das Kalkwerk,* the disintegration of the main character.

The absolute and final cold deprives everything of life. This is Bernhard's most telling image; the frost freezes the violence of movement, takes everything to its death: animals are frozen to death in the ice, brought down the river with their limbs torn asunder. Strauch too has the cold inside him and outside; finally he disappears, presumably destroyed by the frost. 'Der Frost is allmächtig . . . besitzt alles', says Strauch. . . . (pp. 349-50)

The novel is not without its short humorous episodes, however. This weird humour grows out of the fanaticism of the text, out of the exaggerated and constantly occurring extremes of expression. It is dependent on the total immersion in the text that Bernhard is capable of obtaining from his readers. After about twenty pages of subjection to Strauch the painter tells of the authoritarian upbringing by his grandparents.

> Er sei als Kind bei seinen Großeltern aufgewachsen. Streng gehalten in Winterzeiten. Da habe er oft tagelang stillsitzen und Wörterzusammensetzungen auswendig lernen müssen. Als er in die Schule eintrat, wußte er mehr als der Lehrer. . . .
>
> (p. 350)

The inevitable conclusion of his avid learning as a young child necessarily leads to knowing more than the teacher, but this is a conclusion unexpected at the close of a Bernhard thought: one expects disaster, destruction or something equally 'verheerend'.

In *Verstörung* he has weeded out many of the *longueurs* and interpolations of *Frost* and has managed to concentrate more on the central theme. Nevertheless, the form of the work has still not the straightforwardness of *Das Kalkwerk:* Marcel Reich-Ranicki still finds parts monotonous and finds the attempts at psychology spurious. Bernhard's fine command of prose seduces him into unnecessary excursions. The first part of the novel, where the doctor visits various patients on his way to von Saurau, and where the narrator, his son, records the unhealthy state of their own family, seems redundant after one has read the long exhaustive monologue of the Fürst, even if

it is seen as a preparation for the ultimate encounter with the person of highest social standing in this area, and also the sickest.

Nevertheless, considered as an intermediate stage between *Frost* and *Das Kalkwerk, Verstörung* shows a clarification of Bernhard's intentions after *Frost* without sacrificing the dark imagery of the first work, and, at the same time, it contains some of the continuity so remarkable in *Das Kalkwerk.*

The doctor's student son has returned home from his university studies to be taken by his father on his rounds. They visit patients, all of whom are in stages of acute physical or mental suffering. There is no relief. The doctor's own family too in the person of the daughter, is the victim of disorders. The characters isolate themselves in a landscape which itself is isolated. Contact with the outer world is broken off: the industrialist has shut himself up in his house and allows no pictures, no reading matter to enter it. He writes perpetually and destroys what he has written; the miller in the gorge, 'der unter der Haut verfault', has two sons and a Turkish workman who are haunted by a cage full of screeching exotic birds . . . , the young Krainer boy, crippled and insane, is kept in a cage in his bedroom, his body is disintegrating and emits a horrific stench—'was er sprach, war genau so verkrüppelt wie er selber'—. At last father and son reach Hochgobernitz which overlooks the gorge and much of the surrounding countryside. The Fürst is engaged in an endless monologue which, we gather, will end in suicide, the direction taken by his father before him and perhaps by his son after him. He speaks of decay and corruption of the state, of Europe, of the world, of the self-destructive violence of nature itself, of his vain relationships with other men inside and outside his family, of his son, who is at the moment studying in London, but still under the spell of Hochgobernitz. Family relationships again play such an important rôle in Bernhard's work: the closest, most natural relationships are the most dangerous, the most destructive, almost as if they pose problems that the characters, and even perhaps the author, are afraid to tackle. They eventually take refuge in a world of unending fantasy, and in a world of ultimate chaos; Saurau: 'Ich habe den Eindruck, als wäre es in jedem Augenblick natürlich, daß die Welt auseinanderbricht'. . . . He adds: 'Die Menschen sind nichts anderes als eine in die Milliarde gehende ungeheuere auf die fünf Kontinente verteilte Sterbensgemeinschaft.' Suffering is having to endure the waiting for chaos. As with Strauch the only contact he has with the outer world is through newspapers; the only visitors allowed into the castle are the newspaper deliverers. He wishes for no contact, he is preparing for the absolute end. One is reminded of Kasack's 'immer später ist Einsamkeit'.

The ending of the novel is loose, hardly an improvement on the ending of *Frost.* One has to wait for *Das Kalkwerk* for Bernhard to achieve a satisfactory conclusion. *Das Kalkwerk* is free of the gratuitous images of the earlier novels. We know the final catastrophe from the first page, and Bernhard, by making it a murder instead of supposed suicide, presents an act artistically and psychologically more consistent with the violence and aggression latent in his style. *Das Kalkwerk* must rank as one of the finest and most worthwhile German novels of today through its single-mindedness, its most individual style, and, in places, its crazy humour.

Johannes Kleinstück (*Die Welt*, 29 Oct. 1970) refers to the remoteness of the narrator, 'der sich aufs Hörensagen verläßt und an der Grenze des Verstehbaren stößt'. This is important: the narrator in Bernhard's novels has become increasingly distant from his subject: in *Frost* the student confronts Strauch directly, in *Verstörung* the father is the intermediary, in *Das Kalkwerk* the narrator quotes reports of observers, Fro and Wieser, who themselves are mere shadows in the text. The remoteness is reinforced by the constant use of the subjunctive and makes the extremes to which the text goes seem more plausible.

Kleinstück also refers to the dominant obsessiveness of the narration to the exclusion of other factors:

> geklärt wird dadurch nichts, wir wissen nicht,
> ob sich die Konrads hassen oder lieben, ob sie
> in hassender Liebe aneinander gekettet sind,
> wir tun keinen Blick in ihr Inneres, wir wissen
> nicht einmal, ob sie so etwas wie ein Inneres
> besitzen.

He is, I think, wrong to expect these factors; they are the very factors which Bernhard does not investigate as this would detract from the central preoccupation of the novel: the remoteness of the lives of two people, whose life, as reported, has turned into a series of ritualized obsessions, and whose relationship ends with an act of violence, itself obscure in detail.

Like Johannes Kleinstück, Gudrun Tempel (*The Times*, 4th February 1971) sees *Das Kalkwerk* as a totally nihilistic work. This view is not consistent with the text: Konrad's life and work failed, not because life and work must, in themselves, fail, but because he lacked certain qualities, which Thomas Bernhard defines as necessary in order to avoid failure: 'Furchtlosigkeit vor Realisierung (. . .) Furchtlosigkeit einfach davor (. . .) die Studie auf das Papier zu kippen'. . . . *Das Kalkwerk* is less nihilistic, more positive in utterance than *Frost* or *Verstörung.*

From the first page the reader is thrown into the whirlpool of the language, taken up in the reports of Fro and Wieser on Konrad, who 'am Ende der konradschen Ehehölle' shot to death his crippled wife. The reports, sometimes contradictory or fragmentary, trace the helter-skelter existence of the Konrads up to the day of the killing. They have moved from place to place through many parts of the world seeking somewhere to rest, where Konrad can at last apply himself to his studies on the human hearing. They end up buying, at an extortionate price from a nephew, a disused limestone works which had fascinated Konrad as a child. He had always wished to return there, and once there he sets about isolating himself. He plants high shrubs round the works and forbids the snowplough to clear the path to it in the winter. Isolated he tries to complete his studies, yells words at his wife from various distances to find her threshold of hearing, and tests his own very sensitive hearing. However, the interruptions are continual: despite everything visitors arrive and his wife claims constant attention. His work is never completed, never even properly started. He is driven more and more to distraction, loses his sense of reality and kills his wife, hoping for peace at last. This is Bernhard's first thorough-going study of a person, and perhaps because of this his study has a validity greater than in the previous novels: he deals with a central human problem: the inability of an ordinary man to create for himself and the distraction which results from his frustration. This matter is conveyed in a language whipped up to greater and greater extremes of expression, constant repetition of such emphatic words as *tatsächlich, selbstverständlich* and *nurmehr,* and the working out of obsessions. Here everything seems part of the whole; there are no excrescences in the text.

The novel ends with one of Bernhard's finest and most committed passages. Konrad is a prisoner of the law, his life has disintegrated. Bernhard comments on his failure and on the qualities necessary to avert it. . . . (pp. 350-53)

With *Das Kalkwerk* Bernahrd seems to have gone as far as possible in the direction he has taken in his work since 1963. Two short stories, published in 1971, *Der Wetterfleck* and *Am Ortler,* add nothing new. After his latest novel it is hard to see where Bernhard can go next. (p. 353)

D. A. Craig, "The Novels of Thomas Bernhard—A Report," in German Life & Letters, *Vol. XXV, No. 4, July, 1972, pp. 343-53.*

J. W. LAMBERT

When [Thomas Bernhard] was awarded the Austrian State Prize he accepted with the words 'Everything is ridiculous when one thinks of death'. The Minister of Education stormed out of the hall . . .' Can't say I blame him. On that showing Herr Bernhard is a silly show-off; on the showing of *The Force of Habit* [*Die Macht der Gewohnheit*] he is a plodding and derivative writer with no light to throw on the old ideas he nurses—I was going to say at such length, but in fact, though it seemed much longer, the piece lasted barely two hours, an expensive ordeal for the audience as well as for the company. It would seem that Bernhard intended to write a play about the eroding power of dedication and about the stifling pressure of past masterpieces—two perfectly legitimate subjects, had they arisen out of the characters of his imagination, so that we could have embraced them and their dilemmas. Perhaps he has no imagination; certainly he hasn't exercized any. Here is a caravan, headquarters of a circus whose performers are all miserable (perhaps because they never change out of the clothes they wear in the ring). They are subject to the will of the ringmaster, an elderly man with an artificial leg . . . ; and his will is that every day, when not actually juggling or clowning or tightrope-walking or leopard-training, they should, though miserable musicians, join him in rehearsing Schubert's 'Trout' Quintet. This they sullenly do, all except the pianist-animal-trainer, who, as usual, gets drunk, first kicks the piano, then shoots it, then collapses and is thrown out of the caravan. Everybody else leaves except the ringmaster, who—the only good moment of the entire piece—switches on the radio to hear a first-rate professional performance of the music which has been defeating him for twenty-two years. It would, I can see, be possible to write a wry comedy around this scenario. Unfortunately Herr Bernhard has not been able to provide any comic illumination, and has killed his play stone dead by a most astonishing simple-minded mistake. He was himself trained as a musician, a piece of music is his centrepiece: well enough—but he has also tried to write lines patterned like music, so that where in a given musical passage a phrase of several notes might be repeated several times, he has repeated a given verbal phrase several times—notably 'Augsburg tomorrow', which recurs to screaming-point, its irritation value in no way diminished by the fact that the cast persist in pronouncing it Augsberg (Brecht's birthplace at least deserves better than that). . . . 'We must not forget the misery that was our childhood—every childhood' is a line of sloppy, sentimental self-indulgence all too typical of Herr Bernhard, the sort of dramatist who gets Beckett a bad name. (pp. 34-5)

J. W. Lambert, in a review of "The Force of Habit," in Drama, *No. 123, Winter, 1976, pp. 34-5.*

BETTY FALKENBERG

In a way and to a degree unequalled by any of his contemporaries, Handke, Kroetz, the entire Graz or "Viennese Group" (Artmann, Beyer, Achleitner) together, the work of Thomas Bernhard is unsettling. Long excluded from their ranks (Bernhard, a native Austrian, was denied publication in the "organs" of both groups), he still remains, despite the belated recognition of his genius, the loner he always was.

Long before literary critics began speculating about the influence of Wittgenstein on Handke's ambivalence towards language, Bernhard had incorporated the Wittgenstein skepsis into his prose. "Words," says the protagonist of his novel, *Limeworks*, "are made to degrade thought, yes, he would even go so far as to say words were there to do away with thought."

The hero of *Korrektur (Revisions)*, Bernhard's most recent novel . . ., shares certain biographical facts with the master. Both are Austrian scientists who feel stifled by their native homeland. . . . The hero of *Korrektur* reads and rereads Wittgenstein "because he thought to recognize himself in the writings of Wittgenstein who came from the same countryside and who had always been such an acute observer of that countryside." Madness and suicide are endemic to the families of both, as they are, indeed, to post-Hapsburg Austria itself.

But it is not so much in statement as in style that Bernhard can claim his forebear. His dogged rejection of ordinary speech in favor of a quasi-scientific bloodlessness is one of the starkest examples in contemporary prose writing of pounding out an overriding obsession through seeming objectivity. . . . Bernhard's prose is, moreover, the unclouded mirror—for all its seeming quirkiness it is not murky—of his thought. Its rhythms are integral to that thought; its breaths and breathlessnesses are comparable to the long lines of a long Mozart aria. Bernhard has an infallible ear for cadence, for building up tensions to the breaking point and then releasing them for just an eighth-note rest before going on. He also appreciates the comic effect of a comma. In fact, everything in Bernhard's prose serves a rhythmic as well as a narrative function. Take his device used to set up distance between author and reader, material and interpretation. It might be called—not station-identification, but narrator-identification—and it arises out of another device characteristic of him, namely to tell his story through the account of at least one, but generally two, third persons. After pages and pages of what may remind some of Faulkner's, or more likely, Beckett's pauseless prose, Bernhard will interject a punctuating note: "So Fro," or "So Wieser." After a while these punctuating elements work like refrains, refrains which can then be varied: "So Konrad to Fro," or "as Konrad supposedly said to Fro," or finally, "as Konrad already in October said to Fro." Coming, as they generally do in the midst of some thoroughly horrific episode, then casual banality offers a moment of comic relief. It is a tiny trick, but it is brilliant. It jolts the reader and causes him to reflect on the absurdity of all things, even, or especially, the *condition humaine*, in all its sordid as well as petty ramifications. Because all Bernhard's books, all his plays, are really about one thing: death. Death in death, death in life, the futility of all human contact or attempts at understanding, the senselessness of all existence and the cruelty of creating new life, the stupidity of all human beings, the futility of all systems, political or religious, both encompassing as they do the same corruption and stupidity to be found everywhere else. If there is one thing which can bind people together—and the nature of that bond is at best ambi-

valent—it can only be the awareness of the total hopelessness of all human endeavor in the light of the fact of death. (pp. 269-71)

Bernhard's latest novel, *Korrektur (Revisions)*, may be viewed as an almost perfect inversion of the theme of *Kalkwerk (Limeworks)*, in which the protagonist is hindered by psychological blocks from putting down on paper the results of a scientific study on hearing which he has been carrying around in his head for decades. *Kalkwerk*, in turn, harks back to the still earlier novel, *Verstörung (Disturbances)*, in which a mad prince paces his study, dreaming of the life he never lived, the scholarly essays he never completed. (p. 271)

If, in *Kalkwerk*, ruination is the result of noncompletion of a project, in *Korrektur*, ruination is the precise result of the completion of the projects, both the actual building and the chronicling. On completion of the cone, Roithamer's sister dies, only death being able to contain such sublime joy. And on her death, Roithamer, reviewing both his scheme and the written account of it, comes to the shattering conclusion that nothing short of total revision can eradicate the errors contained in the work. (p. 272)

Limeworks ends with its hero giving himself up to the police after being found, half-frozen to death, in the sewage dump near his house. For the hero of *Korrektur* there is no alternative to suicide. His only freedom consists in choosing how and where.

His choice is significant and pulls the threads of the entire novel together. Among the formative experiences of his childhood, as described first by his friend and literary executor in a long, discursive passage, notable for its beautiful rhythmic structure, his long walk through the woods to school emerges as *the* decisive experience. In fact, he tells us, an early literary effort of the hero's was itself devoted to a description of this walk, and was entitled "The Clearing." That Roithamer should choose to hang himself from a tree in the clearing is more than a literary nicety. In our beginning is our end. Every word, every deed shall be eradicated. "Clearing." So ends the book.

Some critics have argued that there is no justification for the division of *Korrektur* into two parts (the *only* division other than commas and periods to be found in the entire 362 pages), on the grounds that there is no difference in the material presented in the two parts. But in part two, where the narrator withdraws, and Roithamer is permitted to tell his own tale, albeit filtered through his notes, a far more impassioned tone breaks through; he rails against the various members of his family with a venom verging on paranoia, until, at the very end, he brings himself up short, recognizing the need for correction, if not reconciliation. It is this dual movement in part two, first forward and then back, that gives the book its tremendous momentum. Moreover, it is the contrast—the balance and beauty of construction of part one poised against the torrential outpourings in part two—which causes the reader to revise his own judgments of the hero, from that of an idealistic scientific spirit to a sick human being obsessed with hatred to a final acceptance of both sides of his person. It is this very tension between the two parts, finally, that gives the book its rich texture and unexpected overtones.

Many themes echo and re-echo throughout the pages of *Korrektur*. The most striking, perhaps because of its uncanny resemblance to Joyce's obsession with that same theme, is the love-hate to the motherland, "the old sow that eats her farrow." (pp. 272-73)

Another phrase from Joyce, from the notebooks, comes to mind in connection with Bernhard: "centripetal writing." Or, put differently, in musical terms, the fugal working out of themes. Even in the handling of tiny details, a larger pattern of symmetry, that can only be perceived in retrospective perusal of all Bernhard's novels up to now, emerges after *Korrektur:* just as a fugue does not merely progress forward, but returns always to its center, amplified.

In addition to the already cited passages from different novels with corresponding resonances, a few others make this point abundantly clear. In describing the purposely deceptive landscaping of the grounds around the Limeworks to increase its inaccessibility, Bernhard writes, "The actual thing is always actually different, the precise opposite of what it actually is." *Korrektur* ends with the speculation by Roithamer, on his last train ride from London back to Austria: "All he had written about Altensam (his home village), and everyone there, was different, other, than he had described it." And from *Verstö-rung:* "Probably everything that I think is different from what I think it to be, I thought."

Or again, the themes of solitude and ruthlessness in the pursuit of one's goal: ruthlessness toward all human beings but especially toward oneself is the *sine qua non* of all creative work. Madness is the dog barking at one's door, but until one has finished the job, one must close one's ears to it. (pp. 273-74)

Kroetz, the young Bavarian playwright, calls his work "A drama built on silences. A theater of the inarticulate." This description may again be applied to Bernhard's use of dialogue—with one difference. Bernhard does not limit his notion of inarticulateness to one social class as does Kroetz, but believes it inherent in human communications altogether. Bernhard's characters are not really individuals, and their speech is not really dialogue, but a monomaniacal talking past one another. They exist as stylized versions of mental and physical basketcases, cut off from the very selves out of whose mouths the words appear to come.

By bleeding his characters of their individuality, by antiseptically draining their speech of all contemporary jargon, Bernhard achieves a pristine quality that is strangely modern, deriving its very power from its unsayingness. (p. 275)

Again, as the work of Bernhard grows, and the total pattern emerges ever more clearly, it yields a fascination over and above that which might accrue to any of the individual parts. Unlike Gide's novels, which argue with each other, or Yeats's *Ego Dominus Tuus,* Bernhard seeks no antiself. Nor does he write to "find" his self. His apparent cancelling out of prior attitudes or viewpoints with each new book is inherent in, and consistent with, his view of the ultimate senselessness of all attitudes or viewpoints. The two sides of the equation balance; there is merely a narrowing down: to zero equals zero. Finally, language itself petrifies, breaks down. (This process, namely of the breakdown of language, has been utilized, indeed capitalized on, by the "new" German film makers who have their characters talk not merely inarticulately, but inaudibly as well. Small wonder that the rash of Kaspar Hauser plays and films has hit Germany so markedly of late.) In Bernhard plays, the sparse texts appear as vertical blocks, like stone slabs, unevenly hewn, with lots of space between. In the novels, the horizontal reigns; pages shed margins, paragraph indentations disappear. In terms of his own dialectic, it is all the same. An empty room can be as claustrophobic as a Biedermeier parlor. Or, in the words of Pascal, as quoted in the motto to *Verstörung,*

"The eternal silence of these infinite spaces terrifies me." And wherever one is, one is alone. (pp. 276-77)

Betty Falkenberg, "Thomas Bernhard," in Partisan Review, *Vol. XLVII, No. 2, 1980, pp. 269-77.*

RICHARD GILMAN

Bernhard, an Austrian like Handke, is nearly 50 years old and for some time has been recognized in the German-speaking world as an extraordinary, if hard to classify, new fictional voice. Three of his novels have been published in the United States (several of his plays are in the process of being translated) and they have been almost totally ignored. The newest of his novels to be published here, his most important work up to the time of its appearance in Germany (1974), came out months ago with not even a mention in *The New York Times Book Review* or *The New York Review of Books* and, with the exception of an admiring and intelligent piece by Betty Falkenburg [see excerpt above] in the current *Partisan Review,* only scattered notices in a few small literary journals. This is in spite of the fact that this book, *Correction (Korrektur),* is astonishingly original, a composition of strange new beauty. Or, more likely, it's because of that.

Bernhard is difficult, to be sure, presenting the same kind of resistance to easy understanding that Beckett once did (and for many audiences continues to do) or as Handke does now. Allowing for wide technical and thematic differences, they are the writers whom he seems to me most to resemble, a more remote connection being to his Austrian predecessor, Robert Musil, and, still more distantly, the German Hermann Broch.

It is the acute sense these writers have of language as being radically untrustworthy, of one's having to outwit the words one uses at the same time that words remain the substance of wit and everything else, that distinguishes their work from our own more accepting, more straightforward literary practices. (p. 85)

There is one other element that has to be taken into account in any consideration of Handke and Bernhard, and that is the enormous influence on them of their fellow Austrian, Ludwig Wittgenstein. . . . In Bernhard's case, the influence is simultaneously both more direct and less so; that is to say, he has a strong temperamental affinity with the great philosopher and has absorbed much from him intellectually, but his work is less a transposition of Wittgenstein into literary and esthetic modes, as some of Handke's tends to be, than it is a sort of parallel utterance running alongside the master's.

Should one not have known of the complex relationship between Bernhard and Wittgenstein, it would be established immediately by *Correction,* whose protagonist is in fact modeled in detail after the philosopher. All the basic facts of the latter's life are here, placed later in time (Wittgenstein's dates are 1889-1951), while the book is set roughly in the present). Roithamer, the central character, who has committed suicide just before the narrative begins, is a brilliant Austrian scientist—his work is in genetic mutations—who has spent much time studying and teaching in England, as Wittgenstein did. Like the latter, Roithamer inherited a large fortune which he quickly gave away; like him, he has designed and built for his sister a strange, austere house and, like him, too, his family has a history of suicide.

At one point, Bernhard tactically separates the two—"he thought he recognized himself in them, the writings of Wittgenstein, a native of the same region as Roithamer and always a keen observer of Roithamer's regional landscape.'' But the identity is beyond question. Besides the physical facts there are the psychic and temperamental ones: Roithamer has Wittgenstein's pessimism about human life, his intolerance for stupidity and lies, his neurasthenia and, as Norman Malcolm tells us about Wittgenstein in his memoir of the philosopher, his tendency to be ''tortured'' and ''exhausted'' by abstract thinking.

But, despite all this, *Correction* is no more a fictionalized biography of Wittgenstein than Mann's *Dr. Faustus* is of Richard Strauss, whose life it borrows. As Mann's novel is ''about'' the life of art and imagination, Bernhard's is about the life of thought. Or rather, it's a literary construction whose elements are the violence mental processes do to us, the unreality they bring about; it's a tale in which thinking is the tragic mode of being. The Wittgenstein figure, through whom Bernhard organizes his own experience and perceptions, has reached the limit of intellectual possibility, the way in an older literary mode the tragic hero reaches a moral limit. (pp. 85-6)

The structure of *Correction* is simple and austere. The book is divided into two parts: the first, called ''Hoeller's Garret,'' and the second, ''Sifting and Sorting.'' There are no other divisions of any kind, no chapters, no paragraphs. . . .

The novel's first section consists mainly in the narrator's memories of Roithamer and knowledge of his circumstances, filled out by the journals and notebooks. The second section begins in the same manner, but gradually the narrator's voice gives way to Roithamer's, speaking through the papers. . . .

By this shift the narrator moves us more and more into the character's (Roithamer's) mind. But the narrator is also a character, of course, and the device serves to remind us of the *literary* action going on: Roithamer's mind at work, the narrator's, Bernhard's—three voices fused into a single expressiveness. In the end we and the narrator are fully inside Roithamer's head, obsessed with his obsessions, feeling his pain, aware of his awarenesses, and we feel ''ruined,'' annihilated by the remorselessness, the incontrovertibility of such thought, the way the narrator had feared. . . .

Gradually, the reader begins to grasp what Bernhard is doing, what instigates all this loathing and terror and what they serve. *Correction,* one comes to see, is no local, particular tale, not someone's pathological story but a profound meditation, or, since that implies a lofty detached enterprise, rather a literary invention violently suffused with thought, whose subject (if I can begin to do justice to it) is this: the fact that we are inserted into a world we haven't made, and consequent on that, the great gulf between what we are and what we are made to be, the effort we make to think our way through the discrepancy, together with the desperate inadequacy of the means we have—language. (p. 86)

Correction is something exceedingly rare among novels of recent years: a paradigm of consciousness and not simply a product. That it's a consciousness of despair and hopelessness doesn't mean the book induces them in us. Bernhard has said that ''the art we need is the art of bearing the unbearable,'' and his novel joins that small group of literary works which nobly help us to do that. (p. 88)

> Richard Gilman, *''The Eloquent Compromise with Silence,''* in The Nation, *Vol. 231, No. 3, July 19-26, 1980, pp. 85-8.*

MARTIN ESSLIN

In the German-speaking world, and in the whole of continental Europe, Thomas Bernhard . . . is generally accepted as one of the leading literary figures of his time, the author of a remarkable series of short stories, seven major novels and ten successful plays, yet in the English-speaking sphere, he is still practically unknown. One of his plays. *Die Macht der Gewohnheit (The Force of Habit),* has been translated, was briefly performed at the National Theatre in London in 1976, and proved a resounding failure. But apart from that, his name has hardly been mentioned.

And, admittedly, Bernhard is a strange and bewildering writer. His deep pessimism, the blackness of his humour, his predilection for a basically monologic form, both in the novel and the short story, and in the theatre, point to a kinship with Beckett; yet there are very profound differences between them as well. Bernhard is a wholly original writer whose roots might perhaps be sought in Kleist and Stifter (as the sources of the remarkable purity and directness of his style in his prose and the free verse of his dramatic works) as well as in the German expressionist theatre, Wedekind and Strindberg, rather than in any contemporary models. (pp. 367-68)

[Bernhard's theatre] is devoid of plot in the conventional sense. It is, essentially, a theatre of images, static situations that are merely gradually elaborated and intensified. . . . (p. 371)

[In each of his plays] there is an almost total absence of surprise, suspense or development. The opening scene, the opening image tells us all. And yet audiences are held by them. Why?

Above all, perhaps, because the images themselves are visually compelling: a stage populated by paraplegics in wheelchairs, a wagon filled with costumed circus performers trying to rehearse chamber music, ridiculously vain VIPs sitting next to the wax images of their authentically great predecessors—these are images interesting enough to be contemplated at length, even if the dialogue is endlessly repetitive. Indeed, repetition is the main verbal device employed by Bernhard to achieve an almost hypnotic effect. . . . All of Bernhard's plays are written in [a] characteristic form of unrhymed free verse without punctuation signs. Only the occasional appearance of a capital letter at the beginning of a line indicates a new sentence. (pp. 372-73)

[Perhaps] Bernhard—trained musician that he is—adopts a musical principle of construction. He uses words in endlessly varied repetition as musical structural elements: a phrase . . . is stated, inverted, varied, repeated and then repeated again in its inverted form. Then a new structural element is brought in . . . and combined with the first one, the new combination inverted and varied, till another fresh element is introduced and added to the previously used elements . . . and after a while the earlier *motif* becomes sparser and is finally dropped—but only to reappear suddenly and unexpectedly at a later stage. In most of his plays, moreover, Bernhard uses certain phrases as constantly recurring *leitmotifs:* in *The Force of Habit,* for example, the sentence ''tomorrow in Augsburg'' (referring to the circus's next stop on its tour) occurs on almost every page. Simple as it is, it carries a multitude of associations and overtones in a number of different contexts: it is used as an indication of the transitoriness of the present situation and a hope of better things to come (''tomorrow things will go better''); it also functions in the opposite sense, in connection with phrases expressing contempt for Augsburg as a filthy second-rate provincial city (''another hopeless place tomorrow''); it is used as a threat when, for example, Caribaldi tells his granddaughter that tomorrow in Augsburg he will buy her the textbooks she will have to learn by heart; and the phrase—the last one spoken in the play—functions as the final expression of hopelessness and defeat when Caribaldi utters it as he sinks, discomfited, into his armchair. And for those in the know, it carries an additional malicious overtone: for Augsburg is Brecht's home town and thus exemplifies an epic theatre of plot and meaning, everything that Bernhard's theatre exphatically tries *not* to be.

The use of repetition as a musical, structural element differentiates Bernhard's utilisation of this device from that of other contemporary dramatists—notably Pinter—who are mainly concerned to show that real speech in real situations *is* largely repetitious. In Bernhard's case, there is no pretence to naturalism. His dramatic language—he uses quite different devices in his narrative prose—is strictly rhythmical. Each line of verse contains one rhythmical element; at the end of each line there must be a pause for breath. There is no *enjambement*. Every new sentence indicated by the use of a capital letter must start at the beginning of a line.

But, without ever pretending to naturalism, Bernhard also uses his rhythmic structural pattern to indicate the disintegration of human speech and communication. Language frequently literally *crumbles* in the mouths of his characters, dissolves into crumbs of half-expressed meaning. (p. 374)

The stylisation of halting, panting and half-completed speech into poetic patterns has only one striking parallel in classical German literature—in the work of Kleist. It is not without significance that in *The Hunting-Party* the writer (who is shown as writing a play about a hunting-party and thus clearly represents Bernhard himself) refers to Kleist when he tells the general's wife that the general seeks to draw him into conversations about his writing:

> About literature he wants to talk
> for example about Heinrich von Kleist
> but I
> do not like talking about it.

Nor is it without significance that Heinrich von Kleist committed suicide. Suicide is one of Bernhard's main themes, both in his narrative prose and in his plays.

Even though in [the dialogue between the writer and the general's wife in the opening of the second scene] . . . , both characters appear to be speaking to each other, nevertheless the basic structure remains essentially monologic. As the writer's half sentences are never finished, their meaning remains known only to himself. And indeed such passages of relatively equal interaction of two characters are rare in Bernhard's dramatic *oeuvre*. The essential pattern is that of a dominant speaker holding forth to a second character who either is completely speechless or only occasionally answers a question or makes a monosyllabic remark. (p. 376)

Throughout all these plays, form and thematic content are strictly one: there is no genuine dialogue in Bernhard because his chief characters are entirely enclosed in separate inner worlds. There are no love scenes or love interests in any of Bernhard's works—narrative or dramatic—because monologue does not allow genuine intereaction between human beings. Any interaction that takes place is thus purely mechanical, as that between puppets. Bernhard's earliest dramatic efforts were written for marionettes. He regards and deliberately designs his characters as basically no different from puppets—simply because he is convinced that people in real life are, with very few exceptions, barely conscious, let alone able to act otherwise than as merely propelled by mechanical instincts and reflexes; that, in fact, living human beings, in the mass, are no better than marionettes. In the epigraph to *The Hunting-Party*, Bernhard quotes Kleist's famous treatise on the puppet theatre: "I inquired after the mechanism of these figures and how it was possible to govern their individual parts and points without having myriads of threads on one's fingers, in the manner required by the rhythm of their movements or their dance." Clearly his own solution for producing this kind of movement or rhythm of his puppets is to create a pattern of rhythmical, intersecting monologues utted by puppet-like characters.

In the real world, the chief triggers for the mechanism that actuates man, the marionette, and makes him twitch and jump are madness and disease. Both in his narrative prose and in his plays, Bernhard never stops stressing that point. Life itself is a disease only curable by death. Cripples and madmen merely exhibit, more plainly and therefore perhaps more frankly, what all men suffer from beneath the surfce. And even "genius is a disease," as the doctor asserts in *The Ignoramus and the Madman*.

In Bernhard's short stories, novellas and novels, this point of view is relentlessly expounded in deep seriousness. Yet his dramatic work is different: the themes are the same, but the atmosphere is ambivalent. The artificiality of the prosody, the clarity of the musical structure combined with the compression and exaggeration caused by the absence of the subtler halftones of the *internal* monologue of the novels or their long passages of reported speech, produces a strangely disturbing effect. Is this theatre stark tragedy? Or crude horror-mongering melodrama? Or is it intended to be comic, almost farcical?

Here, I believe, lies one of the sources of the peculiar fascination of Bernhard's theatre. In West Germany, where he has had his most spectacular triumphs, most of his plays, notably *A Feast for Boris, The Force of Habit* and *The Hunting-Party*, have been received with solemn seriousness, although *The Force of Habit*, for one, is actually subtitled "comedy" by the author himself. The West German theatre public, following the West German critics, tends to look for deep significance and profound philosophical and social meaning. One might say that this public veritably wallows in self-laceration, gloom and tragedy. I should venture to suggest that as an Austrian—and the Austrian tradition of theatre is one of pure entertainment, light-hearted amusement—Bernhard is tempted to make fun of this tendency of the German theatre-going public. . . . Bernhard's theatre thus does not merely seem to me to be basically comic in intention, but arguably the chief comic effect produced by it is that of the audience solemnly taking it as tragedy. The person who is really amused by it the one who has the best laugh, is the playwright himself. These plays are, at least in one important regard (they are, of course, so complex and multilayered that they also display many other intriguing aspects), aggressions against the solemn, educated audience—the "Bildungsbourgeoisie"—as it only exists in West Germany today. As the unnamed hero of the story *Watten* puts it: "We live in a cabarettistic world, in which the high art of imagining life as well as the even higher art of Life and Existence itself are being derided. When I wake up I connect with my name a cabarettistic existence. Every day I commit suicide in a cabarettistic manner. Philosophy cabarettistic. Religion cabarettistic. A war, a huge heap of corpses, dear Sir, a whole mendacious continent, today they are but a joke."

Despair thus turns into derision, and that derision crystallizes in Bernhard's theatre, which can be seen as a savage aggression against the public itself. Bernhard's work is full of remarks displaying a burning hatred not only of the masses of humanity in general, but of the theatre audience in particular. . . . Is he, in piling horror upon horror, repetition upon repetition, venting his outrage upon the spectators, cocking a snook at their readiness to read deep philosophical profundities into what are often quite clearly parodies of famous plays (think of the numerous parallels between **The Hunting-Party** and *The Cherry Orchard*, **Minetti** and *King Lear*) or accumulations of grotesque images of that audience's own humourlessness?

The clearest indication of this derisive aggression against the audience is furnished by **Immanuel Kant**. Here the audience is presented with Immanuel Kant crossing the Atlantic on a luxury liner accompanied by his wife. Everyone knows that Kant died before the age of luxury liners and that he never married. Yet a modern, earnest theatre audience, in the age of the Theatre of the Absurd, is prepared for everything. After all, we have seen Hamlet in modern dress, the Trojan women of Euripides as Vietnamese war victims. There might, after all, be a profound meaning in putting the greatest of all German philosophers into our own time. . . . So will the great Kant not utter great truths even in this anachronistic allegorical modern theatrical situation? He does make pronouncements like:

> Everything that is
> is
> everything that is not
> is not
> The world is the flip side
> of the world
> Truth is the flip side
> of the truth . . .

Here the author clearly is testing the audience's capacity to remain solemnly interested in what is deliberate flood of derisive nonsense unleashed upon them. Will they remain in eager expectancy to receive a final allegorically encoded massage? Is the author polemizing against Kantian philosophy? In the last scene, abruptly Bernhard shows that the man on whose lips the audience has been hanging because he called himself Kant is a harmless madman. . . . And, indeed, the chief characters of *all* of Bernhard's plays are plainly mad: the Good Lady; Caribaldi; the mad doctor and the ignoramus; the president; the bloated, animal-headed VIPs with their bitchy show business talk; Minetti; Kant; the cantankerous world reformer; Hoeller, the complacent ex-Nazi judge. The writer of **The Hunting-Party** is the solitary exception, but he is writing a play in which improbable horrors are accumulated for an audience who will take them for tragedy while they are in fact parody, farce.

Bernhard's theatre, if this analysis is correct, can thus be seen as a gigantic practical joke against the "consumers of culture," the solemn, pretentious German theatre audience. Bernhard is—or presents himself in his public persona—as a confirmed misanthrope whose hatred of mankind, of course, includes self-hatred. . . . Bernhard's main impulse appears as a destructive one. He presents himself in public as an arch destroyer. In an interview which predated his emergence as a major playwright he said, talking about his work as a writer of fiction: "I am . . . not a teller of tales, I basically hate stories. I am a destroyer of stories, I am the typical destroyer of stories." There is doubtless a similarly destructive motivation behind his activity as a playwright.

But if we are faced here with a gigantic act of provocation . . . , an enormous rude gesture at the audience—and the critics who indulge in solemn exegesis of that rude gesture—what is its value?

Seen from the angle from which it is here contemplated, Bernhard's theatrical *oeuvre* can be valued as an exuberant comic creation, a grotesque Dance of Death, an exuberant release of destructive impulses, of Swiftian *saeva indignatio,* an impassioned Philippic against all the pretentiousness and folly of his civilization. What make this outburst of misanthropy and self-hatred remarkable and puts it into proximity to such similar outpourings of misanthropy as Goya's or Daumier's grotesques or the visions of Hieronymus Bosch is not their misanthropy or the hatred they exude but the artistry with which these impulses are hammered into shape. Bernhard's theatre is essentially a *mannerist* theatre. If his characters are puppets, all the greater the skill with which they perform their intricate dance; if his subject-matter is venom and derision, all the more admirable the perfection of the language in which the venom is spat out, the intricacy of the patterns it creates. (pp. 377-83)

Martin Esslin, "A Drama of Disease and Derision: The Plays of Thomas Bernhard," in Modern Drama, *Vol. XXIII, No. 4, January, 1981, pp. 367-84.*

FRANCIS MICHAEL SHARP

The historical past forms a particularly important backdrop for the first volume of Bernhard's autobiographical works, **Die Ursache** (**The Cause**; 1975). It spans the years from 1943 to 1946, which the adolescent Bernhard spent in his native Salzburg as a boarding-school student. The analytic intent of the author is to lay bare the origins of what has been called his catastrophic world view, his bitterness toward Austria and Salzburg, his anger at institutionalized education and religion, his uncompromising hopelessness and misanthropy. He is particularly incensed by the memories of the hypocrisy of this period, during which he witnessed the effortless transition from the fascist administration of his school to an equally authoritarian and repressive Catholic administration. . . .

Suicide or escape are the inevitable alternatives toward which the tensions in Bernhard's life build in **Die Ursache**. Catharsis comes on the day when the fifteen-year-old youth decides to find employment rather than return to school. In **Der Keller** (**The Cellar**; 1976), the second volume of the trilogy, Bernhard depicts this decision as one for life over death. For the following three years as an apprentice in a grocery store, feelings of personal usefulness and satisfaction temporarily dispel the gloom of the previous ones. Bernhard sees this period as a return to the self from the alienating schoolroom and as an emergence from social isolation. He had earlier learned from his grandfather, a minor writer, the demands for solitude placed on the artistic and intellectual personality. His mentor during the apprenticeship years, the store's proprietor, teaches him the lessons of social intercourse with the inhabitants of Scherzhauserfeldsiedlung, an impoverished quarter of Salzburg. There is even a place during these years for emotions such as hope and happiness.

The final volume of Bernhard's autobiographical trilogy demonstrates what fragile and fleeting moments these are in human existence. For a motto to this book, **Der Atem** (**The Breath**, 1978), Bernhard chose a passage from Pascal: "Since men were unable to overcome death, misery and ignorance, in order to be happy they came to an agreement not to think of them."

Bernhard, now eighteen years old, spends the greater part of the time recorded in these pages in a condition too near death to be able to ignore it. After he had contracted a dangerous lung ailment working at the grocery store, he delayed having it treated until it was almost too late. When he finally was taken to the hospital, he was placed in a room full of patients waiting to die. Death became for him an everyday occurrence during the extended period which he spent in this *Sterbezimmer*. (p. 603)

Bernhard was forty-four years old when *Die Ursache* appeared, relatively young to have begun an autobiography. His chief motivation, he explains, was the fear that a further passage of years would entirely erase the bitter subjective reality of the time and put the truth beyond reach. . . . He constantly reminds the reader of the unbridgeable distance which he already feels toward that truth. Working from scraps of memory and apparently without a diary, Bernhard brings our attention to the difficulty in merging his feelings as an adolescent and his present thinking into a written form that corresponds to his pat experience. . . . Another motivation underlying his turn to autobiography stems from an imperative that introspective writers have responded to for centuries: Know thyself. Calling on Montaigne as his spiritual model, he demands of himself a brutally honest self-inventory, finding among his thoughts some which he claims to be unpublishable. . . . The complementary formulation of this imperative appears in another passage, again under the spiritual auspices of Montaigne, in which he declares that his greatest fear is to be misunderstood (*verkannt*) by those who know him only by name. . . . To know one's self and to prevent this self from being "falsely known" are considerations present to some degree either explicitly or implicitly in all autobiographical writing.

Bernhard considers all of his writing as disturbance and irritation and himself as the perpetual *Störenfried* or disturber of the peace. . . . After returning in numerous prose and dramatic works in the sixties and seventies to familiar constellations of characters and landscapes, to basic themes and motifs, he may have foreseen an inevitable weakening of this effect. Before the three volumes of his autobiography began to appear, one critic suggested that he had reached a point at which only a direct articulation of his *Leidensprozes*, his process of suffering, unadorned by fiction and spoken in the first person, could return full credibility to his work. Bernhard's autobiographical works do indeed seem like a reply to this critic's suggestion. They function as an authentication, an existential basis of credibility to avoid the fate of the unheeded Cassandra, his ancestress in legend. (p. 604)

> *Francis Michael Sharp, "Literature As Self-Reflection: Thomas Bernhard and Peter Handke," in* World Literature Today, *Vol. 55, No. 4, Autumn, 1981, pp. 603-07.**

STELLA P. ROSENFELD

Die Kälte is the fourth volume of what promises to be a lengthy series of autobiographical reminiscences. As in its predecessor, *Der Atem* (1978 . . .), here too the author treats only a brief period of his life and offers a detailed chronicle of his illness. . . .

Die Kälte is as much a metaphor for the hopelessness of human existence, for life as a sickness unto death, as it is a personal account of suffering. It abounds with recognizable truths and powerful descriptions and impresses the reader with its com-

plete honesty. Yet the awkward, long-winded, monotonous style and the lack of compassion for the very human condition that seems to be at its core make *Die Kälte* a tedious and dreary book. Indeed, if it were not for the occasional intimations of familial attachments and friendships, it could be termed cold, even callous. Paradoxical as it may seem, the book is nevertheless strangely fascinating and compelling.

> *Stella P. Rosenfeld, in a review of "Die Kälte," in* World Literature Today, *Vol. 56, No. 2, Spring, 1982, p. 326.*

JOHN SIMON

An Austrian who detests Austria and Austrians, a human being who confronts humanity with the greatest mistrust, a writer who puts his faith in writing even while his every sentence attests to his doubt of its efficacy, a man for whom life is at best grotesque and the grave is the goal cannot help attracting the brighter children of a century that flirts with torment and skirts doom. Such a writer is Thomas Bernhard, the 53-year-old poet, playwright, novelist and storyteller, whose following among literati, intellectuals and cultural fellow travelers grows steadily while the rest of the world blithely ignores him.

Three of his novels—**"Gargoyles"** (whose German title, **"Verstörung,"** a word coined by Mr. Bernhard, is bleaker but untranslatable), **"The Lime Works"** and **"Correction"**—have been available in English translations. Now, so is the novella **"Concrete"** (meaning the building material, not the opposite of "abstract"), first published in German in 1982. . . .

"Concrete," which is easier going than some of Mr. Bernhard's work, has minimal action. Rudolf, a well-to-do but always unwell musicologist, has been working for 10 years on his magnum opus, a study of Mendelssohn but, unable to think up the lead sentence, he hasn't written a word. Nothing but notes. He has published little—he considers publishing a crime—and is, clearly, a hypochondriac. His sarcoidosis is not that serious an illness and responds to prednisone (called Prednisolon in German and rendered by the otherwise able translator, David McLintock, as "prednisolone"). Rudolf lives in a country house in a village, Peiskam, where, apart from visits from his housekeeper, he receives only Elizabeth, his hated sister. . . .

But gradually, as Rudolf ruminates—the novel is a set of his notes—the hatred for his sister yields to love-hate, and, finally, to a symbiosis very much like love. Her involvement with the Catholic clergy, her sexual activities, her wheeling and dealing are viewed with a kind of admiring scorn; eventually she is even granted a considerable intellect. The bond is one of "being impossible, erratic, capricious and vacillating,' which "always got on other people's nerves and yet has never ceased to fascinate them and make them seek our company [there's the standard Bernhardian paradox]—fundamentally because we're capricious, erratic, vacillating and unreliable [there's the not-quite-repetition]."

Otherwise **"Concrete"** records Rudolf's meditation on work, intensive but nonproductive; society, omnipresent but mad, stupid and cruel; and life, minimal and mostly pointless. . . .

Is Rudolf one of the walking dead? Mr. Bernhard's characters are drawn to death, either jaggedly harrying themselves toward it or helplessly drifting into it. There is no actual talk of suicide in **"Concrete,"** but the hero of **"Correction"** writes, "We're a nation of suicides . . . but only a small percentage actually kill themselves . . . even though we hold the world's record for suicide." In **"Gargoyles"** a character remarks, "Everything is suicide. What we live, what we read, what we think: training for suicide." But in what may be Mr. Bernhard's finest work to date, . . . [his] autobiographical volumes not yet available in English, he says, "I absolutely had the feeling of being saved when I recognized the possibilities of complete aloneness and took possession of them." Does Rudolf have this chance? Or can he at least claim what the hero of Mr. Bernhard's short story **"Jauregg"** avers, "So every evening . . . something sets in that does not let me despair, although I would *have* to despair, although in truth I *am* desperate."

No wonder Rudolf favors Mendelssohn, of whom Schumann wrote, "He is the most radiant musician, the one who most clearly saw through the contradictions of our age and first reconciled them." But can Rudolf write his book? "Time," he feels, "destroys everything we do, whatever it is." . . . In a speech he gave accepting the Anton Wildgans literary prize, Mr. Bernhard said, "When we're on the traces of the truth without knowing what this truth is, which has nothing in common with reality save that truth we do not know, then it is foundering, it is death on whose traces we are." Yet Wildgans, the Austrian poet-playwright in whose name the prize is given, was an optimist. Not so Mr. Bernhard, the narrator of whose first novel, **"Frost,"** reports on "expeditions into the jungles of aloneness." **"Concrete"** is such an expedition—a small one, through a small jungle. But the aloneness is enormous.

John Simon, "The Sun Never Rises on Rudolf," in The New York Times Book Review, *July 1, 1984, p. 9.*

Elizabeth Bishop

1911-1979

American poet, short story writer, editor, and translator.

Bishop's reputation as an accomplished poet rests on a small but significant body of highly crafted verse. Describing nature and experience with meticulous detail, Bishop often employed unusual metaphors and surreal images to portray an unsettling world. Critics frequently compare Bishop's subtle wit and close attention to detail to that of her friend and mentor, Marianne Moore. Bishop received the Pulitzer Prize for poetry for *Poems: North & South; A Cold Spring* (1955), the National Book Award for *The Complete Poems* (1969), and the National Book Critics' Circle Award for *Geography III* (1976). In addition, in 1976 Bishop became the first American to receive the Neustadt International Prize for literature.

Due to her father's death and her mother's nervous breakdown, Bishop spent her childhood with relatives in Nova Scotia and Massachusetts. After graduating from Vassar College in 1934, she traveled extensively in Europe and North Africa before settling in Key West, Florida. In 1951 she moved to Brazil, where she resided for fifteen years before returning to the United States to teach at Harvard University. Not only have these experiences imbued Bishop's poetry with varied settings and imagery, but travel is a central metaphor in her work, often symbolizing the search for self. In Bishop's poetry, dislocation, loneliness, and constant doubt are associated with such a search, but an acceptance of hardship prevails. In the title poem of her collection *Questions of Travel* (1965) Bishop wonders whether or not it was wise to leave the stability and familiarity of home to travel abroad. The poem implies that without continual risk and uncertainty there can be no spiritual growth. The importance of self-discovery is also emphasized in many of the poems in *Geography III* (1976). The most famous of these, "In the Waiting Room," concerns young Elizabeth's sudden awareness of both the division and connection between herself and the world.

The nature of reality is a prominent theme of the poems in *Poems: North & South; A Cold Spring*. In "The Map" a land map is used to symbolize the difference between objective reality and reproductions of it. The poem suggests that because works of art are slanted by the creator's subjective perceptions, they are as much guides to that individual's imagination as to the objects or ideas being imitated. Similarly, in "At the Fishhouses" and "Cape Breton" Bishop expresses the elusiveness of ultimate reality.

Bishop is considered a master of descriptive verse. Her calm, understated tone and the ease with which she gradually shifts from observations of ordinary objects to philosophical insights are also highly regarded. In his poem "For Elizabeth Bishop 4" Robert Lowell refers to Bishop as an "unerring Muse who makes the casual perfect." Although her poetry is often personal, critics note that Bishop avoids self-pity and egoism and extends her themes from the specific to the universal. Bishop's works of fiction, which are fewer than her works of poetry, have been praised for similar qualities; critic and poet D. J. Enright remarks that "like her poetry, Elizabeth Bishop's

© Thomás Victor 1984

prose is precise, cool, unexcited, flat, with never a trace of pointing up."

Published posthumously, both *The Complete Poems: 1927-1979* (1983) and *The Collected Prose* (1984) have elicited retrospective analyses of her works and have reinforced the widespread critical opinion that Bishop's opus is an important contribution to recent twentieth-century literature.

(See also *CLC*, Vols. 1, 4, 9, 13, 15; *Contemporary Authors*, Vols. 5-8, rev. ed., Vols. 89-92 [obituary]; *Something about the Author*, Vol. 24; and *Dictionary of Literary Biography*, Vol. 5.)

ROBERT LOWELL

[*The essay from which this excerpt is taken originally appeared in* Sewanee Review, *Summer 1947.*]

On the surface, [Elizabeth Bishop's poems in *North & South*] are observations—surpassingly accurate, witty and well-arranged, but nothing more. Sometimes she writes of a place where she has lived on the Atlantic Coast; at others, of a dream, a picture, or some fantastic object. One is reminded of Kafka and certain abstract paintings, and is left rather at sea about the actual subjects of the poems. I think that at least nine-tenths of them fall into a single symbolic pattern. Characterizing it is an elusive business.

There are two opposing factors. The first is something in motion, weary but persisting, almost always failing and on the point of disintegrating, and yet, for the most part, stoically maintained. This is morality, memory, the weed that grows to divide, and the dawn that advances, illuminates and calls to work, the monument "that wants to be a monument," the waves rolling in on the shore, breaking, and being replaced, the echo of the hermit's voice saying, "love must be put in action"; it is the stolid little mechanical horse that carries a dancer, and all those things of memory that "cannot forget us half so easily as they can forget themselves." The second factor is a terminus: rest, sleep, fulfillment or death. This is the imaginary iceberg, the moon which the Man-moth thinks is a small clean hole through which he must thrust his head; it is sleeping on the top of a mast, and the peaceful ceiling: "But oh, that we could sleep up there."

The motion-process is usually accepted as necessary and, therefore, good; yet it is dreary and exhausting. But the formula is mysterious and gently varies with its objects. The terminus is sometimes pathetically or humorously desired as a letting-go or annihilation; sometimes it is fulfillment and the complete harmonious exercise of one's faculties. The rainbow of spiritual peace seen as the author decides to let a fish go, is both like and unlike the moon which the Man-moth mistakes for an opening. In **"Large Bad Picture,"** ships are at anchor in a northern bay, and the author reflects, "It would be hard to say what brought them there / Commerce or contemplation."

The structure of a Bishop poem is simple and effective. It will usually start as description or descriptive narrative, then either the poet or one of her characters or objects reflects. The tone of these reflections is pathetic, witty, fantastic, or shrewd. Frequently, it is all these things at once. Its purpose is to heighten and dramatize the description and, at the same time, to unify and universalize it. In this, and in her marvelous command of shifting speech-tones, Bishop resembles Robert Frost.

In her bare objective language, she also reminds one at times of William Carlos Williams; but it is obvious that her most important model is Marianne Moore. Her dependence should not be defined as imitation, but as one of development and transformation. It is not the dependence of her many facile contemporaries on Auden, but the dependence of Herrick on Jonson, the Herberts on Donne, or of Pope and Johnson on Dryden. Although Bishop would be unimaginable without Moore, her poems add something to the original, and are quite as genuine. Both poets use an elaborate descriptive technique, love exotic objects, are moral, genteel, witty, and withdrawn. There are metrical similarities, and a few of Bishop's poems are done in Moore's manner. But the differences in method and personality are great. Bishop is usually present in her poems; they happen to her, she speaks, and often centers them on herself. Others are dramatic and have human actors. She uses dreams and allegories. (Like Kafka's, her treatment of the absurd is humorous, matter of fact, and logical.) She hardly ever quotes from other writers. Most of her meters are accentual-syllabic. Compared with Moore, she is softer, dreamier, more human and more personal; she is less idiosyncratic, and less magnificent. She is probably slighter; of course, being much younger, she does not have nearly so many extraordinarily good poems.

Bishop's faults leave her best poems uninjured. . . . A few of the shorter poems seem to me quite trivial. On rereading them, one is struck by something a little pert, banal, and over-pointed—it is as though they had been simplified for a child. Occasionally the action seems blurred and foggy especially when she is being most subjective, as in **"Anaphora."** In others, such as **"The Map," "Casabianca"** and **"The Gentleman from Shallot,"** she is self-indulgent, and strings a whimsical commentary on an almost non-existent subject.

Few books of lyrics are as little repetitious as *North & South.* It can be read straight through with excitement. About ten of its thirty poems are failures. Another ten are either unsatisfactory as wholes, or very slight. This leaves **"Roosters"** and **"The Fish,"** large and perfect, and, outside of Marianne Moore, the best poems that I know of written by a woman in this century. (pp. 186-88)

> *Robert Lowell, "From 'Thomas, Bishop, and Williams',"* in Elizabeth Bishop and Her Art, *edited by Lloyd Schwartz and Sybil P. Estess, The University of Michigan Press, 1983, pp. 186-89.**

BONNIE COSTELLO

[The essay from which this excerpt is taken was written in 1977.]

In Elizabeth Bishop's poetry, geography is not for adventurers looking out from a center at the horizon, not for imperialists seeking to appropriate that horizon. Rather, it is the recourse of those hoping to discover, out of the flux of images, where they are and how to get home again. Bishop's poetry accepts our uncertain relation to other times, places, and things, suggesting we have no "self" otherwise, and no home.

It is in this context that I would like to discuss the pervasiveness of the impersonal and the interrogative in her work. I want to show that, paradoxically, for Bishop, questions are assertions. However open-endedly, they structure experience and self-awareness. Like compasses, they point to something absolute we can neither see nor get to; yet in their pointing, they show us where we are. These questions, posed to an impersonal world, turn inward when it refuses to reply. Questions about the world become, then, obliquely, questions about ourselves. While the personal begins in assumptions about the self, the impersonal usually undermines or ignores the self. But in Bishop's poetry the impersonal is not depersonalized because its form is interrogative rather than negative.

These impersonal and interrogative modes tend to promote a feeling of disunity and disorientation, but for Bishop these are precisely the conditions conducive to discovery. Not surprisingly, travel is her major metaphor. Almost every poem treats the experience of travel ambivalently, for while finalities may be static or illusory, constant change is unsettling. Bishop does not resolve this ambivalence, but she eases it by offering her characters, and her readers, fleeting but calming moments of coalescence. (pp. 109-10)

The epigraph to *Geography III,* from *First Lessons in Geography,* begins with questions and answers; but the answers are soon dropped and only the questions continue. They are, we learn, firmer and more real than the answers. Bishop was always a student of geography, but her third level of geography steps back, slightly, from all the travelling, charting, and measuring, to consider the motives and impulses behind these activities. She still asks, Where is Nova Scotia? and Where is Brazil? but in the latest work she opens up previously implicit questions: *"What is a Map?"* and *"What is Geography?"*, versions of: What am I doing? and What and where am I? (p. 110)

The seven-year-old heroine of **"In the Waiting Room,"** the first poem in *Geography III,* asks no questions at first, having little trouble knowing who or where she is.... But wintery Worcester recedes into twilight, and the apparent hierarchy of time and space goes with it. Her aunt *seems* to be inside a long time, while she reads and studies the photographs of far-off places in the *National Geographic*. Then, the hinges of distance and duration come loose and the constructed self flaps precariously. The very layout of the magazine presses ordered differences into explosive proximity, forcing a violently widened definition of the human. The decorously English, well-protected "Osa and Martin Johnson / dressed in riding breeches, / laced boots, and pith helmets," stand side by side with the vulnerable and contagious "dead man slung on a pole," "babies with pointed heads," and "black, naked women" with "horrifying" breasts, creating a "perspective by incongruity" on humanity.

The child doesn't articulate her fascination, of course, but the very fact that she is "too shy to stop" implies that she is somehow brought home to herself here. She fixes her eyes on "the cover: / the yellow margins, the date" as a way of avoiding contact, but these form a fragile interface. The date, which should be a way of protecting boundaries, becomes rather, a sign of contact between this strange world and her own. She loses her balance over the side of the cover, and in a sudden moment of undifferentiation between Aunt Consuelo and herself, a cry "from inside" the dentist's office seems to come literally "from inside" her mouth. "I—we—were falling, falling, / our eyes glued to the cover / of the *National Geographic*, / February, 1918." She clings to the cover as to the rung of a ladder which has come loose from the structure supporting it. The bits and pieces of the personal ("three days / and you'll be seven years old") no longer have much meaning.

The intensity and strangeness of the experience derives not only from the slip into undifferentiation, but from the sense of difference preserved. This is not a pure moment of symbiosis, for there is always an emphasis on how "unlikely" this likeness is. The similarity between Osa and Martin Johnson and the "black, naked women" is never expressed except in the fact of juxtaposition, although the image of the volcano forces them together by its implied threat to human life. Similarly, the difference between the child and her "foolish, timid" Aunt is preserved even while it is denied by the cry of pain. This sense of differences is especially clear in the awkwardness of the child's attempts to come to terms with the experience: "you are an *I*, / you are an *Elizabeth*, / you are one of *them*." Making self both subject and predicate, she still preserves the difference.

A shocking experience of identification, as we have seen, creates a simultaneous loss of original identity, and this loss is never overcome. The inscrutable volcano, the inside of the child's mouth, the dentist's chamber, are all figures for the abyss the child has discovered, and as she peers into it she is full of questions, another and another—why? what? how?—until she is thrown back into the exclamatory "how 'unlikely'" and it is clear they will never be answered. But the transformation of question into exclamation does create a sense of recognition, even if it is the permanently strange that is recognized. We get only a "sidelong glance," not fulfillment or total recognition. Yet, for a moment, this glance does begin

to organize the dualities toward some unutterable simplicity. The questions mediate between absolute difference and undifferentiation, between stillness and total flux, and in this way, however fleetingly, accommodate the self most. The experience in the dentist's office never attains a new, more genuine orientation. But in a fundamental way, the speaker is "brought home to herself" by moving through these questions, even while they are left unanswered. Indeed, many of Bishop's characters lose themselves to find themselves. Like the speaker in George Herbert's "Love Unknown," which Bishop has juxtaposed with this poem, the young Elizabeth is made "new, tender, quick" through her sudden disorientation. It serves as a kind of baptism. In one sense, then, the child experiences a traumatic leap into the impersonal, the unfamiliar. But in a more profound sense, she discovers the personal. Somehow she would have been less herself, finally, if she had picked up *Dick and Jane*, a mirror of her own complacent sense of herself, rather than the *National Geographic*. Probably both were there for her on the waiting room table. But the inquisitive mind goes toward what is not obviously of the self, and it is clear that even then, Bishop was a traveller at heart. (pp. 111-13)

We have seen that Bishop constantly questions her surroundings, and inevitably in the process, questions her perspective. The usual comfort of home is, of course, that we can take it for granted, but for this very reason Bishop is never quite "at home." In the poem under discussion she is, in fact, in a "waiting room." There is certainly no place more impersonal. But precisely because she is not "at home," discovery is possible. A waiting room has very little definition as a place in itself—it is not a home or a destination, but only a transitional space where transitional time is spent. The object of those gathered there, what binds them, does not take place in the room they share but elsewhere, individually. And because it has no function in its own right, it is a place where anything can happen.

Most of the enclosed places Bishop describes are waiting rooms in one way or another (the most extreme being a wake). Her ports, islands, bights, are not microcosms of, or escapes from, history; they contain the tides of unity and discontinuity, of presence and absence, with much the same incompleteness as any wider experience of flux. But while they do not frame or displace the world, do not define us as a home does, they do become places to encounter the world in a focused way. (pp. 114-15)

Bishop's characters never appear in places of origin or destination. Her poems are not without idealized dwellings, but these are only viewed from the outside, in a speculative attitude.... The proto-/crypto-dream-house of **"The End of March"** where otherness is happily contained in self-reflection, in the "diaphanous blue flame ... doubled in the window," is "perfect" but "boarded up." The reality of the beach strollers is temporal, and so is their knowledge. Their vision of the house remains conjectural.... (p. 115)

We have been dealing with the mode of the impersonal primarily in terms of theme, setting, situation. But of course the term is most applicable to a discussion of the speaker. Personal narration is precluded by Bishop's view that the self is amorphous in an amorphous world. Instead, we get a variety of distancing techniques, which bring order to the poems without belying their vision of flux, and without lending privilege to a single perspective.

Often these homeless figures are presented by a detached, third-person narrator, who sees their familiar structures foundering but can imagine a larger womblike mystery. The **"Squatter's Children"** "play at digging holes," at creating roots in the wider, mysterious world which is more meaningful than the "specklike house," the shelter from which their mother's voice, "ugly as sin," calls them to come in. The description repeatedly reveals their vulnerability. Their laughter, "weak flashes of inquiry," is not answered; their "little, soluble, / unwarrantable ark" will not sustain them far. And yet their questioning, digging natures are never really criticized. The narrator intrudes to affirm and reassure their "rights in rooms of falling rain." They are, in a sense, housed in the obscurity of the storm, even as the ark of their selves founders.

Above the mist, from where this impersonal narrator views the landscape, humans look as insignificant as Brueghel's Icarus. Among other things, the impersonal mode puts humanity in perspective. We are continually reminded of a reality that goes on quite aside from our human frame of reference. In **"Cape Breton,"** signs of humanity are almost completely absorbed by the vaster landscape. . . . In this deeply impersonal world, where the "thin mist follows / the white mutations of its dream" humanity looks slight and transient indeed. And yet, as in Brueghel's paintings, the human element is privileged, as a focus of interest if not power.

These detached narratives are among the most placid of Bishop's poems precisely because they put human confusion and loss, as well as human authority, "in perspective." By looking from above, they locate humanity in its wanderings. In a way they can be seen as acts of self-location. The tiny figures are our surrogates and thus soften our own pain in the midst of uncertainty. In **"Squatter's Children"** the narrator speaks directly out of a perspective from which obscurity no longer threatens. The children are safe in their unawareness, the speaker in a higher awareness. (pp. 117-18)

The impersonal, distanced narrator, then, admits a certain stability where experience is troubled. But Bishop never lets this perspective get complacently ironic. A "believer in total immersion," she continually returns to write poems from a more limited, more bewildered point of view. She enters the consciousness of characters lost in a world bigger than themselves or their ideas and lets them speak out of their limitations. We are invited into an intimacy with these speakers, but the impersonal mode is still doubly preserved. These are masks, not Bishop's own voice, or ours. And it is precisely the problem of the personal that these poems engage. In the dramatic monologues of **"Rainy Season; Sub-Tropics"** for instance, Bishop makes experience particular, while at the same time juxtaposing contradictory views in order to show the limits and errors of each. (p. 118)

We have seen how Bishop protects the reader from the disorientation she depicts, first by impersonal narration and second by a series of masks from which we feel an ironic distance. But in *Geography III* these masks are dangerously familiar. The narrative distance of **"In the Waiting Room"** was not between a character and a creation simply, but between the poet and a memory of her past self. There, the problem of memory became, indirectly, another aspect of the instability of time and place. Crusoe of **"Crusoe in England"** is the most realized of Bishop's first person narrators, and here she allows us almost no ironic distance. Because he is human, because he is less certain in his delusions, because his is the only point of view presented, we are shipwrecked with him. Self-admiring but out of proportion, cut off from his surroundings, he is like the tropical creatures, but more aware of the relativity of his

own dimensions. And his attempts to find himself are inquisitive and creative, even if they don't entirely succeed. This is the longest poem in Bishop's [*Geography III*], one that brings together a great many of the themes, motifs, and images of her other work. Here again is the shipwreck, the self and its structures foundering in an impersonal reality of empty volcanoes, waves that close in (but never completely), mist, dry rock, inscrutable cries of goats and gulls. The island is an odd combination of elements from Cape Breton, scenes in the *National Geographic,* South America, all places where characters have earlier lost themselves in order to find themselves. Here again the speaker begins by putting questions to an outer world, but turns them inward from frustration. Like other characters, Crusoe tries to construct meanings "out of nothing at all, or air" when the world won't provide them; as before, such constructs fail to satisfy or protect. But more powerfully than before the experience is affirmed, despite discomfort and struggle, because of the creative, inquiring and self-reflective attitude it provides. (pp. 119-20)

The first theme of Crusoe . . . is that human order imposed on the landscape never "takes" as real presence. But neither does the landscape answer our questions about its objective order. (p. 122)

When the mind fails to find external objectifications it necessarily turns inward for its comfort. Bishop's position on such gestures is ambivalent. On the one hand they are surrenders to solipsism; on the other hand, they are all the meaning we can manage. From **"Crusoe"** it seems that self-explanation, achieved with self-awareness and humility, is justified. Like the Toad, Snail, and Crab [in **"Rainy Season; Sub-Topics"**], Crusoe begins explaining himself to himself; indeed, like the Snail he carries his own house around with him. But unlike the tropical creatures, he does more than complain or flatter himself; he attempts to construct a home out of the alien materials. Since his surroundings cannot be appropriated, and fail even to register his existence, he creates his own world to reflect himself in. Where love is not offered externally, he discovers self-love: "I felt a deep affection for / the smallest of my island industries." He rejoices over "home-brew" (imagination?) and his weird flute (poetry?).

But as a hero of self-consciousness, Crusoe sees the limits of his creations, and this in turn limits his ability to rejoice in them. . . . Bishop does not finally negate these inventions: by confronting an impersonal world in an inquisitive attitude, we do not verify our own values or self-images, but neither do we replace these constructions with anything else. What we gain, what is missing without this experience of disorientation, is a clearer awareness of the relative nature of our identities and our creations. Such self-consciousness is positive, though it may be disturbing in that it disrupts our notion of the genuineness and discreteness of the self. Finally, to locate ourselves in the world, we need *both* to carve out definitions and to know their limitations. (pp. 122-23)

At the time of the narration, Crusoe is, as the title indicates, "in England," home again. We would expect that homecoming to be the subject of the poem, and yet all but three stanzas deal with Crusoe's experience of shipwreck on a strange island. The point the title makes, of course, is that England is no more "home" than the place of miserable empty volcanoes. In this version of the Crusoe story, civilization is not exalted over nature. . . . Here, he desires that continual struggle he so much hated before. . . . Nostalgia persists as part of the human character, transferred now to the former center of pain. He has moved from questions of place and purpose to questions of the past, as he tries to locate himself now in terms of his former hardships. In England the objects of his past have lost all the moisture of vitality; they are empty symbols. For Crusoe the island is "un-rediscovered, un-renamable." He feels the failure of imagination to give presence to the past: "None of the books has ever got it right." And yet the story *he* tells does become authentic, even in reviving images of desire. For all his world-weariness, Crusoe does succeed in gathering a sense of self precisely *in* images of desire.

Clearly, Bishop does not believe in settling down. We never "find ourselves" in any stable location, but rather in transit. As all her critics point out, travel is her natural, dominant metaphor for the human condition. (pp. 125-26)

In many ways at once, the poem **"Questions of Travel"** is central in Bishop's work, for it both comments on and repeats the structure of the other poems. It again deals with travel, and with the feeling of being lost, overwhelmed by change. It is structured in a series of observations that generate questions rather than answers. And again, the questions move increasingly inward, so that the quest for the external world becomes a quest for the self. The self-reflection at the end of the poem is affirmative in mood, even while it is interrogative in form. (pp. 127-28)

[The poem] finally asks, not only: "Should we have stayed at home" but: Where is home? Home seems to be in question, or rather, in questioning.

But travel without pause is tiring and unsatisfying. The problem of these poems becomes how to present moments of rest and coalescence which nonetheless preserve the sense that our condition is inherently restless. Bishop's solution is to create places, objects, figures representing a unity around which we collect ourselves, but at the same time symbolizing our transience. The double function of these images satisfies our ambivalence about travel. The self is kept expansive even while it experiences a needed coalescence.

The "strangest of theatres" at which the characters of **"Questions of Travel"** arrive, for example, reflects their own condition of motion and confusion. The "streams and clouds keep travelling, travelling, / the mountains look like the hulls of capsized ships." The waterfalls even look like "tearstains." Surely the "strangers in a play" these travellers are watching are themselves. . . . Imagining an absolute other is always a way of imagining an absolute self. Perhaps this is why we are attracted in **"Questions of Travel"** to the "inexplicable old stonework, / inexplicable and impenetrable, / at any view, / instantly seen and always, always delightful." There is no limit here, but neither is there complete flux. Another poem, **"The Fish,"** makes clear that these moments of sudden awareness depend upon the extension as well as the retention of difference. Here the narrator confronts, embodied in a fish she has caught, a universe of other parasitical life, and an infinite past of other similar encounters, thus locating herself in relation to other life and history.

All these are examples of the sudden feeling of home. The strange is suddenly familiar; history and change are brought into immediate focus and coherence. But of course, time and space cannot really be concentrated; the poems draw us back into extension. Though victory fills up the little rented boat in **"The Fish,"** it is not properly ours, and we must let the fish go. "The power to relinquish what one would keep, that is freedom," wrote Marianne Moore, and it seems to be a maxim

Bishop took to heart. The pain of loss and confusion is never trivialized in her poems, and yet it is overpowered by a sense of the value of process. "The art of losing's not too hard to master / though it may look like (*Write* it!) like disaster." In mastering the art of losing we master ourselves.

Possession is not the highest of goals for Bishop, but rather, engagement with the world and with one's self through inquiry, even when distance and difference result. . . . In the human world distances are not . . . easily overcome; questions persist beyond all presences. And yet there is no preference for the nonhuman here. Acts of memory may indeed aggravate our losses, but they may also, like brief encounters with the strange, offer experiences of a sudden coalescence of feelings and associations. (pp. 128-30)

[**"The Moose"**] brings together all the elements—disorientation, dream, travel, sudden strange appearances, memory—which the other poems, in various combinations, introduce. All are elements that help us lose ourselves in order to find ourselves. In **"The Moose,"** the stability of the homeland is transformed into a locus of gentle flux, and the journey begins, travel in space corresponding here to travel in time, to memory. The passengers are again surrounded by fog, by a drowsy confusion, but as the distant narrator, looking sympathetically down on them, knows, it is a homey kind of confusion, softening the "hairy, scratchy, splintery . . . impenetrable wood[s]." Out of this oblivion we overhear a conversation "in Eternity," about pain and loss, where things are "cleared up finally," where an unqualified "yes" is possible. This is not the voice of the people on the bus, nor do they hear it except in a vague dream, and yet it belongs to them as their heritage. And as the moose emerges from the wood, simple in her otherworldliness, an emblem of all that the Grandparents have accepted, the passengers do not understand the relation they have to it, and yet they are moved by it. Strange as it is, it is also "homely as a house / (or, safe as houses)." It offers them a sudden feeling of liberation but also of placement. They coalesce for an instant around this mystery. And like the experience in the waiting room, this one is never defined but only embraced in a question the travellers ask, a question about their own natures and identities:

> Why, why do we feel
> (we all feel) this sweet
> sensation of joy?

The impersonal and the interrogative are essential and pervasive characteristics of Bishop's style, linked by their common source in her uncertain, exploratory relation to the world. Inherent in them are certain aesthetic problems with which she has had to grapple. Since these poems lack the intimacy which urges our attention in other lyrics, they risk our indifference or our disbelief. In her early poetry, Bishop tries to surmount this problem by contriving a "we," "I" and "you" who interact, but only distantly. The impersonal requires that images speak for themselves, and at times in the early work, they are too reticent. But the details that introduce **"The Moose"** accumulate quietly, so that even while we are taken by surprise when events suddenly lift into dream, we are not disturbed because we have been guided by a silent ordering presence. Bishop does not falsify her sense of our situation by interpreting all the details she sets adrift towards us. But neither do we feel entirely alone in the wilderness she creates.

At its weakest, the interrogative mode seems a tic, as pat as any assertion it might overturn. In **"The Map"** and in **"The**

Monument,'' some of the questions seem contrived. But in **"Filling Station,"** **"Faustina,"** and **"First Death in Nova Scotia,"** the questions emerge from a change of consciousness; in *Geography III,* they always seem genuine. We come to poetry with the desire for wholeness and order, and the poet of the interrogative mode must somehow satisfy that need without reducing experience to simple answers. When it works, this is Bishop's greatest poetic achievement: to give us satisfaction even as she remains elusive and reticent, even as she reveals that the question is the final form. For through the impersonal mode she makes the questions our own, our most valued possessions, the very form of our identity. (pp. 131-32)

> *Bonnie Costello, "The Impersonal and the Interrogative in the Poetry of Elizabeth Bishop," in* Elizabeth Bishop and Her Art, *edited by Lloyd Schwartz and Sybil P. Estess, The University of Michigan Press, 1983, pp. 109-32.*

ROBERT PINSKY

[The essay from which this excerpt is taken originally appeared in The New Republic, *November 10, 1979.]*

In Elizabeth Bishop's bizarre, sly, deceptively plainspoken late poem **"Crusoe in England,"** the famous solitary looks back on his life near its end, recalling his isolation and rescue in ways deeper and more unsettling than Defoe could have dreamed. After painting the hallucinatory, vivid island, with hissing volcanoes and hissing giant turtles—an unforgettable terrain—Bishop's Crusoe muses on the dried-out, wan relics of a life. It's tempting, after Elizabeth Bishop's sudden death a few weeks ago, to understand that passage as a master-artist's commentary on the mere furniture of personality and biography—the facts, the manuscripts, the ups and downs of public reputation. . . . In the perspective of loss, and actual feeling, artifacts and art can seem withered remnants. In their modesty of outward manner, and their immensely proud awareness of their own power, Bishop's poems always show us, and never tell us, that they are the exception: in her poems, isolation is suspended, as the artifact rises from the dust to unfold its living soul.

She could afford her indifference toward celebrity, and her cool amusement at the literary museum of biography and criticism, because her work was unequaled in its particular intensity. Rereading Bishop's ***Complete Poems*** [1969], and the more recent *Geography III* (1976), I find the emotional force and penetration of her work amazing. In a way, she had to write *Geography III,* and especially its first two poems (**"In the Waiting Room"** and **"Crusoe in England"**) in order to teach us the fuller extent to which her poems were not merely what critics and fellow-poets had always called them—''perfect,'' ''crafted,'' ''readable,'' ''exquisite''—but profoundly ambitious as well.

The critical cliché for years was to praise Bishop for her ''eye''— a convention she mischievously, perhaps a bit contemptuously, abetted by remarking that her poems were ''just description.'' The purpose of the ''eye'' and of the description (as **"In the Waiting Room"** makes explicit) is for Bishop an act of fierce self-definition: she saw the world with such preternatural clarity in order to distinguish herself from it. . . . She wrote so well about people and places because she had a powerful motive, embattled; that motive, in nearly all the poems, is to define oneself away from two opposing nightmares: the pain of isolation, and the loss of identity in the mass of the visible world.

In other words, ''description'' in Bishop is not the notation of pretty or quaint details, but the surest form of knowledge; and knowledge is the geography of survival. (pp. 255-57)

> *Robert Pinsky, "Elizabeth Bishop, 1911-1979," in* Elizabeth Bishop and Her Art, *edited by Lloyd Schwartz and Sybil P. Estess, The University of Michigan Press, 1983, pp. 255-58.*

RICHARD WILBUR

[Elizabeth Bishop once] told me that Poe's best poem, for her taste, was a little-known piece called ''Fairy-Land.'' Years of re-reading that poem have brought me close to her opinion, and have led me to see that her fondness for it was based on a true affinity. ''Fairy-Land'' is a charming dream-vision, written in a transparent style unusual for Poe; at the same time, its weeping trees and multitudinous moons are repeatedly and humorously challenged by the voice of common sense; out of which conflict the poem somehow modulates, at the close, into a poignant yearning for transcendence. All of the voices of that poem have their counterparts in Elizabeth's own work.

Reticent as she was, Elizabeth Bishop wrote several autobiographical pieces in which she testified to a lifelong sense of dislocation. That is, she missed from the beginning what some enjoy, an unthinking conviction that things ought to be as they are; that one ought to exist, bearing a certain name; that the schoolbus driver should have a fox terrier; that there should be a red hydrant down at the corner; that it all makes sense. (pp. 10-11)

If the world is a strange place, then it readily shades into dream. So many of Elizabeth's poems take place at the edge of sleep, or on the threshold of waking, lucidly fusing two orders of consciousness. Some of them are written out of remembered dreams. And then there are superb poems like **"The Man-Moth,"** in which a tragic sensibility is portrayed *under the form* of dream. In a later poem, **"The Riverman,"** her capacity for navigating the irrational enabled her to enter the mind of a witch-doctor, and visit the water-spirits of the Amazon. All this has little to do with the influence of French surrealism, I think; as her Robinson Crusoe says of his artifacts in *Geography III,* Elizabeth Bishop's poems are ''homemade.''

In another kind of poem, she sets some part of the world before her and studies it with a describing eye, an interrogating mind, and a personality eager for coherence. This is the kind of poem, written in a style at once natural and lapidary, in which her stunning accuracies of perception and comparison make us think of her friend and early encourager, Marianne Moore. A sandy beach ''hisses like fat;'' she sees on a wall ''the mildew's ignorant map;'' on a gusty day in Washington she notes how ''Unceasingly, the little flags / Feed their limp stripes into the air.'' One could go on quoting such felicities forever, and it is such things which have led the critics to use the words *wit, delight, precision, elegance* and *fastidiousness;* at the same time, her descriptive genius has led some to say that her poetry is a poetry of surfaces. . . . But in fact her poems, for all their objectivity, are much involved in what they see: though she seldom protests, or specifies her emotions, her work is full of an implicit compassion, and her friend Robert Lowell justly ascribed to her a tone ''of large, grave tenderness and sorrowing amusement.''

That expression ''sorrowing amusement'' is wonderfully exact, and of course it would be quite wrong to overstress the sorrow part of it. If she was afflicted by the absurdity of things, she also took delight in everything curious, incongruous, or crazy; that's one reason why she was the best of company. (pp. 11-12)

When she looked in her poetry for ultimate answers, she generally expressed the search in the key of geography, of travel. And she always reported that such answers were undiscoverable. . . . In and out of her poetry, she lamented her want of a comprehensive philosophy; yet I cannot be sorry that so honest a nature as hers refused to force itself into a system, and I question whether system is the only way to go deep into things.

Though she had no orthodox convictions, and wondered at such certainties in others, Elizabeth Bishop had religious concerns and habits of feeling. I think of her poem about St. Peter; I think of the "pure and angelic note" of the blacksmith's hammer in her story **"In the Village,"** and the way that story ends with the cry, "O, beautiful sound, strike again!" . . . Above all, I think of her poem called **"Twelfth Morning:"** it is a poem about Epiphany, the day when things are manifested, and its opening lines say:

> Like a first coat of whitewash when it's wet,
> the thin grey mist lets everything show through . . .

One thing that comes through the mist is a sound from the shore, the sound of "the sandpipers' / heart-broken cries," and that I take for a sign that grief is a radical presence in the world. But there is also another phenomenon, a black boy named Balthazar who bears the name of one of the Magi, and on whose head is a four-gallon can which "keeps flashing that the world's a pearl." The vision of Balthazar and his four-gallon pearl is qualified by amusement; nevertheless it is a vision. It seems to me that Elizabeth Bishop's poetry perceives beauty as well as absurdity, exemplifies the mind's power to make beauty, and embodies compassion; though her world is ultimately mysterious, one of its constants is sorrow, and another is some purity or splendor which, though forever defiled, is also, as her poem **"Anaphora"** says, perpetually renewed. (pp. 12-14)

> *Richard Wilbur, "Elizabeth Bishop," in* Ploughshares, *Vol. 6, No. 2, 1980, pp. 10-14.*

RICHARD MULLEN

Some of the enchanted mystery which permeates Elizabeth Bishop's poetry arises from her preoccupation with dreams, sleep, and the borders between sleeping and waking. Her poems contain much of the magic, uncanniness and displacement associated with the works of the surrealists, for she too explores the workings of the unconscious and the interplay between conscious perception and dream. Although she draws very little from the surrealists' extreme experiments in technique, she does inherit the liberating bequest of their imaginative breakthroughs, and in an original and unobtrusive manner, she assimilates various surrealist aspirations into her poetic practice. (p. 63)

Although Bishop shares the surrealists' interest in the unconscious, her methods for incorporating oneiric qualities into her poetry differ fundamentally from their approach. She does not seek to subvert logical control, and she refuses to accept the "split" between the roles of conscious and unconscious forces in our perception of the world. Unlike the surrealists, she does not endow the unconscious with a revolutionary power to re-

make experience. Instead, within her poems the realm of dreams, like our waking perceptions, remains problematical. (pp. 63-4)

Another link between Bishop's poetry and the surrealists' discoveries is her delineation of the "otherness" of objects. Within her poems, one finds an awareness that, somehow, whatever seems recognizable to her calm, eclectic consciousness is only part of what is there. However, her techniques for evoking the enigmatic qualities of things differ from the surrealist process of dissociation. To discredit conventional perception, the surrealists deliberately placed the object in an unexpected surrounding and obtained a new source of aesthetic energy. This procedure, whether verbal or plastic, was essentially dissociative. Unlike the surrealists, Bishop rejects the shapeless poetics accompanying the derangement of consciousness, and she enhances the mysterious oddity of things by her unique prowess for ingenious association.

Many of her poems can be explicitly identified as verbal recreations of a dream; for example, **"The Weed," "A Summer's Dream," "Sleeping Standing Up," "The Riverman,"** and **"Some Dreams They Forgot."** However, in other poems, such as **"Chemin de Fer," "Cape Breton," "Squatter's Children," "First Death in Nova Scotia,"** and **"The Bight,"** the reliance on visual detail is so dominant that the created settings also seem oddly dream-like because they radiate with a disturbing ambiguity similar to the manifest content of dreams. From one perspective, the visual imagery in her poetry is grounded in exact and precise observation of natural detail, yet the uninterrupted accumulation of those details often forms settings which seem to emerge from a dream as well as to encompass the external world. (pp. 64-5)

Bishop was intrigued by the *frottage* technique [used by Max Ernst with the surrealist aim of breaking "loose from the laws of identity" by advocating uncontrolled association and by ascribing greater importance to the imaginative apprehension of an object rather than the object itself]. . . . Although this interest in Ernst's techniques for composition should not be over-amplified, it does indicate her sympathy for the surrealist sensibility and provides a means for comprehending the complex way in which this awareness is implemented in **"The Monument."**

The poem is eighty lines of free verse marked by occasional approximate rhymes. An objective and detached description of the visual qualities of the monument begins the poem and continues throughout, interrupted by four quotations from a second unidentified person (ll. 31-34, 40-45, 47-49, 54-58) and various speculations about the purpose, origin and nature of the object by the original speaker. The description of the box's visible features concentrates on the geometric properties of contiguous details. Its shape, angles, texture, slant and perspective are mentioned, much as one might describe the formal abstract elements of some twentieth-century sculpture. Indeed, the monument does resemble a piece of so-called junk sculpture in both its haphazard construction and mundane material, as described by the unappreciative second speaker. . . . It also resembles some Cubist sculpture because its intersecting geometric planes create a multifaceted surface which eleminates front, back and center. The monument is described following the line of sight—first bottom to top. (ll. i-ii) and then vice versa (ll. 11-17). The emphasis on surface description in this first part of the . . . [poem] plays against the later speculations about its purpose. This thematic distinction is emphasized grammatically—the visual description is written in the indicative mood while the speculation is placed in the subjunctive.

"It is an artifact / of wood" which "may be solid," "may" contain the bones of its creator, and "may" have been painted.

Twice in the poem the first speaker interrupts the account to correct the description. . . . Bishop uses this rhetorical device of correcting herself within the poem (epanorthosis) quite frequently. By halting and rebeginning in this way, she colors the tone of the poem with some of the rambling and discursive qualities of natural conversation. The device also gives the impression of accidental or spontaneous composition, an effect which indicates a feature of her surrealist awareness. Like so many twentieth-century poets who desired to bring the colloquial and spontaneous into their language, Bishop recognizes the power which such expansive informality can add to a poem. However, it is typical of her controlled sensibility that this rambling openness is presented through the sheath of a classical rhetorical device. It is also indicative of her poetic talent that she is able to utilize rhetorical forms so artfully that her naturalness does not seem stilted even though it does not issue from the exposure of her personal feelings. Nor does the seeming spontaneity arise from the derangement of consciousness so exalted by the surrealists.

This colloquial and matter-of-fact description of the monument's surface contrasts with the curiously dream-like perspective of the poem. . . . (pp. 67-9)

The ambiguous blending of subject and object and foreground and background within the poem enhances the dreaminess of the scene. As in many other poems, Bishop uses "and" to subvert causal connection: "there is no 'far away,' / and we are far away within the view." This illogical displacement of perspective applies not only to the observer but also the "sea" which is simultaneously too far away to hear, yet so close it can be described, along with the sky and sunlight, in terms of its fibres, grains and splinters—as if one were examining it under a magnifying glass. This dream-like condensation of distance employed while describing the setting of the monument also owes something to surrealist painting techniques; specifically, to the use of a background foreign to the objects presented. (pp. 69-70)

The setting may be surrealistically-oriented; however, the poem itself is not. Although it contains many pictorial elements, it is, like all poems, made of words. And within Bishop's poetry, despite the specific surrealist parallels here, there is never the attack on the Word itself which underlies all surrealist verse. (p. 70)

Bishop rejects the surrealists' attack on the conventions of language. Accordingly, she never employs the radical juxtaposition of verbal elements which permeates so much surrealist poetry. She does not break clauses, phrases or words into fragments; rather she stays within the confines of accepted linguistic and poetic conventions. In short, she uses syntax and grammar for her own needs rather than eliminating them as useless anachronisms.

As a poem, **"The Monument"** exhibits some of the methods which Bishop uses to capture the enigmatic qualities of objects. The monument is a pile of boxes; it might contain various secrets which are not apparent to our eyes. The dream-like rearrangement of the setting charges the poem with surrealist possibilities, yet the impulse of the poem, expressed through the dialogue, attempts to reconstruct the conscious associative elements of the monument. Although it owes something to the surrealist tradition of the poetic picture with its radiant metaphorical potential, it does not rely exclusively on dissociative

techniques. The poem is set up as an argument, and this argument is resolved in the final lines by a declaration of the monument's aesthetic value. . . .

The second work to be examined in relation to its surrealist features is **"Rainy Season; Sub-Tropics,"** a series of three interlinking prose poems which display some resemblance to the writing of Francis Ponge. Like Bishop's poetry, his work captures the "thingness of things" in poems which tilt, magnify and upset rational perspectives through the delineation of particular natural detail. (p. 71)

Recognizable thematic concerns of her poetry—the confrontation between human desires and natural impenetrability, the need for self-protection, painful isolation within a homeless environment, and the bordering worlds of land and water—are carried over into the three meditations through the first person narration of the assorted creatures, all chosen from the older and lower orders of the animal kingdom. Such personification is rarely effective in twentieth-century poetry, yet Bishop successfully recreates the oddities of our experience within the ironic, incisive monologues. One of the richest qualities of her writing is her unfaltering ability to fuse description and narration into an alloy which accentuates the strengths of each contributing element. (pp. 72-3)

With the exception of **"12 O'Clock News,"** these three monologues are the only prose poems Elizabeth Bishop published, and although they constitute only a small part of her entire corpus, they contrast with the other poetic forms she employs in *The Complete Poems* [1969] and *Geography III* which rely heavily on strict rhymes and stanzaic patterns. A question thus arises about the choice of form: what is gained by writing in a mode which eliminates end rhyme, stanzas and the poetic line? (p. 73)

Trying to express the "undulations of the psyche" through a means unfettered by the formal structures of verse composition, Baudelaire initiated the attempt, which the surrealists later heralded, of exploring the creative possibilities of the unconscious through a mode which de-emphasized the artificial imposition of conscious controls.

By writing **"Rainy Season; Sub-Tropics"** as a group of prose poems, Bishop has attempted to draw on the special powers of this form. Yet within these three poems, the daylight clarity of consciousness dominates through the use of declarative language and crystalline imagery. Certainly, the rhythmic elusiveness of these poems uncannily exposes the "prickings of consciousness," but the language in the monologues releases its power through an admirable simplicity. In this series, as well as throughout her writing, Bishop's use of language imbues her poems with this unmistakable sense of everyday reality. The concreteness of the sensory detail, permeating both dreams and waking, is anchored within a grammar which reinforces this simplicity. Here, as elsewhere in her poetry, short simple sentences are dominant. An elementary vocabulary also adds to the uncomplicated texture of the language, as does the straightforward, colloquial syntax.

This simplicity of language belies the oddity and mystery of the monologues. The intense paranoia of the speakers and the wry pungency of their observations coalesce through the rhythmic pacing of the poems—a rhythm as persuasively effective as any formal metrical measure. (pp. 73-4)

By eliminating the artificiality of the poetic line, Bishop increases the chilling immediacy of the speakers' meditational flow as they muse on the eerie conditions of their primeval struggles. As in **"The Monument,"** a fusion of description, narration and setting blurs the common distinctions between conscious and unconscious. These strange voices speak with such controlled eloquence and the foreground details of the setting stand out in such minute clarity that one forgets the background behind the scene is a dank, impenetrable forest. (p. 74)

In her poems, Bishop utilizes her own idiosyncratic kind of artistic displacement, and it is much less radical than that of the surrealist writers. Often, as in **"The Monument," "Rainy Season; Sub-Tropics"** or **"The Weed,"** this displacement appears in a traditional manner in the isolation and unease experienced by a subject within a narrative setting. In her poetry one does not find the grotesque oneiric distortion which may occur, for example, in painting by Dali or Magritte or poems by Breton or Aragon. Instead, she prefers to investigate natural displacement, the "always-more-successful surrealism of everyday life," by describing the oddities of events or incongruities of detail which appear before her questioning gaze and which hint at some displaced meaning. This predilection for scrutinizing natural displacement permeates her poems.

Her use of tilted, shifting perspectives is one way she draws attention to the quirkiness of our limited visions. (pp. 77-8)

Sometimes it is proportion which seems somehow out of balance. In **"Rainy Season; Sub-Tropics"** both the toad and snail ask pity because they are "too big." In **"Questions of Travel"** "there are too many waterfalls here." In **"Chemin de Fer"** the railroad ties are described as "too close together / or maybe too far apart." . . .

Sometimes the oddity of contiguous details is emphasized, creating the impression that displacement occurs in routine ways throughout the scenes she observes. It can appear in the countryside of Cape Breton or the exotically foreign jungles of Brazil. . . . (p. 78)

All of these examples indicate a specific use of displacement; namely, to accentuate the odd confrontation of internal and external worlds. Bishop's poetry delineates not only the confluent forces and ambiguities of interior conflicts expressed in dreams (as in **"The Weed"**), but also the elements of our waking struggle with external realities. Her landscapes may well possess qualities of dreamscapes, but simultaneously they are marked by an unusually rich appreciation of the natural world. Breton wrote that for the surrealists, there were no objects, only subjects. They had no interest in the natural world per se. Throughout Bishop's poetry, this strangeness of our subjective selves, the queer struggle between conscious and unconscious, is projected outward into a world where the "thingness of things" dominates. She often relies on accumulated visual images in order to blur the distinction between subject and object within a dream-like atmosphere which pushes beyond the "split" between conscious and unconscious. Yet at the same time she emphasizes a sense of displaced meaning in order to contradict this fusion by accenting the discrepancy between the inner and outer realms. (pp. 79-80)

> *Richard Mullen, "Elizabeth Bishop's Surrealist Inheritance," in* American Literature, *Vol. 54, No. 1, March, 1982, pp. 63-80.*

JASCHA KESSLER

I have been thinking about the paradox of poetry's ability to show itself forth even while its maker seeks to remain hidden in it, because a book titled *The Complete Poems: 1927-1979,* by Elizabeth Bishop, has just been published. . . . [Elizabeth Bishop] was praised to the skies by Robert Lowell and Randall Jarrell, two poets who were quite tough, very acute readers. Lowell said: "I don't think anyone alive has a better eye than she has: The eye that sees things and the mind behind the eye that remembers." And Jarrell said, "They have a sound, a feel, a whole moral and physical atmosphere different from anything else I know. They are honest, modest, minutely observant, masterly. . . . The more you read her poems, the better and fresher, the more nearly perfect they seem. . . . These are what poems ought to be!" [See *CLC,* Vol. 4.]

As for Elizabeth Bishop's "eye," her friend and model, Marianne Moore, and a younger poet who also works in that mode, May Swenson, have an "eye" just as good, and often better, I think, most readers would agree. As for their "sound," their "moral and physical atmosphere different from anything else," that may be the dustjacket blurb Jarrell supplied in 1964 that offers us the clue to Bishop's work and hidden character. If I were to try to characterize Bishop's difference from Moore, I would say Moore is rather complexly elaborate, a sort of Yankee moralist in Baroque clothing, ornately decorated by literary and natural history allusiveness; and Swenson is, also, verbally elaborate and "scientifically objective and descriptive," so to speak, and impersonal almost always, except for a few emotional outbreaks when she allowed herself once in a very great while to talk about family or self. In Bishop there is something very bitter and strange at the core of her work, something frozen, and denied, and a great deal withheld by an iron will. Why are these three poets alike? What is *not* in their work? All three are women, to make a broad guess, who refused to gaze upon Eros, the god of Love; and it is precisely that lack, which is to my mind an essential lack, that marks them as strange, frozen, and ultimately deficient as poets. Not that they are not each passionate, in their own ways; but their passion, their powerful and energetic passion, is one that has gone profoundly awry, deflected by the force field of some dark and hidden star that, unknown though it is, nonetheless reveals itself by the very form and patterns and quality of their concerns and their work. The best poetry of personal statement in Bishop's *The Complete Poems* is that of the great Brazilian poet, Carlos Drummond de Andrade, which she translated; and another clue to Bishop lies in a wonderful poem from the French of Max Jacob, "Hell is Graduated." There is nothing as good, one thinks, in all of Bishop's own work. Her translations say what she herself never would, or could say, perhaps.

Not that Bishop is not an excellent poet, and not that she is ever anything but a first-rate model when it is a matter of saying in clear, resonant, crystalline language what it is she sees in nature, in the garden, the forest, the city landscape, the jungle and the shore. No one who wants to read and/or write poetry will not learn something about language and craft from her firm, clear expression. . . .

Bishop was always concerned with what she terms *losing;* in the poem titled **"One Art,"** she says: "The art of losing isn't hard to master." In fact *losing* becomes synonymous with the practice of life itself. What is it Bishop knew she had constantly lost, and would always lose? and even while she found the scenery of the world, or what she could take of it, and from it, images for poems? There are many fine poems in this book, always crafted superbly, that will, when read, reread and contemplated, begin to shadow forth her secret loss, and all the losses that followed from it, losses that she concealed and transformed into the art of her poems, which besides being masterly, as Jarrell put it, are also often cold and cruel, not merely long- and silent-suffering, or stoical if you will. I would say that Elizabeth Bishop's lifework, which like May Swenson's poetry, offers us products of disciplined and thoughtful observation of the world we see and hear, and so parallels the kind of detached gathering we think of "scientific," also does with the world what only art can do: it tells us something of its maker, and tells us much more than the maker wished to say, or even perhaps knew. If we care to try to apprehend this rather cold poet . . . , we have the opportunity now, with the publication of Elizabeth Bishop's *The Complete Poems: 1927-1979*. . . .

> *Jascha Kessler, "Elizabeth Bishop: 'The Complete Poems: 1927-1979'," in a radio broadcast on KUSC-FM—Los Angeles, CA, February 23, 1983.*

DAVID BROMWICH

Elizabeth Bishop's steadily widening audience and her endurance among the readers she has once claimed are the reward of constancy to an ideal object. Her reputation is founded on perhaps 25 poems, among them **"Love Lies Sleeping," "The Unbeliever," "The Shampoo," "Over 2,000 Illustrations and a Complete Concordance," "Arrival at Santos"** and **"First Death in Nova Scotia."** Altogether that looks like a modest achievement until one considers that most of the larger poetic reputations of the past century have been founded on similar evidence. The difference is that Bishop's masterpieces stand in a higher ratio to her work as a whole. She published little, because she would not release a poem that fell short of a complete conception; and what strikes one most in reading her poems again [in **"The Complete Poems: 1927-1979"**] is the way they answer each other across pages or volumes, so that each plays its part: **"The Bight,"** for example, earning our esteem for the sake of its much fuller picture of the dream house sketched in **"The End of March"**; the figure of streets coupled to stars, a mystery in **"Going to the Bakery,"** somehow clarifying a similar figure in **"Love Lies Sleeping."** . . .

[Marianne] Moore's influence on Bishop was real though narrow, like the influence of Edward Arlington Robinson on Robert Frost. An original-minded author can profit incalculably from this sort of dependence: the respect one feels for the master of an earlier generation who has shown an unshakable interest in one's own fate. The result in Bishop's case was more than elective affinity and less than discipleship. Of the poems in **"North & South,"** only **"Casabianca"** is a simple imitation; **"The Man-Moth"** presumes an audience trained by Moore; **"Wading at Wellfleet"** uses her discipline with traces of her diction, but the sustained metaphor of the sea as chariot gives the closing lines a power that belongs uniquely to Bishop's fable. . . . So too with a later poem like **"Visits to St. Elizabeths."** . . .

Throughout her career Bishop aimed to bring morality and invention together in a single thought. One can feel this especially in **"The Weed,"** with its Herbert-like meditation on the birth of a new feeling; in **"The Armadillo,"** which shows the complicity of esthetic pleasures in any grand spectacle, even a scene of suffering; in **"Roosters"** and **"The Fish,"** those guilty and strangely conciliatory professions of human strength. The best example is the rhetorical turn several stanzas before the end of **"The Moose,"** in which the poet, having overheard a conversation in a bus about somebody's life, pauses

to recollect the different voices that told similar stories in her childhood and quietly weighs the inflections of the ageless mutterings of sympathy. . . . (p. 7)

In four poems above all—**"The Map," "The Monument," "At the Fishhouses"** and **"The End of March"**—Bishop announced her task as a poet and confirmed her dedication to it. Varied as they are, these poems have the authority of self-portraits, and they depict her, poignantly at times but always masterfully, as a creator of more than secondary imaginings. Her errors, or wanderings from fact, have for her the finality of fact, and her wish is to make a reader see them that way. (p. 30)

From her very first poems, Bishop's fascination for travel was an interest in seeing the place the map told of, the "lion sun" that you meet after turning away from a dream house "littered with correspondences." She speaks too of the dangers of travel for those nourished on art: The title of **"Brazil, January 1, 1502"** alludes to the landing of the conquistadors, who brought to the New World what she calls elsewhere "an active displacement in perspective." A "tapestried landscape" was all European eyes were prepared to see in the jungle. The actual landscape, with its terrors, somehow evaded them. . . .

In contrast with this, the other poems Bishop wrote about South America seem done from a traveler's perspective, as if the poet herself, four and a half centuries later, found the natives recalcitrant to all but esthetic treatment and yet had determined not to let them retreat. The poor of Brazil, her adopted country, were illegible and therefore marvelous to her. But for the same reason they were too rich for her poetry: Her portraits of them are half-bodied, insubstantial and oddly toneless for a poet usually so sure of tone. **"Manuelzinho,"** the longest and best-known poem of the group, is an affair of careful high spirits; yet it is a monologue, and Bishop's effort to dissociate herself from the speaker is awkward and perfunctory. . . .

Of the poems written since **"Geography III,"** **"Pink Dog"** is the most unexpected: a description, full of perverse gusto, of a "depilated dog" with teats hanging to the sidewalk who advises her in instructive tercets to "Dress up! Dress up and dance at Carnival!" An elegy for Robert Lowell also appears in this section. It is rather foreshortened, with an eloquence in the last two stanzas to which the preceding ones have not built a path, but it has great interest as an act of personal friendship that refused to be translated into a gesture of critical sympathy. Lowell's compulsion to change his poetry by rewriting the same poems is compared with nature's seasonal returns: Even the birds seem to say, *"repeat, repeat, repeat; revise, revise, revise."* . . . The remaining new poems in [**"The Complete Poems: 1927-1979"**], **"Santarém"** and **"Sonnet,"** confirm one's feeling that in her last years Bishop was working with undiminished powers, even if none of what emerged has the distinction of **"The End of March," "In the Waiting Room," "The Moose," "Crusoe in England"** or **"Five Flights Up"**— the poems that appeared together in **"Geography III."** It seems almost an impertinence to add that of the poets of her generation, with temperaments often more conspicuously adaptable than hers, Elizabeth Bishop alone now seems secure beyond the disputation of schools or the sway of period loyalties. Like all great poets, she was less a maker of poems than a maker of feelings. (p. 31)

> *David Bromwich, "Morality and Invention in a Single Thought," in* The New York Times Book Review, *February 27, 1983, pp. 7, 30-1.*

ADRIENNE RICH

I have been fascinated by the diversity of challenges that *The Complete Poems, 1927-1979* raises, the questions—poetic and political—that it stirs up, the opportunities it affords. In addition to the four volumes published in her lifetime, this edition . . . includes late poems which appeared in magazines after *Geography III* (1976), some posthumously published late poems, eleven poems written between the ages of sixteen and twenty-two, some uncollected later poems, and translations. Part of the value of such a collection is the chance it gives to see where certain obsessions and motives begin to take hold and how they work their way through a lifetime of poems; how certain echoes sound and die away, how style metamorphoses over time. This collection offers not just challenges and questions, but very deep pleasure. In her later work especially, Bishop is difficult to quote from because her poems are so often hung on one long thread; the progression of language and images does not readily separate into extracts. By the same token she is a wonderful poet to read aloud.

Criticism of Bishop in her lifetime was mostly appreciative of her powers of observation, her carefully articulated descriptive language, her wit, her intelligence, the individuality of her voice. I want to acknowledge the distinction of all these, the marvellous flexibility and sturdiness of her writing, her lack of self-indulgence, her capacity to write of loss and of time past without pathos and with precision, as in poems like **"Sestina," "The Moose," "Filling Station," "First Death in Nova Scotia," "At the Fishhouses."** I want to pay this homage and go on to aspects of her work which I have not yet seen discussed. In particular I am concerned with her experience of outsiderhood, closely—though not exclusively—linked with the essential outsiderhood of a lesbian identity; and with how the outsider's eye enables Bishop to perceive other kinds of outsiders and to identify, or try to identify, with them. I believe she deserves to be read and valued not only for her language and images, or for her personality within the poems, but for the way she locates herself in the world. (pp. 15-16)

The child made "different" because parentless, the emigrant who thinks she would—understandably—"rather have the iceberg than the ship," the woman writing, consciously or not, "against the male flood" (Woolf's phrase), the lesbian writing under the false universal of heterosexuality, the foreigner who can take little for granted—all inhabit Bishop's poetic voice and eye. Outsiderhood is a condition which most people spend (and are often constrained to spend) great energy trying to deny or evade, through whatever kinds of assimilation or protective coloration they can manage. Poetry, too, can serve as protective coloration; the social person who is the poet may also try to "pass," but the price of external assimilation is internal division.

The pain of division is acutely present in some of Bishop's earliest poems, notably in **"A Word With You,"** written when she was twenty-two, a tense, panicky, one-sided conversation during which a whole menagerie gets out of control. . . . (p. 16)

Poems examining intimate relationship are almost wholly absent from Bishop's later work. What takes their place is a series of poems examining relationships between people who are, for reasons of difference, distanced: rich and poor, landowner and tenant, white woman and Black woman, invader and native. Even in her first book she had taken on the theme of the Black woman's existence in a white world. The poem **"Cootchie"** addresses the fate of a Black woman who has died, presumably by drowning, perhaps by suicide. The white woman she has worked for is literally deaf but also self-absorbed; she will not "understand." . . . [**"Songs for a Colored Singer"**] is a white woman's attempt—respectful, I believe—to speak through a Black woman's voice. A risky undertaking, and it betrays the failures and clumsiness of such a position. The personas we adopt, the degree to which we use lives already ripped-off and violated by our own culture, the problem of racist stereotyping in every white head, the issue of the writer's power, right, obligation to speak for others denied a voice, or the writer's duty to shut up at times, or at least to make room for those who can speak with more immediate authority—these are crucial questions for our time, and questions that are relevant to much of Bishop's work. What I value is her attempt to acknowledge other outsiders, lives marginal in ways that hers is not, long before the Civil Rights movement made such awareness temporarily fashionable for some white writers.

Brazil, a multi-racial, yet still racist and class-fragmented country, clearly opened up a further range of understanding for Bishop. Her earliest poems about Brazil grasp the presence of colonization and enslavement. . . . Some of Bishop's best Brazilian poems are exercises in coming to terms with her location as a foreign white woman living as part of a privileged class in a city of beggars and rich people. I am thinking of **"Faustina," "Manuelzinho," "The Burglar of Babylon," "Pink Dog."** (pp. 16-17)

[It] is only now, with a decade of feminist and lesbian poetry and criticism behind us, and with the publication of these *Complete Poems,* that we can read [Bishop] as part of a female and lesbian tradition rather than simply as one of the few and "exceptional" women admitted to the male canon. Too often, the "exceptional" or token outsider is praised for her skill and artistry while her deep and troubled connections with other outsiders are ignored. (This is itself part of the imperative to be assimilated.) It is important to me to know that, through most of her life, Bishop was critically and consciously trying to explore marginality, power and powerlessness, often in poetry of great beauty and sensuous power. That not all these poems are fully realized or satisfying simply means that the living who care that art should embody these questions have still more work to do. (p. 17)

Adrienne Rich, "The Eye of the Outsider: The Poetry of Elizabeth Bishop," in Boston Review, *Vol. VIII, No. 2, April, 1983, pp. 15-17.*

ROBERT PINSKY

The eerie clarity and brilliant surfaces of Elizabeth Bishop's work have always been easy to see. Her first book, *North and South* (1946), contained poems that have been widely memorized, imitated, turned to as antidotes for slackness, and anthologized: **"Wading at Wellfleet," "The Man-Moth," "The Monument," "Florida," "Roosters,"** and **"The Fish"** are among these early poems—not bad for a first book.

But though the achievement and the reputation increased with the publication of *A Cold Spring* (1955, Pulitzer Prize), *Questions of Travel* (1965), and *Complete Poems* (1969, National Book Award), the whole force and unique daring of Bishop's poetry may not have been visible until her last book before her death in 1979, *Geography III* (1976). In the light of that book, all of her work seemed to change. The poet who might have seemed lapidary and self-effacing emerged as a radical explorer of selfhood's very nature. Critics like Helen Vendler and Harold Bloom, and fellow artists like John Ashbery, have begun to show us the nature of Bishop's accomplishment.

Now, *The Complete Poems, 1927-1979,* including translations, uncollected poems, juvenilia, and occasional verses as well as a small number of new poems, shows the magnitude of this immensely readable, yet somehow oblique and elusive poet. It is an exciting, challenging corpus. Within her limitations—she was not prolific, she lacks boldness of scale—Bishop is original without the obvious rhetorical noises that sometimes pass for profundity.

Bishop is a lyric poet of solipsism yearning toward love, of metaphysical doubt acknowledging worldly charm and variety. But her isolated self is too proud to strut; and her doubt is too gravely absolute for certain heroic or Whitmanian manners. On the rare occasions when she reaches for the high style, the grandeur is based on a negative assertion, as in the conclusion of **"At the Fishhouses,"** where the water is

> Cold dark deep and absolutely clear,
> element bearable to no mortal.

The negative assertion, moreover, is tempered by the provisional counterpoint of supposition and simile, which further qualifies the sublime, limiting how much can be known even of the familiar.... [Other lines say the sea] is *like* what we *imagine* knowledge to be. The simile and ... the qualifying adverb ("then *surely* burn your tongue") are hallmarks of Bishop's style and outlook. She reminds us that she is making or positing connections between separate things.... A steady fury with the very idea of falsehood leads her to make every connection explicitly an invention, and her own invention. That a person can be known, or the intensely visible world understood, is always left partly in doubt.

Thus, the poet of gaiety and reticence also denies—all but arrogantly—that one person is likely to know another, or indeed that one particle of experience is more than provisionally linked to any other.... (pp. 24-5)

Nothing is more conventional in modern poetry than the valuing of metaphor above simile. The stark, unostentatious way Bishop's work reverses that convention is characteristic; she is too sure and proud to explain or to show off—partly because what she is sure of is the limitation, as of simile. The reader is free to misunderstand, or not, but italicizing rhetoric or self-explication will not be provided. Similarly, it is possible to make the false assumption that she describes the separate parts of the world, the sensory particulars, out of love for those physical details. But in fact, *The Complete Poems 1927-1979* records at least as much rage as love toward that merely visible, carefully recorded array of distinct things. That is, for all the pleasure of the eye, the poet's drama also includes the mind separating itself from the sensible world that nearly drowns the individual—as in the dizziness of **"In the Waiting Room"**—and the mind separates itself by seeing and naming all that is not itself. The extraordinary power of sight yearns to "look itself away." Each acute observation or similitude that the self makes as it regards the world is also a defiant, negative definition of one's own boundaries.

In *Geography III*, her last work except for the four poems published after the book appeared, the separate self is associated with the figure of the island. In **"Crusoe in England"** the speaker has the nightmare of imagining all the other separate

imaginations, each isolated subjectivity demanding the impossible, to be known:

> I'd have
> nightmares of other islands
> stretching away from mine, infinities
> of islands, islands spawning islands,
> like frogs' eggs turning into polliwogs
> of islands, knowing that I had to live
> on each and every one, eventually,
> for ages, registering their flora
> their fauna, their geography.

Along with the other allegorized geographical feature of the volcano—the essential Bishop totem, molten rock pushed up from under the seemingly still surface—islands embody something in the poet's nature that is not merely pessimistic and enclosed, but antisocial. (The lines preceding the ones I've quoted narrate Crusoe's dream of slitting a baby's throat.) But even the lines about islands express the opposed, charitable and social side of the poet, and bring to mind the fact that—beside all that I have said—she is also a love poet (**"Casabianca," "Chemin de Fer," "Insomnia," "One Art"**) and a poet of funny, charitable social comedy (**"Filling Station," "Manners," "Letter to N.Y.," "House Guest," "12 O'Clock News"**). I don't think any modern poet of her stature has a better sense of humor.

If the reticence of simile and the isolated, volcanic island suggest Bishop's philosophical orientation, her social person is represented by quite different aspects of her writing. The poems often give a mysterious glamor and sweetness to the ordinary and domestic (the almost Norman Rockwell quality of people saying goodbye at a bus stop while "a collie supervises") in a way that suggests a feeling of being ineffably an outsider, a tourist from some other star, in relation to the banal customs of middle-class life. (pp. 25-7)

The peculiar nature of Bishop's version of a Romantic theme—the self isolated in a world unlike it—was clarified by *Geography III*. That book might be described as the autobiographical writing of a nonautobiographical writer; it hovers near personal account without entering the terrain of memoir—much less "confession"—for very long. Yet it is entirely intimate and inward. (p. 27)

[Here] is a poet whose subject was the self, and whose work, on the level of personality, takes that self (in a way) for granted, without a moment of extraneous self-regard or anxious preening. (p. 28)

Robert Pinsky, "Geographer of the Self," in The New Republic, *Vol. 188, No. 13, April 4, 1983, pp. 24-8.*

PETER KEMP

Obligingly, the titles of Elizabeth Bishop's volumes of poetry [included in *The Complete Poems, 1927-1979*]—*North and South, Questions of Travel, Geography III*—chart the range and nature of her literary world. Geography engrosses her. Fascinated by the foreign, she maps it in poem after poem....

Even when attempting other subjects, Elizabeth Bishop finds it hard to tear herself entirely away from her attachment to the geographical. A poem about queasy thoughts in a dentist's waiting-room soon has its protagonist's eyes 'glued to the cover / of the *National Geographic*'. In **'12 O'Clock News',** there is what amounts to an early exercise in the currently modish 'Martian' school of writing, with the implements of the writer's trade seen in terms of topography: her lamp becomes a 'full moon'; the typewriter is an 'escarpment'; sheets of manuscript represent 'a slight landslip' where 'the exposed soil appears to be of poor quality: almost white, calcareous, and shaly'.

Such visual conceits are among Elizabeth Bishop's favourite techniques—used especially often to capture aqueous effects. . . .

Yet, for all its lustrous accuracy of metaphor, Elizabeth Bishop's poetry is eventually dulled by predictability. There is a readiness to rely on the same stylistic tics—particularly repetition. (p. 25)

This mannerism is perhaps symptomatic of a more general penchant for sameness, which limits Elizabeth Bishop's writing. Paradoxically, in view of the author's taste for travel, her poetry ultimately conveys a sense of narrow horizons. Travelogue and topography are virtually fixed features. Outside of this range, she seems uncertain. When treating of people instead of places, for example, the poems are likely to fall into off-putting coyness, punctuated by winsome little cries—'Oh! It has caught Miss Breen's / skirt! There!'—or arch imagery: as when Marianne Moore is conjured up 'with heaven knows how many angels all riding / on the broad black brim of your hat'. It is when confined to the sphere of geography that Elizabeth Bishop shows at her best. Her bulletins from abroad are perhaps as depth-less as a postcard, but they are also as picturesque. . . . Brightly responding to the earth's surface, Elizabeth Bishop ensures that, if her poetry is superficial, it is sumptuously so. (p. 26)

Peter Kemp, "Rainbow, Rainbow," in The Listener, *Vol. 109, No. 2811, June 2, 1983, pp. 25-6.*

ELIZABETH HARDWICK

[In *The Collected Prose*] one will find Elizabeth Bishop's mastery of a moderate tone, find it even in the most searing fictions based upon painful recollections of her early life. One will note the characteristic curiosity, in her case often a curiosity about the curious, and it will be muted, as in her poems, by a respect and tolerance for what the curiosity discovers. There is also, here and there, the unusual visual sharpness that prompts her to challenge, as in a duel, the expected adjectives of description. She finds the words to make her victory convincing. . . .

Poets can, of course, write prose. They can write it as well or as ill as they write verse. . . . (p. 32)

Elizabeth Bishop's prose, as we read it collected and whole, gives me the idea that she set about the writing as an enterprise, something she would do from time to time with the prose part of her mind. It was the same mind that wrote the poems, but that does not alter the fact that certain of her stories were composed in the generally acceptable manner of the time. I think particularly of **"The Baptism," "The Farmer's Children," "Gwendolyn,"** and **"The Housekeeper."** (pp. 32-3)

These stories are a skillful blending of the parts; they know how to give information, how to dramatize a scene, and how to reach the popular drift of "epiphany" at the end. . . . The stories are genuine. You learn from them, and your emotions are solicited by the fate of the characters and the construction of the scene. They are fine examples of the kind of fiction still

offered weekly and monthly by the more thoughtful magazines, and indicate to me that Elizabeth Bishop certainly could have been a fiction writer had she wished it.

Little in that to amaze. What is startling, on the other hand, is that her best prose fictions (**"The Sea & Its Shore," "In Prison," "In the Village"**) are aesthetically radical, rich, and new in conception and tone. They are "experimental," as we used to say. In the late 1930s the fiction in the little magazines often struggled with the challenge of Kafka. It was possible to come up with an abstract and fixed situation of interest, but to uncover the mobility of the abstract is a rare gift. The static must move the mind, the invention, in a swirl of significance both intellectual and emotional. Much must happen from the point of stasis: otherwise there is a nullity, and with so much stripped away there is boredom.

"The Sea & Its Shore" is a magical instance of creative invention. . . . This little treatise and speculation on floating print, wind-tossed paper, fragments of literature, private letters, nonsense, mysterious truncations, arrives from the wonderfully resonant center of the given idea. The contemplation of the prodigality and expendability of print by way of the man on the beach and his stick with the nail in it is a pure and serene fiction exemplifying what we mean by inspiration.

Two stories are of great autobiographical interest and one, **"In the Village,"** is a brilliant modern short story. The first, **"The Country Mouse,"** was left unpublished, although it is a finished work. It is not more revealing and heartbreaking than the other; one might wonder why it was withheld. . . .

[Until] the age of seven Elizabeth Bishop lived with her mother's family in Nova Scotia. At the age of seven she was suddenly removed to Worcester, to the father's family, taken from a simple farm and small maritime village to the well-to-do manufacturing Bishops of Massachusetts.

"The Country Mouse" tells of this removal. "I had been brought back unconsulted and against my wishes to the house my father had been born in, to be saved from a life of poverty and provincialism, bare feet, suet puddings, unsanitary school slates. . . ." In her new home she was miserable. . . . The last paragraph of the story underlines the year 1918, the recognition that she at seven years was doomed to her identity, to her "I, I, I," as a poem has it. The story ends: "Why was I a human being?"

"In the Village" tells of the mother's return from the mental hospital when the girl is five years old. A seamstress is brought in to make a new dress that will signify the end of the black and white mourning clothes. In the midst of the fitting the mother screams, the scream of a new collapse and the destruction of hope. . . .

The story then becomes something else, a brilliant rendering and ordering of certain fresh fictional possibilities. It becomes a sort of sonata of sounds filled with emotion for the child. The scream is balanced by the sound of Nate, the blacksmith, at his anvil. "*Clang.* The pure note: pure and angelic." Another sound enters like a patch of color on a canvas. *Whack.* The little girl is taking the family cow through the village to a grazing space. *Whack* goes the child's directing stick when the cow meanders about and must be gently brought into line. (p. 33)

The sweet sounds of pastoral life, the timbre of the lost paradise, and the sound of lost hope in the scream are elements smoothly woven into an original fictional tapestry. The degree of composition is great—the pauses, the contrasts, the simplicity of it so very complicated. The story is true, but it cannot be accurate because of the artfulness.

"The Country Mouse" is finely written, but written in a spirit much closer to the documentary, to the statement. "My mother was not dead. She was in a sanitorium, in another prolonged 'nervous breakdown.'" And "I had been brought back unconsulted." For a sensitive and reserved nature, autobiographical accuracy is a greater deterrence to publication than the deeper and more disturbing transformations of experience by art. So, **"The Country Mouse"** lay in the drawer and **"In the Village"** was published. (p. 34)

Elizabeth Bishop was indeed a perfectionist. She was also a natural writer with an unusual patience; nothing appears to have been excavated with visible sweat and aching muscle. And yet perhaps it was that the great natural gifts seemed too easy, and she must wait to make everything just so in tone and rhythm, without insistence. (p. 35)

Elizabeth Hardwick, "The Perfectionist," in The New Republic, *Vol. 190, No. 11, March 19, 1984, pp. 32-5.*

NATHAN A. SCOTT, JR.

When [Elizabeth Bishop] accepted the Neustadt International Prize for Literature at the University of Oklahoma in the spring of 1976, she spoke about how all her life she had "lived and behaved very much like . . . [a] sandpiper—just running along the edges of different countries and continents, 'looking for something.'" Which is not unlike what her poetry is doing, what indeed it *has* to be doing, since there is no controlling myth to chart and guide its motions: it is forever turning to this and that and something else and saying (as does the final line in the great poem **"The Monument"**), "Watch it closely." . . . [Since] her poetry is unregulated by any metaphysic wherewith the things and creatures of earth might be ordered into a system of total meaning, it must be continually searching for significances, looking here and looking there till (in the final phrase of **"Over 2,000 Illustrations and a Complete Concordance"**) it has "looked and looked our infant sight away." We dwell, as she sees it, in a world whose variousness is beyond all calculation, a world of continents and cities and mountains, of oceans and mangrove swamps, of buzzards and alligators and fireflies, of dews and frosts, of light and darkness, of stars and clouds, of birth and death, and of all the thousands of other things that make up the daily round of experience. And, amidst "the bewilderingly proliferating data of the universe," a poet of her stamp must take it for granted, as John Ashbery says, that "not until the senses have all but eroded themselves to nothing in the process of doing the work assigned to them can anything approaching a moment of understanding take place." The attention bestowed upon whatever comes one's way must be so pure, so absolute, so intransitive, as to allow us to hear (as she phrases it in her story **"In the Village"**) "the elements speaking: earth, air, fire, water." And, in this way, even without myth or metaphysic, we may win through to knowledge, fundamental knowledge. . . . (pp. 255-56)

Indeed, the posthumously issued *Complete Poems* might well have been given the title that Bishop chose for her book of 1965, *Questions of Travel,* for, in its search for significant particulars, the poetry is constantly moving from Wellfleet, Massachusetts, to Paris, from Florida to Nova Scotia, from New York to Brazil, and on to still other scenes and regions. "There are in her poems," says David Kalstone, "no final

visions—only the saving, continuing, precise pursuits of the travelling eye." Which may well be why, as one moves through her work from her first book *North & South* (1946) to *A Cold Spring* (1955), *Questions of Travel* (1965), *Geography III* (1976), and on to the last poems, one has no sense of any progress or growth, as one does in contemplating the whole career of Eliot or Auden or Lowell: poem after poem is recording utterly discrete perceptions, and though, taken poem by poem, her work is powerfully unified and cogent, the poems altogether seem to be an affair of "Everything only connected by 'and' and 'and'" (**"Over 2,000 Illustrations . . ."**).

So, for the reader tackling Elizabeth Bishop's poetry for the first time, it makes little difference where one begins, since, in whatever one turns to, one finds oneself in the hands of a poet who is saying, "But surely it would have been a pity / not to have seen" this or "not to have pondered" that—as she does in the beautiful poem called **"Questions of Travel."** . . . [The] tone in which the closing question of the poem [". . . should we have stayed at home, / wherever that may be?"] is asked clearly indicates that this poet wants it to be answered in the negative. For she takes a skeptical view of Pascal's injunction that we forswear the temptations of *divertissement* and remain quietly in our own chamber. (pp. 257-59)

It is . . . with an unblinking clarity that Elizabeth Bishop views the world, and she has no recourse to any kind of sentimental pastoralism. Her way of rendering the natural order would have made it wholly appropriate for her to say, with the French writer Alain Robbe-Grillet, "Man looks at the world, and the world does not look back at him." Yet, hard as it is, for all its blazoned days, she bestows upon it and all its creatures an attention so passionate that very often the distinction between the self and the not-self seems nearly altogether to have been dissolved. . . . (pp. 260-61)

Elizabeth Bishop did, to be sure, have a great admiration for George Herbert, but her own idioms would suggest that she was perhaps far more immediately influenced by Hopkins and Stevens and Marianne Moore than by the Metaphysicals in general. Certainly she was most insistent on her neutrality in regard to any form of religion. Yet, again and again, her own style of thought moves from a "composition of place" or object to reflection on its anagogical import and on to a "colloquy" either with herself or with her reader. The central masterpiece in *A Cold Spring,* **"At the Fishhouses,"** presents a case in point. The setting of the poem is a town in Nova Scotia, in the district of the local fishhouses. And the "composition" of the scene, for all its apparent casualness, is wrought with the utmost care. . . . (p. 262)

Thus it is that, with a most deliberate and meticulous kind of literality, the scene is "composed" with such an exactness as will lock us up within the closet of that which is to be meditated. At a later point in the poem the speaker declares herself to be "a believer in total immersion," and this is what she wants for us: total immersion in the tableau presented by [the] old fisherman weaving his net on a bleak, cold evening down at the waterfront where everything seems to have been either iridized by the sun or plastered and rusted over by the erosive power of the sea. Indeed, it is not until we have been fully drawn into this scene that the poem allows it to quiver into life: the speaker offers the old man a cigarette, and they begin to "talk of the decline in the population / and of codfish and herring," as "he waits for a herring boat to come in." . . .

[Having] been made to contemplate the "cold dark deep and absolutely clear" waters of the sea, waters "bearable . . . to fish and to seals'' but ''to no mortal,'' the scene is at last fully composed, and thus the meditation begins, issuing finally into a colloquy with the reader who is directly addressed as ''you''. . . . (p. 263)

By this point the lone fisherman and his shuttle and net have quite faded into the background, and the speaker has realized that what most urgently asks to be pondered is the sea itself, ''dark, salt, clear.'' And the rippling sibilance with which it is described—''slightly, indifferently swinging above the stones, / icily free above the stones''—does, as it echoes the rising and falling of the waters, make for a very intense realization of the briny, inscrutable abysm beyond the land's edge. But the *result* of this meditation is the grave recognition that the sea is much like something in the affairs of human life with which we must reckon, and thus the poem is ready to eventuate in the final colloquy which the speaker addresses at once to herself and to her reader. ''If you should dip your hand in, / your wrist would ache immediately, / your bones would begin to ache. . . .'' ''If you tasted it, it would first taste bitter, / then briny, then surely burn your tongue.'' And then, with what is for her an uncharacteristic explicitness, Bishop specifies the referent of which the sea is a symbol: ''It is like what we imagine knowledge to be. . . .'' Here it is that the poem at its end formulates the idea to which it would have the ''whole soul'' give heed, that a truly unillusioned awareness of our place and prospect is won only by facing into the cold, hard, bedrock realities of our mortal condition and that, however circumspect and sober it may be, even at its best it remains something ''historical,'' something needing to be revised over and again, flowing and flown—like the sea. So to render Bishop's final lines is, of course, to betray them, but it is, one feels, to something like such a conclusion that she is brought on that cold evening in a Nova Scotia town, down by one of the fishhouses where an old man sits netting, as he waits for a herring boat to come in.

Now it is undoubtedly her deep formation by the kind of meditative discipline underlying this poem that accounts for the extraordinary sympathy with which Elizabeth Bishop approached a world which, however intently it is scanned, seems not to look back at us. In this connection one will think of such poems as ''The Weed'' and ''Quai d'Orléans'' and ''Rooster'' in *North & South*, ''The Riverman'' and ''Sandpiper'' in *Questions of Travel*, and ''The Moose'' in *Geography III*. And certainly one will think of the beautiful prose poems, ''Giant Toad'' and ''Strayed Crab'' and ''Giant Snail,'' that make up the sequence called ''Rainy Season; Sub-Tropics.'' . . . [In ''Giant Snail''], like Wordsworth, [Bishop] is looking steadily at her subject, but—again, like Wordsworth—not from a merely analytical, matter-of-fact perspective: on the contrary, she is facing a wordless creature with so much of affectionate responsiveness that not only (in Coleridge's phrase) does ''nature [become] thought and thought nature'' but there occurs even an interchange of roles, the snail becoming a speaking *I* as the poet becomes a listening *thou*. And the result is a well-nigh preternatural commingling of love and awe before the sheer otherness of the things of earth.

Perhaps the most notable instance in Bishop's poetry of this genius for empathy is the great poem in *North & South* that has been so frequently anthologized, ''The Fish.'' (pp. 264-66)

Elizabeth Bishop's remarkable powers of sympathy are not, however, reserved merely for fish and snails, for birds and weeds, for rocks and mountains, for the insensible or subhuman things of earth: they also extend far into the realm of what

Martin Buber called ''the interhuman,'' and she presents many poignantly drawn and memorable personages. Her readers will tend perhaps most especially to recall the Brazilian portraits in *Questions of Travel* which focus not on people of importance but on the humble and the lowly, on those who perch ever so lightly on some narrow and incommodious ledge of the world. . . . [There] is ''Manuelzinho,'' with its account of a young man— ''half squatter, half tenant (no rent)''—who is supposed to supply the poet with vegetables but who is ''the world's worst gardener since Cain.'' . . . Manuelzinho is shiftless and improvident and unreliable, but, with his ''wistful face,'' this ''helpless, foolish man'' is irresistible: so Bishop says: ''I love you all I can, / I think.'' (pp. 268-69)

The poem, like so many of Elizabeth Bishop's finest statements, asks for no ''explication'': its plea is unmistakable, that, whatever the particular legalities may be, we give our sympathy to this poor devil who has never had any large chance at life or liberty or the pursuit of happiness and for whom the world has always been like a wilderness. And it is a similar triumph of moral imagination and fellow feeling that one encounters again and again in such poems as ''Cootchie'' and ''Faustina, or Rock Roses'' and the beautiful poem in *Geography III*, ''In the Waiting Room.''

The immaculate precision of her language has led many of the commentators on her work to speak of Elizabeth Bishop as a ''poet's poet''—which is a bit of fanciness that, prompted by however much of appropriate admiration and respect, may be more than a little questionable. For the tag ''poet's poet'' tends to suggest an imagination sufficient unto itself, taking its own aseity for granted and, with a royal kind of disdain for the world, making poetry out of nothing more than the idea of poetry itself. But nothing could be further from the sort of métier to which Bishop kept an absolute commitment, for she was a poet without myth—even about the poetic vocation itself. And, as she makes us feel, when she in the act of composition crossed out a word and replaced it with another, she did so not for the sake merely of the particular mosaic of language being fashioned but because the stricken word did not adequately render this or that detail of something she had *observed*. Which is to say that her primary fidelity was to the Real and to Things. And though there are numerous poems—like ''The Burglar of Babylon'' and ''Visits to St. Elizabeths'' and ''In the Waiting Room''—that find their space in the realm of ''the interhuman,'' she was most principally a poet of the subject-object relationship.

So it is something like ''Cape Breton''—one of the most perfect poems of our time—that presents her characteristic manner and method. (pp. 270-71)

One commentator has suggested that '''Cape Breton' is a glimpse into a heart of darkness,'' and this indeed is what the poem seems to be peering into, the dark, uncommunicative, and unknowable noumenality at the heart of the world. The speaker is *looking* at this landscape as intently and as piercingly as she can—but it does not look back at her: whatever there is of meaning remains hidden, and on this quiet Sunday morning ''the high 'bird islands''' and the weaving waters and ''the valleys and gorges of the mainland'' and the road clambering along the edge of the coast and the man carrying a baby ''have little to say for themselves.'' All is enveloped in mist, and the scene is overborne by ''an ancient chill.''

Yet, recalcitrant though the world may be, Elizabeth Bishop could find nothing else to depend upon except what she could *see* and *observe;* and thus she seems never to have been inclined to reach what was at one point Stevens' exasperated conclusion, that "reality is a cliché" which the poet had better try to do without; on the contrary, she represents a constantly unquerulous, and sometimes even exuberant, submissiveness to the hegemony of *l'actuelle,* always taking it for granted that (as Jacques Maritain says in his book *The Dream of Descartes*) "human intellection is living and fresh only when it is centered upon the vigilance of sense perception."

Unlike Stevens, it was not her habit to discuss her poetics in her poetry, but the endlessly absorbing and subtle poem called **"The Map"** conveys, for all its indirection, perhaps the best inkling to be found anywhere of how she viewed her special responsibility as a poet. She is looking at a printed map, and she notices how the land which is "shadowed green" appears to lie in water. But then she wonders if indeed the land may not "lean down to lift the sea from under, / drawing it unperturbed around itself." May it not be the case that the land is "tugging at the sea from under?" And, as she gazes at this map, she marvels at the transforming perspective that the mapmaker's art casts upon the surfaces of the earth. . . . (pp. 272-73)

Now, of course, the unspoken premise of the poem is that the cartographer's craft is a mode of art. And his images, like those of any true artist, practice a very radical kind of metamorphosis upon the things of earth: they make the peninsulas of the land appear to be "flat and still"; they render the waters of the sea as calm and quiet, when actually they are roiled with agitation; they make it appear that Norway is a sort of hare running south; and—in, as it were, a spirit of frolic—they organize themselves into highly intricate patterns of figuration that belong to the order of the metonymic. Yet the cartographer's "profiles investigate" topographical actualities: he is not free to rearrange at will the contours of geography: he must be faithful to the given literalities of nature. And thus he supervises a very "delicate" art indeed—an art, as Bishop may be taken to be implying, not unlike that of poetry itself.

So it is *amor mundi,* never *contemptus mundi,* that one feels to be inscribed over her entire work. Though on occasion (as she suggests in **"Wading at Wellfleet"**) she considers the sea to be "all a case of knives," she loves it nevertheless. Though the "huntress of the winter air" (in **"The Colder the Air"**) consults "not time nor circumstance," she admires "her perfect aim." And, as she tells us (**"The Imaginary Iceberg"**), she'd "rather have the iceberg than the ship." Like the black boy Balthazár in **"Twelfth Morning; or What You Will,"** she thinks "that the world's a pearl," and thus her poems want (as she says of the crude artifact being described in **"The Monument"**) "to cherish something" and want to say "commemorate." Hers, as Robert Mazzocco says, is "the middle range, the middle style." "History as nightmare, man as a cipher"—these "*de rigueur* subjects . . . [she] subverts." And thus she has never claimed the wide popularity that is more easily won by those writers who offer some kind of existentialist *frisson.* But her deep influence is easily to be traced in the work of such poets as Randall Jarrell and Robert Lowell and Richard Wilbur and John Ashbery and James Merrill. And in **"The Map," "The Monument," "Roosters," "The Fish," "Cape Breton," "The Armadillo,"** and scores of other poems she appears as one of the most remarkable poets to have graced the American scene, no doubt not a major figure—not in the range of a Frost or a Stevens or a Carlos Williams—but one whose legacy will long be a bench mark against which false sentiment and specious eloquence will be severely judged. (pp. 274-75)

Nathan A. Scott, Jr., "Elizabeth Bishop: Poet without Myth," in The Virginia Quarterly Review, *Vol. 60, No. 2 (Spring, 1984), pp. 255-75.*

MICHAEL HOFMANN

If Molière is right, and everything that isn't verse is prose, and everything that isn't prose is verse, then, with *The Collected Prose* of Elizabeth Bishop (companion-volume to *The Complete Poems,* out last year, from the same publisher), we shall have seen all we shall ever get to see of this wonderful author's work. . . . If the excellence of the *Prose* is quite unsurprising, then it should only be observed that it is not a separate excellence from that of the poems.

The virtues of the prose are the virtues of the poems: observation, wit, decorum, a sinuous intelligence and above all what Randall Jarrell called her 'moral attractiveness'—no abuse, no indiscretion, no protests. If this sounds prim, it isn't: it's only an indication of how far things have gone the other way. . . . The prose is odd and pleasant and sympathetic. . . . The subjects are largely those familiar from the poems: her family, her native Nova Scotia, life by the shores of the Atlantic, in Massachusetts and Brazil, paintings, human portraits and 'questions of travel'. The *aller-et-retour* form of many of the poems is discernible in some of the prose, in **'To the Botequim and Back'** and **'A Trip to Vigia'**. Sometimes, there are detailed correspondences between the poems and the prose: it is the same scene from childhood in **'The Country Mouse'** and **'In the Waiting Room'**. Or correspondences of genre: the realistically elaborated story **'The Sea and Its Shore'** is charmed from its hypothetical premise in just the same way as **'The Man-Moth'** from its newspaper misprint. Both are abstract fantasies indebted, it seems to me, to Kafka. Or again, one might identify two distinct styles in Bishop, in her prose as in her poems: a loose, probing, 'spoken' style and a stately 'high style', literary, fixed, almost artificial, hinting at Victorian prose and at Defoe. These similarities and others make the division of Bishop's prose into the two categories 'Memory' and 'Stories' rather factitious: after all, no such division is made among her poems.

If one imagined a square with admiration and sympathy, amusement and dignity as its four corners, the whole of Elizabeth Bishop's work would be situated inside it. Take for instance the account of only her second meeting with Marianne Moore, an outing to the circus at Madison Square Garden. Miss Moore was carrying

> two huge brown paper bags, full of something. I was given one of these. They contained, she told me, stale brown bread for the elephants, because stale brown bread was one of the things they liked best to eat. (I later suspected that they might like stale white bread just as much but that Marianne had been thinking of their health.)

In a way, the scene is 'a gift', just as the remarkable Miss Moore and her mother are 'a gift', but how easy it would have been to collapse it into sentimental farce. Instead, all the parties involved, and not least the elephants, whose wishes are solicitously though never intrusively guessed at, are treated with the utmost respect—a smiling respect, though, not stiffness or stuffiness. Elizabeth Bishop marries generosity of spirit with generosity of style ('one of the things', 'just as much'): how well her memoir earns its title—itself an acknowledged and admired borrowing from Miss Moore—'**Efforts of Affection**'.

It is this kind of tact and attention—one should perhaps call it grace—that is maintained throughout this collection, and makes it so delightful and rewarding. Whenever it really matters to her, Elizabeth Bishop has the ability to procure for herself the reader's utter, unreserved belief, most obviously when she is writing, as a child, about her childhood. This, just as fraught with difficulties as the type of scene with Miss Moore, is managed with equal assurance. It is, I think, because Bishop is always so committed to the moment and the scene she is describing, and free from any ulterior purpose, that she is both so engaging and so trustworthy. (pp. 33-4)

There is so much more I would like to say about her: her ingenuity, her freakishness, her tendency to personify objects and places (another sign of generosity, for she doesn't do the opposite and reify people in the way, say, Dickens does), the wonderfully candid way she allows herself to be scrutinised and laughed at, just as she, in her writing, laughs and scrutinises. The freedom of her manner: 'he gave me his name and asked me to print it; here it is: Manoel Benicio de Loyola, "diamond-hunter of Curralinho".' The way virtue and virtuosity seem to be inextricably bound up in her work: Miss Mamie in '**Mercedes Hospital**' who 'has the local reputation of a saint'.... I have helplessly and purposely left out of my account all mention of Elizabeth Bishop's masterpiece '**In the Village**' that concludes [*The Complete Prose*], which, even without it, would be wholly admirable. If only there were another to come. (p. 34)

> *Michael Hofmann, "Four Square," in* New Statesman, *Vol. 107, No. 2768, April 6, 1984, pp. 33-4.*

PAUL BAILEY

Robert Giroux, the editor, mentions in his introduction [to *The Collected Prose*] a remark Bishop once made to him on the subject of the confessional poets: 'You just wish they'd keep some of those things to themselves.' He cites the example of that seemingly cheery *villanelle* '**One Art**' ('The art of losing isn't hard to master'), written towards the end of her life, to demonstrate her freedom from self-pity. It is one of the ironies of her often fiercely reticent art that one senses her isolation and pain most keenly when he is celebrating the uniqueness of other creatures—people and animals—and the warm climates she sought in her maturity.

Elizabeth Bishop is that rarest of writers—a constantly attractive presence. She is all of a piece in her prose and her poetry—the same care has been generously lavished on the composition of both. She is always sharply observant in her shyness....

The most beguiling essay in [*The Collected Prose*] is the long memoir of Marianne Moore entitled '**Efforts of Affection.**' ... Bishop wittily, tactfully captures Marianne Moore and her fearsome-sounding mother in their cramped apartment at 260 Cumberland Avenue, with its bowl of nickels (later dimes, finally quarters) for subway fares on a bookcase by the front door. It was considered bad manners to refuse one of these upon leaving.

'The exact way in which anything was done, or made, or functioned, was poetry to her,' Bishop says admiringly of Moore. No wonder they remained so devoted to one another. A similar curiosity informs all the non-fiction in this collection....

A strain of autobiography runs through all the eight short stories included here, even '**In Prison**,' which has a male narrator. The final story, '**In the Village**,' is set in Nova Scotia, where Bishop was raised. A child hears a terrible scream—his mother's, presumably. She seeks reassurance in other sounds, one in particular the *clang* the blacksmith makes as he shapes a horseshoe. Elizabeth Bishop searched for and lighted on any number of consoling sounds in her exquisite art, any number of soothing cadences. Most other poets of her time contented themselves merely with imitating screams.

> *Paul Bailey, "Art of Reticence," in* The Observer, *April 8, 1984, p. 22.*

MUTLU KONUK BLASING

The poetry of Elizabeth Bishop sustains seemingly contradictory commentary: she is an autobiographical poet with an impersonal touch; a surrealist given to meticulous observations of natural facts; a formalist whose poems are open-ended accumulations of detail. Bishop's work resists analysis in terms of such romantic and modernist oppositions as art and life, subject and object, dream and reality, experiment and convention. While she revises the dualistic thinking of her predecessors, her strategy reverses that of other postmodernists: in her work, it is not art that is reduced to experience, but experience that tends to be reduced to art. The "objective" world of experience in Bishop is never a natural source but always an already represented world, and this given, original distance informs her poetry. For Bishop's uniqueness does not lie in her peculiar sensibility, as the largely descriptive criticism of her work—encouraged by her own irreverence toward theoretical discussions of poetry—would suggest.

For a more adequate assessment of Bishop's poetic, which remains consistent throughout her career, we might start with a poem like "**The Gentleman of Shalott**." Here, she rewrites Tennyson's "The Lady of Shalott," revising its opposition of reality and imagination. Tennyson's "Lady" represents the psyche as dwelling in an islanded, inner space of reflection, and such a figure implies a mutually exclusive relationship between the inner and the outer. (pp. 341-42)

In Bishop's "revision" of the poem, the dichotomy of inner and outer disappears; the bilateral symmetry of the human body renders her "gentleman" a mirror image of himself. ... Bishop internalizes the mirror, replacing the subject-object duality not with a unity but with a duplication at the source. The dividing line lies within, and the "center" is itself a reflection. ... With the internalization of the duplication, which preempts the inside-outside dichotomy, the spatial and temporal distinction between an original (nature, fact, or experience) and a subsequent reproduction (a copy, reflection, or art) vanishes. It is impossible to tell which side is the original and which the duplicate; since the "modesty" of the postromantic, peripheral man questions the need for two of him, however, only one side can be him, and the other must be a mirror image. There must be a duplication, then, but it is an atemporal, ahistorical doubling. (pp. 342-44)

"**The Gentleman of Shalott**" has significant implications for Bishop's poetics, for the confusion between the original and the representation, the uncertainty and alienation, are built into the "gentleman." Duplication, the formative principle enabling his existence, constitutes the beginning of discourse; it constitutes also the end or limits of discourse, for the "original" is itself a "reflection." If one starts with two halves without an historical order of priority and lateness, one inhabits a metaphor, the two terms of which—the tenor and the vehicle—are simply equal and coeval in a world "littered with old correspondences." . . . Indeed, the implications of **"The Gentleman of Shalott"** go beyond the poetic. The bilateral symmetry of the body and binary logic—which also demarcates and duplicates in order to generate distinctions and meanings—are themselves mirror images. In this hall of mirrors, the dialectic between Tennyson's and Bishop's poetics, or even the distinction between ladies and gentlemen, may be reduced to the same central pattern, thereby reducing physiological "distinctions" themselves to human duplications. The limitation of this arrangement is solipsism, hinted at by the disappointment registered in the enjambment of "his hands can clasp one / another." Yet the precariousness of the gentleman's position exhilarates: "The uncertainty / he says he / finds exhilarating." The line "he says he" both sets his limits and sets him free. The solipsistic flanking of "says" with two "he" 's suggests that the saying itself is the center that divides and duplicates; it is the spine of the duplicitous "book" that he inhabits, binding his fiction and his fact.

Bishop's poetry as a whole questions the priority of experience over representation. For example, her use of letters as visual images to depict nature suggests that representation may even be prior to the original. (pp. 344-45)

"The Map," which begins *The Complete Poems,* shows why she is interested less in landscape than in its representation on a map, of which her poem is yet another representation. The naiveté of the observer in the poem points up the thoroughly conventional nature of cartography. Representational artifacts, which help us navigate in the world, express a consensus and must be conventional. Yet representation liberates as well as limits. The rift between the original and its representation constitutes an "exhilarating" uncertainty that leads to discovery by prompting questions one could not put to a landscape alone or to a map as a merely conventional artifact. Only when the map is seen as a new landscape equal to its original is there room for questions and answers, thoughts and feelings. (p. 346)

By questioning the priority of nature, Bishop can inhabit a reflected and therefore thoroughly human world. For representations counter nature: they "re-verse" the world, turn it around, and right its wrong. (p. 349)

Mutlu Konuk Blasing, " 'Mont D'Espoir' or 'Mount Despair': The Re-Verses of Elizabeth Bishop," in Contemporary Literature, *Vol. 25, No. 3, Fall, 1984, pp. 341-53.*

Marilyn R(uthe) Bowering

1949-

Canadian poet and novelist.

Surreal and vividly imagistic, Bowering's poems frequently resemble myths and dreams. Bowering writes many poems from the point of view of a primitive female persona and infuses her work with the myths and symbolism of the Canadian West Coast. Her poetry collections—*One Who Became Lost* (1976), *The Killing Room* (1977), and *Giving Back Diamonds* (1982)—often depict extreme emotions, especially anger and violence.

In addition to her collections of poetry, Bowering also wrote *The Visitors Have All Returned* (1979), a structurally experimental novel in which each chapter is only loosely connected to the others. Like her poetry, this work has received mixed critical reviews.

(See also *Contemporary Authors,* Vol. 101.)

Photograph by Michael Elcock

M. TRAVIS LANE

One of the most useful things poets can do for their art is to invent a speaker who creates in his or her or its point-of-view feelings, flesh, and world—the symbolic values of the poem. . . . Such poetry tends to be uncommonly strong and illuminating, and we have some fine examples of it in . . . *One Who Became Lost,* by Marilyn Bowering.

With the exception of a few excellent poems . . . (**"Café"** and **"The Monastery of Hosios Louikas"**), the best poems in [this book] . . . are not spoken by a poetic speaker who represents either the average human sensibility or even the average poetic speaker. Instead the speaker is woman-in-nature—a primitive, an animal, a witch, a goddess—some sort of natural, female force. Bowering [has] . . . an interest in recreating a point-of-view vitally female at the level of dream, totem, and myth. [She is] . . . rewriting the fairy tales, creating a world view without the dualism that has traditionally split the world into male-positive-aggressive and female-negative-passive. For [her] . . . nature is not that simply divided; both male and female alike are aggressor and victim, and for them nothing, not even the earth, is passive. (p. 156)

[*One Who Became Lost* is] a substantial and well-organized book divided into three coherently grouped sections. . . . Actually Bowering brings us two books, for her title, from the small central section, works also for the untitled first but not at all for the titled third section, *Slave-Killers.* The title section of *One Who Became Lost,* set in its center, does suggest for the first section the theme of the search for the original, primitive self and, for the third section, an aspect of what was found in this self. The title poem is a moderately good poem on the loss of childhood, but is preceded by a finer, longer untitled poem about inheritance, original sin, or the discovery of the ancestors and archetypes in the subconscious. The first section repeats in various terms, and not without reminiscence of Roethke, the themes of loss of identity, fear of loss of identity, loss of childhood, the drawing explorations into the worlds of

darkness—the past, our dreams, and the fearful edges of our consciousness. (p. 157)

Bowering is very much interested in violence as part of the psyche, as part of what is nature in us. She is also [consciously interested] . . . in the hostilities of the man-woman relationship. But she does not limit her perceptions of her character's responses, and she does not make a simplified villian out of the Male or out of the Female. Her sense of reality prevents her from simplified emotions even as it tempts her towards extreme ones. And thus two problems, both of which require more from the reader than the reader, lazy fellow, is often willing to yield.

First, Bowering does wish to be free to deal with the expression of emotion that in reality is scream. Whether she spells it ''ai'' or ''eee,'' it will sound right in the voice of any good actor and look a little odd on the page. The poems have to scream at these points; Bowering is right. If the reader is a good, well-behaved reader and reads these poems in order all the way through, by the time he or she comes to them, he or she will be sufficiently drawn into the material so that these screams will work. But the person standing in the bookstore idly dipping through these pages may not be so drawn. And, second, since Bowering builds complexly out of dream materials, the structure of her poems may be as inobvious as that of a dream; we tend to feel her meaning before we can attempt to paraphrase it; a casual reader may doubt there is structure at all.

Yet Bowering's poems are beautifully structured; they are not surrealist messes. Poems that speak through dream imagery rather than through rationalized description and commentary are structurally nearer to painting or music than to prose, and we look for their structure in terms of themes and variations rather than terms of argument. Or again, we can understand them as we do a film by Bergman or Fellini, with the back of our mind, trusting our instincts—this *feels* right. (p. 158)

> *M. Travis Lane, "'The Hidden Dreamer's Cry': Natural Force As Point-of-View," in* The Fiddlehead, *No. 112, Winter, 1977, pp. 156-60.**

DOUGLAS BARBOUR

Marilyn Bowering's *One Who Became Lost* is a strong second book from this young poet. Not all the poems work, but all make their presence felt. Bowering's poems are intensely emotional, and the dominating emotions are anger/(hatred) and love. Many of the poems have the violent juxtapositions of mood and movement associated with dreams, and, indeed, the dream is a central concept in this book. The other central concept is myth, as seen in both the poems from Greece and the poems from the Queen Charlotte Islands with their various allusions to Indian mythology. Although I began this collection with a certain small sense of boredom, Bowering slowly brought me further and further under the spell of her often terrifying visions. When rhythm and language unite as they do in the best of these poems, the result is a true testament to the turmoil of the human heart. *One Who Became Lost* represents a big step forward for this young and as yet unheralded poet.

> *Douglas Barbour, in a review of "One Who Became Lost," in* The Dalhousie Review, *Vol. 57, No. 2, Summer, 1977, p. 356.*

ROBERT BILLINGS

[Susan] Musgrave and Plath seem to be the major influences on Marilyn Bowering. *The Killing Room,* Bowering's first full length collection, is filled with the same sharp edges of both diction and sentiment, and the same working and reworking of myth. . . . Bowering's world is a vicious place, a place where if gentleness exists at all, it is only one more element of the violence. Bowering's personae are caught in violence; they sometimes accept it, sometimes rage against it, and sometimes commit it themselves. This is a world of knives, of warmth cut from the body and held, jealously; of "defamation of the beautiful" and actually wanting "to be lost / in winter." The key to the book is, I think, **"Winter Harbour"**, in which Bowering makes the harbour represent a number of contradictory human impulses: "no Spring to melt the ice floes", 'no unfulfilled desires", "no need." But the point is that such integration is only fantasy: "in some year / we may have enough prayers" (**"Armistice"**), but for now the search goes on, "sprouting or reaping" still "nourish us." There are times in the book when jarring rhymes undercut Bowering's sincerity and the intensity of her world; but for the most part the simple diction, and the combination of immediate presentation and abstraction ("Power is breadth / and being") effectively expose a world in which "'Morality' / means us lying dead." (pp. 101-02)

> *Robert Billings, in a review of "The Killing Room," in* The University of Windsor Review, *Vol. XIII, No. 2, Spring-Summer, 1978, pp. 101-02.*

CHAVIVA HOSEK

The Killing Room by Marilyn Bowering is presided over by the voice of a witchy female, a *persona* we may recognize from the work of other contemporary poets, most notably Atwood, Musgrave, and MacEwen. At its best this can be a peculiarly compelling kind of poetry; at its worst it can seem like mystification to no apparent purpose. The voice of the witchy female seems to specialize in mysterious narratives which are meant to be highly symbolic, full of secret, inaccessible knowledge about blood and bones. This volume as a whole and many individual poems in it have too much in the way of symbolic events and not enough hints of where interpretation might go, not enough statement in relation to myth. For all their attempt at rich suggestiveness, the poems therefore seem thin. . . . [In Bowering's poetry] the voice suggests that it possesses ancient and shared knowledge, yet the poems often read like personal mythology.

I fear my response to this volume is rather bad-tempered. Part of the reason for this reaction is that the poems give so little in the way of aural satisfaction. If we are to live in the realm of magic, why can't we get some of the goodies? Poetry is made of words and sounds, not only of potential meanings. Many of the individual sentences in this poetry are flat and almost deliberately bleached. This may be an attempt to make them more suggestive, but instead they seem merely poverty-stricken, and neither narrative nor texture is memorable in many of them. The speakers of the poems seem almost totally self-involved, brooding on some unstated injury or loss. . . . The most satisfying poems are **"Raven II"** and **"Frog's Woman,"** which have an almost oriental feeling about them, and **"The Origin of Man,"** which has an intelligible narrative, consistent imagery, and a sound pattern that reinforces the narrative. (pp. 162-63)

> *Chaviva Hosek, in a review of "The Killing Room," in* The Fiddlehead, *No. 118, Summer, 1978, pp. 162-63.*

DOUGLAS BARBOUR

The poems in *The Killing Room* are often powerful but it is a power of despair, of acceding to death in all its forms without fighting back. 'Death is wide' and 'there were signs / I was not safe' mark the parameters Bowering's imagination works within here. The cover drawing of a starving girl-child seems only too appropriate, for Bowering's people starve from lack of love and friendship. . . . So the women of **'Married Woman's Complaint'** and **'Rose Harbour Whaling Station, 1910'** *allow* the violence their men work upon them, and that is the reason for despair. No doubt Bowering feels that such bitter violent lives are and were lived, but her representation of them is so starkly absolute, so lacking in psychological exploration, that no hope at all remains. Towards the end, there are a few poems which at least begin to work with this deadly material in new, more open ways. The brilliant **'Winter Harbour'** is a powerful evocation of frightening yet enticing transcendence through death and is simply the best poem in the book. Marilyn Bowering is a talented writer, but this collection is too bleak for most readers to find enjoyable or even salutary.

> *Douglas Barbour, in a review of "The Killing Room," in* The Dalhousie Review, *Vol. 58, No. 3, Autumn, 1978, p. 567.*

JANET GILTROW

Marilyn Bowering's *The Visitors Have all Returned* is "experimental" fiction, but its innovations draw it towards poetry. Bowering presents action elliptically; consequently her chapters have the structural status of poems collected to address a unifying theme. In *The Visitors* the speaker's theme is her detachment from her husband and, eventually and ominously, from her daughter, and her resort to private images of ancient, childless figures traversing a mythic pastoral.

When the plotted connections among narrative units are missing, prose loses some of the ordinary signs of coherence and cohesion. Bowering supplies this deficiency with relentless reference to the narrator, a young woman of inwardly spiralling self-consciousness; the stylistic outcome is an extraordinarily heavy incidence of first person pronouns. A second feature of Bowering's style is related: she writes simple sentences unencumbered by qualifying appositives or verbals. This dearth of ornament parallels the speaker's detachment from her surroundings, for it argues her indifference to audience, and a carelessness about exhibiting any persuasive elaboration that might attract a reader into her world.

Can prose succeed without the conventional materials of cohesion and attractiveness? If the reader can take to this speaker, in all her focussed self-interest, then *The Visitors* works. (pp. 137-38)

Janet Giltrow, "Explorers & Runaways," in Canadian Literature, *No. 87, Winter, 1980, pp. 136-38.**

BRUCE WHITEMAN

On the front cover of Marilyn Bowering's new book of poems there is a photograph of the poet. She is, as the acknowledgements inform us, wearing an expensive dress from Creeds and expensive jewellry designed by Tony Calvetti of Vancouver. If the poet as *Vogue* model seems an unpromising beginning to a book, the remark of Zsa Zsa Gabor which gives it its title ("I never hated a man enough to give diamonds back") certainly does not instill confidence nor help to dispel the feeling that there is less here than meets the eye. That is too bad, because although the collection overall is rather weak, due largely to the limitations of Bowering's interests and the small range of her voice, *Giving Back Diamonds* does nevertheless contain some fine poems. **"Under the Influence,"** for example, is a taut and effective poem, perhaps (as Bowering says) "something outside myself is using me to tell you." There is nothing like an instance of spiritual possession to make a poet honest.

Bowering's poems are by and large verbal explorations of her emotional life, and that accounts both for her strengths and weaknesses. Too often her feelings find expression in words which, one can only suspect, come too easily to the tongue and are, at any rate, certainly not good poetry. . . .

There is a dialectic in Bowering's poetry between the self and the outside world of events and other people, but it is a movement which ultimately returns the poem to the writer's ego. Mythic stories and imagery drawn from nature are employed as emblems or object lessons for personal experience, as in **"Penelope's Hall."** . . .

[In this poem], as in much of *Giving Back Diamonds,* the concern is with relations between men and women, an important subject, needless to say, but one which becomes tiresome when it continues as the main point of reference. The lightweight quality of the book's title gives an inadequate indication of the perceptiveness of which Bowering is sometimes capable; but it is, unfortunately, rather accurate in pinpointing the collection's shortcomings.

Bruce Whiteman, "Some Fine Poems," in The Canadian Forum, *Vol. LXII, No. 726, March, 1983, p. 30.*

JOHN OUGHTON

[In *Giving Back Diamonds*] Bowering does give diamonds back, moulded from the coal of her experience. . . . Bowering's lines are honed, her words deliberately and deceptively simple. Like her West-Coast colleague Susan Musgrave, Bowering is fascinated by elemental things—bones, blood, the pull of the grave—but she prefers a finesse where Musgrave would go for the grand slam. Bowering writes elliptically, sparely, from a sensibility that might serve as a model for the younger woman poet, both delicate and tough. . . .

The poems indeed have a logic of their own, mirroring and amplifying each part and then ringing changes before the echo sours. The best ones have the impact of a dream or fairy tale. . . .

Occasionally she removes a bit too much of the connective tissue between idea and image, making the poem difficult for the reader to explore: the two serial poems **"Mary Shelley"** and **"Sea Changes"** suffer from this. But most of the single poems are, without flashy effects, singular. (p. 25)

John Oughton, "Three Graces," in Books in Canada, *Vol. 12, No. 4, April, 1983, pp. 25-6.**

Malcolm (Stanley) Bradbury

1932-

English novelist, critic, short story writer, editor, dramatist, scriptwriter, and essayist.

A university professor whose major academic interest lies in contemporary literature, Bradbury is known for both his critical works and his satires of academic life. Much of Bradbury's fiction takes place in university settings in England or America and incorporates themes of social dislocation and liberalism.

Bradbury is one of England's most respected authorities on the modernist tradition in novels. *The Social Context of Modern English Literature* (1971) is a kind of modernist handbook which examines the intellectual responses of writers to historical and cultural changes. In *Possibilities: Essays on the State of the Novel* (1973) Bradbury advocates naturalism but also calls for a flexible approach to what he terms the "new problematics of realism." *The Modern American Novel* (1983) is an introductory study of American writers from 1890 to the present.

Bradbury's first novel, *Eating People Is Wrong* (1959), is a comic depiction of English provincial university life. In this work a British professor who considers himself a liberal humanist experiences a midlife crisis of conscience. *Stepping Westward* (1965), a lampoon on the differences between English and American culture, centers on a liberal, socially awkward British professor invited to lecture at an American university. *The History Man* (1975), perhaps Bradbury's most critically acclaimed work, was described by Margaret Drabble as raising "some very serious questions about the nature of civilization without for a moment appearing pretentious or didactic—a fine achievement." *Rates of Exchange* (1983), a cultural comedy about language and its contradictions, involves a professor of linguistics abroad in a mythical Eastern European province. Rachel Billington called the novel "one of the most exciting, original and worthwhile novels to appear in Britain recently."

(See also *Contemporary Authors*, Vols. 1-4, rev. ed.; *Contemporary Authors New Revision Series*, Vol. 1; and *Dictionary of Literary Biography*, Vol. 14.)

© *Jerry Bauer*

C. P. SNOW

I am very interested in how this book ["**Eating People Is Wrong**"] goes down in the United States. For several reasons, I am sure the author is one of the most intelligent and gifted of up-and-coming English novelists. I am also sure that the difficulties of writers getting read across the Atlantic—in either direction—are becoming, not less, but greater. . . .

I say all this because Mr. Bradbury's novel, which is extremely funny, packed with intelligence and moral feeling, and *au fond* original, does present some difficulties of setting for American readers. It is basically a story of people trying to find meaning in their lives, and in particular trying to find meaning through the right love relation. That, of course, is the same in Sioux Falls as in Mr. Bradbury's English town. But Mr. Bradbury, like several other English writers of his generation, has chosen to place his people in an English provincial university; and this may muffle some of his effects, unless U.S. readers have now got to terms with "Lucky Jim." Oxford and Cambridge are international symbols, but the English provincial universities, particularly in their effect on their brightest alumni, such as Mr. Bradbury, are not easy for Americans to apprehend. You have universities all conceivable shapes and sizes, but you have not anything deeply interwoven with the intricacies of the English class structure, which is in many ways a tedious subject for you and, God knows, often even more tedious for us. The essential feature of Mr. Bradbury's background is that a high proportion of all the faculty are disappointed to be teaching where they are, instead of at Cambridge. They feel lost and without either status or purpose. . . .

The people, though, would be just as viable in an American faculty. They are Mr. Bradbury's great triumph. He knows them, cares about them, does not sentimentalize them, and gives each, even the absurd, his measure of respect. That is why it is important that he gets read. Professor Treece is forty, a faded young man such as we have all known, still preserving in a faded but honorable fashion the relics of his liberal youth. He is a very good chap, without enough energy to cut a way through life; he likes girls, but his vitality is not overmastering and he gets lost in labyrinths of personal relations. . . .

The whole of this central theme is treated with both originality and depth, and Mr. Bradbury is a natural novelist. It is fair to say that, though much of the comic decoration is extremely effective, it does not come from the same level of originality. Mr. Bradbury, who is himself an academic, has, like Amis and Wain and a good many other youngish English writers of the Fifties studied Eng. Lit. and adopted certain modish forms of farce. There is in fact a hilarious chapter in his novel where a young academic novelist-poet, as much a drip as any of the young academic novelist-poets' own characters, arrives to give a lecture. That is fun, but some of this knockabout *faux féroce* writing is getting altogether too derivative—one of the occupational dangers of this whole school of writing in England either in prose or verse. Too many scenes have filtered through Waugh, Wodehouse, William Cooper . . . , come out in "Lucky Jim," and are continuing to come out, even in a book which, at a deeper level, is as much on its own as Mr. Bradbury's. Still, that doesn't matter much. His is a really interesting talent, odd, perceptive, melancholy, and tender. I should be ready to take a fair-sized bet on his future.

C. P. Snow, "No Faculty for Finding Love," in Saturday Review, *Vol. XLIII, No. 15, April 9, 1960, p. 29.*

MARTIN TUCKER

Hail the bumbling, fumbling conquering hero. Malcolm Bradbury has written a first novel [*Eating People Is Wrong*] that is sloppy, structurally flabby, occasionally inane, frequently magnificent and ultimately successful. It is as if Dickens and Evelyn Waugh sat down together and said, "Let's write a comic novel in the manner of Kingsley Amis about a man in search of his lost innocence who finds it." The result is one of the most substantial and dazzling literary feasts this year.

Bradbury's novel starts out as a well-made satire of Welfare-State Academia, a genre becoming almost as indigenous to England as Mrs. Gaskell and the three-penny dreadful. About a third of the way through, the novel changes course to become an undergraduate-style lampoon with cardboard characterizations of poker-faced English beats and eccentric, highly-sexed college teachers. The last part of the book redeems all, for here Bradbury shows an increasingly tragic awareness of the comic shortcomings of life once the protective veil of satire is snipped off. This traffic between the clever and the profound, the serious and the flippant is never halted. . . . It is inevitable that Bradbury's book will be compared to Kingsley Amis' *Lucky Jim.* Both are novels about the deadly torpor of British provincial university life, and the deadly silly attempts to relieve or disguise that torpor. Both open in the same manner. . . .

Bradbury is also indebted to Amis for the amusing placement of a mild teacher between two aggressive females. In *Lucky Jim,* the hero succeeds with one woman only when another woman is chasing him. At 40, Bradbury's hero, Treece, finally summons up enough courage to seduce a woman, only to have another woman barge in on them.

Both novels also utilize the same device for their climax. Amis has Jim deliver a speech for the university at an important town-gown affair; the speech is naturally a fiasco of hilariously appalling degree, and Jim sinks to the platform dead drunk. Bradbury gives the speech not to the hero but to a new character, someone not unlike Amis himself, an angry-young-man novelist who has been invited to the university for an important social-literary celebration.

Yet Bradbury is by no means a pilferer. He refers to Amis by name and by allusion. . . . But when plot incidents are forgotten, Bradbury and Amis are worlds apart. Amis' book ended with Jim freed from the stagnant ocean of convention that engulfs the university town; Jim is on his way to London and freedom. It was a clever escape, an amusing plot contrivance that got Jim his freedom, but as a solution to the problem Amis opened up, it could not be taken seriously: Jim is ready for new picaresque adventures in London, for in never really facing himself, he has kept the possibility of surprise available at every moment. But Bradbury's novel goes much further afield than Amis ever intended. Bradbury progresses from the ridiculous to the tragic, as Waugh did in *Vile Bodies.* He shows the insane amusements of his milieu only to close with that milieu's lack of resources.

What Bradbury is writing is a morality drama. At 40, Treece begins to review his life and wonders how much of a man he has been. (p. 19)

Treece is supposed to represent the old liberal who no longer "fits" into the new doctrinaire leftism. The political theme however is as relevant or irrelevant as any other part of the bigger question Bradbury is dealing with—the question of commitment. . . . Treece lacks the sense of commitment which gives meaning to any artist, and . . . being a liberal humanist, Treece is committed to his virtue—honest doubt—which grows more painful as the years pass.

In any society Treece would be a passive liberal. Just as he is nothing without a society to give him meaning, so he is a welcome, necessary and unnoticed addition to any society he enters. He is the eternal questioner: everyone listens to his questions, but no one tries to answer them, including himself. His questions are never meant to be answered: that is his tragedy. . . .

You may be depressed by the conclusion, but you can also expect some of the brightest comedy in years. *Eating People Is Wrong* is often foolish; it is more often magnificent, and it certainly marks the debut of a first-rate talent. (p. 20)

Martin Tucker, "'You Must Expect to Be Depressed'," in The New Republic, *Vol. 142, No. 16, May 2, 1960, pp. 19-20.*

THE NEW YORKER

["**Eating People Is Wrong**"] is full of jokes and witticisms of almost every description, but there are no funny situations, and the few comic episodes that occur are much too light, and perhaps also too tired, to stand up against the predominant, tragic predicament that is Treece's life. Treece's predicament is tragic, but his story is not a tragedy, because it is lacking in the act—the proof of life diminished or increased at whatever cost—that is required to complete the movement that starts with the first sentence of this book. What we have here is aimlessness inside countless circles of busy, monotonous aimlessness, and even if this spectacle were more richly decorated than it is with jokes and puns and so on, it would not be good enough. Mr. Bradbury has created a serious and very human character, and has obscured him with jugglers. (p. 97)

A review of "Eating People Is Wrong," in The New Yorker, *Vol. XXXVI, No. 22, July 16, 1960, pp. 96-7.*

EDWIN MORGAN

Malcolm Bradbury's first novel *Eating People Is Wrong* had a well-deserved success as a witty examination of the liberal conscience in a middle-aged professor at a provincial university. His new book [*Stepping Westward*], which attacks the same theme from a different angle, is just as entertaining, with some truly hilarious moments, and a lot of very sharp observation. This time the hero, James Walker, is a wilting provincial writer, thirtyish, going to fat ('bird-eyed, balding' according to *Time*), with three 'promising' novels behind him and a yearning for spiritual revitalisation.... Much of the comedy of the book rises out of the hard job America has prodding open this inert, tweed-suited, non-car-driving limey into some semblance of assertion and commitment.

In one sense the attempt fails, since the hero returns home to his wife ... without having completed his year, but in another sense he turns the tables on America by mildly refusing to sign a loyalty oath and becoming the storm-centre of a controversy which delights his American sponsor, Professor Froelich. A fruitful clash of English and American liberalisms is what Froelich had hoped for and what the serious passages in the novel are concerned with.... Yet Walker's various defeats and insufficiencies as he shambles across the States ... don't cancel a certain respect he rouses both in Froelich and in the reader. Anti-hero or not, he sometimes reminds us that what America claims to offer him for his rebirth is what Saul Bellow's Henderson had to leave America to find. Apart from the fact that too much time (a third of the novel) is spent getting the hero across the Atlantic, this is a fresh, stimulating, and very amusing book. (p. 191)

> Edwin Morgan, "Shambling Man," in New Statesman, *Vol. LXX, No. 1795, August 6, 1965, pp. 191-92.**

A. S. BYATT

[*The Social Context of Modern English Literature*] treats literature as a social product: it occupies "a middle ground between literary study, sociology and intellectual history." It is broadly concerned with the "modernization" of the social world and the ideas of a distinctively "modern" literature.

Professor Bradbury studies the intellectual response to large changes: the concentration of men in cities, the machine, shifts of administrative power. He also describes the changes that affect the production of the literary work: writers' finances, periodicals, publishing, media. Much of his book's considerable value is due to the careful relation of hard, limiting facts to complicated ideas.

He gives a balanced and intricate historical account of the writer's idea of his function in a liberal society. Throughout the modern period (1870 to now) he discerns a tension between an excited hopefulness, a feeling that the artist is a free man, rid of the old pressures of inherited values and orders—and an apocalyptic despair, a sense that institutions are now blank and anonymous, that values and art itself are essentially subjective and ephemeral, and that freedom itself is only a meaningless lack of relation to anyone or anything.

These are the grand clichés of literary chatter. Malcolm Bradbury treats them with enough knowledge and respect to show their operation as real forces in men's work and lives. He sees a hardening of scepticism and a thickening of uncertainty after the great creative period of Lawrence, Eliot, Conrad, Yeats, and Joyce, all of whom were able to create a style from a despair, an orderly product from an intuition of blankness or chaos. For them, detachment from the social process, or even the desire to destroy or undo the existing culture were a function of the need to create new and durable values centered in their work itself....

Professor Bradbury's discussion of the interlay of tradition and innovation, gaiety and despair, has an impressive detachment and balance, even to the shaping of his sentences. His discussions of egalitarian culture is by contrast vehement. He ends with an impassioned stand on behalf of what Henry James called "the beautiful difficulties of art", of ideas which in literature are not simply ideas but "part of a differently realized world of experience". It is on behalf of this world that he so mistrusts its parody in the differently realized images of the mass media. In these later sections he uses words like purity, disinterestedness and mystery with a conjuring authority which is curiously impressive after the ordered dryness of the earlier part of the book.

It is worth remarking in this context that he does not really discuss what ought to be, if it isn't, a cultural force for high culture—the great increase of organized study of literature. He tells us that English literature was only really an object of study in this century, and, in another place, almost without comment, that good modern writers, if they went to university at all, usually read classics or history, not English....

Malcolm Bradbury is one of the few good creative writers in the university literature schools. He could have told us more about their effects—whether they are inhibiting, or stimulating or neutral. F. R. Leavis believed they should be the custodians of value. I had hoped they were at least what Professor Bradbury says barely exists—"places to find sophisticated discussions of literary practice". Professor Bradbury writes almost as if it is generally accepted that they are purveyors of the bland levelling culture and its dubious malaise.

Writers and readers have been driven to hysteria, lassitude or cramping dogmatism by thinking too much about the concepts in this book. Professor Bradbury's virtue finally is that he knows what he is talking about. His style has the solidity and finish that comes from ideas thoroughly thought through. And that is something to be grateful for.

> A. S. Byatt, "Creating a Style Out of Despair," in The Times, *London, September 9, 1971, p. 10.*

JOHN SPURLING

It may well be ... that the period of bitterly opposed [literary] factions is already over, that novelists are starting to put sides to middle, borrowing elements of naturalism, modernism, symbolism and even criticism with cheerful insouciance. In his new book of essays [*Possibilities*], Malcolm Bradbury—himself both novelist and critic—suggests as much. True, he is not an impartial witness; he seems to hold much the same attitude towards the *nouveau roman* as Professor Weightman, calling it "dehumanised, *chosiste*" as though he too had failed to read Simon's or Sarraute's novels except through a cloud of Robbe-Grillet's theory. He also concentrates mostly on English and American novels and probably for that reason tends to equate humanity with liberal humanism. Nevertheless, for all he often appears to be no more than another advocate for naturalism (which he calls "realism"), he does make a genuine attempt to occupy the middle ground.

He reminds us, first, in an essay called "The Open Form", of the immensely varied history of the novel . . . and he argues that at this particular moment in its history "in a good number of our writers there is a desire to resist formal wholeness." If I read the essay right, he is suggesting that the making of new fiction depends not on the continuous invention and development of new means of expression, but on the constant recycling of old means. Stated so baldly, this may sound suspicious: are we merely to read Nathalie Sarraute as if she was Dostoevsky or Rilke instead of as if she was Robbe-Grillet or Butor? But I don't think this is Professor Bradbury's point. He is really calling for a more empirical approach to all writers, whether of the "crystalline" or "journalistic" type, for an approach which would so far as possible release writers from their period and genre and would place less emphasis on the history of literature with its accompanying list of -isms, and more on the actual means deployed by each individual writer to support his fiction. In other words, he considers that novelists have more freedom of form at their disposal than, for instance, poets, and that critics should make some effort to appreciate the fact. (pp. 68-9)

He proceeds to take both bulls—the bull of fiction as autonomous art and the bull of fiction as journalism—by the horns and, banging their heads together in the politest possible way, concludes that "while we must regard novels as verbal constructs, which they inescapably are, we must see what is constructed not alone as a self-sustaining entity but a species of persuasion—the writer handling material for the reader to engage him properly in the world of this once-and-for-all work."

I am not altogether convinced by the content of Professor Bradbury's argument. It seems to me rather too early in the history of the novel to be able to judge whether all the possible changes of form have yet been explored. . . . It may be that contemporary novelists are simply swinging back like a pendulum from extreme crystallisation towards journalism, as Professor Bradbury detects; or it could be that they are going through a phase of retrenchment after the bold experiments of the first half of this century so as to experiment still more boldly in the future. Again, I think that Professor Bradbury's lack of sympathy with the non-naturalistic novel has led him to underrate the real adjustments critics have to make in their own thinking every time a new novelist of stature puts a bomb under their existing poetics. There is a distinction between the "experimental" writer like B. S. Johnson, who cuts a hole in his page or shuffles up a novel in a box, and the writer like Nathalie Sarraute, or perhaps Firbank, who entirely alters the fictional mode of perception. I don't think Professor Bradbury makes this distinction.

But I am attracted by his temperate tone of voice and by the fact that he offers at least a chance of reconciliation between the factions; and perhaps therefore a chance for the writers to be reappraised in terms of their fictions rather than their theories or the movements to which they have been assigned. "A species of persuasion" may not be a very exact definition of the novel, but it is surely a sane and restorative notion. . . . Criticism remains a personal matter between critic and writer. . . . After all, manning the barricades for one group of writers against another not only plays into the hands of professional critics but makes one feel distinctly uneasy: there are so many writers one doesn't like on the same side, and so many one does like on the other. (pp. 69-70)

> *John Spurling, "Unman the Barricades," in* Encounter, *Vol. XLI, No. 6, December, 1973, pp. 66-70.**

MARGARET DRABBLE

The hero, if so he could be called, of **"The History Man"** is a predatory, unprincipled and ruthlessly fashionable sociologist, Dr. Kirk. . . . The description of the evolution of this representative contemporary figure, and of his equally representative wife Barbara, is a small narrative masterpiece, occupying one short chapter but spanning the changes of the last 15 years. . . .

Bradbury writes brilliantly about the way in which our concepts of ourselves determine every detail of our lives—the clothes we wear, the food we purchase, the houses we live in, the people we choose to sleep with, the manner in which we sleep with them. One of the reasons why this novel is so immensely readable is its evocation of physical reality: it may be a book about ideas, but the ideas are embodied in closely observed details. . . . Consciousness of Freud enabled, indeed obliged novelists to dwell on the workings of the unconscious; consciousness of sociology has enabled all of us to read new meanings into objects, and Bradbury catches extremely well the anxiety of those self-aware people who know that their every choice, their every word or movement, transmits a message, and defines them as this or that kind of person.

It is a hard, uncomfortable world, appropriately described in the present tense since these are *present* people. . . . Bradbury refrains here from moral comment: his tone as narrator is impeccably detached, politely pleasant. A thoroughly civilized writer, he has written a novel that raises some very serious questions about the nature of civilization without for a moment appearing pretentious or didactic—a fine achievement. (p. 3)

> *Margaret Drabble, in a review of "The History Man," in* The New York Times Book Review, *February 8, 1976, pp. 2-3.*

GEORGE STEINER

Malcolm Bradbury is a master of enumeration. **"The History Man"** . . . is packed with ludicrous or gloomy taxonomies. The female lead, Barbara Kirk, is . . . a promoter of Women for Peace, the Children's Crusade for Abortion, and No More Sex for Repression. The glass-and-concrete English academe in which her husband teaches burgeons with notices for all seasons. They include the Women's Lib Nude Encounter Group, the Gaysoc Elizabethan Evening: With Madrigals. . . . Each year, campus fashions change in delicate modulation with the spirit of the day. . . . At the party that is the crux of the novel we find young guests in Afghan yak, combat wear, wet-look plastic. The fauna ranges from bearded Jesuses and long-haired androgynes to girls with pouting plum-colored mouths. . . .

These lists define the brittle, hectic landscape of Bradbury's comedy, which is England in its current dishevelment. Open your door and the jetsam of a broken culture tides in. . . . Howard and Barbara Kirk welcome them all. It is their business to conduct life on the broad and rushing front of involvement, of high-finish immediacy. (p. 130)

The Kirks embody a characteristic but fairly complicated piece of English domestic history. Bradbury calls them "new people." Howard is a representative product of the opening of educational-social doors in the fifties. . . . Barbara has made it to higher education owing to a Socialist teacher of English who has pushed an inherently bright but timid girl out of the gray ruck of family expectations. . . . England is shifting into the swing of the sixties. Marx, Freud, the Beatles are loud in the land. The young look back in anger on the bleak suffocations of their roots and upward scramble.... Sexual experiment and mutual license are the most evident gestures of the new dispensation. But the revolution is general: in diet and clothes, in mobility and dreams.

Howard's sociological study "The Coming of the New Sex" is a success. It is a work in consort with the times—a little weak, perhaps, on documentation, but robustly in tune with the energies and challenges of the permissive scene. (Bradbury's handling of the "adult-liberal" idiom of the London reviewing tribe is immaculate.) An offer is made by the new university at Watermouth. (pp. 130-31)

The moves are familiar: marital abrasions in the groves of academe, departmental Machiavellianism with a dash of ideology, the carapaces of the old and the pimples of the young. There are moments in which Howard and Barbara almost come to question their own dynamic vulnerability, the ecumenical welcome they have extended to the spirit and demon of the age. Windows have been broken and things said which are nearly irreparable. But brightness does not fall from the air. (pp. 131-32)

It is not the plot that matters. Malcolm Bradbury has an acute sense of the autonomous spiralling of language in a society in which anything can be and very nearly everything must be said. The world of the Kirks is one of vehement confession. (There is irony in their name.) Language streams outward, from the bedroom, from the sociological questionnaire, from the lips of the guru. The game of being is the game of words: probing, corrosive, charged with generational tension and frankness as never before. "Historical inevitability," breathes Miss Callendar, the young instructor in the dark-blue trouser suit, as she yields to Dr. Kirk. And the reply comes pat: "Marx arranged it."

The result is an intense stylization. For all its acid and beautifully gauged actuality, **"The History Man"** is very much in the manner of Henry James. It has the same density of convention, the same alertness to the flick of intonation.... All in all, this is one of the funniest, most intelligent novels to come out of England in a long time. (p. 132)

George Steiner, "Party Lines," in The New Yorker, *Vol. LII, No. 11, May 3, 1976, pp. 130-32.*

NICK TOTTON

It must be ... self-admiration that leads Malcolm Bradbury to fill a third of **Who Do You Think You Are?** with poor and loutish parodies of other writers, many of whom are a good deal better than himself. Mr Bradbury is of the opinion that random exaggeration and distortion, plus vulgarity, are a substitute for really understanding the forces which generate a writer's idiosyncracies; this opinion is false.

Having finished with the parodies, a reader may turn back to the stories to see just what it is that Mr Bradbury so much prefers to Murdoch, Durrell, Spark and company. To complicate matters, Mr Bradbury's own stories are really rather good, and often extremely funny. In **'A Goodbye for Evadne Winterbottom'**, for example, he cunningly exploits the central character's 'liberal', trimming evasiveness, giving him a prolix dexterity that makes his voice a marvellous narrative instrument, while at the same time displaying his personality. This is a kind of real economy of structure at which Mr Bradbury excels....

There is a certain glibness, it is true, in the relentless placing and typing of characters—a bit surprising in view of the title story's argument that such a taxonomy is insupportable. Sometimes Mr Bradbury lets his anti-modernist ideology dominate. But by and large the comedy of these stories is humane and humanist, able to attain a respectable seriousness.

Nick Totton, "In Short," in The Spectator, *Vol. 237, No. 7736, October 2, 1976, p. 22.**

MARTIN GREEN

Stepping Westward is a great advance over Malcolm Bradbury's first novel, **Eating People Is Wrong;** in fact, it shows a really significant comic talent. (p. 53)

But I don't want primarily to appraise [**Stepping Westward**] here. I want to reflect on some of its themes, both as Bradbury handles them, and as they exist (in the reader's mind) outside his handling of them. Just what makes him a significant comic talent, of course, is that he puts his finger on material in the reader's mind that stimulates one to this sort of thinking. These themes may be described as some American psychological types and their environment, or the differences between all that and the English equivalent. But in fact, as Bradbury fictionally defines those types, they are something much more sharply challenging and richly suggestive than "types"; they are a discovery of his own, and a discovery for us of our own experience.

The story tells how James Walker, a literary, married Englishman, comes to America on a creative writing fellowship to a Western university, and there encounters a different idea of being a writer and being married. This idea, which is essentially the same mode of being in two different contexts, is in fact his "America." He finds it very exciting and very inviting, and much larger than the English equivalents. But he himself does not measure up to it, and at the end of the book he goes back to England, which means his "large domestic wife" and his writing of querulous comic novels.

The American idea or mode of being is embodied first in Julie Snowflake, a student at somewhere like Wellesley, who meets Walker on the ship from England, visits him during the Christmas vacation, takes him off with her to California, and finally rejects him. This is the sexual, would-be-marital, mode of the idea. In its literary-intellectual version, the American idea is embodied in Bernard Froelich, a member of the English faculty at Benedict Arnold University, who gets Walker the fellowship, who persuades him to refuse the loyalty oath the university imposes, and who exploits the resultant scandal to advance his own interests.

Bradbury has drawn both these figures very well, it seems to me. It is the things they say that are best—very accurate, very funny, very interesting and impressive bits of behavior, but he also knows the house they live in, the books they read, the food they eat, and so on. The writing about them is on a different level from the straight satirical description of institutions and streets and Americana. Bradbury is always sharp in his observation, but when he deals with Julie Snowflake and Bernard Froelich he is doing more than observe. He is responding to an idea, and the surface reality interests him also as the expression of something within, about which he has many powerful and conflicting feelings. (pp. 54-5)

Walker represents England, and English liberalism, we are told. Bradbury offers us some quite elaborate analyses of those concepts. I am unconvinced. Politically, Walker is a lower-middle-class conservative, it seems to me; ideologically, he is a romantic pessimist with a horror of the technological future; and I don't see anything valuably English about those categories. (I mean, of course, that *his* England does not impose itself on me as even comically authentic.) But Walker does represent his kind of negativeness quite vividly, and thereby gives full value to the American positiveness. He "brings out" the other characters. And since this American quality is so powerful even when not brought out, is so much a feature of the cultural scene, Walker's experience does represent that of Englishmen (among others) when in America. (pp. 57-8)

What Froelich has, what "America" has, and what Walker has not, is an egotism of the body. This American type, though involved so much in intellectual activities, is dedicated to self-expression and self-enforcement in immediate relationships, tests of strength, and direct sensual-emotional contacts. The English equivalent expresses himself and enforces himself much more through his identification with cultural abstractions—in Walker's case, through his writing.

One of the puzzling things about Walker, as a person, is the completeness (the 100% quality) of his self-negation. He has *no* convictions, *no* opinions, no power to assert himself, no power to cope with the world or with other people; the reader wonders how he holds together. And yet we are told that Froelich "envies and admires" him; and Julie seeks him out and gives herself to him. Why? Because of what he has written, in both cases. And that is obviously not a matter of mere talent, if we separate that off from the personality it expresses. We need only turn to the book flap to remind ourselves, with a glance at Bradbury's own career history, how much seriousness, industry, energy, ambition, and sheer force of will go into becoming what James Walker is. This too is self-creation, and of a kind that impresses the other two.

Julie and Froelich, though so much more impressive in their social performances, even as people of intelligence, are probably not going to achieve anything in the world of literature, or of any other kind of "abstract" activity. They put a lot of their energy into such activities, but not of the best *kind* of energy. Froelich is going to be chairman of his department. He is writing a book on the plight of the twentieth-century writer, and we are given to understand that it will be just another such book. All that inventiveness in immediate contacts becomes sterile academicism in the world of thought. And I think the reader knows instinctively that Julie too will always be able to express herself in the world of immediate contacts too completely to need, or be capable of, any large-scale venture into abstractions. (pp. 58-9)

There is much stress on Walker's paleness, flabbiness, paunchiness, physical uninterestingness, and on these being English qualities in him. The attractiveness of Julie, and of American girls in general, is located in their physical firmness, litheness, springiness. Much is made also of his clumsiness, his gracelessness, his lack of physical coordination—his ineptitude in the swimming pool and at changing a tire. Julie's first attempt to reform him is an attempt to teach him to "relax physically." And after his few months in America, Walker does become browner, leaner, fitter, more interesting physically—and the mere approach to the boat home sets him sneezing again. America is the land of bodies, as Dr. Jochum, a European wiseman, tells Walker. (p. 59)

America is finally the land of freedom, of anarchy, in every cultural, moral, and sexual way. The campus buildings are a riot of architectural styles, the students are extravagantly sophisticated and extravagantly naive, the married couples on the faculty swap partners for the night. A part of Walker's fascination with America is his sense that anything goes; right and wrong are irrelevant there. . . .

Not that Julie Snowflake and Froelich represent moral and intellectual breakdown; quite the reverse, and it is the novel's generosity and justice toward them in this way that is one of its best features. (p. 60)

The Americans that Julie and Froelich can be said to represent must be primarily the intellectuals. But in a longer perspective, surely a great deal of the country can be said to be, as it were, focused through them. They are experimenters, morally, socially, and intellectually. Their personality style promises to be able to handle difficult and conventional situations—to be able in ten minutes to establish them as what they are, with total strangers, unprotected and unsponsored—to be able to sell themselves. And this is what nonacademic America seems to Walker, a series of alarmingly difficult and unconventional situations. (pp. 61-2)

And surely Bradbury has the right to identify America with this kind of personality structure, in which the ego is located much more in the area of direct emotional-sensual relations, direct and "childish" affections and hostilities, and every kind of cultural abstraction is distrusted, from formal manners to state socialism. It presumably has something to do with the much more permissive system of child-rearing in America. This is the America that erupted in the Berkeley students' movement, and this is the America one can place in opposition to the official personality of Communist Russia. (p. 62)

Walker represents an opposite type at least half against his own will. He believes in American-style "freedom" before he comes to America, despises his own domesticity, and is only halfhearted about the English virtues of politeness, detachment, not hurting people, and so on. He sees England much as his American friends see it, as a damp dugout for the damp of soul, a national funk hole. And at the end he completely accepts Julie's indictment and dismissal of him. And it is in the completeness of his failure that the punch of Bradbury's story lies.

Julie and Froelich were attracted to Walker partly by his negativeness; in their world he is a curiosity of almost pornographic interest; he is a nudist among knights in armor. They took him into their favor, offered to play the games of life with him, promoting him over the heads of a hundred other people nearer their own size and weight. The moment they forgot to give him extra advantages, the moment they began to use both hands, he was hopelessly outclassed. He was knocked to the floor and trampled under foot. Bradbury is saying that this is likely to happen every time between an Englishman and an American—at least, as long as the Englishman accepts the American standards, the superiority of the psychological structure that is described as "American." And that Englishmen should do that seems to be part of American cultural dominance today. (p. 63)

•　•　•　•　•

I wrote the preceding remarks in 1965, immediately after reading *Stepping Westward*. Now, in 1972, it seems worth adding a few more, which derive from the events of the seven years that have passed since then. It is now *not* true that Englishmen "must" accept American cultural standards or psychological structures.

In America, a great deal has happened that can be summed up by saying that we have entered upon an age of revolution. A considerable number of bright young people have made up their minds that a revolution must happen, and everyone who thinks has been forced to declare himself for or against the idea, and to say why. The American personality type that Bradbury presents as material for comedy has begun to deal in death. Its love of freedom has ceased to mean mostly sexual license. It has taken on political functions. (pp. 63-4)

For perhaps the most interesting thing that the seven year lapse measures is the way "reality" has changed while the literary conventions have not. (By "reality" I mean that consensus view of America which is powerful and general enough to force itself on a writer as much in touch as Bradbury.) I have read several other British comic novels since 1965 that took the same angle on America as *Stepping Westward* did. Some of them were published slightly before, but essentially they were contemporary with it, and David Lodge's *Out of the Shelter* was considerably later. Two of them, Julian Mitchell's *As Far As You Can Go* and Kingsley Amis's *One Fat Englishman* were of comparable literary interest with *Stepping Westward,* and Andrew Sinclair's *The Hallelujah Bum* was at least lively. In all of them (they form a distinct genre of modern British fiction) the view of America and the way its idea contrasts with the English idea is the same. In them all the central character, who represents the novelist, comes to the U.S.A., responds reluctantly to its various challenges and invitations, gradually makes up his mind for it as opposed to England, but (usually) returns home nevertheless, feeling unable to meet those challenges adequately. And though they do not deny the tragic elements in the American situation, they respond more to the comic elements. They see even the tragic as comic, in the sense that it is another manifestation of the whole country's size and vitality, its oppositeness to the smallness and claustrophobia of Britain.

Of course the heroes do not all represent the same England as Bradbury's Walker does. . . . The differences between the heroes illustrate the range of British types involved in this imaginative encounter with "America" during the sixties.

Moreover, during these years we also saw America produce comic work that corresponds to the British, in the sense that it issues from the identity that Bradbury attributes to Froelich— I mean the comedy of Heller and Pynchon and *M.A.S.H.* and above all John Barth. *Giles Goat-Boy* is surely the supreme manifestation of that aggressive, extrovert ebullience, that harsh, gross body-humor, which Bradbury describes as "America."

But both these styles seem to have been by-passed by events. America is no longer triumphantly comic, for its citizens or for its visitors. (pp. 64-6)

Moreover, among the Englishmen I have recently met over here, more and more seem to have that sense of themselves, and of their style as Englishmen, in America. They move through the thundering ruins of this great, gaudy, wicked Hollywood set, this *Day of the Locust* scenario, openly keeping a tight hold on their integrity—publishing a sense that they belong to a tight little tradition, unambitious and untriumphant, but simple, solid, cautious, durable. It is a vastly more attractive posture than that of James Walker. Morally they have every advantage. Imaginatively, however, I suspect that the disintegrated looseness and openness of the comic heroes of the sixties promised more in the way of new life for British comedy. (p. 66)

Martin Green, "Transatlantic Communications: Malcolm Bradbury's 'Stepping Westward'," in Old Lines, New Forces: Essays on the Contemporary British Novel, 1960-1970, edited by Robert K. Morris, Fairleigh Dickinson University Press, 1976, pp. 53-66.

MALCOLM BRADBURY

The History Man is a novel about dehumanization; behind the book is a strong visual analogy, of a flat, hostile landscape, not our good old friend, of multi-storey car parks, block buildings, blank walls, treeless spaces, run-down city scapes, a graffiti-scarred new university which could, if events require it, be well converted into a factory, a world in which it is hard to put in the person. The characters, too, are hard objects, and there is no entry into their psychology or their consciousness: they manifest themselves by their speech and their actions. There is one ostensibly sympathetic character, who speaks for humanism; she is a deception to the reader. The central figure, Howard Kirk, the radical sociologist who, four years after the revolutionary season of 1968, when onerous reality seems wonderfully to lift, tries to sustain his transforming passion in an inert world. But he believes that privacy is over, and the self is no more than the sum of the roles that it plays. Howard acts, but otherwise, in a world where speech-acts and ideas cannot affix themselves to a sense of value in action or history, passivity is the norm. Accidents become important, and so do happenings, those chance events that arise when we give a party or juxtapose students in a classroom. There are no purposeful plots, except Howard's; he plots in a plotless world, hoping to serve the radical plot of history. The dominant tense is the present, diminishing the sense of historical or personal rootedness, making the world instantaneous; the text is hard, presented in long paragraph blocks which immerse the agents and their speech. The mode is irony, and neither the world nor its personages are our good old friend. And realism moves toward a harsh abstraction. (p. 207)

Malcolm Bradbury, "Putting in the Person: Character and Abstraction in Current Writing and Painting," in The Contemporary English Novel, Stratford-Upon-Avon Studies, No. 18, edited by Malcolm Bradbury and David Palmer, 1979. Reprint by Holmes & Meier Publishers, Inc., 1980, pp. 181-208.*

JOHN WALSH

Although he claims, in the Introduction [to *All Dressed Up and Nowhere to Go*], to having never been an Angry Young Man in the 1950s (they were all ten years older than he), Malcolm Bradbury's stance in this collection of witty sociological essays is precisely that of the provincial, anti-establishment, pooh-poohing intellect associated with Amis, Osborne, and Wain in their prime.

First published in 1960 and 1962, his two books, *Phogey! How to Have Class in a Classless Society* and *All Dressed Up and Nowhere to Go or the Poor Man's Guide to the Affluent Society,* collected here in a new edition, are masterly studies in the never-had-it-so-good Britain that emerged from the post-war decade of austerity, and discovered coffee bars, geometric furniture, American slang, beehive hairdos, Swedish glassware, sun-lounges and sociology . . . then tried to work out a British life-style to go with the new toys.

Bradbury's central victim is the 'phogey', (a conflation of foggy, phoney, and old fogey), an imperial throwback, a mean-spirited, wary, insular, super-conventional, know-your-place traditionalist that lurks within the psyche of every Brit (even, it sometimes appears, within Mr Bradbury himself). His brisk anatomising of this stuffy figure's beliefs and responses to external stimuli are marvellously entertaining; and he identifies types (The Hanging Judge, The Genial Administrator, The Lady Academic, The Good Sport) with a gimlet eye for detail.

Elsewhere in the volume, Bradbury turns his attention to some modern developments in those large issues, wealth and class. . . . And if, like him, you find both the trappings and assumptions of consumerist society getting too much to bear, you can adopt his guerilla tactics of voluntary poverty, provincialism and the agrarian life.

Mr Bradbury's essays, as one would expect from the author of *The History Man,* are unfailingly elegant, even when at their most polemical, full of new-minted wisdom . . . although their ostensible subject is 20 years old, and manage to make many serious points while dazzling the reader with wit.

> John Walsh, in a review of "All Dressed Up and Nowhere to Go," in Books and Bookmen, No. 327, December, 1982, p. 31.

MARTIN AMIS

It is not every year that Malcolm Bradbury writes a novel. It is every decade that Malcolm Bradbury writes a novel. Already he has called **'Rates of Exchange'** 'a novel for the early eighties,' just as '**"Stepping Westward"** was my novel for the early sixties.' Given such ambitions, it's no wonder that Bradbury's books are notoriously slow to get off the ground—and, in the present case, slower still to land.

'Rates of Exchange' begins with a cod history of Slaka, the imaginary capital of an imaginary East European state. This teasing sketch is written with such ravenous drollery that you can almost hear the author rubbing his hands and smacking his lips at the prospect of the feast to come. Page 13 sees the hero, the laconic linguist Petworth, warily circling Slaka Airport. . . .

The opening wedge of prose would seem to be an elaborate dramatisation of culture shock. . . . Bradbury's apocryphal language—acknowledged here as the fruit of a collaborative classroom project—is an impressive artefact but an unwieldy one, often imperilling the novel's sense of balance.

Anyway, given so many pages in which to recuperate, and so carefully acclimatised by the official guide, the reader finds that his culture shock is dwindling into a long series of mild surprises. All novels, as Professor Bradbury will confirm, are official tours through invented countries; and, as a guide, Bradbury is perhaps rather too finicky and oversolicitous. He doesn't want us to miss anything. 'Poor Petwit, I am sorry. For you there is no story at all,' some cultural janitor tells the hero on page 129, as the novel belatedly embarks on its familiar itinerary: lunches, lectures, romance with lady novelist, entanglement with literary placeman Plitplov (a version of Bernard Froelich in **'Stepping Westward'**), brush with comic ambassador and his nymphomaniac wife. The comic ambassador, a farcical stutterer, must be one of the most outrageously unfunny characters in modern fiction: 'Perhaps you'd care for a pee, care for a pee a peach brandy? . . . Well, how about a sort of piss a sort of Piesporter?' But then, too, the novel does a lot of stuttering on its own account.

Take the 15-page wait at Slaka Airport. Here, Petworth expects the official machinery to fulfil its function of 'meeting and greeting.' Yet 'there has been no meeter to meet him, no greeter to greet him.' A few pages later there is still 'no meeter, no greeter.' A few pages later he is 'waiting for his meeter to meet him, his greeter to greet him.' A few pages later 'the process of meeting and greeting' has yet to begin. If this is deliberate, why is it deliberate?

Similarly, the prose is littered with the lazy adjectives 'small,' 'little,' 'vast,' 'big,' 'fine' and 'great'—especially *great*. This last epithet must put in two or three hundred appearances. Again one allows for a calculated effect. But then *great* goes away for a spell. But then *great* returns, in spades. . . . No doubt, or just possibly, this is deliberate. Great. But why?

Bradbury is a deliberate writer. As is the case with his stablemate David Lodge, Bradbury's modernity is courteous and straightforward, almost apologetic, part of the expository thrust of his fiction. This seems to be the English way. Bradbury tells you what he is up to, and so do his characters. . . . Bradbury has set up the many neat polarities implicit in his title, and these themes are ably and ingeniously dispatched. But the novel's air of teachability is greater than its spontaneous life.

At least two other Westerners have stepped eastward in the recent past: John Updike in 'Bech: A Book' and Saul Bellow in 'The Dean's December.' Comparisons are odious—also unflattering. Bradbury does not match Updike's seriocomic swiftness or Bellow's troubled, meditative realism. True, he is going for something rather more abstract, rather more 'readerly'; but in the end **'Rates of Exchange'** is uneconomical—prohibitively so.

Bradbury is a novelist with one voice, one register: it is cold, amused, detached, donnish, pedagogic. . . . **'Rates of Exchange'** is his first venture outside the academic milieu. In the real world, in 'a novel for the early eighties,' that voice sounds somewhat strained; it drones, and stutters, and goes on a bit too long.

> Martin Amis, "A Slowcoach in Slaka," in The Observer, April 3, 1983, p. 29.

ROGER LEWIS

[In Malcolm Bradbury's *Rates of Exchange*] Slaka is a volatile state in the Soviet orbit. Its 'history is a mystery' because at various times it has been conquered by every tribe in existence. This quirky Ruritania is in permanent flux: the grammatical structure of its language alters overnight (the populace obediently setting aside time in which to change placards), there are several financial systems, and the world beyond the capital is shrouded in mystery. It is a landscape in which gross confusion stems from an attempt to be organised.

Into this world comes Dr Petworth, a minor academic from an even less exalted institute of higher education, a linguist despatched by the British Council on a culture tour. Much of his life has been spent exporting 'the ideal British product': the English language. Almost permanently on the move from country to country, he can discern only the drab similarities of his destinations rather than the exciting differences. As genteelly crumpled as his lecture notes, Petworth is menopausal, almost always fatigued, and never fights back when riled. Our hero in *Rates of Exchange,* with his paper-clips and Fontana Modern Masters, would seem almost wholly unappealing. Bradbury's success, however, is to conduct us behind the ungalvanic facade so that we come to realise that the meekness is in fact virtue. Petworth, 'a speech without a subject, a verb without a noun, certainly not a character in the world historical sense', is nevertheless the only still point in a convulsively turning world.

Into his latest novel Bradbury has hurled all his pet hates, coming to terms with what bores him by making it comic: airports, immigration controls, . . . couriers. His world is one where irritating fads breed like Ionesco's chairs. This would pall were Bradbury not able to turn it into a theatre of the absurd. . . . [In] his novels he writes as a critic (where he gives the impression of being a wry commentator on his characters' activities rather than the inventor of them) and in his criticism he is enormously creative (making imaginative connections and absorbing himself in what he writes about). He plays one role under the guise of the other.

To depict Slaka he develops a style that easily allows both farce and seriousness. Intermingled with the jokes is a subtle disquisition about freedom and privacy. There is no unemployment in Slaka because everybody is officially occupied spying on everybody else. Rooms are abristle with sonic lugs and behind every mirror lurks a member of the secret police who minutely scrutinises one's ablutions. Watched in this way the citizens become actors, learning to disguise their real emotions with such skill that they don't know what an authentic feeling would be like. In this bizarre world of duplicity and stratagem the mild-mannered Petworth appears a subversive warrior. His gentle honesty, in the midst of such mendacity, seems like dissident troublesomeness. He is temperamentally unsuited to barter on this psychological rate of exchange.

> *Roger Lewis, "Merely Players," in* New Statesman, *Vol. 105, No. 2716, April 8, 1983, p. 24.**

FRANCIS KING

What is best in [**Rates of Exchange**] is not the plot, which is essentially thin, nor the characters, who are essentially stereotypes derived from other Iron Curtain novels, but the exhilarating vigour of its author's intellect and style. I particularly enjoyed those passages in which, in the manner of Fielding—a novelist whom he resembles in his mixture of humanity, frankness and irony—Mr Bradbury buttonholes the reader as 'cher lecteur' and then delivers to him what is, in effect, a dazzlingly clever mini-essay in a style notable for the crispness of its imagery and the athleticism of its pace.

> *Francis King, "Professional, Foul," in* The Spectator, *Vol. 250, No. 8074, April 9, 1983, p. 26.*

HERMIONE LEE

To cover all of twentieth century fiction in 200 pages is no easy task; Professor Bradbury's survey [**'The Modern American Novel'**] does it smoothly and well. The necessary chronological structure is livened up by the trick of starting each decade with a key moment. . . .

The literary 'isms' of these decades are clearly defined. . . .

Bradbury is surely right to take Crane's 'The Red Badge of Courage,' Norris's 'McTeague' and Dreiser's 'Sister Carrie' as the crucial turn-of-the-century novels, to give prominence to the innovations of Gertrude Stein and Dos Passos, to promote Henry Roth's 'Call It Sleep' (1935) as a major precursor of later Jewish-American fiction, and to rate Pynchon as the outstanding writer of the early Sixties group that included Barth,

Heller, Vonnegut and Kesey. There is an interesting comparison of James and Dreiser; there are expressive passages on writers such as Hemingway and Dos Passos, and some good quips about Wolfe's portentousness, Stein's gargantuanism . . . and Vonnegut's 'sentimental folksiness', and there's also a very useful bibliography.

Bradbury gives short shrift to women writers. . . .

Still, as a reference book this is impressively informed and strongly directed. As a literary work for sustained reading, however, it is heavy going. As in his just-published novel, **'Rates of Exchange'** (similarly preoccupied with the fate of language and character in the modern 'pluralist' universe), Bradbury's vocabulary is knowingly modish and tiresomely repetitive. Over-insistent key words—'psychic,' 'mythic,' 'discontinuous'—make all the writers sound alike.

In the 'post-modernist' period this language comes into its own: 'signs seem to outrun signification,' there is 'a crisis of intertextuality,' 'the novelist lives in a world of unattached signifiers,' the novel offers itself 'as a form of de-creation leading to re-creation,' 'the sign has floated free of the signified,' the text is 'functioning by an elaborate and often expository discursiveness working on the interface between two levels of experience.' This is the language of **'Rates of Exchange,'** and these are the post-structuralist terms in which Bradbury renders the world and the book. It may be that Bradburese is the most authentic critical currency of the late twentieth century, but a lot of it leaves me, I'm afraid, with a bad attack of *la nausée*.

> *Hermione Lee, "Reader's Digest," in* The Observer, *April 24, 1983, p. 31.*

DAVID MONTROSE

A critical record, in a mere 186 pages, 'of the achievement of American fiction since the turning-point of the 1890s', Malcolm Bradbury's [**The Modern American Novel**] resembles, at first glance, a literary equivalent of those whirlwind tours that promise the delights of 12 capitals in seven days. . . . The book should be judged for what it is: a compact introduction for rookie undergraduates.

Given the incidence of bibliophobia on our campuses, the book had to be, above all, brief and comprehensive. Depth is, therefore, a necessary victim. Nor is comprehensiveness taken so far as to embrace writers who do not fit into the academically-conceived tradition of 'the Modern American Novel'. There are no more than fleeting references to such notables as William Styron, Gore Vidal, and Flannery O'Connor. . . . E. L. Doctorow, John Irving and Don DeLillo, having emerged too recently yet to be set authors, receive similar treatment. And there is no room whatsoever for even the leading practitioners of that distinctively American form, the private-eye novel.

> *David Montrose, in a review of "The Modern American Novel," in* New Statesman, *Vol. 105, No. 2720, May 6, 1983, p. 23.*

JOEL CONARROE

[**Rates of Exchange**] manages to be funny, gloomy, shrewd and silly all at once. Much of it, especially the first hundred pages or so, reads less like fiction than like a meticulously detailed journal kept by a jaundiced traveler with total recall. To anyone who has ever done time in that funny, gloomy place called Moscow the book will afford innumerable shocks of recognition. To everyone else it will provide comic but nevertheless reliable exposure to a land of astonishing inefficiency, awful food, rampant paranoia, and surprisingly hospitable (and lovable) people. . . .

[The book is], more often than not, engaging, even though Bradbury, like all compulsive wits (and especially the British sort), sometimes lets his cleverness get in the way of his story.

His protagonist is Angus Petworth, a middle-aged linguist who travels from London to "Slaka," where he gives some rarefied lectures on the English language. . . . To call him an antihero is seriously to understate the case—Petworth is a scarecrow with a passport. He neither acts nor reacts, and his conversation is less than memorable. It is Bradbury's curious triumph to make of this colorless nonperson a center of attention, to show how, a blank, he becomes the object of desire for a number of people who project onto his vacant persona their own frustrated erotic hopes. . . .

Bradbury's satirical targets are legion. One running joke (a bit too long-running) has to do with language, butchered by everyone Petworth meets, e.g., "Oh my English, I wish it was gooder." . . . Language is Bradbury's theme—he also amuses himself at the expense of the "more fashionable thinkers of the Structuralist persuasion," and of Russian speech, reduced to a series of made up words, as in "Burs'ii Proly'aniii" (government bank), or "Prif'sorii Universitayii."

A minor pleasure (or perversity, depending on your point of view) derives from Bradbury's depiction of America and Americans. When he reveals that he has traveled in the States, Petworth is bombarded with questions: "Do they have topless seminars now in the university, the topless physics, the topless mathematics? How is your ego and your id?" . . .

So much for us! But then since everybody in the book, the British included, is made to look foolish we can forgive Bradbury his stereotypes. We can forgive him, too, his occasional prolixity and his tendency to strain after comic effects, can, in fact, ignore these things and just listen to the music. The novel (or journal, or compendium of cartoons) is full of winning characters and hilarious scenes. Anyone who thinks this sad old world of ours can do with an occasional laugh will find it satisfying.

Joel Conarroe, "Malcolm Bradbury: A Safari to Slaka," in Book World—The Washington Post, *November 20, 1983, p. 3.*

RACHEL BILLINGTON

Malcolm Bradbury, the author of **"Rates of Exchange,"** has always been concerned with defining the value of language. He once wrote that the novel "may resemble the real world in many respects and may appeal to a common recognition of society, reality, humanity; but it is a world made of *language.*" . . .

Although he has always used campus life and campus characters for his fictional world, he has never been what one might describe as an intellectual writer. His favored weapon has been the traditionally English sword of irony and satire, though his technique merges often (and very successfully) into the broader strokes of comedy and even farce. He simply loves language, using it with sharpness and energy. **"Stepping Westward,"**

his second book, made hilarious fun of an Anglo-American professional exchange. His last novel, **"The History Man"** (1975), was celebrated in England as an indictment of the excesses of the academic revolution of the 1960's. Its celebrity grew after it was adapted into a popular television serial.

"Rates of Exchange," which was a finalist in the prestigious Booker Prize competition in Britain this year, is a very different sort of book. Suddenly, here the professor of English is the theorist. This densely written book, in which dialogue appears on the page in unparagraphed chunks, is a novel about an idea. It is an astonishing tour de force. Mr. Bradbury has invented an entire country, essentially mythic although Eastern European in origin, to sustain a proposition laid out before us in various forms in the course of the book.

"What, after all, is our life," the author asks near the start, "but a great dance in which we are all trying to fix the best going rate of exchange, using our minds and our sex, our taste and our clothes?" Trust nothing, he tells us, nothing is fixed, nothing is what it seems; "trust only the novelists, those deeper bankers who spend time trying to turn pieces of printed paper into value, but never pretend that the result is anything more than a useful fiction." This leads us to the most essential and most misleading "rate of exchange"—that in language.

Although the story line is simple, the novel designed to convey these ideas is frequently tough going. (p. 15)

"Rates of Exchange" is a novel by a supremely confident writer. This is both its strength and weakness. Mr. Bradbury dares to create a dominant author's voice and does this in an age when most novelists seem to want a cloak of invisibility. This voice, setting out the theme of the novel, leads us through the first 60-odd pages. Petworth, the protagonist, is hardly allowed a thought, although he is gradually being moved . . . from England to Slaka via airport, airplane and then airport again. The level of writing is excellent, and yet, in the light of the whole novel, this part appears a self-indulgence that Mr. Bradbury should have written, perhaps, for his own use and then put away. The novel, though substantial, should not have to bear what is in effect a long introduction.

His confidence shows again, appropriately so, in his use of the spoken word. Whatever their theme, how many writers would dare to put most of their dialogue in a Slakian kind of nonsense English? Sometimes, of course, the result is amusing . . . but it does not make for fluid reading. As with the opening pages, one admires and yet reserves commitment.

Mr. Bradbury is essentially a comic writer, a man gifted with the power to produce laughter. So comedy is possibly the clue to a final judgment on the book's success or failure. There are many funny jokes based on wordplay and puns and a few extremely funny scenes in **"Rates of Exchange."** However, in general, the tone is too bleak for laughter, the author's grip too tight on the reader's neck. Even the characters, brilliantly inventive though they are, seem too much under the thumb of their master for any heartbreaking moment of truth. (pp. 36-7)

While **"Rates of Exchange"** may not be an altogether successful work, it is nevertheless one of the most exciting, original and worthwhile novels to appear in Britain recently. (p. 37)

Rachel Billington, "Tongue-Tied Linguist," in The New York Times Book Review, *November 20, 1983, pp. 15, 36-7.*

Anita Brookner

1938-

English novelist and critic.

Brookner's three novels are considered sensitive, well-crafted stories about what Robert Taubman calls "the subjugation and defeat of an intelligent heroine." Brookner's first novel, *A Start in Life* (1981), tells of a middle-aged academic's unsuccessful attempt to free herself from her clinging parents. *Providence* (1982) is the story of a scholar of Romanticism who finds her life dull and disappointing but is unable to change. *Look at Me* (1983) generated the most substantial critical response. This story of a timid medical librarian who fails at love and withdraws into her writing as a substitute for living was generally praised as a thoughtful study of alienation.

ANNIE GOTTLIEB

Anita Brookner's first novel, **"The Debut"** [published in Great Britain as **"A Start in Life,"** is less in the Romantic tradition than ironic]. . . . Its English heroine, Ruth Weiss, is a 40-year-old academic whose timid attempts to seize life are overwhelmed by her aging yet childish parents and by the weight of European culture they impose upon her. In her childhood world, youth was the anachronism. Her parents and the books that surrounded her embodied the vitality of the past, the perverse appeal of decay (the chilling portrait of Ruth's deliquescent mother is right out of Christina Stead). The wisdom and folly of the past seem to mock her efforts toward a new beginning; what's the use, it's all been done. An omniscient weary narrator watches with pity and irony as Ruth tries to fuel her brief rebellion with literature. Balzac was right, she decides, Dickens was wrong; the bad have a good time, the virtuous are wallflowers at the ball. And off she goes to Paris to have affairs.

But Ruth seems to be a renunciant by fate or nature. She lacks the robust sexual selfishness that would allow her to take from others. Or perhaps the demands she makes of life are too pure, so that what other people take isn't worth much to her and renunciation becomes the idealist's instinctive escape from disappointment. For whatever reason, Ruth ends up back in London caring for her widowed invalid father in a manner more companionable than incestuous. For those who are at ease in the hyperliterate atmosphere of English novels—and especially for those who can also read the occasional French phrases—this is a precise and haunting little performance. (p. 14)

> Annie Gottlieb, "Three Hapless Heroines," in The New York Times Book Review, *March 29, 1981, pp. 14-15.**

NICHOLAS SHRIMPTON

[*A Start in Life* is] the sort of book which gives feminist writing a good name. *A Start in Life* sets the experience of a modern woman academic, working on Balzac, against the plot of *Eugénie Grandet*. The craftsmanship is, if anything, almost too sedulous. But it produces a very pungent fable about the sacrifice of daughters to the needs of their elderly parents.

© Jerry Bauer

> Nicholas Shrimpton, "Bond at 70," in New Statesman, *Vol. 101, No. 2618, May 22, 1981, p. 21.**

ROBERT TAUBMAN

Kitty in ***Providence*** is the sort of heroine an author invents in order to subject her to a life of disappointments. These are mitigated for her by academic interests—hers in the Romantic tradition, her lover's in French cathedrals. The novel is warm and delightful about donnish life, exhibiting its own kind of donnishness in a sentence like 'The dog was very old, and did not seem particularly viable.' But Kitty's plight is to be half-French, and her common sense, her clothes sense and her solid affections are all on her French side. She lives in Chelsea, but her England is a fantasy constructed around a dead soldier-father and a lover she cannot picture. . . . Worse: the lover is indeed as near as one can get to a fantasy Englishman, a professor with a pleasant vague smile, 'wandering around with a cup in one hand and a saucer in the other, a signet ring just visible on the finger beneath the saucer'. Ruth, in Anita Brookner's first novel, was in love with a professor with 'a neutral, faintly resigned presence': but Kitty's case is even more hopeless. Maurice is not only English, but specifically upper-class Gloucestershire; and Kitty loses him to a girl in her own seminar, out of the same Gloucestershire top drawer, who does what Kitty can't and wouldn't ever do—wear her brother's pullovers. *Providence* is absolutely a love story, and restates, without accounting for, the fact that neither reason nor objective grounds for liking or disliking have anything to do with falling in love. Kitty, an expert on the Romantics, only confirms the 19th-century stereotype: one thinks of Lucy Snowe in *Villette*. Yet Kitty doesn't get as much support from her author as Lucy Snowe. It's made to look only ironical that she is intelligent and sensitive and teaches two strenuous seminars on Romantic love in *Adolphe*. But one wonders why Anita Brookner should spend so much delicacy and irony on situations which she has planned from the start will come to nothing. This is now her second novel about the subjugation and defeat of an intelligent heroine. (pp. 18-19)

Robert Taubman, "Submission," in London Review of Books, May 20 to June 2, 1982, pp. 18-19.*

ELAINE JORDAN

Frances, who begins to write her own story (which we have just read) on the last page of *Look at me,* is tougher than many reviewers have made her seem. Her melancholy retrospect shows a bravery of wit. More than this, she has her revenge. 'Look at me' has two ranges of tone: sad ('just look at me now') or demanding attention with the gaiety of self-assertion. What Frances is denied is not simply love, but good manners. It is the public devaluation of her by the group she so admires that devastates her. When she regains composure, she will seek them out again, apparently meekly, but with an undeclared purpose: 'I needed them for material.' This is not how a well-mannered person should treat her acquaintance, but look at the previously admired Alix Fraser: 'Alix stubbed out her cigarette in the remains of her yellow custard and smeared red over her wide mouth.' This is not a novel of scenes but a meditation on experience in the French tradition.

One problem is how far Frances is presented ironically. The sharpening of her self-knowledge often seems excessively depreciatory, while her bedazzlement by the aura and gusto of the Frasers can hardly be shared by the reader: we can't look at them, and the author doesn't give them marvellous things to say—they are just abominable. It is hard to know whether this is because the writer's early experience of them is constantly attended by the sadism of revenge or whether she just cannot capture in words what makes them so fascinating. (p. 23)

Elaine Jordan, "Travelling," in London Review of Books, April 21 to May 4, 1983, pp. 22-3.*

STEPHEN HARVEY

For the heroine of Anita Brookner's novel [*Look at Me*], life is a bitter pill, and no wonder. Endowed with private means, she lives with an elderly housekeeper in the London mausoleum/flat in which her mother expired after a lingering illness. For fun Frances has entombed herself in a medical library, where she curates a collection of prints and engravings depicting Disease Through the Ages. Her girlhood friend is a soft-spoken cripple, and her closest attachment is to a trio of vivacious sybarites who ignore Frances when they're not ridiculing her. But Frances's dreariest fate, if she only realized it, is to be trapped inside her own precious, suffocating self.

And since she is the narrator/protagonist of this introverted book, the hapless reader is trapped right along with her. Frances characterizes herself as a self-effacing observer, who longs to

act and be noticed. "I needed to learn, from experts," she sighs, "that pure egotism that had always escaped me"; if you ask me Frances does just fine in that department on her own. Rarely has a novel been so cluttered with the first-person-singular-pronoun; Frances's "I" appears 34 times on page 123 alone. Moreover for someone who prides herself on acuity of vision, her description of the supporting characters dominating her rich interior life is remarkably hazy. . . .

The real problem is that Anita Brookner doesn't derive much fun out of Frances's suffering either. If Brookner had betrayed some inkling that her protagonist really deserves no better than she gets (or gives), this might have been an arresting, ironic novel. But *Look at Me* seems intended to be read as a delicate tragedy of alienation—the slow descent of a guileless misfit, intelligent enough to understand her lot, and too passive to change it. By the end, Frances has repaired to her mother's deathbed and pledged to become a novelist, to use writing as a substitute for living. *Look at Me* is precisely what a woman like Frances would come up with—schematic, self-conscious fiction which is a substitute for literature.

Stephen Harvey, in a review of "Look at Me," in The Village Voice, Vol. XXVIII, No. 27, July 5, 1983, p. 46.

JULIA EPSTEIN

The heroine of [*Look at Me*] . . . catalogues images in a medical library—images of melancholy, of madness, of nightmare, of disease and affliction. Pictures by Géricault, El Greco, Durer, Goya, a gallery of morbid visions, pass through her hands daily ("our collection is rather naturally weighted towards the incalculable or the undiagnosed"). Her function in the world, as she defines it, is to maintain her files: to nod, to smile politely, to fetch and carry, to observe, to record, to be one of the "watchers at the feast."

Not a very promising heroine. But *Look at Me* is a nearly impossible achievement, a novel about emptiness and vacancy, about the shambling tread of the aged and the emotionally rigid, about the sort of apparently dull person whose idea of chic is "a pale grey dress with a white puritan collar and a black bow at the neck." Brookner makes that person riveting in her ragged self-knowledge, her ability to look in a mirror, see precisely what others see, and know the image to be false. . . .

To write a novel about writing a novel is hardly new. But Brookner alters the frame slightly, so that her subject is not the writing but the gathering and absorbing and sifting of quotidian detail, meals and disappointments, through the sieve of language and into the moiling cauldron of the imagination. Her novel is not so much self-reflexive as self-digesting, its material imaged and converted into prose even as it unfolds in Frances' life.

In *Look at Me,* Anita Brookner has accomplished what Flaubert once set out to do: to write "a book about nothing," which is to say a book about language, a *Bouvard et Pécuchet* of the soul. *Look at Me* is simultaneously a tragedy of solitude and loss, and a triumph of the sharp-tongued controlling self. Brookner's first novel, *The Debut,* marked off some of this territory, but with a sulkier and a more tentative hand. In *Look at Me,* Brookner unveils a portrait of the melancholic woman, "overpowered by her inability to take the world's measure . . . a garland in her tangled hair," as she unveils a narrative voice in full sail.

Julia Epstein, "Images of Melancholy," in Book World—The Washington Post, *July 24, 1983, p. 6.*

FRANCES TALIAFERRO

In the past two years, Anita Brookner's novels *The Debut* and *Look at Me* have delighted readers here and in Great Britain. With *Providence,* . . . she effectively claims her territory as a writer. "Territory" may, however, be too large a word to suit these politely agoraphobic works. With several other British novelists of past and present, Anita Brookner shares a love of order and pattern, a discreet sense of humor, and a piquant awareness of manners, as well as a rather small canvas. These are novels for a disciplined sensibility—not the excesses of the groaning board but the light sufficiency of the luncheon table; not Wagner crashing through the symphony hall but Brahms suffusing the chamber with rational poignancy.

Jane Austen's world comes congenially to mind, although we would not immediately group Anita Brookner's heroines with Emma Woodhouse—"handsome, clever, and rich," secure in her provenance and her social context. Brookner's young women are certainly clever and usually have a small, liberating independent income, but of their "handsomeness" they are never confident. The exemplary Ruth Weiss of *The Debut,* a Balzac scholar, is haunted by Eugénie Grandet's self-assessment: *"Je ne suis pas assez belle pour lui."* Ruth, Fanny Hinton of *Look at Me,* and Kitty Maule of *Providence* are excellent women—dutiful daughters, passable cooks, occasional wits, and considerable scholars—but all of them are observers and outsiders. None considers passion her prerogative. In all of them, femininity is lodged useless: *Je ne suis pas assez belle pour lui.* They exist most fully in their yearning for impossible, inaccessible men who we know will never seriously look at them, and this yearning shapes each novel's small plot.

Anita Brookner's books are oddly timeless, not only because they record such unchanging human situations as the filial quandary and the shifts of friendship, but especially because they move in almost total disregard of feminist expectations. They want so little, these blameless heroines! Not for them the voracious professionalism or the zipless fornication that preoccupy their sisters in fiction. Brookner's women live mild lives of professional competence and romantic longing for those handsome men who are not good enough for them. . . .

These mild women tend to be both literate and literary. Seduced early in life by books, they live and breathe the conventions of literary romance and then feel faintly deceived when life fails to imitate art. Ardent, single-minded, and chaste at heart whatever their sexual status may be, they are the votaries and victims of courtly love. (p. 75)

Providence has many of the Brooknerian virtues that distinguish the other two novels: elegant prose, ironic humor, a delicate astuteness about character, and a fine sensitivity to the oddities of various social groups. Anita Brookner, an art historian, writes with painterly attention to detail; her novels also have a rich bookishness that sends the reader panting to the library to discover the books that Brookner's heroines take for granted. But in comparison with *The Debut* and *Look at Me,* with their satisfying and worldly complexity, *Providence* seems somewhat limp: a short story stretched beyond its natural elasticity, requiring a tension that its improbable ending cannot provide. . . . It might be best to view *Providence* as an introduction, and then settle down to the pleasures of reading and rereading the small *oeuvre* of this excellent writer. (pp. 75-6)

Frances Taliaferro, in a review of "Providence," in Harper's, *Vol. 268, No. 1605, February, 1984, pp. 75-6.*

KATHLEEN KEARNS

Kitty Maule is a watcher, reserved, intelligent, and controlled. The subject of her scrutiny, and of . . . *Providence,* is her life. It is an interesting enough life, in a modest sort of way, and Kitty knows precisely what it contains and what it lacks. . . . She can catalogue her yearnings for religious faith, and see how she should go about winning the man she longs for. She is a keen observer, but by the end of *Providence* it is clear that she has gotten it all wrong.

The novel is full of missed signals; Kitty is so absorbed in her deficiencies that she cannot see them for what they are. . . . [Whenever] she does feel the stirrings of faith, or even of spontaneous emotion, she quickly suppresses them. She smothers whatever is "too dangerous to contemplate," or too intimate to be revealed incautiously. Even her impatience with restraint is restrained. . . .

When soul-searching becomes too distressing, Kitty immerses herself in her work. Not surprisingly, she is professionally concerned with the Romantic Tradition and the tension between intellectual repudiation of the existence of God and desire for a spiritual sign. Brookner is thus able to construct an elaborate intellectual framework for Kitty's crisis, a framework that becomes problematic for both Kitty and the novel. (p. 39)

At . . . [certain moments] it is difficult to distinguish Brookner's perspective from Kitty's. Having set up the parallels between her character's obsessions and corresponding theoretical issues, she seems a little unsure of how to proceed. In her last novel, *Look at Me,* she exposed the ironies of her characters' predicaments with agile wit. Here, though, she is often too absorbed in presenting her themes to make clear how she feels about Kitty's cosmic preoccupations. The most casual conversation is loaded: in a railway car a chaperone dreads arriving in Paris with his rambunctious charges and sighs, "God help me," to which Kitty responds, "Why should God help you?" An uncomfortable sense emerges that Brookner wants to be critical of her tiresome heroine, even make fun of her, but can't quite bring herself to do it. (pp. 39-40)

Kathleen Kearns, in a review of "Providence," in The New Republic, *Vol. 190, No. 12, March 26, 1984, pp. 39-40.*

Rosellen Brown

1939-

American novelist, poet, and short story writer.

A respected author of poetry and prose, Brown began her career as a poet and has since incorporated poetic elements in her fiction, which is dense with metaphor and imagery. In both her novels and her poems she writes of marriage and the family, although she has also drawn on her experience as a Civil Rights worker in the 1960s in a book of poetry, *Some Deaths in the Delta* (1970), and a novel, *Civil Wars* (1984).

In her first and second novels, Brown uses two narrative voices to portray the protagonists' dual perspectives. *Autobiography of My Mother* (1976) explores the antagonistic relationship between a mother and her daughter, with alternate chapters narrated by first one and then the other. *Tender Mercies* (1978), which centers on a family's struggles to adjust after the wife is paralyzed by an accident caused by her husband, is written in two distinct styles: the husband's story is narrated in straight prose while the wife's is rendered in imagistic stream-of-consciousness, consisting largely of dreams and memories, and resembling prose poems.

In *Cora Fry* (1977), Brown again fuses fiction and poetry. This cycle of poems tells the story of a New England housewife who is frustrated in her marriage but ultimately decides not to leave her husband. Brown said in an interview that her purpose in *Cora Fry* was "to take a woman's experience and see how it is kaleidoscopic, how every tiny piece of her life can be set against another and made to create the illusion of the whole life."

In *Civil Wars* Brown returns to the southern location of *Some Deaths in the Delta*. The protagonists are an unhappily married couple who were Civil Rights activists in the 1960s. The title refers to several instances of civil war: the American Civil War of the 1860s, the Civil Rights struggles of the 1960s, and the perennial conflicts between the sexes and the generations within a family.

(See also *Contemporary Authors*, Vols. 77-80.)

Photograph by Layle Silbert

THE NEW REPUBLIC

Poets so often are apologetic these noisy days, and Rosellen Brown is no exception. She apologizes for the fact that "poems are not action," and contests what she has written with "real events." Well, though one can understand what she is getting at, she is wrong. Her poems [collected in *Some Deaths in the Delta,*] are an event, and the work and love that went into them a form of action. At least one phase of the so-called civil rights struggle is over. But for a few years a certain torch glowed in the South, and men and women and children came to it and felt its heat and helped hold it up for the world to see. Rosellen Brown was among those who came: white, a Yankee, she . . . took part in many efforts to make the South a place where "liberty and justice for all" can be found. As the title of her book suggests, the task is an enormous one. . . .

[Those] who leave and go North find another hell up there, as the second part of this collection of poems emphasizes. For the author eventually returned to New York, and learned (as have so many others before her) that once awakened, the old kind of sleep comes hard. Mississippi made her a less satisfied New Yorker. Now she is not only a damn Yankee, but perhaps a touch un-American. She wants us to measure up to those young Americans of both races she knew in the South in the middle sixties. Though she spends many of her lines setting down the sad ironies and outright evils which plague life in the South, she lets us know from time to time that there is no escaping those ironies and evils, certainly not by crossing the Mason-Dixon line. In doing so she demonstrates a willingness to avoid ideological rancor and rhetorical postures of one sort or another. She loves the people she spent so much time with, and in these poems gives voice to their "life"—their hopes, doubts, assets, handicaps. She has a right to feel that only the successive storming of various Bastilles are *acts,* but no doubt in many towns of the Delta there are individuals who have been in the past grateful for what Rosellen Brown the teacher and social activist has meant to them—and who are now grateful that she has chosen to speak out so intensely and honestly on their, on America's behalf.

A review of "Some Deaths in the Delta," in The New Republic, *Vol. 164, No. 8, February 20, 1971, p. 31.*

JOHN ALFRED AVANT

Rosellen Brown's poetry deals with racism and violence in Mississippi and with the grimness and desolation of city life in the North, specifically Brooklyn—themes that are still painfully valid in reality but have become almost banal when used as subject matter for poetry or fiction, unless the expression is particularly strong or fresh. The quality [of *Some Deaths in the Delta*] is uneven; Brown rarely seems sure of herself as a poet, for the poems tend to slip out of her grasp. I like some of her humorous asides . . . and some verses have an effective simplicity. . . . In its suggestion of uncommunicated rage, most of this volume seems insufficient as a liberation of the poet's feeling; the erratic *Some Deaths in the Delta* is ultimately unsuccessful, but promising.

> *John Alfred Avant, in a review of "Some Deaths in the Delta and Other Poems," in* Library Journal, *Vol. 96, No. 12, June 15, 1971, p. 2088.*

ROBERT B. SHAW

Poems of social protest have perhaps more built-in drawbacks than any other kind. To mention only two disadvantages, they run the risk of appearing frivolous in comparison to the issues that have provoked them; still more dangerously, they run the risk of sounding self-righteous. Rosellen Brown has had considerable success in eluding these difficulties [in *Some Deaths in the Delta*]. . . . She is unsparing and sardonic. . . . It may be that her first-hand experience has added vividness to the poems. Many poets who deal with social topics have little connection with them beyond the newspapers, and their poems show it. In any event, Rosellen Brown is finally successful because she refuses to allow committedness to outweigh craft in the making of a poem. Her sensibility is as disciplined as it is radical. Other poets intent upon treating social issues might profit from reading her. (p. 348)

> *Robert B. Shaw, "The Long and the Short of It," in* Poetry, *Vol. CXIX, No. 6, March, 1972, pp. 342-55.**

MARGARET WIMSATT

[*Some Deaths in the Delta*] might have been subtitled, is certainly about, "The Impact of the Deep South on a Nice Barnard Girl." . . . She manages to record sensations without slipping over into either condescension or sentimentality. . . . But sometimes . . . [her lines] are flat: "He is a black general now— / never planned to join up but / got drafted / because things rolled the way they did," is perfectly nice colloquial prose. And sometimes her sympathy overrules her judgment, as when she prints out as poetry a freshman essay by one of her (obviously bright and sensitive) Tougaloo students. (This is the sociofallacy: that we must admire these verses because their source is so remarkable. It rears its ugly head all over the place these days.) But wherever she is, in Jackson, back home in Brooklyn, or reading a poem about the Bedouin, she is a recording instrument of great depth and sensitivity.

> *Margaret Wimsatt, in a review of "Some Deaths in the Delta," in* Commonweal, *Vol. XCVI, No. 1, March 10, 1972, p. 22.*

ANATOLE BROYARD

A middle-class woman comes home to her apartment in a "multi-ethnic" neighborhood in Brooklyn and finds a burglar going through her jewels. She has already survived so many similar catastrophes that she can afford to be casual about this one, so she says to the burglar's back, "Who are you?" Adapting himself to her tone, he says, "You got a lot of junk, you know?" . . . Here's a good story [from the collection **"Street Games"**], appropriately called **"The Only Way to Make It in New York,"** but Rosellen Brown spoils it by tacking on an apocalypse—an earthquake in California—that drove the woman, her husband and daughter to Brooklyn. She doesn't need the earthquake—it is just an excuse for some fancy hallucinating, when all the time her story is right there in Brooklyn, present, concrete, deft, economical. When you have a life in Brooklyn—or anywhere in New York—an earthquake in California is just a Technicolor Cinerama extravaganza, full of sound and fury, signifying nothing. Leave well enough alone, Mrs. Brown. Quit while you're ahead.

She makes the same mistake in **"How to Win,"** a chilling story of a mother who has a hyperactive child, an innocent monster of energy, a furious prisoner of perpetual motion. Musing on him in his devastations, she wonders how this happened to her to him, to our specials. He is a "possessed" child, not of witchcraft, but of psychology books, which only serve to deepen the mystery. Then his mother discovers that, at his school, they "walk on his neck," break his spirit, "teach him how to lose." We get a sermon on the suffocation of education, and there goes the broken spirit of a promising story.

"Why I Quit the Gowanus Liberation Front" is a fine satire on the efforts of a group of emancipated whites to "integrate" their semirenovated neighborhood. Semirenovated is the telling word here, connoting a limbo where the twain shall never meet, where no amount of foreign aid will ever win over the have-nots. A street fair is proposed: it will shake everybody together, like a black-and-white frosted from the candy store down the block. . . .

But Mrs. Brown still doesn't know when enough is enough. The narrator is so drugged or dragged with the "decadence" of his life that he has to flee wife and family. He "scales gates" in his getaway. He carries a suitcase crammed with symbolism. It is already coming apart at the seams, and so is the story. . . .

Whoever condemned literature to a life sentence of hard labor, anyway? So many of our "serious" writers are becoming lugubrious, are approaching what might be described as the "official" art of the liberal establishment. The gaiety we see on TV rock 'n' roll programs or on the dance floor of the Cheetah, the wit, the invention, the transcendence—why doesn't someone write *these* down? In **"Street Games,"** Mrs. Brown sometimes comes close. She has the eye, the ear, she knows what the have-nots have that you don't. But perhaps she has been too well educated. . . . Perhaps she has been alienated by high culture, by the creative writing theory that catastrophe is the only proper subject for the contemporary short story. She may have forgotten how to dance. If she is not careful, she will be joining the Gowanus Liberation Front.

> *Anatole Broyard, "Some Semirenovated Stories," in* The New York Times, *June 18, 1974, p. 37.*

JANE LARKIN CRAIN

Each of the fourteen short stories in [*Street Games*] deals with the lives of the people living on a block in Brooklyn. . . . Even the shortest of these works conveys something of what the reader can regard as the fundamental outline of a particular life. In **"Gold,"** a little girl simply takes a walk through her neighborhood, and one feels as if one has participated not just in her fantasies but also in the total ambience of dirt and frustration from which she dreams of escaping. In another, longer story, the main character moves between the squalid and chaotic existence of a "commune" on George Street and her parents' townhouse in Brooklyn Heights. . . . With sometimes brutal but consistently evocative imagery, Mrs. Brown manages to depict a particular strand in current parent-child relationships, a familiar brand of post-adolescent panic and disaffection, the violent self-pity of the girl's brilliant but aimless Puerto Rican boyfriend. Mrs. Brown's point of view is never merely spectatorial; even when the stories are told from an exterior perspective, one has a powerful sense of receiving knowledge about the complex substance of her characters' everyday experience—as they themselves perceive it. To be sure, Mrs. Brown concentrates almost unwaveringly on the stormier, more wrenching aspects of the experience of life represented, but her stories seek to enlarge rather than to diminish the people portrayed in them, and it is from this impulse of her writing that the primary seriousness and effectiveness derive.

> Jane Larkin Crain, in a review of "Street Games," in Saturday Review/World, Vol. 1, No. 21, June 29, 1974, p. 19.

JEAN STROUSE

"Do you think there could be something like victims without crimes?" asks a woman in Rosellen Brown's *Street Games*. "Does someone always have to get blamed?" She is writing a letter to her dead junkie husband (**"A Letter to Ismael in the Grave"**), and struggling to figure out whose fault he was, but she is asking the questions for everybody in this tough, painful, funny, perceptive book.

Street Games is more than a collection of stories. It is a neighborhood of real people who wander in and out of each other's lives in the semirenovated "200" block of George Street in the Gowanus section of Brooklyn. Things happen. People hurt. They blame someone, no one, themselves.

Rosellen Brown takes a lot of risks. Her stories are intensely felt but not sentimental or old-fashioned; they are about class and sex and race without being politically rhetorical or didactic. They work because, though she writes about human suffering, Rosellen Brown is interested not in misery or blame or histrionics, but in everyday life. She gets you inside people and beyond them at the same time. She moves in behind their eyes like a literary ventriloquist and writes with their voices, telling more about them than the words they use because she pays such fine attention to shades of expression, to the feelings behind what people say.

Some of the stories are overwrought. Sometimes a literary phrase creeps in where it doesn't belong, or an image is played out too far. But the risk of coming too close to poetry is worth taking, since in this kind of writing the line between what works and what doesn't is so elusive. Rosellen Brown is traveling out of her own experience into the voices of other people's thinking and feeling, talking and seeing. When she succeeds, and she usually does, the voice evokes the world it inhabits.

The woman in a story called **"How To Win"** talks explicitly about this problem of getting inside somebody else's head—only she poses it not as a writer but as the mother of a hy-perkinetic six-year-old. . . . But only paranoid schizophrenics and a few behavioral scientists believe that you really can see into somebody's thoughts. Good writers, actors, mothers, doctors, friends, and teachers can make good guesses—and Rosellen Brown's are first-rate.

She is most successful where (here *I'm* guessing) she is most familiar. Two of the strongest voices in the book belong to white, articulate, middle-class people. (p. 40)

The epiphanies in *Street Games* are writ small. They sneak up on you the way some new small truth about your life does, and they don't have anything to do with who deserves them or with the fixing of blame. Yes, there are crimeless victims, and what gives life to these stories is not the placing of blame but the way the characters cope with pain and loss, fear and victimization. (p. 41)

> Jean Strouse, "Crimeless Victims," in Ms., Vol. III, No. 3, September, 1974, pp. 40-1.

ANATOLE BROYARD

Anyone who goes through a good deal of modern fiction must have had this experience so often that it seems like a recurrent bad dream: You read a novel that shows considerable evidence of talent, intelligence, awareness and technical skill, a book that addresses itself to urgent and timely themes—and when you have reached its last page, you find yourself wondering what you are supposed to feel. You have been given plenty to think about, but that's not the real business of fiction, which is to put you in a posthypnotic trance, where your will is no longer your own and you are suffering or are thrilling to the vicissitudes of someone else's life.

For 270 pages of Rosellen Brown's first novel, I assumed that she had something original and startling up her sleeve, that she was going to find a way to fuse her two main themes into a single chord that would sound the hope or doom of mothers and daughters in our day and age. Because it was impossible to accept in any glad sense either the mother or the daughter in **"The Autobiography of My Mother."** I supposed that Miss Brown was going to tune the tension between them, to rewrite the equation somehow, show me a resolution I never thought of. Everything pointed this way: What other reason could there be for describing such a total antagonism between parent and child but to show us how we would have to learn to live with it or die of it.

Gerta Stein, the mother, is a 72-year-old lawyer who has devoted her life to "the defense of indefensible and unpopular people." She does this because she loves principles, not people. . . . She sees nothing in the here and now, but everything under the aspect of eternity.

Gerta once had a husband, but since her passion found greater satisfaction in court than in bed, she got rid of him. The price she paid for having briefly lost sight of herself was Renata, her daughter. Renata is the kind of young woman who would not know what to do with herself if she did not have a mother to distinguish herself from in every possible way. She is a parody of every psychoanalytic theory of rebellion, a negative parasite that hates what it feeds on.

Gerta, the mother, has a compulsion to be in the right, and she generally is, which makes her about as interesting as a computer. This leaves Renata nothing but a boring wrongheadedness to get through her life with. The reader is hard put to choose between them. . . .

To be sure, Miss Brown's book raises a number of interesting questions, but it is part of the complacency of some modern novelists to believe that they need only ask interesting questions—no answers are required. Answer may be too strong a word. A novel need not give us answers, but it should, perhaps, question the questions until they bleed a little. . . .

There are good things in the book, I must not forget to mention that lots of smart wisecracks about the opposing camps; a scene before a Congressional committee . . . ; a talk show on which Renata and Gerta appear together and do their respective numbers.

In fact, Miss Brown is so lively sometimes that I'm almost tempted to say that it's not her fault that her novel isn't better—society is to blame. But no, it hasn't quite come to that yet.

Anatole Broyard, "Questioning the Questions," in The New York Times, May 26, 1976, p. 37.

LAURIE STONE

In her ingenious book of short stories, **"Street Games,"** Rosellen Brown explored the anxieties of the residents of a Brooklyn block. It was an impressive work. . . .

Assault and anxiety are still Brown's subjects in her first novel, **"The Autobiography of My Mother,"** but her focus has narrowed to the occupants of a single dwelling on the Upper West Side. (p. 7)

Three generations of Stein women in one household create the kind of tension that precedes breakdown. Gerda and Renata cannot stop judging one another by the opposing standards that have made of each of their lives, in its way, a suffocating and dead-ended half-life. Like Grace Paley, Rosellen Brown has a talent for writing the things that very intelligent people say and think when they are slowly going crazy. Renata cannot say what she feels—that she wants, desperately, to gain her mother's acceptance; and Gerda cannot feel the things she says. Each woman talks to the reader instead, in alternating narratives, and gradually, powerfully, the interlocking stories of mother and daughter unfold. (pp. 7-8)

As Gerda becomes more emotionally unmovable, Renata grows increasingly inert. The war between the women becomes a struggle over the child, and in her terrifyingly understandable ignorance, Gerda makes plans to gain custody of Tippy. This decision and its consequences form the shocking and yet completely logical climax of a novel about the unresolvable and deadly connections between mothers and daughters. These connections are nowhere in contemporary fiction better dramatized than here.

"The Autobiography of My Mother" is a bitter, funny, stringently unsentimental novel of rare merit. Rosellen Brown's strength lies in the steady but often dazzling accumulation of facts and details. She writes with great candor and ease, never retreating for one moment from her conviction that family is an accident from which the victims can never recover. That they try to, nevertheless is what makes this novel dramatic and even hopeful. Renata's story is half of **"The Autobiography of My Mother,"** because she feels doomed to share her mother's life, to repeat it. But Renata's return home, in spite of the anger and futility behind the action, is also the first step in being able finally to leave home for good. (p. 8)

Laurie Stone, in a review of "The Autobiography of My Mother," in The New York Times Book Review, June 20, 1976, pp. 7-8.

ANNE LAKE PRESCOTT

If maternity ever seemed simple, it no longer does. Our madonnas look more hassled than serene, and our pietas show us gazing not at a child but into a mirror. In her subtle and moving first novel [*The Autobiography of My Mother*], poet and short story writer Rosellen Brown explores this ambivalence and puzzlement with cool-eyed sympathy. . . .

Many novelists would . . . [be content with] pointing to the generation gap and the outlines of personality which separate us from each other. But Brown is after something more difficult to understand and describe—the recurrence of pattern within a family despite changes of style and condition, a recurrence that both women in part perceive and that explains the title. . . .

"Autobiography" is long on character and incident, short on plot. It is clever rather than witty, sharply observant rather than satirical. Many episodes are touching; a few others, such as a quasirape, are to me unconvincing (Brown is least persuasive when most lurid). The language seems stiff at times, but then both narrators suffer from stiffness of heart.

The novel's chief strength lies in the author's delicate insistence on the contradictions within each woman. Aimless Renata is an acute observer; chilly Gerda has her commitments and a few moments of chivalrous passion ("Am I not to be allowed my paradoxes?"). Brown could have made her another monstrous modern mother, and indeed Gerda is not a parent one would wish on anyone—although it is a relief to read about a mother who passes out the guilt to her daughter not with chicken soup but with exhortations to get a job. A monster-mother would be useful as an "explanation" of how Renata got that way: poor girl/ambitious mother/no love/compensation. But Brown resists the negative as well as positive simplifications we bring to each other; she allows her creations their full measure of paradox.

Anne Lake Prescott, "Rock-a-Bye Mamas," in The Village Voice, Vol. XXI, No. 25, June 21, 1976, p. 43.

EVE OTTENBERG

"The Autobiography of My Mother" does exactly as the title suggests: it makes two separate people and identities into one Rosellen Brown focuses on the psychological warfare between an unusual mother, Gerda Stein, and her very disturbed daughter, Renata. Their confrontation clearly and efficiently reveals how emotional ambivalence in a family upsets the members.

Gerda's and Renata's alternating monologues compose the novel. As their voices mesh, their struggle begins to look like that within one person rather than that between two. . . .

Out of these tangled identity questions Brown unravels the central problem for both mother and daughter—ambivalence. Love and hate mingled together keep these women from understanding each other. **"The Autobiography of My Mother"** also emphasizes the difficulty of self-knowledge. Caught in an unhappy pattern, these people over-simplify and ignore their own motives. Ultimately Gerda rationalizes legally removing her grandchild from the custody of her daughter. She never perceives the irony that she, an oblivious, insensitive parent should see her daughter as an unfit mother.

Despite her many subtleties, Brown's humor is usually direct, as are her ideas and lively images. Her subject matter—the lives of confused, depressed people—does limit these talents. But **"The Autobiography of My Mother"** does highlight Brown's ability to crystalize the delicate interconnections of love and identity.

> *Eve Ottenberg, in a review of "The Autobiography of My Mother," in* The Christian Science Monitor, *August 16, 1976, p. 22.*

JOSEPH EPSTEIN

[Rosellen Brown] has powers of phrasing, of insight into feeling, of evocation; she has learning and she is, novelistically, ambitious, setting—and bringing off—a difficult section of her novel in a pre-Nazi Germany that she cannot have known firsthand but has to have grasped wholly through imagination and intelligent reading. Rosellen Brown has almost everything a novelist should have except, in *The Autobiography of My Mother,* a real story. Her extremely intelligent book might more accurately have been entitled Two Characters in Search of a Novel.

The two characters, a mother and a daughter, are each remarkable. An old world figure, the mother resembles someone not altogether unlike the late Hannah Arendt, though in a more activist strain. . . . European, cerebral, with a mind honed to cut fine distinctions, thinking in an English that makes the requirements of precision that only a well-educated foreigner can bring to the language, she is a most fascinating construction. . . . As for the daughter, she is very near to a human disaster. A floater out on the sea called counter-culture, she has lived in hippy squalor, sleeping round, picking up then dropping one or another interest, eventually becoming a professional incompetent, a title which she earns indisputably by having a child out of wedlock by a Trotskyist whose fingers smell of cat food. (A nice touch, that last.) Such are Miss Brown's two characters, mother and daughter—not exactly a page out of the Christmas J. C. Penney Catalogue.

The setting is claustral, as perhaps it should be for female combat; but more than claustral, it is a bit menacing, as the upper-west side of Manhattan can often be. The novel proper begins with the daughter showing up at her mother's legal office with her child. No men of any moment appear in the book. The two women know each other too well, which doesn't make conversation between them any easier; this and the fact that neither is what the other had in mind for a mother or daughter. Many valuable things about women—also about Woman—get said in Miss Brown's pages; and if at times one is inclined to label this a "feminist" novel—an insulting label—it is finally better than that. Yet for all her talent Miss Brown's novel wants a sense of direction. Hers is a book that offers the object lesson that subtle portraiture, keen psychological insight, and splendid writing—rare and blessed things though they are in themselves—are not sufficient to produce a novel of the first class. It is only at the very end of *The Autobiography of My Mother* that, through a twist with a fatal air of contrivance to it, something like a plot emerges. The effect is rather like hearing a joke splendid in the telling capped by a weak punch-line. Still, her novel does make one indisputable point, and this is that Rosellen Brown is a novelist worth reading. (pp. 599-600)

> *Joseph Epstein, "Is Fiction Necessary?" in* The Hudson Review, *Vol. XXIX, No. 4, Winter, 1976-77, pp. 593-604.**

VICTOR HOWES

[The title character of *Cora Fry*] is a young wife with two children named Nan and Chip, and a husband she thinks of as Fry. No first name. Not that she doesn't love him, but well, she doesn't trust him yet, and she feels trapped in her marriage. . . .

Cora lives in rural New Hampshire. She has always lived there, and she is growing vaguely restless. Watching the lives of others on TV has fed her uneasy wants. . . .

What Cora wants for Cora is what Greta Garbo always said she wanted, it's "luscious freedom / it's not to be needed. To be just alone. . . .''

But the luscious freedom to be alone is not for Cora. When her husband, Fry, takes a night's shore leave from marriage. Cora tries to escape. She moves out. She wrecks her car. She takes the children on the bus to Boston. Then, her anger vented, she returns home. To her worried, welcoming Fry, who "sat still / and worried / swayed in the tidal pull / that brought me home / and still could drown us all."

That tidal pull is what this stream-of-consciousness poem/novel is all about. The tidal pull of the seasons, the sexes, the social norms. Poet Rosellen Brown here pays homage to the ambiguous ties of home and family. Caught in the annual round of gardening, preserving, caring for her husband and children, Cora Fry longs to break loose, envies the muskrat who gnaws himself free from the trap, but cannot emulate him.

Cora, Ms. Brown seems to be saying, is New England to the core. Honest, frank, unromantic, tradition-bound, good. No Anna Karenina she, to spoil her life in pursuit of passion. No Emma Bovary, no Hedda Gabler, no histrionics, only quiet desperation. Even desperation sounds too dramatic. Quiet acceptance.

She's sound as an apple, Cora is, and in consequence, her inner monologue is often prosaic. One can't wax very poetic over putting away the children's rubber boots. Still, Cora has her moments, and it is Rosellen Brown's creative intuition to let us see that deep down inside, like all apples, Cora hides a star.

> *Victor Howes, "'Cora Fry' Tests 'the Tidal Pull'," in* Christian Science Monitor, *March 9, 1977, p. 23.*

ROCHELLE RATNER

Cora Fry works because Brown has found a persona close to herself: the spirit of a woman in a small New England town, half pioneer, half modern. Brown is secure enough as a poet to let the words stand on their own, to know when she's said enough, not to explain or justify what she's said. She's strongest where she's most alone, working from the primitive parts of herself. The poems leave a lot unsaid, they make us stop and think, relate them to our own life. At times some of the modern images seem a little surface, but they also serve to show the reader this isn't really grandmother's old days; the poet still has to exist right here. . . . Brown knows what she's doing, and she does it well.

*Rochelle Ratner, in a review of "Cora Fry," in
Library Journal, Vol. 102, No. 6, March 15, 1977,
p. 713.*

CHRISTOPHER LEHMANN-HAUPT

[Rosellen Brown] writes in her second novel, **"Tender Mercies,"** an arabesque, Faulknerian prose . . . which ordinarily tries the patience by making metaphor the familiar landscape of action without justifying the style of metaphor. Complicatedly beautiful.

However, in **"Tender Mercies"** she has created such a powerful dramatic situation that almost no degree of stylistic ornamentation could diminish it. Dan Courser, in a moment of coltish exuberance, has swung the hull of a boat he is steering over his swimming wife, and caused her to be paralyzed from the neck down. Now, at the beginning of the novel, he has snatched her from a rehabilitation center and driven her home, with her two young children to their house in New Hampshire, where they will begin the awesome journey across the gulf of their mutual resentment and guilt.

I'm still not certain that the style of **"Tender Mercies"** is specifically apt to its dramatic situation, or that it serves to make of that situation any sort of resonant metaphor. Laura, the crippled wife, thinks, feels, and dreams in imagistic italics, which surely reflect a tenuous grip on the real world, but the third-person narrative that embodies Dan's point of view is sometimes at odds with his supposedly rough-hewn Yankee style. Still, the prose does serve to filter what in blunter language might have been unbearably painful. And it gives Miss Brown scope to make of a brutal situation an often touchingly pointed drama.

*Christopher Lehmann-Haupt, in a review of "Tender
Mercies," in The New York Times, November 24,
1978, p. C25.*

MARY KINZIE

In Rosellen Brown's *Cora Fry,* a long cycle of poems narrated by the woman of the title, we find many things that may remind us of Frost, rural loneliness, for example; but we do not find . . . [Frost's] particular compression and resonance. . . . The voice and consciousness of Cora Fry are too weak to echo long after her. Brown's characters don't seem to have any place to begin from, any point of solitude, selfhood, or inwardness. Not quite in touch with things, they are brutal and grasping, prodigiously lonely, and pathetically modern. They are either imprisoned in their houses or hurtling someplace in their cars and consequently have no connection to those corners of the landscape where the human traces blend back into the earth. . . . The highway runs like a ribbon through Rosellen Brown's book, and it is no surprise that Cora Fry has a bad, perhaps a deliberate, car accident two-thirds through the book.

Cora Fry is the story of a woman who sees only a few things, and those, only intermittently. The housewifely poems sound like Sylvia Plath. . . . Some of Cora's poems about her husband also resemble those in *Ariel*. . . . The analogy with Plath makes sense because, like her, Cora is a woman emerging from herself during the Fifties and Sixties; and, like Plath, she doesn't quite reach the surface. History touches Cora rarely; the shock waves in her world are more local in origin. But unlike Frost and other American Romantics like William Carlos Williams, the poems in *Cora Fry* do not get very deeply inside the local,

either. The complications of perception and conscience that mark Frost and Williams have no place in this world, which is not only godless and dry, but dull. When, to brave this problem, Cora or her author try to sound lyrically rich and suggestive, as in the squash poems or the one about an old woman going through garbage cans, the poems just sound foolish; the consciousness does not play or examine, but turns briefly on itself and then lets go. . . . (pp. 98-9)

But every so often the right note is struck. Reunited with her husband after trying to leave him, Cora notices that he walks in a peculiar, stiff way as if during her absence he had "Sat still / and worried, / swayed in the / tidal pull / that brought me home / and still could / drown us all." Rosellen Brown is also fairly good at describing rather ugly domestic scenarios [as in the poem which begins:]

> "Fry," I said
> when he touched me on
> my breast. "Do you think
> of women,
> other women, when
> you're touching me there?"
>
> (p. 99)

There are some fine observations here, the husband blinking in the dark, his inability to shrug properly in this position, his coarse and chilling assurance, "No one you know." But the analogy with the "butterfly / kiss" Cora gives her daughter is a false step, a descent into sentimentality.

One also wonders what principle of realism or surprise is behind the poet's choice of line breaks; I don't know the answer in this case nor in any other in the book. The jaggedness of the lines seems to mirror the tenuousness of Cora's courage, the frailty of her will, and perhaps a foregone conclusion on Brown's part about her character's importance: Cora Fry was born to go under. This persona cannot fight back, and can hardly remember events in the past; in minor ways Brown tries to remember for her. The first poem in the book, a bit portentous but also touching, says:

> I want to understand light years.
> I live in Oxford, New Hampshire.
> When, then, will the light get to me?

Get to her, we must ask, from where? Cora suffers her marriage to Fry, has two children, a car accident, an affair, leaves Fry, comes back to him, and in the last poem in the book we are answered: the light doesn't come from anywhere, it's all manmade. . . . (p. 100)

Between the question about light years and the extinguished stars on the rug, what lies stretched out upon the rural tarmac is what E. M. Forster called "the tapeworm of time," the simple and not necessarily logical sequence of events in a story: one thing happens, and then another thing happens, and the minor characters come and go, and that's all the meaning there is to it. There are a number of voices, often finely caught, in *Cora Fry,* but no conversations; Brown's is not a world in which people can really talk to each other. She uses the basic convention of the long monologue, with here and there a lyric slipped in. . . . The poems do not sound like one person's, and perhaps this is Rosellen Brown's point—that this life is patched together and its errors and lapses irrevocable. (p. 101)

*Mary Kinzie, "'What Are You Doing Up There in
Those Grapes?'" in Parnassus: Poetry in Review,
Vol. 7, No. 1, Fall-Winter, 1978, pp. 96-116.**

PATRICIA CRAIG

It is not entirely an original device to place a handicapped person at the centre of a piece of fiction; perhaps, however, it may be seen as a kind of reaction to all those tales of domestic life in which troubles proliferate in conditions of absolute normality: . . . [The heroine of *Tender Mercies*] is in a spectacular predicament: she is paralysed from the neck down, as the result of an accident caused by her husband in a moment of thoughtlessness. The theme of the novel is rehabilitation, in a wide sense; it's a difficult subject, rife with unease and emotion, full of dangers, for the novelist, of lapses of taste and errors of form. (p. 62)

The details of the situation are distressing, the feelings of the characters are complicated by guilt and a special variety of bitterness, so highly charged it's almost converted into a positive force. One possible tone of conversation is a defensive smartness with an undercurrent of acid; *Tender Mercies* is not a book about futile indulgence. At the worst moments the husband, the culprit, resorts to a desperate clowning.

It's a difficult subject, but the author has achieved a density of language and feeling which represents an efficient fusion of manner and matter: this is reality on a special plane. Just occasionally the sensitive touch becomes a little too marked and showy; it is simply going too far, for example, to present the thoughts of maimed Laura in a format which degenerates into poetic incoherence. But on the whole the narrative method works well; the subtle approach may lead to its own kind of inflations . . . but it contributes style, a quality unexpected and valuable in the context. (pp. 62-3)

> Patricia Craig, "Cripples," in New Statesman, Vol. 98, No. 2521, July 13, 1979, pp. 62-3.*

LYNNE SHARON SCHWARTZ

[*Civil Wars*], a densely packed and morally scrupulous chronicle, occupies a place long vacant and waiting. It belongs to our recent history. It is both political—an account of civil rights activists living through that moment's ambiguous, often deadening aftermaths—and literary—part of a group of realistic novels, many but not all by women, that insist on the family as a social model and potently depict it as strained by the opposing demands of private and public values. Love and work, our perennials.

In her first novel, **"The Autobiography of My Mother,"** Miss Brown wrote about the political rigors of one generation's giving way to, or indirectly leading to the personal fragmentation of, the next. In **"Tender Mercies,"** her subject was a marriage tested by a dreadful accident. In **"Civil Wars,"** these themes are re-examined and recombined, emerging more wisely pondered, more tensely wrought. The cast of characters is larger, and the Southern landscape, physical and spiritual, is richly rendered.

Jessie and Teddy Carll and their children, Andy, 14, and Lydia, 11, are the last white family living in a lower-middle-class neighborhood in Jackson, Miss., in 1978. . . .

Teddy's bigoted sister and brother-in-law are killed in an auto accident, inexplicably leaving their two children in the Carlls' care. Not only a bigger house but a more spacious way of life must be found, one that can accommodate a grief-stricken boy of 8 and a silently exasperating, fastidious girl of 13, both brought up on epithets like "nigger" and the latter closer to

breakdown than anyone dreams. The ensuing struggles to make room in every sense are the "civil wars" of the triple-edged title.

In the narrowest reading, the novel is about the demise of a marriage—a civil pact, after all. But the gradual fraying of the bond between Jessie and Teddy has its place in a complex net of broader issues. What is left for a hero is an unheroic age, especially when he suspects, and his black friends tell him, that it was never "his" movement at all? At what point do dedication and sacrifice become fatuous and self-serving? Is it noble or simply arrogant for a man to have "more anxiety for the world than for himself" (from the Kafka epigraph)? Ultimately, this lucidly courageous book asks not only about heroes stuck in memory's groove but about us. Are we a people surviving, like Jessie's father, at "the bottom of the barrel," living not on "the ideals but the sloughed impurities of the ideals?"

Those large questions are handled in the domestic rather than the epic mode. For Jessie, the "personal" and the "political," words whose meaning has been diminished by slogan, are never polarities to be yanked together by force but exist naturally intertwined as she goes about her life, "her yoked forward movement." I know of no contemporary novel that devotes such respectful care to the actual work of a woman raising a family, in this case almost single-handedly. Everything is unabashedly shown, from draining the spaghetti to finding a dancing school to the time-consuming talks addressed to the needs and wants of bewildered children, all four drawn with a vivid attention to character rarely given the young in our fiction. . . .

Rosellen Brown's approach to her characters is exhaustive. She knows and tells all—their smug and foolish earnestness that becomes courage when challenged, their self-absorption that becomes selflessness in time of need, their true and false heroics. Her style is dense, her tone wry as she records the flux of Jessie's inner life. Intricacies of perception, emotion and thought are assessed by a skeptical intelligence coupled with a thorough devotion to the subject. This very thoroughness sometimes works to the detriment of the story. A poet as well as novelist, Miss Brown is prodigal with metaphor and analogy; on occasion she seems unable to resist the call of her own talent, indulging in skillful but superfluous paraphrase. True as her words are, fewer would have been better.

Any work so clearly of the heart and spirit takes immense risks, this one particularly. It dares to be about ideals and the perils awaiting those committed to them, and it dares to dwell on the most quotidian of matters, with critical scenes taking place in the kitchen and the family car. It directly confronts the sorely ambivalent position of a white family enmeshed in the fight for black people's rights. At a time when fiction by women seems perversely misunderstood, one can only hope that **"Civil Wars"** will be recognized as a brave and fine work.

> Lynne Sharon Schwartz, "End of a Movement, End of a Marriage," in The New York Times Book Review, May 6, 1984, p. 15.

ANN HULBERT

Now that the 1960s generation has come of middle age, a little nostalgia for the old activist days seems to help take the edge off the big chill of life in the 1980s. In the therapeutic thaw, however, memories have a way of turning muddy. The essence of the era, to judge from versions of it offered by recent movies and fiction (and politicians), was a warm communal spirit—just what's missing these days. The actual political causes that brought together all the hopeful, youthful bodies generally get skimpier treatment; so do the private pursuits that have since split up the members of that generation, who are older and more encumbered now.

Rosellen Brown's large novel about two veterans of the Civil Rights Movement is a remarkable exception to such selective recollections of the 1960s. Not that there isn't muddiness in this ambitious novel, an epic of sorts. There is, literally: *Civil Wars* ends with a flood. And there is figurative murkiness as well, but it comes from delving into the ambivalent truths of the past and present, not from skimming too quickly over the styles of the times. In *Civil Wars,* as in her striking first novel, *The Autobiography of My Mother* (1976) and her acclaimed *Tender Mercies* (1978, no relation to the movie of the same name), Brown aims to confront her characters with unwieldy circumstances and see how resilient they turn out to be. Her own style is vigorous and graceful as she unfolds her episodic plot. In scene after carefully lit scene, Brown explores rather than blurs the relations between the past and the present, between private lives and larger forces. (p. 37)

Jessie and Teddy's struggle, an undeclared but serious one, is not the only battle Brown stages between the claims of the public, active realm and those of a more private sphere. In her first novel, *The Autobiography of My Mother,* civil rights lawyer Gerda Stein wins fame crusading for her clients' freedom, only to come home to face a daughter whose will seems paralyzed. In *Civil Wars,* Brown explores the tensions between public and private history on several different scales. She points to the disharmony between the internal and external politics of the Civil Rights Movement, which is recollected and reappraised in the course of the novel. In the background, she sketches in earlier schisms as well, the result of competing familial and social values. (pp. 38-9)

These marital, familial, and political wars—all cool or cold as the novel opens—heat up in the face of disaster, a familiar device in Brown's fiction. . . . At stake in the crisis of this divided house are ideological principles and day-to-day practices.

To set out the novel's thematic structure is not, however, to suggest that *Civil Wars* is schematic. On the contrary, it's of the loose and baggy monster school, and some of its many episodes are flat and almost sentimental. But most of them are the product of the best kind of intellectual and emotional patience, for Brown's inclination is Keatsian, and she filters her narrative through Jessie's equally ambivalent vision. ''If your sympathies exist two at a time . . . they call you soft, and they always will,'' Jessie muses, defensive about her half-doubts and uncertainties. Thanks to her ease with ambiguity, there is unusual tension and texture in the novel's political and familial dilemmas. It's only the Carlls's marital troubles that fail to get such rounded treatment.

As Jessie reflects on the political past, she finds that her and Teddy's years on the march look more complicated rather than less. In retrospect, she dwells on the divisiveness, not the harmony, of the internal politics of the movement. . . . (p. 39)

Jessie also thinks back on some of the public rhetoric, which bothered her in passing then but looms larger now. . . . The lesson . . . the novel as a whole teaches by the accretion of social and psychological detail [is] that the categories of victim, victimizer, and savior are misleading ones, as reductive almost

as master and slave, denying the independence of all. It's not the sort of lesson that translates into political positions or leads to saintly action, but the kind that keeps ideological delusion at bay.

Jessie confronts familial, as well as political, facts with few formulaic conceptions. . . . [She] views the children in her life with unpossessive clarity. It's the girls, not the clear-eyed boys, who are hardest to read. Helen, in fact, is a morose mystery, her adolescent soul bared in diary entries that punctuate the narrative. But even with her troubled surrogate daughter and with her own intense Lydia, Jessie is able to step far back and visualize the invisible. . . . (pp. 39-40)

Such moral sympathy, however, seems to escape Jessie when it comes to her husband. After the opening chapters, in which Jessie's ambivalence toward Teddy is well modulated between impatience at his posturing and insight into his predicament, she loses the depth of vision that guides her so well on political and familial terrain. . . .

Too often, Brown offers no corrective to Jessie's uncharacteristically reductive view of her husband. Poor Teddy carries on as a caricature, ever flatter as the novel progresses and he turns away from the family to politics, first dabbling in action (he aims to stir up an implausible boycott in a nearby black town), then in theory (he plans a book setting out an even less plausible reassessment of the Movement).

Jessie too loses her shadows in his presence.

> She sounded like a television commercial, she
> knew, the contemptuous kind she most de-
> spised. . . .

Jessie's analysis is striking, as always, but she's right, the bickering between them belongs to a less fully imagined medium. It's Teddy who articulates their conflict, accurately but crudely, as he's about to take the kids off to boycott with him. ''I'm teaching them there are larger groups than the family that you can swear loyalty to. . . . I am teaching them that women tend to take a narrow view of anything that threatens their beloved family.'' Beneath the civil wars between the races and generations seems to lurk the longest lasting battle of them all, between the sexes.

That struggle, somewhat surprisingly, is the only one Brown fails to bring into her fine-grained focus, to consider with the ''concentration'' she celebrates in her fiction. By that word, which she uses often, she seems to mean the energetic fusing and focusing of emotion and thought that others have called imagination or sympathy—a crucial moral linking that lets the locked-in self escape and see others from their own center out. Her protagonists have it or aspire to it, and their lives are complicated in the best sense. Brown has it too, and her concentration is the generous, rigorous power of a well-schooled intelligence—a soul, Keats would call it. Her fiction opens onto worlds of pains and troubles and truths that aren't simple. (p. 40)

Ann Hulbert, ''In Struggle,'' in The New Republic, *Vol. 190, No. 18, May 7, 1984, pp. 37-40.*

JEANNE McMANUS

Civil Wars, should the title mislead, is not an evocation of the Old South. It is a startling, chilling introduction to the New South, where social upheaval has taken out all the sugar and left the sting. . . .

[*Civil Wars* is an] unfailingly well-written book, a story that could just as easily be named *Tender Ironies* in an echo of Brown's second novel, *Tender Mercies*. . . .

It takes a new cadence to tell this novel of the New South, and Brown's rhythm is consistently strong. Her prose is packed, of course, with irony, and with a bitter but very real humor. Out go the back roads and magnolia-scented symbols of the Old South and in come the expressways and startling emblems of the New South. Brown conjures it beautifully. . . . (p. 9)

Her characters could easily have fallen into a new brand of stereotype: the middle-aged civil rights workers could have been laughable, forever sitting around and listening to Pete Seeger albums. Instead, they are treacherously good, leading the reader to an expectation then taking a sharp turn. Teddie is a complex ascetic, with his own battles raging inside, a front-lines radical whose purity of purpose is tarnished by his chauvinism and egotism. Jessie is a sympathetic heroine, but there's a bit of nagging and some middle-age, middle-class compromising that keep her driving a jagged unpredictable path.

But Brown's characterization is at its finest with Helen, the pale, blond orphaned 13-year-old who reveals her tortured self only through her diary, page after page of which Brown has captured with the perfect voice of a teen-age girl. Everything from Helen's tortured poetry to her girlish crushes spills out so realistically that the reader feels uncomfortably voyeuristic, as if he'd hung around the school yard and picked up ages that had blown out of a young girl's notebook.

Civil Wars is an intensely political novel, but it is not burdened with its politics. North versus South, Young versus Old, Black versus White, Right versus Left, Rich versus Poor: everywhere Brown's jackhammer cadence and deep convictions keep the novel driving hard, through battle after battle in a New South where there is no peace. (pp. 9, 17)

                    Jeanne McManus, "Mississippi Breakdown," in Book World—The Washington Post, *May 27, 1984, pp. 9, 17.*

VIVIAN GORNICK

Rosellen Brown is a novelist of marriage and the family. Her subject is the lives of men and women as husbands and wives, mothers and fathers. Her story is how the immediate world looks to one of her characters at a moment when attachments that have taken years to knit themselves up threaten to unravel. Her method is to pay concentrated attention to what her character registers during the time of crisis. *Tender Mercies,* Brown's last novel, was set in Vermont among hippie dropouts leading marginal country lives, and *Civil Wars* is set in Mississippi among ex-civil rights workers whose lives are equally uncentered. In each novel the social setting feels accurate and persuasive, but the single-minded attention paid to a moment in the kitchen or the bedroom while a marriage is coming to pieces is Brown's real context. This attention is her metaphor. It is what gives her the patience and the skill necessary to make her writer's intelligence move forward. This new novel is a fine example of the increased authority of her prose. . . .

Throughout *Civil Wars,* we are inside Jessie's head. The way she sees—how she orders experience, interprets motive and event—is the way we see. Her thoughts about how their life came to be as it is are peripheral—a stream of pride, confusion, and regret about the Movement that does not run very deep. Her thoughts about the children are alive with tenderness and concern. Her thoughts about herself apart from her husband and children are remarkably unformed. Her thoughts about Teddy are central. Jessie's continual rumination on who and what Teddy is—the shrewdness of her observations, the shades of distinction over how the Movement first pushed him into and then out of shape—gives character to the prose, provides the novel with texture and pain. . . . He is there on the page because Jessie's thoughts have given him dimension.

Jessie also endlessly appraises, judges, and scorns Teddy—for living in the past, being insensitive to the present, without energy for the future. Intelligent as she is, Jessie begins to sound like a passive scold who could drive anyone (male, female, husband, reader) away. As the narrative progressed, I found myself thinking: Lady, get yourself a life of your own. Leave this poor bastard alone already.

Civil Wars is the work of a writer who respects her craft. Rosellen Brown has lived a long time with Jessie and Teddy: she understands the weight and shape of the prose required to render the feel of their lives, and she has given them their due. I believe the Carlls are trapped. I see them squirming around inside their limitations, am persuaded they cannot break free of a dream-ridden past. However, they lack a vital piece of wisdom—they do not know that their failure to grow into separate adults must pull them apart despite the long woven years together. And unfortunately the author seems to know only as much as her characters. Brown writes without the detachment (the consciousness, if you will) necessary to penetrate the meaning of the Carlls' pain and bewilderment. She takes Jessie and Teddy at face value, presents them as they'd present themselves. In a writer who makes such brilliant use of the close up, this lack of distance is troublesome.

                    Vivian Gornick, "The '60s Are Over," in The Village Voice, *Vol. XXIX, No. 25, June 19, 1984, p. 47.*

John W(ood) Campbell, Jr.

1910-1971

(Also wrote under pseudonyms of Don A. Stuart, Karl Van Campen, and Arthur McCann) American science fiction novelist, short story writer, essayist, and editor.

Campbell has been called perhaps the single greatest influence on modern science fiction, both as a writer and as editor of *Astounding Science Fiction*, one of the most honored magazines in the genre. Campbell's "space operas" were considered to equal, and ultimately to surpass, the achievements of E. E. Smith, the most popular science fiction pulp writer of the 1930s. Many of these early stories touted the beneficence of machines as facilitators for human achievement. This preoccupation with "hardware" was faulted for stressing an impersonal, technocratic elitism over concern for humankind as a whole. Campbell eventually moved away from his highly popular but largely one-dimensional super-weapon tales to stories which concentrated upon and promoted the benefits of scientific ideas and technological inventiveness.

Campbell's reputation was built upon such action-invention stories as the "Arcot, Morey and Wade" series, including *The Black Star Passes* (1953), *Islands of Space* (1957), and *Invaders from the Infinite* (1961), and the "Penton and Blake" tales in *The Planeteers* (1966). Although *The Mightiest Machine* (1947) and *The Moon Is Hell* (1951) were noted for their technical advances in realism, Campbell also wrote mood pieces published under the name Don A. Stuart. Among these are some of his most respected works: "Twilight" (1934), "Night" (1935), and "Who Goes There?" (1938). This last is considered a classic of science fiction and it has been filmed twice, as *The Thing from Another World* and *The Thing*. A departure from previous work in its attention to plotting and characterization, "Who Goes There?" is among the last pieces of fiction Campbell wrote. Works published later, including the stories in *The Incredible Planet* (1949), a collection of his "Aarn Munro" series, and the posthumous *The Space Beyond* (1976), are thought to have been written in the early 1930s.

In 1937 Campbell became editor of *Astounding Stories*, later titled *Astounding Science Fiction* and then *Analog*. He retained this position for 34 years. *Astounding* was the leading science fiction magazine until the 1950s and, despite diminished significance in light of the challenges from new magazines, it remained respected and influential. The magazine won eight Hugo Awards under Campbell's leadership. Its prominence was due to Campbell's insistence on continual improvements in the content and physical quality of the publication. Campbell assembled a group of writers and shaped their work with many of his own story ideas and suggestions for stylistic refinement. Although, as E. F. Bleiler remarked, Campbell was sometimes considered "arrogant, dictatorial, and condescending," he was also respected for the help he offered his writers and the careful attention he gave to all submissions. Under his tutelage, Isaac Asimov, Robert Heinlein, A. E. van Vogt, Theodore Sturgeon, Lester del Rey, and many others were given a showcase.

Campbell's principal writings after he became editor of *Astounding* were his frequently controversial editorials. He wrote

of nearly every sociological subject from a scientific viewpoint. His own background in science often prompted hypotheses which engendered long-running dialogues between Campbell and his readers, some of whom were scientists. Many of these writings are included in *Collected Editorials from Analog* (1966). As his interest in various kinds of pseudoscience increased, most notably his strident defense of L. Ron Hubbard's "dianetics", his credibility with readers became strained.

Although Campbell's place in science fiction as a writer has been variously assessed in recent years, he is credited with the initial advancement of science fiction into a position of increased acceptance and respect as a literary genre.

(See also *Contemporary Authors*, Vols. 21-22; *Contemporary Authors*, Vols. 29-32, rev. ed. [obituary]; *Contemporary Authors Permanent Series*, Vol. 2; and *Dictionary of Literary Biography*, Vol. 8.)

SAM MOSKOWITZ

There is a school of thought that holds that the dramatic Orson Welles *War of the Worlds* scare, on the evening of October 30, 1938, provided the real basis of the science fiction magazine boom of that period. That the program may have helped give impetus to the spate of new publications is quite possible, but that it inspired them is impossible, since four new magazines . . . had been publicly announced as forthcoming *before* the date of the program.

Until wartime paper shortages curtailed publishers' optimism . . . [fifteen additional science-fiction magazines] would be added to the list. By contrast, before the boom there had been but four magazines in publication, and one of them was predominantly supernatural. . . . (p. 336)

The demands of this widening market naturally attracted to the field many authors who had never written science fiction, as well as lured back others who had been absent for a long period. Most important, it encouraged the development of new talent, writers destined to remake the form of science fiction.

The key figure in this process is John W. Campbell, editor of *Astounding Science-Fiction*. Campbell . . . had become the editor of *Astounding Stories* in 1937. Though only twenty-eight, he was regarded then as one of the half-dozen greatest living writers of science fiction. He had established his first reputation by composing great super-science epics which involved action on a galactic scale and which he laced through with hundreds of provocative ideas. When the popularity of that type of story began to ebb, he adopted the pseudonym Don A. Stuart and specialized in delicate mood pieces directing sympathy toward the works of man, displaying the creations of the human mind and the manifestations of research and discovery as fundamentally benevolent and trustworthy. He also underscored the need for incorporating some cementing philosophy as an ingredient of science fiction, in the process engaging in a high degree of experimentalism in presentation of ideas which had a substantial influence on the writers who followed him.

The magazine he edited was stable, profitable, and the accepted leader in its field. It paid top rates and was regarded as a prestige publication. The editor of such a magazine was in a position to assume literary leadership and shape the direction of the entire field. This Campbell proceeded to do.

It was a peculiarity of Campbell's outlook that he was forever mentally hypothesizing his own universes, philosophies, "natural" laws, to fit whatever tidbits of information intrigued him at the moment. If he ran across a seeming paradox, he fabricated his own train of highly imaginative logic to explain it. Frequently, some relatively minor research would have revealed that the answers were already known and documented, but Campbell was always suspicious of pat theories and, besides, he found them rarely as fascinating as his own.

This was an attitude made to order for a successful science fiction writer. Campbell, as a result, was a fount of ideas that never ran dry. These ideas he fed to his authors at such a prodigal rate that it can be truthfully said most of them owed as much of their success to him as they did to their own talent. (pp. 336-38)

> Sam Moskowitz, "The Future in Present Tense," in
> *his* Explorers of the Infinite: Shapers of Science Fic-
> *tion, World Publishing Co., 1963, pp. 334-50.**

SAM MOSKOWITZ

Campbell was a true giant in popularity among those authors who had grown out of the science-fiction magazines. *The Mightiest Machine* . . . epitomized the type of story that had created his followng. Mighty spaceships move at speeds faster than light from star system to star system, warping themselves through another dimension at the whim of Aarn Munro, a mental and physical superman, descendant of earthmen raised on the surface of the planet Jupiter. He custom-contrives universe-shaking energy weapons to combat alien fleets in universe-wide battles. Like Edward E. Smith, Campbell was undeniably a literary Houdini in the mind-staggering art, convincingly manipulating stupendous forces on a cosmic scale.

Time was running out on macrocosmic spectaculars like *The Mightiest Machine;* changes were occurring in plotting and writing science fiction that were to make the story a period piece before it was completed; yet its impact was so profound on a youthful Englishman, Arthur C. Clarke, that nearly twenty years later he would use a race similar to [Campbell's villains] . . . in his greatest critical success, *Childhood's End.* . . .

Notwithstanding, Campbell's major contribution in both story-telling and influence was yet to come. More than is true of most writers, his early life and background shaped the direction he would take in specific plot ideas as well as in method. (p. 28)

[As a student of physics and chemistry at MIT, Campbell's reading tastes instinctively gravitated toward science fiction.] When science-fiction authors' imaginations showed signs of breaking out of the confines of the solar system, Campbell was enthralled. Smith's *The Skylark of Space* established a lifelong admiration for that author and an immediate desire to emulate.

Stemming from his awareness that science-fiction authors frequently made obvious scientific errors, his first writing attempt, a short story called *Invaders from the Infinite,* was aimed at correcting one of the more widespread misconceptions: that there would be a problem in heating an interplanetary ship in space. The story, sent to AMAZING STORIES, was accepted. Elated, Campbell pounded out a longer story, *When the Atoms Failed,* and that, too, was accepted. His enthusiasm waned, however, as the months passed and neither story appeared. . . . Campbell decided to visit T. O'Conor Sloane, the editor who had been in correspondence with him, and straighten out the matter. (pp. 31-2)

[Sloane] made the embryonic author at home and then owned up to the fact that the manuscript of *Invaders from the Infinite* had been lost. . . .

Well, his career would have to be launched with *When the Atoms Failed.* . . . (p. 32)

Sloane more than made up for the disappointment by carrying an illustration for *When the Atoms Failed* on the cover of the issue in which it appeared and beginning the blurb of the story: "Our new author, who is a student at the Massachusetts Institute of Technology, shows marvelous ability at combining science with romance, evolving a piece of fiction of real scientific and literary value."

The story did contain original ideas. First, though the idea of thinking brains in robots had been used frequently before, the concept of a stationary supercalculator, like today's Univac, hd not appeared in the magazines. Scientists in science fiction, never sissies, previously disdained to use even an adding machine in whipping together mathematical concepts destined to change the very shape of the cosmos. Not so Steven Waterson, Campbell's hero, who, improving on the Integraph, an electrical machine capable of calculus in use at MIT in 1930, built himself a pre-space-age electronic "brain" to aid in his problems.

Secondly, it delved into the greater power to be derived from material energy—the actual destruction of matter—as opposed to atomic energy. This knowledge enables Steven Waterson to defeat a group of invading Martians, force the nations of the earth to scrap all their weapons, and set himself up as "president" of the planet. (pp. 32-3)

[*The Metal Horde,* a sequel to *When the Atoms Failed,*] attempted to show what would happen if calculators were refined to the point where they could reason. Scientist Steven Waterson, in the course of the story, defeats and destroys a thinking machine . . . that has traveled through space for 1600 years accompanied by a brood of obedient mechanicals intent upon setting up a world of machines on Earth.

Elements of J. Schossel's *The Second Swarm* . . . are apparent in this story and in *The Voice of the Void.* . . . This novelette tells of a ten-billion-year-old civilization on Earth, confronted by the final cooling of the sun, which utilizes "phase velocity" as a means of going faster than light and escaping to another system. (pp. 33-4)

Utilizing this principle, earth ships, in an attempt to colonize planets around the star Betelgeuse, fight a series of battles with sentient force-creatures in that system. Though mindless, the force creatures adapt to a series of ever-more-potent weapons and give the earth men quite a tussle before they are exterminated. (p. 34)

The names (Arcot, Wade, and Morey) of a group of characters in *Piracy Preferred* . . . provided the label for a major series that was to catapult Campbell to the top rank among science-fiction writers. In the world of 2126, a super criminal, Wade, with the technology to make his high-speed rocket ship invisible, uses a gas that will penetrate metal and temporarily paralyze all who come in contact with it, for his antisocial activities. He puckishly leaves stock certificates for Piracy, Inc., in the amount of the money he steals.

A team of young geniuses—Richard Arcot, a physicist; William Morey, mathematician and son of the president of Transcontinental Airways—in company with John Fuller, a design engineer, chase the pirate into an orbital trap around the earth. The culprit is permitted to join the group instead of being punished. (pp. 34-5)

The group, in a ship powered by a new discovery which causes all molecules to move in the same direction and uses the power derived from the heat so created, takes off for the planet Venus in *Solarite.* . . . There they find two warring races and side with one against the other, employing Wade's invisibility device and paralyzing gas in the process. When the enemy fathoms the secret of invisibility and uses it against them, pellets of radium paint are employed to locate them, whereupon they are finished off with a molecular-motion weapon. . . .

[In 1930 *The Black Star Passes*] focused attention on Campbell and launched him on his first high wave of popularity, which was to challenge that of E. E. Smith. (p. 35)

In *The Black Star Passes,* an ancient race of hydrogen-breathing creatures living on a planet circling a vagrant dead star sweeps close to our solar system and decides to transfer to a fresh planet, Earth. In thousands of words of thrilling action (and many thousand dull words of scientific gobbldy-gook) they are defeated by the team of Arcot, Wade, Morey, and Fuller and retire to their retreating star. However, the battle has instilled them with new spirit and they are determined that the next star they pass they will conquer.

The *Islands of Space* . . . [1931] was Campbell's first full-length novel and he let out all the stops. Exceeding the speed of light by bending the curvature of space, Arcot, Wade, and Morey in their good ship *Ancient Mariner* tour a succession of worlds, finding new wonders and challenges on each. Finally, lost in an infinity of light, they seek to find a race that can guide them, and in the process they help decide a war on a world ten-million light years away from earth.

The novel that followed, *Invaders from the Infinite* . . . [1932], represented the apex of approval for Campbell's super-science stories. This time, a tremendous ship manned by canines that have risen high on the evolutionary ladder lands on Earth to seek help against a universal menace. In the *ne plus ultra* of intergalactic ships, *Thought,* Arcot, Wade, and Morey search the far-flung star clusters for an answer to the danger, finally discovering it after as pyrotechnic a series of space battles as has ever appeared in science fiction. Especially gripping is one episode illustrating the power of suggestion on the course of a battle, when emotions are magnified and projected by a special device. (pp. 35-6)

[Eventually, Campbell decided to try markets other than AMAZING STORIES.] He sold *The Derelicts of Ganymede* to WONDER STORIES [in 1932]. . . . The story is a satiric slap at the questionable ability of a business tycoon to come out on top if he lets a young man start on even keel.

This was followed by *The Electronic Siege* . . . featuring Captain Don Barclay, a physically powerful and mentally extraordinary Jovian prototype of Aarn Munro, who breaks up an illicit medical experimental station on a planetoid. He brought Don Barclay back again in *Space Rays* . . . to aid in the capture of a space pirate. Hugo Gernsback, the publisher, was moved to write a special editorial instead of the customary blurb for this story. Titled "Reasonableness in Science Fiction," it offered the opinion that Campbell was obviously writing a science-fiction burlesque:

> If he has left out any colored rays, or any magical rays that could not immediately perform certain miraculous wonders, we are not aware of this shortcoming in this story. . . . We were tempted to rename the story 'Ray! Ray!' but thought better of it.

The truth was that Campbell wasn't burlesquing anybody. This was the way he always wrote. (pp. 36-7)

Subtly, though, a change was taking place in Campbell's thinking and writing. It was first evidenced in the introductory passages of *The Black Star Passes,* where an atmosphere of hopelessness and sympathy was engendered for the great people of a dying planet now thousands of years on the decline. It began to take form in *The Last Evolution* . . . , in which the courageous battle of thinking machines to save their creators from a cosmic menace, climaxing in the evolution of the mechanisms into energy consciousnesses of pure thought, raises them to an allegorical heaven. Our machines will be our friends to the last, inevitably outlive us, progress beyond us, and possibly even go to their just reward, Campbell suggests.

The Last Evolution marks the point of transition in Campbell's writing career, the change to stress on mood and writing technique from the superscientific action characteristic of past Campbell stories. (p. 38)

[He] set out to write a story in which mood and characterization would predominate and science would play a secondary role.

He had in mind a story that would "sing," that would figuratively serve as a symphonic mood piece in words set to a science-fiction theme. This was the story; *Twilight.*

Seven million years from today, it is the twilight of man. A mighty civilization served by faithful automatic machinery continues to function: "When Earth is cold, and the Sun has died out, those machines will go on. When Earth begins to creak and break, those perfect, ceaseless machines will try to repair her—." No drive, no progress lies in the dwindling human race. Only stagnation. The man from our day, visiting this future, programs machines to work on the creation of a mechanism with built-in curiosity. The story suggests, as did *The Last Evolution,* that even if man goes, the machines can build their own civilization.

Despite Campbell's popularity, every magazine of early 1933 rejected the story and it went back into his files. Then, in late 1933, F. Orlin Tremaine assumed editorship of ASTOUNDING STORIES and began a drive for leadership in the field.

A high point in his dramatic bid was securing the third story in E. E. Smith's "Skylark" series, *The Skylark of Valeron.* The logical next step was to obtain Campbell, the leading contender for Smith's popularity. Tremaine wrote to Campbell, asking if he had a superscience story along the lines that had established his popularity. In 1933 Campbell had sold *The Mightiest Machine* to Sloane at AMAZING. Over a year had passed and Sloane had not published this story, nor had he yet scheduled another Campbell novel, *Mother World.* Campbell got Sloane to return the story and submitted it to Tremaine, who purchased it immediately.

Heartened, Campbell dusted off *Twilight* and sent it in. Tremaine went quietly mad about it and couldn't get it into print fast enough.

Twilight . . . could not be published under Campbell's own name for two reasons. First, most obviously it would destroy the build-up in progress for *The Mightiest Machine.* Secondly, it was so different in approach that it would disorient the readers accustomed to a certain style of story from Campbell. The problem was solved with a pen name, Don A. Stuart. . . . (pp. 36-8)

[Other authors had written earlier works with similar themes, yet] mood had never been the primary purpose in the presentations of the civilizations and cities of these other authors. Nor had anyone so completely attempted to canonize the machine. Over and over again, Campbell's message remained clear: The machine is *not* the enemy and ruination of man; it is his friend and protector.

Don A. Stuart bid fair to eclipse Campbell in popularity as a result of this single story, *Twilight.* Its appearance was to alter the pattern of science-fiction writing. (p. 40)

Stuart appeared again with *Atomic Power* . . . , a story in which men prevent the structure of our solar system from being blown up by atomcrackers in the macrocosmos. The lead story of the issue was the first installment of *The Mightiest Machine,* and a third story by Campbell in the same issue, *The Irrelevant,* resulted in months of debate in the readers' column, since he presented a theoretical evasion of the law of conservation of energy. This was published under the pseudonym Karl van Kampen. . . . (pp. 40-1)

[*Blindness,* published under the Stuart pseudonym,] was a poignant sketch of a scientist who loses his sight in space to bring the world the blessings of atomic energy, only to learn that inadvertently another discovery of his provides a cheaper power source. He dies embittered because the world does not want his atomic energy.

One of the most remarkable and underrated performances under the Stuart name was *The Escape* . . . , written as the result of an argument with a would-be writer as to whether or not it was possible to write a successful love story in the framework of science fiction. A girl who runs off with a boy she loves to escape marrying the selection of the Genetics Board is finally captured and brought back and psychologically reconditioned to "love" the "right" man. This remains one of the finest love stories science fiction has yet produced.

With *The Mightiest Machine* receiving reader accolades, Campbell thought sequels were in order. He wrote three, continuing the adventures of Aarn Munro and his companions. The first, a 15,000-word novelette, *The Incredible Planet,* utilized the well-worn device of losing his characters in space thus enabling them to stumble upon a world whose inhabitants have remained in suspended animation for 400 billion years; a second sequel, *The Interstellar Search,* finds the earthmen aiding a planet whose sun is about to become a nova; and in the final story, *The Infinite Atom,* they arrive home in time to block an invasion by creatures whose previous visit to earth gave rise to the centaur legends. (p. 41)

The three sequels to *The Mightiest Machine* eventually were published as . . . *The Incredible Planet,* in 1949.

Campbell was forced to give full emphasis to Don A. Stuart in a series which he called "The Teachers," but which never was so labeled, beginning . . . with *The Machine.* In this story, a thinking machine that has provided every comfort for men leaves the planet for their own good, forcing them to forage for themselves. (p. 42)

[*The Invaders*], a sequel to *The Machine,* describes a mankind reverted to savagery, easily enslaved by the Tharoo, a race from another world.

[*Rebellion*] finds the human race, through selective breeding, becomes more intelligent than the Tharoo, driving the invaders back off the planet.

The foregoing were not primarily mood stories, but they were adult fare—the predecessors of an entirely new type of science fiction.

In *Night,* a sequel to *Twilight,* . . . Campbell stirringly returned to the mood story. A man of today moves into the inconceivably distant future, when not only the sun but the stars themselves are literally burnt out. At his presence, machines from Neptune move to serve him, but he recognizes them for what they are: "This, I saw, was the last radiation of the heat of life from an already-dead body—the feel of life and warmth, imitation of life by a corpse," for man and all but the last dregs of universal energy are gone.

"You still wonder that we let man die out?" asked the machine. "It was best. In another brief million years he would have lost his high estate. It was best." Campbell had matured. A civilization of machines, he now understands, is but parody, movement without consciousness. It is not and can never be "the last evolution." (pp. 42-3)

Campbell's most successful story in 1936 was *Frictional Losses* . . . , under the Stuart byline, in which a method of eliminating friction proves the ultimate weapon against invaders from outer space.

WONDER STORIES had been sold by Gernsback to Standard Magazines and now appeared as THRILLING WONDER STORIES. Campbell arranged with the editor, Mort Weisinger, for a series of stories under his own name, built around the characters of Penton and Blake, two fugitives from Earth. The best of the group was the first, *Brain Stealers of Mars* . . . concerning Martians capable of converting themselves into an exact replica of any object or person. They provide a knotty problem for the visitors from Earth. This story and those that followed had the light note of humor and the wacky alien creatures which Stanley G. Weinbaum had recently made so popular.

Closest in quality to *Night* and *Twilight* proved to be *Forgetfulness,* . . . in which earthmen landing on a distant planet assume that a race is decadent because it has deserted the automatic cities and mighty power devices that man, in his current state of progress, associates with civilization.

Influential as well as entertaining was his novelette of the Sarn, *Out of Night.* . . . A matriarchial society of aliens who have conquered the earth and have ruled it for 4,000 years are challenged by Aesir, a black, amorphous mass vaguely in the shape of man, ostensibly personifying humanity's unified yearnings past and present. This device was picked up by Robert A. Heinlein in *Sixth Column,* where it helps to route the Asiatic conquerors.

Cloak of Aesir, a sequel, demonstrated the use of psychology in driving the "people" of the Sarn from their domination of Earth, and terminated the short series in ASTOUNDING SCIENCE-FICTION for March, 1939. (pp. 43-4)

From the memories of his childhood [Campbell] drew the most fearsome agony of the past: the doubts, the fears, the shock, and the frustration of repeatedly discovering that the woman who looked so much like his mother was not who she seemed. Who goes there? Friend or foe? He had attempted the theme once before, employing a light touch, in *Brain Stealers of Mars.* This time he was serious. *Who Goes There?* . . . deals with an alien thing from outer space that enters the camp of an Antarctic research party and blends alternately into the forms of the various men and dogs in the camp. The job is to find and kill the chimera before, in the guise of some human being or animal, it gets back to civilization.

An impressive display of writing talent, *Who Goes There?* is in one sense one of the most thrilling detective stories ever written. The suspense and tension mount with each paragraph and are sustained to the last. Reading this story inspired A. E. van Vogt to turn to science fiction with *Vault of the Beast,* a direct take-off on the idea. (p. 45)

A few more Stuart stories would sporadically appear. *The Elder Gods* . . . , a swiftly paced sword-and-sorcery tale, was written as a last-minute fill-in. . . . Together with *The Moon Is Hell,* a short novel of stark realism drawing a parallel between the survival problems of Antarctic and moon explorers, it made its appearance . . . in 1951.

Fifteen years after he had quit writing for a living, Campbell still displayed excellent technique in *The Idealists,* a novelette written expressly for the hard-cover anthology *9 Tales of Space and Time.* . . . Scientists aren't always "good guys," was the point he made, and a high degree of technical development does not necessarily carry with it maturity in dealing with different cultures.

But for all practical purposes, Campbell's writing career ended at the age of 28 with *Who Goes There?* As one of the first of the modern science-fiction writers, he had a profound influence on the field. As editor of the leading, best-paying magazine, he taught, coerced, and cajoled his type of story. As a result, for the more than a quarter-century since he ceased writing, older readers have been haunted by half-remembered echoes in the plot structure of hundreds of stories and in the lines of scores of writers. It is not strange if sometimes readers shake the hypnotic wonder of the wheeling cosmos from their minds and demand: "Who goes there?" (pp. 45-6)

> *Sam Moskowitz, "John W. Campbell," in his* Seekers of Tomorrow: Masters of Science Fiction, *World Publishing Co., 1966, pp. 27-46.*

DAMON KNIGHT

In the pantheon of magazine science fiction there is no more complex and puzzling figure than that of John Campbell, and certainly none odder. Under his own name, . . . he wrote gadgety, fast-moving, cosmic-scaled science fiction in the E. E. Smith tradition, and became, after Smith himself, its acknowledged master; as "Don A. Stuart," he began a one-man literary revival which eventually made that tradition obsolete. As editor of *Astounding,* he forced the magazine through a series of metamorphoses. . . . More clearly than anyone, Campbell saw that the field was growing up and would only be handicapped by the symbols of its pulpwood infancy; he deliberately built up a readership among practicing scientists and technicians; he made himself the apostle of genuine science in science fiction. . . . (pp. 34-5)

In the hasty, ill-composed and ill-considered introduction to . . . *Who Goes There?,* Campbell says of the first Don A. Stuart story, **"Twilight,"** that "it was entirely different from any science fiction that had appeared before." He ought to have added, "in Gernsback's *Amazing Stories* or any of its successors"; so qualified, the statement would have fallen at least somewhere near the truth.

"Twilight" is what Campbell says it is, a pure mood story—and as such is the lineal descendant of H. G. Wells' "The Time Machine," Rudyard Kipling's "A Matter of Fact" (both circa 1890), Stephen Vincent Benét's "By the Waters of Babylon" and many others. By the late thirties, . . . magazine science fiction was fast settling towards a dismal status as just another variety of pulp; Campbell's great achievement was to rescue it from its own overspecialized preoccupations and start it back toward the mainstream of literature. Although he later tried to nudge the pendulum the other way, the movement has continued; the revolution is a success.

The second Campbell-Stuart collection, *Cloak of Aesir,* contains seven stories that justify the author's cheerful boast: every one is a landmark in science fiction history. The germs of countless later stories are in them; indeed, it seems reasonable to doubt that the field ever could have developed as it has if they had not been written.

All these stories belong to what might be called the "Oh, yeah?" school of science fiction, though they are so cloaked in the Stuart mood-writing and in what still seems to me, in some of them, a real beauty, that probably few people realized it till Campbell himself pointed it out.

"Forgetfulness," for instance, is nothing at bottom but an irreverent iconoclast's-eye view of the proposition, "Machine civilization represents progress.'' So is **"The Machine"**; and **"The Invaders"** takes a similar look at "It would be awful if the Earth were conquered from outer space.'' **"The Escape"** is a "tragic" love story with a happy ending—and Campbell defies you to prove it isn't.

Campbell, a capable writer, never has been a stylist, and he didn't alter his natural prose style, with its short, blurted, agrammatical sentences, for the purpose of creating "Don A. Stuart." What makes the difference is partly the tone—a kind of high-pitched sing-song—and partly the point of view, a subtle thing that resists exact definition. The visual quality of every writer's work differs somewhat from every other's; probably it also differs, at least as widely, between one reader and the next, so that if I say that the Don A. Stuart quality, to me, is like a series of images shifting in and out of focus through a pearl-gray haze, nobody else is likely to sit up and say, "That's exactly it," least of all the author; readers who aren't visually oriented will not even know what I'm talking about. But the quality does exist and, I should think, is capable of being detected in some form by almost everybody; it's an important factor in making these stories what they are.

Clearly enough, the Don A. Stuart stories were only one experiment among many to Campbell; but modern readers may find in these two volumes [*Who Goes There?* and *Cloak of Aesir*] his most important and lasting contribution to the literature. (pp. 35-6)

> Damon Knight, "Campbell and His Decade," in his In Search of Wonder: Essays on Modern Science Fiction, *revised edition, Advent: Publishers, 1967, pp. 34-46.*

THEODORE STURGEON

John W. Campbell Jr., escaped from MIT and, a fine traditional sf writer himself (and for a time, as Don A. Stuart, a superb fantasist), took over the editorial chair of *Astounding Science Fiction* thirty years ago. In less than a couple of years he attracted to himself and the magazine (the same thing, really) a nucleus of extraordinary writers. A few had been around for a while—Simak, Leinster, Lieber; the others he discovered or invented or, it sometimes seems, manufactured. Pratt and deCamp, L. Ron Hubbard . . . , van Vogt, del Rey, Heinlein, Hamilton—Campbell, through these men, created what has been called a Golden Age of sf.

He was a superb and provocative teacher of science and of fiction. "Give me a story about aliens," he would challenge, "in which they think as well as a man but not like a man." He would return a story because it turned upon the fission of light metals or a compound of argon, and would explain to you in five or six or seven single-spaced pages why this was not possible—and give you something which would really work, and which in some cases, as with our nuclear energy technology, ultimately did. He conveyed his preoccupations with power (all kinds), superiority (*our* kind) and scientific probability up and down and across the disciplines, so forcefully to his disciples that they produced a body of Campbellian literature on which the entire field pivoted, and which profoundly affects it to this day. The same pressures which produced that first golden explosion also seem to have squirted, like appleseeds, his early converts into other areas; no matter—he discovered/invented/manufactured more, and as *Astounding* became *Analog* . . . the magazine went right on being what it had been since Campbell took over: Campbell. (p. 266)

Theodore Sturgeon, "I List in Numbers," in National Review, *Vol. XXII, No. 9, March 10, 1970, pp. 266-67.**

RICHARD LUPOFF

An illuminating moment in the schism between the science fiction establishment and its foes came about in 1967 and 1968, when the science fiction community, like the rest of American society, engaged in loud debate over the Vietnam war. Starting at the Milford Conference in August 1967 (an annual science fiction writers' workshop) the proposal was made that science fiction writers express themselves on the issue of the war. (p. 26)

The final result was not one but two statements, which appeared as paid advertisements in 1968 issues of *The Magazine of Fantasy and Science Fiction* and *Galaxy Science Fiction*. An examination of the signers of the two statements is illuminating as to the state of science fiction, a state which has continued to evolve since 1967-68 but which has not been *essentially* altered since then.

The "war" ad carried 72 signatures including those of Poul Anderson, Leigh Brackett, John W. Campbell, Hal Clement, L. Sprague de Camp, Edmond Hamilton, Robert A. Heinlein, Joe L. Hensley, R. A. Lafferty, Sam Moskowitz, Larry Niven and Jack Williamson. The "peace" ad carried 82 signatures including those of Isaac Asimov, Peter S. Beagle, James Blish, Anthony Boucher, Ray Bradbury, Terry Carr, Samuel R. Delany, Lester del Rey, Philip K. Dick, Thomas M. Disch, Harlan Ellison, Philip José Farmer, Harry Harrison, Damon Knight, Ursula K. LeGuin, Judith Merril, Joanna Russ, Robert Silverberg, Kate Wilhelm and Donald A. Wollheim. (pp. 26-7)

What is more significant is the fact that *every* author or editor who signed the "war" ad was a traditionalist. Whatever else divides these traditionalists, they are united by their engineering mentality and its preference for violent, repressive solutions to the political problems posed in its novels. These people seem convinced that the application of the right materials and the right forces will solve any problem. It is obvious in their fiction.

The late John W. Campbell was a clear example of this mentality. A former engineering student at MIT, Campbell rose to prominence as a science fiction writer in the 1930s. He wrote a number of impressive mood pieces and some intriguing intellectual puzzle stories. (One of the latter, **"Who Goes There?"** was adapted for the screen as *The Thing:* it is one of the classic 1950s science-fiction-as-paranoia films . . .).

But Campbell hit his stride in a series of superscientific technologically oriented novels like **The Black Star Passes** (1930) and **The Mightiest Machine** (1934). In these stories human values are absent, technology is glorified, force and destruction are implicit in the solution of all problems. While Campbell was the editor of *Astounding Science Fiction* magazine (from 1937 until his death in July 1971, although the magazine was renamed *Analog*), he "discovered" and guided the development of many of the leading authors of the late 1940s and '50s, contributed much to the development of science fiction, and boosted the circulation of his magazine to close to 100,000 copies, triple that of its nearest competitors.

Unfortunately, with the passing of time, Campbell fell increasingly prey to assorted crackpot and rightist notions. In 1947 he introduced to his readers L. Ron Hubbard's *Dianetics*, "the new science of the mind." The literature and procedures of

Dianetics reveals it to be little other than a simplified version of orthodox Freudian theory—but restated in engineering-like terms, and offered with absolute guarantees of success. Later Campbell promoted the Hieronymous Machine—a device for concentrating psychic energy—and the Dean Drive, a sort of perpetual motion machine for powering spaceships. Still later Campbell's editorials "proved" that slavery was a desirable institution, that nonwhites are inherently inferior to whites, that the whole ecology/environmentalist movement was hysterical silliness, and that the four students killed at Kent State brought it on themselves and deserved what they got. (p. 27)

> *Richard Lupoff, "Science Fiction Hawks and Doves: Whose Future Will You Buy?" in* Ramparts, *Vol. 10, No. 8, February, 1972, pp. 25-30.**

RICHARD HODGENS

[*The essay from which this excerpt is taken was originally published in a different form in* Film Quarterly, *Winter 1959.*]

[*The Thing from Another World,* a 1951 film released in the United States as *The Thing,*] was based on a short novel by John W. Campbell, Jr., . . . [entitled] **"Who Goes There?"** The story is regarded as one of the most original and effective science fiction stories, *subspecies* "horror." Its premise is convincing, its development logical, its characterization intelligent, and its suspense considerable. Of these qualities the film retained one or two minutes of suspense. The story and the film are poles apart. Probably for timely interest, the Thing crashed in a flying saucer and was quick-frozen in the Arctic. In Campbell's story "it had lain in the ice for twenty million years" in the Antarctic. In film as in source, when the creature thaws out it is alive and dangerous. In **"Who Goes There?,"** when it gets up and walks away, and later when it is torn to pieces by the dogs and still lives, the nature of the beast makes its invulnerability acceptable. But there is little plausibility about the Hollywood Thing's nine lives. . . . Instead of the nearly insoluble problem created in Campbell's story, this Thing is another monster entirely. He is a vegetable. He looks like Frankenstein's monster. He roars. He is radioactive. And he drinks blood.

Probably Campbell's protean menace was reduced to this strange combination of familiar elements in the belief that the original idea—the idea which made the story make sense—was too complex. This was probably incorrect, because monsters since that *Thing* have imitated the special ability of Campbell's Alien, although with far less credibility . . . and there is no indication that anyone found them difficult to understand. (pp. 82-3)

The Thing is a most radical betrayal of its source, but since the source was generally unfamiliar, and since the idea of a monster from outer space seemed so original (though the monster itself had blood brothers in Transylvania), the film earned both critical approval and a great deal of money. In addition, it fixed the pattern for the majority of science fiction films that followed, for it proved that some money could be made by "science fiction" that preyed on current fears symbolized crudely by any preposterous monster. . . . (p. 83)

One should realize that, like them or not, the invaders in Wells's *War of the Worlds,* the stranded Alien in Campbell's **"Who Goes There?,"** or the parasites in Heinlein's *Puppet Masters* . . . are a different sort of monster from those of most SF films. They may be symbols too, but first they are beings. Campbell may invent a creature that evokes a complex of ancient fears—

fear of the ancient itself, the fear that death may not be final, that evil is indestructible, and fear rising from the imitation motif, fear of possession, of loss of identity, all the fears that gave rise to tales of demons, ghosts, witches, vampires, shape-shifters. But in **"Who Goes There?"** it is a realistically conceived being that evokes these fears and creates the suspense, not an impossible symbol; and the story is not hysterical, but a study of man under stress. (p. 88)

> *Richard Hodgens, "A Brief, Tragical History of the Science Fiction Film," in* Focus on the Science Fiction Film, *edited by William Johnson, Prentice-Hall, Inc., 1972, pp. 78-90.**

LESTER del REY

Back in the very early days of science fiction, everyone knew it was impossible to make a living in the field. There were only two SF magazines being published. . . . Furthermore, no science fiction *books* were being published; so once a story appeared in a magazine, there would be no further income from it.

Writing science fiction was a hobby, not a career, and nobody questioned that obvious fact—nobody but John W. Campbell! Against all logic, he not only determined to make science fiction his life's work, but he succeeded. It took three careers to achieve his goal, during which he became almost single-handedly the creator of modern science fiction. And eventually, others with less genius or less folly found it possible to follow the trail he blazed. (p. 1)

In those days, the science-fiction stories had almost no literary value. They were crudely written, at best, and there was little attempt at characterization. The people were merely used as props to discuss the heavy use of superscience and to make the simple plots work. The important things in science fiction were the wonders of future science and the unlimited possibility for human progress. The best-liked stories dealt with adventures far out in space, where men discovered other somewhat human races and warred mightily with evil invaders of monstrous form.

Campbell took the formula and carried it to its ultimate. His science began at the far edge of current theories and went on from there at breakneck pace. By the end of 1934 he had written six novels. . . . In these novels, his heroes roamed all space and beyond into other universes. New inventions seemed to be created on every page. In the end, his heroes could even create entire universes just by "thinking" into their ultimate machines.

I have included in this volume ["**The Best of John W. Campbell**"] only one short story from this period: **"The Last Evolution."** . . . It shows all the crudity and lack of characterization of the period. But it also shows the scope of Campbell's imagination and his originality. As far as I know, this is the first story ever to deal with robots as more than complex tools or slaves for human convenience. It would be another ten years or more before other writers could accept Campbell's concept of possible evolution.

By the end of 1934, however, Campbell had used up almost every possibility to be found in the old formula. He wrote a few "John W. Campbell, Jr." stories after that, but the enthusiasm was gone. He could have gone on repeating himself, since his stories were still as popular as ever, but he was never content to be a follower—even of himself. (pp. 1-2)

It's hard to be sure, but Campbell's early work does not indicate that he was a naturally gifted writer in the usual sense. But he could learn. . . . So he set about mastering the ability to write science fiction as it had never been done; and because the story turned out to be unlike anything else he had written, he chose to publish it under the pen name of Don A. Stuart. Thus his "Stuart" career began before his "Campbell" one was ending.

The result was **"Twilight,"** a story that was chosen in 1970 by the Science Fiction Writers of America as one of the great classics of the literature. However, the story was hardly an instant success. Every editor in the field turned it down, until F. Orlin Tremaine became editor of *Astounding Stories*. It finally appeared in the November 1934 issue, when the readers gave it almost unanimous praise and demanded more from this "new" writer. . . . By the end of 1935, Stuart was even more popular than Campbell.

Stuart, as Campbell later put it, was an annoying kind of writer. He refused to take the standard axioms for granted. When everyone knew that something was so, Stuart began questioning it. Every science-fiction reader wished for a day when machines would make everything easy for everybody; that would be utopia, of course. So Stuart wrote **"The Machine"** to show how things might really be.

One of the standard horrors of science fiction was the idea of an invading race taking over Earth. Stuart took a good look at that in **"The Invaders."** But suppose the invaders made slaves of the people of Earth; everyone knew that slavery was the worst thing that could happen to people. Well, maybe; Stuart decided to examine that proposition and see just what was the worst that could happen to whom. This story was entitled **"Rebellion."**

These three stories were planned together under the general title of "The Teachers," though that was never actually used for them. But one way or another, they all have the common theme of someone teaching a lesson to someone else, though just what the results might be wasn't as certain as it might seem.

"Blindness" is a strange examination of the idea that the discovery of simple, cheap, atomic fusion power would be the greatest of boons to the human race. It is also a moving story of a man who makes a tremendous sacrifice for science—and what his reward may be. And **"Elimination"** looks at man's ancient wish dream to know what the future may bring.

Campbell, as Stuart, was leading science fiction away from the old, accepted dreams of science fiction. He was blazing the way toward a time when a writer must look at every postulate and examine it as if it were a new idea. But he was doing far more. He never forgot that he had begun by trying to give the feeling and humanity to his stories that had been lacking. More than his ideas, the quality of his writing excited all who read them.

Perhaps this is best shown in **"Forgetfulness."** On the surface, this story is a bit like **"The Invaders"**—an alien race comes to Earth to find mankind living a simple, pastoral, almost childlike life, surrounded by the remnants of a magnificent civilization it has forgotten. It's all handled simply, directly, and with a feeling on the part of the alien that the reader can share. (pp. 2-4)

"Out of Night" and **"Cloak of Aesir"** really go together to make up a short novel. Again Campbell gives us aliens and struggling humans—but there is no simple right and wrong, no obvious warfare, no previously overused cliché situation. And at the end, as one sits with the Sarn Mother, it is the emotional resolution that remains, not the simple chain of events.

"Who Goes There?" is a suspense story, something neither Campbell nor his alter ego, Stuart, had tried before. . . . [It] was chosen by the Science Fiction Writers of America as first among the greatest novellas of all time.

In only ten years, John Campbell had become two of the greatest writers of science fiction. And then (except for one short fantasy novel written to fill a magazine he edited) both careers came to an end, as he began a third which was to be even more influential than any amount of writing could have been— so influential, indeed, that a crater on Mars has now been named *Campbell* to honor him.

Toward the end of 1937, he was asked to be the editor of *Astounding Stories*. . . . As a writer under either pen name, Campbell had been one of the best; but as an editor, he quickly became *the* greatest. If that is a personal judgment, it is one shared by most writers and editors in the field. (p. 4)

> *Lester del Rey, "Introduction: The Three Careers of John W. Campbell," in* The Best of John W. Campbell *by John W. Campbell, edited by Lester del Rey, Nelson Doubleday, Inc., 1976, pp. 1-6.*

DAN MILLER

In the pantheon of science fiction, Campbell ranks slightly higher than a deity, yet most readers new to SF know little of the basis for his reputation. This definitive collection of short fiction [*The Best of John W. Campbell*] is a partial remedy. . . . The anthology shows Campbell's growth from a writer of competent pot boilers into a mature craftsman of a sophistication and professionalism seldom found in early science fiction. Highlights include **"Twilight,"** everybody's idea of an SF classic; **"Forgetfulness,"** about the evolution of knowledge; and **"Who Goes There?,"** a suspense-horror story considered one of the best SF novellas of all time. The celebration of Campbell's other achievements—as editor of *Astounding* and *Analog* magazines for 34 years until his death in 1971—requires a full-length biography. Meanwhile, this collection will be warmly received.

> *Dan Miller, in a review of "The Best of John W. Campbell," in* Booklist, *Vol. 73, No. 1, September 1, 1976, p. 23.*

ALGIS BUDRYS

It's becoming increasingly obvious that we need a long, objective look at John W. Campbell, Jr. But we're not likely to get one.

When he was alive, Campbell was mind-numbingly complex but greatly influential because he could be seen taking major actions which could be labelled simply. Between 1932 and 1938 he made himself the co-equal of E. E. Smith among fabulists of technological optimism. "Superscience fiction" realized its full potential at his hands, and created a body of readers who, some years later, would include writers who sincerely believed that SF was technological in basis.

At the very same time, he was incubating "Don A. Stuart," who, beginning with the short story, **"Twilight,"** and then in a brief but energetic succession of other short work . . . set an example which shocked many of his colleagues into re-evaluating their fundamental ideas of what could be written as pulp magazine science fiction. And he created a body of readers who, some years later, would include new writers who believed the essence of good SF was moodiness and the inclusion of alien characters who talked like thanatopsical eighteenth century English gentlemen.

In 1938, for his pains, he received the husk of *Astounding Stories of Super Science* and by 1940 could clearly be seen to be that almost nonexistent creature, an editor. Within the exact meaning, SF has never had another. . . . (pp. 46-7)

Within a small group of persons in our time—Harold Ross, Helen Gurley Brown, Hugh Hefner, Ben Bradlee, a very few others—Campbell stands as tall as any in that company. None of them could do the trick any better than he could. With minor exceptions, most of them insignificant, all newsstand SF between 1940 and about 1960 was either apparently Campbellian or, when not, consciously and sometimes painfully not.

Galaxy's entire early success was founded on giving relief to writers who hadn't been able to live with Campbell or live without him. (pp. 47-8)

[*The Magazine of Fantasy and Science Fiction*], as our name might indicate, was launched to satisfy Anthony Boucher's longing for Campbell's lost *Unknown*. . . . [Boucher] established a certain special tone which this magazine has never lost. Nevertheless, it was Campbell who had founded *Unknown,* along with the idea that newsstand SF could fluently incorporate both pseudotechnological and magical fantasies from the imagination of the same basic set of contributors. . . .

[Until the 1950s] Campbell operated alone upon the hearts and minds of his writers and of his readers, who firmly believed that any newsstand SF not in *astounding SCIENCE FICTION* was a sometimes interesting but always lesser sort of thing.

Campbell's monopoly of ideas, techniques and thumb-rules thus extended itself to his own analytical faculties. If he understood it, it existed. Nothing else existed. To converse with Campbell for any length of time, it was necessary to make the same assumptions. Once made, they permitted a relationship either harmonious or not, but viable. (p. 48)

The major features of his individuality were footed in a code of manners or, better, the concept that there was a code of manners somewhere, absolute and refined out to the last decimal place of objectivity, so that a gentleman's principal duty consisted of discovering and mapping it, guided by his increasingly educated basic instincts.

In that light, the emergence of moody, sometimes querulous, often eironiphilic Don A. Stuart from universe-wrecking John Campbell makes some sense. Superscience fiction demands protagonists of unwavering moral rigor; intelligences which at a snap can detect the essence of evil and bend all their energies to expunging its taint wholesale forthwith unrelentingly. The fast-action format requires it, just as it simplifies all interactions into Total-Good-versus-Total-Evil for the sake of plot celerity. This is the further consequence: Since the villains, to be convincingly dangerous, must be as technologically capable as the heroes, but the heroes win, the reader and writer must collaborate in the unspoken assumption that right and might are indistinguishable. The mightiest machine is the goodest machine. . . .

There is a detectable specific link between the prewar economic depression and the nature of the "modern" science fiction of the 1940s. More specifically, there is a link between John W. Campbell, Jr., universe-wrecker, and John W. Campbell, Jr., editor—ie., universe-definer. That link is Don A. Stuart, child of the effect of the Depression on Campbell the writer of successful, comparatively lucrative pulp fiction of questionable aspiration and juvenile logic. (p. 49)

It's not that I think Campbell deliberately created Stuart for the purpose of worrying at the problem of understanding problems. That's not how creation works. (p. 50)

But Stuart was assigned the natural study of problems. Beginning with **"Twilight"** and throughout his career, Stuart dealt with or at least catalogued such questions as, for one, the effect on problem-solving Humanity of solving the problem of building problem-solving machines; for another, the situation in which the researcher is the last to realize the true practical value of his incidental discoveries; for a third the problem of not being able to recognize valid information on advanced information-gathering systems when equipped with inadequate means for evaluating information; for a fourth the problem of not being able to distinguish at any given moment between two statically identical affects, one genuine and one equally genuine but not immutable. Etc. It is also noteworthy that all Don A. Stuart stories can simply be described as allegories of failed communication. Clearly, they come from some single, though complex sector of the man's self-image, and probably represent his major intellectual preoccupation of the late 1930s.

When, in late 1938, he was given *Astounding* to work with, what we soon got was the result of a confluence of factors that had been in considerable tension. . . . [Goodbye] not only to John W. Campbell, Jr.'s superscience fiction, but to all superscience fiction except for that of E. E. Smith, Campbell's preceptor and only rival in that art, . . . and goodbye to "Don A. Stuart," the writer, (but Hello! Hallo! Halloo! to John W. Campbell, Jr., editor, preceptor, problem definer, who to the end of his days editorialized exactly as Stuart plotted, and who cuffed and snarled at his writers or charmed them with his great warm bulk, and drove them from tree to tree of his choosing, some of them no doubt thinking that they were simply cooperating with him, and that they were fully his equals, even if as yet slightly smaller versions of him).

Obviously, no one who knew him well enough to work for him at any length could have retained an objective view of him. . . . (pp. 50-1)

A long-standing fact that is only emerging into common unconsciousness since his death is the really large number of major talents who could never relate to him or could work with him only at a distance, or lost their ability to work with him. (p. 51)

And some of the people he'd been publishing right along, for one reason or another, were as mediocre or as bad as his rejects. He was not infallible; or, rather, his standards are not immediately perceptible by others.

But, obviously, no one who failed to feel his effect, or who rebelled against his effect, or lost interest in his effect, is apt to understand matters well enough to tell us exactly what he did and how he did it. (pp. 51-2)

This is no more than the difficulty history has with any major figure. But by its very nature, the dimension of the difficulty in some way measures the pervasive importance of the man. (p. 52)

So from where to begin to understand John Campbell? I would start with two novels: *The Black Star Passes,* and *The Moon is Hell,* and next I would go to *The Best of John W. Campbell.*

Lester del Rey knew Campbell well. But don't expect any definitive or comprehensive analyses of JWC in the introduction [see essay above]. . . . Instead, he gives a chronological account of Campbell's professional life, sticking to the established facts, accounting for the evolving nature of the stories collected here.

These begin with "The Last Evolution," offered as a sample of Campbell, Jr., superscience writing, and then progress through "Twilight," "The Machine," "The Invaders," "Rebellion," "Blindness," "Elimination," and "Forgetfulness" to "Out of Night" and "Cloak of Aesir," and finally "Who Goes There?" which is the finest SF suspense novella ever written. There is one editorial, to illustrate that side of John's work. (pp. 51-2)

It's striking that—as del Rey says, not in so many words—Campbell was sometimes a visibly workmanlike writer. The opening paragraphs of "Elimination" are ludicrous as literary technique. And his idea of what constitutes mood and feeling was derived not from life but from a book by someone else.

But neither of these features makes any difference to Campbell's hard-driving storytelling ability, or to any reader's potential ability to enjoy this work. Except for "The Last Evolution," and a few text references to propeller-driven aircraft and that class of minor anachronism, nothing here would be remarkable if published for the first time today, except in the sense that it would be remarkably competent. If Don A. Stuart had never existed in this field, they would be dynamite, and sometimes beautiful.

So if you read this book, you will have the essence of what Campbell was able to do to his field as a writer. What he did to other writers—as an editor and as a grey eminence—is best found out by listening to them. . . . (p. 53)

Algis Budrys, in a review of "The Best of John W. Campbell," in The Magazine of Fantasy and Science Fiction, *Vol. 51, No. 6, December, 1976, pp. 46-53.*

ALGIS BUDRYS

[Recently,] Roger Elwood walked into a bookstore and was introduced to an old friend of John Campbell's. . . . [During the course of the conversation] it developed there were three hitherto unheard-of, unpublished, forty-year-old JWC, Jr. novellas. The guess was they had probably been intended for Hugo Gernsback and shelved when Campbell was hired by *Astounding.* . . .

The novellas are *Marooned, All,* and *The Space Beyond.* They are now out, under a nice Sternback astronomical painting, as *The Space Beyond,* . . . and represent the most important SF event ever made available for . . . [the price]. (p. 27)

The writing is pure pre-Stuart Campbell, right down to the eccentric punctuation. . . . *Marooned* is a sort of capsulized *The Moon Is Hell,* set aboard an exploratory vessel trapped in Jupiter's atmosphere with no way to break free, the food and air running out, and the internal temperature dropping. Fortunately, there are three Campbellian heroes on board, and not only is the problem solved but their flanged-up inventions will

be worth a fortune by virtue of transforming modern technology.

All is the prototype on which Heinlein wrote *Sixth Column.* And *The Space Beyond* is a superscience interstellar war opera, very reminiscent of *The Black Star Passes* and similar productions, but with peculiarities. For instance, Campbell, unlike E. E. Smith, tended to back off from depicting personal violence; he could burn a fleet anytime, but one-on-one mayhem at close range is much less often seen in his work. *The Space Beyond* is thus somewhat atypical, although still clearly pre-ASF Campbellian. (p. 28)

The stories make pretty good reading on their own account, if you are a superscience fan and have developed the necessary selective blindness toward visibly forthright technique. And then they are very interesting as milestones along an honorable road trod by SF and by John Campbell. Finally, they tell us rather more about Campbell the editor than we knew before.

They are almost certainly not final drafts. *Marooned,* for example, contains many hasty sentences, such as one which superficially appears to read that painting a spaceship black will help it radiate heat. The opening passages are inappropriately flippant, and the pacing of the end pretty obviously shows it's three AM; get it all down somehow and smooth it in the next run-through. (p. 29)

Marooned has obvious echoes of *The Moon Is Hell,* and on slim evidence I would guess it predates that novel. It tosses off several ideas which appear full-blown as key events in the longer story. It's thinkable that their casual treatment might instead result from a feeling that they'd been fully handled once, but I have to decide that Campbell would not have written *Marooned* if he had already written *The Moon Is Hell.* He would, I think, have used some other plot in which to convey his stunningly picturesque vision of Jupiter and the central idea which yielded the image of the floating ocean.

It certainly predates "Stuart's" *Who Goes There?,* in which the pervading misty cold aboard the trapped ship recurs even more convincingly. I would guess that something about those passages fascinated Campbell's mind, so that he reached back for them several years later.

He reached into *All* with both hands. If you outline the plot developments in what I think is the most recent of these three stories, you could lay that diagram right over a diagram of *Sixth Column.* It would be interesting to learn whether Heinlein was given a copy to read, or whether Campbell conveyed all this secondary as well as primary invention simply in conversation or in correspondence. The closeness of the resemblance transcends the usual effect of Campbell casually sowing ideas broadcast, which in this particular case also resulted in Fritz Leiber's less but still openly derivative *Gather, Darkness!* as well as such tertiary evolutions as Dianetics, the modern Science of Mental Health.

All three of these stories abound in notions, thoughts, and offhand mentions which later turn up again and again in "modern science fiction," sometimes under the short-lived Stuart byline, usually under someone else's. (pp. 29-30)

[What] seems particularly clear is that Campbell had an intellectual *floreat* in the early 1930s which was even greater than anyone had hitherto known; a major portion of his public greatness in the 1940s derives from far more private visions during his apprenticeship in and immediately after his college years. What he seems to have spent most of his time perfecting in the "golden age" was the manner in which he let the world see what had been stored up over the previous decade.

Algis Budrys, in a review of "The Space Beyond,"
in The Magazine of Fantasy and Science Fiction,
Vol. 52, No. 3, March, 1977, pp. 27-30.

JACK P. RAWLINS

[*The essay from which this excerpt is taken was originally pre-sented as a lecture at the Eaton Conference on Science Fiction and Fantasy at the University of California, Riverside, in 1980.*]

[In trying to determine the relationship between fantasy and science fiction, fantasy] honors the emotive side of the self, what I call the nighttime perspective. The extreme alternative is literature devoted to the exercise of the daytime powers of the intellect. Here my quintessential specimen is John Campbell's **"Who Goes There?"** The dramatic situation is much like that of [*The Invasion of the*] *Body Snatchers*, but the art teaches us a very different response. Again, an alien thing capable of swallowing humans and making perfect replicas has gotten loose. Some members of the population have already been processed; some have not. How can the thing be stopped?

The scientists of **"Who Goes There?"** respond, not with screams (or at least the first screams are immediately frowned upon and regretted as counterproductive), not with pell-mell running, but with a cool, scientific determination to gather data, learn the physical properties of the monster, and thus control it. . . . [The] data produce hypotheses that are systematically tried, the results are used to form better hypotheses, and finally a test is devised to discriminate human from nonhuman. The test is applied to all members of the population, the monsters among us are killed, and the danger is thwarted.

I have tried to suggest by my dry prose the tone of all this—more like a dissection than a drama. The nightmare is very present—in fact, Campbell stresses that the monster looks *just like* a bad dream—and this likeness allows Campbell to state his theme, the theme of all works of this genre: that the nightmare is *not* best met by running, screaming, and shouting, but by logic, the scientific method, and hard, unsentimental sense. Those who respond with emotionalism are gently locked up so that cooler heads may get on with the job at hand.

Campbell's people are quite aware that they live by the scientific method and that in the method lies their salvation. Listen to them *discuss* the likelihood of their comrade Connant's having been swallowed, in Connant's presence:

> "What about Connant in the meantime?" Kinner demanded. . . .
>
> "He may be human—," Copper started.
>
> Connant burst out in a flood of curses. "Human! *May* be human, you damned saw-bones! What in hell do you think I am?"
>
> "A monster," Copper snapped sharply. "Now shut up and listen. . . . Until we know—you know as well as we do that we have reason to question the fact, and only you know how that question is to be answered—we may reasonably be expected to lock you up."

Connant realizes his incarceration is the logical course, and he submits. Time and again Campbell's people are put into situations that invite an emotional response in this way, and we witness them rejecting the emotional response for a more constructive alternative. . . . "Fantasy" sees reason as an inflexible commitment to normalcy as the only reality; "science fiction" sees reason as the ultimate flexibility—if the data say you may be a monster, you may be, however much like Connant you look.

And in Campbell's world reason does not fail us, because the universe is thoroughly reasonable. When it becomes apparent that there is a monster on the loose, Campbell's people gather for a lecture from Blair, the biologist, and he says it plainly: "This isn't wildly beyond what we already know. It's just a modification we haven't seen before. It's as natural, as logical, as any other manifestation of life. It obeys the same laws." And the implication is carried as much by Campbell's tone as by his plot: if we know our biology well enough, we *need not fear*. Fear, like all other emotional responses, is counterproductive to the business of understanding and controlling the universe. **"Who Goes There?"** is not really scary. Readers who come looking for a monster-movie "kick" feel as though they walked in on an anatomy lesson. Campbell's characters are not emotionally engaging, and he does not want them to be. They strike us as the ultimate engineers—dull in the face of wonders. (pp. 162-64)

"Sense of wonder" is a conventional phrase describing a basic science fiction energy, but I am suggesting that Campbell's mode—which I will call for the moment "science fiction," in quotation marks—trains us in the opposite point of view: far from encouraging us to wonder at alien experience, it suggests we move through wonder as quickly as possible and get down to work, analyzing the alien with the same dispassionate curiosity we would give to any other new lab specimen. If we assume that "science fiction"' strives to maximize wondrousness, we shall often think it misfires. **"Who Goes There?"** seems to squander opportunities for awe. But the monster is not a mind-trip; it is a problem in chemistry. Those who are sensitive to the wondrousness are useless to others who are trying to get a complex task (saving the world) done in a short time.

Written science fiction has always advertised itself as "astounding," "amazing," and the like, yet it has always been populated by heroes who, like the heroes of **"Who Goes There?"** are strong because they are immune from the debilitating power of imagination. . . . "Science fiction," purveyor of wonders, paradoxically celebrates the soul who can gaze at wonders and not be too stirred.

For these reasons Terry Carr has called science fiction "the most rigorously rational form of literature we have ever had." People unfamiliar with science fiction and familiar only with its reputation for wondrousness often give the title "most rational" to detective fiction in the Sherlock Holmes tradition, but wrongly. Holmes and his descendants are indeed dedicated to the principle that *all* worldly experience can be fully known via the rational intellect—that any human experience, no matter how apparently "fantastic," is capable of rational analysis. But literature from Campbell's perspective is the Holmsian principle taken a logical step further: *any* experience, whether in a far galaxy or on another spacetime continuum, is obedient to the laws of logic and science and is therefore fully knowable by the scientific method. We see Holmes' methods effective out beyond the Dog Star, as well as in London's back streets.

"Who Goes There?" and its genre, then, are more than an alternative to *Body Snatchers*'s endorsement of the nighttime response; they are an indictment of it. They are *anti*fantastic—a polemic against the notion of fantasy per se, as *Body Snatchers* is a polemic against reason's claim to all knowledge. Campbell argues that the fantastic is never really fantastic at all when fully known—it is only the familiar laws of nature repackaged. The sense of fantasy, in these terms, is a juvenile indulgence of our emotional selves. Campbell asks us to grow up.

Two kinds of art instruct us to respond with two different parts of ourselves, the emotive and the rational, and each kind sees responding to the alien with the other side of the self to be counterproductive. And the status of objects in the two universes is correspondingly different. In "fantasy," objects have primarily figurative status, whereas in "science fiction," the thing is *a thing,* a literal object. And again, each genre presents the alternative as a fundamental error: in "fantasy," people often have to be taught that the object is an externalization of their internal reality—it is, in short, a metaphor—whereas, in "science fiction," to see the object as a projection of the self is next to madness. (pp. 164-65)

"Who Goes There?" is constructed to disabuse us of any tendency to read figuratively; the work of art teaches us how to read it best. The monster is purposely made to look as much like a metaphor as possible; it looks like a conventional nightmare, and its way of operating perfectly matches the central myth of our paranoid age: I am surrounded by things that look like people but really are not, and they are trying to steal my soul. Campbell's people are thus invited to misinterpret the monster as a metaphor, a manifestation of their emotive selves. But it is not. The monster is an external, objective fact—those who lose sight of that go quickly mad. For Campbell, the fundamental act of sanity is to recognize that the furniture of the world does not *represent* anything beyond itself. "Science fiction," however densely populated with mind-boggling products of the imagination, is paradoxically the most extreme form of realistic art there is. (pp. 165-66)

Jack P. Rawlins, "Confronting the Alien: Fantasy and Anti-Fantasy in Science Fiction Film and Literature," in Bridges to Fantasy, *George E. Slusser, Eric S. Rabkin, Robert Scholes, eds., Southern Illinois University Press, 1982, pp. 160-74.**

THOMAS J. REMINGTON

Introspection is a bug-bear that affects most genres of popular culture once the purveyors and consumers of the genre begin to take themselves seriously. Usually this introspection takes as its points of departure attempts to define historically just exactly what the genre *is;* then through the establishment of rules for inclusion and exclusion it tries to demarcate those practitioners who belong (or don't belong) in the genre.

Science Fiction has been experiencing such growing pains for some time now. . . . (pp. 58-9)

The clearest example is *Astounding Science Fiction: July, 1939,* a facsimile reprint of "the first 'great' issue" of that classic SF pulp "produced under the editorship of John W. Campbell, Jr." . . .

For SF historians, the association of John Campbell's editorship with *Astounding* stands as *the* event in the "Golden Age" of science fiction. Campbell's *Astounding* is revered for giving birth to much of the early work of such major SF authors as Robert Heinlein, Theodore Sturgeon, Isaac Asimov, and A. E. van Vogt. The particular issue here reprinted contains, in fact, the first stories published in *Astounding* by both Asimov and van Vogt.

But the sensitive reader will be quick to surmise that, for all the hoary legends citing it as the mother lode of the Golden Age of SF, *Astounding* was no Megalia Nugget. . . .

None of this is to say that this facsimile edition of a 40 year old pulp has no value; it does, but the value is hardly esthetic.

Like the Blickling Homilies, to cite a random example, the facsimile does much more to establish a context that it does to arouse literary excitement. Thus it goes far to moderate the credulity of the modern student of SF who keeps hearing the old buffs moon about the times "when every issue of *Astounding* was a great new adventure." The book *does* exemplify what science fiction was in the early days of the "Golden Age," and in that sense, at least, scholars and historians may cheer its publication. (p. 59)

Thomas J. Remington, "SF: Mapping the Territory," in The North American Review, *Vol. 266, No. 2, June, 1981, pp. 58-62.**

Albert Camus

1913-1960

Algerian-born French novelist, essayist, dramatist, short story writer, and journalist.

Camus is one of the most important literary figures of the twentieth century. In his highly varied career Camus consistently, often passionately, explored and presented his major theme: the belief that people can be happy in a world without meaning. Throughout his novels, plays, essays, and stories, Camus defended the dignity and decency of the individual and asserted that through purposeful action one can overcome the apparent nihilism of the world. His notion of an "absurd" universe is premised on the tension between life in an irrational universe and the human desire for rationality. Camus's position on this dilemma, demonstrated most clearly in his essay *Le mythe de Sisyphe* (1943; *The Myth of Sisyphus*), is that each person must first recognize that life is "absurd," that is, irrational and meaningless, and then rise above the absurdity. Although this world view has led Camus to be linked with the Existentialists, he himself rejected that classification. Well regarded for his style as well as his ideas, Camus is also praised as a fierce moralist whose faith in humankind did not waver. He was awarded the Nobel Prize for literature in 1957.

Camus was born into poverty and finished school only by earning scholarships and working part-time jobs. At the Lycée d'Algiers he studied philosophy, but the tuberculosis Camus contracted before entering the university prevented him from pursuing a career as an academician. Instead, he became a journalist and immersed himself in the Algerian intellectual scene. His interest in the theater was already evident, for he helped found a theater group, adapted works for the stage, and collaborated on an original play. His first two books, *L'envers et l'endroit* (1937; *The Wrong Side and the Right Side*) and *Noces* (1938; *Nuptials*), are collections of lyrical essays detailing his early life of poverty and his travels through Europe. Also written at this time, but not published until much later, is Camus's first novel, *La mort heureuse* (1971; *A Happy Death*). This work, although less stylistically developed than his later works, touches on the themes of absurdity and self-realization which recur throughout Camus's writings. In 1942 he moved to Paris and became, along with Jean-Paul Sartre, an intellectual leader of the French Resistance.

Taken together, *The Myth of Sisyphus* and his novel *L'étranger* (1942; *The Stranger*) represent Camus's development of the concept of the absurd. Camus perceived the story of Sisyphus, who was doomed to push a rock up a hill only to see it continually roll back down, as a metaphor for the human condition. For Camus, life, like Sisyphus's task, is senseless, but awareness of the absurdity can help humankind overcome its condition. Meursault, the protagonist of *The Stranger,* shoots an Arab for no apparent reason, but he is convicted not so much for killing the man as for refusing to conform to society's standards. Because he acts only on those few things he believes in, Meursault is alienated from the society that wants him to make a show of his contriteness. Approaching his execution, Meursault accepts life as an imperfect end in itself and, although he wants to live, he resolves to die happily and with dignity.

Cultural Service of the French Embassy

While writing these works Camus remained active in the theater, directing and adapting works by others as well as his own. Of his four original dramas, *Caligula* (1944) is often considered his most significant. It recounts the young Roman emperor's search for absolute individual freedom. The death of his sister/lover shocks him into an awareness of life's absurdity, and as a result he orders and participates in random rapes, murders, and humiliations that alienate him from those around him. Most scholars see *Caligula* as a parable warning that individual liberty must affirm, not destroy, the bonds of humanity. *Le malentendu* (1944; *The Misunderstanding*), the story of a man's murder by his sister and mother, is often considered Camus's attempt at a modern tragedy in the classical Greek style. *L'état de siège* (1948; *The State of Siege*) has been viewed as a satiric attack on totalitarianism and an allegory demonstrating the value of courageous human action. The plague that ravishes the town and brutalizes its citizens is stopped only when one character sacrifices his life for the woman he loves. Many scholars argue that the attack on ruthless governments reflects Camus's experience living under the Nazi occupation of France. *Les justes* (1950; *The Just Assassins*) portrays a revolutionary who refuses to throw a bomb because his intended victim is accompanied by a young nephew and niece. This work, many scholars assert, further emphasizes Camus's strong sense of humanity: the end does not justify the means if the cost is human lives.

Critical reception to Camus's plays is mixed. Most critics agree that the overriding concern with intellectual and philosophical issues in Camus's dramas makes them stiff, formal, and lifeless. Many also argue that the characters in these plays are too often merely representatives of specific ideologies. Camus is admired as a director and innovator and his plays are generally well regarded as texts, but the consensus among scholars is that Camus's work for the stage is inferior to his fiction.

La peste (1947; *The Plague*) is a novel which deals with Camus's theme of revolt. Complementing his concept of the absurd, Camus believed in the necessity of each person to "revolt" against the common fate of humanity by seeking personal freedom. Dr. Rieux, the protagonist of *The Plague*, narrates the story of several men in a plague-ridden city. The characters react in different ways, but eventually they unite in their battle against the plague. This emphasis on individual revolt is also the subject of the long essay *L'homme révolté* (1951; *The Rebel*). Examining the nature and history of revolution, Camus advances the theory that each individual must revolt against injustice by refusing to be part of it. Camus opposed mass revolutions because he believed they become nihilistic and their participants accept murder and oppression as necessary means to an end.

Camus's belief in the supremacy of the individual lies at the heart of one of the most publicized events in modern literature: Camus's break with his long-time compatriot, Jean-Paul Sartre. These two leading figures of the postwar French intellectual scene had similar literary philosophies, but their political differences led to a quarrel in the early 1950s which ended their friendship as well as their working relationship. Sartre saw the Soviet purges and labor camps of the 1940s as a stage in the Marxian dialectic process that would eventually bring about a just society. Camus, however, could not condone what he perceived to be the Communists' disregard for human rights. Played out in the international as well as Parisian press, the debate was popularly conceded to Sartre. The effect on Camus was disheartening and his fall into public scorn cast a long shadow over the remainder of his career.

In following years Camus suffered from bouts of depression and writer's block. His reputation was further damaged when he took a central stance on the issue of Arab uprisings in his native Algiers. Both the French government and the Arabs denounced him, and the furor extracted an additional toll on his emotional well-being. His next novel, *La chute* (1956; *The Fall*), is a long, enigmatic monologue of a formerly self-satisfied lawyer who suffers from guilt and relentlessly confesses his sins in order to judge others and induce them to confess as well. Some scholars noted a new tone in this work and suggested that Camus had bleakly submitted to nihilism by asserting that every person shares the guilt for a violent and corrupt world. Many argued, however, that Camus's essential love and respect for humanity is a major element of the novel; they viewed his wish for a common confession as an attempt to reaffirm human solidarity.

When Camus published his first collection of short stories, *L'exil et le royaume* (1957; *The Exile and the Kingdom*), many critics detected a new vitality and optimism in his prose. The energy of the stories, each written in a different style, led many scholars to suggest that Camus had regained direction in his career and established himself as a master of short fiction with this collection. In the following years Camus worked around political quarrels, family troubles, and ill health to begin work on a new novel, *Le premier homme*. He worked diligently and

with great hope for this text, but before it was completed he was killed in an automobile accident.

In spite of marked fluctuations in Camus's popularity—his rise to literary fame in the 1940s occurred as rapidly as his fall from popular appeal in the years preceding his death—his literary significance remains largely undisputed. His work has elicited an enormous amount of scholarly attention and, two decades after his death, he continues to be the subject of much serious study. A defender of political liberty and personal freedom, Camus endures not only as a significant contributor to contemporary literature, but also as a figure of hope and possibility.

(See also *CLC*, Vols. 1, 2, 4, 9, 11, 14 and *Contemporary Authors*, Vols. 89-92.)

In this volume commentary on Albert Camus
is focused on his plays.

HAROLD CLURMAN

Consideration of ["Caligula and Three Other Plays"] by Albert Camus provokes a paradox. They are important without being good. Only one of them, it seems to me, really demands a stage production. This is "Caligula"—a play which marks a date in the French theatre. The significance of this play is related to Camus' position in literature today. Though he writes with both grace and a moving accent, his main contribution resides in his message. His work is a series of parables. He is a moralist: a man who seeks to extract a line of meaning and a principle of conduct from the turbulent contradictions of our times. His aim is to distill hope from the heart of despair. . . .

Camus' work for the theatre, which begins with the somber fatalism of "The Misunderstanding" (1943) [also published as "Cross Purposes"], proceeds in "Caligula" (1945) to the dramatization of the flaw in an amoral revolt against the universal injustice of life and finally moves on to "The Just Assassins" (1949), dealing with the earliest Russian revolutionists. In the avowed morality play, "The State of Siege" (1948), evil is presented as a form of political dictatorship. The total impression these plays make, despite their defects as organic drama, is one of spiritual vigor and integrity. We hold Camus in high esteem because in his own way he represents "a moment in the conscience of mankind."

> *Harold Clurman, "The Moralist on Stage," in* The New York Times Book Review, *September 14, 1958, p. 12.*

HENRY POPKIN

So honest a man as Camus is obviously at a disadvantage in so dishonest an institution as the theater. His sincerity has become a legend, but it has prevented him from becoming a successful dramatist. The Nobel Committee commended his "clear-sighted earnestness," and Harold Clurman called him "a moment in the conscience of mankind." Obviously, this is not a man who can easily lend himself to the subterfuges of the stage, who can say of his playwriting, as Henry James did: "Oh, how it must not be too good and how very bad it must be!" I can not think of a better application of the term "defect of his virtue''; Camus's strenuous virtue is the key to his plays and to his defective sense of the theater. Explicitly forswearing ''psychology, ingenious plot-devices, and spicy situations,'' he requires that we take him in the full intensity of his earnestness or not at all.

Simple in plot, direct in argument, oratorically eloquent, his dramas are like few other modern plays. . . . Camus differs significantly from his many French contemporaries who have put ancient myths on the modern stage. The others have turned conventional myths—at least their antiquity has made them seem conventional—into instruments of iconoclasm. Obviously stimulated by French neo-classical drama, Cocteau, Giraudoux, and Sartre became the debunking inside-dopesters of ancient mythology; they made Oedipus into a young man on the make, Electra into a rather addled termagant, Zeus into a tyrant. They overturned or exposed the classical stories. But what Camus does is to begin with a sufficiently cynical legend—the history of Caligula or the murder of the prodigal son . . .—and to dramatize it as forthrightly as possible, with no tricks, no sneers, no ''modernization.''

Both circumstances and characters are very carefully selected to perform only what the play requires. Nothing is ever thrown in for good measure or for any incidental purpose. We never encounter in these plays the casual bystanders whom a Broadway dramatist might permit to wander in. What characters there are have strict requirements imposed upon them. Camus primarily demands that his protagonists possess freedom, the capacity for exercising free choice. He has to go far to find his free men. His preference sets Camus off from his contemporaries in the theater; some of this difference is implicit in the contrast Eric Bentley once drew between ''Strindbergian'' and ''Ibsenite'' actors. The Strindbergian actor is less restrained: ''His emotions come right out of him with no interference whatsoever and fly like bullets at the enemy.'' But Ibsen, not Strindberg, is the father of modern drama, and, consequently, modern stage characters keep their neuroses in check—or at least in balance. Camus's characters tend to be Strindbergian. Some of Strindberg's unbalanced heroes earn their freedom at the expense of their sanity; one of Camus's heroes, Caligula, pays just this price for freedom. Criminal purposes inspire the principal motivation of *The Misunderstanding* and so liberate the characters from ordinary scruples. The protagonists of *The Just Assassins* are also on the far side of the law, revolutionaries who have put aside the usual inhibitions and are in the act of measuring their freedom. The most dynamic figure in *State of Siege* is, like Caligula, in possession of supreme political power and subject to no regulation by sanity. Camus's characters tear right into the issues, and they ignore small details. Just as Lear's ''Pray you, undo this button,'' could not have occurred in Racine, it also would be an unlikely line in Camus. Everyone in these plays is ready for action—or, more often, for argument. Nothing may intervene to distract, irritate, or enchant us, to explain the characters or to provide context for the events. (pp. 499-500)

The language of these plays is lofty and pure. It reflects the complaint Camus once lodged against our time: ''For the dialogue we have substituted the communique.'' The dramatist sets out to remedy this situation, but his dialogue tends to become, especially in *The Just Assassins* and *State of Siege*, a formal exchange of weighty remarks which too clearly expose the dramatist's designs on us. Hardly anyone else in the modern theater lectures us quite so directly. . . . The result has its merits as oratory and as dialectic, but it is deficient as drama.

The defect of Camus's plays bring to mind the virtues of his fiction, in which the method of narration always keeps up from colliding too abruptly with his themes and, above all, his ideas. . . . The danger of becoming a pamphleteer in fiction must have been clear to Camus and must have compelled him to use technique as a shield for his ideas. But, in his plays, collisions are head-on; except in *Caligula,* we miss the theater's equivalents for the sophisticated method of his fiction. (p. 503)

Henry Popkin, ''Camus As Dramatist,'' in Partisan Review, *Vol. XXVI, No. 3, Summer, 1959, pp. 499-501, 503.*

WALTER KERR

Kenneth Haigh, as the emperor Caligula, announces in the first few moments of the play [''**Caligula**''] . . . that he is going to be the first ruler ever to ''use unlimited power in an unlimited way.'' He is going to kill whom he likes, ravish what wives he chooses, declare famines on the instant, turn himself into a golden-wigged Venus, try absolutely everything on his unfettered march toward the impossible. He learns, shortly before he plunges from a tower to the knives that finally await him, that when everything is possible, nothing is.

Has Albert Camus' play fallen into precisely the same trap, or is it the current performance that makes the evening seem like the four whirring wheels of a high-powered automobile racing immobile on ice?

Of promised power there is plenty. . . .

Yet there is a treadmill under foot. One crime is really not more shocking than the last. When the first bloodied body has been carted away, or the first deliberately insane law handed down to the empire, we have grasped—to the full, apparently—the uttermost limits of one man's absolute freedom. The murder of Scipio's father does not distress us more than the slaughter of Cassius' sons; when they follow one another, scene by scene, the footfall is familiar, the measured tread monotonous.

In short, drama itself seems to observe the law that our moon-maddened hero must discover for himself. If there are no limits to what a character in a play may do, then the play itself is without intelligible boundaries—without a pattern that forms, without a forward movement that we can either desire or yearn for. The sky is open to us, but the sky has no shape.

The fact that the late Mr. Camus's play has been enormously successful in France, however, leads to other questions. Is there somewhere in the performance a secret, insistent, almost imperceptible reduction in size? . . . It is always possible that a play about absolutism has not been done absolutely enough—with the anvil stroke and the untroubled resonance of a monster utterly sure of himself. . . .

But in precisely what way should we laugh when Caligula appears on a half-shell in corkscrew curls, when he paints a suppliant's fingernails and then his bald head, when a prissy old patrician purses his lips in a deadpan moue out front? The play means to touch the outrageous, the unspeakable, the ultimate defiance of all human value in these passages. But the light titters that spring up in the auditorium suggest that only a casual, rather flighty, cynicism has been arrived at, not the soul-destroying and mirthless laughter that might accompany sheer negation.

Between the impossibility of moving forward when there is no forward to move to, and a certain readiness of tone and style that thin out a satanically majestic experiment in living, **"Caligula"** continually stirs interest and then finds its temperature falling

*Walter Kerr, "First Night Report: 'Caligula'," in
New York Herald Tribune, February 17, 1960.*

RIMA DRELL RECK

Albert Camus' expression of "tragedy in modern dress" portrays men struggling with the emotional and psychological facts of alienation by means of man-made justice. Caligula (from the play of the same name, written in 1938, first performed in 1945), apprehending the alienation inherent in the human condition, exercises absolute power to match the absurdity of the world, inevitably to find the same terrible face of self-separation in his own mirror. Martha, Jan, and their mother, in *Le Malentendu* (1944), murder and misunderstand in a search for self-definition under "the injustice of sky and climate." The Plague divides the men and women of *L'Etat de siège* (1948) from their own dignity and, in the end, from their lives, by exercising a justice as logical and inhuman as Caligula's; and the terrorists of *Les Justes* (1949) attempt to redeem the myth of absolute justice with their lives, sacrificing the relative truths which alone are available to man. Those who seek self-identity fail to recognize the futility of such a task in an absurd universe. Those who deal in justice misunderstand the "pathos of distance" between mankind and the good. (p. 42)

Alternating between a desperate lyricism which is well known to readers of his nonpolitical essays (*L'Envers et l'endroit, Noces, L'eté*) and the enigmatic parables of his widely known *récits* (*L'Etranger, La Peste, La Chute*), Camus' plays embody his thought in dramatic action at once tantalizing and obscure. Gabriel Marcel's judgment, that the theater of Camus fails as a dramatic presentation of his ideas, is frequently echoed, and not always, one must note, by critics who are primarily concerned with the possibilities of financial success. "The essential words," wrote Robert Kemp, theater critic for *Le Monde*, "are pronounced at moments when the drama, the brutal drama . . . absorbs the spectator's nervous energy. It is a fine art, no doubt, to mingle thus action and thought, not to separate them," but, he concludes, "the most meaningful words pass so quickly and remain so mysterious that they only brush our consciousness." Germaine Brée questions the strength of the concrete situation to carry the full weight of the thought. To date, the only major staging of Camus in America has elicited mixed comment, but the accusation of oratory mixed with soliloquy, theatricality with intellectualism, seems to predominate. (pp. 42-3)

The theater is for Camus [as he wrote in his *L'Envers et l'endroit*] a place where each spectator has "a rendez-vous with himself," where he can experience a self-definition occasioned by the soliloquies of "those large figures who cry out on the stage." (p. 43)

Plays, however, are not restricted to soliloquy alone. Camus, at various times actor, playwright, producer and adapter, was aware of this fact, meeting it with varying degrees of success. He experimented with group movement, contrast, *divertissements* in *Caligula*. He envisaged a striking red-and-black setting for Faulkner's world in his adaptation of *Requiem for a Nun*, and in an all-out effort, together with Barrault, to "make a myth intelligible to the audience of 1948" in *L'Etat de siège*, he offered "a spectacle whose avowed intention is to combine all forms of dramatic expression from the lyrical monologue to collective theatre, passing through pantomine, simple dialogue, farce and the chorus." The play, one should note, was Camus' least successful and one of his few creations to be criticized on artistic grounds. Visually superabundant, at times even noisy and hurried, *L'Etat de siège* with its simple allegory, in which the Plague evidently stands for bureaucracy and the collapse of human values in society, fails to offer enough for the mind. Camus' most successful plays have been *Caligula* and *Les Justes,* which, though widely different in presentation, share a common theme. The reason for the relative failure of *Le Malentendu* is a matter for speculation; it is the most tightly knit, classic of the plays. The language is beautiful, simple, and the moments of greatest intellectual intensity do not always occur during those instants of intense physical action which made Kemp regret a conflict between watching and understanding. One possible answer may lie in what appears to be the utter nihilism of the play. But the same accusation has been leveled against *Caligula,* which nevertheless had over 400 performances in Paris. (p. 44)

Caligula and *Le Malentendu,* which appear to Philip Thody to represent a world without values, where the absurd reduces all actions to equal insignificance, become, in the light of Camus' conception of drama, artistic testimonies to the essential alienation and grandeur of the human condition. Having relinquished at last "the illusion of another world" which sacrifices human values, the dramatist's thought can "spring forth in images . . . in myths . . . myths with no deeper meaning than that of human suffering and like it, endlessly fertile. Not the divine fable which amuses and blinds, but the face, the gesture and the terrestrial drama in which are embodied a difficult wisdom and a passion with no tomorrow." The enigma, divine for Aeschylus, is earthly for Camus. "The smile of Apollo" is transformed into the agony of the medieval crucifix and, in the modern world, the absurd joy of the suicidal Kirilov as he writes his false confession or the stony face of Martha as she seeks liberty in the unwitting murder of her brother (*Le Malentendu*). (pp. 44-5)

Human alienation is intensified by those who live according to absolute, transcendent values which have no meaning in the world of Camus. Total peace, absolute justice, inexorable logic—all misunderstandings of the essential nature of man, which is eternally and pathetically distant from supreme ends. "An unpunished crime, the Greeks believed, infected the city," notes Camus. And he adds, "But condemned innocence, or crime punished too much, in the long run soils it no less." The modern tragedy stems from a misunderstanding, a fatal misunderstanding not of the divine ways of the gods, but of the finite, physical way of man. Camus' great ideal is *la mesure,* the familiar golden mean, in which man is both related to his natural environment, the earth, and to man and all that the concept man implies—mortality, responsibility, compassion. When the essential balance is disturbed, the scales jangle and dance in the frenzy which is modern history.

Caligula, the earliest of Camus' plays, tells of Rome's young emperor who, driven to despair by the realization of life's absurdity, asks for the moon and plays god with the destinies of his subjects. (pp. 45-6)

Caligula decides to make men "live in the truth" by eliminating contradiction and chance, by exercising his liberty absolutely. He becomes the embodiment of disinterested evil, and dissipates the meaning of life for his subjects by behaving with an inexorable, destructive logic which murders for an ideal—demonstrating life's utter meaninglessness. His logic is the more blinding because it is, in fact, irrefutable. Far from being a detestable villain, Caligula is the most pitiable character in the play. Most cursed because most clear-sighted, he puts men to death arbitrarily in order to make them understand what he has himself understood too well, "that it's not necessary to have done something in order to die.''. . . (p. 46)

Caligula's passion for the impossible is stronger than the passion of those around him for life. Absolute liberty is always exercised at the expense of someone, he notes, and admits this is unfortunate. Absolute liberty is destructive of relative justice. Caligula is as outspoken as the Plague in *L'Etat de siège* and Clamence in *La Chute*. All three conceive a rigorously logical attitude before the problem of suffering in an apparently meaningless world. Though Caligula cannot be refuted in logical terms, the very fact that men cannot live every minute with absurdity finally rouses them to revolt. (pp. 46-7)

A sense of alienation underlies the actions of all four characters in *Le Malentendu*. The over-all "misunderstanding" which unites them is a common belief that a place exists where one can find total self-definition. (p. 48)

Martha and her mother are practiced murderers, but Jan complicates their impersonal routine by speaking openly to them in an attempt to force a recognition from their side. . . . The two women justify their habit of murder in much the same way that Caligula legitimates his limitless exercise of power: life is more cruel than they are. The identity which Jan seeks will be found in his function as victim, an ironic definition, certainly, but one which is central to all resolutions in the play. (p. 49)

Martha is perhaps right in her over-all view of the human condition, but she has not understood the lesson of her brother's death; victim and murderer are equally pitiable; and could they understand this, human justice would begin. The round of misunderstandings is endless as long as man in his essential state of alienation continues to add to the injustice already in the world.

L'Etat de siège allegorizes the plague as a specific injunction against modern bureaucracy and all forms of totalitarianism. As Camus distinctly states in his "Avertissement," this play is in no way meant to be an adaptation of his novel, *La Peste*. . . .

While lacking the dramatic and intellectual complexity of Camus' other plays, *L'Etat de siège* presents characters who strongly recall Camus' *récits* and strongly suggests several of his central themes in simplified forms. (p. 50)

The Judge, Victoria's father, is a coward willing to turn against his own to save himself from disease. He reminds us of Clamence of *La Chute*, *le juge-pénitent*, without ironic self-awareness. Camus' dislike of judges is nowhere as strongly evident as in this play. But the judge is no more unjust than some of his intended victims. (p. 51)

Whereas Diego conquers his fear by a resurgence of his sense of human dignity, Victoria, who is the heroine of the play, is at no time afraid. She wants her life and her love and is willing to risk anything to retain these simple human values. When she dies, Diego realizes too late that his desire to help his fellow man has allowed her death to occur, and offers his life in exchange for hers. The bargain is accepted by the Plague, who has begun to lose his power, and Victoria triumphs in sorrow, vindicating the values which absolutes threaten, fleshly love and the transient beauties of the earth.

In *Les Justes* a small group of terrorists plans and carries out the assassination of the Grand-Duke Sergei Alexandrovitch in Moscow in 1905. Kaliayev, who throws the bomb and is arrested and hanged, and Dora, who makes the bomb, are the central characters. . . . Kaliayev and Dora are not monumental sacrifices to the terrible burden of free will. Instead, they are torn between a misconceived sense of duty toward absolute justice and an overwhelming pity for human life. Only one of the terrorists, Stepan, is single in his purpose. He wants the revolution to succeed, because he loves justice more than life. (pp. 51-2)

Only in the fourth act is Camus' total irony unveiled. Until his imprisonment, Kaliayev is still able to believe that dying for an ideal can justify it. A prisoner, Foka, enters his cell and in a friendly conversation it is revealed that Foka has killed three men in a drunken rage. When he learns that Kaliayev has killed a grand-duke, for which the penalty is hanging, he tries to leave suddenly. Kaliayev forces the revelation that Foka is the hangman, whose sentence is shortened by a year for each man he hangs. The line between victim and executioner grows thinner. Finally, the widow of the Grand-Duke comes to visit Kaliayev in prison, believing that only a murderer can understand her experience of despair and absurdity. Kaliayev refuses to ask God's forgiveness, as she entreats. As long as he is to die, he is not a murderer. Absolute justice, to which he offers his life, will exonerate him.

The final act shows Dora and the revolutionaries waiting to find out if Kaliayev has betrayed their ideal and repented or if he has, instead, died. Dora, in her anguish, begins to doubt the moral position of the just assassins. "If death is the only solution, we are on the wrong path. The right path leads to life, to the sunshine. One cannot always be cold.'' . . . Perhaps taking responsibility for all evil in the world is not a gesture of sacrifice, but one of pride, pride which will be punished. At last, she hears the painful account of Kaliayev's death—he has not betrayed their ideal. However, the report of his final horrible cry brings Dora to the brink of absurdity. Her only consolation is a decision to be the next one to throw a bomb. Exaltation and oblivion will fill the void left by the death of human values. (pp. 52-3)

In the theater of Camus characters search for self-identity through the pursuit of absolutes. They are portrayed as fatally failing to understand that self-identity is illusory and unattainable, that the static resolution they desire is a denial of the very nature of man, which is eternally separated from clarity and from justice. Weighing consciousness against oblivion, reason against submersion in life, responsibility against evasion, Camus' plays express a true humanism which maintains a precarious balance. Each excess increases the alienation of man from himself and the alienation of man from man. In a world where the criminal is no further from justice than his prosecutor, the only things worth striving for and preserving are those which recognize man's limitations. In a theater where each man has a rendez-vous with himself, Camus creates a gesture at once supplicating and defiant before a world in which all men are guilty. (p. 53)

Rima Drell Reck, "The Theater of Albert Camus," in Modern Drama, *Vol. 4, No. 1, May, 1961, pp. 42-53.*

ALBERT SONNENFELD

Nowhere but in France, it seems, do men of letters whose greatest talent clearly lies in other genres devote so much of their creative energy to the theatre. The Golden Age of Corneille and Racine, kept alive by an ever-growing number of French repertory companies, stands constantly before the writer, challenging him to try to rival its inaccessible perfection. . . . Albert Camus' passion for the theatre was lifelong, from his participation in the *Algerian Worker's Theatre* in 1936 to his tragically short reign as director of a government sponsored avant-garde company in 1959. In the midst of the virtually unanimous acclaim accorded him as novelist and thinker during his last years, Camus continued to see himself primarily as a man of the theatre in search of new approaches to the technical problems of the stage. And in a brief program note written for his Paris production of *Requiem for a Nun,* he admitted that his greatest ambition was to create a form of tragedy indigenous to our age. In each of his own plays there is, as Germaine Brée has pointed out, a solitary hero marked for destruction by a fatality which he himself has created. This seems to be the stuff of which tragedy is made. It is now generally acknowledged, however, even by those whose unrestrained admiration for the man has often paralyzed their critical faculties (one reviewer wrote that "to read Camus is to want to shake his hand") that Camus did not realize his ambition.

The technical flaws in Camus' works for the stage are apparent to every reader or spectator. *The Misunderstanding (Le Malentendu)* is weakened by unconvincing dialogue. The characters speak in those polished aphorisms ("He has gone into the bitter house of eternal exile . . . neither in life nor in death is there any peace of homeland.") which look fine in print, in the novels of Gide, Malraux and Camus himself, but which sound strangely hollow in the theatre, where abstraction is the playwright's greatest enemy. *Caligula* . . . fails because of Camus' predilection for the theoretical, for misplaced lyricism and pretentious rhetoric. Nothing much happens on the stage during *The Just Assassins (Les Justes);* the characters pursue those endless philosophical debates, so gripping in the novels of Dostoyevsky but so deadly here and in Camus' stage adaptation of *The Possessed. State of Siege (L'Etat de Siège),* a dramatization of the myth of the plague, is his most ambitious and least successful play. Written for Jean-Louis Barrault, it contains a variety of dialogue ranging from lyrical to burlesque, stylized choreographic movements by the chorus, complicated lighting effects, and music by Arthur Honegger. (pp. 106-07)

In spite of his enviable achievements as adaptor and director, Camus ultimately failed as playwright because he consistently tried to force into the dramatic form themes and situations perfect for his prose narratives but totally alien to the stage. For Camus, as for so many French novelists before him, the theatre proved to be an irresistably attractive but stubbornly hostile medium.

The author of *The Stranger* counted himself among those writers "whose works form a whole where each illuminates the other." Camus' two major novels, *The Stranger* and *The Plague,* are therefore each complemented by two plays and a book of essays treating essentially the same theme. A more forceful statement of his preoccupation with unity is the proud confession, in *The Myth of Sisyphus,* that "no artist has ever expressed more than a single theme in different guises." Exile or revolt are the themes that have most frequently been assigned to Camus' work; both are equally applicable since the central character in the novels, the four plays and even the essays has invariably been both an exile from the mass of humanity and a rebel against the meaningless pattern of life of that humanity. There is another theme which is far more important, however,

because it leads not only to the core of Camus' philosophy but to his choice of literary techniques as well. Each of his novels and plays tells of an intellectual or spiritual metamorphosis. Without exception, his heroes, or the author himself in the case of the early poetic essays, undergo a series of experiences which lead, often abruptly, to an almost clairvoyant understanding of the human predicament, a subsequent inner transformation, and perhaps a new course of action. (pp. 107-08)

In his very first book, *L'Envers et l'Endroit,* published in 1937, and as yet unavailable in English (the best translation for the elusive title would be "The Right and Wrong Side"), we find Camus already committed to the technique implicit in the basic theme of inner metamorphosis. "If I've walked a lot since this book, I haven't walked very far," he wrote in a preface to a recent edition. These lyrical essays, almost short stories really, are written in the first person and tell of the narrator's encounters with loneliness, frustration and death: an old woman, half paralyzed, is left to spend the evening alone when her family goes to the movies; an old man talks desperately to three young men in a café, afraid to stop because his audience might abandon him; a mother is too sick with fever to assuage the anguish of the young son spending the night in vigil at her bedside. Each of these visions of suffering leads the narrator further along the path toward understanding. The tone, while clearly sympathetic, remains objective. . . . It is a foreshadowing of Camus' basic narrative pattern that the narrator, after playing the role of observer in the two opening essays, turns to the monologue to analyze his own existence. His feeling of total estrangement during a visit to Prague forces him to examine his conscience and to realize that his present predicament is symptomatic of a more fundamental human condition. Experience has led to awareness, to understanding. The fog of indifference created by daily routine is dispelled: "Man is face to face with himself: I defy him to be happy." Again, a change in narrative tone, from objectivity to lyricism, provides the alternative to despair. In the brilliant light of the Italian sun, the narrator is reinitiated into the world of beauty and hope. He finds inscribed on the façade of a villa the motto which sums up all of Camus' work: *In magnificentia naturae resurgit spiritus.* This stylistic and thematic tension, between the naked and prosaic inner drama of man's conscience as he observes, and participates in, the meaningless despair of daily routine, and the world of the sun which only poetry can communicate to the readers, is at the heart of Camus' work. "For the absurd man," he wrote in *The Myth of Sisyphus,* "it's no longer a matter of explaining and deciding, but of experiencing and describing." (pp. 108-09)

The extremely thorny problems of stage technique posed by this emphasis on the inner awakening of a character troubled Camus throughout his career as dramatist. In *Révolte dans les Asturies,* a play written "collectively" by Camus and some friends for the *Workers' Theatre* in 1936, he is already experimenting with new approaches to point of view. "The spectator is to be the center of the spectacle," he wrote in the preface. "The play takes place in a square in Oviedo. The spectator must feel he is *in* Oviedo, not *in front* of it; everything goes on around him and he must be the center of the tragedy." In other words, the spectator is to see through the eyes of the miners during their unsuccessful uprising. He is to share fully in their emotional reactions as they are gradually defeated by the Legion, represented on stage by an enormous loud-speaker. This experiment, based largely on the theories of Antonin Artaud whose work exerted a profound influence on Camus' conception of the theatre, was a failure because, in Camus' own words, "it introduces action into a frame that is not suited to it: the theatre." This is an extremely revealing admission by Camus; though he dispensed with the experimental implications of Artaud's theories in his later plays, he continued to make the same mistake. (p. 111)

Reviewing the first performance of *Caligula* for *Le Monde* in 1945, the influential drama critic Robert Kemp wondered whether there were any characters in the play: "When I listen to *Caligula,* I can't stop thinking about Albert Camus. . . . I never wonder: What is Caligula going to do? What are Cherea and Scipio thinking of?—but: what does M. Camus want to say?" The characters of Camus' most successful play, written in 1938, are acting out his own inner drama. From self-satisfied complacency Caligula is shocked into awareness of the absurd, into a futile quest for the absolute and finally into the realization that absolute idealism is the twin of nihilism. In his preface for the American edition of his plays, Camus called *Caligula* a "tragedy of the intelligence."

As the curtain rises, a group of patricians is awaiting word of Caligula who has been absent for three days since the death of his beloved sister Drusilla. During this time Caligula's personality has undergone a complete transformation, for he has realized that death obviates all human values as well as life itself and that consequently nothing has meaning except death. The audience, however, does not see this change taking place. . . . Thus when Caligula finally appears on stage, pensive and distraught, the audience sees him as strangely aberrant and cannot understand that through suffering he has discovered what Camus sees as an absolute truth: the absurdity of life. Caligula's constant glances in the mirror and his dramatic gesture of erasing the image of his past self from the mirror lose their impact in the theatre. The dramatist is unable to make us realize that the reflection in the mirror is of the Caligula who existed before the curtain rose. (pp. 111-12)

The complacent patricians who believe in the validity of their social and religious institutions need, in Caligula's words, "a teacher who knows what he's talking about." And the Emperor's violent parodies of religion, justice and fate constitute his pedagogical method. "He forces everyone to think. Insecurity, that's what makes one think," Cherea says. But because theatrical time, as opposed to novelistic time, precludes the kind of leisurely realistic treatment of social institutions exemplified by Meursault's description of his mother's funeral, Caligula is forced to resort to such an extreme caricature of religion in the Venus scene, to cite but one example, that the audience cannot feel the relevance of this scene to its own institutions. We are too far removed from prosaic reality here to acknowledge the veracity of Caligula's, and Camus', discovery that our lives are governed by sham and pretense. (p. 112)

Camus' attitude toward Caligula is ambivalent. While he admires the Emperor for having reached that level of awareness which enables him to deny the gods (and by gods Camus means all abstract belief from table manners to justice), he despises him for denying man. The audience is supposed to share this attitude. At first, by his sharp caricatural treatment of the complacent patricians, Camus tries to force us to see these social parasites through Caligula's eyes and to accept the necessity for his unmasking of their hypocrisy. As his actions grow more excessive, our sympathy should shift to Caligula's friends, Scipio and Cherea, and to his mistress Caesonia who counsel moderation. But because we were never really convinced of the validity of Caligula's theory of the absurd and because the increasingly degenerate nature of his acts of violence is re-

vealed indirectly, through the patricians' complaints against what has been transpiring off stage, we are not conscious of the gradual disintegration of Caligula's personality. We thought he was mad when he first came on the stage; what we hear about his capricious fondness for murder merely confirms our belief. (pp. 112-13)

The scenes best suited to the stage are those where Camus' preoccupation with the "tragedy of the intelligence" is least apparent. Caligula's abrupt changes of mood, from touching, almost childlike, humility to the most ruthless sadism, permit the actor to display his virtuosity. The Emperor's terrifying solitude as his assassins approach comes close to being "great theatre." He shatters the mirror when it reflects his own horrible image. And yet, though the symbolic link to the mirror of the opening scene is obvious, the impact of this dramatic gesture is attenuated because we never wholly understood the change that had taken place in Caligula. His last speeches, in which he admits his guilt but simultaneously proclaims his triumph at being one of the few in history to have grasped the finality of death and the absurdity of life, are beautifully written; but the audience is unable to accept Caligula's insight because it did not witness each step of his itinerary of self-discovery.

The plot of *The Misunderstanding,* the first play by Camus to be produced in Paris though it was written more than four years after *Caligula,* had already been delineated in the second half of *The Stranger.* Under the mattress of his prison bed, Meursault found part of an old newspaper clipping which told of a strange murder. A young man who had left his native village in Czechoslovakia to seek his fortune returned twenty-five years later to be reunited with his mother and sister who were innkeepers there. When his mother failed to recognize him, the son, now a rich man, decided as a joke to take a room at her hotel. During the night his mother and sister bludgeoned him to death, took his money and threw his body in the river. (pp. 113-14)

In expanding this extremely slight plot into a three act tragedy, Camus found himself obliged to deëmphasize action and to turn instead to the inner drama of Jan, Martha and the mother (the victim and the two assassins) as they proceed inexorably toward the violent dénouement. He uses two types of scenes to reveal his characters' most secret thoughts: conflicts between characters (Jan trying to convince his wife Maria that he should go through with his game of disguise, Martha struggling to overcome her mother's tired yearning for religion and sentiment); and conflicts within a character conveyed largely through monologues (Jan resisting the temptation to disclose his identity, the mother hesitating at the moment of the crime). The dramatic efficacy of these subsurface tensions evaporates in the face of Camus' inability to create convincing human characters whose actions are motivated by something other than his own philosophical theories. The audience never understands, for example, the reasons for Jan's persistent refusal to reveal his identity to his mother and sister. "I came here to bring my fortune and, if I can, happiness," he explains to his wife who had urged him to let his heart speak, to say spontaneously "Here I am." Nowhere does Camus even supply Jan with a good reason for undertaking his game of anonymity in the first place. With each scene marking yet another opportunity missed, the audience in exasperation rejects the validity of Jan's inner struggle, realizing that he withholds his identity for a philosophical reason completely external to his own personality. He is the nameless stranger, modern man, who can gain his true identity only through a spontaneous manifestation of the kind of love which in this world is absent if not impossible. (pp. 114-15)

Equally perplexing are the reasons for Martha's career in murder. Early in the play she explains that she needs to rob only one more victim to be able to escape to a land where "the sun kills all questions." As in *The Stranger,* the sun is the real instigator of murder.... As for her personality, she is impervious to any warm human emotions, and it is difficult to see her obsessive need for sunlight as anything but Camus' own favorite symbolism. Nor can the audience fully understand Martha's coldly detached cruelty until she offers a philosophical explanation of her behavior at the end of the play. Unable to reach the land of the sun, just as Caligula was denied the moon, Martha sees her crime as a revolt against the absurdity of a "life that is more cruel than we are," a revolt which like Caligula's proves futile. This "absurd" is never conveyed to the spectator, however, if one excepts the continuing game of mistaken identity. (p. 115)

The Misunderstanding has been called the tragedy of lack of communication. Whereas Meursault was able to show his detachment from humanity by extended description and laconic indifferent conversation, a character in a play must talk and the characters in *The Misunderstanding* are incredibly prolix, though they talk at cross-purposes. This is aggravated by Camus' choice of such a flimsy, untheatrical plot. His failure to create an effective language of the theatre, however, is the main cause of defective characterization. The mother, supposedly a simple woman wavering between sympathy and cruelty, cannot act out her inner struggle in silence as in a novel.... The sudden intrusions of lyricism in Martha's speeches in praise of the sun ("No, I prefer to picture those other lands over which summer breaks in flame, where winter rains flood the cities, and where . . . things are what they are.") only serve to remove the dialogue even further from human dimensions. Only Maria, Jan's distraught uncomprehending wife, speaks in other than metaphysical terms, and this is possible because for her there is no inner drama. She is the personification of marital devotion; she never quite realizes what has been happening and is totally oblivious to the philosophical assumptions which led to the murder.

Unlike *Caligula* which had undeniable visual appeal, *The Misunderstanding* is almost totally devoid of stage action. To maintain spectator interest, Camus was forced to resort to an embarrassing amount of that kind of theatrical effect which is more appropriate to melodrama: the passport that Martha does not bother inspecting, the mother's arrival just after Jan had swallowed the drugged tea, Jan's decision to return to his wife at the very moment that the drug is taking effect. (p. 116)

The Plague, Camus' second and most ambitious novel, poses even more complex technical problems for *State of Siege* and *The Just Assassins,* the two plays which complement it to form, with the essay *The Rebel,* a tetralogy on the theme of revolt. *The Stranger* told of one person's encounter with the absurd and of his subsequent inner transformation; *The Plague* tells of a collective reaction to a collective problem. Now it is an entire city facing the absurd, and the isolation of individual inhabitants is but a fragmentary symptom of the quarantine imposed on the city as a whole. In *The Stranger* the first-person narrative forced the reader to see with Meursault's eyes and to share in his reactions to experience; the use of the third-person in *The Plague* makes the objective "chronicle" of the suffering of the city of Oran possible. It is not the "author" who acts as chronicler, however, but Doctor Rieux, the central character, whose occupation requires travel throughout the plague-ridden city and makes him a privileged witness of the private dramas taking place in extremely diverse sectors of the population. The focus of the novel is therefore wide.... This broad range of action, with its emphasis on crowd scenes and frequent shifts in locale, will prove to be an insurmountable obstacle to Camus' attempt to adapt the myth of the plague to the limited spatial potential of the stage in *State of Siege.* Moreover, the plague is at its most insidious not at the dramatic moment of a victim's death but in its slow, almost imperceptible power to demoralize the still healthy population. The relaxed pace of narration needed to convey this gradual disintegration is possible only in the novel.

Though some critics have professed to see that amorphous entity the city of Oran as the real hero of *The Plague,* the central theme of revolt depends to a large extent on the inner drama of Dr. Rieux. "*La Peste* is a confession," Camus wrote in Sartre's review *Les Temps Modernes* when asked to explain his use of the third-person, "and everything is calculated to make this confession all the more complete since its form is indirect." Dr. Rieux, like Meursault, continually finds himself face to face with the absurd, here symbolized by the plague, and comes gradually to understand first his own and then the city's predicament. It is highly revealing of the consistency of Camus' novelistic art that the crucial scene in which Rieux achieves true awareness is one based primarily on point of view and change in tone. (p. 117)

State of Siege is not a direct adaptation of the novel but rather an attempt to recreate the myth of the plague as "total theatre," a synthesis of drama, ballet, mime and music. Camus' first task was to find a way to put the plague on stage that was both theatrically feasible and dramatically convincing. Obviously, the slow accumulation of physical details possible in the novel was out of the question; nor could the setting of the play shift rapidly enough to follow the spreading of the plague. Realizing that there was no possibility of conveying the plague's symbolic role as an impersonal and totally destructive force to the theatre audience, Camus decided to make the plague a character in his play. The universality of the symbol is lost when the plague, wearing the grey uniform of a Nazi officer, appears on stage to prescribe new codes of behavior to the citizens of the city of Cadiz in a four page inaugural address. The greatness of Camus' use of the myth of the plague in the novel lay precisely in the extraordinary variety of associations, religious, literary and historical, which it summoned up in the reader's mind. The theatre audience, however, forgets the myth of the plague entirely; on the stage there is a very sarcastic but not unlovable petty bureaucrat always accompanied by a secretary whose function is to keep up-to-date the list of the inhabitants of Cadiz.

Since *State of Siege* like *The Plague* tells of a whole city's reaction to enslavement by the enemy, Camus had to cope with the always difficult problem of putting crowd scenes on stage. His task was complicated by the fact that the crowd of citizens of Cadiz is not "part of the decor" but is in effect one of the central "characters" in the play. Camus unfortunately elected the most obvious solution to his problem when he created an enormous cast which included nameless voices, five messengers, beggars, gypsies, women of the town, men of the town and guards. As a result, the stage is cluttered, and the occasional choreographic movements by the crowd only partially attenuate the general impression of chaos. The silent, patient suffering of the widely dispersed population, so moving in the novel, is clearly impossible to realize in the theatre. (pp. 118-19)

The difference between novelistic time and dramatic time is the greatest stumbling block to Camus' adaptation of essentially novelistic conceptions to the exigencies of the stage. As the plague makes its presence felt throughout the city, scores of domestic and personal dramas of separation and physical anguish ensue. The novelist can take the time to make even the minor participants in the collective suffering seem like full-dimensioned characters. . . . In the play, the tempo is of necessity to rapid for such development of minor characters. These tend to become dehumanized abstractions, speaking in the stock phrases of their particular occupation. (pp. 119-20)

The core of dramatic interest in **State of Siege** is the gradual emergence of Diego as a rebel. Continuing the pattern established in his earlier works, Camus sees the choice confronting his hero in the contrast between the prosaic and the poetic, between the absurd and nature, between the sea and the bureaucratic organization imposed on the city by the plague. Only a wind from the sea can rid the city of its enemy. Camus seems to lose all stylistic control when composing dialogue; the carefully restrained lyricism which makes his descriptions of nature so effective in his novels becomes a veritable flood of imagery in the plays. . . . It is Diego's love for the sea which leads him to rebel. He asks a boatman to take him to the ships lying at anchor outside the harbor of the quarantined city. Just as he is about to embark on this illegal trip outside the city limits, the Plague's secretary arrives on the scene to prevent his departure. Diego refuses to yield even under threat of punishment, and the secretary admits reluctantly: "". . . the machine has always shown a tendency to break down when a man conquers his fear and stands up to it. I won't say it stops completely. But it creaks, and sometimes it actually begins to fold up."" Armed with the knowledge of the power of revolt, Diego tries to convince the citizens of Cadiz to follow him. Unlike Rieux who by his own exemplary action against the plague succeeded in winning the participation of others in his health brigades, Diego, whose revolt consisted of saying ""no"" to the plague, relies on words. (pp. 120-21)

Camus said of **The Just Assassins** that never before had he felt himself so little the author of his own play. He adhered closely to both the plot and the dialogue furnished by Boris Savinkov's *Souvenirs d'un terroriste,* and it was thanks to the severe limits imposed by his given material that he partially avoided his usual pitfall: excessive abstraction in the dialogue. Savinkov's memoirs of the 1905 revolution provided Camus with a specific historical context and a universally understandable ethical question: Are ideals corrupted when unworthy means are used to bring about their realization? The play is not predicated on the audience's *a priori* acceptance of Camus' personal notion of the absurd.

Yet, in spite of the relevance of the moral issue of ""ends and means,"" the very issue which led Camus to break with Sartre, **The Just Assassins** seems verbose, if not boring. This may be due in part to the rather lifeless quality of the French translation of the dialogue in Savinkov's book. But there is another reason more consistent with Camus' repeated failures in adapting narrative material to the stage. The action never takes place on the stage; the characters only describe it and philosophize about it. (p. 121)

Camus probably realized that he was taking a chance in basing his entire play on a delicate moral problem. An essay would seem to be a more appropriate form, but the essay did not offer the dialectical situation that Camus needed to shock his audience into an awareness of the complexity of the ethical problem facing the revolutionary. In a play he could stage a series of debates between characters holding opposing views. These are absorbing at times because of the relevance of the subject under discussion, yet one wonders how much more effective these debates would be in a novel. In *The Brothers Karamazov,* for example, the danger of excessive theorizing in the lengthy discussions on evil between Ivan and Alyosha is avoided by Dostoyevsky's careful alternation of action and dialogue. And reading philosophy is certainly less painful than hearing it. Moreover, Dostoyevsky knew that the most secret torments of man are only partially revealed by what he says; the most significant inner drama takes place in silence, in the mind or soul. Camus the novelist was fully aware of this, and the ""drama of the intelligence"" of his narrator-heroes is not brought out in their usually laconic conversations with other characters but in their solitary meditations which only the reader witnesses. Just one of Camus' narrators, Clamence in his last novel **The Fall,** is garrulous; he talks to escape solitude and the inner drama that would inevitably ensue.

If Camus' failures have been emphasized here, it is only because his stature as novelist and moralist is so apparent as to need no further confirmation. His failure as dramatist can be defined by a simple truism: in the theatre silence is impossible. To write a good play, a dramatist must create effective dialogue; and this is precisely what Camus was unable to do because he continually transported novelistic techniques into the theatre. How ironic that what is perhaps his finest work for the stage should be the adaptation of someone else's novel. In spite of its disastrous Broadway run, **Requiem for a Nun** at times comes close to being the modern tragedy that Camus so desperately wanted to write. ""Faulkner,"" Camus wrote in his preface for the French translation of the novel, ""had solved, in his own way and without being aware of it, a very difficult problem. How to make characters in modern dress speak a language which is contemporary enough to be spoken in our apartments and unusual enough to suggest tragic tone?"" Thus it is that in the crucial scenes of **Requiem for a Nun,** those in which the main characters reveal their most secret thoughts, Camus retained almost all of Faulkner's dialogue. This constitutes his own admission of failure, and one can only speculate whether the **Don Juan** which Camus was writing at the time of his death would have marked the beginning of his career as a creator of modern tragedy. (pp. 122-23)

Albert Sonnenfeld, ""Albert Camus As Dramatist: The Sources of His Failure,"" in The Tulane Drama Review, *Vol. 5, No. 4, June, 1961, pp. 106-23.*

JAMES H. CLANCY

[*The essay from which the following excerpt is taken originally appeared in* Educational Theatre Journal, *October 1961.*]

One of the most frequently noted aspects of the contemporary theatrical scene is the triumphant arrival of unintelligibility as a major feature of many highly regarded plays. Ionesco, in his *Bald Soprano,* indicates both by the irrelevancy of his play's title and by the repetitive no-sense of his dialogue that though his play may have meaning he is dedicated to the belief that that meaning shall not be achieved by intelligible devices. His meaning exists beneath the action and the dialogue and he faithfully, and successfully, shatters the normal, intelligible form of both so that the spectator is refused the possibility of deriving meaning by a rational or intelligible process. (p. 160)

The effect of such theatrical efforts was for some time, however, extremely tangential to the main line of theatre art and it is only recently that unintelligibility has come to be reckoned as a major force in modern drama. (p. 161)

Exciting and valuable as this foray into the unintelligible is, it is not this aspect of the modern theatre that demonstrates its greatest break with the past or its most striking contribution to a possible drama of the future. Such a contribution is rather to be seen in that branch of the modern theatre that may be said to concern itself with new ideas of purpose and refurbished accent on the human will.

This theatre, as might be expected of an art that aims at unintelligibility as well as meaning, is more complicated than the theatre of no-sense. Two major phases of it may be distinguished, however, and although any such arbitrary division is more useful than accurate, it is not amiss to consider the new theatre of ideas as being represented by the otherwise opposing points of view of such authors as Bertolt Brecht and Albert Camus. (p. 162)

Camus and Brecht participated (perhaps unconsciously) in a revolt against the late nineteenth century theatre of ideas not because it contained ideas (the basis of Ionesco's objection), but rather because the ideas it contained no longer seemed to be of central importance. As Brecht points out in the Introduction to his *Little Organum,* "everything had been emptied out of the contemporary theatre." It reflected "false images of the social scene on the stage (including those of naturalism so-called)." (p. 163)

A new idea of the world was necessary to complete the revolt against the naturalistic theatre of the last part of the nineteenth century, and a new theatre of ideas was necessary to express this revolt. The work of both Albert Camus and Bertolt Brecht is central to this new theatre of ideas.

The theatre of Camus, which more directly concerns itself with philosophical issues than does that of Brecht, illustrates one of the directions taken by the new theatre in a re-evaluation of man's relationship to the world. [A] quotation from *Caligula* . . . illustrates the basis from which this change was accomplished: "Men die and they are not happy." The fundamental assumption about the world is no longer, as with the naturalists, that it is material, measurable, predictable, but rather that it is unpredictable, lacks congruity, is, in a special sense, absurd.

The world of things (Sartre's *en-soi*) looms large in this new world, but man is no longer considered as a thing among things. The world of things is not man's world. The absurd is felt when man's desire that the world should be explicable is seen to be opposed by the fact that the world cannot be made explicable in human terms. Camus sees the absurd as a clash between the world's "irrationality and the desperate hunger for clarity which cries out in man's deepest soul. The absurd depends as much upon man as upon the world."

This is what Caligula understands. This is why he feels that the world is insupportable and that he needs "the moon, or happiness, or immortality; something foolish, but something that is not of this world."

But both the moon and happiness are out of his reach, as he considers them out of the reach of all men in a world where incomprehension, misery, and solitude are masters, and so, in

this world where it is impossible to justify moral values, he turns to pure evil . . . in order to equal the gods, who only evidence themselves by their cruelty. (pp. 166-67)

Martha, in *Cross-Purpose,* has, like Caligula, dedicated herself to evil because of a world that is absurd in its cruelty, its isolation, its indifference. Her defiance, like Caligula's, is hopeless and non-fruitful. (p. 167)

[In the world of Caligula and Martha] evil is not measurable, man's nature not predictable. Evil is senseless, as is good. No moral values exist in a world that is absurd in its essence. Man exists among things, but he is not of these things, and he evidences his manhood by rebellion against a world that he can neither understand nor control.

The outlook, in *Caligula* and *Cross-Purpose,* is pessimistic as opposed to the implied optimism of the earlier theatre of ideas, but even if the vision is essentially more repugnant it is at the same time more engrossing and more personal. Camus is not presenting a world of "others," he is not dramatizing what happens to a group of people with a certain environment, a specific heredity. He is dramatizing his despair, his anguish. From the basic tenets of the play, Caligula's defeat is his, as it is ours, as it is everyman's. Camus, and his characters, and his audience, are all confronted by the same problem. If his play touches you at all, it is apt to touch you profoundly, for Camus and you have not so much observed the same phenomena as you have become engaged in the same activity. You and he are at the center of the play. What you have participated in may be a thesis play rather than a play of character, but it is intensely human because the thesis concerns you and not others.

The recognition of the absurdity of the world and man's need to rebel against it are not, however, the concluding notes of Camus' theatre. Many will maintain that his most effective work for the theatre was done when he did not advance his argument beyond these steps, but his plays are works of art and as such they followed his development as a man and reflect the increasing enrichment of his point of view.

The new conclusion that was to be expressed by Camus in the theatre in such plays as *The Just* is clearly formulated in his *Letter to a German Friend,* published in 1944. In this essay, Camus remonstrates with a Nazi for having drawn Caligula's conclusions from Caligula's premise. He blames the Nazi for adding to the injustice of the world that he sees around him. For Camus,

> . . . man must affirm justice in order to struggle against eternal injustice, create happiness in order to protest against a universe of evil.

He remonstrates with the Nazi for having chosen injustice, for having, as did Caligula, thrown in his lot with the gods. As for himself, says Camus, "I have chosen justice, in order to remain faithful to the earth."

Five years after the publication of this "Letter," Camus presented the same problem dramatically in *The Just.* In this play, Kaliayev recognizes, as did Jan in *Cross-Purpose,* that one thing that must be reached for in a world of absurdity is happiness for others. "One cannot be happy," says Jan, "in exile." Kaliayev accepts becoming a criminal only in order that the world will finally "be covered with the innocent." For him there is no individual salvation, no happiness in solitude. For these reasons he is, unlike Caligula, "un meurtrier délicat," a scrupulous assassin. (pp. 167-69)

Camus' theatre gathers its force by replacing the outworn ideas of the naturalistic theatre by newer ideas based on a re-evaluation of the situation of man and the meaning of the universe. It is a theatre founded on the dark premise of no-sense, against which man, because he is man, is forced to revolt; a world of no-values, in which man must strive, no matter what the failure, to establish value; a tragic but human-centered world in which "revolt is justified by failure and purified in death." (p. 169)

James H. Clancy, "Beyond Despair: A New Drama of Ideas," in Essays in the Modern Drama, *edited by Morris Freedman, D. C. Heath and Company, 1964, pp. 160-73.**

F. C. ST. AUBYN

The critics have long since demonstrated that while Camus was not an existentialist, Sartrian or otherwise, there are nevertheless existential elements in his thought. I am not interested here in assessing how few or how many of his ideas are existential and certainly I have no intention of making of Camus an existentialist in the face of his own express statement to the contrary. Nor am I occupied by the unlikely problem of the possible influence of Sartre on Camus. I should like to show, however, how Sartre's ontology, which evolved simultaneously with the early writings of Camus, can be used to illuminate Camus's major literary works. (p. 124)

Obviously the various characters of Camus do not live and think in a static world or in the same emotional, geographical, chronological world. My point of departure is, therefore, the relationship between being-for-itself and the death of the other since it supplies us with the central idea necessary for a unifying interpretation.... This is not to say that Camus's plays and novels can be reduced to a single concept. Such an oversimplification would deny Camus's literary output one of its most significant aspects, its evolution. Nevertheless when Camus speaks in his essay 'Réflexions sur la guillotine,' a determined and passionate plea for the abolition of capital punishment ... we realize that the rupture of ... solidarity by the death of the other provides the primary impetus for the action of most of Camus's works. An interpretation of the effects of the death of the other in the light of Sartre's remarks could give added meaning to these already meaningful works.

In *Caligula,* the first version of which was finished in 1938, we find the death of the other precipitating the whole action of the drama.... As a result of the death of Drusilla, the emperor's sister and mistress, Caligula initiates his reign of the impossible which can only end in his own destruction. Early in the first act Caligula attempts to explain to his faithful servant Hélicon the meaning of this death for himself: 'Cette mort n'est rien, je te le jure; elle est seulement le signe d'une vérité qui me rend la lune nécessaire.' When Hélicon asks the emperor what this truth is, he replies: 'Les hommes meurent et ils ne sont pas heureux.' Death, then, is for Caligula the sign of a truth, the absurd truth of the human condition.... (pp. 124-25)

On another level, however, Camus's treatment of the death of the other in *Caligula* can be said to illustrate Sartre's ontology, especially when the enigmatic ending of the play is taken into consideration. Caligula must first establish the universal guilt of all, that guilt of which Sartre treats when speaking of being-for-others. According to Caligula's implacable logic, 'On meurt parce qu'on est coupable. On est coupable parce qu'on est sujet de Caligula. Or, tout le monde est sujet de Caligula. Donc,

tout le monde est coupable. D'où il resort que tout le monde meurt.' ... One is guilty simply because one is being-for-others. All are guilty because all are subject to the same being-for-others. For Sartre, death is the phenomenon of a personal life, that is, a life which does not begin again. All being-for-itself is subject to the same phenomenon of death; thus, since we are all subjects of Caligula, we are all guilty and we all must die. Caligula has forgotten for the moment that he too is being-for-itself. (pp. 125-26)

Once the guilt of others has been established, Caligula must realize the supreme desire of man, which is, according to Sartre, to be God. The fundamental project of human reality is to metamorphose itself into the ideal of a consciousness which would be the foundation of its own being-for-itself by the pure consciousness it would have of itself, that is, to metamorphose its being-for-itself into being-in-itself-for-itself. (p. 126)

The emperor later forces the Roman poets to improvise in one minute a poem on the subject of death.... The suffering young Scipion, who refuses both to help Caligula because he has had his father killed and to take part in the emperor's assassination because he understands him so well, easily wins the contest. Scipion departs, leaving Caligula alone with his loyal but uncomprehending mistress Caesonia. When Caligula realizes that to be logical to the end he must kill her also, he says: 'Quand je ne tue pas, je me sens seul. Les vivants étes tous là, vous me faites sentir un vide sans mesure où je ne peux regarder. Je ne suis bien que parmi mes morts'.... Caligula's universe is empty because, according to Sartre, the look of the other steals his world from him, decentralizes the world which he is attempting to centralize. Only by eliminating the other's look can he refute the objectivity he is for the other. Only by reducing others to a thing, an object, a being-in-itself, only by killing them can Caligula deny others the limit which their being sets to his freedom. He is happy among his dead because the perfect isolation, the perfect solitude would be that of the being-for-itself which exists alone in a world of objects, of being-in-itself.

Why then does Caligula say: 'Mais tuer n'est pas la solution'? Because his efforts are reduced to treating the other as an instrument, because he can never touch the other except in his being as an object. Even if Caligula could abolish the other, he could not eliminate the fact of the other's having been.... The existence of death, Sartre maintains, alienates us wholly in our own life to the advantage of the other. To be dead is to be a prey for the living. Death is a triumph of the point of view of the other over the point of view we are towards ourselves. The unique characteristic of a dead life is that it is a life of which the other makes himself guardian. In this sense Caligula is an objective and opaque being which has been reduced to the single dimension of exteriority. In this capacity he will continue to pursue his history in the human world and in this sense he is indeed still alive. (pp. 126-28)

Again in *Le Malentendu,* written in 1942-1943 and staged the following year, the death of the other has taken place before the curtain rises. Already in the first scene the mother and daughter have begun to bear only with difficulty the guilt of the death of all the others they have murdered. If they have managed to avoid their guilt up to this point it is because they have successfully reduced the other to a thing in their own minds.... The mother is nevertheless aware that through murder she has ruptured the human solidarity against death and separated herself forever from all others. (p. 133)

The mother and daughter as we-subjects have a common goal, a collective rhythm as Sartre would call it. They are working together for the day when they can escape their dreary Moravia. . . . They are both searching for respite and release from their own guilt. They would both like to reduce themselves to being-in-itself, to a thing. The we-subject relationship remains however an experience of a psychological rather than an ontological order. It in no way corresponds to a real unification of the being-for-itself of the mother and daughter. The entrance of the old servant in the role of the third immediately transforms their relationship from we-subject to us-object. With the appearance of the third the mother and daughter are precipitated into the world as us-objects, a transformation they experience in shame as a community alienation. The old servant is the witness to their guilt. (pp. 133-34)

Much like Caligula and Meursault, Martha is determined to leave the world unreconciled. . . . Her tragedy, as well as that of her mother, is that she finds in suicide exactly what she had been seeking, the peace of being-in-itself. . . . When Maria on her knees begs God to have pity on those who love and are separated, that is on a human group, it is the old servant who as the unrealizable third answers, the third who is on principle distinct from humanity and in whose eyes humanity is wholly object. The third is, according to Sartre, the one who is third in relation to all possible groups, the one who in no case can enter into community with any group. In Sartre's dialectic this concept is one with the idea of God. The old servant's resounding 'Non!', which closes the play, is the pitiless response of the third where the human condition is concerned. We are all condemned to death and, whether we seek it in suicide or find it in innocence, the result is beyond repair and inevitably the same for all. (p. 134)

Camus's *L'Etat de siège,* finished in 1948, seems, as Germaine Brée says, 'a little outside the main line of development of his work'. For me it is the most abstract and least compelling of his plays. The spectacle can nevertheless be said to illustrate Sartre's ontology in several ways. The action does not truly begin with the passing of the comet in the prologue but with the first death of the other from the plague, that of the actor. Up to this point the people of Cadiz have experienced only the psychological we-subject and are, as a matter of fact, experiencing it at the very moment when they are all united in witnessing the death of the third who is the actor. In the face of the Plague personified and the rupture of human solidarity against death they begin to experience the ontological us-object. (p. 136)

The citizens of Cadiz attempt to flee their community alienation as us-objects in the face of the Plague by insisting upon their own transcendence while reducing the other to an object by killing him. In so doing they are of course violating human solidarity. . . . It is finally Diego who, in substituting his own death for that of Victoria, in choosing his own death to save the liberty of the city, makes the right choice. . . . Thus it was Diego who in spite of his solitary experience as the other in love finally assured the human solidarity of the people of Cadiz through love.

Obviously the primary concern of a group of assassins would be the death of the other. So it is in *Les Justes,* which was produced in 1949. Kaliayev, chosen to throw the first bomb, knows that he will not hesitate before the humanity of the Grand Duke because he has reduced him to an abstraction, to a thing . . . But when the time comes Kaliayev fails because the Grand Duke is not alone, his wife and niece and nephew are unex-

pectedly with him. It is the look of the other, the look of the children which arrests his hand. . . . Kaliayev had not foreseen the children. He had not reduced them to being-in-itself in his mind as he had their uncle. (p. 137)

Certain similarities can be noted between the scenes in which the priest visits Meursault in his cell and the scene in which the Grand Duchess visits Kaliayev in his. Both come with a kind of pardon and forgiveness and both come with religion in their mind and heart. And both are refused. The Grand Duchess is as much with the others as the priest, but in a different way. As a member of the oppressing class she is the third and serves only to unite Kaliayev more strongly with his comrades, with the oppressed. In the closing scene Kaliayev's death is described. We know that, like Meursault, he refuses the ministrations of a priest. His girl friend is sure that he must have walked happily and calmly to the scaffold. Once again the plot has moved from the death of the other to the death of self. (p. 138)

[The major creative works of Camus] demonstrate an amazing consistency in their fundamental attitude towards the death of the other and the subsequent death of self. This obsession of Camus, the death of the other as a literary theme, must be carefully distinguished from the theme of the death of self which, again as a theme, uses a radically different perspective. . . . It would be difficult to maintain that Camus, as an artist, did not think beyond his major characters. The treatment of the projection of the themes leaves the themes inviolable, open to as many interpretations as there are readers. The point of juncture between Camus's obsession and Sartre's ontology is found in the latter's . . . remark: 'La mort de l'autre me constitue comme objet irrémédiable, exactement comme ma propre mort.' In treating Camus's works in such a light, one is no longer treating the themes as literary themes but as philosophical projections which are as true for human beings as they are for characters in a novel or play. Since Sartre and Camus read and studied many of the same sources it is not surprising to find that Camus's creative works and Sartre's ontology are mutually illuminating. What is surprising is to observe that in this one instance at least Camus's works are even better illustrations of Sartre's existentialist phenomenology than the latter's own creative works. Certainly many of the ideas expressed in Sartre's philosophical treatise bring a new light to bear on Camus's works. The fact remains that Sartre is primarily a philosopher while Camus was essentially a moralist. As a moralist Camus wrote: 'Ni dans le coeur des individus ni dans les moeurs des sociétés, il n'y aura de paix durable tant que la mort ne sera pas mise hors la loi.' Camus was of course speaking literally of capital punishment. That death can never be put beyond the law from an existential viewpoint both Sartre and Camus, both the philosopher and the moralist, would agree. At this point excessive metaphysical anguish finds its corrective in the rigorous but compassionate ethics of the humanist who was Albert Camus. (pp. 140-41)

F. C. St. Aubyn, "Albert Camus and the Death of the Other: An Existentialist Interpretation," in French Studies, *Vol. XVI, No. 2, April, 1962, pp. 124-41.*

D. M. CHURCH

When *Le Malentendu* was first produced at the Théâtre des Mathurins in 1944, it was not a complete success, but neither was it a complete failure. (p. 33)

The play has primarily been treated by critics in the most obvious way: that is, as a symbolic representation of certain of Camus's philosophical ideas. The more or less allegorical nature of *Le Malentendu* has been frequently discussed. However, the problem of the expression of these ideas has often been neglected. This is an unfortunate situation because the play is essentially a work of art. The metaphysical ideas contained in it have been fully discussed in a much more direct manner in the author's essays. Any examination of these ideas would naturally be more appropriate in a criticism of these essays; and consequently, the treatment of this play, along with any of his other plays or novels, should deal primarily with the problem of artistic expression.

This problem is closely related to the creation of a modern form of tragedy that greatly preoccupied Camus. . . . Since we are dealing with an author who manifests a lifelong passion for the theatre, this problem becomes extremely important in relation to his works as a whole. And since he seems to imply that man's tragic condition is essentially the same in all ages and that only the artistic expression varies, it is logical to assume that the major interest of *Le Malentendu* for present and future literary critics should be its place in the development of the author's and the epoch's theories of modern tragedy.

First of all, in what sense is *Le Malentendu* tragic? We find many clear indications in a lecture on the future of tragedy that Camus delivered in Athens in 1955. Tragedy, for Camus, is essentially punishment without crime; it is the clash of two forces that are both in the right. The tragic hero rebels against a certain order or power, which in turn strikes down the hero because he has revolted. . . . *Le Malentendu,* then, fits into this general scheme of tragedy in the sense that the main characters, and especially Jan and Martha, are engaged in a fatal struggle with a legitimate order; that is, in an impossible fight to surpass their own particularly human limitations.

Reino Virtanen compares this play with the general folk legend from which it derives and the different literary treatments it gave rise to and points out significantly that 'Camus has understood what others failed fully to realize—in this story the tragic function belongs not to the victim but to the assassin'. This is not completely true, since Jan is also a tragic hero; but it is important to realize that Martha and her mother are tragic figures and that it is their downfall that really closes the play. (pp. 33-4)

There is room for a comparison of *Le Malentendu* with the classical Greek tragedies, centred more especially on the theme of recognition of the brother in the three extant Electra plays. In Camus's play the final recognition is achieved by means of a token—the passport—a means that Aristotle did not consider very strong. But recognition by this means is quite common in the Greek plays too. Much more important, however, is a comparison of the dramatic atmosphere which accompanies the recognition—or, in Camus's case, the lack of recognition. . . . It is . . . rewarding to make the comparison with Euripides' *Electra;* in this play the atmosphere of the recognition scenes is almost identical with the dramatic movement of *Le Malentendu.* As Friedrich Solmsen has put it:

> [In the Euripides play] the whole pattern of this episode is a movement toward the desired event, then away again, then there is another turn which takes us closer and closer, almost infinitesimally close to what we expect in great suspense, and this is again followed by a move-

ment away from this point. . . . There is always this arising of hopeful chances, words are spoken that might lead to the discovery; [there is] always the same picture of humanity, of men or women so intent on finding what they desire, striving and struggling so desperately for it, and [who] when they are face to face with their happiness [and] would only have to reach out and grasp it, . . . are blind.

These words could very easily have been written about *Le Malentendu.* In this attempt to create a modern tragedy Camus remains close to the traditions of the ancient Greek variety. (pp. 34-5)

[However, it] might in fact be doubtful whether *Le Malentendu* is a tragedy at all. It is perhaps rather a melodrama with philosophical overtones.

Whether or not the action of the play falls within the realm of tragedy, the basic problem of language still remains. . . . [One] of the major stylistic processes of the play is ambiguity and, with it, a certain bitter irony. Camus's intention was evidently to reconcile tragedy and modern language by giving simple everyday conversation tragic undertones within the context of the intrigue through double meaning. It would seem, however, that this process defeated its purpose by wearying the spectator. One soon grows tired of looking for a double meaning in practically every sentence that is uttered. The problem is further complicated by the fact that there are several different types of irony or ambiguity used in the play. These will be considered separately.

First, there is what we shall call the author's irony. This is a process that consists in putting into a character's mouth words that have a definite ironic ambiguity of which the character himself could not possibly be aware. (pp. 35-6)

A closely related process is that by which Camus expresses indirectly certain philosophical ideas. Here again he puts more meaning into the characters' words than they themselves are aware of. A very precise and down-to-earth statement in the context of character and situation can take on much more profundity when considered in the context of the metaphysical ideas that the author is trying to present. . . . What is involved . . . is not so much ambiguity as . . . two different levels of meaning on which [a] conversation can be interpreted. This technique has become much clearer and much more striking in the revision of the play. Roger Quilliot mildly reproaches Camus for the way his characters seem to vary in their symbolic function, causing our attention to jump back and forth from the characters as real people to their meaning in the philosophical scheme of the play. In the 1958 version, the author has somewhat diminished this effect by eliminating many direct and conscious metaphysical statements from his characters' speeches. . . . The new version is much simpler and thus more intense than the older. All the philosophical ideas of the first are implicit in the second, but in the latter Jan no longer steps out of character to express them. He remains a believable character, and the spectator draws out the deeper meanings in his simple, matter-of-fact speech. (pp. 37-8)

How does one explain such revision? Perhaps Camus decided that too many ambiguities would tend to bewilder the spectator. Perhaps he thought that, if he lessened them, those that remained would be more effective. Perhaps these constant allusions and double-meanings gave more lucidity and perspicacity to the characters than he wished them to have. Perhaps he decided that such a technique was too close to the *jeux d'esprit* which he disliked in the works of such dramatists as Giraudoux. And perhaps it was a combination of several or all of these reasons that occasioned the omissions. Of course, there are still many ambiguous statements left in the revised version. But, for the most part, these fit well into the very nature and theme of the play, as the title itself suggests. They help to translate the basic theme of lack of communication between men. And more than that, they are useful and artistic in the wedding of symbolic meanings with the natural elements of a more or less realistic action. (p. 40)

Closely connected with the process of ambiguity and the use of an image to express a more profound idea than would normally appear on the surface is the problem of characterization. Camus is definitely not interested in presenting a complex psychological portrait of the people in his play. Although we would hesitate to call Jan, his mother, Martha and Maria symbols in the purest sense of the word, we cannot help but consider them as representative of certain attitudes in the context of the author's philosophical thought. A complete psychological analysis of the characters would destroy this function; if they are to carry across on the stage the message that Camus has in mind, they must be simple and, consequently, universal. (p. 41)

An essential element in the communication of the message in *Le Malentendu* is the characterization of the old servant. He exists on a different level from the other characters, serving an almost entirely symbolic purpose. In the earlier versions he has an extremely small role, so small in fact that many people failed to understand his meaning and were greatly troubled by his appearance in the play. Camus was evidently aware of this misunderstanding, for he greatly augmented and, consequently, clarified the servant's role when he revised his play. At the beginning of Act I, scene ii, stage directions are added to show that the old man definitely sees Jan and Maria. . . . He knows, then, all the time that Jan is not a lone traveller. . . . Later . . . , when Jan hands Martha his passport, the 1958 version has the old man come in to distract Martha so that she will not read it. . . . This change evidently makes the action more believable, but it can also be interpreted on a deeper level. In Act II, scene viii, Camus has changed the directions to have the servant follow Martha and her mother into Jan's room. . . . Then when Martha is searching her brother's pockets, he adds indications that the passport falls behind the bed, and the servant picks it up and carries it out without the two women noticing it. . . . But once again the revision has deeper significance. The author has made it very clear that the old man knows all along about the plot and is probably aware of Jan's identity before the murder. Such changes have evidently been made in order to emphasize and clarify the servant's symbolism; it is much more obvious in the 1958 version that he represents the indifferent world in which the characters find themselves.

After having discussed the various problems of ambiguity, symbolism and imagery, we shall return to the basic stylistic problem involved in *Le Malentendu,* that of the language of modern tragedy. . . . The dominant style of *Le Malentendu* is characterized by simplicity. Its bareness has reminded certain critics of the style of *L'Étranger.* . . . The staccato rhythm and simplicity of the scene where Martha fills out the questionnaire concerning Jan's identity is but a slight exaggeration of the dominant tone of the play. In revising the text, Camus has taken pains to simplify the style still further. . . . The simplicity and sobriety of the style sometimes seem inadequate to express the extreme emotions and profound meanings of the play. But, on the other hand, is this not a more natural method than the declamatory style of the traditional theatre? This is a difficult problem and one which, as we find in the unpublished Notebooks, continued to vex Camus. . . . (pp. 43-4)

This does not mean, however, that the dry sobriety of tone is constant throughout the play. Camus makes subtle use of rhythm for variety. For the most part rather choppy or staccato, the cadence becomes slower and more complicated as the discussion moves to a deeper level. The most remarkable variety in the style comes during the few moments when Martha throws off restraint and expresses a sort of lyric *élan.* . . . In a strange poetry, mingled with desperation and greed, Martha's ardent speeches mark the highest points of the play. For all their bitterness and desperation, they are not entirely unlike some of the more lyrical passages in the essays of *L'Envers et l'Endroit* and *Noces.* Yet, at the same time, they are completely in character; in fact, they may have much to do with the fact that many consider Martha the strongest character in the play. In both the aesthetic and practical senses, they do much to emphasize and render more effective the general tone of the play.

We may now arrive at some conclusions about the principles that Camus develops in *Le Malentendu* concerning the problems of the modern tragedy. . . . A natural conversational tone, characterized by simplicity and even understatement, is used to bring the play closer to real life. But many ambiguities and ironic statements facilitate a deeper interpretation of the text. Psychologically simple characters, including one who exists almost entirely on the symbolic level, also help to bring out the universal tragic elements. A restrained but masterful use of images, as well as sparsely scattered lyrical passages, give tragic depth to the style. But one must admit that these processes have not been completely effective. The constant shifting from one level of meaning to another has a tendency to bewilder if not annoy the spectator. The constant double-meanings often seem artificial and even border on the precious. The characters, with the possible exception of Martha, have been so simplified that they do not seem to be properly motivated and, consequently, do not really live on the stage. Many of these problems were solved by the time that Camus adapted Faulkner's *Requiem for a Nun,* another important experiment in modern tragedy. Most important, he has discovered a vital principle inherent in the very nature of the theatre—'Rester vrai tout en jouant large'. It is obvious that *Le Malentendu* has an important place in the development of Camus's dramatic theories and in the general theatrical evolution of the age. Camus and his contemporaries learned much about the nature of modern tragedy from both the successes and failures of this experiment. (pp. 45-6)

> *D. M. Church, "'Le Malentendu': Search for Modern Tragedy," in* French Studies, *Vol. XX, No. 1, January, 1966, pp. 33-46.*

E. FREEMAN

Les Justes is the third and last of his original plays which Camus considered to be attempts at modern tragedy (that is to say, together with *Le Malentendu* and *L'Etat de siège,* but excluding *Caligula*), and is frequently regarded as one of his most successful pieces of writing for the theater. Many accounts of the play appear to be based on an implicit acceptance of its claim to be a modern tragedy. The heroic, exalted atmosphere and the astringent dialogue and structure are admired, and epithets such as ''truly Cornelian aura'' provide the final accolade. But just as in Corneille's theater the border line between tragedy and tragicomedy is frequently in dispute, so in *Les Justes* the author's moral ardor can be sensed to be in such an uneasy relationship with his artistic judgment that an objective critic is roused to examine the play's claim to being tragedy. Is it indeed this so much as a play in an inferior genre: melodrama? (p. 78)

An examination of *Les Justes* as a modern tragedy according to the classic formula will . . . depend to a large extent on the degree to which the tragic antagonists are equally ''just.''

The other two principal prerequisites of tragedy which Camus stressed [in a lecture given at Athens in 1955] are particularly relevant to the political and philosophical subject matter of *Les Justes*. The first is a classical Greek concept which has also been much appreciated by French tragedians, probably more than in any other Western European theater: the necessity of *mesure* in human conduct, or, to use the terms that echo throughout Camus's works, the importance of observing ''la limite qu'il ne faut pas dépasser''. . . . In *Les Justes* Camus is asking: What is the limit to the violence one can commit in the pursuit of just ends? To what extent is one justified in descending to the level of one's brutal and unscrupulous enemies if there is no other effective means of bringing about justice and democracy? . . .

The second characteristic of tragedy is more controversial and raises the whole question of tragedy as a cultural and philosophical phenomenon. According to Camus—and few would disagree with him here—great tragedy has flowered only twice, and briefly on each occasion: in Athens in the fifth century B.C. and in Western Europe during the late Renaissance. (p. 79)

Thus far, Camus is not very original, but where he does enter on new—and disputable—territory is in claiming that the climate is equally suitable for tragedy in the twentieth century. . . . The modern tragic hero will not be a later version of the Renaissance figures, taking on the same forces as Dr. Faustus. Those battles have been won: for Camus it is the liberators themselves, the spiritual descendants of Descartes and Robespierre, who have become the tyrants. The modern tragic hero, in short, will be pitted not against feudal, Christian (''right-wing'') society, but against those who themselves defeated those forces in (predominantly Eastern) Europe in the first half of this century. Camus's theory of modern tragedy, at least as far as *Les Justes* and *L'Etat de siège* are concerned, is in fact irrevocably linked with his polemic against totalitarianism, particularly Stalinism, which dominated his art so considerably from 1945 onward.

Les Justes is crucial to this whole debate in so far as it is a conscious effort at creating tragedy along classic lines and is at the same time set in the home of dialectical materialism during the time of transition. In order to understand the exact nature of the tragic dilemma which Camus wished to portray in *Les Justes,* it is necessary to examine in some detail the sources and genesis of the play. We shall then be in a position to come to certain conclusions about the well-known difficulty of reconciling history, tragedy, and political commitment in general, and Camus's attempt to do so in particular.

One of the first references to *Les Justes* occurs in the second volume of Camus's *Carnets,* in an entry for the middle of June, 1947, where the working title ''Kaliayev'' is used. At this time Camus was preparing the subsection of *L'Homme révolté* entitled ''Le Terrorisme individuel,'' and came across the historical figure of Kaliayev in Boris Savinkov's *Souvenirs d'un terroriste.* Camus saw in Kaliayev just what he needed for *L'Homme révolté:* a rebel with integrity, a man who, unlike the far better-known historical figures of Bakunin and Nechayev, refused to extend revolutionary action beyond certain limits, and who found a unique solution to the difficult ethical problem of tyrannicide. . . . The characters of Dora and Kaliayev (''Yanek'') are clearly conceived from the outset, and a long sketch for their love scene in Act 3 is in fact the first working note for the play. This is important. Kaliayev is to be championed in *L'Homme révolté* as the ideal rebel, who must possess normal human emotions as a safeguard against the dehumanizing logic of Hegelian historicism. He must form a complete contrast with the terrifying robot visualized by Nechayev and Bakunin in the revolutionary catechism. . . . Camus was repelled by the inhuman extremism which characterized many of the anarcho-nihilists and bolshevists who, as he was to assert in *L'Homme révolté,* were the ancestors of the Stalinist tradition. Alternating with such entries are jottings for the play (as yet untitled) which show how Camus sought to emphasize the gulf between the ideal and the real terrorists of the day, and the consequent ''déchirement'' which this caused for Kaliayev and Dora. . . . (pp. 80-2)

From the fall of 1947 onward, Camus worked concurrently on *Les Justes* and *L'Homme révolté,* merging them completely in an article entitled ''Les Meurtriers délicats,'' in which he extolled the historical terrorists who were in the process of becoming the protagonists of his play. In 1903 the Revolutionary Socialist Party formed a terrorist group known as the Organisation de Combat under the leadership of Azef and then of Savinkov. There followed a wave of assassinations constituting the second reign of terror, some twenty years after the first, which had resulted in the death of Alexander II in 1881. . . . Of royal personages the Grand Duke Sergei, uncle of Nicholas II, was the only victim; he was blown up by a bomb thrown by Kaliayev in February, 1905, in exactly the same circumstances as those that make up the plot of *Les Justes.* At the very beginning of the article, Camus stresses the moral scrupulousness of the assassins. . . . (p. 83)

[On] his first attempt, Kaliayev checked himself as he was about to throw the bomb when he saw that the Grand Duke was accompanied by his wife, nephew, and niece. Historically, Kaliayev's action was approved by the whole group, even though it placed them at great peril. . . . This was consistent with their conduct generally. . . . Savinkov vetoed a bomb attack on Admiral Dubasov in a train because it might endanger innocent passengers. At another time, when escaping from prison, he agreed with his comrade that if necessary they would fire at the officers of the guard, but shoot themselves rather than fire at ordinary guardsmen. The essential attraction of these terrorists for Camus, therefore, was that they had a strict sense of a *limit* beyond which they would not extend violence.

Once this is known, it is possible to appreciate the importance of an original feature of *Les Justes* relative to the source material. Stepan Fedorov has no prototype in the *Souvenirs* and is quite foreign to the spirit of ''Les Meurtriers délicats.'' . . . Whereas Kaliayev, Dora, Annenkov, and Voinov were modeled with varying degrees of accuracy on historical figures (Dora being Dora Brilliant and Voinov being Voinarovsky), Stepan was not—at least as far as the Organisation de Combat was concerned. Significantly, although Kaliayev, Dora, and Annenkov were referred to in Camus's first notes by their Christian names, Stepan was known only by the descriptive names "le Tueur" and "le réaliste." He is thus a representative figure, standing for the ruthless "jacobin" spirit of the extremist revolutionary according to tradition. (pp. 83-4)

Camus was perfectly aware that he was fitting an a priori philosophical dialectic to a historical situation, and went so far as to assert: [the fact that the plot is basically authentic does not mean *Les Justes* is a historical play].... He had done exactly the same thing with *Caligula*. The difference between the two plays—and in my opinion one of the reasons for the superiority of *Caligula*—is that *Les Justes* (like *L'Etat de siège* of the same period) is openly didactic, whereas *Caligula* is not.... This didacticism, this moral and philosophical commitment, has prevented Camus from interpreting the assassination of the Grand Duke Sergei with a degree of perspective sufficient to create an artistically coherent "modern tragedy." For despite Camus's attempt to prove that *Le Justes* is not a historical play—thereby claiming for it the universality which tragedy must have—and despite also the undoubted impression it gives of being a preconceived debate fitted to a convenient historical event (rather in the manner of Anouilh's *Becket*, for example), the fact remains that *Les Justes* is nevertheless modeled on historical circumstances with a fidelity that is against all the traditions of French tragedy. It is true that Camus has created Stepan to reinforce the absolutist-relativist antithesis, and in this respect Stepan serves the same function as Cherea in *Caligula* (although as the opposite term of the antithesis). It is true also that Camus has generalized and conceptualized the crucial issue of redemptive suicide. But, apart from this, Camus adheres as accurately as possible to the known facts of the assassination, particularly in the central debate over Kaliayev's refusal to kill the children. This fidelity to the facts vitiates the whole aspiration of the play to the status of tragedy.

A play that is based on the premise that there is a limit beyond which human action must not pass can be tragic only to the extent that it portrays a protagonist who, perhaps through some form of hubris (but not essentially), loses sufficient control of himself to move from *mesure* to *démesure*. In *Les Justes* there is some confusion as to what constitutes the limit separating the two concepts. That is to say, in the terms of Camus's political philosophy, what is the point at which justifiable and reasonably ethical revolutionary activity becomes unjustifiable brutal terrorism, aiming at quick results, ostensibly because of concern for the oppressed, but in truth, according to Camus, motivated by hatred of the oppressor and little more? Is it murder, or is it only certain kinds of murder? In *Les Justes* there are two limits. The first, which is intensely personal to the author, is the total sanctity of life. Camus's early note for the play suggests that *all* murder constitutes a limit.... To all intents and purposes the assassins have already gone beyond this limit at the outset of the play by having firmly resolved to assassinate the Grand Duke. It is clear from the importance which Camus attached to the idea of redemptive suicide that the tragic action in the play is the assassination itself, which is only the consummation of the movement of tragic involvement which began for Kaliayev, Dora, and the others the day they compromised the purity of their ideals by finally resorting to terrorism.... As is shown most acutely in Kaliayev and Dora, they are living in a hell on earth, that irrevocable state of damnation which was for Dostoevsky "the suffering of being unable to love." In the theater, however, the play, as tragedy at this level, is compromised for those who do not grasp Camus's premise—that the characters, having arrogated to themselves the power of life and death in any circumstances whatsoever, have already fallen into a metaphysical limbo. The

point is all the more easily lost in the theater for any spectator who is not a total pacifist, since the assassination of a supposed tyrant does not *automatically* inspire revulsion and metaphysical anguish.

The real limit in the play at the obvious dramatic level is an extension and refinement of the first—the killing of children. Camus has now moved from the absolute position of a Tarrou (all execution is wrong) to a relative position (some executions are wrong) which turns *Les Justes* into an ostensibly more accessible political play about the ends versus the means.... Once one accepts that this is the real limit in the play between *mesure* and *démesure*, the play loses its tragic appeal. Having to assassinate a man who, if not outrageously tyrannical himself, is a leading representative of an inhuman and despotic system, *and succeeding in doing it without exceeding a crucial ethical limit* (the distinction between a culpable adult and an innocent child) makes Kaliayev not a tragic figure in any dramatic sense, but rather the exemplary hero of a didactic melodrama exactly as defined by Camus.... Not only exemplary, but lucky, since Fate sees to it, just as in the historic circumstances, that he is not faced a second time with the dilemma of deciding whether or not to kill the children. One feels that Anouilh or Sartre, each for different reasons, would not have allowed Kaliayev to escape so lightly.

Out of respect for the essential facts of the historical incident, Camus has not weighted circumstances heavily enough against Kaliayev for his ideals—his sense of limits—to be strained to breaking point. Kaliayev is allowed to be what Camus obviously believed him to be in real life: the ideal rebel, the perfect anti-Stalinist before the letter. He is too humble, too scrupulous, too flawless to be tragic in the accepted dramatic sense. (pp. 86-9)

Stepan is in fact the crux of Camus's dilemma in *Les Justes*, a dilemma that originated in Camus's attempt to do three things at once: (1) create a modern tragedy in accordance with a number of basic aesthetic principles; (2) make a statement about a twentieth-century disease of the political mind; and (3) remain reasonably faithful to the historic circumstances of 1905 (although Camus stressed that he was not writing a historical play, evidently he was not prepared to alter the details sufficiently to make Kaliayev a tragic hero in a truly classic and dramatic sense). The fundamental weakness of *Les Justes* as an attempt at modern tragedy is that there are two structural antagonisms, both potentially tragic but, as handled by Camus, pulling against each other and dissipating the tension. First, there is the play about 1905: Kaliayev and friends versus the established forces of czarist Russia. In Hebbel's terms, an individual representing a new order challenges the old order: he is crushed, but not without making his mark. Nine playwrights out of ten, basing an attempt at modern tragedy on the assassination of the Grand Duke Sergei in 1905, would have structured their play on this conflict. Camus, however, is the one playwright in ten who, anachronistically, saw this historic event as the occasion for a statement about Stalinism and political expediency in general. He thus created a rival antagonism: Kaliayev the idealist, the creator, the poet versus Stepan the realist, the destroyer, the killer.

But this back-dated vision of Stalinism is not the order of the day; it is not the force that crushes Kaliayev. In strict dramatic terms it is an intrusion, a propaganda digression revealing the extent to which Camus's political obsessions of 1946-1948 impaired his artistic judgment.... Our conclusion then must be that the pretensions of *Les Justes* to modern tragedy are vitiated by the fact that the play contains two parallel, antithetical structures which overlap but never coincide: Kaliayev versus czarism, and Kaliayev versus ur-Stanlinism. The first is tragic but not dramatic; the second, dramatic but not tragic. The two could have coincided only if Camus had had sufficient courage to discard the strict historic framework of the assassination. (pp. 89-90)

As it is, *Les Justes* is ''tragic'' only in a loose, philosophical sense (in so far as the assassination of the Grand Duke, like all execution, however well reasoned, is physically and spiritually degrading); but in strict dramatic terms *Les Justes* is scarcely more tragic than the *Oresteia* would have been if Orestes had drawn the line after exacting his just vengeance on Aegisthus and decided to spare Clytemnestra. For Aeschylus, it was evil to kill one's mother, but in certain circumstances—such as at the command of Apollo—it was inevitable, and tragic. For Camus, it is evil to kill children. And so children are not killed. Camus would not have their blood on Kaliayev's hands any more than Nahum Tate in the eighteenth century would have Lear's aberration culminate in the death of Cordelia. Thus for three acts Camus points his play in the right direction for a genuinely dramatic and tragic consummation, builds up to a potentially tragic climax—and then commits what can best be compared to coitus interruptus. The last two acts are an anticlimax in every way. At the end of the play Kaliayev inspires in us a warm glow, which may have much to do with moral approbation, but which has none of that combination of pity, terror, and aesthetic pleasure which is the quintessence of tragic emotion.

It is tempting to talk of a failure of the imagination on Camus's part, but it is in fact all too easy to misunderstand his purpose in *Les Justes*. If he did not contemplate making any radical alteration to the facts of the 1905 assassination, it was because the plot he dug out of Savinkov was already richly suggestive for his all-important antitotalitarian polemics of the years immediately following 1945— and that was enough for him. Ironically, it is conceivable that if Camus had backed up his claim that he was not writing a historical play with greater conviction, and had brought Kaliayev, under pressure, to commit the atrocity I have proposed (which would have made it a much more Sartrean sort of play), he might, by implication, have made his point about Stalinism with greater effect, and at the same time achieved that synthesis of drama, tragedy, and ethics which eluded him throughout his life. (p. 91)

> *E. Freeman, ''Camus's 'Les Justes': Modern Tragedy or Old-Fashioned Melodrama?'' in* Modern Language Quarterly, *Vol. 31, No. 1, March, 1970, pp. 78-91.*

E. FREEMAN

It was shortly after seeing a performance of *Les Possédés* during its provincial tour that Camus was killed. Those close to him believe that at this time he was just emerging from his long and difficult period of sterility and reappraisal—he is known to have been working hard on a novel, *Le Premier Homme,* for example. As far as the theatre is concerned, he confided to Germaine Brée in 1959 that he was toying with the idea of a play linking Don Juan-Sganarelle and Faust-Mephistopheles which he regarded as 'two aspects of the same dichotomy'. But it seems certain that no fragment of this or any other late work for the theatre by Camus exists. . . . Whether, once the Algerian War was over, and with his own theatre to work in

amid the very different theatrical atmosphere of the 1960s, Camus would have gone on to produce a quantity of work of any significance makes interesting speculation, but is in the last resort doubtful. And so what finally is to be our assessment of the Camus whose last completely original work for the theatre was performed in 1949? Few critics, and even fewer theatre people, now believe that Camus's plays will enjoy the viability which seems assured for the work of dramatists such as Shaw, O'Casey, Pirandello, Brecht and Anouilh, although this stature appeared within Camus's grasp after the success of *Les Justes.* Two questions must be asked: to what extent has Camus succeeded in creating the modern tragedy with which he was obsessed throughout his career, and how successful is his work as *theatre,* independently of whether it constitutes a convincing form of modern tragedy?

In answer to the first question, it seems to me that Camus does not make a really effective dramatic exploitation of the advantages which his political and philosophical theories would appear to give him. . . . A predilection for the tragic theme of a conflict between a powerful individual (e.g. Antigone) and an invincible order, or representative of order (e.g. Creon), and a passionate concern for the importance of not transcending limits, more or less equating to the classical horror of *hubris*—overweening pride or *démesure*—these would appear to leave Camus just as richly endowed in dramatic theory as Corneille and Racine. And so they do. But Camus's practice is not really a logical extension in dramatic terms of his theory. His theatre has the absurd as its premise, and this fact has far greater dramatic significance than the actions which result from it on the stage. Even if one agrees with Guicharnaud that Camus's plays, like those of Sartre, are 'crammed with action or the expectation of action', the fact remains that his tragedy is one of situation. It is metaphysical not psychological, and as John Cruickshank has observed, does not present 'flawed' heroes in the Elizabethan sense. Camus was convinced—strangely so in an experienced man of the theatre who revered Sophocles and Shakespeare—that metaphysics and psychology were incompatible in tragedy; and for him psychology in fact was anathema in any guise in any sort of play.

Unfortunately this conception of metaphysical tragedy has resulted in an excessively abstract form of expression. One of the best examples of this is Camus's handling of the mask, a favourite theatrical device of French dramatists since the Renaissance. . . . The mask, the instrument of inscrutability, the totally impenetrable screen around the personality, and cause of doubt, misunderstanding and murder, is the perfect metaphor of the absurd. In *Le Malentendu,* the blackest of his plays, Camus implies that this is the natural order of the world. (pp. 148-50)

[A] vision of a world in which 'no one is ever recognized' dominates all four plays. It should be noted that in each one Camus makes a very sparing literal use of the mask—some form of disguise or game of pretence. Caligula disguises himself as Venus; Kaliayev (off stage) as a street-hawker; Jan assumes the name of Karl Hasek; and Diego wears 'le masque des médecins de la peste'. There is, however, a considerable disparity between the brief and functional uses of the mask at a literal level and its application at the metaphorical level to stress the impossibility of communication, understanding and love between human beings. It is not just in *Le Malentendu* that Camus presents a despairing picture of a world in which the normal persona of human beings is the mask of tragedy. Once the mask is in place, it stays on. Only once does Camus manage effectively to exteriorize the transformation which has befallen the wearer, and that is in the powerful Act I curtain to *Caligula.* (p. 151)

An awareness of Camus's idea of how the fact of the absurd can affect the human personality is . . . essential for an understanding of the structure of his plays. Every main character from the first, Pèpe, to the last, Stavroguine, has become literally and metaphorically *figé*, fixed, blocked in time. In this respect—and coincidentally and not at all as a result of any 'influence'—Camus is perhaps more fundamentally Pirandellian than the scores of French dramatists who have made such ostentatious use of the Italian's more superficial plotting and characterization techniques since 1923. The trouble is that he hardly ever succeeds in rendering the mask/absurd metaphor concrete on the stage. The skill with which Anouilh, Giraudoux and Sartre manipulate *personae* is lacking in Camus, if not actually repugnant to him. One feels that Camus's commitment to his thesis—that alienation imposes masks of deception and insensitivity upon the real self—was too sincere. He was not dispassionate enough to use this classic device in a way which might legitimately please and intrigue in the theatre. Criticism after criticism of Camus's theatre offers the opinion that it is 'too intellectual', too obviously the work of a desiccated manipulator of ideas. On the contrary, the converse might just as easily be argued. Camus is indeed an intellectual dramatist in the sense that he believed the theatre ought to be a serious and non-commercial affair, a medium for important statements about the human condition, but hardly an intellectual in the matter of form. He does not possess the ability to stand back from his theme and present it objectively by means of illusion, perspective, juxtaposition of details in the classic manner of French dramatists since the seventeenth century. It is significant that two of Camus's plays which are considered to be among the most successful, *Requiem pour une nonne* and *Les Possédés,* are adaptations which retain most of the 'popular' elements of the original novels: physical violence, mystery, dramatic irony, flashbacks. Camus could not avoid the action which is a key feature of the scenarios provided by Faulkner and Dostoevsky, although he did, as we have seen, create a very different atmosphere in each case. I doubt whether, if he had lived to begin a new cycle of plays in the 1960s. Camus would have learned the lesson of these successes, namely that his ideal modern tragedy need not be static, totally verbal and interior. For Camus's abhorrence of technical virtuosity, psychological theatre and the well-made play stem from an intellectual disdain on his part which made him equate popular and 'theatrical' elements with inferior theatre. (pp. 153-54)

[Camus defined *Caligula*] as a 'tragedy of the intelligence' but made repeated attempts in the successive versions to make the play more human by modifying and developing the characters of Hélicon and Scipion for example, and making the character of Caligula more sympathetic. And yet, as Albert Sonnenfeld has argued in a detailed discussion of Camus's 'failure' as a dramatist [see above], it is very difficult for the audience to estabish contact on any sort of human level with the hero. The problem is . . . that of communicating to an audience the real experience of the absurd, one of the effects of which is the impossibility of communicating anything to anyone. The task is feasible *à la rigueur* in the novel or cinema, but not in the theatre, as Martin Esslin has argued, unless the dramatist adopts a radically 'anti-cartesian' approach to dialogue, characterization and dramatic structure. Although . . . Camus appeared to be on the verge of a breakthrough with the character of 'le Vieux', the problem is one which he did not make any con-

sistent attempt to solve. The highly experimental (and brilliantly successful) prose style of *L'Étranger* has no counterpart in the plays. Split asunder by this gulf between form and theme, Camus's theatre constitutes one of the greatest paradoxes of the transitional decade 1940-50. (pp. 155-56)

The time has now come to make a résumé of the main aspects of Camus's dramatic style, making allowance for the difficulty of synthesizing the work of such a highly personal artist who never repeated the exact theme and form of any work, either in the theatre or in any other medium.

Taking theme first, all of Camus's original plays and most of those he adapted or translated are based in some measure on the premiss that our human condition is absurd. Violence and repression are common features. The inevitability of death is a source of unparalleled anguish (*Caligula*), as is the arrogation of the power of life and death over other people (*Les Justes, Requiem pour une nonne*). Even when enjoying social and material success, man is haunted by an eternal quest for some physical or metaphysical goal, the exact nature of which is not always clear to him (*Le Malentendu*). Chance frequently takes what seems to be almost a malevolent course, thwarting all attempts to achieve happiness (*Le Malentendu*) or arbitrarily destroying that which already exists (*Caligula*). The protagonists are generally alienated from their physical background and from those human beings one would expect to be closest to them (*Le Malentendu, Un Cas intéressant*). The fact of the absurd can strike not merely individuals but whole sections of society. Civilized society is then split asunder in a conflict characterized by cowardice and treachery, and nihilistic collaboration with the absurd (*L'État de siège, Révolte dans les Asturies, Les Possédés*).

All of Camus's plays are based on conflict. The manifestations of the absurd constitute one of the terms—the general condition or existing order, against which the heroes of Camus's plays react, or rebel. The heroes, the antithetical term, are animated by a sense of 'revolt'. In *Le Mythe de Sisyphe* revolt designated a state of spiritual tension based on a lucid scrutiny of the absurd, and culminated in a curious form of stoic happiness. But in the theatre Camus handles revolt in a much more moralistic manner. Revolt must be creative and relative, not destructive and absolute (revolution). It must be based on a recognition of values, a 'qualitative' ethic, that is to say a scale of ethical priorities involving the totality of mankind. The rebel may not therefore combat the absurd with all the means at his disposal, and must be prepared for the anguish of making value-judgments about other people, whose claims to life are no less great than his own. At all times the rebel must be aware of a *limit*, beyond which he must not pass, on pain of redeeming transgression with his own life. And yet the absurd presents a terrifying paradox. It is in itself a total experience: life is never the same again. People of intelligence and sensitivity are tempted to make a total reaction, since the 'logic' of the absurd in the mind of whoever fully experiences it requires that the whole basis of society be transformed and an awareness of the absurd be universalized. (pp. 156-57)

The form that Camus's plays take is conditioned by these linked themes of the absurd and revolt. At its most profound level of interpretation Camus's theatre is metaphysical tragedy in which a basically noble and sensitive individual is pitted against an invincible and inscrutable order. It is characterized by a state of tension which is frequently independent of what happens during the course of the play. As a representation of human action on the other hand, Camus's theatre is strictly speaking not tragedy in any recognized formal sense so much as melodrama according to his own definition: a simplistic presentation of right and wrong. This explains the heroic and Romantic aura of much of his characterization. Theme dominates form: what the play is saying is more important than the way in which it says it. Camus has no time for theatrical games. He has something to say and he gets on with it. His characteristic plot is therfore linear, situated on the brink of a crisis, and is developed in a straightforward and chronological manner. (p. 157)

In characterization, too, Camus shows the same tendency to stress general rather than particular features. This explains the inescapable impression of rigidity that many of Camus's characters make. Rather than individuals they represent types of social and philosophical positions: revolt (Diego, Pépe, Kaliayev), 'revolution' (Stepan, Caligula, Martha), cynical nihilism (Nada, Skouratov, Hélicon), proletarian indifference (Foka), vile bourgeoisie (the judge, the grocer, the chemist), the eternal feminine (Dora, Maria, Caesonia, Victoria, Pilar), the young idealist making his first contact with reality (Scipion, Voinov), the mature relativist (Cherea, Annenkov) . . . the list could continue until every character in Camus's theatre is categorized.

Camus's dialogue is consistent with this philosophical conception of character and setting. He regarded language as the main problem in modern tragedy, and sought to create a stylized, neutral idiom which would nevertheless be recognizable as the language of the twentieth century and yet at the same time sufficiently 'distanced' and elevated to create what he considered to be the proper aura of tragedy. With the exception of his immature apprentice-piece, *Révolte dans les Asturies,* his dialogue is polished, correct, even literary. In his search for modern tragedy Camus had no time for naturalism, and, much though he was affected by Hemingway and Faulkner in the novel, one feels he would have wished to derive nothing at all from their fellow American Arthur Miller in the theatre. (pp. 158-59)

Camus thus tried to harmonize all the elements of form to accord with his metaphysical and somewhat abstract themes. The universal and symbolic implications of his plays are stressed at the expense of the historical and concrete. With their elevated and unified tone, purity of language, minimization of physical detail, and concentration upon theme to the exclusion of superfluous humour, anecdote and scenic ingenuity, Camus's plays are thus much more authentically classical in form than those of his contemporaries. And yet there is always something lacking too. That vital spark of human warmth, of truly theatrical tension when a dramatist who is the complete master of his effects grips his audience exactly as he wishes through his characters, glows sporadically in *Le Malentendu* and *Les Justes* and perhaps comes near to being sustained only in *Caligula.* Despite the fact that, given the right production in the right place, these three plays can and occasionally do work well (and even *L'État de siège* appears to have had its moments in German translation), it remains true that in the last resort Camus's theatre reads far better than it acts. Thus by the standards the author set himself it is unsatisfactory, not to say a failure. (p. 160)

Incommunicable metaphysics, disparity of form and theme, faulty theatrical judgement, philosophical complexity and abstraction, cloying didacticism and failure to develop a sufficiently personal and artistically appropriate language to bear the weight of the play: these are the principal criticisms of Camus's theatre. Yet it would be quite wrong to regard it as a total failure. (p.163)

The real merit of Camus's theatre lies in the sphere of theme rather than form, in so far as it is possible to separate the success of one from the failure of the other. Camus's theatre constitutes the most sincere attempt in its genre to create philosophical theatre mirroring the metaphysical anguish of our age. At the same time it combats the nihilism to which such speculation can lead, and in this respect the author follows clearly in the tradition of the great French moralists. Camus's theatre is unequalled for the probity and passion with which it defended human values during a decade in France when they had never been more fragile. (p. 164)

E. Freeman, in his The Theatre of Albert Camus: A Critical Study, *Methuen & Co. Ltd., 1971, 178 p.*

Philip Caputo

1941-

American novelist, journalist, and nonfiction writer.

Caputo has achieved success with works that draw upon his experiences in Vietnam. Caputo was among the first American soldiers to arrive in Vietnam in 1965; the sixteen months he spent in combat there provided the material for his critically acclaimed first work, *A Rumor of War* (1977). Upon his discharge from the Marine Corps in the late 1960s, he became a journalist and, as a reporter for the *Chicago Tribune*, returned to cover the fall of Saigon ten years after he first arrived in Vietnam. The dual perspective of a soldier and a foreign correspondent enabled Caputo to write with an insight uncommon among chroniclers of the Vietnam War.

Hailed for its candid depiction of the excitement as well as the horror of combat experience, *A Rumor of War* received overwhelmingly positive reviews. One critic claimed Caputo's memoir is "unquestionably the very best work to appear on the Vietnam War," and William Styron noted that "some of Caputo's troubled, searching meditations on the love and hate of war, on fear, and the ambivalent discord that warfare can create in the hearts of decent men, are among the most eloquent I have read in modern literature."

Caputo's second work, a novel entitled *Horn of Africa* (1981), shares with *A Rumor of War* the exploration of violence in human nature. His next novel, *DelCorso's Gallery* (1983), is set in Vietnam and Lebanon and incorporates Caputo's journalistic experiences in these countries. Although his novels have been less enthusiastically received than *A Rumor of War*, Caputo's work is widely praised for its vivid and insightful descriptions of human violence and its compelling, persuasive narratives.

(See also *Contemporary Authors*, Vols. 73-76.)

© Thomas Victor 1984

THEODORE SOLOTAROFF

["**A Rumor of War**," Caputo's personal account of the Vietnam War, is] the true story of the transformation of one of "the knights of Camelot," whose "crusade" was Vietnam and whose cause could only be "noble and good" into a vindictive, desperate and chronically schizoid killer in a war he had come to realize was futile and evil. As Emerson put it, "the lengthened shadow of a man is history": Caputo would no doubt agree, for the course and character and damage of America's involvement was registered on his altered body, mind, nerves and spirit.

The causes and stages of his transformation form the spine of his narrative. It begins with Caputo's account of his summers at Quantico, where officer's training differed little from the fabled sadism of Marine boot camp. (p. 9)

With each month he appears to have more fury to burn, more moral numbness to account for in needlessly destroyed villages and hamlets. He wrestles with the mockeries of the "rules" of engagement. . . . He concludes that military ethics seemed to be a matter of killing people at long range with sophisticated weapons. But the actuality was the official American strategy of "organized butchery." In his final month of duty, the commander of his half-decimated company is offering a can of beer "and the time to drink it" for any enemy casualty.

Caputo's book is not as relentless as I am making it seem. It is not meant to be one long damning indictment, or an endless chronicle of demoralization and brutalization. There are the repeated accounts of the tender, unshakable loyalty and concern of men bonding together not just for survival but to preserve their humanity. There is their gentle behavior as well as brutal: Two grunts rubbing salve on a baby's jungle sores while their officer threatens to pistol-whip the uncooperative mother. There are the close, brilliant accounts of the exhilaration and tension of combat: the heightening of the senses and mind to a pitch of acuity. There is the almost "orgasmic" pleasure of leadership when Caputo's company responds perfectly under the stress of battle. There is the transcendent moment when Caputo's virus of fear disappears. . . .

Indifferent to his own death, he is still ravaged by anxieties and deleriums of violence about his steadily dwindling company. When a village boy reports that he knows of two Vietcong in an adjacent hut, and when nothing is done about it, Caputo frantically decides to snatch them. He sends in a team of his most reliable sharpshooters: "If they give you any problems, kill 'em." As he then admits, "In my heart I hoped Allen

102

would find some excuse for killing them and Allen had read my heart.'' When the two bodies are duly brought in, one of them is the boy who gave the information.

What was Caputo's degree of guilt? By the time one reaches this culminating incident, we believe him when he says, ''Something evil had been in me that night.'' One also believes him when he says, ''The war in general and U.S. military policy in particular were ultimately to blame for the death of Le Du and Le Dung.'' One wants to see Caputo exonerated, as he was. For the ultimate effect of this book is to make the personal and the public responsibility merge into a nightmare of horror and waste experienced humanly by the Caputos and inhumanly by the politicians and generals. Out of the force of his obsession with the war and his role in it, Caputo has revealed the broken idealism and suppressed agony of America's involvement. **''A Rumor of War''** is the troubled conscience of America speaking passionately, truthfully, finally. (p. 21)

Theodore Solotaroff, ''Memoirs for Memorial Day,'' in The New York Times Book Review, *May 29, 1977, pp. 9, 21.*

WILLIAM STYRON

One of the indispensable features of Caputo's narrative [*A Rumor of War*] is that he is never less than honest, sometimes relentlessly so, about his feelings concerning the thrill of warfare and the intoxication of combat. At least in the beginning, before the madness. After sixteen months of bloody skirmishes and the ravages of disease and a hostile environment, after the psychological and emotional attrition, Caputo—who had begun ''this splendid little war'' in the jaunty high spirits of Prince Hal, was very close to emotional and physical collapse, a ''moral casualty,'' convinced—and in 1966!—that the war was unwinnable and a disgrace to the flag under which he had fought to such a pitch of exhaustion.

There is a persuasive legitimacy in this hatred of a war when it is evoked by a man who has suffered its most horrible debauchments. But perhaps that is why we are equally persuaded by Caputo's insistence on a recognition that for many men, himself included, war and the confrontation with death can produce an emotion—a commingled exultation and anguish—that verges on rapture. It is like a mighty drug, certainly it approaches the transcendental. After becoming a civilian, Caputo was engaged for a long time in the antiwar movement. But, he says, ''I would never be able to hate the war with anything like the undiluted passion of my friends in the movement.'' These friends, he implies, could never understand how for him the war ''had been an experience as fascinating as it was repulsive, as exhilarating as it was sad, as tender as it was cruel.'' Some of Caputo's troubled, searching meditations on the love and hate of war, on fear, and the ambivalent discord that warfare can create in the hearts of decent men, are among the most eloquent I have read in modern literature. (p. 3)

What Philip Caputo demonstrates . . . in his ruthless testament is how the war in Vietnam defiled even its most harmless and well-meaning participants. His is the chronicle of men fighting with great bravery but forever losing ground in a kind of perplexed, insidious lassitude—learning too late that they were suffocating in a moral swamp. (p. 4)

Caputo writes brilliantly about . . . [the] early days around Danang, that period of eager expectation before the horrors descended and the war began to taste like something incessantly

loathsome on his tongue. Even then, in that time of cautious waiting—a stationary war of skirmishes and patrols and skittish engagements with the Viet Cong—it was not pleasant duty, but after all this is what Caputo had bought and bargained for: the unspeakable heat and the mosquitoes, the incessant clouds of dust, the boredom, the chickenshit from upper echelons (often described with ferocious humor, in the spirit of *Catch 22*), the dreary nights on liberty in the ramshackle town, the impenetrably lush and sinister mountain range hovering over the flyblown domestic landscape, already smeared with American junk. . . .

Boredom, inanition, a sitting war; drunken brawls in Danang, whores, more chickenshit, the seething lust for action. All this Caputo embroiders in fine detail—and then the action came in a powerful burst for Caputo and his comrades. Suddenly there were pitched engagements with the enemy. There were the first extended movements into enemy territory, the first helicopter assaults, the first real engagements under heavy fire, and, inevitably, the first shocking deaths. War became a reality for Caputo; it was no longer a film fantasy called *The Halls of Montezuma*, and there is great yet subtle power in Caputo's description of how—in this new kind of conflict, against a spectral enemy on a bizarre and jumbled terrain (so different from such textbook campaigns as Saipan or even Korea)—the underpinnings of his morale began to crumble, doubt bloomed, and the first cynical mistrust was implanted in his brain. These misgivings—which later became revulsion and disillusionment—did not arrive as the result of a single event but as an amalgam of various happenings, each one repellent, which Caputo (as well as the reader) begins to perceive as being embedded in the matrix of the war and its specifically evil nature. . . .

In this book Philip Caputo writes so beautifully and honestly about both fear and courage, writes with such knowing certitude about death and men's confrontation with the abyss, that we cannot doubt for an instant that he is a brave man who fought well long after that ''splendid little war'' became an obscene nightmare in which he nearly drowned. But he was dragged downward, and indeed the most agonizing part of his chronicle is found not in the descriptions of carnage and battle—as harrowingly re-created as they are—but in his own savage denouement when, driven into a raging madness by the senseless devastation he has witnessed and participated in, he turns into a monster and commits that mythic Vietnam-stained crime: he allows the murder of civilians. Although he was ultimately exonerated, his deed became plainly a wound forever engrafted on his soul. It seems the inevitable climax to this powerful story of a decent man sunk into a dirty time, in a far place where he was never intended to be, in an evil war. (p. 6)

William Styron, "A Farewell to Arms," in The New York Review of Books, *Vol. XXIV, No. 11, June 23, 1977, pp. 3-4, 6.*

D. KEITH MANO

What can be said? This is the hardest review I have ever had to write. Okay: there are three options. I can hang it up now, at sentence four. Or I can tell you that *A Rumor of War* is the most daunting and significant personal account yet generated by our great dishonor, Vietnam—which *Rumor* is: full stop: no qualifications—and end my assessment, my responsibility, there. Yes, but would that be enough? Would you read it? Oh, I'd like to have authority over your life. For just this moment.

To hit you across the mouth, take your first-born child, invalidate your credit cards, whatever, if you don't read *A Rumor of War*. Now. I am that sick with passion for this book.

Or, option three, I can tell you what happened to Marine Lieutenant Philip J. Caputo in Vietnam. My review might then astonish you—but never as the book would astonish. Because its force depends on a slow acceptance: an acceptance, by you, of Lieutenant Caputo—half fearful soldier, half courageous soldier; half cynical, half enthusiastic—and, after three hundred pages, you will accept. (p. 1001)

Caputo hasn't written a leftist harangue (though I could easily have forgiven him for that). Indeed *Rumor* is more or less apolitical. It transcends the hawk-dove face-off. It's about young men under unreasonable stress: more persuasive for that. Caputo qualifies: the credentials are impeccable.

Take his brilliant analysis of heroism: "Yet he [any soldier] is also attracted by the danger, for he knows that he can overcome his fear only by facing it. His blind rage then begins to focus on the men who are the source of the danger—and of his fear. It concentrates inside him, and through some chemistry is transformed into a fierce resolve to fight until the danger ceases to exist. But this resolve, which is sometimes called courage, cannot be separated from the fear that has aroused it. Its very measure is the measure of that fear. It is, in fact, a powerful urge not to be afraid any more...." That, I hazard, can stand as the simplest, most accurate, description of bravery, its curious metabolism, ever written....

No man can write about war unless he is first willing to acknowledge that special exhilaration: the exhilaration of a good kill. And today, for obvious reasons, you don't chance upon many people who are willing to acknowledge it in themselves. Caputo is: and through those last fifty pages—*hypocrite lecteur, mon semblable, mon frère*—he will acknowledge much more than that....

Philip Caputo announces the finish, the unplanned obsolescence, of our conventional military force. There is no other possible conclusion. Army, Navy, Marines: they might as well be retrained as doormen or elevator operators or museum guards. America will never fight another counterinsurgency war. In fact, I doubt whether we will ever undertake any kind of conventional war again. At present we're fortunate if we can defend Bayside, Queens, let alone Mexico City or Taiwan or even Tel Aviv. You see, war is murder now. It's not the terrain you choose to defend, it's the terminology. And they, our opposition, have chosen the words: murder, not war. Man *v.* man, ambush *v.* ambush, Marine *v.* so-called "civilian." War is personal: it guest-appears on TV: Vietnam QED'd that. And we cannot accept the term "murderer." Unless we are willing to murder—are you, baby?—let us agree to disband, let's beat our swords into IBM shares. *A Rumor of War* convinced me of that. It will convince you. (p. 1002)

> D. Keith Mano, "Best of Season," in *National Review*, Vol. XXIX, No. 34, September 2, 1977, pp. 1001-02.

THE VIRGINIA QUARTERLY REVIEW

It is difficult to know where to begin an analysis of [*A Rumor of War*, a] first-rate memoir of a Marine lieutenant's experience with war. It is unquestionably the very best work to appear on the Vietnam war and one of the finest pieces of American writing on war from the ground in this century. The fascination

of Caputo's account is not that his experiences were typical or his reactions to the war commonplace among veterans—both of these interpretations would be only partly true. What Caputo has done is to capture the sounds of men at war as no other American writer has ever done.... If there is any book published last year that ought to be read by everyone, it is this one.

> A review of "A Rumor of War," in The Virginia Quarterly Review, Vol. 54, No. 1 (Winter, 1978), p. 25.

RANDALL KENNEDY

In *Horn of Africa* Philip Caputo endeavors to present a "personal vision of the nature of violence and to show what happens when a certain kind of man is placed in a condition in which he is free to exceed the bounds of acceptable human conduct." Jeremy Nordstrand is this "certain kind of man." An imperious figure with bear-like strength, Nordstrand and two other US intelligence agents undertake a secret mission to Ethiopia. Its purpose is to smuggle arms to a warlike Islamic tribe, the Beni-Hamid, to help them fight the central Ethiopian government. Nordstrand's motivation, however, has nothing to do with the purposes of his superiors. He joins the mission hoping to find a place where he can follow his murderous impulses without restraint. (p. 46)

Through ruthlessness he achieves his goal of moral outlawry. When Moody, the mission's appointed commander, tries to discipline Nordstrand, the tables are turned and Moody is humiliated by physical and psychological torture. On another occasion Nordstrand proves his immunity to compunction by shooting and beheading five prisoners, an act that propels him, in [his accomplice Charlie] Gage's apt description, beyond "the tug of society's moral gravity."

Nordstrand's savagery, along with his knowledge of modern warfare, wins him the worshipful admiration of the Beni-Hamid. After leading them to victories over the Ethiopians, he is inducted into their tribe, a ceremony he relishes as a final shedding of his Western cultural inheritance. But his triumph is short lived. He is blinded by disease and crippled by a leg wound. Without his leadership the Beni-Hamid are routed and the agents forced to flee. In a final, harrowing encounter with the desert, a trek in which survival calls for drinking water out of dead camels' bellies, Moody kills himself and Gage kills Nordstrand. "I took out my pistol and shot him," says Gage. "Twice. Twice in the head."

Horn of Africa is a novel without heroes, a chronicle suffused with bitterness and a sense of doom.... Caputo's tale is a searing attack on American values, an up-to-date elaboration of D. H. Lawrence's famous judgment that "the essential American soul is hard, isolate, stoic and a killer."

Caputo's damning portrayal of Nordstrand and his cohorts is overlaid by an equally dim view of the Beni-Hamid and the other tribes and factions which claim to constitute a liberation movement. Though the rebels fight in the name of self-determination, Caputo pictures them more as bandits than as revolutionaries. (pp. 46-7)

The political sensibility behind Caputo's examination of power and its dangers is essentially anti-political. Evil adheres to every brand of politics encountered in *Horn of Africa*. Indeed the more sincerely someone embraces politics the more evil he becomes....

Horn of Africa is an ambitious work meant to last beyond the vagaries of a single literary season and to say something of permanence about the human condition. Caputo succeeds when he describes the psychological effect of violence upon its perpetrators and victims, a subject of which he proved his mastery in *Rumor of War,* a powerful account of his experiences as a soldier in Vietnam. The scenes of combat and torture that dot *Horn of Africa* bring to a sharp focus his vision of human wickedness and the weaknesses that nourish it. (p. 47)

Caputo runs into trouble, however, when he too obviously strives to make *Horn of Africa* weighty. He puts Nietzsche into his narrative by propping a paperback copy of *Beyond Good and Evil* into Nordstrand's hands and filling his mouth with drivel about supermen. And while Caputo never expressly mentions Conrad, his influence hovers over *Horn of Africa*. It is an obtrusive presence that Caputo encourages. His description of the Nile seems to parody Conrad's description of the Congo. Conrad called his imagined journey to the interior of the Congo *The Heart of Darkness*. Caputo speaks of a section of Vietnam as "the Forest of Darkness." Conrad's Kurtz uttered "The horror! The horror!" as he was about to die. Caputo's Nordstrand screams "I see! I see!" at that same penultimate moment. This evocation of literary ancestors produces unnecessary contrivance. Nordstrand's philosophical rantings are neither articulate nor profound; they are simply a device for explicating ideas and motives that Caputo, with the more subtle tools of dialogue and characterization, had already made clear. Moreover, his image of the Nietzsche-obsessed Vietnam veteran suffers from staleness: Robert Stone used it effectively several years ago in his novel *Dog Soldiers*. The pall of overuse similarly spoils Caputo's manipulation of Conradian motifs. (pp. 47-8)

Finally, there is a problem that Caputo himself identifies in the author's note preceding his novel, where he confesses to committing "literary imperialism" in writing *Horn of Africa.* Referring to himself, he observes: "what arrogance to place a non-existent province on the map of one of Africa's oldest nations, and then populate it with an imaginary black-Arab tribe." Caputo's note distinguishes him as one of the few writers who have had the sensitivity to articulate misgivings about portraying black Africa through the lens of a white Western consciousness. . . .

Caputo is right . . . in calling our attention to the presence of literary imperialism. He is wrong, though, when he suggests that the problem resides in the peculiar hubris of artists, their insistence upon allowing their imaginations to roam freely over alien lands. For the problem lies in something far more common—a cultural chauvinism that afflicts not only artists but also, and perhaps more importantly, their audience. The problem is that white observers for centuries have offered writings about Africa which represent neither factual reportage nor inventive creation, but mere confirmation of settled biases. Caputo, unfortunately and despite his disclaimers, is part of this long tradition. On the one hand he ratifies an iconography of Islam that is both familiar and demeaning. Employing a set of popular images, he reduces a complicated religious culture to a flattened stereotype: the fanatical, incompetent, and treacherous Moslem. On the other hand he posits a judgment on African history which echoes with Western condescension. Disdainful of Africa's past, Hegel wrote over a century ago that it "is no historical part of the world." Commenting on Africa's prospects, V. S. Naipaul recently declared that "Africa has no future." Disturbed by Africa's present, Caputo

conjures up a hateful wind that whispers "No hope. . . . No hope." (p. 48)

Randall Kennedy, in a review of "Horn of Africa," in The New Republic, *Vol. 183, No. 17, October 25, 1980, pp. 46-8.*

D. KEITH MANO

Philip Caputo last wrote *A Rumor of War;* indisputably the most consequential and terrific Vietnam memoir: alone, it almost made our involvement there worthwhile. Still, I don't see why Caputo should be penalized (or rewarded) for former brilliance. Every reviewer from the *NYT* to the *Block Island Bivalve* will compare *Rumor* and *Horn of Africa*. Oh, there are coy parallels; the temptation is like a ripe carbuncle. Yet, for our purposes, *Horn*—novel, not memoir—was written by Phil X.

And Phil X can write well enough. In *Horn* he has glued together a very big protagonist. Fine with me: hell, *Moby Dick* was no take-out from Arthur Treacher's: I prefer a large subject. But Nordstrand, the overreacher, the Hwang-Do expert Mr. Kurtz, the spiker of human morality, is rather like Piltdown Man: myth made from three or four semi-persuasive forged bones. Nordstrand will trog into fictional Bejaya (near Sudan / Ethiopia and, after this book, probably eligible for UN membership) on a rogue CIA mission. His intent, however, is to become Lawrence of Bejaya and, eventually, rule over mucho sand. . . .

Mr. X has the defect of his considerable virtues. *Horn,* though this may sound unlikely, is too intelligent: too structured and accurate: too industrious. X, for instance, has 20-20 hearing where dialogue is involved. Egyptian and Ethiopian, Greek and hash seller blow garlic or *kat* in your ear: camels break most articulate wind. But the three CIA men—Nordstrand, Gage, and Moody—are playing *No Exit* in a boisterous crowd. They seem to be one expressionist person. (p. 1340)

And X is an excellent conservator of detail: nothing has been left uncatalogued. His thing-imagery is quite fine. . . . X is obsessive, though: he will want to explain everything, perhaps because he was once a correspondent (damn, I'm not supposed to know that) and doesn't trust the readership. Consequently, *Horn* is overlong by at least 15 per cent: half the opening section could be cut, and a lot of diary. Fiction can stand silences; fiction actually requires them. But X will tell all: and when description becomes interior his prose is eyeless. . . . Perfunctory writing, better omitted. Sand, a Kalashnikov rifle, Bejayan factions, clothing: they flourish under that sort of reportorial nosiness. But you can't send wire-service copy from inside someone's head.

Don't misread me. *Horn of Africa* is sometimes a compelling book. I mean only that it is more often a compulsive book. I was impressed: but frequently the way a captive seaman might be, by force not by art. Nonetheless, I await Phil Y's next. (pp. 1340-41)

D. Keith Mano, "Starting Over," in National Review, *Vol. XXXII, No. 22, October 31, 1980, pp. 1340-42.*

PETER ANDREWS

Tales of adventure set in Africa, with their prefabricated plots and pasteboard heroes, have become so much the special preserve of hack novelists that the genre has been all but spoiled for serious writers. Philip Caputo's [*Horn of Africa,* a] story of African gun running and clandestine warfare, begins in such a conventional way that it took me a few more pages than it should have to realize that it is the genuine article: a real novel stuffed with excitement and filled with sharply drawn characters, written by a tough, sinewy writer who has something more important on his mind than finding a new tax shelter. . . .

As is to be expected from the author of **"A Rumor of War,"** the finest memoir of men at arms in our generation, the battle scenes are brilliant. Mr. Caputo knows the muddled horror as well as the shameful exhilaration of combat, and he has the skill to put you at the center of it and rub your nose in the stink of it.

More important, he knows how to create characters who fix themselves in your mind. (p. 12)

Except for Gage, whose only cause is to have none, each character constructs an elaborate rationale about why he is there. But the fact is, they all participate in a filthy little war because each of them needs something out of the conflict. Colfax needs a more important job better suited to his talents. Moody needs redemption for past sins. Gage merely needs to know what it is that truly frightens him. Nordstrand needs to do battle on the last empty space left on earth and fulfill his own vision of himself. Gage, who needs the least, survives best.

Dealing with scenes that are at once so banal and so grand is hellishly difficult for any writer. But Mr. Caputo—perhaps because this is his first novel and he may not know how hard a job it is—wades in and brings it off splendidly.

"Horn of Africa" is far from flawless; Mr. Caputo is still finding his way as a novelist. When he backtracks to give us Nordstrand's early history and show us a monster in the making, his powers recede to the merely ordinary, and sometimes less than ordinary. It is mostly a dose of pop psychology about an unhappy childhood illuminated by minor injustices—as if Raskolnikov were the product of a social worker's indifference. Mr. Caputo sometimes rushes in to drive home a point the reader is capable of getting without tutoring; but saying that he has written a book with some extremely rough patches is like complaining that Pete Rose overruns a base now and again. That is the way he plays the game and the source of his particular excellence. Philip Caputo has the talent to become a major American novelist. (p. 46)

> *Peter Andrews, "A Filthy Little War," in* The New York Times Book Review, *November 2, 1980, pp. 12, 46.*

R. Z. SHEPPARD

Philip Caputo (*A Rumor of War, Horn of Africa*) is one of the more successful enhancers of the factual, largely because he writes intensely about his own experiences, which were dramatic and perilous. Caputo, 42, served with the U.S. Marine Corps in Viet Nam during the mid-'60s. He returned ten years later to cover the fall of Saigon for the Chicago *Tribune.* As a journalist, he also rode camels with Eritrean rebels in Ethiopia and was shot in both feet by Muslim militiamen in Beirut.

Substantial parts of *DelCorso's Gallery* are set in Viet Nam and Lebanon; the novel is not only about war but also about the relationship between morals and aesthetics. Nicholas Del-

Corso, the proletarian hero with a limp caused by an old wound, acts as if the good and the beautiful are inseparable. He is an award-winning news photographer who, like a Hemingway bullfighter, prefers to work in close. The moment of truth occurs in the darkroom when the faces of the anguished and the dead resolve beneath the surface of the developing solution.

Unlike P.X. Dunlop, his rival and former mentor, DelCorso does not doctor his work for effects. He believes that to dodge in shadows or turn bright noon into a moody twilight is to romanticize war's brutality. Dunlop, on the other hand, brands his ex-protégé's snapshots sensationalist. Author Caputo clearly sides with DelCorso and with an ethic that combines the redeeming social value of photography with the woozier aspects of Zen: "His intimacy with his camera had to be such that his use of it at the decisive instant was reflex action, an immediate union of the tangible and intangible, of hand and eye, mind and heart."

The novel's central rivalry climaxes in Beirut, though not before DelCorso tussles with guilt, a bruised class conscience and the bitter truth that he would rather chase wars than stay home with his wife and children. From the reader's point of view, this is a good thing. A domesticated DelCorso, brooding about integrity, mortgage payments and marriage, proves to be unbearable. Abroad, he is the subject of an old-fashioned, manly novel, crisply written with plenty of locker-room banter and bang-bang.

> *R. Z. Sheppard, "Snapshots," in* Time, *Vol. 122, No. 13, September 26, 1983, p. K11.*

JOE KLEIN

Philip Caputo has written a celebrated memoir (**"A Rumor of War"**) and a novel about the meaningless horror of modern war (**"Horn of Africa"**). He works the same territory again in his new novel, **"DelCorso's Gallery."**

Nicholas DelCorso, a Vietnam veteran turned combat photographer, wants to show the public the true face of war. It has become an obsession with him, an attempted expiation of a momentary sin of callousness, a crusade that seems inexplicable and tasteless to P. X. Dunlop, his former mentor. (pp. 14-15)

With bemused revulsion, he watches DelCorso photographing mangled corpses. Their rivalry, the emotional center of this book, reaches its climax in Beirut, a place so awful that even the professional action junkies, the war correspondents, have difficulty sustaining their macho existential pose. . . .

Mr. Caputo writes with all the subtlety of a punch to the gut, but his descriptions of combat photographers and correspondents at work are right on the money. Like his hero, though, the author seems far more comfortable in ravaged Beirut than in the putatively civilized professional world of New York. His attempt to describe DelCorso's marriage to a cool Irish-American aristocrat isn't nearly so compelling as the battle sequences. Mr. Caputo remains very much a Marine—a bit awkward when it comes to domesticity and philosophizing but a tiger in the field. (p. 15)

> *Joe Klein, in a review of "DelCorso's Gallery," in* The New York Times Book Review, *November 13, 1983, pp. 14, 16.*

Aimé (Fernand) Césaire

1913-

West Indian poet, dramatist, and essayist.

Césaire's notability as a major Caribbean literary figure derives from his long surrealist poem *Cahier d'un retour au pays natal* (1939; *Return to My Native Land*) and also from his role in formulating, along with Léopold Senghor and Léon Damas, the concept of négritude. Concerned with the plight of blacks in a world dominated politically and culturally by Western values, Césaire and other supporters of négritude urge blacks to reject assimilation and to honor instead their own racial qualities and roots. The ideals of négritude permeate Césaire's work and have also greatly influenced his successful political career.

Born and raised on the West Indies island of Martinique, Césaire studied in Paris in the late 1930s. It was here that he associated with Senghor, who later became the president of Senegal and a poet of renown, and Damas, a French Guianan whose poetry is well respected. Their work on *L'etudiant noir*, an influential publication among black students which promoted the common heritage of all blacks, led to the origination of négritude. In 1939, Césaire returned to Martinique and became involved in politics, serving as mayor of Fort-de-France. He also became one of Martinique's three deputies to the French parliament in 1946. Césaire espoused Communism initially but renounced it in 1956, finding it incompatible with his long-standing goal of independence for Martinique from French and foreign domination. In addition to politics and writing, Césaire founded the review *Tropiques*, significant for its intellectually challenging ideas about culture and politics and its advocacy of surrealism.

As with négritude, Césaire adopted surrealism as a tool to free his writing from the conventions of French literature. Jean-Paul Sartre recognized his purpose when he wrote: "Surrealism, a European poetic movement, is stolen from the Europeans by a black who turns it against them." Among the poems written by Césaire in the surrealist tradition are *Return to My Native Land, Les Armes miraculeuses* (1946), *Soleil cou coupé* (1948; *Beheaded Sun*), *Corps Perdu* (1950; *Disembodied*), and *Ferrements* (1960). Critics note that he moved away from surrealism in his drama and in his collection of revised poems, *Cadastre* (1961).

Césaire's first long poem, *Return to My Native Land*, is regarded by many critics as his masterpiece. The poem was published in Paris in 1939 but went virtually unnoticed. It was rediscovered and endorsed by André Breton, who met Césaire when he visited Martinique during World War II. Breton wrote that the poem was "nothing less than the greatest lyrical monument of our time." Sartre's essay on négritude in *Black Orpheus* also directed attention to Césaire's work. The three movements of *Return to My Native Land* are composed in pounding, discordant rhythms. The first surveys the demoralizing conditions of Martinique caused by colonialism; the second involves Césaire's conscious attempt to free himself from European attitudes and to regain his négritude; and the third is his celebration of his black heritage.

© Lütfi Özkök

Believing that drama would be more accessible to the people than the surreal, sometimes hermetic poetry he had been writing, Césaire turned to writing plays in the late 1950s. *La tragedie du Roi Christophe* (1963; *The Tragedy of King Christophe*) and *Une saison au Congo* (1966; *A Season in the Congo*) continue to propound négritude and voice Césaire's anger but utilize a more conventional dramatic structure. In the first play, Henri Christophe, the Haitian king who presided over the decolonization of Haiti in the early nineteenth century, discovers the loss of humanity caused by years of tyranny. *A Season in the Congo* also views history from the perspective of a black leader, centering on the martyrdom of Patrice Lamumba, leader of the newly independent Congo Republic. A third play in the collection was to have been a portrait of Malcolm X. *La Tempête* (1969), Césaire's adaptation of Shakespeare's play *The Tempest*, explores the relationship between Prospero, portrayed as a decadent colonizer, and his slaves.

In addition to a study of Toussaint L'Overture, the Haitian revolutionary liberator, two other nonfiction works exemplify Césaire's concerns. *Discours sur le colonialisme* (1950; *Discourse on Colonialism*) denounces colonialism as a civilizing force, and *Lettre à Maurice Thorez* (1956), a widely publicized pamphlet, explains Césaire's reasons for leaving the Communist Party. *Aimé Césaire: The Collected Poetry* (1983) demonstrates Césaire's unusual and highly emotional fusion of négritude, surrealism, and love for his native land and his African roots.

(See also *CLC*, Vol. 19 and *Contemporary Authors*, Vols. 65-68.)

JEAN-PAUL SARTRE

[*The following is excerpted from a translation of Jean-Paul Sartre's seminal essay on negritude, "Orphée Noir," which Sartre wrote as the introduction to Leopold Sédar-Senghor's* Anthologie de la nouvelle poésie nègre et malgache de langue française *(1948). The translation by John MacCombie first appeared in the* Massachusetts Review *in 1965.*]

[If the poems in *Anthologie de la nouvelle poésie nègre et malgache de langue française*] shame us . . . , they were not intended to: they were not written for us; and they will not shame any colonists or their accomplices who open this book, for these latter will think they are reading letters over someone's shoulder, letters not meant for them. These black men are addressing themselves to black men about black men; their poetry is neither satiric nor imprecatory: it is an awakening to consciousness. (p. 7)

[Race] consciousness is based first of all on the black soul, or, rather—since the term is often used in this anthology—on a certain quality common to the thoughts and conduct of Negroes which is called *Negritude*. . . . There are only two ways to go about forming racial concepts: either one causes certain subjective characteristics to become objective, or else one tries to interiorize objectively revealed manners of conduct; thus the black man who asserts his negritude by means of a revolutionary movement immediately places himself in the position of having to meditate, either because he wishes to recognize in himself certain objectively established traits of the African civilizations, or because he hopes to discover the Essence of blackness in the well of his heart. Thus subjectivity reappears: the relation of the self with the self; the source of all poetry, the very poetry from which the worker had to disengage himself. The black man who asks his colored brothers to "find themselves" is going to try to present to them an exemplary image of their Negritude and will look into his own soul to grasp it. He wants to be both a beacon and a mirror; the first revolutionary will be the harbinger of the black soul, the herald—half prophet and half follower—who will tear Blackness out of himself in order to offer it to the world. . . . In the anthology which I am introducing to you here, there is only one subject that all the poets attempt to treat, more or less successfully. From Haiti to Cayenne, there is a single idea: *reveal* the black soul. Black poetry is evangelic, it announces good news: Blackness has been rediscovered.

However, this negritude, which they wish to fish for in their abyssal depths, does not fall under the soul's gaze all by itself: in the soul, nothing is gratuitous. The herald of the black soul has gone through white schools . . . ; it is through having had some contact with white culture that his blackness has passed from the immediacy of existence to the meditative state. But at the same time, he has more or less ceased to live his negritude. In choosing to see what he is, he has become split, he no longer co-incides with himself. And on the other hand, it is because he was already exiled from himself that he discovered this need to reveal himself. He therefore begins by exile. It is a double exile: the exile of his body offers a magnificent image of the exile of his heart; he is in Europe most of the time, in the cold, in the middle of gray crowds; he

dreams of Port-au-Prince, of Haiti. But in Port-au-Prince he was *already* in exile; the slavers had torn his fathers out of Africa and dispersed them. (pp. 11-12)

However, the walls of this culture prison must be broken down; it will be necessary to return to Africa some day: thus the themes of return to the native country and of re-descent into the glaring hell of the black soul are indissolubly mixed up in the *vates* of negritude. A quest is involved here, a systematic stripping and an "ascèse" [the ascetic's movement of *interiorization*] accompanied by a continual effort of investigation. And I shall call this poetry "Orphic" because the Negro's tireless descent into himself makes me think of Orpheus going to claim Eurydice from Pluto. Thus, through an exceptional stroke of poetic good luck, it is by letting himself fall into trances, by rolling on the ground like a possessed man tormented by himself, by singing of his angers, his regrets or his hates, by exhibiting his wounds, his life torn between "civilization" and his old black substratum; in short, by becoming most lyrical, that the black poet is most certain of creating a great collective poetry: by speaking only of himself, he speaks for all Negroes; it is when he seems smothered by the serpents of our culture that he is the most revolutionary, for he then undertakes to ruin systematically the European knowledge he has acquired, and this spiritual destruction symbolizes the great future taking-up of arms by which black men will destroy their chains. (p. 13)

The fact that the prophets of negritude are forced to write their gospel *in French* means that there is a certain risk of dangerously slowing down the efforts of black men to reject our tutelege. Having been dispersed to the four corners of the earth by the slave trade, black men have no common language; in order to incite the oppressed to unite, they must necessarily rely on the words of the oppressor's language. And French is the language that will furnish the black poet with the largest audience, at least within the limits of French colonization. . . . And since words are ideas, when the Negro declares in French that he rejects French culture, he accepts with one hand what he rejects with the other; he sets up the enemy's thinking-apparatus in himself, like a crusher. This would not matter: except that this syntax and vocabulary—forged thousands of miles away in another epoch to answer other needs and to designate other objects—are unsuitable to furnish him with the means of speaking about himself, his own anxieties, his own hopes. The French language and French thought are analytical. What would happen if the black spirit were above all synthetical? The rather ugly term "negritude" is one of the few black contributions to our dictionary. But after all, if this "negritude" is a definable or at least a describable concept, it must subsume other more elementary concepts which correspond to the immediate fundamental ideas directly involved with Negro consciousness: but where are the words to describe them? (p. 14)

Only through Poetry can the black men of Tenanarive and of Cayenne, the black men of Port-au-Prince and of Saint-Louis, communicate with each other in private. And since French lacks terms and concepts to define negritude, since negritude is silence, these poets will use "allusive words, never direct, reducing themselves to the same silence" in order to evoke it. Short-circuits of language: behind the flaming fall of words, we glimpse a great black mute idol. It is not only the black man's self-portrayal that seems poetic to me; it is also his personal way of utilizing the means of expression at his disposal. His position incites him to do it: even before he thinks of writing poetry, in him, the light of white words is refracted, polarized and altered. This is nowhere more manifest than in his use of two connected terms—"white-black"—that cover both the great cosmic division—"day and night"—and the human conflict between the native and the colonist. But it is a connection based on a hierarchical system: by giving the Negro this term, the teacher also gives him a hundred language habits which consecrate the white man's rights over the black man. The Negro will learn to say "white like snow" to indicate innocence, to speak of the blackness of a look, of a soul, of a deed. As soon as he opens his mouth, he accuses himself, unless he persists in upsetting the hierarchy. And if he upsets it *in French,* he is already poetizing: can you imagine the strange savor that an expression like "the blackness of innocence" or "the darkness of virtue" would have for us? That is the savor which we taste on every page of this book.... (pp. 16-17)

[For example, throughout one of the poems,] black is color; better still, light; its soft diffuse radiance dissolves our habits; the *black* country where the ancients are sleeping is not a dark hell: it is a land of sun and fire. Then again, in another connection, the superiority of white over black does not express only the superiority that the colonist claims to have over the native: more profoundly, it expresses a universal adoration of *day* as well as our night terrors, which also are universal. In this sense, these black men are re-establishing the hierarchy they have just upset. They don't want to be poets of *night,* poets of vain revolt and despair: they give the promise of dawn; they greet

> the transparent dawn of a new day.

At last, the black man discovers, through the pen, his baleful sense of foreboding:

> Nigger black like misery

one of them, and then another, cries out:

> Deliver me from my blood's night

Thus the word *black* is found to contain *all Evil* and *all Good,* it covers up almost unbearable tension between two contradictory classifications: solar hierarchy and racial hierarchy. It gains thereby an extraordinary poetry, like self-destructive objects from the hands of Duchamp and the Surrealists; there is a secret blackness in white, a secret whiteness in black, a vivid flickering of Being and of Non-being which is perhaps nowhere expressed as well as in this poem of Césaire:

> My tall wounded statue, a stone in its fore-
> head; my great inattentive day flesh with
> pitiless spots, my great night flesh with
> day spots.

The poet will go even further; he writes:

> Our beautiful faces like the true operative
> power of negation.

Behind this abstract eloquence evoking Lautréamont is seen an extremely bold and subtle attempt to give some sense to black skin and to realize the poetic synthesis of the two faces of night. When David Diop says that the Negro is "black like misery," he makes black represent deprivation of light. But Césaire develops and goes into this image more deeply: night is no longer absence, it is refusal. Black is not color, it is the destruction of this borrowed clarity which falls from the white sun. The revolutionary Negro is negation because he wishes to be complete nudity: in order to build his Truth, he must first

destroy others' Truth. Black faces—these night memories which haunt our days—embody the dark work of Negativity which patiently gnaws at concepts. Thus, by a reversal which curiously recalls that of the humiliated Negro—insulted and called "dirty nigger" when he asserts his rights—it is the privative aspect of darkness that establishes its value. Liberty is the color of night.

Destructions, *autodafés* of language, magic symbolism, ambivalence of concepts: all the negative aspects of modern poetry are here. But it is not a matter of some gratuitous game. The black man's position, his original "rending," the alienation that a foreign way of thinking imposes on him, all oblige him to reconquer his existential unity as a Negro—or, if you prefer, the original purity of his plan—through a gradual "ascèse," beyond the language stage. Negritude—like liberty—is a point of departure and an ultimate goal: it is a matter of making negritude pass from the immediate to the mediate, a matter of *thematicising* it. The black man must therefore find death in white culture in order to be reborn with a black soul.... It is not a matter of his *knowing,* nor of his ecstatically tearing himself away from himself, but rather of both discovering and becoming what he is.

There are two convergent means of arriving at this primordial simplicity of existence: one is objective, the other subjective. The poets in our anthology sometimes use one, sometimes the other, and sometimes both of them together. In effect, there exists an objective negritude that is expressed by the mores, arts, chants and dances of the African populaces.... The poetic act, then, is a dance of the soul; the poet turns round and round like a dervish until he faints; he has established his ancestors' time in himself, he feels it flowing with its peculiar violent pulls; he hopes to "find" himself in this rhythmic pulsation; I shall say that he tries to make himself "possessed" by his people's negritude; he hopes that the echoes of his tam-tam will come to awaken timeless instincts sleeping within him.... The black men of Africa ... are still in the great period of mythical fecundity and French-language black poets are not just using their myths as a form of diversion as we use our epic poems: they allow themselves to be spellbound by them so that at the end of the incantation, negritude—magnificently evoked—may surge forth. This is why I call this method of "objective poetry" *magic,* or charm.

Césaire, on the contrary, chose to backtrack into himself. Since this Eurydice will disappear in smoke if Black Orpheus turns around to look back on her, he will descend the royal road of his soul with his back turned on the bottom of the grotto; he will descend below words and meanings,—"in order to think of you, I have placed all words on the mountain-of-pity"—below daily activities and the plan of "repetition," even below the first barrier reefs of revolt, with his back turned and his eyes closed, in order finally to touch with his feet the black water of dreams and desire and to let himself drown in it. Desire and dream will rise up snarling like a tidal wave; they will make words dance like flotsam and throw them pell-mell, shattered, on the shore. (pp. 17-20)

One recognizes the old surrealistic *method* (automatic writing, like mysticism, is a method: it presupposes an apprenticeship, exercises, a start along the way). One must dive under the superficial crust of reality, of common sense, of reasoning reason, in order to touch the very bottom of the soul and awaken the timeless forces of desire: desire which makes of man a refusal of everything and a love of everything: desire, the radical negation of natural laws and of the possible, a call to miracles; desire which, by its mad cosmic energy, plunges man back into the seething breast of Nature and, at the same time, lifts him above Nature through the affirmation of his Right to be unsatisfied. Furthermore, Césaire is not the first Negro to take this road. Before him, Etienne Léro had founded *Légitime Défense*. . . .

However, if one compares Léro with Césaire, one cannot help but be struck by their dissimilarities, and this comparison may allow us to measure the abyss that prevents a black revolutionary from utilizing white surrealism. Léro was the precursor; he invented the exploitation of surrealism as a "miraculous weapon" and an instrument for reconnaissance, a sort of radar with which one probes the depths of the abyss. But his poems are student exercises, they are mere imitations: they do not go beyond themselves; rather, they close in on each other. . . . (p. 21)

The purpose of surrealism is to rediscover—beyond race and condition, beyond class, behind the fire of language—dazzling silent darknesses which are no longer opposed to anything, not even to day, because day and night and all opposites are blended in them and suppressed; consequently, one might speak of the impassiveness and the impersonality of the surrealist poem, just as there is a Parnassian impassiveness and impersonality.

A poem by Césaire, on the contrary, bursts and wheels around like a rocket; suns turning and exploding into new suns come out of it: it is a perpetual going-beyond. It is not a question of the poem becoming part of the calm unity of opposites; but rather of making *one* of the opposites in the "black-white" couple expand like a phallus in its opposition to the other. The density of these words thrown into the air like stones from a volcano, is found in negritude, which is defined as being *against* Europe and colonization. What Césaire destroys is not *all* culture but rather *white* culture; what he brings to light is not desire for *everything* but rather the revolutionary aspirations of the oppressed Negro; what he touches in his very depths is not the spirit but a certain specific, concrete form of humanity. With this in mind, one can speak here about *engaged* and even *directed* automatic writing, not because there is any meditative intervention but because the words and images perpetually translate the same torrid obsession. The white surrealist finds within himself the trigger; Césaire finds within himself the fixed inflexibility of demands and feeling. . . . Césaire's words are pressed against each other and cemented by his furious passion. Between the most daring comparisons and between the most widely separated terms, runs a secret thread of hate and hope. . . . In Césaire, the great surrealist tradition is realized, it takes on its definitive meaning and is destroyed: surrealism—that European movement—is taken from the Europeans by a Black man who turns it against them and gives it rigorously defined function. . . . Césaire's originality lies in his having directed his powerful, concentrated anxiety as a Negro, as one oppressed, as a militant individual, into this world of the most destructive, free and metaphysical poetry at the moment when Eluard and Aragon were failing to give political content to their verse. And finally, *negritude-object* is snatched from Césaire like a cry of pain, of love and of hate. Here again he follows the surrealist tradition of *objective* poetry. Césaire's words do not describe negritude, they do not designate it, they do not copy it from the outside like a painter with a model: they *create* it; they compose it under our very eyes: henceforth it is a thing which can be observed and learned; the subjective method which he has chosen joins the objective method we spoke about earlier: he ejects the black soul from

himself at the very moment when others are trying to interiorize it; the final result is the same in both cases. Negritude is the far-away tam-tam in the streets of Dakar at night; voo-doo shouts from some Haitian cellar window, sliding along level with the roadway; the Congolese mask; but it is also . . . [a] poem by Césaire, . . . [a] slobbery, bloody poem full of phlegm, twisting in the dust like a cut-up worm. This double spasm of absorption and excretion beats out the rhythm of the black heart on every page of this collection.

What then, at present, is this negritude, sole anxiety of these poets, sole subject of this book? It must first be stated that a white man could hardly speak about it suitably, since he has no inner experience of it and since European languages lack words to describe it. I ought then to let the reader encounter it in the pages of this collection and draw his own conclusions about it. But this introduction would be incomplete if, after having indicated that the quest for the Black Grail represented—both in its original intention and in its methods—the most authentic synthesis of revolutionary aspirations and poetic anxiety, I did not show that this complex notion is essentially pure Poetry. I shall therefore limit myself to examining these poems objectively as a cluster of testimonies and to pointing out some of their principal themes. Senghor says: "What makes the *negritude* of a poem is less its theme than its style, the emotional warmth which gives life to words, which transmutes the word into the Word." It could not be more explicitly stated that negritude is neither a state nor a definite ensemble of vices and virtues or of intellectual and moral qualities, but rather a certain affective attitude towards the world. (pp. 22-5)

[Here] is what Césaire tells us about it:

> My negritude is not a stone with its deafness flung out
>   against the clamor of the day
> My negritude is not a dead speck of water on the dead
>   eye of the earth
> my negritude is neither a tower nor a cathedral
> it plunges into the red flesh of the ground
> it plunges into the ardent flesh of the sky
> it perforates the opaque pressure of its righteous
>   patience.

Negritude is portrayed in these beautiful lines of verse more as an act than as a frame of mind. But this act is an *inner* determination: it is not a question of *taking* the goods of this world in one's hands and transforming them; it is a question of *existing* in the middle of the world. (p. 25)

Jean-Paul Sartre, "Black Orpheus," translated by John MacCombie, in The Black American Writer: Poetry and Drama, *Vol. II, edited by C.W.E. Bigsby, 1969. Reprint by Penguin Books Inc., 1971, pp. 6-40.**

CLAYTON ESHLEMAN AND ANNETTE SMITH

Although Césaire was by no means the sole exponent of negritude, the word is now inseparable from his name, and largely responsible for his prominent position in the Third World. This neologism, made up (perhaps on the model of the South American *negrismo*) by latinizing the derogatory word for black (*nègre*) with an augmentative suffix, appeared in print, probably for the first time, in the *Notebook of a Return to the Native Land:* "My negritude is not a stone, its deafness hurled against the clamour of the day / my negritude is not a leukoma of dead liquid over the earth's dead eye / my negritude is neither tower nor cathedral." What was negritude then? A subsequent passage of the *Notebook* answered the question: negritude "takes root in the ardent flesh of the soil / it breaks through the opaque prostration with its upright patience." In more prosaic terms, it signified a response to the century-old problem of the alienated position of the blacks in history. Once upon a time, the blacks inhabited their homeland: a whole continent. And then, there was the diaspora which all over the world left the blacks enslaved or colonized, with neither a present nor a future nor even a language of their own. (p. 5)

The negritude movement . . . set as its initial goal a renewed awareness of being black, the acceptance of one's destiny, history, and culture, as well as a sense of responsibility toward the past. (p. 6)

In the fifties negritude was to become as much of an arena as *engagement* had been in the 1940s. In retrospect, there were deep differences in the way various people conceived it—too many to do more here than just allude to some of the positions. Senghor was understood—perhaps wrongly—to consider black culture as the product of a black *nature*. If as a result of some covenant with nature, black Africans were a chosen race, they were bound to be both more secure about their roots and less alienated than deported blacks. Senghor's poetry and many contemporary African novels tend to prove this point. Césaire seems to have shared Senghor's view in the early part of his career—and he was later to be criticized for it by a younger generation of black intellectuals. In an interview with Jacqueline Leiner in 1978, however, he maintained that for him black culture had never had anything to do with biology and everything to do with a combination of geography and history: identity in suffering, not in genetic material, determined the bond among black people of different origins. If history had made victors of the blacks, there would not be what he called elsewhere "a greater solidarity among black people."

But whether innate or acquired, the characteristics of black culture on which all interpreters of negritude agreed were antipodal to the Western values of rationalism, technology, Christianity, and individualism. They spelled not the control of nature by reason and science but a joyful participation in it; not its control by technology but a coexistence with other forms of life; not the Christianity of the missions but the celebration of very ancient pagan rites; not the praise of individual achievement but the fraternity and communal soul of the clan, the tribe, as well as the love of ancestors. "A culture is born not when Man grasps the world, but when he is grasped . . . by it." Let us insert here that for Césaire (as for many other non-African blacks) the African heritage had been acquired through books and espoused spiritually—which made it perhaps an even more aggressive ideal. (pp. 6-7)

The idea was also to find a theoretician in the High Priest of postwar French letters, Jean-Paul Sartre. His essay, "Orphée Noir" ("Black Orpheus") [see excerpt above], which served as an introduction to Senghor's *Anthology of the New Black and Malagasy Poetry* (1948), gave negritude an existential and Hegelian imprimatur in a period when every aspect of intellectual life had to be viewed in those terms. . . .

Sartre's definition of negritude was not the last one. It was, in fact, to become the touchstone of most subsequent definitions. Later exponents of the concept found Sartre too race conscious and not sufficiently class conscious. What they wanted was a classless society in which all races would be equal, and not a raceless society. Some (like Césaire himself more recently) felt that the concept of a black essence reeked either

of determinism or of mysticism and that negritude would cease to exist in a world with more equitable economic conditions. (p. 7)

From our perspective, there is no easy answer: negritude is a dynamic concept. How relevant it was and will remain in the future depends on the situation and history of each particular colonized group. Politically speaking, as a number of African nations acquired their autonomy in the fifties and sixties, negritude lost some of its spark. Culturally speaking the future is open. Possibly some black literature will be written in native vernaculars; or, on the contrary, it is conceivable that young nations might lose their inferiority complex to the point where using the literary tools of their former masters will no longer be an issue. It is true that negritude was at its most potent in countries colonized by the French, that is, in which there existed a rigorously structured and policed official language. Former colonies in which the official language is English seem less sensitive to the problem. Some countries, such as Cuba, have chosen to emphasize the hybrid aspect of the culture and to promote a *mestiza* literature. Finally, black literature might be lured by its own success into joining the mainstream of Western literature. (p. 8)

When all is said and done, an introduction should answer the question: why read Césaire? Why read poems that require long exegeses, which stern readers have in the past deemed, at best, a brilliant intellectual game, at worst, arrogantly obscure, and riddled with typographical, grammatical, or semiotic idiosyncrasies? We would like to reply that these flaws are not, in the case of Césaire, artificial and derivative tricks but simply occasional alterations inherent in sustained profundity and abundance. In the long run, only being "inside" a poem can truly expound Césaire's poetry. It is impossible, of course, to reconstitute a paradigm of what can only be an individual and multiform experience. But, were we pressed to do it, we would say that the first element characteristic of Césaire's poetic voice is its solemnity. . . .

A second characteristic might be an exquisitely subtle blend of ferocity and tenderness. It is plain that Césaire is a master at turning the screw: a poem like **"Fangs"** depicts suffering as "map of blood map of the blood / bled raw sweated raw skinned raw. . . ." (p. 18)

Finally, another characteristic is Césaire's ability to surprise. We are delighted by this "truly wild disappearance / tropical as an apparition of a nocturnal wolf at high noon" which abruptly succeeds the quasi-epic tone of **"Visitation"**; a "pretty nymph sheds her leaves amidst the manzanilla milk and the accolades of fraternal leeches" at the end of the otherwise grim **"Day and Night."** . . . Césaire has the ultimate cleverness to appear surprised himself by his surprises, thus making them more credible. It is as if, in spite of him and almost behind his back, the world in its boundless luxuriance performed magical tricks for the common pleasure of writer and reader. (p. 19)

We have chosen these three characteristics because together they seem to speak to the contemporary psyche better than would a homogeneous voice: the prophetic to our need for certainty and authority; the mixture of cruelty and tenderness to our need of being alternatively object and subject; the surprise to the child in us. We prefer to think of ourselves as unresolved. We also prefer to think of ourselves as fabricators of meanings, and the "courage of the imagination" Césaire requires of his readers amply fulfills the *bricoleurs* in them.

Those still unconvinced by the aesthetic case must not overlook the equally compelling historical and moral one. In the *Tragedy of King Christophe* Césaire has the main character say that one has to demand more from the blacks than from any other race: more work, more faith, more enthusiasm, more persistence. As one looks back over Césaire's amazing career, it appears that he has lived up to his hero's ideals and even added one to the list: vision. On the black child from the slums of Basse-Pointe an almost messianic role was bestowed. For he was to become a bridge between the twain that, in principle, should never meet, Europe and Africa. Thus he symbolizes and sums up what is probably the twentieth century's most important phenomenon: the powerful surge next to the old and the new world, of a third world both very new and very old. Rather than aiming at the lowest common denominator between the two cultures, Césaire sought to fulfill his Africanism with "the zeal of an apocalyptic wasp," and the adjective here conveys adequately the extreme quality of this choice. As he pointed out again in his recent interview (*Le Monde*, December, 1981), however, it was by borrowing European techniques that he succeeded in expressing his Africanism in its purest form.

Césaire seems to have been constantly driven by the vision that the end result of this Africanization would be an elemental man in whom all mankind would recognize itself. Thus he claimed to have demonstrated Hegel's idea that the universal is not the negation of the particular, that it is by going deeper into the particular that one reaches the universal. In making the universal man black (and vice versa) Césaire was paradoxically putting the finishing touch to an image of man toward which Europe itself had been groping in the wake of Rousseau, Diderot, and the Enlightenment and which continued to develop through nineteenth- and twentieth-century anthropology. In expanding Man's image, he gave the white world, which had educated him, a hundredfold more than what he had received from it. And, as a bonus, he gave a more genuine meaning to the traditional claim of the French language to be a universal one. (pp. 19-20)

Negritude may well be, as we suggested before, politically outdated. Césaire himself (in the haunting and hieratical **"Lay of Errantry"**) hints that Africa's glory may be only an ancient tale in a now closed wizard's book. But perhaps it is precisely there, in its visionary status, that lies the real beginning of negritude. For the Africa of oil wells, supertankers, commodity markets, gigantic dams, and labor problems may need its guiding light even more than it needs tractors, guns, and capital, if it is not to become just another alienated industrial world. Negritude has the potential to remain, according to Camus' prophetic paradox, the end that, in turn, shall be justified only to the extent that the means are justifiable.

Césaire's career as a political figure or as a poet is far from completed. He is still at the helm of his native island and in the interview in *Le Monde* mentioned above he announces the forthcoming publication of another collection of poems, **"Moi, laminaire."** He might surprise us in both these domains. But we venture to say that in neither will it be by revolutionary stances. To him, revolution and violence were only a phase. The readjustment of his political goals so as to focus on the development of Martinique and on local issues and the increasingly elegiac tone of his poetry are symmetrically significant of his present position. (p. 20)

> *Clayton Eshleman and Annette Smith, in an introduction to* The Collected Poetry *by Aimé Césaire,*

> *translated by Clayton Eshleman and Annette Smith, University of California Press, 1983, pp. 1-28.*

KARL KELLER

Cesaire at 70. Marxist revolutionary. For a quarter century, representative from Martinique (near Grenada) to the French Assembly. For four decades, father-apologist for the ideology of negritude. Leading Third World intellectual. French playwright and surrealist poet. "Whoever would not understand me," he writes, "would not understand any better the roaring of a tiger." Now perhaps, with [*The Collected Poetry* by Aime Cesaire], we can begin to understand this tiger. . . .

One now sees that there are two styles in Cesaire's life work, two minds at work: the influence of Andre Breton and other surrealists, encouraging him to take at random the mythologies and landscapes of black Africa and the Caribbean in defining negritude; and the influence of American black poets of the Harlem Renaissance, encouraging him to take images of glory from slavery and segregation in making his definition. The surrealism liberated *him*, but I'm not sure how effectively it served Cesaire in liberating the Third World ("my colonized hells")—and that has been one of Cesaire's motives.

As surrealist, he could write of "this mouthful of stars revomited into a cake of fireflies" and of "this knife stab of a vomit of broken teeth in the belly of the wind" and feel that he was breaking up old forms, old minds—making "a sport of nigromancy," he calls it. But these bursts, beautiful and barbarous, called more attention to him as maker than they did to the world he wanted to make. For decades he found the surreal aesthetically revolutionary, but in the face of the torture and the suffering, he has pretty well abandoned it as a luxury. . . . Cesaire shocked with his surrealism but probably had more of an effect as shocking champion of negritude, the international brotherhood of all black men. . . . This side of Cesaire caught on all over the world—but less as a man with a program than a man with an exemplary voice.

Cesaire's more political poems make connections—with the reader, with systems of thought, with history, with society. He calls them "sublime excoriations of a flesh fraternal and whipped to the point of rebellious fires." (pp. 1, 10)

The most recent poems of Cesaire, especially his **"Ferraments,"** are more politically aggressive, louder, more anxiously reaching for an international audience, more the shouts of the atoning liberator. . . .

Cesaire, like Whitman, waits for a response from his people, waits for new life from them, waits for them to follow him. . . .

As Cesaire himself has moved from his early platforms on through to reform, from the hope of the artful to the uses of art to inspire hope, he has, in various ways, been trying to say that there is, in the awful, awe-filled blackness of blackness, plenty of light. (p. 10)

> *Karl Keller, "A Radical Poet with a Political Program," in* Los Angeles Times Book Review, *December 4, 1983, pp. 1, 10.*

MARJORIE PERLOFF

[What] will surely be considered one of the most important translations from the French in 1983 [is Clayton Eshleman and Annette Smith's *The Collected Poetry* by Aimé Césaire].

The appeal of Césaire's poetry depends, I think, on its particular blend of a native vitalism, a violent energy that celebrates the irrational, the strange, even the bestial, with a French sophistication, wit, and learning. If, as Eshleman and Smith note, the poetry is "a perpetual scene of dismemberment and mutilation," if it goes so far as to celebrate cannibalism as that which "symbolically eradicates the distinction between the I and the Other, between human and nonhuman, between what is (anthropologically) edible and what is not, and, finally, between the subject and the object" . . . , it is also a self-consciously literary poetry, full of echoes of Rimbaud (especially the Rimbaud of the *Saison en enfer*), Lautréamont, Baudelaire, and Mallarmé. Again, if Césaire's rhythms are influenced by African dances and voodoo rituals, his syntax is so Latinate and his vocabulary so esoteric, that it brings to mind the reference shelf rather than the tribal dance. (p. 43)

Césaire's is nothing if not an explosive poetry. The *Notebook of a Return to the Native Land,* for example, is a 1,055-line exorcism (part prose, part free verse) of the poet's "civilized" instincts, his lingering shame at belonging to a country and a race so abject, servile, petty and repressed as is his. A paratactic catalogue poem that piles up phrase upon phrase, image upon image, in a complex network of repetitions, its thrust is to define the threshold between sleep and waking—the sleep of oppression, the blind acceptance of the status quo, that gives way to rebirth, to a new awareness of what is and may be. Accordingly, it begins with the refrain line, repeated again and again in the first section of the poem, "Au bout du petit matin . . ." ("At the end of the little morning," a purposely childlike reference to dawn, which Eshleman and Smith awkwardly render as "At the end of the wee hours"), followed by a strophe that characterizes the poet's initial anguish, an anguish always laced with black humour. . . .

Here we have the hallmarks of Césaire's style: impassioned direct address ("Va-t'en"), name-calling ("gueule de flic," "gueule de vache"), parallel constructions that aren't quite parallel ("les larbins de l'ordre et les hannetons de l'espérance"), hyperbole ("la force putréfiante des ambiances crépusculaires"), oxymoron ("dans mes profondeurs à hauteur inverse du vingtième étage des maisons les plus insolents"), violent imagery ("sacré soleil vénérien"), and above all the chant-like rhythm created by the repetition of word and sound, as in "je nourrissais . . . je délaçais . . . j'entendais" or in "de l'autre côté du désastre, un fleuve de tourterelles et de trèfles."

There is really nothing comparable to this mode in American poetry. In the long catalogue poems of Allen Ginsberg and Imamu Baraka, we find similarly impassioned repetition, parallelism, hyperbole; again, in a sequence like Galway Kinnell's *The Book of Nightmares,* we meet imagery of perhaps equal violence and stringency. But Césaire's poetry is quite different from Ginsberg's on the one hand or Kinnell's on the other in its curious conjunction of an intense realism (in the course of the *Notebook,* the topography of Martinique, its climate, architecture, and inhabitants are graphically described) with a surrealism that seems so inevitable it may almost escape our attention.

Who is it, for instance, that the poet meets "Au bout du petit matin"—a cop or a "bedbug of a petty monk"? Or both? If the former, then the paradise lost he cannot attain is one of a primitive society that had not learned the need for law-enforce-

ment. If the latter, the enemy is primarily Christianity. These are, of course, part and parcel of the same complex for Césaire, but the point I am trying to make is that his is a language so violently charged with meaning that each word falls on the ear (or hits the eye) with resounding force. (p. 44)

What strikes me as especially remarkable [in *Cahier d'un retour au pays natal*] and in Césaire's surrealist lyrics in *Les Armes Miraculeuses* . . . of 1946 is the total absence of sentimentality or self-pity. He can see himself as [victimized] . . . without casting about for a scapegoat. For, as the "I" comes to realize in the course of the poem, "Nous vomissure de négrier" ("We the vomit of slave ships") must exorcise our own cowardice, fear, and hypocrisy before change can take place. . . . (p. 45)

Marjorie Perloff, "The French Connection," in The American Poetry Review, *Vol. 13, No. 1, January-February, 1984, pp. 40-5.*

SERGE GAVRONSKY

[If] his orientation had been solely French, Mr. Césaire would not have been able to return from "exile" in France and find his originality as a poet. What a reader discovers in his early epic poem, "Notebook of a Return to the Native Land" [in "Aime Cesaire: The Collected Poetry"], is a concerted effort to affirm his stature in French letters by a sort of poetic one-upmanship but also a determination to create a new language capable of expressing his African heritage—a "'Black' French which even while being French would carry the 'Negro' mark," as he once defined it to the Haitian poet René Depestre. The poem's dazzling syntactical and lexical inventiveness combines elements of African and Haitian history (in 1804 Haiti became the first black republic) with reflections on contemporary racism in Paris and a vast display of botanical, zoological, medical and classical erudition, not to mention African and Creole terminology. Of course, the influence of European poets and thinkers is also there, but the rhythmic insistence of the lines reminds the reader of an African oral tradition, one that can easily be set to music. For these reasons, the poem has reached an audience far beyond France. . . .

If none of his other collections of poems (including the most recently published, "Moi, Laminaire . . . ," which is not in this edition) have been able to duplicate the erudition, ideological commitment and linguistic playfulness of "Notebook," each has reaffirmed Mr. Césaire's reputation as a poet. He is able to deal with classic Surrealist strategies involving a whole range of unexpected associations—at times the consequence of automatic writing, as in "Miraculous Weapons" (1946) and "Solar Throat Slashed" (1948)—as well as with political ideas and purely lyrical turns, as in "Ferraments" (1960) and "Noria" (1976). When the poet calls himself a barbarian, the reader should be reminded of the connotation "primitive" but also of the condition of the black in a white world. . . .

With the publication of this collection of Mr. Césaire's poetry, his influence will no longer be limited to negritude. He has found his rightful place among the major French poets of this century.

Serge Gavronsky, "Black Themes in Surreal Guise," in The New York Times Book Review, *February 19, 1984, p. 14.*

Amy Clampitt

19??-

American poet.

Clampitt received critical acclaim for her first major collection of poetry, *The Kingfisher* (1983). Several critics suggested that Clampitt is the most important new poet on the American literary scene. Her richly descriptive verse, enhanced by striking imagery, varies in technique and deals with such topics as love, death, and the passage of time. Many critics applauded the skill with which she shifts from light set pieces to somber reflections on modern life. Clampitt began her career with small press publications and her poems have also appeared in several prestigious literary magazines.

(See also *Contemporary Authors*, Vol. 110.)

© *Thomas Victor 1984*

HELEN VENDLER

Amy Clampitt writes a beautiful, taxing poetry. In it, thinking uncoils and coils again, embodying its perpetual argument with itself. The mind that composes these poems wants to have things out on the highest premises; refinement is as natural to it as breathing. Like all poetic minds it thinks in images, drawn here from an alluring variety of origins—nature (from Iowa to Greece), religion (from Athena to Christ), science (from geology to entomology), art (from manuscript illumination to Beethoven), and literature (from Homer to Hopkins). Clampitt is unself-consciously allusive; the poems are rich with geographical and literary texture, a texture that supports and cushions and gives body to the meditation—sometimes eager, sometimes resentful—that forms the main strand of each poem.

Clampitt's poems, the best ones, are long, as painful ruminations have to be. Clampitt is a woman in middle age contemplating, in retrospect, a difficult Iowa childhood and adolescence, a move East and travels in Europe, and, in the present, love and friendship, periods of happiness on the Maine coast, and recently the death of parents. This life is very discreetly presented, in ways almost bare of anecdote; and yet the intensity of response in Clampitt's language suggests a life registered instant by painful (or exalted) instant. If Iowa has not had a poet before, it has one now. . . .

That a poem beginning with the barbedwire fencing in an Iowa woodlot should end (after its savage weather report in the middle) with the philosophical conundrum of identity, is surprising, but only until one sees how typical such a proceeding is in Clampitt, where one thing is sure to lead to another. I take **"The Woodlot"** as typical because it, like most Clampitt poems, seems at once unpredictable and conclusive, straying into an expressionist fantasy with the storms, distilling a purity of feeling with the violets, and raising fundamental questions of a metaphysical order in its conclusion.

All of these qualities are displayed in Clampitt's several bravura pieces in this volume, of which the most transfixing is her three-part piece "Triptych": its parts are called **"Palm Sunday," "Good Friday,"** and **"Easter Morning."** These poems are about the human inclination to cruelty and to victimage,

sometimes in the name of love, sometimes in the name of art, sometimes in the name of religion. (p. 19)

If Clampitt often leaves us exhausted by her headlong and pitiless investigations into the roots of behavior—which by themselves would be only horror stories if they were not mediated by her exquisite lines—she can also revive us by the way she can lose herself in the *visibilia* of the world. In a one-sentence fifty-line poem on fog, named, as a painting might be, **"Marine Surface, Low Overcast,"** she takes on the specific task of the poet who wants to represent as many lusters and hues and transitions as a painter can. These old rivalries between painting and poetry renew themselves in each generation, and many notable recent poems . . . have renewed questions about aesthetic illusion in painting and poetry.

Clampitt's debts in her descriptive poems—to Keats's luxurious lingerings, to Hopkins's Ruskinian notebooks and poems, and to Marianne Moore's scientific notations—are joyfully assumed. Among the interesting new things in Clampitt's descriptive vocabulary, visible in her **"Marine Surface,"** is a whole lexicon of the diction of women. This lexicon (which did not particularly interest Dickinson, Moore, Bishop, or Plath) is a natural resource for Clampitt. It appears here in words relating to cloth, thread making, and fashion (herringbone, floss, déshabille, spun, fur, stuff, train, rumpling, suede, texture, nap, sheen, loom, fabric), in other words connected to household activities (churn, stir, solder, whip to a froth) and household objects (buttermilk, velouté, looking-glass, sheets, basin). . . .

The inventions of the natural world are so manifold, Clampitt makes us see, that only by responding to their prompting, in their marvelous changes, can "pure imagining" equal them. Testing the feasibility of invention in language against the changeableness of natural appearance is the tireless work of the writer who values the visual world (and many do not). But it is not just visual "rendering" (by whatever analogies) that makes visual poetry "work." Poetic diction has its own laws that must be satisfied along with the requirements of the eye. Poetic diction demands that words be linked one to the other so that it will seem that they "grew" there by natural affinity. The tried-and-true linkage by sound is most beautiful (as here in "albatross' and "floss") when there is some disproportion— as here in word length and semantic category—between the members, so that alliance does not resemble identity. . . .

[In] Clampitt's poems, words, like neurons, put out branches to other words; the synapses thus formed are commands to the reader's processing apparatus to close the gap, to make the fleeting association. All of this linguistic patterning must accompany accurate visual rendition, or the poem will lack the fuel to make itself go. It is literally by such small electrical jumps that a poem refuels itself for the next inch of travel down the page. Clampitt has luxury to spare in this quarter, as she varies her fabric from sheer to thick, extending and diminishing her musical line, damasking her surface with pattern.

All this decorative change of pace is indispensable in poetry, in the sparest as well as in the most ornamented. But poems also, like essays, benefit from interesting thoughts; and like novels, they benefit from interesting incident. Clampitt's intellectuality and her curiosity about life give her the virtues of the essayist and observer of event. The two long elegies in memory of her parents admit us to precincts of deep feeling, intermingled with intense thought. (p. 20)

Though Clampitt published two small books before *The Kingfisher*, the advance in this collection over those preceding it is dumbfounding. When we read a book of American poems by a contemporary writer, we often forget that America will be remembered, when we are all dead, by the memorials of its culture; in them others will find out what we felt at what we saw (as Stevens puts it). Embodying their century, the minds that produce cultural objects are intellects "engaged in the hazardous / redefinition of structures / no one has yet looked at," as Clampitt says in **"Beach Glass."** A century from now, this volume will still offer a rare window into a rare mind, it will still offer beautiful objects of delectation; but it will have taken on as well the documentary value of what, in the twentieth century, made up the stuff of culture. And later yet, when (if man still exists) its cultural terminology is obsolescent, its social patterns extinct, it will, I think, still be read for its triumph over the resistance of language, the reason why poetry lasts. (p. 22)

Helen Vendler, "On the Thread of Language," in The New York Review of Books, *Vol. XXX, No. 3, March 3, 1983, pp. 19-22.*

PAUL A. OLSON

The Kingfisher is a book of tough stuff, full of dirt and doctrine. Since dirt and doctrine are the stuff of Great Plains Poetry and literature in the medieval period (where I have tried to plant my flag), I can treat what Clampitt does by describing how she handles the dirt of the prairie and the visionary lights of medieval religion. She is first a poet of dirt, not of space or history after the manner of Charles Olson and the New Poundians. . . . The transformation of guilt into dirt and of expiation day (or judgment day) into washday bespeaks both the religion and the region.

Part of Clampitt's capacity to handle prairie-plains themes and her sort of religious insight comes from the combination of capacity to handle extended syntactic structures having a disciplined rhythmic character while moving across the dirt comprising prairie space-and-time as if it were a sea frozen by the syntax into almost permanent form. **"The Quarry"** begins with an account of the limestone quarries of Le Grand, Iowa seen as the Eocene sea; its fossil remains become schooner cut bluestem, burr oak, willow wisps and the body of De Soto returned to the Mississippi to become sea fossil again. In that flux of fossil, water, grass and again fossil, the one perdurable fact which emerges from present cultural life appears to be the greed which we have hardened into civilization: the plow driving "straight into the belly of the future" to create the "stilted El Dorado" of the Iowa capitol's golden dome. Until gold and greed appear in the poem, its prosody is a dance of modestly used alliteration and assonance combined with an iterative pairing of words ("this grid . . . this hardening lymph of haste"; "the lilt and ripple" of night birdsong; "the wickiups / now here, now there"; the Indian world "hemmed in or undermined" by treaties). Then with the plow the rhythm thrusts on spondees and iambs. I have been told by New Critics wearing their shining badges (For the Defense of Art) that imitative form is an offense in poetry, but in these poems it works. (pp. 99-100)

Always the natural world is turning into the religious and vice-versa, and always the religious is here and now as well as history. The speaker in the poems is, by her own account, an Anglican or Anglican *manqué*, but the poems turn the concept of the sacrament and the sacramental, common enough in Anglican tradition, into the notion of a sacramental universe, Bonaventure's *vestigia dei*, a place where everything may or may not be sacrament. Plant and animal curiosities observed with a taxonomist's eye for detail appear and blaze or drift into ugliness or nothingness until one cannot distinguish whether the revelations are natural or divine. (p. 100)

If the sacramental is also the natural, the "scientific," in Clampitt's world, so also is the departure from sacrament which is the original fault. **"Good Friday"** is the massacre of the innocent in the survival of the fittest: the death of Charles Darwin's daughters amid his wife's Wedgwood pieties, the celebration of cruel pieties in a bourgeois overstuffed world, and Olduvai where the pharisee, the killer and the innocent were all present. Clampitt's poems persistently render the savagery of human nature: of love or lust gone only recriminative (**"The Kingfisher"**; **"A Hairline Fracture"**) of child-mother and child-icon relations gone flat across the centuries from Greece to Israel to Vietnam to the poet herself (**"A Procession at Candlemas"**); the savagery of Jewish children burning in vision and in actuality (**"The Burning Child"** which apparently also plays off Robert Southwell's poem, "The Burning Babe"); the softer savagery of decadent fathers seeking to seduce their daughters, with fine living, away from their own fine living in the artifice of eternity which is the convent.

Yet sometimes at the height of the deliberation over such savagery built in by evolution, the poet sees something like the descent of the Whitsun dove in the yellow capped bird of **"A Procession at Candlemas"** or the "Kingfisher" of the title poem which is all fire and beauty and suffering. . . . And this creates both the social conscience and the sense of tragedy.

The poetry is of a difficult sort—like Donne's metaphysical stuff the product of an effort to understand a science-interpreted world in terms of the verities of personal experience and to wrestle with a Christian dogma gone superstitious through struggling with it all. The wrestler is a self that cannot let go of vision, of direct experience, or of science. Hence in part the tangled syntax. Hence in part the prosody of a kind that Dante might have called shaggy. The product is an intellectual poetry like Donne's in some respects. At times the poetry lets go of the natural scene to rise to a kind of mystical statement worthy of Hopkins or of Sir John Davies at his best. . . . (p. 101)

> Paul A. Olson, "The Marryings of All Likeness," in Prairie Schooner, *Vol. 51, No. 1, Spring, 1983, pp. 99-102.*

EDMUND WHITE

Amy Clampitt, who has just made one of the most brilliant debuts in recent American literary history, can do everything with words but tell a story—and stories are what she wants her poems to be. In *The Kingfisher* she takes up (or intends to take up) narratives involving great public themes—religion, politics, history, the Nazi holocaust, self-immolation as a form of protest, nuclear devastation, even the anguish Israel stirs in the Jewish pacifist. She also addresses (or wants to address) decisive personal moments—a dazzling glimpse of art ordering the disarray of life (**"Dancers Exercising"**) or, conversely, a dark vision of the terrifying disorder just behind the comforting insulation of the quotidian (**"A Hairline Fracture"**).

But her talent is neither narrative nor dramatic, and the plot of her poems is often left to the copious notes at the end of the book. . . .

In Clampitt's work, one senses not awkwardness but rather a strange fusion of an ambition to narrate and a talent for suppressing the tale, the talent betraying and transforming the ambition. In fact, her manner of writing a poem is actively antagonistic to the chore of telling a story. Her poems make me think of Schiller's remark that "even when the poet is himself the subject, if he would describe his feeling to us, we never learn of his condition directly and at first hand, but rather how he was reflected on it in his own mind, what he has thought about it as an observer of himself." And it is these reflections that Clampitt renders with exemplary vigor and courage.

A characteristic poem is **"Beethoven Opus 111."** Here Clampitt sets up a pair of opposites, the composer and her own father, a Midwestern farmer. Having started with these antipodes, she then shuttles back and forth between them, discovering all the ways in which they are joined. . . .

Typically, there is no mention of someone playing the piano. Instead, Clampitt shows us the profit to be had from flouting rules: she mixes metaphors with Shakespearean gusto and overwhelms us in a percussive flurry of satisfying overstatement. She is gorgeously guilty of the so-called "fallacy of imitative form" in the way her prosody imitates Beethoven's music. (p. 485)

"A Procession at Candlemas" fuses three distinct elements: the Purification of the Virgin; a mother dying in intensive care while her daughter drives toward her along Route 80; and an intricate fabric of allusions to birth and death in ceremony and in reality around the world and throughout history. A passage from **"Rain at Bellagio"** serves as a motto for the poet: "reining / the fragments of experience into one process— / being-and-becoming fused, a single scheme."

Narrative is by its very nature linear (from the past toward the present), economical (a small cast of characters), hierarchical (details subordinated to events), impulsive (the forward motion engendered by suspense or mystery) and causational. What Clampitt writes is circular, diffuse, vertiginous and organized through simultaneity. Her method is the one appropriate to our experience. She is not one of Schiller's "naïve" poets but a "sentimental" one, that is, one who refracts every mote of received light through the shattering prism of her sensibility. In the abundance of her imagination she has reminded at least one critic of Keats, but her anxiety—the anxious *luridness* of her perception—is incomparably modern. (p. 486)

> Edmund White, "Poetry As Alchemy," in The Nation, *Vol. 236, No. 15, April 16, 1983, pp. 485-86.*

RICHARD HOWARD

Of these 50 poems [in *The Kingfisher*], 14 have appeared in *The New Yorker,* consecrated there by the most fastidious editorial taste now (and for the last 25 years) operative in the world of commercial periodicals; in her own high middle ages, Amy Clampitt has had her first book published ninth in the Knopf Poetry Series, consecrated there by the most fastidious editorial taste now (and for the last four years) operative in the world of commercial publishing; embellished with commendations from Richard Wilbur and Helen Vendler, who has since reviewed the book at length in *The New York Review of Books* [see excerpt above] . . . this poetry is doomed to success.

Of course, success is perhaps the showiest way we have of ignoring our poets—thrusting them into the neglectful limelight where they can writhe—as if the sound were turned off on a brilliant screen—until someone rescues them from the pillory of acclaim. . . . Pathetically, I can only add to this syndrome of camouflaging celebrity, for I too enjoy and admire these poems at just that pitch of enthusiasm which sets them beyond the pale—or the murk—where poems usually *take*. It seems to me that *The Kingfisher* has given me more delight (what Roland Barthes calls *jóuissance*, not *plaisir*) than any first book of poems since the first book of poems I read by A. R. Ammons. Amy Clampitt does things in her own way, but of course unless we can say what that way is, it is not perhaps really doing them. I shall try.

It has to do with some readily identifiable devices. Syntax, for one thing . . . : the poem is wreathed around its grammar, often being one very long sentence, submissive to the voice, observant of the local inflections, but governing the weight of the lines on the page, *down* the page, so that we know throughout that we are within a governance, the thrall of grammar, which is the same word, if you trace it far enough "back," as glamour. . . . Clampitt's other main device, or at least one you can collect for yourself by merely glancing at her page, is her science of enjambment (replacing rhyme by unwonted suspensions). . . . Clampitt ends her lines—breaks them open—in such a way as to show meanings not otherwise evident. The sense strikes against the ends of lines and their beginnings like a river defining itself by its entertainment now of one bank, now of the other, and this axiological enclosure becomes her signature, Clampitt's way of ensuring the meaning by every method that comes to hand. (pp. 271-73)

In a culture like ours, near to drowning in its own garbage, [Clampitt] functions with a certain ecological security: waste not, want not, especially when it is out of others' waste that you can make up your own wants. Not surprisingly, there are fifteen pages of notes—not teasing, as in Eliot or Empson; not merely identifying, as in Moore; but midwifely: "the scheme may be clearer if this poem is thought of as a meditation in the form of a travelogue." One advantage about publishing your poems when you are so evidently a grown-up (which means, of course: uncertain, as no adolescent can afford to be, about what being a grown-up means) is that you don't have to be nervous about being hard, obscure, or even just complicated. You just go ahead and tell how to get on with it. These poems are enormously allusive (nor does she reveal that we need to remember "milk of Magnesia" is a classical reference as willingly as she explains her Catholic ones: "clean as a crucifix— a thrift . . . that looks like waste"), and they are expansive too—from Iowa to Greece by way of Italy, France, and England, with flying visits to Africa and Tenochtitlán. I suppose that is one way of saying (not claiming) that the poet is "major," "strong," "relevant"—whatever the current cant for the poet who shoulders others out of the way: Clampitt expects you to be prepared to deal with *anything* in her poems, and if you are not, she will help you. What she calls the "hazardous redefinition of structures / no one has yet looked at" is what we can listen for, look to initially, in her poems. They will reward us as only the new poet can, by making us re-order the old poets, and adding herself to what it is we can do to the world ("everything that is the case") by perceiving it. I shall praise *The Kingfisher* best by saying that its poet jeopardizes her second book extravagantly: I have never waited for *the next installment* with greater qualms, yet with greater confidence. (pp. 274-75)

Richard Howard, "'The Hazardous Definition of Structures'," in Parnassus: Poetry in Review, *Vol. 11, No. 1, Spring-Summer, 1983, pp. 271-75.*

PETER STITT

The Kingfisher is Clampitt's first volume, in many ways an almost dazzling performance. (p. 430)

The interlocking of vowel and consonant sounds is as impressive as the range of the diction, the way the words function to broaden implication as they echo, reflect, and refract one another.

I began this book as I recommend you begin it, at the back, by reading the notes. Besides making individual poems easier to read, this exercise will introduce you immediately to certain important facets of Clampitt's sensibility. For one thing, we notice an interest in the life sciences—biology, ornithology, oceanography, anthropology—along with literature, mythology, history, and the classical world generally. One result of all this learning (facts, book facts, what are you?) is a tendency towards pedanticism, an overloading of the poems with accurate detail at the expense of feeling, emotion. Clampitt seems to prefer the past to the present, material already covered in books to that drawn raw from life. To say this is neither entirely accurate nor entirely fair—her best poems are those which describe natural events, and while these poems are often filled with learned allusions, they also reflect a good deal of close

observation of nature itself. But her weakest poems are generally those that deal with the most contemporary facets of human (as opposed to animal or vegetable) life, poems such as **"A Procession at Candlemas,"** which purports to relate a cross-country drive on Interstate 80, but which shows no real sympathy with, and thus no ability to describe, either the people encountered or the life lived. (p. 431)

The book is quite long and has a thoughtful structure, based on water, earth, fire, and air as metaphorical components of existence. These four medieval elements function better as images than as ideas, however; despite her learning, Clampitt is primarily a descriptive, rather than an intellectual, poet. This is why the book, for all its bulk, still seems rather thin; reading it is a bit like eating a gallon of bouillon at one sitting; you are filled up and feel heavy, but an hour later wonder where all that substance has gone. The heaviness in these poems lies in detail and texture rather than in thematic content. . . . (pp. 431-32)

Peter Stitt, "'Words, Book Words, What Are You?'" in The Georgia Review, *Vol. XXXVII, No. 2, Summer, 1983, pp. 428-38.**

RICHARD TILLINGHAST

It is hard to think of any poet who has written as well about the natural world as Amy Clampitt does. **"The Kingfisher"** opens with nine splendid poems about the New England seashore—its weather, its tidal flora and fauna, and its effect on the observer. But this is not to be thought of as "nature poetry" if that term suggests the vague outlines, suffused with metaphysical half ideas, of Wordsworth and the American Transcendentalists. One is led to imagine the writings of an expert naturalist with a poet's virtuoso command of vocabulary, gift for playing the English language like a musical instrument and startling and delightful ability to create metaphor—to invoke a spectrum of previously unthought-of but apt associations beyond the scope of ordinary human imagination.

When you read Amy Clampitt, have a dictionary or two at your elbow. Her curiosity and lovingly precise attention to the world, both natural and man-made, have their logical extension in her knowledge and choice of words. Thus, "blue willowware / plates go round the dado"; "eiders" seen on the water are characterized by that delightful, old-fashioned adjective "trig"; a turtle is seen as "domed repoussé / leather with an underlip of crimson"—and "repoussé," once pictured, forever enriches one's notion of a turtle's shell. . . . This use of words, while dazzling, even overrich for some palates, is not done out of sheer ostentation. I have mentioned the way the vocabulary serves the poet's sharp eye. In turn the recherché words become elements in Miss Clampitt's extremely musical verse.

In conventional nature poetry, the natural world is so thoroughly expropriated by the concerns of the human observer that it often hardly has room to breathe. At the other extreme, the pure naturalist can so isolate nature from the human that the sense of man's relation to nature is lost. I admire in Amy Clampitt's seashore poems the way they entwine the human with the natural without suffocating nature. (pp. 12, 30)

Richard Tillinghast, "Nature, Fantasy, Art," in The New York Times Book Review, *August 7, 1983, pp. 12, 30.**

PETER PORTER

Amy Clampitt is in the line of remarkable American women poets—Emily Dickinson (see Ms Clampitt's **'Lindenbloom'**), Marianne Moore and Elizabeth Bishop (see the rest of her book *passim*). She ranges from Dickinson's transformations of reality to Moore's and Bishop's beautifully imagined and tensely described surfaces. She is a virtuoso of the here and the palpable.

It is probably only my temperament which causes me to lose patience occasionally with her plethora of description [in *The Kingfisher*]. She can paint you in words surfaces as touchable as Alma-Tadema's marble, but you wonder whether her effects may not be as empty as his often are. . . . [The line-breaks in Clampitt's poetry seem highly arbitrary.] This is almost fashion writing in verse, its precision a sort of supreme accessorising of nature. After a while, the closeupness and professionalism induce myopia.

Such detailing is a received style in poetry today: we are being challenged to reinterpret, re-see even, the world about us. Yet it is all too easy to overdo, too readily inflated. In **'Beach Glass'** the bell on a buoy is said to be 'deaf as Cassandra / to any note but warning.' This is a nearly redundant simile. Elsewhere the poem, though embodying a familiar notion that glass, made from sand, returns to sand by the action of the sea, gains a fine onward-moving impetus. And Ms Clampitt's worst habit, of marching densely assembled phrases forward like dragoons, can occur in otherwise well-wrought pieces, such as **'Botanical Nomenclature,'** where the progress of the poem has to support 'stemrib grisaille edge-tasselled / with opening goblets.' Like many writers, she understands her own temptations, referring in one place to her fondness for 'fleeing instead / towards scenes of transhumance.'

The poems in the second part of *The Kingfisher* are less devoted to 'transhumance.' Some of them are attractive and warmly personal. . . . In these poems she is less likely to overload the ark. Despite my carpings, I enjoyed the book. Its tone is surprisingly friendly, a sort of Episcopalian laving-on of eyes.

Peter Porter, "Painting in Words," in The Observer, *June 17, 1984, p. 22.**

Robert (Lowell) Coover

1932-

American novelist, short story writer, dramatist, and poet.

Coover uses his fiction to startle and fascinate the reader. He believes, with John Barth, that literature has reached a state of "exhaustion." In his search for new literary approaches, Coover produces works in which the distinction between fantasy and reality becomes blurred. By taking standard elements from fairy tales, biblical stories, or historical events and placing them in a distorted context, Coover strives to deconstruct the myths and traditions which people create to give meaning to life. Robert Scholes has cited Coover's work, along with those by Barth, Donald Barthelme, and W. H. Gass, as examples of "metafiction," a term he defines as writing that "attempts, among other things, to assault or transcend the laws of fiction. . . ."

In the novel *The Origin of the Brunists* (1966), Coover describes the formation of a religious cult, the Brunists, after the survivor of a coal mine disaster, Giovanni Bruno, claims he was saved by divine intervention. In this work Coover investigates the human need to create myths, to impose order and purpose on chaos and inexplicable tragedy. Coover's second novel, *The Universal Baseball Association, Inc., J. Henry Waugh, Prop.* (1968), takes this theme somewhat further. An expansion of Coover's short story "The Second Son" (1962), this novel portrays a lonely, middle-aged accountant who devises a world for himself through a table baseball game. In obvious parallels to God, J. Henry Waugh creates the players, their histories, and their futures. The plot climaxes when the dice dictate that a favorite player must die; at this point Waugh has become so involved with the game that the "reality" of his life merges with the "reality" of the game. Coover blurs the lines between the two "realities" and leads the reader to question which of the two worlds is "invented."

Coover's next work, *Pricksongs & Descants* (1969), is a collection of short stories, some of which were written early in his career. By making readers aware that they are reading fiction and by subverting myths, Coover attempts in this book to induce an appreciation of new patterns. In *Pricksongs & Descants* Coover takes stories from the Bible ("The Brother," "J's Marriage"), fairy tales ("The Gingerbread House," "The Door"), and familiar everyday events ("Panel Game," "The Babysitter") and twists them into original, unexpected shapes. "The Brother," for example, relates the story of Noah's brother, who helps build the ark and then is left by Noah to drown. Along with other pieces, *Pricksongs & Descants* contains "Seven Exemplary Fictions" with a prologue in which Coover explains his literary intentions. He contends that "great narratives remain meaningful through time as a language-medium between generations, as a weapon against the fringe-areas of our consciousness, and as a mythic reinforcement of our tenuous grip on reality. The novelist uses familiar mythic or historical forms to combat the content of those forms and to conduct the reader . . . to the real, away from mystification to clarification, away from magic to maturity, away from mystery to revelation. And it is above all to the need for new modes of perception and fictional forms able to encompass them that I . . . address these stories."

Coover's next novel, *The Public Burning* (1977), brought him wide recognition. In this novel Coover uses facts from the 1953 conviction and execution of Julius and Ethel Rosenberg and brings in then-Vice-President Richard Nixon as narrator. Creating bizarre scenes full of perversity and violence, Coover attempts to point out how destructive American self-concepts are. As he said of the book: "I originally felt back in 1966 that the execution of the Rosenbergs had been a watershed event in American history which we had somehow managed to forget or repress. . . . I was convinced, one, that they were not guilty as charged, and, two, even had they been, the punishment was hysterical and excessive. . . . [It] was important that we remember it, that we not be so callous as to just shrug it off, or else it can happen again and again." Due to the controversial subject of *The Public Burning*, Coover had great difficulty getting it published and faced an onslaught of negative reviews upon publication. Concurrently, however, some critics praised the book as brilliant.

A Political Fable (1980) is an expanded version of Coover's story "The Cat in the Hat for President" (1968). In this novel Coover presents the Dr. Seuss character, with all his zany antics, as a presidential candidate. Despite its broad farce, the book ends with the cat's murder and the symbolic death of artistic, creative energies. *Charlie in the House of Rue* (1980) is a novella which Coover attempted to write in the style of a silent film. Beginning in a slapstick mode, the book soon becomes surreal and horrific as the Chaplinesque protagonist accidentally hangs the heroine and frantically and unsuccessfully tries to save her. Here Coover manipulates such techniques as pratfalls and sight gags to show their inherent violence. *Spanking the Maid* (1981) is an experimental work in which the story is built around multiple repetitions of a single scene. A recent collection of short stories, *In Bed One Night & Other Brief Encounters* (1983), demonstrates Coover's talent for transforming standard occurrences into extraordinary events and for focusing on the act of writing itself.

Although the esoteric nature of Coover's writing has limited his readership, he has received significant scholarly recognition. Throughout his career his novels, stories, and plays reflect his comments in a 1973 interview: "Artists re-create; they make us think about doing all the things we shouldn't do, all the impossible, apocalyptic things, and weaken and tear down structures so that they can be rebuilt, releasing new energies. Realizing this gave me an excuse to be the anarchist I've always wanted to be. I discovered I could be an anarchist and be constructive at the same time."

(See also *CLC*, Vols. 3, 7, 15; *Contemporary Authors*, Vols. 45-48; *Contemporary Authors New Revision Series*, Vol. 3; *Dictionary of Literary Biography*, Vol. 2; and *Dictionary of Literary Biography Yearbook: 1981.*)

PETER S. PRESCOTT

Like a child who pats a pile of wet sand into turrets and crenelated ramparts, Robert Coover prods at our most banal distractions and vulgar obsessions, nudging them into surreal and alarming forms. His fictions—novels, stories and, in ["A Theological Position"], plays—sound at times like incantations which, as they progress, mount to frenzy. What began slowly, seemingly grounded in homely realistic details, lurches, reels a bit, becomes possessed by manic excitation; the characters' faces dissolve to reveal archetypal forms beneath; time and direction come unglued; the choices a writer makes to send his story one way or another are ignored so that simultaneously all possible alternatives occur and, at the end, as often as not, we find our laughter contracting in our throats because some of Coover's stories can be fearsome indeed.

From fantasies that crowd our minds in idle moments Coover's best tales come. At first simple distractions, the fantasies assume control. . . . A baby-sitter arrives and, for a moment, her employer is distracted by lust. Images gnaw at the corners of this man's consciousness; certain scenes recur, theme and variations, as the pace accelerates. Which are "real," which imagined? Where, in fact, is the point of departure, the tonic note? (p. 97)

This is Coover's most intriguing skill: while casting his stories loose from time and realism, he maintains the form and pace that narrative requires, shaping from banal details stories and symbols that have the timelessness, the compelling but oblique reality, of myth. He plays, too, with literary stories that have the qualities of myth, revising them to remind us of the eternal attraction of the gingerbread house even if, behind the cherry door, there is a "sound of black rags flapping." (pp. 97-8)

In the longest play [included in "A Theological Position"], "The Kid," the conventions of the Western, often satirized before, are given a scathing beating. Every line spoken, every stage direction, is a cliché . . . ; the Kid is a psychopath pro-

grammed to respond only to certain stimuli, particularly Injuns, and the local hero has to be ceremoniously sacrificed. In [the title] play, the "theological position" is that virgin birth is no longer possible and therefore the priest had better have sex with the pregnant maiden; toward the end, only the players' genitals are talking, which should have been funnier, or more profound, or something. Never mind, Coover takes extraordinary risks and deserves forgiveness for his failures.

The remaining two plays are better. Both are monologues. In one ["**Love Scene**"], a director, perhaps God, urges two actors to show some feeling in their love scene, but they respond only with impassive motions. A scene with intriguing reverberations: perhaps Coover is suggesting that the first attempt to create love failed, or that love cannot respond to the clichés this director uses. . . . Coover's effect here, as elsewhere, derives in part from the deliberate artificiality of actors. . . . (pp. 98, 100)

The other monologue, "**Rip Awake,**" may be Coover's "Emperor Jones." Rip Van Winkle toils up his mountain again, half dreading, half looking forward to his next encounter with the little men: "I mean. listen, I don't entirely regret them twenty years." Rip is in bad shape. He can't remember things well, can't sleep now, wonders whether the dwarfish bowlers get their importance from him or he from them. He worries about the Revolution: did it really happen, and if so and he slept through it, does he need his own? Are the "little buggers" in fact real? Anyway, Rip is, as he says, "proceeding back up the mountain to rassel with the spooks in his life." Internal or external, *those* are real, and that is what Coover writes about so well. (p. 100)

Peter S. Prescott, "Lumps in the Throat," in Newsweek, Vol. LXXIX, No. 20, May 15, 1972, pp. 97-8, 100.

B. H. FUSSELL

Parodic language is Coover's meat and potatoes. Words are where the action is and what the action is, so much so that the pieces [in *A Theological Position*] seem better adapted for radio than for stage. Coover's problem as a potential playwright is how to translate his large talent for sound effects into equally potent gesture and visible action. He solves the problem of a main action by exploiting in each piece a burlesque re-enactment of some form of ritual sacrifice, moving from the myth of Movie Western in *The Kid* to Christian myth in the title play. In *A Theological Position,* a sort of Chaucerian fabliau, the main comedy depends upon the radical incongruity between what the Priest is doing (screwing the wife) and what he is saying (persuading the husband by Thomistic argument that the Immaculate Conception is impossible). . . . But the play's—and the Priest's—climax depends upon the precise location of an answering voice—*Her CUNT speaks.* After which, so does the Man's—and the Priest's—Prick, in a travesty of the miraculous tongues of the Holy Ghost. What is so concrete for the aural and visual imagination, however, is more problematic for the literal concreteness of the stage. (p. 756)

B. H. Fussell, "On the Trail of the Lonesome Dramaturge," in The Hudson Review, Vol. XXVI, No. 4, Winter, 1973-74, pp. 753-62.*

ROBERT SCHOLES

Metafiction assimilates all the perspectives of criticism into the fictional process itself. It may emphasize structural, formal, behavioral, or philosophical qualities, but most writers of metafiction are thoroughly aware of all these possibilities and are likely to have experimented with all of them. . . . [Consider] four works of metafiction by four American writers: John Barth's *Lost in the Funhouse*, Donald Barthelme's *City Life*, Robert Coover's *Pricksongs and Descants*, and W. H. Gass' *In the Heart of the Heart of the Country*. All four of these books are collections of short pieces. This is not merely a matter of symmetry. When extended, metafiction must either lapse into a more fundamental mode of fiction or risk losing all fictional interest in order to maintain its intellectual perspectives. The ideas that govern fiction assert themselves more powerfully in direct proportion to the length of a fictional work. Metafiction, then, tends toward brevity because it attempts, among other things, to assault or transcend the laws of fiction—an undertaking which can only be achieved from within fictional form.

The four works chosen here are impressive in themselves: the products of active intelligence grappling with the problems of living and writing in the second half of the twentieth century. . . . Each of the four books, taken as a whole, emphasizes one aspect of metafiction which may be related to one of the aspects of fiction and criticism. . . .

Lost in *the Funhouse* (formal)	*City Life* (behavioral)
Pricksongs *and Descants* (structural)	*In the Heart of the* *Heart of the Country* (philosophical)

These four books, of course, do not fit into the four categories described above like pigeons into pigeonholes. Their metafictional resourcefulness alone would ensure that. But each one does take a distinct direction, which can be designated initially and tentatively by the above diagram. (pp. 114-15)

[In *Pricksongs and Descants* Coover is] less directly concerned with the conditions of being than are Gass and Barthelme, and more immediately interested in the order of fiction itself. . . . Both descants and pricksongs are contrapuntal music. They run counter to the *cantus firmus* of behavior. But to run counter is not to run free. These songs must speak to us finally about reality, however roundabout their approach. (p. 118)

[Coover] sees contemporary man as living in a contracting universe, forced to re-assume "cosmic, eternal, supernatural (in its soberest sense) and pessimistic" perspectives. In such a world the writer must use

> the fabulous to probe beyond the phenomenological, beyond appearances, beyond randomly perceived events, beyond mere history. But these probes are above all—like [Don Quixote's] sallies—challenges to the assumptions of a dying age, exemplary adventures of the Poetic Imagination, high-minded journeys toward the New World and never mind that the nag's a pile of bones. (*Pricksongs* . . .)

Coover, like Gass, senses an order beyond fiction and beyond phenomena, which may be discovered. But where Gass seeks to move through behavior to essence, Coover makes the parallel move through form to idea. This is why some of the most successful things in *Pricksongs* are reworkings of fairy tales which probe into the human needs behind them.

Gass thinks of a "real" Hansel and Gretel "who went for a walk in a real forest but they walked too far in the forest and suddenly the forest was a forest of story with the loveliest little gingerbread house in it" (*In the Heart* . . .). But Coover thinks of a fictional Hansel and Gretel who find in a gingerbread house the door to reality. . . . This gingerbread house is a garden of sexuality, with its phallic chimney and cherry-red door. Sex itself is the door that connects fictional form and mythic idea: which is why these tales are called pricksongs and descants, or "death-cunt-and-prick songs," as Granny calls them in the opening story, **"The Door."** Apertures and orifices are as dominant in *Pricksongs* as mirrors and containers are in the *Funhouse*. Coover's technique is to take the motifs of folk literature and explode them into motivations and revelations, as the energy might be released from a packed atomic structure. **"The Door"** itself is a critical mass obtained by the fusion of "Jack the Giant-Killer," "Beauty and the Beast," "Little Red Riding Hood," and other mythic fictions. In the heavy water of this mixture there is more truth than in many surface phenomena. Granny is aware of this as she ruminates on the younger generation's preoccupation with epidermal existence. . . . Granny is witch and wolf, wife and mother; she is the old Beauty who married the Beast—"only my Beast never became a prince"—she is temptress and artist, a Scheherazade who has "veils to lift and tales to tell"; she is initatrix into the mysteries of her own degradation and transfiguration:

> for I have mated with the monster my love and listened to him lap clean his lolly after. . . . I have been split with the pain and terrible haste of his thick quick cock and then still itchin and bleedin have gazed on as he lept other bitches at random and I have watched my own beauty decline my love and still no Prince no Prince and yet you doubt that I understand? and loved him my child loved the damned Beast after all. . . .

The "flux and tedium" of phenomenal existence is not reality but the thing which hides it. For Coover, reality is mythic, and the myths are the doors of perception. Like a mind-blown Lévi-Strauss, he is concerned to open those doors.

Coover's mythic vision can be defined partly by its distance from Barthelme's perspective on myth. Usually a fabricator of assemblages of "flux and tedium," in "The Glass Mountain" Barthelme gives us a fairy tale of sorts. It seems there is this man climbing—grasping in each hand "a sturdy plumber's friend"—a glass mountain "at the corner of Thirteenth Street and Eighth Avenue." In one hundred numbered sentences and fragments he reaches the top with its "beautiful enchanted symbol."

> 97. I approached the symbol, with its layers of meaning, but when I touched it, it changed into only a beautiful princess.
>
> 98. I threw the beautiful princess headfirst down the mountain. . . . (*City Life* . . .)

This is myth enmeshed in phenomena. The "symbol" in the story symbolizes symbolism, reducing it to absurdity. It becomes an object with a sign on it that says "beautiful enchanted symbol." The magical transformation of "symbol" into "princess" is simply a change of signs. Barthelme is like a comic magician who removes a sign labeled "rabbit" from behind a sign labeled "hat" in a parody of all magic. But when Coover gives us a magician putting a lady in a hat in the last story of *Pricksongs,* she is a real lady in a real hat:

> Pockets handkerchief. Is becoming rather frantic. Grasps hat and thumps it vigorously, shakes it. Places it once more on table, brim up. Closes eyes as though in incantations, hands extended over hat. Snaps fingers several times, reaches in tenuously. Fumbles. Loud slap. Withdraws hand hastily in angry astonishment. Grasps hat. Gritting teeth, infuriated, hurls hat to floor, leaps on it with both feet. Something crunches. Hideous piercing shriek. (*Pricksongs* . . .)

Magic is real. The fairy tales are true. Beast and princess are not phony symbols for Coover but fictional ideas of human essences. Barth and Barthelme are the chroniclers of our despair: despair over the exhausted forms of our thought and our existence. No wonder they laugh so much. Coover and Gass are reaching through form and behavior for some ultimate values, some true truth. No wonder they come on so strong. All four are working in that rarefied air of metafiction, trying to climb beyond Beckett and Borges, toward things that no critic—not even a metacritic, if there were such a thing—can discern. (pp. 120-23)

> *Robert Scholes, "The Range of Metafiction: Barth, Barthelme, Coover, Gass," in his* Fabulation and Metafiction, *University of Illinois Press, 1979, pp. 114-23.**

KIRKUS REVIEWS

"The Cat in the Hat for President": that was the title of this satire [*A Political Fable*] when first published in 1968 (in the literary magazine *New American Review*)—and that's the single, inspired, ferocious joke (dated not one whit) that keeps most of these 88 miniature pages roaring along. . . . [The] Convention turns into a circus: first a catchy slogan starts appearing everywhere ("Let's make the White House a Cat House"); next, an irresistible campaign song fills the air ("So go to bat for the Cat in the Hat! / He's the Cat who knows where it's at! / With Tricks and Voom and Things like that!"); then funny hats, gorgeous cheerleaders, cute gags—and finally the arrival of the Cat himself, who pulls Seuss-like stunts, wreaks cartoon havoc, wows the crowd, and wins the nomination on the first ballot. . . . But the Cat's antics . . . eventually get out of hand . . . and he's skinned alive by an angry mob. True, Coover pushes this finale into the sort of excess and literalism that so thoroughly undermined *The Public Burning:* "While the Cat burned, the throng fucked in a great conglobation of races, sexes, ages, and convictions; it was the Great American Dream in oily actuality . . ." But otherwise the sheer awful exuberance of the central absurdity here—which somehow, paradoxically, tempers Coover's naked loathing with Seuss' more good-natured mania—works to perfection: a devastating, across-the-board swipe at presidential imagery and campaign hype, perhaps even righter for Election '80 than it was for the more issue-centered nightmares of '68. (pp. 724-25)

> *A review of "A Political Fable," in* Kirkus Reviews, *Vol. XLVIII, No. 11, June 1, 1980, pp. 724-25.*

JEROME KLINKOWITZ

If the Cat in the Hat were to publish novels for adults, they would probably read like the works of Robert Coover. A ma-

gician with both words and circumstances, Coover writes of American absurdities with a crazy infectious rhythm that makes his nonsense convincing. . . .

The Cat in the Hat books our kids love portray . . . infantile dreams of messing up Mother's household, a mad unleashing of every childish whim. *A Political Fable* does the same for us adults who've been living with presidential politics for the past eight months.

The Cat in the Hat for President? "I can lead it all by myself!" exclaims his slogan, and his campaign tactics add just that final touch, that one last straw, that breaks the spell of rationality that keeps the whole spectacle of our presidential elections on this side of lunacy. . . .

And what, after all, happens in a Cat in the Hat charade? After the punning, messing up, and mortification at Mother's discovery of the hijinks, nothing much at all—everything is swept up into the Cat's magical cleaning machine, and the page is clear for another book's adventure.

Like presidential campaigns, the Cat in the Hat books succeed each other like the turning of seasons, and the insight into ritual—as always, Coover's greatest gift—is the more serious side of this ludicrously funny book.

> *Jerome Klinkowitz, "Cat in the Hat for President!!!" in* Book Week—Chicago Sun-Times, *July 27, 1980, p. 13.*

CAROLE COOK

[*A Political Fable*] is not exactly a new book. In fact, it is stretching things to resurrect in hardcover a short story that, when published in *New American Review No. 4* in 1968, ran to 39 pages. . . . It's not that the fable, in which the renowned Dr. Seuss character gets the presidential nomination because of his charismatic magic tricks, doesn't hold up. But . . . *A Political Fable* seems more a trip down memory lane than a universal satire. The increasingly demonic nature of the Cat in the Hat, the stoned-out double talk and sloganeering, the haywire absurdity embraced by officials and public alike recall those days of Turn On-Tune In-Drop Out and Hell-No We-Won't-Go. It's still a dandy short story but, to cite another 1970s chestnut, it isn't Relevant.

> *Carole Cook, in a review of "A Political Fable," in* Saturday Review, *Vol. 7, No. 12, August, 1980, p. 66.*

CHARLA GABERT

Charlie in the House of Rue is a miniature tragicomedy which takes as its point of departure the character and conventions of a Charlie Chaplin film. The leading character is not only named Charlie, but he also physically resembles Chaplin. . . . Charlie falls into the same straits as his namesake, employs characteristic gestures (e.g., twirling his cane), and possesses the same elastic naivete. As the story progresses, however, we are drawn away from our preconceptions about a Chaplinesque Charlie and into the dream-like, funhouse world of Coover.

The aesthetic problem of translating literature into the medium of film is a commonly discussed one, but Coover's opposite task is equally difficult and interesting. Like Joyce's experiments in *Ulysses* in writing prose that resembles other nonverbal media (such as the fugue), Coover's words create the texture of a silent Charlie Chaplin movie.

The text preserves certain formal aspects of film: visually precise rendering of actions, sudden shifts in scene, and the juxtaposition of ostensibly unrelated images. Coover utilizes only the present tense to simulate the immediacy of a live performance—of things seen rather than told—and to divorce the action from any antecedents or future results. Written in a consistently descriptive prose, the text captures physical motion with the same precise, literal accuracy that a camera does. Sentences are rhythmically related to the movements they refer to, ranging from short and curt to long and breathless. "He stands, brushes himself off, smiles apologetically up at the lady, sets the vase back gently on the balustrade, mops his brow, straightens his tie, leans back in exhaustion, and knocks the vase to the tiled floor, where it shatters in a thousand pieces." Or: "He waves at her. He jumps up and down. He throws her a kiss." Since virtually all the action of the story is physical, Coover varies his prose to differentiate movements and to break the activity into meaningful units. In so doing, he emphasizes not only the visual quality of a silent film, but also the underlying pacing and tempo that are fundamental to all films—the rhythm that is created by the movements of the camera, the length of each shot or scene in relation to the whole, and the repetition of discrete images or motifs.

The unique characteristics of silent films—absence of dialogue, and exaggerated gestures approaching pantomine—particularly dominate our expectations and shape the text. Charlie's psychological isolation and the primitive level of communication with other characters are economically expressed by the absence of speech, resulting in the impression that the "house of rue" is really a soundless vacuum. Coover has also drawn upon familiar conventions of horror film to reiterate the connection of his text to film: the shot of an emaciated white hand emerging from a coffin to push back the lid; the idea of a victim trapped in a house that is actively hostile; the silent scream which cannot be heard and is terrifying for that reason.

Although most of the familiar elements of a Chaplin film are on display—Chaplin as comic victim and mischievous prankster, the slapstick antics of a well-intentioned but clumsy buffoon, the pretty but unapproachable girl—the crucial element of humor is missing. . . . Without the laugh to cushion his fall, Charlie gets hurt; without the humor to win us over, Charlie looks malicious.

The narrator's voice is, for Coover, unusually circumspect and unobtrusive. In his earlier work of short fictions, *Pricksongs and Descants,* Coover did not hesitate to emphasize the author's controlling, inventive role and to point to the choices involved in the creative act. The multiplicity of overlapping, contradictory events, and the prismatic quality of the plots, required the presence of a self-consciously inventive narrator, who proclaimed his arbitrary power and worked to subvert the idea that a single reality was being portrayed. In *Charlie in the House of Rue,* however, Coover defines the narrator's role in terms of the passive, uniquely cinematic act of viewing, using it to further create for the reader the experience of watching a silent Chaplin film. Although Coover tracks a linear, narrative course through a kaleidoscopic series of events—which are related thematically rather than causally—the narrator's complete separation from the internal thoughts and feelings of his characters allows him to function as a "speculative spectator," who reads motives and meanings into Charlie's gestures and facial expressions much as a movie audience would do. The traditional concept of the narrator as a storyteller with some degree of insight into his characters recedes in importance; what replaces

it is the viewpoint of an observer who watches and records events (over which he has no acknowledged control) as they unfold.

The nature of the events in *Charlie in the House of Rue* suggests, in fact, that no one is in control, least of all Charlie, who bounces from room to room like a pinball, buffeted by his own fears and desires, as well as by the constantly shifting rooms, objects and people. Assembled from a cast of easily identifiable stock figures, the people he encounters are little more than cartoon characters who function symbolically, almost allegorically—the policeman representing ineffectual authority, the sexually aggressive maid unbridled lust. These characters present us with no past or future, primarily because they cannot and do not speak. Their silence locks them into a reality that is visually compelling but ontologically empty; their actions are stylized, obsessive, and redundant. Each character exists in a separate realm—maid in the bedroom, woman in white in the foyer—while Charlie shuttles between them; when they vanish from Charlie's sight, they seem to disappear altogether. As the story progresses, they lose any semblance of being independent actors, and by the end, they are simply part of the hostile environment. Initially indifferent and unresponsive to Charlie, they grow increasingly aggressive, and attack him or try to thwart him. But even these actions resemble motiveless, gratuitous acts that are prompted not by their feelings or personal reactions to Charlie, but by an inexplicable stimulus outside of them.

The surreal environment that exists inside the house is a landscape littered with dreamlike symbols, objects that change into something else at their own volition. Charlie throws a pie into an old man's face, but the face turns out to belong to the mournful woman in white, the last person Charlie wants to injure; her eyes are actually the old man's, but they soon metamorphose into the maid's bare behind. . . . As the chaos grows more violent around him, Charlie too becomes more frantic in his futile effort to gain control of the unpredictable activity threatening to engulf him.

The "house of rue" exists solely as an interior space, a world unto itself which is as claustrophobic as a sound stage. The space is never defined clearly; doors and rooms disappear and materialize as Charlie leaves and enters them. His presence in the house is never explained, his entrance is never recorded, but it is clear from the beginning that the house is an alien environment in which he is first an intruder, then a prisoner. As a metaphor for the psyche, the house contains the forces that Charlie unintentionally sets in motion as a prisoner of his own fears and desires, which the house's inhabitants merely reflect and exemplify. The concept of rue refers not only to the remorse and regret that Charlie feels for accidentally causing the woman in white to be hanged, but also to his growing recognition of himself as a moral force, someone who is not only sorry but who must suffer for his sins.

The contradiction between the other characters' initial indifference to Charlie and their subsequent hostility toward him suggests that they are emissaries sent to punish Charlie; it is not only internal guilt, but external retribution that he cannot escape. Indeed, the house is like a Kafkaesque torture chamber in which Charlie unwittingly finds himself judged, declared guilty, and punished, without even realizing that charges have been brought against him. (pp. 60-3)

The last half of the story follows Charlie's desperate, ineffectual efforts to save the woman in white. As she dangles in the foyer, Charlie careens from room to room, searching for something to cut the rope. (p. 63)

Charlie's progress from a state of playful innocence to one of fatal tragedy proceeds inexorably, despite his ostensibly random movement from one room, one situation, to the next. In confronting his own cruelty, he forfeits his familiar status as the eternal victim and assumes the role of victimizer. At the same time, as he falls prey to forces beyond his control and suffers the guilt of the woman's death, we see him as a modern anti-hero who lacks the resources to shape his own destiny. It is here, in the expansion of Charlie's character from the pathetic to the tragic, that Coover most clearly departs from the "Little Tramp" character. By the time we reach the conclusion, the sentimental ending of the silver screen will no longer suffice. Instead, Coover gives us Charlie clinging in mid-air to the woman's corpse as the lights go out around him—a black-humored inversion of a typical ending in which Charlie and the girl are finally united, then plunged into eternal darkness by the shrinking circle of the lens. (p. 64)

> Charla Gabert, "The Metamorphosis of Charlie," in Chicago Review, Vol. 32, No. 2, Autumn, 1980, pp. 60-4.

RICHARD ANDERSEN

Coover's fictions clearly emphasize their author's interest in providing his readers with the kinds of metaphors that are necessary for a healthy imagination. Unfortunately, Coover says between the lines in every story he writes, people today have lost their desire for the thrill of discovery. They have become comfortable with having their conventional viewpoints confirmed through a limited range of artistic forms that have outlived their usefulness. Each of Coover's stories, then, invites its reader to relinquish one or more of his traditional approaches to art and participate with its author in an exercise of wit that frequently juxtaposes what is fantastic in life with the everyday.

The principal method through which Coover liberates readers from sensibilities that have been deadened by the familiar is irony. Irony enables Coover and his readers to distance themselves from traditional forms without isolating themselves from the human content of those forms. As a result, Coover's readers have the opportunity and pleasure of tearing down many of society's inherited approaches to art and life without losing their concern for humanity's condition. The result is a healthy sense of humor and the awareness of a developing consciousness.

In his first novel, *The Origin of the Brunists,* Coover presents his readers with a fascinating interplay of realistic and artificial modes that enable his readers to enjoy his mockery of traditional narrative forms while simultaneously employing its conventions in vitally new ways. Similarly, Coover undercuts man's dependency on religion and history while revitalizing his interest in fiction as a way of ordering his universe. *The Universal Baseball Association, Inc., J. Henry Waugh, Prop.,* like *The Origin of the Brunists,* is primarily concerned with man's need to create order through fiction. . . . The fictions may be highly artificial, as in the case of games or mathematical formulas, or they may be more subjective, such as when they appear in the forms of myth, religion, and history. When man forgets his role as a creator of fiction, however, and begins to accept the works of his imagination as fact or truth, he finds himself

imprisoned and manipulated by the very perspectives that he constructed.

In the twenty-one fictions collected in *Pricksongs and Descants,* Coover focuses his attention on reinterpreting familiar stories, which have been traditionally revered for the human truths they contain, and emphasizing the variety of technical and imaginative possibilities available when art and life are free from limiting conventions. The nature of reality, Coover seems to be saying, is so complex that any single way of interpreting it must necessarily be false. Hence, the problem of nature's multiplicity becomes its own solution. For art truly to represent nature, it must be variable as nature itself.

Having recast the appeal for originality and multiplicity that unified *Pricksongs and Descants* into the four one-act plays that comprise *A Theological Position,* Coover returned to his interest in *The Public Burning,* a new view of the events surrounding the executions of Julius and Ethel Rosenberg that makes as legitimate a claim to truth as any objective statement of the facts:

> The truth for a narrator is not the same as the truth for a journalist, historian, or scientist. The author's truth comes out of a set of metaphors—even if sometimes he gives them names and calls them characters. So that in a work of fiction you can have a sense of terrible truth about a thing that doesn't seem to relate at all to the so-called real world. Normally, though, the metaphors *will* relate to the real world—language itself, after all, is a product of that world—and so fiction will have a second standard of truth. That is, the metaphors themselves have in the first place some *need* to arise, and the word "truth" is probably as good as any to describe why this is so. . . .

Reworking history, as he has done with myths, legends, and fairy tales, may represent a new arena in which Coover can explore further the interests that have been of primary concern to him since *The Origin of the Brunists:* "Like in the creation of myths, I sometimes transpose events for the sake of a kind of inner coherence, and there's a certain amount of condensation and so on, but mainly I accept that what I'm dealing with here is a society that is fascinated with real data, facts and figures, dates, newspaper stuff. I can't mess around too much with the data here lest I lose contact with that fascination." Nevertheless, "my own inclination as a writer is to move more and more in that direction, condensing, moving facts around, juxtaposing living and dead persons, myth and history. That would seem a useful and proper way to write about the past". . . . (pp. 141-43)

However Coover chooses to reinterpret history, his readers can be assured of accomplished and inventive stories that deal absurdly and metaphysically with the human condition without losing their sense of humor. (p. 143)

> Richard Andersen, in his Robert Coover, Twayne Publishers, 1981, 156 p.

JON ZONDERMAN

Robert Coover has turned Chaplin on his head. In *Charlie in the House of Rue* Coover has placed the Little Tramp in a house where his timing, no matter how perfect, can not draw from the other characters the slightest response.

At first, the Tramp is merely annoyed by this. But Coover doesn't just pose for us the "what if nobody responded" question. He goes a step further and sets the supporting characters on their own courses.

The beautiful woman, whom the Tramp is mystified and made humble by, tries to commit suicide. While attempting to keep her from her course—jumping off the top of the staircase—the Tramp accidentally pushes her over the edge, where she dangles by the rope around her neck while he scampers around the foyer and second storey trying to get her down. Even Charlie grabbing for his baggy pants to keep them up, then his derby to keep it on, then his pants, then his derby, pants, derby, pants, derby, can't bring humor to this grisly scene.

The bald man, yes, the ubiquitous bald man with the thick mustache and suspenders, whose pate is used for everything, including an ashtray, gives the Tramp his comeuppance by standing at the kitchen table, looking into the soup that he has been sullenly staring at throughout the story, and promptly urinating into it. . . .

The lights are always going out on the Tramp, and he finds himself in a place he never thought he'd be. He strikes the man, only to find it is the woman. . . . By the three-quarter point of the book, the story is moving at breakneck speed, yet there is no more slapstick to the pratfalls. It is no longer Chaplin, not even Olson and Johnson.

Once again, Coover has created a character beyond the edge, one who has taken his lunacy to the point where it turns on him.

Charlie has none of the political overtones of *The Public Burning,* where a crazed Richard Nixon goes out of his mind persecuting the Rosenbergs. The book stays away from religion, the theme of *The Origin of the Brunists,* Coover's first novel, which won him a William Faulkner Award in 1966. In *Brunists,* a Pennsylvania small-town newspaper editor turns the survivor of a mineshaft accident into a new messiah.

Charlie is closest to *The Universal Baseball Association Inc., J. Henry Waugh Prop.,* in which a man devises a dice-roll baseball game to amuse himself, only to have it envelop him to the point where his reality becomes that of the league, the games and the players.

The thread that runs through all Coover's work is the notion of America gone haywire, the fiercely independent character, always in control, suddenly out of control, no longer a part of the world around him. In Coover's world, not only do Americans have no history, but no reality. They are merely the lines of type in a newspaper, the statistics in a baseball record book and, finally, fleeting images on a moving-picture screen.

> *Jon Zonderman, in a review of "Charlie in the House of Rue," in* The American Book Review, *Vol. 4, No. 2, January-February, 1982, p. 24.*

GEORGE LEONARD

Denis Johnston wrote of Samuel Beckett that his works were "algebraic, in that his characters have the quality of X. And what X means, depends not upon him, but upon us." The Godot that bums wait for isn't simply God, but anything humans wait for that will solve everything. . . .

Robert Coover, in his new novella ["**Spanking the Maid**"], has adopted Beckett's algebraic method. There is a "maid"

and a "master," but they're as stylized as Beckett characters and will stand for any master-slave relationship you think fits.

The maid enters, tries to be perfect, fails; the master spanks her. She tries again, gets spanked again. Some of it sounds like Samuel Beckett rewriting "The Story of O": "And what has she done wrong today? he wonders, tracing the bloody welts with his fingertips. He has forgotten. It doesn't matter.". . .

We're not gaining Samuel Beckett but we are losing Robert Coover. He's a writer of great natural energies and they keep bursting out here, undercutting the Schopenhauer theme. It's odd to watch a novelist trying to be dull—and failing.

Coover has always found life bizarre, the opposite of monotony. His previous fables include a gang of media-wise politicians who prey upon the public's nostalgia for a childhood hero. . . . They run The Cat in the Hat for President. (Is it so different?)

And what about Coover's master of reality who made up an entire league of ballplayers who played ball games in his head? . . .

Robert Coover, we miss you.

> *George Leonard, "Robert Coover Tries on Beckett's Garb," in* Los Angeles Times Book Review, *May 30, 1982, p. 4.*

JOHN O'BRIEN

[*Spanking the Maid*] is a failed attempt to employ the methods of the *nouveau roman;* the repetitions, the variations upon images, the structural loops, the shifts in perspective, all seem wearily imitative, forced, and pretentious. Each morning a maid enters her employer's bedroom, and each morning she is spanked for her failures. . . . [There] is an implicit invitation to see how the book is constructed. . . . [However], the machinery creaks, sputters, and grinds; the tricks are telegraphed, even to the ending in which the employer and maid exchange roles. Finally, I began to suspect that some grand metaphor was rearing its ugly head. Or a fable: the man and his maid are supposed to represent the relationship between man and woman, between husband and wife, children and parents; or between artist and society, or artist and critic. No matter how well the artist does some things, so the fable might go, the critic will spank him for not doing others.

Spanking the Maid can be seen as new and inventive only if one forgets a dozen or so French novelists of the past 30 years. It is a simplification of the techniques of the French writers, and should not be viewed as much more.

> *John O'Brien, "Inventions and Conventions in the New Wave Novel," in* Book World—The Washington Post, *August 15, 1982, p. 10.**

LARRY McCAFFERY

[The] fiction of Robert Coover is tightly unified by its metafictional impulses. In examining the concept of man-as-fictionmaker, nearly all of Coover's works deal with characters busily constructing systems to play with or to help them deal with their chaotic lives. Some of these systems are clearly fictional in nature. . . . Yet Coover's work is filled with hints that other, less obviously artificial systems—such as mathematics, science, religion, myth, and the perspectives of history and politics—are also fictional at their core. Indeed, in most of Coover's fiction there exists a tension between the process of man creating his fictions and his desire to assert that his systems have an independent existence of their own. For Coover, this tension typically results in man losing sight of the fictional basis of his systems and eventually becoming trapped within them.

In developing this view of man-as-fiction-maker, Coover is hoping to illuminate not only the process through which narrative art is created but also the broad base of metaphor through which the universe is comprehended. His application points in the same direction as the study of the use of metaphor in so many other areas of investigation, such as anthropology, mathematics, linguistic analysis, the various metasciences, and so on. Each of these disciplines has tended to analyze its own structures as useful models or symbolic systems created by man—either consciously or through some sort of innate structuring agency within him—and then applied to the world. In his fascinating study, *The Myth of Metaphor,* Colin Turbayne has examined Descartes's mind-body dualism and Newton's universe-as-machine analogy as examples of the way in which metaphors gradually instill themselves as ontological verities. The process Turbayne describes for "undressing" such hidden metaphors is very similar to what Coover is aiming for in his fiction:

> First, the detection of the presence of the metaphor; second, the attempt to "undress" the metaphor by presenting the literal truth, "to behold the deformity of error we need only undress it"; and third, the restoration of the metaphor, only this time with awareness of its presence.

If we substitute Coover's concept of "fiction" for Turbayne's closely related term, "metaphor," we have a close approximation of Coover's method. For both Turbayne and Coover, the point is not at all *to do away* with metaphors and fictions; those forms that are still useful can continue to be applied and even admired as aesthetic objects—but this should be done with awareness of their true nature. This awareness does not hinder their utility, but it does permit us to break up more freely those forms which have lost their usefulness and to replace them with fresher, more vital constructions.

It is partially Coover's distrust of rigid, dogmatic attitudes of all kinds which leads him to dedicate his prologue to *Pricksongs and Descants* (perversely placed in the middle of his collection) to Cervantes. As explained by Coover, Cervantes's fictions "exemplified the dual nature of all good narrative art; . . . they struggled against the unconscious mythic residue in human life and sought to synthesize the unsynthesizable, sallied forth against adolescent thought-modes and exhausted art forms, and returned home with new complexities." Mistrusting absolutes of any kind and feeling that the complexities of reality are as inexhaustible as the number of perspectives we bring to bear on it, Coover directs much of his work at breaking the hold of these "unconscious mythic residues" (themselves a form of fiction) over people. One strategy used for this purpose is to use "familiar or historical forms to combat the content of those forms". . . . Thus Coover often creates his fictions out of precisely the sort of familiar myths, fictions, cliché patterns, and stereotypes whose *content* he hopes to undermine. This undermining is achieved at times by overt parody or irony, and at other times by allowing the elements to freely engage and contradict one another. But at all times Coover hopes to deal

with myth and fiction making on their own grounds (hence the metafictional character of all his works), and to use the energy stored within these mythic residues to break up the hold which they have and to redirect their forces.

Cervantes also represents for Coover a writer who felt the need to challenge the literary conventions of his age and who, in doing so, successfully created a narrative form capable of sustaining these challenges. Thus Coover observes, addressing Cervantes, "Perhaps above all else your works were exemplars of a revolution in narrative fiction, a revolution which governs us". . . . In *Don Quixote* Cervantes combined what Coover calls "poetic analogy and literal history"—a combination which is usually credited with having given birth to the novel. Ironically, many of the conventions initiated in part by Cervantes have today become just as dogmatized as the stifling conventions of the romance in Cervantes's time. If Cervantes opened up a new world for narrative fiction, this world has alarmingly begun to shrink once more. (pp. 25-8)

[Like] so many other contemporary writers and critics, Coover feels that relying on any one set of conventions (like those of realism) will lead inevitably to a dead end—much as relying on any single perspective will produce only a false perspective. Realizing that modern audiences have grown suspicious of many of the conventions of realism, Coover often adopts strategies which will allow him to deal with these suspicions openly. We find him experimenting with new or unusual narrative methods, but just as often we find him resurrecting the forms, techniques, and subject matter of past traditions which have lost their conventionality and staleness because of disuse.

One result of this insistence on form is that the metafictional quality of Coover's fiction derives as much from the *process at work* as it does from the content. His fiction can also be termed "self-reflexive" in the sense used by Roger Shattuck—that is, it "endlessly studies its own behaviors and considers them suitable subject matter. . . . It is not art for art's sake, but art about art . . . it strives to be its own subject." This self-directed aspect of Coover's work means that it is not only possible to view many of his fictions—including his three novels—as allegories about art, but that in many specific passages we discover that the text is discussing itself as it proceeds. Thus even in his first novel [*The Origin of the Brunists*], which of all his works seems the most realistic and concerned with social commentary, Coover's real subject remains the relationship between man and his invented creations—the creations we have broadly termed "fictions." (pp. 28-9)

Larry McCaffery, "Robert Coover and the Magic of Fiction Making," in his The Metafictional Muse: The Works of Robert Coover, Donald Barthelme, and William H. Gass, *University of Pittsburgh Press, 1982, pp. 25-98.*

JOHN BROSNAHAN

[*In Bed One Night & Other Brief Encounters* includes short] takes displaying Coover's prodigious literary technique. A conventioneer's high jinks in a stream-of-consciousness mode; non-sequiturs on the interstate; and the wisdom of fresh starts: all become opportunities for Coover's manic and inventive invasion of the modern mind.

John Brosnahan, in a review of "In Bed One Night & Other Brief Encounters," in Booklist, *Vol. 80, No. 2, September 15, 1983, p. 134.*

CARYN JAMES

Robert Coover's stories are mind games with a heart. *In Bed One Night and Other Brief Encounters* humanizes language games and literary theorizing, and, remarkably, does so by using cartoonish characters and a nearly anonymous narrative voice. While these nine very short pieces don't amount to much in themselves, they are miniature demonstrations of the control Coover displays in his more substantial work. Like a literary juggler, he keeps all the parts of his fiction in motion, balancing rhythm, word play, and the central image of the author creating his story. Or does the story create the author?

"Beginnings," written in 1972, masterfully explores this question. "In order to get started, he went to live alone on an island and shot himself," reads the first line. What he starts is the story we're reading.... This circular undercutting of cause and effect is the most facile part of **"Beginnings."** Reaching for substance, Coover brings the author-character to life, making him implausible, mundane, unique, and universal. The island becomes a postlapsarian Eden, complete with Eve (this time she's the one who gives up a rib), children, and the distractions and rewards of family life....

Though the more recent works are slighter, they share some characteristic Coover effects. "here's what happened it was pretty good" is the first line of **"An Encounter." "The Old Man"** starts, "this one has to do with an old man." Such stories belong to the second generation of metafiction: Coover not only writes about self-conscious storytelling, he assumes that we are aware of his self-referential posture. There's no need to introduce us to the pervasive but protean "he," the author-character at the center of most of his fiction....

"In Bed One Night" is a literary slapstick in which several strangers are assigned to share the same bed—social security cutbacks seem to be the problem. An old lady searches for her dentures, her one-legged brother lies at the foot of the bed, a drunken worker fucks a fat woman, and a skinny Oriental cowers, as the owner of the bed registers his shock: *"wha—?!* he cries out in alarm." Coover skillfully orchestrates this pandemonium in a breathless, unpunctuated style. Even when his comic technique is so emphatically in the foreground, he keeps an eye on the complexity of authorship. In his most farcical moments or his most deft and restrained moods, Coover is relentlessly energetic about one question. His fiction insists on asking where its own creativity comes from, and just as insistently answers that it exists only in the active process of writing and reading.

Caryn James, in a review of "In Bed One Night and Other Brief Encounters," in VLS, No. 22, December, 1983, p. 4.

A(rchibald) J(oseph) Cronin

1896-1981

Scottish novelist, dramatist, and nonfiction writer.

Cronin's internationally best-selling novels examine moral conflicts between the individual and society. His heroes, who include doctors, missionaries, and small-town newspaper editors, are idealists in pursuit of justice for the common citizen. Although Cronin's novels are set in the twentieth century, they remind critics of works by the Brontë sisters and Thomas Hardy. Like those earlier novels, Cronin's are moralistic and feature dramatic plots, powerful themes, and memorable characters. Some of his novels have been made into films.

When in his thirties, Cronin abandoned a lucrative medical career to become a writer. His literary debut, the novel *Hatter's Castle* (1931), was a popular and critical success. Percy Hutchinson proclaimed it "a restoration of the English novel," having "the stuff of greatness." Other early successes included the novels *The Stars Look Down* (1935), *The Citadel* (1937), and *The Keys of the Kingdom* (1941). *The Stars Look Down* recounts the struggles of miners during a strike in a Welsh coal town. Cronin draws an unsentimental picture of the losses suffered by both the workers and the company when basic human values are neglected. *The Citadel* was controversial among the British medical community due to its examination of the conflict between medical ethics and what must be done to survive in a competitive field. *The Keys of the Kingdom* is the story of a priest who must temper his individuality in order to fulfill his commitments to the church.

In addition to *The Stars Look Down* and *The Citadel*, Cronin wrote several other novels that are based on his personal experiences. *The Green Years* (1945) and its sequel, *Shannon's Way* (1950), recount the life of an idealistic young man who, upon entering medical school, is supervised by an unscrupulous department head. The young man later begins to practice in a clinic in a rundown urban area and finds his work unexpectedly rewarding. *A Song of Sixpence* (1964) is an autobiographical novel that, according to Cronin, comes closest of all his work to representing his true literary aspirations.

(See also *Contemporary Authors*, Vols. 1-4, rev. ed., Vol. 102 [obituary]; *Contemporary Authors New Revision Series*, Vol. 5; and *Something about the Author*, Vol. 25 [obituary].)

HUGH WALPOLE

To say that [Dr. Cronin's] first novel ["**Hatter's Castle**"] is causing a sensation is putting it most mildly. He has been reviewed . . . almost in terms of hysteria. Wherever I go I find that his book is being read—not merely read, but devoured. People sit with their feet on the fender . . . and their noses in the page almost as they have not done since the days of Dickens.

And yet Dr. Cronin's novel can very easily be criticized. It will be criticized on every side. It will be said that it is imitative . . . , it will be said that it is old-fashioned, melodramatic and that the general catastrophe is far too thorough to be true. All these criticisms can be made with justice. . . .

[The chief reason that] "**Hatter's Castle**" is having so sensational a career is that Dr. Cronin, in writing it, has been afraid of nothing. He has not been afraid lest people should call him a fool, he has not been afraid of the hackneyed situation (he has a fine scene of the errant daughter thrust into the stormy night by her irate father. . . .), he is not afraid of melodrama . . . , and he refuses altogether to be subjective. He tells you nothing at all about Dr. Cronin except that he knows obviously about women's pains and diseases.

The result of this indifference to comment is a terrific creative force! You may, when the book is closed, look back and let play with your superior mind, but while the narrative proceeds you are absolutely held. Dr. Cronin has a superb narrative gift and he can create character like Thomas Hardy. He is *not* Thomas Hardy. He writes very often badly, he does not suggest the larger destinies, he has none of Hardy's wonderful poetic beauty, but the wife of James Brodie is worthy to be set beside the Mayor of Casterbridge: he would not be ashamed of her company.

Now enough of these comparisons. The fact is that the triumph of "**Hatter's Castle**" is another step in the return of the objective novel to English fiction. . . .

Hugh Walpole, "London Letter: June," in New York Herald Tribune Books, *June 28, 1931, p. 9.*

PERCY HUTCHISON

Except for "Wuthering Heights" and "Jude the Obscure," it would be impossible to cite another serious novel in English so cumulative of horror as **"Hatter's Castle."** There have, of course, been scores of stories written with the deliberate purpose of making the reader's hair stand on end and chills course up and down the spine. But the creation of such works is a kind of game, in which the writer is abetted by the reader; entertainment is the purpose of the author's tour de force. **"Hatter's Castle"** we take to be no such book. Dr. Cronin, we are convinced, has gone about his work scarcely less seriously than did Emily Brontë; his delineation of James Brodie [the protagonist] is clearly intended as portraiture, and the novel, therefore, is not to be judged from the standards set up by Poe and Stevenson. We say all this at the outset, for Dr. Cronin, in ways that will be made apparent, is so little of an artist that his work fails as a whole by reason of an over-emphasis which lends an air of artificiality when, if we are right, exactly the opposite was intended. . . .

James Brodie is Scotch-Irish, the scene of the story is Scotland, and the period a half-century ago. This last makes Brodie a bit more plausible, for the tyrant father (witness Patrick Brontë) was more in evidence then than he is today. But James Brodie is more than a mere tyrant, he is a pathological case, controlled by delusions of grandeur and later by the demon of drink. Thus, at the outset, the central character of the narrative is placed outside the human pale; he is largely irresponsible, and if the horror at the suffering which innocent persons are forced to endure at Brodie's hands is thereby increased, and pity for them augmented, the actual effect is vastly less than the novelist desired, because the cumulative catastrophe is seen as one of those "acts of God" against which there is no insurance. If Mary, wanting but a few months to become a mother, is kicked bodily out of the house, and the over-wrought Nessie is goaded into hanging herself, the reader may, indeed, weep, but he weeps as for one struck by lightning or overwhelmed in shipwreck. . . .

It is proof of Dr. Cronin's inability to maintain artistic control of his concept and his material that when he finds the death of [Dennis Foyle, whom Mary loves,] necessitated by the plan of his narrative, he cannot compass the event except by another burst of melodrama, as if he had not enough of melodrama behind him and before. To have Dennis go to his death with an entire trainload of people when a bridge gives way in a storm is to produce precisely the opposite of the effect required at the moment, for it attracts an attention which should remain concentrated on the tragedy of poor Mary, a tragedy which is immeasurably to deepen.

It is possible that Dr. Cronin, listening to old wives' tales in the Highlands, may have heard of a father who, fancying himself injured by a daughter's indiscretion, actually kicked her from his door. But only an imagination akin to Emily Brontë's could have made use of it. The girl, all but mortally hurt, drags herself to a cow-shed, where she gives birth to her infant. Found by an old woman, who summons Dr. Renwick, Mary is eventually saved. The child is not. Mary then disappears from the story, going to take service in London, and is only brought back into the narrative toward the close on the piteous appeal of Nessie that her sister return to her.

If we have shown certain of A. J. Cronin's failures it is only felt that something should be said of what is not only the finest passage in the book but one of the finest of its kind in the history of the English novel. Reference is to the profoundly

stirring and exquisitely lyric scene of Mary's surrender. That Dr. Cronin surpasses the similar scene in "Tess" all who read the two must agree, although, of course, some measure of excuse will be found for Hardy in the Victorian canon that in literature a young woman must be deprived of her will by a draught of wine. But Tess and Mary are sisters in their spiritual innocence; and Dr. Cronin is to be congratulated on a word-picture superior to that done by the novelist he so patently has taken for his master. . . .

The increasing insanity of James Brodie, if one can endure that sort of thing, is carried on with a cumulative effect that is masterly as a literary achievement. Nessie, frail of body and nervously unstable, is held to her books by her father with a paranoiac persistency that is coldly devilish. The university offers an annual money prize for the best work done by a school pupil, and Brodie is possessed with the fixed idea that Nessie can and will be the winner. When she falls she can bear up no longer. Her father has made her do lessons in a cold room; she has been ill fed; she has been allowed not a moment's respite, and her mind breaks. When Mary, whom Nessie had sent out of the house on a pretext, returns, she finds the little girl's lifeless body dangling from a beam in the kitchen. Dr. Renwick comes, and although he can do nothing for Nessie he does take Mary away, having learned that he loves her. Thus one gleam of light enters the dour tale at the last, although Renwick is badly done, being merely a puppet of the author's directing. But it is possible that some injustice is done Dr. Cronin here, for the melodrama of Brodie has so deafened the ears that one can scarcely hear the subdued notes of the Renwick-Mary episode.

What is to be said of **"Hatter's Castle"** in conclusion? It is not a masterpiece, but it is, unless signs fall, the work of a novelist who is destined for the seats of the mighty. In the first place, A. J. Cronin has resolutely turned his back on the allurements and artificialities which have so often in recent years diverted the English novel from its great tradition of portrayal of human life and human lives. Putting to one side the romantic work of Joseph Conrad and the work of John Galsworthy as belonging more especially within the genre of the comedy of manners, **"Hatter's Castle"** is the most important work in English fiction in decades. For it is a restoration of the English novel as it began with Fielding and Richardson and Smollett. It is not so complete a restoration as one could desire; the faults are too many and too glaring. But it has the stuff of greatness. And the author has shown an apprentice hand that should grow in sureness and strength.

> *Percy Hutchison, "'Hatter's Castle', a Novel in the Great Tradition," in* The New York Times Book Review, *July 19, 1931, p. 4.*

DOROTHY VAN DOREN

Not since "Wuthering Heights" have we had a horror story that so completely satisfies all the requirements of the genre [as does **"Hatter's Castle"**]. Hatter's Castle is the home of a great, blustering, egocentric paranoiac, a hatter in a small Scottish town fifty years ago. James Brodie is convinced of his noble birth; he is a large, handsome man, domineering, brutal, deluded with visions of his own grandeur. The tale of his downfall, which is brought about by the destruction or death of every member of his family save one, makes the book. At the end he is a skeleton of his former self, destroyed by drink, by the failure of his last hope, by his own vast, vain aspirations and desires. (p. 113)

This, of course, is not a cheery tale. But the horror story is meant not to cheer but to harrow, and Mr. Cronin has faithfully fulfilled his task. He has done more. His story is differentiated from the ordinary example of its class in two ways. One is his successful combination of romantic terror and realism. When it is necessary to present a scene of unhappiness or desolation or sordidness, no pains are spared to make the picture clear. None of the elegant circumlocutions which sheltered the reader of earlier tales is employed. A spade is described as it is, and if filth clings to it, then the filth is given its proper name. Moreover, Mr. Cronin, incredibly enough, inspires pity in the reader for James Brodie. . . . He might have been a cheap, stock-company villain, brought to his comeuppance by the forces of goodness and righteousness. He is, instead, a tragic figure, destroyed by his own great vices, a man of strength brought to dust, an Oedipus putting out his own eyes through his own folly.

It is this fact that distinguishes Mr. Cronin from other writers who have attempted the same feat, that, indeed, makes him with this, his first novel, a novelist to be watched and reckoned with. His Mary is all that is beautiful, good, tender, and pure; she is not ridiculous. His Brodie is the embodiment of all villainy; he is nevertheless tragic. Black is black, with Mr. Cronin, and white is blinding white. But because of his frankness and his courage, because he is not afraid of the heights and the depths of his characters, he achieves something of the mighty eloquence that must be in all novels before they are great. (p. 114)

> Dorothy Van Doren, "Death, Destruction, and Power," in The Nation, Vol. CXXXIII, No. 3447, July 29, 1931, pp. 113-14.

FRED T. MARSH

Dr. Cronin's second novel ["Three Loves"] is less powerful but more convincing than its predecessor—"Hatter's Castle"; it is less fantastic and more modern; less gripping, perhaps, but more moving. In short, it is not so extraordinary a feat of virtuosity, imitative but effective, but it is a more genuine piece of work. Both novels are laid in Scotland near Glasgow. The time of "Three Loves," which centers on the turn of the century, is a generation later. And the second, like the first, is essentially a psychological drama, based on the life of a single individual—although melodrama is freely used to heighten effects. The writing is smooth and flowing, failing in emphasis, however, and lacking in original distinction. . . .

In "Three Loves" Lucy Moore is another strong person in a small sphere. She clutches at life instead of letting it flow around her. She seizes, refusing merely to accept. She butts her head against stone walls and dies unyielding. The objects of her love must succumb to her boundless emotional vitality, be purged and recreated in her flames. Her husband first, then her son, and then Jesus are to be molded in the heat of her love. She must manage, rule, order, dictate, out of her devotion. She must possess and they must acquiesce in that possession. Just as James Brodie [in "Hatter's Castle"] had to dominate or die, so Lucy Moore must possess, emotionally, or perish. And in both instances the ruling passions develop increasingly until they become psychopathic. Dr. Cronin, with a physician's logic, follows the course of human motivations to their extreme conclusions. . . .

The book has a few exceptionally strong passages. The episodes involving Miss Hocking, whose queerness suddenly develops into mania, are of unusual interest and in their symbolic significance add luster to the novel. . . . The last third of the book is a bold piece of representation in its picture (not at all sensational) of convent life. The author's approach toward religion is obviously that of an unsympathetic, essentially hostile rationalist.

"Three Loves" is a sound, serious and moving novel, made of stronger stuff than most of the English novels, which are said to be reviving the Victorian tradition. This is not to say that its author is another Hardy, or that his novel, touching on a similar theme, is a new "Sons and Lovers."

> Fred T. Marsh, "The Pride of Possessiveness," in New York Herald Tribune Books, April 3, 1932, p. 5.

PERCY HUTCHISON

Radically as Dr. Cronin's new novel ["Three Loves"] differs in plot and episode from "Hatter's Castle," so indelibly does this author impress his personality on his work that one will recognize the same hand behind both. Nor is this all, for in one particular is there similarity. In the first of the two books it is a man's stubbornness, an uprightness that leans backward, that eventually accomplishes his ruin. In "Three Loves" it is a woman's stubbornness. Here, however, the analogy ends. In "Hatter's Castle" James Brodie breaks most of the lives about him, and his own defeat is unrelieved by anything that could be called a victory. Lucy Moore, on the other hand, although she brings sufficient pain to others, and a major portion of pain to herself, does to no one irreparable injury; and there is something of victory in her own ultimate defeat. "Three Loves" is, therefore, a softer book than was "Hatter's Castle."

But the adjective is to be used only in the comparative degree, for by no stretch of the imagination might even the present work be called a wholly gentle story. It would appear that Dr. Cronin has seen too much of human beings to be deceived into finding them other than they mostly are. Goodness and badness, capacity to yield and inability to yield, weakness and strength, insight to love wisely, and the blindness that makes wisdom in love impossible—all of these Dr. Cronin finds inextricably woven and tumbled together in the people about him. Consequently, he is a clairvoyant novelist; and welcome on that account.

From the title one might easily be led to expect either a romance or one of those analytical studies so much indulged in today. But "Three Loves" is neither. Lucy Moore, a Scotch Highland lass of the Murray clan by birth, is happily married, and the first of the trio of "loves" is her husband. The second is her son—a child at the outset of the story. And the third is God. That people ofttimes are bruised by love is a common thesis of the novelists. But Dr. Cronin has turned things about. Lucy is not bruised by love, she bruises herself on love. In the stubbornness of upright pride she batters herself to pieces against her surroundings, as James Brodie, in "Hatter's Castle," battered himself to pieces.

Lucy Murray, to judge from the story, was a winsome lass when she married the Irish lad, Frank Moore. Their little boy, Peter, was a likable youngster. In the opinion of her kinsfolk Lucy married beneath her family. On the whole, however, this attitude seems to have been adopted by them as an excuse for not helping her in time of financial distress rather than to have had any foundation in fact: Moore was sober and industrious, kind and measurably understanding. Perhaps it is Dr. Cronin's premise that the more easygoing disposition of the Irish prevents them from fully understanding that dourness so prevalent among the Scotch, a premise that was hinted at more than once in **"Hatter's Castle."** . . .

[Later,] Frank meets his death when the small boat he is in is run down in the fog. Incidentally, the short and swift narration of the events taking place behind the wall of mist, the pathos (for Lucy is aboard the craft that cuts Frank down), the deftness of sentence and the economy of description, all combine to render this one of the memorable things in recent fiction.

Bereft of her husband, Lucy centres her whole life upon the little boy, placing him in a school in Ireland, and slaving to support herself and him. . . . When her former employer, old Lennox, asks Lucy to marry him, and she refuses, more than one reader may be tempted to feel that the novelist has taken an unfair advantage of his heroine. For, even if narrow and, perhaps, a little close, nevertheless Lennox was friendly and kind and sufficiently generous so that Lucy would have been assured of comforts and Peter of the university career which had begun to seem impossible. To those, however, whose reading has been among the novelists of the ultra-modern school, Lucy's attitude is readily understandable, for the reason that those novelists have dwelt insistently on the mother-son complex. And it might have been well had Dr. Cronin taken a leaf from their textbook here and made the mother's psychology more clear than he does. Perhaps in his capacity of physician he had so often come into contact with such exaggerated and purblind maternal jealousy he failed to perceive that a reader might not realize at once that Lucy's refusal is due to her fear that a step-father might in some indefinable way come between herself and the boy.

It may be imagined that it will be the purpose of the author of **"Three Loves"** to have Peter go to the dogs. But it is not. Subsisting on an incredible paucity of shillings a week, Lucy puts Peter through the university (he had won a small scholarship) and he is graduated in medicine. Lucy, although only a few years over 40, has by this time worn herself to the bone, and is an object of great pity. Truly, Scotch stubbornness is a fearsome thing. And the more is she to be pitied, for a second time does her pride render her blind. Because of her insane fear of losing her hold on Peter she tries to prevent his marriage. So he carries it through secretly. It is an excellent marriage, but she was adamant against it. And again she meets defeat at the hands of pride. In her extremity she turns to religion.

Subtly aware of all the forces that have been working for so long within this woman of his creative imagination, Dr. Cronin lets it be known that Lucy's "vision" is due largely to undernourishment and although he will push her to the length of courting, as it were, martyrdom by seeking to join a religious order dedicated to the most rigorous discipline, it is clear he holds no brief either for or against that phase of the religious life. But he understands it, and the pages that deal with Lucy's convent life, an unusual situation for a novelist to handle, are done with understanding, delicacy and beauty.

Again it is Lucy's stubbornness that defeats her. She cannot, in the way she has elected, give herself to her third love, religion. As she managed Frank, and then Peter, so she must manage God. Gently, nay, with tenderness, nevertheless with firmness, Lucy, emaciated, and with a heart fatally deranged

from her long struggle with hunger, want and disappointment, dies without again meeting Peter to whom she would return. Victory? Yes. Though a pyrrhic one. For Lucy has been of that indomitable company that never surrenders. Perhaps, however, there is something of irony intended also. Like James Brodie, Lucy Moore is not one we should either wish to be or to come into contact with!

"Three Loves" is a novel "of parts," as our elders might have said. And A. J. Cronin has again demonstrated that he has something to contribute to English fiction.

> *Percy Hutchison, "Dr. Cronin's Portrait of a Stubborn Woman," in* The New York Times Book Review, *April 3, 1932, p. 6.*

PERCY HUTCHISON

In **"Grand Canary"** we have the third venture by the author of **"Hatter's Castle"** and **"Three Loves"** in the field of fiction. A. J. Cronin, it will be recalled, is a London physician who has deserted medicine for the novel—not, we take it, because he likes medicine less, but because he likes authorship more. And just as **"Three Loves"** differed radically from **"Hatter's Castle,"** so does the new narrative differ from both. . . .

Those who read Dr. Cronin's earlier novels recognized that the author had a flair for direct narration which placed him apart from the general run of modern novelists. At the same time, perhaps because of his long experience in the sickroom, he had also a human understanding likewise somewhat rare. The combination compelled the reader to look forward to subsequent books with keen expectancy.

On the score of narrative only, **"Grand Canary"** marks, perhaps, an advance. And in respect to two of the characters, certainly, namely, Dr. Leith and Lady Fielding, there is something of the penetration, the depth of analysis, which marked the preceding novels. But in its total effect the new novel has not the impact of either **"Hatter's Castle"** or **"Three Loves,"** though this is not to gainsay the possibility that **"Grand Canary"** may not win more adherents for the author than he has won before. If it does so it will be because of its freer style.

Yet we wonder if Dr. Cronin may not have been the victim of his critics. With a man leaping so suddenly into all but the forefront of advancing novelists, it was inevitable that he should be confused as to the direction in which he should seek most assiduously to advance. **"Grand Canary"** exhibits something of this confusion. Moreover, one fears that it exhibits also certain crotchets which the author has nourished. And for the exhibition of these crotchets Dr. Cronin—moved solely by an ideal—has created, not living men and women, but puppets of his direction. . . .

Yet if the reader is hereby moved to expect anything like [convention] . . . , let him at once disabuse his mind. One thing Dr. Cronin is not—he is not conventional; possibly because he knows from empirical experience that a combination of elements does not always give the expected result. The relationship between Dr. Leith and Lady Fielding is a delicate, original and moving contribution to modern literature, which seems in general to hold that once a man and woman are thrown together there can be but one outcome. This part of the book— the main part, and its justification—we leave to the reader to discover.

Where we think that the author has erred is in his secondary characters. There are too many of these; their actions are unimportant and their contribution to the story is negligible. Justifiable objection will be raised against the missionary, Robert Tranter. Undoubtedly there are hypocrites in all walks of life; but in a novel hypocrisy may not be treated casually; it should be given adequate treatment, so that the novelist may justify himself, or it should not be handled at all. The same is to be said of other minor characters in **"Grand Canary."** . . .

Hence one's fear that Dr. Cronin has become the victim of his critics. He has been told he should be less concentrated, that he should be more diffuse. **"Grand Canary"** proves that diffuseness is not this novelist's forte. Yet another explanation is possible. It may be that each of these several characters (not excluding Dr. Leith and Mary Fielding) is a type, that each stands for a group the author has met with in the medical practice he has now abandoned, and that, in this novel, he has got rid of them once and for all. We hope so. And reiterating that **"Grand Canary"** shines as exceptional narrative, we await Dr. Cronin's next novel with interest.

> *Percy Hutchison, "Dr. Cronin's Gift for Narrative,"*
> in The New York Times Book Review, *May 14,*
> *1933, p. 6.*

GRAHAM GREENE

Undoubtedly an aesthetic pleasure can be gained from reading Dr. Cronin, the pleasure of observing a certain kind of novelist flowering with a superb unconsciousness. [In *Grand Canary*], pressed between two covers, is a perfect example of the Popular Novelist. Viewed in this light his defects become positive qualities. One is inclined to praise his inability to create a plausible human being, for one real character would break the book and Dr. Cronin's importance as an Awful Example. A long literary pedigree is of importance to characters in a novel of this class; it is a badge of respectability, an assurance to the reader: "You have met us all before in the best of company. There will be nothing to shock, nothing to disturb you, nothing to give you ideas." So in *Grand Canary* we have the missionary seduced by a loose woman, the boxer with a "seductive Irish voice" who reads Plato (spelt Playto to indicate the brogue; but how does Dr. Cronin pronounce the name?); the cockney bawd; the sardonic, embittered doctor, won back to hope in life by the love of a good woman whom he nurses through the yellow fever. Their physical appearance is minutely described—"chiselled" features, "strong" teeth, sometimes "firm" teeth, sometimes "perfect" teeth, almost always "white" teeth; they "hiss" words, their eyes blaze. This is all fair barnstorming, board-rattling stuff, but the popular novelist must also know how to write grandly. On these occasions the English language loses any meaning whatever for Dr. Cronin. Literary phrases run riot. He turns berserk, reckless of consequences. "Slowly before their eyes the day languished as with love, swooning towards the arms of the dark." Dr. Cronin is liable to turn nature on with a tap at the most unnecessary moments. When the missionary succumbs to the loose woman ("He stumbled inside the cabin. He closed the door.") the next chapter opens with supreme irrelevance: "But night succumbed in turn to morning and all the warm beauty of the darkness drooped into the ocean like a languid hand."

It is extraordinary how obscure the Popular Novelist can be without losing his public (Dr. Cronin speaks somewhere of a silence which is "lingering yet chaste," of "omniscient winds,"

and his principal characters are frequently having visions "which words could never formulate"). This is sometimes explained by what is called the narrative gift. He may not be able to create character; he may not have much of a story to tell, but how quickly it is said, how cleverly he tells it. This is not true of Dr. Cronin, whose characters all tell each other what they know already as in old-fashioned plays, and it is difficult to understand how a narrative gift can ever be said to exist apart from any merit of style, story or character.

> *Graham Greene, in a review of "Grand Canary,"*
> in The Spectator, *Vol. 150, No. 5473, May 19, 1933,*
> *p. 728.*

PERCY HUTCHISON

One of the most interesting of present-day literary figures is A. J. Cronin, the London physician who at the age of 34 suddenly abandoned an increasing practice to become a writer of fiction. Seldom has a first novel received the acclaim accorded Dr. Cronin's **"Hatter's Castle."** In his fourth venture, **"The Stars Look Down,"** there is to be found the same fearless handling of his theme, the same impressive understanding of men and women and motives, which made the first novel noteworthy.

It is important, this fact of A. J. Cronin's medical career, for it throws light both on his point of view and his method. In **"Hatter's Castle"** he did not get entirely away from his consulting room. James Brodie, the central figure of the story, is so clearly a pathological case that the novel, in spite of its terrific dramatic impact, fails of universality. **"The Stars Look Down,"** while far from being kid-gloved fiction, has nothing of the pathological. But the characters, even down to the least important, are, as in the earlier book, realized with the same startling accuracy, the accuracy of a physician summing up a patient. A reader, while he could but hate James Brodie, was compelled to acknowledge the truth of the portrayal. There is the same fidelity of portraiture here. And because the pathological has been avoided, there is a universality **"Hatter's Castle"** lacked. Dr. Cronin inspires confidence in a reader.

The background of **"The Stars Look Down"** is an English coal mining town. The span of the story is the thirty years between 1903 and 1933. There are strikes and lockouts, and the war. But the war is seen only on the home front, with manufacturers making legitimate and illegitimate profits, and the armistice more a disruption of an established order than a poultice for the wounds of a nation. The underlying theme is the struggle between labor and capital. But Dr. Cronin is neither a crusader for one nor a defender of the other. He is the physician surveying an unbalanced organism, and, as it were, reporting it in his files, together with his diagnosis. But he is a physician who refuses to prescribe, fearing, perhaps, that the remedy may be worse than the disease. The social organism must always be unbalanced, is apparently his view, hence the tolerance inherent in the title. The stars will go on looking down and beholding just about the same scrambled pattern of human goodness and human frailty.

The opening of the novel is pathetic drama. The workers at the Neptune have been out on strike, and starvation stares the men and their families in the face. Starvation breaks the strike and the men go back. Dr. Cronin's picture of the pinched faces of the elders, the thin shoulders of the children, women fighting for a loaf of bread, boys and men snatching at the leavings in

CONTEMPORARY LITERARY CRITICISM, Vol. 32

the slaughter-house that ordinarily would be thrown away, is unforgettable in its horror. . . .

At the time of the strike there is, among the younger men in the mine, one named Joe Gowlan, handsome, able, but a petty thief, a seducer of women, and a man without heart or scruple. Dr. Cronin tries pretty hard to keep Gowlan in hand, but it will be the opinion of many that not at all times is he successful. Joe every now and again becomes dangerously near a machine-made villain of melodrama. Naturally, there are many such as he in the world—too many. But Dr. Cronin has not completely learned the novelist's art of selection and discrimination. Gowlan should not both succeed by a ruse in turning Jenny, the girl pregnant by him, over to David for a husband and also be the one (having become a millionaire in the war) to drive Arthur Barras into poverty. He might very well have done all this in life, but in a novel it is just a little too much piling up of villainies for a literature that has gone beyond the "Duchess of Malfi" stage.

On the other hand, few novelists have exceeded Dr. Cronin's striking ability to keep a complicated story clear at all times and also swiftly moving. He is uncannily like Dickens in this. "The Stars Look Down" has almost as many characters as some of the Dickens novels, has almost as many different histories advancing simultaneously, or interacting one upon another. (p. 1)

The ending of the book has something of the calmness of a benediction: David, who had served a term in Parliament as Labor Member from Sleescale, is defeated by Gowlan, the omnipotent industrialist and war profiteer. Arthur Barras, once the owner of Neptune, gets a job as underviewer in the mine, and David goes back to work in the pits. Lest this should seem to the reader a bit strained, the author reminds us that when Labor's great experiment in governing England gave way before the country's desire for change, many a man who had been raised from dock or pit or railway yard went back to his original task. Life is a whirligig, says Dr. Cronin in effect. The stars in their diurnal course look down on pretty much the same sort of a world now and forever.

With the possible exception of overdrawing in the character of Joe Gowlan, or, rather, in the author's permitting him to commit so many villainies, this comes close to being a great novel. It is a finer piece of work than "Hatter's Castle." It touches human lives more broadly and is better balanced.

"The Stars Look Down" is an exhaustive and deep reading of life, varied with contrasting characters, kaleidoscopic in its changes, almost breathless in pace. But again this writer comes back to Dr. Cronin the physician in Dr. Cronin the novelist, for it is in his training as a physician that his power as a novelist lies. Many of the pages are perfervid enough in incident or emotion. Yet a peculiar calmness, an all but Olympian serenity, seems to pervade the book. Dr. Cronin, turned fictionist, has the capacity of his earlier profession to be dispassionate without being cold. Hence, along with its calmness, the book exhibits an extraordinary vitality. It is impossible to conceive of a reader laying aside "The Stars Look Down" once he has started the tale. It is equally impossible to conceive of any reader not recommending the book far and wide. It is certain to take its place among the leading novels of the year. (p. 23)

Percy Hutchison, "The Clash of Capital and Labor," in The New York Times Book Review, *September 22, 1935, pp. 1, 23.*

ELEANOR CLARK

Judging only by the stature and intricacy of ["**The Stars Look Down**"], one would incline to think of the author's career as meteoric. This has not been the case. Like most great achievements the book is the culmination of lesser endeavors, experiments in the medium embodying a restricted philosophy, a personal moral. It is the logical development from "**Hatter's Castle**," Dr. Cronin's first novel. . . . "**Hatter's Castle**" was a passionate but unsatisfying book, both in style and subject matter more imitative of the Victorians than integral to our own world. Its interest was chiefly pathological and the suffering described was of a world apart, understandable only as the conclusion drawn from a possible but peculiar premise. One was conscious of a straining to be forceful as if the author were trying to overcome in himself a natural remoteness from human problems.

In this new novel, the remoteness is of a different kind. It is the detachment that comes from complete immersion in the life around one, and it makes the book one of the few in recent times in which an author has dealt with the whole riot of confusion and goodness and waste of life in the modern world, trusting his own vision and without the hypocrisy of a vicarious belief. But there is another side to this quality of detachment; there is in it something of the inadequacy of the cynic. Such a book should print a gigantic question mark on the mind. Instead, the author seems to be giving an answer, a personal answer better suited to the range of his earlier work and leaving one with the impression that the only arms against the sea of troubles presented here are reticence and a cup of tea.

For the purpose of analysis one might call the general theme of the novel the struggle between capital and labor. Actually it is broader, the struggle between those who are not willing to compromise their sense of values in order to prosper under the present system, and those for whom no compromise is necessary, who have in themselves the brutality of the system. . . .

It is impossible to summarize the various threads of story, or the many moods and power of the book. When new social standards come as they must to shove the framework of this story into history, the book will be alive still and memorable for its insight and swiftly moving scenes: the lust and cruelty of Gowlan's maneuvers, the poor relation with the tin of crackers by her bedside, the grotesque downfall of Barras, and the tenderness of the scene in which David, after a defeat in the House, watches the death of his wife Jenny, generous, faithless Jenny dying with a teacup in her hand and her little finger crooked "polite." It is so much of life and in a form so subtle that one forgets, reading, that a pattern has been imposed to make life credible. One may even forget the only thing that has been left out of this pattern, which is the ability in people to refuse defeat and to look down on such drama with something more than the neutrality of stars.

Eleanor Clark, "One of the Few," in The New Republic, *Vol. LXXXIV, No. 1088, October 9, 1935, p. 250.*

MABEL S. ULRICH

For the theme of ["**The Citadel**"], his fourth novel, Dr. Cronin has drawn on his experiences in the study and practice of medicine and has given us a vivid portrait of an intelligent, hardheaded young physician struggling to gain a foothold in his profession. A theme hardly unusual enough to cause the British medical lions to rear on their hind legs as they did and yelp a passionate protest. The crux of the matter lies of course in the fact that the author in its telling committed the unpardonable offense of dragging from the medical fraternity's closet its own privately sequestered skeletons. (p. 5)

The conflict between medical honesty and a competitive society is only the primary theme of this novel. Its secondary and "feminine" theme is that of married love. To the love story of Andrew and Chris the author has brought the extraordinary understanding of women's psychology to which his earlier novels have testified. Level-headed, clear-seeing Chris has as much steel in her backbone as has Andrew. Hard work and poverty have no terrors for her. The passionate integrity he brings to his science she brings to human relations—above all to her man. From him she will accept no compromise of principles, not even when love itself is at stake. They love, squabble, and make up with refreshing realism, always aware, as is the reader, of the reality of the spiritual and physical support each gives the other.

Like the author's previous novels, "The Citadel" has a satisfying solid and three-dimensional quality. "I keep telling myself never to take anything for granted," says Andrew of his medical code—which, one feels, may well be Cronin's own, and account in part at least for the structural solidity that distinguishes all his work. But it is its content rather than its literary excellence that has aroused controversy in England. Is it indeed a fair picture of the medical profession? Many American readers will no doubt object that the canvas has too much shadow, that while all in the know must have met in professional experience the counterpart of every one of Cronin's silly, ignorant, and money-loving physicians, there exists a far larger proportion than the novel suggests whose skill and integrity merit respect and trust. Cronin of course would be the last to deny this, but for his special ends he has chosen to take these for granted. What he has set out to do—and has done admirably—is to cut through the romanticism that still surrounds the medical profession, and boldly expose the potentialities of charlatanism and dishonesty inherent in a system whereby a large group of men must depend for economic security on the real or fancied suffering of others. And what he has to say about this situation applies not alone to England, but to the world over.

To American doctors the novel's main interest may well lie in the differences in methods of medical procedure in the two countries. Among them it will undoubtedly arouse conflicting opinions. But all who enjoy a good novel for its own sake will find it an engrossing, finely written story that needs no justification whatever. (p. 6)

Mabel S. Ulrich, "Doctor's Dilemma," in The Saturday Review of Literature, Vol. XVI, No. 20, September 11, 1937, pp. 5-6.

ALFRED KAZIN

Six years ago Dr. Cronin came in like a lion, to the fanfare of a critical acclaim that bracketed his name with those of Ibsen, Hardy and Charlotte Brontë. British fiction, so thin and nervous since the war, seemed a little more human. Here, it was generally felt, was a doctor who had deserted the surgery because of a genuine literary compulsion, a man whose first book was a solid and resounding tragedy, a writer who seemed able to plow his way through the sickliness and the corruption of trivial

realism. Dr. Cronin wrote competently; it was obvious that he wrote passionately; and whatever one thought of his claim to greatness, there was a general, pleased feeling that some one solid had arrived.

In those six years the resemblance to Ibsen, Hardy and Charlotte Brontë has become increasingly invisible. Dr. Cronin's big, square novels, published with such becoming regularity, have varied in quality; but in all of them the matter has been less imposing than the moral. The truth seems to be that Dr. Cronin has first-hand ideas and second-hand skill. In "The Citadel," as in "The Stars Look Down," one is excited by his great moral earnestness, his flat insistence on facing the central problems of British economy and culture; but as the book goes on that earnestness becomes a whispered indignation, almost a doggedly pessimistic insistence on the tones of dourness. Characters are added to each other faithfully; the action is blocked out; the story moves along, sometimes with inordinate rapidity; but always, despite one's interest, despite the automatic pleasure taken in "a good story," the end result seems trivial.

That triviality, it seems to me, is due largely to Dr. Cronin's conception of character. The men and women in "The Citadel" are not entangled in evil, shaped to some human modest design; instead they confront life and themselves with uniform emotions and a uniform speech. Dr. Cronin's characters fall a little too easily into two widely separated classes. He has people like Andrew Manson, who wanted to be ascetic and profound, a virtuous physician; and he has society doctors who are all black against Andrew's white, who, a little too sharply, tell you that they are quacks or weaklings or racketeers, while Andrew remains pure and always delightfully, forgivably weak. He has women like Christine Manson, who is Leora Arrowsmith minus the gayety and the erratic humanity, but who is, nevertheless, a treasure of a wife; and he has dark-gowned, softly smiling ladies of leisure who tempt Andrew as if he were Christian and they the demons of Anti-christ.

The story of Andrew's ascent from a grubby, unfashionable Scots medical school to a life of pure endeavor, will remind many of "Arrowsmith," if only because both Andrew and Martin have corresponding wives, jobs, friends and corresponding failures in the attempt to buck commercial medicine. There the two books part. . . . ["Arrowsmith"] is a book that tingles with the joy of life, a novel written around a problem and not pushed after it; and its strength lies in the contagious zest of its characterizations, in a Gottlieb, a Leora, a Puckerbaugh; but there is not a character in "The Citadel" whom one remembers as anything but a sad-faced participant in an atonal drama. . . .

Andrew's material success and spiritual failure in London form the crux of Dr. Cronin's book. It is in this section that Dr. Cronin expends most of his indignation and takes so many potshots at the medico as villain. Andrew's spiritual crisis, alas! is utterly unmoving. We suspect it because it is so transparently an aberration. Essentially ascetic and selfless at heart, Andrew's sudden greed and extravagance represent not a movement, a phase, but a falsely dramatic stage of decline, a stage about which we know too much while it lasts. Dr. Cronin is forced to take recourse to bathos; the conflict between Christine, who wants to be poor but devoted, and Andrew, who wants money, is stilted. . . .

When Andrew reforms, of course, and decides to be self-respecting, if poor, his remorse flows over, and from one extreme he runs right into another. Christine, like Leora Arrowsmith, dies suddenly in the midst of a crisis, and Dr. Cronin is ready for Andrew's culminating act of defiance. It is a heroic bit, done with great spirit, and it is a declamation that releases Dr. Cronin's opinion of British medicine, its organization and its individuals; but it is only a declamation, a paragraph of rhetoric set against honest but ineffectual fiction.

Alfred Kazin, "Dr. Cronin's Novel about the Medical Profession," in The New York Times Book Review, *September 12, 1937, p. 6.*

OTIS FERGUSON

Here is another of those fascinating excursions, by way of fiction, into the regions of men at work, under the conditions of life—**"The Citadel."** As fiction it has excellent living stuff in whole blocks of pages; and there are blocks where the events necessary to the main design are too abrupt and pat for their necessary effect. But I shouldn't care to judge this novel under the ordinary fictional rules until the term fiction has been widened to include credits for large experience, a balanced judgment thereon and story-teller's knack for recreation thereof; and narrowed to rule out all this review-supplement bosh of credit for Industry and Effort, especially of credit for Correct Conduct along the line of this or that ideology, take your pick. Cronin's novel has above everything else the quality of absorbing instruction, the illusion of seeing through a clear glass certain workings of the world, and the feeling that under its serene air of happen-so there is a detailed particular truth which both verifies and extends whatever of universal truth a person may know.

Otis Ferguson, "Men at Work," in The New Republic, *Vol. LXXXXII, No. 1190, September 22, 1937, p. 195.*

MARY ROSS

In **"The Keys of the Kingdom"** as in his preceding novel, **"The Citadel"** Dr. Cronin tells the story of a man who faced life directly, without cant and with the will to serve his fellow men. The priest in the present story, like the doctor in the widely discussed earlier novel, is an individualist in the sense that his conscience, not his self-interest must be his guide. In the Church, as in the medical profession, that necessity entails courage, disillusion, often personal disadvantage and disappointment. . . .

This story of the life of a priest shows the conflict between an individualist and an institution—a conflict not unlike that between Andrew Mason and the medical profession in **"The Citadel."** The position of the priest is in some ways simpler than that of the doctor, since Francis had forsworn marriage and personal ambition such as that which compelled Andrew's decisions. Both men, however, have the qualities which distinguish the individualist who is not a mere iconoclast—simplicity, logical directness and faith in one's goal, not the desire to change for change's sake nor the will to dominate.

As readers of Dr. Cronin's earlier novels will anticipate, his present story has vigor and drama. It also has beauty, gentleness and humor. **"The Keys of the Kingdom"** is, I believe, a more appealing and more memorable book than any the author has written heretofore. Hingeing as it does on questions which deeply involve the faiths of many people, it seems likely that it will be even more widely discussed than **"The Citadel."** It

seems likely also that whether the reader shares the faith of Father Francis or the kindly and honest agnosticism of the Scottish doctor who died fighting the plague at his side, he will find excitement and comfort in this story of the life of a good man.

Mary Ross, "A Most Appealing and Memorable Book," in New York Herald Tribune Books, *July 20, 1941, p. 1.*

KATHERINE WOODS

[**"The Keys of the Kingdom,"** the] new novel by the author of **"The Citadel,"** is a magnificent story of the great adventure of individual goodness. And yet it is an essential trait of its hero's character that he could not have thought of the word "magnificent" as in any sense applied to his achievements, or the word "great" to his life. He saw himself as a man of puny strivings, and humility was in the very sinew of his saintliness, along with courage and brotherliness and truth. Just so, innately, was Francis Chisholm a man of great adventure. And the novel with a modern saint as hero sharpens a mercilessly perceptive wit in the portrayal of a sinner also, and stabs us to the examination of universal values, in an engrossingly dramatic story about a Roman Catholic priest who went to China as a missionary. . . .

Through the first third of its progress, **"The Keys of the Kingdom"** sustains an excellent pace as a better-than-average novel which offers a sincere and skillful, though not extraordinary, development of a difficult but not especially unusual theme. The saint moves along a trying way, harassed by others' rigidities and his own self-doubt. The sinner's feet have begun their sure climb upward. A wretched complication of domestic tragedy has been handled with delicacy and daring. And A. J. Cronin is supplying, in short, an acceptable successor to his widely read book of four years ago. Then suddenly the reader is caught and held in the excitement of tense incident. And **"The Citadel"** is forgotten. What cannot be forgotten, now, is the whole strange close-knit episode of the false miracle. From that first climax **"The Keys of the Kingdom"** steps to a road apart. It runs its course, now, in unflagging, mounting interest and in far-reaching significance, with the subtlety that conceals subtlety piercing to fundamental question through gripping event. . . .

No one who has read Dr. Cronin's earlier work needs to be told with what compact dramatic skill event has followed event and idea has been held safely back from the edge of symbolism. But **"The Keys of the Kingdom"** is a better book than **"The Citadel,"** as its greater human warmth and vitality touch a broader significance with more profundity and finesse. . . .

Underlying the whole course of this novel is the difference between good and evil in ordinary men. There is almost nothing here of what the world calls vice. And the book's outstanding sinner is very ordinary indeed. The Anselm Mealy pricelessly portrayed in this story is a successful career man in his church: he would have been equally successful in any business, profession, or office where roseate self-confidence, extrovert geniality, facile enthusiasm and shrewd executive ability moved within the spiritual closed-circle of material satisfaction and untroubled self-approval, to assure their happy possessor's popularity and gain. Anselm's unctuous piety is as sincere, and as inevitable, as his clichés; his gross self-seeking is as unconscious as his lack of sympathy: he is simply incapable of sympathy, or of anything else that requires sensitiveness, spiritual understanding, or naked lonely thought. It will be unfortunate if **"The Keys of the Kingdom"** is read as "attacking the church" (any church) and discussed from that point of view primarily. Certainly Dr. Cronin is attacking worldliness and bigotry and over-organization, and the claim of man-made standards or establishments to stand between man and his God. But the breadth of his attack is against the ancient deadly evil of intolerance and greed and arrogant complacency, wherever they may be: in church, class, nation; in you and me. And he is telling us too how the sure values without which there can be no real brotherliness grow in loneliness and question from the soil of humility to true spiritual power.

A second reading of **"The Keys of the Kingdom"** has left this reviewer even more absorbed and impressed than the first. It is not a flawless book: it has perhaps some redundancy of disaster, some overemphasis. But its human force grows in retrospect. And especially, reading the eventful story again, one is struck by the subtlety of thought which slowly gathers its thrust and polishes its steel.

> Katherine Woods, "A Modern Saint Is the Hero of A. J. Cronin's Novel," in The New York Times Book Review, *July 20, 1941, p. 5.*

WILLIAM Du BOIS

For his seventh novel in fourteen years Dr. Cronin offers us **"The Green Years,"** a slice of Scotch-Irish autobiography that teems with quiet charm and the special brand of heartache that this painstaking author is so adept at fashioning. The fact that the movies have already paid a record price for the rights should surprise no one: like **"The Citadel,"** which won the critics' prize for that year, and **"The Keys of the Kingdom,"** which is yet to be released, it offers a ready-made scenario for the trials, and the ultimate triumph, of a starved but valiant youth. Dr. Cronin's meticulous hand (which made **"The Citadel"** a kind of super-blueprint of every young doctor) has taken his own boyhood and made of it a mirror in which we may see reflected the frustrations of youth. Here, once again, is the loneliness and the blind ecstasy of adolescence—and the sense of release when adolescence is outgrown and life is faced at last.

Like most successful patterns, the story line of **"The Green Years"** is simplicity itself to the casual eye. An 8-year-old orphan boy crosses the Irish Sea from Dublin to live with his Scotch grandparents. Levenford, so far as the author pictures it, is a combination of factory town and Main Street, plus a conventionally dour outlook; Lomond View, the Leckies' "semi-detached" villa in the suburb, is dominated by the twin Scotch virtues of parsimony and silence. Papa's soul is a closed purse that has grown foul with rust; Mama is a gentle drudge, too busy to do much for her not-too-welcome grandson; Kate, the frumpy schoolteacher-daughter, is tortured by a spinster's unfulfilled dreams; Murdoch, the slightly scrofulous son, is scratching out his brains to pass his Civil Service tests.

But upstairs in his frowsy bedroom is Grandpa—and Grandpa, from Robie's first day in Lomond View, is the boy's delight. . . .

Sometimes the drabness creeps up and stifles the drama. Sometimes, for all of Dr. Cronin's planning, his catalogue of poverty seems a mere catalogue—and little more. The death of Gavin, Robie's boyhood friend, on a railway crossing seems merely a gratuitous blow of fate—similar to Christine's death in **"The**

Citadel." . . . And the final solution of Robie's despair is redeemed from pure corn only by the author's quick curtain.

But the fact remains that **"The Green Years"** is a stirring and even eloquent story of boyhood—always providing the reader is willing to join Dr. Cronin midway in his narrative. Dissenters will complain that they have met Mama and Murdoch elsewhere—that young Robie is cold and not too convincing Copperfield—that Grandpa, for all his flourishes, seems a vague blend of Micawber and Bergerac. But dissenters have no business in the stalls while this maestro is performing.

> William Du Bois, "Scenes from a Frustrated Boyhood," in The New York Times Book Review, *November 12, 1944, p. 3.*

NATHAN L. ROTHMAN

[**"The Green Years"**] is not one of Dr. Cronin's more effective novels. To get right down to the truth, it is rather a weak and tentative effort, lacking both the assurance and the dramatic outline which are generally characteristic of his work. Some of this lack of tone is certainly the result of design rather than accident, since the story is simply an account of a boy's growth from eight to eighteen. Such a tale would be expected to ramble, to unwind like a kitestring rather than to expand from any dramatic center. Yet even here, in the history of a youth, some position must be taken by the writer other than that of friendly narrator. He may take a youth's view of life, give it to us through eyes drowned in new sight, ears and nostrils assailed with the wonderful, agonizing freshness of sensation. Or he may give us the man's view, looking backward, with some vision be it bitter or proud, just so long as there is an achieved vantage point from which all past and present falls into place and has meaning. You do not need to be Joyce or Wolfe to do either of these things; it would be enough to reach for them.

Dr. Cronin's Robert Shannon is neither one thing nor the other. His is not the hot, immediate experience of youth, nor the remembered pantomine, long ago played, now understood. Robert has none of the spirit of youth, none of the spine of maturity. He seems in fact to have been created expressly to appeal to our least critical sentiments, a cautious, affecting little man of sugar and water, sweet and harmless, no visible character. . . . crosses are piled upon his back to show how he can bear them and walk his ten years—yet somehow it seems that nothing has happened. There is not the feeling of real suffering, or its surmounting, here. You need more of a character for that. It comes down to this, then: that young Robert Shannon is not a successful, living creation, and not all the adventures in unhappy Scotland will make him so. The other characters about him are similarly unrealized. . . . The book is altogether a mild, even soothing affair, despite its unhappy circumstances. This is a combination of effects that may indeed please many readers.

> Nathan L. Rothman, "A. J. Cronin Creates Robert Shannon," in The Saturday Review of Literature, *Vol. XXVII, No. 47, November 18, 1944, p. 22.*

C. V. TERRY

"Shannon's Way" is not billed as a sequel to Dr. Cronin's last novel, **"The Green Years."** It may be read as an entity in itself, and judged on its own doubtful merits. As a sequel, it seems a pale coda to the first volume—or, should we say, a tenuous suspension-bridge to other episodes in Robie's glum saga? As a self-sufficient account of a young Scotch doctor's struggle to make a name for himself as a researcher, his lonely ragings as he trods his chosen path, and the standard females who console him en route, it is a sketchy scenario indeed—something that Dr. Cronin might have jotted down on odd bits of paper with a blunt pencil, and never endowed with a third dimension. . . .

Since Dr. Cronin never takes the time to dramatize [Robie's individual pursuit to isolate an influenza bacilli] properly, or even to explain the chase in terms the layman might understand, one's interest diminishes at a rather startling rate.

The familiar Cronin formula is followed rigorously throughout—with no real variation in the monotony. First, of course, we have the bull-headed, opportunistic Department Head—who sacks our hero promptly when he discovers that he's been using those Bunsen burners for his own ends. Next, the scramble for a livelihood in drab corners—a rural "fever-hospital," a slum-clinic, the residency at a plush-lined sanatorium for mental cases, where Robie meets, suffers, and lives down the meanness of humankind. Finally, and just as inevitably, the Big Frustration (when an American researcher beats him to the deadline), and the Big Recompense (when *the* girl, and *the* job he's always wanted, tumble willy-nilly in his threadbare lap).

Throughout, of course, he's sustained by the love of one of those model girl students that apparently exist only in the pages of medical novels, the sultry ardors of a nurse at the mental home, the homespun affection of a few Greenyear leftovers. All of it is told just as baldly as this story-line would suggest—and with little attempt on the novelist's part to warm one's interest in his sullen hero.

> *C. V. Terry, "Scotch Sour," in* The New York Times Book Review, *July 18, 1948, p. 12.*

LON TINKLE

["**The Spanish Gardener**"] is a compact and neat parable whose simple moral is well worth restatement for our times. The sermon, so to speak, in "**The Spanish Gardener**" is one already familiar to Dr. Cronin's readers: namely, that simple, direct affections and honest acts can be corroded and destroyed by distrust and by too much introspection. Or, put more aphoristically and a little less exactly, to the impure in heart all things are impure.

Dr. Cronin begins his story with a firm discipline, in a tone as dry and detached as Somerset Maugham's. Throughout, "**The Spanish Gardener**" is in fact as attentively carpentered as any novel by Maugham himself. But the detached mood soon disappears: Dr. Cronin has targets to scourge and no intention of remaining above the strife. His story is as predictable as the resolution of a given algebraic equation. (p. 20)

All [the] characters are developed so skimpily, however, as to be mere puppets manipulated adroitly by Dr. Cronin's sure hand. Even the events exploited betray the fact that the author's mind was concentrated on his moral. Here again are the stock devices of the hurried and unexpected out-of-town trip, the placing of stolen articles in an innocent pocket, the villain's moll whose lies indict the virtuous, the Eden-like retreat in the mountains, the pure hearts, existing in the midst of squalor.

The relationship the author places his characters in is not so much superficial as artificial. And in the end, the freight of intended meaning is too heavy for such thin, pallid creations. (p. 21)

> *Lon Tinkle, "Serpent in Eden," in* The Saturday Review of Literature, *Vol. XXXIII, No. 36, September 9, 1950, pp. 20-1.*

JOHN BARKHAM

The Germans have a word for a writer who lets his hair (and standards) down. They call him "unbuttoned." Dr. A. J. Cronin must have been in very unbuttoned mood when he wrote "**Beyond This Place**" an old-fashioned melodrammer of the kind popular *circa* Ouida and Marie Corelli. That is not to say it isn't worth propping up in your hammock this summer, or that it won't be a best seller. The answer is yes in both cases. It's just that Dr. Cronin has elected this time to tell a suspenseful tale without regard for people or probabilities.

The book . . . opens in a British town on a deceptively peaceful note, with Mrs. Burgess, a gray-haired "widow," welcoming her clean-limbed son, Paul, from medical school. He needs his birth certificate for a vacation job, and she can't give it to him. Why? There is a mystery here and Paul soon learns that his real name is Mathry, and that his father has done fifteen years of a life sentence for the murder of a prostitute.

After the first shock Paul goes to the scene of the crime, determined to find out what his father did. Thereafter the author leads him a long and fateful chase picking up the threads of a crime forgotten by all but the man doing time for it. . . .

All ends happily, except that Dr. Cronin leaves some loose ends lying around. What, for example, happened to Lena Andersen, the beautiful blonde who loved Paul and nursed him through illness? She walks out of the story.

Dr. Cronin's sense of theatre has not deserted him. His menaces are satisfying. Some of the scenes are vivid thumbnails. . . .

Plot is all, and it is played out skillfully enough to keep the reader going from cover to cover. But the characters are monochrome figures—Paul pullulating with self-pity and the others merely making automatic gestures to move the story along. They speak in a stilted style. . . .

Button up that overcoat, Doctor. It's time to get to work again.

> *John Barkham, "Even the Judge Was a Conniver," in* The New York Times Book Review, *July 19, 1953, p. 5.*

CHARLES LEE

A. J. Cronin, one of the world's most popular novelists and least competent critics, has this to say about "**Beyond This Place**," his newest book: "It is probably the most exciting novel I have ever written." . . . The fact of the matter is that all nine of Dr. Cronin's previous brain-children are better proportioned and more intelligent. . . .

"**Beyond This Place**" suffers from the major fault of having been "constructed," to use the good doctor's own word, to fit a crusade. It issues from irritation, not from intensity; it is shaped by artifice, not by art. In its grotesque attack on the present system of trial by jury . . . the book reads like badly diluted Dickens, passionate urgency all but gone and humor totally absent. In support of his attack Dr. Cronin concocts a fantastically irregular murder trial with which to berate the judiciary process, ignoring the fact that his own "trial" of the courts is monstrously loaded and overlooking entirely the fact that in law (as in medicine) some lamentable margin of error must be allowed for the imperfections of humanity. Like many crusaders, Dr. Cronin is vehement in assault, but fuzzy as to the nature of his reforms.

The story, set in Northern Ireland and the Midlands city of Wortley in 1936, deals with the strenuous efforts of young Paul Mathry to obtain the release of his father, Rees, from Stoneheath Prison, where he has spent fifteen years of a life sentence for a murder which he did not commit. The circumstantial evidence on which Rees has been convicted is so faulty that only an author would try to get away with it; the prison so cruel (Rees is never allowed a visitor) that it would seem Dr. Cronin missed the real target of a crusade; the language with which he reports these dismal events so Victorian that one wonders why the whole business wasn't set in 1876 instead of 1936. . . .

The characters are as stereotyped as the language, the original prosecutor in the case (Sir Matthew Sprott) being an engine of knavery and the heroine (Lena Anderson), confusingly described as a Juno, a Madonna, and an Amazon, the misunderstood victim of a British raping party (what a picture of England Dr. Cronin draws!). Rees's villainous truculence toward his family is only the final touch of the bizarre in a novel that also features a purse made of human skin and a hitherto unrecorded illusion of the great magician Harry Houdini, an appearance at Wortley's Palace Theatre just nine years after his death.

> Charles Lee, "Fraying Margins of Error," *in* The Saturday Review, *New York, Vol. XXXVI, No. 30, July 25, 1953, p. 14.*

JOHN BARKHAM

Dr. Cronin's novel ["**A Thing of Beauty**"], his best since "**The Citadel**" almost twenty years ago, is an object lesson in the power a writer can infuse into a story when he becomes deeply involved in its theme. In his last book, "**Beyond This Place**," Dr. Cronin was the professional story teller, standing aloof from his characters and spinning his tale with a craftsman's competence but a personal disinterest. In his new book, the story of an English painter persecuted for his art, he writes with a crusading fervor that makes this one of the most moving novels of the year.

Never overtly pleading his cause, Dr. Cronin leaves it to his story to drive home its moral with quiet ferocity. I laid down this gripping book vowing never again to be a Philistine about avant-garde art. . . . Clearly Dr. Cronin feels very strongly about this, and his book should make all but the stoniest of readers share his indignation. . . .

[The story] is recounted with sustained drive and a fine economy of means. Dr. Cronin disdains aimless scene-setting or atmospheric mood-making: every word either advances the plot or throws light on character. His story is none the less powerful for being predictable, and in its finest passages it reaches heights of real eloquence.

The book's moral seems irresistible; for an upperclass Englishman to become a true artist, he must break out of his stifling milieu and make contact with humanity on broad, lower levels. Yet in making the transition, as Desmonde does, he forfeits recognition by the very class from which he springs. Dr. Cronin

sums up the irony of this cycle in a peroration faintly tinged with bitterness.

"**A Thing of Beauty**" . . . is close enough to truth to make one ashamed of man's recurrent myopia. The reward of the innovator in art, Dr. Cronin seems to be saying, is a fine funeral or an imposing statue.

> John Barkham, "Persecuted for His Art," *in* The New York Times Book Review, *May 20, 1956, p. 4.*

ANTHONY BAILEY

Mr. Cronin has a reputation as a "professional novelist" or a "good story-teller" and his latest book [*A Thing of Beauty*] has the lulling effect those terms imply. I picked it up, remembering that *The Citadel* had given me, at the age of fourteen, a strong desire to be a doctor and to save humanity. And I thought that intellectual fashions one adopts at a later age had, perhaps, made me unfair to writers of this kind. But I was wrong. This book is a sedative.

It purports to be the story of a great painter's life and it is no compliment to say that Mr. Cronin gets as near to depicting Genius as Henry James did in *Roderick Hudson*. James' first attempt, however, did have some subtlety to recommend it; Mr. Cronin's book has none. It is, first of all, one of those chronicle novels that seem to be demanded by women's monthly magazines in which no development of character is required but instead "interesting characters" and much local color. . . .

The infuriating thing about this sort of book is that one can tell oneself that it's manna for the masses only for so long; and there comes a point where one rebels out of simple embarrassment. Of course we know that, if we aren't treated to a happy ending, Stephen will die of TB and his name will live on. . . . His father will eventually come to realize that there may be something, even though he can't quite grasp what, in the creative life; and then there's compassion and posthumous forgiveness. But this isn't the creative life which is here recounted, and nowhere is there any insight at all into what could possibly engage or destroy the inquiring intelligence. . . . [That] this sort of tawdry nonsense should be foisted off as the artistic life by an author who can write pages of even semiliterate English is, if not an insult, at least a sort of confidence trick.

Mr. Cronin's prose is perhaps an indication of his quality. It is that pseudo Pre-Raphaelite English which dwells on "maidservants" and the vintages of Port. Everything is "delicious," from spring weather to good working-class tea.

Why, then, take this book seriously at all? As I said, partly because it seems to be a lie. Partly, too, because there is something sad in finding that after all one was right about this kind of book.

> Anthony Bailey, "Struggles of the Artistic Life," *in* Commonweal, *Vol. 64, No. 14, July 6, 1956, p. 353.*

PETER GIRVIN

Oddly, "**The Northern Light**" seems but a skeleton Cronin novel. Obviously this able and experienced writer has observed the problems of a provincial newspaper . . . so that he knows what occasionally happens to them when somebody wants to acquire them. Furthermore, his characters are credible, even when their creator is most sentimental about them. But the richness of detail, the solidly woven warp and woof of living that have been so typically Cronin in previous novels, are wanting from **"The Northern Light."** Here is what might be called a dwarf specimen of a species that is typically larger and more luxuriant in habit.

Peter Girvin, "But the Paper Came Out," in The New York Times Book Review, *May 25, 1958, p. 5.*

THE NEW YORKER

["**The Judas Tree**" is a] silly book about a very rich, retired Scottish-born doctor and his guilty conscience. The doctor, David Moray, . . . has established himself in Switzerland, where he lives very well. . . . The serpent, conscience, slithers into this paradise when a chance word pinches David's memory and reminds him of the Scottish village where, thirty years earlier, he wronged and then abandoned a good young woman. He decides to go back to the village and see whether a little gift of money and a kind word might smooth her feelings, even at this late date, but on arriving in Scotland he finds that his lost love is not elderly and not humble and not sad but dead and buried, and no longer able to satisfy his appetite for gratitude and admiration. There is, however, her daughter, twenty years old, very religious, and quite penniless, who is the purest hypocritical spirit to appear on the literary horizon since Little Eva. . . . What follows is lots and lots of doom, performed to the mission-bell music that is so well suited to Mr. Cronin's coy, parsonage prose. (pp. 208-09)

A review of "The Judas Tree," in The New Yorker, *Vol. XXXVII, No. 34, October 7, 1961, pp. 208-09.*

JOSEPH CLANCY

There are no bad stories; there are only bad novels. Take [*The Judas Tree*] for example. . . . Such a story could make a good or a bad novel but in A. J. Cronin's case, it has made a bad one.

The reason is clear. Everything hinges on the characterization of the doctor: he must be subtly and convincingly drawn. Mr. Cronin fails; for instead of action rooted in character, he gives us facets of character invented to fit the action. We are constantly aware not so much of the fact that Dr. Moray is charming, guilt-ridden or self-deceptive as the fact that Mr. Cronin is trying very hard, and by the most obvious means, to convince us that he is.

The publishers warn us that this is a "devastating" novel and more "realistic" than any of Mr. Cronin's previous works. The realism seems to consist of a few timid vulgarities in the dialogue and a few self-conscious attempts at graphic sexual descriptions. The reader need have no fears. Cronin is still well to the right of D. H. Lawrence and Henry Miller in such matters and is, indeed, so unsure in managing them that this, not the speech or action, becomes embarrassing.

This story needed either more "realism" or less; most of all it needed realism in depicting the human soul. What it also needed was a different author. . . .

Joseph Clancy, in a review of "The Judas Tree," in The Catholic World, *Vol. 194, No. 1163, February, 1962, p. 318.*

RICHARD SULLIVAN

Cronin is a writer of the natural, easy sort. Let us not go in for fantastical comparisons; but he works in the high tradition of Dickens and Scott. He tells a story with such gripping intensity that, reading, you feel glad that this is a book you must stay up until 2 a. m. to finish. In the morning, knowing how things came out, you feel sad that there is not more to read of this enthralling novel.

Dr. Cronin's novels in the past occasionally have been marked by lapses into sentimentality or melodrama. None has been a downright poor novel, but a few have been shaky. **"The Green Years"** was the best of them, until this one.

"A Song of Sixpence" is a first-person narrative told by a bright Scotch-Irish boy, surrounded by fascinating persons—all, in a true sense, Dickensian characters—in and out of his immediate family. The time span goes from early childhood to graduation from the university as doctor of medicine beginning his practice. It covers some early years of this century, intimately, freshly, thru the narrator's period of growing up.

Economic, social, and religious pressures descend upon him. He is variously poor, intrusive, and Catholic among people who, early in this century, in Scotland, are not disposed to accept him. But he rises. And if there is a touch of Horatio Alger maneuvering in his rising, there also was such a touch in "Ivanhoe" and "David Copperfield."

The book is exceptionally readable and engaging. It tells a story in the old high tradition of the novel. Dr. Cronin does not play about with the language stylistically or structurally. He is not an innovator but a traditionalist, not an experimenter but an experienced writer with a sound eye and ear for prose.

Let us not make fantastical comparisons, but—in his tradition—Dr. Cronin writes compellingly, as did some of his very popular predecessors.

Richard Sullivan, "A Storyteller of the Natural, Easy Sort," in Chicago Tribune, *September 20, 1964, p. 5.*

JAMES G. MURRAY

Given Dr. Cronin's considerable reputation and some fourteen titles on which it is based, [*A Song of Sixpence*] obviously requires a notice. It does not, however, deserve one. For this is a bad book, not in the sense of being a good book that has failed, but in the sense of being a second-rate book that does not meet the requirements of its lower estate. And the reason for this has something to do with the matters of honesty and sentiment, or—more simply—with honest sentimentality.

The reader is told (on the book jacket, it is true, but in the author's words) that "of all my novels . . . *A Song of Sixpence* is to me . . . the real thing." Further, the author speaks of being "deeply moved" and "carried away" by the narrative because here he "was truly expressing" himself. One takes it, then, that Cronin sees his book as a fictionalized account of his boyhood in the Scottish highlands, a boyhood in which the usual emotional difficulties of growing up were complicated by a would-be writer's sensitivity, by the uniqueness of his Catholicism in a completely Presbyterian community, and by the poverty and loss he knew upon his father's death.

There is a book somewhere in that stuff of memory. It could be shaped into straight autobiography—except that Cronin published his a number of years ago. And it could also be turned into a decent piece of fiction, provided of course that the sentiment in such material could be stopped just this side of the maudlin. But the author wanted it both ways, and simply did not have the talent to manage a genuine autobiographical novel. For to work in that mined field, authors—unlike Coleridge's theatregoers and poetry readers—must not entertain a willing suspension of disbelief. And yet, as his quoted words attest, Cronin took himself and his memories too seriously.

The artist in the man should have known what the man in the artist was not able to discern: that his story, if true, did not have sufficient individuality to interest or to be of interest to anyone but himself: that his story, if invented, did not have anything in it to differentiate it from a hundred other middle-brow novels of slick sentiment and sentimentality.

I have nothing against the latter. In many ways and for a variety of reasons, I believe, an honest, unpretentious tear-bath of a book for the unsophisticated is better than one that aims higher but falls short—or one, such as this, that wrongfully uses art to supply the defects of reality, and reality to substitute for the truth of art. Remembered or not, all Cronin's characters in this book, including its hero, are extraordinarily naive clichés. Created or not, his sequential incidents (plot?), syrupy descriptions (background?), and intrepid moralizing (theme?) suggest not the fruits of a creative imagination but the flotsam of a memory not so selective as it once was and never particularly stimulating in the first place. (pp. 458-59)

James G. Murray, in a review of "A Song of Sixpence," in America, *Vol. 111, No. 16, October 17, 1964, pp. 458-59.*

ROBERT BURNS

This curiously old-fashioned novel [*A Song of Sixpence*] is Doctor Cronin's fourteenth, published 35 years after his first, **Hatter's Castle**. This record demonstrates that Cronin is a prolific writer who has made few concessions to the ephemeral tastes of literary reviewers. *A Song of Sixpence* is traditional Cronin as much as **The Citadel** and **Keys of the Kingdom** but I must confess that I found it pleasant reading.

Set in his familiar pre-war Scotland, *A Song of Sixpence* traces the coming to manhood of Laurence Carroll, an unbelievably unspoiled youngster of Dickensian cast. The events of his life, although catastrophic in themselves are not nearly tortuous or agonizing enough to satisfy most contemporary novelists. And drastically unlike the latter, Cronin posts only exterior forces toward the development of his characters. The Freudian struggles so essential to most modern novelists are not for him. He eschews the counterpoint of the Id and the Superego so completely that when Laurence suffers "a nervous breakdown," it comes without warning both to him and to us. Significantly, his convalescence is suggested in terms of the recovery of his motor functions; psychotherapy, even self-administered, is never suggested. (p. 74)

As a stylist Dr. Cronin is . . . conventional but he writes with the effortless grace of a polished professional. As he guides his characters through their actions, he is unquestionably *there* making all the arrangements, calling all the signals at every turn. He is able to do this unobtrusively, however, because of an assurance that is almost completely free from self conscious introspection and questioning. Like their master, his characters seem hardly ever to question or probe. Isn't it enough that external events are happy or sad, evil or good, frightening or

benign? These alone cause the characters in *A Song of Sixpence* to react, to change and sometimes to develop. So even if Dr. Cronin's style is noticeably dated, it is long enough to reach from the body to the ground. It is clearly adequate to accomplish Dr. Cronin's limited purposes.

What estimation, then, does *A Song of Sixpence* deserve? On one level it is a pleasant if superficial novel for people with nostalgia for old-fashioned drug stores and band concerts in the park. On another, it may be escapist fare for some of the many who occasionally tire of the existentialist struggle to survive among countless messages and overwhelming decisions.

Neither of these estimates, having been said, are necessarily jibes. *A Song of Sixpence* is certainly not a major novel, not even an important one, but Dr. Cronin is a master of his trade with the skill and discipline to make his novels something more than literary period pieces. And if sterner critics might find Cronin's latest book superfluous, it can be argued that calorie counting has not made whipped cream obsolete and that there is place for lagniappe so long as we do not mistake it for meat and potatoes. (pp. 74-5)

Robert Burns, "Another Key, Another Kingdom," in The Critic, *Vol. XXIII, No. 2, October-November, 1964, pp. 74-5.*

EUGENE J. LINEHAN, S. J.

Superior Slovene Vodka, made entirely from rye and green rye malt, is the **"Pocketful of Rye"** which entitles this little novel of A. J. Cronin. The Vodka is an attempt at escapism on the part of the hero, Laurence Carroll: young physician. He has reread Thompson's famous "Hound of Heaven" and the running proves to be as futile as the hero of Thompson's poetry. Carroll has a conversion of Hollywood proportions in a tiny Swiss Church as he dialogues with the Blessed Sacrament. The twin voices which he imagines is explained by the parish priest as a dialogue with conscience, the Catholic conscience which few ever escape. This turns the physician back to his Scottish home and to real acceptance of obligations. It's a bit pat, but the story tells well and its message is a needed one for most of us. . . .

[The] author is a man of style and the novel can stand on its own as a good, tight little tale which encourages all of us to face ourselves a bit more honestly.

Eugene J. Linehan, S. J., in a review of "A Pocketful of Rye," in Best Sellers, *Vol. 29, No. 15, November 1, 1969, p. 285.*

JEREMY BROOKS

Dr Cronin is not merely not believable [in **The Minstrel Boy**]: he is committing truthlessness with the unctuous confidence of a money-lender committing robbery. This story of the rise, fall and redemption of a young and beautiful Catholic priest with an exquisite singing voice and a taste for the ladies is sentimentally snobbish about music, religion, food, wine, gardening, travel, sex, money, Ireland, clothes . . . you name it, Dr Cronin has a snobbery for it.

Jeremy Brooks, "Spine-Chiller," in The Sunday Times, *London, May 11, 1975, p. 41.**

PATRICIA GOODFELLOW

Cronin's easy storytelling art is [in *Desmonde*] applied to the true story of his lifelong friend Desmonde Fitzgerald. Desmonde is a brilliant singer with a strong other-worldly bent that leads him to the heights and the depths during a checkered career as priest, night-club singer, movie actor, missionary in India, and perennial spiritual quester. Desmonde's downers are generally caused by his uninvited attraction to the opposite sex. Cronin plays himself throughout—a prosperously devout and loyal friend who recounts Desmonde's progress with an odd mix of disapproval and wonder. Cronin's universe is morally black and white, defined by Catholic orthodoxy and the social assumptions of perhaps a half century ago. However, *Desmonde* is an enjoyable narrative of a half-rogue, half-saint which should please traditionalists.

> *Patricia Goodfellow, in a review of "Desmonde,"*
> *in* Library Journal, *Vol. 100, No. 16, September 15,*
> *1975, p. 1651.*

Joan Didion

1934-

American novelist, essayist, journalist, scriptwriter, and short story writer.

Didion is respected both as a novelist and as a writer of personalized, journalistic essays. The disintegration of American morals and the cultural chaos upon which her essays comment are explored more fully in her novels, where the overriding theme is individual and societal fragmentation. Consequently, a sense of anxiety or dread permeates much of her work, and her novels have a reputation for being depressing and even morbid.

Didion's essays have appeared regularly in such periodicals as *The Saturday Evening Post, National Review, The New York Times Book Review*, and *The New York Review of Books* and have been collected in two volumes, *Slouching Towards Bethlehem* (1968) and *The White Album* (1979). In the title essay of the latter volume, which concerns both the national chaos of the summer of 1968 and her own nervous breakdown at that time, Didion wrote, "an attack of vertigo and nausea does not now seem to me an inappropriate response to the summer of 1968." This essay illustrates the emphasis which Didion places in all her writing on the relationship between personal and national dissolution. Many critics hold Didion's essays in higher regard than her novels, but Didion claims that she "never wanted to be a journalist or a reporter" and that reportorial assignments serve for her primarily as sources of material for her novels.

Didion's first novel, *Run River* (1963), is a story of family strife set in California, Didion's native state. Lily McClellan, the central character, is typical of the complex, fully developed female protagonists Didion is noted for creating. These are women who try to find meaning in a world which no longer recognizes the importance of personal and collective morals and who attempt to maintain ties with a past which has no place in the present. Central to *Run River* is the portrayal of California as the last frontier of American idealism and the place most representative of the country's cultural disintegration. The vision of the United States as an amoral society is mirrored in the breakdown of a family. Didion uses this microcosmic technique in all of her fiction, including three short stories written in 1964 and collected in a limited edition volume, *Telling Stories* (1978). These stories are noted for their foreshadowing of the themes which appear in her later novels.

Geographical locations play an important role in emphasizing themes in Didion's fiction. The setting for Maria Wyeth's nihilistic crisis in *Play It As It Lays* (1970) is the artificial world of Hollywood, where people use one another to advance their own status. Boca Grande is the imaginary Latin American country in which Charlotte Douglas awaits the arrival of her outlaw daughter in *A Book of Common Prayer* (1977). A country without a past or a future, torn apart by frequent, violent uprisings, it mirrors Charlotte's internal disorder.

The political turbulence and violence which have lately been endemic in Latin America resurface in *Salvador* (1983), Didion's account of her two-week stay in El Salvador. The essays in *Salvador* are concerned not with facts about the conflict but

© *Jerry Bauer*

with the fear that pervades daily existence in such a place. Like her earlier journalism, these essays are written from an extremely personal point of view through which Didion conveys her own fear and repulsion. In the novel *Democracy* (1984), Didion returns to her concern for the loss of traditional values and the absence of viable new ones. The story can be read on several levels: as a murder mystery, as a love story, and as an exposure of the fraudulence of public life. The various threads interweave to form a picture of America's political decline and moral decay. Somewhat disarmingly, Didion provides the narrator with her own name, forcing the reader to question the fictional nature of the other characters.

(See also *CLC*, Vols. 1, 3, 8, 14; *Contemporary Authors*, Vols. 5-8, rev. ed.; *Dictionary of Literary Biography*, Vol. 2; and *Dictionary of Literary Biography Yearbook: 1981*.)

KATHERINE USHER HENDERSON

Few contemporary American writers are "American" in all the ways that Joan Didion is. Although she has visited Europe often, she has never written an essay on Europe, nor do we find a single European character in her fiction. Not only are all of her major fictional characters born and raised in the

United States; they also bear no marks of European nationality, carry no memory traces of European traditions. (p. 140)

In both her fiction and her essays, Didion sees the American character as often arrogant, often nostalgic, but invariably and quintessentially romantic, and thus deluded. Her more nostalgic characters are ever looking backward to the simplicity of childhood, finding there the source of the myth they are currently living: Maria Wyeth learned from her father that material success is life's easy and natural goal; Lily McClellan learned from her parents that no harm could come to her or her family in the Sacramento Valley. Her other characters have woven different myths: Charlotte Douglas, that all change is progress, that history moves people inevitably toward the greater good; Grace Strasser-Mendana, that every problem is susceptible of scientific solution. These illusions are characteristically (although not exclusively) American, and Didion also sees as characteristically American the tenacity with which they are held and the naiveté with which they are expressed.

Against these romantic myths Didion portrays the reality of the emptiness of material success, the disintegration of the family, and social and economic revolution that do not, in any moral sense at least, constitute progress. Her characters must either recognize this reality (a recognition that may produce madness, as it does in the case of Maria Wyeth) or be destroyed by it, as Lucille Miller and Charlotte Douglas are. Among Didion's heroines only Lily McClellan and Grace Strasser-Mendana have the resilience to confront the realities of chaos and evil and still find something in life worth affirming.

Seeing herself as "American" as anyone, Didion is constantly testing her own illusions against reality. . . . Although brought up with the same illusions as many of the people she writes about, Didion, unlike most of them, is ultimately an antiromantic realist.

Didion's writings are American in their characters, in the myths by which these characters try to live their lives, and in their tension between a vision of nature and God as benevolent and a conflicting vision of nature and the supernatural as fraught with danger and evil. Didion sees in Americans the dissonance produced by a naive confidence that they have a covenant with God coexisting with a fear of omnipresent evil and imminent doom; stemming from our Puritan heritage, this dissonance is familiar to readers of nineteenth-century American literature, for it is a dominant note in the fiction of Hawthorne and Melville. (pp. 140-42)

Nature is sometimes beautiful in Didion's writings . . . , but it is always latent with terror as well, for it can subdue man, reducing him to insignificance. Like the Mississippi River in Mark Twain's *Huck Finn*, the Sacramento River in *Run River* represents not only time, but also the power and mystery of nature to which man is subject. The forces of nature in Didion's writings—the Santa Ana winds, a forest fire burning out of control—often have the majestic, destructive power that Melville attributed to the great white whale. As Ishmael wonders whether the destruction of the *Pequod* reflects upon the evil of Moby Dick or the evil living in the sailors' hearts, so does Didion stress the same mystery. . . . Like the heroes of Hawthorne and Melville, Didion's heroines inhabit a world in which good and evil are not merely social or political, but part of the impenetrable universe itself.

Whereas Didion certainly sees the subjects of her fiction and essays as American, she would probably be surprised to hear her work described as "woman's literature," especially since she has publically rejected the tenets of the women's movement. Yet all three of her novels are dominated by a woman's point of view, and all three portray in detail women's feelings about experiences that are exclusively feminine: childbirth, motherhood, abortion, menstruation, sexual submission to male demands. The relationship between mother and daughter is important in all three, and overshadows all other bonds in *Play It As It Lays*. . . . All of Didion's heroines are mothers, and all are deeply involved with their children.

Although men in Didion's fiction often lack the power to express love or other emotion, they have a power to act, to change the real world, that women do not. (pp. 142-44)

Didion's women are fully realized characters; we may or may not like them, but we understand why they behave as they do. Her male characters are often shadowy by comparison; the reasons for their actions are often far from clear. Everett McClellan is convincing in many parts of *Run River,* but we never understand why, given his eagerness to settle down and become a rancher, he enlists in the army, leaving Lily alone with two babies and a querulous old man. Leonard Douglas is superb as a witty, harassed lawyer, but his behavior at crucial points in *A Book of Common Prayer* is also puzzling. He clearly cares enough about Charlotte to keep track of her, to go to New Orleans when their baby is born; why on earth does he allow her to drift about Central America with a dying baby? On one level the answer to these questions is obvious: Didion wished to manipulate the plots of the novels to isolate her heroines. But she could have given her male characters more plausible motives for their behavior, especially in the case of Everett, whose point of view dominates whole sections of the novel.

Didion's fictional women engage her immense talents as a realistic novelist; she draws each of them with fine, sharp brush strokes that reveal every dimension of their personalities, every connection between character and action. Although her men cannot be called flat characters, they do not fully compel the reader's credence, for their behavior is often inconsistent with their character as Didion has presented it.

A few feminist critics rejected Didion's first two novels because Lily and Maria are passive, traditional women who yearn for the stability and emotional closeness of the family, submit to men sexually, and, with the exception of their mothers, are uncomfortable with other adult women. However, feminist criticism today is less likely to dictate to writers the kinds of characters they should create. In "Women's Literature," Elizabeth Janeway sensibly suggests that women's literature is not confined to that written by avowed feminists, but rather includes all literature that presents "women's experience from within," describing and evaluating it "in terms which can be various and individual but which are inherently the product of women's lives." Didion's fiction fits this definition. . . . (pp. 144-45)

While Didion's experience as a woman has been transformed and expressed through her fictional characters, her essays, with few exceptions, are not written from a woman's perspective. The voice in the essays is that of an American, a Californian, a writer, even a "migraine personality," but seldom a woman writing of explicitly feminine experience. There are a few exceptions: "John Wayne: A Love Song" could not have been written by a man, and one of the themes of "On Going Home" is the double mother-daughter relationship. Yet nowhere in the essays do we find what appears everywhere in the fiction, what

Didion has called "the irreconcilable difference" of being a woman: "that sense of living one's deepest life underwater, that dark involvement with blood and birth and death." Female experience as Didion conceives of it is not only personal and sexual, but also uncontrolled. In her fiction she can distance herself from and exercise control over this experience in a way that would be impossible to achieve in her autobiographical essays.

Although not written from the particular perspective of a woman, Didion's essays appeal to most feminists for several reasons. They assume that a woman is just as involved in the larger society as a man and that her ability to observe and analyze that society is as keen as his. Many of them belong to the journalist's tradition of aggressive, even intrusive reporting. They embody many qualities traditionally considered "masculine": bluntness, precision, objectivity, and a complete absence of sentimentality. One must be glad that Didion does not restrict herself to feminine experience in her essays; although many women are currently writing about every aspect of women's experience, there are few writers—male or female—with her dramatic ability to present and evaluate American culture.

In both her essays and her fiction Didion seeks to render the moral complexity of contemporary American experience, especially the dilemmas and ambiguities resulting from the erosion of traditional values by a new social and political reality. To this end, she violates the conventions of traditional journalism whenever it suits her purpose, fusing the public and the personal, frequently placing herself in an otherwise objective essay, giving us her private and often anguished experience as a metaphor for the writer, for her generation, and sometimes for her entire society.

In her fiction, on the other hand, Didion has found that a traditional form and structure better suit her purpose. Unlike many other contemporary novelists, she creates real settings, characters that behave with some consistency, plots that have a beginning, middle, and end. In her few pieces of literary criticism Didion defends these traditions against the "new fiction" of Kurt Vonnegut, Joseph Heller, and Bruce Jay Friedman. Lacking plot, structure, or consistent point of view, the new fiction, Didion feels, allows the author to abnegate his responsibility to make a moral statement. . . . (pp. 145-47)

In several different pieces she cites *Madame Bovary* as a model to be emulated: realistic in its smallest detail, traditional in structure and plot, it is a model that Didion aspires to, for it is the kind of novel that she believes comes closest to the truth. When she speaks of the truth, Didion thinks not of a political or religious truth—of any ideology—but of a setting forth of moral ambiguity, an ordering of life's moral complexity. To this end, style and artifice are not the enemies of truth, but the means to approach it. . . . (p. 147)

Implicit in Didion's view of the writer's responsibility is her conviction that, however multiple and ambiguous it may be, truth exists and can be approached by the writer with the courage and skill to project a coherent, realistic vision. Her own vision reveals to us the moral condition of contemporary Americans, living by illusions as fragile as fine china, clinging to shards of broken dreams, yet often redeemed by an immense potential for love and commitment. Thus, while preternaturally attuned to every false note in American culture, Didion yet holds out to us the possibility of integrity, integrity based on rigorous and continual self-scrutiny. "Style is character," she

has said. The care that she devotes to every paragraph, the years spent on a single novel, the endless revisions, the novels and essays begun and laid aside—all attest to her struggle for integrity. We accept her criticism of us because it stems from the same drive, "to fight lying all the way." For Didion, integrity of style and integrity of character are one. (pp. 147-48)

Katherine Usher Henderson, in her Joan Didion, *Frederick Ungar Publishing Co., 1981, 164 p.*

DAVID LEPPARD

El Salvador calls everything into question. Among foreign visitors there is an endemic paranoia, a profound sense that every moment harbours the possibility of a violent death. Deploying her full rhetorical weaponry, Joan Didion's [*Salvador*] takes us on a journey to the heart of the Salvadorean darkness. It evokes the unspeakable insanity effected by a well-intentioned imperialism gone terribly wrong. . . .

Her critics will object that two weeks is insufficient time to make an expert of anyone. The objection is valid; but it entirely misconstrues Ms Didion's purpose. *Salvador* deliberately refrains from offering an economic, social or political analysis of the causes of the war; and in this sense, admittedly, it has only a partial truth to tell. It concentrates instead on capturing the atmosphere of a particularly horrific place at a particularly horrific time, to the exclusion of past or future concerns.

Dissolving the simple dichotomy of Left and Right, the book possesses a remarkable capacity for blending penetrating social documentary with the literature of apocalypse. . . . It constitutes a black tourist guide through the *noche obscura* of the Salvadorean nightmare: the apparently safe Sheraton Hotel, where two US agrarian advisers were assassinated; the death dumps at El Playon and the Puerta del Diablo; the city morgue. (p. 23)

This is a powerful and highly articulate indictment of the pervasive political repression which has become institutionalised in El Salvador today. This indictment reaches its highest pitch in Joan Didion's description of the unfinished cathedral in San Salvador, where Archbishop Romero was drilled through the heart with a .22-calibre dumdum bullet while saying mass. (pp. 23-4)

David Leppard, "Salvadorean Nights," in The Listener, *Vol. 109, No. 2806, April 28, 1983, pp. 23-4.*

MARK FALCOFF

Salvador is an exhaustive and picturesque catalogue of all the vices of Salvadoran society, juxtaposed with descriptions of the relentlessly optimistic posturing of U.S. embassy officials in San Salvador and the staff of our military and AID missions. Miss Didion utilizes her pen as a sort of zoom lens, shifting rapidly and in close focus from decomposing corpses on a country road to the sinister features of troglodyte generals and corrupt politicians, from the squalor of rural villages to the false glitter of roller discos and Miss Universe pageants. Folded into these sketches . . . are excerpts from the U.S. and Salvadoran press, from official documents, and also from "documents" of less readily ascertainable authority.

Since Miss Didion is a writer of exceptional talent, the impact is precisely what is intended: to convince us that El Salvador is the quintessential Heart of Darkness—a black hole into which even the best of deeds and intentions are bound to disappear. . . . Miss Didion does not believe that things would get better if the United States abandoned El Salvador—indeed, quite possibly they would get considerably worse. But she wishes us to know that this *is* the nature of the beast; once we have absorbed this knowledge, we need not trouble our hearts (or our consciences) about the future.

Obviously, this is a far more alluring position for an intellectual to adopt than the more chancy ''progressive'' notions about El Salvador mindlessly retailed by radical nuns, out-of-work diplomats, and ''peace'' activists—with Miss Didion, at least, one is insured against any eventual embarrassments. Small wonder that *Salvador* has been greeted with almost unreserved praise by the prestige press, including reviewers who did not particularly like her earlier work, *A Book of Common Prayer,* a novel that was far more sophisticated in its views of Latin America (and, also, more mordant in its depiction of American liberals) than *Salvador.*

With *Salvador,* however, there are two big problems. One has to do with the facts, the other with Joan Didion. There are some serious inaccuracies in the text, and many, many more half-truths. (p. 66)

What is even more disturbing about *Salvador* than Miss Didion's disingenuous use of facts and fugitive quotations is the way in which she makes the tiny republic of El Salvador into a mirror reflecting her own basic contempt for liberal democracy and—why not say it?—the American way of life. . . .

Perhaps the most outrageous passage in the entire book is the one mockingly describing a large American-style shopping mall in downtown San Salvador. . . . (p. 68)

Although this passage has been singled out for special admiration by reviewers who share its attitude of sneering disdain, Joan Didion is nevertheless right: beach towels with maps of Manhattan *are* the future for which El Salvador ''presumably [is] being saved.'' They represent choice and opportunity, prosperity and freedom—things Miss Didion possesses in sufficient abundance to hold them cheap, particularly when others reach out for them. Her disparaging comments about elections and land reform, her thinly-veiled clericalism, and her contempt for the middle class and its works all come together here. (p. 69)

El Salvador is a country with more than its share of inequality and injustice, and constitutional democracy—even in the limited Latin American sense—may never ''take'' there. But it is one thing to acknowledge these harsh realities and seek to work around them; another to write off an entire country, along with one's own national values. The latter spirit is the spirit of *Salvador,* of Miss Didion, and—so it would appear—of the literary culture in which she makes her home. (pp. 69-70)

> Mark Falcoff, ''Two Weeks,'' in Commentary, *Vol. 75, No. 5, May, 1983, pp. 66, 68-70.*

JOHN PILGER

[The] apocalyptic obsession of Reagan and others before him has been usually exported [to Central America] without the knowledge and approval of most of the American people, many of whom would oppose its imposition if only they knew that such criminal stupidity ran counter to the interests of their own nation. In *Salvador* Joan Didion *seems* to be making this point; elsewhere in the rush of her stylish prose such basic truths, which her readers need to know, are missing. As a journalist I can understand that perhaps only an exceptional novelist can

encapsulate an epoch; and in this respect *Salvador* is a lost opportunity. (p. 20)

Joan Didion's book is certainly compulsive reading as a portrait of the macabre. But as it progresses the doubts and questions pile up. What is Joan Didion for? What is she against? Indeed, why did she go to El Salvador? If, as I read in the *Washington Post,* the book is merely about the 'mechanism of fear' and how it worked on the author herself, then perhaps it succeeds within those confined limits: that is, as an indulgent literary exercise in atmospherics and little else. My difficulty is that, having been to El Salvador and to many places like it, I have minimal interest in The Perils of Joan who . . . becomes the recipient of myriad, menacing Latin stares and the captive, it would appear, of the American embassy and of Reagan's man with the death squads. His name is Deane Hinton and, according to the author, he gives 'the sense of a man determined not to crack'.

Alas, my negative thoughts persist when I read that Joan has described her El Salvador sojourn as 'a total immersion experience'. In Marin County, California, HQ of the Me Generation, a Total Immersion Experience might well be performed, if not in El Salvador then in a hot tub with company; and the suspicion nags that this book is the Me Generation having one more vicarious fling. And I would not so much mind that had the author taken off her shades just long enough during her two weeks' Total Immersion Experience to observe the lives of the ordinary people of El Salvador and their epic, melancholy struggle to defend themselves against Reagan, Deane Hinton, goons, malnutrition, malaria, and the economic legacies of the likes of Major-General Smedley Butler and his Marines.

If the author went to the trouble of trembling at road-blocks, why did she not venture into the heart of El Salvador—into the villages where people's courage and tenacity to survive ought to be humbling or inspiring to an outsider from Consumerworld. Some of the bravest people I have met live in El Salvador; but Joan Didion gives us no sense of their *fight*. . . . If these remarkable common people exist at all in her book, they are merged with all the other demons in her *noche obscura,* in which *everybody* is sinister. She sees El Salvador as so many others saw Vietnam—as a war, a 'domino', a 'nightmare'—almost always as a threat to *themselves,* almost never as a community of human beings. (pp. 20-1)

Did the author talk to the Slum Dwellers' Association or to the Christian Peasants' Association, or to any of the numerous groups which comprise the resistance and have done so, like the two mentioned, for half a century? Assaulting the liberal emotions, turning the centre-left stomach, pricking the conservative conscience, having fun with fear, will no longer do. Those who wrung their hands over the 'nightmare' in Vietnam did all that; and the nightmare went on. (p. 21)

> John Pilger, ''Having Fun with Fear,'' in New Statesman, *Vol. 105, No. 2720, May 6, 1983, pp. 20-1.**

JUAN E. CORRADI

In places where life is reasonably ordered, the violence that rages in the Third World is masked by a propensity to integrate it in some favorite sequence of meaning. . . . It is rarely, if ever, depicted as a terrifying impasse, as horror, a catastrophe of meaning. The politician's speech, the journalist's story, the social scientist's account do not reach the "heart of darkness." Only a writer in full command of her craft can recreate it on the page. Joan Didion's *Salvador,* a lean and splendid book, pierces ideological fictions and takes us to the outer and almost unbearable limits of what we call "politics," "society," and "culture"—to the point where those rational notions turn into terror, obscenity, and hallucination. . . .

From the immense distance of definitions, terror appears as the arbitrary use, by organs of political authority, of severe coercion against individuals or groups, the credible threat of such use, or the arbitrary liquidation of such individuals and groups. But from the writer's notes something more ominous makes itself felt that defies all definitions: a process of corrosion that eats the soul as relentlessly as it consumes bodies. . . .

If this short book seems bottomless, it is because Joan Didion's phrases bring forth the peculiar state of hypnotic abeyance that is the essence of terror. She achieves this effect through the careful notation of detail and the unabated watchfulness over language. She refuses both analysis and synthesis, she rejects abstractions and eschews conclusions. Instead, she reports on these as discursive operations performed by near and distant actors while they seek to mask, or neutralize, or routinize a truth that is everywhere in evidence but impossible to face: objective and abject, like a corpse. (p. 387)

When Joan Didion paints the paraphernalia of terror—the vehicles, uniforms, weapons, the methods of extrajudicial execution, the dumping sites, the local words that are as twisted as the bodies . . .—the effect is not mysterious, as in a *chiaroscuro,* but hyperreal. She does not give us a plot to unravel, an interpretive key to unlock the horror, a solution: "This was a story that would perhaps not be illuminated at all." She keeps the narrative on a plane where incidents and objects multiply and cram the space. The only rule that governs situations seems to be the lewd proliferation of the lurid. . . .

Joan Didion tells us something about terror that escapes other accounts and most analyses, namely, that it is *obscene,* for obscene is anybody and anything that has lost distance, perspective, a sense of its own limits, something exiled from its natural conditions of meaning, radically out of context. . . .

There is a linguistic supplement to this plethora of abjections: it is comprised of fragments from the discourse of the actors— fragments from President Magaña and from President Reagan, from present Ambassador Hinton and former Ambassador White, from embassy officials, Salvadoran officers, from the grandson of a legendary dictator, from nuns and priests and university professors. Didion places the quotations side by side, or next to the brute facts of life and death, so skillfully that, without recourse to commentary, they testify to the mendacious loquacity of a condition where language is called upon, most of the time, not to illuminate truth but to dream it as it ought to be, to improve its appearance, to formulate ramshackle mythologies, to lure us into the realm of shadow-boxing, of pure symbolic action. (p. 388)

There is much in this book that will provide ammunition to thoughtful critics of the Reagan administration's policies in Central America. But I should like to suggest that, in the end, this is beside the point. It would be a disservice to Joan Didion's real achievement to reduce her statements to even the most reasoned critical analyses of the current political situation in El Salvador. Even the most lucid political commentary belongs only to the moment. A good book belongs to literature and, as such, survives, triumphs over the occasion of its production. . . . *Salvador* has the unmistakable aura of true literature in its prosody, in its imagery, its testimony.

Because it is written at a slight angle from more conventional discourses, because it flies too slowly, sometimes too high, some other times too low over that little nation that is smaller than San Diego county but nonetheless commands the attention of the world, this book is strangely remote from the bustle of the moment. It thus hints at other truths than those we negotiate and ingest every day. (p. 389)

Juan E. Corradi, "A Culture of Fear," in Dissent, *Vol. 30, No. 3, Summer, 1983, pp. 387-89.*

ANNE TYLER

The literary critic Frederick Karl was recently quoted as saying that Joan Didion "diminishes whatever she touches." It's a remark that becomes more interesting when you twist it into a compliment: Joan Didion writes from a vantage point so remote that all she describes seems tiny and trim and uncannily precise, like a scene viewed through the wrong end of a telescope. That cleared space where she stands, that chilly vacuum that could either be intellectual irony or profound depression, gives her a slant of vision that is arresting and unique.

Democracy, her fourth novel, is narrated by an "I" who is apparently Joan Didion herself, untransformed. . . .

And what is her story? Well, Jack Lovett, a world traveler whose business dealings don't bear close investigation, meets Inez Christian in Hawaii on her seventeenth birthday. They have a brief affair and then part. Inez marries Harry Victor, who eventually becomes a U.S. Senator. Over the next twenty years, she and Jack Lovett run into each other by chance here and there, in various far-flung corners of the world. There's a hushed-up scandal when Inez's father murders Inez's sister and the sister's male guest. Inez abandons the role of politician's wife and goes away with Jack Lovett. There's the beginning of another scandal when Jack Lovett's business dealings come into question, but by then he has died of natural causes.

End of story.

Some story, you say.

But what gives these "fitful glimpses" (as Joan Didion calls them) shape and direction is the eye that observes them—that eye looking through the wrong end of the telescope. In many ways, the strongest character in this novel is the narrator herself, with her cataloguing of clues, her conjectures, her obsessive fascination with the various participants. We never physically see her or understand her position, exactly . . . but she casts an aura of loneliness over all she describes. She might be a foreigner, even an observer from another planet—one so edgy and alert that she ends up knowing more about our own world than we know ourselves. (p. 35)

Now, the question is, what does all this amount to? Are freeze frames of a handful of people at various moments over a couple of decades really going to come to anything? Where do we get a sense of motion?

But it may be that the reader's journey here is not toward a happy ending, or even an unhappy ending, but toward adopting the narrator's vision of the world. In this vision, every act is random and baffling, "circumstantial," and human beings are ciphers to be studied as intently as distant stars.

You close the book and say, "Was that *it*?" And then you say, "Well, really." And then you go off, feeling vaguely dissatisfied, and look for something with a little more point to it. But later, bits and pieces of *Democracy* come back to you—pictures, still photos. (p. 36)

> Anne Tyler, "*Affairs of State*," in The New Republic, *Vol. 190, No. 14, April 9, 1984, pp. 35-6.*

MARY McCARTHY

"**Democracy**," a novel, takes its title from Henry Adams's "Democracy," subtitled "An American Novel." . . .

I have found it hard to make out what connection there can be between Joan Didion's "**Democracy**," opening with a memory of the pink dawns of early atomic weapons tests in the Pacific, and Henry Adams's "Democracy," which deals with the dirty politics of the second Grant Administration. And, leaving aside Henry Adams, I do not quite see how democracy comes into the Didion tale except for the fact that two Democratic politicians (both Vietnam-war opponents) and a C.I.A. man play large roles in it. For Adams, "democracy" had become a coarse travesty of the ideal of popular rule, indissociable from the gravy train and the grease spots on the Congressman's vest. For Miss Didion too, the term is rich in irony, though corruption by now is so universal that it can no longer be identified with a party or tendency or grand ideal betrayed. (p. 1)

The Didion novel, which arrives at its climax in March 1975, while the character "Joan Didion" is teaching . . . at Berkeley and the Vietnam War is winding down, can be described as a murder story set in Honolulu—a murder without a mystery in that the elderly "blueblood" killer of a nisei politician and of his own "socialite" daughter proudly announces culpability from his room in the downtown Y.M.C.A. I have put "blueblood" and "socialite" in quotation marks to indicate the colonial, road-show quality of the island's palmy social life, which always seems to have an airport (once dockside) lei around its neck. (pp. 1, 18)

As I say, in "**Democracy**" no mystery is made about the murder. . . . "Cards on the table," the author declares, introducing herself to the reader on page 17. Yet despite an appearance of factuality achieved by the author's total recall of names, middle names, dates, by perfect chronometry of arrival and departure times and stereophonic dialogue of imaginary newsworthy figures, "**Democracy**" is deeply mysterious, cryptic, enigmatic, like a tarot pack or most of Joan Didion's work.

One way of looking at that work is to decide that it has been influenced by movies; hypnotized by movies would be more appropriate. . . . Like the camera, this mental apparatus does not think but projects images, very haunting and troubling ones for the most part, precisely because they are mute. Even when sonorized, as has happened here, they remain silent and somewhat frightening in their stunned aversion from thought. This powerful relation to film, stronger than that of any other current author, must account for her affinity with Joseph Conrad, whose tales and romances . . . seem to have anticipated film, like an uncanny prophecy.

What was new in Conrad was the potency of an image or images, often inexplicable in purely reasonable terms. . . . Certainly one senses Conrad in Miss Didion's "**Democracy**"; he has passed through this territory, making trail blazes. The novel seems closer to "Heart of Darkness" than the literal-minded movie "Apocalpyse Now" did, which was also trying to talk about the end of Vietnam and unspeakable "horrors," located upriver in the film. One odd development in "**Democracy**," though, as compared with any Conrad text, is that the narrator—in Conrad usually the immensely talkative and indeed (dare I say it?) too garrulous Marlow—has been virtually silenced. What the character "Joan Didion" offers us is mainly brisk narration, impossible to construe as comment or rumination, unlike Marlow's chatter, but I shall come back to "Joan Didion" later.

For the moment, I want to forget about the cinematic influences and effects—the freezes and rapid fades and the humming sound track that make themselves felt in whatever she has done since "**Run River**" (1963)—and concentrate on examining the construction of this particular book as book. Yet here too I am reminded of what one might call an allied art. The construction of "**Democracy**" feels like the working out of a jigsaw puzzle that is slowly being put together with a continual shuffling and re-examination of pieces still on the edges or heaped in the middle of the design. We have started with a bit of sky (those pink dawns); now and then, without hurry, a new piece is carefully inserted, and the gentle click of cardboard locking into cardboard is felt—no forcing. Despite the fact that the pieces are known to us, face down and face up, almost from the start, there is an intense suspense, which seems to be causeless . . . , suspense arising from the assembly of the pieces, that is, from the procedures of narrative themselves. "This is a hard story to tell," the author says on page 15. It is a hard story to listen to, boring in the primal sense of the word—"making a hole in or through with a drill." Some parts of it are painful in their own right, shocking . . . , but what mainly hurts is the drilling, the repetition, in short, the suspense of waiting for the narrative line to be carefully played out, the odd-shaped piece inserted. (p. 18)

What is a live fact—Joan Didion—doing in a work of fiction? She must be a decoy set there to lure us into believing that Inez Victor is real in some ghostly-goblin manner, as real anyway as the author herself is. For that purpose, the classic narrator, the fictive "I," could not serve, evidently. Or just seemed dated in a deconstructing universe. Before the end of the novel, in a flash-forward, the author is represented as actually flying to Kuala Lumpur to see Inez Victor, who by that time is working in a camp for refugees, having separated from Harry Victor and their children, Adlai and Jessie, and all their world. Does this mirror a real journey that Joan Didion has pressed into service to meet a fictional need (to end the novel), as other authors are apt to do with loose material that happens to be lying around?

In current theories of fiction, much attention is given to the role of the narrator, considered as sheer verbal device, without correspondence to any anterior reality. Yet if I understand Joan Didion right, here she is doing the exact opposite, inserting an attestable fact—herself—into the moving sands of fiction. I am not sure what the result of the undertaking is. It may well be to diminish the fictional likelihood of "Inez Victor" while leaving the reader to wonder about the reality of "Joan Didion."

In fact, the problem of "originals" haunts this peculiar fiction, intentionally, I should guess. It is an eerie lighting effect, making the strange appear familiar and the familiar strange. At times Harry Victor seems meant to recall one of the Kennedys (most likely Bobby) or all of them. (pp. 18-19)

I have noted the cinematic quality of Joan Didion's work and the relation of the present construction to puzzles, specifically of the jigsaw kind. I might also have compared the narrative line to a French seam—one big stitch forward, one little stitch back, turn over and repeat on other side of cloth—valued in dressmaking for its strength and for hiding the raw edges of the cloth. Still another set of correspondences is discernible in literary reminiscences and allusions, beginning, obviously, with the title: Henry Adams, Hemingway, Mailer, Orwell, Wallace Stevens, Delmore Schwartz, A. E. Housman, W. H. Auden, Kierkegaard. The ending must be a pointed reference to Eliot, and on page 16 one has met some lines in italics followed by the words "So Trollope might begin this novel."

This is part of the book's knowingness—not an altogether pleasant quality. The knowingness makes a curious accompaniment to the celebrity theme, for Joan Didion clearly does not care for the celebrity circuit and one of the attractions Jack Lovett has for her—and possibly for Inez too—is that he is not in Who's Who, does not have his name on his whiskey bottle in a Hong Kong restaurant. . . .

Still, to be known and to be knowing are not so far apart. Everyone in **"Democracy"** is some kind of insider. It is not merely the Harry Victors and their entourages; the author herself has some complicity in the insider-outsider game—seven years at Vogue leave their mark. In the milieu of this **"Democracy,"** not just people but places and times can be poker chips. . . .

For all its technical mastery and on-target social observation (Miss Didion is wonderful not only at hearing her characters but at naming them—take "Inez"), there is a depthlessness in **"Democracy"** as there was in **"A Book of Common Prayer."** We would need to know a Harry Victor from the inside looking out to feel his real hollowness; it is tiring just to listen to his sound track playing over and over. This is true for most of the characters, though with the bit parts the effect is stunning. . . . To my mind, the best character is Billy Dillon, Harry Victor's aide, who has the good fortune—which is also the reader's—of being a consciously funny man.

But, finally, what is one to make of Jack Lovett, inscrutable by profession from beginning to end? Whatever one decides, one must applaud the author's nerve in making a C.I.A. agent in his 60's the love interest and *parfit gentil knight* of her book. Actually, this is a romantic, even a sentimental novel, with the C.I.A. man and the Congressman's wife as a pair of eternally faithful lovers, constantly separated and constantly reunited till his death. . . . That Inez Victor (and her creator) clearly prefer a C.I.A. agent to a famous liberal senator may indicate a preference for action over talk or just a distaste for United States hypocrisy—the larger aims of Harry Victor and of "the store" being at bottom the same. Maybe those are the "cards on the table" that were promised when we first met "Joan Didion" in that early chapter.

Possibly. As I said to start with, the book is deeply enigmatic. For the reader willing to sweat over them, there are a number of half-buried puzzles. . . .

Perhaps all the elements in the puzzle are out of movies. Perhaps Joan Didion is just wishing that she were an old-time screenwriter rather than a novelist. If that is it, I am irritated. To be portentous, one ought to be deeper than that. I feel a bit like Alice when she heard the Duchess speak calmly of "a large mustard mine near here." Of course, the Duchess could speak calmly because that was Wonderland. And possibly that is the right way to take this latest Joan Didion—calmly, not setting out to solve sphinxine riddles, not looking for influences

and analogues, not hoping for the author's sake to exorcise the malign shadow of Hemingway, certainly not asking how Wendell Omura got on Janet's lanai or how, precisely, old Hem, than whom no more elitist writer ever took up pen, could illustrate in his sentence structure any idea of democracy. Just let it go. (p. 19)

> *Mary McCarthy, "Love and Death in the Pacific,"
> in* The New York Times Book Review, *April 22,
> 1984, pp. 1, 18-19.*

THOMAS R. EDWARDS

Joan Didion is one of those writers—Norman Mailer, Mary McCarthy, and Gore Vidal are others—who are so good at the higher journalism that their status as novelists may sometimes seem insecure. Do they, we may wonder, keep writing fiction out of professional pride, as if only the novel could truly certify their literary talent and seriousness? Are not their novels, however fine, shadowed by a suspicion, however baseless, that the form is not quite the best form for such powers?

Certainly *Democracy,* Didion's new novel, opens with an ominously awkward display of self-consciousness about the basic moves of fictional narrative:

> The light at dawn during those
> Pacific tests was something to see.
> Something to behold.
> Something that could almost make
> you think you saw God, he said.
> He said to her.
> Jack Lovett said to Inez Victor.
> Inez Victor who was born Inez
> Christian.

This self-revising fumbling with the identity cards that novels are supposed to slip quietly under the door seems a little like having a magician confess that the rabbit came not from the empty hat but from inside his vest. "This is a hard story to tell," complains the last sentence of this first chapter, and the manner of this opening makes one wonder if for Didion the old game is still good enough to play. . . .

Despite the authorial shufflings, a story begins to get told, as if impelled by the stubborn conventions of narrative itself, the odd necessity of continuing once you have, for whatever reason, started. The devices of anti-fiction don't disappear. "Call me the author," the second chapter begins, followed by a glimpse of a writer named "Joan Didion" (done in the manner not of Melville but, of all people, Trollope) who is struggling to get her story started: "Consider any of these things long enough and you will see that they tend to deny the relevance not only of personality but of narrative, which makes them less than ideal images with which to begin a novel, but we go with what we have."

So indeed we do, but counter-illusion has begun to generate its own, second-order kind of credence—if this narrator is the Joan Didion who went to Berkeley, worked for *Vogue* in 1960, now lives in Los Angeles but travels to far-off places as a reporter, and so on, then Inez Christian Victor and Jack Lovett and the other people in this book may be real after all, since Joan Didion says she knew them. Maybe she does have nothing up her sleeve.

For a critic this is good material, but most readers of novels want the puppets to come to life, and in *Democracy* they blessedly do so before long, despite the continuing maneuverings of the author. . . .

The devastating personal and public consequences of the loss of history are Didion's theme. The significant relations of events wash away in a flood of facts, those equally circumstantial details that news reporting democratically represents as being about equal in import. . . .

Vietnam is the most dramatic recent evidence of where an appetite for imperium can lead democracy; but the larger subject must be the evanescence of thought and moral judgment in a world of ceaselessly unsortable information. (p. 23)

Democracy is absorbing, immensely intelligent, and witty, and it finally earns its complexity of form. It is indeed "a hard story to tell," and the presence in it of "Joan Didion" trying to tell it is an essential part of its subject. Throughout one senses the author struggling with the moral difficulty that makes the story hard to tell—how to stop claiming what Inez finally relinquishes, "the American exemption" from having to recognize that history records not the victory of personal wills over reality (as people like Harry Victor want to suppose), but the "undertow of having and not having, the convulsions of a world largely unaffected by the individual efforts of anyone in it."

This grim message supports the assumption that a novel by another American pessimist, Henry Adams's *Democracy,* is somewhere in Didion's mind. . . . Both novels deal with the perilous maturing of a political culture which the national rhetoric ceaselessly represents as vigorous and young. . . .

With due allowance for the distances between Quincy and Sacramento, Henry Adams and Joan Didion may have something in common. In both of them, irony and subtlety confront a chaotic new reality that shatters the orderings of simpler, older ways. Both face such a world with an essentially aristocratic weapon, the power to dispose language and thought, at least, against those empowered to dispose just about everything else. And both, I suppose, understand that such a weapon is only defensive, and that it may not suffice. (p. 24)

> *Thomas R. Edwards, "An American Education," in The New York Review of Books, Vol. XXXI, No. 8, May 10, 1984, pp. 23-4.*

ISA KAPP

The steady drizzle of bitter memories in [*Democracy*] keeps directing the reader to "one night outside Honolulu in the spring of 1975 . . . when the C130s and the C141s were already shuttling between Honolulu and Anderson and Clark and Saigon . . . bringing out the dependents, bringing out the dealers, bringing out the money, bringing out the pet dogs and the sponsored bar girls and the porcelain elephants. . . .'' From this string of scornful images we can tell that the American system of government is going to have the ignominious fate of disappointing Joan Didion.

It's not the first time we have been privy to Didion's vexations of the spirit, and we have by now grown accustomed to the tone of sad concern for our national well-being that insidiously infiltrates so much of her prose. She collects (and sells) ominous symptoms as if they were sea shells. She becomes mournful over trifles, and has obviously persuaded herself that mourning becomes her. Indeed, she first hoisted herself to public attention on the bootstraps of one of the world's best-known

pessimistic poems, Yeats' "The Second Coming," explaining that she called her book of essays *Slouching Toward Bethlehem* because "The widening gyre, the falcon which does not hear the falconer, the gaze blank and pitiless as the sun: these have been my points of reference."

Play It As It Lays, Didion's second novel, was fraught with implications that American society is atomized and loveless. Packed, as if it were a carry-on airplane bag, with divorce, drug addiciton, abortion, a neurally handicapped child, vagrant sex, sadism, and mental breakdown, the book testified more clearly to ailments within than without. Why did this series of disasters recommend themselves to her imagination as a likely fictional plot? Although pessimism is no doubt an inalienable right, we sense that hers is not only borrowed but unearned.

Primed for disabuse, Didion has swooped like a homing pigeon toward those places that confirm it. . . . [Accusatory] rhetoric is pretty much the extent to which she responds to any social predicament that distresses her. . . . Yet to many readers (and reviewers), eager for the kicks of dissent without its grubby chores, that posture passes for genuine political involvement and, worse still, political wisdom.

In fact, apart from her two weeks in El Salvador . . . and her interviews with sometime revolutionary celebrities like Eldridge Cleaver and Huey Newton, Joan Didion has few credentials as political journalist, and even fewer as moral critic. For *Democracy* she shamelessly lifted the title of Henry Adams' still timely Washington novel. Adams was at least knowledgeable about social and political relations in the capital during Grant's Administration, and about the particular temptations a susceptible senator might fall prey to. The insinuation of ubiquitous corruption saturates Didion's *Democracy* —like a bottled salad dressing—yet the book is not about the substance of politics, or even its strategies, at all. (pp. 6-7)

Actually, there is no story—only spatters of disillusion and distaste. Didion starts hinting early on that a murder will take place, and in time, Paul Christian, father of Inez, goes haywire and shoots his daughter Janet and her lover, a congressman from Hawaii. But don't inquire too deeply into motives—it's just the same nasty concentration of unhealthy feelings that Didion understands so well.

A curious mix of detachment and bathos, *Democracy* reads as if some loner had clipped out all the newspaper stories and fan magazine gossip about a film star, and then imagined the star to be a close friend. There's a tremendous focus on photos, interviews and clothing, with the author simultaneously disdaining voyeurism and lapping it up. (p. 7)

If it takes a while to unravel Didion's purpose, we finally realize that *Democracy* is about her constructing a plot around newsworthy subjects. Perhaps that is why her main characters are represented in space-saving code words and significant phrases. . . . But when it comes to herself—she constantly pops up in the narrative—Didion pulls a real switch, resorting to full-length sentences, and earnestly briefing us on her state of mind, her favorite authors, her progress on her novel. . . . (pp. 7-8)

She goes on to furnish a fond recollection of a course she gave at Berkeley "on the work of certain post-industrial writers." Orwell, Hemingway, Adams, Mailer—Didion is always putting herself into imaginary association with the greats. . . . For all her promptings, the only literary ancestry I can actually discern is a rather unseemly mating of Gertrude Stein and Raymond Chandler.

By her own standard of language as the mark of political integrity, character and accomplishment, Didion must surely at this point be extremely worried about herself. What are we to make of a formulation like this: "Harry Victor's phantom constituency was based on comfort and its concomitant uneasiness"? Or, "no unequivocal lone figure on the crest of the immutable hill"? . . .

Didion's main writing success has been in pieces of first-person reportage. An irrepressible narcissist, she loves the first person; she also likes facts. Give her the weather, the numbers displayed on aircraft, snatches of conversation . . . and she gets them just right. In life, lack of pretense appeals to her. But give her a novel to write and she turns coy, smug, fashionable, imitative, distraught—a chameleon, and a great pretender. (p. 8)

Isa Kapp, "Unearned Pessimism," in The New Leader, Vol. LXVII, No. 9, May 14, 1984, pp. 6-8.

JOSEPH EPSTEIN

I do not have the attention span to sustain a lengthy depression, but I have of late been reading two novelists who do: Renata Adler and Joan Didion. I think of them as the Sunshine Girls, largely because in their work the sun is never shining. . . . Miss Adler and Miss Didion are slender women who write slender books heavy with gloom. (p. 62)

Democracy, Joan Didion's most recent novel, is, as its narrator, a woman calling herself Joan Didion, calls it, a "novel of fitful glimpses." It is Miss Didion's richest novel since *Run River.* By richest I mean that there are riches on every page: lovely details, sharp observations, risky but always interesting generalizations, real information—many of the things that I, for one, read novels in the hope of discovering. "Let the man build you a real drink," one character says to another, and with that single sentence, a sentence of a kind for which Miss Didion has a splendid knack, she calls up a whole way of life, in this instance that of the business-class country-club stage of culture.

Miss Didion can build you a real character, too, and *Democracy,* slender though it is as a novel, is filled with interesting characters, major and minor. (p. 66)

Democracy is doing two things at once. It is telling the love story of Inez Victor and Jack Lovett, and it is providing an account of the fraudulence of public life, in its political and celebrity realms, and both are subtly done. Its criticism of left-wing politics, in the person of Harry Victor, is devastating. . . .

But it won't do to slip Miss Didion into a political box. She doesn't much like what has happened in America. Yet she doesn't much like it anywhere else either. Set for the most part during the Vietnam years, her novel, perhaps intended to bring Henry Adams's novel *Democracy* (1880) up to date, dwells on the decline of American power and the decay of American life. But then Miss Didion is, by temperament, drawn to decline and decay.

Good as *Democracy* is, one cannot help feeling it would have been better if Miss Didion had left out the character called Joan Didion, the novelist. Throughout the novel, this Joan Didion drops in to tell you about the difficulties and limitations of narrative. . . . There is a sense in which, because of the fragmented way she tells her story, Miss Didion must have felt called upon to bring her own novelistic problems into the book. Yet one also feels that she is pleased by the modernist note that this device demonstrates.

Why make narrative seem so difficult? The trick used to be to make telling a story as straight and smooth as one could. Now it seems to be to make it as tortuous and jagged as possible. I think Miss Didion would have done better, to borrow a phrase, to have played her story as it lay, and not to have undermined it with accounts of the unreliability of narrative.

With its deconstructionists in literary criticism, its ordinary-language and other philosophers, and its novelists, our age may one day come to be known in intellectual history for its role in the advancement of techniques to prove that reality doesn't exist. Along with their natural gifts of dark temperament, our Sunshine Girls, Renata Adler and Joan Didion, are joined in this enterprise. It is more than a mite depressing. (p. 67)

Joseph Epstein, "The Sunshine Girls," in Commentary, Vol. 77, No. 6, June, 1984, pp. 62-7.*

José Donoso

1924-

Chilean novelist, short story writer, essayist, poet, and critic.

One of the leading figures of the contemporary "boom" in Spanish-American literature, Donoso is best known for his ambiguous and complex antinovel *El obsceno pájaro de la noche* (1970; *The Obscene Bird of Night*). With the publication of this work, Donoso's slowly growing reputation greatly increased, and although he has continued to write prolifically, producing novels, short stories, poetry, and a critical study entitled *Historia personal del "boom"* (1972; *The Boom in Spanish American Literature*), *The Obscene Bird of Night* is still widely regarded as his single most impressive work.

Donoso's work prior to *The Obscene Bird of Night* is relatively realistic and conventionally structured when compared to his avant-garde masterpiece and later fiction. Although his first and second novels—*Coronación* (1957; *Coronation*) and *Este domingo* (1966; *This Sunday*)—differ stylistically from his later fiction, they foreshadow Donoso's predominant themes: the decay of society, the emotional disintegration of the individual, and the eventual deterioration of the boundaries between nightmare and reality, chaos and order. *Coronation* depicts the hollow life and psychological decline of a wealthy young man and his repressive relationship with his cruel, dying grandmother, who lives in a world of fantasies and illusions. *This Sunday*, like *Coronation* and many of Donoso's subsequent works, contrasts the sexually vigorous lower class with the emotionally sterile upper class. In developing the entanglement and interdependency between an unsatisfied bourgeoise and her lower-class lover, Donoso portrays, as Gerald Kersh notes, "something of squalor and nobility in the culminating psychic crash, in the settling dust of which patrons and patronized alike appear as the shadows of a dream."

Like *Coronation* and *This Sunday*, *The Obscene Bird of Night* consists of two disparate social settings—an established family estate and a deteriorating residence of deranged servants—between which the protagonist oscillates. An aura of delirium permeates the novel: characters change identities; fantasies and dream sequences weave through the labyrinthian narrative; and the protagonist himself eventually succumbs to madness. The highly complex structure and the multiple layers of meaning of *The Obscene Bird of Night* give rise to its ambiguity and varied critical interpretations.

Donoso's later works, including *Tres novelitas burguesas* (1973; *Sacred Families*), a collection of three novellas, and his recently translated *Casa de campo* (1978; *A House in the Country*), share with *The Obscene Bird of Night* a foreboding, sinister examination of individuals struggling against internal and external disintegration. Although Chilean society figures prominently in many of his works, Donoso's established international reputation attests to the universal application of his fiction. As Kirsten F. Nigro notes, Donoso's novels "are more than commentaries on Chilean society in progressive stages of decay; they are monstrous visions of diseased and withered souls."

(See also *CLC*, Vols. 4, 8, 11 and *Contemporary Authors*, Vols. 81-84.)

Photograph by Layle Silbert

GRANVILLE HICKS

[*Coronation*] describes the last months in the life of Misiá Elisa Grey de Abalas, a woman of ninety-four, once a great beauty, now a bedridden skeleton attended by two aging but faithful servants, Rosario and Lourdes. She claims to be descended from royalty, and insists that she is a saint as well as a queen. Her saintliness, however, is intermittent, for she has terrible fits of temper in which her language becomes "obscene, virulent, desperate." . . .

Almost the only person to share with the devoted servants the responsibility for looking after Misiá Elisa is her grandson, Don Andrés. . . . Now in his fifties, Don Andrés has his own apartment, but from time to time, however reluctantly, he visits the old lady. Largely because of her influence, he has grown up to be afraid of life and has withdrawn himself from it as far as possible. (p. 27)

The book might be regarded as an account of the decay of the upper class. Misiá Elisa, so old, so useless, so given to self-deception, so quick to inflict pain on others, could be taken as a symbol, with Andrés displaying the impotence of his class. (pp. 27-8)

Donoso, it is clear, takes a dark view of the human condition, and yet the book does not succeed in giving the reader a tragic sense of life. This is in part because the author relies so heavily on direct analysis of psychological states. The portrayal of Don Andrés, in particular, is close to a case history of regression. Despite the fact that the author has studied in America and teaches English literature, he seems to be under the influence of the French psychological novel.

In part, however, he is quite successful. Misiá Elisa in her bad mood is the incarnation of malice. . . . The old servants provide an effective sort of chorus, and one can only be amused by their high jinks at the end. (p. 28)

> *Granville Hicks, "Death Would Not Wait on Feeling," in* Saturday Review, *Vol. XLVIII, No. 11, March 13, 1965, pp. 27-8.*

ALEXANDER COLEMAN

José Donoso brings to ["**Coronation**"] . . . a caustic and satirical bent for the macabre. Not since the appearance in this country of Muriel Spark's "Memento Mori" have the foibles of the senile been exposed in such a mordant and, in the end, comic fashion. It is a cruel and amusing book, the satire no less effective when flaying the useless aristocracy than when examining the anguish of an old family tottering on the brink of catastrophe.

Donoso's [is a] withering, gruesome book. . . .

> *Alexander Coleman, "The Dictatorship of Senility," in* The New York Times Book Review, *March 14, 1965, p. 5.*

F.W.J. HEMMINGS

[*Coronation*] is best described as a 19th-century novel, even though the people in it telephone their grocery orders to supermarkets and may, if they have the fare and the wish, fly to Europe. Everything about it is redolent of naturalism in its heyday: the clear-cut stratification of society into slum-dwellers driven to crime and fastidious, cultivated rentiers, with only a parasitic servant class in between; the Buddenbrooksian theme of a great family in decay; the shuddering Schopenhaueresque preoccupation with personal annihilation; and at the centre of the web, the old mad woman in a rambling, shuttered, antiquated house, Tante Dide or, better, Miss Havisham; indeed, by accident or design Señor Donoso has given the old lady's maid-companion the name Estela. Yet the book wears no air of pastiche; one is almost convinced that Chile may be just such an anachronistic preserve; and *Coronation* has the immeasurable advantage that it retains that thickness and solidity of colouring which the novel had, one feared, lost for good round about 1890. (p. 971)

> *F.W.J. Hemmings, "Dirt," in* New Statesman, *Vol. LXIX, No. 1788, June 18, 1965, pp. 970-71.**

PETER VANSITTART

[*Coronation* is] a richly-textured academic novel, academic certainly not through any lifelessness but because its technique is traditional and conversational, conditioned by the leisured lives of its characters and leading to an elaborately contrived climax. Don Andres, an aging Chilean gentleman, does not have to work. French history, his collection of walking sticks, politics, occupy him together with visits to his ninety-four-

year-old grandmother, a wearying but essential link with the stylish well-grained past.

Beneath the placid sunny afternoons, however, nothing is really well. Andres's existence is merely elegant absence of death. Terrified of mortality and whole-heartedness he has never risked taking a bite out of life. The old lady herself is only apparently harmless. Cloudy with sexual fantasies she is capable of spasmodic and disconcerting insights, particularly venomous when a teenage maid moves into the ornate decrepit mansion. Croaking out malice about Estelle and himself she jogs Andres into awareness of his own futility, which the girl could surely redeem. She, of course, has very different needs. The result is rueful comedy, with moments of the macabre rather than the tragic. (p. 791)

> *Peter Vansittart, "Taking It Easy," in* The Spectator, *Vol. 214, No. 7147, June 18, 1965, pp. 791-92.**

GERALD KERSH

The reviewer who gets spiritual refreshment out of pecking holes in books is not likely to have much fun with *This Sunday*. Turn it whichever way you like, it presents a clear-cut, uncompromising facet. I don't imply that it is gemlike in any precious sense of the term; only that it is so tight-textured and true-surfaced as to be, critically speaking, almost beak-proof. . . .

José Donoso, scorning gimmicks and working with the small, hard stuff that is so difficult to come by, has produced a rare and curious book—an unspectacular original. . . . Donoso has demonstrated without fireworks that it is possible to write a lean and supple kind of prose without aping Hemingway, to dive deep without Dostoevskian ballast, to be evocative without effeminacy and poetic without ambiguity. . . .

This Sunday is peopled by characters with wills of their own, who go to the devil in their own ways, rough-hewing their own ends and making a wretched job of it.

To understand isn't necessarily to forgive. José Donoso is intelligently compassionate, and sane pity is the voice of doom; *This Sunday* is, therefore, high tragedy, deadly and inexorable. Any honestly perceptive study of emotional interdependence is bound to tend that way. . . .

Man is a complex of shifting centers of gravity and inconstant triangles of force; and so it follows that any essay in divided human tensions must end as a study in breaking points, which is just what Mr. Donoso's short and potent novel turns out to be.

Misiá Chepa, the *bourgeoise* whose husband sees her as a multi-teated bitch dying to be milked, needs to be needed. She can't stand unless she is heavily leaned upon. The jailbird who wants to be wanted, and whom Misiá chooses as her spiritual counterpoise and prop, hasn't the seasoning or the grain to take her weight. There is something of squalor and nobility in the culminating psychic crash, in the settling dust of which patrons and patronized alike appear as the shadows of a dream, and out of which only the children seem to emerge as real.

Here is a very fine novel. . . . [The] author is a first-rate artist. . . .

> *Gerald Kersh, "Study in Breaking Points," in* Saturday Review, *Vol. L, No. 49, December 9, 1967, p. 30.*

OLIVER T. MYERS

It might be that *This Sunday* is too much like *Coronation,* not only in characters and milieu but even in some of the plotting. As a novel *This Sunday* comes off better. But what Donoso has been giving us (here and foreshadowed in some earlier stories, a few written originally in English) is the portrait of a decaying society, nostalgic for a glory that had never quite existed, with the other classes lacking the moral and psychological dominance to succeed except through violence. The relations between master and servant will elicit comparisons with the modern American South, but without the complication of race. The strength of the household servants, of the poor, of the criminal, is contrasted with the enervation of the well-to-do, but is insufficient for any real accomplishment.

But this cannot be said to be Donoso's theme. It will be apparent in *This Sunday* but becomes disturbingly obvious when traced across earlier writings. Donoso does not write about adults. The most fully realized characters in what I've read of him are the young, the innocent or overly wise children, the adolescent bursting with (or from) sex; or the middle aged, prematurely senile from menopause or ennui; or the very old, who have outlived too many generations. We don't see child-parent relationships, a generation is skipped, we are made to feel the remoteness of the grandchild from the grandparent.

The central figure of *Coronation* is a man in his 50s still under the thumb of his nonagenarian grandmother. The first-person narrator of *This Sunday* hardly speaks of his parents; it is the grandparents that we see through his eyes and then, alternately, through their own. (pp. 351, 353)

Donoso has created a more horrifying nightmare for his victims in this latest work than in *Coronation,* which at times was merely grotesque. He has now a surer hand with delineation of oddity (the aging grandson's prized walking-stick collection in the earlier novel was silly; here, the deaf grandfather attempting Handel's *Harmonious Blacksmith,* imitating Cortot's *tempo,* tells us much more). He finally succeeds in making us know the full complexity of the immature and the post-mature mind with remarkable economy.

Donoso's *This Sunday* is scarcely longer than a novella. But we can take from it as much experience of human decay as we can bear. (p. 353)

> Oliver T. Myers, "Youth & Age in Chile," in The Nation, *Vol. 206, No. 11, March 11, 1968, pp. 351, 353.*

KIRSTEN F. NIGRO

[José Donoso] has emerged from the generation of 1950 as Chile's most widely acclaimed contemporary novelist. . . . [He] is now considered a major figure in the great "boom" of the Latin American novel along with others like Fuentes, García Márquez, Vargas Llosa, and Cabrera Infante.

What is peculiar about "el fenómeno José Donoso" is the scarcity of critics who have really studied him in great depth. Those who have done so have focused attention mainly on what is most obvious in his novels: the continued development of a single theme—the decay of a rigidly structured Chilean society. Old and crumbling ancestral mansions, aging servants, families who spiritually and physically crucify each other, congenital insanity, insinuations of incest, the rank odor of things gone old and sour—these are the elements in Donoso's novels

which lead some critics to believe that he is "un recio novelista y cuentista preocupado por la decadencia del clan familiar" or of specific social classes.

It is true that Donoso's novels can be read as chronicles of domestic and class disintegration. *Coronación* and *El obsceno pájaro de la noche* depict the final stages of moral and economic ruin in once-aristocratic families. *Este domingo* paints a similar picture, only this time within the framework of dehumanizing middle-class values. In *El lugar sin límites* a symbolic family, housed in a brothel, represents disease and corruption at its worst, especially among Chilean landowners. For this reason some critics consider Donoso a naturalist obsessed with death and decay. They have called him a writer with a message, bent on exposing a society in decadence. . . . (pp. 216-18)

Since Chile is very much present in Donoso's novels, and since he often devotes long passages to the accumulation of descriptive detail, other critics call him a realist, a master painter of Chilean customs and language. . . . Even outside Chile Donoso has been the object of . . . traditional interpretations. The Uruguayan critic Mario Benedetti has praised Donoso for describing with realistic precision the different types in Chilean society. . . . (p. 218)

Other critics have applauded Donoso for depicting skillfully the upper and lower strata of Chilean society, for placing them in direct contraposition to underscore their differences as well as the ties, mostly sexual, which bind them together. They have commented that structurally his novels are perfectly balanced and reflect the "oposición de clases" which is their major theme. Donoso has been called "traditional," perhaps mainly because his first three novels are not overly experimental and because they "unquestionably give every evidence of a modest and perfectly calculated kind of realistic literary practice" [see excerpt by Alexander Coleman in *CLC,* Vol. 11].

But Donoso is deceptive, and his so-called realism is a mask, a disguise which has fooled many of his critics, who are still equating realism with nativism and universalism with all extremes of experimentation. Of course, *El obsceno pájaro de la noche,* a totally schizophrenic and chaotic novel, can by no stretch of the imagination be called "traditional" or "realistic." For those who have seen Donoso as a rather conservative writer, that work would represent an abrupt about-face. But nothing is farther from the truth. Donoso's novels present a clear line of progression in chaos, a creative trajectory which begins in the crumbling mansion of Misiá Elisita Abalos in *Coronación* and terminates in the disconnected and labyrinthine nightmare of *El obsceno pájaro de la noche.* The chaos has always been there, but behind a false façade of realism which many critics have not penetrated.

The chaos in Donoso's novels can best be described as grotesque. . . . The grotesque, however, is not a distorted reflection of reality in a concave mirror; the grotesque reflects a reality which is already distorted and fragmented.

Although critics are still far from agreeing on a definition of the grotesque, Wolfgang Kayser, in his study of *The Grotesque in Art and Literature,* reaches various conclusions with which I agree for the most part. Kayser tells us that the grotesque is an estranged world. It is not merely a strange or alien world, like that in a fairy tale. It is our world which is transformed, and we react with terror or surprise because we no longer feel it to be reliable. . . . (pp. 218-20)

In other words, the grotesque depicts a world without all the comfortable illusions of structured reality. Kayser insists that the process of disintegration must be experienced on a physical level and that the grotesque does not concern itself with man's individual actions or with the destruction of moral order. But Kayser has dedicated very little of his study to the more recent manifestations of the grotesque, where it is man, with his moral and psychic aberrations, who is an active participant in, if not the creator of, a world of grotesque dimensions. Consequently, the grotesque in contemporary fiction tends to depict a corrosive process which encompasses not only physical but psychic reality as well. (pp. 220-21)

Kayser also insists that grotesque chaos must be brought about by demonic forces which remain beyond human comprehension, a theory with which I cannot agree. There is in fact an outside force, beyond man's control, which also directs this disintegrative process, but it is not totally incomprehensible. What helps to undermine order in the grotesque, at least in Donoso's novels, is an "irresistible process implacably grinding down whatever sense of structure has been raised as an ordering principle against it," a process known as entropy, a law of physics which determines that in man and his universe there is "a tendency to sink back into that original chaos from which [they] may have emerged." Entropy takes chaos one step beyond into formlessness and stasis, to a total leveling of all material distinctions and ordering principles.

The grotesque has many ways of projecting or symbolizing this entropic process, all of them employed by Donoso in his novels: psychological fragmentation, spiritual or physical atrophy and hypertrophy, ambiguity or inversion of sexual roles, symbolical substitution, insanity, and human travesty. Donoso makes use of these to depict the agonizing obliteration of man's personal identity, a spiritual dismembering which throws his world into chaos. (p. 221)

His four novels, therefore, are more than commentaries on Chilean society in progressive stages of decay; they are monstrous visions of diseased and withered souls. His characters are victims of frustrated sexuality and morbid obsessions which erupt into violence to shatter the monotony and rigidity of their individual lives. They are engaged in an endless and futile battle against the encroachments of chaos from without and within. Although bound for sure destruction, they do their best "para no presenciar ese desmoronamiento del orden natural mediante la intrusión del absurdo" ["to keep from witnessing that slow destruction of the natural order brought about by the intrusion of the absurd"]. In the end, they are defeated. (p. 222)

The chaos in *El lugar sin límites* is the same inexorable force which leads to death and insanity in *Coronación* and *Este domingo;* it also explains El Mudito's mysterious metamorphosis into a pile of ashes at the end of *El obsceno pájaro de la noche.* This grotesque chaos does not operate to expose the decadence of a rigid and hierarchical society, as some critics believe. In Donoso's novels all order falls to pieces because it is a reflection of a false myth, of the mistaken concept that man possesses an internal symmetry. When seen in this light it seems limiting to consider Donoso a *costumbrista,* or a realist, or to read his novels only in search of some social message. His novels do have a central thesis indeed, one that he develops obsessively and which he summarizes by stating, "No creo—es decir, no puedo decir que no creo porque no creo es una afirmación y no me atrevo a afirmar nada—pero en fin, *creo que no creo* que exista una unidad psicológica en el ser humano." ["I do not believe—that is to say, I cannot say that I

do not believe because I do not believe is an affirmation and I do not dare to affirm anything—but finally, *I believe that I do not believe* that a psychological unity in the human being exists."] It is in this context that his work is best understood and that it is a reflection of what Alvin Greenberg has called the "modern novel of disintegration." Consequently, the critic who would analyze Donoso's novels on the basis of time-worn critical approaches in vogue when the novel was a structured reflection of a seemingly structured reality is denying other possible meanings of that writer's work. (pp. 231-32)

> *Kirsten F. Nigro, "From 'Criollismo' to the Grotesque: Approaches to José Donoso," in* Tradition and Renewal: Essays on Twentieth-Century Latin American Literature and Culture, *edited by Merlin H. Forster, University of Illinois Press, 1975, pp. 208-32.*

PHOEBE-LOU ADAMS

Mr. Donoso's three long short stories [collected in *Sacred Families*] are located in and about Barcelona, but his characters are internationally familiar. They belong to that artistic intelligentsia whose members are never as talented or as brilliant as they like to believe. They are, in short, prosperous phonies busily deceiving themselves and each other, and their lives are a mixture of pose and dream. Mr. Donoso's system in these tales is to carry the pose, or the dream, or both into literal action which necessarily becomes bizarre fantasy. . . . [These are] amusing stories, clever, malicious, and provocative.

> *Phoebe-Lou Adams, in a review of "Sacred Families," in* The Atlantic Monthly, *Vol. 240, No. 3, September, 1977, p. 96.*

G. R. McMURRAY

José Donoso's *Historia personal del "boom"* [*The Boom in Spanish American Literature: A Personal History*] provides readers of English with information about the so-called Boom in Latin American fiction of the 1960s as well as some insights into the life of Chile's best-known living writer. In this slim volume Donoso makes no pretense of serious scholarship, but rather evokes personal recollections of major events between 1955 and 1970. The most important of these are: the Cuban Revolution, which served to unify Latin American intellectuals; the publication by Seix Barral of Mario Vargas Llosa's experimental novel *La ciudad y los perros* (1962); the founding of the literary journal *Mundo Nuevo;* and the resounding success of García Márquez's *Cien años de soledad* (1967), which brought the Boom to its peak. The end of the euphoric period came with the arrest of Cuban poet Heberto Padilla in 1971, an act that shattered the solidarity among Latin American men of letters.

Donoso's feelings of cultural asphyxiation in Chile emerge as the principal reason for his self-imposed exile in the United States and Spain since 1965. Glimpses into his professional development are provided by his remarks on several of his colleagues: among others, Carlos Fuentes . . . , Mario Vargas Llosa . . . , and Ernesto Sábato. . . .

Written with a flare for the dramatic and interlaced with irony, these memoirs convey the intellectual excitement of the Boom along with its lighter moments. They also help to explain why contemporary Latin American literature is appreciated by an ever-expanding international audience.

G. R. McMurray, in a review of "The Boom in Spanish American Literature: A Personal History," in World Literature Today, *Vol. 51, No. 4, Autumn, 1977, p. 600.*

ALFRED J. MacADAM

Metonymy is oriented toward keeping things moving, while metaphor is oriented toward finality, just as the instinct of self-preservation is in obvious conflict with the idea of suicide. (p. 110)

It is precisely [the] idea of metaphor versus metonymy, of continuance versus closure, that is enacted in José Donoso's *El obsceno pájaro de la noche* (1974). The narrative is concernd in this case with itself, with keeping itself moving, keeping alive despite its own tendency to end. Donoso's text, for our purposes, combines elements from Sarduy, Onetti, and Lezama: the idea that the characters are nothing more than permutations of the poles of narrative, metaphor and metonymy, the idea that these poles are in opposition, and the idea that the only possible subject of the narrative is the narrative itself, that the text is a self-consuming, self-generating verbal object.

Such a text is, of course, monstrous.... Monstrosity is an essential part of satire, monstrosity understood as an exaggeration of any kind which renders the distorted object grotesque. But this distortion transcends the comic, the parodic, and the satiric (in the sense of that which pokes fun at something else) because it erases the relationship betwen the real (the normal) and the grotesque (the distorted version of the real). Satire ... seems to be saying, "You may see or be tempted to see a relationship between the real and the unreal here, but you must forget that relationship, forget the idea of mimesis or representation." ... Like the reality of dreams, satire utilizes elements similar to things in the "real" world but organized in a form, a language, different from that of reality. To see satire exclusively in terms of carnival inversions or as a means whereby we see behind everyday reality is to simplify it, reduce it. (pp. 111-12)

[There is a part of the literary tradition] which sees the artist as a kind of outlaw, the kind of author Cervantes imagined in Ginés de Pasamonte or Shakespeare in Autolycus. A. Bartlett Giamatti [in his essay "Proteus Unbound: Some Versions of the Sea God in the Renaissance," in *The Disciplines of Criticism,* edited by Peter Demetz, Thomas Greene, and Lowry Nelson, Jr.] has carefully delineated this figure in Renaissance literature as that of Proteus, and Proteus is certainly the name one would be inclined to ascribe to the satirist, who, as verbal *magus,* weaves a labyrinth of words to make us aware of the horror of order, the very order consecrated by the divinely inspired *vates.* That the satirist's vision is ironic or dark is certainly often true; but without darkness, light is insignificant or blinding.

Proteus, the demonic element in language, its powers to seduce, to fool, is at the center of *El obsceno pájaro de la noche,* where once again art, artist, and text are fused. (pp. 112-13)

In addition to Proteus, two other literary metaphors may serve as aids to reflection on *El obsceno pájaro de la noche,* the Ptolomaic cosmology and Mary Shelley's Dr. Frankenstein. The Ptolomaic cosmology, as Dante used it, saw the universe as a series of concentric spheres: to this world-within-world concept Donoso adds, in the cosmology of his text, the ideas of the microcosm and reversibility. The idea of the microcosm,

related to synecdoche, suggests that the fragment constitutes a minute recapitulation of the whole. (In the Renaissance, man was often spoken of as a microcosm because he seemed to be the entire universe in miniature.) *El obscuro pájaro de la noche* is composed of successive story layers ..., each one a version or metaphor of the next, an arrangement which suggests that the reader will eventually reach a center that will give him a perspective on the rest, a vantage point from which the relationship of all the parts may be seen. But this idea is replaced by that of reversibility, the idea that the peeling off of the successive layers brings the reader no closer to the center and that at a certain point the process reverses itself. Instead of getting to the center, the reader finds himself again at the beginning.

The Ptolomaic system is repeated throughout the text by the idea of enclosure. The first scene of the book takes place in the Casa de Ejercicios Espirituales de la Encarnación de la Chimba, a combination convent and old-age asylum. The old women in the convent are continuously putting things into packages, tucking the packages away, just as they themselves have been tucked away in the cloister, just as a dead body is put inside a coffin, as bad memories are repressed. The pattern established here makes all acts of enclosure—the sexual act, the gestation of a baby, wearing clothes, binding a text within covers—metaphors for each other. The narrator, who speaks to us from within various *personae* or masks, encloses himself within various identities, each one breeding another: the book encloses the pages, the words are enclosures we fill with meaning, the totality is enclosed within an interpretation. The closer we come to the text the further away from us it moves; at best we can see the layers as the narrative's own desperate attempt to create the illusion of infinite space, to keep on moving despite the fact that it is doomed, limited by its own nature, that of any book.

The kind of artist-creator depicted in Mary Shelley's *Frankenstein, or The Modern Prometheus* (1816) prefigures in many ways the narrator in *El obsceno pájaro de la noche.* Frankenstein, like Donoso's narrator, is a sick creator: he is in love with himself or with versions of himself, thereby compounding narcissism with incest; he creates out of season, in the fall, and he despises what he creates. The body that Frankenstein (the ultimate *bricoleur*) creates out of pieces taken from corpses seems to him beautiful as he creates it, yet becomes hideous when alive. Frankenstein at first flees it (represses its existence) when it comes to life and then spends the rest of his own life trying to destroy it. This antagonism between the creator and his creation may seem quite typical of romanticism, but it has further reaching ramifications. In Donoso's text ... the conventional distinction between art and artist (the monster and Frankenstein) disappears, and the narrative itself is seen as a monstrous creator, incapable of doing anything except narrating, creating stories in its own image.

What the narrator (he has several names, but we see him first as the convent janitor, Mudito, the mute) says is in effect irrelevant. What matters most is the telling itself, the imposition of order (grammar) on arbitrarily chosen things (signs), and the equally arbitrary identification of certain segments of the discourse with certain names, and other parts with other names. The teller here is what he tells; the constant shifts of identity, of enclosure, are therefore nothing more or less than the ebb and flow of the discourse itself. It is always *in medias res,* wherever it happens to be, and it always ends with a death, a loss of voice. The final scene of *El obsceno pájaro de la noche* is one of total dispersion: a crone (a witch? a sybil?) empties over a fire, whch consumes everything, the sack in which the narrator (by now nothing more than a disembodied voice) has been sewn: "In a few minutes nothing remains under the bridge. Only the black spot the fire left on the rocks and a blackened tin can with a wire handle. The wind knocks it over, it rolls along the rocks and falls into the river." . . . The speaking mute (the text) is destroyed . . . [but] there is no idea that a prophesy has been fulfilled, only the notion that the only death of the text, of the narrator/narrative, is silence. (pp. 113-15)

Donoso's text dramatizes the problem of the artist as only satire can: the artist is not a personality but a function, not a human being but an activity. It is not who but what the narrator is that is at stake here. . . . Machado's mad narrators leave texts that justify their meaningless lives; Bioy's anonymous diarist shows how the literary character becomes a text; Cortázar's Oliveira is nothing more than a plot seeking its resolution; Cabrera Infante's figures are nothing more than the pale transcriptions of an author/character, and so on. It is from language these texts come and to it they return. It fell to Donoso to delineate that trajectory in full, in its most tortuous and monstrous gyrations. (p. 118)

> *Alfred J. Mac Adam, "José Donoso: Endgame," in his* Modern Latin American Narratives: The Dreams of Reason, *The University of Chicago Press, 1977, pp. 110-18.*

GEORGE R. McMURRAY

Although Donoso is known primarily as a novelist, he has also published a total of seventeen short stories, all of which were written between 1950 and 1962. These artistically drawn, psychologically penetrating studies of middle-class mores deserve critical acclaim for their intrinsic literary merit, but they are especially important here because they contain in embryonic form many of the thematic preoccupations developed at greater length in the novels.

["**China**"] focuses nostalgically on the past as well as the inevitable loss of innocence and imagination that characterize adulthood. . . .

"**Veraneo**" (Summertime) also sets forth the loss-of-innocence theme, but even more important, it probes the complexities of human relationships and suggests the demise of one of man's most basic institutions, the family. The plot is sketched mainly through the actions and dialogues of adolescents and servants spending a summer at a beach resort. (p. 34)

Domination, dependence, and the fusion of identities in ["**Veraneo**"], though important, are overshadowed by another theme which recurs in many of Donoso's subsequent works and which is introduced here in the form of a house symbol. (p. 35)

An integral part of the plot, [the] dilapidated house symbolizes the "false family," a term Donoso uses to indicate a negation of the archetypal, close-knit family unit, which has been eroded by time, infidelity, and hypocrisy. The decaying structure also conveys, through magical moments of beauty, the nostalgia for childlike innocence, imagination, and delight that emerged from "**China**" and that will make its final appearance in *This Sunday*.

"**Ana María**" presents another interpretation of the false-family and fusion-of-identity motifs. Here an impoverished old man and his barren wife have given up all pretense of love after thirty years of marriage while, at the other extreme, a young couple with a three-year-old daughter, Ana María, are interested solely in sex. Left to wander aimlessly through a densely wooded garden, the child becomes friendly with the old man who works on a construction site nearby. When the latter finds himself unemployed and abandoned by his embittered spouse, he goes to bid the child a fond farewell. However, upon being confronted with her beautiful, hypnotic eyes, he offers no resistance as she leads him away to an uncertain destiny.

The bonds of friendship between the old man and Ana María result from their mutual loneliness and illustrate Donoso's belief in the magnetic attraction often felt between unlike human beings. Their unique relationship . . . anticipates the kind of symbiotic unions evidenced in some of the author's future works. . . . (pp. 35-6)

"**Dos cartas**" (Two Letters), albeit one of Donoso's least distinguished pieces of short fiction, touches on a theme that assumes major proportions in much of his subsequent literary production, i.e., Chile's rigidly stratified social structure which imprisons the middle and upper classes in a stifling atmosphere of conformity. One of the protagonists of "**Dos cartas**" is a young Chilean lawyer named Jaime Martínez who approaches the pinnacle of success in his profession with the uneasy awareness that his family's prominent position "has made him a prisoner without giving him stability" and that "he had not chosen his profession and way of life but rather . . . they were imposed on him and therefore he was a prisoner of dissatisfaction and anxiety." . . . In the case of Martínez, the strict adherence to conventional behavior, the excessive stress on the so-called rational side of life and the suppression of all emotions bordering on the irrational merely inflate his conscious ego and enhance his professional success. In Donoso's best fiction, however, the darker, instinctive side of existence surges forth and either alters or controls the destiny of his characters. (p. 36)

The dichotomy between the rational and the instinctual spheres of the mind is nowhere more evident in Donoso's works than in "**Paseo**," perhaps his finest story. The protagonist, an unattractive, strait-laced spinster named Mathilda, supervises the household of her three brothers, all of whom are successful lawyers in an unnamed port city. The strictly, indeed fanatically, observed routine of their existence is interrupted by the appearance of a white, mongrel bitch that follows Mathilda home from Mass on a rainy day and little by little wins her affection. One night she takes the dog for a walk and never returns.

An outstanding artistic achievement more than anything else, "**Paseo**" immerses its reader into a fictional realm fraught with irony and contrapuntal overtones fluctuating between rigid logic and terrifying ambiguity. This story also represents a focal point in Donoso's total literary production because of the fact that its social and psychological implications become obsessions in the novels. The Chilean author's excessively rational middle- and upper-class characters generally lead sterile, routine lives, suffer from varying degrees of neuroses, and often depend on their contacts with the more instinctive and sexually vigorous lower classes for infusions of vitality. This marked difference in character traits between classes recalls Freud's contentions that culture results from the repression of instincts, that neurosis is a necessary product of culture, and that the higher the culture the higher the degree of repression and neurosis. (p. 38)

Donoso is of the opinion that daily routine carried to excess constitutes false rituals which substitute meaningless activity for living and . . . bring death into life in order to eliminate the terror of nothingness. Routine activity and strict, rational behavior in **"Paseo"** not only isolate the characters from each other but, in the case of Mathilda, make her vulnerable to the mysterious forces of life she has always suppressed. Her strange behavior and ultimate disappearance evoke elements of the psychology of Carl G. Jung who, like Freud, has attributed many of modern man's neuroses to the split or "dissociation" of his rational conscious from the darker, unconscious levels of his psyche. . . .

In Donoso's works symbols frequently become obsessions that take hold of his excessively rationalistic characters and little by little consume them. The mongrel bitch in **"Paseo,"** for example, . . . would seem to embody Mathilda's repressed instincts, a call to adventure given in response to her over-powering unconscious needs. Indeed, when she first meets the dog and turns suddenly to send it on its way, the look that passes between them appears to contain a "secret commitment" and Mathilda's "peremptory 'psst' had the sound of something like a last effort to repel an encroaching destiny." . . . (p. 40)

"Paseo" sets forth what might be considered a classical existential situation, on the one hand a perfectly ordered, seemingly placid life and, on the other, a crisis which erupts with diabolical force, stifling reason and submerging the individual into an abyss created by his—in this case her—own obsessions. Mathilda's alienation from the instinctual inner self makes her not only a casualty of the illness Jung has diagnosed in his analysis of the contemporary psyche, but also a precursor of the obsessed, irrational figures populating Donoso's subsequent fiction. (p. 41)

[An] example of surrealism in Donoso's short fiction is **"Una señora"** (**"A Lady"**) which presents the Freudian will-to-kill obsession and, simultaneously, exposes the dark side of the psyche. While riding a streetcar one day, the narrator sits briefly next to an ordinary looking, middle-aged woman in a green raincoat. The next evening he is convinced he catches sight of the same person again and, during the following weeks, imagines he meets her frequently on the street. When he does not see her for some time, he begins to search for her obsessively and even falls ill from thinking about her. One morning he awakens certain that somewhere in the city she is dying and that evening, when all the noises of the neighborhood suddenly cease, he feels equally certain of her death. The next day he follows the funeral procession of a woman whose demise he has seen announced in the newspaper and, after the burial service, takes a stroll through the cemetery, feeling strangely at peace with himself. This ending, by means of which the narrator imposes his subjective interpretation of the world on objective reality, suggests the surrealists' attempt to break through the outer limits of the rational consciousness in order to discover a more comprehensive "surreality."

The author's preoccupation with the nature of reality, including its metaphysical aspects, is perhaps best expressed in his short fiction by his most enigmatic tale, **"La puerta cerrada"** (**"The Closed Door"**). The setting, like that of [**"Una señora,"**] is a boarding house and home for a false family, in this case a young widow and her son Sebastián Rengifo. Sebastián is considered odd because of his inordinate fondness for sleeping, an activity that leaves him no time for normal relations with other people. He confesses that he always dreams of a magical

world of light, truth, and happiness but that as soon as he awakens a door shuts out what he has just envisioned. His overriding ambition is to open the door so that he can fuse his dream world with everyday reality. In the office where he is employed his supervisor, Aquiles Marambio, predicts a bright future for him but advises him to be more outgoing with his co-workers in order to improve his professional prospects. Sebastián informs Aquiles that he prefers sleeping to socializing and explains his preoccupation with the closed door. Although Aquiles scoffs at him, their discussion leads to a bet that when Sebastián dies, if he has a smile on his face—an indication that he has been able to open the door—Aquiles will pay for his funeral. Upon the death of his mother, Sebastián immediately resigns from his position in order to spend his time sleeping. Years later, impoverished, ostracized, and still striving to realize his ambition, he is overtaken by death at the entrance to Aquiles' home. Because of the radiant smile on his face, his former supervisor feels obliged to defray his funeral expenses.

The principal questions raised by this tale are what, if anything, the protagonist, the closed door, and the world beyond it represent. Sebastián evokes the sensitive, imaginative dreamer whose rejection of conventional values sets him apart from his fellow men. (pp. 46-7)

Sebastián's striving to open the door also recalls the surrealists' ideal of achieving a total reality by erasing the line between the real and the imaginary, an ideal illustrated by his desire "to bring the happiness of his dream world into this life, into this reality." . . . (p. 47)

In view of his isolation, sensitivity, and obsessive efforts to unveil a perfect, all-encompassing reality, Sebastián also brings to mind the dedicated artist whose lifelong search for beauty becomes a metaphor of modern man's quest for the missing God. (pp. 47-8)

The religious fervor of his endeavor is . . . implied at the end of the story when, upon returning from church, Marambio Aquiles' young daughters discover Sebastián's body in the doorway of their home. At first they are frightened by the sight of death, but then the serenely happy expression on his face elicits the following exchange:

> "Look, Daddy, how beautiful! It looks as if he had seen . . ."
>
> "Shut up, don't say such stupid things!" exclaimed Marambio, furious.
>
> "It looks as though he were seeing . . ." . . .

But before they can say anything more, Marambio pushes them into the house and closes the door.

The little girls' suggestion that Sebastián has seen God may be much closer to the truth than their philistine father is capable of imagining, for if artistic perfection does indeed constitute Sebastián's concept of God, the smile on his face would seem to indicate that the moment of death became for him the supreme moment of aesthetic revelation, i.e., the moment in which he at last achieved the absolute beauty or the total reality he had sought all his life. The closed door, then, symbolizes not only the insurmountable barrier between objective reality and subjective art, but also the separation between society and the artist. Whatever its interpretation, **"The Closed Door"** stands out as one of Donoso's most significant and fascinating tales. Its harmoniously fused singleness of action and multiplicity of suggestion anticipate the combination of unity and complexity so characteristic of his novels.

Irony has played an increasingly significant role in modern literature, particularly in the present century, and because of its complex, multifaceted, and elusive nature, it has become one of the most controversial concepts in aesthetics. (p. 48)

Donoso, like many contemporary writers, utilizes irony as a means of coming to grips with, and asserting a measure of independence from, a paradoxical world devoid of absolutes. Virtually all of the Chilean author's short stories contain elements of irony, but in several it emerges as a basic ingredient and in one, **"Fiesta en grande,"** its omnipresence becomes oppressive and constitutes a flaw. This tragicomedy's situational irony stems from the contradictions between the protagonist's high aspirations and the cruel blows of fate that lie in store for him. In the opening scene Alberto Aldea, sporting a flashy new necktie, eagerly awaits the opportune moment to impress his office colleagues with the news of his pistol-shooting championship. Their enthusiastic invitation to celebrate his triumph contrasts sharply with the descriptions of his drab home life and his anxiety, generated by timidity, over the thought of a fiesta. His moments of prestige come to an abrupt end during the absurd incident in the country after which his domineering mother confiscates his pistol with the intention of throwing it into the river on her way to Mass the next day. Alberto's dream, replete with Freudian symbols, and his resultant terror of being left alone without his mother complete the annihilation of his illusions and, perhaps, of his entire personality. The end result of this accumulation of ironic events is an excess of cruelty that transforms farce into tragedy and amusement into exaggerated pathos. (p. 49)

Donoso's masterpiece of irony in his short fiction is **"Paseo."** ... This story differs from the others ... in that it utilizes verbal as well as situational irony, i.e., the words themselves, in addition to the occurrences, convey a duality of meaning. Here a point of view is adopted midway between the author and the action, the first-person narrator recalling an episode that occurred many years previously, during his childhood. Moreover, not only is he reporting ironically his juvenile reactions to the series of extraordinary events, but he also admits he was a mere bystander, never an active participant, and that his imagination and memory may have deceived him. Through the use of these devices, the author achieves a remarkable degree of detachment, casts doubt on the narrator's reliability, and thus charges his tale with an extraordinarily heavy dose of irony.

Verbal irony in **"Paseo"** stems principally from the mature narrator's tongue-in-cheek recollections of his childlike reactions to the adult members of his family. Thus, the boy, his aunt, and her three brothers become victims of irony, all of them confidently unaware of the dangers lurking beneath the surface and around the edges of their perfectly ordered universe. (pp. 51-2)

The casual reader of Donoso's short fiction is likely to be impressed by its many characteristics of nineteenth and early twentieth-century realism: the presentation of Chilean customs, especially of the middle and upper-middle classes; the succinct, analytical style; the impeccably structured plots; and the traditional literary techniques. However, as critic Alexander Coleman has warned [see *CLC*, Vol. 11], to see nothing more than "a perfectly calculated kind of realistic literary practice" in

the stories is "to hide their insidious and quite beautifully disguised thematics."

Donoso is a masterful creator of dialogues, visual scenes, and moods, all of which lend vitality to his psychological portraits and enrich the texture of his fictional fabric. In most of the stories the reader's sensibilities are engaged by terse conversations and sensual descriptions that unmask the protagonists and set the stage for character or plot development. (p. 53)

The majority of Donoso's tales are linear in structure, with every detail aimed at a steadily rising climax and rapid ending. **"The Güero," "Charleston," "Paseo,"** and **"The Dane's Place"** develop plots in circular form, beginning at the end and then chronologically retracing the entire course of events. Only three stories [**"Dos cartas," "Santelices,"** and **"Ana Maria"**] deviate from the above formula. (p. 54)

The Chilean author's manipulation of the narrative point of view in his short fiction is, like his treatment of language and time, traditional and carefully executed. Of his fourteen most important stories, seven are told in the first person by the protagonist or a witness-narrator, six are related by a third-person narrator, and one, **"Dos cartas,"** alternates between these two methods. In his stories told in the third person Donoso varies aesthetic distance (the appropriate distance between the reader and the fictional material) in order to control the reader's involvement and achieve maximum effect. Thus, the omniscient narrator's point of view is often replaced by that of one of the characters whose mind serves as a highly polished mirror to reflect the fictional world the author wishes to represent. When filtered through the consciousness of a so-called third-person reflector, this world is brought closer to the reader who tends to identify more readily with the character and share his dramatic situation. Two stories illustrating the use of the reflector technique are **"Fiesta en grande,"** in which the timid office clerk Alberto Aldea is dominated by his mother, and **"Santelices,"** the tale of the sadomasochistic boarding-house dweller who leaps to his death from his office window. The tragic lives of these protagonists achieve greater poignancy due to the fact that much of what happens to them is presented from their points of view. (pp. 54-5)

Virtually all of Donoso's short stories leave an impression of unity, a quality achieved not only through stylistic, technical, and structural devices, but also through the incorporation of recurring symbols, images, and rhythmic speech patterns which integrate language with plot, expand meaning, and lend texture and resonance to the material. (p. 56)

Although the literal sketches of Donoso's short fiction impart an overall impression of traditional realism, his characters' placid lives are frequently disturbed by impulses over which they have little or no control. Their irrational emotions tend to prevail in the later works, suggesting the author's deepening disenchantment with the rigidly conceived world of reason which he lampoons by uncovering the other face of reality. In the process of carrying out his attacks against false values based on absolutes, he has evolved a more subjective style and experimented extensively with avant-garde novelistic architecture, point of view and treatment of time. The result is a shift to metaphoric expression which through implication and comparison lends depth and ambiguity to objective reality. These aesthetic preoccupations tend to minimize the importance of the Chilean scene and elevate the works in question to a more abstract realm of universality. Thus, whereas *Coronation, This Sunday* and most of the short stories convey an unmistakable flavor of Chilean reality, in *Hell Has No Limits* and *The Obscene Bird of Night* the setting and culture of the author's native land, though ingeniously integrated into the fictional texture, are blurred through a prism of poeticized myth and fantasy. In a somewhat similar but more straightforward manner, the Barcelona setting of *Sacred Families* provides a backdrop for numerous scenes typifying upper-middle-class life throughout the occidental world.

Donoso is not always suitable fare for the casual reader seeking light entertainment. Though illuminated by occasional flashes of wit, irony, and fantasy, his gloomy portraits of man alone in an inhospitable universe not only convey a nostalgia for past innocence, the loss of which has contributed to the metaphysical crisis of today, but also suggest a world headed for total destruction and oblivion. The corrosion of long-established institutions is brought more sharply into focus by the protagonists who, as outsiders, impart a strong dissatisfaction with prevailing conditions and seek to liberate themselves from their oppressive environments by a wide variety of means. (pp. 148-49)

The Chilean author might be described as an eclectic, having been impressed by various individuals and movements but always having shunned direct intellectual and ideological involvement. Thus, although his works illustrate the existentialist concepts of the absurd and the ever-evolving self, he rejects the more positive elements of this philosophy, recognizing little beyond despair. Likewise he joins the surrealists in their belief that Freud's irrational realm of the unconscious can be just as real as objective reality, but the surrealists' aspirations of ameliorating the human condition through their artistic endeavor would more than likely strike him as naïve. Without intending to suggest any direct influences, one can draw similarities between Donoso and some of his favorite American and European authors. Like Faulkner's, his fiction depicts vestiges of a society that has seen better days; his symbolic representations of the subconscious suggest Virginia Woolf's intuitive method; his recreation of past reality through sensory perceptions attests to his familiarity with the works of Proust; his expert manipulation of the point of view perhaps results from his avid reading of Henry James; the houses which enliven his works evoke Dickens' vividly drawn mansions; and Humberto Peñaloza's mutations and bizarre visions bring to mind Kafka's famous protagonist of *The Metamorphosis* who turns into an enormous bug.

Donoso's concern for the individual trapped in the confines of outmoded traditions and hypocritical conventions is shared by other prominent contemporary Chilean writers such as Carlos Droguett, Enrique Lafourcade, Antonio Skármeta, Alfonso Alcalde, Fernando Alegría, Jorge Edwards, Jorge Guzmán, and Guillermo Blanco. Their repudiation of existing conditions is expressed by a variety of reactions ranging from Droguett's violent rebellion to Skármeta's triumph through action and Donoso's revolt through the magical world of the inner self where reason and logic tend to disappear. In this frame of reference his monument of grotesque fantasy, *The Obscene Bird of Night,* is unique in Chilean letters and a significant event in both Latin American and world fiction. (p. 150)

Some readers may be depressed by Donoso's recurring insinuations of impending doom, but few will fail to appreciate his astonishing imagination, aesthetic sensitivity, and profound insight into the terrifying realities lurking beneath the surface of today's world. (p. 151)

George R. McMurray, in his José Donoso, *Twayne Publishers, 1979, 178 p.*

RONALD SCHWARTZ

If Severo Sarduy's novels may be considered "coldly elusive," José Donoso's are "boldly hallucinogenic." . . .

Donoso's novels do not primarily describe places, events, and characters from the outside, but cram all of these elements into worlds of words, a world aware of its own verbal nature. More often then not his novels are complex and his characters fragmented and difficult to identify or distinguish from one another whether through their own dialogues or channeled through the consciousness of a narrator. Donoso's greatest gifts are his glorious flights of imagination, the frank revelation of his consciousness, the portrayal of his aesthetic sensations, and his profound insights into the realities elucidated through his startling prose. Language is the center of Donoso's novels, and Donoso abandons traditional plot, character, and thematic development in order to depict today's world in his own meaningful, spontaneous way, much in the spirit of the anti-novelists. (p. 100)

Students of literature will puzzle over [*The Obscene Bird of Night*] for years to come, but . . . a later work of Donoso's, *Sacred Families*, [is] a lesser phantasmagorical world, one characterized by a more traditional technique and also more in the realm of straightforward storytelling: an "anti-anti-novel," if you will, a form that perhaps marks the new direction for Latin American novelists and narratives for the 1980s.

A shorter, less dense work than *Obscene Bird, Sacred Families* has had little critical exposure in the United States and abroad and is worthy of scrutiny. Although the novel is set in Barcelona, Donoso is perennially concerned "with unraveling all the threads that compose the fabric of Chilean society," in [Emir Rodríguez] Monegal's words. All of his works, whether written in Chile or in exile, deal explicitly with Chilean life of the twentieth century. Donoso's themes are fairly constant throughout his fictions: the alienation, spiritual and emotional disintegration, and rebellious nature of his protagonists. *Sacred Families* is a series of three novellas (or one longer novel utilizing the same characters) that explicitly treats the theme of possessive materialism within the lives of three urban haute-bourgeois protagonists: a doctor, a dentist, and a model. The novellas are not only linked thematically, but certain characters weave in and out of the fabric of the intrigue that is set primarily in contemporary Barcelona.

Chattanooga-Choo-Choo is a flight of fantasy narrated by Anselmo, a doctor-artist-playboy, who sleeps one night with model Sylvia Corday. Sylvia's husband Ramón, an architect, assembles and reassembles his wife, providing her with new face masks in his own quest for sexual domination of women. After a party one night Sylvia and Anselmo sleep together clandestinely, and in some quirky, surrealist maneuvering, Sylvia dismantles Anselmo's genitals with vanishing cream, taking revenge on him and her husband for using her sexually. Disturbed that his wife Magdalena might discover his missing member, Anselmo despairs until his next meeting with Sylvia. The wives, however, also have the power to dismember their men. At the conclusion of the novella Sylvia tells Magdalena that an error has occurred . . . she has Anselmo's "package" and Magdalena has Ramón's. The women then reassemble their respective husbands, complete with missing parts; the men then reenact the 1940s song "Chattanooga-Choo-Choo" in a parody of the Andrews Sisters begun by Sylvia and Magdalena at the party a few nights before.

Donoso here is critical of male domination and female submissiveness, resulting in a pro-Women's Liberation tale told in surrealistic terms. His portrait of a haute bourgeoisie that replaces religious values and moral convictions with easy love, sex, drugs, camp, the gay scene and ventures into superficial nostalgia, is complete. Donoso is a master at mood, creating a sensuous atmosphere that pervades the entire tale. He also has a sharp eye and critical ear for the shallow, hypocritical repartee at the parties reeking with synthetic atmosphere. Most fascinating is the grotesque world he creates, as the reader always waits for the unexpected to happen, in this case, husbands dismantling their spouses and packing them and their private parts away. (pp. 106-07)

Green Atom Number Five, another tale of dismemberment and disintegration, deals with friends of Anselmo and Magdalena, Roberto and Marta Ferrer, an older, childless couple, apparently well adjusted, who are transformed grotesquely into a pair of snarling savages because of a series of thefts that leave them materialistically and spiritually bankrupt. (p. 108)

[This] surrealistic parable à la Cortázar recalls Alain Robbe-Grillet's obsessions with inanimate objects; Donoso depicts what happens to two people who have always led orderly lives and the consequences of dispossession, pretentiousness, and sexual sterility.... An omniscient novelist, Donoso dissolves the tale, leaving the childless, despoiled couple in absolute nakedness and despair. Their physical disintegration also signifies their psychic and moral decay, since Donoso believes that material objects cannot fulfill or be used as substitutes for real feelings even with the labyrinth we know as materialistic society. Donoso also points out that—in the words of G. R. McMurray—"the horror of man's rigidly ordered reality ... is surpassed only by his horror of chaos as shown by the frightening disintegration that follows the disappearance of Roberto's painting."

Donoso's final novella, *Gaspard de la Nuit,* receives its name from Maurice Ravel's famous musical work and reunites Sylvia Corday (who had made Anselmo's sex organ vanish and sang "Chattanooga-Choo-Choo") with Paolo, the gay decorator, celebrant at Anselmo's house, designer of Roberto and Marta Ferrer's vanished apartment, and reveler at other parties given by Barcelona's haute bourgeoisie. *Gaspard* relates the story of a teenage boy, Mauricio, visiting his now divorced (reassembled) mother, Sylvia Corday, the current mistress of Raimundo del Solar. Mauricio rejects all of her efforts toward reconciliation and occupies himself by whistling the melody of the title by Ravel.... Similar to *The Obscene Bird of Night, Gaspard* moves us once again into the world of schizophrenia. In what is probably the most complex of the three novellas in this collection (but not necessarily the most likable), Donoso returns to brilliant storytelling, pulling out all the stops in an effort to create another short, perceptively psychological masterpiece dealing with the themes of conformity and fantasy.

Gaspard is a tale of psychic rebellion. Mauricio (named after Ravel, he says) tunes out the Barcelona high life with his frequent trips to the zoo at Villvidrera, refuses offers of a stereo, a Vespa motorbike, hippie shirts, and amulets to the chagrin of his fashionable but selfish and desperate mother, anxious to go away to the country or beach with her lover and not be saddled with her sixteen-year-old son. Organized into five sections, Mauricio has a history of abject loneliness, having been raised mostly by his grandmother and absentee wealthy father in Madrid. In subsequent sections we see Maurice, now on vacation with his mother in Barcelona, unable to make contact with "Jackie-O," a woman wheeling a baby carriage who wears sunglasses in the Kennedy mode. Next Mauricio is followed by a brown-suited older man, who, identifying the melody of *Gaspard* through Mauricio's whistling, sends the youth fleeing from a homosexual encounter. Mauricio's happiest moments come in the Villvidrera Park area, where he makes contact with a co-ed group of Catalonian teenagers playing soccer, a beetle (shades of Kafka), and a supposed raggedy street urchin, his exact double, with whom he evidently changes roles. And Donoso leaves us with a supposed prince-and-the-pauper denouement.

What is fascinating about this novella is Donoso's ambiguous ending. Is the street urchin really there or is he a figment of Mauricio's schizoid personality? When the new Mauricio arrives home, he integrates perfectly into Sylvia Corday's lifestyle, perhaps fulfilling the wishes of the lighter side of his nature. What is disturbing, however, is Donoso's clinging to the notion of a darker side of Mauricio's personality, assuming an identity that went against his nature. Ravel's music is the link between Mauricio's abject loneliness ... and his quest for a new, totally schizophrenic personality.... (pp. 108-10)

Gaspard remains an enigma, the tale of a mental depressive, perhaps anorexic, whose personality split reveals ambivalent urges to dominate and destroy, which are, in reality, perhaps an individual's reaction to social conformity and crass materialism, the values of the upper middle class in today's Barcelona (or Santiago)....

Unlike *The Obscene Bird of Night, Sacred Families* represents a traditionally story-oriented performance by Donoso, with tightly controlled events leading to unexpected climaxes.... (p. 110)

Donoso has used his talent and ingenuity, his sense of surrealism and satire to put a new face on the literature of disintegration. All of his fictional works deal with characters who pass fragmented lives or are unable to communicate or are trapped by a conformist society or who suffer mental, emotional, spiritual, psychic, or geographical isolation.... Donoso's view of the human condition may be so dark and pessimistic that he might ... be called the Balzac of Chilean letters—Balzac, because Donoso's works give us a broad canvas of society, the violent underside of a conventional bourgeois world that is his perennial theme. (pp. 110-11)

Donoso's fiction, projected beyond his native Chile, has elevated his career—and those of some of his fellow Chilean novelists—to international perspective. But it is Donoso himself, because of his insightful, stylistically deft prose, who has achieved recognition of universal stature. (p. 111)

> *Ronald Schwartz, "Donoso: Chilean Phantasmagoria," in his* Nomads, Exiles, & Emigres: The Rebirth of the Latin American Narrative, 1960-80, *The Scarecrow Press, Inc., 1980, pp. 100-11.*

ALFRED J. MAC ADAM

If Henry James had allowed the perversity he merely suggests in his writings actually to appear, he might have written [*La misteriosa desaparición de la marquesita de Loria*] by José Donoso. Instead of Isabel Archer's passage from innocence to experience in *Portrait of a Lady,* we would see her innate corruption emerge as she became more deeply immersed in a corrupt world. There would be no innocence, only ignorance; and the hypothetical Isabel Archer's education would lead her from solitary narcissism to a sexual chaos devoid of rules or love, animated by passions and the need to satisfy them.

La misteriosa desaparición de la marquesita de Loria is that text. It traces the life of Blanca Arias: her marriage to an adorable but impotent *marqués,* her widowhood of barren sexuality, and her "mysterious disappearance." Although he set the novel in early twentieth-century Madrid, Donoso has actually written a moral allegory that combines the Gothic novel, James and Laclos. . . .

In *El lugar sin límites, El obsceno pájaro de la noche* and *Casa de campo,* the idea of sacrifice is paramount: the sacrifice of la Manuela in the first, of Humberto Peñaloza in the second and of the rebels in the third. In all three a repressive order (political or sexual) effaces the identity of the opposition. Here the victim is not innocent; but innocent or not, she is devoured by a world she cannot comprehend. An extraordinary text.

> *Alfred J. Mac Adam, in a review of "La misteriosa desaparición de la marquesita de Loria," in* World Literature Today, *Vol. 55, No. 2, Spring, 1981, p. 281.*

ALFRED J. Mac ADAM

José Donoso [with *El jardín de al lado*] once again shows himself to be a master of the least understood of the major literary forms, the novella. . . .

The novella is a most self-conscious form and *El jardín* a splendid example: it provides hints both about itself and about the genre. First, it is self-reflexive: art and the production of art are themes to which it returns constantly. This has a decided effect on the protagonists: they are presented in terms of a myth or archetype of the writer, in a way analogous to Mann's *Death in Venice.* Here Donoso studies a failed writer's inability to cope with life, which has deprived him of a controllable, comprehensible milieu. Finally, *El jardín* relates art to death and exile: in order to become an artist it is necessary to withdraw from life and then turn experience into art. . . .

Donoso has written a witty and melancholy text that includes statements about exile, Spanish-Spanish American relations both in art and politics, and the state of Spanish American fiction in the post-boom. A wonderful book.

> *Alfred J. Mac Adam, in a review of "El jardín de al lado," in* World Literature Today, *Vol. 56, No. 3, Summer, 1982, p. 490.*

ALBERTO BLASI

Poets often write dramas and novelists often write poetry at some time during their careers, but not always with such results as *Murder in the Cathedral* and *Chamber Music.* Yet these plays and poems hold considerable significance for a deeper understanding of the artist's entire production and offer specific insights into his private world. This is the case with José Donoso's poems. The eminent Chilean novelist . . . is fond of autobiographical communication, as witnessed by his articles, a previous book and lectures on the Donoso subject. The present collection of thirty poems [*Poems de un novelista*] is enriched by a twelve-page introduction by the author aimed at explaining why he felt compelled to write such a book and what personal circumstances inspired the verse. . . .

Nearly all of this poetic material illuminates Donoso's intimacy with and vision of life in Spain and elsewhere. His desolate, keen and ascetic point of view is its primary subject, many of these insights having been previously coined in his narrative work. A personal tendency toward poetic asceticism and a long career in the codification of narrative discourse result in a remarkable text situated in that zone between poetry and prose.

Echoes of César Vallejo and Octavio Paz are detectable in this book, but analyzed as a whole—that is, as an interaction between the introductory essay and the poems—it should be considered a personal and valid item in its author's list of works. It illustrates, illuminates and perhaps confesses the writer's main obsessions, serving as a critical tool for a keener insight into Donoso's most important novels. . . . [The] collection is indispensable as a key to his inner self and as a map to the suffocating, anguished, mythical world of his creation. The elegy of "la tía Victoria de la Clara" and the compassionate interpretation of the ritual killing of a pig will remain in the reader's mind, apart from any other considerations, as "poetry" in the best sense of the word.

> *Alberto Blasi, in a review of "Poemas de un novelista," in* World Literature Today, *Vol. 57, No. 1, Winter, 1983, p. 73.*

STANLEY REYNOLDS

The great virgin literary landscape of Latin America for a long time lay unspoiled, beckoning European writers with a taste for the exotic . . . to use it to build a complete little world for themselves. No one knew Latin America and therefore they were as free to invent as science fiction writers. . . . [The] European reader wanted exotica from Spanish and Portuguese America; the US reader wanted treacherous greaseballs and sexy dames.

They certainly got it. Those of us who knew Latin America first-hand waited and, generally speaking, we are still waiting for the realistic novel. Borges, it has always seemed to me, is as festooned with exotic literary flowers as any European hack sitting at home imagining Latin America.

Not a single lover of the bizarre is going to be disappointed by José Donoso, the Childean heir to Borges and Márquez. [*A House in the Country*] is not only self-conscious "strangeness" run riot but also post-Modernism gone nuts. Like a Russian novel there is a cast of characters listed at the front, including 33 cousins, not one of whom has the same name. . . .

A House in the Country is surreal, a fantasy, a mess really, but there is something grand about the game Señor Donoso is playing with the reader ("In an earlier version of this novel . . ."). If I am looking for documentation about Latin America I have only to go to UNESCO, Amnesty International or the CIA; this is the novel as a toy, a plaything and it is mind-spinning, wonderful stuff, which also does indeed deal with revolutionaries, dictators and reigns of terror. Highly recommended to those good readers who enjoy being baffled, puzzled and amazed.

> *Stanley Reynolds, "The South American Way," in* Punch, *Vol. 286, No. 7481, April 18, 1984, p. 59.*

Zoë (Ann) Fairbairns

1948-

English novelist.

Fairbairns is a feminist writer whose novels examine from both a historical and a contemporary perspective the inequalities and difficulties women have faced. She has been commended for creating strong characters, male and female, who reflect women's struggles, and for avoiding being didactic or simplistic.

Benefits **(1976) is a futuristic story set in the closing years of the twentieth century, when women are subject to compulsory birth control. As an Orwellian government attempts to institutionalize motherhood, selective breeding begins and women's role in society is vastly reduced.** ***Benefits*** **has been praised as a meaningful political fable, and Fairbairns is recognized for her skill in balancing her characters.**

Stand We at Last **(1983) has been called Fairbairns's most accomplished novel. This work follows five generations of English women through their struggles to gain personal and political freedom. Elizabeth Grossman asserted that Fairbairns tried to cover too many topics and failed to explore the passing time periods in depth, but other critics applauded Fairbairns's historical research and declared that** ***Stand We at Last*** **was a convincing portrait of women's issues over the last hundred years.**

(See also *Contemporary Authors,* **Vol. 103.)**

NICHOLAS SHRIMPTON

[*Benefits*] begins as a brisk tract on the campaigns for abortion on demand and the retentions of child benefits. It then suddenly transforms itself into a zany dystopia, set in the closing years of the 20th century. In part this is a satirical reversal of current arguments against legal abortion, since the woman of the future's right to choose is inhibited by compulsory birth control and she resorts to back-street doctors in order to become pregnant. But there is also an attempt to pursue a serious political hypothesis. A new government begins to pay women substantial salaries for rearing their own children. This seemingly desirable step leads immediately to the exclusion of women from the job-market, and ultimately to a policy of selective breeding. By the end we seem to be back with the old Welfare State, some of its warts and all. As a vision of the future the book suffers from the extreme narrowness of its focus. As an argument it is confused by its author's inability to resist distractions. Zoe Fairbairns writes excellent jokes. But she does need a tighter framework in which to set them. (p. 559)

Nicholas Shrimpton, "A Dash of Kim," in New Statesman, *Vol. 98, No. 2534, October 12, 1979, pp. 559-60.*

VICTORIA GLENDINNING

[*Benefits*] is a feminist novel: it is about the women. It is complex and ambitious, and in some of its aspects has nothing to do with imaginative literature. It is a short novel that is remembered as a long one, because it is jampacked and because it covers a period of thirty years from 1976—*ie* it is a projection of what could happen to women, and therefore to all society, in the immediate future. . . . In *Benefits,* the intimacy of personal stories meshes grindingly with the exposition of ideas. But for all that it should be read.

The central theme emerges only gradually from dialectic, incident, reports of legislation and robust cinematic set-pieces. . . . Nearly every female type, the home-maker, the uncommitted, the lesbian, the bisexual, the power-hungry, the good, the bad, the boring and the mad, are represented in the course of this thirty years' war; you could make this book mean what you want it to, since everyone can find her own position stated, and without irony, by somebody.

But what it begins to be about—and was about all along, one realises—is the attitude of women to childbearing. Not to be allowed to have a baby is as monstrous as not being allowed to prevent one. The 'Benefit' of the title is the state wage paid to women who have children—a social measure many would now be in favour of. But the post-1984 government find they can control the population by denying Benefit to women they consider undesirable. The wheel turns full circle; the Victorian concept of 'deserving' and 'undeserving' suits the social and genetic engineers perfectly. . . . The personal is *not* political, it seems; women are innately anarchic and infinitely various. 'What do the women want?' asks the future government in bewilderment, as the whole sex comes out in revolt. They all want something different, depending on their age, experience, temperament, intelligence, and biological proclivities. They are united only in wanting to have babies how and when they choose.

Where does this leave the women's movement? In fractions and factions. This is the problem Zoë Fairbairns leaves unsolved. Perhaps her strength—as many women's—lies in Keats's negative capability of 'being in uncertainties, mysteries, doubts, without any irritable reaching after fact and reason'. *Benefits* is a serious novel but not a work of art; it might, however, make a powerful film, with a cast of thousands of women and children; and a few parts for male actors with worried faces; and the tower-block, ambiguous symbol of generation, overshadowing them all.

> *Victoria Glendinning, in a review of "Benefits," in* Books and Bookmen, *Vol. 25, No. 2, November, 1979, p. 44.*

ANGELA McROBBIE

Fairbairns' 600-page family saga [*Stand We at Last*] succeeds admirably in sweeping the reader into its narrative; nor does it at any point read as though written to a formula, despite its explicit intention to present a feminist reworking of the genre....

[The] expectations of the traditional saga are overturned (no direct descendants and no inheritance); and yet there *is* a legacy, as Fairbairns goes to great lengths to demonstrate—a legacy which works its way down through the suffragette movement to feminism today. *Stand We at Last* should be read not only by feminists but also by our mothers' generation; it summons a strength through broken spirits and a pride despite apparent imprisonment. Its sadness lies, I think, in its absences—those of youth and the compensation of a rich family and community culture, something not necessarily irreconcilable with the aims of the Women's Movement.

> *Angela McRobbie, "Dependence," in* New Statesman, *Vol. 105, No. 2708, February 11, 1983, p. 31.**

ELIZABETH GROSSMAN

Stand We at Last is billed as a feminist saga and it is: a tale of women of ordinary circumstances whose lives have been bound by convention and the accidents and politics of sex and birth. And although the novel accomplishes what it sets out to, involving us in the fate of its many heroines and occasionally painting a vivid scene, its contrivance hinders its success. It reaches out at too many incidents of history, stretching itself thin to cover so much time and ground. Its landscape is rendered plainly and more convincingly than its dialogue, which is so obviously designed to convey a message. Sprawling over more than a century, *Stand We at Last* makes its point—sincerely, but not in a particularly original or unusual way. Its plot and characters may well satisfy those fond of the genre, but others may feel time would be better spent with Dickens, Gaskell, or Eliot.

> *Elizabeth Grossman, "A Feminist 'Thornbirds'?" in* Ms., *Vol. XI, No. 9, March, 1983, p. 34.*

AUDREY C. FOOTE

The title introductory poem "The March of Women" and the author's preface all declare that this large novel [*Stand We at Last*] has a feminist theme and purpose. But those who expect militant propaganda will be surprised by Fairbairns' even-handedness, good humor and, above all, lively narrative skill with which she devises a large cast of convincing characters, both female and male, and places them within a well-depicted historical framework that extends for over a century.

That history is often harsh, but the fiction is humane. The major characters, mostly lower-middle-class English women from 1855 to 1970, endure and usually prevail against the universal as well as particular privations and troubles of their times and class.... Yet while the laws, institutions and customs are often repressive or demoralizing to these women, blame is almost never placed on their individual lovers, fathers, husbands or even employers. Interestingly, the men characters are often shown as more generous, better tempered than their mates. Moreover, while the women are indeed usually disadvantaged by their society, the author suggests that attainment of independence is ultimately within their grasp.

As this is very much a novel and not a tract, any pattern among these varied lives is only partial; rather, certain designs occasionally repeat: girlish energy and ambition are somehow foiled or burn out; discouragement and depression follow, and then abandonment to often embittered dependence, usually but not always on men.

> *Audrey C. Foote, in a review of "Stand We at Last," in* Book World—The Washington Post, *March 6, 1983, p. 4.*

S. M. MOWBRAY

The title [*Stand We at Last*] comes from a Women's Movement hymn which also includes the discouraging line 'Life, strife, these two are one'—an apt enough comment for the central characters of this novel. It is a kind of Women's Lib. family saga.... The five heroines have a terrible time. Illegitimate children, VD, destitution, forced registration as prostitutes, rape, infidelity and desertion by their menfolk, and of course the pains of childbirth—these are only a few of their troubles. The most intrepid of the book's heroines is Sarah, who works her fingers to the bone in Australian exile and finally goes down gloriously in the *Titanic;* the most irritating is Jackie, who loses her virginity under the influence of marijuana and throws up a career in medicine to be a drop-out relying on the charity of the Women's Centre.

The author was poetry editor for *Spare Rib* and is involved in running a feminist library. The history in her book is well researched and, in spite of the catchpenny sensationalism, it fills a gap in the ranks of fiction relevant to the Women's Movement.... Readers who enjoyed Zoë Fairbairns's last novel, *Benefits* ..., which was set in the future, will salute her versatility and professionalism. It is perhaps not her fault that the shoulder-to-shoulder march of feminism as depicted in this novel, with its automatic approval of such issues as abortion and its closing of ranks against men, ultimately appears an oddly pathetic victory.

> *S. M. Mowbray, in a review of "Stand We at Last," in* British Book News, *June, 1983, p. 389.*

James (Martin) Fenton

1949-

English poet and critic.

An accomplished and significant poet, Fenton writes in several distinct styles. His fascination with information and vocabulary has led him to write "found poetry," which John Bayley describes as "a static composition evolved out of large and yet delicate quantities of semi-quotation." Fenton has based found poems on various sources, including anthropology, science, and history, and even, in the case of "The Pitt-Rivers Museum, Oxford," on the contents of a museum. He also writes light verse: some of these poems are topical, such as "Letter to John Fuller," which satirizes A. Alvarez's criticism of poetry; others, such as "Kingfisher's Boxing Gloves," are nonsensical in the style of Lewis Carroll. In a third category are Fenton's analytical, political poems, many of which relate to war. Fenton's poetry reveals his proficiency in difficult and unusual English literary forms. For this reason, and because of his attention to detail and his creation of mysterious, imaginary landscapes, many critics compare Fenton with W. H. Auden, whom Fenton has acknowledged as a major influence.

Fenton's first literary success came at the age of nineteen, when he gained recognition for his sonnet sequence *Our Western Furniture* (1968), a satirical, anti-imperialist poem about Commodore Perry's mission to Japan. The poem was first published in pamphlet form and was later one of the most critically acclaimed poems included in Fenton's first full-length collection, *Terminal Moraine* (1972). *Terminal Moraine* was hailed by critics for its technical accomplishment, literary erudition, and intelligent treatment of serious subjects.

During the years between the publication of *Terminal Moraine* and Fenton's second major collection, *The Memory of War* (1982), Fenton worked as a journalist, traveling extensively in Indochina and in Germany. Some of the poems based on his experiences were published in various periodicals and in pamphlets entitled *A Vacant Possession* (1978), *German Requiem* (1981), and *Dead Soldiers* (1982). Shortly after returning to England, Fenton published *The Memory of War,* which includes poems from his entire career, and *Children in Exile* (1983), which contains eight new poems in addition to all of *The Memory of War*. Fenton is now the theater critic for London's *Sunday Times* and has published a collection of his reviews, *You Were Marvellous* (1983).

Fenton's work elicits warm admiration from critics, although early reviews noted that technical virtuosity sometimes dominates his poetry. Many critics see an improvement in Fenton's later work; in his war poems he communicates feelings of sorrow and desolation while still making the most of his gift for satire and language. Two of his most highly praised war poems, written in different styles, are "Dead Soldiers," a bitterly humorous poem which comments on the devastations of war by using images of a feast which takes place on a battlefield, and "Children in Exile," a serious, straightforward poem about Cambodian refugee children who cannot escape nightmares of the horrors of the Pol Pot regime. In Julian Symons's opinion, "Fenton's work, ironic, elegant, aware

of yet always a little detached from the suffering it deals with, is the truest social poetry of our time."

(See also *Contemporary Authors*, Vol. 102.)

JULIAN SYMONS

['**Our Western Furniture**', one of the poems in *Terminal Moraine*], is an astonishing piece of work. Fenton's theme is the commercial opening-up of Japan in the mid-nineteenth century by Commodore Perry, and he uses it to provide all sorts of brilliant pictures and to strike off a variety of attitudes. The sequence shows Japanese and American reactions to each other, Perry's dreams of the distant country after his return, his death, and in the final sonnet a non-moral reflection on history's contradictions. . . .

Such a writer gives the impression of being so accomplished that he has nothing to learn. It is true that with all this ingenuity and inventive power goes a certain quirkiness, a determination to have fun, which is exhilarating but has its dangers. A long poem called '**The Fruit-Grower in War-Time (and some of his enemies)**' uses passages from a book on fruit-growing to point the moral that the dusts or washes used to destroy bugs are also indirectly destructive of our own life-patterns, and that the larger implications of this are horrifying. . . .

Admiring the poem, one is still inclined to ask whether the same thing couldn't have been said more directly, and without so much quotation from *Tree Fruit Growing,* as one questions the dragging-in elsewhere of terms about fungi like 'a pezizaform hairy sporochodium'. But perhaps this is being a bit crabby—I suppose similar complaints might have been made about early Auden. The thing to emphasize is the real achievement of **'Our Western Furniture',** and the promise of development implicit in almost everything Fenton has written since then. (p. 139)

Julian Symons, ''Down to Earth,'' in London Magazine, *Vol. 12, No. 3, August-September, 1972, pp. 138-41.**

DOUGLAS DUNN

Fenton works for the front half of the *New Statesman,* and is said by the blurb to be a member of International Socialism. He has kept this from the part of him that writes poems; *Terminal Moraine* is uncommitted and affable.... On the evidence of a poem like **''The Kingfisher's Boxing Gloves'',** Mr Fenton seems to be a cross between a Parisian dandy and the heavyweight champion of Oxford. This poem has been praised in another paper for its obscurity. The poet notes for us that it has come ''from the French.'' It has in fact been rendered from Mr Fenton's French: the poem was written in that language and then brought back to English. Brilliant? Fatuous? The fatuousness of brilliance? I'm not sure which. There can be no doubt, however, about the poem's pleasing accuracies.... (pp. 59-60)

More satisfying is **''The Pitt-Rivers Museum, Oxford'',** a poem about ''the fabled lands where myths / Go when they die . . .'' or ''this boxroom of the forgotten or hardly possible.'' Fenton uses the grotesque or strange exhibits—a musical whip, a dowser's twig—as catalysts to his sense of humour; but the poem transforms the museum and its chaotic piles of souvenirs into a darker place—where ''The lonely and unpopular / Might find the landscapes of their childhood marked out. . . .'' The moral drama which a reader might experience in the poem—partly the result of cadence as well as imagery—is taken a step further:

> Go
> In groups to giggle at curious finds.
> But do not step into the kingdom of your promises
> To yourself, like a child entering the forbidden
> Woods of his lonely playtime:

That simile is used with mastery. It brings all the atmosphere built up throughout the poem suddenly to bear on the poem's true subject—self-delusion through imagination. A poem of this length on that theme would work hard to avoid being a moral tract. At an early age, Fenton already knows how to handle the standard but always difficult moral subjects with originality.

Fenton is clearly ''influenced'' by Auden, especially later Auden. Easily identifiable Auden touches can be seen in **''Pitt-Rivers Museum''**—rhythm, syntax, and, in **''South Parks Road'',** the shape of the stanza as well as some of its details.... He has immense potential, but the **''Open Letter to Richard Crossman''** in shaky *ottava rima* is an ominous sign; his talent seems to me the kind that could be swindled out of fulfilment by too much journalism, of which light verse can be a part. His effort to sound genial and wise makes him sound a thousand years old; and his displays of erudition, the cultural glee with which he seizes the recherché or historical, remove him almost as far as it is possible to go from the kind of subject he deals with interestingly in the *New Statesman*. But what he has written so far is enough to make **Terminal Moraine** one of the most interesting débuts for many years. (p. 60)

Douglas Dunn, ''To Still History,'' in Encounter, *Vol. XXXIX, No. 5, November, 1972, pp. 57-64.**

CRAIG RAINE

[In *A Vacant Possession,* Fenton's] starting point is Auden's statement: 'Present in every human being are two desires, a desire to know the truth about the primary world, the given world in which we are born, live, love, hate and die, and the desire to make new secondary worlds of our own or, if we cannot make them ourselves, to share in the secondary worlds of those who can.' Those who can, do; those who can't, leech. Fenton can. His fictional worlds impose themselves on us (and on him) as they might on the mind of a madman—which is why the poems are prefaced by an extract from *Rasselas* where the astronomer complains that he has suffered 'chimeras to prey upon me in secret'.

'Song', for instance, continues the nonsense mode of 'Lollipops of the Pomeranian Baroque' and 'The Kingfisher's Boxing Gloves' in his previous collection. It is a short humoresque that examines the night-life of slugs and spiders.... 'Song' is, however, distinguished from other nonsense poetry by the way in which it constantly flirts with meaning: we almost take it seriously because it almost takes itself seriously. The other poems, though very different in tone, are partly about the relationship of the purely imagined to the real. The last, 'In a Notebook', repeats the same description of a Vietnamese village during the war but offers two alternative endings, the first imagined, the second real. Here, the imagination is seen to be irresponsible. Elsewhere, it is compelling, inventive, a brilliant liar.

'Prison Island' is obviously a fiction, full of poignantly urgent political advice that has been superseded by time, yet delighting in its own dubious status. How can we be moved by the merely invented, it seems to ask. The text of the poem is a letter from a political prisoner on one of the Lipari islands off north Sicily to a friend on the mainland.... But if the poem is the letter, how can it include information about its fate after it was sent? This deliberately gives the fictional game away and allows Fenton his implicit question: how can we be troubled by a chimera? . . .

'A Vacant Possesion' begins once more with an empty house, but this time the poet is moving in, with bewildering imaginative speed. The furniture is, of course, purely mental, as the sudden time changes make clear.... Once again, though, we're convinced by the detail (a mixture of the ordinary and the bizarre) until our disbelief is quite suspended by Fenton's final trump: the narrator goes into his bedroom for something he's forgotten, then can't remember what it is. Given the poet's carte blanche to invent, what could be more convincing than this 'failure' to do so?

Craig Raine, ''Secondary Worlds,'' in New Statesman, *Vol. 96, Nos. 2492 & 2493, December 22 & 29, 1978, pp. 882-83.**

LAWRENCE SAIL

All five poems in James Fenton's *A Vacant Possession* show the expertise evident in his first collection, *Terminal Moraine*—but the mood is very different. There is a feeling of desolation, of loneliness and hurt, which is both moving and disturbing. Even the opening poem, "Song", the closest in spirit to *Terminal Moraine,* has an undertone of menace, and the path described in the final stanza offers little reassurance. . . . (p. 59)

It is the theme of friendship, with its obverse of loss and betrayal, which links these poems. Both the title poem and "Prison Island" depict situations haunted by unreality and inadequacy. "Nest of Vampires" suggests that even childhood, in retrospect, has forbidden mysteries whose solution could only be unpleasant. "In a Notebook" reinforces the twin trap of hollowness and encirclement implied in the pamphlet's title, by re-using lines from the first three stanzas to construct the fourth. The fifth stanza seems to close the circle almost completely, with its grim answer to the question asked at the end of "Song"—

And I'm afraid most of my friends are dead.

These are sombre poems, but they have a fine and honest intensity which commands respect. (pp. 59-60)

> *Lawrence Sail, in a review of "A Vacant Possession," in* Poetry Review, *Vol. 68, No. 4, January, 1979, pp. 59-60.*

PETER PORTER

[Fenton] projects force and conviction . . . , and has done so since his earliest poems appeared at the beginning of the Seventies. After 'Terminal Moraine' (1971), his poetic course has been chequered, but now he has swum into clear view with ["The Memory Of War"], a book made up of the strongest parts of his earlier work and several striking new poems of weight and length. . . . [It] is not too soon to hail his achievement and celebrate his voice.

What is he saying in his poems, or, put another way, what is the nature of the force inherent in his invention? The answer won't come pat. He is political in a sense, writing about war-devastated countries, such as Germany and Cambodia. He has taken over Auden's playful extensions of psychoanalysis and finds in social pictures maps of moral decrepitude ('The Pitt-Rivers Museum, Oxford'). He is master of the palimpsest, putting bits of scholarly arcana together, which he calls here 'Exempla,' and making elaborate collages, such as 'Chosun,' a masterpiece built up from bizarre detail taken from a nineteenth-century book on Korea. He is always brilliant when he writes Nonsense Verse. Each poem in the section 'The Empire of the Senseless' is beautifully poised. His light verse, represented by 'Letter to John Fuller,' deflates hysteria in the wittiest of numbers. Then there are his Horatian, discursive poems, which create imaginary landscapes of exile and loss, as in 'Prison Island' and 'A Vacant Possession.'

Reading Fenton *in toto* makes you appreciate the enormous importance of the arbitrary in art. Even the most telling detail has to submit to the gift of the maker: he brings it to life by choosing it and giving it neighbourhood. Our minds respond to the lapidarist in him, to the pleasure of this piece going there, and this detail set against that other. We test it on our ear and our feelings. Fenton is a magician-materialist—he assembles, he juxtaposes, and he makes art out of his chosen matter as a witch-doctor fashions fetishes. His assemblages bring with them tragedy, comedy, love of the world's variety, and the sadness of its moral blight.

> *Peter Porter, "Out of the Anteroom," in* The Observer, *July 18, 1982, p. 31.**

MICHAEL CARLSON

The impact of James Fenton's best poems comes from the surprise of encountering the unexpected within his otherwise careful formal strategies. This seeming contradiction is a two-edged sword, however, for in Fenton's poetry there is also a distance between the poet and the poem, which is created by artifice, and which robs his most accomplished verses of their effect.

The Memory of War begins with a sequence of poems titled 'A German Requiem'. . . . The poet is presented as the observer of decay, the chronicler of a process of fading. From this stance comes the poet's detachment, for though he is himself a builder, he is working in a style which has been subject to considerable decay; he uses this fact consciously in the echoes he evokes. It is a war with memory, as much as a memory of war.

This tradition which Fenton follows was once described by Donald Davie as being 'decadently subtle', tending to accept scenes or historical situations as givens. The poet fits experience into an accepted world-view, rather than forging his own outlook. Such verse is more at home with decay than exploration; each striking image stands out against a reflective background, in which the intuitive collides with the academic.

In 'Dead Soldiers', the spiritual centrepiece of this book, Fenton superbly portrays the insanity of war through the use of images that are chillingly out of place. But, as if to soften that assault on the reader, the poem is given an historical setting that makes the unique situation into an historical given. The poem is further distanced by the use of a journalist narrator whose detachment for the excesses of Prince Chantaraingsey renders further images anecdotal. The poem emerges with the quality of observations left to percolate on the back burner of the poet's imagination, where, steeped in his skill, they have slid, inevitably Hobbesian, into their own state of decay.

Some poems seek different solutions. 'A Vacant Possession' shows form following function in a stately decline . . . while 'The Skip' uses humour to cover similar ground more effectively. But the danger of distancing becomes more obvious in Fenton's nonsense verse; written with such detachment it resembles an exercise too easy to be taxing.

The best example of the problem comes in the section entitled 'Exempla', which includes a series of found poems, mostly unearthed in the Pitt-Rivers Museum. At first, it seemed a piece of formal daring: in a slim collection gathered over 14 years, the inclusion of a large number of found poems was a leap away from the formal constraints which appeared to be holding Fenton's energy back. But reading the found poems, one wonders eventually whether they too have been transformed into decay, or whether other events, like the war in Cambodia, have not been transformed into the poetic equivalent of index cards in the Pitt-Rivers. (pp. 25-6)

Fenton's poems are immaculately crafted, but the skill of 'The Fruit-Grower in Wartime' is, in the end, merely wry, and

Fenton perhaps could be compared to one of his own found poems, **'What the Frog's Eye tells the Frog's Brain':**

> He does remember a living
> Thing provided it stays within
> His field of vision and he is not distracted.

Poets of James Fenton's talents should be more distracted. (p. 26)

Michael Carlson, "The War of Memory," in The Spectator, Vol. 249, No. 8048, October 9, 1982, pp. 25-6.*

JONATHAN RABAN

Fenton is as clever and ingenious as anyone around, but he is alone among his contemporaries in having a great deal to write *about*. He has all the civil virtues, the wit, the technical cunning, the seductive fluency but he has subordinated them to something much larger and more powerful; a vision of recent history, and his own personal place in it, that is at once intellectually demanding, morally and politically complex, wide in its human sympathies, and shot through with a sane and sober humour. Fenton's poems have a very high relative density. . . .

[The] poems in **"The Memory of War"** date back as far as his student days at Oxford. . . . His work then was sprightly, cultivated, domestic; thoroughly Oxonian in manner, even down to its nervous brushes with International Socialism. A jaunty air of fun-over-the-teacakes clings to Fenton's early poems. . . . Fenton was entertainingly tough on the notion that poetry had any pressing business with madness and despair; certainly his own verse at the time, with its nursery and suburban references, its elegant metrics, was far too well-bred to flirt with such extremities.

Yet, ironically, his poetry really came alive after he had himself gone to an historical extremity. . . . He left literary London to set up house in Cambodia. Journalism paid his fare (I assume), but Fenton apparently lived through that war more as a local inhabitant than as a foreign correspondent. His Cambodian poems, at least, have no truck with the shallow detachment of reportage. They are resonant with articulate bewilderment and sorrow—not "war poems" so much as poems that find, in the particular savaged landscape of Cambodia, sufficient pain, destruction and loss to make themselves at home. The gentle lullaby rhythms of **"In a Notebook"**, with its lovely colouring-in of domestic life in Fenton's riverbank village, suddenly stiffen in the last stanza. . . . The poem's raw material is an enormity. Fenton's response is to honour it with all the technical finesse at his command—with metrical poise, an unruffled verbal exactness, the care of the instinctive miniaturist. . . .

With its rapidly shifting locations and its large family of characters, **"A German Requiem"** creates the illusion of extraordinary space and inclusiveness within a very tight form. In fewer than 80 lines, Fenton manages to build something that feels cathedral-like, vaulted, tall, full of echoes and dark cloisters of implication.

Much of Fenton's strength comes from this ability to conjure what is tacit and make it fill the spaces between the lines. His longer poems are collages of crystallised detail, stories in solution. Each poem is like a Henry James novella recast as a puzzle, with only the most shimmering incidents left standing. The pleasure is that, like all good puzzles, they do eventually

unravel: on second or third reading, everything suddenly slides into sharp focus. . . .

The glancing, elegantly fractured form that Fenton's poems take, with their ellipses and sudden electric connections, answers to a view of life that is stylish, wary, provisional, always intelligent, never breast-beating.

Jonathan Raban, "Visions of Historical Extremity," in The Times, London, October 10, 1982, p. 45.

HILARY SPURLING

The best British theatre critics have generally been, like James Fenton (who [in **You Were Marvellous**] is clearly offering himself for judgment only by the highest standards), provocative, opinionated and bookish rather than theatrical by training. But Fenton's peers in the past—Cibber, Hazlitt, Shaw, Beerbohm, Tynan—have also nearly all been wits, smooth, sharp, cutting, often killingly funny and, to a man, dab hands at description.

Fenton belongs to an altogether more puritanical tradition. Evocation is not his forte. His verdicts, often just and sometimes memorably offensive . . . are always magisterial. His style is high-minded, heavy-handed and, when it comes to performance, direction and design, so uninformative that his column reads at times like an end-of-term report. . . .

For Fenton, the theatre holds nothing in the way of fashion or frivolity, little passion and absolutely no sensuous appeal. . . .

But the great virtue of this eccentric critic is precisely the seriousness with which he takes himself, his trade and the theatre which it is his delight to study and evaluate. He thinks, reads, compares, weighs and judges, in a word he ponders; and, in an age so conditioned by and to snap judgments, ponderousness has its points. Fenton brings a clear and concentrated intelligence to bear on matters not usually thought worth assessing at this level. Above all, he minds about the theatre so much, with such energy and earnestness, that it seems ungrateful to ask for a touch of something worldlier as well; or, as Fenton says himself, 'once again, the *Observer* is demanding the impossible.'

Hilary Spurling, "A Serious Business," in The Observer, July 31, 1983, p. 25.

ARNOLD WESKER

[*This essay was originally published in* The Listener, *August 25, 1983.*]

James Fenton's nature doesn't appear to be vindictive, though wiser playwrights would run miles from such a risk as I now take. I declare my interest: two of my plays have been the subject of his comments. Those for *Caritas* I'd heard were not favourable and did not read. The practice of the craft is pain enough without subjecting oneself to the cruel ephemerality of a reviewer's opinion. When I've written this I'll read it and add a postscript. Those for *Annie Wobbler*, my latest play, were generous.

Criticism is crucial to democracy. So crucial it must be checked and weighed and constantly open to counter-criticism. Assembling one's critical opinions after only four years may seem like immodest haste to claim posterity's attention, but four years *is* four years. The problem of evaluating theatre is that no one dares make, or quite knows, the distinction between the lovely lady, showbiz, and the embarrassing slut, art. Criteria become jumbled. 'You were marvellous' is a showbiz expression. It does not reflect Mr Fenton's serious criteria. Where are we?

The cosy argument is that artists hate criticism. Not true. We are relentlessly self-critical, and most of us have at least one acerbic friend whose criticism is invaluable. Criticism from colleagues involved in theatre is constant up to and beyond first nights. The Penguin editions of my plays are full of changes.

Newspaper reviews, on the other hand, render the artist victim of a dangerous deception for which I know no remedy. It can only be identified. The nature of the deception is this: reviews are merely individual opinions whose importance is magnified out of proportion by print, which has magic properties and carries awesome authority. Like a teacher's report. Teachers must always be right, they've been appointed. The child can only ever be wrong.

Fenton, in his postscript [to *You Were Marvellous*,] honestly concedes the possibility of being, and claims the right, to be wrong. It's disarming. But jejune. 'We must be true to our anger, true to our enthusiasms, true to our excitement, true to our boredom,' he insists. It can only ever be a half-truth. Behind his anger, his enthusiasm, his etc., etc. is the *Sunday Times*. We are not pitted only against him but against an institution. Reviewers like to delude themselves they have a public who trusts them. But did anyone change papers because Fenton took over from Levin?

There's more to the deception. Aware of it or not, the public regards artistic activity as presumptuous. Unfavourable reviews play to their gallery. Artists acclaimed by time are safer. Living ones work in a continual state of original sin from which only a good review can redeem them. They're a kind of criminal; the public must be protected. The reviewer is St George, print his sword! The reader, who thrills to a good thrashing, is on his side before he begins.

If artists feel a depressing sense of injustice confronted by an adverse review, it's not because they've been criticised but because they've been criticised humiliatingly in public by an overwhelming institution whose sleight of hand appears to deal, omnipotently, in 'the truth', and against which they have no appeal.

A story illustrates my point. [My play] *Caritas* had just opened. At a friend's house I met an elderly, cultured woman I'd met before. We usually discussed theatre and she'd confide how much she admired my work. I didn't need to ask had she seen my new play, I *told* her she hadn't. 'It was because of Fenton's bad review wasn't it?' I added. She apologetically confessed I was right. 'But why,' I asked her in despair, 'why did you trust him rather than me?' I reminded her how often she'd told me she'd admired my work. 'Why didn't you give me the benefit of the doubt after 25 years of writing?' She mumbled something about 'he wrote in such a way that I felt it wasn't for me'. She could have had no idea of the helpless, dispirited feeling with which she left me.

Two problems attend the reading of an entire collection of theatre reviews in one go. First, you need to have seen the productions to measure the opinions offered. Criticism of a play frequently bears little relationship to the experience of it. Second, to have the critical note ringing in your head without the pauses of living, loving and laughing is a kind of torture, like the water-drip. Reading only one a week, it's possible to

recognise Mr Fenton as a normal, intelligent human being with opinions like other normal, intelligent human beings, sometimes persuasive, witty, well written, other times not. He's informed, seems to take more trouble than duty calls for, has winning breathless enthusiasms, and pure hatreds like other normal, intelligent human beings.

And this is why we despair. It *is* just another opinion; as intelligent or flawed as those of countless acquaintances. The sense of injustice comes from knowing one is condemned not on merit but by the accident of A's appointment rather than B's.

In my opinion Fenton missed the intention of *Amadeus* which, as a self-confession of mediocrity and a hymn of praise to genius, makes it a far more interesting and moving work than he perceived. (And I write as someone who doesn't normally respond to Shaffer's kind of theatre.) He was right to applaud *Duet For One,* and to come away depressed from *Cats;* but he was uninteresting about Barton's distressing *Merchant of Venice,* and did not achieve in his review of *The Greeks* what his introduction claims was his intention: a record of the production's details. I disagree with this opinion, agree with the other. So what?

Few who work in the theatre rate a reviewer's opinions. They care only to survive the new round of unsubstantiated, shorthand comment rushed and subbed and laced with human fallibility. When asked whether they are pleased with good reviews, they reply 'Relieved, rather.' They've lived with a production at such proximity that they know it for its *real* strengths and weaknesses. Reviewers confuse sentiment for sentimentality, and declare something doesn't work when they mean they don't share its intellectual or moral assumptions. Or don't understand them! They miss subtleties of structure, speech rhythms, textural patterns, ironies, echoes, links, the way actors and directors can either betray a text's intentions or, through cunning directoral manipulation, give text a substance it doesn't possess. Theatre people can damn and praise their work far more accurately.

Mr Fenton declares: Critics unite! 'In order to begin work, we need the right to be wrong, the right to be unfair, the right to be overenthusiastic.' But at whose expense? And what curious reasoning claims 'the right to be unfair'? It rings bravely but I hear the tiniest crackle of sententiousness. A year to write a play, a year before it's produced, then those unassailable reviews claiming the right to be unfair. Two years of work wiped out, two years more to wait. Such considerations cannot be dismissed as 'tough luck—that's showbiz.' Livelihoods, cracked confidence, pain are involved. Each time a new, young critic takes over we brace ourselves fearing he is going to flex his muscles on us, beat a drum calling the crowds' attention— 'Over here! over here!' Mr Fenton must be aware he's doing more than simply exercising his right to be wrong when he writes of Shaffer: 'Mozart is depicted in an offensive and banal way because he is seen through the eyes of a very, very bad dramatist indeed—perhaps the worst serious English dramatist since John Drinkwater.' Could he cross his heart and deny that one tiny part of his ego rubbed its hands together, smacked its lips and murmured: 'That'll make 'em sit up'? *Postscript.* I've read Mr Fenton's review of *Caritas.* It is a very illuminating case history of misreading. I have a theory that if you tell people what they're reading, *that* is what they'll read. Tell them here is a play by Wesker and they'll find what they *imagine* is to be expected of Wesker. I recently wrote a bawdy comedy which was sent to managements as the work of a

Cambridge professor of philosophy. Responses reflected what they'd been told. Similarly Mr Fenton seems to have an image of me as a certain kind of writer.

Caritas is about an anchoress who asks to be immured, hoping for a pure life of divine revelation. She finds she has no vocation for such a life, begs release, is denied it and goes mad. 'Caritas is extremely badly written,' says Mr Fenton. I say it is extremely well written. More, in view of the misery of young people inextricably attached to fanatical notions which have imprisoned them, I think *Caritas* as a metaphor for self-delusion is also an important play. Who is to be believed? After a quarter of a century writing plays (directing and viewing them too) it is just possible I knew at least as much about it as Mr Fenton. How could readers decide? His review acted as a kind of censor to the play. Criticism of critics reads sourly. Self-defence involves immodest assertions. Catch 22.

Asking 'What was Mr Wesker after?' Fenton, unwaveringly confident—and why shouldn't he be? there was no one to challenge him—replies: 'The answer is only too clear from the text . . . an image of repression.' He *expected* me to be writing about repression and that's what he saw. The text is only too clearly about a girl who *asks* to be immured, not who is *forced* into it. The image is of self-imprisonment. Setting it against the background of the Peasants' Revolt I was choosing not another 'image of repression' but, again as the text clearly states, another image of self-destruction. Both the anchoress and the peasants sought worthy ends, both betrayed those ends through excess, dogma, fanaticism. Mr Fenton, still blinded by his preconceptions, suggested I changed the setting from Surrey to Norfolk in search of 'grittiness'. Readers cannot be expected to know my connections with Norfolk through marriage, *Roots, The Wedding Feast;* a responsible theatre critic should. I knew one dialect, not the other. 'He has obviously done very little research.' Why does Mr Fenton assume so? He doesn't know me. He didn't ask. In fact I researched it in great detail, as my many notebooks testify. All art is selection. He means he doesn't respond to what I decided to put in and leave out. He should say so. Insults diminish the value of his opinions. . . . This is not only a defence of my play; such a case-history enables us to evaluate Mr Fenton's reliability as a reviewer. Other playwrights could no doubt put similar cases.

Dear Mr Fenton, I concede your right to be wrong (though not unfair, come, come, sir!), even to be paid for it. But be aware others pay a hidden price for your luxury. The life of a play is postponed, a bank overdraft grows, time is wasted recovering. *Caritas* is one of my most original plays. Years must pass before it can be reevaluated. Many of us work hard, seriously, responsibly. We take risks, we treat our audiences intelligently, prod their laughter at rich rather than facile levels. These reviews, whatever the lapses, reveal a responsible intelligence that we need to encourage us to continue taking risks. Don't go into competition with us or demean yourself with pyrotechnic insults. And remember, *we* have to continue working after *you* have become bored with our art . . . and have moved on to other interests.

Arnold Wesker, "'Individual Opinions Magnified Out of Proportion by Print','' in his Distinctions, Jonathan Cape Ltd., 1985.

JULIAN SYMONS

There are three poetic Fentons, two of comparatively minor interest. One offers botanical, psychological or medical "exempla" taken from books or other printed work as poems, rather in the whimsical manner of the surrealists exhibiting "found objects" as art. Another produces light verse that is always lively, sometimes funny, and often marked by a deadly topicality. . . .The third Fenton, however, has fulfilled what **"Our Western Furniture"** promised, in a dozen magnificent poems. It is notable that almost all of them have their origins in his Cambodian and German experiences.

The title poem of [**"Children in Exile"**] is one of them. In elegant, almost casual four-line stanzas Fenton tells the story of four child refugees from Pol Pot's Cambodia. . . .

"Children in Exile" is not exactly a narrative poem, but it "tells a story" in a way that is so unfashionable to-day as to be called bold. The directness and simplicity of speech, the rhetoric firmly under control, are necessary to the story's telling, but Fenton has other styles equally effective, like the linked prose passages of despair and destruction in **"Lines for Translation into Any Language"** or the unstressed symbolism of **"Wind"**. . . .

"Dead Soldiers" and **"In a Notebook"**, with its various images of peace destroyed by war . . . are particularly fine. In such poems Fenton fulfils what the socially conscious poets of the Thirties intended but hardly ever achieved. They wanted to write about war but not to experience it, and ended up producing poems chiefly about their own feelings. Fenton's work, ironic, elegant, aware of yet always a little detached from the suffering it deals with, is the truest social poetry of our time.

Julian Symons, "A War Poet of Our Time," in The Times, *London, November 20, 1983, p. 38.*

STEPHEN SPENDER

James Fenton is a brilliant poet of great technical virtuosity. His poetry is plunged in the real life of the kind that we see on television screens, read about in the newspapers, and (a happy few) discuss at High Tables. In the first two sections of [*Children in Exile: Poems 1965-1984*] there are poems about recollections of the bombing of Germany in 1944 and 1945, about Vietnamese refugees haunted by terrible memories of their bombings, about his own experiences as a political journalist visiting Vietnam in 1972-73. After these poems of great immediacy, there are poems in the manner of Auden's poetry of psychoanalytic parables mixed with an ominous sense of the neurotic forces moving thorugh contemporary history. In this section Fenton, like Auden, seems to be drawing strongly on memories of his own Anglican upbringing in Yorkshire. . . .

In this phase of Fenton's poetry, as with Auden's in the 1930s, one feels, at one and the same time, that the poet has created within the poem a mysterious world with mysterious laws which work by their own logic, and yet also that there is a need of some ideology or system of belief which would make everything clear. One feels, too, that there are occasional references to some private area of the poet's life—perhaps to childhood memories—which are withheld from the reader. The feeling of Auden in some of these poems is so strong that it seems more like identification with his work than imitation of it. But because Fenton, as it were, takes over Auden, it also becomes Fenton's own world. . . .

Some of Fenton's greatest successes belong to this section of the book—the evocative poem **"Wind"** and the wonderfully sustained **"Chosun,"** a poem about the relationship of an elaborate mythology or theology to the lives of Koreans. This, incidentally, is an example of one aspect of Fenton's poetry: that it is packed with information, anthropological, scientific, and political. Fenton is also obsessed with vocabularies, particularly the scientific, which in his fifth section, called "Exempla," he turns into a kind of elaborate parody of scientific definitions—serious parody, if you like, because he shows how admirable, if absurd, they are. . . . (p. 31)

I want to emphasize the lightness, fun, and gaiety of some of Fenton's work, because without the wit, his most serious poems might seem weighed down by their subject matter, which is intensely political—not so much in being partisan or ideological, as in being saturated in the *terribilita* of the contemporary political world scene. Here he cetainly parts company with Auden, for Auden renounced the whole connection of his poetry with the world produced by politics. He did so, I think . . . because he thought that it was indecent for the inner dream worlds created by poetic imagination to take as subject matter the outer world of a nightmare reality which results from modern power politics. . . .

Fenton, I am sure, is fully aware of these objections to writing poetry about the horrors which fill newspapers and television screens. It is no reflection on him to say that he comes to the reader armed with credentials and a deliberate strategy. The credentials are that he has been involved as a journalist in the places he is writing about. And he is honest in writing poetry in which the poet is journalist, reporter—simply that, and not one who parades his poetic heart on his sleeve. . . .

In these war poems Fenton does not adopt a poetic persona, but that of someone whom he is addressing who is not a poet but who may be taken to share Fenton's view about the matters discussed. The most successful poem in the book is that which provides its title, **"Children in Exile."** This is dedicated to

friends of his living in the Italian countryside near Florence— an American publisher and his wife—who have adopted a Cambodian family with its four children, rescued from being the victims of Pol Pot. . . .

The real horror of Cambodia is filtered through the realistic dreams of the children who have been saturated in that horror. In **"A German Requiem,"** a sequence of poems about a bombed German town, or towns, Fenton writes about the inability of the people living there to remember the horrors. Forgetting becomes a kind of diminution and magnification of them, both at the same time. (p. 32)

Here Fenton's strategy for imagining our terrible contemporary realities in poetry is rather like that of a photographer who photographs a scene, placing two or three filters across the lens in order to concentrate the scene by giving it some hallucinatory quality.

In several of these poems, Fenton is, then, clearly political. Clearly, too, he is not detached. He has political sympathies. In his poems about Germany and Cambodia, one feels these sympathies—liberal and socialist, I should guess—but at the same time a kind of absence of any ideology where, with Brecht, there would be communism, with Auden, Christianity. That there is this absence, especially of communism, probably throws some light on our time. Surely in the 1930s, Fenton would have been writing the kind of poetry that John Cornford (or even Auden) attempted to write, about the Marxist historical-materialist interpretation of contemporary history. One feels that in the end—perhaps because it has become impossible for someone like him to hold such a belief today—Fenton is driven back onto his own humanity. (pp. 32-3)

Stephen Spender, "Politics and a Poet," in The New Republic, *Vol. 190, No. 19, May 14, 1984, pp. 31-3.*

Dario Fo

1929-

Italian dramatist.

Fo is one of the world's most widely produced contemporary playwrights. Critic Suzanne Cowan notes, "To give a full account of Dario Fo's theatrical career would really be tantamount to writing a history of post-war Italy, because his work can only be understood as a continuous, uniquely creative response to the major social and political development of the past thirty years." Politically, Fo is a proponent of proletarian revolution, but he eventually broke with the Communist party when he thought that its aims were diverging from the best interests of the working class. Artistically, he advocates taking advantage of Italy's heritage of popular theater, including in his works elements of the circus, the minstrel show, puppetry, mime, regional dialects, and *commedia dell'arte*. Richard Sogliuzzo explains how these two concerns work together: "In Fo's theatre, the medium is undoubtedly the message: a proletarian revolution to be accomplished by utilizing theatrical traditions born of the people." Fo and Franca Rame, his actress-wife and sometime-collaborator, have toured their plays extensively in Europe, usually playing the lead roles themselves. However, the strong political nature of their work has until recently prevented their plays from being produced in England and the United States. The couple have twice been denied permission to enter the United States.

The zany humor for which Fo is noted has always been integral to his work, but his political commitment developed gradually. Shortly after the end of World War II, Fo began performing original one-man comedy shows in nightclubs and other commercial theaters. His first nationally known production, *Il dito nell'occhio* (1953), attempted to convey Marxist ideas, but they were mostly obscured by the visually spectacular, circus-like aspects of the show. When Compagnia Dario Fo-Franca Rame, the Fos's first touring company, was established in 1958, social satire was their forte; only later did they turn to political satire. During this period, the couple also performed on television in a popular comedy revue, but they were eventually censored for being too vocal about their leftist political views. Around the same time, Fo produced *La signora e da buttare* (1967), which was a turning point in his career. His first explicitly political play and his last to be produced in a commercial theater for many years, *La signora e da buttare* has a circus setting, a frenetic pace, and many gesture and movement gags. The title means "the lady is for the scrapheap" and refers to the circus owner, who represents American imperialism and capitalism.

In response to the turbulent political and social climate of the 1960s, Fo vowed to "stop playing the jester of the bourgeoisie." He renounced commercial theater entirely in favor of a theater which could act as an instrument of social change. In 1968 he and Rame formed another touring troupe, Nuova Scena, under the auspices of the Italian Communist Party. To appeal to his new proletarian audience, Fo simplified his works. Many were allegories which used puppets to represent political movements. In *Grande pantomima con bandiere e pupazzi piccoli e medi* (1968), a satire of Italian history during the twenty-five years following World War II, a beautiful woman, rep-

© Jerry Bauer

resenting capitalism, is born out of a giant monster puppet, fascism, and seduces a giant dragon puppet, communism. Although Fo was working with the Communist party at this time, he did not hesitate to criticize its bureaucratic structure and its tendency towards reform rather than revolution. The Party withdrew its support from Nuova Scena, and in 1970 Fo and Rame formed a new company, Il Collettivo Teatrale La Comune.

La Comune's goal was to raise the consciousness of the working classes, to encourage them to overthrow the bourgeois state, and to bring about a socialist government. Plays from the La Comune period tended to be highly topical. For instance, *Guerra di popolo in Cile* (1973) is about the people's war in Chile, *Fedayn* (1971) concerns the Palestinian problem, and *Morte accidentale di un anarchico* (1970; *Accidental Death of an Anarchist*) is a farcical rendering of the cover-up which followed the police murder of anarchist Giuseppe Pinelli. Because of their topicality, most of the La Comune plays were short-lived, but *Accidental Death of an Anarchist* has achieved sustained and international popularity. It is Fo's first play to receive a professional production both in England and in the United States. Because La Comune performances relied extensively on improvisation and audience interaction, published texts of these plays tend to be unrepresentative of what is seen onstage.

In recent years, Fo has collaborated more extensively with Rame and produced strongly feminist plays. These works concentrate on family and male-female relationships yet retain their political context. The couple's most successful collaboration has been *Tutta casa, letto e chiesa*, a series of eight monologues, some serious and some humorous, which focus on the position of women in society. The pieces have been performed in the United States and England in various combinations and under such various titles as *One Woman Plays* (1981), *Female Parts* (1982), and *Orgasmo Adulto Escapes from the Zoo* (1983). Another Fo comedy which is both domestic and political, *No se paga! No se paga!* (1974; *We Won't Pay! We Won't Pay!*), is about housewives who organize a supermarket boycott to protest exorbitant prices. In a 1984 interview, Fo compared the male-female relationship in the family unit with the bourgeois-proletariat relationship in society. He explained the personal nature of the later plays by saying, "In the face of the failure of revolutionary ideals, the basic problem is how people relate to one another."

GEOFF BROWN

[*Accidental Death of an Anarchist* produces] situations which are half farce, half nightmare and completely deplorable. The play is steeped in fact, drawing on the death of railway worker Giuseppe Pinelli, a noted anarchist, who was arrested for his part in the bomb massacre at the Agricultural Bank (14 dead) and later 'fell' (ie was pushed) to his death from the fourth floor of the Milan police headquarters on 16 December 1969.

However, Fo's play . . . also demonstrates that Italy is the home of *Commedia dell'arte,* that ancient popular brand of theatre with its broad physical clowning revolving around the activities of well-known stereotypes, from the lustful greedy old man Pantalone to the darting acrobatic servant Harlequin. And it was a shrewd move of Dario Fo . . . to apply the genre to contemporary political ends. On the one hand, it gives the mass audience something to latch on to and enjoy apart from the slogans and dialectic: characters who collide with each other, get their fingers trapped in filing cabinets or assume silly disguises with wooden legs, wooden hands and joke cigars, are funny whatever their political stance. On the other hand—and this may not be intentional—the framework of popular farce makes political theatre's natural, yet wearying, insistence that characters adopt fixed, embattled positions seem like an essential comic strategy. Hectoring, humourless political theatre may be a joy to the converted (and anathema to those converted in the opposite direction), but it can be simply annoying to the millions of confused waverers.

It would be difficult to be very annoyed here. . . . This is obviously planned as a show with spirit rather than polish. And the unfolding plot has its own powerful fascination—with the Maniac impersonating a legal luminary sent to investigate the police reports of 'accidental death' and letting the cock-eyed band of inspectors and superintendents condemn themselves by their own tangled words and actions. (pp. 30-1)

> *Geoff Brown, in a review of "Accidental Death of an Anarchist," in* Plays and Players, *Vol. 26, No. 8, May, 1979, pp. 30-1.*

J. W. LAMBERT

I went off to see *Einer fur alle, alle fur einen* . . . with no great hopes. . . . But Signor Fo, however dubious his political com-

mon-sense has been in the past, tells us in the programme that he soon grasped the fact that documentary and . . . didactic plays were death to real theatre. And this piece is a splendid example of how to make political theatre enjoyable. It deals with the Italian scene between 1911 and the outbreak, as one may call it, of Fascism. The stage casually embodies a lorry taking away those arrested, a police station replete with easily distracted police chief, a dress-shop, and a modest home. It shows us the petty authorities of the old regime turning into the petty but lethal tyrants of the new. But it does all this with an exuberant mixture of fun and good-humoured satire. The shade of Beattie Bryant hovers over the young bride getting a dressmaker's assistant to take her through a Communist catechism as she tries on her wedding-dress; joyful bursts of rum-ti-tum, and launchings into 'O sole mio', send up Italian triviality with infectious glee; the example of Brecht and Weill injects a few pointed and extremely tuneful ballads. . . . At times affectionate, at times bitter, often lurching into excellent farce (I hope I may be allowed to quote my favourite line, when the hero is being disguised as a widow—'Watch it girls, his arse is his Achilles heel'), the piece is never, never sour.

> *J. W. Lambert, "Globetrotting Theatre," in* Drama, *No. 133, Summer, 1979, pp. 12-20.**

JOHN LAHR

Dario Fo, the Italian comedian and playwright, whose hilarious *Accidental Death of an Anarchist* . . . savages the brutality of the Italian police, uses the clown's hijinks to do gorgeous battle with officialdom. . . .

As a clown and an activist, Fo has discovered in farce a strategy for emotionally detaching both audience and actors from the tragic issues his plays debate. "In farce," he says, "you have the possibility of going beyond the character. You can comment on the situation while you're in it." Political laughter wants to disenchant; and farce's artificiality keeps the audience from being spellbound. The play becomes not only a criticism of life but of theatre.

Fo introduces a maniac into police headquarters and lets him turn the tables on authority to put the story right while spelling out the establishment's "strategy of tension." True to archetype, this prankster is a man of many names and disguises, a poltergeist in baggy pants ("I can injure without visible signs"), who frees his comrades by throwing their police files out of the window.

The maniac is a whirlwind of comic invention. He shares with all tricksters the seeming ability to detach parts of his body from himself. As in Joe Orton's *Loot* (Fo's brother in mayhem), the maniac's false eye falls out and they have great fun finding it. And as if to clinch the purity of Fo's comic impulse, the clown's emblem—his vestigial phallus—miraculously appears in the form of the maniac's wooden leg, at once a literal and figurative "third leg" which is always banging up against the detectives. . . .

With sight gags, pratfalls and the occasional boffo burlesque exchange ("I gave three lectures a week. Roman Law. Ecclesiastical Law. Denis Law . . ."), the maniac gets down to the trenchant business of picking the police testimony to pieces. He impersonates a judge trying to get the record straight; but the real court of appeal is laughter. It's a good test for the clown's malicious appetite for revenge. By the end of act one, the police, terrified of losing their jobs, have come up with three different versions of events, each more preposterous than the next. (p. 559)

It's wonderful mayhem, with the maniac in complete control of his bumptious mischief. He tells them "to show a human heart behind the tangle of lies you have left in your wake." He forces them to sing, and they must sing a song of anarchy ("We have but one thought, revolution is in our hearts"). It's a noisy, rousing song; and the first act ends with its delicious irony. As Shaw wrote in *Misalliance:* "Anarchism is a game at which the police can beat you."

Political theatre and the clown's protean personality find their apotheosis in Fo's shrewd finale. Amid the tumult of confused identities, violent chases and biting one-liners. Fo is debating all sides of the question of reform or revolution. (pp. 559-60)

The clown may not be the right person to follow to the barricades, but no one has a better strategy for making subversive ideas irresistible on stage. The clown substitutes playfulness for polemic, imagination for gullibility. Although the West End venue slightly mutes its high spirits, *Accidental Death of an Anarchist* is a loud, vulgar, kinetic, scurrilous, smart, sensational show. In other words, everything theatre should be. (p. 560)

> *John Lahr, "A Playful Polemic," in* New Society, *Vol. 51, No. 910, March 13, 1980, pp. 559-60.*

BENEDICT NIGHTINGALE

[In *Accidental Death of an Anarchist*] Fo's method is to manoeuvre the police into becoming increasingly desperate with their own verbal petards. Was the suspect so badly bullied that he committed suicide? No, he wasn't, it was a very good humoured interrogation. Did he jump out of the window from sheer happiness, then? Well, no, not exactly.... So the questions continue until the truth is blurted out: Pinelli was pushed.

It is a sombre conclusion. An atrocity has been committed, and one that we ourselves can hardly dismiss as a hot-blooded Mediterranean aberration.... And yet the inquisitor is a blend of trickster and clown, whose iconoclastic glee and eccentric camouflage (at one point, believe it or not, Long John Silver minus only the parrot) both proclaim his origins as the *zanni* of Italian commedia dell'arte; the police are strutting or tumbling grotesques, a ripe bunch of gorgonzola Cheeses; and one of the play's many comic ideas actually turns out to be a variation on the *Python* sketch about the killer joke, which it is death to hear....

In short, it's funny, but always purposefully so. We listen to the cross-examination of Fo's villains for some of the same reasons we listen to the arguments in a Stoppard play, because we are ribbed and jollied into doing so; and the cross-examination has real content. However, there's also a danger that such a style may disguise the nature of the pill it's sugaring, and perhaps this happens at the play's end. I, for one, don't like someone manipulating me into the position of cheerfully consenting to the murder of my social enemies, even if those enemies (as a wittily horrific dénouement makes clear) would cheerfully murder you and me, should we get to know too much about them. Dario Fo is said to be distressed by some of the recent actions of the Red Brigades, and would not, I am sure, give his personal imprimatur to the assassination of Aldo Moro. But it may be that a play like this, tolerating and even encouraging political violence, yet extracting the nastiness

from it by a burlesque presentation, makes such events marginally more likely.

> *Benedict Nightingale, "Calls-to-Arms," in* New Statesman, *Vol. 99, No. 2556, March 14, 1980, p. 405.**

MEL GUSSOW

If you are deflated by thoughts of inflation, if you have ever looked at the price of food in the supermarket or glanced at a menu in a restaurant and decided that we had suddenly moved to a different, less rewarding monetary system, then Dario Fo's **"We Won't Pay! We Won't Pay!"** should fill you with laughs of recognition.... Mr. Fo's manic farce should be obligatory viewing for anyone battling, i.e., succumbing to, the high cost of living.

For the purposes of his incautious cautionary tale, Mr. Fo, who is Italy's most celebrated and most controversial contemporary playwright, takes a typical Italian family, typical, that is, from Vittorio de Sica movies. Giovanni works, Antonia scrimps. He shouts, she slaves. She lives to cook his dinner and he carries chauvinism as a tattoo on his heart.

One day Antonia and her sister housewives, fed up with rising prices, stage an impromptu strike in a supermarket....

What ensues is a madcap travesty of kitchen-sink comedies, which also manages to shoot satiric darts at the police, government bureaucracy, unions, the welfare state and masculine domestic privilege. **"We Won't Pay!"** has the outrage of that moment in the movie "Network" when Peter Finch shouted, "I'm mad as hell, and I'm not going to take this anymore."

Such is the impact of Mr. Fo's humor that he seduces an audience into responding to the most indelicate comic situations. Try to keep from smiling when Giovanni tells the crazy tragic story of a dog with an electronic hearing aid. The performance I attended was filled with older matinee ladies. Many of them seemed about to capsize with laughter, with only the merest squirm of embarrassment at Mr. Fo's occasional spiciness. The fact is that he tickled them in their pocketbooks....

In common with Mr. Fo's **"Accidental Death of an Anarchist,"** a long-running London comedy hit about the violence that government can inflict on concerned citizens, **"We Won't Pay!"** is the work of a social reformer with a fractured funnybone.

> *Mel Gussow, "'We Won't Pay!' Comedy on Consumerism," in* The New York Times, *December 18, 1980, p. C30.*

VARIETY

A play about inflation could hardly be more topical, and although it was written in 1974, Dario Fo's Italian farce, **"We Won't Pay! We Won't Pay!,"** is as up-to-date as the morning paper's supermarket ads. There's an abundance of laughs in this leftwing blast at economic imbalance....

"We Won't Pay!" shows a masterful hand at farcical plotting and comic characterization, plus a distinctively European political underpinning. Few American playwrights have much overt commitment to any political viewpoint, left, right or center, so Fo's radical anticapitalistic didacticism is at least fresh....

It's also very funny. The story turns on a consumers' revolt by lire-starved workingclass housewives in Milan who pilfer large quantities of overpriced food, then try to hide it from investigating cops by stuffing it under their dresses and claiming pregnancy. The central femme character, an Italian cousin of one of Brecht's proletarian heroines, is also forced to hide the booty from her law-abiding factory-worker husband. In time, however, the husband sees the radical light, and the play concludes as the characters herald imminent Socialist Utopia. . . .

The labyrinthine plot developments are smoothly meshed into the author's propagandistic theme, which is nitty-gritty Marxist.

Humm., in a review of "We Won't Pay! We Won't Pay!" in Variety, *December 24, 1980, p. 62.*

EDITH OLIVER

There is every indication of comic ingenuity in **"We Won't Pay! We Won't Pay!,"** a farce. . . . [A director's note in the program says], "In this play there are a number of stories, which are related to the socio-economic conditions of inflation, retold within the structure of a household comedy. . . ." Fortunately, Fo—whatever his odd theories about drama, and whatever his political allegiances—is much friskier than his director. There is indeed a number of tales in **"We Won't Pay!,"** but they are more snippets and broken threads than long strands. Like all farces, pre- and post-Marx, the play is a matter of abrupt turns of action, quirky notions, and, even in translation . . . a smattering of funny lines. At the opening, the housewives enter, loaded down with bags of food looted from a local supermarket. Much conversation about inflation and rebellion. A policeman enters, and we're off—into a scramble of false pregnancy (the falsity being rice, pasta, a bottle of olives, and other provender concealed under a belted coat); premature birth (the bottle of olives breaks); the summoning of an ambulance; rabbit-head-and-birdseed soup; the Pope and the Pill (along with off-the-cuff, and inept, impersonations); unpaid bills for rent, gas, and electricity, and their consequences. Everybody is broke, and everybody is spunky; there is no question about our sympathies.

Edith Oliver, in a review of "We Won't Pay! We Won't Pay!" in The New Yorker, *Vol. LVII, No. 1, February 23, 1981, p. 88.*

BENEDICT NIGHTINGALE

The rude view of Dario Fo is that he is, in the current jargon, an unabashed pill-coater. That is, he inveigles us into swallowing his radical nostra by plastering them with funny lines, entertaining business, and farcical rough-and-tumble ultimately derived from the *commedia dell'arte*. It sounds pretty indigestible, not to say dubiously therapeutic; and so it would no doubt prove in practice, if his humour really were external rather than innate, imposed rather than intrinsic. As it happens, though, the rude view isn't the fair one. More often than his critics care to recognise, the humour is functional, not decorative. What mainly amuses us about Fo's *Accidental Death of an Anarchist* is also what shocks and disturbs us: the increasingly distraught antics of the Milanese cops as, prodded, needled and mocked by an updated version of the 16th-century *zanni*, they devise increasingly idiotic excuses for the defenestration of a political prisoner.

The same can be said for the bulk of the feminist monologues . . . [which constitute **One Woman Plays**. In **Waking Up,** a] wife leaps out of bed late for work, erroneously dusts the baby's bottom with parmesan cheese, finds she's lost the house-key, and launches into a blundering search which comically but also pointedly demonstrates the pressures under which she's expected to live. Even the last-gasp denouement, that it's really Sunday and the factory is closed, is rather more than the sort of punch-line that used to end revue sketches in the days when revue sketches used to have ends. Similarly, another overwrought wife isn't just indulging in verbal horseplay or Stoppardesque parody of newspaper headlines when she jokes about 'orgasm' sounding like a cross between an orang-outang and a cataclysm: 'nun at zoo attacked by crazed orgasm.' She's coping with her own nervous feeling about something she's never experienced.

These are tiny examples; but they and others cumulatively produce an identikit picture it would be self-indulgent to call paranoid, anachronistic or (a subtler objection) less relevant to Britain than to macho Italy. This capsule woman is expected to go out to work, yet also cook, clean, look after the tots, and treat her husband's whims as sacrosanct. Sex is a wham-bam business, leaving her feeling like a pinball machine without the freedom to go into tilt when crudely manhandled. If she resists, she's an uptight bitch; and when she finds herself a more considerate, egalitarian lover, he hasn't the self-control to save her from pregnancy, parturition, and reactivation of the cycle that consigns her to domestic serfdom. . . .

[The] plays are rather more than comically-couched whingeings and blubberings on behalf of the victim sex. Indeed, another justification of the funhouse style is that it at once suggests and reflects a pep, a resilience, in their protagonists. . . . And in the evening's coda, a terse and distinctly unfunny version of **Medea,** resilience becomes defiance, and a brand of defiance which reminds us that the jokesmith Fo is also the somewhat chilling revolutionary who ended **Accidental Death** by recommending the murder of admittedly corrupt policemen. Jason, treacherous husband, is responsible for laws which 'imprison us women in a cage and hang children round our necks to keep us quiet'. So he and they must be resisted in the ultimate way, by exemplary infanticide. 'Die and let a new woman be born,' rasps [one character] . . . , and she repeats, in case we missed the point, 'a new woman! A new woman!' It's a resounding call to arms, a ringing declaration of belief in the grand feminist end; but it would, I suspect, echo more happily in the ears of most humane people if the means, weapons and victims recommended weren't children.

Benedict Nightingale, "Bitter Pill," in New Statesman, *Vol. 102, No. 2624, July 3, 1981, p. 22.**

BENEDICT NIGHTINGALE

[In **Can't Pay? Won't Pay!** (also performed as **We Won't Pay! We Won't Pay!**), the] fun, though considerable and expertly staged, spirals too far beyond what it more or less remains in **Accidental Death** and **One-Woman Plays,** the logical reflection, illustration and exploration of subject and theme. Specifically, would the 'respectable' CP member really convince himself that the stolen vegetables his rebellious wife has stuffed up her jumper are actually a pregnancy transplant? He and his friend emerge as morons, scarcely the Fo view of workers. Whether for this reason, its tendency to repetition and prolixity, or something else, the play's political clout proves less than we've come to expect of a writer whose very name has a combative ring, akin to Agamemnon Enemy or Xerxes Thug. (pp. 23-4)

Benedict Nightingale, "A Spare Man," in New Statesman, Vol. 102, No. 2629, August 7, 1981, pp. 23-4.*

VARIETY

In these wide open, permissive, seen and heard it all before '80s, is it possible for a play to be "a direct political intervention" in or a "radical criticism" of society? Italian wife-and-husband playwriting team Franca Rame and Dario Fo make a good case for the possibility, though it isn't entirely convincing and is probably more valid in Italy where women are more restricted by men, state and church than in the U.S.

"Female Parts" is made up of two farcically satirical one-act plays, **"A Woman Alone"** and **"The Same Old Story."** . . .

The two plays . . . are avowedly feminist. They go beyond propaganda, however. Written with vigor and lusty humor, they have theatricality and dramatic life. Though not for Broadway, there should be a place for them off-Broadway, at more-daring regional theatres, and on campuses.

"A Woman Alone" is the more obvious of the two. In it a dizzy blonde wife, locked in her apartment by her husband, unburdens herself to the new tenant opposite her window. . . .

There's nothing new as feminism goes, but the play makes valid points, and is often riotously funny. It's probably 10 minutes too long for its content, and it could easily degenerate into noisy hysteria. . . .

"The Same Old Story" is shorter, bolder, far more imaginative and more genuinely jolting. It takes place on a small wooden platform that substitutes for, among other things, a bed and an examination couch. Alone and fully dressed in tights, boots, fatigue jacket and headband, . . . [the central character] skillfully avoids obscenity while simulating copulation with a militant-radical comrade, an examination for pregnancy prior to a possible abortion, childbirth and sordid other matters.

It's not drawing-room comedy and won't be seen on network tv but it's often honest and funny and, again, vividly illustrates feminist beliefs. . . .

Rame and Fo may be political, radical critics of society. More important, they are real playwrights. . . .

Mart., in a review of "Female Parts," in Variety, August 4, 1982, p. 62.

FRANK RICH

The plays [which make up **"Orgasmo Adulto Escapes from the Zoo"**] are uncompromising in their convictions. And yet we sit . . . [in the theater] with the sinking sensation that **"Orgasmo Adulto"** isn't provoking the laughter, thought or outrage it intends. . . .

The concerns of all eight pieces are similar. As the actress explains in a chatty, relaxed prologue, **"Orgasmo Adulto"** is "an entertainment about the condition of women"—or, more specifically, about how "we're all prisoners of the male organ." The characters are usually oppressed wives and mothers who strike back as best they can at the male "devil" and the "tail" that this devil wears "in front."

This is reasonable subject matter, but the Fo-Rame approach to it here seems limited and tired. Most of the plays . . . express a dogmatic, Freudian determinism reminiscent of Lina Wertmuller films like "Swept Away" and "Seven Beauties": The imagery of castration and excrement predominate as we continually witness the wages of male sexual aggression. Worse, Mr. Fo and Miss Rame don't cloak this theme in the scabrous black humor that might rehabilitate it. The mode is more often conventional (and obvious) farce, typified by a gag in which a woman slams a door on her lover's most vulnerable appendage.

The other ideological aspects of **"Orgasmo Adulto"** are also primitively stated. Unlike Caryl Churchill, who finds novel ways to dramatize her connections between capitalism and male supremacy, Mr. Fo and Miss Rame gives us a radicalized, overlong slice of "I Love Lucy" slapstick in which a wife who has "everything" in the way of housekeeping appliances is literally a prisoner in her own home. . . .

As was the case with the other Fo play thus far seen in New York, **"We Won't Pay! We Won't Pay!,"** it's possible that something has been lost in the English adaptation. . . . Maybe, too, the distance separating Italy's socio-sexual landscape from ours is just too vast. . . . American audiences may find themselves listening to unsophisticated lectures that don't travel well. Such matters as a woman's right to abortion or to a liberated role in lovemaking are melodramatically argued as if they were taboo topics never broached in a theater before. In a similar manner, simulated sex and scatological language are italicized constantly, apparently on the rather sexist assumption that men will be startled to see a woman engage in such ostensibly male prerogatives. . . .

The material's repetitiveness can emerge as a deadening whininess; the attempts to tap into the plays' indigenous, folkloric Italian roots are intermittent.

Frank Rich, "Estelle Parsons in 'Orgasmo Adulto'," in The New York Times, August 5, 1983, p. 3.

MEL GUSSOW

As playwright monologist and public personality, Dario Fo is an impertinent iconoclast, provoking officialdom at the same time that he is tickling his audience. Among contemporary playwrights who are concerned with the theater of politics—writers as diverse as Fernando Arrabal, David Hare and Caryl Churchill—Fo has distinguished himself not only as an author but as a performer of his own work. Imagine a cross between Bertolt Brecht and Lenny Bruce and you may begin to have an idea of the scope of Fo's anarchic art. In common with Brecht, he is seeking social change; in common with Bruce, he is often scatological and blasphemous. . . .

Though the Fo-Rame sketches [in **"Adulto Orgasmo Escapes From the Zoo"**] were supposedly written in the 70's, to American eyes they seem decades out of date—simplistic outbursts against woman's incarceration in bed and kitchen by boorish men. Perhaps more than anything, they are an indication of the repressive state of women in Italy.

Only two of the eight pieces are of more than marginal interest, **"A Woman Alone"** and a brief, folkloric version of **"Medea."**

The other six monologues are a potpourri of vaudeville skits, attenuated confessionals and small jokes. . . . As explorations of the obsessions of singular women, they are not, for example, in a class with Jane Martin's "Talking With." There is, in fact, a limit to the performance artistry that anyone . . . can bring to bear on such insubstantial reflections.

Fo is funniest and most challenging in the plays he has written by himself on more broadly political subjects—in **"We Won't Pay," "Accidental Death"** and **"About Face."** These three could be regarded as a kind of informal trilogy, as *discorsi* on consumerism, corruption and capitalism. Each is concerned with the subjugation of individuals by ruling authority, with the battle between the haves and the have-nots. Though they are originally addressed to the Italian populace and derive from specific local events, they achieve a more general perspective in performance. . . .

The most recent of the trio, **"About Face,"** is filled with scandalous assaults on governmental and bureaucratic interference. As with many of Fo's plays, it begins with a fact—in this case, the kidnapping of former Prime Minister Aldo Moro—and then does a leap into fantasy. Fo imagines that the wealthy Agnelli has been snatched by the Red Brigades, is hurt in a traffic accident and is mistaken for the Fiat worker who rescues him. In plastic surgery, he is given a replica of the rescuer's face, and the evening becomes a careening comedy about mistaken identity, medical quackery, industrial pettifoggery and myopic constabulary. Along the way, Fo suggests that the plutocrat might have engineered his own kidnapping, which would have been a case of "self-terrorism." Acting as theatrical caricaturist, Fo reaches his hilarious high in **"About Face"** when a mob of secret agents bug an apartment by hiding inside the furniture. (p. 3)

When one reads Fo, it is difficult to envision this scene and the full panoply of his humor. In performance, **"About Face,"** . . . becomes the theatrical equivalent of an animated cartoon. In contrast to other politically concerned playwrights, Fo is more scenarist than dramatist. In that sense, he can be compared with the San Francisco Mime Troupe, which, led by a playwright, devises scenarios on public issues and elaborates on them in production. (p. 11)

> Mel Gussow, "*Dario Fo's Barbed Wit Is Aimed at Many Targets,*" in The New York Times, *August 14, 1983, pp. 3, 11.*

JOHN SIMON

I am not very fond of one-man plays. Or one-woman, one-trained-seal, one-anything plays. . . . Generally speaking, there is something demoralizing about going to theatrical solos—like being invited to dine off paper plates.

There are, however, exceptions: if the performer is great, the material is marvelous, or the situation, though dramatic, calls for a monologue—say, the story of Jonah. A little of all three of these conditions obtains in *Orgasmo Adulto Escapes From the Zoo.* . . .

[These] eight plays are definitely not Communist propaganda; they are feminist propaganda. They are monologues for women. . . . There are three incidental male roles, but they are non-speaking, because the men are dumb in every sense, as well as deaf to reason. (p. 42)

Contrasto for a Solo Voice is about a peasant lass who contrives, for one night at any rate, to take (I am using a euphemism; the plays revel in obscenity and scatology) her lover rather than be taken by him. *The Freak Mamma* is about a crazy-seeming mother who enters a church and goes to confession in the hope of escaping the pursuing cops, and tells of a series of transformations she underwent while watching over her Red Brigades son, which took her from Communism to Maoism, from punk to radical feminism.

These, [along with *Waking Up* and *A Woman Alone*], are the chiefly comic plays. The more serious ones include *We All Have the Same Story,* a symbolic fairy tale about the dual nature of woman as factitious angel and repressed hellion, and about how she must come to terms with her suppressed rebelliousness by releasing and digesting it before she can be whole. *Monologue of a Whore in a Lunatic Asylum* is the extorted confession of a factory-worker-cum-whore much abused by men, whom a woman doctor has strapped into a sort of psychiatric electric chair that, with mild shocks, forces her to tell the story of her politicization into a violent anarchist feminist. *It Happens Tomorrow* offers the immobile, spotlighted face of a woman, while her impersonal voice on tape relates her torture as a political prisoner, resulting in near-death. *Medea* is an alleged rural Italian version of the story told by Euripides, often couched in words closely approximating the original, but placing the emphasis on a more contemporary feminist interpretation of the celebrated infanticide.

As feminist agit-prop for the Italy of the seventies (when most of these pieces were written), this may have been pretty incendiary stuff; for today's America, it is rather passé. Though anti-E.R.A. women may still find it shocking, the rest will consider it mild and obsolescent, as flat as yesterday's beer or yesteryear's revolutions. The men in the audience, being of the kind that frequents such entertainments, find the anti-male jokes and tirades (many of them deserved) hugely amusing, especially if they have a simplistic sense of humor. The more serious playlets (each evening contains two), which have moments of wry merriment, tend to be more interesting because they function more clearly on two levels. Though the comic ones, in turn, have some serious elements in them, these are not enough for an added dimension. On the whole, the satire—sexual or political—is broad and sophomoric; still, there are flashes when something happens: A joke comes alive, a homely truth hits home, an absurdist situation takes on a hallucinatory, surreal reality. But, alas, what vastitudes of stale cake between the raisins *d'être.* (pp. 42-3)

But, seriously, dear Franca Rame and Dario Fo: One-character plays—is that what theater is fo'? (p. 43)

> John Simon, "*Eight,*" in New York *Magazine, Vol. 16, No. 32, August 15, 1983, pp. 42-3.*

ROBERT BRUSTEIN

Dario Fo is a high-spirited Italian dramatist in an Aristophanic tradition who writes plays as if Karl Marx and Groucho Marx were contending for his soul. The result of this unlikely struggle is a species of left-wing political farce, a rare theatrical form regularly practiced in this country only by the San Francisco Mime Troupe. Fo has two reigning passions, not always well integrated in his work—a passion for justice and a passion for the absurd. In *We Won't Pay! We Won't Pay!,* for example, a play about a consumer's strike in a proletarian district of Milan, he alternates hilarious adultery comedy with such long-winded anticapitalist tirades that even those who share his political position wish he'd get off the stump and back to his raunchy high jinks.

With *Accidental Death of an Anarchist* . . . , however, he has found a most congenial parable, where politics is the root of the comedy rather than a didactic graft or transplant. The absurdity in this play is human organization itself. Fo's targets are the corrupt practices of government bureaucracies and state-sponsored agencies, and he has a delicious time ridiculing the evasions and lies of civic functionaries. As a result, *Accidental Death of an Anarchist* is more radical than even Fo may have intended, for the satire embraces all inhibiting systems, including those of the Eastern bloc. Despite his Communist rhetoric, Fo is, like most comic artists, an anarchist, his enemy being any structure that would restrict the exuberant physical life of humanity. (p. 25)

[The] thin plot is really a pretext for an extraordinary series of riffs and ripostes, as the Fool lampoons, satirizes, and generally unbalances his ludicrously outclassed antagonists. A clone of Groucho, his mockery is a compound of nerve, wit, gall, and energy, as he mangles syntax and logic, confirming the surreal relationship between words and objects. It was Antonin Artaud who first noticed affinities between anarchism and farce—in an essay written, as a matter of fact, on the Marx Brothers. Identifying what he called "the dangerous aspect of all these funny jokes." . . . Artaud saw the liberating nature of laughter and the revolutionary impulses of anarchism to be one and the same. In *Accidental Death of an Anarchist,* Fo acknowledges similar links as he conducts a revolt of the body against the state, assaulting all restraints—moral, social, or political—on the irrepressible nature of free men. (pp. 25-6)

Robert Brustein, "Exploding an Anarchist Play," in The New Republic, *Vol. 191, No. 25, December 17, 1984, pp. 25-6.*

Antonia (Pakenham) Fraser

1932-

English biographer, novelist, scriptwriter, and short story writer.

Born to "the literary Longfords" of England (historian Francis Pakenham, Earl of Longford, and Elizabeth Longford, author of several historical memoirs), Fraser's interest in writing has culminated in several best-selling historical biographies set in the seventeenth century. Critically valued for their depth of research and sympathetic character portraits, Fraser's biographies attempt to free their subjects from the dry factual analyses common to many academic discussions. She also writes mystery novels which center on a liberated heroine, Jemima Shore, as well as short stories, juvenile books, and scripts for radio and television.

Fraser burst upon the literary scene in 1969 with her critically acclaimed *Mary Queen of Scots,* a thoroughly researched attempt to uncover the woman whose image has become distorted. Some critics contend that her treatment of politics is uncertain in places. Many debate the conclusions regarding Mary herself; Roy Strong states that the biography depicts "a dim and stupid woman," while J. P. Kenyon contends that it shows Mary to be politically and intellectually astute. Fraser's second biography, *Cromwell, Our Chief of Men* (1973), was also reviewed as unpolished in its treatment of political events but generally successful as an attempt to "humanize" such a historically biased figure. *King James VI of Scotland, I of England* (1974) is a less extensive work of scholarship which Alden Whitman nevertheless finds to be "thoroughly readable as a character study." *Royal Charles: Charles II and the Restoration* (1979) attempts to correct the historical portrayal of another prominent royal figure. Some critics believe Fraser's assessment of Charles is overly favorable. Critics praise Fraser's recent history *The Weaker Vessel: Woman's Lot in 17th Century England* (1984) as a pioneering overview of the repressive state of women's lives during that era. The book is based on memoirs, diaries, and character studies representative of the period.

(See also *Contemporary Authors,* Vols. 85-88 and *Something about the Author,* Vol. 32.)

Photograph by Mark Gerson

V. G. KIERNAN

Women have been great purveyors of historical novels, but [*Mary, Queen of Scots*] is emphatically not one of them. Everything in it is carefully documented, and what is romantic in the story stands out more effectively because the handling is always realistic and critical, imagination working on facts instead of on fantasies. Sources of information about Mary are numerous, and if few new ones have been found, or are likely to be found, the known ones have been meticulously used. It is typical of the author's thoroughness to have had a search made in the Vatican archives for a document probably non-existent. There are many sorts of history, on the other hand, and it may come more instinctively to women, denizens of the narrow intense aquarium of the family, to see it as a conflict of individual wills and destinies rather than of mass forces and

movements. What we are given is a many-sided account of Mary and her court, her few friends and many enemies, rather than of Scotland in the time of Mary. . . .

A great deal in Mary's story is, in the ordinary Elizabethan's understanding of the word, tragic. It abounds in violent reversals of fate, crime and punishment, the fall of princes, battle and death. . . . What this book will convince many readers of is that somehow the story remains tragic for us too, in our altered world and with our altered minds. . . .

Mary 'thoroughly enjoyed the business of ruling'. Whether her political endowment went much beyond a taste for power and a love of intrigue emerges less clearly. A comparison with Isabella of Castile, that young woman who not long before had succeeded in taming another faction-torn country, might have been instructive. . . .

[Mary] is given credit, repeatedly, for a virtuous disposition, a 'profound disgust of immorality in sexual matters'. What can at any rate be agreed is that she was not, in the modern cant sense, much given to romance; she had the royal virtue of being prepared, for political advantage , to marry anyone, young or old, handsome or hideous. (p. 616)

To set out to narrate events often narrated before, and by writers from Walter Scott downward, is to face an exceptionally severe test. Lady Antonia comes through it with remarkable success, neither giving way to the temptation of sewing purple patches nor relapsing into the pedestrian. Episodes like Rizzio's murder, and then Darnley's, or the escape from Loch Leven, are told with careful detail, and with a working up of dramatic tension never allowed to topple into melodrama. . . . The style is always fresh and sensitive, with an occasional touch of wit, and there is a quick eye for history's graphic minutiae. . . . There is an eye too for its incongruities. Few of these could be more striking than the spectacle of Mary, the dethroned prisoner, and her warder Lord Shrewsbury's wife Bess of Hardwicke, . . . sitting together embroidering. On its own lines, it is hard to see how this book could be bettered.

> *V. G. Kiernan, "Exquisite Princess," in* The Listener, *Vol. LXXXI, No. 2092, May 1, 1969, pp. 616-17.*

A. S. BYATT

Antonia Fraser's new biography [*Mary Queen of Scots*] corrects many myths, endorses a few, and satisfies our double curiosity about Mary, both as a queen and as a real woman. Lady Antonia sees history as an art, not as an impersonal science, which does not mean that she is not thorough. . . .

Her book is very long but consistently gripping, and much of its success depends on the creation of a real world of physical and emotional detail. . . . But the dramatic highlights—Darnley's murder, Mary's flight to England—have the narrative sweep and flow, and appeal to the imagination in the way they should.

Elizabeth appears little; she is presented, deliberately, largely as the shadowy queen and cousin of Mary's own dangerous fantasy of the friend over the border who would help and understand. But the inevitable contrast of fates and symbolic roles is illuminating. . . . Lady Antonia's impressive indictment of Mary's Scottish lords, measured and understood though it is, makes it clear that it was impossible for Mary to represent in any meaningful way a Scotland divided by faction amongst nobles brutal, violent, practising witches, and—even by the standards of the time—greedy, short-sighted and inconstant. . . . Honour seemed to mean nothing more than primitive clan loyalty, itself easily blurred by political intermarriage. Mary tried to govern: she made sensible steps towards religious tolerance, including talking to Knox, who reduced her to hysterical 'owling'. But Elizabeth became the incarnation of the Just Virgin, the immortal Astraea, whose return to earth after the bloodshed of the Iron Age indicated a new Golden Age. Mary could not sustain the representation of justice without a man. And that had its difficulties.

It was Mary who wished 'that one of the two were a man, to make an end of all debates' and then she and Elizabeth might marry. I used to believe that Elizabeth's sexual isolation, her use of cold-blooded political flirtation and genuine loyal friendship for her advisers, contrasted beautifully with Mary's passionate subjection to Bothwell. . . . Lady Antonia's careful analysis of her feelings and behaviour makes it clear that this stereotype was very much a political myth. . . .

[Mary's] captivity increased the nervous illness she suffered from when action was impossible, and Lady Antonia exposes tactfully the 'attrition in her powers of judgment' that increased with her distance in time from the real world. Lady Antonia concentrates attention on Mary's desperate situation in the years of imprisonment and sees her inefficient plotting as a captive's legitimate attempts to free herself.

This inevitably produces an image of Elizabeth as the secure and powerful persecutor, murdering her cousin for political reasons. But Elizabeth was afraid, and with reason, of assassination; as she told Mary herself, she had known what it was to be the innocent focus of religious rebellion under Mary Tudor, and had had the sense to keep her hands clean. It is ironic that it was Elizabeth who learned early to live with the fear of execution, and Elizabeth who had learned in her own early imprisonment what Mary had not needed to know—to control herself, her thoughts, her servants, in silence, so as to survive. (p. 693)

Sympathetic historians have simplified [Mary's] character—not a complex one—for iconographical purposes, and made a saint of her, which she was not; she was more courageous than devoted, and I should like more evidence before I quite accept Lady Antonia's view that her character showed greatness by changing and deepening in adversity. That other symbolic role—the Scarlet Woman—does, however, seem to have been very much a deliberate creation of the lords, to back up their dethronement and imprisonment of her. . . . Throughout this book I kept turning back to Shakespeare's powerful political images too. . . . The strongest impression left after reading *Mary Queen of Scots* is of the unexpected literal truth of that Scottish play about butchery, blackness, greed, witchcraft, political chaos and the slaughter of innocents: *Macbeth*. (pp. 693-94)

> *A. S. Byatt, "Daughter of Debate," in* New Statesman, *Vol. 77, No. 1992, May 16, 1969, pp. 693-94.*

ROY STRONG

It is a long time since we had a fully fledged biography of Mary Queen of Scots, and this splendid new one by Antonia Fraser (*Mary Queen of Scots*) . . . is full of surprises. . . .

[It reveals] the one thing about the Queen which had never occurred to me: not that she was a cunning Jezebel, a Catholic saint or even a romantic heroine, rather that she was in truth a dim and stupid woman, caught up in a drift of events she was incapable of understanding, let alone controlling.

She remains, of course, a legendary beauty. . . . She was, as Antonia Fraser points out, the Mannerist ideal of feminine perfection in the flesh, tall and willowy with reddish fair hair. This ravishing loveliness had gone by her mid-twenties, and she rapidly degenerated into a sad, matronly figure with sharp features topped by false hair. . . . Throughout her life she was a person who, in Cecil's words, could give 'winning and sugared entertainment of all men.' This fatal wayward charm explains much about her, as indeed—a point excellently stressed in this biography—does her bad health, probably caused by porphyria. Mary had two miscarriages, one of twins, and was continuously prone to sickness, swooning and the aches and pains connected with dropsy and rheumatism. . . . But these sad physical aspects of the Queen were not compensated by an intellect of any great power.

Mary seems to have had no eye for human character at all. Her career is littered with appalling blunders. . . .

Well educated in the renaissance tradition, Mary was little more than a Guise puppet, a pretty court débutante who found herself Queen of France on the sudden death of her father-in-law in a tournament. Antonia Fraser points out that the usual belief that she was at loggerheads with her mother-in-law, Catherine de Medici, is incorrect. The reason for this is clear enough. Mary was not nor ever would be of the same calibre as Catherine. . . . Even her own cousin, Mary Tudor—another failure and someone with whom she shared moody melancholy, emotional fixations and swooning—was far more politically capable. (p. 648)

This book is . . . a compelling exposé of the dangers of power in the hands of the intellectually feeble and emotionally uncontrolled. Antonia Fraser tells us about the years of exile in England when, even cut off in isolation at Chatsworth, Tutbury or Sheffield, Mary continued her political bungling. Some of the endless plots are so crazy that they read like a compilation manufactured by a cross between W. S. Gilbert and Edgar Allan Poe. When, eventually, Secretary Walsingham rigged a plot against her with the most blatant crudity, it characteristically never crossed her mind that this was happening. . . . Festooned with rosaries, she faced the executioner convinced that she was dying a Catholic martyr. The last hours were played out with a moving splendour—proud grand gestures to her foes, tender embraces for her grief-stricken attendants, admirable composure on the scaffold, a wonderful climax when she divested herself of black to reveal herself in the liturgical crimson of the martyrs. All these unforgettable moments of high drama and emotion, however, must not obscure the fact that she died not because she was a Jezebel, a monument to Catholic sanctity, or the object of her cousin's vindictiveness, but as a victim of her own stupidity. (pp. 648-49)

Roy Strong, "Mary, Mary, Quite Contrary," in The Spectator, *Vol. 222, No. 7351, May 16, 1969, pp. 648-49.*

C. V. WEDGWOOD

[In *Mary Queen of Scots*], Antonia Fraser has diligently compiled and sifted everything that is known of [Mary], trying to reach the truth behind contemporary slanders and later legends. She has given particular attention to Mary's medical history, and is able to show that she was subject to periods of nervous collapse under stress, in which her vitality and her judgment forsook her and she fell into a kind of apathy. One such collapse (naturally enough) followed the shock of Darnley's murder. Antonia Fraser interprets her marriage to Bothwell . . . as being performed in a state of almost tranced acquiescence. . . .

Antonia Fraser sees Mary as essentially of a maternal disposition. She loved the sickly little Dauphin with a motherly solicitude. Darnley, too, was younger than she was, and she fell in love with him when nursing him through an illness. Furthermore, though she remained to the end an attractive woman able to inspire love in others, her own love life was over by the time she was twenty-five. This is hardly the story of a *grande amoureuse*. (p. 70)

All in all this is a compassionate and often illuminating account of Mary as a woman. The happiness of her sheltered youth at the French Court, when she seemed almost a spoiled child of fortune, makes a tenderly sunny prelude—and an effective contrast—to the hardships and problems of her brief years as ruling Queen in Scotland, while the effect of her long imprisonment in bringing out the greater depth and seriousness of her character is sensitively indicated.

Had Mary been a private individual the book would be wholly convincing. But Mary's life was engulfed by political forces which neither she, nor for that matter any of her contempo-

raries, had the power to dominate, although other rulers were on the whole more successful in their efforts. Mary's tragedy lay in her inability to meet the stresses and demands of the world in which she was unavoidably destined to play an important part.

In describing the upheavals of western Europe in this epoch of violent religious conflict and economic change Antonia Fraser is notably less successful than she is in drawing the personal portrait of the Queen. Her account of events . . . is brief and superficial—enough to make the sequence comprehensible but never deep enough to explain the significance of the forces with which Mary had to contend. Ultimately this is a weakness in the biography of a woman who, in spite of many qualities and a good intelligence, so tragically failed as a ruler. Yet it seems churlish to complain that something is missing in a book which is so full of interesting detail and so rich in human interest. (pp. 70-1)

C. V. Wedgwood, "The Real Mary Was a Woman," in The New York Times Book Review, *November 23, 1969, pp. 4, 70-1.*

KEITH THOMAS

Cromwell's career is traced in great detail [in *Cromwell: Our Chief of Men;* published in the United States as *Cromwell: The Lord Protector*]: from the first dishevelled appearance of the rough Huntingdonshire squire in the House of Commons, with blood specks on his neckband, through his victories at Marston Moor Naseby and Preston, to his apotheosis as Lord Protector. At all points the author reveals a transparent desire to be accurate and fair. [Antonia Fraser] deals scrupulously with those aspects of Cromwell's life which still arouse deep passion, notably the execution of Charles I and the massacres at Drogheda and Wexford. She also emphasises dimensions of the man which centuries of royalist propaganda have tended to efface. . . .

Antonia Fraser has an eye for picturesque detail and likes a good story. She devotes a lot of space to the numerous legends which still surround Cromwell's career, some of which she regards as possessing poetic truth, however false otherwise. She picks over all the old chestnuts: Cromwell's Jewish ancestry; his coloured descendants; his mistresses; his pact with the Devil; the ruins he knocked about. . . . This posthumous mythology is so wide-ranging because Cromwell touched so many aspects of our national life. (p. 760)

The serious student of the period may . . . find it less rewarding than he had hoped. This is not because of its minor inaccuracies or its numerous misprints. Antonia Fraser is not equally at home with all aspects of the period. On economic matters, on political ideas and on radical movements she is often uncertain and sometimes confused. But factual mistakes are inevitable in a book of this size, and the real reason for one's misgivings lies elsewhere.

The weakness of *Cromwell* stems from two doubtful assumptions on which the book is constructed. The first is that it is possible to write biography without getting involved in history. Antonia Fraser tells us that she has no intention of competing with 'the living giants of 17th-century research who stalk the land'. Her aim is to rescue Cromwell the man. But one cannot appraise Cromwell the man without committing oneself to a clearer view of the relationship in which he stood to the heroic events of the time: one has to consider how far he was the representative of forces larger than himself, whether he controlled events or was controlled by them. This she never tries to do. The second assumption is that the best way of re-creating Cromwell the man is to pile up as much detail as possible about all his actions and behaviour, and to add everything which can be found out about the world in which he lived, in the hope that the resulting compilation will speak for itself. But of course it does not. Antonia Fraser offers no overall analysis of Cromwell's psychological make-up and development, no systematic discussion of his objectives. Any underlying view of the man is concealed by the welter of irrelevant detail. The brief summary with which she concludes her long narrative does not reveal the 'totally unexpected Cromwell' promised us by the publisher's blurb. Instead, it merely restates the familiar paradoxes of Cromwell's temperament: his mixture of decisiveness and inaction, of physical violence and spiritual interlocution, of cataclysmic rage and cheerful insouciance. Had she lingered longer at the critical moments of decision and uncertainty in Cromwell's life she might have produced a more illuminating account. But by concerning herself only with his surface behaviour and by treating all events as of equal weight she leaves the reader no clearer about Cromwell's psychology than about his historical importance. She never probes into the underlying reasons for his decisions; and even the grounds for his refusal of the kingship are left unexplored.

The lack of penetrating analysis thus prevents the book from making an original contribution to the study of Cromwell, whether as a man or as a public figure. . . . [Readers] anxious to penetrate the man himself will do best to turn to the Protector's own words (of which Antonia Fraser makes disappointingly little use). Carlyle's edition of Cromwell's letters and speeches did more than any formal biography has ever done to alter popular views of this most perplexing figure. (pp. 760-61)

> *Keith Thomas, "Everybody's Cromwell," in* The Listener, *Vol. 89, No. 2306, June 7, 1973, pp. 760-61.*

G. R. ELTON

S. R. Gardiner called Cromwell the greatest of Englishmen, but when he came to write his little book on Oliver's place in English history the phrase acquired no substance. More recent studies also never achieve anything much better than adequacy. . . . Oliver, in the end, defeated [all his biographers]. He has now defeated Lady Antonia Fraser who, drowning in the morass, drags the reader after her.

[*Cromwell, Our Chief of Men*] is certainly the biggest book on Cromwell—well over 700 pages of it. It rests on honest and hard work; it embodies solid reading in printed materials and some acquaintance with unpublished manuscripts; its prose, never meretricious, varies from the competent to the unexciting. Reading this interminable book is made no easier by occasional lapses in grammatical structure and a cavalier attitude to commas. The author is not always certain of her words: 'unexceptional' for 'unexceptionable' contrasts with 'inimicable' for 'inimical.' We find Cromwell incurring the focus of public attention and settlers called upon to upstake themselves: both sound obscurely painful experiences.

The book's chief faults are two—poor organisation and a lack of psychological penetration. The first accounts for its inordinate length. This is not really a biography of Oliver Cromwell but a relentless history of his times written around him. Of course, we cannot understand Cromwell without understanding

what happened in his lifetime, and a person so much the cause of action in himself and other calls for the inclusion of much general history. But in obeying these demands Lady Antonia keeps losing the thread: where she should summarise, allude or adumbrate, she recites, expounds and comments. Her book lacks intellectual discipline, and even its virtues of sense, modesty and care cannot in consequence make it readable.

The problem of psychological insight is never easy in historical biography, but in Oliver's case it is crucial because he has a way of appearing to each searching student as a reflection of his own bundle of predilections. The extraordinary difficulty of depicting a man so manifestly demonic is assuredly an excuse for ultimate failure in explaining him, but this biographer does worse than she need have done. She is much too honest to play about with dubious psychologising, though now and again she uses terms which she does not seem to grasp with any precision. An author who can say that a person suffered from what "in modern language" would be called a nervous breakdown, cannot at least be accused of modishness, but when a tiresome journey in Russia is called traumatic that taint begins to appear. 'Paranoiac' and 'psychosomatic' are flashed about a bit too readily. Lady Antonia is, of course, aware that Cromwell's personality was very unstable and she rightly draws attention to his frequent terrifying rages; but, despite talk of "the dark night of the soul," she never persuades me that, being evidently nice, sensible and a bit downright, she comprehends the violence and frustration at the heart of the man which, failing too frequently, he strove to control. As for his religion, the conscious core of him, we get a valiant attempt to expound it, but the understanding of puritanism here displayed is from the outside—and is that of an earnest and not very perceptive student. . . . Lady Antonia makes no attempt to exculpate the man and especially permits a combination of sympathy for the Irish and a critical attitude to the sources unusual in her to dominate the most repulsive phase of the great man's public life; but with all her piling of detail and painting of shadows she still fails to lay bare his inner reality. . . .

In the end it remains uncertain whether Cromwell possessed greatness, intellectual power, insight and foresight, the ability to define tasks precisely—or whether he really rose so high because he did not know where he was going and never matched inner force to the situation into which events and the animal drive of his being catapulted him. This biography brings us no nearer to solving the puzzle.

> *G. R. Elton, "Cromwell—Still Elusive," in* The Spectator, *Vol. 230, No. 7563, June 9, 1973, p. 715.*

C. V. WEDGWOOD

Antonia Fraser's richly detailed biography ["**Cromwell: The Lord Protector**"] does full justice to Cromwell's public career. She is particularly good on Ireland, excusing nothing that cannot be excused, but explaining the irrational fear and hatred of the "Popish Irish butchers," intensified by years of pamphlet propaganda, which lay behind his excesses. She is also perceptive in her study of his political doubts and changes of opinion in the critical middle years.

Though she treats his actions fully, Antonia Fraser's true interest lies elsewhere. She has sought, she says, "to rescue the personality" of Cromwell, to detach what he truly was from the almost overwhelming weight of 17th-century scholarship which now surrounds him and his epoch. To rescue his personality? It is the modern phrase. In Cromwell's time they might have substituted the word "soul," for this is very much what she means.

Let it be said at once that she has been as nearly successful in this difficult task as anyone can hope to be. The great quality of her **"Mary Queen of Scots"** was her sympathetic elucidation of personality. But Mary Stuart is easy compared to Cromwell. In the first place, as Cromwell was not born in a royal family, no one at the time took much notice of his early and formative years. Material is scanty and of uncertain value for the whole of this period. In the second place, his particular brand of religion, what Antonia Fraser calls "the life-long dialogue he carried on with himself concerning the intentions of the Almighty," is unsympathetic and often incomprehensible to the 20th century. But she has read herself into a real understanding and sympathy with it.

Little by little, with careful elucidation and quotation, she lets us follow the development of this troubled, neurotic man who experienced a conversion (preceded by a near nervous breakdown, she suggests) in his thirties, and thereafter, convinced that by strenuous prayer he could tap the sources of the Almighty's will, was enabled to lead armies, to take fearful decisions (though often only after torments of prayer and doubt) and to steer a distracted nation out of the wilderness. It is an extraordinary story and she unfolds it with true understanding.

To end on a lighter note, she is a delight to read on the more homely side of his family life and on the minor triumphs and tribulations of the Cromwell family as their unexpected greatness was forced upon them.

> C. V. Wedgwood, in a review of "Cromwell: The Lord Protector," in The New York Times Book Review, October 28, 1973, p. 7.

BLAIR WORDEN

Antonia Fraser's enormous biography [*Cromwell: The Lord Protector*] succeeds in what I take to be its aim: it can be read with pleasure and profit by almost anyone who can afford it, however well or ill acquainted with Cromwell's period. The pleasure might have been doubled, and the profit scarcely diminished, if the length had been halved; but even the most knowledgeable of seventeenth-century historians may feel awed by the thoroughness of Lady Antonia's research. . . .

There are, as one might expect, no startling discoveries, for the challenge to Cromwell's modern biographers is less to unearth new evidence than to make fresh sense of the old; and none of Lady Antonia's perceptions can be said to be very original. Nevertheless, the book is distinguished by narrative skill (especially marked in the accounts of military campaigns) and by unerring good sense. No biographer has dealt so sensitively or so persuasively with Cromwell's friendships and family relationships, a theme which illuminates the public as well as the private man. The factual errors are mostly trivial. There is an occasional tendency to lean on unreliable sources, but otherwise Lady Antonia's judgments command respect even where one dissents from them.

These are admirable qualities. They are, indeed, qualities that reviewers always seem to find themselves describing as admirable. The trouble is that Oliver Cromwell was a great man, and this book, for all its merits, does not begin to convey the measure of his greatness. Why not?

To answer that the limitations of any book reflect the limitations of its author would be as inadequate as it would be ungallant. A writer capable of a book as good as this is capable of a better one. It is true that Lady Antonia does not seem to be abreast of the more esoteric of academic controversies, and that there are those who will imagine that this matters. . . .

Other deficiencies, perhaps, are more serious. Lady Antonia, more at home with Cromwell the soldier than with Cromwell the statesman, shows little grasp of the way politics works or of the political circumstances in which Cromwell operated. Consequently, like many of his other biographers, she is weaker on the 1650s than on the 1640s. A general criticism of the book is that the background of the story is notably less impressive than the foreground. In this respect Cromwell is a much tougher biographical challenge than Mary Queen of Scots, the subject of Lady Antonia's previous book, and at times one senses that she feels out of her depth. When her confidence wilts, her prose tends to wilt too.

These are disconcerting weaknesses, of the kind reviewers always call disconcerting. But they do not answer our question. Similar criticisms could be made, with far more force, of the one indisputably great work to have been published on Cromwell: Thomas Carlyle's edition, first printed in 1845, of Cromwell's letters and speeches. . . .

No one would wish Lady Antonia to have imitated Carlyle's histrionics. He made appalling mistakes, as editor, as historian, and as biographer. But somewhere in the recesses of his mind— that sulphurous mixture of rigid Scottish Calvinism and woolly German Romanticism—a bond was forged between Carlyle and his subject; and from that bond came a depth of inspiration missing from all biographies of Cromwell before and since. (p. 24)

Of course, [Lady Antonia] could not pretend to Carlyle's genius; but she can pretend to talent. Need she imprison it in so nerveless a literary genre? No safe biography of Cromwell could be a satisfying one. The question to which Lady Antonia really addresses herself is not whether Cromwell was a great man, but whether he was a nice man: the kind of man, in fact, whom the general reader could safely invite to dinner. We know the answer from the start. There are black marks, it is true; but the judicial murder of Charles I and the massacres at Drogheda and Wexford, events for which Oliver is severely rebuked (and in her treatment of these Lady Antonia is at her most perceptive), are the only large blemishes on what otherwise, as the almost headmistressish concluding paragraphs make clear, has been a most satisfactory semester.

Yet the fact—from which Lady Antonia is not the only modern historian to avert her gaze—is that in many respects Cromwell was not a nice man at all. (pp. 24-5)

The springs of greatness are often elemental, and hence morally neutral. Cromwell's greatest feats owed as much to his vices as to his virtues. The virtues were, in fact, quite extraordinary, but we cannot grasp their stature if we doctor Cromwell's whole personality for the benefit of those who, as George Eliot put it, "are incapable of assimilating ideas unless they are administered in a highly diluted form." We need always to set them against what Lady Antonia euphemistically calls "the darker side to his nature." Cromwell's virtues were not born in him: they were earned. His achievement was to tame himself, and to appreciate the magnitude of the process we have to know the beast he tamed. (p. 25)

Blair Worden, "Rugged Outcast," in The New York Review of Books, *Vol. XX, No. 18, November 15, 1973, pp. 24-6.**

DAVID UNDERDOWN

Antonia Fraser's massive biography, **"Cromwell: The Lord Protector,"** attempts, she tells us, to rescue the personality of Oliver Cromwell from the obscurity into which . . . it had fallen." The author draws heavily on, and pays generous tribute to, the mass of recent, more analytical scholarship on the English Revolution of 1640-1660. . . . It is fluently, but not vividly written, with an integrity that spurns shortcuts and oversimplifications, and is based on careful research in the sources, including a few relatively unfamiliar ones. Biographies of Cromwell—good, bad, and indifferent—abound, but there is in fact no earlier one which provides a straightforward, detailed narrative of the man's career on anything like this scale.

Cromwell's ambivalences have always fascinated historians. . . . The tension between the man of action and "the man of introspection" is at the center of Lady Antonia's character-analysis. She brings together a good deal of evidence about Oliver's medical history, noting the frequent bouts of depression and psychosomatic illness during periods of indecision, often followed by spells of manic activity. Perhaps over-cautiously, she shies away from anything like a full-scale psychological interpretation. But if this is no trendy piece of psycho-history, it is still a convincing portrait of a complex human being: the family man who loved music, country sports, and sometimes crude practical jokes, as well as the pious Puritan general, the devious politician, and the sometimes brutal fanatic of the Irish campaign.

The other central paradox which runs through the book is a political one: the paradox of the revolutionary in power. This raises perhaps the crucial question about Cromwell: was he a revolutionary who aged into conservatism, or was there always a basic dualism in his political nature, between the traditionalist country squire and the committed Puritan reformer? Lady Antonia inclines to the former solution, holding that Cromwell traveled the long road from radical opposition to Charles I in the 1640's to the conservatism of the Protectorate. (pp. 317-19)

Yet there is a case for the other alternative, and in some ways it offers a better insight into the apparent contradictions of the revolution, contradictions which Cromwell himself personified. On Lady Antonia's own showing, much of Cromwell's record before 1653 is consistent with the conservatism of the Protectorate. She is not altogether happy in her handling of the intricacies of parliamentary politics, but she recognizes that at no time was Oliver in the same camp as republican firebrands like Marten and Ludlow. In the tortuous negotiations with Charles I in 1647 she notes Cromwell's "honest endeavours to preserve the middle ground," and her account of his hesitations over the King's trial (followed by one of those characteristic surges of determined action) is excellent. Swayed though he might often be by flashes of intoxicating godly exaltation, even in the 1640's Cromwell retained the values of the Huntingdon gentleman. . . . (p. 319)

Readers of [Lady Antonia's] earlier **"Mary Queen of Scots"** will be aware that she is an accomplished biographer, and **"Cromwell"** exhibits no diminution of her skill. In what she intended she is eminently successful. The biography that would completely integrate Cromwell the person with Cromwell the statesman, however, still remains to be written. Given the endless complexity of the man and his times, perhaps it never will be. (p. 320)

David Underdown, "Fraser's Cromwell," in The Virginia Quarterly Review, *Vol. 50, No. 2 (Spring, 1974), pp. 317-20.*

C. G. THAYER

This unpretentiously splendid study [*King James VI of Scotland, I of England*] is beyond praise, but deserves it anyhow. It is a different sort of book from Lady Antonia's earlier studies of Mary Stuart and Cromwell in that it relies for the most part on secondary sources and original documents more or less readily available. That is to say, it is modestly introduced as not being a work of original scholarship and research. But having written so brilliantly about the mother, Lady Antonia can hardly be expected to write amateurishly about the unfortunate son. She has used her knowledge and resources with extraordinary shrewdness to produce a book every bit as sympathetic as the long out-of-print biography by Charles Williams, and a good deal more professional, in the best sense.

Rather than aiming to present new facts about James (and perhaps there are not many to be unearthed), she has offered a modest reassessment of the old ones, and, more important, she has done much to undermine the ludicrous lack of understanding of her subject that began in his own time. . . .

Inevitably, many readers will find Lady Antonia's account of James's years in Scotland the most interesting part of the book; and with some justification, since Scottish affairs from 1567 to 1603 are on all levels something to boggle the mind. (p. 122)

But what is most important about this book is the extremely persuasive argument that James I was in fact a far better monarch than he has been credited with being. With all his grotesque self-indulgence . . . , he was a fundamentally decent and generous man whose passion for peace, anathema to his more violently fire-breathing subjects, can be readily appreciated without recourse to psychoanalysis. James's foreign policy . . . was perfectly rational and intelligent, if finally unsuccessful. Not Solomon himself, armed with all the weapons of authority and divine kingship could have prevented the outbreak of that disgusting tragedy, The Thirty Years' War. James tried and was for a time successful. He deserves the moving praise of his present and best biographer. (p. 123)

C. G. Thayer, in a review of "King James VI of Scotland, I of England," in The Ohio Review, *Vol. XVI, No. 2, Winter, 1975, pp. 122-23.*

SHIRLEY STRUM KENNY

Antonia Fraser's *King James VI of Scotland, I of England* is a tribute to the king and to the age. At political matters, however, James was not adept, and Fraser's attempt to arouse "greater understanding and therefore greater sympathy" for a king she finds worthy of the "great position" of first monarch of Great Britain consequently falters. His political successes, such as they were, resulted, according to Fraser, from his indecision and inability to act. When he did act it was to embroil himself in scandal or intrigue. . . . As statesman James displayed none of the judgment or even taste that characterized his literary and intellectual pursuits. On the basis of his political maneuvers, it is difficult to agree with Fraser that his subjects "were not so badly served by him after all."

The brevity of the ''biographical essay,'' as Fraser calls it, a text that runs scarcely more than 100 pages in all, makes it impossible for her to give a three-dimensional portrait of James—she had no intention of supplanting the full-length studies. . . .

Shirley Strum Kenny, ''Great Position,'' in The New Republic, *Vol. 172, No. 12, March 22, 1975, p. 25.*

ALDEN WHITMAN

The first King of Great Britain (self-proclaimed until Parliament agreed), James Stuart has had a deservedly unenviable reputation owing to his family background, his bisexuality, his unsettled religious allegiances and his ''juggle-and-rule'' politics. This view of James is only slightly ameliorated by Lady Antonia Fraser [in her *King James VI of Scotland, I of England*]. . . .

It would be difficult to be entirely partisan to James, and Lady Antonia stops short of adulation; but she clearly seeks to put the best gloss possible on him and on his son Charles I, to whom she refers as ''the Martyr King.'' . . .

Skirting the basic conflicts in British life, Lady Antonia has produced a rather hollow essay—gorgeous on the outside, lavish in illustrations, felicitous in presentation, yet withal lacking in essential understanding of James's reigns. On superficial levels, nonetheless, she has cleared away some of the unjust accusations leveled against James that have persisted over the years. . . .

Lady Antonia writes about . . . James's personal life with insight and understanding. She is properly sympathetic, I think, in delineating the forces that shaped his character and in showing that he was not hard-hearted in agreeing, in effect, to his mother's execution. . . . James, even in his teens, was quite aware of survival. . . .

Although Lady Antonia's essay is not infused with profound political insights, it is thoroughly readable as a character study. . . .

Alden Whitman, in a review of ''King James VI of Scotland, I of England,'' in The New York Times Book Review, *March 30, 1975, p. 16.*

SUSANNAH CLAPP

Antonia Fraser's tale of convent capers [*Quiet as a Nun,* is] a heavily propertied but lightly written thriller. The proceedings are presided over by one Jemima Shore, television interviewer and one-time convent girl who has an eager eye for nunnish delights and deprivations, and remains relatively cool when confronted with kidnapped schoolgirls, candleless chapels and whispered warnings. Since the novel's villains turn out to be almost poignantly recognisable for what they are, her no-nonsense attitude is eminently justified, and carries the novel calmly over the wilder sensationalisms suggested by its title. But a certain amount of more vigorous action, and rather fewer general reflections ('How quickly autumn passed! Like every pleasure, it seemed momentary'), might have made a pleasant book more exciting.

Susannah Clapp, ''Whirligig,'' in New Statesman, *Vol. 93, No. 2410, May 27, 1977, p. 719.**

DANIEL COOGAN

[In *Quiet As a Nun,* Lady Antonia Fraser] has created a suspenseful story, though without much success at masking the outcome. Her private investigator, Jemima Shore, of whom we at no point get any real description, seems to be an alter ego of Antonia Fraser herself. Murder in a convent would seem to be a sure-fire recipe for a thriller, especially when combined with secret passages, ghostly walks and child-abduction. But the thrills (at least as felt by this reviewer) are at best only mild, and the potentially fascinating background is treated with such unfortunate superficiality as to be disturbing rather than contributive. . . .

There is a strange incongruity between the personality of the ultra-modern narrator-heroine, a kind of British Barbara Walters, a nationally known TV personality, and the medieval ambience of the Convent of Blessed Eleanor, where she does her sleuthing.

The strength of the book lies in the little vignettes of characterization that dot its pages, such as that of the child Tessa Justin. The protagonists—Jemima and the murderers—emerge with much less clarity.

The solution to the mystery that troubles the good nuns, accomplished by the joint efforts of one of them (whom Jemima, for a while, suspects of complicity) and Jemima herself, has long been at least partially obvious to the reader. The neat device of killing off the culprits in a convenient automobile accident is too slick and comfortable and tidy for me. (p. 223)

To be fair, I must admit that I read *Quiet as a Nun* in one sitting, with great absorption. But, when I had finished, I was disappointed. The disappointment centered, I think, on dissatisfaction with the unprepossessing heroine, to whom, despite their circumstantial similarities, Lady Antonia has given none of her own undoubted charm. (pp. 223-24)

Daniel Coogan, in a review of ''Quiet As a Nun,'' in America, *Vol. 137, No. 10, October 8, 1977, pp. 223-24.*

PETER STANSKY

There have been comparatively few biographies of Charles II, and Lady Antonia makes up for the lack [in *Royal Charles: Charles II and the Restoration*]. She is refreshingly unpretentious, as when she explains why she will keep her notes to a minimum: experts on the period already know the sources, and the general reader will not be interested. She makes no claim to have gone beyond the printed sources and secondary works—a huge bibliography in any case, including such splendid material as the diaries of Samuel Pepys and John Evelyn. She has worked hard and thoroughly—in some senses almost too much so, in that she seems determined to tell us all she knows about Charles II.

In her evenhanded progress through his 55 years, there might have been somewhat more differentiation and selectivity. An old-fashioned biographer with a modern sensibility, she does not hesitate to linger over the glorious set pieces in the life and does them full justice. . . . (pp. 1, 30)

Lady Antonia is sympathetic to her subject: understandably, she sees nothing wrong in his time-consuming devotion to sex and sport. She provides vivid pictures of his various mistresses. . . .

The difficulty, however, is that Charles is depicted as almost too good to be true. . . .

It is not that Charles is claimed to be perfect, but whenever there is a choice of interpretations, the favorable one is almost invariably chosen. What has previously been recognized as a positive affection for vice, a triumph for debauchery, is now depicted as a rather charming laxity. A king whom others have seen as lazy and merry is now shown as sober and serious, even though he had a public mask of "cynicism, gaiety, indifference." Most of his behavior that might appear cruel and arbitrary is excused as normal in the context of the times. . . .

What others have seen as political confusion or, in the older interpretation, a move toward arbitrary government, Lady Antonia depicts as a more conscious policy. She does a fine job in sorting out a potentially confusing story and tells it with admirable effect, despite a few misjudged attempts to be "with it," resorting to the latest slangy phrases and livening up things with contemporary comparisons that now seem apt enough but will serve to date the book. (p. 30)

But the general verdict, as one might expect of a "labour of love," is highly favorable. (p. 31)

Peter Stansky, "An Oddly Modern Figure," in The New York Times Book Review, *December 9, 1979, pp. 1, 30-1.**

J. H. PLUMB

[Charles II] was tender, kind, overwhelmingly generous, and totally disillusioned. On this aspect of his character Antonia Fraser is both fresh and original [in her *Royal Charles: Charles II and the Restoration*]. For her, rightly, he is no "Merrie Monarch" but a cynical, melancholy man, a lover of the flesh but always conscious of the fleeting nature of its satisfactions. . . . His character, as well as the events of his life, make him a splendid subject for a biography and Antonia Fraser's book does him justice.

This is a far better book than either her *Mary Queen of Scots* or *Cromwell,* good as they were: the narrative is stronger, tenser, better structured; her perceptions of character go deeper and carry conviction. As always, Antonia Fraser has done her scholarly homework. . . . The result is the best biography of Charles II yet available: indeed it is one of the best historical biographies for some years. (p. 43)

I think Antonia Fraser slightly misjudges Charles's long-term political aspirations and, indeed, she is often unsure when dealing with the intricate political conflicts of his reign, such as relations with the French and the City. But no other writer has been so convincing on the monarch himself. And I think that Antonia Fraser has never written better—her style is here freer, wittier; her judgments of men and women and their motives deeper. She is becoming a formidably good historian and biographer. (p. 44)

J. H. Plumb, "Un-Kinglike King," in The New York Review of Books, *Vol. XXVI, No. 20, December 20, 1979, pp. 43-4.*

W. D. BLACKMON

Antonia Fraser, undaunted by the overwhelming weight of historical opinion, sets out in her latest book [*Royal Charles: Charles II and the Restoration*] to do what Charles Stuart himself could not do: make Charles II of England a great king. Lady Fraser has an excellent reason for such an attempt—everything bad that could possibly be said about the King's dissipation and laziness has already been said, both by his contemporaries and later biographers. Fraser's attempt to restore Charles to favorable public opinion is a fascinating blend of painstaking (and interesting) historical research and a flamboyant writing style, but, in paying court to Charles, her research is often slanted and her prose, in the manner of an apologia, elaborate, tangled, and a bit embarrassed. (p. 122)

At Charles's death, Fraser's final advice to the reader is "Let his royal ashes lie soft upon King Charles II," and my final advice to Fraser's potential reader is that the book is, as was once said of the King, "of many virtues and many great imperfections." (p. 123)

W. D. Blackmon, in a review of "Royal Charles: Charles II and the Restoration," in The Denver Quarterly, *Vol. 15, No. 1, Spring, 1980, pp. 122-23.*

PATRICIA CRAIG and MARY CADOGAN

Debonair Jemima, a past pupil of the convent (though she's not a Catholic) and now a successful television interviewer and presenter of her own programme, is the heroine of two detective novels by Antonia Fraser. In *Quiet as a Nun* (1977) she is summoned to the school to investigate queer goings-on. A cry for help is sent out by her old headmistress Mother Ancilla, and soon Jemima is back in the world of bells, statues and rosary beads. It takes 'an outsider's eye to see clearly what perhaps we, so close to it all, have missed'. 'Jemima,' says Mother Ancilla, 'you've got to tell us. Why did she die?' 'She' is Rosabelle Powerstock, or Sister Miriam, who has starved to death in a ruined tower in the convent grounds (a prop straight out of the *Schoolgirls' Weekly*). There are political reasons for her death, as it turns out: she owns property, including the convent and its lands; and she has fallen under the influence of a person who holds fanatical views about the redistribution of wealth. The disrupter of the convent's peace is Alexander Skarbek who actually roams its corridors at night got up as the Black Nun, a legendary figure that proves convenient for his distorted purpose. At one point in the eventful narrative he traps Jemima in a crypt replete with the bones of nuns; it is a fearful spot, but the resolute investigator never loses heart. (p. 235)

[Eventually, the mystery is solved and] the property justly disposed (it remains with the convent). Jemima the Protestant, the modern heroine, the independent woman with a married lover, can admire the nuns for the qualities of faith, order, composure and kindness which she sees in them. It's a romantic view.

When Jemima visits the Northern Highlands (*The Wild Island,* 1978) she is soon writing to Mother Agnes (promoted after the death of Mother Ancilla): 'I find myself in a very odd situation here.' She's not exaggerating: her host Charles Beauregard has been found drowned shortly before she arrives, and she is surprised to hear him referred to as His Late Majesty King Charles Edward of Scotland; a crackpot royalist organization has the island in its grip. (pp. 235-36)

Jemima, in fact, has done very little practical detecting in this novel, and her plea ('I'm a television reporter, not a detective') is not much of a defence from the reader's point of view. As a character, she is meant to stand for a fairly uncommon type:

the harassed celebrity, continually at the mercy of those who attribute mysterious powers of judgement and action to the television performer. The title of her programme, 'Jemima Shore—Investigator' (a parody of American 'private eye' jargon), is apt to be taken literally; though the subject of her weekly investigations is always a social question of great import. There is a double irony in the fact that the title has stuck to her, so that people always expect her to put their troubles right. She is willing to do her best; but the sheer magnitude and opacity of the mysteries facing an investigator on Eilean Fas (the Wild Island) are enough to stump anyone. In the end, nothing but curiosity, 'at once her best and her worst quality', drives Jemima on; and she fails to draw a logical conclusion from the facts as she observes them. (pp. 236-37)

The rules governing strict detective fiction have been relaxed, and increasing realism in one department is matched by increasing fantasy in another. The events described in both these novels are quite preposterous—convent life at its most unorthodox; Scottish nationalism gone haywire. Engagement with real social issues (schemes to provide housing for the poor and lunatic brands of nationalism do of course exist) actually lessens their credibility, since these are never treated seriously. But no miracles of elucidation are performed by the heroine; and in this respect at least she has moved closer to the plausible and unostentatious, qualities required of the modern, straightforward character. Indeed, the concept of the heroine has shifted from the extraordinary to the ordinary, at least in middlebrow fiction. *Apparent* ordinariness, which we find in the Miss Silver type of sleuth, won't do. Jemima Shore is really just the focus of interest in the books, not the powerful outsider who has got everything under control, the behaviour of other people as well as her own. She is as startled as anyone when the truth comes out, though she is quick to see how it makes sense of everything that had seemed puzzling.

There is no room for complication in Jemima's nature when incessant adventures are taking place around her; but . . . her sanity is striking in the face of so much dottiness and criminal lunacy. The genre doesn't demand more than a clear outline for its central characters, about whom facts are presented plainly and without emotional fuss. Antonia Fraser has brought the Gothic mystery up to date, simply by transcribing its charnel atmosphere in very forthright terms. Her briskness, with its underlay of mild humour, works all the time to dispel the clouds of murk she's for ever summoning up, and the result is jolly and blithe in defiance of the subject. . . . (pp. 237-38)

> *Patricia Craig and Mary Cadogan, '''A Curious Career for a Woman'?'' in their* The Lady Investigates: Women Detectives and Spies in Fiction, *St. Martin's Press, 1981, pp. 223-46.**

HARRIET WAUGH

The first mystery in Antonia Fraser's detective novel, *Cool Repentance,* is why it is not set in Ireland. The characters give off such a strong whiff of decadent Anglo-Irish flesh that it seems perverse to have located them somewhere in rural-England-by-the-sea. Anyway, despite the eccentricity of the setting, it starts off excellently.

Christobel Herrick, whose fate is at the centre of the novel, is a prematurely retired famous actress about to be enticed back on stage by an ambitious, pseudish director. . . . She has recently returned to her husband's home after a protracted desertion of a humiliating kind: she had run off with the stable

boy, the son of the domestic servants of the house. The stable boy had used her as a stepping-stone to becoming a pop star, ruined her career, then deserted her, only to die in a motorbicycle crash. Christobel has now returned to resume her role at the centre of the household as though she had never left it. Her husband, Julian, seems as adoring as ever, but is he? . . . What does their governess, the aunt of the stable boy, feel about having her place in the household usurped? And, most important of all, what do Mr and Mrs Blagge, the parents of the spoilt stable boy feel at having to serve the woman they blame for their son's death? These are the questions that intrigue Jemima Shore, Antonia Fraser's prissy detective. . . .

As can be seen, this is an excellent recipe for murder and, until a badly described second death, is glorious fun. Unfortunately at this point the story loses some of its zest, and though the ending is genuinely surprising the psychology behind the first murder makes an unconvincing Molotov cocktail.

> *Harriet Waugh, ''Thrillers,'' in* The Spectator, *Vol. 248, No. 8033, June 26, 1982, p. 28.**

LOIS POTTER

The Weaker Vessel is a celebration, not a lament. The women whose lives fill its crowded pages include not only royal mistresses, actresses, great heiresses, and the rare (mainly childless) creative artists and writers, but the ordinary maids, wives and widows whose quieter achievements can be deduced from the family papers of the period; fittingly, the final chapter is given over to the role of the midwife. Lady Antonia has avoided the lurid and often-told stories of the Essex divorce and the Castlehaven scandal (though the adventures of Lady Roos and the witty Lady Catherine Sedley make a good substitute); she has looked, on the whole, for the encouraging and heart-warming. . . .

Unlike Lady Antonia's other works, *The Weaker Vessel* lacks the unifying element of a single central figure, though she is skilful in indicating the dynastic relationships which link characters in different parts of the book. Her arrangement of the material—partly thematic, partly chronological, with chapter titles that are decorative rather than informative—encourages the reader to treat it as a bedside book rather than to seek a sustained argument. Much of the material does speak perfectly well for itself, and the author's reluctance to argue a case is partly a matter of tact, though at times it also suggests the same kind of diffidence that she notes in female writers of the period.

In fact, this extremely enjoyable book does have a serious argument. Lady Antonia stresses the crucial role of education in improving woman's lot, shows considerable sympathy for the idea of a ''lay convent'' for Protestant women (perhaps a woman's college?), but also notes the dangerous contempt which clever women in this period often felt for their own sex. In her final chapter, she draws attention to the cyclical pattern of woman's history in the seventeenth century. The Civil War gave many of them an opportunity to discover hidden strengths and talents. . . . But the Restoration, like other post-war eras, reimposed traditional ''female'' values, and in some ways (the improvement of university education, the intrusion of men into the specifically female area of midwifery) actually widened the gap between the sexes. ''As with all forms of liberation, of which the liberation of women is only one example, it is easy to suppose in a time of freedom that the darker days of repression can never come again.'' This warning, I think, is worth any amount of righteous indignation.

Lois Potter, ''Breaking Silence,'' in The Times Educational Supplement, *No. 3544, June 1, 1984, p. 22.*

BLAIR WORDEN

[In *The Weaker Vessel*] the varieties of social opportunity and experience in the Stuart age indicate the difficulties posed by Antonia Fraser's subtitle, 'Woman's Lot in 17th-Century England'. A better choice might have been 'Meetings with Remarkable Women', for her book has little place for the ordinary or for the silent. In some ways, it is true, 17th-century women did have a common lot. Whatever their class, they were held to be inferior to men, intellectually, morally and spiritually. Institutions and the law, as we would say, discriminated against them. Yet in society they shared little beyond their formal disadvantages. Historical inquiry which treats people as members of a class—a class, moreover, which constitutes a rather sizable proportion of the population—does not always make them more interesting.

We need a more elastic and less anachronistic vocabulary. We talk of 'attitudes to women'—and invite the phrase to cover not only abstract statements about female characteristics but the full range of unfathomable personal feeling. The 'attitudes' we identify prove often to belong to a broader mental context from which they cannot be separated without distortion. Thus Fraser says that the 17th century had 'a distinct feeling of guilt' about 'romantic love'. Women and men alike 'shuddered away from the concept of love'; 'ever with love came guilt.' But her examples are of people feeling guilty not about loving each other but about disobeying their fathers, to whose acknowledged authority over female and male alike there were few bounds. Fraser's evidence cannot tell us anything about attitudes to affection until we have established what it tells us about attitudes to patriarchalism. There is a confusion, too, in Fraser's identification of 'love' with 'romantic love' (compounded when she muddles 'romantic love' with the cult of 'platonic love'). What the 17th century 'shuddered away from' was not love, on which it set a high value, but the human inclination to mistake emotional intensity for depth. Fraser's examples are helpful only when we set them in the context of the period's mistrust of 'the passions', of which sexual passion was only one.

How do we give a history to sexuality, a subject which in our own lives is so continuously capable of confounding our reasoned certainties? Where self-knowledge is inevitably precarious, historical knowledge is unlikely to be secure. To learn about the formal status of past women is not necessarily to learn much about the operation or the balance of past sexual power. A major surprise of Fraser's book is her decision to draw so little on the imaginative literature of the time. Simple and obvious questions ask themselves. Why is there so large a gap between the depressed condition of women apparently prescribed by sermons and by social commentaries and the authority which women exert in Shakespearean or Restoration comedy? And why, if romantic love was so alien a sentiment, was there so large and avid a readership for romantic fiction? . . .

It is hard to see how the generalisations now sometimes advanced about the emotional limitations of 17th-century people could be made by any historian acquainted with the period's manifold expressions of the pain of enforced marital separation and of the grief of marital bereavement. Whatever the mistakes of Fraser's book, that scowling error is not among them. . . .

Did the 17th century bring changed perceptions of womanhood? The expanding range of diaries, private letters, biographies and autobiographies—the material which makes Fraser's book possible—reflects a growing interest in human observation and in individual psychology. At the same time, the scientific revolution modified or modernised traditional opinions. By the end of the century it seemed harder to think of women as witches, easier to explain menstruation in medical than in Biblical terms. Yet on the subject of change Fraser offers curiously little help, even though she gives her book a chronological arrangement. Tentatively she suggests that parents became less strict in imposing marriages upon their children, and that marriages across the classes were on the increase: but her evidence seems decidedly thin. . . .

Fraser has read widely: but her references to 'recent research' must be taken with a pinch of salt. She has absorbed little that has recently been written on 17th-century women, and for social history she is over-dependent on Peter Laslett's book of 1965, *The World We Have Lost,* whose warmest admirers would hardly call it authoritative. Even so, Fraser has succeeded strikingly in imposing order and clarity upon a mass of material. She gives us a rich and colourful gallery of portraits. . . . There is a series of real-life adventure stories, enlivened by a spot of whipping here and of wall-jumping there. She is especially interesting on the contrast between the closing of doors to women in activities which required formal education and the ease with which they could operate in the business community—above all, perhaps, in the printing and publishing trades. Here Fraser might have found room for the bookseller Abigail Baldwin, whose eventful life has been described by Eleanor Rostenberg.

But that would have made *The Weaker Vessel* even longer; and like most of Fraser's books, it is much too long already. It contains many points, but no argument. As one struggles through her 470 pages of text one begins to hunger for intellectual edge and shape. Still, if Fraser's prose is not incisive, it at least has qualities of lucidity and vigour. She writes better than the average academic.

Blair Worden, ''Sexual Whiggery,'' in London Review of Books, *June 7 to June 20, 1984, p. 16.**

Max (Rudolf) Frisch

1911-

Swiss dramatist, novelist, diarist, and journalist.

Frisch is considered among the most prominent contemporary writers of German literature. His work is influenced thematically and stylistically by the German Expressionists, particularly dramatist Bertolt Brecht. Like the Expressionists, Frisch informs his plays and his novels with disjointed time sequences and shifting senses of reality. In doing so, he examines the existentialist idea that the course of one's life depends upon personal decisions and actions. Frisch suggests that although each person has the potential to be unique, individual identity cannot be realized until one acts upon that potential. In lieu of personal identity, Frisch implies, individuals who fail to act are doomed to adopt the definitions placed upon them by society. In all his work Frisch emphasizes the importance of establishing identity and exerting will over fate. In his plays he also explores the issue of social responsibility by questioning the degree to which intervention is required to prevent totalitarianism.

Like his countryman, dramatist Friedrich Dürrenmatt, to whom he is often compared, Frisch interprets Swiss neutrality during World War II as a reluctance to take a moral stand. Many of his plays are attempts to explain why the Holocaust was not prevented and examine the feelings of guilt experienced by observers who might have intervened. A parable play, *Biedermann und die Brandstifter* (1958; *The Firebugs*), concerns a hypocritical industrialist who, feigning liberalism, allows two hoodlums to occupy his household. The pair proceed unhindered to burn down an entire town, even after they have stated their intent and stored fuel in the industrialist's attic. Similarly, another parable play, *Andorra* (1961), examines citizens of a fictional village who use their prejudices to justify a murder. Implicit in these as well as his other plays is the idea that the individual's acceptance of stereotypical, socially defined roles is the basic cause of modern corruption and alienation.

Frisch further develops this theme in his fiction. His most widely read novel, *Stiller* (1954; *I'm Not Stiller*), is the story of an unsuccessful sculptor who attempts to change the course of his life by adopting a new identity. Frisch's acclaimed novel *Mein Name sei Gantenbein* (1964; *A Wilderness of Mirrors*) also concerns a man who experiments with various identities but fails to express his true personality. In *Blaubart* (1982; *Bluebeard*), a falsely accused murderer grows to doubt his innocence and believe the prosecution's accusations. Michael Butler notes that in *Bluebeard* Frisch again reveals his "life-long obsession with the problem of identity and the fatal propensity of human beings to thrust crippling definitions on each other." Frisch offers little hope for improving the bleak situations he portrays. Some of his works, in fact, suggest an inclination toward human self-destruction. Frisch's play *Die chinesesche Mauer: Eine Farce* (1947; *The Chinese Wall*) and his novel *Homo Faber* (1957; *Homo Faber: A Report*) depict intellectuals unable to prevent disasters brought on by technological advancements.

Frisch's nonfiction is also considered important to his work as a whole. During the 1940s, when he interrupted his career

as a writer to work as an architect, Frisch wrote several newspaper articles concerning urban planning. These are considered significant because they project his socialist views. Also of interest are Frisch's diaries, which include *Tagebuch, 1946-1949* (1950; *Sketchbook, 1946-1949*) and *Tagebuch, 1966-1971* (1972; *Sketchbook, 1966-1971*). These diaries reflect many of Frisch's literary themes and artistic ideals.

(See also *CLC*, Vols. 3, 9, 14, 18 and *Contemporary Authors*, Vols. 85-88.)

CHARLES W. HOFFMANN

Persistent though it may be . . . the view that the dramatist Frisch is the essential Frisch is, I think, wrong. For one thing, it can be demonstrated—though I do not propose to do so here—that the things which most often claim Frisch's attention are matters better suited to the private world of the introspective novel than to the social world of the stage. *Andorra* is, of course, an exception. Of more obvious importance is the simple fact that, aside from *Andorra* and *Biedermann und die Brandstifter*, Frisch has not written a *new* play since the early fifties. He has rewritten and revised his earlier dramas, but the mature Frisch has turned increasingly to prose fiction; and in *Stiller, Homo faber,* and *Mein Name sei Gantenbein* he has created three of the most important novels of the past decade. Taken together, these books are perhaps the most meaningful recent German writing in their particular genre: the psychological novel.

Their significance does not lie so much in Frisch's narrative technique. The structure and the plot development in *Stiller* and *Homo faber* are essentially traditional, and only in *Gantenbein* does Frisch move onto experimental, new narrative ground.... The significance of the works lies, rather, in the astonishing accuracy and depth of psychological insight with which the experiences of his typically modern heroes are viewed and presented. His characters are engaged—often against their will and rarely successfully—in what Frisch considers to be the most urgent concerns of living. And while these ''urgent concerns'' are not profound new discoveries, the psychological understanding that Frisch has for what motivates his characters is rare, indeed. Finally, since most of us can see ourselves in the central figures, the importance of the novels lies also in what they can help us to recognize about our own inner selves. It would be going too far to call Frisch's intent ''therapeutic''— but I suspect not *much* too far. (pp. 93-4)

I do not consider the novels to be in any sense a trilogy; and when I compare them to each other I do not mean to imply that Frisch intentionally fills out in one what he left sketchy or incomplete in another. This is not the case. Each novel is unique; and though they sometimes complement each other, as do *Stiller* and *Homo faber* particularly, this is because Frisch tries in each to bring the central character into psychological focus. (pp. 94-5)

The first concern of Frisch's heroes is the examination of self, and the novels rest on a series of assumptions that Frisch makes (though not always explicitly in the works themselves) about this examination. If man is to develop the ability to live productively with his fellow human beings, he must first look at self. Indeed, until he has done so, he has not even begun to be human, for, though the awareness of self may be what tortures man, it is also the essence of his humanity. Unless he tries to find out what makes him act the way he does, he must remain alienated from self and unfree. One might then expect man to engage willingly in the search for self. But self-discovery is threatening and painful and difficult, while the state of unconscious, alienated, ''unfree'' living is at least familiar and thus less menacing. It may well be an unpleasant state, but it is also an easy one. Hence, man is not apt to search for his self unless he is forced to do so.

This is more or less the starting point for Frisch's novels. His characters are confronted with circumstances which make the refusal to look at self no longer possible, or at least so threatening that self-examination now becomes the easier path. Each of them has been jarred loose from a familiar and essentially unconscious pattern of behavior by a severe psychic crisis. And since this crisis has been brought on by the old pattern, the character is forced to grant the shortcomings of his previous actions, his previous self, and to search for something better to put in their place. In each of the novels a different phase of this process is examined, and in each different results are achieved. (pp. 95-6)

Since none of the three heroes come to know self completely, none completely achieves the new orientation of personality, the new character structure which for Frisch is synonymous with inner freedom. None attains the emotional independence

which will enable him fully to follow the voice of reason and health and well-being.

All of them, however, eventually look for inner freedom; all come to recognize that they are not free; and all have at least the desire to become so. Again, their success varies in degree. (p. 98)

Frisch's ultimate purpose in all three novels is, in my view, to give new and imaginative expression to this old truth: that men must learn the difficult way of love if they are to escape from loneliness and isolation. Or, to be more precise, his purpose is to show how men fail in the attempt to escape, for Frisch is pessimistic about modern man's chances for success. In all the novels there are only two characters who achieve it, who do learn to love: the district attorney Rolf in *Stiller* and Rolf's wife. Not only are these secondary characters; they also appear in the earliest of the three books. Since then, since 1954, Frisch has not created a character who succeeds. (pp. 100-01)

Of the three main characters—Stiller, Faber, and the narrator in *Gantenbein*—none solves the problem of relatedness. To be sure, Stiller, when we first see him at the beginning of the novel, has already come a long way from the narcissistic and thus thoroughly destructive orientation that had once cut him off from his wife, Julika, and from his lover, Sibylle.... To a large extent he has conquered the feelings of failure and of insufficiency which poisoned those relationships, and now during his imprisonment he also learns he cannot insist that others see him as he wants to be seen. But though he is finally released from his real prison, he is unable to gain complete freedom from the symbolic prison of self. Stiller's new attempt to live in union with Julika is thus doomed, despite his genuine eagerness to make the marriage work this time. To my way of thinking, it is doubtful whether anyone could succeed with so fragile and so withdrawn a woman as Julika, but Frisch holds Stiller himself responsible for the ultimate failure to break out of his isolation.

After showing us in this first novel a character who tries and fails, Frisch shows us in the second a man who never tries. Walter Faber has pretended to escape from the fact of aloneness by shutting his eyes to it. His attempt to live as if life were predictable and readily controlled has forced him to avoid relationships with any real depth to them. Relatedness may be a noble goal; but the search for it involves risk and uncertainty, the necessity of having to choose between values, frustration, and almost certainly some heartache. This makes relatedness too problematic and too complicated to fit into Faber's scheme of things. The contacts he has permitted himself to have with others have been superficial and harmless; and as a result he has only stood on the outside of life. (pp. 101-02)

In *Mein Name sei Gantenbein* [Frisch] approaches the problem in a different and, again, a conjectural way. Assuming one were not bound to a fixed, real identity but free to experiment with a variety of identities, could he perhaps find a role that would make union with others and the overcoming of separateness possible? To a large extent the novel can, I think, be seen as Frisch's probing for an answer to this implicit question and the constant trying on of identities as a weighing of various possibilities for relating to other people. The fact that the pretended blindness of Gantenbein is the novel's central motif bears out the view that this is Frisch's primary concern. Of all the roles the unnamed narrator tries on, he likes the role of Gantenbein best, because it seems to offer the most opportunities for harmonious living with others. . . . Gantenbein he seems to be able to love creatively, productively; as Gantenbein he seems to come close to finding happiness. [But] in the end this happy state of affairs proves to be illusory. Even when the narrator endows one of his imagined selves with the attributes that seem to lead to relatedness, he finds himself unable to escape from isolation. (pp. 102-03)

In *Stiller,* the hero never attains freedom or relatedness because he is unable to transcend self, and the crucial point in this failure has not yet been identified. Since Stiller himself never really seems to grasp the point, Frisch does not make it very evident for the reader either, though the situation seems relatively clear until the final section of the novel. (p. 103)

[Frisch] sets Stiller's ultimate bondage in an implicit religious framework. . . . In the figure of Stiller—or so it seems to me—Frisch has drawn an extreme portrait of modern secularized man, unable to believe in any higher instance outside of himself and so forced to take on the role of being his own Saviour. Without an absolute source of strength and direction in which to put his faith, he demands of himself the performance of tasks that men once reserved for gods. And in this sense the novel becomes a demonstration of the psychological disaster—self-idolatry—which has been made possible by man's loss of spiritual belief. Frisch, of course, does not call for a facile return to faith. His portrayal of Stiller is essentially sympathetic, and this means that he wants simply to show how difficult it must be for man to transcend self when self is the only thing in which he can believe.

In Walter Faber, the hero of the next novel, Frisch again paints the portrait of modern man, but this time one who idolizes technology, statistics, machines, "progress." And *Homo faber* is written to show that such idolatry leads, even more clearly than Stiller's self-idolatry does, to psychological catastrophe. It has blocked Faber from all awareness of self, from the chance to become free and to escape from loneliness. The events related in the book now force him to see the error of his living, but recognition comes too late to lead to change. (pp. 106-07)

Walter Faber—who, as *homo faber*, stands, of course, for modern technological man in general—is not only afraid of life because it is disorderly and uncontrollable. He also denies life by approaching it as though it were something mechanical. The process of growth disturbs him and that of organic decay he finds obscene. For him the proper study of man is not man, but cybernetics. He not only is attracted to machines rather than to living beings; he also believes that people are inferior to machines because they are made of less durable material and are more subject to structural stress. Just as he tries to treat his emotions as though they were things, so, too, human beings are things for him. And this means that Walter Faber's attitude is death oriented, rather than life oriented. He is a destroyer rather than a creator, and for this the destruction of the daughter he created [Sabeth] is a fitting symbol. Walter himself overcomes this orientation in the tragic, but nevertheless *human* affair with Sabeth. But if it takes a catastrophe of these dimensions to awaken modern man, then the book is a gloomy prediction of where his consciousness is taking him. Narcissism, the danger in *Stiller,* has been replaced by necrophilia.

The portrait that Frisch paints in his last novel, *Mein Name sei Gantenbein,* is obviously quite different from the ones we have seen. It is more complex and more individualized, but above all it is a composite portrait. It is something like those Picasso paintings which break up a face into fragments, each of which is a plane observed from a different angle. Picasso's artistic intent is to show the subject not as he is seen from just the front or just the side, but as he appears from various vantage points at the same time. Frisch's literary portrait is designed to do something similar: to demonstrate that a person is the sum not only of a few actual experiences he has had, but also of all the possible experiences he is capable of imagining.

The form in which Frisch has chosen to realize this intent—the narrator's experimentation with the various selves he might be—makes *Mein Name sei Gantenbein* essentially a static book. It must largely do without the thing that provides the temporal structure for most novels: plot. Instead, the progression of this book is associative; one episode gives way to the next when the narrator tires of the role he is playing or is frustrated by it and is eager to try on a new role. This means that *when* an episode begins and ends is even more important than the content of the episode as such. We learn what moves this unnamed narrator by examining the selves he imagines, but we learn even more if we focus on the moments when a role becomes unsatisfactory and a different one is created to take its place. This way of looking at the novel makes it easier to accept the fact that widely divergent and often openly contradictory personalities are united in one character. But it also makes the task of the critic more difficult, and much space would be needed if one were to propose an interpretation for the several hundred moments of association in the novel. (pp. 109-11)

It is, of course, impossible to know where Max Frisch will go now after this brilliant demonstration in *Mein Name sei Gantenbein* of the apparently insoluble dilemma of man's relatedness: that to love, one must be blind, but to be blind to others is to be alone. It is idle to try to guess what his next portrait of man will look like. But we can be reasonably confident that there will be another portrait, for surely we have not heard the last from Frisch on our search for self, on our struggle to be free, and on our one hope for escaping loneliness: love. (p. 113)

> Charles W. Hoffmann, "The Search for Self, Inner Freedom, and Relatedness in the Novels of Max Frisch," *in* The Contemporary Novel in German: A Symposium, *edited by Robert R. Heitner, University of Texas Press, 1967, pp. 91-114.*

ARRIGO SUBIOTTO

In a more direct, less complex and ambiguous manner than Dürrenmatt, Frisch made a worthy, honest attempt in his plays (more private themes dominate his prose writing) to state and analyse some of the uncomfortable problems left in the wake of the Second World War. Above all he tried to elucidate the process of 'how it came about', 'how it could come to this', with guilt, inevitably, as the central motif in every case. Frisch subtitled his second play, *Nun singen sie wieder (Now They've Started Singing Again),* written in 1945, 'Attempt at a Requiem': in the German soldiers who shoot helpless hostages and the Allied airmen who bomb defenceless civilians he portrays and deplores the mentality that sees the enemy as totally black and satanic. But the humanistic pacifism of this play lacks a trenchant cutting edge—at most it is to be found in the flagellation of the 'culture as alibi' syndrome which Frisch also inveighs against in his *Tagebuch.* The character of the schoolmaster mouths the hollow phrases about beauty, truth and greatness while condoning the shabby deeds of war. Here are the germs of a critique proper to the writer—unmasking the manipulation of consciousness through language which induces ready-made opinions and a distorted apprehension of reality in the service of vested interests. Frisch's skill and awareness in fulfilling this task become of overriding significance in *Biedermann* and *Andorra*. (pp. 183-84)

[The protagonist of *Biedermann*] is a wealthy hair-oil manufacturer, Gottlieb Biedermann (a modern commercial philistine parodying Everyman), who through fear, cowardice, hypocrisy, guilt feelings and pretended liberality allows a pair of disreputable, brazen characters to insinuate themselves into his household. With barefaced effrontery, coupled with threats and cajolery, they proceed to stack the attic with cans of petrol and openly proclaim their intention of setting fire to the house and town. Biedermann refuses to believe they are serious. . . . With the undeviating, single-track logic of a morality play the plot unfolds until the final holocaust, when the spectator recalls the lines of the firemen's chorus in the opening

> Many things catch fire,
> But not every fire
> Is caused by inexorable fate.

This contemporary fable lends itself to many interpretations. Although it has several Pinter-like elements—the mundane setting in a private house, the irruption into this 'safe' world of disturbingly provocative outsiders, the colloquial dialogue concealing an ominous content—it can be related in allegorical manner to specific political and historical themes, while a Pinter play explores the startling subtleties of personal human relationships. *Biedermann* can be seen as a metaphor of Hitler's legitimate 'seizure of power' or of the way in which the nations of the world are playing with nuclear bombs as deterrents. . . . It also offers a 'model' of liberal societies allowing freedom of action, in the name of liberty, to extremist elements in their midst (whether of right or left) whose avowed aim it is to destroy those societies. The model can even fit the contemporary situation of many advanced industrial states which depend heavily on immigrant labour and at the same time close their eyes to the dangerously explosive social stresses they are fostering.

The warning note sounded in *Biedermann* was followed in 1961 by *Andorra,* another parable, this time explicitly generated by the phenomenon of anti-semitism and its catastrophic expression in Nazi Germany. Andorra has nothing to do with the country of that name; indeed, the setting is virtually a village, where every individual might expect to be accepted for his true value as a person. Instead, the opposite is revealed to happen. The Teacher passes off his illegitimate son as a Jew whom he had saved as a child from the 'Blacks' in the neighbouring country. With mounting pressure from the 'Blacks' on Andorra, the inhabitants demonstrate their latent anti-semitism by detecting in the youth Andri all the preconceived semitic traits they covertly hate. Gradually he is forced into conforming to this false image until the point comes when he actively and defiantly identifies with it. An invasion by the 'Blacks' leads to his sacrifice, almost as a scapegoat, and only after his death do the townspeople realize their separate and collective guilt in distorting reality to fit their rigid prejudices. An epic technique reminiscent of Brecht is used effectively to keep the issue alive: between scenes all the people who had actively or tacitly participated in Andri's persecution, the Priest, the Soldier, the Doctor, the Carpenter, etc., appear one by one in a witness-box to exculpate themselves from what happened 'in the past'— a procedure that has been gone through *ad nauseam* by Germans since the Second World War. With masterly sensitivity Frisch exploits the banal clichés that serve to cloak the true attitudes of people in their social relationships. The Doctor mouths the unspoken thoughts of latent racism everywhere and at all times, for the fate of the Jews is only one of many models, useful for being historically specific. . . . It would be mistaken to view *Andorra* principally as an indictment of anti-semitism; of greater concern to Frisch is the threat to the individual. More frightening than the persecution of Andri is his own gradual acceptance of the role of the Jew; slowly he withdraws from his own identity to conform to a stereotyped image until he too accepts this as his true self. The parable is a cry of warning to beware of preconceived notions and role-playing that obscure and distort the freshness and vitality of the individual identity. In this respect the theme of *Andorra* lies in close proximity to much of Frisch's prose work. The novels are largely about the threats that surround personal identity and constitute a continuous search by Frisch for certainty.

The significance of his latest play, *Biografie, ein Spiel,* which was first performed in 1967, is that Frisch has apparently abandoned 'public' themes about the individual's guilt and responsibilities in society, and turned instead to his own doubts and self-questionings as an introverted 'specimen'. Kürmann, a behavioural scientist, makes use of that freedom the stage has to offer of repeating, altering, experimenting, to investigate the possibilties of altering the course his life has already run. Under the supervision of a sort of compère, called the Recorder, he enacts variants of past scenes, especially of the key encounter with Antoinette, his future wife. Ultimately, Kürmann comes to realize that all the permutations he tries out in the conviction that 'he knows exactly what he would do differently' are no improvement on the real events, imperfect though these were, and that none of them has the vibrant quality of actually having been lived. Appropriately, the form of the drama is 'experimental', dispensing with the normal plot along a temporal co-ordinate in favour of rehearsals of variant possibilities—the technique of repeated laboratory experimentation. In both theme and form Frisch married in this play the modern technological age of cybernetics and computers with the intensely private world of erratic and unique individual experience.

Frisch, like Dürrenmatt, has been a major force in German drama for the generation since 1945. Both have capitalized on their Swiss nationality to contribute a detached, critical and authoritative view of German topics, at the same time wrestling with the constraints of a restrictive minor state that militate against breadth of vision. Despite their biting criticism of bourgeois forms of culture and their deeply felt social commitment, they clearly reject the communist state in which their individual voices might scarcely be allowed to speak. In devising ingenious models to articulate international concerns these two Swiss dramatists have depicted the weaknesses of individuals and societies with theatrical insight and skill. They have also achieved a combative stature that totally belies the cautious neutrality which we have come to associate with their country. (pp. 185-88)

Arrigo Subiotto, ''The Swiss Contribution,''in The German Theatre: A Symposium, *edited by Ronald Hayman, Barnes & Noble Books, 1975, pp. 171-88.**

ANDREW MOTION

What's in a name? The answer, according to **"I'm Not Stiller,"** is a tyrannical past, and the novel doesn't waste any time before beginning to argue its case. In the opening pages a man claiming to be called White is arrested while crossing the Swiss border and accused of being Anatol Ludwig Stiller, a sculptor who disappeared six years previously. But when White denies the charge and is thrown into jail, the novel is only able to develop by the most subdued kind of immediate action. It turns, instead, to reminiscence and reflection.

The result is an intelligently persuasive analysis of identity and reality, but it can hardly help being dogged by temptations which often beset fictions set in prison. The hero, with little to distract him from himself, becomes increasingly boring; and the story, with such an obvious set of equivalents for the human condition to draw on (time is a prison and we're all doing life sentences) becomes increasingly inert under the weight of symbols and parallels.

As Stiller (for it is he all along) is interviewed by the public prosecutor, various figures appear from his past to elucidate the present. . . .

Stiller is eventually persuaded to stop denying his true name, and the explanation for his disappearance emerges, when he is taken to see his former studio. In a violent destructive frenzy, he smashes the examples of his work which remain there—but seeking finally to abolish the past only convinces him that he is powerless to escape it. The effect is described by the prosecutor in a postscript which occupies the final quarter of the novel. . . .

'As long as a person does not accept himself,' the prosecutor blandly explains, 'he will always have the fear of being misunderstood and misconstrued by his environment.' The remark gives an indication of Max Frisch's ambitious intention, which is to explore a crisis in the character of a country, Switzerland, as well as an individual. But the prosecutor's tone, with its legitimate detachment and omniscience, allows the novel's lurking dogmatism to appear. Perhaps when **'I'm Not Stiller'** was first published . . . , this was necessarily curtailed. In the complete version, it is tediously overbearing.

> Andrew Motion, "Dragging Out a Life Sentence," in The Observer, July 25, 1982, p. 30.*

MARION GLASTONBURY

The possibility of self-knowledge with and through others is [Max Frisch's] perennial theme. The elusiveness of shared truth torments his protagonists. Increasingly bewildered by love at cross purposes, they retreat into solitude, take stock of the past, and stand condemned by their own memories. . . . [The] imprisoned narrator in *I'm Not Stiller* . . . denies that he is guilty as charged but confesses to several murders in the name of 'White', an American citizen of German descent. . . .

As the initial mystery is gradually resolved, we are made aware of further perplexities. Court proceedings to set the record straight are clearly a bureaucratic farce; so what *are* the laws of personal relations and where is justice to be found? What do we owe each other in marriage, kinship and common humanity? How much is each one of us worth, and what can we call our own in an age of technical reproduction when, as televiewers, telehearers and teleknowers, we perceive everything at second-hand? Vicarious experience encompasses the globe, and the interior has already been laid bare by Proust, Jung, Kafka and Thomas Mann.

The weight of these giants and their legacy of philosophical and psychological analysis must be borne by their heirs in Europe, interpreters of the human condition who have lost faith in the dignity and coherence of character, and in the romantic pre-eminence of the self. . . . [The] generic Frisch hero [is] a martyr to history, socially powerless, trapped in the misconceptions of others, and desperate to save his life by losing it. Accordingly, he plunges into simple stories of the New World, melodrama and burlesque, gangland yarns and jungle adventure, tribal myth and the legend of Rip Van Winkle. These elemental forms, ardent fantasies and popular entertainments, untrammelled by doubt and introspection, have their counterpart in the occasional stark gestures and bursts of energy with which characters try to stop the world when they want to get off. Breaking the endless journey from self-justification to self-censure and back again, the narrator acts on impulse, chooses authenticity, becomes momentarily himself, 'free from the fear of doing the wrong thing'. . . .

[Frisch's] novels are more solid, less solipsistic than a summary of their ideas might suggest. A single consciousness contains multitudes: in fathoming it, Frisch evokes the complex reality of a dangerous and enthralling world.

> Marion Glastonbury, "Breaking Out," in New Statesman, Vol. 104, No. 2681, August 6, 1982, p. 23.*

D. J. ENRIGHT

'I try on stories like clothes,' says the narrator of ["**Gantenbein**"] . . . , now reissued with its English title changed from **'A Wilderness of Mirrors.'** In this rather more engaging replay of the 'identity mystery' secreted in **'I'm Not Stiller,'** two different identities and two life-stories are invented for a dead stranger. He could have been Gantenbein, who pretends to be blind, or Enderlin, who is having an affair with Gantenbein's wife—or possibly both gentlemen are having an affair with the wife of Svoboda.

Versions and variations proliferate: one female character starts as an actress and is recast as a contessa; another is a manicurist who declines into a call-girl (found strangled with a cord). Frisch touches explicitly on his obsession, his speciality, when the narrator confesses that he too often feels that any book not concerned with preventing war or creating a better society is senseless and inadmissible. . . .

My feeling is that here, as elsewhere in Frisch, for all the incidental insights and vividnesses, the ponderous machinery is out of proportion to the final product.

> D. J. Enright, "Germanic Tales," in The Observer, March 13, 1983, p. 33.*

RICHARD GILMAN

Max Frisch isn't an easy writer to classify. He's Swiss but in no sense a regionalist; he's neither comfortably traditional nor avant-garde in his style or styles. At his best, he's what we might call sharply contemporary, with an edge of nervous informality and a kind of rueful sagacity. He's been versatile to the point of sometimes seeming glib—his plays, written mostly in the 1950's and 60's, are especially notable in that respect—but he's also full of unexpected felicities; Max Frisch surprises.

His true achievements lie in a few novels, the relatively early **"I'm Not Stiller"** (a cult book for its admirers, of which I'm one), **"Homo Faber"** and the recent **"Man in the Holocene,"** along with his several volumes of autobiographical **"Sketchbooks."** These volumes of personal reflection complement his best fiction, which, without being confessional in any flagrant sense, is characterized by a strain of what I would call moral autobiography. . . .

["**Bluebeard**"] ought to enhance Mr. Frisch's reputation for fertile unpredictability of theme and manner, although it doesn't quite match "**Man in the Holocene**" in that respect. The earlier book, which incorporated drawings and swatches of geological information into the story of an old man marooned in an Alpine village by an avalanche, is Mr. Frisch's most adventurous experiment in style. "**Bluebeard**" is extraordinarily elegant but stylistically narrow, sober and entirely without adornment. Still, its virtues make it at least as arresting as its predecessor.

Henry James once described Ibsen's plays as being about "thinkable things"—meaning that, in contrast to so much intellectually impoverished drama, they nourish the mind. "**Bluebeard**" is a novel about thinkable things that is easily separable from so much contemporary fiction of bland domesticity or intellectual gigantism, fiction on whose surface the mind can't find a point of attachment.

"**Bluebeard**" is an extremely short "tale," as Mr. Frisch calls it, even shorter than "**Man in the Holocene.**" Like Samuel Beckett, Mr. Frisch seems to be paring away his stock of expressiveness, moving toward a purer means as he nears his mid-70's. The book is made up in large part of remembered excerpts from the transcript of a fictional murder trial, interspersed with remarks, comments and reflections by the accused man. (p. 9)

The fascination of this novel lies in the fact that Schaad's formal guilt comes not to matter. What we follow is the arc of his effort to live with his acquittal and what it releases in him: a complex, subtle and disturbing cluster of truths about himself that spread far beyond the simple, bounded fact of the crime. Again and again Schaad talks about what "helps" and what doesn't during his life under the shadow of the murder. "What helps is billiards," he says, and "walking helps for a while." "Traveling abroad is no help at all," he says, and "I have also tried movies, of course, but I rarely stay to the end, I cannot take scenes of violence." And then there's alcohol, which "is also no help."

This sounds at first like the depiction of a quite understandable state of mind, that of a person wrongfully accused of a serious crime and acquitted under a cloud. Or it could be the state of mind of an actual murderer. But one isn't far into the book before it becomes clear that Mr. Frisch is up to something more interesting and problematic, something intellectually and morally dangerous. He wants to render the elusive relationship between the world of things said and done and believed—history itself, in particular moral history—and truths that can't be pinned down, proved or established beyond doubt, especially shadings of guilt and innocence.

By "help" Mr. Frisch doesn't mean assistance in forgetting. Schaad isn't so much trying to forget as to live in the face of ambiguity, uncertainty and, above all, the discrepancy between public perception of him and what he knows or suspects about himself. (p. 26)

[In "**Bluebeard**," Frisch juxtaposes] extremely precise physical descriptions with passages from the trial full of emotion, accusation and judgment. This works to undermine our natural but constricting interest in the murder case and shifts it toward the truer story, the inward one.

Schaad is a man whose moral nature cannot be dealt with by any sort of trial or verdict. He is more than simply a suspect in the case; like all human natures, his is intrinsically suspect. The name Felix Schaad seems derived from *Schadenfreude*, meaning pleasure in another's harm, but it could refer to Schaad as both harmer and harmed or, in another connotation of *schaden*, as damaged.

At any rate, one aspect of his sense of guilt clearly concerns his relations with women. . . .

The autobiographical element in Mr. Frisch's fiction is at its most direct in "**Montauk**," an account of an amorous weekend spent by an aging writer and a much younger woman; the characters are so recognizable that its designation as a novel seems dubious at best. Whatever its genre, "**Montauk**" is very revealing of its author's attitude toward women, which, depending on one's generosity, can be described as either old-fashioned European masculine superiority or very contemporary male chauvinism. And there are traces of this attitude in "**Stiller**" and other books of Mr. Frisch's.

"**Bluebeard**" is clearly not the author's life thinly disguised, but it seems to me that it isn't totally an aloof invention either. The [book's last] words "You are in pain" are, I think, addressed not only to the narrator but to the author as well and may refer both to moral uncertainty and ontological suffering. For the novel isn't the story of a soul in torment over a specific act but an investigation of the relative nature of moral and experiential truth. In this regard it reminds me of two very different works: Camus's "The Stranger" and Claude Chabrol's movie "Just Before Nightfall." . . . Short, almost laconic, beautifully shaped, "**Bluebeard**" will stay in my memory, barbed and unsettling. (p. 27)

Richard Gilman, "Who Killed Wife No. 6?" in The New York Times Book Review, *July 10, 1983, pp. 9, 26-7.*

SVEN BIRKERTS

The precision-minded Swiss have never been famous for grand gesture or passionate utterance. It is as if exposure to the mighty contours of the land has over generations pruned back the national soul and turned its energies inward. . . .

Out of this mountain fastness comes novelist, dramatist, and perennial Nobel candidate Max Frisch . . . , whose career has been one long assault upon repression, self-satisfaction, and bourgeois right-mindedness. Frisch—the Swiss who would not be Swiss—has done everything in his power to throw off the burden of his heritage. In the forty years since he quit architecture for writing, he has expressed himself with great inventiveness upon a single theme: the near-impossibility of living truthfully. He determined early on that the will to self-deception acts on the character as powerfully and almost as inevitably as gravity acts on the body. From his first major novel, *I'm Not Stiller* . . . , right up through the just-published novella, *Bluebeard,* he has argued that the self is not a given, that love is anything but the voluptuous surrender in a TV ad, and that it was the imperialistic ego that Blake named as "The invisible worm / That flies in the night." (p. 32)

For all its formal alteration, Frisch's work reveals an underlying consistency. The structural and stylistic shifts mark his maturing, the varying of his concerns, his need for increasingly direct statement. The man grows, but he is the same man. (p. 33)

Slim, as exquisitely crafted as any of his other works, [*Bluebeard*] is at once a stride forward and a return to certain former tendencies. Dr. Felix Schaad has been acquitted of the murder of Rosalinde Z., a prostitute and one of his seven former wives. The narrative consists of the obsessive replaying of the trial in Schaad's mind. Try as he may, he cannot silence the testimony. (pp. 34-5)

It is not clear from the testimony or Schaad's behavior whether he has or has not committed the crime. What does emerge from the various accounts is that he has lived his life as a supremely egotistical creature. As the testimony comes to an end, Schaad quite suddenly breaks. He rushes back to his home town and makes a confession at the police station. The town is nowhere near the scene of the crime, though, psychologically speaking, it is the very place. . . . Having made the confession, Schaad drives his car into a tree in an unsuccessful suicide attempt. While he is in the hospital, news comes that the real murderer has been arrested. But this makes no difference to the now-speechless Schaad. He has discovered his guilt. He did not murder Rosalinde, but he could have. The murder was a specific event, but his guilt is a condition of the soul. . . .

Bluebeard has been executed with the sharp geometrical inevitability of a perfect combination shot. Frisch is not so much returning to earlier themes as he is bringing the preoccupations of a lifetime under a more calculated and intense pressure. Eliot's remark, that each new masterpiece changes our relation to the masterpieces of the past, can be applied to this newest addition to Frisch's oeuvre. *Bluebeard* suggests that Frisch's zeal for serious, difficult subjects has not abated, that those of us who prophesied silence were premature. His tidings are no cheerier than usual, but we have never looked to Frisch for cheer. He has always been there to remind us that there is no simple prescription for truthful living, and that happiness is that point in geometry where parallel lines melt. (p. 35)

Sven Birkerts, "A Swiss Master," in The New Republic, *Vol. 189, No. 2, July 11, 1983, pp. 32-5.*

JIM MILLER

["**Bluebeard**"] shows Frisch to be in dazzling command of his meticulous literary powers. The hero is a hapless Don Juan named Herr Doktor Schaad. We meet him in the aftermath of a spectacular trial in which he has been accused of strangling a Zurich prostitute—his sixth wife. Acquitted by the jury, Schaad persists in trying himself in the courtroom of his conscience. Therein lies the drama in this laconic little fable about guilt and innocence in an Age of Bureaucracy.

Through a sequence of terse flashbacks we relive Schaad's ordeal. A long parade of witnesses—secretaries, psychiatrists, ex-wives—offer conflicting testimony. Depending on the speaker, the doctor appears meek, harmless, ill-tempered, tight-lipped, humorless, hypersensitive, a selfless philanthropist, an alcoholic philanderer. The prosecutor bullies him into rehearsing his dreams and confiding that perhaps he was jealously protective of his wives. Evidence gathered from his own private notebooks makes him seem insanely suspicious. . . .

Shaken by the trial's public exhumation of his private character, his medical practice in ruins, Schaad can neither repair his confidence nor escape a nagging sense of guilt. He tries shooting pool, feeding swans, strolling city streets—all to no avail. As he ruminates endlessly, the cold objectivity of remembered courtroom dialogues melts into a fevered fantasia of impersonal inquisition and inward remorse. . . .

Where, in fact, does justice lie? Is Schaad the innocent victim of a perfectly civilized form of judicial torture, a man driven mad by the methodical investigation of his conduct and character? Or did the jury mistakenly acquit a sadistic strangler, an heir to Bluebeard, the legendary wife slayer? For the answer, you'll have to consult Frisch's clever puzzlebox of a tale—and be prepared for a surprise ending. (p. 70)

Jim Miller, "Trial by Inner Jury," in Newsweek, *Vol. CII, No. 3, July 18, 1983, pp. 69-70.*

ROBERT M. ADAMS

Max Frisch, who has revived (and revised) the story of Bluebeard in a short, quasi-parabolic book [*Bluebeard*] is a versatile Swiss man of letters with a practiced talent for deliberately fragmented and enigmatic writings. *I'm Not Stiller,* his first, best-known, and still best book, studied a divided personality, one element of which was intent on repudiating the other; its theme of guilt disintegrating a nonpersonality only vaguely aware of what was being done to it would provide a constant pattern for Frisch's work. *Homo Faber* was a fable of technological man brought to destruction by the ancient Fates—as well as by an inopportune itch for slender easy young things. *Man in the Holocene,* though ostensibly about a single senile citizen overwhelmed by his past and fading out in the Ticino, was full of portentous echoes about the deteriorating human condition. Thus one can hardly help reading *Bluebeard* for its overtones, especially since its texture as a narration is diaphanous and full of holes. . . .

In short, the book, like several of Frisch's previous narratives, is an extended exercise in tantalizing and bafflement; it systematically withholds information, gives contradictory information, gives irrelevant answers to requests for information, or gives deliberately trivial information (as about a childhood rabbit named Pinocchio). The author is particularly evasive in defining the mental processes of his characters, either by professing frank ignorance or by silently ignoring them. (p. 14)

[*Bluebeard*] is sparsely written, mostly in dialogue, with few transitions and hardly any introductions; characters appear (sometimes from beyond the grave), testify or decline to testify, and dematerialize. Locales and periods change phantasmagorically. . . . The particularly revolting character of the murder seems to saturate the book's atmosphere; and of course the verdict, handed down at the beginning of the book, is really no verdict at all. So the book is spooky, even if it is not a mystery, and confirms the sense one gets from Frisch's career as a whole that he's a skilled contriver of mind-entangling labyrinths, after the fashion of Kafka and Borges.

On the other hand, there are some *Mitteleuropa* preoccupations that hover around *Bluebeard,* to which the unsuspicious American reader might be alerted by a glance at the recently reissued *Sketchbooks.* Frisch as a German Swiss is much exercised by the question of German war guilt, by the atrocities of the concentration camps and the fearsome destructiveness of the Hitler regime. . . . The historic record, for those who can stand to look into it, is searing; the wound on the moral conscience of the West seems likely to be unhealable.

It was Jules Michelet who called Gilles de Rais, the avatar of Bluebeard, a *bête d'extermination;* I do not know if Herr Frisch had in mind this phrase, or the awful parallel it has come inexorably to imply, when writing his story. But the shape he has given it provides a perfect model of the way inherited guilt can be shifted almost magically onto a faceless foreign scapegoat invented for the occasion. The Greek who in Frisch's novel appears from nowhere at the last moment to assume the burden of the murderer's guilt is hidden under multiple anomalies; he is a student in Zurich without knowing German; he is old, he is young; he has no motives, no tangible presence, no connections or relations. He exists simply as a negative neutral *Ausländer* onto whom Dr. Schaad (whose name implies ''harm'' or ''damage'') off-loads his guilt.

Frisch's book has been enormously popular in Germany. . . . Outside its particular social setting, one can hardly think it would amount to much. But Frisch's special gift for enclosing within a frame of deep guilt and shame a lot of vacant and undefined space, into which the reader's native feelings can insinuate themselves, has clearly dovetailed, in some complex and perhaps duplicitous way, with a historic situation. The book may well prove to have been an important symptom: diagnosticians of the future, with the happy advantage of hindsight, will no doubt tell us what condition it portends in that great, troubled, and now divided nation which is still struggling through nightmares to find its soul. (pp. 15-16)

> *Robert M. Adams, ''Shaggy Dog Fable,'' in* The New York Review of Books, *Vol. XXX, No. 14, September 29, 1983, pp. 14-16.*

DAVID MYERS

Both Frisch and Dürrenmatt, the terrible Swiss twins of moralistic postwar drama, have shown themselves fascinated over the last forty years with the tragicomic analysis of evaded ethical responsibility. The guilt of their protagonists has commonly had allegorical overtones for the whole of Western civilization. These male protagonists are violently expelled from the ostensible harmony of their cowardly lives. They are forced into tragic introspection that reveals they are *en mauvais foi* with themselves. Their lives culminate in the moving confession of guilt and failure. This is so with Dürrenmatt's Ill in *Der Besuch der alten Dame* and with Trapp in *Die Panne,* just as it is with Frisch's teacher in **Andorra.** Frisch's **Biedermann und die Brandstifter** is a farcical but still allegorical variation on this theme.

Frisch's latest novel **Blaubart** reads like an absurd inversion of these plays in a minor domestic key. The main character Felix Schaad does not achieve tragic stature through his obsession with a guilt that he has largely invented. He simply renders himself neurotically ineffectual, paranoid, and suicidal. The fact is that he is no more guilty of the ultimate sin of lovelessness than his seven egoistic wives.

In the original seventeenth-century legend, Bluebeard is a comic hyperbole of bloodthirstiness and perverted lust. Frisch parodistically inverts this legend, mocking its psychological superficiality. This is the same technique that he used in his play **Don Juan oder die Liebe zur Geometrie.** . . . Felix Schaad, like Frisch's Don Juan, is the unhappy victim of twentieth-century woman's social and sexual liberation. Felix is in fact a frustrated romantic monogamist who overloads the marital sexual union with almost mystic significance. He thereby makes prosaic marriage so overtense that it becomes hellish. His seven wives betray and exploit him until he is left a quivering wreck. (pp. 59-60)

Most of the novel takes the form of a legalistic cross-examination of witnesses. At times this technique becomes circumspect, repetitive, and even trivial. Each cross-examination is like a fragment of a jigsaw puzzle that is never really put together. The reality of actual courtroom scenes is freely interspersed with surreal fantasy as Felix Schaad's overdeveloped conscience cross-examines what is left of his libido and sublimation mechanism. This application of dry legalistic jargon to Felix's dreams and his libido should have produced more humor than it does in this somewhat self-important novel. Frisch's analysis of Felix's sexual problems owes a great deal to Sigmund Freud just as his analysis of Felix's guilt obsession shows the influence of Franz Kafka's *Der Prozess.* In the end, **Blaubart** can best be seen as a fairly poker-faced farce on bourgeois sexual neuroses in the 1980s. Marital and sexual malfunctions are seen by Frisch as the symptoms of a society that is narcissistically frigid and without direction or idealistic commitment. The comic dupe is Bluebeard himself, Felix Schaad as the oversensitive male seeking his elusive salvation in self-inflicted guilt. In fact he saves no one, least of all himself. (p. 60)

> *David Myers, in a review of ''Blaubart,'' in* The International Fiction Review, *Vol. 11, No. 1, Winter, 1984, pp. 59-60.*

Günter (Wilhelm) Grass

1927-

German novelist, poet, dramatist, essayist, illustrator, and nonfiction writer.

Grass is generally regarded as the most significant German writer to emerge in the post-World War II era. He established his reputation with three novels, known collectively as the *Danzig Trilogy,* which present various reactions of the German people to the rise of Nazism, the horrors of war, and the guilt that has lingered in the aftermath of Hitler's regime. These concerns are evident in his most famous novel, *Die Blechtrommel* (1959; *The Tin Drum*), in which the protagonist Oskar Matzerath willfully stunts his growth, perhaps as a response to the horror and chaos he observes. Grass is especially renowned for his exuberant prose style and creative stylistic techniques. In his novels, he combines meticulously plotted, realistic detail and absurd developments to create startling effects. His works accommodate a playful, childlike tone as well as bizarre and grotesque action. Grass has also gained respect for his poems and plays, but his accomplishments in these genres have been overshadowed by the international success of his novels. In recent years, Grass's focus on contemporary aspects of German culture and society reflects his active interest in German politics.

Grass's creative imagination and his artistic sensibilities are strongly rooted in his childhood experiences. The takeover of his home city Danzig by the Nazis was a major force in shaping his youth. Living under Nazi rule, Grass became a member of the Hitler Youth. He saw combat in World War II and became a prisoner of war while still in his teens. The noted Grass scholar Michael Hollington suggests that one reason Grass's fiction often centers on perversions of youth, such as Oskar's refusal to grow, is that Grass's own childhood was twisted by Nazi indoctrination and war. From his mother Grass learned the superstitions and myths of the Cassubians, an old Slavic race whose folklore deals with people who survive through cunning. This influence is revealed in characters who, like Oskar, rely on wit rather than physical stature. When Grass began writing in the years following the war, these elements fused into an original vantage point from which he could examine the culture and history of his people.

The *Danzig Trilogy* is partly composed of autobiographical material, as it depicts life in Danzig and the city's experiences with Nazism. The themes of guilt and responsibility figure prominently in these works. *The Tin Drum,* the first novel of the trilogy, brought Grass international fame. Regarded as a stylistic tour-de-force, this picaresque novel combines fantasy and realism, innocence and terror to capture the wildly erratic personality of its protagonist and the brutal events he witnesses. *The Tin Drum* is also rich in allusions to the New Testament and various myths and mixes prose and poetry. *Katz und Maus* (1961; *Cat and Mouse*), set during the war, relates the story of an alienated Danzig youth who seeks social acceptance and personal meaning by becoming an athlete and later a soldier; however, his aspirations end in failure and humiliation. Although some critics assert that the novel's allegorical and symbolic substance are too plain, others praise Grass for sensitively capturing the torment and guilt of his

protagonist. *Hundejahre* (1963; *Dog Years*) incorporates satire, parody, and an examination of linguistics in relating the story of three young men who each respond differently to the rise of Nazism. Grass also includes autobiographical elements in his later novels; many of these works voice his political beliefs. *Aus dem Tagebuch einer Schnecke* (1972; *From the Diary of a Snail*), *Der Butt* (1977; *The Flounder*), and *Das Treffen in Telgte* (1979; *The Meeting at Telgte*) met with varying degrees of success, and most critics continue to view the *Danzig Trilogy* as Grass's premier achievement.

Grass's poetry, though it receives less attention that his prose works, is generally well regarded. The tone of his poetry has shifted from exuberance and playfulness in his early work to a more restrained examination of moral and political issues. Critics most often praise his command of the language and his linguistic experiments. Grass has also written several plays which, although they are considered powerful, have met with modest success. Several of them have been linked with the Theater of the Absurd due to their startling imagery, black comedy, and bleak view of existence.

Kopfgeburten: oder Die Deutschen sterben aus (1980; *Headbirths or the Germans Are Dying Out*) is representative of Grass's novelistic concerns since the *Danzig Trilogy*. This work, which was inspired by his travels through Asia and by his interest in the German elections of 1980, follows Grass as he imagines the making of a film about a West German couple who debate the pros and cons of bringing a baby into an unstable world. During the course of the book, Grass ruminates on what the world would be like if there were 950 million Germans instead of Chinese. Grass also examines such topics as the reuniting of East and West Germany and various issues pertaining to the elections of 1980. Critical reception to this novel was mixed. Several reviewers objected to Grass's discussion of issues of personal interest within the framework of a novel. Others, however, applauded Grass's attempt to coalesce his interest in politics and literature.

(See also *CLC*, Vols. 1, 2, 4, 6, 11, 15, 22 and *Contemporary Authors*, Vols. 13-16, rev. ed.)

MAX KNIGHT

When Günter Grass's **"Tin Drum"** was published, Hans Magnus Enzensberger said it was a dish on which reviewers would gag for a decade. Grass's poems, available to Americans for the first time in [*Selected Poems*] are the dessert. The freewheeling German romps with gusto through the brambles of his imagination, sticks his tongue out provocatively, or bewilders his audience with an innocence that is only slyly feigned.

The poems are as iconoclastic as the novels, but tamer—they shock by juxtaposition and gaps in continuity rather than by Rabelaisian disregard for sensitive readers' stomachs. Grass's more notorious personal fetishes from the novels (worms, eels, floating corpses) do not appear in this selection, but the more genteel (chickens, cooks) do. . . .

Grass has said his poetry was influenced by Rilke, Garcia Lorca and Ringelnatz; little of Rilke is discernible, but a touch of Lorca's daemonism is there, with a larger dose of Ringelnatz's buffoonery; most of it, however, is Grass. As in the novels, Grass plays hide and seek with his readers, allowing them to understand (or not understand) his poem "on two levels," interlarding them with symbols yet denying symbolic intent.

Freud once said that sometimes even a cigar is just a cigar; are, then Grass's cherries, midges, blackbirds really just cherries, midges, blackbirds? Surely his gold teeth are no ordinary gold teeth, since they are "plucked from the dead" (in Auschwitz?), since caries "long has lurked behind the toothpaste" (of sweet German official statements covering up guilt?), and since one has to "open his mouth" (to admit the Nazi enormities?).

> Max Knight, *"Romp through the Brambles," in* The New York Times Book Review, *August 14, 1966, p. 5.*

MICHAEL HAMBURGER

[*This essay from which this excerpt is taken was originally published in* Dimension, *Summer 1970.*]

When I ask myself what makes Günter Grass so outstanding a phenomenon as a poet, the first answer that occurs to me is: the circumstance that he is so many other things as well, an outstanding novelist, playwright, draughtsman, politician and cook. In an age of specialists such diversity of interest and accomplishment could well be suspect, as indeed it is to some of Günter Grass's critics. Yet the more one looks at Grass's diverse activities the more clearly one sees that they all spring from the same source and centre; also, that the unfashionable

diversity is inseparable from his achievement in each of and other, fields, because the whole man moves together, within the area of his dominant tensions and concerns. I am far from wanting to claim that this area, in Günter Grass's case, is unlimited: but it is strikingly and decisively larger than that of most other poets in our time, and that is one reason why Günter Grass's poetry is so difficult to place in terms of literary history, trends and genres.

In the early nineteen-fifties, when Grass was writing the poems collected in his first book, *Die Vorzüge der Windhühner*, Gottfried Benn was still advocating what he called 'absolute poetry', 'words assembled in a fascinating way' and not subject to moral or social criteria. On the other hand, and on the other side, Bertolt Brecht was still advocating a kind of poetry to be judged by its moral and social usefulness. Benn's emphasis was on self-expression, the enacting of inner states; Brecht's on the rendering of external and communal realities. If we ask ourselves to which of these sides Günter Grass belonged as a poet—and almost all the better poetry written by German writers of Grass's generation follows a line of development that can be traced back to that crucial divergence—we come up against one aspect of Grass's capacity to embrace and balance extreme opposites. Shortly after the publication of *Die Vorzüge der Windhühner* Grass wrote three short prose pieces which appeared in the periodical *Akzente* under the title 'Der Inhalt als Widerstand' ('Content as Resistance'), in which imagination and reality, fantasy and observation, are treated not as alternatives but as the generators of a necessary tension. The middle piece, a brief dramatic account of a walk taken by two poets, Pempelfort and Krudewil, presents the extreme alternatives. Pempelfort is in the habit of stuffing himself with indigestible food before going to bed, to induce nightmares and genitive metaphors which he can jot down between fits of sleep; the quoted specimens of his poems place him in the line of development which includes German Expressionism and the Surrealism that was rediscovered by German poets after the war. Krudewil, on the other hand, wants to 'knit a new Muse', who is 'grey, mistrustful and totally dreamless, a meticulous housewife'. This homely and matter-of-fact Muse points to the practice of Brecht, who drew on dreams not for metaphors or images, but moralities. Grass's treatment of these two characters is good-humouredly and humorously impartial. Those who misunderstand Grass's moderation, and moderation generally, as either indifference or weakness, when it is the strength of those who don't lose their heads in a crisis, could regard this piece as an early instance of Grass's equivocation; but Grass would not have bothered to write the dialogue if he had not been deeply involved in the issues which it raises.

Before turning to Grass's poems I want to touch on one other prose piece, published nearly ten years later in the same periodical, when Grass had become a celebrated writer and a controversial public figure. It is the lecture 'Vom mangelnden Selbstvertrauen der schreibenden Hofnarren unter Berücksichtigung nicht vorhandener Höfe' ('On the Lack of Self-confidence among Writing Court Fools in View of Non-existent Courts'). . . . Grass came out in favour of a position half-way between what the radicals understood by commitment—the subordination of art to political and social programmes—and the essential demand of art itself for free play of the imagination, the freedom which Grass identifies with that of the court fool or jester. If a writer is worried about the state of affairs in his country and elsewhere, Grass argues—and there can be no doubt at all that Grass himself cares about it passionately—the best way to do something about it is the way of political action proper—the kind of action which Grass himself has undertaken on behalf of the political party which he supports. (pp. 134-36)

Grass is not only an anti-specialist but an anti-ideologist. Even his theoretical pronouncements are nourished and sustained by his awareness of complexity, an awareness which he owes to first-hand experience. In his imaginative works, including his poems, the mixture has not remained constant. Just as in his prose fiction there has been a gradual shift away from subjective fantasy to observed realities, a shift parallelled in his plays, it is the first book of poems that shows Grass at his most exuberantly and uninhibitedly clownish. This is not to say that these early poems lack moral or metaphysical seriousness, but that the element of free play in them is more pronounced and more idiosyncratic than in the later poems, in which the clown has to defend his privilege of freedom, a special freedom begrudged to him by the moralist and the politician.

It has become something of a commonplace in Grass criticism to note that his imagination and invention are most prolific where he is closest to childhood experience, by which I mean both his own, as evoked in the more or less autobiographical sections of *Die Blechtrommel* and *Katz und Maus* or in the more or less autobiographical poem **'Kleckerburg',** and childish modes of feeling, seeing and behaving. Almost without exception, the poems in Grass's first book owe their vigour and peculiarity to this mode of feeling, seeing, and behaving. These early poems enact primitive gestures and processes without regard for the distinctions which adult rationality imposes on the objects of perception. They have their being in a world without divisions or distinctions, full of magical substitutions and transformations. To speak of surrealism in connection with those early poems tells us little about them, because they are as realistic as they are fantastic, with a realism that seems fantastic only because it is true to the polymorphous vision of childhood. As far as literary influences are concerned, Grass's early poems are far less closely related to the work of any Surrealist poet than to that of a Dadaist, Jean (or Hans) Arp, whose eye and ear had the same mischievous innocence, giving a grotesque twist to everyday objects and banal phrases. In his later, post-Dadaist work, Arp also adapted his unanchored images and metaphors to increasingly moral and social preoccupations, not to mention the metaphysical ones which, much like Grass, he had always combined with his comic zest.

Most of the poems in *Die Vorzüge der Windhühner* deal in unanchored images, like the 'eleventh finger' which cannot be tied down to any particular plane of meaning or symbolism, but owes its genesis and function to a complex of largely personal associations. Such unanchored and floating images were also carried over into Grass's prose, especially in *Die Blechtrommel,* and some of them had such obsessional power over Grass's imagination that they recur with variations in his poems, prose narratives, plays and drawings. . . . The substitution practised by Grass in these poems also includes drastic synaesthesia, as in the many poems connected with music, orchestras, musical instruments. Sounds are freely transposed into visual impressions and vice versa, as in **'Die Schule der Tenöre'** ('The School for Tenors'). (pp. 136-37)

I shall not attempt a lengthy interpretation of this poem which would amount to a translation of it into the terms of adult rationality—terms irrelevant to the poem, in any case. In my context it is enough to point out that its subject —or content, to link up with Grass's early contribution to poetics—is little more than a sequence of kinetic gestures, derived in the first place from a personal response to the singing of tenors, but proceeding by a series of free substitutions and transpositions. These substitutions and transpositions observe no distinctions between one order of experience and another, between aural and visual phenomena, between what is physically plausible and what is not. As in surrealist writing, metaphor is autonomous; but, though one thing in the poem leads to another by associations that are astonishingly fluid, the poem is held together by an organization different from automatic writing in that the initial phenomenon is never quite left behind. (p. 140)

But for the wit and the more ingenious allusions in poems like **'The School for Tenors'** they would belong to a realm of clown's and child's play which is amoral and asocial. Yet even in **'The School for Tenors'** satirical implications arise from references to historical phenomena like seaside resorts, shrapnel and, above all, to audiences in an opera house. The very short, almost epigrammatic pieces in the same collection present Grass the moralist looking over the shoulder of the clown and child, not least incisively in **'Familiär'** (**'Family Matters'),** which has the additional irony of judging the adult world from a child's point of view—a device most characteristic of the man who was to write *The Tin Drum,* as well as later poems like **'Advent'.** (p. 141)

Very few of Grass's later poems are as exuberantly playful as most of those in his first collection; but just as the moralist was not wholly absent from the early poems, the clowning fantast and the polymorphous sensualist keep popping up in later poems seemingly dominated by political and social satire. The creative tension permits, and indeed demands, a good deal of movement in one direction; but it does not break.

In Grass's next collection, *Gleisdreieck,* it is the poems that touch on divided Berlin which give the clearest indication of how fantasy interlocks with minute observation in Grass's work. The elaborate documentation that preceded the writing of *The Tin Drum* is one instance of a development that can also be traced in the poems and the drawings, from the high degree of abstraction in the drawings done for *Die Vorzüge der Windhühner* to the grotesque magnification of realistic detail in the drawings done for *Gleisdreieck,* and on to the meticulous verisimilitude of the clenched hand reproduced on the cover of the third collection, *Ausgefragt.* (pp. 141-42)

The underlying seriousness of Grass's clowning—as of all good clowning—is even more evident in *Gleisdreieck* than in the earlier collection. Without any loss of comic zest or invention Grass can now write existential parables like **'Im Ei'** (**'In the Egg')** or **'Saturn',** poems that take the greater risk of being open to interpretation in terms other than those of pure zany fantasy. One outstanding poem in *Gleisdreieck* has proved utterly untranslatable, because its effect depends on quadruple rhymes and on corresponding permutations of meaning for which only the vaguest equivalents can be found in another language. Grass himself has a special liking for this poem, the sinister nursery rhyme **'Kinderlied',** perhaps because it represents the most direct and the most drastic fusion in all his poetry of innocence and experience. This artistic fusion results from the confrontation of the freedom most precious to Grass, the freedom of child's play which is also the court jester's prerogative, with its polar opposite, the repression of individuality imposed by totalitarian political régimes. (pp. 142-43)

No other poem by Grass has the same combination of simplicity and intricacy, extreme economy of means and extreme wealth of implication. Apart from the taut syntactic structure and the rhyme scheme, the poem is untranslatable because no single word in English has the familiar and horrible connotations of a German word like 'angezeigt'—reported to the police or other official authority as being ideologically suspect—or 'abgeworben'—the bureaucratic counterpart to being excommunicated, blackballed, expelled, deprived of civil rights, ceasing to exist as a member of a corporative and collective order that has become omnipotent. (pp. 143-44)

It is characteristic of the state of West German literature in the late sixties that Günter Grass's third collection of poems, *Ausgefragt,* gave rise to political controversies rather than to literary ones; and the collection does contain a relatively high proportion of poems that respond directly—perhaps too directly in some cases—to political and topical issues. Some of them, like **'In Ohnmacht gefallen'** (**'Powerless, with a Guitar'**), were bound to be read as provocations or correctives aimed at the radical left. . . . (p. 144)

Compared with Grass's earlier poems this one gives little scope for playfulness. An almost Brechtian literalness and austerity seem to contradict Grass's resolve to keep the court fool separate from the politically committed citizen. Yet I think it would be wrong to read this poem primarily as a polemic against the radicals. The gravity of its manner suggests that Grass is quarrelling more with himself than with others, that he is rendering a painful experience of his own. The old exuberance re-asserts itself elsewhere in the same collection, even in thematically related poems like **'Der Dampfkessel-Effekt'** (**'The Steam Boiler Effect'**) which *are* primarily polemical. . . . Perhaps the happiest poem of all in *Ausgefragt*—happiest in two senses of the word—is **'Advent'**, since it blends social satire with the freedom and zest which—in Grass's work—appertain to the world of childhood. (pp. 145-46)

Whatever Günter Grass may do next—and he is the most unpredictable of artists—his third book of poems points to a widening awareness; and this means that he is unlikely to take his realism and literalness beyond a certain point. His involvement in the practical business of politics has imposed a very perceptible strain on him, but his essentially unpuritanical temper has ensured that the creative tension between innocence and experience, spontaneity and self-discipline is always maintained. Another way of putting it is that, unlike the ideologists and radicals, Grass does not want to carry politics over into private life or into those artistic processes which have to do with personality. If *Ausgefragt* is dominated by public concerns, it also contains this short poem, **'Falsche Schönheit'** (**'Wrong Beauty'**): . . .

This quiet
life,
   I mean the period from yesterday to Monday morning,
      is fun again:
I laugh at the dish of parsnips,
our guinea pig pinkly reminds me,
cheerfulness threatens to flood my table,
and an idea,
   an idea of sorts,
      rises without yeast;
       and I'm happy
         because it is wrong and beautiful.

Ideas that make one happy because they are 'wrong and beautiful' have no place in the austere post-Brechtian verse written by so many West and East German poets in the nineteen-sixties. When he wants to be, Grass can be as realistic as they are; but

the court jester's freedom includes the right to be fantastic, playful and grotesque.

Grass's insistence on this freedom has a special importance against the background of a general crisis in West German literature, precipitated by its increasing politicization. While East German poets like Wolf Biermann and Reiner Kunze have been defending the individual against encroachments on his privacy on the part of an all-powerful collective, or of an all-powerful bureaucracy that claims to represent the collective, many West German writers have done their best to deprive themselves of such personal liberty as they enjoy. . . . Those who have followed critical opinion in West Germany over the years will be familiar with statements about what can no longer be written: love poems, because love is a form of bourgeois self-indulgence; nature poems, because we live in a technological age; confessional poems, or poems of personal experience, because they are poems of personal experience; moon poems, because, as Peter Rühmkorf suggested well before the first moon landing, cosmonauts are better qualified to deal with the moon than poets. Needless to say, all those kinds of poems have continued to be written, even if they have been written in new ways. (pp. 147-49)

Günter Grass, in any case, has not worried too much about what can and cannot be written, according to the latest theoretical appraisal of the state of civilization. He has written what he was impelled to write, with a prodigal energy which—even in poems—has involved the risk of error, of tactlessness, of 'wrong beauty', of bad taste. It remains to be seen whether Günter Grass can maintain his energy and spontaneity as a poet not only in the teeth of the ideological constrictors, to whom he has made no concessions, but also as he moves farther and farther away from childhood and the peculiar imaginative sources of his art. Since there is a limit to the fruitful tension between the politician and the clown, or between any kind of arduous practical involvement and the state of openness which poetry demands, it is my hope that conditions in Germany will soon make it unnecessary for Grass to assume responsibilities that ought to be borne by persons without his unique talents as a writer and artist. The tension, as I have tried to show, was there from the first, even when the clown seemed to have it all his way, and the moralist in Grass had not yet involved him in party politics. There is no reason why it should cease if my hope is fulfilled, since in poets practical experience is transmuted into awareness, and innocence is never lost, but renews itself within the awareness. (p. 149)

Michael Hamburger, "Moralist and Jester: The Poetry of Günter Grass," in his Art As Second Nature: Occasional Pieces, 1950-74, *Carcanet New Press, 1975, pp. 134-49.*

MICHAEL HOLLINGTON

In approaching Grass as a poet and a dramatist, it is extremely difficult to forget that Grass has gained pre-eminent recognition as a novelist: in what follows I have not attempted to do so. Certainly the most immediate kind of interest that these works are likely to arouse for admirers of Grass's novels lies in the large number of parallels or anticipations of images and themes explored in the prose works. Standing by themselves, they would not have made Grass a significant contemporary writer— the body of lyric writing is too slender. . . .

My own satisfaction in reading these works comes chiefly from the discovery of how closely Grass's work—even when it is at its most 'absurd'—reflects contemporary social and psychological realities. Political themes are apparent from the very start, and while the poems and plays, like the work in general, display a clear development in the direction of increasingly overt political subject-matter, the gain in directness often entails a loss in effectiveness. Certainly in the case of the poems, it seems to me that the most powerful political statements are made through the medium of a symbolic language. (p. 88)

'. . . Lyric poetry has always offered me the chance or opportunity of taking stock, of putting myself in most particular question.' Grass's familiar existentialist phrasing of the 'challenge' of lyric poetry suggests the difficulty of assessing his poetic output—contained in three volumes published between 1956 and 1967 and collected in . . . *Gesammelte Gedichte (Collected Poems)*—in isolation from the work as a whole or more latterly, from his political involvements. The reader confronts a writer with very little interest in the 'purity' of literary genres and a great deal of expressed mistrust or even contempt for 'formalist' writing. (p. 89)

Grass's first volume of poems, *Die Vorzüge der Windhühner (The Advantages of Windfowl)*, which appeared in 1956 (it was also his first substantial appearance as a writer), declares its surrealist playfulness in its title. What are 'windfowl?' How can they be said to have 'advantages'? Over what? (p. 92)

There is awkwardness and self-consciousness [in the title poem]—the 'rinds of dreams' are predictably hard, and the 'key of allegory', even if it's a joke cliché, is a ponderous one—but little to suggest indifference to poetic form. Grass follows modernist masters (like Pound and Eliot, for English readers) in using syntactic pattern and repetition as the bolster of free verse . . . in supporting this structure through assonance. . . . This shapely syntactical clarity liberates metaphor from the need to respect normal logical categories, dissolves mental props like 'tenor' and 'vehicle', so that the birds are both feeders and food, both perceivers and perceived, both the objects that the poem describes and that description itself (*'Feder'* provides a pun, meaning both 'feather' and 'pen'). The line of poetic descent, from Symbolism via Surrealism, is manifest.

These images provide an introduction to the mythological system of the volume . . . a network of recurrent associations that provides the larger unifying structure of the poems. (pp. 93-4)

[Many] of the poems carry Grass's common mythic structuring of recent German history—an idyllic beginning, set in the distant past, is rudely shattered by calamity, and then follows a period of flight and retreat into protective corners from which the lyric subject observes the chaos outside. There is an overall ironic perspective that resembles the novels to follow: the poet's imagery effects a 'making strange' of the familiar objects of everyday life, mocking that desired bourgeois safety and comfort that is designed to separate the interior world of the house from the fearsome forces of nature or history outside. He uses himself as exemplary subject.

Read in this way, the poems of this volume form a coherent sequence with clear affinities to *The Tin Drum*. The presence of related images—glass-shattering voices, dwarfs, hunchbacks, Polish flags and hairy triangles—is not in itself as significant as the desire to combine these images into something like a coherent narrative. Perhaps Gottfried Benn was right when in 1953 he advised the author of these poems to turn to prose, and Grass may have acknowledged the wisdom of this advice when he published some of the poems separately under the title *Short Stories from Berlin*. The narrative tricks of *The*

Tin Drum are often to be glimpsed—that initial gambit of involving the reader, for instance, by putting in his mouth a question about the advantages of windfowl and then proceeding to answer it, anticipates the first chapter of the novel (which is obviously more aggressive in its way of grasping our attention). Yet the most obviously narrative poems in the collection are those set in the form of parables, which suggest once again that Grass was not altogether immune to the Kafkaesque fashions of German writing in the fifties. (pp. 95-6)

Grass's second collection of poems, *Gleisdreieck (Triangle Junction)*, which appeared a year later than *The Tin Drum*, seems to me his finest. The concrete realities that the poems address, reflected only through the code of associative images in *The Advantages of Windfowl*, now moves forward into prominent focus; the title refers to a Berlin underground station where lines from the two sectors of the city form a triangular junction. Buildings are going up, built over the rubble of war-damage—this is now the Berlin of the somewhat belated postwar reconstruction; with a kind of remarkable prophetic insight in pre-wall Berlin, the opening poem ('five strophes of three lines each') concerns the building of 'fire-proof walls'. These are associated with a kind of whitewashing: they are 'immaculately sawn out', one of them carries Persil advertisements, a boy rueing the loss of his rubble-playground throws a snowball. . . . In a fine parable-style poem with a Brechtian title, **'The Ballad of the Black Cloud'**, the builders leave behind lime, which is eaten to good effect by an 'immaculate' hen who lays her brood in the builder's sand; the black cloud is an ironic apocalypse threatening the security of the brood in the sand, but passing by—not without disturbing effect:

> And no-one will ever be sure
> What came of those four eggs
> Under the hen, under the cloud,
>
> What happened to them in the builders' sand.

In another powerful conception, **'The Great Rubble Lady Speaks'**, the lament of the rubble lady is drowned by the sentimental sounds of a *Biedermeier* society comfortably reinstalled. . . . (pp. 98-9)

The poetic persona of these poems, however, registers the hollowness of this return to 'normality', the secret anxieties that it attempts to mask and suppress. The everyday world opens up sudden chasms of anxiety: in the poem **'Friday'** for instance, the poet brings home fresh herrings to cook (the poem takes as its subject the ritual of composing a poem), unwraps them from their newspaper-wrapping, only to find that the newspaper contains news of crisis and disaster. In [**'Saturn'**], one of the finest poems in this volume, where Grass is at the peak of his powers, each everyday object or action becomes strange and monstrous. . . . Once more, the poem's formal structure is tight and economical, setting up a pattern of expectations and working variations upon it (the influence of Brecht is again apparent). (pp. 99-101)

Ausgefragt (Cross-Examined) is Grass's third substantial volume of poems (it came out in 1967). It is the most uneven of the collections, containing some first-rate work, sometimes larger and more ambitious than the earlier successes, and also some less satisfactory and questionable poems. Many of the poems are markedly different in style from those in the previous volumes; at the outset, they announce an aggressive departure to fresh fields and pastures new:

> Enough of similes,
> chewing the cud and splitting hairs,
> of waiting for my gall to write.

There are gains and losses. Gone indeed are some of the more pretentious gestures of *The Advantages of Windfowl*, the comparings of worries to watches: the language is generally crisper, more natural and conversational. But also gone from some of the poems at least is the kind of taut economy that distinguishes the best poems of *Gleisdreieck*, the capacity to structure tightly round a single image or group of images. Many of the political poems, of which the most famous are those contained in the section 'ZORN ARGER WUT' ('ANGER VEXATION RAGE') are unconvincing. These poems, attacks on fashionable protests, protestors and protesting poets, are uncertain in their tone: at times they engage complex and meaningful problems concerning the worth and effectiveness of literary protest, bringing themselves (poems protesting against protests) dynamically into the issue. At other times their sarcasm is crass and their propositions dubious. . . . (pp. 102-03)

[The] political poems are related to a concern that runs through all Grass's poems, the relation between the writer in the process of formulating his phrases, and the realities he wishes to convey. In *Advantages of Windfowl* this concern is made apparent in frequent images of the printed text itself, the shape of the type on the page: the pair of poems **'K, der Käfer'** (**'K, the beetle'**) and **'V, der Vogel'** (**'V, the bird'**) are the most obvious examples, using the shape of the letters as visual emblems of the experiences described, the one about a beetle on its back like the letter K on its side, the other developing its images out of the wedge-shaped letter V and the silhouette of birds in flight:

> V, the bird, a wedge
> tears open an apple, lays bare a brain,
> inserts the gorges of mountains . . .

In *Gleisdreieck* poems like **'In the Egg'** ask Platonist questions about language, whether we live in a cave of language, and whether words are not about things but merely about other words. . . . (p. 104)

Grass thus displays his adherence to a modernist myth of language—its mistrust of the abstract written sign and its attempt to concretize words through a maximal use of their physical presence on the page. It is well known that Grass does his writing in a standing position, as if he were wielding a chisel and working at a sculpture as he had done as an art student, and that he writes the first drafts of his works in longhand; his narrative are likewise conscious of the physical act of writing (Brauxel/Amsel disapproves of Matern's habit of writing directly with a typewriter, Oskar equates black marks on white paper with guilt). It is particularly striking that each volume of poems is accompanied with drawings of the animals and objects that are so frequently the subjects of these works. These drawings have an important role in realizing the meaning of the poems, mediating the gap between the abstract signs of language and the concrete realities of experience.

At the heart of Grass's work is a mistrust of language as a deceitful structuring of reality. Harry Liebenau, the budding poet of *Dog Years*, whose penchant for pretentious metaphor and redundant statement makes him a plausible author of *The Advantages of Windfowl*, senses the frustration of trying to fit a static verbal formulation to the dynamism of experience: 'In fifth I coined the expression: "The new soloist leaps so slowly a pencil could follow." That is what I still call leaps that are skilfully delayed: leaps that a pencil could follow. If only I could follow leaps with a pencil.' . . . In the novels, Grass's strategy is to unmask the inadequacy of language by inventing

multiple, patently artificial verbal patterns. In some of the best of his poems he adopts an opposite strategy, concentrating on making the language as minimal as possible. (pp. 105-06)

Michael Hollington, in his Günter Grass: The Writer in a Pluralist Society, *Marion Boyars, 1980, 186 p.*

ELISABETH FINNE AND WES BLOMSTER

"I'm curious about the 80s," comments Günter Grass in his latest book [*Kopfgeburten*]. His curiosity is shared by the readers of Grass and of his creative countrymen who currently populate the German literary scene. One aspect of this curiosity regards the role which Grass himself will play within German literature in the decade which has just opened. The observations which follow concern the problem of representation in contemporary German writing: to what degree can a present-day writer represent his nation, and, if the question is of possible validity, who among German writers might serve this representational function in the present decade? Despite the evidence which negates the writer as the representative of a pluralistic society, it is not unreasonable to claim this status for Günter Grass. (p. 560)

Despite these many factors which speak against the assignment of a representative role to any German writer in the 1980s, it is clear that one man will continue in a position of central importance to German society during this decade. Even if his position requires redefinition of representation, Günter Grass seems destined by work and character to be present actively at every intersection of art and politics in his country.

A review of major turning points in Grass's career emphasizes the changing nature of representation. Grass will probably never again know the solidarity with any generation of Germans manifested in his march down Berlin's Kurfürstendamm in January 1967, arms locked with students chanting "Ho-Ho-Ho-Chi-Minh." This liaison ended with the police's killing of the student Benno Ohnesorg before the West Berlin Opera in June of that year. (That demonstration, it is recalled, protested the presence of the late Shah of Iran in Berlin.) This began, in turn, the series of macabre and tragic events which continues in Germany today. Terrorism and violence—forces of which Grass disapproved totally—brought to the headlines the names of Rudi Dutschke, Andreas Baader and Ulrike Meinhof. Today Grass lives largely in isolation. His alienation from such organized political forces as the New Left, however, does not contradict his position as a representative writer.

In another sense, Grass is today the victim of his own early popularity. "To become a classic in our time . . . may involve being condemned to ineffectuality," Michael Hollington has observed [in the foreword to his book, excerpted above]. While Grass, at a previous point in his career, "represented to the intelligentsia . . . the 'active conscience of Germany,'" he is now "widely mistrusted as a treacherous establishment liberal." One scholar has concluded that "he is no longer of contemporary relevance." His representative position is consequently denied.

Hollington defines two reasons for widespread lack of interest in Grass within Germany. The guilt of the Nazi period, to which Grass devoted so much energy, is a dead issue for a generation of readers totally postwar in orientation: "Liberal democracy has for them no value in itself, as it had for Grass and his generation, brought up in the Nazi period." A more general reason involves "a very widespread deterioration . . . of the vitality of the liberal humanist tradition." . . .

The analysis is correct; yet it underscores the necessity that Grass be seen as the representative writer of Germany today. Precisely for the reasons stated above, Grass grows increasingly important as the mediator between Germany past and present. Current lack of concern for these two issues—the Nazi past and the humanist tradition—does not make them unimportant. The current upsurge in neo-Nazi activity in the country, combined with beginning economic troubles, will reaffirm the centrality of these problems and—if there are eyes to read—will focus renewed attention upon Grass's endeavor. Grass is beyond doubt literary Germany's most significant link between past traditions and modernity; he is simultaneously both the roots and foliage of that creative continuity upon which the spiritual well-being of the nation depends. . . .

Grass will remain a controversial figure; the Right will see him as dangerously leftist, and the Left will view him as an impotent intellectual liberal. It is precisely this position, however, which qualifies him as the representative writer of a society torn by contradictions and lacking that common denominator which seemingly validated the representative function of writers in previous epochs. (p. 562)

In the discomfort which he causes, Grass is something of an heir of Heine. For him there are neither taboos nor sacred cows; he permits himself detours around nothing. Indeed, there are some in the troubled Germany of today—haunted by the black myth of professional persecution or *Berufsverbot*—who assert that open admiration of Grass would involve the risk of unemployment. This suggests that Grass is the representative of an intellectual underground within his own nation; a significant truth might be contained in this assertion.

Two final perspectives demand consideration. Today Grass commands more attention in the rest of the world than any other living German writer. Even if the pluralistic society within which he works is unable to view him as its representative, he certainly is this in the eyes of the world. Looking also at divided Germany, Grass has recently advanced the thesis that modern Germany involves indeed two states; they compose, however, one cultural nation. . . .

Günter Grass's entire mature life has been a translation into reality of the metaphor of the two beer mats—his creative effort and his political involvement—offered late in *Aus dem Tagebuch einer Schnecke (From the Diary of a Snail;* 1972). Grass will continue to juxtapose opposite truths; impossibility will continue to confront impossibility in congenial coexistence. He will weave further personal experience, speculation and the reality of contemporary Germany into an often rough but coherent tapestry out of which the turbulent history of the twentieth century can be read. To saddle him with the designation "representative writer" might well be as unwelcome to him as the concept of the writer as the conscience of the nation once was. Nonetheless, Grass is there; he is beyond doubt the most representative writer of Germany today, and there is reason to assume that he will continue his effort undaunted throughout the eighties. Indeed, it has been suggested that Grass might well be viewed as the Sisyphus of this decade; Grass himself affirms: "I'm not going to quit." . . . (p. 563)

Elisabeth Finne and Wes Blomster, "The Federal Republic in the Eighties: On German Representation," in World Literature Today, *Vol. 55, No. 4, Autumn, 1981, pp. 560-64.*

JOEL AGEE

There are ropewalkers, lion tamers, and clowns among novelists; also bareback riders, trapeze artists, strong men, and illusionists; and once in awhile an impresario will appear who commands a whole circus, as Günter Grass did a few years ago with *The Flounder,* the three-ring, cymbal-clashing, sawdust-kicking entertainment he gave himself as a fiftieth birthday present. *Headbirths* is a much more modest performance, a mere juggling act—but let that "mere" not imply any disparagement of the art of juggling, or of Günter Grass's command of it. Anyone who can keep two approximately equal handfuls of real-life and fictional characters smoothly circulating and even conversing in the same narrative space, without giving any impression of artificiality, has earned my respect; and Grass throws in at least a dozen other items of widely disparate bulk and shape—the Christian Democratic and the Social Democratic parties of Germany, for example; the Chinese and the Berlin walls; a novel-in-progress called *Headbirths;* Orwell's slavish decade (is it ours as well?) and Camus's defiant Sisyphus; hunger in Asia and a vacuum-sealed German liverwurst that survives the combined ravages of time, tropical heat, the probing slice of a border inspector's knife, and Günter Grass's whimsy. Time and time again he considers dismissing the sausage from his plot, just as a master juggler will seem to drop one particularly unmanageable rubber ball, only to cradle it on his foot or in the nape of his neck for a while and toss it back into the general whirl.

The novel (but is it a novel?) begins with a frightening event that took place three years ago in Shanghai, the city where 11 million out of 950 million Chinese live. Günter Grass was walking in the street with his wife, Ute, surrounded by countless identically dressed bicycle riders, when suddenly he was "hit by an idea, a speculative reversal: *what if, from this day on, the world had to face up to the existence of nine hundred fifty million Germans. . . ."*

The italics are mine, but I believe Mr. Grass would agree that the terrifying implications of such a thought cannot be emphasized strongly enough. (pp. 30-1)

Back in Berlin a month later, after brief stopovers in Singapore, Manila, and Cairo, the Grasses encountered, much to their surprise, precisely the inverse strain of speculation in the political debates of the day: the Christian opposition, led by Franz Josef Strauss, was attacking the Socialist-Liberal government for preventing the Germans from multiplying properly. A sizable portion of the sixty million alleged Germans living on German soil were foreigners, they declared. Discount these foreigners—the only natural and obvious Christian-Democratic thing to do—and the most devastating of all future-shocks will present itself: *the Germans are dying out.* Five English words sum it up, but who can sum up the consequences? . . .

Mr. Grass, a committed Social Democrat, thinks the unthinkable with a charm and lightheartedness that seem calculated to irritate the hell out of Franz Josef Strauss and his followers. He even wants to make a movie of it—and a comedy at that! He discusses the idea with Volker Schlöndorff, the filmmaker . . . ; why not incarnate the whole dilemma in the story of two nice blond northern German representatives of the Liberal-Socialist coalition who want nothing more than to produce a baby but are held back by political scruples? Schlöndorff likes the idea: conception has taken place—the headbirth is on its way.

Part of the pleasure of reading this book is watching Mr. Grass's two homunculi take on an ever more human appearance; it's a little like watching a photograph coming to life in a chemical bath. At first we see little more than a gray shimmer of sociopolitical definition: we learn that they are "indefatigably self-reflecting veterans of the student protest movement." That they are teachers, both of them. That they met at a sit-in against the Vietnam War or the reactionary Springer press, or both. That he is a Social Democrat, while she belongs to the FDP (Free Democrats). That they own a cat. That their mutual love is on an even keel. That she takes the Pill regularly. That they want and don't want a child. Individual features begin to emerge, bit by bit: a set of names to begin with—Dörte and Harm, with a common surname, Peters. They walk, argue, plan, and converse: about having and not having a child, naturally, and also about the world's stockpiled dangers and multiplying disasters, which are the principal reason for Dörte's continual popping of the Pill. (p. 31)

So it goes, back and forth, from nowhere to nowhere, while Dörte and Harm, these headbirths, travel to Asia and back with "Sisyphus," an agency that organizes worldwide slumming tours for the socially conscious. Gradually, page by page, we watch Herr and Frau Peters take on the color and feeling of breathing, believable characters. Well, *possible* characters, since the film hasn't been made yet. Or will it be a book? Günter Grass is not sure. No one's sure of anything any more, with the possible exception of Franz Josef Strauss and his followers. Our young couple's dithering over their possible baby is just one small, private, prototypical instance of an extremely popular Central European parlor game (that's what Grass calls it, but actually it's played on our shores as well), "Ontheonehand-Ontheotherhand." . . . Harm and Dörte agree that "on the one hand the environmentalists are right; on the other, they'll get Strauss elected." And if Strauss gets elected, what will their child's future be like? On the other hand. . . .

But which other hand? Mr. Grass has at least four, like Shiva. Out of the blue, another theme has arisen. Actually, it's been there all along, more or less unnoticed—a theme that doesn't concern Harm and Dörte at all, or Franz Josef Strauss, for that matter, though it does prick him into some furious remarks (in real life, not fiction) about "rats and blowflies." He means writers and, by extension, those who take them seriously. There are no two ways about this subject, as far as Günter Grass is concerned, and this despite the East-West frontier: there is, he says, only one German culture, one single German literature written by East and West German rats and blowflies "who gnaw at the consensus and shit on the newly laundered tablecloth." (pp. 31-2)

Günter Grass is a vigorous and colorful stylist; he is as inventive in his use of words as he is in his manipulation of themes; his sentences sparkle with puns and wordplay, they delight with satirical feints and stabs. (p. 32)

> *Joel Agee, "950 Million Germans?!" in* The New
> Republic, *Vol. 186, No. 15, April 14, 1982, pp. 30-2.*

RICHARD GILMAN

Famous writers tend to become institutions, or rather to institutionalize themselves. As designated seers or gadflies, they take on the burden of everyone else's conscience and poke around in all sorts of public business. Tolstoy ended as a writer of this kind; Camus, more subtly and gracefully, was one; Norman Mailer works hard at it. Today there is no writer more swollen with self-importance or, if that's too harsh, more convinced of his responsibility for the whole of his culture than Günter Grass, who has begun to think of himself as identical with the fates of German literature, German politics and German mores.

As his prophet's beard grows longer, Grass becomes duller, quirkier and more self-indulgent. . . . Grass's latest book has been translated into English: Once again I can imagine its appeal to his zealous adherents at home, but it doesn't travel well.

Headbirths, whose subtitle is **The Germans Are Dying Out** (an echo of Peter Handke's play about capitalism, *They Are Dying Out*), is an exceedingly odd book—short, haphazard, erratic in theme and tone; it suggests something thrown together between blockbusters, just to keep the old hand in. Superficially, it has to do with a trip Grass and his wife took to China and India in 1979 with Volker Schlöndorff, the director of the film version of **The Tin Drum**. . . . Grass and Schlöndorff used the occasion to plan a movie about a young German couple, both schoolteachers, who make roughly the same trip in the interest of "broadening" their sense of the underdeveloped world.

Grass's invented couple, two of his "headbirths," came of age in the 1960s, members of "a generation that had committed itself to the principle of refusal: resolved to throw off all sexual and social restraints." But since that time "they have found themselves knee-deep in prosperity-determined consumerism and pleasureless sex," so that, Grass implies, all that's left to them are the rhetoric and empty gestures of liberalism. In their ambivalence about having a child—"yes to baby/no to baby" is the way Grass describes it—they represent, literally, the sterility of liberalism or rather . . . the sterility of the fashionable, intellectually pretentious liberalism of Helmut Schmidt's ruling coalition.

Grass uses the couple and the projected movie as pretexts for a wide, rambling, unwitty, at times nearly incoherent attack on a great many things German. He hates the new interest in "culture" and religion. The Germans, he writes, "rummage about for spiritual values which, to exclude intellectual refinements, they call fundamental values. Ethical concepts on clearance. Every day a new idea of Christ is thrown on the market. Culture is in. Readings, lectures, exhibitions are taken by storm. Perpetual theater festivals. Music ad nauseam. Like a drowning man, the citizen grasps at books."

Well, here's another book for him to grasp at. It is a little graceless for this writer who has been piling things onto the culture to complain now that there's too much of it. But Grass has become so much an institution that he operates on automatic pilot. The "headbirths" keep coming: literary notions, extraliterary notions, political critiques, social cavils, proposals of every kind. (pp. 502-03)

Occasionally Grass shows an awareness of how unproductively irritating he can be, as in the section where he defends his literary career while at the same time acknowledging some of its peculiarities. And there are a few moments of genuine feeling, in particular his mourning the death of a friend, the writer Nicolas Born, who died at 45 just after Grass's return to Germany. But the lofty, hectoring tone predominates. And what are we to do with a passage like this: "good old capitalism and good old communism . . . thanks to their tried and true enmity, they are becoming . . . more and more alike; two evil old men whom we have to love because the love they offer us refuses to be snubbed"? Strained, unfunny, the passage is a typical "headbirth," advancing neither the cause of literature nor that of political understanding. (pp. 503-04)

Richard Gilman, "On the One Hand . . . ," in The Nation, Vol. 234, No. 16, April 24, 1982, pp. 502-04.

JOHN SUTHERLAND

Headbirths is a novelist's diary or quarry, unprocessed working materials published long before their time. . . .

Grass is fashioning a new discourse and claiming (or repossessing) new territories for modern fiction. It's evidently not easy, and may indeed be impossible. A dominant myth alluded to is that of Sisyphus's sterile labour, and the main plot of *Headbirths* ostensibly chronicles an ambitious novel-film collaboration which never got off the ground, and of which the present book is the meagre relic.

The title indicates Grass's principal conceit: that of the birth of Athena from the forehead of Zeus. This stands for the creation of new material forms, social, political or artistic. The idea is twisted ingeniously this way and that in the course of the work. *Headbirths,* for instance, is dedicated to Grass's admired fellow novelist Nicolas Born, who apparently died during its writing from a tumour of the brain (head death). . . .

The overarching—and, presumably, historical—event in the novel is a business tour by Grass and Volker Schlöndorff (director of *The Tin Drum*) to various Third World locations. Seething India, Java or China are preferred for the film they have vaguely in mind. If the project comes off, it must, however, be shot in July-August 1980, after the election contest between Schmidt and Strauss in which they are both interested. . . .

Grass devises a film scenario for Schlöndorff, and plays with it in the provisional form of what might perhaps become a novel instead. It centres on a model German teacher couple, Harm and Dörte Peters, from Itzehoe, Holstein. They worry their heads perpetually about whether or not they should have a baby. . . .

These creatures of Grass's mind carry with them (as Grass himself did) a one-kilo, lightly smoked, coarsely cut, liver sausage. This sweaty talisman has no 'deeper meaning', Grass notes. It is merely anchorage, a nod towards the Brechtian rule that *'Man ist was er isst.'* Besides which, no head ever invented or gave birth to a liver sausage. By contrast with their cargo of delicatessen concreteness, Grass's couple exist only *in potentia*—'unjelled', as he puts it, half-way between the headbirth of the novelist and that of the film-maker: 'if I neglect the features of Harm and Dörte Peters, outfitting him with no squint and her with no gap between her front teeth, it's for a reason. Schlöndorff will fill these clearly circumscribed blanks with the facial expression of two actors.' . . .

Running through the scenarios and digressions of *Headbirths* is an extraordinarily frank personal essay. 'By a dubious stroke of luck', the novelist was born in 1927. But the current purge of an older, unluckier generation of German writers with Nazi pasts leads him to speculate on his own career had he been born ten years earlier, in 1917. In an eerie bio-bibliography of this tainted self, he provides an oeuvre which runs from the late Expressionist, rhapsodic poetry of his Hitler Youth period, through the post-Stalingrad 'poetry of lasting significance', to the 'fresh start' mode of de-Nazified 1947. All of which pertains to Grass's main literary-historical datum: that the ideology of National Socialism has laid waste the German language as extensively and less reparably than bombing laid waste the country's cities. If the German writer wants a tradition, he has to make it up out of his own head. In this book, Grass manages to do that very well. (p. 18)

John Sutherland, "Nationalities," in London Review of Books, May 6 to May 19, 1982, pp. 18-19.*

JOHN UPDIKE

Critics who urge upon American writers more social commitment and a more public role should ponder the cautionary case of Günter Grass. Here is a novelist who has gone so public he can't be bothered to write a novel; he just sends dispatches to his readers from the front lines of his engagement. His latest work, **"Headbirths; or, The Germans Are Dying Out"** . . . is topical and political with a specificity that warrants a prefatory Publisher's Note:

> *Headbirths* was written in late 1979, shortly after Günter Grass returned from a trip to China and just before the German elections of 1980. Candidates of the two major parties contending for power were Helmut Schmidt, the Social Democrat Chancellor of the German Federal Republic, and Franz Josef Strauss, Bavarian Prime Minister and head of the opposition party, the Christian Democrats. Günter Grass's commitment was and is to the Social Democrats and their party head, Willy Brandt.

Got that? Then you are ready to take a brief ride on the roller coaster of Grass's mind as it goes clickety-clack, clickety-clack, *wheeeee!* on the ups and downs of such issues as nuclear plants, the low German birthrate, the early middle age of the protest generation, the union of the two Germanys, the importance of the German language and its writers, and capitalism and its clear inferiority to an ever so dimly apprehended "Democratic socialism"—themes already stirred into such bubbling stews as **"The Flounder," "Local Anaesthetic,"** and **"The Meeting at Telgte."** The pot this time holds a few dollops of fiction, as Grass shares with the reader his efforts to imagine a movie about the Asian adventures of Harm and Dörte Peters, hypothetical schoolteachers from Itzehoe in Holstein. (p. 129)

It is hard to imagine an American writer of comparable distinction publishing a book so unbuttoned in manner, so dishevelled in content, so ingenuously confident of his readership's indulgence. Saul Bellow, his head as spinning with ideas as Günter Grass's, yet dresses them up in fictional costume, in "The Dean's December," or else presents them straightforwardly as journalism, in "To Jerusalem and Back." These are clean headbirths; Grass gives us pangs, placenta, and squalling infant all in a heap, plus a damp surgical mask and a bent forceps. He tells us about his trip to China, and about the dying of the poet Nicolas Born, an old friend and fellow-participant in unofficial East-West writers' meetings held in East Berlin for four years ending in 1977. He rehearses political speeches for the coming Strauss-Schmidt campaign, he pleads for hopeless causes like a "National Endowment . . . a place where every German can look for himself and his origins and find questions to ask," he pontificates about the Germans ("They always insist on being terrifyingly more or pathetically less than they are"), he imagines himself as born ten years earlier and turning his pen to pro-Nazi rhapsodies, he proposes that East and West Germany swap systems every ten years ("The

Democratic Republic would have an opportunity to relax under capitalism, while the Federal Republic could drain off cholesterol under communism''), he writes cascades of little editorials already dated by their sneers at Carter (''a bigoted preacher in Washington'') and their focus on Iran. He spouts off, in short. Like a psychiatrist patiently auditing a stream of free association, the reader listens for the telltale note, the clue to the monologuist's real concerns. (pp. 129-30)

''Headbirths'' appears to be really about Turks. The Chinese that Grass visits and admires, the Indians and Balinese that disquiet Harm and Dörte, the millions and millions of them, are Turks of a different color. The Turkish Turks are already in Germany; the eighties will bring the others in. ''In the course of the eighties,'' Harm Peters orates to a frightened crowd of cement workers in Lägerdorf, ''Asia will discharge its demographic pressure and flood the European continent. I see them by the thousands, by the hundreds of thousands, silently trickling in, and here, yes, here in Itzehoe, in our very midst.'' In Grass's cinematic vision, the beer halls and women's clubs fill with ''Indians, Malays, Pakistanis, and Chinese, with Asia's overflow, until Harm and Dörte find themselves applauded by predominantly foreign audiences, while what's left of the native Germans, intimidated, lose themselves in the enthusiastic mass.'' A mere eighty million industrious, frugal, politically earnest, unprolific Germans cannot possibly survive in such a human sea: ''Europe is dissolving into Asia.'' That is the anxiety, symbolized by the Turks invited into Germany for their cheap labor and now looming as an unbanishable presence. . . . **''Headbirths; or, The Germans Are Dying Out,''** beneath all its merry guff, holds an authentic pang as Germany surrenders its barbaric old notion of racial purity and sizes up its modest place in a mongrel world. (pp. 130-31)

John Updike, ''The Squeeze Is On,'' in The New Yorker, *Vol. LVIII, No. 1, June 14, 1982, pp. 129-34.**

Thom(son William) Gunn

1929-

English poet, critic, editor, and essayist.

An English poet who has lived in the United States since 1955, Gunn has combined in his writing characteristics of both formal, traditionally structured poetry and relaxed, modern free verse. His subjects range from metaphysical conceits to motorcycle gangs and LSD, and at the center of his work there is a tension between constraint and energy that Gunn describes in *Moly* (1971) as "a debate between the passion for definition and the passion for flow." As a student and beginning poet at Cambridge in the early 1950s, Gunn shared many concerns with such writers as Donald Davie, Philip Larkin, and others who have been collectively referred to as The Movement. Like Movement poetry, Gunn's early work displays a predilection for tightly rhymed and metered verse and a rejection of the neoromanticism favored in England in the 1940s. The poems in his first collection, *Fighting Terms* (1954), were written at Cambridge and reveal his attempt at stylistic sophistication and hard realism. Gunn's admiration for the man of action, which recurs throughout his career, is evident here in the many images of soldiers and war. In 1954, Gunn moved to California and enrolled at Stanford University, where he studied under the poet and critic Yvor Winters.

Gunn's life in the United States has strongly influenced his work. Although such dominant concerns as the quest for personal identity and meaning in human existence have remained constant, his topics, imagery, and style have changed, as well as his philosophical approach. His second collection, *The Sense of Movement* (1958), like *Fighting Terms,* displays a formal construction and examines the existential premise of a valueless world in which the individual creates meaning through willed action. However, the influence of American culture begins to emerge and in Gunn's next collection, *My Sad Captains and Other Poems* (1961), this influence becomes explicit.

My Sad Captains is divided into two thematically and stylistically different sections and is considered a major transitional volume. The first half continues in the mode of Gunn's previous volumes, stressing violence, roughness, and action with tight, formal control. The second section marks the beginning of Gunn's movement from metrical verse to syllabics and eventually to even more relaxed free forms. The change in technique is mirrored in the emergence of new poetic concerns: Gunn's metaphysical contemplations are abandoned in order to record experiences in and perceptions of the physical world. Nature begins to figure prominantly and Gunn's combative stance toward the world is softened. The poems begin to express a recognition that emotional contact beween humans is both possible and desirable. Gunn's next collection, *Touch* (1968), expands on this sense of hope and possibility. The poems are written mostly in free verse or a combination of free verse and syllabics, a style which is seen to reflect Gunn's developing optimism.

In the early 1960s Gunn taught at the University of California at Berkeley and became involved with the radical counter-

Fay Godwin's Photo Files

culture in San Francisco. His experiences with LSD and his new insights provided the material for many of the poems in *Moly* and *Jack Straw's Castle and Other Poems* (1976). This was a period of almost ecstatic discovery for him, and these two volumes reflect his growth as he embraces the community of humankind while also acknowledging the pain and trauma of deeply sharing oneself.

The Passages of Joy (1982) contains what many critics consider his most revealing poems. They explore his English heritage, and in several poems Gunn speaks openly, for the first time, about his homosexuality. As Gunn's style continues to relax, some critics express regret over his departure from formal literary traditions, but his poems are frequently praised for their heightened clarity and directness and for the precision of Gunn's control. In 1982 Gunn also published his first collection of essays, *The Occasions of Poetry.* This volume contains critical analyses of the work of other poets as well as autobiographical pieces. Although Gunn continues to be better known in England than in the United States, he undoubtedly belongs to the Anglo-American tradition which includes such notable poets as T. S. Eliot, Ezra Pound, and W. H. Auden.

(See also *CLC,* Vols. 3, 6, 18; *Contemporary Authors,* Vols. 17-20, rev. ed.; *Contemporary Authors New Revision Series,* Vol. 9; and *Dictionary of Literary Biography,* Vol. 27.)

P. R. KING

[Thom Gunn] shared the belief of The Movement poets that poetry should be well made and craftsmanlike, utilizing traditional rhythms and rhyme schemes. Many of his early poems expressed fairly complex ideas within intricately extended metaphors, a style which helped earn him the label of 'a modern metaphysical poet', especially as these poems were often concerned with matters of love and passion, one of the traditional themes of the seventeenth-century metaphysical poets.

Now that he has published six volumes of poetry this view seems somewhat limited and cannot provide a full account of his strongly individualistic voice. . . . Many of his poems, particularly his best ones, are linked closely to his life and experiences and especially to his exploration of his sense of himself and the possible attitudes and commitments he might embrace. There is a sense in which his poetry might be seen as a continuously developing attempt to understand the intellectual's condition in modern life and to explore the divisions, conflicts, tensions and problems that he faces. His poems explore aspects of the rift between thinking man and acting man, between body and mind, self and others, self and the natural world.

In Iris Murdoch's novel *The Time of the Angels* there is a character called Pattie, a black servant who suddenly finds that after years of loneliness, grinding work and poverty, after the experience of an aching lack of companionship and affection, she is able, under the gentle touch of another's love, to let the bitterness and cold egocentrism of her earlier self melt into a new sense of identity. Her new self is able to respond to others. It is described at the moment of rebirth [as 'some sudden amazing freedom']. . . . This 'sudden amazing freedom' and its accompanying sense of completeness in responding to another is a perfect description of the goal towards which the poetry of Thom Gunn moves. . . . (pp. 77-8)

It is hardly a characteristic most easily perceived at first glance and particularly not if the reader concentrates only on the early, better-known poems. In these, Gunn's famous concern with the world of the leather-jacketed ton-up boys, and his apparent mistrust of love which almost amounts to scorn, prevents the deep groundswell of this theme being seen at a superficial glance.

Fighting Terms (1954, revised 1962), as its title suggests, promotes a tough, hardened stance towards the world and personal relationships. In the various situations and *personae* of these poems the individual, even when he is in love, is seen to occupy an embattled position. Poems like **'Lofty in the Palais de Dance'** or **'The Beachhead'** adopt an aggressive pose. They are not immediately personal poems, even when dealing with personal emotions. Gunn wears a series of masks and looks at a number of situations, writing as if from within a different character. (pp. 78-9)

[The poems in this volume] have a strict structure (frequently a six-line stanza based on an iambic rhythm) with carefully developed imagery and fastidious rhymes which emphasize the intellectual control and sharp consciousness shared by the protagonists of the poem who try to overcome their detached nature by burying themselves in action. *The Sense of Movement* (1957) takes this theme further and uses a theory of pose as its vehicle. Gunn developed this theory while a student at Cambridge. He maintained that, since everybody seemed to behave quite differently with different people and in different circumstances, it would be best to be fully aware of this and to control such

roles consciously. A poet, particularly, might use such a theory to write from outside his own personal experience. We can see this conscious adoption of different poses in both the first two books, but it is in the second that the theory is used to explore facets of contemporary life.

Many of the poems both employ the theory and at the same time hint at its limitations. The pose particularly pursued is that of the Hell's Angels motorbike gang member (these poems were written in the period of the James Dean-style tough-guy rebellion). Its best presentation is the most heavily anthologized of Gunn's poems, **'On the Move'**.

This poem describes a gang of ton-up toughs, 'the Boys', who race their motorcycles across the landscape, tearing noisily from one barely noticed town to another without any clear sense of direction. Around this central description Gunn weaves a series of ideas that convert the motorcyclists into a symbol for a particular response to life. (pp. 83-4)

[The Boys' solution to a sense of meaningless is generalized] into an image of modern man who, it is claimed, is born amid movement and who cannot properly control this very movement he is committed to because he has no sense of final goal. All he can do is commit himself to the ongoing action. (p. 85)

In **'On the Move'** Gunn successfully employs images from contemporary culture, but only in part to help him explore the motives for the behaviour of the rebellious youths that anonymously populate many of his poems. His real concern is to make them symbolize not just their own generation but a whole way of possible confrontation with our modern world. Whether the motorcyclists could actually see themselves in the way Gunn sees them is beside the point. What matters is the articulation of the poet's possible stance towards his world—a world which he sees in this poem as giving no sense of absolute value to man. (pp. 85-6)

It is in such poems [as **'On the Move'**] that Gunn laid the groundwork on which his early critics erected an image of him as the 'tough-guy intellectual'. Yet this label neglects the fact that he has been a self-conscious writer from the very beginning, always aware of his limitations. **'On the Move'** contains its own distancing comment on the posture it decribes. This sense of the limits of the pose becomes increasingly explicit in the next book; meanwhile the remaining poems in the 1957 volume create a sense of modern man 'condemned to be an individual' in that he must explore the limitations of thought and of the world in which he lives, a world in which he can no longer wrestle a meaning from the historically meaningful traditions but must instead test all values through his own sense of the possibility of man. (p. 86)

The images that predominate in this volume are of toughness, hardness and self-discipline. Their connotations suggest a view of man imprisoned within his individual self, unable to know himself through any inherited value system and unable to lay hold of authentic life except by self-control and conscious exploration of his sense of apartness from nature and his fellow human beings. This exloration can be achieved only through action and commitment in which the action is the greater part of the meaning. It is not an achieved philosophy in which a man could rest for long, and Gunn himself was unable to rest in it, as we shall see. . . . There is a price to be paid by those who try to will desire and control energy and action by disciplined order. In **'The Beaters'** there is a suggestion of the dangers involved. The enemy is seen as necessary in order to provoke the required discipline, and the implication is that life can be lived only by continually promoting its own adversary. This is a dangerous stance which leads inevitably to a split between people and a division within the individual. *My Sad Captains* (1961) takes the examination of this danger further and consciously elaborates it in the first half of the book, while in the second half the first suggestions of a different direction begin to emerge.

In the first part there are still poems on motorcycle gangs ('**Black Jackets**') and tough heroes ('**The Byrnies**'), but these are somewhat forced compared with earlier ones. . . . For a much more impressive presentation of the strengths and weaknesses of this pose of the isolated individual creating his own morality by force of will and self-discipline, we must turn to '**Claus von Stauffenberg**' and '**Innocence**'.

'**Claus von Stauffenberg**' concerns the Second World War German army officer, a maimed veteran of many successful campaigns who became a member of Hitler's staff and who was part of an unsuccessful conspiracy to assassinate the Führer. He is thought to be the man who planted the bomb which, in fact, led to his own death and not the death of Hitler. The poem suggests that, although the act is a failure in terms of its own goal, it succeeds in another way; for the act and man lodge in our memories, in history itself, as an image of the courageous individual action of a man who kept firm hold of his sense of morality while those about him who were most powerful were systematically deranging humanistic values. (pp. 88-90)

It is written in a cool, spare language with a traditional four-line stanza in iambic rhythm and rhyming *abab*.

This form is shared with '**Innocence**', a poem that explores the other, darker side of the self-disciplined will. Again the subject concerns Nazi Germany, this time describing how a young boy grows through his Nazi youth to become a soldier on the Russian front killing partisans. (p. 90)

We have in this poem a strong image of the warped self. It uses a ballad-like stanza but does not so much tell a narrative as describe a sequence of conditions which are both commented on and placed at the same time. It reveals the limitations that result from the development of self through action that has no regard for any goal. The innocence is turned into a dangerous egotism that reduces man to his physical self and, paradoxically, blinds him to the bodily suffering of another. . . .

In these two poems we see the two separate selves of the poet as portrayed in the early books. In *My Sad Captains* it is as if Gunn has arrived at the point where he is able to see both the strengths and weaknesses of this divided self but is as yet unable to heal the rift. That is why the book ends with the title poem which is a valediction to these early heroes. However, a more hopeful change is seen developing in the poems of the second half of the collection which immediately precede this valediction. These show the influence of Gunn's decision to live in California, several of them being about his life there. They also show a move towards looser rhythms and forms. Many are written not in traditional forms but in syllabics. These are composed of lines of equal numbers of syllables (usually six, seven or nine) and with a rhythm of two main stresses and two subsidiary stresses to each line, the stresses occurring in irregular sequences. It is a rhythm more American than English (it has been perfected by William Carlos Williams and Marianne Moore, although W. H. Auden has made good occasional use of it). Its freedom shadows the freer themes of the poems. (p. 92)

These poems are frequently about the Californian landscape with its eucalyptus and giant redwood firs and, especially, the peculiar clarity of light which typifies California. There seems here to be the beginning of an openness towards a new sense of delight and awe in the presence of nature which has not previously appeared in the poetry of someone who earlier celebrated city scenes because they are 'extreme, material and the work of man' ('**In Praise of Cities**'). (p. 93)

In '**My Sad Captains**' Gunn takes leave of his tough-guy pose. Whatever meaning he once found in it he now recognizes as significant only for the individual who experiences it—it contains no power to relate that individual either to nature or to others. The old heroes are stars that 'turn with disinterested / hard energy', shining with a light which, however brightly it appears in the firmament, cannot cast any real illumination across the dark universe. It is in the 1967 volume that, as the title *Touch* suggests, we see the poet exploring how contact can be made with nature and with other people. The centre of the book is the long poem sequence '**Misanthropos**', arguably one of Gunn's most effective poems. In it he imagines a solitary man in a bare landscape, apparently the sole survivor of a holocaust. In some poems he is described from outside by an observer-narrator, in others he speaks with his own voice. (p. 94)

This is a fine poem, full of variety but with strict control of the developing theme which traces a whole movement of possible thought and describes the incredibly difficult leap from 'the imprisoned self' (as Martin Dodsworth describes it) through the mysterious and irrational, to the touch of human sympathy. (p. 98)

In '**Back to Life**', the last poem of the book, we discover an ending with this . . . realization: that there is no way in which man can completely merge with others—he is condemned to remain solitary—and yet this very recognition shared by all is the only redeeming possibility for communication. In the poems of this volume we see the protagonist experiencing his sense of touch, not just physically but also in the sense of 'getting in touch' with others, sympathizing with and understanding someone beyond ourself. Although the sense of the other is vague and shadowy in many of the poems, it does nevertheless provide the first experience at the feeling level of the protagonist's responses in his fumbling search for genuine communication. *Moly* (1971) is the collection in which Gunn wrote of his experiences with the drug LSD. (pp. 98-9)

In their form [the poems in *Moly*] return to carefully developed structures and frequently employ traditional metre and rhyme schemes. This refelcts Gunn's feeling that careful ordering is necessary to balance the content. . . . Clearly the book suggests that a new freedom—even revelation—has been obtained through the drug, but it is not advocating its wholesale use. LSD/Moly signifies the need for an openness to experience and the need to articulate a new vision.

The nature of this vision can begin to be seen when we realize that many of the poems are concerned with transformation (many poems in Gunn's books describe changes in a person). Some of the central poems are to do with half-men, half-beast creatures ('**Moly**' and '**Tom-Dobbin**'), and others concern the transformation of vision ('**The Colour-Machine**', '**Three**'). (p. 99)

The final poems of the book are about the attempt to merge with surroundings in a meaningful unity through the effect of the drug. '**The Garden of the Gods**' creates a mythic sense of divinity, a magical nature which is a rich profusion of delights and the source of fecundity in man. It is a beautiful description of an Eden-like garden in which 'It was sufficient, there, to be', an existence in which meaning-as-explanation was superseded by meaning-as-simply-experience. The conscious mind becomes perception within a fully living body. (p. 101)

In *Jack Straw's Castle* (1976), Gunn continues the theme of the previous book in poems written after the LSD experience which, benefiting from the liberation which that experience wrought, attempt to translate it into the events of ordinary reality. There are poems suggesting how life may be lived with an intimate sense of relation to our world, but they are realistic in measuring the possibility of failure to do this and the consequences flowing from it. The kind of success that can be achieved, and the recognition of the inner self's properties which must be given their full weight if that success is to be gained, are dealt with in the two long poems on which the book is centred.

'Geysers' adopts an irregular, fragmented line which represents the *experience* of the subject matter, rather than commenting on it from outside. The subject is an account of camping out in the hills above a group of warm water geysers in Sonoma County, California. As the campers move among one another, they go down to join strangers in a primitive communal bathhouse, taking part in what becomes a drugged, bisexual orgy. In this experience their conscious wills are subordinated to their feelings and desires. . . . In this poem the divided self which has formed the staple image of so much of Gunn's poetry, even when the attempt to touch was made, becomes at last a unity. The experience that is evoked is impossible to describe and can only be *felt* as read. It is possible that the weight and effect of the poem as Gunn might wish a reader to experience it can be brought out only for someone who has been prepared by reading all the previous poems. But it remains the one poem of his that has come closest, not to describing, but to *enacting* the desired experience. In many ways it is the freest of all his poems.

In the title poem of the volume Gunn uses looser forms again, although they are not as free as in 'Geysers'. He takes up the children's rhyme and employs it to symbolize the poet's mind (his conscious, subconscious and unconscious selves) in describing the rooms of the house/castle in which he lives. Much of the poem is concerned with a nightmare that turns the rooms into hellish horrors with images of the demonic murderer Charles Manson bobbing up wherever the poet looks. In these horrors, drawn from real life, Gunn seems to be suggesting a recognition of feelings, desires and responses that he possesses deep down in his normally buried self which, when brought to the surface, reveal us all as implicated to some degree in the pain and suffering that a man like Manson creates. (pp. 102-03)

'Jack Straw's Castle' ends on a positive note, like many others in this collection. It is an acceptance that our sense of identity is given significance precisely through the existence of others and that by trusting in their reality and their goodness we may achieve our own power of touch. In this book a new freedom has been acquired. The divided self may not be entirely healed, but at least that part of the self which is conscious, detached and willed is finally able to merge with experience and become 'as if' something beyond its own boundaries. A striking example of this is the poem 'Yoko'—a *tour de force* in which Gunn writes as if he was a dog speaking of his love for his master and his joy-in-the-world that he experiences when out walking with his master. It is virtually the only complete poem

of Gunn's entire output in which he writes as if from inside the skin of a subject totally different from himself. The nearest poem to it is '**Considering the Snail**' but there the snail is commented on, not just re-created. In '**Yoko**' the poet *is* the dog. It is not a pose or a disguise, but rather a true creation of another world that is felt, not willed. (p. 105)

Gunn's poetry is the account of an existential quest, a pursuit of a sense of personal identity and meaning in a world where the traditional supports for life's meaning are being questioned. It is a quest that may not yet be finished: a resolution that so far has been perhaps more often stated than enacted would imply this. Nevertheless it is a quest which in its manner of proceeding has produced some fine poems that articulate the genuine response of a late twentieth-century man to the possibility of identity. Slowly he has moved towards a position where he is beginning to be able to convert those forces ranged against the individual, even death, into something positive. Taken as a whole the poems of Thom Gunn repudiate the criticism of someone like Alan Brownjohn who has said that Gunn idealizes 'the brutal, the irrational and the wilful'. In so far as some early poems may appear to do this, these may be regarded as the few failures of Gunn's work. But if the poems are taken together, in support of one another, the reader can discern a deliberate moving away from the early fantasies and false poses towards a more hopeful, more realistic acceptance of self and the world in which the whole is always greater than its parts. (p. 106)

> *P. R. King, "'A Courier After Identity': The Poetry of Thom Gunn," in his* Nine Contemporary Poets: A Critical Introduction, *Methuen, 1979, pp. 77-106.*

CLIVE WILMER

Gunn is quite consciously a writer of contrasts, who has drawn on a wide range of influences and modes. But his work none the less impresses the careful reader with its underlying consistency. He made his name, after all, as a master of rigorously traditional verse forms, and he continues to excel in them, but he has since become hardly less accomplished in a variety of 'open' forms and the verse is no less shapely. His approach is at root impersonal: his first person, like Ralegh's or Jonson's or Hardy's, is unquestionably that of a particular man, but a man who expects his individuality to be of interest in so far as it is a quality the reader shares with him. . . . His work, which has done much to dispel the critical orthodoxy that abstract language is inimical to poetry, has become over the years increasingly sensuous in detail, reflecting preoccupations that were there from the beginning, though not at first as qualities of the language. For this most chaste of modern poets is a philosophical hedonist—rather like Camus, of all modern moralists the one he appears to value most.

The most interesting contrast of all, perhaps, is connected with his sense of the past. What strikes us most immediately in Gunn's poems—what made him famous in fact—is their contained energy. Yet he is also, without fallng into academicism, a highly literary poet, and his literariness, far from being a limitation, may well be the main source of his strength. Gunn's vulnerability, as Donald Davie has said in praise of him, has much to do with his renunciation of the 'glibly deprecating ironies' that insulated so many of the fifties' poets from the full range of poetic possibility. In order to escape such 'facile knowingness' and the phase of British culture that it expressed, Gunn went back to the youth of English poetry 'to discover that phase of British English—Donne's, Marlowe's, above all Shakespeare's—in which the language could register without embarrassment the frankly heroic'. And in his mature work, says Davie, 'The Renaissance styles—of life more than of writing—are invoked . . . not to judge the tawdry present, nor to keep it at arm's length, but on the contrary so as to comprehend it in a way that extends to it not just compassion but dignity. . . .' The only tradition in the English language that shares this verbal innocence is that of American poetry since Whitman, with all its vulnerability and spaciousnes. Gunn, who has lived in the United States since 1954, has nourished himself on that tradition too—so it is perhaps no accident that most of the essays in [*The Occasions of Poetry*] deal with American or Renaissance writers. (pp. 11-12)

[Gunn's] criticism is interesting for what, indirectly, it tells us about his poetry, but it is still more valuable for the way his own experience of writing illuminates what he reads. He is, quite simply, a marvellous 'reader' of other men's verse. The aspect of literary practice which engages Gunn's critical intelligence most frequently and most fruitfully is the relation of a poet's words to the subject matter that calls them forth. (p. 13)

The occasions of poetry . . . are only starting points. They constitute the 'shape' of experience, but the task of a poet is to seek out its 'content'. Gunn employs a variety of related metaphors to describe the journey between the two: exploration and adventure, and the related images of looting and conquest. These metaphors unite poets as diverse as Robert Duncan and Yvor Winters. (p. 14)

If the process of poetry, then, is adventure or exploration, its goal must be 'understanding'. This is a word which recurs so often . . . that we are justified in suspecting its meaning to be less obvious than we might at first have thought. . . . 'The process of understanding', says Gunn, amounts to something 'more than the business of comprehending the text . . . Understanding means taking (the poems) to heart, means—ultimately—*acting* on them.' Of course, he is referring not to the business of understanding life but to the effect of literature. But to apply the word 'understand' to experience at all is, in a sense, to draw an analogy between life and books. If we study life, we can learn from it; our chances of acting on experience are improved. (p. 16)

In recent years, Gunn's interest in American poery has moved away from the traditionalism Winters stood for towards the more loosely informal writing that acknowledges Pound and Williams as its masters. [*The Occasions of Poetry*], which begins with an essay written in 1965, may be read in part as a record of that shift in emphasis. During this period Gunn seems to have broadened his use of the word 'understanding'. For Jonson and Winters it was the *sine qua non* of poetry and implied a reduction of experience to generalized formulae. Gunn now argues that poetry is 'an attempt to *grasp*, with grasp meaning both to *take hold of* in a first bid at possession, and also to *understand*'. A grasp of particulars is now quite as important to him as the formulation of propositions, and it entails a concreteness of language that twenty years ago had seemed beside the point. This has nothing to do with metaphor or symbol or correlatives for private emotion. What he values is the precise rendering of physical fact *as it is,* in all its 'thinginess'. Yet when he says of Gary Snyder, the master of this kind of writing, that 'like most serious poets he is mainly concerned at finding himself on a barely known planet in an almost unknown universe, where he must attempt to create and discover meanings', we realize that Gunn has not moved far

from the Wintersian position, for he sees Snyder's poetry as a matter of exploration, discovery and understanding. . . . In attempting to notate the particulars of experience accurately, Snyder guides us gently into territory we all share. Language, after all, is a common property. When we are persuaded, through language, of the truth of a perception, we have entered the realm of generality: we have stumbled on meaning. Gunn's special talent as a critic lies in his ability to show how, as we read, we move in this way from occasion to meaning. (pp. 16-17)

Clive Wilmer, in an introduction to The Occasions of Poetry: Essays in Criticism and Autobiography *by Thom Gunn, edited by Clive Wilmer, Faber and Faber, 1982, pp. 11-17.*

JAY PARINI

[Rule and Energy, two] potentially counterdestructive principles, exist everywhere in [Thom Gunn's] work, not sapping the poems of their strength but creating a tense climate of balanced opposition. Any poet worth thinking twice about possesses *at least* an energetic mind; but it is the harnessing of this energy which makes for excellence. In Gunn's work an apparently unlimited energy of vision finds, variously, the natural boundaries which make expression—and clarity—possible. (p. 134)

[Gunn's early poems] reflect his British heritage and the interest in "formalist" poetry characteristic of poets identified with the so-called Movement. "What poets like Larkin, Davie, Elizabeth Jennings, and I had in common at that time was that we were deliberately eschewing Modernism, and turning back, though not very thoroughly, to traditional resources in structure and method," says Gunn. (pp. 134-35)

The traditionalist bent of Gunn's first book, *Fighting Terms* (1954), tugs in opposition to his rebellious themes. The poet most often invokes a soldier persona, an existential warrior in the act of self-definition. (p. 135)

Among the accomplished poems from this early phase of Gunn's career is **"Tamer and Hawk,"** which treats of the Rule/Energy conflict in tightly rhymed trimeter stanzas. . . . The poem is a swift, bold stroke; its central conceit is a subtly worked-out metaphor—the hawk is possessed by but in turn possesses the tamer. . . . The theme of possession and control, of the positive and negative aspects of any intense relationship (whether between man and woman or poet and his language), has rarely found more distinct expression. **"Tamer and Hawk"** is equal to anything in Gunn's later volumes, and it points the way to the direction of his next book.

The Sense of Movement (1957) fulfills the promise of Gunn's first book, displaying a new range of assimilated (or half-assimilated) voices and refining, somewhat, the central metaphor of his work—the conflict of intellect and emotion. (pp. 135-36)

Much of *The Sense of Movement* was written while Gunn studied at Stanford under Yvor Winters, and these poems reflect his teacher's aesthetic to some extent. To Winters, says Gunn, poetry "was an instrument for exploring the truth of things, as far as human beings can explore it, and it can do so with greater verbal exactitude than prose can manage." Yet Gunn's notion of poetry goes well beyond the narrow strictures of Winters, admitting a wider range of feeling. Indeed, his belief that reality inheres in the particulars of experience almost works against Winters's dedication to abstract reason. Gunn's poetry is not intellectual, finally; rather, it explores concrete reality in a sensuous manner. (p. 138)

My Sad Captains (1961) can, without strain, be called a "watershed" in Gunn's career. Its two parts neatly separate the early style (formal poetry about the creative will and self-determination) and the later, freer style (largely concerned with the interplay of man and nature and the necessity of love). Gunn never abandons metrical verse, but the echoes of Yeats and others disappear. *Captains* is possibly Gunn's strongest book to date. (p. 139)

From here on, Gunn will aim more to describe than to prescribe experience. The poems in Part II, written in syllabics, move beyond the rigid expectations of formal verse; syllabics force on the poem a nerve-wrackingly regular irregularity: the reader *feels* the arbitrary restraint of a given number of syllables per line. When syllabics work, the effect is stunning, unsettling: the lines seem cut off like fingers, raw, unbandaged. (p. 140)

The thirteen poems in Part II are a cluster of Gunn's best work, marked by a passionate eye for detail and sustained by a new exactness of diction; his imagery has a new sharpness, the poems glitter like cut glass. **"My Sad Captains,"** the title poem, completes the sequence; it is Gunn's farewell to the past, to his obsession with heroism. It constitutes a deeply felt elegy to his old self. . . . [It] is a tender yet fiercely self-critical piece . . . , a resolution to approach life and art from now on with greater flexibility and humaneness.

This new direction finds direct expression in *Positives* (1966), a unique event in Gunn's career, a collaborative sequence of poems and photographs done with his brother, Ander Gunn. (pp. 141-42)

I find the poems in *Positives* tense and unconstrained at the same time; their language adheres firmly to the images evoked, images which move from birth to death, from childhood to old age, always with compassion and wit. Although Gunn's sympathies lodge clearly with the downcast of the world, those on the fringe, there is an acute worldliness about these poems, an ironic bite that redeems them from sentimentality. . . . (p. 142)

The following year Gunn published *Touch* (1967), establishing what I take to be his "mature" style—a mixture of free verse, syllabics, and metrical verse in poems largely concerned with what Wallace Stevens called a poet's "sense of the world." Gunn writes, movingly, of personal love, of sunlight, of his pity for mankind, of himself among others. . . .

Gunn's message is important and fresh. The efforts at self-definition which obsess his early personae reach outward here in the greater effort simply to be human, which involves (as Bertrand Russell said beautifully) "the longing for love, the search for knowledge, and unbearable pity for the suffering of mankind." (p. 143)

While **"Misanthropos"** is Gunn's centerpiece in *Touch,* I prefer many of the other poems, such as **"Snowfall," "In the Tank,"** and **"The Produce District,"** poems of exact observation, marked by a deep sense of controlling intelligence. They point the way toward *Moly* (1971), Gunn's most personal book to date.

Most of these poems evoke Gunn's Californian experience in the late sixties, "the time, after all, not only of the Beatles but of LSD as well," he writes. His fascination with LSD is apparent from the title; Moly was, of course, the magical herb given to Odysseus by Hermes to protect him when he entered

Circe's house. The poet's drug experiences opened to him new veins of reality; his concern with perception takes on a stunningly new dimension; for LSD presented Gunn with intensely fresh visions of both the physical world and his own nature. The old problem of Rule and Energy became all the more acute as well. . . . (p. 145)

Gunn uses formal meters and rhyme to restrain, precariously, the strange new feelings which attend this widening of consciousness. In a brief statement prepared for the Poetry Book Society . . . the author writes of *Moly:* "It could be seen as a debate between the passion for definition and the passion for flow." These terms, of course, recollect Rule and Energy: the poet's feelings are intense and threaten to overwhelm him, but his intellect (and the imagination) modify and restrain this passion with equal force; always, the balance of opposites is sought after. There is constantly in this new work that sense of "continuous creation" mentioned in **"Touch,"** a rare and irrepressible life-force beyond constraint but trapped, temporarily, by the artist in his poem. (p. 146)

In a sense, *Jack Straw's Castle* (1976) is an extension of *Moly.* The poems spring from the same source, that quasi-mystical sense of "continuous creation." These latest poems examine, especially in the eleven-part title sequence, the consequence of heightened self-consciousness and the necessity of human community and communication. Gunn ranges widely here, from his English past to his Californian present, but a strange new continuity obtains, as if the poet's life had ceased from previous linearity. Past and present now inform each other—exist simultaneously in the Bergsonian *durée* of the poem.

"The Geysers," a four-part sequence, is the heart of *Jack Straw's Castle,* and its language is richly descriptive, physical, imagistic. . . . The poet loosens, gradually, his grip on self-consciousness, and the poetry itself loosens; meters break down as barriers break. . . . An attitude of benevolence and communal love emerges as a solution to self-confinement.

Yet its obverse, self-entrapment, obsesses the poet in the title poem, **"Jack Straw's Castle."** Whereas self-containment was, in his earlier books, seen as a positive move in the direction of existential self-definition, now only anxiety attends this limitation. . . . Within the metaphorical castle, hero Jack examines each room in turn, especially the cellars. One cannot be sure whether these are *real* rooms or the rooms of each dream; "dream sponsors" occur, such as Charles Manson and the Medusa, adding to the nightmarish quality of the poem. In fact, the poem may be thought of as a descent into the infernal regions of the unconscious mind. Jack drops into levels of subliminal mentality, digging away roots, delving into the foundations of selfhood, entering into a pure world of necessity. . . . (pp. 148-49)

It is finally the urge to contact a reality beyond the castle's boundaries which brings the sequence to its tensely beautiful and haunting conclusion. Jack wakens to realize that someone is in bed with him; he is no longer alone. . . . Is it a dream or not? He shrugs: "The beauty's in what is, not what may seem." And in any case, "With dreams like this, Jack's ready for the world." So the poem ends, not conclusively, but with some optimism.

In essence, the sequence re-creates in miniature the entire journey Gunn has undertaken from *Fighting Terms* to the present, from self-consciousness to an outward turning; he recognizes the possibilities for love, for attachment to the beautiful and terrible flux of "continuous creation" in which all that matters is what Dorothy Parker, referring to Hemingway, called "grace under pressure," what I call a delicate balance of Energy and Rule.

The final section of *Jack Straw's Castle* exhibits some of Gunn's finest work to date.... From metrical to free verse, Gunn shows himself capable of mastering his experience, of translating *chronos* into *mythos,* of creating a language at once energetic and supremely under control.

Already Gunn is a poet of considerable status in contemporary British poetry. He has added to the language a handful of lyrics which may well survive the terrible winnowing process of time. And surely his struggle for existential self-affirmation, his reaching beyond self-confinement into the realm of community and love are central to our time if we do not wish to become barbarians. His effort to rule by intelligence the natural energies which lead, too often, to self-mutilation and, worse, the destruction of others, is exemplary. Thom Gunn is, in short, an essential poet, one for whom we should be grateful. (pp. 150-51)

> *Jay Parini, "Rule and Energy: The Poetry of Thom Gunn," in* The Massachusetts Review, *Vol. XXIII, No. 1, Spring, 1982, pp. 134-51.*

DONALD DAVIE

In the past, I have been persuaded by those like Colin Falck who have thought Thom Gunn's distinctive and great achievement was to have re-established creative connections with at least one aspect of Shakespeare, and with some of Shakespeare's great contemporaries, notably Marlowe and Donne. Gunn, I believe, liked this notion, and Clive Wilmer endorses it in his excellent and too brief Introduction to *The Occasions of Poetry* [see excerpt above]. It is disconcerting to have to acknowledge that in Gunn's very fine collection of poems [*The Passages of Joy*] this dimension of his writing is no longer evident. In none of these 37 poems, as I read them, is there any longer evidence that their author has been attending to the songs from Shakespeare's plays, to Donne's Songs and Sonnets, or Marlowe's translations and imitations of Ovid: they are 'contemporary' in an altogether less complicated and more obvious way. Although the title of the collection and an epigraph to one poem come (surprisingly) from Johnson's 'Vanity of Human Wishes', in all other respects these poems seem to remember not much before Whitman, and certainly nothing before Stendhal or Keats. Clearly, if Gunn has indeed been one modern poet with a sympathy for the English Renaissance, that was far from being as central to his achievement as some of us thought. For the achievement is still there: *The Passages of Joy* is as fine a collection as he has ever published, and if it lacks the resonances that some of us have come to expect and delight in, it provides others that many readers may well prefer.

And after all the signs were always there, if we had cared to look. Rereading in *The Occasions of Poetry* Gunn's essay on Ben Jonson, one notices for the first time how difficult he finds it to enter into Jonson's world. The difficulties can be surmounted, and mostly he surmounts them, after very plainly and helpfully and not without erudition pointing them out to his readers. One difficulty he does not surmount, I think, is his inability to share Jonson's Christian piety. But more revealing in relation to his own poetry is the difficulty he has with the famous forthrightness of Jonson's not necessarily Christian affirmation.... 'Jonson,' Gunn comments, 'like so many of his contemporaries, looked up to the moral chastity

of someone who *knew* what was right to do (and did it) rather than having to learn it from experience.' The implication is rather plainly that whereas this 'looking up' was a possibility for Jonson and his contemporaries, it is no longer possible for us, or not for those of us who write poems. And sure enough, when we turn to what Gunn writes about his own poems and about 20th-century poetry, we see that a Keatsian 'proving upon the pulses' is for him axiomatic....

Gunn has always been a highly intellectual poet: but that is not quite the same as saying, what seems to be also true, that he is a poet of and for the intelligentsia. The reason for this, for his having no choice in the matter, has been widely known for a long time, but in these two books he takes great care that none of us should be in any doubt about it. He is a practising homosexual, and in poem after poem here he proves on his pulses, from experience, that so far as he is concerned homosexual practices (even, in some circumstances, of a notably promiscuous and mercenary kind) constitute 'what is right'. Among the essays, one on **'Homosexuality in Robert Duncan's Poetry'** makes the same point....

Clive Wilmer calls Gunn 'this most chaste of modern poets'. He does not have in mind Gunn's subject-matter.... 'Chaste', as Wilmer uses the word, refers to Gunn's style, and in that sense it is exact. That has always been what is singular about Gunn's work: the combination of unchaste subject-matter (one can be unchaste in other matters than sex) with a remarkably chaste, remarkably lean and unadorned, style. This fruitful tension is more marked in *The Passages of Joy* than ever before, chiefly because unusually many of the poems are in unmetred verse, where the tautness of formal control can show itself only in a diction that is, as always with this poet, terse and rapid and non-sensuous. Yet, enamoured though he is of liberation ..., he has never fallen for the simple-minded liberationist arguments for free verse as against metre; and the alternately rhyming pentameters in a poem called **'Crossroads'** splendidly vindicate his belief that 'in metrical verse, it is the nature of the control being exercised that becomes part of the life being spoken about.' Similarly (that same fruitful tension in another key), though he idealises the Sixties, he doesn't like, and never did, a kind of writing that came in with that disgraceful decade:

> For several weeks I have been reading
> the poetry of my juniors.
> Mother doesn't understand,
> and they hate Daddy, the noted alcoholic.
> They write with black irony
> of breakdown, mental institution,
> and suicide attempt, of which the experience
> does not always seem first-hand.
> It is very poetic poetry.

This is a fair example of the firmness that Gunn's chaste diction can manage in free verse, but the acerbity (relatively rare in Gunn but always welcome and well managed) gives it an adventitious lift. A purer example, because free of such special effects, is the last poem in the book, **'Night Taxi'**, which resists quotation precisely because its 65 lines of unmetred verse support one another totally, so that no excerpt from them carries any punch on its own. And surely just that effect is what is meant, stylistically, by 'chaste'....

The most scholarly essay in *The Occasions of Poetry* is also the longest and the best, on Fulke Greville. Here not only is the learning impressive and well marshalled, but the critical intelligence is at full stretch as nowhere else. The criticism is methodical and trenchant in the manner of Gunn's old teacher, Yvor Winters: but it discriminates far more patiently than Winters did. I do not scruple to call this essay 'masterly', with a mastery that is likely to be overlooked because Greville is a poet who has never appealed to many, and probably never will. Gunn confronts that in Greville which he too finds unappealing: 'The preceding outline ends as a description of attitudes that I find at best sterile and at worst obnoxious.' . . . What is exemplary is Gunn's insistence, and his demonstration, that in poem after poem Greville can and does validate poetically ideas that remain, in the abstract, obnoxious. This seems to represent an exertion of sympathy beyond what six years later Gunn was able to manage for Greville's contemporary, Jonson; whether or not Gunn can nowadays enter into pre-Enlightenment ethical attitudes, in 1968 he certainly could.

He did so by way of Camus, in whose image of *'le malconfort'*—'the cell where one cannot stand, sit, or lie'—he finds an exact analogy to Greville's 'that strait building, Little-ease of sin'. Gunn applauds Camus for saying, *'Il fallait vivre dans le malconfort,'* for 'the determination to live with that sickness, fully acknowledging it and accepting it as the basis for our actions'. 'Greville,' Gunn says, 'could not make such an acceptance.' The rigour of this is extraordinary: Gunn calls us to live in Little-ease, while denying ourselves the Christian consolation that even the notoriously bleak Calvinist Greville could fall back upon. Obviously for an unbeliever like Gunn neither sin nor depravity can have, strictly speaking, any meaning: but that distinction is quite consumed in his conviction that Greville's Little-ease, whether or not we call it 'sin', is the state in which we all live, and have to live. That is borne out by Gunn's poems. Let no one be deceived by the title: *The Passages of Joy* isn't in the least a joyous book. The steely temper of it comes clear as soon as we return the phrase to its context in **'The Vanity of Human Wishes'**:

> Time hovers o'er, impatient to destroy,
> And shuts up all the Passages of Joy.

The life in Gunn's poems is life in Little-ease; and he persuades us while we read that this is true whether we are 'straight' or (the pathetic incongruity of the word!) 'gay'.

> *Donald Davie, "Looking Up," in* London Review of Books, *July 15 to August 4, 1982, p. 19.*

PETER KEMP

'I can try / At least to get my snapshots accurate,' Thom Gunn remarks in one of the poems in his new collection, *The Passages of Joy.* The critical essays assembled in *The Occasions of Poetry* pay tribute to other poets who have done so. Crisp bits of verbal photography are frequently held up for admiration. Keats is praised for his 'sharp-eyed exactness'; Hardy, congratulated on the 'clarity of . . . [his] images'. William Carlos Williams—in some ways the key exhibit—is enthused over as though he were a flawless camera lens: 'clear delineation . . . perfect accuracy'.

Gunn aims at achieving similar results. Cloudiness caused by out-of-focus rhetoric or 'confessional' over-exposure is deplored in the essays. The poems brilliantly snap up a collection of high-definition images. But there's more to them than mere Nikon precision. . . . [Gunn] invests his own sharp images with depths of significance: 'every detail brightened with meaning'. Sometimes this is accomplished by the angle from which things are viewed. More usually—it is Gunn's favourite technique—two pictures are creatively juxtaposed.

Juxtaposition increasingly characterises Gunn's writing. Bringing together techniques learned from both English and American poets, he also shows a taste for coupling the literary and the *louche*. . . . His latest writings show an imagination amiably hospitable to hustlers and Hardy, Keats and Castro Street, S/M paraphernalia and sonnet sequences. The manner of his poetry is carefully played off against its matter, the former becoming more chaste as the latter gets raunchier.

With impeccable control, *The Passages of Joy* often depicts kicking over the traces. Gunn's imagination alertly cruises through leather bars, round all-night partyings, past towel boys, rough trade and urban cowpokes. Linking solicitude and soliciting, a number of poems pore attentively over San Francisco studs. . . . (p. 21)

This is the side of Gunn's personality that relishes high-adrenalin stimulation—butch insignia, wild-side sex. Frequently, in this new book, it is ranged against its opposite. **'New York'**, for instance, opens with high-risk alfresco sex but cosily concludes amidst sleepy domesticity. **'Hide and Seek'**, the title and subject of one poem, and a recurrent motif in others, encompasses both extremes: going covertly out on a limb; being eventually drawn back into everyday community. **'Talbot Road'** uses the game to staple together two companion pictures set on Hampstead Heath: Gunn, as a boy, by day, sedately playing hide and seek; Gunn, as a man, by night, romping through rougher rituals.

This poem also engineers a confrontation between his adolescent and present selves. Such eerie *alter ego* meetings are common in Gunn. His poems are full of scenes in which one aspect of his life or personality stares at its opposite. Dichotomies intrigue him: day and night, trust and risk, indoors and outdoors, streets and vegetation.

And there is a fissure through his attitude to pleasure. Part of Gunn hankers after a hippie Eden, some great bounce-around of nude togetherness. . . . But another part—that which pins a monitory epigraph from Johnson on to this new book of poems—is grimly aware of the casualties of hedonism.

The Passages of Joy abounds with reference to the transience of fun. . . . Presley, charismatic rebel in an earlier poem, is brought on again—but now as a sorry object-lesson: 'almost matronly', a dropsical zombie numbed by painkillers.

Numbness and unfeelingness always provoke Gunn's distaste. Here, besides drug-clotted Presley, he shakes his head over a comatose cousin, a stupefied alcoholic, and some 'heavy' office-girls who 'sweat into their double knits' as they 'belch and munch' their way through lunch. Attempting to disparage crudity and animus, this latter piece topples embarrassingly into what it derides.

Usually, though, Gunn sustains a fine poise of style and attitude. *The Passages of Joy* offers some of his most sensitively powerful poetry—pieces like **'June'**, where he focuses on Oriental poppies blooming in a San Francisco yard. With Imagist precision—vivid and meticulous—he itemises the process of their bursting into flower.

Blazing with sensuous evocation, the lines also glow with rich significance. The flare of floral splendour turns into a delicately handled image of erotic heat. The uncanny natural concord of the poppies—blossoming simultaneously—becomes a fertile emblem of human sexual harmony. In poems like this, Gunn triumphantly unites the graphic and the resonant. He is able, as he says of Isherwood, 'to present complexity through the elegance of simplicity'. (p. 22)

Peter Kemp, "Gunn's Views," in The Listener, *Vol. 108, No. 2773, August 12, 1982, pp. 21-2.*

JOHN LUCAS

I am sorry to say that *The Passages of Joy* seems to me an utterly cliché-ridden collection. There are clichés of phrase: the poet speaks of being 'buried' in his work, he remembers a friend's 'boisterous sense of fun', he 'tingles' with knowledge. There are clichés of thought, of which the poem to Elvis Presley is a particularly unfortunate example.... But above all, it is the cliché of manner that hurts this volume. There are two such manners. One is the laid-back, free-form, West Coast style of the majority of the poems, which is so slack as to be almost enervate, and which therefore works only when it mimes its subject matter as in **'Slow Walker.'** ... The other is that tight, formal style with which Gunn began and which now has about it a kind of metallic heaviness, a lack of rhythmic grace which Yvor Winters sanctioned ... but which is in fact fatally dull. The trouble with *The Passages of Joy* is that the voice we are required to listen to finds it very difficult to say anything that is new, plausible or engaging. (p. 21)

John Lucas, "Pleading for the Authenticity of the Spirit," in New Statesman, *Vol. 104, No. 2682, August 13, 1982, pp. 20-1.**

MARK CALDWELL

Thom Gunn's new book of poems [*The Passages of Joy*] comes clean with a companion volume of essays [*The Occasion of Poetry*], as if someone were trying to package him as an august poet and critic—the gay Matthew Arnold of his time. Even their titles have parallel ambiguities. What's an Occasion? What's a Passage?

As an essayist, Gunn is modest and generous, belying the hype. Some of his essays—like those of Rod Taylor, Dick Davis, and James Merrill—are "occasional" in that they're short, casual, slight, even fugitive, floating away into thin air on their own gracefulness. Yet the longer pieces on Fulke Greville and Thomas Hardy are "occasional" in a more satisfying sense: here Gunn unassumingly puts his intelligence wholly at the service of the occasioning subject, which is never a mere pretext for self-analysis or sermonizing. He's well worth reading when he explains how Greville, a late Elizabethan and Jacobean courtier and poet, appropriated and transformed the different kinds of poetry made available to him by the cultural ferment of the 1590s. Or the way Hardy adapted the taciturnity of English folk ballads, cutting away connective tissue and explanation to let events speak starkly for themselves.

Note that stress on "experience," not meddled with by the writer's ego, as the stuff of the good poem.... Gunn wants to avoid the self-involvement of confession, to make the act of writing a testimony to what he calls "the particulars of the present" transient and elusive, but significant just because they exist: parts of an individual's life, but somehow transcending it.

This, I think, suggests both the strengths and weaknesses of Gunn's poetry, here and elsewhere. He never quite explores

his idea that writing affirms experience, never seems quite aware of how complicated the connections are, or how yawning the gulfs that can open up between experience (whatever *that* is) and the apparently simple but really eldritch act of turning it into blobs of ink on a page. His poems sometimes have a trustful way of taking intractably weird things and pulling all their teeth out, either by making them into ressuringly general emblems of the human condition, or by fitting them to traditional iambics or quatrains, which in another writer might point up their strangeness but which in Gunn more often just domesticates them.... [The poems in *The Passages of Joy*] are smart, sincere, humane, but tamer than Gunn's own experiences suggest they ought to be.

Mark Caldwell, in a review of "The Occasions of Poetry: Essays in Criticism and Autobiography" and "The Passages of Joy," in The Village Voice, *Vol. XXVII, No. 43, October 26, 1982, p. 55.*

DANA GIOIA

Gunn is a very versatile writer both technically and thematically. *Games of Chance* allows the reader to study one side of him in isolation. These eleven new poems, all written in free verse, show Gunn in a reflective mood. Like an operatic tenor whose voice has darkened with age, Gunn is moving into new roles in his recent work, and though he may move among the same scenery as before, he now sees it from a different perspective. He shows the same curiosity as ever, but it is now tinged with cynicism, as in **"Expression,"** where Gunn turns his attention to the work of young poets.... (p. 491)

Elsewhere Gunn strikes a more tender note. In **"Elegy"** the memory of an acquaintance who shot himself becomes a general lament for all of his dead.... But ultimately Gunn undermines whatever tenderness he shows with the bitter reminders of reality. In **"As Expected"** the slow gains a young man makes with a ward of retarded adults are destroyed by his successors. Or in **"Adultery,"** a variation on the Elizabethan echo poems that have always fascinated Gunn, a wife's carefully orchestrated lie is rendered pointless when Gunn suddenly reverses the points of view and reveals how little her husband cares for her. *Games of Chance* is a powerful book. (pp. 491-92)

Dana Gioia, "Poetry and the Fine Presses," in The Hudson Review, *Vol. XXXV, No. 3, Autumn, 1982, pp. 483-98.**

JOHN MOLE

The play of intelligence has always been a distinguishing mark of Thom Gunn's poetry, and his critical essays [collected in *The Occasions of Poetry*] show that it is what he values most in the poetry of others. Writing on the early work of Gary Snyder—a significant signpost en route to his own Americanisation—he singles out a poem which is "about feeling the cleanness of the senses" and goes on to observe that "cleanness, exactness, adequacy are the first impressions we have of the language and the rhythms ... rhythms at one with the perceptions, neither their servants nor their masters." It is this kind of firm grace, a lyrical pact between servant and master, the practice of an efficient sensibility, that Gunn has always seemed to go for. In his strongest poems he has achieved a balance of rule and energy where, with an increasing confidence in the handling of free verse and syllabics, the celebrated pose has gradually relaxed into a more mature poise.

The poems I like most in *The Passages of Joy* are, in the words of one of them, exercises ''in stance, and / in the muscle of feeling.'' They are full of teasing questions of identity, and often turn on a moment of complex interplay experienced as a creative tension. . . . Gunn's continual alertness to the need to be ''loose but in control'' (or, as he reverses it in the sonnet **''Keats at Highgate''**, ''perhaps not well-dressed but oh no not loose'') keeps the reader involved with his search for that fusion of passion and intellect which, for him, is the essence of a good poem. His scenarios have increasingly become the streets and bars of San Francisco or New York but they are not just those of a convert to the American way of life excited by local colour. They are occasions for the exploration of ''the cool source of all that hurry / and desperate activity'', just as in the autobiographical sequence about living in London, **''Talbot Road''**, his memories weave their way between impressions of remoteness and pressing activity. . . . When, though, the poems become merely a part of that ''live current'', when they are loose to the point of hanging out—as in some of the pieces which seem to do no more than celebrate *coming* out—they seem very limp indeed. The freebooting innocent abroad, preoccupied with the ''warm teasing tickle'' in the cave of a handshake which takes his mind off toothpaste, offers whimsical glimpses of the gay life but fails to make them more than a faintly embarrassing catalogue of local thrills. The gap between Gunn's best and worst poetry remains a vast one, and points to a paradox he has not yet resolved. (pp. 63-4)

John Mole, ''Modern Languages,'' in Encounter, *Vol. LX, No. 1, January, 1983, pp. 60-6.**

A(lbert) R(amsdell) Gurney, Jr.

1930-

(Has also written under pseudonym of Pete Gurney) American dramatist, novelist, and scriptwriter.

Gurney's dramas depict the lives of America's upper-middle class and are often compared with the stories of John Cheever. Born into an affluent family in Buffalo, New York, Gurney writes satirically of his background, simultaneously defending and exposing the WASP culture. He wrote his first one-act play, *Love in Buffalo* (1958), while attending the Yale School of Drama and continued to compose one-act dramas throughout the 1960s. Gurney's first full-length play, *Scenes from American Life* (1970), consists of a series of episodes tracing Buffalo's social elite from the 1930s to the near future. Gurney achieved his first solid commercial success with *The Dining Room* (1981). Inspired by Thorton Wilder's *The Long Christmas Dinner*, Gurney's play examines upper-middle class life through a number of vignettes set within a dining room. Explaining the source of his subject matter, Gurney reveals, "I'm looking back over my shoulder with some fondness and bemusement—and sometimes amazement—at the strange ways I lived."

(See also *Contemporary Authors*, Vols. 77-80.)

© *Thomas Victor 1984*

Martin Gottfried, in a review of "Scenes from American Life," in Women's Wear Daily, March 26, 1971. Reprinted in New York Theatre Critics' Reviews, Vol. XXXII, No. 13, June 13, 1971, p. 271.

MARTIN GOTTFRIED

I don't know whether A. R. Gurney, Jr.'s **"Scenes From American Life"** can really be called a theatre piece. . . . But whatever it is called it is mostly a lovely entertainment, gently satirical and nostalgic. . . . [It] is a cozy, perceptive view of America, past and present, that in its own way untangles the leaves, flowers, underbrush and weeds of our culture to show the roots of this country.

In more than a dozen quick scenes, Mr. Gurney draws line sketches of Buffalo life over the past forty years: . . . antisemitism at the country club; shopping trips to New York; choosing between a coming out party and a college education; an encounter group; tennis sociology; well-meaning ladies fighting the elm blight; church sermons.

Some of these scenes are shorter than others, some more like cartoons than others. The characters often run through many of them though there is no real continuity. The time settings are interwoven so that a Second World War scene may be followed by a Depression sequence and then a reference to McCarthyism.

There are also looks into the future and these are the weakest. In an effort to be relevant as well as nostalgic, Gurney describes a future of military dictatorship and it is inconsistent with the tone and writing level of everything else, not to mention being trite and irrelevent to his "play's" personality. Satire, after all, is based on fact while future projection is fiction, and Gurney is much weaker as a creative writer than he is as a humorously critical one.

His dire predictions detract from the production but they don't spoil it. . . .

EDITH OLIVER

["**Scenes from American Life**"] is both satire and valedictory. It is a cluster of scenes—some of them as brief as sketches—about the lives of the well-connected and the well-to-do in Buffalo between the early thirties and what is probably the middle eighties, by which time the country has been taken over by the military and we have become a Fascist state. It must be said at once that the author's underlying pessimism and apocalyptic outlook in no way dim his wit and his sense of fun; along with the comedy there is sadness, and even tragedy, shown or implied, in **"Scenes from American Life,"** but the play is never bleak, and heaven knows it is never dull. (pp. 95-6)

[Mr. Gurney] is himself from Buffalo, and he seems almost to have chosen his scenes at random while rooting through his memories rather than to have made them up, and then to have arranged them according to some private scheme of his own. The form of the play is elusive, to say the least. As we shuttle back and forth in time, there are comic scenes and pathetic ones and harsh ones. (p. 96)

Edith Oliver, in a review of "Scenes from American Life," in The New Yorker, *Vol. XLVII, No. 7, April 3, 1971, pp. 95-6.*

SANDY WILSON

Until I went to see *Children* . . . I had no idea how conditioned I had become to modern play-writing. During the first couple of scenes four characters appeared: a Mother, her daughter, her son and the son's wife. Their relationships were made quite clear and they conversed about a straightforward situation . . . in a realistic setting. . . . Then the Mother suddenly made a remark about erosion: in time, she said, the garden and then the house would slide into the sea.

'Aha!' I thought to myself. 'I've got it! These are not real people at all, nor is that a real house. This is a Symbolic Play, and the people and the house represent the Condition of Present-day America.' But the play continued, the characters went on behaving like real people, and the subject of erosion was not brought up again. Shortly the conversation turned towards Sex. . . . 'Aha!' I thought again. . . . But no. The play continued, the situation developed, and, although there was a little cuddling between the brother and his wife (his *wife*?), hardly a button was unfastened.

'Well,' I thought, 'there's only one course open now. . . . [Someone] is suddenly going to stop in mid-speech and say, "I'm sorry. I simply can't go on with this. It's a load of crap," whereupon the stage manager will come on and remonstrate. And then the whole thing is going to turn into a discussion about Watergate, or Northern Ireland, or Racialism, or Property Speculation (Yess, yes, that's it! Someone mentioned selling the house!!).' But, for God's sake, the play just went on. . . . 'Heavens!' I thought. 'Can it be? Can it *possibly* be? Is this that dear, forgotten, old-fashioned thing, a Good Play? I do believe it is. I do believe I am actually . . . watching a Good Play. I am not going to be bored, or baffled. I am not going to be preached at or bludgeoned over the head with statistics and propaganda. And I am not going to be shocked, brutalised, outraged or assaulted. Oh, thank you, thank you, thank you!' (p. 36)

Children is simply what it sets out to be: a soundly structured piece, absorbing, amusing, occasionally exciting and finally very moving, about the tensions of a middle-class American family on a July the Fourth week-end. It makes no breakthrough, it neither attacks the audience or seeks to justify itself, and I don't suppose it will give such critics as the swinging old gentleman on the *Sunday Times* much of a charge. In fact I would not claim that it is a great play, or even a very original one, since it explores territory which has already been fairly well trodden by, amongst others, Lillian Hellman, Arthur Miller and William Inge, more ambitiously and perhaps more memorably. But if anyone is still prepared to sit down calmly and enjoy what is, I repeat, a Good Play, then let him go to *Children.* (p. 37)

Sandy Wilson, in a review of "Children," in Plays and Players, *Vol. 21, No. 8, May, 1974, pp. 36-7.*

MARTIN LEVIN

You might take ["**The Gospel According to Joe**"] for yet another vulgarization of the Christ story. Well, you would be wrong. Yes, A. R. Gurney Jr. superimposes the story of Jesus on post-modern times. Joseph (a quondam salesman of storm windows) and Mary (a worker in a day care center) are sequestered in the barn of "a dude commune" where the infant Jesus is born. And thenceforth the little book consists of one calculated anachronism after another, sometimes with metaphorical confusion. . . . But Gurney is no more concerned with the Bible per se than George Orwell in "Animal Farm" was concerned with zoology. Gurney's search is for earthly, not spiritual illumination. To this end, he narrates the Gospel, through Joseph, as a commentary on the human family. The effect is warm, wry and as inconclusive as man's future.

Martin Levin, in a review of "The Gospel According to Joe," in The New York Times Book Review, *May 26, 1974, p. 18.*

MARTIN GOTTFRIED

A. R. Gurney's ["**Children**"] means to be about the childhood relationships that are never outgrown—those between siblings, those between child and parents. It is an excellent subject but Gurney has explored it only in an illustrative way and even then, he's wandered. This play spends most of its time dealing with another subject—one without the dramatic possibilities of childhood, one more bland: that subject is emotional repression among WASPs. . . .

[The play's] house is meant to be a symbol of upper middle class WASP roots. It is being bequeathed by a widow to her grown children on the occasion of her imminent remarriage. That occasion is coincidental with the 4th of July weekend, though it is no coincidence. For their declarations of independence, or lack of it, are at stake this weekend.

The mother's independence is related to her remarriage; her son's is related to outgrowing jockhood; her divorced daughter's independence will be declared if she can finally live with the man she has long loved, but of whom the family always disapproved.

It is the play's scheme to have all these dreams dashed by the conditioning of family relationships but in the process of introducing social color, Gurney instead blames their unhappiness on a general WASP way of life he feels is emotionally repressive.

I think this is because he is more relaxed writing on subjects than for people. The scenes in which the WASP way of life is knocked are the ones that work; those that mean to indicate family ties are less dramatic. That is why the play's emphasis is shifted from children to familiar disapprovals of white Anglo-Saxon social rules and games. . . .

Gurney is a talented writer. Five years ago his "**Scenes From American Life**" successfully presented the promise of a dramatic intelligence directed toward the middle class that is too often ignored by our stage. That intelligence and interest are present in this work. "**Children**" seems more sociological than artistic. Its style is without personal signature. And finally, it isn't a necessary play. The author has come up with a good subject, but he didn't dramatize it as if the stage was a necessity to its expression.

A necessity to be on the stage is fundamental to theatrical worth. Without it, a play needn't be a play and if it needn't then it oughtn't.

Martin Gottfried, "Gurney's Wandering 'Children'," in New York Post, *October 26, 1976. Re-*

printed in New York Theatre Critics' Reviews, *Vol. XXXVII, No. 25, Dec. 6, 1976, p. 95.*

MEL GUSSOW

A young wife turns to her husband and says, "Here I am in your mother's outfit, you're in your father's bathrobe, and we're living in your family's house." In A. R. Gurney Jr.'s [**"Children"**] . . . , the family—rich, rule-bound and very WASPish—is a sustaining but also a stunting force.

Though the children now have children, no one has matured, just as values have frozen on this conservative landscape, a grand house on a New England island, where everyone has always spent summers together. . . .

"Children" begins brightly: grown-up children wryly bicker, and their mother futilely tries to maintain her equilibrium. There is a universality in the interwoven anxieties and grievances. These concerns are endemic to this family and, as audiences will note, they are endemic to other families as well.

Mr. Gurney has a great deal to say about the strictures of close family bonds, the loss of individualism and gamesmanship and cleanliness as a way of life, and, up to a point, he says it very well.

The play falters with the return home—and the nonappearance on stage—of a prodigal son, the misanthropoic Pokey. Pokey is not only the catalyst, he is also the most fascinating character in **"Children"**—an abrasive, willful creature who is seeking identity outside the family. The others are gradually revealed as self-defeating, mutually enervating and even foolish.

Structurally, Mr. Gurney's intention is clear. By reducing Pokey to a presence, he can focus on the family itself. But our curiosity about this outsider is piqued. The fact is that Pokey would enliven the play—as would three other major characters who are also studiously kept off stage. Too much of the drama is unseen—acts of violence, emotional as well as physical.

In the climactic scene, the author appears to have second thoughts about excluding characters. He suddenly introduces Pokey behind a screen door, where dimly and silently . . . he lurks while his mother unburdens herself of a litany of her mistakes. The scene is itself a mistake, and convinces us of what we have been suspecting all along: the play is overly ambiguous. Like Pokey, it remains in the shadows.

We are never sure where the author's allegiance lies or who should be the receiver of our sympathy. At first he seems to side with the mother, then briefly with the daughter, and finally seems to settle with Pokey, although all of this character's acts seem mean and petulant.

"Children" is based on a short story by John Cheever, not the one named "The Children," but "Goodbye, My Brother." The original is a perfect sketch of an idyllic family holiday upset by the arrival of an objectionable "changeling" brother. Mr. Gurney has taken the setting and basic points in the plot and has altered almost everything else, including the names. What Mr. Cheever viewed fondly, even poignantly, Mr. Gurney considers vainglorious.

Mel Gussow, " 'Children,' New Gurney Play, Begins Brightly, Then Falters," in The New York Times, *October 26, 1976, p. 47.*

THE VIRGINIA QUARTERLY REVIEW

This thoroughly enjoyable novel [*Entertaining Strangers*] is a devastatingly funny and highly sophisticated dissection of the academic life. It will be an enlightening revelation to those who naïvely think that pure sweetness and light prevail behind the ivy towers of a University. Despite their scholarly insights and cultural references, professors are shown to be subject to all the human frailties of bad character, excessive ambition, and destructive jealousy. The hilarious description of a typical faculty meeting is itself worth the entire price of the book.

A review of "Entertaining Strangers," in The Virginia Quarterly Review, *Vol. 53, No. 4 (Autumn, 1977), p. 142.*

JOHN SIMON

That stimulating writer A. R. Gurney Jr. has come up with *The Dining Room,* in which an elegant, old-fashioned (though not genuinely antique) dining room serves as the real and symbolic setting for countless, not directly related lives—or, rather, telltale fragments of them—forming a passing parade of Wasp America—preppie, post-preppie, and anti-preppie—from its heyday to its present, precariously eked-out survival. The dining room is the scene of much more than merely eating—of assorted fun, sadness, contentment, and rebellion—as a modus vivendi goes from viable to friable.

One problem here may be excessive trickiness. In Thornton Wilder's *The Long Christmas Dinner,* from which this play seems to derive, there is, although stylized and accelerated, a consecutive progression and confinement to one family. Gurney, however, jumps back and forth in time, around in place (this only *seems* to be the same dining room), and ever onward with new dramatis personae. Moreover, we get double exposure, as one unrelated episode slowly dissolves into another. (pp. 81-2)

There is no denying that Gurney has been in better form before—notably in the not dissimilar *Scenes From American Life*—yet even at his second best he is observant, thoughtful, and, when most unflinchingly satirical, still unabatedly humane. (p. 82)

John Simon, "Malle de Guare," in New York Magazine, *Vol. 15, No. 10, March 8, 1982, pp. 81-2.**

GERALD WEALES

The central character of Gurney's [*The Dining Room*] is the setting. It is a well-appointed dining room, old style, one that conjures formal family meals and all that that implies in both negative and positive senses. The room represents not a particular home or family, but a host of such dining rooms peopled by families in varying degrees of stability or disintegration. . . . In the opening sequence, the father, a stickler for routine, offers his idea of personal and political propriety as substantive truth, but does so against the discordant voice of his very respectful son whose teacher has just told him that there is something called a Depression going on out there. What the play shows is the way "out there" enters the dining room, disrupts the family structure, renders the room obsolete, reveals the canker on the rose. It is a world in which adultery, homosexuality, heavy drinking, parental bullying, youthful rebellion are recognized but not acknowledged, kept in their place which is certainly not in the dining room.

Since Gurney has adapted a John Cheever story for PBS and since **Children** (1974), one of his most accomplished plays, was suggested by a Cheever story, some reviewers have seen Gurney as operating in Cheever territory. So he does, but it is Gurney country, to. The analogy is most useful if it draws Cheever admirers to Gurney, for the two writers share not simply the same geographical and psychological areas, but the same tone of ironic dismay, the oblique comedy of necessary loss. In one of the sequences in the play, an Amherst student gets his aunt to demonstrate the table service that was once used for formal dinners; he explains, as he snaps away with his camera, that it is his anthropology assignment, his contribution to a series on the eating habits of vanishing tribes—this one the WASPs of the American Northeast. If the play were no more than that joke implies it would be a relatively simple exercise in polite satire. At one point, in a teasing scene with a stockbroker turned furniture repairer, a woman gets under the table for the first time, thinking that a dining room table is "something special," and discovers that it is "just wood" underneath. The strength of the play lies in the way it uses its accumulation of situations to suggest that the table is more than "just wood," that the obsolescence of the dining room represents not only the casting off of the family gathering as often unwilling shared pretense but the loss of values as well. (pp. 243-44)

Gerald Weales, "Goodbye to All That: Loss Is More," in Commonweal, *Vol. CIX, No. 8, April 23, 1982, pp. 243-44.**

ROBERT BRUSTEIN

[*The Dining Room*] dramatizes the domestic crises that usually afflict families during lunch and dinner. The problem is that neither the crises nor the families are particularly interesting; the play seems more an exercise in WASP sociology than an act of theatrical imagination.

To be fair, the playwright is less interested in dramatic confrontations than in depicting, through a technique of kaleidoscopic time warps, the manners and morals of a dying aristocratic class. The play is full of convincing nostalgia for the passing of a decent old world, and tolerant resignation (less convincing) over what is coming to replace it. "Some Irish fellow or Jewish gentleman will be sitting in that chair—and your grandson will be back at the plough," remarks one crustacean before remembering to add, "and that won't be such a bad thing either." It is the noblesse oblige of Renoir's *Grand Illusion,* where the aristocratic French officer ends up sacrificing his life for Jewish and working-class comrades, though he feels much more kinship with his noble German counterpart. I was more persuaded by another scene in which a young Amherst student, "studying the eating habits of various vanishing cultures—the WASPs of Northeastern United States," is thrown out of the room by his Aunt Harriet, who threatens to "cut off his anthropological balls."

Much more affectionately, Gurney is also studying the eating habits of vanishing Americans. As played by a cast of eight, who transform (sometimes too cutely) into children, young people, middle-aged people, and oldsters, *The Dining Room* is a short course in what to do with finger bowls, how to make butter balls, and when to use the Waterford crystal. . . . The playwright recognizes the futility of mourning dead manners, so his elegy is often tempered with a shrug. The writing is refined, deliberate, and economical; it is also, unfortunately,

thin and colorless, as if the maid had substituted water for the ink. (pp. 27-8)

Robert Brustein, "Plays of the Transition," in The New Republic, *Vol. 186, No. 19, May 12, 1982, pp. 25-8.**

JOHN SIMON

Some plays are too small for the theater, for television, for anything except the author's memory, his heart, and a bureau drawer. Such a one is A. R. Gurney Jr.'s *What I Did Last Summer* . . . , an amiable, not unintelligent, intermittently amusing, but finally utterly tepid miniature that only those bursting at the seams with goodwill can clasp to their bosoms or bursting seams.

It is a memory play about the author's fourteenth summer at an aestival colony on the Canadian side of Lake Erie near Buffalo, the site of other Gurneyana. Charlie's father is in the Pacific (the time is 1945); his mother, Grace, is harried and lonely and has had a tiny affair. . . . Charlie, seeking gainful employment, wanders onto the property of Anna Trumbull, nicknamed the Pig Woman, who is part Indian and semi-outcast. She is an artist *manqué*—which, as Bonny explains, is an art teacher with no students—and a bourgeois-despising eccentric. . . .

If you are not exactly ravished by the story so far, don't expect much more from the actual play. Gurney is a civilized writer who manages to navigate a reasonably steady course between period oddities and conversational bromides, between bits of Pirandellianizing and an occasional sharply perceived, brightly rendered incident or verbal exchange. The proceedings never sink into dreariness, but they never rise above mild poignancy or modest zestfulness. When, at the end, the audience-addressing Charlie declares that he wrote this play when he turned sixteen . . . I am inclined to take him at his word. There is only so much a gentle play about a boy's coming of age under the tutelage of a sweetly doomed oddball can do for us these days, and this one doesn't even quite do all of that. Gurney has proved himself more at home with satire; this sort of thing he might as well leave to Lanford Wilson. . . .

If you are the sort of theatergoer thankful for small favors, here, certainly, is a small one. (p. 76)

John Simon, "Summer of '45," in New York Magazine, *Vol. 16, No. 7, February 14, 1983, pp. 76-7.*

EDITH OLIVER

Even though A. R. Gurney, Jr.'s **"What I Did Last Summer"** is non-vintage Gurney and doesn't take off on its own, there is considerable pleasure in it. The play . . . is set in a beach resort on Lake Erie during the final summer of the Second World War, and it tells the story (among several stories) of a fourteen-year-old boy named Charlie—the "I" of the title—who escapes the resort, his family, and his summer Latin homework to become the hired boy and eventually the disciple of an elderly art teacher named Anna Trumbull, herself a former summer colonial. (p. 104)

In form, **"What I Did"** is composed of small, self-contained incidents, as were such vintage Gurney plays as **"The Dining Room"** and **"Scenes from American Life,"** and most of the incidents are entertaining and believable enough. One trouble may lie (I'm not sure of this myself) in the character of Anna, on whom so much of the action hinges. She seems synthetic, made up, too "right" in her opinions on social matters and the environment, to say nothing of realizing potential. At one point, she tells Charlie that they can go out and look at the stars or go inside and read the poems of— And under my breath I said, "Not Yeats," one second before she said, "William Butler Yeats." (p. 106)

> *Edith Oliver, in a review of "What I Did Last Summer," in* The New Yorker, *Vol. LIX, No. 1, February 21, 1983, pp. 104, 106.*

JOHN SIMON

Shaw, as he himself put it, wrote "plays pleasant and unpleasant"; Anouilh, in his own words, produced "black plays" and "rosy plays." A. R. Gurney Jr. . . . should also devise some such hortatory distinction; his black or unpleasant plays are much more interesting than his pleasant or rosy ones (which, by the way, is not true of Shaw or Anouilh). *The Middle Ages,* which ought to be designated "ever-so-slightly-shocking pink," is subtitled instead "A New Comedy," which is a misnomer. . . .

The play covers a near quarter century in the lives of four persons. The pivot is Barney, the charming ne'er-do-well elder son of Charles Rusher, the urbane president and patriarch of said club, who is being buried in the first scene but who, in characteristic Gurney playwriting fashion, returns in all but the last one (which, chronologically, follows on the first) to enact the gradual humanization of a benevolent Wasp despot by his son, his daughter-in-law, and changing times. . . .

[In *The Middle Ages*] Gurney shies away from true and troubling psychological and social issues (although he does throw in some facile liberal-going-on-radical window dressing), he is obliged to write situation comedy and turn the entire play into an extended coitus interruptus that, alas, belongs on television. . . .

There are, as always in Gurney, some droll situations and a sufficiency of funny lines; still, in the shadow of previous Gurneyana that have assiduously raked over the same terrain, they yield diminishing delight. . . . Place *The Middle Ages* beside *Arms and the Man* and *Thieves Carnival,* and you'll see how Anouilh and Shaw, despite the intervening years, have maintained their comic bite—preferable by far to this sheepishly toothless grin.

> *John Simon, "Middling Stages," in* New York Magazine, *Vol. 16, No. 14, April 4, 1983, p. 66.*

EDITH OLIVER

[The action in **"The Middle Ages"**], like the action of most of Mr. Gurney's plays, is a matter of small scenes, usually funny yet with a bittersweet undercurrent, and it tells the story of the enduring, seemingly hopeless love between a man named Barney and a woman named Eleanor. . . .

The play, of course, reflects many circumstances outside the club, and becomes a kind of indirect social history of these last forty eruptive years. The mood is comic throughout, even when the most sober matters are touched on, and the ending is highly satisfactory. . . .

When I saw it last spring, I knew I liked it as much as Mr. Gurney's **"The Dining Room,"** but I didn't realize until the

second time around that it cuts even more deeply into emotions and is, if anything, even funnier.

> *Edith Oliver, in a review of "The Middle Ages," in* The New Yorker, *Vol. LIX, No. 7, April 4, 1983, p. 100.*

RICHARD GILMAN

A. R. Gurney Jr. has a wonderful name for the kind of work he does, an unmistakably American name from its initials to its "Jr." What Gurney does is write the most thoroughly American middlebrow plays of any of our dramatists; if "middlebrow" is too strong a word, I'll call him the poet laureate of middle-consciousness.

I use that term to indicate both that his plays fall in the center of the technical and thematic spectrums of American drama and that they never rise much above a modest level of wit and perceptiveness, or ever fall much below it. Moreover, in a theater increasingly dominated by writers from minority religious and ethnic backgrounds, Gurney speaks for, or to, or with the voice of what is still our largest population bloc. Gurney is a WASP—he has rather excessively been called the John Cheever of the theater—who celebrates the cultural and moral virtues of his heritage (specifically in its Eastern, more or less educated and more or less upper-class aspects), mourns their decline and pokes fun at their present perversions.

He doesn't do any of these things with notable force or invention, true, but neither is he often flaccid or wholly derivative. His plays are usually about ordinary people to whom nothing extreme or spectacular happens; structurally, they combine traditional naturalism with some mildly avant-garde (or, more accurately, erstwhile avant-garde) techniques.

None of the plays I've seen is Aristotelian: most of them range back and forth in time, over periods as long as forty years, and some have multiple settings. Gurney is given to scenes flowing into one another or overlapping, and to such other somewhat shopworn expressionist techniques as naming characters "the girl," "the father," "the policeman" and so on. His most interesting play using these methods, or anyway his most diverting idea for a play, is *Who Killed Richard Cory?,* which starts with Edwin Arlington Robinson's famous poem and spins a psychic and sociological drama from its lines. . . .

[*The Dining Room* and *The Middle Ages*] display most of Gurney's methods and concerns. They wander around in time— *The Middle Ages* begins in the mid-1940s and ends in the late 1970s—their scenes are connected not by narrative progression but by a ruling idea, and they deal with aspects of WASP life.

The notion behind *The Dining Room* is that WASPs are fading out as a distinctive cultural grouping, and that this is both amusing and saddening. . . . The room itself is supposed to function as a metaphor for upper-bourgeois life: The dining room was once the center of proper domestic existence, but how many families use it now? In an early scene an architect tells a young couple who've bought the house that they ought to convert the room to some other use. (p. 552)

But too often the room wobbles out of its metaphorical or symbolic status, as in a scene where a son learns that his mother is having an affair, a discovery that could as easily have been made in another room. And too often what Gurney gives us is obvious or sentimental; even at his best, when he's "touching," it's the lightest of strokes.

The Middle Ages takes place in the "trophy room" of a men's club in an unnamed Eastern city. A fable about love and propriety, or the lack thereof, among you-know-who, its chief dramatic elements are the protracted pursuit of his sister-in-law by the black sheep scion of a leading family and the scion's conflict with his father. Along the way, Gurney has some sociological fun at the expense of aristocratic foibles and prejudices—among the son's antics that shock the father is his inviting some black friends to use the club's pool. But the play, while never inept and seldom boring, hasn't much energy and offers no surprises. It's right in the middle. (pp. 552-53)

> *Richard Gilman, in a review of "The Dining Room" and "The Middle Ages," in* The Nation, *Vol. 236, No. 17, April 30, 1983, pp. 552-53.*

JOHN SIMON

Do we really need an updated, edulcorated, and cutesy stage version of *The Aspern Papers*? A. R. Gurney Jr. evidently thought so, for that is what he gave us with **The Golden Age**. Tom, a young part-time teacher and would-be writer, infiltrates the Upper East Side brownstone that Mrs. Isabel Hastings Hoyt shares with her mousy granddaughter, Virginia. . . . As Tom . . . starts to write a book about the Golden Age—the age of his beloved F. Scott Fitzgerald—he becomes convinced that Mrs. Hoyt was Fitzgerald's mistress and the model for Daisy, and that the (as he sees it) important missing sexual chapter of *The Great Gatsby* must be, in manuscript form, somewhere in this house. . . .

It is all awesomely precious and coy and shaggy-doggy, with unbelievable characters and plot, and cheap tricks the foremost of which is the black notebook that may or may not contain the *Gatsby* chapter and that Tom is always on the verge of securing only to be foiled and foiled again in best comic-strip or TV-serial fashion.

Everything here is slippery, reversible, double-bottomed—even the tone keeps changing—and the game is not witty enough to be worth the candle. (p. 93)

> *John Simon, "Brass, at Best," in* New York Magazine, *Vol. 17, No. 17, April 23, 1984, pp. 93-4.**

BRENDAN GILL

In the program accompanying **"The Golden Age,"** . . . we learn that the play was "suggested" by Henry James's novella "The Aspern Papers," but "suggest" is perhaps too passive a term for what is to be observed onstage. The greater part of the amusement we gain from the play comes from the author's own evident amusement in working out parallels to—and divagations from—the enchanting original work. Author and audience are like so many agreeable, well-bred guests at a party in some big house in the country; outside, it is rainy and cold, and we have gathered by the library fire to compose a game that will while away a couple of hours between luncheon and teatime. What fun to construct a new toy out of James's old one! Well, yes and no, and in the end I fear it is mostly no—the Master remains so vigorous a presence that the fun falters and the game quails and shrivels in the very act of being carried out. The three characters who set the toy plot spinning at first threaten to seem merely impertinent, but little by little they dissolve into irrelevance; when a patrician dowager picks up a shotgun and commands a young scamp to strip to the skin, we are closer to Jules Feiffer than we are to James.

The setting of "The Aspern Papers" is a dusky, moldering house in nineteenth-century Venice; the setting of **"The Golden Age"** is a brownstone in contemporary Manhattan. The owner of the house is Isabel Hastings Hoyt, the aforementioned dowager. She is said to be eighty and hard up, but neither she nor her house gives off what James once called "the unmistakable stamp of poverty." . . . Writing nearly a hundred years after James, Gurney is far more explicit than James was in dealing with the sexual aspects of the odious bargain that the three people set about striking; as Mrs. Hoyt joyously recounts her memories of the high jinks of the past, certain low jinks take place in the present with her not very fastidious connivance. What was allusive and shadowy in James is baldly and bleakly spelled out in Gurney; the essential unpleasantness behind the comedy emerges as a taint. . . .

> *Brendan Gill, "High Jinks and Low," in* The New Yorker, *Vol. LX, No. 10, April 23, 1984, p. 116.*

Ronald Harwood

1934-

South African-born English dramatist, novelist, biographer, short story writer, and scriptwriter.

Harwood is best known for *The Dresser* (1980), a play that focuses on the complex relationship between Sir, an aging, egocentric actor, and Norman, his dresser. This play is loosely based on Harwood's experiences with the touring company of actor-manager Donald Wolfit. Harwood began with Wolfit's company in 1953, having come to London two years earlier to study acting. The five years which Harwood spent with Wolfit's company came at the end of the era during which professional touring repertory companies flourished. Harwood has memorialized the era both in *The Dresser* and in the biography which Wolfit asked him to write, *Sir Donald Wolfit, C.B.E.: His Life and Work in the Unfashionable Theatre* (1971). These are considered Harwood's most important works.

Harwood's first novel was inspired by an incident of racial violence which occurred in his native South Africa in 1960. *All the Same Shadows* (1961) is the story of a Cape Town Zulu houseboy who is exploited by the whites he encounters. A later novel, *Articles of Faith* (1973), traces racial prejudice through five generations of a prominent white family in South Africa. Among Harwood's other novels are *The Girl in Melanie Klein* (1969), a humorous work set in a luxury mental hospital, and *Genoa Ferry* (1976), a mystery-thriller. He has also written many plays for television and several for the stage, as well as adaptations of novels by J. B. Priestley, Evelyn Waugh, and Aleksandr Solzhenitsyn.

(See also *Contemporary Authors*, Vols. 1-4, rev. ed.; *Contemporary Authors New Revision Series*, Vol. 4; and *Dictionary of Literary Biography*, Vol. 13.)

© *Jerry Bauer*

ROBERT PICK

When Alan Paton published "Cry, the Beloved Country" thirteen years ago, he called it a "story of comfort in desolation." There is small comfort in [*George Washington September, Sir!*], the present novel about *apartheid*. The desolation of the urbanized South African natives appears to have grown with their growing loss of *naïveté;* lasting degradation has only served to sharpen sensitivity. Nor has the wretchedness of their status blunted the urgency of their human needs. This, at least, is the picture that emerges from Ronald Harwood's book, his first novel. . . .

Mr. Harwood, who shows himself a very skillful writer, does justice to the complexity, as well as the honesty, of his engaging hero. If one considers the limitations of George's idiom, the powerful pertinence of his account is nothing short of amazing. And so is its sustained suspense. Not until well along in the narrative does one realize that Jannie, a colored brothel keeper who approaches the boy after his first brush with the police, plies him with drink and money and offers him Nancy, a beautiful Zulu girl, has more in mind than using the two young people as models for the pornographic photos he sells to "Europeans." The sordid frame-up that follows, and the tragedy that engulfs George—a tragedy born in the fear that rules his land—are fully convincing.

THE TIMES, LONDON

On the battlefield at night, a man cries out. Why? Because, he replies simply, "I had this vision; I saw God".

This is the difficult situation that confronts the characters in *Private Potter* [a television play by Mr. Ronald Harwood and Mr. Casper Wrede]. . . . Difficult obviously, but in what sense? Not, surely, in the way that the authors suppose. Whether or not there is any truth in what Potter says, whether he did have (or thought he had) a vision, his offence against Queen's Regulations is clear enough. The only question is whether or not he is fit to stand trial.

But in this play the superiors are almost as neurotic as Private Potter (always supposing he is neurotic, of course); in scene after scene voices are raised, wills clash, and everybody gets very worked up trying to decide if Potter is a lunatic or a saint—as though that made any difference from the Army's point of view. Only the intervention of . . . a down-to-earth Army surgeon with a thoroughly practical view of the situation prevented us from believing the whole world had gone mad.

"Battlefield Visionary," in The Times, *London, April 7, 1961, p. 18.*

The way the author finally leads his much-tried protagonist out of his inner conflict is too adroit to be persuasive. It is a false note; but it comes at the very end, too late to spoil a poignant and, at the very least, most readable novel.

> Robert Pick, "Tragedy Born of Fear," in The New York Times Book Review, *September 10, 1961, p. 52.*

BRIGID BROPHY

[*The Guilt Merchants*] takes a theme which might have appalled Dostoievsky: the guilt of the Nazis who administered the concentration camps, and the guilt of Jews who still pursue justice or vengeance. He begins with an admirably imagined South America . . . where an ex-Nazi is rumoured to be hiding and where an Israeli agent arrives incognito to hunt him down. But when it comes to working it out Mr Harwood seems to take fright at his theme and ignobly settles for a well-made commercial novel. By the dénouement he is letting his characters utter the melodramatics ('And when I admitted it to myself I died quietly inside') of one of those 'problem plays' which comfortingly raise no problem at all. (pp. 717-18)

> Brigid Brophy, "Antoniona," in New Statesman, *Vol. LXV, No. 1678, May 10, 1963, pp. 717-18.**

HASKEL FRANKEL

The girl in Melanie Klein is Niobe Grynne brought to The Nest bald and mute; and with her arrival Mr. Harwood is off on one of those off-beat tempests in teapots that seem to be a British specialty.

For until Niobe's arrival life at The Nest was as peaceful as life can be in an asylum, even one that looks like a country estate. Prior to Niobe, The Nest seems to have had only three patients. . . .

Hugo, Wassler, and Nora are a relatively contented threesome, who busily clean a swimming pool that will never be filled and play Nest Tennis, a game of their own invention. . . . (Nest Tennis is Ronald Harwood's happiest invention and provides a lovely *Alice in Wonderland* touch, a touch this novel could use more of.)

How the seemingly mad unravel what happened to Niobe Grynne (christened Naomi Green) and the aftermath comprise the bulk of the novel. Mr. Harwood's style is light, humorous, and suspenseful enough to keep the reader interested if not passionately involved. However, the question of sanity is what intrigues one with *The Girl in Melanie Klein.* Who is sane and who is insane? Is one to believe Niobe's story? If so, she is sane. But then again, should we believe Hugo's retelling of the story? Remember, he is our narrator. Niobe could be sane; we know that Hugo is mad. Or do we? After all, Dr. Lipschitz is in charge of Hugo's case, and there are some nagging doubts as to the doctor's mental stability. But that takes us back again to Hugo's reportage on Dr. Lipschitz.

It is this sort of puzzle-box approach that makes *The Girl in Melanie Klein* quietly tantalizing and something more than a suitable vehicle for a Peter Sellers screen romp. If you can imagine one novel as being both sunny and Pinteresque, *The Girl in Melanie Klein* is it. Or perhaps I too am mad.

> Haskel Frankel, "Madness in the Nest," in Saturday Review, *Vol. LII, No. 17, April 26, 1969, p. 58.*

HASKEL FRANKEL

[*The Guilt Merchants* is set in El Pueblo], a South American town of no size or importance. . . . But if El Pueblo is uninteresting, some of its citizenry are most interesting, particularly Carlos Anido. He is a Jewish survivor of Weisering, one of the worst of the Nazi concentration camps. Anido seems almost a Job-like figure. His present is not much happier than his past. . . .

The mystery about Anido is the locked room he rents near the center of town, which no one else has ever been inside, but from which voices have been heard speaking German.

To El Pueblo comes Sidnitz, an Israeli agent who for sixteen years has been searching for Wilhelm Brullach, the murderous commandant of Weisering, though he does not know what the man looks like or even if he is still alive. The action of this novel . . . begins with the arrival of Sidnitz. *The Guilt Merchants* moves in swiftly on the reader like some dark storm cloud heavy with the threat of violence. Unfortunately, the mood does not sustain or build. Extraneous characters creep in to drain away power. What purpose is served by Anna, Cordonez's wife? That she is unfaithful to her husband with Sidnitz serves no purpose in the novel other than to lengthen it and to inject a sexual scene. And why is she a Jewish convert when her husband is not anxious to have people in town know of his Jewishness? . . .

But what hurts *The Guilt Merchants* most is its descent from a novel of character to a story in which characters are forced into a theatrical plot. Can one really believe the super fireworks that pour forth when Brullach and Sidnitz are about to meet? And that Sidnitz does not want to capture Brullach? Or the fate ultimately imposed upon Brullach as punishment? This is melodrama, gaslight vintage.

Because a theater audience is captive, there is a possibility that *The Guilt Merchants* might work on a stage. But with a novel the reader is in charge. The pace is his. The words are permanent and visible, and one can examine them at his own pace. It hurts Mr. Harwood's story. (p. 47)

In short, Mr. Harwood has done himself no great service with *The Guilt Merchants.* Its powerful beginning only heightens the ultimate disappointment. The novel's one virtue is the proof it offers that Ronald Harwood is a writer, but readers of *The Girl in Melanie Klein* already know that. (p. 48)

> Haskel Frankel, in a review of "The Guilt Merchants," in Saturday Review, *Vol. LII, No. 40, October 4, 1969, pp. 47-8.*

SHANE STEVENS

[Many] questions are raised and solved in Ronald Harwood's *The Guilt Merchants.* Unfortunately, not all of them are solved satisfactorily, at least for this reader. This is partially so because the characters do not come sufficiently alive.

Guilt is, of course, a fascinating subject and much can be said about its universality. But in fiction this must be handled deftly and when characterization is rendered incomplete for purposes of structure, the novel suffers. In *The Guilt Merchants,* everyone has his say but after a while we are no longer listening. Perhaps because the story is over long before the ending, and all that is left is the working out of a psychic puzzle of dubious value or interest.

Shane Stevens, "Pursuit of the Past," in Book World—Chicago Tribune, February 8, 1970, p. 13.

ERIC SHORTER

[*Sir Donald Wolfit*] is a good book. It deserves to thrive. It is not a great book and considering that it describes the life of a great actor perhaps it ought to be. But great books about great actors are much rarer than great acting. Let us therefore be grateful that Mr. Harwood, who was himself once in Wolfit's company, has done such a good and sensitive job on an actor whose legendary egoism and megalomania obscured for many playgoers the true value of his art. . . .

He was born, somewhat humbly in Nottinghamshire, after his time; and though the early part of Mr. Harwood's story is not any more engaging than the early parts of most biographies it illuminates occasionally the man to come, as in the account of Wolfit's schoolboy tendency to display exaggerated signs of exhaustion after sprinting 220 yards. (p. 73)

Wolfit's style and crusading spirit—the belief in the value of classic drama, the need to take it to all and sundry—marked him off as an outsider. . . . His failure to fit at the Old Vic must have surprised nobody, though his power there as an actor was plain.

To that power—especially the Wolfit voice, whose range was constantly surprising—Mr. Harwood pays full tribute. The *Lear* and the *Tamburlaine* are vividly recalled. So is the sheer amount of acting then required of a young player to win his spurs. (pp. 73-4)

We shall not look upon [Wolfit's] like again—though I could wish to look on better editing, fewer repetitions and more accurate spelling . . . than this generally very careful and perceptive study of the last great actor-manager offers.

And if that sounds solemn, let me remind the reader of those many green room anecdotes, based on the actor's pomposity, to which Mr. Harwood devotes a late endearing chapter, and the dependence during *Lear* on a supply in the wings of Guinness and grapes. (p. 74)

Eric Shorter, "Great and Unfashionable," in Drama, No. 103, Winter, 1971, pp. 73-4.

LEONARD BUCKLEY

Is the lady a dipsomaniac? Is she just eccentric? Or is she a tramp? Our curiosity is gripped at once [in *The Guests*] as she lurches carefully from her bedroom, stops to consider what is missing in her appearance and then goes back to put on her skirt.

But whatever the explanation is of her oddness she is clearly about to give a dinner party. There are spurts of annoyance and satisfaction as one light in the dining room will not come on but another does. She lays out the name-cards round the table. She pats her hair. She dithers as a waiting hostess will. Then she opens the door to her first guests and in a moment she has plunged into those overbright exchanges that make up a social occasion. You cannot, of course, help noticing that the exchanges are all one-sided. She is making up the guests as well. . . .

As an exercise in loneliness all this would have been poignant enough. But gradually we perceived something else beyond. Like their presence at the dinner table the people themselves

were imaginary. There had never been a family or a husband. "I did not know I had a sister until I met Peter", the lady confided. But Peter, like the sister, was make-believe.

In short Mr Harwood had given us a slice of life in which there were several layers of reality to be peeled. [*The Guests*] was impressively done.

Leonard Buckley, in a review of "The Guests," in The Times, London, December 11, 1972, p. 6.

PETER PRINCE

Ronald Harwood is a South African and his new novel [*Articles of Faith*] is concerned with the tragic clash of races in his homeland. I almost wrote 'inevitably concerned' for it's difficult to imagine any serious South African author who wouldn't feel moved to comment in more or less depth on his country's racial tragedy. There is a danger here, however, as in any literary tradition—the *québécois* writers of French Canada offer another example—where authors feel duty-bound to reflect their society's overwhelming interest in a particular political or cultural concern. Conscious that he is in the service of crucially significant ideals, it's only too easy for a writer to slacken in his attention to such mundane matters as strong and individual characterisation, intelligent plotting, credible dialogue, and all the other nuts and bolts that help distinguish a novel from a political polemic.

Happily, *Articles of Faith* almost never drifts into that trap. I did say 'almost never': there are times in this epic novel, which traces the dismal history of Southern Africa over the past 180 years, when Mr Harwood's characters tend to settle a bit into cardboard representatives of the various ethnic groups who have ruled or pillaged or perished in that sad land. There is the boorish Dutchman, the ineffectual Englishman, the liberal Jewish lawyer, dense black masses of superstitious 'Kaffirs': altogether looking just a suspicion like yet another appearance by the grand old troupers of South Africa's long-running horror show. But against this, time and again the book snaps into life through Mr Harwood's shrewd and inventive perceptions, so that a broadly familiar historical tale becomes fresh and almost surprising in his hands.

Peter Prince, "Out of Afrika," in New Statesman, Vol. 86, No. 2226, November 16, 1973, p. 744.*

RONALD BLYTHE

[Ronald Harwood] sprawls, but it is an ever-inquisitive, restless and striking motivation which forces [*Articles of Faith*] into its heroic size and shape. No lag, nothing redundant. Its indictment is that Cape colonists have for generations, furtively, mixed their blood with that of the Xhosa and Khoikhoi nations, on a scale which makes the current miscegenation laws a humbug. . . .

Harwood displays a society lacerated by sexual guilt. His account of the reduction of the Xhosa and Khoikhoi, dubbed respectively Kaffir and Hottentot by the crude Dutch, is dramatic and deeply moving. The conflict in the book is created by the use of faith as vision ar.d love versus the use of faith as political expediency. The size of the problem is measured against the size of the land. A curious and unforgettable moral and physical panorama is unrolled. *Articles of Faith,* a splendid novel, is a tragedy about recalcitrant statements concerning God.

Ronald Blythe, "Spellbound," in The Listener, *Vol. 91, No. 2337, January 10, 1974, p. 56.**

TERRANCE EDWARDS

From 1794 right down to 1972 ["**Articles of Faith**"] sweeps across the South African scene, distilling something of its history, much of its prejudices and fears—and perhaps a few of its hopes.

It is through the lives of successive generations of the white family Henning that this anguished nation's growth is traced. . . .

Always the family is in trouble. And nearly always the thread of trouble, of tragedy, stems from the propensity of the family's male members to miscegenate with slaves, servants and acquaintances of the colored races.

The house of Henning, it is clear, will continue on its course and to continue to come to grief. For "Henning" read "South Africa."

From one point of view, "**Articles of Faith,**" with its broad scope, intricate plot, and sometimes sensitive style, gives many useful insights into South Africa's malaise.

However, I found myself more than a little irked by its affectedness and more than a little saddened that another South African writer—obviously endowed in this case with great talent—had been diverted into merciless exploitation of the race theme.

In a word, Mr. Harwood gets in the way of the story. In places he unabashedly writes what amounts to political diatribe, and the book's purpose and structure is marred by inaccuracies seemingly included for shock and propaganda value. . . . [One] is left with unhappy conclusions about Mr. Harwood's intentions.

In the end, the novelist's celebration of his moral superiority mars his examination of South Africa's great and painful racial complexity.

Terrance Edwards, in a review of "Articles of Faith," in The Christian Science Monitor, *May 29, 1974, p. F5.*

MYRNA BLUMBERG

Ronald Harwood is a bold writer with an inquisitive conscience. In his new novel, *César and Augusta,* he explores a struggle that many people have ridiculed: goodness attempting to accomodate eroticism honourably. He has also chosen to reinterpret two complex musicians who had the highest aspirations, who were adored, revered, neglected, laughed at in France, taken up in Britain as the precursors of modern music, then often set aside again with exasperation and evasion. His hero César Franck, it has been said, made even Liszt blush.

Mr Harwood relives a few years in Franck's life with great imaginative sympathy. His writing is outstandingly readable and intelligent, and he is unusually open on human catalysts in life and art and how it sometimes takes two or more people to make one functioning artist.

In 1875, when the novel begins, he has become professor of organ at the Conservatoire where he is never entirely accepted, and the happy chief organist at the church of Sainte-Clothilde where he is obsessively teased and beguiled by the beautiful, partly-Irish singer, Augusta Holmes. . . .

In the novel he abandons Augusta as if she were a disused tuning fork but his longing for domestic tranquility and to meet the scruples of his faith should not be underestimated. He does also suffer recurringly from an inability to trust his feelings to others. There are biographical papers on him that are not available to the public and Mr Harwood's intuitive appreciation of him is remarkable. . . .

Unlike Ronald Harwood's *Articles of Faith,* which is set in South Africa and whose power is in its breadth of perceptions, *César and Augusta* has little of the political and social belligerence in Paris after the Franco-Prussian war: a fine artistic decision as Franck removed himself from any extremes of action. The nine stories in *One. Interior. Day.* make more use of Mr Harwood's sense of hilarity but also follow one man's resolve to be faithful to talent and ethical relationships. . . .

Edward and his generous wife are in most of the stories and Edward's self-honesty is impressive as he develops from a theatre-loving boy in Cape Town to a writer dashing around England, Italy, Los Angeles. Ronald Harwood's refreshing contribution to humorous writing on the pagan film world is his thoughtful composure, his justice to non-materialism.

Myrna Blumberg, in a review of "César and Augusta" and "One. Interior. Day.," in The Times, *London, April 6, 1976, p. 19.*

THE TIMES, LONDON

The Genoa Ferry is devious and exotic. It is a stylish, beautifully written and often very exciting story, set (presumably) in Gadaffi's Libya. Martin Fisher is summoned to North Africa, supposedly by his sinister, domineering brother, and finds himself lost in a labyrinth of sexual and political intrigue; his own bewilderment may well be shared by the reader. With its atmosphere of menacing, death-haunted carnival, *The Genoa Ferry* kept reminding me of the film *Black Orpheus:* I enjoyed it enormously, but I would be hard pushed to say exactly what it is all about.

A review of "The Genoa Ferry," in The Times, *London, October 21, 1976, p. 17.**

DAVID MAYER

That [*The Ordeal of Gilbert Pinfold*] ultimately fails as a play is in no way a fault of any performance nor of . . . [the] direction. Nor can all the blame be laid at the door of Ronald Harwood who adapted Waugh's penultimate novel, though Harwood is open to criticism both in the manner of his adapting and for failing to recognise the sharply confining limitations of his source. Waugh himself is the culprit, both as a novelist and a scenarist, for although he had lost none of his adeptness as a prose stylist and story-teller, Waugh as usual projected himself in lightly disguised form to the centre of his novel. . . . But unlike his previous novels, where the Waugh personae are a part of a variegated bustle, Waugh as Pinfold is solitary star, almost the sole performer. . . . The 'real' characters of *Pinfold* are as shadowy and intangible as the hallucinations that visit Waugh's stand-in. Translated to the stage and given voice and body, they remain indefinite and, worse, uninteresting. Pinfold alone feeds our astonishment, and that in steadily diminishing quantities.

Harwood labours with the text to mixed effect. In some instances, the author's third-person voice has been translated into the first-person but without a corresponding change from narrative to dramatic action. And there are more troubling distortions: an episode devised by Waugh to show Pinfold as a species of tatty staked bear failing to fight off a snapping mongrel pack of interviewers from the BBC Radio is reversed into a triumph, a truculent Nabokovian don making mincemeat of his interrogators. On the few occasions that Harwood trusts his own powers as a dramatist and turns a mere suggestion into a scene, as he does when Pinfold arrogantly boasts of his political connections to his fellow diners, Pinfold's self-destructive urges and the forces behind his irrational fears are agonisingly visible. Harwood solves the problems of giving credibility to ethereal voices and creating characters whose identities slip back and forth between the worlds of substance and fantasy, but the author has not made these interesting, at least not for very long.

> *David Mayer, in a review of "The Ordeal of Gilbert Pinfold," in* Plays and Players, *Vol. 2, No. 25, November, 1977, p. 25.*

NEWGATE CALLENDAR

["**The Genoa Ferry**"] falls into no easy category. It is part murder mystery, in which a man tries to ascertain the facts about the death of his stepbrother. It is part travelogue, in which the smells and rottenness of a North African city are vividly described. It is partly a novel of ideas, with much attention paid to a grubby set of characters and their motivations. The ending is sheer Grand Guignol. And the whole book is full of alienation symbols. Whether or not Harwood was inspired by some of the North African stories of Paul Bowles, "**The Genoa Ferry**" is an unusually gripping piece of writing that can rank with the Bowles books. (p. 36)

> *Newgate Callendar, in a review of "The Genoa Ferry," in* The New York Times Book Review, *November 20, 1977, p. 36.*

NIGEL WILLIAMS

In Ronald Harwood's new novel, *César and Augusta,* it is gentleness that proves a strength. The book is set in the France of the 1870s, and concerns César Franck's sudden, late flowering as a composer. Alone with a shrewish wife . . . , Franck seems the archetypal teacher until a passionate young woman called Augusta Holmes cons her way into his composition class, posing as a man. Harwood charts the relationship between the dry, nervous old man, and his tempestuous, awkward pupil in a well-structured narrative, and shows how the girl inspired Franck to compose the first of his major works, the Piano Quintet. . . .

The book is never less than readable and often something more. Franck, with his hatred of Wagner ('a touch of German sausage in the chords') and his suppressed sexuality, is a living and attractive central character, not a dummy in historical costume, and Mr Harwood writes well about the experience of listening to music.

It is his obsession with and concern for art that informs the same author's volume of short stories, published in tandem with this novel. *One. Interior. Day.* deals with the art of the writer adrift in the world of the movies. All the stories are recounted by Edward Lands, a stiff-upper-lip Britisher with high standards and a happy marriage. There could have been an interesting tension between Lands and the Nathanael-West-style weirdos he encounters, but, as in *César and Augusta,* the characters are fighting their stereotypes, and less successfully than in the novel.

> *Nigel Williams, "Dreeing the Weirdos," in* The Listener, *Vol. 99, No. 2553, March 30, 1978, p. 419.**

ROSALIND WADE

It was a bold and imaginative decision on the part of Ronald Harwood's publishers to issue simultaneously two such widely different examples of his work as *César and Augusta* and *One. Interior. Day.* (p. 45)

One of the main points of interest about *One. Interior. Day.* is that the two books could be so different. No matter how closely an author may identify with historical characters, the fact that he is interpreting rather than creating obliges him to be reticent to some extent about his own reactions and experiences. In these nine stories about the film industry, Ronald Harwood is even more involved than is customary, for the outline of life as lived by the chief character, Edward Lands, is charted by the well known landmarks of Ronald Harwood's own professional career.

This does not inhibit progress as severely as might have been anticipated. The strange no-man's land between reportage and creativity produces a curiously tantalising world of semi-make believe. One longs to know more about Edward and his wife in their day-to-day routine at home; why they remain such easy prey to the dupes and charlatans and what is going to become of them in the end. The lightish humour and gentle etching in of character might well have been undertaken merely in order to prove the author's versatility. Certainly, they are a startling contrast to the savage emotions which tear César and Augusta apart. (pp. 45-6)

> *Rosalind Wade, in a review of "César and Augusta," in* Contemporary Review, *Vol. 233, No. 1350, July, 1978, pp. 45-6.*

DAVID MAYER

What mars . . . Ronald Harwood's *A Family* is its tired structure and laboured profundities couched in the sort of dialogue where each time a character says anything at all, It Means Something Significant. The structure of *A Family* is cast from the late 19th-century mould, wrought by Ibsen and his contemporaries and seized by such 20th-century authors as O'Neill and Miller, where the arms of the past reach in to snatch at the present, a stalled Newtonian machine years later kicked suddenly into life so that every past action is reciprocated by its long-delayed reaction.

And as the play's main spring is a war-time memory, repressed and unacknowledged for 33 years, of a father's . . . heroic and disastrously misguided attempt to rescue his son from wartime Italy, where the son . . . , even then a lad big enough to know his own mind, had, on fleeing a German POW camp, joined a partisan guerrilla band and fallen deeply in love with a local girl. The ensuing complications, enforced liberation and the girl's suicide, all awkwardly recalled in lumpish flashbacks, may be physical, but the reactions are deeply psychological. . . . Happiness, suggests Harwood, is a resolved Oedipal conflict, and gives us . . . [the father] as a crusty and meddlesome Laius with a deaf-aid and parachutist's kit, eventually struck down by his son, not at a Delphic crossroad, but in the claustrophobic bosom of a Jewish family knit together by skeins of fear, hatred and recrimination. In *A Family* all is revealed, all is explained. The machine never falters. (pp. 29-30)

David Mayer, in a review of "A Family," in Plays and Players, *Vol. 25, No. 10, July, 1978, pp. 29-30.*

ANTHONY CURTIS

Mr. Harwood is a serious writer with a number of novels to his credit and a biography of Donald Wolfit, . . . but he is also a writer who has made a good living out of films and television and has learnt how to discipline himself to the requirements of those media. *A Family* seems to have been written by two Mr. Harwoods in a not altogether harmonious collaboration. Harwood I, the serious artist, is fascinated as many British playwrights have been before him, by the love-hatred which a closely-knit family group inspires in its members. He has something to say about what happens when someone in his generation, and someone in his children's generation, tries to break away from the crippling embrace of the family to live their lives as private individuals in complete autonomy. He sits down and works out a draft of the idea which he then shows to Harwood II, the film and TV writer. (p. 49)

As with all collaborations the final result is a compromise not wholly pleasing to either party but efficient enough to hold an audience for an evening in which curiosity and admiration alternate with embarrassment and puzzlement. Harwood I's original idea—a rather moving and frightening idea—that in the end we love the tyranny of the family more than we love our freedom, is overlaid by a lot of cheap comedy and melodrama, pencilled in at the behest of Harwood II, and the whole thing is riddled with contradictions at both the realistic and the psychological levels that come perilously close to robbing the play of its seriousness. (p. 50)

Anthony Curtis, in a review of "A Family," in Drama, *No. 130, Autumn, 1978, pp. 49-50.*

FRANK RICH

The dark and jagged set of Ronald Harwood's play **"The Dresser"** is the ratty backstage area—moldy dressing rooms, cramped corridors and wings—of a crumbling theater somewhere in the British provinces. The time is 1942, and the stink of death is in the air. Outside, there are howling sirens, signaling another Luftwaffe bombing raid. Inside, skulking about the gloom, are Mr. Harwood's central characters—two men who seem to have scant reason to live.

Sir . . . is an aged Shakespearean actor-manager, now reduced to touring third-rate towns with a war-depleted troupe of "old men, cripples and nancy-boys." His mind and body are failing fast, yet tonight he is to give his 427th performance as King Lear. Norman . . . , his dresser, is supposed to ready Sir for the show, yet he's scarcely better off. A sepulchral, middle-aged homosexual who's spent 16 years in near-feudal servitude to his master, he seems to gain his sole spiritual nourishment from the pint bottle he keeps in his back pocket. Whatever friends he has are long gone, ghosts left behind at other lonely theaters along the road.

But while Sir and Norman are pathetic, they're bound together by a common cause: an audience is in the house, and the show must go on. **"The Dresser"** . . . is about how Sir, Norman and the rest of their fleabag company somehow rise above air raids and personal calamities to perform their "Lear." If it's a stirring evening—and it most abundantly is—it's not because Mr. Harwood has written a flawless play, or one that runs particularly deep. It's because this writer and his two glorious stars burn with a love of the theater that conquers all.

Why do Sir and Norman go on with the show? Because, for them, the stage really is the one safe haven where even the dreariest realities of life can always be escaped. As we watch these theater people practice their total childlike faith in the transcendent powers of make-believe, we rediscover that feeling in ourselves. The primal impulse that makes Sir and Norman go on is the same one that first sent us to the theater as an audience.

Mr. Harwood does more, too. A one-time dresser to the late actor-manager Donald Wolfit, the playwright has crammed **"The Dresser"** with perfectly observed, devilishly entertaining backstage lore. Sir's hammy provincial troupe is the final, seedy inheritor of the 19th-century theatrical tradition epitomized by Vincent Crummles's roving company in "Nicholas Nickleby"—and it's just as hilarious in its noble yet chaotic pursuit of the Bard. Most important, Mr. Harwood has written a moving, platonic love story for Sir and Norman—two irascible men who can't live without each other any better than they can live without the theater.

It is the author's conceit—sometimes too explicitly stated—that Sir and Norman's private backstage drama parallels the onstage one between Lear and his fool. The crotchety old star sees himself as royalty—even if, to his eternal displeasure, he has yet to be knighted—and he regards Norman as a peon who exists only to do his every bidding. But now that Sir is in decline, he needs the dresser as a nursemaid and confessor—a role the younger man plays very well, even as he bridles at his boss's parsimony and abuse. Yet Norman needs Sir, too: when the old actor takes to the stage, the dresser basks in his performance as if it were his own. Once their theatrical tradition—and wartorn England itself—fall into ruin, it's only a matter of time before the men come together in madness and affection. (p. 128)

[The] frailties of the play are . . . visible. Mr. Harwood tends to explain his jokes and, especially in an Act II confrontation between Sir and his long-suffering actress wife . . . , to announce his emotional points. His ending . . . is sentimental melodrama, not tragedy. Luckily, these real weaknesses are usually counterbalanced by the author's wit and high-charged theatricality. (pp. 128-29)

Frank Rich, "'Dresser,' a Monarch and His Loyal Vassal: The Show Must Go On," in The New York Times, *November 10, 1981, p. C7.*

ROBERT BRUSTEIN

Ronald Harwood, who once looked after Donald Wolfit's doublet and hose, has fashioned a theatrical patchwork about this legendary British actor-manager and his times. It is called *The Dresser* . . . and, as a work of drama, it is agreeable, contrived, predictable, and sentimental, which is to say, much like those rickety vehicles (*The Bells, The Count of Monte Cristo*) such vagrant actors used to chauffeur when they didn't have Shakespeare sitting in the garage. The most amiable thing about *The Dresser* is its affection for the seedy backstage mores of circuiting rep companies, expressed in an alternately fustian and bitchy style. I can see the play being performed annually at the Garrick Club in London or the Player's in New York, for it is soaked in the same kind of boozy anecdotes that retired actors like to pour out while waving shotglasses of Old Grand Dad over their soiled cravats and egg-spattered velvet smoking jackets.

Set in 1942 during the Blitz, *The Dresser* is nostalgic for a period when the show went on despite the fatal illness of the principal performer, the loss to National Service of the younger male company members, or the bombs being dropped on stage by what the Wolfit figure irately calls "squadrons of Fascist Bolsheviks." As in most nostalgia trips, however, the landscape seems vague, if not somewhat fuzzy—particularly in its image of human relationships. *The Dresser* works best as an isolated character sketch; it needs more tailoring as a play. The exposition is lumpy, the plot stitching is visible, the supporting characters are threadbare. The most potentially interesting dramatic issue—the resentment felt by a self-sacrificing underling toward his self-regarding employer—is raised without being resolved, because Norman, the dresser, is simply not conceived with sufficient depth or truthfulness.

Harwood has a better handle on "Sir"—as his histrionic hero is called, perhaps in ironic recognition that, unlike his real-life model, he will never win a knighthood. Sir is treated as a temperamental, self-dramatizing, plummy old thesp, who seduces his apprentices and manipulates his company and crew. What redeems the old ham is his flamboyant spirit and his love-hate relationship with the stage. (pp. 21, 24)

When Sir expires quietly on his dressing room couch, Norman explodes in rage against "the old sod," but lest this moment of truth betray the obligatory reconciliations, he is also given

the chance to pour out his grief ("You think you loved him? What about me?") before cradling his head under the dead man's arm, and singing "The Wind and the Rain," to a counterpoint of sobs from the audience.

There are hints of Fool-Lear parallels throughout the evening, but one hopes against hope the author will have sense enough not to make them explicit. To suggest a correspondence between the most remorseless tragedy ever written and this treacle-drenched artifact is not just presumptuous, it is a serious tactical error, reminding us how little the author has invented apart from backstage color. *The Dresser* is a drama of failed opportunities, not least of them Mr. Harwood's, who had the knowledge and the experience to tell a true story of the stage, but didn't have the courage. One has only to remember the rages of the actor-hero in the Osborne-Creighton *Epitaph for George Dillon* . . . to see how this play invokes a condition without ever really investigating it. For all the theatrical chat and internecine rivalries in *The Dresser,* we never discover (as we do so poignantly in O'Neill's *Long Day's Journey*) the true qualities of a "third-rate actor-manager on a tour of the provinces," aside from his rodomontade and self-pity. We don't even learn how a routine actor like Wolfit could sometimes rise to be a great one. . . .

In our culture, the actor's life is indeed tragic (so is the dresser's). Here it is merely an occasion for green-room jokes and bathetic scenes. (p. 24)

Robert Brustein, "The Naked and the Dressed," in The New Republic, *Vol. 185, No. 23, December 9, 1981, pp. 21, 24-5.**

Mark Helprin

1947-

American novelist and short story writer.

Helprin blends elements of fantasy with realistic social settings to create imaginative, fable-like works with moral implications. His protagonists typically undertake sundry comic adventures through which they gain a humane perspective of life. With *A Dove of the East* (1975), a collection of his early short stories, Helprin established a reputation for inventing extravagant plots and characters. His first novel, *Refiner's Fire: The Life and Adventures of Marshall Pearl, A Foundling* (1977), relates a young man's escapades around the world through a series of heroic exploits that some critics likened to works of the picaresque-romance tradition.

For many critics, *Ellis Island and Other Stories* (1981) marked Helprin's arrival as an accomplished author. In these stories, Helprin emphasizes common moral concerns more strongly than in his earlier work. His recent best-selling novel, *Winter's Tale* (1983), mixes fable and myth with romance, history, and a network of literary allusions. The story centers on the struggle of a mythologized Manhattan to become free from poverty and crime. Peter Lake, the novel's hero, moves in picaresque fashion from one adventure to another while pursued by evil forces. As in his earlier works, Helprin eschews realism in favor of a fantastic pursuit of his utopian vision.

(See also *CLC*, Vols. 7, 10, 22 and *Contemporary Authors*, Vols. 81-84.)

ROBERT TOWERS

One can understand the impatience of writers with the demands and constrictions of realistic fiction. Many of them perceive it as an exhausted mode, though realism (like a sick king who has had to surrender whole provinces) still holds a position of shaky dominance. . . . Is the situation ripe for a romantic revival such as seems to be occurring in music and painting? Instead of attempting painstakingly to create an acceptable simulacrum of the world as we (at least some of us) experience it, or to forge verbal artifacts that are sufficient unto themselves, wouldn't it be more exhilarating to restore our atrophied sense of wonder, to write about a magnificent white horse that can soar like Pegasus, to conjure up a band of troll-like criminals in perpetual pursuit of a saintly orphan who is both a burglar and a master mechanic, to describe a fantasized New York City with all the resources of an unashamedly poetic prose?

Mark Helprin obviously thinks so. He has made romantic forays before, in several pieces from *Ellis Island and Other Stories* (a collection much admired by a number of reviewers and prize-givers) and in his first novel, *Refiner's Fire,* in which the narrator's adventures seem as whimsically arbitrary as those of any knight-errant. Now, astride a huge, fire-breathing dragon of a novel, Helprin has mounted an all-out assault on the ramparts of realism, brandishing the sword of fantasy and shouting his battle cries: ''Vision! Apocalypse! Ecstasy!'' The boldness, not to say chutzpah, of *Winter's Tale* may well leave the reader stunned. . . .

© Thomas Victor 1984

Escaping from his master's stable in Brooklyn, the stallion [Athansor] crosses the Williamsburg Bridge and makes his way to the Battery, at which point the imagery becomes positively incandescent. . . . At the Battery, the horse rescues a man fleeing from a sinister gang dressed in bowler hats and heavy coats—and so we are launched on a phantasmagoric flight. . . . (p. 122)

The fleeing man is Peter Lake, the burglar-mechanic ''hero'' of the novel, a man who appears, disappears (presumably dead), and many decades later reappears (transformed) in the course of a time scheme that extends from the early years of this century to the advent—at once catastrophic and life-renewing—of the third millennium. His pursuers are the Short Tails—men ''with strange bent faces, clifflike brows, tiny chins, noses and ears that looked sewn-back-on, and hairlines that descended preposterously far''—and their cruel leader, Pearly Soames. The horse, Athansor, has a habit of appearing at crucial moments to aid the forces of Good in their struggle with the persistent forces of Evil, represented by the marauding Short Tails. This dynamic interplay of forces—call them Eros and Thanatos, if you like—is embodied in scores of characters (emblematic figures, really, for Helprin has no interest in psychological realism) and myriad episodes and images; it supplies whatever narrative energy the book possesses.

Confronted by superabundance, I will mention only a few of the figures and elements that are woven into the fabric of

Winter's Tale. There is Beverly Penn, the beautiful, elusive, and ailing daughter of a newspaper publisher; for a short time before she dies, she is married to Peter Lake, who is forever afterward haunted by her image. Hardesty Marratta is a stalwart young man who spurns his father's millions, retaining only a golden salver on which is inscribed an Italian motto celebrating the perfectly just city—one of the themes that runs throughout the novel.... Then, there is Praeger de Pinto, who is also inspired by the ideal of the just city, and becomes mayor of New York at the city's moment of apocalypse. And finally, representing man's unremitting drive toward transcendence, there is Jackson Mead, the eternal builder of bridges, who, as the millennium approaches, arrives in New York harbor in a towering ship, determined to erect the greatest bridge of all— one that will extend from the city into the empyrean.

Helprin's fantasy-spinning apparatus works prodigiously. He invents not only a fabulous New York City—a towering, tunneling metropolis raised upon contrasts and oppositions—but also the Bayonne Marshes, a region inhabited by a primitive and unkempt tribe of Baymen, and the Lake of the Coheeries, "so far upstate that no one could find it," where in winter the village is covered by thirty feet of snow. He invents a special weather for New York, including a great white cloud mass that surrounds the city, cutting it off from the hinterlands, and a series of arctically severe winters during which the Hudson River is frozen its entire length and travel is possible only by skates, sleigh, or ice boat. There must be at least twenty descriptions of winter—lyrical or grotesque set-pieces, in one instance involving complex snow palaces, whose rooms serve "as impromptu restaurants, hotels, shops, and inns," and thousands of tents pitched on the ice.

Not only settings but countless episodes display the fecundity of Helprin's imagination. (pp. 122-23)

Furthermore, nearly every image, every incident, seems to cry out for thematic interpretation.... A large body of literature and folklore seems to underlie the imagery of the novel. In the evocations of the variety, squalor, and sublimity of New York, Walt Whitman's "Crossing Brooklyn Ferry" and Hart Crane's "The Bridge" will spring to the reader's mind. The noble horse Athansor will remind some of the noble lion Aslan in C. S. Lewis's Narnia series: the Bayman called Abysmillard ("Sores marched around his body and were visible through all his matted and well-manured hair—as were the occasional living things that sometimes poked from within") will remind others of some creature in the Tolkien sagas. *Winter's Tale* is exceedingly bookish in its inspiration.

Does it succeed as a novel? My answer must be a slightly qualified negative. A number of Helprin's inventions are spectacular, and some of his effects are richly suggestive. But frequently they seem more willed than inspired. Again and again, I had the sense that my responses were being coerced, that the author was trying to batter me into an acceptance of the book's visionary and poetic powers.... Too often one is made conscious of the effort to whip the language into flame. Occasionally the results verge on the ludicrous, and the novel sinks under the weight of excessive purple and gold.

It is, of course, possible that *Winter's Tale* will become a cult object, embraced by those adolescents of all ages who are especially prone to magical thinking and to a craving for instant transfiguration. But I doubt it, for the novel contains a more serious weakness than any hitherto mentioned. For all his inventiveness, Helprin has failed to provide his fabulous material

with a proper fable—the compelling story that is essential to romantic fiction, whether it be an epic by Tolkien or a subliterary effusion by Barbara Cartland or by one of the purveyors of shopping-mall gothic. In the absence of a sustaining narrative interest, I regularly felt myself succumbing to the tedium of yet another set-piece, dazzling or otherwise. (p. 123)

Robert Towers, "Assaulting Realism," in The Atlantic Monthly, *Vol. 252, No. 3, September, 1983, pp. 122-23.*

ANATOLE BROYARD

I know a divorced father with literary aspirations who makes up interminable bedtime stories for his 7-year-old son on the one night a week the boy sleeps at his place. The stories are picaresque, filled with adventure, magic, love and violence. They also contain surprisingly beautiful digressions, in which the father seems to be confiding his undisguised hopes and fears to his son. The boy is restless listening to these stories, but he realizes that his father needs to tell them.

I'm reminded of this man by Mark Helprin's new novel, "**Winter's Tale**," in which he appears to be divorced from himself. Abandoning the delicacy, precision and economy of his last book, "**Ellis Island**," he seems to be telling us all an interminable bedtime story in this garrulous new work. Perhaps he was aiming for the picaresque, but it seems to me that we are past the time for the picaresque. It requires a structured society to which a charming rogue can oppose himself, but in a world like ours, which is itself picaresque, there is no opposition, no tension.

"**Winter's Tale**" seems to be an extension of the weakest story in "**Ellis Island**," the title piece, which is a surrealist fantasy full of the kind of fictional leaps and bounds that are commonly taken for spontaneity or inspiration. An author kicking up his heels seems to gladden readers' hearts, as if they felt more comfortable with him when he is less scrupulous about art.

"**Winter's Tale**" is about "the millennium"—isn't all serious fiction about millenniums?—and once again the reader is menaced with the spectacle of general deterioration. The book, all 673 pages of it, is like the morning-after debris left by a wild and expensive party....

"**Winter's Tale**" attempts a grand design, and when grand designs don't work, they become grand confusions or pandemoniums. Almost every good writer has unpublished pages, reams of them, that he had to write and then reject in order to clarify or purify himself. Some writers choose to publish them, and who is to say no if the machinery is there? I hope that Mr. Helprin feels better for it and that in his next book, he will again be as good as he was in "**Ellis Island**."

Anatole Broyard, in a review of "Winter's Tale," in The New York Times, *September 2, 1983, p. C20.*

BENJAMIN De MOTT

Arriving late at an elegant London dinner party, the narrator of "**Tamar**," a short story in Mark Helprin's "**Ellis Island, and Other Stories**," is seated at the "children's table," as a kind of genteel punishment. (The time is close to the start of World War II; the narrator is in London on a mission that fails—raising escape funds for European Jewry.) The teenagers in attendance are new to him and charming—lively, intelligent, dream-ridden. Amused by their chatter, the narrator finds himself under compulsion to entertain. He launches a ''long story about Palestine,'' then races on—his imagination freed—''because they were children, more or less''—to wilder stuff. ''I spoke of impossible battles . . . of feats of endurance which made me reel merely in imagining them, of horses that flew, and golden shafts of light, pillars of fire, miracles here and there . . . anything which seemed as if it might be believed.'' (p. 1)

I connect **''Tamar''** with **''Winter's Tale,''** Mr. Helprin's utterly extraordinary new book (his second novel and fourth work of fiction) for two reasons. The first involves simple literary sleuthing: The substance of the story-hour performance described in a few paragraphs in the tale is extremely close to the substance of the nearly 700 pages of **''Winter's Tale.''** Pillars of fire, impossible battles and feats of endurance abound in the book. A flying horse is a central character, and, like the man in the story, the novelist whips about gleefully among a dozen modes of the fabulous—tall tales, fairy tales, sci-fi, animated cartoons, what you will.

The other reason for connecting **''Tamar''** with **''Winter's Tale''** concerns the book's potential uses. A piercing sense of the beautiful arising from narrative and emotional fantasy is everywhere alive in the novel. And because the novelist commits himself throughout to the pursuit of nourishing truths—truths of justice, hope and cheer remote from the more fashionable truths of alienation and despair—**''Winter's Tale''** stands forth in its own right as restorer and comforter. The witty responsiveness necessary to a full experience of the book is doubtless more likely to turn up in urban readers than elsewhere; a primary ambition of the work seems to be, in fact, to teach its audience how to understand—i.e., how to inhabit to some purpose and with some joy—a great city. But in the end, the wisdom in these pages is in no respect whatever parochial. The affirming voices that one is reminded of are those of Blake and Whitman. (pp. 1, 21)

It's not through any of [the] unique natures, though, or through an account of the touching, hilarious, strikingly variegated personages of the book that one best approaches the golden core of **''Winter's Tale.''** Nor can one possess the work merely by studying the touchstone passages in which description and narrative soar highest. . . . (p. 21)

No, the heart of this book resides unquestionably in its moral energy, in the thousand original gestures, ruminations, Woola Woola writing feats that summon its audience beyond the narrow limits of conventional vision, commanding us to see our time and place afresh. Is it not astonishing that a work so rooted in fantasy, filled with narrative high jinks and comic flights, stands forth centrally as a moral discourse? It is indeed. And although I would insist that it's the vividness of the ideal in this book that's the source of its moral weight, and although it's clearly the fantasies that carry the ideal, I do not pretend to know why or how the marvelous concord of discords in Mr. Helprin's **''Winter's Tale''** is achieved. I can testify only to the force of the book's summons to wider vision, to the strength of its command to see anew and to the pivotal significance of the author's reflections on the city itself in driving us toward awareness of his fundamental seriousness.

Heeding his summons, obeying his command, means sustaining steady alertness to the ranges of contradiction that must be embodied in any human being laying claim to a vital life in a metropolis. The obligation, as spelled out in **''Winter's Tale,''** is to shed indifference and apathy, to realize the suffering

through which one walks—the suffering of small children living and dying like beasts, against which Peter Lake cries out to a self-made publisher, Isaac Penn. But the obligation of equal urgency is to feel at every moment, without complacency or stoniness, the icy sliver of truth in Penn's answer: ''Who said that justice is what you imagine? Can you be sure that you know it when you see it, that you will live long enough to recognize the decisive thunder of its occurrence, that it can be manifest within a generation, within ten generations, within the entire span of human existence?''

''Winter's Tale'' tolerates no beamishness, will not let its readers simplify their being. It insists that its audience live along the nerves of Hardesty Marratta's repugnance at Manhattan—''the entire population . . . rushed about here and there, venting their passions—struggling, kicking, and shuddering like marionettes.'' But the book insists equally that its audience live into the moment when ''the wind changed, the light came out, and (Hardesty) was caught up in some sort of magic. For no apparent reason he suddenly became king of the world. . . . The city seemed to have no middle ground.''

And, above all, it requires that we think our way toward the ideal city, toward a sense of what such a place could and should mean, toward a conception of how the inhabitants might become worthy of such space: ''To enter a city intact it is necessary to pass through . . . gates far more difficult to find than gates of stone, for they are test mechanisms, devices, and implementations of justice.'' One gate is that of ''acceptance of responsibility,'' another is that of ''the desire to explore,'' still another that of ''devotion to beauty,'' and the last is the gate of ''selfless love.'' It's in the development of this theme that **''Winter's Tale''** rises to the level of significant affirmation.

I understand that praising an author nowadays as an affirmer can harm him; books that discover justice in the world are exposed to the same suspicion stirred by positive-outlook scams such as television's ''good news break.'' And Mr. Helprin has a record. Gifted as a wish fulfiller, as in numberless other ways, he's created, in his earlier work, a large gallery of admirably indomitable, entirely improbable winners. And the population of his winners' gallery is considerably expanded by **''Winter's Tale.''** Good and evil lock horns time and again in this work, and evil does not prevail. Men and women of virtue and intellect are regularly awarded honors. Children who die untimely deaths are miraculously raised from the grave. Smoke-cloud disasters such as the burning of Manhattan at the time of the millennium are themselves found not lacking in silver linings.

But disasters without immediately visible silver linings occur in **''Winter's Tale''** and, to repeat, there is no whitewashing of Metropolis. If the author's theory of justice requires us to think in broader time frames than the ordinary professional historian or Marxist theorist is accustomed to imagine, and if his reasoning slides off occasionally toward incoherence, the grand argument of his work—its general impression of life, its challenge to the suffocating dogma that good hope in a writer inevitably signifies obliviousness—remains indismissible.

There's far more that I would wish to say about the book—so much more that I find myself nervous, to a degree I don't recall in my past as a reviewer, about failing the work, inadequately displaying its brilliance. The canniness of the balancing of fantasy and realism, the capacity of these Dickensian presences to bring to mind, subtly, contemporaries and near-contemporaries from Rupert Murdoch to Howard Hughes to Thomas Pynchon, the excitement scholars will find in interpreting Mr. Helprin's extension of the line of American imaginers who have grappled for longer than a century with the meanings of technology. . . . Not for some time have I read a work as funny, thoughtful, passionate or large-souled. Rightly used, it could inspire as well as comfort us. **"Winter's Tale"** is a great gift at an hour of great need. (pp. 21-2)

> Benjamin De Mott, *"A Vision of the Just City," in* The New York Times Book Review, *September 4, 1983, pp. 1, 21-2.*

PETER S. PRESCOTT

Here's a great, glossy pudding of a novel by an author I'd praised earlier for his vigor, imagination and economy. Kind-hearted critics call disasters of this magnitude "ambitious," but the problem with **"Winter's Tale"** is that it's not ambitious enough. Mark Helprin seems determined to get through his nearly 700 pages on charm and a fuzzy vision of the millennium alone. This means his story doesn't have a conventional plot or credible characters. It offers instead a succession of implausible incidents and a crowd of vaguely mythic figures: heroes and lovable ladies, villains and megalomaniac fools, even a wonder horse, doughty in battle and capable of flight.

Most of the action takes place in Manhattan at the beginning and end of this century. With leaden hand, Helprin assures us that the city is the worst of places—violent, corrupt and despairing, and yet dazzling in its potential for spiritual renewal. If you detect in these words a lack of specificity, you're right: though Helprin thwacks at New York throughout his novel, he never gives us a particularly coherent or significant picture of the place. . . . Halfway into his book, Helprin has still avoided a plot, but he's established a theme. Peter Lake has a "strong feeling . . . that every action in the world had eventual consequences and would never be forgotten, as if it were entered in a magnificent ledger of unimaginable complexity." Note the superfluity of adjectives, a sure sign of a writer in distress.

Helprin endlessly repeats Peter Lake's strong feeling: "Nothing is random, nor will anything ever be." . . . Helprin's novel fails because it leads its reader through hundreds of pages of tired and imprecise language toward an apocalyptic vision that he won't, in the end, define. What are we to make of our hero's lover when we're told that "Her motions flowed in a hundred thousand pictures, each of searing beauty, each on its way through the black cold of archless accommodating space"? Or of a woman who, "traveling through the city for an hour . . . had seen enough to write a thousand encyclopedias of deep praise"? In writing his fantasy, Helprin fell into the fundamental error of assuming that fantasy can be vaguer than realistic fiction. On the contrary: fantasy must be more precise. (pp. 78, 81)

> Peter S. Prescott, *"The Worst of Times," in* News-week, *Vol. CII, No. 12, September 19, 1983, pp. 78, 81.*

SEYMOUR KRIM

Every grateful reader who was exposed to Mark Helprin's recent collection, **Ellis Island and Other Stories,** knew that a fresh voice and vision was on the march. Although the author had brought out two previous books that signaled the gathering of forces of a major talent, it was **Ellis Island** that brought him

to the attention of his first real audience. His combination of the realistic and fantastic intertwining of experience, guided by compassion and a prose style as clear and shining as a northern star, gave hope on two levels: it opened up possibilities beyond realism for a transportation of life that could no longer be contained by the literal, and it gave almost therapeutic faith to those disillusioned and wearied by much serious fiction. Helprin was that rare thing, a first-rate technician who was also a sincere standard-bearer for a new dawn in humankind's endless effort to lift itself out of suffering and injustice. (p. 3)

Helprin has now released the most ambitious work he has yet attempted, a huge cyclorama that covers a hundred years in time and at least an equal number of characters. It's theme is no less than the resurrection of New York from a city of the damned to a place of universal justice and hope. One motto that magically appears and reappears several times during the novel sums up the author's intention: "For what can be imagined more beautiful than the sight of a perfectly just city rejoicing alone?" Only Mark Helprin could present his utopian cause with such eloquent directness, and it would be a hard-hearted reviewer who didn't root for him to cleanse our cynicism and prepare for us this brave new world.

Unfortunately, **Winter's Tale** turns out to be a self-willed fairy tale that even on its own terms refuses to convince. The future that the author wants so beautifully to paint is more truly a nostalgic elegy for a late 19th-century city, when innocent young men and girls had their happiest moments ice-skating, eating "roasted oysters," sitting "by the hearth," driving in horse-drawn sleighs and the like. All the complexity of a 20th-century megalopolis is quaintly and sometimes cutely simplified so that Helprin can mythologize the simple virtues of our ancestors and make them goals of the future. None of the alienation, hostility, electronic bewilderment and minority aggressiveness of an actual New York is allowed to be heard. Even the scenes of brutality and poverty seem to be a stubbornly romanticized version of old New York etchings and photographs, with echoes of Stephen Crane and Dickens in the pictorial writing rather than the more challenging fragmentations of Hart Crane and John Dos Passos.

This kind of single-minded idealism, at the expense of the difficult real, is reflected in a plot which soars so complacently in every direction that ultimately one page reads like another. (pp. 3, 13)

Although this is a novel ostensibly concerned with the resurrection of souls from the veil of materialism—and the moral rebirth of a dying city—the emphasis on funny names, odd costumes and eccentric behavior often makes us feel that we are witnesses to a quaint vaudeville show. There is a split between the high spiritual ambition of the book and an old-fashioned need to hook the audience with external bizarreness, which soon becomes predictable.

Granting all these disappointments, one still must point out that Mark Helprin is no less a spectacular writer than before. Rare talent might be misused but it can't be lost. When he reaches the climax to his cloudsy fable, and New York is burning as preparation for the millennium, he could well be a new and unvulgar Cecil B. DeMille of prose as he engirds the city with words and shows his power with big effects. It takes a far-ranging eye to conceive such a spectacle. It takes an equally rich and uncommon imagination to take on a novel of this perilous scale and import. The writer who takes risks is always more admirable than the miser of small success.

But every indication is that this book should be a crucial intersection in Helprin's career thus far. He has choices to make; inner maps to consult. His refusal to make taut his fantasies with the electric shocks of a commonly understood reality—as in the past—has diffused and muffled the liberating punch of his vision. Worst of all, it made one formerly enchanted reader want to quit before the end. (p. 13)

Seymour Krim, "Mark Helprin's New York Fantasy with Clipped Wings," in Book World—The Washington Post, *September 25, 1983, pp. 3, 13.*

GEOFFREY STOKES

"Words were all he knew; they possessed him and overwhelmed him, as if they were a thousand white cats with whom he shared a one-room apartment." This description, of a character from **Winter's Tale,** is emblematic of the current critical punch-up over Helprin's sprawling, picaresque novel. Are its hundreds of century-spanning, myth-discovering pages finally "overwhelmed" by words, or has Helprin—subtly in control of what seems to be a runaway—taught his old cats new tricks? Like Peter Lake supporting the mayoral campaign of Praeger de Pinto, I vote 12 times with the enthusiasts. . . .

Helprin, extending the factory fugue in **Refiner's Fire,** has launched a full-fledged romantic assault on the lingering grasp of realism. For beyond the flying horses and unspeakable villains, the music-swept love and beady-eyed vengeance, the whir of machinery and silence of ice, the most elaborate cruelties and gentle charities, beyond even the magic geography and limpid chronology, he offers a vision of a city that could "intensify pity, telescope emotion, and float the heart the way the sea is gently buoyant with great ships."

To reach that city—indeed, to transcend it, for such a city would have to be "a cold instrument. And, despite its beauty, it would have to be cruel"—Helprin piles invention upon invention. In addition to his 19th century city (which, god help us, occupies only a fifth of the novel), he gives us: The Rule of the Ermine Mayor; Jackson Mead's bridge into eternity; the great newspaper war between *The Sun* and *The Ghost* (a tabloid so contemptuous of its audience that it had abandoned merely misleading headlines . . . in favor of headlines unaccompanied by any story at all: "'Dead Model Sues Talking Dog'"); the Lake of the Coheeries, "so far upstate that no one could find it," where language has an innocent life of its own; at least two resurrections; a flaming invasion of Manhattan from the City of the Poor; literary references both strange and sly; child's play; the failure and telekinetic rebirth of machinery; a dozen achingly beautiful winter set-pieces and countless thoroughly improbable coincidences.

All of this is rendered in language so inflated, so riskily "poetic" that it threatens at any moment to topple over into preciosity: "The city's fire burns away the mists that frequently obscure it. Then, it looks like an animal perched upon the shore of the river. Then, it seems like a single work of art shrouded in changing galleries of climate, a sculpture of unfathomable detail standing on the floor of an orrery that is filled with bright lights and golden suns." The last speaker, one realizes with something of a shock, is among the apostles of reason and intellection that Helprin has set to balance the voices of ecstatic revelation. And if this represents **Winter's Tale**'s purely intellectual pole, one must surely ask whether Helprin's Road of Excess leads either him or us to the Palace of Wisdom.

I think it does—and not merely because the fecundity of his language batters us into a suspension of disbelief that may be only partly unwilling. The sheer flash of **Winter's Tale** is so striking on the surface that one is tempted to forget its structure, but the structure finally beguiles us.

Geoffrey Stokes, "Garrulous, Windy, Sprawling, Magical," in The Village Voice, *Vol. XXVIII, No. 39, September 27, 1983, p. 43.*

Richard F(ranklin) Hugo

1923-1982

American poet, novelist, editor, and essayist.

Hugo was a poet of the Pacific Northwest, yet his renown attests to a stature greater than that of most "regional" poets. He is noted for the tight, rhythmic control of his language and lines and for the sharp sense of place evoked in his poems. Hugo's images are urgent and compelling; he imbues the many minute or seemingly irrelevant details found in his poems with a subtle significance, thereby creating a tension between the particular and the universal. This tension is considered central to Hugo's most powerful poems.

In his poems Hugo reflected as much upon the internal region of the individual as on the external region of the natural world, and he considered these two deeply interconnected. According to Frederick Garber, "the landscape where things happen to Hugo goes as far into his mind as it goes outside of it"; Hugo's poetry "is about the meeting of these landscapes." The role of the past as a shaping force on the individual predominates. While "failed towns, isolated people and communities imprisoned in walls of boredom and rage," as Michael Allen notes, are often the subjects of Hugo's poems, there is also a pervading sense of optimism, of an uplifting hope, as Hugo puts it, "that humanity will always survive civilization."

Critics have praised Hugo's technical skills, the emotional impact of his compressed images, and the casual, sometimes humorous tone of his poems. In addition to his major collections—including *A Run of Jacks* (1961), *Death of the Kapowsin Tavern* (1965), *Good Luck in Cracked Italian* (1969), *The Lady in Kicking Horse Reservoir* (1973), *What Thou Lovest Well, Remains American* (1975), *31 Letters and 13 Dreams* (1977), and *Selected Poems* (1979)—Hugo also wrote a mystery, *Death and the Good Life* (1981), and a posthumously published novel, *The Hitler Diaries* (1983). His forte, however, was poetry, and his characteristic stance as a self-analytic writer, a perceptive observer, and a Westerner is again evident in his posthumous collection *Sea Lanes Out* (1983).

(See also *CLC*, Vols. 6, 18; *Contemporary Authors*, Vols. 49-52, Vol. 108 [obituary]; *Contemporary Authors New Revision Series*, Vol. 3; and *Dictionary of Literary Biography*, Vol. 5.)

James Schevill, "Experience in Image, Sound, and Rhythm," in Saturday Review, *Vol. XLV, No. 18, May 5, 1962, pp. 24-7.**

JAMES SCHEVILL

[In "**A Run of Jacks**," Richard F. Hugo] writes short, descriptive poetry focusing on places and things. He tends to stress the word and the image rather than the complete experience, so that often wholeness is sacrificed to individual effect. Thus we have at the end of one poem such a statement as, "Tonight the sea will come like the eyes / of all cats in the world stampeding." The word "stampeding" seems too calculated an attempt to shape a striking final image. Too many of Hugo's poems suffer from the quest for a false originality that plagues so many poets today. Yet, at his best, he reaches out into the natural world with an impressive sense of identity. Based mainly on images from his native Pacific Northwest, his poems often strike through to the power of this country torn from its Indian past. . . . (p. 25)

PAUL FUSSELL

[*Death of the Kapowsin Tavern*] brilliantly registers the poet's love affair with the wry, twisted language of Hopkins, Robert Lowell, and Dylan Thomas. Indeed, these poems take startling risks with language, and even where they fail they persuade us that the risks have been worth the taking. The very openings seize the reader and hustle him on into the poems' knotty but honest interiors. . . . The opening of the title poem, about the ruins of a burnt-down tavern, generates from language the sort of sheer excitement that has hardly been equalled since the appearance of Lowell's *Lord Weary's Castle* in 1946. . . . The language, even when in its excess it turns affected and hectic, seems to follow the very curves and mouldings of experience itself. But if Hugo's technique dazzles, his themes disappoint: his confrontations with sinister places, flowing waters, and the perpetual mystery of fecundity become repetitive, and his obsessions with the losses of the past come finally to seem unfresh, automatic. (p. 30)

*Paul Fussell, "How to Sing of a Diminished Thing,"
in* Saturday Review, *Vol. XLVIII, No. 27, July 3,
1965, pp. 30-2.*

THE VIRGINIA QUARTERLY REVIEW

Of the words used to describe Richard F. Hugo's first book of
poems, **"A Run of Jacks,"** perhaps the most repeated was
"powerful." This second book [**"Death of the Kapowsin Tavern"**] is also powerful, with a raw but compassionate strength
that is appropriate to the rough and dying strength of the far
west where the human need for life lingers in the burned ruins
and rotten rivers of a new civilization no better than the old.
These poems are ugly poems often, but of an ugliness which
is its own beauty, a human beauty not of form and grace but
of action and passion. His discovery of beauty in violence and
ugly disaster is the vision of a poet of intense insight; Richard
F. Hugo, too, is a poet of skill matching that vision. (pp. cxxi,
cxxiv)

A review of "Death of the Kapowsin Tavern," in
The Virginia Quarterly Review, *Vol. 41, No. 4 (Autumn, 1965), pp. cxxi, cxxiv.*

E. L. MAYO

Hugo, in these delightful, observant poems [in *Good Luck in
Cracked Italian*], brings back Italy to America so that we see
it not as a tourist trap but as a country of marvellous beauty
that has suffered more and endured longer than America has.
(p. 115)

Time past and time present fuse in many of these poems. The
time dimension, sometimes Hugo's past, sometimes Europe's,
gives pathos and dignity to everything the poet sees and does.
He retains, nevertheless, a sharp eye for the beauties of the
Italian seashore and countryside. His landscapes furthermore
are always peopled, not with tourists or artists or nobility, but
with Italian working people: farmers, fishermen, most of whom
are still desperately poor. (p. 116)

The title of this book is very significant. It tells us that the
poet is trying very hard to communicate with people, in this
case with the Italian people, but that because of some defect
in his accent or idiom what he has to say is not coming through.
From this feeling of inadequacy or self-distrust arises the note
of controlled desperation that we hear all through the poems.
What could be more typical of the predicament of all Americans
abroad? We all have something important we want to say,
about our feeling for them, about America; and nobody will
listen, or if they listen do not seem to understand.

There are, incidentally, no aristocrats, intellectuals (except
Galileo), writers (except Aretino, Keats and Shelley), painters
(except Breughel) in these poems, and these are just mentioned.
To Hugo only the struggling peasants are real; he identifies
with them and tries to penetrate to their basic thought and
feeling. Years ago Santayana accused Browning of painting
"a decapitated Italy." Is this true of Hugo? Not really, because
the poems are primarily pastoral and elegiac in spirit, not dramatic. And if a kind of mutual incomprehension exists between
poet and peasant Hugo transcends it through landscapes as vivid
as anything in Robinson Jeffers, but peopled not with neurotic
Californians but with hard-working Italians many of whom are
not averse to making an extra penny from the stray American
tourist. (p. 117)

[Although] there is a sort of chorus of Italian people in the
background of most of the poems, they are not really presented
individually or dramatically—or perhaps I should say only one
of them is, in **"Maratea Porto: The Dear Postmistress There,"**
in some ways the most beautifully formed and successful poem
of the lot, funny and sad. The postmistress's imperturbable
refrain at the end of each of the six stanzas: "*Niente per voi
today*," summarizes one of the important themes of the book,
the isolation of the American in Europe, and, even more, perhaps, the isolation of the soul in the world.

And yet the book is a kind of liberation—a liberation from the
incompleteness of a memory broken off unceremoniously but
now, here, across the miles and years, completed magnificently. (p. 118)

E. L. Mayo, "A Kind of Liberation," in Northwest
Review, *Vol. X, No. 3, Summer, 1970, pp. 115-18.*

J. D. REED

[*Good Luck in Cracked Italian*] deals with a revisit to Italy,
twenty years after WWII. Unlike most such collections it does
not smack of the "where are the meters and sentiments of
yesteryear?" Here, the young bombardier of twenty years ago
sees an even more terrible world. This intensification of feeling
calls up a new force in a poet whose ability to handle dynamite
was proved in *Death Of The Kapowsin Tavern*. . . . Hugo's
special and abiding force as a poet is landscape, an art in
rejection. He can present land as raw and undeniable as a
welfare check. Italy is perfect country for this kind of presentation, but I think we can all be glad that this fine poet has
done his damned Italian book. Though the book contains some
of his finest poems, they lack sometimes the stark music of
his Northwest poems. Perhaps now he'll concentrate on the
renaming of Montana, and heal more wounds that sing with
such a grace.

*J. D. Reed, in a review of "Good Luck in Cracked
Italian," in* Sumac: An Active Anthology, *Vol. 3,
No. II, Winter, 1971, p. 154.*

RICHARD HOWARD

The Italian interval—wartime service and the return, twenty
years later, to not only the tourist trappings (Keats's grave,
Galileo's chair, Tiberius's cliff) but to horrid Puglia, "a country where we never fail, / grow old or die, but simply move
unnoticed / to the next cold town"—is shown, in this crisp,
level book [*Good Luck in Cracked Italian*], to be a kind of
developing-tank for what has been Richard Hugo's negative
all along, enabling him to conjugate his themes into their final,
obsessive twist: "what endures is what we have neglected".

Turning from the desolations of the Pacific Northwest which
his first two books had constituted as the grounds for his divorce
from himself, the poet easily or at least eagerly sees himself
back in the country of his wartime service. Not that he will
seek to send down roots here, or to succeed: success is never
Hugo's concern. His concern is the unenviable, the unvisited,
even the uninviting, which he may or must invest with his own
deprivations, his own private war. The distinctness of impulse
in the language, the movement organized in single syllables
by the craving mind . . . , this credible richness is related to,
even derived from, the poverty of the places, local emanations
free (or freed) to be the poet's own. Each poem adds its incisive
particulars to the general stoic wreck. . . . But the summarizing

piece, a pendant to the overture, *Docking at Palermo,* and a kind of antiphonal rejoinder to *Sailing to Byzantium,* is the last and largest of Hugo's Italian exposures, fast-shuttered, wide lensed, a fantasia on all the themes of ignorance and refusal and ruin he has been able to afford in his months in "South Italy, remote and stone." (pp. 35-6)

What startles, then reassures in all this canon of the inconsolable, the unsanctified, the dispossessed, is Hugo's *poetics,* the analogy of language to experience. If significance is to be discovered in a world of refusals, then the method as well as the madness must be policed by the negative, by the demands of resistance overcome, rhythm completed, meaning presumed which we call *form.* It is no accident that we must develop a *negative* in order to produce a true *image.* Neither silence nor screaming would generate this utterance, but merely—merely!— that submission to negation, sacrifice, denial and constraint which makes up the entire justice (and generosity) of prosody. One trusts the veracity of Hugo's stoic despair not because matters veer so mercilessly to the bad, but because the verse is managed, is maneuvered so much to the good. As Valéry reminds us, a man is no poet at all if the difficulties inherent in his art deprive him of what he has to say; Richard Hugo is an important poet because they provide him, rather, a means of saying it. (p. 36)

> Richard Howard, "A Beginning, a Middle, and an Ode to Terminus," in Poetry, Vol. CXIX, No. 1, October, 1971, pp. 34-9.*

FREDERICK GARBER

Richard Hugo's poems are infused with an essential strangeness that is both immediate and pervasive, the first and last qualities in all the landscapes where things happen to him. It is comforting to say that Hugo is a regional poet, a celebrator of place who stares out at the Pacific Northwest; but its glance meets his stare as a lighthouse beacon hits the eye of a beguiled fish. Furthermore, the region in which he is located is as much within him as without, and most often in both places at once. The landscape where things happen to Hugo goes as far into his mind as it goes outside of it, and the landscape inside has a relationship with the one outside which words like *contiguity* and *continuity,* separately or together, cannot exhaust. In part the poetry—like that of Stevens or William Stafford—is about the meeting of these landscapes. Thus, if we want to call Hugo a regional poet we have to extend the region he encompasses to include the mind which makes the poems out of those meetings. He and his mind move out from the beaches of the Olympic Peninsula to the house of a just-dead drunk, deep into Italy and out to Montana ranches, into places that are no longer here and others that ought never to have been anywhere. Wherever it goes, this mind is never entirely surprised. Perhaps that means that the strangeness too is as much within him as without, that the confrontations of landscapes are really shocks of recognition. There is, after all, that within himself which can seem as dark as the darkest waters. But Hugo is never that easy a poet. An immense compassion links him to all other men without making him one of them, while his awareness of men as natural objects is wildly overweighed by his sense of them as men. Shocks of recognition are surely there, but his inner landscape is still the mind of a man and not a fish, its strangeness a human strangeness, and his ability to recognize likeness is the property of an isolated but percipient intelligence which watches those like itself at war with each other and with their surroundings.

This intelligence can entice more out of some surroundings than it can out of others, which is not to say that Hugo is limited (the Italian poems show that he is not) but that what he sees is usually seen most clearly in certain conditions. On the whole his is not a citified intelligence: in the city, he has said, it is difficult simply to see any one person or thing for very long, while in the country his sensibility is not flooded or forced to delete in order to understand. To this we ought to add another comment of his, that poets (Hugoesque poets) are conservative about life because they want things to stay long enough for the poets to understand them with full sensibility. And one more remark, published in the *New American Review,* should help toward fathoming the center of Hugo's sense of the world: poets need few things, he said, and among those are "a brief look at something most people ignore." Hugo's imagination hugs immutable starkness and seeks out, with awe, the locale of bare confrontations. The essential Hugoesque landscape is a beach, and the fundamental activity in it is the stare of a man at the alien sea. *Run of Jacks* is therefore not only his first book but his most basic one, for what occurs there is so radical that everything after it, better or worse, has not changed the lineaments of that act:

> Your land ends at this border,
> water and stone, mobile in tide,
> diffuse in storm, but here.
> The final fist of island rock
> does not strike space away. Swim
> and you are not in your country.
> ("**La Push**")

The rhythms in these poems are taut, muscular, nervous, probing what his world sounds like and what it dances to. These lines hold no empty spaces for sounds to echo in, because the landscape (within and without) has no blanks where anything can rest. The immense pressure within Hugo's language, then, renders exactly the intense density of what he sees. He stands in a town at the edge of the sea, facing out from the Olympic Peninsula to the Pacific which begins where all that is like him ends. Here at the margin he can see most clearly the packedness of every fragment of experience, even up to the rim where another kind of country starts. When the density he sees is not only theme but becomes part of the way the poem reaches us— in the rapid jumps from one image to another, in the compacted pressure of the words which are driven into relations by the rhythms—then this kind of Hugoesque poem achieves its complete effect, taking the reader into La Push and all its related landscapes at every possible level of experience. Hugo's compulsion to see density is so instinctive and ineradicable that he seeks for a landscape like this as a place in which to ease the urgency of the instinct. When he and the landscape are in so open a relationship that his imagination meets no barriers, the compulsion can lead him even into the country of elemental foreignness, where he sees the busy density in every scrap of *its* experience. . . . Curiously, the overwhelming amplification which is the city's essential act can (though it doesn't always) blot out Hugo's awareness of the pressure every fragment holds. But even there, especially around the edges, Hugo can exercise the primary forms of his imagination and dance at the recognition of the unremittingly alien: "**First South and Cambridge**" does this brilliantly. And some poems place men of the city just at the boundary where a brute struggle ensues, one which they often lose. The men, their houses and wives, in "**West Marginal Way**" live out all the meanings of the pun to which their street name leads their lives; while "**A District in the City**" puts them at a point where that which is enticingly not of their kind begins to emerge. Still, even in landscapes which are far from these marginal ways this humanized (though not humanizing) imagination cannot put a world together without a man inside of the landscape looking at it. The act of confrontation, after all, goes deep within a mind as well as far outside of it. Sometimes a version of the ubiquitous fat man looks out at the sea, as in **"Cape Alava"** where, "at this westmost U.S. point," a clown sails a stone into the wind. . . . The history of the Northwest has studded the landscape with the leavings of many men who stood up to the edge of things, with the cities behind them and the elementally foreign just at the end of their fingertips. There, trying to turn the foreign into themselves, they grubbed a bleak sustenance which might have built the bones of a city but might equally have gone nowhere at all (as in the great **"Montana Ranch Abandoned"** in a later collection). Men at the edge are finding a place to be, perhaps with the knowing pain of the clown at Cape Alava, often with characters at a more blunted stage of awareness whose sensibilities are as bleak as the lands they hold on to.

Hugo finds these characters here and now, though he does not always find them alive or in anything like a pristine state. In fact, their ability to be found at all depends upon their insignificance: one remembers that this most conservative modern wants "a brief look at something most people ignore." What endures of man may well have survived because men neglect it. Sometimes the shreds alone are sufficient, for here a man has *been*, and if the men who were there knew less than the poet and his doubles know, what is left of those men—stubborn fragments that may be no more than the stumps of a burnedout booze hall—is left partly because they were too uninteresting for most curious stares. In a whole series of poems Hugo stands where they did or where their vestiges are now, himself again at a margin, this time that between past and present, between the memories of others which his imagination lifts into presentness, and the irrevocable immediacy of that presentness. Margins are places where things change into other things, and Hugo's stereoscopic vision (one of his most brilliant repeated feats of the imagination) sees the past and the present and the point of change all together and at once. This is an elegiac conservatism which pores over the past of the enduringly minimal, finding significance in the remains of what is no longer quite viable. The past opens up at the point where he stands, and if Hugo's sensibility is immediate (he claims not to be good at working out of memory) his compassion leaps into the dead worlds of others and rebuilds marginal existences out of monuments. (pp. 58-61)

The move from **Run of Jacks** to [Hugo's second book **Death of the Kapowsin Tavern,**] changes no basic structures at the center of Hugo's experience but there is a shift toward a relative fullness within the immediate present. The past cannot be wiped out: it broods over all of Hugo's moves. But now he is drawn into a fascination with modes of immediate relation to the natural, modes more obviously and externally active than those the fat man endured on the beach (his activity there was of an imagination looking for points of focus). In the **Kapowsin** poems many of the men doing the relating, when not the fat man himself, are the kinds of companions with whom he feels most at ease. This is to say that he is looking less for variety of experience than for possibilities within a special mode, his own, and on a special locale, the edge of a river. The confrontation has shifted from a beach at the margin of a (usually) unmoving sea to the bank of a river, flowing water which carries fish, flotsam and several possibilities of a kind of relationship which is as rich in its limitations as in its depth.

Though there is far more in **Death of the Kapowsin Tavern** than river poems, it is that group which leads off the book and gives it its ground tone, a tone which never leaves, even in a framework of more civil things to which only limited access is possible. This is a difficult world for steelhead and for people. But, though the world may be nicer to steelhead than it is to people, it is nice to people because there are steelhead in it. Steelhead and jacks make possible a mode of communication that can cause the usually unhearing to respond. We can plunge within their surroundings through an extension of ourselves, enter the depths of the vital center and get a response of shuddering struggle which ends either with flight or limpness, but ends only after the harsh tension of communication has been fought through. When a line shoots over the surface of a winter river there is a gesture of silent speech, a radical vernacular through which contact from one side of the edge is made to the other. Its syntax is the lineaments of snare and struggle. Few of these fishermen stand there burning for the kind of marginal sustenance one has to grub out of indifferent matter. They are there at the edge to make points against strangeness:

> These men are never cold. Their faces
> burn with winter and their eyes
> are hot. They see, across the flat,
> the black day coming for them
> and the black sea. Good wind
> mixes with the bourbon in their bones.
> ("**Plunking the Skagit**")

This is exploratory language, as clean in its way as the diction of **Run of Jacks,** again with no open spaces and with a sense that no corner of the world or a phrase is without life. It explores with more ease and confidence, though, with a gradual opening up that is to lead eventually (though not fully in this book) to the composed gift of self in the Italian poems and in those that went back to Montana. Hugo sees what he has always seen, but the immense pressure—which was partly due to a need to keep his world closed off and tight—is no longer there at the limit where the words are just kept from flying apart. The fat man is still a tough guy but flaunts it somewhat less, even in **"Duwamish Head,"** his autobiography. Hugo's consciousness is still elemental and conservative, bound deeply into the enduring forms of confrontation. There is no greater acceptance of marginal struggles in **Death of the Kapowsin Tavern** but there is less imminent hysteria in it about what happens at the edges. Now he wants to work his eyes to their limit, see all the contours of the confrontation, explore what it can mean to men aside from grubbing for rudimentary support from flora. The eye returns from its work, its actions transmuted into a language which is precise and percipient, taut but not strained, ruthless in its quest for exactness of sight and statement. . . . The foreign is no friendlier than before, nor do backs break any less easily; but the eye which watches the line streak over and into the river sees itself, its subjects and objects, in more complex relations which do not exclude compassion but now have to include a warming awe. No one loves anything or himself more or less. Brutality (from that which ignores us) still follows meaningless laws. But Hugo has opened himself up, still with the fat man's occasional self-pity and penchant for self-dramatization—now, though, with a vision whose sharpness precludes neither awe nor (and this *is* new) something like a circumspect regard. One should not exaggerate the extent of this movement or the regard: Hugo loves no antagonists. Yet the relations between men and their opposites on the other side of the edge now have more diversity within them, and that recognition of diversity has come along with an easing of stance and verbal pressure that makes his style suppler in its assertions about itself and what it molds into being. . . . The sweep of truth that pulses through these limber rhythms is deep but restricted. The meeting at the boundary finds profound veracity in the fact of its activity and in the acuity of Hugo's awed vision and language, but the scope of what it can know rarely goes far. Hugo works in a difficult field. He wants to explore the possible relationships but the very business of exploration may well cancel out any chance of understanding: "To know is to be alien to rivers" or so says the fat man in **"Duwamish Head;"** and as he stands where the road ends at Tahola he has less to ask from the sea and therefore learns more of the meaning of waters:

> See the gleam,
> the stars that once were fish and died.
> We kiss between the fire and the ocean.
> In the morning we will start another stare
> across the gray. Nowhere *mare nostro.*
> Don't claim it and the sea belongs to you.
>   ("**Road Ends at Tahola**")

Any truth picked up under these circumstances—and the poems attest to what he has won—comes partly through luck, partly through a cunning that cons out of seas and rivers what they did not know they owned and could give away.

The title of the last section of the book, "Limited Access," carries the scope of this difficult activity into explorations of the relations between men and their own kind, between Hugo himself and those he has known, and between men and the places and art they have made. Men are, in some ways, as diffiuclt to get at as steelhead, but Hugo knows things about the being of roomers in stale flats, a dead drinking companion and a fort that has lost its guns that he cannot even guess at about the inside of the Duwamish. Some scenes in this last section are not unexpected, but the poems of waters have given these poems about men and their places a depth that makes apparent the limited access that exists everywhere that Hugo can reach. Yet there *is* a kind of enlightenment available here and now on a stream's bank. And there is an even fuller understanding possible about people and their places, an understanding whose motive force is the brooding compassion that had been held back in **Run of Jacks** but begins now, as a warm and fertile under-layer, to break through the tough guy's defenses. Access is never less than limited, but no lure can get deeper into the center of a stream than Hugo's compassion gets into the world of his pained kind or the beauty of a place's stubborn oldness. He is an authority on a sort of hurt that people undergo, and he knows that it is not landscapes but other people who are the enemies of the grubby and the unattractive. (pp. 62-5)

In the earlier poems of **Run of Jacks** the voice delineated its world with fantastic exactness but gave little of itself. Many of those poems revealed a gripping of self, a refusal to expose the personality, which echoed here and there in the clenched tensions of the language and occasionally made of those tensions a reflection of the voice's impulse toward a protective hardness. I have already mentioned the easing in the speech of **Death of the Kapowsin Tavern.** This easing occurred when the voice moved from what could have been shrill (though it rarely was) toward the gradual revelation of a personality which owned more confidence about its private complexities. The poetry as a whole was progressing, always tentatively, toward the fuller rendering of a selfhood which knew itself better with

each poem but never stopped seeing and recording what was always apparent to its sensibility.

The poems in **Good Luck in Cracked Italian,** Hugo's third book, record an interlude in which he explores the relationships between the changing voice of the poems and what endured in the content of their vision. He came to Italy with all the guilt hung over from the period of flinging bombs from five miles up, but, even more, with a curiosity about what he had been then and what he can see now of where he was. The chill winds blow in Italy too, on a ground fertile with incidents of marginal confrontation and the monuments in which repose more memories than even Hugo can imagine himself into. He can see all that his sensibility knows best but see it elsewhere than at home, and with a private warmth that expands the scope of both content and response. . . . But there is nothing in this openness of voice which carries on the confessional mode of the fifties and sixties. Hugo is too much a fan of Valéry to keep the poem anywhere else but between himself and the reader, shaping the sound of the voice so that we can believe in it and accept what it says, but never making of the voice a shriek directly out of his own substance. Only Lowell and Sylvia Plath have managed that fierce drive out of substance with consistent success. Their ways were never within the range of possibilities Hugo could have examined. Yet this openness which tempers his urgencies without denying them is not all or exclusive. Nothing he had learned to say or be is left out of the Italian poems because, though they say little about the Northwest, they include everything he had come to see at all points in time and in the spaces of his world and his personality. There is, then, no essential change in style but an accretion of variety and therefore of flexibility, an enrichment of the potentials of mood. Some of the poems in the Italian book echo the sinewy toughness of an earlier mode of voice but now that the toughness is not all that there is it sometimes finds a kind of pleasure even in its own mature seeing. . . . The inner and outer landscapes continue to shift and play against each other but the enrichment of the possibilities of voice is matched by a concomitant complexity in the modulations of the outer landscape. Nothing has changed but much more has emerged as this least Blakean of contemporaries cleanses the doors of his perception and enlarges the range of the window which joins both landscapes. Within that range all that is old in Italy gives fully of itself, not because it is mellifluously Italian (the hurt he knows well is here too) but because nothing in any of his worlds is without reference to the human, and the human in the voice is now triumphantly emergent and aware of the fullest meanings. What these poems completed in the movement of self that began with the earliest poems was taken back to the West, to Montana's towns, streams and Indians. It may be that Hugo had to step out of his home for awhile to complete himself. When he returned from the Italian interlude he settled into subsequent poems with a skilled comfort that found no corners closed off to him. . . . (pp. 65-7)

[Hugo's] true relations are with poets like William Stafford, on whom Hugo has written, and with the great Welshman R. S. Thomas. Both Hugo and Thomas—and Stafford, to some extent—are tied deeply into elemental things that never change, and each stares hard at the people who differ little from those elements. These poets, and a few others like them, hold onto the minimally enduring with a fervid conservatism that has nothing to do with politics and everything with people for whom no change seems possible. These cold pastorals come down from Wordsworth, who taught us all to see starkness with a compassion that cannot bubble but opens a place for warmth where there had been only hardness. Hugo fits in this line, whose significance in our time we ought to recognize, though there are not now many poets who work in it. Of those who do he is one of the best. That should suffice for anyone's distinction. (p. 67)

Frederick Garber, "Fat Man at the Margin: The Poetry of Richard Hugo," in The Iowa Review, *Vol. 3, No. 4 (Fall), 1972, pp. 58-67.*

VERNON YOUNG

Hugo's America is a *post*-frontier landscape-and-community. His poems are elegies for what was already moribund, the ghost towns or the by-passed crossroad villages of the North Central West, Lutheran and impoverished; company towns abandoned by the companies, or relegated by a high-powered economy that had scant mercy for the small farmer fighting drought or the storekeeper who hadn't moved out when the copper mine was exhausted. Whatever sociology or waterless acre of history may be gleaned from Hugo's arid, dehumanized small town is not his frontal subject. His poems are about the *ethos* of the Protestant provincial survivals beyond the American Pale. He doesn't, very often, mourn the *heroic* West, he is too busy celebrating the vestige of it for its own sake, for *his* sake; it is what he grew up in and its limitations, its *grayness* (his only color beside green), its deformed lives and dustbowl psyches, its pitiful diversions—getting drunk, fishing for perch, ogling a whore—are the very objects of his durable affection. (p. 227)

Hugo has the virtue that goes with the limitation of the deliberate provincial—or of, one might say, the hedgehog in that epigram; he knows one thing well, having only a polite curiosity about the life lived anywhere else (his Italy poems, product of the war, all wind up sounding as if he were writing about Montana); he fills his own space, settles for his own vocabulary, constructs his poems from declarative sentences and an increasingly sophisticated use of elision. More than anyone else, he reminds me of the painter, Vlaminck, who determined that by God when people saw a painting in a gallery window they'd know on first sight that it was a Vlaminck! Hugo has identified and certified himself with such an unerring employment of his idiom that there is little to say about his new collection [*White Center*] except that there are no surprises in it, and perhaps we wouldn't want any, that the poems therein speak with the same voice as before, exploit the same geography, express the same feeling of a spectacular human isolation, and are as ardent as ever in praise of drift!

And in that direction I begin to ask tiresome questions. A poem, **"Second Chances"** (in *White Center*), begins,

> I can't let it go, the picture I keep of myself
> in ruin, living alone, some wretched town
> where friendship is based on just being around.

A good poem, yet there is in it, maybe, cause for alarm. He "can't let it go"—and the more he dwells on it, the more often he returns to it in the verses he writes, with, it's true, an astonishing talent for variants on a monochordic theme. Yet the effect of it soon will depend very much on how often you can hear him play it again—the same story, same misgivings. (pp. 228-29)

I do begin to ask: *why*, except for the poem's sake, which for a stretch is adequate reason, this caterpillar identification with failure? *why* the uncritical infatuation with drunkards, whores,

hoboes? Is there not something comically immature in Hugo's persistent sentimentality about ponds he never fished, waitresses he never made (same thing)?

For the moment, it holds. The poems are good. Reread the poems, don't listen to the man. Remember Frost. He was better than he made himself sound when he "addressed" the world instead of writing poems about the only part of the world he had any love of. (pp. 229-30)

Vernon Young, "Two Hedgehogs and a Fox," in Parnassus: Poetry in Review, *Vol. 8, No. 1, Fall-Winter, 1979, pp. 227-37.*

MICHAEL ALLEN

Any understanding of Richard Hugo's West must begin back in the 1890s when three easterners invented the West that has played such an important part in American culture in this century. The West of Frederick Remington, Theodore Roosevelt and Owen Wister grew out of the expansive energies of easterners who made, consciously or unconsciously, a myth of American toughness overcoming the vast potentialities of the West's natural resources. Owen Wister wanted his novel, *The Virginian* (1902), to become a national fable, uniting North and South, East and West; what he created was the figure of male hero who would have few feelings, few human connections and few needs; who would do his job in the wilderness successfully and make that wilderness accessible to eastern expansion. Since Wister, the popular understanding of the West as a region has always been tied to that male hero: the tough man and the vast landscapes are as inseparable as cowboy and horse. (p. 25)

Richard Hugo, taking a similar tough-guy stance and living in a similar landscape as the Virginian, has given us, in **The Lady in Kicking Horse Reservoir** (1973), a poetry which works against this pervasive myth of the West and the western hero.... Where Wister and his friends found beautiful solitude and toughness, Hugo takes that same landscape and expresses the need for human community, for the necessary presence of human feelings to keep a man sane and whole. He has seen the remains of those expansionist energies which Roosevelt and Wister applauded and he has seen them as hardly heroic.... For Hugo, the West is a dream that does not belong to those who would—and do—exploit its land; the dreams of the West are those failed hopes of the poor and the greedy and the wishful who came there to find a better life. To Hugo, the American dream is not the unlimited possibilities of expansion but the ache of need. His landscape, vast and rugged as it still is, is a place where a man's possibilities are limited by that ruggedness and its associated weathers and winds that beat against human enterprise and make those connections between people that much more important.

In Montana then, Richard Hugo's West is born, big and "thick as a fist / or blunt instrument" where "long roads weave and curve / red veins of rage." ... There is less a romance of landscape than there is an education in the realities of space, a sensitivity to the effects that wind and weather can have on human lives and settlements.... (pp. 26-7)

In such a place, humanity barely survives. "With land this open, wind is blowing where there is no wind": the line could have been part of a novel by Wright Morris or Larry McMurtry, so central is it to the contemporary experience of the West, so separated is it from the dream of the West and western expansion. What is open is not always free; there are things unseen in the widest vista. Those shifting capacities of wind, from breeze to dust storm, become a governing metaphor in Richard Hugo's poetry, and lead . . . to the past and what is left of it in the interiors of buildings and the memories of human lives that have survived. . . . What Wister neglected and ignored in his push for a western myth is, in fact, what has endured: those human lives and remnants, those human connections among the poor and the greedy who moved west out of need, not exploitation.

It is the physical and emotional needs of a man that characterize Richard Hugo's western hero. The speakers in his poems are not what Robert Warshow, in "The Westerner," noticed of the many western film heroes that owed their existence to *The Virginian;* the speakers are not gentlemen, nor men of leisure, free to roam because they possess inner or external resources. Hugo's people are the dispossessed, who wander not for adventure but for some better life that lies, all too often, only at the bottom of a drink. . . . (pp. 27-8)

The bar is where the Hugo town has its center; it is the place where those unattainable dreams meet the all-too-evident reality, where love and violence meet and regulars and strangers can share an intimacy isolated from a society that recognizes success and power more than it recognizes human need. **"To Die in Milltown"** contains the day of the town, the life of a man and the region surrounding the town—all from the viewpoint of the bar. (p. 28)

Life in Milltown is the bar, where drinks are "full of sun" and drunks remember girls from their past, "filled with sun," who return unchanged in dreams, that cheat death. Only in the bars are divisions overcome, and tenderness, loss and dream contribute to a shared intimacy. Only in the closed-in space in the car can human feeling gain space and release from the needs of dispossession and disconnection. As the town surrounds the isolated man with divisions, he turns away from the losses which make up society to a dream which makes things whole; such is the process in Hugo's most widely quoted poem, **"Degrees of Gray in Philipsburg."** . . . (pp. 28-9)

Philipsburg is a map to isolation: the streets are "laid out by the insane," go past churches "kept up" from duty and lead to failure. At the center of the town is a jail, as if this is the goal of the poem's map. Certainly the jail provides the emotional center of the poem: isolation surrounded by a town where rage is "the principal supporting business," where history and pollution drive "the best liked girls" to Butte; where the failed mill and "two dead kiln" (an important pun) stand around the jail whose only prisoner is himself a stranger, "not knowing what he's done." The town also represents a human life, a life in which feeling has been lost from defeat "so accurate" that "the church bell simply seems / a pure announcement: ring and no one comes." Defeat, the poem implies, is a condition hard to leave, hard to let go. As the town, so the man is a living defeat, an imprisoned life that will never reach other towns of "towering blondes, good jazz and booze."

In the image of the jail the political, historical and social forces of the town meet and coalesce with those psychological forces in the speaker's broken life. In a way not unlike Wordsworth's idea of the mind "fitted" to Nature, Hugo shows how interior psychology is "fitted" to exterior social conditions. The town inside the self, which imprisons the speaker's psyche in boredom and replays of rage and loss—this is what must die. When it dies, the political and social failures of the town—and of the

speaker's life—can also die, and something new in the man and the town, a new intimacy, can begin.

The old man in the last stanza of **"Philipsburg,"** alive before the jail was built, sparks the fire that leads to escape from this emotional prison. A grim, neglected presence, the old man jokes about his age and his lips collapse as he speaks. As stubborn and standing as the old mill "that won't fall finally down," he survives and laughs even in his defeat. When telling the old man "no," the speaker finds he is talking to himself, rejecting the same town and defeat the old man's laugh rejects: his car still runs; his money is good silver and, what is more, the first woman to come into the poem is "slender and her red hair lights the wall."

Freud would have called it reawakened libido. Jung would have pointed to how the old man figures, in this poem by a man, to rekindle psychic energy to releasing the magic of the encircling prison. Whatever the psychological rendering, the imagery is clear. Inside the walls of the town, the prisonhouse where boredom and rage dominate, there is a flame, a fire, an energy. The waitress may be only a waitress, but the chance for human intimacy, an end to isolation, failure and rage, is like a flame against the wall.

Those failed western towns are proof enough that the western expansion celebrated by Wister and Roosevelt was not all gold. Outside the walls of the bar, the jail, beyond the town festering in its boredom and isolation, lies the landscape which drew those white settlers. Rather than seeing the landscape as potential wealth and actual beauty, Hugo sees the dust and wind as much as the trout streams. And if that wind—that "degrading wind" from "Ovando"—has worn down the opportunities and expansion of America into the West, there is good reason. According to Hugo, that wind is finally not what we commonly call "American"—not, that is, white American. It is Indian, and the converging sympaties and sorrows from that other side of the history of American expansion find an eloquent place in the poem, **"Bear Paw."** . . . (pp. 29-30)

As the poem opens, the wind is white, a metaphor for the armies of the 5th infantry that pursued Chiefs Joseph, Yellow Hand and Looking Glass of the Nez Percé northward as the tribes tried to reach Canada in September of 1877. Hugo, in 1972, is standing at the site near the Bear Paw mountains where Chief Joseph, seeing that his people were dying of cold and starvation, surrendered. (p. 31)

Turning from history, its data and detachment, Hugo demands in the third stanza an acceptance of the suffering: "close enough to struggle, to take blood / on your hands." As if such acceptance were like the "lull in wind" the Indians felt before their defeat, things change: the wind is not "senile" and Looking Glass, long dead, "will not die." What appears as an acceptance of historical fact has been overturned. There is something more than history; there is the wind, the weather itself. What is needed is not history but prayer, not facts learned but surrender experienced, an action taken in the heart that overcomes the isolations and divisions. The last lines of the poem are unmistakably spoken by a white man who compares his surrender of the spirit to that surrender of Joseph and his tribe a hundred years earlier. What this white man surrenders to is not an army with superior weapons and fresh troops but the wind itself, that spirit so thoroughly part of Indian religion, a "lone surviving god" which has filled the Hugo landscape with both defeat and the possibilities of change, a new vision.

In his surrender, Richard Hugo recognizes the necessity of a culture which has more than victories, historical facts and cars that make clouds of dust. In the heart of **"Bear Paw"** one line is resonant with both Joseph's experience and Hugo's: "only the eternal nothing of space." Not the eternal possibilities or opportunities or adventure—there are no metaphoric extensions possible from defeat and dispossession, no place for human heroism and independence, no matter how tough. The nothing of space, that "lull in wind," is as fine and calm a response to manifest destiny and the appetite of American expansion as there could be. There is no newer frontier and no new tough hero to exploit it; there is only human need and the importance of human connection. As Richard Hugo's landscape has developed, it has become that of a man who knows the harsher realities of space, wind and weather that drive people not toward new schemes for wealth but toward each other for warmth.

As if *The Lady in Kicking Horse Reservoir* were preparation, Hugo's next book, *What Thou Lovest Well, Remains American* (. . . 1975), shows a lessening of the images of prison towns (Philipsburg, Hot Springs, Dixon) and of the image of the harsh wind as metaphor of defeat. What Hugo concentrates on is presenting images of individual human beings and their struggle to keep holds on life, on each other, on the sympathies of the poet—and by extension, the reader. Richard Hugo would like his readers to feel the lonely awkwardness of **"The Swimmer at Lake Edward,"** the toughness of a madman's truth in **"Reconsidering the Madman,"** and how it must feel to work for the Trio Fruit Company in Missoula. (pp. 31-2)

Hugo's imagination may be drawn to exploring images of failed towns, isolated people and communities imprisoned in walls of boredom and rage simply because the experience of human community is so deeply valuable to him. In *The Lady in Kicking Horse Reservoir,* he allows himself only a few poems which satisfy this ache for community, and **"Missoula Softball Tournament"** is perhaps the best example. (pp. 32-3)

The problem of how to present community, however, stands central to Hugo's writing as his poetry has moved from those images remaining from the Old West myth—the hardened hero, isolated town, harsh wind—to images from the lives of people who live in something other than the saloon or open range.

Perhaps what is being destroyed is the brutality of need and expansion that shaped the first western myth; perhaps what survives is intimacy. The overall effect is the displacement of the western myth by the image of a society struggling to work, as images of lonely people, of outcasts, the poor, the old, the Indian or neglected fills its pages. It is the image of a society just beginning to be aware of itself as a collection of people, not a thing of walls and tough guys and the wind on the horizon.

Although his sixth book, *31 Letters and 13 Dreams,* is overwhelmingly autobiographical, here Hugo also turns to the image of the West and to the important presence people have in the vast distances of western space. Moments of poetic uplift in the general prose of the letters make definite claims for the people, if not the land or the toughness, of the West. The tough guy is older and wiser. . . . (pp. 33-4)

Hugo fears that both parts of the West—both the tough and brutal, with its accompanying isolation and expanse, and the honest and open, with its acceptance of human cruelty and need—will fade with the changes that an expanding technological society will bring. He would like to see the honest part remain; it is an image of the West less myth than fact, based as it is, not in Wister's novel or in Remington's paintings nor in Roosevelt's rhetoric, but in the memory of a particular historic time in America's past, when the expansion of America's territory and of its economy abruptly halted for awhile: the thirties:

> the forlorn towns
> just hanging on take me back to the thirties where
>   most poems
> come from, the warm meaningful gestures we make,
>   the warm ways
> we search each other for help in a bewildering world,
> a world so terrifyingly big we settle for small
> ones here we can control.
>   (**"Letter to Goldbarth from Big Fork"** . . .)

Those warm gestures hold society together. Those expressions of warmth, of the common and essential connections of feeling, which can only be called social, have not often been part of American poetry. What we often read is political or private poetry that verges on commenting on American society itself. Pablo Neruda could make exemplary poetry that expands outward toward society by writing about a gift of socks, but America has not the social cohesion (natural or forced) as does Chile: the society is just too vast, too full of potential, of unseen, hidden surfaces in its extensive landscape. Perhaps therein lies the enduring gift of the myth of the West: as a western hero once learned how to read that vast expanse of land for its potential values and dangers, so now a very western poet offers to make the western landscape a metaphor for American society. In our vast complexities and sometimes unseen differences, those warm gestures between people, across wide spaces, can overcome the isolation, boredom and loss of community which was the image of that earlier West—a West which has played so important a role in American society for the past century. (pp. 34-5)

*Michael Allen, " 'Only the Eternal Nothing of Space':
Richard Hugo's West," in* Western American Literature, *Vol. XV, No. 1, Spring, 1980, pp. 25-35.*

ANATOLE BROYARD

Richard Hugo is . . . a serious writer, a poet and essayist, and he has managed to hold on to some of his virtues in **"Death and the Good Life."** His hero, Al Barnes, is not only a deputy sheriff, but a poet as well. He may be the only poet in America who has read Rilke but not Baudelaire, but aside from that, he's reasonably disarming.

Barnes is more interested in women's "bottoms" than their breasts, which shows what poetry can do for suspense fiction. Mr. Hugo has a nice old-fashioned Dashiell Hammett-Raymond Chandler fondness for the labored simile. Barnes's police uniform impresses a bartender "about as much as the death of Jean Harlow." A hotel clerk looks "as prudish as Mae West."

The action of **"Death and the Good Life"** is appropriately convoluted. Mr. Hugo would sooner supererogate than fall short. There is a giantess who murders in sexual revenge, a nymphomaniac who uses a maid for sadistic fantasies, a suggestion of sexual vandalism, a case of incest—everything the heart desires in light reading.

Every now and then the real poet peeks through. Mr. Hugo, who lives and teaches in Montana, has a talent for describing small Western towns. In these towns, you can almost imagine **"Death and the Good Life"** happening. And that's all one can ask of crime fiction, isn't it—to be able almost to imagine it, to read an author who is smart enough to stay out of the way and let us lose ourselves in peace.

Anatole Broyard, "Crimes Against Fiction," in The New York Times, *February 7, 1981, p. 31.**

ROGER MITCHELL

[*The Right Madness on Skye*] is a very good effort. That came as a surprise—I think because of two large and unreliable preconceptions of mine about Hugo's work. In the first place, I have always taken his locating and describing of places as evidence in him, at a fundamental level, of a regional realist. He seemed to have much in common with Sherwood Anderson or Edgar Lee Masters, even Edwin Arlington Robinson. Reading my way recently through his other books, however, I saw a Hugo I hadn't seen before, one far less interested in region and regional identification than in what I'm tempted to call myth, a word he sometimes uses himself.... [Most of Hugo is compressed into the last stanza of **"Duwamish No. 2"**]: the sense of private hurt and injury, the loneliness, the ordinariness, all leading to the conclusion that life tends in "one direction only"—a northerly and bitter one—and that it must be lived, essentially, without love. The only consolation is found along the river, which, in Hugo, always implies the complicated, mythical act of fishing.

The most obvious thing about **"Duwamish No. 2"** is that it could have been written about any river. Place, in a photographically regional sense, is unimportant. The phrase in *Right Madness* is "All places are near...." The next most obvious thing is that the key words of the stanza—river, salt, sea, north—are used emblematically, nearly allegorically. In realist writing, words mean first what common usage says they mean, but in this passage the river is first a complex emblem or symbol. As it runs down and out to sea, it is a traditional symbol for the natural, entropic "course" of human life. It is also the place from which life, as in fishing, can be snatched. "Fishing preceded song," says a poem in *Right Madness*. Salt suggests bitterness and tears in this poem almost before it is linked naturally to the sea, and north, as he says in *Right Madness,* is "one direction I've always believed."

It should have come as little surprise that Hugo could write comfortably in and about a place other than his own. He had done it before, of course, in *Good Luck in Cracked Italian,* but that book was so linked to the experiences World War II forced on him that one was not tempted to place it near the center of his writing. Why Scotland, then? A poem from *The Lady in the Kicking Horse Reservoir* hints at an answer. **"Drums in Scotland,"** written on a short visit there in the early seventies, says: "This land / is tough north music." In other words, the Scottish landscape and, as *Right Madness* suggests, the Scottish experience reach Hugo with their abundant evocations of a bleak, deprived, once violent existence. Here, too, half-way around the world from White Center, is a place, like the southern Italy he was stationed in during the war and later returned to, where life is lived with a kind of minimalist intensity.

As a child of the Depression, Hugo has rendered that intensity often in images that we associate with the photography of Dorothea Lange and Walker Evans, the poetry of Carl Sandburg, and the fiction of John Steinbeck. It is quite easy, in fact, to assume—as I did—that Hugo's portrayals of physical and emotional degradation carry with them the unstated liberal and progressive hope for their amelioration.... Passages ... can be found throughout Hugo's work ... [that] reveal a con-

sistent affection for the impoverished, oppressed, and ignored. In *Right Madness,* for instance, we are given several portraits of beggars and displaced crofters, as well as Hugo's delight in playing the role of peasant. All the ingredients for an engaged poetry are there except the engagement. When he said in **"Letter to Hanson,"** "I keep feeling revolutionary / but I have no cause," I tended to discount it. But he said essentially the same thing as far back as his second book in a poem called **"Bad Vision at the Skagit."** ... Hugo does see injustice, if I read his tone correctly, but he sees something else as well, hinted at in the "slow water," "beating birds," and "sun." That other thing, which is linked to nature and natural process, is larger and more important than the injustice. It keeps him from "seeing" the injustice or from reacting as he would like to toward it. It gives him, as he says, bad vision. But it also gives him real vision, and he will not sacrifice that to demands for social justice.

Why? True perception would seem to be its own justification, but there is another reason why Hugo feels "no cause." He has no faith in justice or progress. (pp. 57-8)

At the heart of Hugo's work, alongside a compassion for life's victims, is an undespairing recognition of what he calls in **"Letter to Reed,"** "The degraded human condition," a world "dying from faith in progress." There are poems in *What Thou Lovest Well Remains American,* like **"Starting Back,"** which call for a rejection of civilization altogether. **"Keokuk,"** in the same book, is almost Luddite in its urging to "batter the factory down and live with famine."

To the question, then, what is this prototypical American poet doing on the Isle of Skye, I begin to have more answers than I have room to do them justice.... [Though] Richard Hugo was an outsider and a stranger to that place, he recognized the essentials of its inner life, saw that they were his as well, and quickly made his poems grow there. It is no fluke that the first poem in the book was written from a calendar photograph before he went. Skye is another place where Richard Hugo has encountered the remnants of a peasant poverty and a peasant honesty and fortitude, which are, for him, the final, necessary consolations. (pp. 58-9)

Roger Mitchell, in a review of "The Right Madness on Skye," in The North American Review, *Vol. 266, No. 1, March, 1981, pp. 57-9.*

NEWGATE CALLENDAR

When a poet turns to crime fiction, what do we get? Elegant writing? Avant-garde writing? In Richard Hugo's case, traditional writing. His first mystery is **"Death and the Good Life"** ..., and it introduces a cop named Al Barnes, who operates out of Plains, Mont.

Mr. Hugo has a sympathetic eye for character—starting with Barnes himself, who is a former poet and the most soft-hearted deputy sheriff ever to track down evil. He feels sorry for people in trouble.... But Barnes is not really a softie, and nothing can stand in his way when he is determined to ferret out the truth. Two axe murders lead him to an old murder in Portland, Ore., where, in turn, a baseball game makes him sound the unlikely eureka.

If Mr. Hugo breaks no new ground here, he has nevertheless written a superior book of its kind—complete with suspense, some hectic action and a surprise ending. Using the conventions of a traditional murder investigation, he has brought together a group of realistic characters and developed them with unusual finesse.

Newgate Callendar, in a review of ''Death and the Good Life,'' in The New York Times Book Review, *March 29, 1981, p. 39.*

PETER STITT

Hugo's is . . . a personal, even romantic, kind of poetry; in all his work there is a submerged, shadowy version of autobiography lying just beneath the detailed, descriptive surface. In *White Center* the poet returns to his starting place, the community contiguous to Seattle where he was raised. The early days were not happy ones for this speaker, as he makes clear in a comment on his verse in **"Beaverbank."** . . . (p. 185)

The process revealed by this book is an inherently healthy one, involving the gradual discovery of self, of happiness. The change is revealed most starkly, most dramatically in the beautiful concluding poem of the volume. **"White Center"** is directly about the original neighborhood, the life lived there, and is addressed to the grandmother who raised this man. (pp. 185-86)

In *The Triggering Town: Lectures and Essays on Poetry and Writing,* Hugo comments on the way in which a poet ought to handle the truth of reality in his poetry. When writing about a real place, the poet should not feel obliged to render it with literal accuracy: "You owe reality nothing and the truth about your feelings everything." Hugo's best poems are expressive of the feelings, however much they seem concerned with external imagery. This fact is not always apparent on a first reading, for the feelings are always presented within the context of some external situation. (p. 186)

The Right Madness on Skye [is] a kind of travel book of poems. Beyond very good writing, one thing these books share is Hugo's consistent concern for people whose lives are not magic. He doesn't write about tragic figures—that would be too dramatic; rather, he empathizes with those who know the dreariness of day following empty day, those to whom promotion does not come, those who end up losing in life's many conflicts. The Isle of Skye was thus a perfect place for Hugo to spend several months—the soil is bad both for crops and pasture, the fishing is at best extremely dangerous, the weather is unpredictable and harsh, and the history records a long series of invasions and occupations.

The people of Skye are shrewd and long-suffering; so it has been throughout their history. Many times the island was invaded by barbarians from the north; crops were burned, men killed, women carried off. Later, feudal lords came from Scotland to build their castles and force the islanders into serfdom. More than once the entire population of some smaller nearby island was exiled so the lord could graze his sheep; sent to places as far as New Zealand, many died on the way and none ever returned alive. Richard Hugo is an ideal poet for such an island, such a race of men; he records their landscape and their history with great affection. The best poems here mingle something of the deprivation, exploitation, poverty of their lives with Hugo's sense of his own similar situation. (pp. 186-87)

Richard Hugo has never written better than he does in these two volumes, and he has ever been among our best and most careful craftsmen. The publication of two so strong volumes in a single year is an imaginative tour de force that has rarely been equalled, much less bettered. (p. 187)

Peter Stitt, "Purity and Impurity in Poetry," in The Georgia Review, *Vol. XXXV, No. 1, Spring, 1981, pp. 182-89.*

PETER SERCHUK

For even those who have followed the careful and steady development of Richard Hugo's verse these past ten to fifteen years—in particular since the publication of *The Lady in Kicking Horse Reservoir* (1973)—*White Center* will seem a remarkable achievement. Although the book touches on most of the usual Hugo subjects—the West, the past, small towns and rivers—it moves far beyond the poet's other work in its thematic continuity, its control of language, and its imaginative zeal. What is more important, the book carries with it a tone of greater authority, a more seasoned and stable voice sure of its fifty-odd years of hard survival, yet free of the glorifying narcissism that often plagues our contemporary poetics.

Hugo's trump card in securing this necessary distance from the self lies primarily in his creative process. He hardly ever begins with a specific subject for his poems. Instead he starts with a single image or observation from which he can move in any way language or imagination dictates. He feels no allegiance to some preconceived notion of where the poem is *supposed* to go. His faith is in the inventive or dream process, in the formation of luminous details (either fact or fiction) through which spontaneous language can be generated. For Hugo the formula is clear: the creation of language creates meaning as opposed to preconceived meanings' utilizing language as a vehicle for their expression. (p. 271)

The main focus of this, Hugo's seventh volume of poems, is the poet's childhood in White Center, Washington. Using memory and language as catalysts, Hugo works his way back through manhood, through adolescence, to the emotional center of his life. He stops frequently along the way to chart his progress, to expose contradictions, and to understand what price has been paid for his survival. Frequently ghosts of the past appear, and Hugo is unsure whether to pity or damn them. . . . What is especially impressive is Hugo's honesty, the way he asks himself the same questions over and over in different poems, in different guises, each inquiry revealing another detail of the complicated matrix. He does not try to disguise the myths he has created to survive. Rather he uses them as road markings leading toward that center point. (p. 272)

As the themes of the book fully evolve, we begin to see more clearly what is behind Hugo's journey back to the past: the struggle to accept his present happiness. Hugo has survived, yet he knows that a piece of him lives and dies in the past, sharing the same hard ground with those haunting souls who did not escape. . . . Having survived the need to appease the past, having now worked his way beyond the delusions of pity and shame, he is free to bless and forgive these ghosts one by one. And likewise to accept their forgiveness.

The subject of survival also plays a major role in Hugo's latest book, *The Right Madness on Skye.* On this occasion the subject is survival on the ancient Isle of Skye off the coast of northwest Scotland, where Hugo and his family lived for several months in 1977. Hugo's trip to the Isle of Skye affords him a special opportunity to combine his own personal history with the rich history and mythology of another culture. Like William Carlos Williams, Hugo begins with the local—the locale, sure that all else will reveal itself through this tightly focused lens.

He visits graveyards, castles, villages, and farmlands that seem to beg to have poems written about them. They call out, each with its own history, its own story; and what better traveler to stop and meditate on their long existence than Richard Hugo? He becomes the new cartographer of this once brutalized land, his eyes the new compass with which to survey the terrain, his American language the new medium in which to translate history's ancient tongue. "It's all here / in the names, the sound of broken bone and blood" ("**A Map of Skye**").

There is no middle ground and no compromise. Hugo gives himself fully to his task. Using his sacred dream-life as a bridge, he reinvents the island's history and returns to feudal Skye. He becomes the man of all times, the perfect historian who remembers details from first-hand experience, yet has the objective distance of hundreds of years. He works with the crofters in the fields, lives at the mercy of the feudal lord, becomes a soldier simultaneously in both the conquering and annihilated armies. The dream-life begins to break down when he realizes that he can only return to the past, not change it. He'd like to call back the crofters from their ships, tell them that the repossessed land is theirs again and the crop is good. But no. They do not want their fates to be reimagined. They do not want to be brought back to life only to experience their hard survival over again.... Hugo is left to do what these inhabitants of Skye have done for centuries—ignore pity, accept time and circumstance, develop the right madness for survival, the right madness on Skye. (pp. 272-74)

Richard Hugo is one of only a handful of writers, in poetry or prose, who have developed a successful balance between the spoken and the written language. While maintaining the structural integrity of formal written expression his syntax simultaneously aligns itself to the natural rhythms of speech. These poems seem so easy, so fluid and conversational, that one must be careful not to read them too quickly. They are complex, but it is the invention and meditation that are complex, not the language presentation. How often in our poetry we find writers using language as a barrier to expression. Hugo rejects this notion. Language need not be obtuse to be rich. Hugo has put his full faith behind his language, behind its infinite ability to deliver whatever the dream-life demands; and these new poems prove he has been richly rewarded for doing so. (p. 274)

Peter Serchuk, "Confessions of Travelers and Pilgrims," in The Sewanee Review, *Vol. LXXXIX, No. 2, Spring, 1981, pp. 271-78.**

DAVE SMITH

Reading Richard Hugo's **Selected Poems** one discovers a poet of unusual continuity in vision and execution. There are the benchmarks of change and of some evolution, but he does not show the radical alterations of style or thought which mark his contemporaries such as, say, Adrienne Rich, Robert Bly, James Wright, or Donald Hall. Indeed, the poems he includes here reinforce the sense that Hugo was born to say one kind of poem and knew what it was from the start. This is slightly deceptive. Just as Hugo has always tempted readers to see him as an immediate confessional poet of self-degradation, his **Selected Poems** eliminates work that shows his struggle to create an art characterized by tense passion and tragic joy, an art of the durably made thing. He has, for example, cut nearly 100 poems from his long out of print first three collections, *A Run of Jacks* (1961), *Death of the Kapowsin Tavern* (1965), and *Good Luck in Cracked Italian* (1969). He has cut another eighty-seven

poems from *The Lady in Kicking Horse Reservoir* (1973), *What Thou Lovest Well Remains American* (1975), and *31 Letters and 13 Dreams* (1977), all of which are readily available. I regret that so much of the early work, some of it admittedly weak, was sacrificed for reprinting later work, but that half of his accomplishment which remains is not distinctly different, it is only more clearly accessible.

All poets labor to make increasingly transparent and accurate what they have to say. We do not necessarily agree what this thrust toward clarity means, hence divergent responses to Merwin. Still, poets usually begin in overwriting and opacity. The best slowly win through to a special luminosity that has little to do with being either discursive or imagistic and do so at the point they have manipulated tradition to be adequate and sufficient to their purposes. More than many of his contemporaries, Hugo began and has remained in the middle ground of discourse and image, satisfied to work at being clear at the level of communication while increasing the vivid and resonant images he owns in the power of implication. Reduced to the most absurd distillation, Hugo writes in a private code of the single confrontation of a man with an inevitable fate: he must survive by finding a way home and he will always fail in his attempts. The most characteristically Hugo and, perhaps, the best poem in his first book illustrates what I mean. "**1614 Boren**," a street address, begins:

> Room on room, we poke debris for fun,
> chips of dolls, the union picnic flag,
> a valentine with a plump girl in a swing
> who never could grow body hair or old....

In what is typical strategy for him, Hugo has returned to the scene of a crime, the abandonment of vital life. In the next stanza, having seen a slick picture of a pastoral scene still hanging on the wall of this emptied house, he asks "What does the picture mean, hung where it is / in the best room?" He describes the conventional portrait of trees, house, vines, canals that hides "the world of harm behind the dormant hill." With no transition he jumps to the absent roomers, identifying them only as room 5 and 7, telling us how sordid their lives were, and noting they called this *place* and *house*. Home would be "a joke on the horizon— / bad proportions and the color of disease." Weaving by contrast this ruined address with the picture it yet keeps like a lost secret, Hugo concludes:

> But the picture, where? The Netherlands
> perhaps. There are Netherland canals.
> But are they bleached by sky, or scorched
> pale grey by an invader's guns?
> It can't exist. It's just a sketcher's whim.
> The world has poison and the world has sperm
> and water looks like water, not like milk
> or a cotton highway. There's a chance
> a man who sweated years in a stale room,
> probably one upstairs, left the picture here
> on purpose, and when he moved believed
> that was the place he was really moving from.

That picture of the Netherlands is a calendar cliché and we all know it, but Hugo means for us to see also that it is the netherland of dream as equally phony as the girl who never grows body hair, or grows ugly. But Hugo, if he has brought us back to the debris that realistically all homes become, has no intention of abandoning dream. He believes that dream is the right way to vision, and images of spiritual vision (and blindness) proliferate from beginning to end of the **Selected Poems**. Therefore whoever left the illusion of what home might be has also taken it with him. The nether-world can't exist and yet it does.

"1614 Boren" reveals a great deal more of what is essential to Richard Hugo. We see first, perhaps, that it is a landscape poem in which historical and natural forces operate. The poem is spoken by an objective, observing voice; no "I" or "We," as victim, enters this poem. Yet objects are arranged with telling absences to achieve a clear emotional relationship which in the end generates and earns something like discursive wisdom. Hugo takes the scene and place as a text to be teased toward extrapolation of larger truths. In many of his poems he tells us to "Remember." When he does not say it, he means it, for by his poems he sanctifies and resurrects life. In consequence, his tone is typically somber and on occasion turns preacherly. In fact, this poem is a kind of guided tour through failure that is still wild with possibility and we note that the speaker appears to move intimately here while the poem shows us that he is removed, controlled. Yet he is not unengaged. This speaker moving through the world of the degraded and the real is performing the hypothetical test that I believe is the critical act of Richard Hugo's art. He intends quite simply to know, to see what is real and what is not, what remains and what degrades.

Richard Hugo, in spite of his reputation for pessimism and worse, is a relentless optimist whose examination of the symptoms of personal and communal disintegration has tended to disguise his search for permanent, healthy, and reliable values. He resists rather than cultivates despair and degradation. But he must know experientially, and must express, the full defeats of life if he is to do more than present false pictures of the Netherlands. For Hugo the imagination seems to be a transforming power to create and transfer to his readers a tragic sympathy which leads to joy and freedom. That freedom and joy is inevitably equated with home and home's various trial landscapes. In his search for home there is always a dialectic of voices: one speaker is the credible squint-eyed realist our grandmothers praised for having feet on the ground, the concluding voice of **"1614 Boren"**; the other voice is the dreamer to whom all remains mysterious, unknown, alive, and expressive of secret vitality. In effect, it is the dreamer who cannot leave the picture of the Netherlands. Hugo refuses ever to resolve this dialectic and thus he presents us with no clear answers that may be gleaned from the *Selected Poems* but rather takes the role of both voices in dramatic contention through poem after poem. It will seem heretical to some, but I think that Hugo is not, finally, a narrative poet but a philosophic (and imagistic) poet whose debates are those of the contemporary American spirit, debates primarily of hypothesis and question. (p. 34)

Hugo's poems have undergone only slight changes in style in the nearly thirty years the *Selected Poems* represents. His music has always been insistent and derived from Anglo-Saxon sonic practices. He loves a strongly stressed line, usually three to five stresses, which has a density and intensity that is always willing to risk overwhelming the ear. The quality of his sound is ordinarily determined by frequent alliteration, blunt monosyllabics, interior sound repetitions, jammed and nervy phrasings, and a syntax which alternates an extended weaving with a terse statement. He deploys images as if they were sequential flashbulbs, almost too quickly for absorption. Yet he surrounds these images with commentary that frames as well as shifts them for perception. And over the course of a book, he repeats and modulates his imagery until it becomes a coded language.

His quirky placement of adjectives begins as apparent registration but usually alters to an ethical, moral, historical, or social observation. His lines function vertically, horizontally, and collectively to create description, pointing, and meaning. He has been said to write a boredom of iambics but he is rarely consistent in any meter. Above all he operates stanzaically, as if by paragraphs, using stanzas for changes of perspective, voice, and subject. His stanzas balance the alternating long and short sentences which, with his fervent stresses, accomplish his jumpy and recognizable style. He does not trust very much the music of white space. He is, in words, and has always been a meat and potatoes man. (pp. 34-5)

Having spoken of so much in Hugo that is typical, obsessive, characteristic, and, perhaps, predictable I do not wish to leave the impression that I agree with a scattering of critics who find him a monotonous poet. Truly, he writes a lot and a lot of what he writes comes demandingly in the same cadence and with the same strategies. If he is a predictable poet it is well to remember that his subjects and his sub-themes are also predictable: weather, oceans, rivers, stars, the evidence of failure and love and death, bars, drunks, the dead, and that dominant impossibility of getting home, a quest which beings in self-consideration as well as in definition of the visible world. For Hugo, this quest is the act of search and revelation and, though it helps to be aware of his strategic techniques, ulitmately his interest is in revealing the truth more than in verbal acrobatics.

"Quest for a self is fundamental to poetry," Hugo writes in his collected prose, *The Triggering Town.* But one doesn't find a misplaced self like a favorite fishing rod. The self, like a poem, is a created and then discovered organism of values, definitions, attitudes, and gestures. (pp. 35-6)

For Richard Hugo, the quest for self and the quest for home are virtually synonymous and are the act of survival that is as necessary as it is temporary. If it were possible to draw a paradigmatic figure for his poems, such a figure would show an oscillating process of men who find themselves in places that ought to have provided support for the struggling human spirit and did not. The men themselves vary according to the roles Hugo assigns them, being clowns, drunks, fishermen, lovers, madmen, travelers, etc., but they are all the self dispossessed. They waken as from a hallucinatory sleep and observe a landscape that is suddenly as readable as a sacred text. Often they feel they have come near home and sometimes believe they have reached it. Inevitably they are disabused and sent back to memory and dream where the journey, and the self-creation, must begin once more. Hugo has developed for this experience a poem which requires an energetic and nominational progression of statements which will be altered, questioned, negated, and restated within a single poem until that construction feels complete and unified. In his first two collections the makers of these statements are usually to be found beside western American rivers, in bars, or at the site of decaying towns. In the third collection, *Good Luck In Cracked Italian,* the speaker is a more autobiographical Hugo, an ex-World War II bombardier who has returned to the Italy he occupied. In whatever disguise, as fisherman or comrade or traveler, the man at the center of Hugo's attention continues to observe, to state, to seek his way home. . . . (p. 36)

All the towns of Italy that Hugo visits and all the wonderfully obsessive places of his poems—Kalalock, Kapowsin, Tahola, Maratea, Missoula, Silver Star, Philipsburg, Ten Sleep, Wisdom—are stages upon which Hugo plays out his dual quest. They are not intrinsically important to the particular poem he writes but rather are stages on the map of his progress, a progress that is the spirit's as much as it is in any poet of our time. Indeed, Hugo is fascinated with maps and they recur throughout his work because they spatialize what would otherwise have to be a linear and narrative progression. But his *home* does not lie on any map. It exists inside language alone, in poems, so that language itself becomes not merely the referent of what is real but the literal container and shaper of what is real. To invite all those places into the poem is, therefore, to give them a chance to live, to exercise their values once more in the life of the speaker. This in turn allows the speaker to test his evolving self. In *The Triggering Town,* Hugo writes: "To feel that you are a wrong thing in a right world should lead a poet to be highly self-critical in the act of writing." Of course he means poets ought to feel humility. But he also means that the opposition of communal values and the self's values may lead to home and all that that means. It may lead to a proper vision. It is worth remarking here that this attitude separates Hugo from many of his contemporaries. For them the world is usually wrong, while Hugo imagines himself wrong and the world the victim of his transgressions. Indeed, the underlying conviction of Hugo's vision is that home, which waits only in the imagination, cannot be reached precisely because men continue to violate the spirit. That is, they do not relive to the point of understanding and even forgiveness the acts and moments of their dispossession. But this is exactly what Hugo does in his best single volume, *The Lady in Kicking Horse Reservoir*. . . . (pp. 36-7)

It is that journey to the place which Hugo believes might allow a wrong self the chance of getting right that his dramatis personae continually undertake. Such figures are, reductively, the haves and have-nots. They form a rough society of the beautiful, the rich, the blonde, the sexy on one hand and the ugly, the poor, the lonely, the frustrated on the other. Hugo's women tend to be extremes of happy mothers or girls gone mad. His men tend to be domineering officials (mayors, cops, etc.) or Hemingwayesque survivors. But though he portrays a society of belongers and outsiders, the only finally safe and sanctified characters are those who possess vision and courage. He frequently causes such men to be fishermen, and he is not unaware of the fishermen's traditional role as a quasi-religious art figure, a visionary. . . . [They] are the survivors. They gather in bars and cantinas within the fellowship of shared vision and frontier virtues: courage, loyalty, self-reliance, tolerance, affection— what one expects from home. Bars become, as in **"Death of the Kapowsin Tavern,"** recognizably home as well as "the temple and our sanctuary."

But getting right, for Richard Hugo, is not, as it may seem, a matter of cultivating a Romantic reentry into the companionship of bars or even the solidarity with Nature which seems so much a part of his vision. One cannot fail to see that in the end the picture he hangs on the wall is not a pastoral ideal at all. If towns represent one kind of dispossession and anonymity, Nature is an even more implacable anonymity and it is alien to man. In *The Triggering Town* Hugo writes: "I've found anonymity to be wonderfully seductive. Something pulls some of us back from that tempting disappearance." That something is art. Those who pull back most are those who achieve vision, who learn to value the mysteries of existence, what Hugo calls the "unknowns." Hugo's art, again, requires his spatial depiction of impacted reality in order to suggest, rather than consecutively follow, the journey of the self away from anonymity and toward a substantial existence. Hugo wants to depict the life of the spirit not in mystical phrases and leaps but

in the most realistic terms he can manage, a spiritual realism very much like that of a Bosch or Breughel.

It is this spiritual realism which causes Hugo to construct an almost coded vocabulary. If his tones are usually mournful and celebratory, his words are verbs and nouns jammed together with emotional weight and telescopic accuracy. Who describes death better than Hugo saying "the long starch of his side begins"? Again, in the *Triggering Town,* Hugo speaks of his intention: "You are after those words you can own and ways of putting them in phrases and lines that are yours by right of obsessive musical deed. . . . Your words used your way will generate your meanings. . . . Your way of writing locates, even creates, your inner life." He believes that language is indivisible and organic, that the vitality of life depends literally on the power of words to re-new, re-view, and re-say what would otherwise invisibly degenerate, decay, and disappear into anonymity. Readers of Hugo's poems well know his symbolic code of colors, of dominant grays, the continuous use of wind and cold and north to suggest the forces of dissolution and death, the vitality and deception implied by beautiful waters and grasses and trees, the chilling evidence of minimal survival portrayed in abondoned buildings, rotting farm implements, polluted rivers, girls turned to barking dogs. All these, used repeatedly, form the vocabulary of what he calls "the world / of black dazzle" which only the essentially wild, essentially visionary self can heroically resist. Or, it may be, understand passionately enough to express in poems we must learn to read not as discrete successes or failures but as the long and continuous reading of the landscape of the spirit which is the great accomplishment of this *Selected Poems.* This is the act, as Hugo describes it in *The Triggering Town,* of "receiving, responding, converting and appropriating," an act of scavenging, reviving, of holding on, sticking, using the world, of surviving. He reminds us in his poems that though we are in harm's way if we are alive it is nevertheless our glory and our responsibility to live according to the values that most enhance each other's being. That is to say, Hugo returns us to man's ancient dream of the free and vital self in a home community of selves. That is precisely the point of that abandoned picture in **"1614 Boren"** just as it is the paradox at the heart of the American experiment in nationhood.

Hugo is a particularly American poet in his insistence on the independent self's survival and the need of a home community for self's definitions. Perhaps it is clear by now that I think we most understand his art by viewing him as a player of roles, not as a self-revealing *miserable.* His exaggeration of himself as the most offensive social outlaw proceeds from his need to dramatize the deeply fundamental American dream (and paradox) of individuality and communal identity. He testifies to what Americans have believed to be humanly decent and permanent as well as to what we break by ineptness, ignorance, greed, and malice. He has the spirit of Melville and Warren in telling us how dark a thing man is. His poems depend upon his own hard self-accusations: he drinks too much, he wastes himself, he lacks courage, he is fat, ugly, uneducated, unsophisticated, inferior, an orphan. Who among us isn't all that? Who isn't a wrong thing in a right place? And who doesn't carry imagination's dream of getting right, that particular fervor of our national mission? . . . But Hugo's real genius forces him to say "I did lots of things and I'm myself / to live with, bad as any German." So are we all. And that is why Hugo says "An act of imagination is an act of self-acceptance." (pp. 37-8)

[If] my way of looking at Hugo's poems seems odd, it will appear outrageous to claim that he is a tragic poet in the manner of Yeats, yet I think his poems derive their resonance from the irresolvable confrontation of dream and fact whose dramatic embodiment in strongly musical language releases the human spirit to joy. Though his hob-nailed lines throb through the gray towns of depair, Hugo is neither cynical nor pessimistic, nor even solipsistic. If there is any lingering connection with his teacher Roethke, it is that insistent search for joy in the revelations of the least things in this world, for he knows that only there do the truths remain and only the true poet can draw forth those small songs of enduring vitality. In spite of all his protestations of fear, inadequacy, and degradation, Richard Hugo does not and will not shrink from the risk of being thought a sentimental fool. For him the poem is neither a sigh for silence nor a crafty toy, but the necessary exploration of simple and inexhaustible love that is freedom. . . . The tragic poet of joy is a paradox but not an impossibility. In the debris and folly of human history imagination finds that picture of hope on the wall of **"1614 Boren"** because it put it there, because imagination and song are the homes which sanctify those virtues without which we are less than men. Hugo conquers loss by finding in the world the continuing evidence of love, beauty, courage, fidelity, forgiveness, and passion. He helps us to know and possess our lives. . . .

[Mostly, Hugo thinks] of himself as a carrier of hope. In *The Triggering Town* he writes: "Hope for what? I don't know. Maybe hope that humanity will always survive civilization." Civilization, many of us are always saying, is what we lack. Hugo knows better, knows that this is the anonymity which buries the fierce individual, and knows that the poet does not speak to crowds but to the single beleaguered spirit. This is the speech of survival that is like a drumbeat. (p. 38)

> Dave Smith, "Getting Right: Richard Hugo's 'Selected Poems' and 'The Triggering Town'," in The American Poetry Review, Vol. 10, No. 5, September-October, 1981, pp. 34-8.

MICHAEL S. ALLEN

Rejected. Humiliated. Degraded. Again and again when speaking in interviews, autobiographical essays, and poems, Richard Hugo brings these words into the discussion of his life. Besides offering, as Roethke had, a psychological theory for writing from obsession, Hugo also talks freely about the psychological problems in his past, covering the bleak areas of his life with an evenhandedness free from self-pity or posturing, admitting the power of emotional forces that we are sometimes born with and sometimes learn to submit to too easily. His talking about such matters in interviews and essays provides a basis for understanding the importance of those poems scattered throughout his work that refer to loss and degradation. Poems like **"Between the Bridges," "Neighbor," "The Way a Ghost Dissolves," "No Bells to Believe," "Duwamish,"** and others from *A Run of Jacks* (1961) contain a presence of hurt that cannot be missed. They stand as a tacit admission of the importance, for survival in this world, of integrating and making whole a sense of self.

Hugo's problems are always tied to specific forces—economic, regional, historical, personal—that make the grist for the mill of his poetic obsessions. Hugo is very much *the* American Depression poet, coming to prominence forty years after that great economic shock haunted his childhood and that of a whole generation of Americans. The Depression shaped his consciousness of need, leaving a background from which he struggled to escape. . . . Poverty haunts him, with its unglamorous ache; it infests the town he carries with him, wherever he goes, as in this poignant opening to one of the best of his "letter poems," **"Letter to Levertov from Butte."** . . . This town may be Butte, Montana, but the town that Hugo carries with him is Seattle, more specifically, Hugo's working-class neighborhood just outside Seattle, White Center. He carries that town with him since what he sees, in any town, is an organization of human society that allows the hurts of poverty to ruin people's lives.

Next to White Center, when Hugo was growing up, were two other working-class neighborhoods, Riverside and Youngstown, where Hugo had most of his early friends. There, near the Duwamish River, the boys saw every day "the castle, the hill, West Seattle, where we would go to high school.". . . [West Seattle represented] the eternal presence of the ideal: the social acceptance and economic confidence that are just out of reach. The ideal could be had with money. Attaining the ideal meant being beautiful and safe, secure in the knowledge of power, and being able to understand and control social and economic realities. Money was the key to power, beauty, and love. Without money, faces were not calm, want was real, and love was something spurred by need.

Beneath the lack of money—the dispossession from society and the things of this world—lay another dispossession: Richard Hugo was born Richard Hogan, the son of a father who deserted his teenaged wife, Hugo's mother; she, in turn, left her infant son to be brought up by her parents. When she later married a man named Hugo, young Richard decided that that would be his surname. Thus a double dispossession lies behind Hugo's early poems. In some ways his first two books, *A Run of Jacks* and *Death of the Kapowsin Tavern* (1965), are haunted by the intertwining of those two emotional scars: his personal tragedy is seen in economic terms, and economic degradation is seen as intensely personal. A poem from Hugo's second book, **"Houses Lie, Believe the Lying Sea,"** indicates the depth at which those two scars join. (pp. 43-5)

[In this poem] Hugo's experience in the abandoned house stands as a paradigm for those other images, scattered through so many poems, of shacks, tenements, peeling slats, and rooms that don't feel right. In such poems as **"Hideout," "Between the Bridges," "No Bells to Believe,"** and **"Kapowsin,"** the houses or buildings stand, sometimes barely, as aspects of failure highlighted by the power and beauty of the natural landscape, often the sea. Critically, an opposition between the poverty of Hugo's neighborhood and the wealth of West Seattle may be implied in such contrasts between ruined buildings and rich natural imagery, but the image of the sea is used in a more complex way. The sea beyond the poor houses is rich, inaccessible, and powerful, and its power is as inaccessible to money as it is to poverty. The poor, in their feeling for their lives and surroundings, do have some claim on the power of the sea; they are tied to it economically and even literally, as they live along the banks of the river that leads to it.

Not merely metaphor, the sea is a tangible presence that demands the attention of all workers in Riverside and Youngstown, fishermen or mill workers. Whatever their fathers do, the boys of those neighborhoods fish and learn that men have fights in taverns by the river. This is the ethic that Hugo, left mainly alone by his grandparents, adopted as a means to survive. An unquestioned power in his life, the sea becomes part of the psychological landscape of his poetry.

Very much a part of the experience of poverty, the almost palpable sensation of being tied to a landscape or seascape that provides jobs, work, and a way to survive has been studied by psychiatrist Robert Coles in his monumental work, *Children of Crisis*. (pp. 46-7)

There are obvious connections between the emotional lives that Coles has described and the life that Hugo has spoken of in his poetry and prose: the same hurt, sense of worthlessness, boredom, need, and momentary release from the necessity of work. Though his life, even during the Depression, was not characterized by the utter desolation of the migrants' lives, Hugo can claim the feelings of the very poor as his own partly through the heightening effect of the personal desertions in his life. With his greater sense of self and easier economic life, he gains strength to look at his and others' poverty and to feel his way to a language that adequately expresses that pain.

For Hugo the pain goes deeper than the poverty that engenders it. The psychological dislocation that arises from a childhood desertion can create the same sense of degradation and unworthiness that underlay the surrounding experience of poverty in his neighborhood. The two worlds, outside the house and inside the home, are connected by that same spoiled water of failure and humiliation. The psychological hurt complements the economic need; the constant burden of work is like the constant search for a sense of self-worth; the anger toward money and prestige parallels the deep internal anger arising from being betrayed and deserted. (pp. 47-8)

As the migrant children do, Hugo must learn to work with what he has. His being reared by his grandparents shaped his sense of self and his relation to the society around him. It also left him with a developed sensitivity to the fragility of life for the old and with the greater sense of boredom for a boy brought up among tired and defeated people. (p. 48)

The presence of the old—whether people, objects, or even ideas— is widespread in Hugo's poetry. At times the land itself is old, something our contemporary culture is losing sight of, like a road along the interstate highway. Certainly houses are old, as in **"Houses Lie, Believe the Lying Sea."** What is old needs attention, affection, understanding, and help. The old have as fragile and precarious an existence as does a young boy; in Hugo's poetry this attention to the old is not the expression of some predisposed ethic but a necessary part of the poet's coming to know himself. (p. 49)

Hugo's sensitivity to the old is tied to an awareness of the abuses of power: "the value of the old" is a problem linked with "the value of the cruel." In this poem, placed in Indiana at a safe distance from Seattle, Hugo can have moments of fun with the problem, can show the mixed feeling of "on that plate, a rose survives the cracks" and "Let's run and love the old and know tomorrow / whatever trails our running leaves in air / a tiny crone will price and call antique." But the poem ends on a more ominous note: an antique doughboy levels his bayonet "level as your frown / when salesmen come . . . their baskets heavy / with those bullets armies wouldn't buy." Behind the play of fragility and the small cruelties of age is something as powerful and as cruel as a pyromaniac and as economically unethical as a salesman trying to foist bad goods on unsuspecting customers.

"The value of the old" is an extension of Hugo's youthful sensitivity to his grandparents. Early in his poetic career he dealt with the important presence of his grandmother in **"The Way a Ghost Dissolves."** With her life bounded by hard work, need, faith, and age, she is seen by Hugo as a ghost. The imagery of the poem, though placed outdoors, reinforces an interior, "close" feeling by playing with those boundaries. . . . The ghost dissolves in an essentially passive acceptance of whatever comes. Behind the work is the earth's reaction, "provided," as if all of the woman's activity is circumscribed by that agrarian patience that has often given more to the land than it has gained in return. Hugo claims the life of this ghost as his own future.

> I will garden on the double run,
> my rhythm obvious in ringing rakes,
> and trust in fate to keep me poor and kind
>
> and work until my heart is short;
> then go out slowly with a feeble grin,
> my fingers flexing but my eyes gone gray
> from cramps and lack of oxygen.

The verbs outline the life set forth in the whole poem: "garden," "trust," "work," "go out," "gone." Early in his career Hugo sees his life locked in the same heartless working routine his grandparents had survived.

"The Way a Ghost Dissolves" is a touching and frightening poem: frightening in that such a life will be lived again, contained by a force so strong that a man can see his life set before him, closed in the same way that age closes the lives of us all. Such an emotional condition is nearly barren, even ghostly. Indeed the last image of the poem is simple suffocation. Surely there is some other life to imagine, something else for a young man to do.

There is: in the neighborhood outside the house where boys played themselves to toughness, jeering at Greek fishermen, hiding in abandoned mills, and finding fights. Many men have known this world while growing up. . . . (pp. 50-1)

One remembers an earlier Hugo statement: "When we were kids, making a living, even finding a job, was tough." For a boy who feels the effects of poverty and rejection, such an image can become the vehicle for several unspoken feelings: in a world where survival is a constant question, being tough can mean being someone who cannot be destroyed, who is not hurt deeply by the dangers that happen daily; someone who can go on, tap some power beyond that of normal beaten-down reality, and win. This tough, self-reliant masculinity grows to be a central image in Hugo's poetry: the archetypal western loner, so self-reliant, American, and tough that his emotional life feels gray like a jail, as in **"Degrees of Gray in Philipsburg."**

But there is a dimension to masculine toughness that gains clairty when . . . compared to the guiding image of **"The Way a Ghost Dissolves."** A young boy must survive not only the tough world of poverty but also the passive acceptance of such a defeated life. . . . [In his poetry Hugo shows anger, an instinct to fight in whatever way he can to protect what self-worth he has.] That anger is a defense is now a psychological truism, but it is defense at the bottom line and therefore an emotional state that the poor know well.

"Neighbor" offers a masculine parallel to **"The Way a Ghost Dissolves"** and shows anger turned on itself in the image of a drunk lying flat in the garden that Hugo's grandmother worked devotedly. . . . It's funny, this parody of socially accepted manners, and Hugo makes the fun gentle and polite. As in any number of comic sketches, the drunk wants only to be liked and is so compliant that he has to be "helped and held." But this compliance masks—as Karen Horney pointed out in her famous study, *Our Inner Conflicts*—a lot of anger, a hatred so severe that a man may kill himself emotionally by bending over to deny its existence.

Getting drunk is a way to survive the hurt of poverty and the sense of worthlessness that develops into self-hatred. As Hugo imagines the scene, he identifies with the drunk, helps him, knows his habits and the shack where he lives. Later Hugo came to realize that **"Neighbor"** had been "no idle curiosity, no chance subject for a poem. I felt I might very well end up that way, and to this day the idea isn't unattractive." Such a statement demonstrates the depths of Hugo's sense of defeat and indicates the depth of struggle he has had with alcoholism. In this poem, resignation, defeat, and need combine to unlock a further area of the landscape of the imagination. (pp. 52-3)

[Anger] is just beneath the polite and comic surface; as it emerges we feel how well Hugo has unlocked this inner landscape, to bring the reader that mixture of disdain and sympathy evident in the final stanza.

> I hear he's dead, and wait now on my porch.
> He must be in his shack. The wagon's
> due to come and take him where they take
> late alcoholics, probably called Farm's End.
> I plan my frown, certain he'll be carried out
> bleeding from the corners of his grin. . . .

Most of the language is almost casual, but there is an underlying care: the wagon is "due to come," and the unseen officials will take the neighbor "where they take / late alcoholics"— the assonance and word choice are gentle, in fact, polite. They add a heavy irony to the casual prose of "probably called Farm's End," and we remember the drunk at the beginning of the poem, face down in the beets. The frown the poet assumes is protective, a social mask meant to insulate him from the bloody image certain to come into view as the drunk is carried out.

The way **"Neighbor"** carefully traces the connections of inner landscape and social failure shows us how deeply Hugo is aware of the pity and anger that are the emotional condition of the poor. Like the poor in Coles's book, Hugo's drunk feels a resignation and a loss of self-esteem that make him keep his place and be polite. And, as Coles described it, beneath the resignation is rage, directed more often toward self than toward society. The imaginative power of that rage is unlocked in Hugo's poetry. Anger seems to be a force welling from the unconscious, taking landscapes or figures of loss and poverty and making them felt presences, momentarily made whole as that anger raises them up to full height and then allows them to collapse. A major source of Hugo's poetry, that deep rage beneath the surface pity and politeness of the poor is both let loose and channeled in the language of the poems. The drunk does not control his rage; he is controlled and killed by it. The poet, in making the patterns of sound and images that are the poem, controls his own anger by triggering the release of that emotional energy that can kill. It is an imaginative act that asks for and evokes a fundamental sympathy on the part of the reader as the unlocking of the inner landscape becomes an occasion for the sharing of emotional health.

With Hugo's first two books we find a statement and an exploration of the inner landscape of poverty. In *A Run of Jacks* that statement is clear; the emotional scars of poverty are evident. In *Death of the Kapowsin Tavern* the statement takes on larger dimensions and assumes a regional outline that identifies the Pacific Northwest with the landscape of poverty and anger. There are moments, of course, when the burden of past hurt lifts and the sheer natural energy and beauty of the regional landscape are an illumination. But not all discoveries are beautiful and not all illuminations carry with them the confidence that the world is beautiful and right. There are drunks in taverns, rivers full of crud, and shacks where boys leave home early and never want to go back. The energy in Hugo's poetry owes much of its richness to that hurt that carries the weight of pain from the experience of poverty. (pp. 53-4)

> *Michael S. Allen, in his* We Are Called Human: The Poetry of Richard Hugo, *The University of Arkansas Press, 1982, 158 p.*

PETER ANDREWS

To a considerable degree an adventure novel represents a bargain struck between the reader and the author. I am willing to suspend my disbelief to the fullest if it will help the narrative get under way. But the author has to promise me that I will not be made to look like a fool if I do. In **"The Hitler Diaries,"** despite recent events that have made the plot seem prophetic, Richard Hugo fails to live up to his end of the deal and what might have been a promising novel falls apart almost as quickly as the author puts it together.

Mr. Hugo starts with the interesting premise that during the war Adolf Hitler kept a secret diary which has been unearthed and is now being offered to an American publisher for $10 million. The diary contains some political dynamite that starts off a continent-wide string of murders which may have been committed by Communists or Neo-Fascists or both. So far, so good. I am willing to believe that if Mr. Hugo wants me to. But then he goes on to create a spider's web of intrigue and leaves out the spider.

First we have the diary itself, which from the brief selection we are initially offered reads more like lost pages from the Kama Sutra, contradicting, without a word of explanation, everything we know about Hitler. Then, although men are prepared to murder for the diary, no one, including the publisher who is coughing up the $10 million, has time to read it. Or if they do, they don't bother to tell us about it. Finally another paragraph of the diaries is revealed; it contains a reference to a contemporary Kremlin figure so mundane I can not imagine that anyone in the politburo would turn a hair.

Mr. Hugo begins with an international bombshell and ends up with a paper noisemaker at a children's birthday party. (pp. 42-3)

> *Peter Andrews, "Blasting Nasty Nazis," in* The New York Times Book Review, *May 22, 1983, pp. 42-3.**

DAVE SMITH

Richard Hugo, widely considered the preeminent poet of Western America, proclaimed, "those words you can own . . . by right of obsessive musical deed." His subject was the American orphan, himself, refracted by scenes, people, weather, objects and creatures. Reading him is like browsing through second-hand shops with Wallace Stevens and Ernest Hemingway, chanting the mute histories of each cracked mirror and dented spittoon. Hugo felt and voiced the unprivileged, inarticulate world. His poems, although they are rarely outright narratives, tell the tale of the American search for identity and knowledge from the underbelly. One might say of him what he wrote about President Kennedy: "He was not afraid of what we are." His is sometimes clunky, plodding poetry, but his collected work is a surprising, remarkable song of courage that penetrates inner landscapes. In **"Making Certain It Goes On"**—a welcome, stubby, wandering, and final collection—Richard Hugo, like Thoreau, earned the right to look any man in the face.

To Hugo poetry wasn't ethical or moral commentary in lines, but every poem was an instruction. To him the poem was life's harsh music learned in the school of hard knocks. He saw man as cruel, hurt and hurting, incapable of much improvement, and ill-prepared for the little wisdom he can cull from the elements that doom him to the loss and oblivion Hugo called "north." . . .

Against this implacable condition, Hugo set himself to witness what mattered—the struggle to survive with intense feeling, pell-mell energy, utter and immediate honesty. . . . He went continuously home—to all the American homes, as he would have said, we had and never had. (p. 12)

John Updike's Rabbit would have understood Hugo's running. . . . He was on the road for home. Lord, how he looked! I can think of no poet whose verbal and emotional odometer laid on so many miles. His finest individual books, **"The Lady In Kicking Horse Reservoir"** (1973) and **"What Thou Lovest Well Remains American"** (1975), are psychic maps that end in the secret, splendid places we now call "Hugo's." He took us to Silver Star, Wisdom, Ovando, Ten Sleep, Camas and Bearpaw. He rested at waters named Kicking Horse, Pishkun, Sweathouse, Napi, Lone Lake, Taholah and Drummond. In **"The Triggering Town"** (1979), a collection of prose, he wrote: "Take someone you emotionally trust, a friend or lover, to a town you like the looks of but know little about, and show your companion around the town in the poem. . . . You know here you are and that is a source of stability."

He was looking for what he called the "knowns" and, as if his readers were his companions, he was our guide to the permanent, passionate, not yet completely civilized, not entirely homogenized life where we might confront and survive degradation, shame and deterioration. Whether it was bar, grassy bank, or a night softball field, he ran to a place of communion where one might be abused, hated, or loved, but not ignored or anonymous. There one could wail, know names, dance, maybe find women, at least find music and howl back at "weather, that lone surviving god." He took us to see the cruelty, rage, oppression and debris of a town and spirit in **"Degrees of Gray In Philipsburg."** Here all defeats seemed fused in that "ancient kiss / still burning out your eyes" and the world loomed so bad that death appeared seductive in the guise of a lifelong prisoner. Hugo wasn't running toward that. He was running for his life. "You tell him no. You're talking to yourself. / The car that brought you here still runs."

He found his aggressive ring-tailed roaring voice early and never abandoned its drumming iambics or his stark and alliterative sentences that account for so many unusually memorable, epigrammatic lines, such as, "We were renegade when God had gills." And he favored quick cinematic cuts, quirkily placed adjectives and stanzas that function like chapters in fiction. His fulcrum was the hypothesis, "Say your life broke

down." He called his way of writing style and named it "the adhesive force. This adhesive force will be your way of writing." It was, in Ezra Pound's formula, "uncounterfeitable," and unlike most of his contemporaries, Hugo did not seriously alter it in successive books. His form was right for what he wanted—intensity, immediacy, and verbal velocity, the panoramic and the telescopic. He made the poem a state of mind and a force field. Yet he felt it wasn't enough.

In the poems in **"13 Letters and 13 Dreams"** (1977) he extended and relaxed his usual line and admitted prose elements. It is impossible to convey in a review how much information, story, joke, gossip, vitality and, often enough, prattle the book carries. We learn about his hip injury, his interest in civic referendums, his experience with whores, loneliness, barbers, offended bar-owners who read about themselves in his poems in The New Yorker and the final payment of his mortgage (due in 2001). He eats, drinks, fishes, cruises and chatters about Isaac Bashevis Singer, Herbert Gold, Milton, Keats, Mr. Chips, C. C. Rider, and Perry Mason.

After that book appeared he asked me if I thought it was a mistake, recognizing, I think, that its slack structure, garrulous personality and huge appetite were so at odds with the coolly corseted taste of academics and their journals. Flattered that he asked, I nevertheless said it was a mistake. Now, when I read **"Letter to Goldbarth from Big Fork"** where he writes, "Dear Albert. This is a wholesome town. Really. Cherries grow / big here and all summer a charming theater puts on / worthy productions," and drones on like a state brochure hack, I think I was right. But I was wrong. It matters that a poet's work should create a large, unified and resonant image of man. That is why poets have written sequences. **"31 Letters and 31 Dreams"** is Hugo's version of John Berryman's "Dream Songs," Robert Lowell's "History" and even William Carlos Williams's "Paterson." If its music is more the honking and wheezing of a one-man band than we might wish, the image of a man bearing himself with relentless introspection, intelligence, courage and withering good humor is one we haven't yet ceased to need.

Though he would never be a serene poet, his collected poems show Hugo turning toward a calm peace that would mark his best work in **"White Center"** (1980) and **"The Right Madness On Skye"** (1980), and in the 22 new poems in this volume. (pp. 12-13)

Among the new poems included in **"Making Certain It Goes On"** Hugo was still driving, looking, and naming. If we had not noticed before that his great gift was the elegy, we see it now in the poems about Anthony Ostroff, Thomas Wolfe, Zen Hofman and the Confederate graves in Little Rock. Two of his best poems are here—**"Salt Water Story"** and **"Here, but Unable to Answer,"** the only poem which unequivocally addressed and celebrated his father.

There is also one that ought to make granite weep. Long after they were young comrades, Hugo and James Wright fondly called each other Ed Bedford, after a surly tavern keeper they met when the Wrights and Hugos had once vacationed together. Each could laugh at the Bedford in the other, and also love him. In **"Last Words to James Wright"** Hugo is flying to New York for a reading, remembering his great friend whose courage in poetry and struggles with alcohol, depression and cancer had been exemplary. Why should we not hope for a gray town and a clear river where the poets wait and speak with such honor as this poem confers upon us all? . . .

Richard Hugo died in 1982. He did not doubt his work would go on. It will. (p. 13)

Dave Smith, "Lyrics for Life's Harsh Music," in The New York Times Book Review, February 26, 1984, pp. 12-13.

DON BOGEN

Richard Hugo is not well served by this volume of collected poems [*Making Certain It Goes On*]. His eight large books are crammed together here, with poems beginning and ending in mid-page, some annoying typographical errors—including an abrupt change in the typeface of one poem—and a welter of blurbs cluttering the dust jacket. The title, with its fashionable gerund and open-ended tone, seems almost a parody of current literary fads. As a phrase, "making certain it goes on" is awkwardly colloquial and vague—making certain *what* goes on? As a title for twenty years of a man's work, it lacks dignity. Yet even with a cleaner format, more stringent proofreading and a sensible title, such a collection would not display Hugo's work to its best advantage. Hugo published a great amount of poetry during his lifetime, an average of a book every two and a half years between 1961 and 1980, and his verse underwent few major stylistic or thematic developments. Bringing all his poems together in a lump like this exaggerates the essential sameness of much of his work.

Hugo wrote mostly about places and himself. This combination of subjects can make the collection seem dully repetitive: the poet in the rain forest, the poet at the beach, the poet leaving the Italian village, etc. A number of the pieces, particularly those set in nature, do not rise above the level of verbal post-cards. (p. 324)

The lyricism of Hugo's poetry is balanced by his insistently colloquial tone. Like others of his generation, Hugo worked to develop a poetic voice that would sound authentic and nat-ural, not academic. There is, unfortunately, a typical pose that comes along with this, that of poet as regular guy, sensitive but not particularly artistic or intellectual. After several poems this stance can become annoying. . . . There is an awkward element of self-pity in some of Hugo's work, especially the poems about bars, dance halls and other scenes of failed ro-mance. The stance of poet as regular guy creates problems in happier pieces as well. The letter poems of *31 Letters and 13 Dreams* (1977), most of which are to friends and well-known fellow poets, can be disturbingly ingratiating, especially when Hugo catalogues his own and his friends' successes in middle age. Lines like "Dear Vi: You were great at the Roethke festival this summer / in Portland" and "Dear John: Great to see your long-coming, well-crafted book / getting good re-views" are rhythmically slack and colorless—they could be snippets from anyone's mail.

But *31 Letters and 13 Dreams* exaggerates the weaknesses of Hugo's typical pose and style. In his best poems, he leaves such posturing behind and engages fundamental social issues: alienation, community, loss. No one has written more evoc-atively of a certain kind of American place: the mean small towns of an indifferent Western landscape, in which the raw-ness of our history is most exposed. . . . It is a land of failures—economic, social, personal—and the poet delineates the mar-ginal lives of its inhabitants with humor, acceptance and lyric grace. . . . [In his] poems on decaying Western scenes, Hugo is the consummate American elegist, consoling us for the blasted places of our history and reminding us that human warmth can still survive.

Hugo's laments for Silver Star, Philipsburg, Drummond and other washed-out towns are thoughtful and moving, but the attitude of consolation may finally be a little too easy. His work is considerably stronger, I think, when it adopts a more critical approach to the pain of history. In certain odd poems throughout his career—a study of Mission Carmel in his first book, a look at a cemetery in Elkhorn from the work of the mid-1970s—Hugo confronts a suffering more deeply rooted than the malaise of lonely shopkeepers and former mill hands. His response is not sympathy and acceptance but controlled anger and clarifying irony. . . . Hugo does some of his best work with subjects whom simple pity cannot help.

This more complex work culminates in his last two books, *The Right Madness on Skye* and *White Center*, both published in 1980. Though the latter includes a few postcard pieces and some fairly predictable consolations, it also shows a new per-spective that transcends the typical stance of Hugo's previous work. Much of *White Center* is about the intractability of the past, its resistance to the distortions of nostalgia or self-ac-commodating verse. . . . *White Center* is, finally, a book that rejects things: glamorous self-dramatizing gestures, the preoc-cupation with beautiful losers in small towns, boozy myths of sensitivity. The emotional force behind this rejection invigo-rates a good deal of the writing. . . . (pp. 324-25)

In *The Right Madness on Skye* Hugo's increased self-awareness adds perspective to his studies of battles, ruined castles and crumbling Scottish graveyards. Easy poetic sympathy for the oppressed is replaced by a more accurate vision of what art can and cannot do. . . . Recognizing the limits of imagination, Hugo attempts more complex and thoughtful poems in this book, and the result is his tightest and most uniformly suc-cessful volume.

There is a tomblike finality about any posthumous collection, but it is especially distressing when the poet's last work was his best. Richard Hugo's accomplishments tend to get lost in the sheer bulk of *Making Certain It Goes On*. Yet there are important poems here. What we will come to value in Hugo's poetry, I think, is not his easygoing pose and the repetitive work it produced but the moments of clarity that delineate human loss. (p. 326)

Don Bogen, "American Elegies," in The Nation, Vol. 238, No. 10, March 17, 1984, pp. 324-26.

LEX RUNCIMAN

Written after Richard Hugo's lung surgery in 1981, and com-pleted just before his death in October of 1982, the poems of *Sea Lanes Out* are dominated by two competing yet comple-mentary impulses: a sense of mortality on one hand, and per-sistence on the other. The mortality finds its expression in elegies, for Harold Herndon (owner of the Milltown bar of Hugo's earlier famous poem), for Hugo's father, for Zen Hoff-man "in his powered wheelchair," for the "Confederate Graves in Little Rock," for Hugo's childhood house "now a church parking lot. . . ." Against such destructions and provoked by them are the facts of memory, the effort to remember, and Hugo's insistence that imagination can assert people amount to more than we know. It is such acts of imagination which finally dominate these poems, many of them ending in images of persistence and even of wonder.

The poem **"A Death in the Aquarium"** is an instructive example. The facts of the poem's narrative are few but they are clear: an unidentified man has shot himself "in full sight / of the red Irish lord and the rare / albino sea perch." No note is found, no identification, no explanation; "a year later the case was filed unsolved." The poem closes with a series of unanswered questions, questions which in their phrasing assert our kinship with this unidentified man, a kinship both biological and amazing. . . . (p. 51)

As emotionally difficult as this last book is to read—and for those who knew Hugo, or studied with him, or heard him, it is a difficult book to read because it is last—to do so is to confirm again Hugo's complex genius for place. Characteristically Hugo's poems appropriate a place in order to belong to it and in it. They accomplish, though frequently at great psychic cost, what Hugo refers to in **"Distances"** as the "trick." When learned, it allows us to "live in this world, neighbor to goat, / neighbor to trout. . . ." For Hugo, a writer whose poems reveal little of conventional religious belief, landscape is the constant, the source of faith. (pp. 51-2)

Those writers whom we think of as having in some fundamental way defined western American literature are more often fiction writers than poets: A. B. Guthrie, Wallace Stegner, Zane Grey, Frank Waters—the list is not much longer. Richard Hugo's last chapbook, *Sea Lanes Out,* confirms his rightful place among such names. Whether the landscape be Italy or Scotland, Montana or Washington, Hugo has always been a poet of landscape, and a westerner. His rivers, roads, towns, houses, and bars are homes only grudgingly, often indifferently, and only after struggle on the part of those who would be home there. It is Hugo's interior landscape—that intensity of struggle amid bleak revelations—which informs and defines the country of these poems, country which, ugly or not, Richard Hugo never failed to love. (p. 52)

> *Lex Runciman, in a review of "Sea Lanes Out," in* Western American Literature, *Vol. XIX, No. 1, May, 1984, pp. 51-2.*

Susan Isaacs

1943-

American novelist, editor, and critic.

Isaacs is known for the wit and satire of her fiction which explores such subjects as suburbia, marital relationships, and the quest by women for self-fulfillment. Critics attribute her best-selling status and popularity to her accurate rendering of contemporary dialogue, sharp observations about human nature, and her use of comic one-liners to evoke the absurdity of modern living and trends.

(See also *Contemporary Authors*, Vols. 89-92.)

© *Thomas Victor 1984*

KIRKUS REVIEWS

The real mystery about this mystery-comedy-romance [*Compromising Positions*] is how it ever got to be a Book-of-the-Month Club selection. Admittedly, first-novelist Isaacs and her housewife-detective-narrator, Judith Singer, come across with easy wit and likable smartsiness when introducing Judith's Long Island upper-middle-suburbs milieu—the milieu also of Casanova dentist Bruce Fleckstein, whose mysterious murder has Judith all keyed up. And, as curious Judith starts digging up more and more about Dr. Bruce's kinky conquests (including some of Judith's best friends!), we're ready to breeze happily through another blood-and-fluffer, pleasantly forgettable even if the mystery itself happens to be a third-rate puzzle. Isaacs, however, has other ideas. She wants us to take Judith's amateur sleuthing seriously and realistically, to accept it as her way of fulfilling herself. . . . Unfortunately, this welding of the formula mystery-comedy with the self-realization novel is so unconvincing that we end up siding with pompously disapproving husband Bob, who seems to be in one book while Judith dabbles in another, fulfilling herself by wearing her bullet-proof vest as bait in a trap for the killer. The stuffy husband bit and the female lust bit . . . have been done better—and to death—by the Sue Kaufmans and Erica Jongs. And better mysteries are a dime a dozen. In fact, the only things that are Isaacs' own here are that sweetly satiric tone and a sure ear for contemporary dialogue; we look forward to hearing those sassy sounds in far better, less clumsily contrived, books ahead.

A review of "Compromising Positions," in Kirkus Reviews, *Vol. XLVI, No. 3, February 1, 1978, p. 125.*

JACK SULLIVAN

The trouble with "page-turners" is that we often turn the pages quickly because they are awful. We are motivated not so much by "suspense" as by self-preservation.

In ["Compromising Positions"] however, we are motivated—at least for a while—by verbal dexterity and sheer cleverness. . . .

Set on Long Island, the novel satirizes not only thrillers but also suburbia. The narrator is housewife Judith Singer, mother of two, who involves herself in a conventionally grisly, lurid murder mystery because it is "better than facing two weeks' accumulation of laundry" and it is "a change from Sesame Street and chicken pot pies."

It is also a change from a marriage in which the heroine's "usual I'm-not-in-the-mood signal is a mighty yawn as we ascend the stairs. At that moment, we achieve a tacit understanding and he heads for the pajama drawer." If there is an occasionally strident note of knee-jerk feminism in all this, Miss Isaacs' overall aim is so precise, her one-liners so wonderfully funny, that we can hardly complain. . . .

This is deliciously mean stuff, and it is unfortunate that Miss Isaacs doesn't have the nerve to sustain it. She gradually allows her heroine to become bogged down in an elaborate murder case that is as tedious as her laundry and her husband. Miss Isaacs is so good in her opening scenes that when the tone moves from spoofery to straight ratiocination, we're simply not in the mood.

Jack Sullivan, "Solving a Murder Beats Doing Laundry," in The New York Times Book Review, *April 30, 1978, p. 15.*

CHARLES J. KEFFER

[*Compromising Positions*] is a delightful story for several reasons. First, the story line is interesting and suspenseful. Even when it is clear at the end who committed the murder, an unusual twist appears. Secondly, this is somewhat of a socio-logical study. The lives of the people of Shorehaven are bared before the reader. The characters who populate this story and the community are varied: from a religious, almost fanatical, Catholic, to the inane, lonely woman who succumbs to Fleck-stein's overtures, to Judith Singer herself who finds her life with husband, Bob, and two small children basically uneventful and unexciting. Third, for those who like it, there is a little bit of simple romance. Most importantly, there is a writing style that is witty and creative. There are numerous occasions when Ms. Isaacs uses that unique turn of phrase which is most appropriate for the situation. Some readers may be taken aback slightly by some of the language and by an underlying philo-sophical orientation which seems to say that everybody's life is theirs to lead as they see fit. On balance, however, it's a book that I would recommend highly. I can't wait for her next one.

Charles J. Keffer, in a review of "Compromising Positions," in Best Sellers, Vol. 38, No. 5, August, 1978, pp. 151-52.

PUBLISHERS WEEKLY

[Close Relations] is a delightful read. The novel is both a witty analysis of big-city politics, family relationships and the singles scene in Washington and New York—all this accurate, astrin-gent and candid—and a fairy tale love story in which the her-oine finds her Prince Charming almost despite herself.... Isaacs's depiction of ... [the heroine's] family is mercilessly irreverent and wickedly funny. Her ear for dialogue is perfect, especially in the scenes in which her family lecture Marcia on the dangers of a relationship with an Irishman, unleashing a barrage of ethnic slurs that are cruelly hilarious.... The novel is a risible romp throughout—the snappy dialogue yielding up laughs on every page, the love story tender and satisfying, the plot pulsing with adrenalin.

A review of "Close Relations," in Publishers Weekly, Vol. 218, No. 4, July 25, 1980, p. 145.

SUSAN CHEEVER

Susan Isaacs' second novel Close Relations ... focuses on a bright-but-confused woman in her mid-thirties struggling to come to terms with: (a) her commitment to a high-pressure job, speechwriter to William Paterno, president of the council of the City of New York; (b) the kind of sexual appetites which have traditionally been a male prerogative—at least in litera-ture, and (c) a difficult relationship with a gorgeous man who allows her to live with him, but considers marriage out of the question.

The story of Marcia Green is set against a background which is almost a genre by now—the comic Jewish family intent on pressuring her to stop fooling around with that gorgeous creep (needless to say, he's Irish Catholic), and settle down with a nice Jewish boy....

Isaacs deals with this situation with borscht-belt humor which borders on the manic.... She has a lively eye for detail and a tart descriptive style that make this same old story easy to read....

Although the story is punctuated with flashbacks describing a variety of workaday sexual encounters—he did this to me, he

did that to me—Marcia's sexual attraction to the gorgeous Jerry Morrissey is both lyrical and funny. Her lust for him, described in language which limns the clichés of male lust, is sad (because you know he doesn't love her) and hilarious (because of Isaac's witty tone)....

She also succeeds in nailing the hothouse vulgarity and op-pressive pressure tactics of a certain kind of Jewish family once and for all (I hope). And her main character, in spite of a lot of kvetching, is alive enough so that it's easy to care what happens to her, and a cinch to be pleased when what happens is better than anyone ... could have imagined.

But here is the bad news about this funny, readable book. Isaacs' story seems to be constructed entirely to gratify the reader's simplest desires. If she had an original point to make, or a section of real experience that she wanted to describe, it's been lost in the shuffle. This is a book with three happy end-ings, all of them a little hard to believe. Everyone gets her man, and everybody turns out to be right.... There is one good thing about plots which aim to please the reader though. They do.

Susan Cheever, "A Heroine with Chutzpah," in Book World—The Washington Post, August 31, 1980, p. 4.

KATHA POLLITT

You can't blame Susan Isaacs for not wanting to make her second novel Compromising Positions II, but I can't help it, I do. In Compromising Positions, a fed-up, witty, very likable suburban matron tracks down a killer and in the process dis-cards her sexist husband in favor of a sexy cop. The result was a perfect read—it had romance, feminism, murder, and social satire—and since it came out, I've been waiting for a sequel, starring our heroine and her new love as the Nick and Nora Charles of Shorehaven, Long Island. This is not that book.

In Close Relations, Isaacs gives us another wisecracking, ami-ably neurotic heroine—Marcia Green, a 35-year old divorced speechwriter for a New York City councilman—and she places her once more between two men, one nice, one not so nice. This time, though, instead of car pools and PTA meetings, the backdrop is a Democratic gubernatorial primary, and the central question is not who killed the dentist, but this: Will Marcia be able to overcome her loathing for her family long enough to see that the man they are crudely and coldly and for all the wrong reasons pushing her to marry is in fact Mr. Right?

It's a premise as contrived as that of any mystery story. Isaacs is a clever writer, though, and diverts us with her sharp ob-servation of the world in which her characters move. (p. 80)

Jerry Morrissey ... is the fellow that Aunt Estelle, Uncle Julius, and Marcia's widowed mother all want her to dump: He's Irish—i.e., anti-Semitic, unsteady, prone to violence and drink—and anyway, he'll never marry her. The Green-Lin-denbaum clan is easily the crassest, most bigoted Jewish family to appear in print since the Portnoys, and Marcia's need to rebel against them prevents her from seeing the truth: Jerry may be great in bed, but he's conceited and bossy, and he doesn't love her. David Hoffman, on the other hand, is crazy about her, and he's also Jewish, pleasant, smart, kind, and very rich. Will Marcia grow up and grab him? What do you think?

Isaacs's point, of course, is that you don't have to be miserable to be happy. It does, however, help to be rich; in the world of *Close Relations,* only the very wealthy are reasonable and humane, able, say, to enjoy classical music—everyone else is an ethnic grotesque. That bothered me some, and so did the many moments when Marcia's love for David, who really is very nice, seems indistinguishable from her growing eagerness for the way of life she will lead as his wife. Her belated discovery of the joys of luxury is all very well as far as it goes, but do we really want to call it maturity? A novel—even a fluent, frequently clever one like this—needs more to sustain it than the protagonist's realization that having lots of money is heaven on earth, particularly when you don't have to earn it yourself. If I didn't remember that the heroine of *Compromising Positions* cast her lot with a lowly policeman, I'd suspect Isaacs of being a bit of a snob.

> *Katha Pollitt, "Women in Love, and Out: 'Close Relations',"* in New York *Magazine, Vol. 13, No. 39, October 6, 1980, pp. 80-1.*

MICHIKO KAKUTANI

[Susan Isaacs's literary models in **"Almost Paradise"**] appear to be Erich Segal, Judith Krantz and Janet Dailey. To be sure, she has some of their tricks down pat: she manages, in the course of the book, to range over some three generations and two continents, tangle her characters in lots of messy relationships and compromising positions, and for good measure, throw in some incest and a lengthy deathbed scene.

All this should make for fast, if not exactly edifying, reading, but it doesn't. The reader knows from the second page what is going to happen, and the only suspense that remains has to do with how many clichés Miss Isaacs can pack into the remaining 480-odd pages. The characters not only speak in clichés—since much of this book takes place in the movie world, "you're going to be a big star" is a favorite expression—but most of them *are* clichés, devoid of any inner life and equipped with only the most obvious of emotions. . . .

As for Miss Isaacs's style and narrative approach, the first sentence of the book should give you a pretty good idea of where **"Almost Paradise"** is headed: "Jane Cobleigh," it reads, "was on a British Airways Concorde, flying faster than sound to try and reclaim her husband."

> *Michiko Kakutani in a review of "Almost Paradise," in* The New York Times, *Section 3, February 1, 1984, p. 23.*

JONATHAN YARDLEY

Almost Paradise is a commercial novel with aspirations to be something more—aspirations that, unfortunately, it fails by a wide measure to fulfill. Susan Isaacs is an intelligent writer and a perceptive observer of social customs, and if you close your ears to the clanking machinery of her third novel you are likely to be diverted by it. But she wants to do more than provide a mere entertainment. She wants to make a Statement about marriage à la mode; the trouble is that the marriage around which the novel is constructed is so improbable, and the novel itself is so weighted down with the clichés of schlock fiction, that Isaacs' good intentions eventually get swallowed up in the fat pudding she has concocted.

The persons to whom these tens of thousands of words are devoted are Nicholas Cobleigh and his wife Jane, *née* Heissenhuber. *Ach du lieber!* Can anybody out there pronounce these names? Of course not, which is the first of the novel's problems. . . . In trying to make Nicholas Cobleigh seem quintessentially Yankee WASP and Jane Heissenhuber seem quintessentially middlewestern Teutonic, she has given them names that turn them, unwittingly, into caricatures—names that, lying so heavily on the tongue as they do, strain the reader's credulity from the moment they first appear.

Apart from their names, they're mildly interesting people. Jane, to whom we are introduced first, is the daughter of Sally Tompkins, a vaudeville and burlesque performer, and her husband Richard Heissenhuber, a Cincinnati bank clerk whom she had mistakenly imagined to have prospects. Sally dies suddenly when Jane is 3, so her rearing is left to Dorothy, the harridan of a stepmother who slinks in a few months later. In this repressive household (her father repeatedly beats her and makes sexual advances) Jane becomes insecure and self-protective; yet she does not completely lose her innate ebullience, and it begins to reappear when at last she makes her escape to Pembroke College, in Rhode Island.

There she meets Nicholas Cobleigh, a student at Brown University. His parents are, like so many others in this novel, an unlikely pair. His father, James, is a handsome, sharp, tough lawyer; his mother, Winifred, is a horsey, absent-minded heir to the considerable fortune of the Tuttles, who "were not as rich as the Rockefellers or the Mellons, but they were rich enough." . . .

It's not love at first sight, but friendship; Nicholas is pinned to another. But as their involvement with the theater intensifies, and as the dimensions of Nicholas' stage presence begin to emerge in full, they grow ever closer. Finally, on what is to be their last night together, Nicholas at last declares his love for Jane—hers for him has been percolating for months—and in almost no time they are married and testing their talents in summer stock. Even though these are the early '60s and consciousnesses are beginning to be raised, Jane does what numberless women before her had; she throws aside her own career so that her husband may pursue his.

Which Nicholas does to startling effect. Within a decade and a half he hits the jackpot. . . . And up to this point his marriage has remained happy, though in somewhat peculiar circumstances: it has been six years since Jane, the victim of a whopping case of agoraphobia, has left their house in Connecticut. This no doubt helps explain why, when his co-star Laurel Blake comes calling with nothing on under her trench coat, Nicholas is willing—reluctant, but willing.

Well. This could go on forever, and in *Almost Paradise* it just about does. We've already done child abuse and attempted incest, right? We've got the agoraphobia, but that's unfinished business; we need a phobia clinic to cure it, and the presiding psychiatrist on whose couch Jane will find satisfactions even greater than those of the mind. We've got the wife who sacrificed her career for that of her husband, but that's also unfinished business: we need a moment of confrontation in which Nicholas tells her, "You just never had the talent," and then her ultimate vindication when she triumphs as—are you ready for this?—the host of a television talk show. We've got the fling with the co-star, but that too is unfinished; we need a marital separation, and a throbbing love for a younger woman, and a moment of truth.

We get it, every bit of it, and that's the real trouble with *Almost Paradise*. Susan Isaacs, who ought to know better, has been unable to resist the clichés of commercial fiction. *Almost Par-*

adise gives the impression of being a novel that was not so much written as assembled. . . . The prose is too accomplished for this to be the work of Rosemary Rogers or Janet Dailey, but the glossy settings and the trendy troubles are right off the paperback best-seller lists.

That being the case, it's difficult to take *Almost Paradise* as seriously as its author and publisher evidently would like us to. It may aspire to being a consideration of the cords and discords of contemporary marriage, but it's really just another "good read." If that's all you want from it, fine; it is considerably more skillfully done than the run-of-the-mill potboiler, and Isaacs does know how to keep a story rolling along. But if you're looking for more than that, look elsewhere.

> *Jonathan Yardley, "Susan Isaacs' Marriage à la mode," in* Book World—The Washington Post, *February 12, 1984, p. 3.*

ANNA SHAPIRO

[If "**Almost Paradise**"] sounds a bit like a novel of domestic bliss, it is exactly that—for a time. This perfect world doesn't last, however; the serpent enters the garden in the form of family scandal, and bliss turns to crisis. Unfortunately, there is an unintentional split between social stereotypes throughout the book. Jane, her mother and the Jewish theatrical agent Murray King are vibrant wiseacres whose posturings only exaggerate their emotional nakedness, while their gentile counterparts (Nicholas and his family) are privileged drips. There are artistic problems with the book—a reliance on such conventional indicators as looks and money, a less than integral structure of events—but Miss Isaacs keeps the plot boiling, and mostly one is reading too absorbedly to notice.

> *Anna Shapiro, in a review of "Almost Paradise," in* The New York Times Book Review, *February 12, 1984, pp. 20-1.*

JANE OPPENHEIM

[*Almost Paradise*] is a novel about a marriage, or about what becomes a "charade of marriage."

Jane Heissenhuber and Nicholas Cobleigh were of such diverse worlds that it is surprising they met at all, which they did as college seniors. . . .

These two were different—in temperament, in interests, in background. Can there be happiness in "a marriage of opposites"? Can a woman give up dreams of her own career to nurture that of her husband? And can a marriage survive separate love affairs? If such questions start to sound like standard soap fare, Susan Isaacs' very direct style and sensitive writing come to the rescue. What she is saying often becomes less significant than how it is being said. The whole is very apt and timely to the decade in which she is writing.

Setting the stage occupies a good half of *Almost Paradise*. Ms. Isaacs has created real people. She devotes over two hundred pages to presenting their (imaginary) genealogy, ancestry and pedigree. By the time the protagonists face problems, the reader knows the three hundred year route that has made Jane and Nicholas what they are, and has deep insight into their psychological make-up.

Susan Isaacs has a fine sense of suspense. Until the very last pages there is no hint of how her story will end. In essence, she is reminding us that life is too short. . . . We always think there will be time—time to make mistakes, time to correct mistakes. But life is not Paradise—it is only *Almost Paradise*.

> *Jane Oppenheim, in a review of "Almost Paradise," in* Best Sellers, *Vol. 43, No. 12, March, 1984, p. 438.*

Milan Kundera

1929-

Czechoslovakian novelist, dramatist, and poet.

Kundera is one of Czechoslovakia's most important authors, even though much of his work has been banned in his own country and he has lived in Paris since 1975. Rejecting the tenets of socialist realism promoted by the Communist regime under Joseph Stalin, Kundera has instead explored the psychology and emotions of his characters as individuals. His fiction is very complex, often presenting events in a disjointed time frame and from the viewpoint of several characters whose sexual machinations are usually central to the stories.

Although many critics focus on the political disillusionment evident in his work, Kundera claims that there has been too much emphasis on this aspect and he especially dislikes being classified as a dissident writer. In an interview, Kundera commented: "If I write a love story, and there are three lines about Stalin in that story, people will talk about the three lines and forget the rest. . . ." It is probable that critics examine the political implications of his work because of Kundera's involvement in the political and cultural turmoils of Czechoslovakia. As a young man he witnessed the Nazi occupation of his country during the Second World War. Kundera became a member of the Communist party that gained power after the war. Although he was expelled for a time, he was reinstated and became an influential member of the group of intellectuals who were demanding greater artistic freedom, a movement that led to a brief period of liberalization known as the Prague Spring. But after the Soviet invasion in 1969, Kundera was labeled a counterrevolutionary, his books were banned, and he lost his position teaching film studies at the Academy of Music and Dramatic Arts in Prague. Kundera left Czechoslovakia in 1975 to accept a teaching position at the University of Rennes in France.

Kundera gained international attention when two of his early works were translated and published in the West. His first novel *Žert* (1967; *The Joke*) is an ironic view of a young intellectual in a Communist country who falls out of favor with the authorities. The French version was introduced by Louis Aragon and helped establish Kundera's reputation in France, where all of his books have been especially well received. *Směšné lásky* (1963, 1965, 1968; *Laughable Loves*), which contains a preface by Philip Roth, is a collection of short stories dealing with desire and seduction.

Kundera began his writing career as a poet, and then turned to drama before writing the fiction which brought him world renown. Although he has stated that he has little regard for either his poetry or his drama, his first play was produced both in Czechoslovakia and in more than a dozen other countries. Entitled *Majitelé Klíčů* (1962; *The Owners of the Keys*), it offers a satiric look at heroism during the Nazi occupation. Kundera's later novels include *Valčík na rozloučenou* (1979; *The Farewell Party*), *Život je jinde* (1979; *Life Is Elsewhere*), and *Kniha smíchu a zapomnění* (*The Book of Laughter and Forgetting*). His recent novel *The Unbearable Lightness of Being* (1984) is set in Czechoslovakia after the 1969 Russian invasion and follows two couples as they redefine their relationships.

© Lütfi Özkök

It has been interpreted as an existential examination of the pain which can result from commitment and the meaninglessness of a life without responsibility. The novel is divided into seven sections and interweaves various themes in patterns reminiscent of musical composition.

(See also *CLC*, Vols. 4, 9, 19 and *Contemporary Authors*, Vols. 85-88.)

LUBOMÍR DOLEŽEL

A follower of the tradition of the multiperspective novel in modern Czech fiction, Kundera made a substantial contribution to the development of its devices and functions.

The story of *The Joke* is conveyed by four *Ich*-narrators. The chief narrator, Ludvík Jahn, is the main protagonist of the novel. Three secondary narrators, Helena, Jaroslav, and Kostka, all have (or had) a close relationship to Ludvík: Helena as his 'victim', Jaroslav as his old classmate, Kostka as his friend and ideological antagonist. (pp. 114-15)

The fundamental problem of the narrative structure of *The Joke* consists in the selection of the narrators. Why were these characters and not any of the others entrusted with the function of narrating? The selection of narrators was not fortuitous but determined, I believe, by the structure and type of Kundera's novel. Typologically, *The Joke* can be designated an *ideological novel* (novel of ideas), i.e. a novel dominated in its structure by the plane of ideas. The narrators of *The Joke* are representatives of various systems of 'false' ideologies-myths; their narrative monologues are *authentic accounts of the social conditions and of the individual directions of the destruction of myths.*

The typological character of Kundera's novel determines the selection of narrators not only in a positive but also in a negative sense, i.e. by eliminating certain potential candidates. Two important agents in Ludvík's story—his 'enemy' Zemánek and his love Lucie—are not assigned the function of narrator. Their contributions to the narrative symposium are not required because they have nothing to say about the destruction of myths. (pp. 115-16)

Lucie's absence from the narrative symposium can be related also to a factor of the plot structure of the novel. In the plot construction of *The Joke,* Lucie assumes the role of 'mystery'. She is the 'goddess of escape' (Ludvík), both by her name, and by her role in Ludvík's personal tragedy. She is a romantic character with a mysterious past and ambiguous motivations. It is obvious that Lucie's own narration, her self-revelation, would destroy the atmosphere of romantic mystery surrounding her personality and actions. (p. 116)

It seems to me that the specific features of the particular narrative monologues reflect various stages of the myth-destroying process which the narrators have reached. Specifically, the structure and texture of the narrative monologue depends on the balance of two functions of narrator, namely the *representational* and the *interpretative* function. We assume that the balance of representation and interpretation, different in the particular narrative monologues of *The Joke,* reflects the narrator's stage in the myth-destroying process.

In Helena's narrative, interpretation dominates over representation. The destruction of Helena's myth occurs solely under external pressures; she herself is incapable of a critical rejection of her myth and its phraseology. Helena's myth remains naive from the beginning to the end. Her faked 'suicide' is a grotesque symbol of the perserverance of a naive myth. Helena's naiveté is also reflected in the style of her narrative. This style is very close to what is called 'stream-of-consciousness style', an uncontrolled, unorganized, spontaneous flow of freely associated motifs, trite phrases and expressions....

Kostka's evangelical myth is just the opposite of Helena's naive ideology. In his narrative performance, however, Kostka is very close to Helena. Interpretation clearly dominates over representation in his narrative. Destruction of Kostka's refractory myth is not completed; it is carried only to the stage of unsolvable dilemmas. Kostka continues to use the terms and phraseology of his impaired myth to interpret his own story as well as the stories of the other protagonists. Because of the dominance of interpretation over representation in Kostka's narrative, Kostka seems to be the least reliable narrator of the symposium. This unreliability is especially revealed in his rendering of Lucie's story. (p. 117)

Whereas in Kostka's narrative the subjective interpretation adjusts the introduced motifs to its own ends, Jaroslav's monologue is built on a parallelism of representation and interpretation. It presents narrated events on two parallel and disjointed levels, that of folkloristic myth and that of 'everyday life'. Jaroslav's archaic myth interprets the motifs of his narrative

in the terms, symbolism and phraseology of folk poetry. At the same time, however, the narrator himself is aware of the inadequacy of such an interpretation; Jaroslav comes to regard his myth as 'dreaming' and 'fantasy'. Nevertheless, he still is not ready to give up trying 'to live in two worlds at the same time'. For others, however, Jaroslav's folkloristic interpretations are almost ridiculous; they create shadows of the narrated events which the participants of these events refuse to accept as authentic.

Jaroslav's narrative monologue is very special in that it gives a systematic, one might almost say, scientific account of his myth and its transformations. This component of the interpretative function (interpretation of the interpretation) explains the density of professional language drawn from history and musical theory in Jaroslav's narrative style.... (p. 118)

Jaroslav's expert treatise on Moravian folklore represents one extreme pole of the stylistic variety of *The Joke,* the other one being represented by the loose and spontaneous style of Helena's monologue....

It is Ludvík who offers the most important contribution to the narrative symposium of *The Joke.* His monologue dominates the narrative structure of the novel not only because it introduces the most important episodes of the action, but also because it presents the most profound and most conscious destruction of a myth. Mythological interpretation is replaced by critical analysis; a perfect harmony between the narrator's representational 'responsibility' and his interpretative function is thus achieved. This state of harmony is facilitated by two essential features of Ludvík's story. First, in no other story is the destruction of myth so closely connected with personal tragedy. Second, Ludvík's character shows from the very beginning both a *Lust zum Fabulieren* and an inclination to self-analysis, to critical evaluation of one's own deeds and words. Ludvík excels in the merciless 'tearing away of veils'.

It is, therefore, not surprising that Ludvík is assigned the role of destroying not only his own myth but also of contributing substantially to the destruction of other characters' myths. (p. 119)

In this connection, I would like to mention specifically Ludvík's depiction of the ceremony of 'the welcoming of new citizens into life' (chapter v). Here we find a meticulous application of the device of 'making strange', an applicaton which in its consistency and sophistication is unique in Czech literature. 'Tearing away of veils' is accomplished here solely by a literary device, by the depiction of the scene from a special angle, from the viewpoint of a stranger who does not understand what is going on. This angle renders all actions, words and emotions void, meaningless and disconnected. Only after this absurd depiction is the 'meaning' of the ceremony revealed (in Ludvík's conversation with the official who performed the ceremony).

Ludvík's passion for the 'tearing away of veils' is reflected in his narrative style through relentless enumeration of dreary or ugly details which, appearing sometimes in parentheses, distort every picture....

It would be a great mistake, however, to call Ludvík's narrative style 'naturalistic'. A more detailed investigation of his monologue would reveal a complex, multilayered texture, where detailed descriptiveness with a bias for ugly details represents only one extreme pole; it is balanced by uninhibited poetic language expressed in rhythmical syntax and in symbolic imagery.... (p. 120)

Up to now we have concentrated on the study of correlations between the narrative and the ideological structure of *The Joke*. The study of these correlations revealed that the form of narrative symposium used in the novel is not mere fashionable whimsy; rather it is a device by which is realized multiple destruction and self-destruction of myths which are, one might say, the real protagonists of this ideological novel. However, the correlations just described represent only one of the functions of the narrative symposium of *The Joke;* other functions can be revealed when studying *correlations between the narrative structure and the structure of fictional time....*

The basis feature of fictional time in *The Joke* is quite typical for modern fiction: the proper chronology of events is done away with and replaced by achronological confrontations and clashes of narrated events occuring on different time-planes, in different time-periods. (p. 121)

All narratives begin in the narrated present . . . and then return, using the device of flashback or reminiscence, to various periods of the narrated past....

There is no need here to follow in detail the time-pattern of the particular narratives and to describe the shifts from one time-period to another. Let us just note that, with a few exceptions, the narratives do not overlap....

Therefore, I do not hesitate to call the overall pattern of *The Joke* a *linear* structure. Moreover, the occasional overlapping and intersections possess, in my opinion, a different function in *The Joke,* a function which can be described on the level of the narrative structure: they show the limits of credibility, the 'reliability' of particular narrators. (p. 123)

Our analysis of the time-structure of *The Joke* would be incomplete, however, if we did not deal with the special status of the last, the seventh, chapter. (p. 124)

Various interpretations of . . . [the] special time and narrative structure of the last chapter of *The Joke* will certainly be offered. In my opinion, the function of this structure is purely rhythmical: an irregular, but generally rapid pattern of alternating narrative monologues is played off against the slow progress and the monotonous repetition of the leitmotif of the chapter—the ancient folkloristic ritual of the 'Ride of the Kings'. These contrasting progressions create a complex rhythmic pattern which provides an appropriate background for the grotesque culmination of Ludvík's story.

Our investigation into the problems of the narrator in Kundera's novel *The Joke* has led us to the core of the novel's artistic structure. It has revealed the ingenious network which mutually links all the principal structural components: the idea, the characters, the action, the time, the narrative form. Study of the narrator cuts across the traditional categories of form and content and gives us a rare opportunity to view the literary structure in its entirety. At the same time, we can observe how the structural network leans in a specific direction by the impact of the dominant structural component, the plane of ideas. In a period governed by collective ideologies, Kundera uses the type of the ideological novel and the form of a collective narrative symposium to ensure the best balance between the aesthetic message and the immanent structure of his novel. Following the narrative symposium of *The Joke,* we travel the peripatetic road leading from the dehumanized mythological past through the tumultuous present of myth-destruction toward a distant, but well-defined ideal of humanity. (p. 125)

Lubomír Doležel, " 'Narrative Symposium' in Milan Kundera's 'The Joke'," in his Narrative Modes in Czech Literature, *University of Toronto Press, 1973, pp. 112-25.*

PHILIP ROTH

[*Philip Roth is credited with bringing Kundera's works to the attention of the English-speaking public. The essay from which this excerpt is taken was originally published as the introduction to Kundera's* Laughable Loves, *1974.*]

I would think that . . . [Milan Kundera] would prefer to find a readership in the West that was not drawn to his fiction because he is a writer who is oppressed by a Communist regime, especially since Kundera's political novel, *The Joke,* happens to represent only an aspect of his wide-ranging intelligence and talent. (pp. 203-04)

But having written *The Joke,* Kundera, for all his wide-ranging interests, now finds himself an enemy of the state and nothing more—ironically enough, in a position very much like the protagonist of *The Joke,* whose error it is as a young Communist student to send a teasing postcard to his girl friend, making fun of her naïve political earnestness. (p. 204)

Well, in Eastern Europe a man should be more careful of the letters he writes, even to his girl friend. For his three joking sentences, Jahn is found guilty by a student tribunal of being an enemy of the state, is expelled from the university and the Party, and is consigned to an army penal corps where for seven years he works in the coal mines. "But, Comrades," says Jahn, "it was only a joke." Nonetheless, he is swallowed up by a state somewhat lacking a sense of humor about itself, and subsequently, having misplaced his own sense of humor somewhere in the mines, he is swallowed up and further humiliated by his plans for revenge.

The Joke is, of course, not so benign in intent as Jahn's postcard. I would suppose that Kundera must himself have known, somewhere along the line, that one day the authorities might confirm the imaginative truthfulness of his book by bringing their own dogmatic seriousness down upon him for writing as he did about the plight of Ludvík Jahn. "Socialist realism," after all, is the approved artistic mode in his country, and as one Prague critic informed me when I asked for a definition, "Socialist realism consists of writing in praise of the government and the party so that even *they* understand it." Oddly (just another joke, really) Kundera's book conforms more to Stalin's own prescription for art: "socialist content in national form." Since two of the most esteemed books written in the nation in question happen to be *The Trial* by Franz Kafka and *The Good Soldier Schweik* by Jaroslav Hašek, Kundera's own novel about a loyal citizen upon whom a terrible joke is played by the powers that be would seem to be entirely in keeping with the spirit of Stalin's injunction. If only Stalin were alive so that Kundera could point out to him this continuity in "national form" and historical preoccupation. (pp. 204-05)

Erotic play and power are the subjects frequently at the center of the stories that Kundera calls, collectively, *Laughable Loves.* Sexuality as a weapon (in this case, the weapon of he who is otherwise wholly assailable) is to the point of *The Joke* as well: to revenge himself upon the political friend who had turned upon him back in his remote student days, Ludvík Jahn, released from the coal mines at last, coldly conceives a plan to seduce the man's wife. In this decision by Kundera's hero to put his virility in the service of his rage, he displays a kinship to characters in the fiction of Mailer and Mishima. . . . However, what distinguishes Kundera's cocksman from Mailer's or Mishima's is the ease with which his erotic power play is thwarted, and turns into yet another joke at his expense. He is so much more vulnerable in good part because he has been so crippled by ostracism from the Party and imprisonment in the penal corps . . . , but also because Kundera, unlike Mailer or Mishima, seems even in a book as bleak and cheerless as *The Joke* to be fundamentally *amused* by the uses to which a man will think to put his sexual member, or the uses to which his member will put him. This amusement, mixed though it is with sympathy and sorrow, leads Kundera away from anything even faintly resembling a mystical belief or ideological investment in the power of potency or orgasm.

In *Laughable Loves,* what I've called Kundera's "amusement" with erotic enterprises and lustful strategies emerges as the mild satire of a story like **"The Golden Apple of Eternal Desire,"** wherein Don Juanism is viewed as a sport played by a man against a team of women, oftentimes without body contact—or, in the wry, rather worldly irony of the Dr. Havel stories, **"Symposium"** and **"Dr. Havel After Ten Years,"** where Don Juanism is depicted as a way of life in which women of all social stations eagerly and willingly participate as "sexual objects," particularly so with Havel, eminent physician and aging Casanova, who in his prime is matter-of-factly told by a professional colleague: ". . . you're like death, you take everything." Or Kundera's amusement emerges as a kind of detached Chekhovian tenderness in the story about a balding, thirtyish, would-have-been eroticist, who sets about to seduce an aging woman whose body he expects to find repellent, a seduction undertaken to revenge himself upon his own stubborn phallic daydreams. . . . [This story], **"Let the Old Dead Make Room for the Young Dead,"** seems to me "Chekhovian" not merely because of its tone, or its concern with the painful and touching consequences of time passing and old selves dying, but because it is so very good.

In **"The Hitchhiking Game,"** **"Nobody Will Laugh,"** and **"Edward and God,"** Kundera turns to those jokes he is so fond on contemplating, the ones that begin in whimsical perversity, and end in trouble. . . . What is so often laughable, in the stories of Kundera's Czechoslovakia, is how grimly serious just about everything turns out to be, jokes, games, and pleasure included; what's laughable is how terribly little there is to laugh at with any joy.

My own favorite story is **"Edward and God."** Like *The Joke,* it deals with a young Czech whose playfulness (with women, of course) and highly developed taste for cynicism and blasphemy expose him to the harsh judgments of a dogmatic society or, rather, expose him to those authorities who righteously promulgate and protect the dogmas, but do so stupidly and without even genuine conviction or understanding. . . . [Where] there is something of an aggrieved tone and polemical intent in *The Joke*—a sense communicated, at least to a Westerner, that the novel is also a *statement* made in behalf of an abused nation, and in defiance of a heartless regime—**"Edward and God"** is more like a rumination, in anecdotal form, upon a social predicament that rouses the author to comic analysis and philosophical speculation, even to farce, rather than to angry exposé. (pp. 205-09)

"Edward and God" does not derive from manifesto or protest literature, but connects in spirit as well as form to those humorous stories one hears by the hundreds in Prague these days,

stories such as a powerless or oppressed people are often adept at telling about themselves, and in which they seem to take an aesthetic pleasure—what pleasure is there otherwise?—from the very absurdities and paradoxes that characterize their hardship and cause them pain. (p. 209)

Philip Roth, "Imagining the Erotic, Three Introductions: Milan Kundera," in his Reading Myself and Others, *Farrar, Straus and Giroux, 1975, pp. 200-09.*

PETER KUSSI

Milan Kundera writes fiction in order to ask questions. Could that have actually happened? Why was he so ashamed of her anyway? Then why did he make it all up? Why did he lie? Why is she so nervous? Has Mirek ever understood her? These questions, part of a dialogue between narrator and reader, or perhaps between narrator and author, are taken from the first pages of Kundera's latest novel [*The Book of Laughter and Forgetting*]. . . . (p. 206)

Kundera interrogates his characters, poses questions to his various narrator-personae, engages his readers and puzzles them into questioning themselves. He is after clarity, definition, with a French faith in lucidity and a Czech mistrust of absolutes. The devil laughs at God because of His inscrutability; angels laugh with God at the simplicity of creation. Kundera, with an ironic smile, constructs fictional worlds in which patient investigation by narrator, characters and readers is rewarded by glimpses into the rules of the game.

Kundera is an astonishingly inventive author who uses a variety of structural ways to question his themes. . . . [In *The Joke*] he used the technique of multiple narration. By cross-examining the accounts of the story furnished by four narrators, Kundera exposed their "overlapping delusions," to use the memorable phrase of critic Elizabeth Pochoda [see *CLC,* Vol. 19]. In prewar Czech literature this technique was favored by Karel Čapek. But whereas Čapek the relativist showed that each man has his own truth, Kundera the skeptic shows that each man has his own falsehood.

A related technique employed by Kundera is the multiple point of view on the author's part, resulting in shifts of perspective and of the relative scale of importance. Kundera's metaphor for this purpose is the movable observation tower. The author discusses it with his readers in [*Life Is Elsewhere*]. . . . The observatory is mentioned again in *The Book of Laughter and Forgetting,* along with several closely related images. . . . In this novel about memory and awareness, background and foreground, past and present, the recollected trivia and forgotten loves are ever shifting and sliding past each other. Russian tanks invade the country, and Mother is thinking about some pears the pharmacist promised her. Shocking. Or is it? In a beautiful image Kundera describes Mother's perspective: "A big pear in the foreground and somewhere off in the distance a tank, tiny as a ladybug, ready at any moment to take wing and disappear from sight. So Mother was right after all: tanks are mortal, pears eternal." . . . (pp. 206-07)

Are tanks more important than pears? Questions, and still more questions. The very structure of *The Book of Laughter and Forgetting* is a question, for, as Kundera explains, the book is not so much a novel as a book of variations—and what are variations if not a spiral of questions about a single theme? In a broader sense, Kundera's prose writings as a whole can be seen as variations on a few related themes: awareness and self-deception, the power of human lucidity and its limits, the games of history and love.

Kundera's fiction is a game of wits in which deception is one of the main strategies. Ludvík, the hero of *The Joke,* feigns love for Helena as part of his scheme of revenge. *The Farewell Party* is a comedy of deception, while *The Book of Laughter and Forgetting,* and many of Kundera's short stories are ironic dissertations on the arts of erotic trickery. The distinctive feature of Kundera's fiction, however, is not merely that his characters resort to guile in order to outwit fate and each other; his heroes and heroines also frequently deceive themselves. In fact, self-deception is such a striking element in Kundera's stories and novels that his protagonists could really be divided into two moral types: those who are satisfied to remain self-deluded and those struggling for a measure of self-awareness.

Self-deception is often unmasked when a character is called upon to take action. In Kundera's world a crucial step is frequently taken without clear motivation or deliberation, impulsively, catching the psyche exposed like a sudden, involuntary glimpse of one's face in a mirror. In *The Farewell Party*—a book about death and birth, yet Kundera's most playful novel—a pivotal point occurs when the pregnant Růžena reaches for a pill held in the palm of her adversary Jakub. Růžena believes the pill to be a tranquilizer, but as Jakub knows perfectly well, it actually contains poison: "Jakub stared into her eyes, then slowly, ceremoniously, he opened his hand." For a moment he is vouchsafed a searing flash of insight into the meaning of his behavior.

> Raskolnikov experienced his act of murder as a tragedy, and staggered under the weight of his deed. Jakub was amazed to find that his deed was weightless, easy to bear, light as air. And he wondered whether there was not more horror in this lightness than in all the dark agonies and contortions of the Russian hero. . . .

In a masterpiece of concise irony, the narrator describes Jakub's meditation on guilt: "The One testing him (the nonexistent God) wished to learn what Jakub was really like and not what he pretended to be like. And Jakub decided to be honest in the face of his examiner, to be the person he really was." . . . Who, then, is Jakub? The one *pretending* to be Jakub, or the one who *decided* to be Jakub? Can someone deciding to be honest at the same time *be* honest?

One form of self-deception to which Kundera's protagonists are prone may be called "bad faith," a moral syndrome reminiscent of the *mauvaise foi* first diagnosed in the modern consciousness by Jean-Paul Sartre. This bad faith is consciously induced self-deception whereby people pretend to themselves to be unaware of certain realities in order to postpone the need for making decisions. (p. 207)

Mauvaise foi is a philosophical concept, and its applicability to literary characters is only implicit. Yet there are remarkable parallels between Sartre's paradigm and several situations in Kundera's novels. In *Life Is Elsewhere* the artist kisses Maman, and "subsequent reflection could not change what had happened but only establish the fact that something wrong had taken place. But Maman could not be sure even of that, and so she postponed solving the problem until some future time." . . . (pp. 207-08)

Similarly, in *The Book of Laughter and Forgetting,* Tamina—perhaps the most attractive and intriguing of Kundera's hero-

ines—tries to suppress her awareness of sexual intimacy with Hugo by concentrating on vacations spent with her late husband, a mental effort Kundera compares to an exercise in irregular verbs. "But why did Tamina refuse to defend herself?" asks the narrator. *He* (not *she*—Czech grammar is clear about the gender of anonymous narrators) is puzzled, for it is not only the protagonists or readers who struggle for awareness; the narrator too begins in a state of partial ignorance and gains knowledge slowly, painfully, as the story progresses. . . .

Why is self-awareness so difficult to achieve? Kundera does not look to Freud for the answer. People fool themselves because truth is elusive and fragmented, and because they are losing touch with memory and history. . . .

The hero of *The Joke* still had a name and a tradition, was rooted in a specific time and place. Memory, in *The Joke,* has an ambiguous significance: the loss of tradition, as exemplified by the banalization of the ancient Ride of the Kings, is to be deplored, but forgetfulness is also a necessary means of healing and reconciliation. Nothing will be forgiven, writes Kundera, but everything will be forgotten.

However, by the time the cycle of novels has culminated in *The Book of Laughter and Forgetting,* (and the 1968 invasion of his land has faded from the world's conscience), amnesia has become for Kundera a clear-cut metaphor for individual and national destruction. After *The Joke* Kundera's novels grow more ahistorical and parodic, with characters designated by first names or occupational categories. *The Farewell Party* takes place in a spa, far from Prague and close to the border of national and geographic anonymity. In *The Book of Laughter and Forgetting* Kundera shifts back and forth from a very real Prague to a painfully recollected homeland and finally to an Atlantis of blissful amnesia, an innocent island suggestive of a miniature America as well as the land of Lilliput.

The discontinuity with the past, the generational amnesia, is reflected in several of Kundera's novels by the search for a missing parent—more specifically a missing father, the *pater absconditus*. (p. 208)

From his high-rise tower in Brittany, from his Paris window, Milan Kundera is still looking east toward Prague, toward his Moravian birthplace, toward the Central Europe he considers his spiritual home. What is there in his work that is descended from Czech literary traditions? The novel of ideas has never taken root in Czech culture, nor has the kind of intellectual game Kundera plays with Eros and politics, fiction and reality. Czech readers are more used to laughing than to exploring the sources of laughter, and pure jeu d'esprit has appeared in modern Czech literature only rarely and belatedly.

Kundera's real literary roots are in the eighteenth century, in the digressive storytellers, in Sterne and especially in the French ironists and Encyclopedists. In his recent works, particularly *The Book of Laughter and Forgetting,* as Kundera leaves the land of Bohemia and views the little figures of the world panorama from an ever higher observatory, his irony often changes to Swiftian satire, and to Swiftian pessimism. Among modern writers, he has expressed an affinity for Thomas Mann, for Anatole France, for the existentialists, for the Central European writers with a philosophical bent. As he put it in a 1963 interview: "Precision of thought moves me more than precision of observation. . . ."

The bulk of Kundera's work has never been published in his homeland, but he does not bewail the necessity of writing for foreigners. He thinks the era of parochial national literatures is over, and he believes in the Goethean concept of a world community of letters. The knowledge that he is dependent on translators has affected Kundera's style, inducing him to make his expression clearer, more decisive, less subject to misinterpretation. . . .

Kundera's purely literary paternity may be European rather than specifically Czech, but he has many qualities which have come to be associated with Czech culture: skepticism, dislike of hubris and gigantism, insistence on a human scale as the ideal measure of values, the use of humor as a means of demystification. Very much in the Czech tradition too is the writer as teacher and moralist. . . . It is hard to say just what effects Kundera's strong political engagement has on his fiction. There is no doubt that his fervor and the associated lyrical emotions he is at such pains to suppress have added power to his high-energy writing and have given his fiction its unusual interplay of polis, Eros and Thanatos. Of course, there is a price to be paid when ironic detachment and inquisitive attitude are replaced by assertions, particularly when those assertions are questionable. Is the cultural impact of the East really so one-sidedly detrimental? What are the origins of the triviality, amnesia, infantility of the modern world? Or its genocidal propensities? As the genially insane physician of *The Farewell Party* so hilariously—and chillingly—shows, superrationality is never very far from irrationality.

In interviews and statements Kundera may engage in polemics, but in his novels, stories and plays this great author's most personal voice sounds a dialogue with the truth. After publication of *The Joke,* Czech novelist and playwright Ivan Klíma wrote: "In his passionate desire to reach the truth, no matter how bitter; to resist every illusion, no matter how modestly formulated; to eradicate all myths, no matter how innocent-looking, Milan Kundera has gone further than anyone in the history of Czech prose." This is still true today. (p. 209)

> *Peter Kussi, "Milan Kundera: Dialogues with Fiction," in* World Literature Today, *Vol. 57, No. 2, Spring, 1983, pp. 206-09.*

FRANCES TALIAFERRO

Milan Kundera's dazzling novel **"The Book of Laughter and Forgetting,"** published here in 1980, was a revelation to xenophobic readers. All preconceived notions of what a "Czech novel" might be were confounded by this extraordinary work, at once political and philosophical, erotic and spiritual, funny and profound. As for the author's intentions, Milan Kundera has commented (in a conversation with Philip Roth) on the peculiar hospitality of the novel form: "Ironic essay, novelistic narrative, autobiographical fragment, historic fact, flight of fantasy: The synthetic power of the novel is capable of combining everything into a unified whole like the voices of polyphonic music."

Now we see that "synthetic power" splendidly at work in Milan Kundera's new novel, **"The Unbearable Lightness of Being."** . . . It centers on the connected lives of two couples. Tomas is the most promising young surgeon at his hospital in Prague. He is also an "epic womanizer" and collector of women. Among the dozens he has slept with, his wife, Tereza, and his mistress, Sabina, represent fidelity and betrayal, the opposite poles of erotic possibility. . . .

In the binary universe of this novel, it is not only lovers who are paired and repaired with old and new partners. Being itself is divided into pairs of opposites. Fidelity and betrayal, soul and body, political oppression and personal feeling balance and modify. . . . Most of all, however, life is both "light" and "heavy." Sometimes we make the "heaviest" life choices in the lightest and most accidental way. Sometimes, recognizing the transitory quality of even the gravest burdens, we experience "the unbearable lightness of being."

"The Book of Laughter and Forgetting" was a series of episodic variations on a theme. **"The Unbearable Lightness of Being,"** a work of larger scale and complexity, is symphonically arranged, so that thematic events are constantly enriched by smaller phrases and motifs. The theme of political "necessity"—centering on the Russian invasion of Czechoslovakia in 1968—is echoed in many small allusions. The "necessity" of Tomas's love for his wife Tereza is signaled by the fact that at the beginning of their acquaintance she is clutching a copy of "Anna Karenina."

The symmetrical composition of that novel is not merely "novelistic." The author explains that we all compose our lives like music, turning chance occurrences into permanent motifs. In the polyphonic music of this novel, Mr. Kundera points out that each voice is singing its own version of two motifs Beethoven named "the difficult resolution": *"Muss es sein? Es muss sein!"* ("Must it be? It must be!")

Necessity is a less memorable theme in Mr. Kundera's work than sexuality. He has observed elsewhere that "a scene of physical love generates an extremely sharp light which suddenly reveals the essence of characters and sums up their life situation." Certainly there is no wiser observer now writing of the multifarious relations of men and women. . . .

Mr. Kundera is not alone in possessing a philosophical sense of humor, a liking for human crankiness, and a political sensibility. What distinguishes him from, say, Kurt Vonnegut? Perhaps one judges Mr. Kundera the better novelist in homage to his country's gallant sufferings—a form of romanticism, incidentally, that the author regards with some amusement. I think, however, that Milan Kundera is the more durable because his world view is the more open. However schematic his "double exposures"—laughter forgetting, heaviness lightness, soul body—his novels do not move according to formula, but acquaint the reader with the complex variations of an intelligence both speculative and playful. **"The Unbearable Lightness of Being"** is his best novel yet.

> *Frances Taliaferro, "Love As Fugue: A Master's Best Novel," in* The Wall Street Journal, *April 27, 1984, p. 26.*

JANET MALCOLM

Kitsch is the enemy of every artist, of course, but it has special menace for the artist who has made his way out of the abyss of "totalitarian kitsch" (as Kundera calls it), only to find himself peering into the chasm of Western anticommunist kitsch. Kundera, who left Czechoslovakia in 1975, after he was expelled from the Communist party for the second time and could no longer publish or teach there, now lives in Paris and works in an increasingly—what to call it?—abstract, surreal, "poetic" idiom.

His need to experiment with form is surely connected to his personal vendetta against the puerilities of "socialist realism" and its "free world" counterparts. . . .

His novels have all the unpredictability and changeability of mountain weather, and are marked by an almost compulsive disregard for the laws of genre. Like a driver who signals right and promptly turns left, Kundera repeatedly betrays the reader's trust in the conventions that give him his bearings in a novel. . . .

Near the end of his novel *Life Is Elsewhere* (1969) [for example], Kundera steps out from behind the curtain of his narrative—the sardonically told story of a mamma's boy, a young poet who develops into a monstrosity of totalitarian kitsch—and speaks of his restiveness under the constraints of the novel form. "Just as your life is determined by the kind of profession and marriage you have chosen, so our novel is limited by our observatory perspective. . . . We have chosen this approach as you have chosen your fate, and our choice is equally unalterable," Kundera says ruefully, and then goes on to wonder whether maybe the novelist cannot welsh on his commitment after all: "Man cannot jump out of his life, but perhaps a novel has more freedom. Suppose we hurriedly and secretly dismantled our observatory and transported it elsewhere, at least for a little while?"

Kundera then proposes to write a chapter that will be to the main narrative what a small guest house is to a country manor, and suddenly, without warning, the reader is thrust into one of the most lyrical and heart-rending scenes in contemporary fiction—a scene between a red-haired girl and a middle-aged man (who appears in the novel for the first time) that is of almost unbearable sadness and tenderness. . . . Kundera describes the scene as "a quiet interlude in which an anonymous man unexpectedly lights a lamp of kindness," and it fades out of the book (which is interesting and sometimes very funny but otherwise never very affecting) like one of those mysterious distinct sounds one hears at dawn and supposes one has dreamed.

In his next two novels—*The Book of Laughter and Forgetting* and [*The Unbearable Lightness of Being*] Kundera attempts to recapture this emotional tone while simultaneously experimenting with surrealist techniques. It stubbornly eludes him in the first book, whose surrealism seems somewhat pathetic and outdated, and whose pathos has an "as if" quality: instead of being moved, one is aware of being *cued* to be moved. But in *The Unbearable Lightness of Being* Kundera succeeds in actually creating the work of high modernist playfulness and deep pathos that he had merely projected in the earlier book.

Like *Ulysses*, it is a book entwined with another book—in this case *Anna Karenina*, a copy of which Kundera, with his characteristic directness, puts under the arm of his heroine, Tereza, as she enters the novel. He draws on *Anna Karenina* not in a literal sense—his Tereza and Tomas and Sabina and Franz in no way "equal" Anna and Vronsky and Levin and Kitty. It is the existential dilemma at the core of *Anna Karenina* that he plucks from the Russian novel and restates in terms of the opposition between heaviness and lightness. When Tolstoy wrote of the vacuous and senseless life of Vronsky and Anna in the country after their forced retreat from society (a life that he had the inspiration of showing through the eyes of the careworn, child-burdened, *"excessivement terre-à-terre"* Dolly, as Vronsky dismissively calls her), he was writing about the unbearable lightness of being. We keep this state at bay with our marriages, friendships, commitments, responsibilities, loyalties and ties to family, culture, and nation; and we float up

toward it every time we commit adultery, betray a friend, break ranks, defy authority, sever a family bond, leave a homeland, or (as Kundera goes beyond Tolstoy in suggesting) attempt to create a work of art. "What then shall we choose?" Kundera writes. "Weight or lightness?" (p. 3)

The Unbearable Lightness of Being has a kind of charmed life. It is like a performance that has gotten off on the right foot. Every door Kundera tries opens for him. In the earlier books, one felt like a passenger in a small plane, swooping and dropping precipitately and heading straight for a mountain; in the present book, one travels by steady jumbo jet. The heavy/light polarity acts as a kind of fixative for Kundera's special sensitivity to the ambiguities and ironies of the position of the Janus-faced political émigré, and to its potentialities as a universal metaphor. (p. 4)

The distinction of Michael Henry Heim's translation lies in the clean precision and elegant leanness of diction through which the novel's taut modernist tone is rendered. In her new novel, *Pitch Dark*, Renata Adler asks (in the voice of the book's narrator), "Do I need to stylize it, or can I tell it as it was?" To point out that "telling it as it was" is itself another stylization is only to restate the question that has haunted fiction throughout this century. In *Life Is Elsewhere,* Kundera used Rimbaud's line *"Il faut être absolument moderne"* as an epigraph. But the modern novelist, unlike the modern painter, sculptor, or poet, cannot absolutely divest himself of realism: the modernist novel is inevitably a hybrid form. Only through the illusion that he is in some sense "telling it as it was" can the novelist sustain the reader's attention and touch his heart. The self-reflexiveness of modern art, its aggressive avowal of materials . . . can extend only partially to narrative literature. Kundera's work deepens our sense of modernism as a force powerfully pulling at the novelist but never quite taking him over the border. (p. 6)

Janet Malcolm, "The Game of Lights," in The New York Review of Books, *Vol. XXXI, No. 8, May 10, 1984, pp. 3-4, 6.*

TOM LIPPI

Set in his native Czechoslovakia, in the aftermath of the "Prague Spring" of 1968, Milan Kundera's latest novel recounts the experiences of two couples and a dog entangled in the emotional and political intrigues accompanying the August arrival of Russian troops and Soviet order. *The Unbearable Lightness of Being* is the story of Tomas, a respected physician who abandons comfortable exile to return to his native land and falls victim to political oppression; of his wife Tereza, at once tormented by and inextricably drawn to her vision of home; of his mistress Sabina, who escapes to a pointless freedom devoid of all commitments; and of her gentle lover Franz, good, true, brilliant and hopeless. The characters are real enough, and the stage upon which they are displayed broad and imposing. But a fifth character in this novel is the author himself.

Kundera . . . is master here, directing the action from on high, an accomplished puppeteer. But frequently the puppeteer's hands appear as he re-directs our attention to the ideas that inspire the performance, indeed away from the mere objects that impersonate them.

These first-person intrusions by the author—occasionally bits like "I have been thinking about Tomas for many years" or "But let us return to the bowler hat"—are slightly puzzling, more so when quoted out of context. But then out-of-context is really all they are. There is no context, no *real* world, in this novel. We are never asked to suspend our disbelief, but rather reminded to cling jealously to it. In its effort to fly in the face of traditional novel form, the book issues a challenge, a quite self-conscious one, to the validity of form. And here style mirrors content.

Validity is on the block in the novel: the validity of involvement, passionate or political, the validity of occupation, of experience, of art. . . . Cast in the pallid light of this perspective, the events and characters portrayed in the novel seem relegated to an existence that seems more ritual than real. . . .

Only the pathetic heroine Tereza seems moved to genuine, unfettered emotion.

Imprisoned by a hopelessly unfailing love for Tomas, Tereza embodies commitment, in Kundera's terms the burden or "heaviness" of being. She is his one "poetic" love, which roughly translates into the one woman in whom he takes more than a merely glandular interest. . . . [He] cavorts like a satyr and returns at night, reeking of other women, to the bed of his one true love.

Tomas, however, is not completely unsympathetic. Something—love, the desire for a good night's sleep—impels him to follow his wife back to Prague, and this act is his undoing. He will not kick himself free of the world completely, cannot disappear like the meaningless Sabina into that voidish lightness of being. . . . Tomas opts for some involvement in the world, as grim as it has become; ultimately he chooses, albeit from a drastically reduced list of choices, "significance." In doing so he chooses, as well, its concomitant despair.

That such a choice need be made, and that, given the constraints imposed upon humanity in the novel, the choice amounts to very nearly an affirmation, speaks to the central image of the book; that of the essential ambiguity, the tragic paradox, that modern life poses. Not only are there no easy choices, but there are no choices without deeply painful consequences. Any response a character makes to the grim circumstances of life is undermined by the impossibility of a genuinely human resolution in a world no longer fit for simple humanity. Accordingly, the author's depiction of the struggle is complex and disturbing, a metaphor for the condition it examines.

> Tom Lippi, "The Tragic Paradox of Modern Life," in Pacific Sun, *Year 22, No. 19, May 11-17, 1984, p. 24.*

BETTY FALKENBERG

[Milan Kundera] has turned interrogation into a literary method. . . . [In *The Unbearable Lightness of Being,* he] holds up to scrutiny four characters whose lives cross in a kind of cat's-cradle, but more broadly this is "an investigation of human life in the trap it has become." . . .

Lightness-weight and fidelity-betrayal are only two of the many questions Kundera dissects. . . . But ultimately, the only questions worth asking are those that have no answers. These "set the limits of human possibilities, describe the boundaries of human existence."

Unfortunately, Kundera also lapses into fuzzy metaphysical musings. . . . [The] ponderous excursis on the musicological-metaphysical *weight* of Beethoven's *Es muss sein,* unlike the lively and fascinating colloquy on Moravian folk music in *The Joke,* seems labored and yields little in the way of insight or information.

In structure, this novel adheres to the pattern of the earlier novel: seven parts, some of which mark returns to previously handled themes, situations or characters. Kundera worries his material in a nervous, circular manner reminiscent of Mahler; he seems never to have done with it. The repeated agitating can be—as it is with Mahler—highly affecting. The themes stick in one's head, humming themselves away. We do well to listen to them.

By temper, subject and method, Kundera is a modernist. With roots in 19th-century formalism, he embodies those elements of the Central and Western European School that we may call Absurd Reality: post-Kafka and post-Brecht. He steps inside, then outside his characters, questioning their motives and—going beyond Brecht in this—questioning his own motives as well.

If *The Unbearable Lightness of Being* does not achieve levitation to the dizzying heights attained in *The Book of Laughter and Forgetting,* it is nonetheless an achievement of a very high order.

> Betty Falkenberg, "Losing Substance," in The New Leader, *Vol. LXVII, No. 9, May 14, 1984, p. 11.*

IAN McEWAN

From the beginning of Milan Kundera's writing career—and even in his early short stories—he has been addressing the problem of how, in [Virginia] Woolf's formulation, the 'granite' of ideas can sit comfortably beside the 'rainbow' of poetic truth, and in [**'The Unbearable Lightness of Being'**] he has triumphed, though at some cost; a metaphysical inquiry into the nature of fate and two love stories, related with Kundera's usual blend of scepticism and compassion, are united in a lucid novel whose exhilarating pessimism is subtly, and perhaps confusedly, challenged by the warmth of the telling.

It is partly the very nature of Kundera's ideas that prevents them from smothering the vitality of this novel, and partly the way he presents his characters. His agnosticism and nihilism allow him a freedom, an absence of commitment, which her passionate feminism denied Virginia Woolf in 'The Pargiters.' The lightness of Kundera's title refers to the insubstantiality, the meaninglessness of an event, or a life, if it cannot be repeated again; transitoriness denies validity to an event, prevents us coming to a verdict. Everything can be 'pardoned in advance and therefore everything cynically permitted.' Lightness in individual lives suggests a freedom from fate, obligation, truth, soaring into the heights—a flight into insignificance. Lightness is associated with vertigo—the desire to fall, to be weak, to yield responsibility.

Weight, on the other hand, is identified with the myth of eternal return which Kundera derives from Nietzsche: 'in the world of eternal return the weight of unbearable responsibility lies on every move we make.' But though heaviness is crushing, 'in the love poetry of every age the woman longs to be weighed down by the man's body.' Weight is therefore an image of 'life's most intense fulfilment'—it brings us closer to the truth, to the inevitability of our fate.

It is between these bleak polarities—unbearable lightness and crushing weight—that Kundera unfolds the lives, and predominantly they are sexual lives, of his four characters. How far does he succeed in guarding the weightless rainbow from the burden of the granite? Like many authors, Kundera is keen to let us know that his characters do not really exist. They are pure artifice.... And yet he introduces one of his principal characters like this: 'I have been thinking about Tomas for many years. But only in the light of these reflections [i.e. of lightness and weight] did I see him clearly.'

It is a clever trick. It is hard not to believe that these characters are not Czech friends of the author. He does not pretend to know everything about them. At times he is protective, at others sceptical. He speculates about them, explores them.... It is precisely because his characterisation is investigative, just like his metaphysical inquiries, that the two modes of writing do not appear to clash; instead they are made to serve the same end—the novel 'is an investigation of human life in the trap the world has become.'

There is, however, a small price to pay. These lovers seem real, but they are also remote. They are more talked about than shown. They are offered as evidence, and we become more involved in the author's relationship with them than in the experiences they undergo....

As in his last novel ['**The Book of Laughter and Forgetting**'], Kundera shows himself here to be a powerful opponent of totalitarian tyranny, but he is also suspicious of Western liberalism, sceptical of anyone who compromises his individuality by joining a political movement. This is the core of his nihilism: tyranny is foul, protest is delusion, silence is death.

And yet this nihilism exposes an interesting contradiction within the author. Among many other delights, the novel contains a scathing exposition on the nature of kitsch—that 'categorical agreement with being.' He asserts that a politics without kitsch is inconceivable and 'in the realm of kitsch the dictatorship of the heart reigns supreme.' However, the end of the book is dominated by an emotional account of the death of Tereza's dog (with chocolates laid in the grave).

Like Sterne, whom he admires, Kundera is really a man of the heart, and those readers who emphasise Kundera's warmth at the expense of his cold, rigorous eye and therefore 'kitschify' are not entirely to blame. There is an unexamined rift in this author between feeling and intellect. It is left to the reader to work at keeping both in view to understand what a dark and brilliant achievement the novel is.

> Ian McEwan, "*Granite and Rainbow*," *in* The Observer, *May 20, 1984, p. 22.*

DAVID LODGE

Twenty years ago, when the *Critical Quarterly* and I were young, and Milan Kundera was writing *The Joke* and wondering, no doubt, whether he would be allowed to publish it, it's very unlikely that I would have been asked, or, if asked, agreed, to write a critical article about a Czech novelist. The defiant, I-Like-It-Here provincialism of the Movement, the jealous guarding of the English Great Tradition by Leavis and his disciples, and the New Criticism's focus on stylistic nuance in literary texts, all militated against taking a professional interest in foreign writing. I was never under the spell of Leavis, but I was a literary child of the 1950s, and, as a critic, I was committed to the kind of close reading that, it seemed, could only be performed on and in one's mother tongue. In *Language of Fiction* (1966) I argued that meaning was as inseparable from verbal form in the novel as the New Criticism had shown

it to be in lyric poetry; and that although prose fiction was more translatable than verse, since in it sound and rhythm were less important, nevertheless there was bound to be such a degree of alteration and loss of meaning in the translation of a novel that the critic could never 'possess' it with the necessary confidence.

I no longer hold this position with the puritanical rigour expressed in the first part of *Language of Fiction*. Exposure to the Continental European structuralist tradition of poetics and criticism has shown me that literary narrative operates several codes of communication simultaneously, and in most of them (for instance, enigma, sequence, irony, perspective) effects are readily transferable from one natural language to another (and even from one medium to another). A flashback is a flashback in any language; so is a shift in point of view, a peripeteia, or an 'open' ending.

This does not entail any downgrading of language in the novel. Kundera himself claims that total commitment to the novel as *verbal* art for which I tried to provide a theoretical justification in *Language of Fiction*. 'Ever since *Madame Bovary*', he observes in the preface to the new edition of *The Joke,* 'the art of the novel has been considered equal to the art of poetry, and the novelist (any novelist worthy of the name) endows every word of his prose with the uniqueness of the word in a poem.' This does not mean that translation is impossible—if it did then a novelist like Kundera, writing in a minority language whose native speakers are forbidden access to his books, might as well shoot himself.... [On the contrary, many] tropes and figures are translatable between most Indo-European languages.

The problem of translation, then, is no longer a disincentive to addressing oneself to the critical consideration of a Czech novelist; and the conscious insularity of British literary culture in the 1950s has long since lost whatever justification it may once have had in encouraging a new wave of writers. But in the meantime, a new critical anxiety has arisen to threaten the project. To write on the fiction of 'Milan Kundera' is almost inevitably to accord that name the unity and substance of an historic individual ...: Milan Kundera, the author. But the liveliest and most innovative discourses of contemporary criticism, loosely describable as 'post-structuralist', have thrown the idea of the author very much into question.

Roland Barthes announced the 'Death of the Author' with characteristic Nietzschean relish back in 1968, at about the same time that Russian tanks were rolling into Czechoslovakia.... [His] proclamation, startling in 1968, is now a commonplace of academic criticism in the fashionable 'deconstructionist' mode, but has had little or no effect on the actual practice of writing outside the academy, which remains obstinately author-centred. Books are still identified and classified according to author. The value attributed to books brings kudos, prizes and royalties to their authors, who are the object of considerable public interest. Poststructuralist theorists, some of whom have been known to collaborate in this process, would no doubt explain it by saying that the institution of literature is still in thrall to bourgeois ideology. (pp. 106-07)

It is, of course, undeniable that the modern 'author' is a comparatively recent phenomenon. The further we peer back into history, the more anonymous and collective the production of stories, lyrics and drama appears. And Foucault is quite right to say that, looking in the opposite direction, 'We can easily imagine a culture where discourse would circulate without any need for an author'. Whether one would wish to live in it is, however, another matter. George Orwell imagined such a culture in *1984*.

The idea of the author which Barthes and Foucault seek to discredit is the product of humanism and the Enlightenment as well as of capitalism. Collective, anonymous art belongs historically to eras when slavery and serfdom were deemed ethically acceptable. Copyright is only one of many 'rights'—freedom of speech, freedom of movement, freedom of religious worship—which the bourgeois ideology of liberal humanism has claimed for the individual human being. Only those who take such freedoms for granted in their daily lives could perhaps contemplate with satisfaction the obsolescence of the idea which sustains and justifies them.

Of course the poststructuralist critique of the bourgeois or liberal humanist concept of individual man does not represent itself as totalitarian, but as utopian. (p. 108)

When *The Book of Laughter and Forgetting* was published, the government of Czechoslovakia deprived Milan Kundera of his citizenship *in absentia*. That a government should be stung into taking such revenge on an individual author is perhaps a good reason for wanting to defend the idea of authorship. If *The Book of Laughter and Forgetting* had been an anonymous discourse, like the anti-government jokes that circulate in all totalitarian states, the politicians would have found it easier to ignore.

One reason why the poststructuralist critique of the idea of the author has been so warmly welcomed in some quarters of academe is that it is presented as a liberation, a critical utopia. 'The Death of the Author, the Absolute Subject of literature, means the liberation of the text from the authority of a presence behind it which gives it meaning', says Catherine Belsey, enthusiastically paraphrasing Barthes. 'Released from the constraints of a single and univocal reading, the text becomes available for production, plural, contradictory, capable of change.' Behind this argument is a quite false antithesis between two models of interpretation, one of which we are told we must choose: either (A) the text contains a single meaning which the author intended and which it is the duty of the critic to establish, or (B) the text is a system capable of generating an infinite number of meanings when activated by the reader. (p. 109)

No one who is seriously engaged in the practice of writing fiction *and* familiar with modern critical theory (I speak personally, but also, I venture to think, for Kundera) could accept either of these positions as starkly stated here. Works of literature—in our era of civilisation, at least—do not come into being by accident. They are intentional acts, produced by individual writers employing shared codes of signification according to a certain design, weighing and measuring the interrelation of part to part and parts to the developing whole, projecting the work against the anticipated response of a hypothetical reader. Without such control and design there would be no reason to write one sentence rather than another, or to arrange one's sentences in any particular order. There would be no ground, either, on which to object to censorship. . . . But once the child leaves home—the book is published—a different situation obtains. It is of the nature of texts, especially fictional ones, that they have gaps and indeterminacies which may be filled in by different readers in different ways, and it is of the nature of codes that, once brought into play, they may generate patterns of significance which were not consciously

intended by the author who activated them, and which do not require his 'authorisation' to be accepted as valid interpretations of the text.

The serious modern writer is, therefore, likely to be just as suspicious of position A, above, as of position B. He (or she) knows that the proponents of A are all too eager to discard the 'implied author' of a text in pursuit of the 'real author', and to ask the latter what he 'meant' by his text instead of taking the trouble to read it attentively. The writer therefore finds ways of evading such questions, or confusing such questioners, by masks, disguises, obliquities and ambiguities, by hiding secret meanings in his text—secret, sometimes, even from himself.

Milan Kundera seems to be a case in point. He was at the very outset of his literary career a victim of the Intentional Fallacy (a fallacy that is committed by imputing and inferring intentions on the basis of extra-textual evidence). Here is a writer with a history of courageous resistance to the dominant ideology of a Communist State, finally forced into exile as the price of his intellectual independence. Must he not be labelled a 'dissident' writer? Since his books refer to the injustices and bad faith of the Communist régime in Czechoslovakia, must this not be what his fiction is *about*? That is precisely how *The Joke* has been received in the West. Kundera records, in the preface to the new edition, that, 'When, in 1980, during a television panel discussion devoted to my works, someone called *The Joke* "a major indictment of Stalinism", I was quick to interject, "Spare me your Stalinism, please. *The Joke* is a love story"'.'

This interjection is itself a statement of authorial intention, which we are not bound to accept. It is, indeed, a consciously simplistic description of *The Joke,* designed to head off a differently reductive reading of the text. But it does point us in the right direction. Kundera's work is ultimately more concerned with love—and death—than with politics; but it has been his fate to live in a country where life is willy-nilly conditioned by politics to an extent that has no equivalent in western democracies, so that these themes present themselves to his imagination inevitably and inextricably entangled with recent political history. But, as Kundera himself put it, repudiating the label of 'dissident writer':

> If you cannot view the art that comes to you
> from Prague, Budapest or Warsaw in any other
> way than by means of this wretched political
> code, you murder it, no less brutally than the
> work of the Stalinist dogmatists. And you are
> quite unable to hear its true voice. The impor-
> tance of this art does not lie in the fact that it
> pillories this or that political regime, but that,
> on the strength of social and human experience
> of a kind people here in the West cannot even
> imagine, it offers new testimony about man-
> kind.

As if to elude being read exclusively in the 'political code', Kundera concentrated subsequently on erotic comedy, often black comedy, in such works as *The Farewell Party* and *Laughable Loves*. In *The Book of Laughter and Forgetting* he returned to the explicit treatment of political material and dealt very directly with the effect of politics on his own life—but in a book so original, idiosyncratic and surprising in form that it offers the strongest possible resistance to a 'single univocal reading'. Whereas in *The Joke* Kundera displayed, at the first attempt, his mastery of the modernist novel, *The Book of Laughter and Forgetting* is a masterpiece of postmodernist fiction. . . . (pp. 109-11)

[A] summary gives some idea of the narrative *content* of *The Joke,* and as a bare story has, I dare say, a certain interest. But it conveys very little idea of what it is like to read *The Joke,* because, there, the information . . . comes to the reader in an entirely different order and in an entirely different mode of discourse. (p. 114)

As we read *The Joke* we necessarily 'make sense' of the narrative by restoring the codes of causality and chronology which have been deliberately 'scrambled' in the text. But this is not to say that the meaning of the text is the *fabula* which we can disinter from the *sjuzet.* On the contrary, the meaning inheres in the hermeneutic process itself: the reader's activity in interpreting and making sense of the story, responding to the clues and cues provided by the text, constantly readjusting a provisional interpretation in the light of new knowledge, re-enacts the efforts of the characters to make sense of their own lives. (p. 115)

The Joke is manifestly a 'modern' novel, but it would be hard to believe that it was composed in the manner Roland Barthes attributes to the 'modern scriptor', who 'is born simultaneously with the text, is in no way equipped with a being preceding or exceeding the writing, is not the subject with the book as predicate'. On the contrary, we have in reading *The Joke* an overwhelming sense of a creative mind behind the text, its 'implied author', who constructed its labyrinth of meanings with love and dedication and immense skill over a long period of time, during which the design of the whole must have been present to his consciousness. *The Book of Laughter and Forgetting,* however, seems, in part, to fit Barthes' prescription/description of the modern text as 'a multi-dimensional space in which a variety of writings, none of them original, blend and clash'. It *is* 'original', but lacks the rich, 'deep', slowly emerging, satisfying aesthetic and thematic unity of *The Joke.* It is fragmentary, disjunctive, confused and confusing; it has an improvised air. Instead of telling a single, unified story, it tells several separate stories, only two of which concern the same character. . . . The kind of 'recognitions' which illuminate *The Joke* are deliberately frustrated in the later book. (p. 116)

The method used to study the form of *The Joke*—inferring the *fabula* and comparing it with the *sjuzet*—will hardly do in this instance. There are too many discrete *fabulas* to cope with, and in any case they are narrated in a rather straightforward summary fashion. The 'deformation' of the *fabula* in the *sjuzet* consists not so much in the manipulation of chronology and point of view as in the disruption of the temporal-spatial continuity of the narrative by the intrusions and digressions of the authorial narrator. This narrator identifies himself quite unambiguously as 'Milan Kundera', and relates several apparently 'true' stories about his own life. Paradoxically, this overt appearance of the author in the text does not make it easier, but harder, to determine what it 'means'. The real author has, as it were, leapfrogged over the implied author, to appear as a trope in his own text, which makes it all the harder to identify the implied author's attitudes and values. These three versions of the author are, obviously, very closely related, but do not quite coincide with each other.

The only way to deal, critically, with *The Book of Laughter and Forgetting* is to review its textual strategies in the order in which they are experienced by the reader. (pp. 116-17)

[The following passage appears near the end of Part Three, entitled 'The Angels':]

> . . . And I ran after that voice through the streets in the hope of keeping up with that wonderful wreath of bodies rising above the city, and I realised with anguish in my heart that they were flying like birds and I was falling like a stone, that they had wings and I would never have any. . . .

This passage has the sublime perfection of a Joycean 'epiphany', but in its astonishing shift from the historical to the fantastic it strikes a characteristically 'postmodernist' note—one that has caused Milan Kundera to be linked with such writers as Gabriel Garcia Márquez, Günter Grass and Salman Rushdie, under the umbrella of 'magic realism'. Kundera uses this technique more modestly and sparingly (and perhaps for that reason more effectively) than they do, but with the same implied justification: that the contradictions and outrages of modern history are of such a scale that only the overt 'lie' of the fantastic or grotesque image can adequately represent them. The power and effectiveness of this passage could not, however, be conveyed by quoting it out of context. It brings together, with devastating rhetorical force, bits of information and symbolic motifs that have been previously introduced into the text with deceptive casualness. It is this periodic *convergence* of diverse and apparently disparate discourses that gives *The Book of Laughter and Forgetting* its unity. (p. 119)

The Book of Laughter and Forgetting contains many . . . enigmas, contradictions, ambiguities, which are not resolved. It never allows the reader the luxury of identifying with a secure authorial position that is invulnerable to criticism and irony. But that it is the work of a distinctive, gifted, self-conscious 'author' is never in doubt. (p. 120)

> *David Lodge, "Milan Kundera, and the Idea of the Author in Modern Criticism," in* Critical Quarterly, *Vol. 26, Nos. 1 & 2, Spring & Summer, 1984, pp. 105-21.*

STEVEN G. KELLMAN

Is it appropriate to begin a review of Milan Kundera with a rhetorical question? Are all questions rhetorical? In a 1980 interview with Philip Roth published as an afterward to *The Book of Laughter and Forgetting,* Kundera said: "The stupidity of people comes from having an answer for everything. The wisdom of the novel comes from having a question for everything." *The Unbearable Lightness of Being,* Kundera's fifth novel, is an unquestionable triumph, a Socratic monologue bearing abundant wisdom. . . .

Why does Milan Kundera write like no one else in the world?

Kundera's father was a prominent pianist, and he himself worked for a time as a jazz musician. Two of the principal figures in his first novel, *The Joke* . . . , Ludvik and Jaroslav, are a clarinetist and a violinist, respectively. Music furnishes the metaphors by which many Kundera characters live. . . .

Human lives in Kundera are composed like music, and his novels are constructed like orchestral variations. . . . [Each] has seven sections. The new novel [*The Unbearable Lightness of Being*] is less a septych, a sequence of seven consecutive episodes, than a septet, a fugue on several characters, ideas, and incidents that recur throughout. In recounting the intersecting lives of Tomas, Tereza, Franz, and Sabina, in Czechoslovakia, Switzerland, France, Thailand, and the United States, Kundera's technique is circular and polyphonic rather than linear and univocal. He described his last novel as "a polyphony in which various stories mutually explain, illumine, complement each other," and might have done the same for his new one as well. In *The Book of Laughter and Forgetting,* he paid tribute to musical variations: "The variation is the form of maximum concentration. It enables the composer to limit himself to the matter at hand, to go straight to the heart of it."

The Unbearable Lightness of Being exhibits this maximum concentration as a set of variations on the experiences of a few Europeans in the aftermath of the Prague Spring, and on meditations the author improvises about them. There's anecdotal matter lurking here. . . . Yet the narrative is curiously detached, the author wryly, wistfully intent on ruminating. In one section, rather than narrate the progress of the relationship between Franz and Sabina, Kundera provides us with "A Short Dictionary of Misunderstood Words." An examination of the lovers' divergent approaches to such terms as "woman," "parades," "cemetery," "strength," and "living in truth" defines their estrangement and makes it intelligible.

Einmal ist keinmal—"If we have only one life to live, we might as well not have lived at all." As an American sage once noted, once is not enough. Kundera reiterates this notion at several points in [*The Unbearable Lightness of Being*] and it is the basis for the lightness he attributes to unilinear human existence, as if weight were a function of simultaneous alternatives. The book's fugal form provides substance through repetition. . . . An ordinary memoir or political statement would have been unbearably light: "The characters in my novels are my own unrealized possibilities," Kundera says. They are his chance to imagine roads not taken and linger over contradictory thoughts on eros, spirituality, contingency, tyranny.

For Kundera, the adversary isn't simply Socialist Realism or the scoundrels who seized power in 1968; it's what he calls a "categorical agreement with being." This cosmic complacency is as much an occupational hazard of dissidence as of sycophancy. For all his fixation on Czech capitulation to Russian brawn, Kundera is only obliquely and warily a political writer. The cultural manifestation of metaphysical smugness, the sanitized version of reality he detests, is kitsch: "a folding screen set up to curtain off death." Kundera asks pointed questions about the dogmas of cheer, of "a world in which shit is denied and everyone acts as though it did not exist," and these questions levitate *The Unbearable Lightness of Being.*

Kundera's novel is written under the sign of the interrogation point. Its catechism is a strategy for besmirching the hygienic systems that diminish its characters' lives. In posing questions—about the characters' relations to one another, to their author, and to the universe—Kundera is writing *no* in lightning to a literary regime that demands a very different kind of prose:

> In the realm of totalitarian kitsch, all answers are given in advance and preclude any questions. It follows, then, that the true opponent of totalitarian kitsch is the person who asks questions. A question is like a knife that slices through the stage backdrop and gives us a look at what lies hidden behind it.

Kundera's ambitions are loftier than tossing verbal stones at Soviet tanks back in Prague or immersing us in the singular lives of one cast of dramatis personae. *The Unbearable Light-*

ness of Being is not entirely devoid of the concrete quiddities that are the chief pleasure of traditional realism. . . . But this spare book dares disturb that universe. "A question with no answer is a barrier that cannot be breached. In other words, it is questions with no answers that set the limits of human possibilities, describe the boundaries of human existence." If a book succeeds in embodying that kind of description, there isn't much more a reader can ask.

Steven G. Kellman, "Disturbing the Universe," in
The Village Voice, *Vol. XXIX, No. 26, June 26, 1984, p. 43.*

NORMAN PODHORETZ

Dear Milan Kundera:

About four years ago, a copy of the bound galleys of your novel, *The Book of Laughter and Forgetting,* came into my office for review. As a magazine editor I get so many books every week in that form that unless I have a special reason I rarely do more than glance at their titles. In the case of *The Book of Laughter and Forgetting* I had no such special reason. By 1980 your name should have been more familiar to me, but in fact I had only a vague impression of you as an East European dissident—so vague that, I am now ashamed to confess, I could not have said for certain which country you came from: Hungary? Yugoslavia? Czechoslovakia? Perhaps even Poland? [In a footnote, Podhoretz comments: "Since then you have taught me that the term East Europe is wrong because the countries in question belong to the West and that we should speak instead of Central Europe. But in 1980 I did not yet understand this."]

Nor was I particularly curious about you either as an individual or as a member of the class of "East" European dissident writers. This was not because I was or am unsympathetic to dissidents in Communist regimes or those living in exile in the West. On the contrary, as a passionate anti-Communist, I am all too sympathetic—at least for their own good as writers.

"How many books about the horrors of life under Communism am I supposed to read? How many ought I to read?" asks William F. Buckley, Jr., another member of the radically diminished fraternity of unregenerate anti-Communists in the American intellectual world. Like Buckley, I felt that there were a good many people who still needed to learn about "the horrors of life under Communism," but that I was not one of them. Pleased though I was to see books by dissidents from behind the Iron Curtain published and disseminated, I resisted reading any more of them myself.

What then induced me to begin reading *The Book of Laughter and Forgetting*? I have no idea. Knowing your work as well as I do now, I can almost visualize myself as a character in a Kundera novel, standing in front of the cabinet in my office where review copies of new books are kept, suddenly being seized by one of them while you, the author, break into the picture to search speculatively for the cause. But whatever answer you might come up with, I have none. I simply do not know why I should have been drawn against so much resistance to *The Book of Laughter and Forgetting.* What I do know is that once I had begun reading it, I was transfixed.

Twenty-five years ago, as a young literary critic, I was sent an advance copy of a book of poems called *Life Studies.* It was by Robert Lowell, a poet already famous and much honored in America, but whose earlier work had generally left me cold. I therefore opened *Life Studies* with no great expectation of pleasure, but what I found there was more than pleasure. Reading it, I told Lowell in a note thanking him for the book, made me remember, as no other new volume of verse had for a long time, why I had become interested in poetry in the first place. That is exactly what *The Book of Laughter and Forgetting* did for my old love of the novel—a love grown cold and stale and dutiful.

During my years as a literary critic, I specialized in contemporary fiction, and one of the reasons I eventually gave up on criticism was that the novels I was reading seemed to me less and less worth writing about. They might be more or less interesting, more or less amusing, but mostly they told me more about their authors, and less about life or the world, than I wanted or needed to know. Once upon a time the novel (as its English name suggests) had been a bringer of news; or (to put it in the terms you yourself use in a recent essay entitled "The Novel and Europe") its mission had been to "uncover a hitherto unknown segment of existence." But novel after novel was now "only confirming what had already been said."

That is how you characterize the "hundreds and thousands of novels published in huge editions and widely read in Communist Russia." But "confirming what had already been said" was precisely what most of the novels written and published in the democratic West, including many honored for boldness and originality, were also doing. This was the situation twenty years ago, and it is perhaps even worse today. I do not, of course, mean that our novelists follow an official "party line," either directly or in some broader sense. What I do mean is that the most esteemed novels of our age in the West often seem to have as their main purpose the reinforcement of the by now endlessly reiterated idea that literary people are superior in every way to the businessmen, the politicians, the workers among whom they live—that they are more intelligent, more sensitive, and morally finer than everyone else.

You write, in the same essay from which I have just quoted, that "Every novel says to the reader: 'Things are not as simple as you think.'" This may be true of the best, the greatest, of novels. But it is not true of most contemporary American novels. Most contemporary American novels invite the reader to join with the author in a luxuriously complacent celebration of themselves and of the stock prejudices and bigotries of the "advanced" literary culture against the middle-class world around them. Flaubert could declare that *he* was Madame Bovary; the contemporary American novelist, faced with a modern-day equivalent of such a character, announces: How wonderful it is to have nothing whatever in common with this dull and inferior person.

In your essay on the novel you too bring up Flaubert and you credit him with discovering "the *terra* previously *incognita* of the everyday." But what "hitherto unknown segment of existence" did you discover in *The Book of Laughter and Forgetting*? In my opinion, the answer has to be: the distinctive things Communism does to the life—most notably the spiritual or cultural life—of a society. Before reading *The Book of Laughter and Forgetting*, I thought that a novel set in Communist Czechoslovakia could "only confirm what had already been said" and what I, as a convinced anti-Communist, had already taken in. William Buckley quite reasonably asks: "How is it possible for the thousandth exposé of life under Communism to be original?" But what you proved in *The Book of Laughter and Forgetting* (and, I have since discovered, in some of your earlier novels like *The Joke* as well) is that it *is* possible

to be original even in going over the most frequently trodden ground. You cite with approval "Hermann Broch's obstinately repeated point that the only *raison d'être* of a novel is to discover what can only be discovered by a novel," and your own novels are a splendid demonstration of that point.

If I were still a practicing literary critic, I would be obligated at this juncture to show how *The Book of Laughter and Forgetting* achieves this marvelous result. To tell you the truth, though, even if I were not so rusty, I would have a hard time doing so. This is not an easy book to describe, let alone to analyze. Indeed, if I had not read it before the reviews came out, I would have been put off, and misled, by the terms in which they praised it.

Not that these terms were all inaccurate. *The Book of Laughter and Forgetting* assuredly is, in the words of one reviewer, "part fairy tale, part literary criticism, part political tract, part musicology, and part autobiography"; and I also agree with the same reviewer when he adds that "the whole is genius." Yet what compelled me most when I first opened *The Book of Laughter and Forgetting* was not its form or its aesthetic character but its *intellectual* force, the astonishing intelligence controlling and suffusing every line.

The only other contemporary novelist I could think of with that kind of intellectual force, that degree of intelligence, was Saul Bellow. Like Bellow, you moved with easy freedom and complete authority through the world of ideas, and like him too you were often playful in the way you handled them. But in the end Bellow seemed always to be writing only about himself, composing endless and finally claustrophobic variations on the theme of Saul Bellow's sensibility. You too were a composer of variations; in fact, in *The Book of Laughter and Forgetting* itself you made so bold as to inform us that "This entire book is a novel in the form of variations." Yet even though you yourself, as Milan Kundera, kept making personal appearances in the course of which you talked about your own life or, again speaking frankly in your own name, delivered yourself of brilliant little essays about the history of Czechoslovakia, or of music, or of literature, *you*, Milan Kundera, were not the subject of this novel, or the "theme" of these variations. The theme was totalitarianism: what it is, what it does, where it comes from. But this was a novel, however free and easy in its formal syncretism, whose mission was "to discover what can only be discovered by a novel," and consequently all its terms were specified. Totalitarianism thus meant Communism, and more specifically Soviet Communism, and still more specifically Communism as imposed on Czechoslovakia, first in 1948 by a coup and then, twenty years later in 1968, by the power of Soviet tanks.

Nowadays it is generally held that Communism is born out of hunger and oppression, and in conspicuously failing to "confirm" that idea, you were to that extent being original. But to anyone familiar with the literature, what you had to say about Communism was not in itself new: that it arises out of the utopian fantasy of a return to Paradise; that it can brook no challenge to its certainties; that it cannot and will not tolerate pluralism either in the form of the independent individual or in the form of the unique national culture.

All these things had been said before—by Orwell, Koestler, Camus, and most recently Solzhenitsyn. Indeed, according to Solzhenitsyn, Communism has done to Russia itself exactly what you tell us it has done to Czechoslovakia and all the other peoples and nations that have been absorbed into the Soviet empire. From the point of view of those nations it is traditional Russian imperialism that has crushed the life out of them, but in Solzhenitsyn's eyes Russia itself is as much the victim of Communism as the countries of Central Europe.

In another of your essays, "The Tragedy of Central Europe," you lean toward the perspective of the enslaved countries in fixing the blame on Russia rather than Communism, and you also agree with the great Polish dissident Leszek Kolakowski when he criticizes Solzhenitsyn's "tendency to idealize czarism." Nevertheless, there can be no doubt that *The Book of Laughter and Forgetting* is anti-Communist before it is anti-Russian. It begins not with Stalin but with the Czech Communist leader Klement Gottwald and the coup that brought Communism to power in Czechoslovakia, and you make it clear throughout that the utopian fantasies in whose service Czechoslovakia is gradually murdered as a nation come from within. It is only when the nation begins to awake and tries to save itself from the slow suicide it has been committing that the Soviet tanks are sent in.

Yet even though in one sense *The Book of Laughter and Forgetting* said nothing new about Communism, in another sense it "discovered" Communism as surely as Flaubert "discovered" everyday life (about which, after all, *Madame Bovary* said nothing new, either). As I have already indicated, I find it very hard to understand how you were able to make the familiar seem unfamiliar and then to familiarize it anew with such great freshness and immediacy. Perhaps the answer lies in the unfamiliar form you created in which a number of apparently unrelated stories written in different literary genres ranging from the conventionally realistic to the surrealistic are strung together only by the author's direct intervention and a common theme which, however, is not even clearly visible in every case.

What, for example, connects Karel of Part II, who makes love simultaneously to his wife and his mistress as his aged mother sleeps in the next room, with Mirek of Part I, a disillusioned ex-Communist who gets six years in prison for trying to keep a careful record of events after the invasion of Czechoslovakia? Then there is the section about the student who rushes off to spend an evening getting drunk with a group of famous poets while a married woman he has been lusting after waits impatiently for him in his room. Why is the fairly straight comic realism of that section immediately followed by the grim Kafkaesque parable of the young woman who finds herself living in a world populated exclusively by little children ("angels") who at first worship and then finally torment her to death?

Whatever explanations subsequent analysis might yield, the fact is that those "brutal juxtapositions" make so powerful an effect on a first reading that they justify themselves before they are fully understood; and here too (at least so far as I personally was concerned) you prevailed against resistance. Nowadays my taste in fiction runs strongly to the realistic, and the enthusiasm I once felt for the experimental has waned as experimental writing has itself become both conventional and purposeless. But just as you have "discovered" Communism for the novel, so you have resurrected formal experimentation. The point of such experimentation was not originally to drive the novel out of the world it had been exploring for so long through the techniques and devices of realism; the point was to extend those techniques to previously unexplored regions of the inner life. What you say of Bartók, that he "knew how to discover the last original possibility in music based on the tonal principle," could be said of what Joyce, Kafka, and Proust

were doing in relation to the fictional principle of verisimilitude. It can also, I believe, be said of you.

But since you yourself compare *The Book of Laughter and Forgetting* to a piece of music, it seems appropriate to admit that in reading it I was not so much reminded of other modern novelists as of the tonal modernist composers who, no matter how dissonant and difficult they may be (some of Bartók's own string quartets are a good case in point), are still intelligible to the ear in a way that the atonal and serial composers are not, no matter how often one listens to their works. Bartók, Stravinsky, Prokofiev, Shostakovich, and your beloved Janáček all found new and striking means by which to make the familiar world of sound seem new—to bring it, as we say, back to life. And this, it seemed to me, was what you were doing to a familiar world of experience in *The Book of Laughter and Forgetting*.

A few weeks after I had finished reading it, *The Book of Laughter and Forgetting* was published in the United States, and to my amazement the reviewers were just as enthusiastic about it as I had been. If you are wondering why this should have amazed me, I will tell you frankly that I would not have expected the American literary world to applaud so outspokenly anti-Communist a book. In France, where you have been living since 1975, anti-Communism may lately have come into fashion among intellectuals, but here in the United States it has for some years been anathema to literary people—and to most other people who think of themselves as liberals or as "sophisticated" or both. Very few of these people are actually sympathetic to Communism, but even fewer of them take it seriously as a threat or even as a reality. They are convinced that no one in the Soviet Union, let alone the satellite countries, believes in Communism any longer, if they ever did; and as for the Third World, the Marxist-Leninists there are not really Communists (even to call them Communists is taken as a sign of political primitivism) but nationalists making use of a convenient rhetoric. Hence to be an anti-Communist is to be guilty of hating and fearing an illusion—or rather, the ghost of something that may once have existed but that has long since passed away.

In the view of most American literary people, however, anti-Communists are not merely suffering from paranoid delusions; they are also dangerous in that they tend to exaggerate the dimensions of the Soviet threat. Here again, just as very few of these people are pro-Communist, hardly a single one can be found who is openly or straightforwardly pro-Soviet. Once there were many defenders of and apologists for the Soviet Union in the American literary world, but that was a long time ago. In recent years it has been almost impossible to find a writer or a critic who will argue that the Soviet Union is building a workers' paradise or who will declare that Soviet domination of the countries of Central Europe is a good thing.

On the other hand, it is now the standard view that in its conflict with the West, or rather the United States, the Soviet Union is more sinned against than sinning. Everything the Soviets do (even the invasion of Afghanistan) is defensive or a reaction to an American provocation; and anything that cannot be explained away in these terms (the attempted assassination of the Pope, the cheating on arms-control agreements, the use of poison gas) is denied. The idea that seems self-evident to you (and to me), namely, that the Soviets are out to dominate the world, is regarded as too patently ridiculous even to be debated; it is dismissed either with a patronizing smile or with a show of incredulous indignation. One is permitted to criticize the

Soviet Union as a "tyranny," but to see it as a threat is both to be paranoid and to feed Soviet paranoia, thereby increasing the risk of an all-out nuclear war.

Given this frame of mind, most reviewers might have been expected to bridle at the anti-Communism of *The Book of Laughter and Forgetting.* But none of them did. Why? Possibly some or even all of them were so impressed with your novel as a work of art that they were willing to forgive or overlook its anti-Communism. Perhaps. But in any event—and this is a factor I should have anticipated but did not—as a Czech who has suffered and is now in exile, you have a license to be anti-Soviet and even anti-Communist. All Soviet or Central European dissidents are granted that license. By sympathizing with and celebrating dissident or refugee artists and intellectuals from the Communist world, literary people here can demonstrate (to themselves as much as to others) that their hatred of oppression extends to the Left no less than to the Right and that their love of literature also transcends political and ideological differences.

If you ask me what objection I or anyone else could conceivably have to such a lofty attitude, I will ask you in turn to reflect on the price that you yourself are paying for being treated in this way. In a piece about the reaction in France to your latest novel, *The Unbearable Lightness of Being,* Edmund White writes: "When faced with a figure such as Kundera, French leftists, eager to atone for former Soviet sympathies, begin to echo the unregenerate anti-Communism of Gaullists." The opposite has been true of the American reaction to your work. Here it has either become yet another occasion for sneering at "unregenerate anti-Communism" or else it has been described in the most disingenuously abstract terms available. You are writing about memory and laughter, about being and non-being, about love and sex, about angels and devils, about home and exile—about anything, in short, but the fate of Czechoslovakia under Communism and what that fate means, or should mean, to those of us living in the free world.

Thus one of your leftist admirers in America assures us that "Kundera refuses to settle into a complacency where answers come easy; no cold-war scold he. He subjects the 'free world's' contradictions to equally fierce scrutiny; the issues he confronts—the bearing of time, choice, and being—transcend time and place." Neither, according to another of your admirers who also puts derisive quotation marks around the phrase free world, do you detect any fundamental difference between the fate of literature under conditions of artistic freedom and what happens to it under Communist totalitarianism: "His need to experiment with form is surely connected to his personal vendetta against the puerilities of 'socialist realism' and its 'free world' counterparts."

What is being done to you here, I have come to see, bears a macabre resemblance to what has been done posthumously to George Orwell. In Orwell's own lifetime, no one had any doubt that the species of totalitarianism he was warning against in *Nineteen Eighty-Four* was Communism. Yet as we have all discovered from the endless discussions of that book occasioned by the coming of the real 1984, it is now interpreted and taught more as a warning against the United States than the Soviet Union. If the word Orwellian means turning things into their opposites ("war is peace," etc.), then Orwell himself has been Orwellianized—not by an all-powerful state in control of all means of expression and publication but by what Orwell himself called the "new aristocracy" of publicists and professors. This new aristocracy so dominates the centers in which opinion is shaped that it is able to distort the truth, especially about the past, to a degree that Orwell thought could never be reached so long as freedom of speech existed.

Like Orwell before you, you are obsessed with the theme of memory, and you believe with one of your characters "that the struggle of man against power is the struggle of memory against forgetting." The power you have in mind is the political power of the totalitarian state, but what the case of Orwell so ironically and paradoxically and poignantly demonstrates is that in the democratic West the power against which memory must struggle is the *cultural* power of the "new aristocracy." This power, with no help whatever from the state (and indeed operating in opposition to the state), has taken the real Orwell, to whom nothing was more fundamental than the distinction between the free world and the Communist world, and sent him down the memory hole, while giving us in his place an Orwell who was neutral as between the United States and the Soviet Union and who saw no important differences between life in a Communist society and life in the democratic West.

Now that same power is trying to do the same thing to you. But of course this is an even more brazen operation. Orwell's grave has been robbed; you are being kidnapped.

When I first thought of writing to you about this, I assumed that you would be appalled to learn how in America your work was falling into the hands of people who were using it for political purposes that you would surely consider pernicious. But now *I* am appalled to learn that you have been cooperating with your own kidnappers. "If I write a love story, and there are three lines about Stalin in that story," you tell the New York *Times Book Review,* "people will talk about the three lines and forget the rest, or read the rest for its political implications or as a metaphor for politics." But in America, once again, the opposite more nearly obtains: you write a book about Czechoslovakia under Communism containing three lines about love and everyone talks about those three lines and says that Czechoslovakia under Communism is a metaphor for life in the "free world" (in quotation marks of course). Or you write a novel, *The Unbearable Lightness of Being,* containing a brief episode in which an anti-Communist Czech émigré in Paris is seen by one of the characters as no different in kind from the Communists back in Prague (both being equally dogmatic), and virtually every reviewer gleefully cites it by way of suggesting that in your eyes Communism and anti-Communism are equivalent evils.

I think I can understand why a writer in exile from a Communist society should wish to turn his back on politics altogether, particularly where his own work is concerned. It is, after all, the essence of totalitarianism to politicize everything, most emphatically including the arts, and what better protest could there be against this distinctive species of tyranny than to insist on the reality and finally the superior importance of the non-political in life? You are, for example, obviously fascinated by erotic experience in its own right and for its own sake, and that is why you write about it so much. Yet it is hard to escape the impression that sex also plays such a large role in your novels because under Communism it became the only area of privacy that remained relatively intact when everything else had become politicized. (Surely too you make fun of orgies and nude beaches because they represent an effort to turn sex into a servant of the utopian fantasies that Communism has failed to satisfy.)

But even greater than your passion for sex is your love of Western civilization, and especially its literature and its music.

If I read you correctly, nothing that Communism has done, none of the crimes it has committed, not even the gulags it has created, seems to you worse than the war it has waged against Western culture. To you it is a war that goes beyond the stifling of free expression or the effort by the state to prescribe the very forms in which artists are permitted to work. It is *total* war. It involves the complete cultural annihilation by the Soviet Union of the countries of Central Europe, and this in turn— so you believe—represents the amputation of a vital part of Western civilization.

You make a powerful case in "The Tragedy of Central Europe" for the proposition that the countries of that area are "the cultural home" of the West. From this it follows that in acquiescing since Yalta in their absorption into the alien civilization of the East (alien because "Russian Communism vigorously reawakened Russia's old anti-Western obsessions and turned it brutally against Europe"), the West has shown that it no longer believes in the worth of its own civilization. The unity of the West was once based on religion; then religion "bowed out, giving way to culture, which became the expression of the supreme values by which European humanity understood itself, defined itself, identified itself as European." The tragedy of Central Europe has revealed that "Just as God long ago gave way to culture, culture in turn is giving way." To what? You do not say because you do not know. "I think I know only that culture has bowed out" in the West.

You do not explicitly add here that you for one are refusing to bow out, but you do tell us elsewhere that your supreme commitment is to the heritage of the European novel. You further give us to understand that as a novelist you mean to keep faith with your Central European heritage in particular— a heritage embodied in a "disabused view of history" and "the 'non-serious spirit' that mocks grandeur and glory." Summing it all up, you once responded to someone who had praised your first book as an indictment of Stalinism with the irritable remark: "Spare me your Stalinism. *The Joke* is a love story. . . . [It] is *merely* a novel."

Your love of culture, then, gives you a double incentive to deny the political dimension of your work. You wish to protect it from the "mindlessness of politicization," and at the same time to be anti-political is a way of *not* forgetting the murdered spirit of Czechoslovakia and the other countries of Central Europe which have now "disappeared from the map."

Even though I do not share your generally sour attitude toward religion, to all this I say: Yes, yes, and again yes. But I ask you, I implore you, to consider that by cooperating with those who have kidnapped your work, you are "bowing out" yourself. The testimony of the dissidents behind the Iron Curtain, whether they languish in prison or now live in the West, has played an immense role in forcing the intellectuals of Europe and America to think about the political values at stake in the conflict between East and West. Now you have come along

and forced us all to begin thinking again (or perhaps for the first time) about the *cultural* dimension of this struggle. This has been the distinctive contribution, and the glory, of your work. Why then should you wish to encourage the agents of the very cultural abdication you deplore and mourn and lament? Why should you, of all writers, wish to be coopted by people who think there is no moral or political—or cultural—difference between West and East worth talking about, let alone fighting over? Why should you allow yourself to provide cover for people who think that Western civilization should not and cannot be defended?

You will perhaps answer in the words with which your essay on the novel concludes: "I am attached to nothing apart from the European novel," and that the "wisdom of the novel" requires skepticism as opposed to dogmatic certainty, the refusal to take sides, the raising of questions rather than the finding of answers. But let me remind you of what you also know—that the novel is devoted to exploring the concrete and the particular. Those on the American Left who have taken you up have been able to do so only by ignoring the novelistic essence of your work, its concreteness and its particularity: by robbing it (to adapt the guiding metaphor of your latest novel) of *weight*, by cutting it loose from the earth and letting it float high into a realm of comfortable abstractions in which all moral and political distinctions become invisible, and everything merges into "the unbearable lightness of being."

In the novel to which you give that phrase as a title, you profess uncertainly as to whether one should choose weight or lightness, but that novel itself, like your writing in general, belies the uncertainty. In your work you have chosen weight, which is to say the burdens of memory and the celebration of a "world of concrete living." Even your flirtation with the irresponsibilities of lightness paradoxically adds to that weight, deriving as it does from the heavy burden you have accepted of keeping the mocking and irreverent spirit of your culturally devastated homeland alive: a spirit that darkens the lightness of the laughter you so value and that throws the shadow of the gallows over the jokes you love to make.

You have declared in an interview that you want all of us in the West to understand what happened at Yalta, that it is necessary for "a Frenchman or an American . . . to know, to reason, to comprehend what is happening to, say, people in Czechoslovakia . . . so that his naiveté won't become his tragedy." It is for the sake of that necessary understanding that I beg you to stop giving aid and encouragement to the cultural powers who are using some of your own words to prevent your work from helping to alert a demoralized West to the dangers it faces from a self-imposed Yalta of its own. (pp. 34-9)

Norman Podhoretz, "An Open Letter to Milan Kundera," in Commentary, *Vol. 78, No. 4, October, 1984, pp. 34-9.*

Penelope Lively

1933-

Egyptian-born English novelist, short story writer, and author of books for children.

An award-winning author of literature for children, Lively is rapidly gaining recognition for her adult fiction as well. Her novels reveal her deep interest in history, time, and memory and their effect on human relationships and individual perceptions of life. For example, in *The Road to Lichfield* (1977), Lively's first adult novel, a young woman's fond memories of her deceased father are suddenly challenged when she learns that he had a lengthy extramarital affair.

While Lively maintains her thematic focus on the patterns of time and the importance of memory in all of her novels, she also explores a variety of other issues. In *Judgement Day* (1980) she confronts the difficulty of believing in a benevolent God when considering life's inexplicable hardships and tragedies, and in *Next to Nature, Art* (1982) she satirizes artistic pretensions. *Perfect Happiness* (1983) centers on a woman who comes to terms with the death of her famous husband.

(See also *Children's Literature Review*, Vol. 7; *Contemporary Authors*, Vols. 41-44, rev. ed.; *Something about the Author*, Vol. 7; and *Dictionary of Literary Biography*, Vol. 14.)

JOHN MELLORS

There is nothing very original about the plot [of *The Road to Lichfield*]. . . .

The book is lifted out of the ordinary by its author's treatment of her two main themes: continuity and memory. Is the past 'something people carry around like a millstone' or 'what they prop themselves up with'? Does memory distort or preserve? . . . Is domestic harmony gained only by 'the deft avoidance of all those rogue subjects that can shatter the smooth passage of a meal'? Penelope Lively has an easy, unobtrusive style, throws light from unexpected angles on large issues, and leaves the reader concerned about her characters' future.

John Mellors, "Acceptance Won't Do," *in* The Listener, *Vol. 98, No. 2520, August 4, 1977, p. 158.**

JOHN MELLORS

In one of the 14 stories in *Nothing Missing but the Samovar*, an elderly spinster makes a habit of walking in Hyde Park: 'She studied her fellow walkers with avid attention . . . She delighted in novelty: eccentricities of dress, perplexing snatches of conversation. She moved up and down the wide paths, across the grass, between the neat flowerbeds, alert and expectant—an inquisitive ghost foraging among the walkers.' It goes without saying that people who write about people are inquisitive, but not all writers have Penelope Lively's knack of effacing herself to a ghost's invisibility. She is as tactful as her cathedral officials in **'Interpreting the Past',** who are careful never to intrude on visitors: 'The past has no right to impose itself on people; it is there to be taken or left, as we see fit.' Penelope

Photograph by Mark Gerson

Lively does not impose her stories on us, and as a result of her unobtrusive skill we see fit to take them, not leave them.

She is particularly good at showing how one generation looks at, or ignores, the activities and preoccupations of another. . . . [One] story, **'Party',** is all about the mingling without mixing of different age-groups. A 63-year-old woman, thinking of her husband, who died ten years ago, feels 'a faint, fragrant gust of sexual memory'. She finds that she has nothing in common with her daughter and her elder grandchildren, but with her 11-year-old grandson she is happy to sit up until morning making model aeroplanes. (p. 174)

John Mellors, "Inquisitive Ghosts," *in* The Listener, *Vol. 101, No. 2595, January 25, 1979, pp. 174-75.**

SUSAN HILL

[In *Treasures of Time*, Lively] reveals a gift for highlighting character-types, picking out revealing details of social behaviour, manner and conversation, and a certain ability to hit a nail ironically on the head. She is technically inventive and assured, and her book reads a little like the work of Elizabeth Jane Howard—a compliment indeed. Yet I do not think she has yet proved that she possesses a talent for writing adult fiction of anything like the high order of her children's books.

273

Treasures of Time is enjoyable, perceptive, shrewd, but it collapses badly, and scurries towards a rather arbitrary conclusion, as though she had lost interest or run out of steam—grown bored, long before her readers. Having created a completely convincing social world, with past and present filled in intrinsic detail, she fails to exploit its full potential. . . . (p. 22)

Her novel concerns the family of a celebrated archaeologist, now dead, and a television profile film being made about his life, work and personality. Mrs Lively goes into some detail about the historical period, and significance of Paxton's researches which, being singularly lacking in any historical sense myself, I read with a rather abstracted interest, and some incomprehension. But to many people, they will add a further dimension to her novel. The accounts of Paxton's character and behaviour, the descriptions of his surviving family, are the most fascinating. . . . Laura Paxton is pretentious, snobbish, stupid, and deeply dissatisfied, bored and unhappy, and Mrs Lively traces her present discontent convincingly back to her childhood, in a series of neatly encapsulated flashbacks, at which she is extremely skilled. Laura's sister, Nellie, was intelligent, plain, devoted to archaeology, deeply in love with Paxton. Now, she is confined to a wheelchair after a stroke, and lives an uneasy life with Laura. . . . [The] portrait of Nellie is the most acute, shrewd and compassionate one of a person with a handicap and affliction, I have read for many a year. How Nellie's thoughts, observations, emotions, memories, exist like an absolutely clear, flowing stream, below the flat rock which has shut down upon her, trapping her in slow, blurred speech and paralysed movement, is most beautifully conveyed.

The other central relationship in the book is between Paxton's daughter, Kate, an awkward, fierce, graceless, defensive girl, and Tom, a thoroughly honourable nice, mature young man, who loves her, and finally, cannot cope with her. (pp. 22-3)

Mrs Lively handles all the separate threads of her book with ease, and there are some delightful vignettes of incidental character, and other worlds, perfectly caught, though she has not yet learned when to be ruthless about removing pleasant, well-conceived and written but ultimately redundant, or irrelevant, episodes. I read her novel in a single evening, immersed in it totally, sorry when it ended so prematurely. (p. 23)

Susan Hill, "Steady Stuff," in Books and Bookmen,
Vol. 24, No. 12, September, 1979, pp. 22-3.*

PATRICIA CRAIG

[An] orthodox television production is the subject of *Treasures of Time*. The overt subject at any rate: Penelope Lively has always been preoccupied with time, continuity and patterns of accretion, and these are no less integral to her adult than her juvenile fiction. History and archaeology provide the means to rationalise the obsession, and these disciplines loom in the background of her new novel. A documentary series is to feature the work of the late Hugh Paxton, celebrated for his excavations at a site in Wiltshire named Charlie's Trump. Relatives and associates of the famous man are invited to take part. His daughter Kate introduces into the group a research student named Tom Rider whose perceptions and presumptions are central to the theme. Tom's moderately sardonic views on the national heritage, the wry conclusions he comes to after spending a day with a party of Japanese tourists, his half-mocking relation with the image of himself as a clever working-class boy—these are among the highlights of a story that is never dull, though it is too often glib and easy-going. It lacks

the build-up of psychic pressure and the clarity of tone which are the hallmarks of her children's books.

Patricia Craig, "Battery Iron," in New Statesman,
Vol. 98, No. 2531, September 21, 1979, p. 429.*

JOHN MELLORS

Penelope Lively gets better with every book. In *Treasures of Time* she raises all sorts of issues about the past. Does a place have an atmosphere given by its history? Or is the *genius loci* entirely subjective, dependent on the onlooker? Tom, the postgraduate student of 18th-century antiquarianism, is asked by a party of Japanese tourists to accompany them round Oxford and its environs—and 'explain'. Almost everything is misunderstood by the visitiors. . . . Tom concludes that 'what you feel about what you see depends not on what it is, but who you are. A place is an illusion.'

When the characters in *Treasures of Time* are forced to re-examine their own and one another's past, identity is shown to be as illusory as place. An elderly spinster has a second stroke and dies. Her sister, apparently a completely self-contained, insensitive person, with a 'knack of instantly putting everyone else at a disadvantage', is shattered by the death. An engagement is broken off, Tom deciding that he is unfitted to cope, for ever, with his fiancée's 'fatal compulsion always to put herself in the least favourable light'. Like Sir Thomas Browne, whom she is fond of quoting, Penelope Lively is ever heedful of 'the wheel of things'.

John Mellors, "Banned Books," in The Listener,
Vol. 102, No. 2630, September 27, 1979, p. 425.*

JOHN NAUGHTON

[*Judgement Day* is about decay]. Set in a credible modern (i.e., socially heterogenous) English village, it chronicles the impact which the arrival of an intelligent young couple has on the circle of dead-heads who manage the affairs of the local church. The focus of the action is a fund-raising project designed to provide the kind of cash needed to restore the ancient fabric.

That this project has a rather ambiguous conclusion is neither here nor there, for Ms Lively's quarry is really the forces of change in British society and their differential impact on different age groups and social strata. . . .

Judgement Day is an impressive piece of work, sharp and surefooted on the nuances of class and of personal conflict. Choosing a modern village . . . was a good stratagem, not only because it provides a natural stage, but also because the fissiparous villagers attain a fragile unity whenever threatened by the onslaught of the wider society (in this case, motorcycling yobbos from the nearest town). If a Martian anthropologist were to ask for a quick guide to the essence of British society in the 1970s, then Ms Lively's book would do almost as well as the entire output of Nuffield College.

John Naughton, "Empty Houses," in The Listener,
Vol. 104, No. 2688, November 20, 1980, pp. 700-01.*

FRANCIS KING

[Penelope Lively's] quality can best be conveyed by saying that she is the kind of writer that Barbara Pym might have been if she had married and had children. The setting of *Judgement*

Day . . . might be that of a Pym novel; and that, at the centre of this village and the events that take place in it, there should always loom up the church of St Peter and St Paul, with a 14th-century wall-painting, the Doom, as 'its glory and surprise', is precisely what one might expect if Barbara Pym had been the author. Also reminiscent of Pym, in its undemonstrative tenderness, tentativeness and frustration, is the relationship between Clare Paling, a newcomer to the village, and the vicar of the church, a lonely and unloved man of 40, who has never married.

But whereas, if this were a Pym novel, Clare would be some churchy spinster, here she is both an agnostic and the possessor of a frequently absent husband and two children. She is cultivated enough to object, on a visit to Matins, to the ghastly flatness and triteness of the Good News Bible in use . . . ; she is sensitive enough to overcome her initial distaste for the vicar and to pity him in his uncertain isolation. She is tough enough to give a tongue-lashing to a callous brute of a man, who parks his car in such a way in front of hers that she is stuck for more than an hour while waiting for his return.

Both she and her two precocious, self-conscious children are perfectly realised; and the vicar, increasingly living in a world of fantasy in which all the unattainables of his barren existence are realised in daydreams, is drawn with the same decisiveness of line and vividness of colour. (p. 24)

The lower-middle class man with whom Clare has her row over the car, his wife, Shirl, and his brassy girl-friend are less subtle and less convincing creations, viewed without either much compassion or, more important, much understanding. Clearly, Mrs Lively finds them a rubbishy trio. . . .

Clare makes a declaration of her credo to the vicar: 'I believe, insofar as I believe in anything, that we are quite fortuitously here, and that the world is a cruel and terrible place, but inexplicably and bewilderingly beautiful.' Is it presumptuous to assume that it is also Clare's creator who is speaking here? Certainly the book is full of the unjust fortuitousness with which human happiness and misery are apportioned, and of Clare's consciousness of the unjustness of this. . . .

This is a book unobtrusively expert in its craftmanship, as the author slips into this character and now into that, in what are often sections of less than half a page. Thought-processes of people as different as the vicar's churchwarden, the doomed child and Clare are cunningly differentiated. There are smooth changes between past and present tense.

Because the whole tone of the narrative is so discreet and because, until the desecration of the church, little that is showily dramatic happens, it would be easy to underestimate the merit of Mrs Lively's novel. But in its constant awareness both of the joy and beauty and of the sadness and hideousness of life, it is a work of real, if self-limiting, accomplishment. (p. 25)

Francis King, "Look Lively," in The Spectator, *Vol. 245, No. 7950, November 22, 1980, pp. 24-5.*

ALAN BROWNJOHN

In Laddenham, a neat village near the light industrial township of Spelbury in the southern English heartlands, Penelope Lively has set a nicely pertinacious account of the secular assumptions and irrational impulses which govern the way many of us live now. *Judgement Day* centres on the relationship the agnostic

Clare Paling forms with a well-meaning and feeble man of God, and his church. . . . The ostensibly tidy lives of the retired, the respectable burghers, the young married and their children, are more complex and fraught than appears; Clare's motives in seeking to graft her goodwill on to this community are more ambiguous than she realises; and the pageant [she plans in order to bring the townspeople together] is doomed to failure when violent forces impinging on village life suddenly erupt to shatter all the good intentions. It might sound like an honourably observant novel written to a formula; but it is much better than that.

It is better than that mainly because its aerial survey of a familiar sector of English existence is done with an almost flawless accuracy, but no inclination to point easy morals. Penelope Lively places every incident scrupulously, arranges the minor faults and decent virtues of her characters in a sequence leading somehow inexorably to frustration and tragedy; and in so doing sorts out ordinary living in the present in England in a way that makes moving sense without thrusting conclusions on the reader. Clare Paling—horrified at the ditching of the Authorised Version by the parson's superiors—has to tell him that words "are all we've got." It is the nearest to a message that *Judgement Day* reaches. But the ending of the novel leaves an unpleasant feeling that even the abiding potency of language is in doubt: Miss Lively's chilling cameo has wider reference than the village green of Laddenham. (p. 90)

Alan Brownjohn, "Breaking the Rules," in Encounter, *Vol. LVI, No. 5, May, 1981, pp. 86-91.**

BRYN CALESS

Penelope Lively exemplifies her name and [with *Next to Nature, Art*] she surpasses her previous achievements in fiction. She has produced a splendid satire on the pretensions of the early 1970s in Britain, and made a number of timely sideswipes for sanity in her cool and didactic appraisal of talent. Framleigh is a 'creative Study Centre' run by Toby, a bisexual *poseur*, who screws money out of what he calls 'ordinary people' who come for week-long courses in art, pottery and sculpture. He is truly one of the most appalling of human beings. Talentless himself, he resents and puts down the glimmerings of merit in others. He is aided by Paula, sculptress and easy of virtue, Greg, American self-styled poet ('the poet *is* the message'), and Bob, potter and lecher, who makes his money out of 'Toby' jugs and honey-pots for the local department stores. These constitute the 'faculty' of teachers, who impart their lofty ideals about 'doing your own thing' and 'being yourself to willing and rather pathetic acolytes—a week at a time. . . . Penelope Lively writes elegant, incisive prose which often conceals the genuine savagery of her attack. Her satire is direct and believable, the wit is profound. This is a splendid novel, with so few faults they are not worth remarking. (pp. 576-77)

Bryn Caless, in a review of "Next to Nature, Art," in British Book News, *September, 1982, pp. 576-77.*

ANGELA HUTH

In *Perfect Happiness* Penelope Lively concerns herself with the subject of loss. This, so often in the past, has proved a dangerous subject, particularly in the hands of women writers. It induces characters with that modern disease of scurrying to find themselves, and delivering us with the unedited findings. It deprives many a writer of all humour.

Miss Lively has achieved a considerable triumph, therefore, in managing to cross such tricky terrain without so much as a stumble. In her exploration of three different kinds of loss, while shirking no gloomy corner, she engages nothing but respect and admiration for her heroines. Her art is to examine their various plights with great sympathy, yet never to swop her role of writer for that of psychiatrist.

Frances Brooklyn, middle-aged and recently widowed, has a practical approach to bereavement. It is, of course, something to be endured, suffered, lived through—there is no escape from its pangs. (p. 22)

On a visit to Venice, near to cracking, she responds to the friendship of a trouser-suited American tourist, Ruth Bowers (a superb portrait, this) the kind of woman for whom the dead Steven would not have cared. She discovers things about her husband's past she did not know. *Perfect* happiness, was it? . . . [After] a while, most touchingly, she finds she has become the love of a kind, bearded gentleman, a feeling she cannot yet bring herself to reciprocate, but time may bring its changes. Possibility of new kinds of light in the darkness is a strong theme of the book.

Frances's sister-in-law, Zoe, a brusque and friendly unmarried lady, a hectic journalist, is left by her lover of ten years for a younger woman. Zoe has a hysterectomy and carries on with her job as merrily as she is able. Aches, but no moans. Then Frances's teenage daughter Tabitha 'furiously intent among the second violins' is abandoned by her boyfriend: she deals as sensibly as her mother with practical aids for the internal void.

The three women represent different shades of loss; their particular sufferings, universally recognisable, are handled with an extraordinary freshness of approach and keenness of observation. . . . In all her wisdom, Miss Lively never depresses through her characters' sadness. *Perfect Happiness* avoids none of the bleakness of its subject, but leaves the reader with a feeling of optimism, encouragement for when our turn comes. It is a marvellous book. (pp. 22-3)

Angela Huth, "Love and Magic," in The Spectator, Vol. 251, No. 8097, September 17, 1983, pp. 22-3.*

JOHN MELLORS

Penelope Lively has chosen to write about the painful problems facing a woman after the sudden death of her husband. . . . The book's title, *Perfect Happiness,* refers to the past. Frances has to adjust to the loss of that happiness and the near-certainty that, at her age, 49, she will find no equivalent.

Perfect Happiness is not depressing. Nor is it sentimental. Frances fights back in two ways. She learns how to summon up, deliberately, past moments of happiness, instead of letting them come at her and knock her off balance. Also, she begins to admit into her life people and possessions her husband had never known. . . .

Penelope Lively has created characters in whose reality we believe and about whose fortunes we care. In very tricky terrain for a novelist she never puts a foot wrong. She knows that those who feel grief do not feel it all the time. They still have to choose what clothes to wear, make scrambled eggs, answer the telephone. The strongest among them will make conscious decisions towards achieving a new independence. When Frances is introduced to people with the words 'Frances was married to . . .', she knows that she must not be 'made to wear Steven

for ever like a regimental brooch'. At the end of *Perfect Happiness,* Frances is 'neither happy nor grieving, looking not backwards into the day but on into the next'. The reader is left the richer for sharing Frances's experience.

John Mellors, "Today's Taboos," in The Listener, Vol. 110, No. 2827, September 22, 1983, p. 25.*

CLANCY SIGAL

[In **"Next to Nature, Art,"** something] is wrong at Framleigh Hall, deep in the Warwickshire countryside. And we soon discover the problem is that the 18th-century manor house is now the Framleigh Creative Study Centre, an "artistic sanctuary." . . . Toby, Paula, his mistress, Bob, a potter, and Greg, a pretentious Yank poet, talk endlessly about art while having almost no talent themselves. But they are shrewd salesmen of the "Framleigh Ideal," and they impress the rather humble and confused nonartists who, fleeing their mundane lives, pay good money to spend a week there. It's a con, of course. As the middle-aged housewife Mary Chambers—the author's voice of English common sense—soon discovers. Cunningly contrasted with the guests and Toby and his self-involved crew of failed artists is the spontaneous play of Paula's small son, Jason, and a prankish village kid named Kevin. . . . Through the children the author seems to be suggesting that adult art is impossible without unselfconscious, even juvenile, play. Penelope Lively . . . is gaining a reputation and an audience for her serious adult books. She deserves both; she has a wickedly comic touch. Her amused, amusing look at England's sub-bohemian culture is clear and sharp.

Clancy Sigal, in a review of "Next to Nature," in The New York Times Book Review, January 1, 1984, p. 20.

FRANCES HILL

The American Jewish immigrants of Bernard Malamud's stories inhabit a world of their own spiritual past and an unanchored present. Anxious, needy, pathetic, blinkered, faltering, kindly, they stumble through life with only the most tenuous links with the places they live in. Penelope Lively's characters are set solidly in and against market towns, Saxon churches, Aldeburgh beaches, High Streets with Smiths, Boots and Sainsburys in them. Yet Malamud's favourite theme—of giving and taking, requesting, withholding, often relenting—also leavens and moulds several stories of Lively's.

In **'The Ghost of a Flea',** Angela, doggedly treading the borderline between madness and sanity, reaches out towards Paul and, when he takes hold, hangs on like a leech. He retains enough freedom to fall in love with another girl but does not shake off his burden. Angela after a while attempts and fails at suicide. Paul and his wife-to-be, 'separated and tethered' by Angela, know at the end of the story that she is part of their future.

In **'The Art of Biography',** Edward Lamprey requests information of Lucinda Rockingham, 'eighty if she was a day', on her late employer, a poet. Miss Rockingham offers Lamprey far more than he guessed she could give. As a result, he spends a whole week in her house, neglecting his girlfriend. She, in turn, finally leaves him. (p. 29)

It is no accident that one of Penelope Lively's main themes in these stories is the one that dominates Bernard Malamud's fiction. Her people, like his, though so differently formed by their personal and cultural histories, stand in similar relations to chance and events. Their lives are governed very largely by circumstance. . . . It is natural that in their helplessness in the face of circumstances both Malamud's and Lively's characters should spend a fair amount of their time pleading with each other and then giving or withholding what is asked. It is natural, too, that both should show human blindness combining with chance to produce ironic, or tragic, results.

Penelope Lively's best story, **'Grow Old Along with Me: The Best is Yet to Be',** is about looking, and not seeing. Sarah and Tony, young and callow, trying to decide whether or not to marry, visit a Saxon church. They express deepest respect for the church's antiquity. But when they come across two old people, locked in a clandestine, passionate embrace, they are filled with contempt, even horror. The story is full of intertwined ironies. (pp. 29-30)

Each of Penelope Lively's stories is beautifully written, full of irony and gentle, pointed humour and perfect descriptions. Characterisation and dialogue are excellent. But **'Corruption'**, **'Customers'**, **'Yellow Trains'** and **'The Emasculation of Ted Roper,'** unlike the stories already described, stay on the surface. **'The Darkness Out There'** is marred by the desire to explain what has already been shown. This is a sure sign of uncertainty and crops up elsewhere in the stories that are less than first-class. **'Venice Now and Then'** and **'The Pill Box'** are 'experimental', the one technically, the other in terms of subject matter, and neither quite works. Penelope Lively still seems to be finding her feet as a short story writer, despite the . . . excellent tales in this collection. (p. 30)

Frances Hill, "Blinded," in The Spectator, *Vol. 252, No. 8123, March 17, 1984, pp. 29-30.**

ALIDA BECKER

[The main theme of **"Perfect Happiness"** is not] just the matter of bereavement, as experienced by her fiftyish heroine, Frances, who, when we first meet her, is "recollecting not in tranquility but in ripe howling grief her husband Steven dead now eight months two weeks one day." The theme is also how the past is changed by the present, the way time intersects with and refracts our feelings, the way the physical world around us can be both a "solace and a mockery." Weighty matters, these. But Mrs. Lively handles them with quiet wisdom, graceful goodheartedness and understated wit. Best of all, she firmly anchors them with an absorbing story and a group of vividly drawn, mostly likable and always affecting characters. . . .

We also view deft variations on the theme of loss through Frances' adopted daughter Tabitha, suffering in the throes of her first love affair, and through Frances' beloved sister-in-law Zoe, a spunky journalist who has never married, has always done precisely what she wanted, and suddenly finds herself regretting everything she had so blithely given up.

All three women look back at what they remember as "perfect happiness, past perfect, pluperfect." Resilient and unsentimental, they manage to make their memories, complex and illusory as they may be, a way of sustaining the present and the future.

Alida Becker, "Life After Loss," in The New York Times Book Review, *October 21, 1984, p. 34.*

Gregorio López y Fuentes

1897-1966

Mexican novelist, short story writer, poet, and editor.

López y Fuentes is one of the principal authors who wrote about the Mexican Revolution of 1910. His works focus directly or indirectly on the Revolution, especially on the ways it affected the Indians. In his first major novel, *Campamento* (1931), he describes one night in a military encampment, concentrating not on individual soldiers but on their group identity and circumstances. His next major novel, *Tierra* (1932), portrays the ten-year struggle, led by the Indian leader Emiliano Zapata, in which the indigenous Indians fight for their right to own land. López y Fuentes's best-known work, *El indio* (1935), described by Isaac Goldberg as a "miniature epic," examines the political and social conditions of postrevolutionary Mexico by depicting life in a remote Indian village. As in *Campamento*, *El indio* employs a "mass protagonist"; individuals remain nameless and are of secondary importance to the characterization of the group as a whole. Many of López y Fuentes's novels, while supporting the aims of the Revolution, are critical of the way the reforms have been carried out. Critics praise López y Fuentes for conveying vividly and accurately the revolutionary era of Mexico.

CHARLES POORE

Willa Cather's famous plea for "the novel démeublé" is more than answered in ["El Indio," an] uncommonly interesting story of Indian life in Mexico. You could not find a tale less cluttered with unnecessary literary furniture—or richer in episodes that make you believe the truth of what you read. . . .

Nothing else you have read about Mexico is like **"El Indio"** [published in Great Britain as **"They That Reap"**]. In Ogden Nash's phrase about another matter, it is sui generis to a fault. The scene is a high, remote mountain village. All the Indians who live there are the characters. They aren't even given names. But you come to know them with an ultimate thoroughness based on seeing how they live day after day, what they do and what they fear and what they hate. Their games are as revealing as their battles. The enemy within the gates is fought as desperately as the invaders—*gente de razon*, which sardonically means people of reason—who come up from the plains below.

The story begins and ends with episodes of invasion. First the wandering plunderers who arrive to look for fabulous hidden caches of gold and who torture the Indians when they cannot find what they want. Then, years later, the men of the new day who bring talk of roads and schools and freedom and who plunge the Indians into the disastrous currents of politics.

Within that long interval there are the stories of many individual lives. . . .

Lynn Carrick remarks in a prefatory note that "any one familiar with the main outlines of Mexican history in recent times will be able to interpret the story in specific terms of what has actually happened and is still happening south of the Rio Grande. But any such explanations would seem pointless and unnecessary. **"El Indio"** can be enjoyed for what it is without straining for symbolism or historical analogies." For that matter, this story could be given world-wide analogies. That's what makes the book ring true. . . .

Gregorio Lopez y Fuentes does not make the fatal mistake of idealizing his people. He shows them as they are. . . .

He has no facile solution to offer for the future of these Indians. But he has a compelling ability to make you see how they live.

Charles Poore, "An Uncommon Story of an Indian Village in Mexico," in The New York Times Book Review, *February 21, 1937, p. 3.*

ISAAC GOLDBERG

Whether **"El Indio"** may properly be called a novel is beside the question; as a matter of definition it is rather a miniature epic. A proud Indian youth is crippled by the cupidity of the white man, equally lustful for gold and for women. The compatriot who discovers him mutilated at the bottom of a gully wins away his sweetheart. A war of sorcerers is waged when the father of the cripple seeks vengeance upon the successful rival. The actors in this drama meet their various deaths by animal ferocity, pestilence, or the rigors of the elements; only the cripple survives. This plot, however, is but the nucleus for the evocation of a conquered race, and the nostalgia that it portrays gives way at last to the promises of education and economic justice.

By this same token a certain unobtrusive allegory inheres in the tale. No person is named; it is as if the identity of the characters, important as they are to themselves and to one another, is merged into the history and the fate of the collectivity. . . .

López y Fuentes has, intuitively, and in generous proportions, both sight and vision. His description of the Indian rite of the "volador," and his account of the huntsman's death at the tusks of the wild peccaries are remarkable for their simple power. From a Hispanic-American culture not at its best in the longer forms of fiction comes now this excellent work that may well be studied by our own writers.

Isaac Goldberg, "A Miniature Epic," in The Saturday Review of Literature, *Vol. XV, No. 8, February 27, 1937, p. 10.*

ERNEST MOORE

In Mexico a new novel is being created. It is simple in art, realistic in subject, and rooted firmly in native Mexican life and culture. Because it is a social novel, written with a vigor new to modern Mexican letters, drawing its inspiration, ideals, and much of its subject matter, from the Mexican Revolution of 1910, it has become known as the "Novel of the Revolution". The word "Revolution" in the title itself indicates the importance of the new novel, for only significant economic and social reforms and the cultivation of national arts and crafts are popularly identified by Mexicans as outgrowths of *the* Revolution.

[There are] . . . three main figures responsible for this literary creation,—Mariano Azuela, Martín Luis Guzmán and Gregorio López y Fuentes. . . . (p. 23)

Gregorio López y Fuentes is the most important, for although he is a newcomer and little known abroad, in Mexico his novels are in great demand. In the United States there is a growing interest in them, several having been very favorably reviewed in newspapers and periodicals. And now his latest work, *El indio,* has just been published in an English translation. . . .

López y Fuentes has rapidly risen to fame in Mexico through his steady output of novels. Each successive work marks an advance in technique and reveals a deeper understanding of the social problems of his country. With Guzmán self-exiled in Spain, and Azuela entering his sixties, López y Fuentes—just turned forty—is likely to become Mexico's most prominent contemporary novelist. Certainly he seems the most promising at this moment. (p. 24)

The reader will recall that the Revolution awakened Mexico to the serious plight into which it had been thrown by four centuries of military abuse, feudal land conditions, and Church corruption. . . . [Toward the end of the conflict the "revolutinary ideals" originating in the people's discontent] . . . were permanently synthesized, and embodied in the Mexican Constitution of 1917. In essence, this notable document insists that labor be granted equality with capital, that land be redistributed fairly among Mexicans, and that the *indio* and the Mexican be made the basic considerations of every social, economic, and cultural manifestation of the nation's life.

These ideas López y Fuentes uses as focal points in his examination of Mexican life. A survey of his novels will show the direction his social criticism takes as well as his rapid development in skill as a novelist.

Campamento marks the beginning of a satire that is to strike deeper and deeper in his later novels at the roots of social evils. Here the thrust is light, yet he manages through a study of revolutionary masses to point out the wide gap between revolutionary ideals and the actual conditions under which people are forced to live during war. He is an objective observer. His descriptions are vivid. The Indian, who in real life turns out to be the chief protagonist in the drama of revolution, is portrayed in this novel as the victim of *all* the warring factions. A nameless Indian guide runs beside the general staff's horses, driven on by the trampling hoofs, until he dies of exhaustion. . . . His death elicits a few pitying remarks from the soldiers. Nevertheless, the same men—most of whom also have Indian blood in their veins—who watch him die with the blood spurting from his exhausted lungs, will witness similar brutality again and again without uttering a word of protest!

In this work of brief span—fifteen hours of life in a military camp—the author relies upon the unities of time and place to integrate his vivid and precise descriptions of the Revolution.

The restless human beings act out their individual rôles of tragedy upon the serene and beautiful stage of the Mexican Valley. Their actions are natural. As individuals they play petty parts; as a group they reach epic grandeur in their tremendous struggles, sacrifices, and accomplishments.

The style of the author is supple, well suited to his task. His pages are crowded with turbulent military masses madly fighting for ideals that are vague but impelling. . . . (pp. 24-5)

Humor, sketches of individuals, descriptions of interesting local customs and crude camp life, and gentle between-the-line irony, all go to make up a thoroughly enjoyable, though loosely woven, novel.

Tierra, his next novel, has been acclaimed by some Mexican critics as his best. . . . The author shows that unlike most *literati* of his country he is not an isolated observer deriving his style and his realism from European fonts, but that he lives intimately associated with the history of his people. Here the author's ideas of the Revolution have grown coherent and are increasingly stressed as the work progresses. López y Fuentes presents the most vital problem of Revolutionary Mexico—the fundamental right of the people to cultivate for themselves the land on which they live. *Tierra,* then, is a thesis novel treating the agrarian problem in southern Mexico.

Designating the chapters by years instead of numbers does not hide the lack of unity in the novel as a whole. This objection is minimized, however, by the directness of the author's approach to his problem and by his critical attitude, sustained throughout the novel. (p. 26)

With the exception of Zapata, who is drawn true to life, the characters are merely outlined. This is a sacrifice made to the thesis and to the rapidity with which the action must move to cover the long period of history here dealt with. Thoroughly readable, the novel is replete with concrete instances of the people's need of land, and with understanding accounts of their struggles to obtain it. They are just now coming into their full inheritance. *Tierra* is *the* agrarian novel of the Revolution.

López y Fuentes writes a social satire of broader scope in *¡Mi general!,* which is in some ways a parallel to Mariano Azuela's *Los de abajo.* Both deal with what may be called the "General cycle". A man of lowly birth rises to fame as a general, rejoices in his success, and then sinks again into oblivion. . . . Both have very simple plots, and both are strong indictments of the time. (p. 28)

Starting as a cowboy, [the protagonist of *¡Migeneral!*] is swept along into numerous political and military offices as the revolutionary movement gathers momentum, rising at last to the military zenith of generalship. Fortune soon frowns and the general, humiliated and in great anguish, slides back to his former obscurity. All the points in his cycle,—rancher, cattle trader, captain, general, deputy, counter-revolutionist, fugitive, body-guard, and cowboy—offer the author opportunities to examine the political corruption, the military "racket", and the cynical side of revolution. The General is interesting as an individual, yet he is more understandable and significant as a type of revolutionary, and it is in this latter rôle that the author has cast him.

Accurate descriptions, scenes of turbulent military life, reveal the author's intimate knowledge of the Revolution. For interest as well as for movement, *¡Mi general!* is easily the equal of *Tierra.* His style has improved in this work in carefulness of detail, while still retaining its conversational flow and its Mexican flavor.

In his latest novel, *El indio,* López y Fuentes turns his satirical pen toward another problem fundamental to all social progress in Mexico—"the incorporation of the Indian into the life of the nation", as José Vasconcelos expresses it. The Indian had appeared in an occasional episode in his early novels as the victim of the class struggle; here López y Fuentes develops fully what he previously had only touched upon, and his novel becomes a brilliant revelation of the actual living conditions of the *indio.*

This is the story of a primitive people living in their rude palm-and-mud huts, practicing their age-old crafts, defending their time-honored customs, a people thrown into unwilling contact with the civilized white men who half-heartedly try to "incorporate" them. In a series of vividly descriptive passages which reveal the author's intimate knowledge of the *indio,* a native community comes to life for the reader. Strong, full-blooded men and women carefully till their meager fields, ply their crafts, fish, hunt, and yet barely manage to supply themselves with enough food to live. Their own work is done in addition to toiling at sugar ovens and on the lands of the local *hacendados,* who use every means in their power to enslave their workers. (pp. 28-9)

López y Fuentes sketches in his symbolic, nameless characters, a people exploited by the landowner and the priest, and lately by the politician. That they are hardy, their capacity to bear their crushing burdens has proved. They will survive, for all their sufferings, says the author. In contrast to their outnumbered and "vanishing redskin" brothers in the United States, they are the bulk of the Mexican population, and they continue to add to their numbers by absorption of the white populace. Eventually they will possess their land and rule their country. It is the author's purpose to help them come into their rightful inheritance, to apply the Revolutionary ideals in their behalf now, not by forcing reforms upon them which they do not understand or accept, but by studying their languages, seeing the good in their customs and traditions, teaching them useful crafts and modern methods in agriculture,—in a word, by restoring their confidence. (pp. 30-1)

López y Fuentes on the basis of his own experience among the *indios* of Veracruz tries to portray Indian life as it really is, neither pathetic nor ideal. For this reason *El indio* contains some of the best descriptive passages to be found in the modern Mexican novel. The pages that describe the death of a hunter attacked by a herd of wild boars, the strange rites of Indian witchcraft, or the curious tribal marriage, fill the reader's mind with vivid images of Mexican folk life. . . .

López y Fuentes shares with other "novelists of the Revolution" the sincere conviction that Mexico offers a wide and fertile field of study for the modern Mexican novelist. But he stands alone in his ability to create a novel that, fusing the critical and the pictorial, scrutinizes the soul of changing Mexico. (p. 31)

> *Ernest Moore, "López y Fuentes, Novelist of the Mexican Revolution," in* The Spanish Review, *Vol. IV, No. 1, April, 1937, pp. 23-31.*

BOYD CARTER

The participation of López y Fuentes in the Revolution was more limited than that of Azuela or Guzmán but sufficiently

committing to give him enough first-hand experience to assimilate its physical details and movement as well as its idealistic and ironical under- and overtones. Moreover, as a native of the state of Veracruz with roots deep in the psychology and customs of Indians and mestizos, as one of the unsuccessful defenders of Veracruz against the U.S. occupying force of 1914, and as an adherent to the Carranza faction, he acquired a set of experiences and perspectives that differed somewhat from those of [other writers]. . . .

The geographical proximity of the state of Veracruz to the state of Morelos facilitated the opportunities of López y Fuentes to study and to understand the rôle of the most pure in motive of the revolutionary figures. Emiliano Zapata, in the eyes of his partisans, the leader *sans peur et sans reproche,* who simplified the purposes of the Revolution to the two demands of *land and withdrawal of federal troops,* could not but appeal to a man of López y Fuentes' sincerity, integrity, generous sentiments, and human sympathies. *Land (Tierra,* 1932) is the story of Zapata from 1910 to 1920. The author solves the structural problem of reducing chronological breadth to compositional unity by having Zapata serve as the hub, the developments of each of the ten years as spokes, and the peons and their echelon leaders as the raw source of power to keep the revolutionary wheel turning. (p. 147)

Land, in theme, execution, and significance merits more attention than *Mi general* (1934) or *Bivouac (Campamento,* 1931). The latter, López y Fuentes' first novel on the Revolution, is an audio-photographic close-up of a military unit as it rests for a few days between engagements. In no novel thus far published on the Revolution does one find such a concentration of details or greater success in distilling dramatic interest from an essentially undramatic and amorphous situation. The author circumvents monotony through stylistic skill, periscopic shifts of focus within the camp, the interlarding of alerts, rumors, arrival of prisoners, and a trial of deserters. His talent in conferring graphic saliency on trivial incidents is such that the killing of a chicken, of a cow, a quarrel, amputation of a leg, bananas stealthily fried behind shutters, the diversified and sometimes promiscuous functions of the women campfollowers, these and scores of other petty happenings acquire an animation that fixes them indelibly in the memory. That López y Fuentes is a writer *"pour qui le monde visible existe"* is amply illustrated on each page. Nevertheless, one feels that behind the façade of his objectivity he finds it difficult to restrain the impulse to sympathize, in the manner of Dickens and Alphonse Daudet, and to interpret analytically like Martín Luis Guzmán. (p. 148)

El Indio, the most widely read of López y Fuentes' novels, ranks at the top of Spanish-American fiction dealing with the Indian. Only Ciro Alegría's *El mundo es ancho y ajeno* has won comparable recognition. Although published three years after *Land, El Indio* precedes it in the chronology of events dramatized and in fact may well be viewed as its companion piece. (p. 149)

> *Boyd Carter, "The Mexican Novel at Mid-Century," in* Prairie Schooner, *Vol. XXVIII, No. 2, Summer, 1954, pp. 143-56.**

JOHN S. BRUSHWOOD

In 1931 there was not one novel of importance published [in Mexico] that did not deal with the [Revolution] . . . in one way or another. (p. 205)

There were two facets to the Revolution, even during its military phase: one was predominantly political and looked toward a genuinely democratic, capitalistic society; the other was social and anticipated fundamental changes in the economic structure. One was middle class, the other was proletarian. The first was the initial and predominant force. The second, whose principal exponent during the military phase was Emiliano Zapata, came later and was in the position of having to exert its influence on the middle-class, political revolt that had already started. (pp. 205-06)

The Revolution had been a combination of heterogeneous forces. It was chaotic; and although sporadic moments of glory were apparent, the tragedy of civil war was even more so. The Revolution as an entity, as an achievement of men in search of freedom from a static society, could not possibly have been felt in the years immediately following, when the sense of tragedy prevailed. Because the interpretation of the Revolution was ambiguous, and its presence persistent, the need to discover its nature arose; and the first step was to look at what had happened.

The wave of novels of the Revolution in 1931 shows several different ways of telling the story, but with some characteristics that are common to most books on this theme: they are lineal accounts, episodic, with sketchily drawn characters. In general, everything—structure, style, characterization, even ideology—is subordinate to each author's need to tell what it was like. (p. 206)

The best novel of 1931 was Gregorio López y Fuentes' *Campamento,* which is important not only for its intrinsic merit, but also for what it forecasts of a distinguished literary career. *Campamento* is less a story than an illumination of a revolutionary encampment. The author's view flashes across the entire scene and reproduces the reality of a night, a moment in the long struggle. . . . The reactions of the revolutionaries are an intensification of ordinary human emotions. They are in a special situation which is becoming commonplace. They take advantage of the freedom that comes from the anonymity of belonging to the revolutionary band. The author accepts their state of anonymity as reality, and focusses his attention on the band rather than on individuals. Individuals do appear, but their real identity is with the group rather than as separate people. What matters in *Campamento* is what "the revolutionaries" do. López y Fuentes cultivated this device of the group protagonist in later novels, and also continued the same flashy style of obvious satire, easy irony, and broad antithesis. His prose is not beautiful, it is "catchy."

A year later, López y Fuentes published *Tierra,* a story of the whole course of the Revolution, with emphasis on the *zapatista* movement. Although this book is not a profound study, it is one of the clearest pictures of what happened from the end of the dictatorship to the end of the military phase of the Revolution. The lineal character of the narrative is emphasized by the use of dates as chapter titles. The real protagonist of the novel is the movement of the Revolution. Its effect on the *ranchería* (where the peons live on a large hacienda) is the central theme. It is mildly disconcerting that none of the characters, not even Zapata, is a protagonist; and it is possible to misread the novel if one tries to make it conform to a more conventional narrative method.

Tierra opens on a scene in which the peons are changing the boundaries of the hacienda. They know that the owner is able to do this because he has the power to influence the necessary authorities. But they are resigned to the facts of life. Several narrative sketches of the peons' life follow: payday, a death, a birth. The effect of these sketches is not surprising. They show the same picture of feudal society under the Díaz regime that is found in many different places, including the novels of José López Portillo y Rojas. López y Fuentes, however, makes a generalization of the condition, instead of allowing for individual differences as his predecessor did. He wins the reader's sympathy easily by quick character sketches that make you comprehend a man's social condition even though you don't know him very well. The peons on Don Bernardo's hacienda are not all stupid by any means. But the author makes it clear that they have absolutely no hope of freeing themselves from bondage. They vacillate between placid acceptance of Don Bernardo's patronizing despotism and unhappy recognition of the obvious inequality. They have no thought of rebellion. They are as static as the ruling class.

For reasons that are entirely unjust, Don Bernardo has Antonio Hernández, a young peon, sent away as an army recruit. When Antonio returns, well before he was expected, he informs the hacienda of the Madero revolt. The news does not impress the peons greatly. The action in the north is far removed from them. But Don Bernardo is frightened because his assumption that the revolt will not amount to much is shaken by the obvious feeling of freedom on the part of Antonio. It costs Antonio some effort to gather a small band, but he does so and wins a few skirmishes. When Madero is successful, Don Bernardo and other *porfiristas* take the lead politically, carefully including Antonio in their company but keeping him in his place. The peons' condition has not changed.

López y Fuentes introduces Zapata into the novel as an ideal and develops him into a legend. Antonio Hernández and his men join the *zapatista* forces. From this point on, the novel contains perhaps an overdose of Zapata's idealistic insistence on immediate redistribution of the land. More effective than Zapata's words is the author's description of the *zapatistas* as a farming army, taking time out from the Revolution to cultivate their crops on land that should belong to them. The Revolution does not give them what they need, and they continue the fight against the post-Revolutionary government until Zapata is killed treacherously. Antonio Hernández, the physical symbol of the Revolution, is killed in battle. Toward the end of the book, the author uses one of his literary tricks very effectively when he says that everyone knows Antonio is dead but no one knows where he is buried, everyone knows where Zapata is buried but no one knows he is dead. Zapata has become a legend. The peons think they see him or hear him ride by, and their hope lives. Even if the Revolution physically ended in Antonio Hernández, its movement continues because the course that has been set cannot be reversed. (pp. 209-11)

López y Fuentes published his last novel of the Revolution, strictly speaking, in 1934. *Mi general* is the story of a humble man who becomes a general during the Revolution and is unable to find a place for himself after the fighting is over. The book adds very little to what the author has already said about the Revolution. (p. 213)

Although the Revolution continued to be . . . [Mexican novelists'] major preoccupation, the works published in 1935 and 1936 show two tendencies away from the account of revolutionary action: description of regional customs, and examination of the social problems that were apparent in post-Revolutionary Mexico. (p. 214)

The desire to tell what happened to the country is similar to the desire to describe the nation's way of life. And it may be a good idea to observe here that, aside from the Mexican Revolution, this kind of *costumbrismo* was common in the novel throughout Spanish America. It was a process of self-observation that amounted to a necessary step toward self-awareness.

Post-Revolutionary *costumbrismo* is different from the novels of the late nineteenth century, because the new *costumbrismo* shows no inclination to cling to tradition. Its intent is more in the nature of an examination than of nostalgic reflection. And, of course, such an examination is only a step away from social protest. (pp. 214-15)

Foremost among [predominant social problems in which one element was unable to defend itself] was the question of the Indian and his position in the changing society.

López y Fuentes turned from the Revolution itself to the problem of the Indian (*El indio,* 1935) in what became one of Mexico's best known and most influential novels. Recognition of the Indian's separation from society was, of course, a part of the Revolution's awakening effect. In earlier literature, when the Indian appeared at all, it was in an idealized interpretation that exalted the virtues of primitivism and gave the Indian enough of the white man's standards to make him acceptable on the latter's terms. Such make-believe could not go on forever.

Mexico is one of several Spanish-American countries that have very large Indian populations. From the moment of contact of the two civilizations, the dominant European tried to ignore the Indian except when he wanted to take advantage of him. . . . Toward the end of the nineteenth century, there began a slow-growing tendency in Spanish America to recognize the social injustice faced by the Indian, and later to take into account the ethnic characteristics that isolate Indian groups. The question is extremely complicated because it involves all kinds of considerations: ethnic, economic, social, political. And we must add to these difficulties the problem of plain human prejudice. The theme has become a major one in twentieth-century, Spanish-American literature, and López y Fuentes' novel set the stage in Mexico.

The people in *El indio* are not referred to by names, but by occupation, social function, or physical characteristics. This technique affects the reader in several different ways, and they are not all good. The anonymity produces a group characterization, and that, apparently, is what the author wanted to do. However, if López y Fuentes intended to spur his readers to active sympathy, he would have done better had he individualized his characters. Anonymity also emphasizes the primitive state of the people, perhaps more than the author intended. And it occasionally produces a ''wise-old-chief-has-spoken'' effect that is dangerously close to the noble savage foolishness of a century earlier.

A slender thread of story, concerning two lovers, connects episodes that the author chose to illustrate the Indian culture. The structure is typical of López y Fuentes. The episodes can be understood as an account of contemporary life, or as symbolic of the history of the confrontation of cultures. White men appear in the isolated Indian village. They look for gold and demand the Indians' help. They abuse the Indians' hospitality. The Indians retaliate and are in trouble. Later, a teacher comes. The Indians are obliged to work for both the Church and the State, to the detriment of their own interests. They observe the existence of two standards of justice, one for the white man and another for the Indian.

López y Fuentes' view of the Indian is the view of a social reformer, not an ethnologist. Basically, the trouble is a question of prejudice. The Indian is not a part of society because he is regarded as ''other.'' The pictures of his life are shown in the *costumbrista* fashion; and although the author shows them with sympathy, he does not really enter into the Indian's being, as some later novelists have done. He sees what the Indian does, but he sees from his own point of view rather than from the Indian's. In general, this point of view does not greatly affect the novelist's intent, but it does have a tendency to make the book picturesque rather than profound. (pp. 215-17)

[From 1942 to 1946, novels] of protest outnumbered accounts of the Revolution. Regionalism is an important factor even in novels where it is not fundamental. Very gradually and subtly the novel probed more deeply into the meaning of the Mexican circumstance. A few books made understanding of the individual primary, and relegated the external social facts to a secondary position; but the common procedure was still to examine the new Mexico and to place people within the scene. The novel was hesitant: there was very little experimentation, yet the need to observe and describe was losing the intensity that characterized it ten years earlier. The nation itself was changing, also hesitantly. In the opposition of introversion and extroversion during the years since the Revolution, national introversion had been the stronger force. Mexico needed to be concerned for its internal problems, and the novels that examined the state of the country are a reflection of this need. (p. 226)

In his second *indigenista* novel, *Los peregrinos inmóviles (The Immovable Pilgrims)*—published in 1944—López y Fuentes changed his position from outside to inside in such a way that the novel would not see the Indian as ''other,'' but would see what ''other'' signified from the standpoint of the Indian. The people are uprooted, disputes arise, divisions take place, the white man imposes himself, the place to settle is found. The crossroads is the center of the world. The Indian stops—indeed, in a sense, he has never gone anywhere—and resists the insistent intrusion of the ''other.'' He sits, defensively, and awaits the attack.

The author's new position anticipated the approach taken by more recent novelists, most notably Rosario Castellanos. Unfortunately, López y Fuentes' efforts did not produce really satisfactory results, because his position is not consistent. The tendency to move inside is modified by the author's apparent desire to see the Indians' story as a gigantic symbol of the history of Mexico. He moves outside to get this view. And he fails because the story is partly related to time and partly removed from time. The reader is prompted to identify the symbolism historically, and then is deceived because symbol and history won't fit together. The result is that, after a first reading, he is likely to feel that he has missed something in a novel that is probably very good. But a second reading shows that he really didn't miss anything at all. The book tries to do two things that are not at all compatible, and the result is failure in both directions. What is left is an abortive attempt to see the world from the standpoint of the Indian, an unsatisfactory symbolism, and a wealth of external information about what the Indian is like. However, the movement toward the interior world of the Indian is sufficient to cast an entirely different light on the problem of his incorporation into society. ***Los peregrinos inmóviles*** emphasizes the egocentricity of the Indian point of view. ***El indio*** showed him living in a different world, but the later novel indicates that the separation of the two worlds is based on the assumption, held by both white men and Indians, that the world in which one lives is reality, and everything else is apart, unrelated, and naturally of little consequence. (p. 213-232)

> *John S. Brushwood, "The Mirror Image (1931-1946)," in his* Mexico in Its Novel: A Nation's Search for Identity, *University of Texas Press, 1966, pp. 205-34.**

Peter Matthiessen

1927-

American novelist, nonfiction writer, short story writer, and editor.

Matthiessen is a novelist and naturalist who writes with conviction and compassion about vanishing cultures, oppressed peoples, and exotic wildlife and landscapes. Combining scientific observation with lyrical, intelligent prose, he explores such concerns as the impact of modern civilization on the natural world and the necessity for commitment to environmental concerns. An extensive traveller who has explored uncharted areas, Matthiessen bases the majority of his writing on his personal experiences.

Matthiessen wrote his first novel, *Race Rock* (1954), while living in Paris, where he cofounded the *Paris Review* with Harold L. Humes. After returning to the United States in 1953, he wrote the novels *Partisans* (1955) and *Raditzer* (1961). In the late 1950s Matthiessen began the travels which have strongly influenced his career. These led him to such places as the remote wilderness areas of North and South America and resulted in *Wildlife in America* (1959) and *The Cloud Forest: A Chronicle of the South American Wilderness* (1961). Matthiessen's fourth novel, *At Play in the Fields of the Lord* (1965), met with considerable critical recognition. This work takes place in the jungles of South America, where a primitive tribe is threatened with extinction due to the encroachment of civilization. William Styron describes this novel as "a dense, rich, musical book, filled with tragic and comic resonances."

During the ten-year span between the publication of *At Play in the Fields of the Lord* and his next novel, *Far Tortuga* (1975), Matthiessen wrote numerous nonfiction works which further strengthened his reputation as an outstanding writer and an observant traveller. *The Shorebirds of North America* (1967) is a nature study written in the flowing style characteristic of much of his work; *Sal Si Puedes: Cesar Chavez and the New American Revolution* (1969) examines the famed American fighter for the rights of migrant workers; *Blue Meridian* (1971) is based on Matthiessen's expedition in search of the great white shark; and *The Tree Where Man Was Born* (1972) exemplifies his powers of observation and his humanitarian concerns as he describes the nature and cultures of East Africa.

Far Tortuga is widely considered Matthiessen's most accomplished work. It relates the doomed voyage of a group of sailors who leave the Cayman Islands to hunt turtles in the Caribbean. The novel is made up of descriptive passages interspersed with blocks of dialogue in Caribbean dialects. Matthiessen does not explicitly attribute the dialogue to specific characters; the reader must identify the characters by their individual speech patterns and comments. Also included are such unusual items as pages with a single word, blots to signify death, and type set in the shape of a ship's mast. Matthiessen was praised for the poetic quality of his prose and for his detached manner of describing only the characters' behavior and not their thoughts. Although overall critical response was mixed, *Far Tortuga* greatly increased Matthiessen's literary stature.

Since *Far Tortuga*, Matthiessen has written several other nonfiction works. *The Snow Leopard* (1978), for which Matthiessen

received a National Book Award, is perhaps his most personal nature book. It relates his 1973 journey to Nepal to observe Himalayan blue sheep and his hope of encountering the rarely-seen snow leopard. For Matthiessen the trip was also a search for peace and fulfillment following the death of his wife. As is true of many of Matthiessen's travelogues, *The Snow Leopard* becomes more than a simple journal of observations by virtue of his personal meditations. In *Sand Rivers* (1981) Matthiessen again records his African travels, this time describing an extended trek into the Selous Game Reserve, one of Africa's largest remaining wilderness areas. *In the Spirit of Crazy Horse* (1983) and *Indian Country* (1984) evidence Matthiessen's interest in the history, culture, and political situation of American Indians. *In the Spirit of Crazy Horse* compares the legendary Indian, whose refusal to live on a reservation resulted in his death, with a modern-day Indian accused of murder. Page Stegner describes this work as "one of the most dramatic demonstrations of endemic American racism that has yet been written—a powerful, unsettling book that will force even the most ethno-pious reader to inspect the limits of his understanding." *Indian Country*, which centers on the struggles of American Indians to defend their land and cultural identity against modern technological society, is based on personal encounters and interviews conducted throughout the United States.

(See also *CLC*, Vols. 5, 7, 11; *Contemporary Authors*, Vols. 9-12, rev. ed.; *Something about the Author*, Vol. 27; and *Dictionary of Literary Biography*, Vol. 6.)

SYLVIA BERKMAN

[With] his first novel **"Race Rock,"** [Peter Matthiessen] assumes immediate place as a writer of disciplined craft, perception, imaginative vigor and serious temperament.

The story he presents is intricate, both in method and in the complex of emotional relationships with which it deals. It is a story of salt shifting tidal waters, so to speak, not only in that its events take place against the shoreline of an ever-various, continual sea but, plunging deeper, in that its prime concern is with the rearranging interflowing briny particles of hate, love, shame and fear that form the groundswell of experience. . . .

Mr. Matthiessen presents his material . . . with dramatic power and acute verisimilitude. He commands also a gift of flexible taut expression which takes wings at times into a lyricism beautifully modulated and controlled.

> *Sylvia Berkman, "The Reluctant Adults," in* The New York Times Book Review, *April 4, 1954, p. 5.*

EDWARD WEEKS

[Peter Matthiessen] is by intention a tight writer: he begins with a situation of tension and screws it to a higher pitch. This is his device in his first novel, *Race Rock* . . . , and I'm sorry to report that the story will be disagreeable to many readers. It concerns four Americans, all in their twenties, who have been attracted to each other since childhood: Sam, who has proved a failure as a painter; Eve Murray, who was his wife; George McConville, a wealthy young broker who has made Eve his mistress and, as she thinks, pregnant; and Cady Shipman, the embittered veteran who in his rough way also attracts Eve. . . .

In the story that follows, Mr. Matthiessen in his counterpoint of present and past seeks to tell you why they have become what they are. But his aims are in opposition: his first and most compelling is to show you the deterioration, no matter how repellent; his second, to recover the integrity of his quartet where he can. It is a losing battle.

The author is at his best in his scenes of direct action: Cady and the cat, the sea wind and the fishermen, the drunken Russian Roulette—here, we say, is a writer, observant and of power. He is beyond his depth when he depicts the elders at their Sunday dinner. And he is very, very, unsure of himself in his similes and metaphors, which clutter up the story and make it self-conscious: "Indoor associations, careening forward like ancient odorous dogs" . . . ; "she wiped a fleck of his laughter from her cheek." . . . The novel arouses curiosity; I want to find out. But in the end, for lack of sympathy, I am left with the bleak question, "So what?"

> *Edward Weeks, in a review of "Race Rock," in* The Atlantic Monthly, *Vol. 193, No. 6, June, 1954, p. 74.*

WILLIAM GOYEN

["Partisans" is] the quest of a young American for his identity in terms of a search for a political hero and guide. It is the hope of this young man, son of a United States diplomat and working for an international wire service in Paris, that in "interviewing" his hero, now purged from the party and kept in hiding before being disposed of, he might clarify for himself his own political and philosophical confusions. The hero's name is Jacobi, the seeker's Sand. . . .

In the end, Sand finds Jacobi who will not divulge his "story" to the interviewer but tells him to go home and continue the struggle of the Great Twentieth-Century War in the name of oppressed humanity.

The author means this novel to be a study of a man of action whose relationship to Party ideology has been destroyed by personal passion. It is a study of failure, too, and of noble aims. He intends his novel, I believe, to be an exploration of the meanings of partisanship and of the search for a clear way of individual action and belief through the confusions of ideologies and groups. Certainly Peter Matthiessen's Jacobi is Idea rather than Man. Yet Sand, as well as such minor characters as Lise and Olivier, seems Idea that speaks of The People rather than human beings involved in struggle with Idea. Perhaps this is the author's ultimate intention. Nevertheless, these ideas are rather like those exchanged in a session after a political science class or by expatriates in a Left Bank café.

The characters seem only mouthpieces. They are not empowered by depth of dramatic conviction—or confusion. They do, however, impress one with this young author's thoughtful attempt to find answers to ancient and serious questions—though here he has only chased them around Paris. One doubts the motivations—or is not convinced or driven by them as Sand is; and so the novel lacks the novelist's authentic magic, it lacks voice. What it ends up being is a temporally chopped-up, sometimes brightly written but more often sluggishly constructed, discursive and youthful treatment of a theme that does not rise into the area of ultimate realities and permanent truths as Mr. Matthiessen intended it to.

> *William Goyen, "Underground Quest," in* The New York Times Book Review, *October 2, 1955, p. 4.*

JAMES FINN

In *Partisans* many of the situations . . . seem contrived. . . .

[Too] often [the] characters do not merely express or even embody the ideas they discuss; they are engulfed by them. In spite of the insistence of detailed, sensuous observation, of personal and idiosyncratic behavior, the characters do not fully emerge from the dialectic in which they are involved. Embattled concepts, not engaged people, are presented to us. We are left with a novel of ideas that does not quite come off.

In spite of such strictures, there is much to be commended in the novel. The scenes which are good are impressive, the descriptions ring true, and the writing has a nervous energy that is suited to the subject and exciting in itself.

> *James Finn, "A Modern Quest," in* Commonweal, *Vol. LXIII, No. 4, October 28, 1955, pp. 102-03.*

ARCHIE CARR

Packed with carefully gathered information, [**"Wildlife in America"**] is a delight to read. Appendices offer factual material on rare, declining and extinct species, a chronology of wild-life legislation, and there is an extensive bibliography. . . .

This is a dramatic, unsettling story, skillfully told in a clean, strong prose not often found in the literature of conservation. The author never veers toward either sentimentality or over-documentation. He remains, in fact, almost too aloof for good propaganda, by withholding explanation of the motives of conservation. He never stoops to tell, in so many words, why we must fight to save wild things, assuming, evidently, that men of goodwill already know, as he knows, how awesome the finality of extinction is. I wonder about this.

Although depletion and waste are prominent in the book they are not by any means the whole story. There is, in fact, a good deal of optimism in it. . . .

Biologists may get querulous over Mr. Matthiessen's falling in with the tendency to restrict the word "wildlife" to animals with backbones, leaving as some unstipulated kind of life all the teeming spineless creatures. There is what seems to me a serious oversimplification in the author's statement that "the basic principles of conservation are now quite clearly understood, and it is only the details of their application which, here and there, are still disputed." Conservation is applied ecology, and the "basic principles" of ecology are not by any means all understood; and anyway, back of them the conservationist is facing the inexorable fecundity of the human race—the most basic factor of all.

Mr. Matthiessen, however, must not be heckled about these things. He is arguing for stop-gap conservation, at the level of saving species from extinction. He is explaining why massive help is needed in this, and he does it without ranting or vaporizing, telling the story as the poignant tale it is, and sad, puzzling dilemma that we must solve at once or have on our conscience forever. If his book is as widely read as it deserves to be, our descendants may be much in debt to Peter Matthiessen.

Archie Carr, "The Need to Let Live," in The New York Times Book Review, *November 22, 1959, p. 38.*

TERRY SOUTHERN

[In *Raditzer* we find] a character distinct from those in literature, yet one who has somehow figured, if but hauntingly, in the lives of us all. It is, in certain ways, as though a whole novel had been devoted to one of Algren's sideline freaks, a grotesque and loathsome creature—yet seen ultimately, as sometimes happens in life, as but another human being. . . .

We see Raditzer, the ordinary seaman, mostly through the eyes of Charles Stark, his shipmate and reluctant mentor, abroad the *U.S.S. General Pendleton* in Pacific waters, late 1944. Stark is that sane and perceptive fellow who used to be played by Herbert Marshall in the movies but who frequently recurs, somewhat younger now, as first-person narrator in *New Yorker* short stories—a cardboard figure and a pretty dull tool actually, with his flagrantly self-conscious "reasonableness" and "normalcy," and his finger-deep introspection. Stark is, in short, a literary ideal; he represents the reader. (p. 170)

Raditzer attaches himself to Stark, and the latter, much to the ire and consternation of the rest of the crew, tolerates the imposition—though, granted, with a rather formidable ambivalence. Raditzer's general demeanor might be described as gregariously anti-social; he is so obsessed with the ugliness others see in him that he is in a constant drive to assert it tenfold—groping desperately, one might believe, for alienation . . . hatred . . . punishment. The greater interest in such a case

as Raditzer, however, does not rest with any standard or complex Freudian equation explaining *him,* but lies in the emotional Rorschach he evokes in others. That is to say, *shall we kill him?*

Close readers will follow an excellent and updated Christ story in *Raditzer,* though this is not to suggest that the tale be limited to allegory, any more than should, say *Miss Lonelyhearts.* . . . [The] novel's best reading, certainly, is not as allegory, but as character portrayal—the familiar face, that strange and furtive face seen somewhere long ago beneath brief lamplight . . . in the army barracks, a subway toilet, the last row of a Times Square movie . . . a rare bird and a very ugly one. But then is it really ugly after all? Perhaps what we sometimes see as "ugly"—in nature, in life, in the human condition—is but the unhappily twisted reflection of a much closer source.

Finally, of course, the book, like all good things alas, is not without fault. There is a great deal in it that is forced, especially at the beginning; much of the dialogue is wooden; the peripheral characters seem unduly dull and inconsequential, though perhaps here all must pale alongside the real-life stench of the hero; and lastly, the book is almost totally lacking in outward drama and suspense. This last fault is a serious one for a book of its format. It is well enough for coarse works of yesteryear's colors to pound along, fat and tardy, but novels of contemporary form should enjoy, above all, sharpness of pace and event. However, one must not cavil; wine, salad and cheese are not essential, surely, to the starving faced with a two-pound T-bone. (pp. 170-71)

Terry Southern, "Christ Seen Darkly," in The Nation, *Vol. 192, No. 8, February 25, 1961, pp. 170-71.*

MARSTON BATES

Peter Matthiessen, novelist and naturalist, started on his way to South America. Five months later he came back—and wrote a book ["**The Cloud Forest**"]. There is nothing unusual about this. Countless gringos have visited South America, and one sometimes gets the feeling that most of them must have written books. Yet Matthiessen's trip was unusual. Somehow he managed to get to parts of the continent that have been seen by very few gringos. And, most unusual of all, he came back with a completely delightful book.

This, to my knowledge, has only happened twice before in this century; and to get this statistic we have to stretch the word gringo to include the British. But comparison with H. M. Tomlinson's "The Sea and the Jungle" and with Peter Fleming's "Brazilian Adventure" is inevitable. Among American writers on South America, Peter Matthiessen is unique.

Mr. Matthiessen, to be sure, can write; and this is always helpful in the case of people producing books. He is master of a clean, dry, straightforward prose that is yet vivid and often aptly picturesque. Beneath this prose, there is an extraordinary perception. How, in these five months and with only rudimentary Spanish, did he get such an intimate "feel" for the country and the people? Having lived for eight years in a little town on the eastern slopes of the Colombian Andes, I think I know the kind of people and kind of country that Peter Matthiessen encountered. But nowhere in "**The Cloud Forest**" did I come across a false note, or find occasion to raise my eyebrows at the reactions of a gringo tourist. (p. 3)

Marston Bates, *"Fortune Smiled on the Traveler in a Unmapped Part of the Earth,"* in The New York Times Book Review, *October 15, 1961, pp. 3, 30.*

LOREN EISELEY

["**Under the Mountain Wall**," a] sensitively written book by Peter Matthiessen, is an engrossing human document that sheds light on the story of man, stone-age or modern. The material is drawn from the 1961 Peabody-Harvard Expedition to Central New Guinea whose members—Matthiessen was one—were the first white men ever to establish close contact with the Kurelu and live among them for several months. . . .

In the world today there are very few men left who could truly be called "stone age" in the sense of being completely untouched by the faint echoes emanating from the larger world beyond their borders. The Kurelu of Central New Guinea, dwelling in the mile-high Baliem Valley, were such a people. Matthiessen, in his Preface, speaks of them as destined to be no more than another backward group "crouched in the long shadow of the white man." Ironically, so fast-paced are present changes that it is now the shadow of Indonesia that will fall athwart these simple natives, whose lands have been transferred under such dubious ethics as may be attributable to the exigencies of the cold war. It is not, of course, as political pawns that Matthiessen has seen the Kurelu, compelling as that phase of their story may be to the political scientist. Nor has he been content to report what could easily have been, in other hands, abstract institutional details of tribal life. Rather, he has brought to his subject the pity and insight that only a truly articulate observer can focus upon scenes so remote from the ordinary, and so barbaric.

The Kurelu with their constant tribal quarrels, their economic concentration upon pigs, their dark feuds in which women and little children are regarded as fair game, are, at first glance, an unlovely and callous lot. (p. 3)

[Matthiessen] observes the untamed power of the warlike, the men-killers, the women-stealers, who are a potential source of trouble and the evokers of wars and feuds. But he also points out other types among the Kurelu: Weneluke, a sensitive, gentle boy who likes to sketch pictures on rock surfaces; Weake, the innocent child cut down in ambush; the wise, the good, the violent.

Now what Matthiessen has described in beautiful and poignant writing is the way of savages—savages without history, who fight with spears over stolen pigs and women—savages who must perpetually guard their lands and working women from watch towers lest enemies fall upon them unaware. Here, however, is where a dark, unspoken thought seizes upon our minds. Here is the source of that powerful observation which Matthiessen does not mention, but which lies hidden in his book: these people are another proof that all mankind is the same. They live in huts, not skyscrapers. Their weapons are bows and spears; nevertheless they are ourselves in miniature.

The gentle who would stay at peace are badgered and abused by the warlike; sly chieftains manipulate for power. Boundaries waver with the will and strength of men to hold them. Always men go armed. Always the most peaceful wayfarer, whether man, woman or child, realizes that around the next bend in the trail a spear may be driven through his body. Still the gentle speak in quiet voices; the artist draws with his charcoal sticks, not for magic but for joy.

In those great tribes that constitute modern nations, many complications have arisen, but still the aggressive and powerful threaten and contend, brandishing unheard-of weapons across the breadth of seas; still the quiet go in fear of the violent, and women and children are afraid in the night. Our ways change but slowly if at all. (p. 64)

Loren Eiseley, *"Miniatures of Ourselves,"* in The New York Times Book Review, *November 18, 1962, pp. 3, 64.*

ELIOT FREMONT-SMITH

["**At Play in the Fields of the Lord**"] has nearly everything—a powerful plot, a rich variety of characters, a perceptive, deeply felt view of man's yearnings and his essential ironic tragedy, and a prose style that is vivid, sensuous and disciplined by intelligence. What it lacks—and, I'm afraid, prevents it not only from being a great novel but also from being even a particularly good one, is a sense, or quality, of necessity. By this I mean, the book does not compel the reader into it; its intensity does not engulf the reader as I think it must in this kind of serious, committed novel (as opposed to an entertainment), but acts rather as a barrier between the world within the book and the emotional involvement with the world that the reader wants so much to have.

Thus, at every page, one is interested, admiring, agreeing even—but not transported, not engrossed. It's like reading Conrad, but without the magic (I have no other word for it). Because of the book's many obvious qualities and because passion is there, powerful though fixed, one's disappointment at being less than absorbed is keen and eventually overriding. . . .

False morality myth, magic, the Noble Savage, man's tragic destiny to corrupt himself and find innocence only in madness, are the subjects of "**At Play in the Fields of the Lord**," a title that conveys not comedy but bitter endless irony. . . .

Mr. Matthiessen tends to speak, perhaps too much, through and around his characters; though some are memorable (particularly one missionary wife from North Dakota, who rises to grace in madness), each has his turn at being controlled by strings. The descriptive writing is lyrical and authoritative. . . .

The intent is there, and the tools. But the magic or whatever it is that transfers caring from author to reader, that makes possible and sustains involvement, is not. Its absence, one very much regrets to say, is fatal.

Eliot Fremont-Smith, *"Once More, the Noble Savage,"* in The New York Times, *November 8, 1965, p. 33.*

JOHN THOMPSON

Far back upstream, so very far back in the jungles of the Amazon headwaters that not even an anthropologist has visited them, live the Indians of Peter Matthiessen's novel, *At Play in the Fields of the Lord*. Perhaps this little naked tribe is the last in the world untouched by civilization. In this story, they are touched and they fall, undone by the fascination their ultimate remoteness exerts on an assortment of Americans. The novel tells how this happens, how by airplane, outboard motor, by jungle trail, the Americans at last bring the first successful contact of the modern world to the savage Niaruna. At every stage of their various journeys, the Americans are tried to the extremes of danger by the piranha-infested rivers, by the filth and disease of jungle outposts, by the treacheries of the local satrap, their enmities for one another, by drink, drugs, madness, by machine gun and rifle and pistol fire, by spears, machetes, arrows, knives, fists, and broken bottles. They are tormented day and night by lusts, racial hatreds, and religious enthusiasms. Some of them die, but some, much altered, survive even the final catastrophe.

At Play in the Fields of the Lord is then, a novel of adventure, and it is, furthermore, to bring in at once the inevitable phrase, a good old-fashioned adventure novel. Peter Matthiessen is not horsing around with the elements of an adventure story, he gives us one straight. The perils of his adventurers, both physical and spiritual, are the elements of the plot, and his plotting is serious, responsible, and so engaging that it is likely most readers will not, need not, be aware in their excitement of how skillful and even ingenious this plotting is. In the first place, the characters assembled here are no accidental or coincidental group, no mere transitory names on a hotel register or a passenger list, come together by chance with their separate fates. Each of them has his own complicated necessity for the push through the jungle to the Niaruna tribe. Their relations with one another, also, are necessary. Their confrontations, quarrels, fights, loves, are each of them necessary stages in the plot. The perils, as I have indicated, are vivid and violent and frequent; but no single adventure seems to be there just for the adventure, for the sake of the thrill, nor because, if the danger is there, our tour must be exposed to it. The events grow out of one another, accumulating in intensity, until in the end every item of character has revealed itself in action, every gun that was hanging on the wall has been proven in discharge to have been no mere ornament, and the basic predicaments of the novel's opening have proven themselves, in their long and complex working out, to have been the true omens of fate, necessity, and action.

Two antagonists compete for the Niaruna, each wanting to save them. One is a soldier of fortune, totally disenchanted and self-debauched, but because he is, of all things, a college-educated American Indian, he is determined first of all to find some "real" Indians, and then, finding them, he is determined to lead them in what might well be a successful military defense of their territory. The other is a missionary, one of an American group determined to save the Indians' souls for Christ. The soldier of fortune, of necessity, becomes a god; the missionary, of necessity, loses his faith and becomes the tool of secular interests. And between them, in their exchanged roles, they destroy the tribe they have so spectacularly risked their lives to save.

To the reader, however, these designs of the plot are not forced in their unfolding. The book remains to the end an adventure story, with the scale and intensity of the action constantly augmenting. This is a considerable achievement. If, having finished this novel, you were to turn back to the beginning and read again a chapter or two, you would see how all this was brought about. The machinery, of course, is there. But it functions always as a related series of elements in a story. And this, I suppose, is what is meant by that phrase, a good old-fashioned novel. . . .

The characters are readily visualized, and always instantly recognizable as they come and go. In a long novel with a dozen or more leading parts, this is no small virtue; an old-fashioned virtue, perhaps, but a genuine one. Sometimes, for all their exotic traits, it seems we recognize them a bit too readily, as though they were type-cast. And we learn probably too much about them, the author has supplied rather more background for each of them than we really require, as he has supplied, in many scenes, a bit more information than necessary. He tells us more than anyone in the scene knows, more than he should know, more than we need to know. These somewhat too-well-known characters, together with one other familiar element, give even to the endless invention and excitement of all the things that happen, to the surprises and reversals of the plot, a very faint aroma of the familiar. Again, it is a good-old-fashioned adventure story.

The other and final familiarity is that of the theme, which is the inevitable destruction of what is innocent and primitive by those who believe, or pretend to believe, that they are out to save it. (p. 20)

John Thompson, "Matthiessen and Updike," in The New York Review of Books, *Vol. V, No. 19, December 23, 1965, pp. 20-1.**

ROBERT M. MENGEL

Highly original in its approach and a beautiful object in its own right, [*The Shorebirds of North America*] devotes itself to its subject, not only with unstinting effort, but also with a refined extravagance recalling the great tradition of the 19th-century luxury works on birds—the Goulds, Audubons, Elliots, and others. . . .

Peter Matthiessen's general text takes the form of a prolonged essay, which has already appeared, with unsubstantial differences, in *The New Yorker*. Mr. Matthiessen is a writer of considerable experience and at his best produces a flowing, poetic style somewhat suggestive of Daphne DuMaurier. He devotes himself to the shorebirds—everything about shorebirds—with unflagging enthusiasm remarkable for its sustained pitch. It is possible, perhaps even probable, that many readers, swept along in this flow, will therefore follow him into areas they would never normally enter, and will acquire, in the process, not only a good deal of generalized and particulate information on shorebirds but, more importantly, a certain insight into what modern field biology is all about. Such readers should be warned that, while Mr. Matthiessen has obviously done an extraordinary amount of reading, he is as clearly not a trained biologist and his text abounds with small factual errors and conceptual near misses (occasionally the misses are wide). This will probably not be very important to many readers and is certainly not worth documenting in detail, but the warning should still be made. The book, fortunately, is abundantly documented, and the author's opinions (not always sound) clearly labeled as such.

Although he has obviously watched many shorebirds in many places (whose names he tends to drop), the author is not as thoroughly familiar with shorebirds in the field as is many a competent amateur, a fact he reveals in various small but telling ways. No alert veteran, for instance, could ever state that the northern phalarope (one of the most diminutive of shorebirds and the size of a house sparrow) is not "much larger than a robin."

As to Mr. Matthiessen's literary art, I have already said that at his best he is good. Opinions would certainly vary but I find his best too rare. In striving for constantly high-pitched effect he strains, becoming more preoccupied with words for their own sake than for their relevance and meaning; a profusion of idiotic combinations, scrambled metaphors and impenetrable meanings result. In this general vein, he coins the pretty and allegorically useful term "wind birds" for shorebirds (itself a pretty and allegorically useful term of long currency). Having coined it, he proceeds to beat it to death, and it can only be silly in his long discourses on reproductive biology, evolutionary history, behavioral adaptations, etc. And I absolutely balk at the description of an oyster as a "dour opponent."

Nevertheless, too few scientists can write better, or trouble themselves to, and Mr. Matthiessen, criticisms notwithstanding, has performed a distinct service in popularizing some important matters.

> *Robert M. Mengel, "Haunting the World's Great Empty, Open Places," in* Book World—Chicago Tribune, *December 10, 1967, p. 5.*

JOHN HAY

[*The Shorebirds of North America*] is one of the finest books of natural history that I have ever seen, regardless of its qualities as an ornithological text, which are considerable. Not the least of the assets of *The Shorebirds of North America* is its feeling of scope, a sense it provides of the worldwide environment in which these "wind birds," in Peter Matthiessen's phrase, have their various being. In other words, this is not just a glossy teaser for the uninitiated; it has authentic unity and depth....

Peter Matthiessen's text has the deftness and balance of a fine writer, it is a mosaic of fascinating information, of observation and description expertly placed. He ranges the field from the fringes of this continent to its interior—not to mention his use of collateral avian associations in many others parts of the world—giving innumerable examples of ways of flight, of mating and nesting, and of distraction and displacement behavior. In a relatively short number of pages we are given the wide realm of shorebirds not only in fact and detail but in their beauty of action, in so far as words can accomplish it.

> *John Hay, in a review of "The Shorebirds of North America," in* Natural History, *Vol. LXXVII, No. 1, January, 1968, p. 70.*

JOHN RECHY

Peter Matthiessen's *Sal Si Puedes* ("Escape If You Can") documents ... [a] list of horrors surrounding the migrant workers: abysmal living conditions, exposure to dangerous sprays, a 1967 average income of less than $1,500, housing codes specifically excluding laborers' camps (officials of the Farm Bureau Federation in Bakersfield, California, admitted to the Housing Authority that they deliberately created miserable living conditions for the migrants so they would leave immediately after the harvest was completed), violations of child-labor regulations (a skinny boy of ten is described struggling to lift a heavy box of grapes), exclusion from Social Security and Workmen's Compensation, filth and illness, an infant mortality rate 125 per cent higher than the national level.

Protesting such conditions, workers led by Cesar Chavez, himself a field laborer, struck the grape growers of California in 1965. The strike was greeted by violence. (p. 33)

"Most good Americans, like 'good Germans,'" Matthiessen says, "have managed to stay unaware of inhumanity in their own country [because] ... misery refutes the American way of life." And he correctly sees the plight of the migrant worker

as part of a multifaceted evil, "related to all of America's most serious afflictions: racism, poverty, environmental pollution, and urban crowding and decay—all of these compounded by the waste of war."

Yet the broad scope of Matthiessen's intentions is marred by a staggering insistence on comprehensiveness, and also by his awe of Chavez.

On the first count, his document becomes so tangled in a labyrinth of labor-union details that the drama of the strike itself is sometimes all but lost. Brilliant descriptive flashes, dramatically built confrontations (the excitement of the picket line, with strikers challenging scabs to cross over) indicate what the book might have been.

Matthiessen's admiration for Chavez is boundless. He sees him as the one who, "of all leaders now in sight, best represents the rising generations." That is not so. Mystical, ascetic, dedicated, Chavez is unquestionably a giant figure in the emergence of *la raza*, much as Martin Luther King is for the blacks. But he is not yet a saint, and Matthiessen seems to attempt his canonization. (pp. 33-4)

[The young militant Chicanos] await the fierce warning from a Chicano James Baldwin and search for their own Malcolm X, their own Eldridge Cleaver. They know that a nonviolent man like Chavez lives under the constant threat of assassination in a lunatic state.

Despite its honest outrage, Matthiessen's book has too much of the sweet, lovely, idealistic, decent wistfulness of Martin Luther King's "I have a dream." The dream has turned into a nightmare. (p. 34)

> *John Rechy, "No Mañanas for Today's Chicanos," in* Saturday Review, *Vol. LIII, No. 11, March 14, 1970, pp. 31-4.*

JAMES FOREST

[In *Sal Si Puedes* Peter Matthiessen] prefers the typewriter equivalent of the cinema verité, shoulder-held camera approach over the rehearsed, Mennen-deodorized, color-enhanced sound stage method.... As a consequence, Matthiessen records everything pretty much as it's happening and being said; and the reader is allowed to share in the surprise of experience with all its jostles, open-endedness and frequent lack of sequential progression. (It isn't until well into the book's second half that much is told of Chavez' childhood—Matthiessen waited for the recollections to surface from a more spontaneous stimulus than a writer's questioning).

The method left me feeling I had been there—walking with Chavez early one August morning along a highway at Delano's edge, eating matzohs and drinking Diet Cola at the end of the fast, picketing with Mexican-American and Filipino strikers (while Mrs. Zapata, a large woman, bellowed *la causa*'s message to the laboring strikebreakers within the vineyard), even talking with furious but thoroughly human growers who believe the strikers are communists. Always, the shoulder-held camera—to which Matthiessen, despite his admiration for the strikers and their cause, refuses to attach ideologically selected filters. (p. 72)

> *James Forest, "Rendering to Cesar," in* The Critic, *Vol. XXVIII, No. 5, May-June, 1970, pp. 72-7.*

JOHN WOMACK, JR.

Of all the recent books on farm-workers, the truest is Peter Matthiessen's *Sal Si Puedes*. It was born in a deathly time, in the wretched summer of 1968, after the assassinations, the riots, and the mournful mud of Resurrection City, when Matthiessen journeyed to Delano to interview "one of the few public figures that I would go ten steps out of my way to meet." Courting disaster, he expected Chavez to "impress" him. If Chavez had, and Matthiessen had taken it, the book would have been only another exposé of one more fraud by one more exhibitionist. But on the quiet Sunday morning when he received Matthiessen at his house, walked with him to early Mass, and drove out to Forty Acres to sit and visit with him, Chavez was just himself—which "startled" Matthiessen. The result is this splendid and inspiring book.

It is not a biography, in style or purpose. Only at random Matthiessen concedes Chavez's past. . . . He does not even suggest why Chavez, hobnobbing with congressmen, hustling mayors and legislators, meeting in "the best motel in town," quit it all in 1962 to settle his wife and eight kids in Delano and start building from scratch without violence a movement that had always before failed, a farmworkers' union.

But Matthiessen does have the man Chavez has become as alive as he can be in print. . . . Because Chavez gave him the nerve to write in praise without idolatry or shame, Matthiessen gives others the nerve to believe that "warmth and intelligence and courage, even in combination, did not account for what I felt at the end of the four-hour walk on that first Sunday morning. . . . What welled out of him was a phenomenon much spoken of in a society afraid of its own hate, but one that I had never seen before—or not, at least, in anyone unswayed by drugs or aching youth; the simple love of man that accompanies some ultimate acceptance of self." (p. 16)

> John Womack, Jr., "The Chicanos," in The New York Review of Books, *Vol. XIX, No. 3, August 31, 1972, pp. 12-18.**

WILLIAM STYRON

[*The essay from which this excerpt is taken originally appeared in 1979 as an introduction to* Peter Matthiessen, A Bibliography: 1951-1979, *compiled by D. Nichols.*]

I read *Partisans* and *Raditzer* with the same careful eye that I had *Race Rock;* as talented and sensitive as each appeared to be, the statement of a writer at the outset of his career, they were, I felt, merely forerunners of something more ambitious, more complex and substantial—and I was right. When *At Play in the Fields of the Lord* was published in 1965 there was revealed in stunning outline the fully realized work of a novelist writing at white heat and at the peak of his powers; a dense, rich, musical book, filled with tragic and comic resonances, it is fiction of genuine stature, with a staying power that makes it as remarkable to read now as when it first appeared.

But before *At Play* was published Peter had to begin that wandering yet consecrated phase of his career which has taken him to every corner of the globe, and which, reflected in a remarkable series of chronicles, has placed him at the forefront of the naturalists of his time. (p. 251)

From what sprang this amazing obsession to plant one's feet upon the most exotic quarters of the earth, to traverse festering swamps and to scale the aching heights of implausible moun-

tains? The wanderlust and feeling for adventure that is in many men, I suppose, but mercifully Peter has been more than a mere adventurer: he is a poet and a scientist, and the mingling of these two personae has given us such carefully observed, unsentimental, yet lyrically echoing works as *The Cloud Forest, Under the Mountain Wall, The Tree Where Man Was Born* and *The Snow Leopard*. In the books themselves the reader will find at least part of the answer to the reason for Peter's quest. In these books, with their infusion of the ecological and the anthropological, with their unshrinking vision of man in mysterious and uneasy interplay with nature—books at once descriptive and analytical, scrupulous and vivid in detail, sometimes amusing, often meditative and mystical—Peter Matthiessen has created a unique body of work. It is the work of a man in ecstatic contemplation of our beautiful and inexplicable planet. To this body of natural history, add a novel like *At Play in the Fields of the Lord* and that brooding, briny, stormswept tone poem, *Far Tortuga,* and we behold a writer of phenomenal scope and versatility. (pp. 251-52)

> William Styron, *"Portraits and Farewells: Peter Matthiessen," in his* This Quiet Dust and Other Writings, *Random House, 1982, pp. 249-52.*

SAMUEL PICKERING, JR.

In comparison to *The Snow Leopard,* which is marred by botanizing amid Eastern philosophy, *Sand Rivers* is straightforward. Although the elephant becomes a symbol, Matthiessen resists making it apocalyptic; it represents the primitive majesty of the natural, something that man has destroyed within himself and is rapidly destroying outside himself.

In many travel books the personality of the author is more important than the ostensible subject of the book. . . . Matthiessen is an ascetic. In attempting to return to the natural or unadorned purity, he has pared his character to the bare bones; and although the safari through the Selous Game Reserve is important for him because he journeys out of our age into a simpler, better time, it would have been more intriguing if Matthiessen were not a true believer. In general ascetics write dull travel books. Spiritual progresses are usually strippings—and after the world, the flesh, and the devil are torn away, little is left that is interesting. The best potential writer of a travel book is the man who indiscriminantly sucks the marrow out of life, not out of a bean pod like Thoreau. Instead of traveling to the heart of darkness to find the light he knows is there, he inhabits the shadows, civilizations between worlds in which contrasts and conflicts are strikingly apparent. The best travel book on Africa in recent years is Edward Hoagland's *African Calliope,* an account of three months Hoagland spent in the Sudan in 1977. Because he lacks Matthiessen's commitment, Hoagland's vision is not clouded by belief, and his celebration of life in the Sudan with all its horrors and blessings is fascinating.

Matthiessen travels into the Selous Reserve with a former warden Brian Nicholson whom Matthiessen describes in detail and with whom he frequently disagrees. Because Nicholson does not allow Matthiessen to indulge in sentimental primitivism at the start of the safari, there is some conflict. Predictably, however, the dangers of the journey bring warden and writer close together. Days in the bush scratch away the crust which the warden affects in civilization, and eventually he is revealed as a disappointed idealist with a heart as soft as Matthiessen's. Matthiessen tells many good stories about Nicholson, and although he quarrels with Nicholson, he likes and admires him. Nicholson has lived that life beyond convention that Matthiessen envies. (pp. 886-87)

Matthiessen is far better than the common run of writers, and *Sand Rivers* is a good book. It is filled with entertaining anecdotes; the descriptions of animals are well done, and Matthiessen is probably on the side of the angels in his wish to preserve the Selous Reserve from man's rapacity and the incompetence of the Tanzanian Game Department. *Sand Rivers,* however, is not extraordinary.... (p. 887)

> Samuel Pickering, Jr., *"At the Beginning and the End of the Earth," in* The Georgia Review, *Vol. XXXV, No. 4, Winter, 1981, pp. 883-88.**

JIM HARRISON

"**Sand Rivers**" is a strange, bittersweet, autumnal book based on a safari into the Selous Game Reserve in southern Tanzania, one of the last great wildernesses left on earth. Once again we have a clear triumph from Peter Matthiessen, who has delivered so many that I am reminded of D. H. Lawrence's insistence that the only true aristocracy on earth is that of consciousness. Whenever Mr. Matthiessen publishes a book, we learn what new lid of consciousness he has popped through. (p. 1)

On its surface, "**Sand Rivers**" is a record of a trek, a march back through time with the deeply disturbing resonance of the future hanging in the air like a death announcement. Mr. Matthiessen is guided by a white Kenyan, Brian Nicholson, the former warden of Selous.... Selous is a "reserve," not to be confused with such famous game parks as the Serengeti or Ngorongoro. There are no accommodations or conveniences for tourists in Selous, an area of some 22,000 square miles... The reserve has an estimated mammal population of 750,000 creatures, a density of animal life that renders all comparisons fatuous....

"**Sand Rivers**" moves from natural history to the novel to some sort of majestic fable. After providing considerable historical background . . . and describing a succession of base camps, Mr. Matthiessen narrates how he and Mr. Nicholson moved off on foot with a half-dozen bearers for a 10-day hike into a totally trackless area. They are a motley group, with Mr. Matthiessen and Mr. Nicholson diametrically opposed on every issue on earth except the survival of this wilderness. Brian Nicholson is the sort of man who makes the most battle-scarred warriors of the movies (say John Wayne) seem like self-indulgent whiners. Mr. Nicholson's racist politics are not attractive, but it has been largely through his efforts that the Selous persists into the present. Part of the fascination and charm of the book is a result of the tensions between the two men....

I underlined nearly a third of the book as quotable: the prose has a glistening, sculpted character to it, especially in the last half....

Finally, as with most of Mr. Matthiessen's work, the sense of beauty and mystery is indelible; not that you retain the specific information on natural history, but that you have had your brain, and perhaps the soul, prodded, urged, moved into a new dimension. (p. 26)

> Jim Harrison, *"Voice of the Wilderness," in* The New York Times Book Review, *May 17, 1981, pp. 1, 26.*

VERNON YOUNG

Matthiessen was invited, in 1979, to join what the sponsor called "the last safari into the last wilderness," namely the Selous Game Preserve, largest remaining wild-life sanctuary on the continent, and to extend the hunt with a walk into territory untrodden by white men before, in the company of an ex-gamewarden, Brian Nicholson, and the eminent photographer, Baron Hugo von Lawick. As anyone who has read *The Snow Leopard* will recall, Matthiessen combines the exhaustive knowledge of the naturalist (he knows the *names* of *everything*—bird, bush and mammal!) with a poet's response to far-out landscapes. Since the country into which he trekked on this occasion is in one of the new African republics, Tanzania, his book [*Sand Rivers*] has the twin appeal of a travelogue and a political footnote. Matthiessen confesses to being a sentimental American who would like to argue the cause of Africa for the black Africans. In view of the damaging evidence that accumulates before his eyes or in the reminders of Nicholson, who has spent a lifetime in British East Africa and lately fought a losing battle against native indifference or mismanagement, he does not insist on his thesis. (pp. 627-28)

Sand Rivers is not a political critique of contemporary Africa; it is among the *journeys back* which have distinguished the trek literature of a hundred years and more, from Mungo Park to Evelyn Waugh and Bruce Chatwin. Yet the political implications which, we gather, Matthiessen and Nicholson not infrequently raised on their long walk, are unavoidable, since the copious animal and bird life which Matthiessen is rehearsing is more than ever before dependent for its survival on human administration, and administration is nothing less than imagination translating the desirable into the operative. Nicholson would like to place his confidence in the occasional Tanzania Game Department official appointed by socialist management who has not been brainwashed to obstruct as a matter of course the "European" experience, but he fears there are not enough of them.... Hence, Matthiessen's narrative, told in the wide-awake terms of a teeming, continuous present, can be read as an elegy for tomorrow, an impression enforced by the autumnal tone of Hugo von Lawick's marvellous pictures, as if the menace as well as the beauty had been photographed just before the last sunset seen by mankind.

Matthiessen, . . . perhaps feeling that he'll never get another chance to name everything as he sees it, tends to load his paragraphs with more rare birds and insects than any but a specialized reader can identify. When he pauses to relate one marvel to another and senses the particular merging into the general, his command of color, sound and substance conjures the resonance of the vast continental space. "Big pink-and-lavender grasshoppers rise and sail away on the hot wind, the burning of their flight as dry and scratchy as the long grass and the baked black rock, the hard red lateritic earth, the crust of Africa." He is wonderful when recreating the alternate silence and clatter of an African night, and uncommon, I think, in any gathering of prose landscape writing is his talent for actualizing the *sounds* of wild life: "The early morning sound of a ground hornbill, the remote dim hooting of a woodland spirit, poo-too, po-to''; the "trilling" of a tiny scrops owl; the "high, eerie giggling" of hyenas; the "nasal, puffing snort" emitted by kangoni; the "peculiar, sneezing bark" made by the impala; the "ominous chinking" of a tinker bird; the "squalling and explosive *chack*" of four boubous chasing through a bush; the "harsh racket" of a roller; the "deep, tearing coughs of a restless leopard," and "the see-saw creaking of the *coqui francolin*."

As one would expect, he records . . . the perpetual co-habitation of life and death, glimpsed at any hour within the same frame. . . . (pp. 628-29)

All this . . . takes on a more haunted interest for the reader who is aware that this region of Africa—comprising Mt. Kenya and Mt. Kilimanjaro, the Serengeti plain, the slave routes to Zanzibar, the sources of the Nile—is alive with associations of past encounters. It was within this area that Speke, in 1861, arrived at the unspeakable kingdom of Buganda (today's Uganda) with its pervert ruler, Mutesa, who buried living wives with their beheaded husbands; where Henry Morton Stanley caught up with Dr. Livingston and, later, travelling north on what he thought was the Nile, found that he was on the Congo. And it is within this quadrangle of territory that a recent school of anthropologists has alleged to have located the home of our immediate ancestor—the killer ape. (p. 630)

> *Vernon Young, "Africa Addio," in* The Hudson Review, *Vol. XXXIV, No. 4, Winter, 1981-82, pp. 625-30.**

ROBERT SHERRILL

[Matthiessen] has had considerable experience observing others hunt all sorts of beasts and fish. This is the first time he has observed manhunts, and there are moments in [*In the Spirit of Crazy Horse*] when I get the feeling that, though he follows the events with meticulousness and gusto, he almost wishes he were back dealing with more admirable predators, such as the lion in Kenya that snapped off a schoolgirl's head *(Sand Rivers)* or the shark that swam off with the bottom half of a Californian *(Blue Meridian: The Search for the Great White Shark).*

Those who have, through his books, accompanied Peter Matthiessen on his wide-ranging adventures know that he is a man of great courage, conscience, insight, sympathy, and tenderness. Those characteristics are seen again in *In the Spirit of Crazy Horse.* But unless I am badly misled by the internal evidence, there has also been a profound change in Matthiessen: he is losing confidence in mankind, and perhaps in himself. In *Sal Si Puedes,* his 1969 book about Cesar Chavez and the United Farm Workers, Matthiessen, after quoting a black migrant farm worker as predicting "the world gonna be great one day," adds that "Cesar Chavez shares this astonishing hope of an evolution in human values and I do too; it is the only hope we have." On the final page of that book, he predicts that sooner or later "the new citizens" who prefer freedom to conformism and fear will "win, for the same reason that other new Americans won, two centuries ago, because time and history are on their side, and passion." But fourteen years later, in this, his first "social issues" book since *Sal Si Puedes,* there is no such note of hope, no assurance that mankind will outgrow its orneriness. (p. 115)

Maybe I read too much hopelessness into *Crazy Horse.* But I am fairly certain of one thing, and I think it relates to his depression: Matthiessen has lost, for the moment at least, his touch of poetry. At its best, Matthiessen's prose is so right that it becomes more than prose, as when he tells us of the song of the whales in *Blue Meridian,* those marvelous oinks, squeaks, grunts, and whistles, "tuned by the ages to a purity beyond refining, a sound that man should hear each morning to remind him of the morning of the world"; or recalls his meeting with the sharks in "a nether world of openmouthed dead staring forms that moved in slow predestined circles";

or paints that primordial scene, in *Sand Rivers,* of "spleen-yellow" crocodiles feasting on a rotting hippopotamus, "swollen a pale purple, that was stranded like a huge rubber toy on a hidden bar out in mid-river." Death and violence have often inspired him before; victims have stirred him to some of his finest writing. But not here. Here there is only prose hardened by unhappiness with a mean system that defies reform. In this respect, I guess, *In the Spirit of Crazy Horse* is a perfect book for our times. (p. 116)

> *Robert Sherrill, "A Warrior's Legacy," in* The Atlantic Monthly, *Vol. 251, No. 3, March, 1983, pp. 112, 114-16.*

CHRISTOPHER LEHMANN-HAUPT

In a letter of his own that he quotes in his latest nonfiction work, **"In the Spirit of Crazy Horse,"** Peter Matthiessen describes the case he treats in this book as "one of the most complex and interesting trials of our time." That may possibly be true. Elsewhere, he compares it to the trial of Sacco and Vanzetti. That too may very well be valid.

But from the point of view of a reader of **"In the Spirit of Crazy Horse,"** the case is not that interesting or momentous. Indeed it is one more in what seems to have been an endless string of similiar cases that we have been reading about ever since the 1960's. To my dismay, in the process of reading Mr. Matthiessen's work, I eventually grew bored.

One wishes it were not so. One does not like to be put in the position of yawning at murder, injustice, conspiracy and the railroading of innocent people. Moreover, there are important aspects to **"In the Spirit of Crazy Horse,"** In it, one of our better nature writers offers a grim but detailed portrait of contemporary Indian life on the reservations of South Dakota. In particular, we get the drama of the reviving warrior spirit in the formation of the troubled American Indian Movement (A.I.M.), led by such charismatic and controversial figures as Russell Means, Dennis Banks and Leonard Peltier.

In long quoted passages, we get appalling autobiographies by people who have spent most of their brief lives in the precincts of despair and madness. We are offered a series of closeup views of events that were at best distantly perceived through the media at the time they occurred. . . .

Most disturbing and controversial of all, Mr. Matthiessen has composed his history so as to reveal how the latest tensions between the United States Government and its native residents are simply further episodes in a chain of events that go right back to such deplorable 19th-century disasters as the reciprocal massacres at the Little Big Horn and Wounded Knee. Needless to add, the Indians in this version are not presented in the erstwhile cliché of pitiless savages but rather as a people provoked to violence by nothing less than the need for its race to survive.

Still, the case on which the whole narrative hinges does not seem all that interesting. So Indians on the Pine Ridge Reservation were attacked by members of the F.B.I., according to Mr. Matthiessen, and two agents were killed. So, he maintains, the F.B.I. fabricated evidence to discredit A.I.M. instead of going after the actual perpetrators. So, he concludes, the real villains behind the latest Indian wars are the corporate interests that want the Indians' mineral and uranium rights and are even willing to pay the price of polluting and poisoning the Western reservations. So what else is new?

Aside from being rather too familiar, Mr. Matthiessen's story is so black and white in its portraits of the good guys and the bad guys that, perversely, one finds oneself dreaming up possible excuses for the bad guys. Could a case possibly be made for the right of the many to prevail over the few in the quest for an energy source independent of the Organization of Petroleum Exporting Countries? Might the persecutors of those Indians who want to return to their native ways be sensing deep in their genes a need for more uniform cultures in the future—a melting pot whose contents will actually melt?

Such speculation is probably nonsense. Perhaps it is mere greed for material profit that lies behind the land-grab conspiracy that Mr. Matthiessen decries. Perhaps it is hatred provoked by deep guilt that accounts for our alleged persecution of American Indians.

But however we account for it all, we have certainly run into it before, with its talk of genocide and colonialism and third world consciousness. It's too bad, because the book makes a persuasive case (as a result of the Freedom of Information Act) that Leonard Peltier may well deserve a new trial following his conviction on two counts of murder in the first degree for the slayings of the two F.B.I. agents. And attention should certainly be paid to the injustices Mr. Matthiessen has tried to document. But because he seems to have lost his perspective and gone on far too long about people and events that don't in his treatment seem to deserve the attention, the reader—this reader, anyway—ultimately loses his capacity for outrage.

Christopher Lehmann-Haupt, "The Troubled Indians," in The New York Times, *March 5, 1983, p. 17.*

ALAN M. DERSHOWITZ

"**In the Spirit of Crazy Horse,**" is really about contemporary America and the way American law is seen through the eyes of American Indians. It is not the tale of a particular tribe or geographically centered culture but rather of a political group spanning the entire spectrum of tribes and geography—the American Indian Movement, or AIM, as it has come to be known. Mr. Matthiessen focuses on the deadly confrontation between AIM and the F.B.I., and specifically on the execution-style murder of two F.B.I. agents at Ogala, S.D., on June 26, 1975, and the events that followed. (p. 26)

The issues of guilt and innocence—both in their technical legal sense and in their broader moral sense—are still vigorously disputed; they form the basis for much of Mr. Matthiessen's narrative. He is at his best when he discusses the complex and compelling moral issues. His theme is that the violence of the American Indian Movement cannot be understood, or judged, in a vacuum; it must be viewed against the suffering inflicted upon the forebears of AIM—and all Indians—over several centuries. But Mr. Matthiessen is at his worst when he becomes a polemicist for his journalistic clients. He is utterly unconvincing—indeed embarrassingly sophomoric—when he pleads the legal innocence of individual Indian criminals. And let there be no mistake: The American Indian Movement—like every militant fringe group—contains its share of violent criminals who seek to glorify their predatory acts under the flag of the movement. A history of discrimination may explain and, in extreme cases, perhaps even excuse criminality. But it can rarely justify it, especially against innocent victims.

The two executed F.B.I. agents were gunned down at close range. They were disarmed, helpless and probably begging for their lives. There were no eyewitnesses, or at least none who would testify, to who murdered them. But considerable circumstantial evidence pointed toward Leonard Peltier, one of the most militant AIM leaders. There can be little doubt that the F.B.I. was out to get Mr. Peltier. Nor can there be any doubt that the F.B.I. desperately wanted to bring to justice the murderers of its agents. The real question—and the one that Mr. Matthiessen answers in the affirmative—is whether the F.B.I. framed Mr. Peltier for killings he may not have committed.

On this issue, Mr. Matthiessen not only fails to convince; he inadvertently makes a strong case for Mr. Peltier's guilt. Invoking the clichés of the radical left, Mr. Matthiessen takes at face value nearly every conspiratorial claim of the movement, no matter how unfounded or preposterous. Every car crash, every unexplained death, every unrelated arrest fits into the seamless web of deceit he seems to feel was woven by the F.B.I. and its cohorts.

This is not to dispute all of AIM's complaints against the F.B.I. Some—such as infiltration of the movement for purposes of engendering internal distrust and dissension—carry indications of credibility. These tactics, indefensible though they are, have been commonly used by the F.B.I. against radical groups of all political persuasions. But other allegations, such as systematic beatings and "contracts" on the lives of AIM leaders, do not seem credible. Mr. Matthiessen surely provides no proof beyond the self-serving claims of the alleged victims and their partisan lawyers. As I was reading Mr. Matthiessen's "legal brief," I found myself wanting to shout at this good-hearted naif, "Don't you know that's the kind of nonsense every convicted murderer tries to get you to believe; I get dozens of these letters every week." But Mr. Matthiessen seems to have been taken in and to have left most of his otherwise excellent critical faculties at home when he interviewed Mr. Peltier and his followers.

Though the book purports at times to present an objective appraisal, Mr. Matthiessen finally acknowledges—near the end—that his "account of the Peltier case argued the position of traditional Indians and their allies in the American Indian Movmement." And at the very close of the book, he describes how "I told Leonard I believed [that he hadn't killed the agents], and I did, and I do." And I wonder. Why does Mr. Matthiessen go out of his way so frequently to make disclaimers such as "my personal opinion of his guilt or innocence [is] of no importance"? And why does he quote one of the AIM lawyers as saying: "I know Bill Kunstler [another of the AIM lawyers] thought they killed the agents, but he believes that they were innocent whether they did it or not"?

In the end, Mr. Matthiessen tries to have it both ways. He says that "from the Indian's viewpoint—and increasingly from my own—any talk of innocence or guilt was beside the point." But he insists nonetheless that the evidence "made it plain that Peltier had been railroaded into jail."

"**In the Spirit of Crazy Horse,**" documents the imperfection of the American legal system, especially when it is mustered against a political group—even one as violent as the American Indian Movement. It is also a tragic account of the self-destructive quality of many of the self-appointed leaders of that movement. Drawn from among the most vocal, the most violent and the most radical native Americans, many of these leaders exploited their newly discovered heritage for their own personal ends. Some have ended where they belong—in jail. Other have simply drifted away. What remains are thousands of poverty-stricken Indians, first driven by years of neglect to accept false prophets of violence and then shorn even of that ineffective leadership.

The tragedy of Mr. Matthiessen's book is that he fails to understand that his heroes—the radicals of AIM—did not act in the selfless spirit of Chief Crazy Horse, that noble 19th-century leader of Indian resistance. They acted more in the violent spirit of Custer. By doing so, they helped to destroy the dream and hopes of American Indians. (pp. 26-7)

Alan M. Dershowitz, "Agents and Indians," in The New York Times Book Review, *March 6, 1983, pp. 1, 26-7.*

RODERICK NORDELL

Even when Peter Matthiessen writes the text in a book full of photographs ("**The Tree Where Man Was Born**," with Eliot Porter's pictures of Africa) he goes for literature as well as information. This is both a strength and possible drawback in the 600 gray, unillustrated pages of "**In the Spirit of Crazy Horse.**"

Matthiessen's literary art pulls you along. There is the resonance with history, as he recalls the 19th-century massacre of Indians at Wounded Knee while describing the past decade's often violent events in the same Pine Ridge reservation area of South Dakota. There is the skilled interweaving of past and present individual voices to tell a story of treachery, corruption, and courage on and off the reservation, in and out of government. There is the distinctive presence of the author's own voice, letting admiration, indignation, and sarcasm glint through. The result: an eloquent recital of wrongs done to the Lakota people, along with latter-day efforts to right them, justice gone astray, and lands plundered for newly found mineral resources in defiance of bygone treaty obligations.

The possible drawback is that the very elements making for distinction may undercut the persuasiveness of the case Matthiessen offers. When he adds more and more to his rich investigative mixture, the clear thread of argument becomes slack. When he lets his mockery of government officials, however justified, edge his prose, there is the danger of indictment being taken for polemic, of assent from the already convinced turning to doubt from readers on the fence.

The likelihood is that unadorned facts would carry the day anyway. . . .

For all the exploration of recent controversy, perhaps the prime contribution of "**In the Spirit of Crazy Horse**" for the reader is its immersion in Lakota life and lore. Here is an author who does not overlook anybody's human failings but who conveys with respect a sense of the achievements, setbacks and spiritual yearnings of people in conditions "almost unimaginable to most Americans."

Roderick Nordell, "Elegant Recitals of Wrongs to Lakota People and Efforts to Right Them," in The Christian Science Monitor, *March 11, 1983, p. 17.*

PAGE STEGNER

On a sultry morning in June 1975 two FBI agents assigned to the Pine Ridge Reservation near Rapid City, South Dakota,

followed a station wagon onto Indian land somewhere between the little towns of Oglala and Pine Ridge, two traditional Lakota Sioux communities thought to be harboring American Indian Movement (AIM) agitators and generally hostile to outside law enforcement agencies. . . . [They] suddenly found themselves parked in a wood-lined field and fired upon from a nearby hill by an unspecified number of angry Indians. . . .

In the Spirit of Crazy Horse revolves around [the murder of the two FBI agents], the ensuing manhunt, the trials of the three men eventually charged with the crimes, and the highly suspect conviction of one, AIM member Leonard Peltier, now serving two consecutive life terms for murder. Through meticulous examination of the evidence presented in court, extensive interviews with the accused, law enforcement agencies, defense lawyers, prosecuting attorneys, prison inmates, traditional Indian leaders, AIM organizers, and in profiles of everybody from the judges who presided over the trials to the witnesses who testified at them (or refused to testify), Peter Matthiessen tells a story that slowly clarifies what probably happened on that hot June morning some fifty miles southeast of Custer's last stand. If anyone beside the actual killer (or killers) can tell the literal truth about the final moments of Coler and Williams, he (or she) has not yet done so.

For the larger issues raised by the book, however, the literal truth hardly matters. The detective story makes absorbing reading, as good as any investigative reporting ever gets, but it is there primarily as a thread on which to hang an inquiry that goes far beyond the murder of two unfortunate men who, through ignorance or arrogance, bad judgment or professional zeal, put themselves in the wrong place at the wrong time. The questions that concern Matthiessen are what created the climate in the first place in which such brutal violence could occur, and why was the federal government so "enthusiastic" in its investigation of the "ResMurs" (Reservation Murders)—an investigation which Arthur Flemming, chairman of the US Civil Rights Commission, was moved to call in a letter of protest to the US attorney general "an over-reaction which takes on aspects of a vendetta." And why, in light of subsequent disclosures of FBI tactics that one appeals court judge called a "clear abuse of the investigative process," and in light of "eyewitness" testimony against Peltier by an alcoholic incompetent who was later shown to be fifty miles from the scene of the crimes, and in light of courtroom proceedings in which critical information was withheld from the jury during their deliberations, was Leonard Peltier extradicted from Canada, tried, found guilty, imprisoned, and denied (as yet) retrial? . . .

The chronicle of our nation's sorry relationship with the Indian is important background for Matthiessen's book, but perhaps because it is not exactly news he devotes only a short section to historical recapitulation, focusing his attention instead on a period of activism that begins with a "Declaration of Indian Purpose" at a conference of sixty-seven tribes in Chicago in June 1961 and ends with the death of the FBI agents at Pine Ridge in June 1975. During this period a number of confrontations took place that exacerbated the suspicion and distrust with which Indians regard whites. These came at a time of reemerging ethnic pride among young red men and women who had begun remythologizing ancestral leaders like Red Cloud, Sitting Bull, and Crazy Horse, and who had begun to take a few of their cues from militant blacks and Chicanos. Suspicion and distrust coupled with anger and pride—a volatile combination. (p. 21)

The psychological climate in which the FBI agents were killed is clearly not the result of simple Indian paranoia. They had good reason to be frightened of armed lawmen. But Matthiessen makes no attempt to excuse murder on the grounds it was provoked. [The FBI agents], he acknowledges, were not just killed in a fire fight; they were coldly executed, and he makes no case for mitigating responsibility for that act. Nor did any of the men indicted for the killings deny that they, along with more than a dozen other Indians, took part in a shoot-out with the FBI agents. They claimed they acted in self-defense. One of the Indians was killed.

At the same time Matthiessen cannot ignore a disturbing question: why did the death of two white men inspire "the biggest manhunt in FBI history" . . . ? (p. 23)

In truth, nobody knows who killed Agents Coler and Williams either, though that did not prevent Leonard Peltier from going to prison for their murder. Maybe Peltier did pull the trigger. Or maybe he was railroaded by a Justice Department so eager to revenge two of their own that they wanted to hang any Pine Ridge Indian they could get their hands on. By Matthiessen's account, there is good reason to think so. (p. 24)

Matthiessen makes . . . [an] argument that Peltier should at least be retried. It is but one incident in Matthiessen's far broader argument that our entire national Indian policy should be retried (and not, it should be said, by a return to 1950s proposals for "termination" of all relations with the Indians favored by James Watt and Ronald Reagan). "Whatever the nature and degree of his participation at Oglala," Matthiessen writes, "the ruthless persecution of Leonard Peltier had less to do with his own actions than with underlying issues of history, racism, and economics, in particular Indian sovereignty claims and growing opposition to massive energy development on treaty lands and the dwindling reservations."

In the Spirit of Crazy Horse is one of the most dramatic demonstrations of endemic American racism that has yet been written—a powerful, unsettling book that will force even the most ethno-pious reader to inspect the limits of his understanding. . . . Leslie Marmon Silko, the Laguna Pueblo writer, commenting on the romantic sentimentality most whites harbor for "the Indian" (the one who isn't armed, drunk, or holding up progress) wrote, "The American public has difficulty believing . . . [that] injustice continues to be inflicted upon Indian people because Americans assume that the sympathy or tolerance they feel toward Indians is somehow 'felt' or transferred to the government policy that deals with Indians. This is not the case." Along with its many other accomplishments, Peter Matthiessen's superb new work should put an end to that assumption. (pp. 24, 31)

        Page Stegner, "Reds," in The New York Review of Books, *Vol. XXX, No. 6, April 14, 1983, pp. 21-4, 31.*

WILCOMB E. WASHBURN

Mix together the following ingredients: a threatened natural environment, endangered plants and animals, and Indians resisting change, and you have the formula for a story that will be bought by an American public quick to applaud those who fight against change when it is perceived as unjust or unnecessary.

Peter Matthiessen, a naturalist and journalist who has only recently (in his *In the Spirit of Crazy Horse*) moved from the natural environment to Indians, has in this book combined both. *Indian Country* is neither history nor social analysis. It consists of personal reminiscences by Matthiessen and his informants. His principal informant, Craig Carpenter, was, in the 1950s, "by his own account, a 'half-baked detribalized Mohawk from the Great Lakes country trying to find his way back to the real Indians.'" In the "spiritual" journeys the two take together, many other detribalized urban Indians, far from their original homes, appear in the guise of "traditional" Indians, usually as "spiritual advisers" to other detribalized Indians.

The pretensions of these Indians to represent the 500 Indian tribes, nations, bands and villages officially recognized by the United States as having governmental character have not been accepted by these governments. The white media, on the other hand, have uncritically treated the tiny handful of individual Indian activists as somehow representing the Indian point of view. Why? Because the Indian activists have learned to phrase their denunciations of the white man and legitimate Indian leaders in terms of stereotypical values familiar to whites (e.g., reverence for "Mother Earth") even though in most cases these activists have only a casual (at best) or cynical (at worst) acquaintance with these values.

It need hardly be stated that Matthiessen's book has no scholarly value except for the light it throws on these detribalized activists and their white supporters and agents. Beginning with Matthiessen's suggestion on the first page that the Indians were named so not because Columbus thought he had arrived in the Sea of India but because he believed he had found a people living in harmony with nature (*una gente in Dios*), we are treated with partisanship, innuendo, opinion and rumor masquerading as fact. One cause involving Indian land after another is spread before us. . . . (p. 10)

In almost every one of [the] disputes concerning Indian land, the picture presented is one in which a handful of beleaguered "traditionals" is battling an insensitive elected "puppet" tribal government established under the authority of the Indian Reorganization Act of 1934, part of the sweeping New Deal revision of Indian affairs undertaken under the leadership of John Collier. The courts, which have vigorously defended and expanded the sovereign character of Indian governments in the last 40 years, are also denounced by Matthiessen when they rule against the pretensions of a handful of "traditionals" in favor of elected tribal governments. The efforts of a few of the "traditionals" to bring their "case" to the United Nations in Geneva, or to Fidel Castro (as Buffalo Tiger of the "Miccosukee Nation" did in 1959) is celebrated. Curiously no mention is made of the indictment and conviction of the U.S. Government (for crimes against the "traditionals") at the so-called Russell International Tribunal in Rotterdam in 1980 by a group of ideological activists sharing Matthiessen's point of view, and presented by one of his informants for *Indian Country,* Tim Coulter of Washington's own Indian Law Resource Center. Coulter's generously funded center affords "traditionals" the opportunity to attack elected tribal governments. (It also represents a few legitimate tribal governments.) Why the omission of the Russell tribunal from Matthiessen's book? Could it be that he realized that the too obvious linkage of the "traditional" cause to the ideological cold war between the United States and the Soviet Union, to say nothing of the absurdity of the charges of genocide, sterilization of Indian women and the like, with which the United States was charged and "convicted," would deprive the "traditionals" of the sympathy Matthiessen carefully seeks to cultivate?

Matthiessen and the few individuals and groups celebrated by him live in a symbiotic relationship. Each one sustains and—one is tempted to say—creates the other. Few would hear about Matthiessen's friends if he and other ill-informed journalists did not amplify their voices and ignore those of the vast majority of Indians opposed to their point of view. Barring this not-to-be-expected miracle, the American people will continue to have Matthiessen's mushy sentiments repeatedly shoved into their faces. (p. 11)

Wilcomb E. Washburn, "Who Speaks for the Indian?" in Book World—The Washington Post, *May 20, 1984, pp. 10-11.*

PAUL ZWEIG

For almost twenty years, Peter Matthiessen has pursued a vanishing world of wilderness and uninhabited spaces in which man is no more than a sparse, gentle guest. In a dozen books of fiction and naturalist reportage, Matthiessen has written about the Amazon jungle and the plains of eastern Africa; he has tramped across the Nepalese Himalayas, and climbed into the high jungle valleys of New Guinea. No one writes more vividly about the complex sounds and sights of a world without man, or where man blends in uncannily as merely another venture in nature's billion-year experiment.

Matthiessen's knowledge of the botanist's and zoologist's lore is encyclopedic. His descriptions of the African savannah or of the inner reaches of the Himalayas may be the best we have. In such remote places, his writing becomes a poetry of nomenclature in all its whimsy and barbarism, but also its curious splendor, as man casts his net of language upon the fluid rhythms of a world that ignores him, or would if man did not have a power of destruction which cannot be ignored. . . .

Matthiessen the naturalist has also been an elegist, chronicling the decline of an older earth of sparse populations hunting and gathering, or planting according to modest needs, in a ritual of respect for the cycles of the year. It is a gentle picture, maybe a purely invented one, expressing as it does a powerful longing: the dream of a reconciled world.

The opening scenes of Matthiessen's newest book, *Indian Country,* take us yet again into this vanishing world, in this case a part of inland Florida. . . . [There is a] sort of lyrical precision one appreciates in Matthiessen's writing: the sense of limitless space, an elusive population of vividly named species, grasses, sky—whole vocabularies of trees. (p. 36)

Matthiessen has two subjects in *Indian Country:* the destruction of America's last open land by the grinding pressure of big industry, in particular the energy industry; and the tragic struggle of the last people on the land to preserve their shrinking territories, and even more, to preserve the holy balance of their traditions, linked to the complex, fragile ecology of the land.

Matthiessen has crisscrossed the country, visiting Indian reservations in Florida and Tennessee, New York, California, the Dakotas, the Southwest. Among Hopis and Navaho, Cherokees, Mohawks and Muskeegees; among countless remnants of tribes that have left powerful names in the sagas of the American past—Sioux, Apache, Comanche—he has stopped to talk, and found distrustful, secretive peoples, who have learned that there is little to hope for from a white man, even a friendly one. They are struggling to keep old traditions intact, amidst the desolation of rugged territories, hostile white neighbors, and energy conglomerates who often conspire with the

Indians' own lawyers to steal the oil and mineral rights of America's last wilderness for pennies an acre.

With patience and impassioned sympathy, Matthiessen has penetrated the "Indian awakening" that has been taking place for more than twenty years on reservations around the country. Repeatedly he has encountered a complex, often bitter political struggle between Indians who have bought the B.I.A.'s offer of welfare money, running water, and electricity—who have moved into tract villages, abandoning traditional settlements located near sacred pools rich with hundreds or even a thousand years of tradition—and recalcitrant, usually minority groups of "traditionals," for whom the B.I.A. (along with other official state agencies) is merely a more cunning face of cultural annihilation. (pp. 36-7)

It is a tragic conflict; both the "traditionals," longing to observe the old "Mohawk Way," and the "Tribals," hoping to manage some integration with white society, live under a destructive shadow. In this wilderness of upper New York State, almost visible from the camp of the "traditionals," a General Motors foundry spews acrid smoke into the air and a Reynolds Aluminum plant wafts "a light warm haze of fluoride effluvium." . . . The Indians are fighting, but they are fighting for a dead land.

Indian Country tells the same desperate story over and over again. . . . In place after place, the rape of the land and the despoiling of the Indians go hand in hand; and all of us are poorer for it. For, in Matthiessen's view, the Indians—those that are left, even half-acculturated, desperately poor, often alienated from their own past—are the spiritual custodians of a relationship to the natural world which we have lost.

The loss may destroy us. The Indians are our conscience; as they are silenced, bought off, discouraged, "terminated," something irrevocable is happening to our country. Those places of silence and ancient emptiness, about which Matthiessen writes so movingly, are vanishing, and with them our own secure place in the world is vanishing too, replaced by factory smoke, by piles of radioactive tailings at the mouth of uranium mines, and by the planet-wide death still barely bottled up in nuclear warehouses. (pp. 37-8)

Indian Country tells the story of many lost battles, and a few battles won. Every celebration of Indian courage and determination, every injunction barring the destruction of yet another tract of glorious country, gives the measure of what, year by year, is being lost. Matthiessen's story is, finally, an unutterably sad one. (p. 38)

Paul Zweig, "Vanishing Tribes," in The New Republic, *Vol. 190, No. 22, June 4, 1984, pp. 36-8.*

PETER NABOKOV

During the past eight years Peter Matthiessen has returned from his travels in Africa or Nepal to discover a hidden network of native American states of mind and places—his "Indian country." These are remote, impoverished, embattled enclaves within or on the borders of the official Indian reservations. There the representatives of what Matthiessen considers the true Indian way of life are still holding out—his "traditionals." . . . [The "traditionals"] are troublemaking idealists from Florida to California who refuse to abandon their old treaty rights, who dream of absolute tribal sovereignty, defiantly resist federal authorities and their own tribal governments, and equate their survival with that of the land they revere.

To Matthiessen these holdouts represent America's last hope as they stand up to the federal Indian bureaucracy, the law enforcement establishment, and the multinational energy consortiums that are poisoning their sacred lands. Matthiessen has no doubt that the white man's frontier crusade to obliterate Indian culture remains very much alive; he seems to regard this collection of magazine pieces as urgent dispatches from censored zones in an American cold war. He is to be commended for caring enough about these beleaguered corners of Indian America to search them out. Again and again he must outwait the suspicious scrutiny of his wary subjects. Through a mysterious string of inside contacts he manages to connect with key people and bring out their desperate stories [in *Indian Country*].

Matthiessen also dips into the morass of cultural and political history behind each of the tribes he visited. He makes an effort to untangle the legal nightmares that are part of every tribe's pedigree, trying to pinpoint the crucial shifts in the power relations between whites and Indians. Finally, as if these tasks have made him increasingly uneasy, he does what comes most naturally to him, evoking the wildlife and landscape that brought him to some of these locations on earlier assignments and still seem to engage his abiding affections. Indeed the book is at its most powerful less in its account of human misery than in its description of environmental ruin. . . .

If Matthiessen's outrage about the environment and his sympathies toward the Indian seem so well directed, why does one sense throughout that something is cripplingly wrong with his voice and his thesis? . . .

To [Matthiessen] what makes his Indian friends authentic is that in spirit they still exist *ab origine*. He would have us see his eleven sketches as pilgrimages to the last strongholds of primeval truth in America. To reach them he takes as his companion that long-suffering intermediary, the mystic scout. As Thoreau had his Penobscot guide Joe Polis, and Leatherstocking his loyal Chingachgook, Matthiessen has Craig Carpenter, who describes himself as a "half-baked detribalized Mohawk from the Great Lakes country trying to find his way back to the real Indians."

As we follow them on backroads and into Indian kitchens we see the reenactment of an old pattern of intellectual exploitation: had the Indians never existed, perhaps white writers would have had to invent them, as a utopian antithesis to everything they disliked or found alienating about their own world. The spectrum of symbolic interpretations to which the defenseless Indian societies have been subject over the centuries has been well delineated in Elemire Zolla's *The Writer and the Shaman: A Morphology of the American Indian*. Since the time of Jean-Jacques Rousseau (not to be confused, as Matthiessen seems to have, with the painter Henri Rousseau) opinions about Indians have swung from deploring them to adoring them. Indian writer Vine Deloria, Jr., maintains that US government policy still reflects this historical ambivalence; in this century he sees the pendulum swing between pro-Indian and anti-Indian legislation and back again as condensed into twenty-year cycles.

Reading Matthiessen's book one has the sinking feeling that he is somehow trapped at the pro-Indian pole of this fixed ambivalence. His loyalties and evocations seem inherited from the earlier writers and approaches which Zolla surveyed. His pious attitudes toward his native hosts too often fall within the "tradition of benevolence," exemplified by the idealistic descriptions of Indians in Thoreau, Melville, and Hamlin Gar-

land. His sense of outrage is often undercut by a mystical romanticism straight out of the "literature of reverence" epitomized by the writings of D. H. Lawrence. And to the broad genre Zolla calls "poetic ethnography," a category embracing fiction and non-fiction, Matthiessen splices the hyperbole and innuendo of radical journalism that often comes dangerously close to branding most whites as insensitive exploiters and most nonradical Indians as sell-outs. . . .

The problem with such lofty sentiments lies in using "The Indian" as a screen on which to project them. For how can one judge the validity of this interpretation of the collective essence of Indian society against those that claim that all Indians are dumb, lazy, savage, or nearly extinct? The problem, of course, is that "the" Indian has always been a fiction, and Matthiessen's promotion of this monolithic stereotype is among his book's major failings. While he pays respect to particulars of culture and ecology when he is visiting Indians, his book's pervasive certainty about what Indianness means leads him to ignore the widely contrasting social, religious, demographic, economic, political, and ecological circumstances found among over three hundred different North American Indian peoples. (p. 44)

In his novel *Far Tortuga* Matthiessen was willing to experiment boldly with prose rhythms and Caribbean dialects, and the risk produced the most brilliant novel I have read about the sea since Joseph Conrad's *Nigger of the "Narcissus."* But his writing here seems strangely cowed as he unhesitatingly takes sides with the Indian factions he dubs as true "traditionals." This reduction of Indian social and political realities to struggles between traditionals and "elected" or "tribal" Indians makes for grievous oversimplification. Today's system of tribal governments was set up during the Indian New Deal in the 1930s by the idealistic Commissioner of Indian Affairs, John Collier. For the tribes that voted to come under Collier's Indian Reorganization Act, the system was intended to restore land and some semblance of power to Indian peoples who were disenfranchised during the late nineteenth century. During the last few decades increasing numbers of Indian leaders have contested the authority of the tribal government apparatus, claiming that it has effectively denied them their sovereign rights as promised in old treaties. They maintain that their tribal council officials are puppets of the government's Bureau of Indian Affairs, and that, by deputizing the opposition, the federal government has turned Indians against themselves and left them vulnerable, once again, to outsiders who want their remnant lands. . . .

Matthiessen seems unaware, however, that this internal tribal dissent over how white to become has persisted since colonial times and that it has always been the part of Indian history that whites have chosen to emphasize. . . . As with most short-term visitors to Indian communities before him, Matthiessen ignores the other, myriad interest groups whose alliances and competitions make contemporary reservation life a far more complex puzzle than the one he presents. He gives little or no attention to the issues that have priority for Indians who live in cities and periodically come back to the reservation or retain voting rights there, to the concerns of mixed-bloods with varying degrees of status and investment in reservation policies, to the interests of college-educated Indians or professionals who have returned home or serve as long-distance emissaries, or to the preoccupations of members of various religious groups that stand together when it comes to tribal issues. For these and other constituencies, Matthiessen's "traditional" versus "tribal" dispute is only one of many tensions that surround them; most would resent an outsider designating them as less "Indian" in spirit or creed because they had other things on their minds. . . .

[The] most intriguing and heartening aspect of Indian survival is the ways that tribes have continually been able to reinvent their identities as groups through the interplay of their inherited traditions, their historical circumstances, their imagined selves, and manipulations of their "image" and expressive symbols. The dialectic between a timeless perspective and the time-bound exigencies of survival have helped to produce the Native American Church, the Shaker Church, the revived Sun Dance, the new inter-tribal sweat lodge ceremony, the California Bola Maru Religion, the Redbird Smith movement, and other examples of native American ability to endure in tormenting times. Matthiessen runs into trouble by applying one exclusive criterion for traditionalism to a spectrum of tribal cultures. It is rather like assessing the degree to which the French or British are more or less European, and then maintaining that Europeanness is a nobler attribute than either of them. Most Navajos, for instance, will be bewildered to learn that their age-old talent for incorporating items from other cultures—whether weaving methods, religious iconography, or pickup trucks—puts them low on Matthiessen's scale of traditional virtue. . . .

Throughout the book Matthiessen offers incomplete, sketchy references; his apparent wariness of [his primary sources] . . . , as well as voluminous anthropological and historical materials on each of the tribes he investigates, seems based either on the constraints of magazine deadlines or the distrust in which many of his Indian informants hold those materials. Yet he might have taken a lesson from Edmund Wilson, whose *Apologies to the Iroquois* was effective as advocacy journalism precisely because Wilson patiently interwove the perspectives of the best academicians, historical scholarship, his own experiences, and native testimony—much of it from vociferous militants.

Matthiessen comes across as an uneasy polemicist and a reluctant war correspondent; he relaxes only when he has animals to watch, hills to climb, surroundings to describe, and one or two people whose inner sensibilities he can quietly respond to across a campfire. . . . Otherwise these reports seem a burden of conscience to him. . . .

What is most interesting about Matthiessen's book is its unwitting perpetuation of the oldest images that whites have used to turn the Indians into symbols of their own deepest longings. Perhaps these images can be replaced only when the conversion of spirit Matthiessen preaches comes to pass. Meanwhile his impassioned confusion of the themes of America as Lost Paradise and the Indian as its Dispossessed Spirit seems evidence of the astonishing power of the myth of "the Indian" to enthrall white imaginations. It is as if, in some cosmic compensation for five centuries of anguish and insult, Indians have preserved a way to imprison their conquerors and still keep their secrets. (p. 45)

Peter Nabokov, "Return to the Native," in The New York Review of Books, *Vol. XXXI, No. 14, September 27, 1984, pp. 44-5.*

Joe McGinniss

1942-

American nonfiction writer, novelist, and journalist.

McGinniss has gained prominence for his nonfiction books on subjects of current interest. His work is based on extensive research and personal involvement. For instance, *Fatal Vision* (1983), his recent best-seller, concerns the trial of Dr. Jeffrey MacDonald, a former Green Beret and "all-American boy" who was accused of murdering his pregnant wife and two small daughters. McGinniss worked closely with his subject, living in MacDonald's California condominium with access to his private papers and records. The result is a comprehensive rendering of the events which led to MacDonald's conviction in 1982.

McGinniss's first book, *The Selling of the President 1968* (1969), exposes how Richard Nixon's political promoters used television to remake his public image. McGinniss gained behind-the-scenes knowledge of the Nixon campaign by presenting himself to Nixon's promoters as a student who was researching a scholarly thesis on the role of the electronic media in a political campaign. *The Selling of the President 1968* brought McGinniss instant fame; the strenuous speaking tour which followed provided material for his only fictional work, *The Dream Team* (1972). In this novel McGinniss presents a self-portrait in the protagonist, a best-selling author who tires of the book-promoting circuit. *Heroes* (1976), a nonfictional account of McGinniss's search for contemporary heroic figures, reveals how deeply the success of his first book and the pressure to maintain that level of achievement affected McGinniss. Although he interviews such notable figures as Eugene McCarthy, George McGovern, Daniel Berrigan, and Arthur Miller, *Heroes* is more an attempt to understand his own confusion and loss of fame than an explanation of the lack of contemporary American heroes.

McGinniss acknowledges that in writing *Heroes* he gained a deeper understanding of himself and was able to move on to less personal material in his next two books, *Going to Extremes* (1980) and *Fatal Vision*. McGinniss lived in Alaska for two years in order to write *Going to Extremes*, which explores why people move to America's last frontier and how they cope, or fail to cope, with their isolation.

(See also *Contemporary Authors*, Vols. 25-28, rev. ed.)

JOHN OSBORNE

[*The Selling of the President 1968*] is the best thing that's happened to Richard Nixon since somebody told him to stop wiggling those fingers. The author, Joe McGinniss, has done the President the immense and obviously unintended favor of showing him to be the normal, temperish, profane, vulnerable adult male that his spokesmen at the White House keep insisting he isn't. They are under the illusion that Mr. Nixon is best served by making him out to be superhumanly calm, beyond disturbance—a Presidential potato. . . . Joe McGinniss informs us—and accurately, I am told by some of the men who figure in this book and who still work for Nixon—that he wasn't like that during the campaign last year. . . .

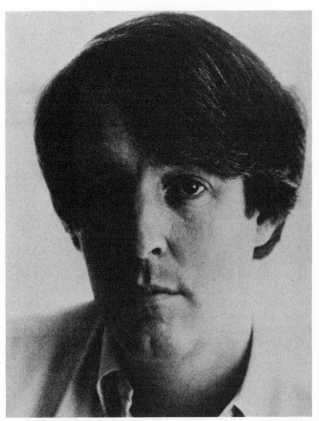

Photograph by Nancy Doherty

[The] campaign staffers who managed the Nixon TV effort last year would have saved themselves a lot of pain and deprived us of the most interesting account yet written of the 1968 race for the Presidency if they had troubled to check on the beguiling young man (aged 26) who presented himself to them in June. As they recall it, he said that he wanted to research and write a studious, philosophic account of the role of the electronic media in modern Presidential politics. No quotes; nothing that would embarrass anybody; a book, they were led to expect, that would deal in soporific generalities and take them and their expertise with stultifying gravity. (p. 26)

I am supposed, I gather, to be frightened by the evidence . . . that enormous thought and effort went into remaking Richard Nixon for television and into projecting an image so different from "the real Nixon" as to constitute a massive fraud upon the electorate. . . . Well, after reading and rereading the McGinniss account, I am reassured. It didn't work. All of that effort, all of those millions spent for television accomplished—what? Essentially the same Richard Nixon whom I followed in person around the country came across to the country through the tube. . . . It is for the unobserved but overheard and intimately quoted Nixon that I value the McGinniss account. It is useful to know that the President has a horror of psychiatrists . . . and that he curses when he's angry. Whatever we have in the Nixon Presidency, we don't have a potato. Maybe Nixon should hire Joe McGinniss. (pp. 27-8)

John Osborne, "Nixon through the Tube," in The New Republic, *Vol. 161, No. 15, October 11, 1969, pp. 26-8.*

L. E. SISSMAN

[Joe McGinniss] has written a sensationally but, I'm afraid, aptly titled book about . . . [a] new phenomenon in American politics. **"The Selling of the President 1968"** . . . is his insider's account of how a group of skillful advertising and television specialists engineered Richard Nixon's television campaign last year. . . .

[McGinniss] has written an admirably clear and brief account of the whole Nixon television campaign, from its beginnings in philosophical position papers largely inspired by the disjunctive *éclaircissements* of Marshall McLuhan to its telethonic climax in Los Angeles on Election Eve. It indicates that the chief intent of the television advisers and technicians was to replace the baleful image of the Old Nixon—cold, distant, minatory, punitive—with a bland and casual new one. (p. 57)

In developing his story, Mr. McGinniss also develops the characters of the Nixon people with considerable skill; we understand both the mechanics and motivations of the campaign and the psychology of the men who ran it. As a bonus, we get a set of dramatic and ludicrous incidents that rise above the level of anecdote because the participants are people we already know and understand. This novelistic method adds a good deal to the book, and so, conversely, does a set of internal memos and campaign documents. My only serious reservation is that Mr. McGinniss, whose repugnance at the distortions of the image-making process is abundantly evident, sometimes goes beyond legitimate editorial comment to speculate moralistically about his characters and their actions, both of which surely speak clearly for themselves. . . . A smaller cavil is that McGinniss now and then writes portentous short sentences in portentous short words, in the manner of Jimmy Breslin or an ad for *Jock*. Nonetheless, it's a good book. (p. 58)

L. E. Sissman, "Television Makes the Man," in The New Yorker, *Vol. XLV, No. 45, December 27, 1969, pp. 57-8.*

ANTHONY HOWARD

A very strange thing happened in the American publishing world last autumn. As the summer ended Mr. Theodore White—that historian laureate of US presidential elections—produced his customary reverential account of the previous year's campaign [*The Making of the President 1968*].

Mr. White's book slowly and surely began its climb up the best-seller lists. . . .

But then something very inconvenient occurred. A slim volume—with its title clearly an ironic crib from Mr. White's—suddenly made its appearance on those same shelves on which *The Making of the President 1968* had previously been standing in isolated majestic splendour. . . . In the very first week in which it was published, *The Selling of the President* showed *The Making of the President* a clean pair of heels in the popularity stakes—and it has never looked back since. . . .

Mr. McGinniss's book is primarily about the television and advertising men who worked on the Nixon presidential campaign—and anyone looking at them at the time who thought (as I did) that they were stern, unbending fellows had clearly got it wrong. In private, it turns out, they sang like canaries. . . .

What plainly most offended Mr. McGinniss was that even Mr. Nixon's closest television advisers accepted the future President as a hollow man—as someone whom they had to fill up with some synthetic stuffing if they were ever to get him elected. Thus far I find it easy enough to agree with him—indeed, if one message comes loud and clear through every page it is of the total, absolute cynicism of the media men of Madison Avenue. At times you almost feel sorry for Richard Nixon. There he is, as it were, at the centre of the stage trying to do his laborious best while these Iago-type figures will insist on whispering across the footlights just how bad he really is. . . .

We can all probably agree that that kind of thing is not very attractive—but how much of an insidious danger really is it? It seems to me that it is here that Mr. McGinniss is in some difficulty, and not least for personal reasons. If the television manipulators and the advertising technicians he is warning us against were as sinisterly professional as all that, then how did it come about that they were so naïve as to admit to all their secrets so obviously a bad security risk? . . . To say the least, the much cracked-up, high-powered Nixon staff does not seem in this case to have been anything like as vigilant as it might have been. (p. 329)

And were the Nixon media men anyway all that successful in marketing their own product? The main danger about Mr. McGinniss's wonderfully entertaining book is perhaps the cumulative impression it contrives to leave that somehow a lot of modern miracle men came along and succeeded in getting a total dolt elected President of the United States. . . . [It] strikes me as a fundamental misreading of what happened.

In the first place, those who packaged Richard Nixon for American television came dangerously near to blowing the whole thing. . . . But secondly (and much more important) was the real Richard Nixon—the original human article carefully disguised inside the expensive package—in himself so unsaleable anyway? Everything that has happened since his election strongly suggests that penny-plain he would have been just right for the mood of the country if only he had been put on the market just as he was. All that was wrong with him as a candidate was that the Madison Avenue boys prevented the American people from getting a real look at him.

And it is over this perhaps that Mr. McGinniss has performed his most ironic service. I am pretty sure that the various human details scattered throughout this book—not least those concerning Mr. Nixon's evident distaste for all the media men who surrounded him—will in the end prove to have done him more good than any of Mr. White's purple prose. (pp. 329-30)

Anthony Howard, "Nixon & the Madison Avenue Boys," in New Statesman, *Vol. 79, No. 2034, March 6, 1970, pp. 329-30.*

JOE FLAHERTY

[In *The Dream Team,* Joe McGinniss] has chosen the world of the racetrack as his motif. When the muses are calling the parade to post, he sprints along at a pretty snappy pace. When he deals with the problems of a successful writer whose career and marriage are collapsing, the going gets as sloppy as a rainy Wednesday at Aqueduct.

The book opens with a prologue concerning two young men who are planning a tour of Southern tracks. The narrator-hero (later to become the best-selling author) goes back in time and convincingly documents his love for the ponies. . . . So far, so good. The reader gets a hint he might be in for one of those hardboiled treats James M. Cain used to serve up. . . .

The story now shifts abruptly to a Saturday in San Francisco. The writer is there on tour—plugging his best seller with his bankroll soaring but his soul descending. He forms a three-person parlay with an aspiring female journalist named Jennifer and a talk-show host, Barnaby Blaine. Barnaby's real avocation is touting horses, with enough paraphernalia to make the Rand Corporation envious. (p. 34)

Jennifer is one of those dismally platitudinous love-children who seem to be serving as beacons for disgruntled older men in literature these days. (pp. 34-5)

The book starts moving again after the trio head for Hialeah. McGinniss builds a surrogate father-son relationship between Blaine and the writer, with the counterpoint of the gambler as a computer and the compulsive romantic.

Blaine is by far the best and most haunted character in the book, and one is jealous of the space denied him and devoted to the insipid Jennifer. . . .

When McGinniss writes about horses or describes tracks, races and jockeys' techniques, he is right on the money. But, sadly, you realize he doesn't really give a damn about Jennifer and the writer's woes; because, if he did, there couldn't be such disparity in the prose style. The other stuff has been added like fruit to a drink at the Fontainebleau, for sheer decoration. It serves the same purpose—to dilute the kick.

In the end, Blaine's betting system fails, and he returns to San Francisco. Jennifer floats off to spread her pollen among the more deserving, and the writer breaks even for the meet and returns to his shadowy wife. It seems as if Samuel Beckett is the chart caller for the human race: nobody really moves. And a novel that could have gone the distance winds up distressingly, in a series of disconnected but impressive sprints. (p. 35)

> Joe Flaherty, "A Betting System that Failed," in The New York Times Book Review, *April 30, 1972,* pp. 34-5.

CHRISTOPHER LEHMANN-HAUPT

The message of Joe McGinniss's first novel, **"The Dream Team,"** is to stay away from fast women and slow horses, but the message isn't what matters here. What matters here is how Mr. McGinniss succeeds in holding our interest through a six-day binge in Miami while old Barnaby tries to handicap the horses at Hialeah, while young Jennifer tries to clutch life to her breast and while the young narrator of their adventures tries to enjoy the fruits of both activities.

The young narrator of **"The Dream Team"** is an author on tour promoting his best-selling book, while his wife and children languish back home in the East. Though his story is a fantasy, we might as well think of him as Joe promoting his first book, **"The Selling of the President."** In San Francisco, near the end of his tour, Joe meets up with Barnaby and Jennifer. . . .

On the spur of an evening of heavy drinking, the three suddenly decide to fly to Miami to take the weather, test Barnaby's system at Hialeah, touch each other, and taste a little bliss. The Dream Team of Mr. McGinniss's title may appear to be "a collection of the smartest, prettiest girl reporters in the country" that Jennifer has ambitions to join, but we know who it really is, as it wings its way into the Florida sun.

But as it wings it way into the Florida sun, Joe gets airsick. When it arrives in Miami, the rain begins to fall. . . . Bit by bit, the pressure mounts, tempers turn edgy, the money trickles away, and the dream turns into alcohol and torn-up pari-mutuel tickets.

What it finally all comes down to is Joie de Vivre in the Flamingo Stakes, with an erratic apprentice-jockey up. Should Joe plunge to recoup his losses, or should he fold his tens and silently steal away? I won't reveal how Mr. McGinniss ends his horse race and his yarn, but it is a bittersweet conclusion to a compelling few hours of reading. And it all goes to show that a little corn isn't necessarily a bad thing.

> Christopher Lehmann-Haupt, "Picking Brains and Race Horses," in The New York Times, *May 9, 1972, p. 39.*

JOHN SPURLING

I enjoyed **The Dream Team** so much that I didn't care whether it was naturalistic or not. Although it's a first novel, its author, Joe McGinniss, is already well-known for his **The Selling of the President** and he has disarmingly made the novel's hero/narrator a best-selling author. . . . Joe McGinniss tells his story nimbly—the matter is light and he keeps the tone light—but it is above all, perhaps, an excuse to communicate his enthusiasm for horse-racing and as such, in the end, almost more of a rhapsody than a farce. Certainly the most memorable scene is that in which the radio interviewer covers the floor of his hotel room with charts of racing form and goes to work with slide-rule and note-books, making allowance even for the weather. His comic obsession, the result of which in the story is only to make the narrator lose still more money, is also the motive force of the novel.

> John Spurling, "Against Nature," in New Statesman, *Vol. 85, No. 2202, June 1, 1973, p. 817.**

ROBERT SHERRILL

[In **Heroes**] Joe McGinniss says he's going to write about heroes and winds up writing mostly about himself and his problems. It's as though you were promised a full account of the kidnapping of Helen and the ensuing wars between Greece and Troy, but instead got only an entertaining account of a crap game inside the Trojan horse.

To be sure, McGinniss does go through the half-hearted ritual of seeking out some headliners—people like John Glenn and George McGovern and William Buckley and Daniel Berrigan—to see if he can find the yeast of heroism. He fails, not only because he has prejudged their failure in a very silly fashion ("The truth was, we did not have heroes anymore because *there were no heroic acts left to be performed*") but also because the kind of hero he was looking for had to measure up to some sort of buttery formula that I certainly don't understand and I doubt that McGinnis does—that is, his concept of a hero was one who "provided a transcendental link between the contingencies of the finite and the imagined realm of the supernatural,'' or who ''unites the course of history and the stream of dreams.'' In defense of McGinniss, let me hasten to add that those are not his quotes; he borrows them.

In making his rounds McGinniss does occasionally—when he stops trying to be a philosopher—reveal his genius for re-creating scenes. (p. F1)

His glance at Buckley is a perfect biographical haiku, and his memories of his seedy palsy-walsy outing with the Vietnam War's most decorated soldier have that marvelous touch that Jimmy Breslin has given to so many similar encounters.

But mostly you get strange autobiography.

Six years ago McGinniss blessed this land with his book *The Selling of the President, 1968*. He became famous and at least temporarily rich. If he did not exactly become a hero to others, he apparently became something of a hero to himself.

Then McGinniss learned just how thin six years can stretch the fame derived from one event, when the interim has been filled mostly with sloth. But he couldn't let go of it; six times in this book—and it is a very small book—he reminds us, as no doubt he was constantly reminding himself, of that faded glory. He has become like a middle-aged member of the Boosters Club who keeps talking about the time he ran 95 yards for a touchdown as a sophomore.

The salvation of McGinniss is: he knows his problem. Or he seems to. There is this scene with Eugene McCarthy at Toots Shor's at which nothing happened—very little happens in this book, which is part of McGinniss's moral—except the craving inside McGinniss's brain to get inside McCarthy's:

> What I wanted to say to him was: ''Look. Once you were at the center of things. Everything revolved around you.... Now it's gone. The moment has passed. It won't be back.'' I wanted to say also that once I had been at the center of things.... Now, I wanted to ask Eugene McCarthy, *What happens next? Where is the center of things? Why didn't we stay there? Will we ever be there again?* (His emphasis.)

What McGinniss needs is for somebody to give him a swift kick, with instructions to quit whining and get back to using his considerable talents as they ought to be used. If he had got around to asking McCarthy such dopey questions, he probably would have got a verbal kick to that effect....

No longer a hero to himself, McGinniss has become a sulky character in his own soap opera. Unfortunately, the kind of ego that most people lay aside in their early twenties has prompted him to transfer his staleness to the world at large. (p. F4)

Robert Sherrill, "Good Men Are Hard to Find," in Book World—The Washington Post, *April 18, 1976, pp. F1, F4.*

EDWARD HOAGLAND

[''Heroes''] is an interesting book which gets better as it goes along and gradually absorbs one once again into a familiar, very current form; the author's search for himself in the guise of fulfilling a much more merchantable assignment. In this case, Joe McGinniss was sent out with a lucrative contract to look for ''the vanishing American hero.'' Even to begin with, for many reasons which he enumerates, he was pessimistic

about finding such a beastie. Apparently he thinks there will never be any heroes again.... But the lucrative part was important to him because his first book, **"The Selling of the President, 1968,"** had made him at 26 the youngest author ever to stand number one on the nonfiction bestseller list—''not counting Anne Frank.'' However, it had gradually dawned on him over the next few years not only that he would never be a great writer but that he would never write so well or successfully again.

On the evidence here, I would say the assumption was premature, but as he traveled about the country, seeking out famous people—a rather unimaginative list, on the whole—he wasn't interviewing them at all. Certainly he wasn't really asking them why there aren't public heroes any more, why they themselves aren't heroes. He was crying out to them boyishly, ''Say it ain't so about me!'' and ''What shall I do with myself!'' A lot of the book is written in extremely short sentences, as by a sick man. Not sick as though heading toward an early demise but sick as in a fainting spell.... The genre is appealing enough, the book brief, and McGinniss makes fun of himself and has the good sense to quote Joseph Campbell on the subject of heroes....

The putative heroes for McGinniss are, of course, from somewhere around that same era when he was Number One, and he keeps asking them, ''Hey, remember me? Include me in!'' Meanwhile he's keeping his wife and children on a string as to whether he'll come home to them or continue to live with his girlfriend.

Nevertheless, the best writing in the book is about his daughter Suzie when she gets sick, and his own father's failures and death. He's good on General William Westmoreland and military reportage too. He's fair and respectful with the various figures who are hard on him, such as a colonel who witnesses his cowardice on the battlefield in Vietnam, and Daniel Berrigan up in Winnipeg, but is generally cruel to those like George McGovern who are nice friendly gentle guys....

McGinniss reaches no conclusions about himself, no catharsis of any kind, and one has the unusual feeling at the end of the book that he'd prefer that we all write in and tell him what our opinion is. Will he wind up like Neil Armstrong—first man to walk on the moon—in Cincinnati teaching school?...

He's a crisp, professional writer, recovering from a dizzying early success, who can dot his book with pretty vignettes, such as at test pilot school shooting a jet through roll after roll in the sky, ''like riding on the feathers of an arrow.'' He has been dogged by a reputation for betraying confidences because of his portraits of McGovern (in a New York Times Magazine article) and Nixon (in his **"The Selling of the President, 1968"**), and he petulantly expresses surprise that Ted Kennedy steered clear of him. I would have, too. But much good writing verges upon betrayal. The point finally turns on whether the betrayal was done in the service of trying to get at the whole truth—whether the decency in the person who feels betrayed has been put in, as well as the sensational lapses. McGinniss has tended to specialize in the confidences and lapses, but I suspect that as another decade goes by and the hunger in him which he chronicles and even tries to purge here has had more chance to cool, he will end up a balanced writer.

Edward Hoagland, "William Buckley Snubbed Him, Styron Lost Some Crabmeat," in The New York Times Book Review, *April 18, 1976, p. 8.*

CHIP BROWN

McGinniss went north in November 1977 to see what sort of people were drawn to Alaska's extreme cold and isolated life where the land was "unchanged by the presence of man" and to explore the effects wrought by the boom economy. He suspected "the irresistible forces of big business, modern technology, and greed" were engulfing the wilderness, the ancient ways of the Alaska natives and the sense of limitlessness and possibility that lie at the heart of the frontier spirit. His purpose, as he set out, was to record "the last days of the last frontier."

To this grandiose assignment, McGinniss brought his formidable reportorial talents and his gliding, seductive writing style. Unfortunately [*Going to Extremes*] . . . is little more than a travelogue of impressions, interviews and vignettes with some of the pleasures of the genre but many of its limitations. Having never been to Alaska before, McGinniss knocked around the state for nearly two years as an unabashed "cheechako"—the slightly disparaging Alaskan term for unseasoned newcomer. On occasion he turns the pose of impressionable ingenue to his favor with flashes of humor. . . .

His astute eye and ear for dialogue serve him well—most impressively in a chapter about a native woman named Olive Cook who is caught between the culture of her village in western Alaska and her new urban life in Anchorage and later in Washington D.C. . . . Olive Cook curses the traditional religious ceremony in the village at Christmastime because it interferes with Christmas from Disneyland on the tube. "You can't even watch real Christmas on TV!" she cries, and in that line, McGinness has captured all of the confusion, ambivalence and despair that haunt Alaska natives trying to live two lives at once.

Absorbing as some of the chapters are, McGinniss fails to tie them together with anything other than the thread of his travels and thus leaves *Going to Extremes* without much narrative momentum. The author also seems reluctant to sum up, to examine and to develop some of the themes latent in his material. Perhaps he was constrained by his pose as a cheerful cheechako.

Whatever, *Going to Extremes* will probably suffer in the shadow of [John McPhee's] *Coming into the Country*. Where McGinniss glanced off a dozen towns, McPhee rooted into one and discerned the power of the land that makes it unthinkable to many Alaskans to live anywhere else.

Yet there is a hint in the last and most sustained chapter—about a wilderness journey into the Brooks Range—that McGinness has come to sense the spell of Alaska. He moves beyond his journalism of snapshots, postcards and grab-bag impressions, impelled to convey the "mystical" feeling that overtook his party in a mountain basin where no person had ever been. (pp. 5, 9)

> Chip Brown, "The Call of the Wild," in Book World—
> The Washington Post, *September 14, 1980, pp. 5, 9.*

PAUL THEROUX

Mr. McGinniss was urged by friends, his curiosity and an issue of The National Geographic to spend a year in Alaska. He was told it was a "raw and wild and stimulating land. . . . It would . . . change, in some way, anyone who ventured there." But [in **"Going to Extremes"**] he reports more rawness than stimulation. After reading this book I feel a sledge of wild huskies couldn't drag me there. **"Going to Extremes"** is a serviceable

title, but "Exit, Pursued by a Bear" would have described the book exactly. The bear was a grizzly sow with three cubs, and had Mr. McGinniss contemplating the topmost branches of a tree.

Mr. McGinniss does not moralize or travel with a theme in mind. Like John McPhee whose route was similar in his Alaska book, "Coming Into the Country," he takes the rough with the smooth. But he lacks Mr. McPhee's intensity and metaphysics, and he has little of Mr. McPhee's high style. Mr. McGinniss's version of a travel book is a plotless chronicle of comings and goings, picaresque reportage: he is Studs Terkel on snowshoes. What another person might find frightful, he considers judiciously, and then moves on. He sees some grounds for hope in a group of hippy-revisionists-turned-disco-jockeys playing Grateful Dead records to the unpeopled tundra. And yet it seems to me that it will take more than the Grateful Dead to soothe the savage Alaskan breast that Mr. McGinniss lays bare in his account of a year trudging around the state. (pp. 1, 34)

"Alaskans" may be a misnomer. One of Mr. McGinniss's problems is in trying and failing to differentiate among the peoples he meets. "A native girl carrying a baby boarded the train," he writes: this is hardly a revealing sentence. In other places he refers to Indians and Eskimos, but it is impossible to tell one from another. I am not asking for clear racial distinctions, but only for a bit of cultural paraphernalia that might help me understand why they go to extremes. Apart from them are the "whites." This might be Alaskan terminology that Mr. McGinniss is adopting, but again it is unhelpful, and there might be blacks there who will take exception to it. This, in a sense, is a dilemma all Americans share: don't make distinctions. We always assume that differentiation means contempt. It has resulted in a lack of subtlety and a rather gimcrack prose style.

Mr. McGinness often writes clearly and well, but just as often he fills a paragraph with sentence fragments. . . . This is obviously not carelessness, but design, but it makes for some rather scruffy prose.

Perhaps that style suits his subjects, the monosyllabic airline pilots and backwoodsmen and the industrial developments, every one of which seems like a blot on the landscape. But it does not serve his intelligence, because for the most part Mr. McGinniss is unflappable and thorough; he takes risks, is patient with the crustiest mountebank, and is about as intrepid as anyone could wish. . . .

But Mr. McGinniss went to extremes, and after an excess of urban Alaskan blight he and some others trekked toward Cockedhat mountain in the Brooks Range in the north-central part of the state. This last section of the book is pretty and unpeopled. . . . (p. 34)

"Go, and look behind the ranges," Kipling wrote in his poem "The Explorer." Mr. McGinniss heeds the advice and gives a graceful ending to a book that is otherwise largely his observation of misdirected energy and of a society that seems to be disintegrating before it has had a chance to form. Mr. McGinniss did not set out to judge or explain, but only to find out what Alaska is. He has succeeded, for nearly everything he says is news. (p. 35)

> Paul Theroux, in a review of "Going to Extremes,"
> in The New York Times Book Review, *September*
> *14, 1980, pp. 1, 34-5.*

MARK KRAMER

Going to Extremes is fine reading. It is thick with whole people, exotic landscapes, the nervous and constant curiosity of an adventurer who knows that the essence of place is more likely found while chatting in barrooms than while viewing the wondrous works of man and nature. (pp. 290-91)

McGinnis has a sharp eye for the rough and beery self-servers, the opportunistic but misfit wanderers who have swelled Alaska's population since the discovery of oil. The vignettes that fill the first sixteen chapters form an exquisite *cinéma vérité* whose unmoderated but soon patent message tells of the destruction of nature and culture by exploitative invaders.

There's not a sentence of preaching in the book. Again and again, with an elegant journalistic jujitsu, McGinnis has his people do themselves in, announce their own poignance, crassness, lostness and, now and then, nobility. . . . [His vignettes are] strongest when dealing with bar friends, less boldly drawn when describing company officials, rural entrepreneurs, former academics who have made new lives in snowbound cabins along Arctic Circle traplines.

Only one thing is missing from McGinnis's journey, and that is McGinnis. There's hardly a glimpse of the man who met all those interesting people and went to all those alien and exciting places. He never talks about himself. With two interesting exceptions, he never hints at why he's chosen his subject, why he's footloose, how he reacts to the sequences he relates, the people he meets. He is conspicuously absent.

Such near invisibility must have been a useful posture for him to assume in the field, when discovering how things really are. It even suits exposition of some complex and orderable subjects whose telling aspects don't require the author to discuss how he banished ignorance and learned what's what.

But this is a travel book. It is a wanderer's chronicle—a lovely and well-worn genre, and a difficult one. And one of its well-settled conventions seems to require the author's tasteful self-revelation, his offering of personal evidence (if the trip is to be thought worthwhile) that travel has indeed broadened him.

Which leads to the two moments of self-revelation. The first is a confession of pain felt atop a high mountain glacier onto which he has flown in a ski-plane. It's a triumphant backpacker's pain, pain evoked by "the inability to look in all directions at once." This is a striking passage, surprising because our unknown host tells what he feels, not what he sees—he is "consumed by immensity and splendor beyond anything I had ever imagined." He does so with a seemingly unconscious sweetness, for it is not done with particular artfulness, just an atypical blurt of astonishment.

The second moment occurs after days of hard hiking. . . . [He has climbed] through an almost intestinal canal of rock into a mile-long grassy meadow, tranquil in the midst of arctic desolation. McGinniss experiences a mystical fullness before "this astonishing display which had seemed to give each of us a deep and sudden private flash of insight into the process of the creation of the earth." . . . [The] experience is invoked, rather than described. He leaves one convinced of the preciousness of pristine wilderness, but frustrated with the host's elusiveness. (pp. 291-92)

Mark Kramer, "Elegant Jujitsu," in The Nation, Vol. 231, No. 9, September 27, 1980, pp. 290-92.

ELIOT FREMONT-SMITH

One trouble with Joe McGinniss's true-crime anatomy, *Fatal Vision* . . . , is that it's 663 pages long. If the prose is a little wooden and the insights less than electric, that's like forever. This isn't the Rosenberg case. The book's great length testifies to the author's earnestness, as well as (perhaps) to commercial savvy; but it's insensitive to the enjoyment of true-crime.

Another trouble is that the central mystery of the book, the engine of suspense, is resolved early on—indeed, for reviewers, before the book even begins, in the publicity rap. The suspense is not whether Jeffrey MacDonald, back in 1970, actually bludgeoned, knifed, and ice-picked his pregnant wife and two little daughters ages five and two to death, but whether McGinniss *thinks* he did. There's a suggestion that McGinniss had doubts at first. But now he's convinced. As was a jury in 1979. Which leaves us with the details. One scrabbles around for them (at least I do), feeling kind of crass. I mean—and I'm aware that it doesn't matter that I know—where *exactly* did the ice pick go in? Stuff like that. . . .

Fatal Vision has blood and gore; the crime scene at Fort Bragg is gone over several times. It also has explanation and endless saga. . . .

The whiffs of tensions arise from the fact that all the while McGinness worked on the book . . . , MacDonald thought McGinniss was out to vindicate him. That's why all the tapes and cooperation; they even lived together briefly before the trial. This sounds more interesting than it is. Of course, for himself, for *us*, McGinniss had to write what he came to believe. But we know what that is from the outset. So what's left are an imagined consternation on MacDonald's behalf when he sees the book in prison, and some vague ethical questions about expectations and obligations that McGinniss only acknowledges. Maybe that's enough. MacDonald is extraordinarily self-deluding; yet exploitation can cut several ways.

It's irony that's supposed to be the backbone of *Fatal Vision,* which isn't the Jean Harris case but isn't exactly low-life, either. MacDonald was handsome, bright, charming, organized, athletic, gung-ho, an all-American winner. . . .

But there's this cloud: he's under indictment for three murders.

Well, you could cut this mustard with a trash barrel. McGinniss wants to be and seem responsible, so he cuts it very slowly, as if the outcome, the truth, weren't immediately apparent. There's wisdom in this, even generosity. True-crime is a bit like sports; you know what happened and still wish to savor it in print the next day. But 663 pages' worth? . . .

I don't like this book, and in the end don't quite know why. It's not a "new" *In Cold Blood* or *The Executioner's Song* . . . ; McGinniss doesn't write like Capote or have the spunk of Mailer. But that's not the problem, or maybe is only part of it. After snobbery (class, rhetoric, lifestyle, etc.), after acknowledgment of McGinniss's *work* (four years on this thing), after realizing that McGinniss may not have anything *importantly* new to say about the culture or our "values" (a tall order, in any case), after absolving him for perhaps overstating his original belief in MacDonald's innocence—after all this and more, all I know is I feel cheap. In both senses: inside myself, and had.

It's as if we were in the thrall of some whirligig that spins around and every so often shoots out a fix of blood and gore. The ice-pick mayhem is what I really want, and the rest should be there, but if not transcendent, short. I don't really *care* about Jeffrey MacDonald—and while it's easy to say that's McGinniss's fault, I'm not entirely sure. I think we're all in a deal together, readers and writers and subjects, and . . . it ain't exactly holy. Maybe that's the meaning of the title, *Fatal Vision*. Otherwise, I haven't a noncommercial clue.

Eliot Fremont-Smith, "The Diet Doc Blues," in The Village Voice, *Vol. XXVIII, No. 38, September 20, 1983, p. 45.*

JOAN BARTHEL

"If we can prove that he did it," the Federal prosecutor told the jury at Dr. MacDonald's murder trial, "then we don't need to prove that he's the kind of guy who *could* have done it." Both these questions are probed in Mr. McGinniss's "**Fatal Vision,**" along with an obvious third question: If he did it, in God's name, why? It's a long, compelling story, with a cast approaching thousands. . . . (p. 12)

Dr. MacDonald's personality emerges in chapters of taped reminiscence inserted throughout the chronological narrative. At first, this device seems cumbersome. The time fluctuations become confusing, and Dr. MacDonald's sexual preoccupations constitute merely a pathetic and basically boring case of arrested adolescence. But as the story moves forward, the first-person counterpoint begins to sound much more significant, and eventually it adds to the book's impact. Other major figures are memorably sketched, especially the couple's parents. (pp. 12, 32)

But even a long story needn't have made such a long book. Some of the reporting is repetitive. The grand jury hearing spans almost 200 pages of verbatim statements. . . .

Mr. McGinniss's compulsion to be comprehensive is understandable. He's re-creating a sensational, controversial case with legal, moral and societal implications. . . . So it's not surprising that he would step with scrupulous precision through the maze of facts, opinions, deceptions, contradictions and inconsistencies.

Indeed, Mr. McGinnis himself, without being intrusive, becomes a genuinely sympathetic character in the book, especially after he admits candidly that he took it on after four years of negotiations between Dr. MacDonald and Joseph Wambaugh had broken down. He confronts recurring questions of guilt and innocence and the ambivalence of love. . . . If his personal epilogue seems a trace overwritten, he's entitled. He has researched and told a complicated story very effectively. And while Dr. MacDonald was back in California on appeal, he made Mr. McGinniss the custodian of the murdered children's baby albums, complete with locks of hair and a baby tooth.

These things happen when reporters become involved in people's lives and deaths, when a writing project evolves into a kind of selective, if unforeseen and not entirely voluntary, human bondage. It is this involvement, finally, that makes "**Fatal Vision**"—even beyond the fascination of the story it tells and even at this length—well worth reading. (p. 32)

Joan Barthel, "The Jeffrey MacDonald Murder Case," in The New York Times Book Review, *September 25, 1983, pp. 12, 32.*

JOSEPHINE HENDIN

Even murder should have dignity. How can we justify the passage of brutality from the police blotter or tabloid to the permanence of a book, except as a necessary step toward restoring meaning and individuality to the victims or the killers? Murder books such as Meyer Levin's *Compulsion*, Truman Capote's *In Cold Blood*, or Norman Mailer's *The Executioner's Song* have looked for meaning even in the unprovoked or random murder of strangers, furthering our awareness of murder as a crisis of morality, psyche, and culture. *Fatal Vision* by Joe McGinniss is different. It takes a crime of intimacy rich in meaning and refuses it significance, coherence, or explanation. (p. 35)

Issues of meaning, or morality, or motive recede when death seems less significant for itself than for the interest it arouses in others. . . . [*Fatal Vision*] renders seven hundred pages' worth of facts and viewpoints as adding up to nothing. It appeals so completely to the desire for pictures without captions that it is virtually a celebration of inexplicability. (pp. 35-6)

The gap between what MacDonald seemed to be and what he did is not a distance McGinniss cares to negotiate. He alternates "The Voice of Jeffrey MacDonald," composed of tapes of MacDonald giving his view of his life, with evidentiary material drawn from the investigations, hearings, and trial, and with interviews of family members, particularly MacDonald's in-laws who began as his supporters and became his accusers. Each person is presented as the star of his own story; no one's words are questioned or challenged. MacDonald and his amazing murders remain irreconcilable, incoherent. Yet it is clear he and his act exist in an elaborate relation of paradox: the slayer of children who is an expert on child abuse, the creator of bloody crisis who expertly redeems others from bloody trauma. These are selves existing in a tight, explicit relationship whose terms, if not conventionally rational, are not inexplicable either. The tragedy invites each reader's explanation. (p. 37)

Belief in inexplicable guilt, like belief in inexplicable innocence, ignores the exploration and judgment in which human understanding takes place. As the prosecutor bypassed such issues by obtaining conviction on physical evidence alone, believing that if he could prove MacDonald killed, he did not have to prove he was the sort of man who could kill, so McGinniss hopes, less successfully, to find a physical cause for the murders. Diet pills, he suggests, might have triggered an uncontrollable rage in MacDonald. Yet he also reveals this possibility is not supported by lab tests taken the night of the murder, which show no traces of drugs or alcohol in MacDonald's bloodstream. . . .

Inexplicability is an intellectual and emotional alternative to dealing with complexity. Eroding connections between self and act, sliding over the nature of an intimacy that culminated in a triple murder, it releases McGinniss from the frustration of having to challenge anyone. Neither MacDonald nor [MacDonald's wife] Colette exist for him as people, only as unfathomable curios. Released from human meanings and connections that sustain individuality and dignity, they seem to exist only on the level of chance, of circumstance. In such a place, de Sade's hope finds a harrowing fulfillment: "Murder only deprives the victim of his first life; a means must be found of depriving him of his second. . . ." (p. 39)

Josephine Hendin, "All-American Atrocity," in The New Republic, *Vol. 189, No. 17, October 24, 1983, pp. 35-37, 39.*

ANN JONES

Joe McGinniss, who had set out to chronicle a case of unjust prosecution [in *Fatal Vision*], changed his mind.

But he didn't tell MacDonald. How in the world could he? McGinniss had lived with MacDonald during his murder trial, and later, during one of MacDonald's preliminary stints behind bars, McGinniss lived in MacDonald's Southern California condo, drank his beer, watched his sunsets and went through his papers. He changed his mind—and went on writing. Consequently, we have here a kind of double story: the story of a killer being inched toward conviction by former supporters who have changed their minds and the story of a writer torn between conflicting moral obligations. . . . McGinniss scarcely mentions his dilemma—what moral allegiance *is* owed to a triple murderer, anyway?—yet it has affected the way he put this book together.

McGinniss keeps himself in the wings and gives center stage much of the time to the voice of Jeffrey MacDonald, letting readers develop their own distaste for him. (p. 472)

McGinniss is a terrific investigator, who obviously went to great trouble to gather this material, but even the reader who is fascinated by the psychiatric evaluation of Jeffrey MacDonald is likely to nod off when the fourth or fifth expert takes the stand to say essentially the same thing the other experts said in page after page of verbatim grand jury testimony.

McGinniss presents so much of the official record, I suspect, so that the reader, compelled as McGinniss was to slog through it, will come out as he did, persuaded from faith in MacDonald's innocence to belief in the certainty of his guilt. This is the device of an uneasy writer who assuages the guilt of his own apostasy by putting his readers through the same conversion, and for the most part it works. But dogged readers, worn down by many a tiring page and by a gnawing sense that the writer should have done a little more of his share of the work, will be filled with relief and gratitude when McGinniss finally shows up in the last seventy pages of the book, speaking in his own sensible voice, describing his own defection, telling at last what to make of all this. Among other things, he speculates on the narcissistic personality, enumerates some of MacDonald's lies and documents his heavy amphetamine use (to lose weight) just before the killings. I would willingly have taken his word for more than this, but McGinniss, oddly enough, seems to have underestimated his own authority as a writer. He has produced a long, surprisingly dull book with some memorable sections, a compilation of impressive but sometimes wearisome material that might have been completely gripping if only he had not been so timid about speaking his mind. (pp. 473-74)

Ann Jones, ''An All-American Killer,'' in The Nation, *Vol. 237, No. 15, November 12, 1983, pp. 471-74.*

Brian Moore

1921-

Irish-born Canadian novelist, short story writer, nonfiction writer, and scriptwriter.

Moore is a respected novelist who uses traditional structure and an unadorned, straightforward prose style. His work is usually praised for its intriguing plots; careful characterization, especially of women; and skillful evocation of place, including Belfast, where he was born, and Canada and the United States, where he has lived. Moore often draws upon his Roman Catholic background to examine themes of spiritual, psychological, and social conflict. His protagonists are generally alienated people who are luckless, displaced, or consumed by their own needs or the needs of others.

In Moore's first novel, *The Lonely Passion of Judith Hearne* (1955), the aged title character assesses her life with bitterness, finding solace in alcohol and her imagination. This novel brought Moore immediate acclaim and recognition, as critics were impressed with his subtle communication of Judith Hearne's desperation. *The Luck of Ginger Coffey* (1960), which won the Governor General's Award, relates the futile efforts of an Irish emigre in Canada to achieve success for himself and financial security for his family.

Moore's later fiction often contains supernatural events and reveals his growing interest in religious and metaphysical issues. *Catholics* (1972) focuses on the conflict between traditional Roman Catholic dogma and the more socially oriented contemporary Catholic church. *The Great Victorian Collection* (1975) examines the difficulty of distinguishing between appearance and reality. In *The Temptation of Eileen Hughes* (1981) a middle-aged businessman becomes infatuated with a twenty-year-old shopgirl whom he desires as an object of worship. Critics praised Moore for his insightful portrayal of obsessive love and the human need for a god-figure. *Cold Heaven* (1983) concerns a woman who sees her husband die in a boating accident. The next day his body vanishes and there are clues suggesting that he has returned to life. Moore investigates spiritual themes and guilt as the woman attempts to understand the implications of both her religious experiences and her marital infidelity.

With each new novel, Moore continues to earn praise for his absorbing narratives and credible characters. As Joyce Carol Oates notes, "His reputation as a supremely entertaining 'serious' writer is secure."

(See also *CLC*, Vols. 1, 3, 5, 7, 8, 19; *Contemporary Authors*, Vols. 1-4, rev. ed.; and *Contemporary Authors New Revision Series*, Vol. 1.)

© *Thomas Victor 1984*

VAL CLERY

Brian Moore is the most extraordinary and the most professional of Canada's writers. In 26 years he has published 12 novels of high literary quality, earning himself a Governor General's Award for fiction with his third, *The Luck of Ginger Coffey*, . . . in 1960. And yet his name is rarely included in those Canlitanies that our critics delight in droning through.

Amongst our literary establishment, it seems almost a breach of good taste to mention that Moore is a Canadian writer.

He has two strikes against him, of course. Not only is he an immigrant, but he is a Canadian *emigré*. More often than not he sets his novels in his Irish homeland or in the United States where he now lives instead of in the true North strong and free. And he has chosen to work out of effete Malibu rather than weather the rough justice of our climate and our literary politics.

There may be more subtle reasons for the disfavour he attracts here. His books have consistently made proper nonsense of the cherished theory that victims and survivors are human phenomena somehow unique to Canadian literature. And it seems to me that his outstanding skill in depicting women is distrusted, and even resented as a trespass, by some of our women writers.

The Temptation of Eileen Hughes will do little to assuage those resentments. Although most of its action takes place in contemporary London, it derives from Moore's homeland, the costive, sad enclave of Northern Ireland. The three most intimately portrayed characters are women, victims and survivors; the two male characters, observed externally, serve only as catalysts.

The Eileen Hughes of the title is an innocent, an attractive bourgeois Catholic of 19 who has never had a steady boyfriend. . . . She has been adopted socially by a well-to-do sophisticated couple [Bernard and Mona] in the small Ulster town where she lives. . . .

Eventually, during a visit to a historic mansion, Bernard blurts out to Eileen the real reason why she was invited on the trip: that he has developed a secret asexual passion for her, which he equates with the courtly love of medieval Provence. He reveals that he has already bought an elegant estate in Ireland in the hope that she will join him and Mona there in a chaste *ménage à trois*. . . .

[A] bare outline of plot can give little sense of Brian Moore's story-telling skill. He is sparse in his descriptions, but manages to weave an immense complexity of character and social background into the dialogue and the interior monologues of Eileen, her mother and Mona. Only once, when Mona is waiting outside the hospital emergency ward for Bernard to recover [after his suicide attempt], does he overload her thoughts with detail, unduly slowing the pace of an otherwise perfectly controlled story.

For all its explicit tragedy, *The Temptation of Eileen Hughes* is in the formal sense a comedy, not of manners but of moralities. The actions and reactions of its characters are overshadowed by the heretical Jansenist notion that sins of the flesh are the cardinal sins, a notion that still haunts the Irish and has long blighted their sensuality and sexuality and love.

Similar tragi-comedies are played out still in small-town Ontario and Quebec and in Atlantic Canada, because the same moral blight was carried here by Irish Catholic immigrants, was imported directly from France and was supplemented by an equivalent Protestant strain, deriving from Luther, Calvin and Knox. We Canadians will never know who we are merely by looking at ourselves in the mirror. We must look back, must know where we came from and what made us. The few writers such as Brian Moore who remind us of our origins are owed a debt and an acknowledgement of their place in Canadian writing.

> Val Clery, "Of Moral Blights and Jansenist Heresies," in Quill and Quire, *Vol. 47, No. 5, May, 1981, p. 30.*

CHRISTOPHER LEHMANN-HAUPT

We enter Brian Moore's tautly dramatic new novel ["**The Temptation of Eileen Hughes**"] . . . through the eyes of Eileen Hughes, a 20-year-old from Northern Ireland on her first visit to London. She's the sort of person who says, "It's grand, really it is," when Bernard McAuley, her employer's husband, shows her into the tiny top-floor maid's room she must stay in because the hotel has neglected to reserve her a room near the McAuleys' suite. . . .

But what is Eileen Hughes doing here with the McAuleys, a Roman Catholic couple from Eileen's home town of Lismore, who are rich where she is poor, worldly where she is innocent, bold where she is shy? . . .

[After] tantalizing us with . . . finely calibrated innuendoes, Mr. Moore reveals the game that is afoot. Bernard McAuley is insanely in love with Eileen. He's worshiped her ever since Mona first hired her to work in one of their stores. He had

meant to bring her to London only to be near her while his frustrated wife hunted up sexual partners.

But when Eileen jokingly lets it drop that she wouldn't mind living in a mansion, Bernard drops his guard and tells her his feelings and his plan. He has secretly bought a big new house in the country and he wants to install Eileen in it along with his wife. How would Eileen like to have her own suite of rooms and a new better-paying job? But far from being flattered or aroused by this proposal, Eileen is terrified and sickened.

From this point on in the story, the suspense builds over whether Eileen will continue to reject Bernard and try to get away from him, or succumb either to pity or the temptation to be discreetly bought. It is not such an easy choice, for though Eileen hasn't a weak or devious fiber in her body, she is growing to like the luxury the McAuleys have treated her to, and Bernard is so enslaved by his worship that he seems on the verge of self-destruction.

But Mr. Moore never tries to milk this suspense. Instead, in scene after elegant scene, he saws the various legs off his plot to keep its surface perfectly balanced. At the midpoint of the story is a particularly well-turned episode that neatly adumbrates the novel's larger shape. Eileen wishes at one point to walk back to the hotel alone. Bernard graciously releases her—into the London Zoo. There Eileen sees children petting lambs and remembers watching sheep being shorn. Eventually noticing that Bernard is following her, she runs from him and leads him into a figurative trap. The questions are neatly posed: Which of the two is in captivity? Who is being fleeced? Who will escape whom? . . . Is Eileen morally right in her treatment of Bernard? Is she a person of real integrity? Or is she what Bernard says she is, "just another example of a wee girl who is taught, 'This is right and that is wrong,' and who believes it without thinking, simply because some priest says it's so."?

Is Eileen's pity called for? Or is Bernard's mad idolatry impervious to the actions of its object? Is Eileen sexually problematic? (After all, even though she's only 20, she's never yet met a man who suited her.) Or is sex irrelevant? (After all, Bernard has long ago lost interest in his wife, and is far more interested in worship than possession.)

Such questions go on echoing. Which is another way of saying that this book is on fire, and goes right on burning one's memory.

> Christopher Lehmann-Haupt, in a review of "The Temptation of Eileen Hughes," in The New York Times, *July 3, 1981, p. C8.*

PETER S. PRESCOTT

More than most novelists, I think, Brian Moore enjoys playing with his readers' expectations. Aha, he seems to say, you thought I was writing about this; now don't you feel a little foolish to discover that I was really up to something else—something more innocent and yet more terrible—all along? His new novel [*The Temptation of Eileen Hughes*] seems at first to have a theme as old as novel writing itself: the seduction of an ignorant virgin by a corrupt man with the compliance of his wife. Not so. Moore's real concern here is with love considered as a potentially fatal disease. It's a theme nearly as old as the other—"Manon Lescaut" and "The Sorrows of Young Werther" spring to mind—but one to which Moore gives an interesting spin: the story is told not from the lover's point of view, but from those of the women involved. (pp. 63-4)

Matters do not turn out well; they never do in this kind of novel. Moore sets up a classic conflict—the predatory rich man accustomed to arranging other people's lives to suit himself stalking the honorable girl for whom concession means escape from a life of genteel poverty—and then devotes most of his story to Eileen's attempts to evade Bernard's attempts at pursuit. Because Bernard is genuinely demented, Moore wisely confines his perspective to those whom Bernard affects. He moves with assurance and apparent ease from third- to first-person narration, gliding in and out of both Mona's and Eileen's thoughts. Moore's prose has always been deceptively simple, never more so than here, yet it accommodates the most complex effects: the scene, for instance, in which Mona's promiscuity is revealed, is done entirely in pantomime, as seen from a distance by Eileen. Poor Eileen: in life, she wouldn't hold our interest for a moment, but such is Moore's art that we are made to care for her—and care what happens to her. (p. 64)

> Peter S. Prescott, "Irish Stew," in Newsweek, Vol. XCVIII, No. 2, July 20, 1981, pp. 63, 65.

JOYCE CAROL OATES

In his long and estimable career, Brian Moore has written a number of novels prized for their storytelling qualities and for a wonderfully graceful synthesis of the funny, the sardonic, the poignant and the near tragic; his reputation as a supremely entertaining "serious" writer is secure. In his best-remembered novels—**"The Lonely Passion of Judith Hearne"** (1956) and **"The Luck of Ginger Coffey"** (1960), my own favorite among his 14 books—he works that indefinable miracle of creating a character in such a way that it is difficult to believe we have not actually known Judith Hearne or poor luckless Ginger. . . .

These highly readable novels succeed most compellingly on an immediate level: rich with convincing detail, communicating the admixture of drollery and sorrow that characterizes "real" life, populated with individuals who speak and act and dream and breathe as if altogether innocent of the fact that they are mere fictitious characters.

By contrast, Brian Moore's **"The Great Victorian Collection"** (1975), a slender parabolic enterprise burdened with a transparent, and surely unsurprising, theme concerning "appearances" and "reality," is puzzling by its very thinness; allegorical in intention, it ended as something akin to anecdote. And now, in **"The Temptation of Eileen Hughes,"** there is another spare message-laden work that appears to address itself in allegorical fashion to an ambitious subject—mankind's need to believe in God, any God. But the new novel is so sketchy, anemic and hurried that one is led to wonder what has gone amiss. For not only is character largely unexplored here—and humor absent—but Mr. Moore tells his story in so perfunctory a manner that it is as if he is merely going through the motions of a narrative this time.

The most engaging character in **"The Temptation of Eileen Hughes"** is the besotted lover Bernard McAuley, who has deluded himself into believing that he has fallen in love with 20-year-old Eileen Hughes, a Roman Catholic who gives the impression less of being repressed than of simply having no personality. . . .

A "failed priest," Bernard succumbs to Eileen's subdued charms because she is so virginal, so innocent, so ignorant—and possessed of such conventional qualities of beauty as a skin of "statue white" and eyes of "clear light blue." Rather like a

Dostoyevskian lover-idolater writ small, Bernard confuses his passion for a religious impulse. "Love, real love, is quite different from desire. It's like the love a mystic feels for God. It's worship," he says. "When you fall in love with someone," Bernard tells Eileen, "really fall in love, it's a sort of miracle, it's almost religious. The person you love is perfect. As God is perfect."

But Eileen thinks, "If only someone her own age, some nice boy, would say to her what Bernard McAuley had been trying to say this afternoon." Her "temptation," then, would be to believe in Bernard; or in her own inflated worth; or to take advantage of the McAuleys by accepting the offer of a managerial position in one of their most prestigious stores. The problem with the novel in dramatic terms is that Eileen is never made to feel any significant temptation; she takes a firm and somewhat prim moral stance from the very first. She knows who she is, and she isn't God, and poor eloquent Bernard cannot woo her, either with his proffered love or his suicidal despair. . . .

Had the character of Bernard McAuley been more thoroughly explored, or had he been given the novel's narrative voice, **"The Temptation of Eileen Hughes"** would have been a painful and probably memorable confessional work with allegorical implications. It might have been a double allegory, referring not only to mankind's need to "believe" in God, but also to the novelist's need to "believe" in his characters. But McAuley is rarely onstage; and when he is, we experience him through the conventional eyes, and in the primer vocabularies, of either his wife or Eileen. Moreover, the tragic mystery of self-destructive, misplaced obsession that McAuley is meant to embody is ludicrously undercut by the intrusion of a genial, low-keyed American pothead named Earl, who seduces Eileen so effortlessly, and with so little evident effect, that she scarcely remembers it afterward.

Presented as a devout Roman Catholic and an "innocent," unhypocritical virgin, Eileen registers a moment of epiphany so simple-minded, and so banal, that one can only conclude that the author has lost all interest in her. . . .

In a more realistic novel, it would mean something that Mr. and Mrs. McAuley are the only Catholics on their block in an exclusive residential neighborhood in Lismore; it would mean something that three Northern Irish Catholics fly to London for a week's holiday. But **"The Temptation of Eileen Hughes"** is as skeletal as a television or film script, in which background footage (in this case, of London) compensates for the foreground anemia. And the doomed Bernard, who might have engaged our deepest sympathy, passes by like an insubstantial image on a screen—committing suicide in one brief bland paragraph, being buried in the next. It would be a pity if a reader new to Brian Moore were to begin reading him with this modest undertaking rather than with one of his earlier, more finished, and far more humanly moving novels, which occupy a special place in our literature.

> Joyce Carol Oates, "A Tale of Love and Idolatry," in The New York Times Book Review, August 2, 1981, p. 3.

FRANCIS KING

Brian Moore must always be a cause both of bewilderment and of envy to his fellow novelists. Whereas other modern Irish writers fizz and flash with stylistic intoxication, he has become increasingly sober. So rarely does he produce an out-of-the-way metaphor or simile that, when he does so, it has an unusually powerful impact. . . .

But, mysteriously, beneath this surface flatness, strange creatures thresh, slither and collide with each other. Many sentences may seem bare, some may even seem banal; but the cumulative impression left by a sequence of them is one of complexity and originality. It is as difficult for another novelist to say precisely how Mr. Moore brings this off as for another dramatist to say precisely how Terence Rattigan accomplished the same kind of feat in a series of plays in which memorable characters come to life out of lines through which no blood seems to pulse.

In *The Temptation of Eileen Hughes,* a married couple and a young girl arrive at an expensive Belgravia hotel from Northern Ireland. The girl, Eileen, imagines that she has been brought along as the friend of the young wife, Mona; but it is in fact the husband, Bernard, who has insisted on having her with them. . . .

His love of Eileen is similar in its passionate asexuality to [his] previous love of God; and in confessing it to her and so approaching too near to her, he fears that, as in the case of his faith in God, he may have destroyed what is of most value to him in the whole world. 'Never seek to tell thy love. . . .' Mr. Moore makes one see this physically unattractive man in his expensive English clothes; and he also makes one both shrink from him, as from some bird of prey, and feel sorry for him in his bondage to an obsession. He must have Eileen solely for himself; and to achieve that objective, he is prepared to make any deal with her or his wife.

Mr. Moore has always shown uncanny empathy in his depiction of women. It is therefore no surprise that Bernard's attractive, corrupt wife, daughter of a failed dentist, should be so convincing. . . .

But the most remarkable creation of all—since simplicity, decency and innocence are things always difficult to make interesting and not insipid—is the girl, Eileen. Her life with her widowed, ailing mother has been narrow and unadventurous. She has met few boys and those that she has met have immediately tried to grope their way to clumsy sex. She is dazzled by the luxury hotel, the hired limousine and the costly meals in restaurants; and inevitably, she contrasts the freedom and splendour of London with Belfast.

At first Eileen sees herself, as we see her, in the role of victim; but, as the book progresses, both she and we come to realise that the reverse is, in fact, the case. She has the couple in thrall and can do with them what she wishes. Her 'temptation' in the title is not merely the obvious one of selling herself to the man who is prepared to pay all that he possesses for her; it is also the temptation to make use of the powers of life-and-death, God-like, she now wields. Whether she succumbs to one or other or both of these temptations, it would ruin the reader's pleasure to reveal.

Particularly subtle is the way in which Mr. Moore enables us to see London through the eyes of this unsophisticated girl; we, too, might be seeing it for the first time, as she walks past Buckingham Palace, explores that desolate waste-land of squalid hotels south of Victoria Station, or ventures into a restaurant of a kind previously unknown to her. But the tyranny of the loved one over the lover—wonderfully exemplified when Eileen runs away from Bernard in Regent's Park and then watches

him, in hiding, as he desperately tries to find her—is the strongest and most fascinating element in a strong and fascinating book.

Francis King, "Victimised," in The Spectator, *Vol. 247, No. 7996, October 10, 1981, p. 25.*

MICHAEL TAYLOR

Brian Moore writes an unfashionably pellucid prose so bare of intensifying metaphor that a simple sentence like "The rain wept in front of her" leaps from the page as though it were a bizarre metaphysical conceit. Ironically enough, I read *The Temptation of Eileen Hughes* in tandem with Anthony Burgess' *Earthly Powers,* a supremely grandiose account of the terrible temptations—both terrestrial and spiritual—battering fallen man, in which a sentence like "The rain wept in front of her" would only be a drop in the deluge of metaphorical expression engulfing each page. Yet one doesn't really need the experience of reading clotted Burgess to be aware of the thin gruel of Moore; nor is it simply a question on my part of indulging a predilection for the knotty over the spare to say how much less there is of Moore in this particular instance than of Burgess. I say "in this particular instance" for, had I been reading an earlier, even sparer novel by Moore, *Catholics,* in tandem with *Earthly Powers,* the contrast might well have worked in Moore's favour: in *Catholics,* the beautiful simplicity of Moore's style, so precisely the right vehicle for the simple gravity of the book's conflict, might well have worked to have made even more noticeable the strain of floridness in *Earthly Powers'* excess.

There is absolutely nothing florid about *The Temptation of Eileen Hughes.* But built like *Catholics,* it gravitates in theme towards *The Doctor's Wife* and *The Mangan Inheritance,* the two most recent books by Moore before this one: in all three, Moore's unfashionably pellucid prose encompasses a perennially fashionable theme—the enticement of forbidden pleasures—though in *The Temptation* the book oscillates between the pleasures of *Catholics* and those of *The Doctor's Wife,* between the enticements of the spiritual and those of the erotic life. The more interesting temptation is the spiritual one. Despite the book's title, the temptation of Eileen Hughes does not establish itself as the driving temptation of the plot except ambiguously (she is the temptation), not only because it is commonplace and she herself something of a simpleton, but also because there is never any danger of her succumbing to it. Eileen in fact is invincible in her romantic ordinariness, determined to resist the strange advances of her employer with all the cruelty of uncomprehending youth, stiffened by an unimaginative upbringing in a small town in Northern Ireland. Set in London in the dog-days of August, where her Irish employer and his wife take her on holiday, the book charts the inevitable defeat of Eileen's employer, Bernard McAuley, in his attempt to be permitted to worship at the shrine of whatever he finds mystical in Eileen Hughes' make-up. The supremely innocent, supremely cruel, young Irish girl resists all the blandishments of power and material wealth laid out satanically for her, but falls—when she's really tempted and high on marijuana—with hardly any struggle to the hyper-ordinary, cliché-ridden endearments of a conventional girl's conventional notion of the romantic American: "he was like an actor in a cowboy film. He was tall and slim with long, dark hair and a long, curling mustache."

The more interesting temptation of course involves Eileen's employer. Indeed, his is the book's dominant characterization:

he is a mysterious and elusive figure whose wife, Mona, after four years of marriage, still finds baffling and frightening—as she frequently tells us, she never knows what goes on inside his head. The only way we get to know what goes on in Bernard's head better than she does is in his pursuit of Eileen and in his explanations to her of why he wishes to shift all his powers of adoration from his wife to his wife's demure employee. (pp. 100-01)

Bernard cannot resist the temptation of telling his saint all that he feels for her—this is the temptation of Eileen Hughes, and as soon as Bernard falls for it, he is a doomed man. As for Eileen herself, she spends most of the time bemused by the grotesque unexpectedness of this side of her employer's personality. And despite a somewhat unconvincing awakening to the reality—and possibilities—of her position after her final visit with Mona, she remains true to her own virtuous lights until the end, though she does not, we notice, attend Bernard's funeral. . . .

I can't help but feel that Brian Moore means more in this book than meets the eye. Most of the time the potential for either an interesting psychological or cultural complexity is thwarted by our being restricted by and large to seeing events through the naive eyes of Eileen Hughes—she is the narrating consciousness for 150 pages out of a 200 page book. The simplicity of the book's style reflects the simple-mindedness of its eponymous heroine—a far cry from the enabling simplicities of *Catholics*. And yet—and yet—the fact that all the principals are embattled Catholics, the occasional reference to the saracen tanks rumbling through the Northern Irish streets, the mad obsession of Bernard itself, the implacable intransigence of Eileen, the desperate promiscuity of Mona, all suggest fugitively another more disturbing meaning behind the disturbingly simple-minded surface of *The Temptation of Eileen Hughes*. Perhaps the real temptation of the book is to turn it into something it simply isn't: to try to transform it into something closer to *Catholics* when really it is what it seems, a spiritualized version of its banal secular counterpart *The Doctor's Wife*. (p. 102)

Michael Taylor, in a review of "The Temptation of Eileen Hughes," in The Fiddlehead, *No. 132, April, 1982, pp. 100-02.*

DAVID MacFARLANE

[In *Cold Heaven,* Brian Moore] quickly has his readers on the edge of their seats. A young doctor, Alex Davenport, and his wife, Marie, spend a brief holiday in Nice, France. While he is swimming in the Bay of Angels, a powerboat tears over him as his wife watches in horror from a paddle boat. She had intended to announce to Alex that day that she was going to leave him for another man; instead, the day ends with the announcement that a skull fracture and a severe concussion have killed the brilliant but selfish pathologist. The next day, however, the straightforward tragedy takes a bizarre turn that will keep reading lights ablaze until dawn. Marie, arriving at the hospital to make the necessary arrangements, is informed that her husband's body has disappeared from the morgue. The bewildered doctors have no explanation. Returning to her hotel room, she discovers that her husband's wallet, his passport, his traveller's cheques and airline ticket have also disappeared. Her belongings have not been touched.

Once the initial mystery has been established, everything that follows becomes a source of suspicion and fear. There are hints

that Alex's research has something to do with his unlikely disappearance. Marie suspects that she is being punished by a wrathful God for her infidelity, and—predictably enough for those familiar with Moore's obsession with Catholicism—it is around that suspicion that the mystery of *Cold Heaven* is constructed. The guilt and intrigue of adultery are blown into nightmarish proportions. No event remains innocent. Even a seemingly innocuous visit to a convent gift shop becomes part of Marie's struggle against her fate. . . .

In *Cold Heaven* Moore's taut and uncluttered style harbors within it a sense of imminent danger that is almost cinematic in its effect. Indeed, his detailed, steady pacing is frequently reminiscent of Alfred Hitchcock. . . .

Brian Moore's strength is his ability to make tangible the unbelievable and the miraculous. His consistently fine prose and the precision of his narrative create a reality in which characters and readers alike are forced to believe the improbable. Moore inhabits a world which is partly that of a religious visionary and partly that of a thriller writer. *Cold Heaven* is a remarkable success because the word "mystery" applies to both.

David MacFarlane, "A Miraculous Mystery," in Maclean's Magazine, *Vol. 96, No. 36, September 5, 1983, p. 49.*

ALAN RYAN

Moore's interests, even in his comic mood, have always tended toward the dark side of human events—terrible temptations, for example, that force a character's will to the edge of a cliff. In earlier novels, he has dealt directly with the surreal and the supernatural—in *The Great Victorian Collection,* a young man awakens in a California motel to find that he has dreamed into existence a huge assortment of Victorian *objets d'art,* and in *Fergus,* the Irish-born writer of the title must confront a motley gang of ghosts from his past—but in most of Brian Moore's writing, one is always aware of larger, and darker, worlds lurking just out of view.

In *Cold Heaven,* the world of the supernatural arrives in a burst of brilliant light that dazzles—and awes and frightens—the reader as well as the characters. (p. 3)

Cold Heaven is that most desirable sort of novel, one that keeps your hands taut on the book and your breath held tight in your chest. At the same time, the entertainment is of a very high order, filled with ideas given powerful dramatic form. Moore's intense exploration of Marie Davenport's dilemma (one of faith and conscience as well as survival and sanity), crystallizes the plight of an ordinary, modern person—a sinner, as it were—faced with extraordinary events, specifically, a miracle. If you or I were suddenly, and unwillingly, vouchsafed a glimpse of the Blessed Virgin ourselves, we would no doubt feel the same way she does.

Brian Moore is, as he has always been, a masterly writer, and *Cold Heaven* is word-perfect. The style is so transparent, so casually brilliant, that the events it narrates seem to be happening in real life, without the intrusion of paper and ink. Moore can paint a character in an easy stroke or two, and it is his believable characters, as well as his stunning subject matter and fascinating ideas, that give this book such tremendous suspense. And it is genuine suspense, the kind that grows out of real concern for the people involved, and out of a need to know *what happens,* because what happens will be hugely important. (p. 5)

Alan Ryan, "A Miracle on the Beach at Carmel," in Book World—The Washington Post, *September 11, 1983, pp. 3, 5.*

FRANCES TALIAFERRO

Brian Moore established his reputation with his first novel, **"The Lonely Passion of Judith Hearne,"** in 1956. The Irish setting gave a special poignancy to this portrait of a sad middle-class spinster resolutely slipping into emotional destitution. Subsequent novels have revealed the author's continuing willingness to pay attention to the dreary and unloved, the lapsed and fallible who would rather have some immediate human affection than wait for God's promised kingdom. . . .

["**Cold Heaven**"] begins in Nice, with a quick and violent boating accident in the Baie des Anges. While Dr. Alex Davenport is swimming, a motor boat crashes into him and leaves him close to death. His wife, Marie, is distraught over the accident and its ironic timing: She had been planning to tell him that day that she intended to leave him for another physician. . . . (p. 11)

Gradually it becomes clear to the reader that Marie has imagined a complex quid pro quo in which Alex's survival depends on her cooperation with "them," and that the paranoid "they" refers to her enemy—God.

Marie is a lapsed Roman Catholic who sees herself as an "unbelieving adulteress." Why, then, did a vision of the Virgin Mary appear to her a year ago on a rocky headland at Carmel, instructing her that the rock must be a place of pilgrimage and that she must tell the priests about it? . . . To what end do "they" continue to send the signs and portents that lead Marie to enact her part?

These questions, which ultimately prove tiresome, are never completely answered. . . . Having a vision seems to teach Marie nothing except that it feels good when it's all over and God leaves you alone. The vision has some practical consequences—a shrine will be built on the rocky headland and the nearby Sisters of Mary Immaculate will be saved from financial ruin—but this benign resolution simply isn't enough to justify all the tedious comings and goings of the plot. "**Cold Heaven**" is irritatingly dominated by logistics: so many trips by taxi, bus and plane, so many hotel and motel and rental-car reservations, so much mileage driven and flown and so many messages left with answering services. They crowd out all but the most rudimentary character development, so that the sympathy one needs to feel for Marie never gets much beyond indifference.

Brian Moore's intentions for this novel are unclear. It begins with promising urgency and looks as if it will turn into a psychological thriller, but the initial suspense declines into anticlimax. To readers who are already disposed to believe in miracles, the Carmel sections may be gratifying, but the unconverted will find neither a satisfying exploration of the psychology of visions nor a fully realized portrait of the sinner who becomes God's unwilling agent. "**Cold Heaven**" is a chilly disappointment, a cheerless novel whose flat characters cannot sustain the weight of its factitiousness. (pp. 11, 38)

Frances Taliaferro, "A Spiritual Quid Pro Quo," in The New York Times Book Review, *September 18, 1983, pp. 11, 38.*

MARK ABLEY

"We have before us the modern mind, intelligent, skeptical, ironical, splendidly trained for the great game of pretending that the world it comprehends in sterilized sobriety is the only and ultimate reality there is—yet a mind living in sin with the soul of Abraham." The German critic Erich Heller wrote those words with reference to Kafka, whose fiction shows both the necessity and the impossibility of religious faith, but they could also be applied to Brian Moore. In *Cold Heaven,* as in *Catholics,* as in *The Mangan Inheritance,* he takes seriously ideas and intuitions that we skeptical, ironical moderns are supposed to have passed beyond. He uses his intelligence to subvert our limited awareness of intelligence. (p. 15)

Moore is unafraid to use the devices and modes of a thriller in a novel intended as "serious" art. He is, after all, a former screenplay-writer for Alfred Hitchcock.

One of the difficulties that many novelists face when arranging their plots is that of coincidence; incompetent writers (and, occasionally, Dickens) make us worry that their strange collection of events could never just have *happened* to occur that way. Brian Moore defies coincidence by denying coincidence; in the world of *Cold Heaven,* nothing is accidental. A bolt of lightning, a repeated dream, the lyrics of an old song, a fat man exercising his poodles near the sea—everything carries a secret meaning. The hand of God, or His agents, or destiny is everywhere. Or at least: it is everywhere in the mind of the central character, who may or may not be deluded. For a novelist—though not for his more thoughtful characters—if God is alive, everything is permitted. The danger is that when a writer chooses to shun probability, leaving his characters at the mercy of an interfering fate, his people may turn into puppets, jerked to and fro on transcendent strings.

Moore gets around this by some clever use of theology. "God doesn't reveal Himself to us in an unmistakable way," a worldly monsignor tells Marie. . . . In the last few pages she accepts that she has free will. Whether she chooses to stay with Alex or to leave him for Daniel is entirely up to her. In the same way, every reader of *Cold Heaven* is free to dismiss the book as the windy nonsense of an expatriate Irishman nostalgic for the certainties of his old faith. Yet for anyone who takes the novel as more than a *jeu d'esprit,* its vision of the supernatural is terrifying: a brutal energy that mocks our pretensions and transcends our ideas of good and evil. Alex's resurrection is little more than a sign from heaven to Marie. The Yeatsian title is apt and well-earned.

Behind the speedy plot and the material wealth of many of its characters, *Cold Heaven* displays a sad and terrible sense of rootlessness, of homelessness. In this, as well as its interest in extramarital affairs, the novel is characteristic of Moore. . . . Perhaps, like many other writers, Moore is a monk *manqué.* Echoing T. S. Eliot, he calls New York an "unreal city." He would never call a convent or a monastery unreal.

Before everything else, however, he is a wonderful story-teller. His books are never dreary and rarely untidy; their excitement is poised, almost serene. Anyone who intends to write a novel for the first or second time could do no better than to examine the style and structure of his fiction, along with that of Graham Greene—from whom Moore has learned, or taken, a good deal. The two priests in *Cold Heaven* are American versions of types that Greene has made famous. At several points this novel recalls one of Greene's most intriguing works, *The End of the Affair,* which also deals with miracles, Catholicism, adultery, death, and a refusal to believe.... The coldness of Moore's heaven is balanced by the warmth he still finds possible on earth. In short, he dares to hope.

Nonetheless, the novel subverts our expectations even at the end. In spiritual terms, enough is resolved; in everyday terms, *Cold Heaven* builds toward a climax that never occurs, a scene Moore chose not to write. This can't be offered as a criticism except by those who are so totally out of sympathy with his preoccupations, or simply with his refusal to dismiss religion as absurd, that the whole book will seem an outlandish failure. The main criticisms I would make are that in the second half of the book the narrative is somewhat breathless, as if Moore were losing patience with the mechanics of his plot, and also that his language occasionally lets him down. (pp. 15-16)

Brian Moore does play a great game of pretending; even if he asks us to believe as many as six impossible things before breakfast, he knows that eyes of sterilized sobriety see nothing. Nothing at all. (p. 16)

Mark Abley, "Beyond Belief," in Books in Canada, *Vol. 12, No. 9, November, 1983, pp. 15-16.*

KERRY McSWEENEY

The dust-jacket of *Cold Heaven* . . . claims that it shows [Moore] "at the very height of his powers." The sad truth is quite otherwise. In Moore's last four novels there has been a falling off in quality, freshness and bite so marked as to suggest that the sixty-two year old novelist is now past his peak. *The Mangan Inheritance* (1979) did have its strong points, including a striking evocation of place. But *The Doctor's Wife* (1976) and *The Temptation of Eileen Hughes* (1981) were slick romantic melodramas centring on adulterous passion, containing a spurious religious overlay, and littered with the tourist-eye detail of hotels, restaurants and airports. So is *Cold Heaven*. It is true that the religious element in the novel is more pronounced and involves apparitional effects that recall *Fergus* (1970) and *The Great Victorian Collection* (1975), two of Moore's most impressive fictions. But the more one ponders the comparison the more the thinness, even factitiousness, of *Cold Heaven* becomes apparent. (p. 32)

What more than anything else makes *Cold Heaven* so disappointing is that Moore has little imaginative or fictive interest in Marie's apparition. Her sketchy characterization includes not a shred of evidence to suggest why she might have experienced this vision. Perhaps it is simply because God moves in mysterious ways. Certainly the evidence in the text leads to this otherworldly conclusion, for when Marie revisits the scene of her vision in the company of two nuns, the Virgin Immaculate appears to all three of them. The trouble is—as Jean-Paul Sartre remarked in another connection—God is not a good novelist. Neither is Brian Moore in *Cold Heaven*.

In introducing supernatural events into prose fiction, the good novelist—Emily Brontë, Hawthorne or Henry James, for example—will allow the reader to suspect that the events may have a naturalistic explanation (scientific, psychological or epistemological). This uncertainty tends to intensify the reader's interest and deepen his engagement with the text. In *Cold Heaven,* on the other hand, there is no reason not to believe that the Virgin Immaculate actually did appear. Since there is no doubt, there is no interest. At the end of the novel, Marie has become the reader's surrogate as she walks away from the site of her vision, pleased that her supernatural matters have

been taken out of her hands by priests and nuns, and anxious to return "to ordinary life, to its burdens, its consequences."

How is one to account for the falling off in the quality of Moore's fiction? I regret to say that commercial success is one possibility. Another is that Moore has allowed his greatest strength as a novelist to atrophy: his widely praised ability to write movingly about ordinary people—to be the loser's advocate, in Mordecai Richler's phrase. This was certainly the principal reason for the distinction of *Judith Hearne* (1955), Moore's first and still his best-known novel. But it is hardly a full explanation, for the central characters of some of his strongest novels—Brendan Tierney in *An Answer from Limbo* (1962) and the title characters of *I Am Mary Dunne* (1970) and *Fergus*—can hardly be described as ordinary. Another explanation is that in his finest novels memory and a sense of the past are quintessentially important—both because Moore's own past experience informs his creations and because the pressure of the past is the determining influence on the present lives of the central characters. Proust says in *Contre Saint-Beuve* that "there comes a time in life when talent, like memory, fails, and the muscle of the mind which brings inward memories before one like memories of the outer world, loses its power." Without this power Brian Moore can still offer professionally packaged fictional entertainment. But he used to offer much much more. (pp. 32-3)

Kerry McSweeney, "California Dreaming," in The Canadian Forum, *Vol. LXIII, No. 733, November, 1983, pp. 32-3.*

RICHARD DEVESON

Brian Moore's *Cold Heaven* proves that a novel can be magnificent even while its central idea remains incredible....

The book is magnificent in a technical sense: the writing (as always with Moore) is beautifully clear; the handling of suspense is masterly; motifs of blue sky and mist, lightning and thunder, serve succinctly both as thriller-like cues and as central poetic symbols. There is lightish relief—such as the worldly Monsignor ('God's golfer') who signs off with his 'Have a nice day'—but this is still vital to the plot. And the pattern of ideas is tight-knit and ambitious without being overbearing: religion and common sense; miracle and medical science; God's commands and free will; marriage and adultery.

The novel remains incredible, to this reader, because Moore— or at least his text—does seem to endorse the supernatural version of the events within it; no room for a non-supernatural version is really left. But even those who are resistant to, or just plain sceptical about apparitions and miracles will find it utterly engrossing reading.

Richard Deveson, "Death-Traps," in New Statesman, *Vol. 106, No. 2749, November 25, 1983, p. 28.**

MICHAEL PAUL GALLAGHER

It is nearly thirty years since Brian Moore's first novel, *The Lonely Passion of Judith Hearne,* proved that here was a significantly new voice in Irish fiction. Of that book Moore has told us that he wanted to explore his own religious unbelief but, preferring to project it away from autobiography, he did so through the question: what if one of my mother's sodality friends were to lose the faith? [In *Cold Heaven*] he is still supremely at home with a feminine consciousness at the centre and he is still weaving dramas of crisis on the flux of belief and unbelief. But this time the temptation has altered in direction: we are now given a totally secular woman being disturbed by evidences of the supernatural. (pp. 131-32)

Ever since the apparitions of *Fergus,* Moore has allowed himself a certain obsession with the ghostly. *The Great Victorian Collection* concerned a "secular miracle", but here he pushes into the further region of a religious miracle. His central question would seem to be whether a miracle can force a person into faith. The official answer is given by Father Niles, the somewhat snoopy journalist who specialises in such matters: miracles are "only signs which solicit belief", never a sign which "*compels* assent". The psychological drama of the novel would seem to validate this distinction, and indeed to rely upon it. Marie undergoes considerable soliciting but ultimately, like many a previous Moore central character, comes to a moment of choice. She asserts her "right not to believe"; and indeed she decides to refuse to *admit* that she has seen and heard an apparition of the Virgin. (p. 132)

If this agnostic victory had been explored by Brian Moore in the fifties, it might have had the satiric edge and anger of *The Feast of Lupercal.* Now the stage is large enough to allow some very sympathetic embodiments of official religion. Although Father Niles is a banal busy-body, and although young Sister Anna is naive, at least two other religious personages can be said to be figures of wisdom in this narrative. Monsignor Cassidy is an honest man, who ultimately respects the freedom of Marie to deny what he knows she has seen: he will leave her out of his official report on the miracle. Quite new in Moore's world is the moral authority accorded to another figure, the shy and elderly mystic, Mother St. Jude.... *Cold Heaven* is about the psychological impossibility of faith even in the teeth of the evidence. In terms of Johannine theology one might say that Marie "comes and sees" but "does not enter". What she sees is an apparition (twice); what her superstition suspects is a controlling deity who is using her in a battle of belief and under threat of some harm to her husband. So far so good. My own hunch is that Brian Moore intended us to recognize another dimension in the soliciting to faith—the eyes of the saint and their impact on Marie: "her expression one of overwhelming reverence joined to a complete and enveloping love . . . a look she (Marie) had never known from any other human being." ... This attraction of holiness is mentioned but it is never faced in the course of Marie's decision to refuse; in a sense it

is easier for her to turn her back on the strangeness of a miraculous apparition, unwillingly witnessed, than to reject the miracle of love in whose presence she enters "a larger feeling, a feeling of peace". That this second potential struggle is never made explicit in her consciousness, is, to my mind, a minor disappointment in what remains a marvellously theological piece of fiction.

But *Cold Heaven* is more than a welcome addition to Moore's corpus. It is probably his best told story to date, approaching something of the thriller in its intensity and yet lightness of touch.... Indeed this novel has as much right to be hailed (in the jargon) as a hermeneutical mystery story as Umberto Eco's bestseller *The Name of the Rose.* In *Cold Heaven* we gradually come to dismiss some of Marie's reading into events as a kind of paranoia: for instance, her husband seems to her either to improve or disimprove in health, depending on whether or not she co-operates with the "orders" of the supernatural, and its representatives. (pp. 132-34)

Many novels ago Brian Moore transcended anger; here he also transcends a merely ironic ambiguity. This is a book that remains open to all the ranges of experience from beatitude to banality. If the novel has a contemplative breadth of sympathy, it has also a passion in its telling that seemed to have diminished into coolness in Moore's last four novels. They were always well-wrought as is *Cold Heaven;* but this time there is an urgency and a breakthrough into new horizons. At the end Marie is left a little sad and yet opting with sureness. She is a mixture of honesty (something of mystery has been seen and heard) and necessary dishonesty (akin to Wittgenstein's famous injunction to remain silent about what one does not know); and to this is joined a capacity to doubt the interpretations of all those "coincidences". What is beyond doubt is that she stood on a strange threshold and looked across at another world, a world where miracle beckoned both as a disruptive threat (the vision) and as a healing depth (Mother St. Jude). She finds the courage to turn from that threshold and to re-enter her "ordinary muddled life", the "known and imperfect existence". And once again Brian Moore has proved himself a master of the drama of two worlds of consciousness, two horizons that clash by night. (p. 134)

Michael Paul Gallagher, in a review of "Cold Heaven," in Irish University Review: A Journal of Irish Studies, *Vol. 14, No. 1, Spring, 1984, pp. 131-34.*

Paul Muldoon
1951-

Irish poet.

Muldoon has a highly individual voice which reflects the vulnerability of life in strife-torn Northern Ireland. Roger Conover has claimed that his poems are about "an ancient faith answering to a modern reason." Among Muldoon's eclectic subjects are the violence of the natural world, the tensions of human relationships, personal memories of childhood and adolescence, and Irish folklore and history. Equally diverse are the structures of his poems, which utilize such forms as "ballad style quatrains," modified sonnets, short lyrics, and dramatic monologues. Most critics caution that Muldoon's colloquial diction is deceptively simple; they often comment about the allusiveness of the meaning of his poems, echoing Seamus Heaney's opinion that what Muldoon has to say is "constantly in disguise."

Muldoon's collections include *New Weather* (1973), *Mules* (1977), *Why Brownlee Left* (1980), and *Quoof* (1983). Each new volume substantiates John Kerrigan's statement that a "combination of visual clarity and verbal panache . . . has become the hallmark of Paul Muldoon."

(See also *Contemporary Authors*, Vol. 113.)

Photograph by Susan Mullally. Courtesy of Wake Forest University Press

HUGO WILLIAMS

[Paul Muldoon] represents a painfully accurate rendezvous for the exacting requirements of traditional skill, youthful experiment and popular demand. But the poems [in *New Weather*], though sometimes competition winners, are rather iced with their own talent. . . . [He has] a punchy inventiveness, a dry, flourished masculinity, which, with low Irish cunning, cleverly disguises and brings up to date for city consumption their essential literariness. Muldoon's detached virtuosity sits uneasily on the shoulders of a twenty-two-year-old, distracting one's attention. But why should this be? Must poets develop backwards now to hold us? Must they unmature? . . . Muldoon's effects seem worked up, the target too aimed for. Yet there is joy in a bullseye. . . . He has an instinctive feel for things which will embody his thoughts, which is fine . . . when his thoughts are not too intent on poetry. When this happens he sees meanings on every street corner and sometimes they are only layabouts lounging there who wouldn't appreciate being in a poem at all. . . . Sometimes [he goes] on to complexify the subject too completely, as if he was rounding up sheep, and all the time his flights managing as if by magic to return home by the foot of the page. (pp. 125-26)

Muldoon is no romantic and when I read fine poems of his like *The Cure for Warts, Vespers, The Indians on Alcatraz, Kate Whiskey, Upriver Incident* or the moving anthem to Brendan Behan *Lives of the Saints,* or any of those where the focus falls on the foreground of the poem, I think perhaps it is his classical sense I am judging too harshly from a (contradiction) romantic master's desk. (p. 127)

Hugo Williams, "Sounding Like Nobody," in Poetry, Vol. 13, No. 2, June-July, 1973, pp. 123-31.*

DILLON JOHNSTON

In his first book, *New Weather* (1973), [Paul Muldoon] distinguishes himself, through his use of metaphor, from Seamus Heaney, whose disciple he is often proclaimed. In contrast to Heaney's elemental analogies, Muldoon's metaphysical metaphors fleetingly reflect correspondences that grow in one's mind into truths or tease one out of thought. Whereas he offers these correspondences ironically or non-committally, they often suggest an innocent pre-Newtonian view of an interrelated universe, an impression enforced by Muldoon's habit of structuring poems on the four elements, with water and air predominant.

"Seanchas" represents his typical use of metaphor. The seanchai is an unschooled oral historian whom the poet visits in rural Ulster. He "can adlib / No other route. If we play back the tape / He may take up where he left off." His flock flows similarly: "their bellies / Accumulate and, are anonymous again. But having shape, / Separate and memorable."

Occasionally, his metaphors are simply facile, so that one critic for *Hibernia,* not above obtuseness, entitled his review of Muldoon's book, "Enchanting Emptiness." Indeed, Muldoon's poems are comprised, in his own phrase, "of carefully appointed mirrors." Sometimes . . . he angles the mirrors by lapsing from parallel structure (**"Thinking of the Goldfish"**)

315

or by creating ambiguous references (**"Vespers"**) or by obscuring the surface being reflected, as in **"Leaving An Island."** . . . [The success of **"Leaving An Island"**] depends less on the metaphors in the second and last stanzas than on a radiant tone which seems to me characteristic of a peculiarly Irish sensuality. In Synge's lyric lines or Clarke's *aisling* poems or James Simmons' love songs, vivid colors and pellucid atmosphere imply a reprieve from asceticism, an impression made explicit by Heaney's "In Gallarus Oratory" where, coming from the sepulchral darkness of the church, the ancient parishioners found "the sea a censer, and the grass a flame." In Muldoon's poem something of Miranda's wonder invades the tone of the instructed youth.

Muldoon is not involved in the descents and excavations that preoccupy Heaney, Montague, Mahon, and Kinsella. In most of his poems he is a tourist or vagrant, moving in, or out, enquiring or taking note. Like Kinsella, Ryan, and Montague, he writes of America with fresh vision. (pp. 15-17)

> *Dillon Johnston, " 'The Enabling Ritual': Irish Poetry in the 'Seventies," in* Shenandoah, *Vol. XXV, No. 4, Summer, 1974, pp. 3-24.**

ROGER CONOVER

Two years after publication, Paul Muldoon's *New Weather* remains the most important first book by an Irish poet since Seamus Heaney's *Death of a Naturalist* appeared in 1966. With this single volume of 36 poems, Muldoon clearly distinguished himself as a major presence in Ireland—not only among the select half-dozen poets in their 20's whose work has managed to outlive its traditionally terminal form of entry (the chapbook series), but also among the Dolmen "professionals," whose reputations were secure even before Muldoon began his apprenticeship. Muldoon, now 24, is still one of the youngest on the scene. But the authority of his first book rules such things as birthdates out of consideration. These poems are the result of continuous age and aging.

New Weather is a sui generic work, even as its title suggests. Muldoon's work is derivative only to the extent that all good poetry is derivative: it is informed by the tradition. His skill is not in imitating others, but in repeating his own sure aims with such astounding accuracy and from such a variety of positions that we gradually recognize a cluster of simple truths in an area that we had always supposed to be the blindspot of our vision. The correspondences that are most striking in Muldoon's work are those which exist between his own poems. His poems are too individual to characterize very effectively in terms of anyone else's work, although on a line-for-line basis any number of parallels might be drawn. The one comparison which has received the most attention deserves notice here, if only to distinguish superficial from profound resemblances, and to detach Muldoon's work from the forced adoption which seems to have been issued upon it from the start. It is a bad critical habit which *assigns* a young poet to a literary parent, but it is a habit whose subscribers have made it a wild rumour in the case of Muldoon.

I am referring to the widespread notion that Paul Muldoon is the other (or younger or next) Seamus Heaney. Unfortunately, the similar *circumstances* of their lives and poems have been mistaken for the very different *conditions* of their lives and poems. It's a neat mistake: Heaney and Muldoon are both from the North, and both received early attention from Faber's prestigious anthologies. In *Introduction 2,* Muldoon dedicated one

poem (**"Unborn"**) among an impressive suite of 14 to Heaney. And there is no doubt that Heaney's work figured significantly in Muldoon's early development as a poet. By the time his first book was published, however, Muldoon had reworked those early poems into a haunting, strenuous music, very much in his own idiom. Except for a shared topography and a common interest in texture, the Heaney-Glob tones had been played out. But when *New Weather* was released, only months after Heaney's third volume, *Wintering Out,* it was inevitable that the Heaney resonances should be re-emphasized.

Taken together, the two Faber books made a nice review package, and reviewers were inclined to indulge in a bit of their own poetry: a landscape which had already been located, peopled and named by Heaney's three volumes was now mythologized and ritualized by Muldoon. Muldoon seemed to be reconstructing the ancient code from which Heaney intuited his secret intelligence from the earth's rhythms. Muldoon was the presiding hierophant over Heaney's dark mysteries. Indeed, the poems themselves seemed to support this collaborative vision. Both poets sensed the presence of deeper rhythms in commonplace routines; both were interested in sources and origins, in the bog past and the pagan past. To both, the earth was damp, female, and mothering, and to both it was a scarred, wounded, plundered treasure of recurring forms. Both shaped poems around the act of birth (and stillbirth), and both favored the uterine state of life.

That brouhaha was two years ago. What it finally came down to was that people who liked Heaney liked Muldoon, mostly for the stony vocabulary of life-behind-the-hedges. But today, Muldoon's best readers may be those who have grown weary of Heaney's textures, but who continue to find in Muldoon the articulation of a deeper structure of which the texture is only the outer skin. Heaney suggests such a structure, but keeps it mysterious. It is Muldoon who comes closest to sounding it out, with his precocious, if not preconscious, instincts. But these instincts are constantly being put to the test of his profound good sense. And that is precisely what his poems are often about—an ancient faith answering to a modern reason.

Taken together, Muldoon's poems reconstitute a strategy of language which restores meaning to reflex and routine. By repeating the accidental meanings of words as well as acts, he reminds us of their derivative content and purpose, of the forgotten sense of what gets repeated. . . . (pp. 127-29)

More often than not, Muldoon begins his poems by making a casual observation or by reporting an unambiguous fact in an utterly straightforward manner. . . . What is important about these beginnings is the sense of what is reserved, even by the ordinary. For too many poets, including the likes of Thomas Kinsella, to be ordinary is to stand in the midst of free-floating detritus. For Muldoon, the ordinary is the clear, the simple, the commonplace. By the end of his poems, Muldoon is discovering the vestige of an ancient ritual in what seemed an involuntary gesture, or he is reading profound lessons from the objects of the natural world. . . . Muldoon's is a poetry which sees *into* things, and speaks of the world in terms of its own internal designs and patterns.

Amputating beginnings and endings of poems is not the best way to discuss an inherently organic poetry, but it does suggest certain patterns which are easily overlooked if the poems are considered one at a time. Muldoon has a wonderful ability to lose himself in the internal activity of an *other's* identity, until, at the end of a poem, he resurfaces to pronounce a final ob-

servation, a secret, which informs and clarifies his own identity. Early in **"Wind and Tree,"** Muldoon writes: "Often where
the wind has gathered / The trees together and together, / One
tree will take / Another in her arms and hold." Four lines later
"They are breaking each other." Muldoon ends the poem with
a perfect statement of the knowledge that he intuits from the
tree: "Often I think I should be like / The single tree, going
nowhere, / Since my own arm could not and would not / Break
the other. Yet by my broken bones / I tell new weather."
Muldoon recognizes, articulates, and heeds the formal intelligence of the natural world without formulizing or abstracting
it. **"Vespers"** could not end with a simpler evocation of natural
form: "The frost has designs on it." (pp. 129-30)

The 36 poems in this volume, "having shape, / [are] Separate
and memorable." At the same time, they organize themselves
into a coherent and unified vision based on Muldoon's unique
conception of the poem. This vision, to the extent that it can
be paraphrased in abstract prose, might be so approximated:

> The identity of a thing is implicit in its form.
> Meaning is internally held, not externally im-
> posed. The trick is to get inside. But for the
> thing itself, the impulse is to resist penetration
> from the outside.

That's a bit formulistic, but it identifies the tension that Muldoon's poems celebrate over and over again with infinite fluidity and grace.

Essential to the vision is a core of imagery which runs throughout *New Weather,* and which stresses internal relationships and
designs. Well suited to the autotelic species of *being* represented by the hedgehog is a whole system of centripetal, concentric images and activities, many of which recall Emily Dickinson's delicious line about the spider . . . who weaves private
secrets into his web, the answers to which only "Himself
himself inform." Like the spider who builds a self-insulating
world out of his own excreta Muldoon's central images and
themes dwell on a nature that is inherently vulnerable and
instinctively protective. This describes a delicate balance which
finds its purest expression in Muldoon's *autophagous,* or self-
devouring, forms. . . . In about two-thirds of these poems,
something is consuming, excreting, chasing, or transforming
its self. (pp. 131-32)

The self trying to live on and within itself lends an atmosphere
of eerie sadness and horror to these poems. But make no mistake. These poems are not *about* horror; the horror is only
dimly perceived behind the interface which separates soft inside
from hard outside, safety from harm. This tension is embodied
in the egg (again, shades of Kinsella), a portean and protein
sac of life which must break out of its own protective skin in
order to become vulnerable, and, paradoxically, in order to
survive. A whole cluster of related imagery points back to the
seminal image of the egg. Consider, for example, "the nest /
That has been pulling itself together / In the hedge's intestine"
(**"Blowing Eggs"**), or "the nests of birds, these obvious con-
centrations of black" which are the hearts of hedges in winter
(**"Hedges in Winter"**), or "the clutch of eggs [that] hatched
out under our heat" (**"The Lost Tribe"**). In each case, the
egg or the egg-variant is protected by "a crown of thorns," a
hedge, briars, a shell, a womb, or some other shield, not unlike
the hooded, armoured exteriors of Marianne Moore's exotic
and sensitive animals. The strict syllabics of a poem like **"The
Lost Tribe"** suggest other affinities with Moore. Muldoon is

constantly dramatizing the danger of exposure, the terror of
being born. . . .

Muldoon achieves two of his best moments when he locates
the interface between a man and a woman at the edge of passion. It is here that the boundary between one's own self and
another self is most starkly confronted. In **"Vespers"** and **"The
Kissing Seat,"** only the thinnest separation exists, but penetration is still resisted despite the temptation to risk it all. . . .
(p. 132)

In the last three poems of the volume, Muldoon writes about
the North. Here again, he focuses on an interface which exists
between innocence and harm. In so doing, he suggests a mythic
North, a North which is not tied to the particular circumstances
of local history. He plunges deep into the past, **"Right across
the Great Plains,"** and re-emerges in a timeless place where
the dead "hold our / Sadness in their eyes, who wished / For
the explosion's heart, not / Pain's edge where we take shelter."
Notwithstanding the more overtly political poems written by
Thomas Kinsella and Seamus Deane, Muldoon's **"The Field
Hospital"** is the best poem on the war in the North that I know.
It is about much more than the North.

Finally, I'd like to close with a proposition. I remarked earlier
that Muldoon's conception of the poem is unique. Nevertheless, he has been influenced along the way. I've made some
offhand allusions to other poets, partly in an attempt to provide
interesting ways of talking about Muldoon in relation to poets
who predate Heaney. An investigation which would really re-
pay someone's efforts would be to consider Muldoon in relation
to Robert Frost. Yes, Robert Frost. Frost's "Spring Pools"
and Muldoon's **"The Upriver Incident"** establish a common
ground which, I suspect, exists on very deep level between the
Master and the master poet. (p. 133)

> *Roger Conover, in a review of "New Weather," in*
> Éire-Ireland, *Vol. X, No. 2, 1975, pp. 127-33.*

COLIN FALCK

In his first book *New Weather* Paul Muldoon seemed to be
controlling a native Irish airiness with a certain determination
to be modern and realistic, but he also showed a reluctance to
engage with much of the recalcitrantly unliterary stuff of modern life (so that when he mentioned 'the water that slopped /
From the system he was meant / To have lagged' one could
wonder momentarily if this was some unusually arcane bit of
allegory). In his new book *Mules* there isn't much blunt banality
either, and what we get instead is a fair number of historical
or remotely-imagined dramatic pieces together with a general
tendency to lapse into the Irishly anecdotal when other subjects
fail. Muldoon's anecdotes incline towards darkly suggestive
hints at mythic depths rather than spelled-out rationality, and
perhaps for this reason have a way rather often of misfiring or
seeming a bit of a try-on. He gives the impression by now (like
Seamus Heaney: one of the best poems here, **'Ned Skinner'**,
is a broodingly Heaneyish tale about the castration of some
pigs) of scraping the folkloric barrel, but at any rate what he
brings out of it still seems recognisably and authentically Irish.
(p. 53)

> *Colin Falck, "From the Penile Colony," in* The New
> Review, *Vol. IV, No. 42, September, 1977, pp. 51-3.**

CHRISTOPHER HOPE

[In *Mules* Paul Muldoon] is evidently aware that however far he reaches, home is where he starts from, and home rules. . . . Muldoon turns a cold eye on a land fit for anti-heroes. Here are poems of the revolutionary, the centaur, vacquero, Virgin, stripper, Bearded Woman, merman: a cavalcade of the great reduced by a quiet faith and suburban constrictions into fit subjects for poems of containment. His language is crisp and refreshingly tart, finely expressing the often difficult relations between his parish and the wider world, as well as the world to come. His poems constitute a profound attack on heroic Irishry not entirely undermined by a sneaking belief in its necessity, and enough terse, spry wit to make the most of the contradiction. . . . He looks to the world beyond while standing firmly in his backyard. It is an honest, unsensational endeavour. But I can't help wondering whether there are not signs of a worrying ambivalence, as if he would break ground without disturbing the soil, as if discretion were the better part of discretion and a keen sense of the inherent contradictions were sufficient to justify the leap into faith, rather too easily granting to himself, as he would to his **'Mules'**, 'the best of both worlds. . . .' (pp. 83-4)

Christopher Hope, "Clive of Indy," in London Magazine, n.s. Vol. 17, No. 4, October, 1977, pp. 79-86.*

ANNE STEVENSON

[Paul Muldoon has written] elegantly turned out pastorals in *Mules*. Here, every cowpat is carefully placed just where you have to notice it for authenticity's sake, yet it is never in the way of a smooth effect. In an eerily subtle study of homosexuality (or so I assume) at his school, Muldoon's snaffled, laconic casualness leads to crude action. . . . (p. 486)

If this poem—called **'How to Play Championship Tennis'**—for reasons of subject-matter and tone sounds a bit Larkinish, more often Muldoon resembles a sleeker, Irish Robert Frost. His frame of reference is earthy, sly, obliquely religious and calculated to astonish as much as it is to please. Understatement is Muldoon's main line, though he deals with equal efficiency in the unexpected. The title poem ends amazingly on a Wordsworthian note. The mule born of Sam Parsons's jackass and Muldoon's father's mare might have sprung from the earth:

> Were it not for the afterbirth
> Trailed like some fine, silk parachute,
> That we would know from what heights it fell.

The ambiguity of 'heights' is tantalising. Does Muldoon mean Heaven or raw nature? Is he mocking Wordsworth or endorsing him? Like Frost, Muldoon is a fine dramatic poet. In **'Ned Skinner'**, the relationship between the hired pig butcher and Aunt Sarah is stabbingly sketched in a few ruthless stanzas. So if one has reservations about Muldoon's poems, they are the reservations one always has about the photographically perfect. (pp. 486-87)

Anne Stevenson, "Snaffling and Curbing," in The Listener, Vol. 98, No. 2530, October 13, 1977, pp. 486-87.*

CRAIG WALLACE BARROW

[*Mules*] will frustrate those wishing Northern Irish poets to lacerate their souls on the bloody realities of Ulster, for in the collection's first poem, **"Lunch with Pancho Villa,"** Muldoon lets a "celebrated pamphleteer" berate the poet-narrator:

> 'Look, son. Just look around you.
> People are getting themselves killed
> Left, right and centre
> While you do what? Write rondeaux?
> There's more living in this country
> Than stars and horses, pigs and trees,
> Not that you'd guess it from your poems.
> Do you never listen to the news?
> You want to get down to something true,
> Something a little nearer home.'

While the poet-narrator has not much more success than Stephen Dedalus in "Aeolus" in answering the seductive call of political journalism in this poem, the answer is clearer, though still oblique, in **"The Centaurs," "The Narrow Road to the North,"** and **"Armageddon, Armageddon."** In **"The Centaurs"** not only William of Orange and Hernan Cortes are conqueror imperialists, but so is Saul of Tarsus on the road to Damascus, a man struck blind by self-righteousness. Without divine intervention in Saul's case, or wisdom, man may follow "isms" or soldiering blindly, like the Japanese soldier stumbling out of the forest 30 years after World War II in **"The Narrow Road to the North"**—"Too late / To break the sword across his knee, / To be right or wrong." The soldier's military life cauterizes the possibility of his return to the life he wants and Muldoon's title connects the soldier's experience to Ulster's. An experience even more at the core of Muldoon's response to the claims of political rhetoric is the seven sonnet-like parts of **"Armageddon, Armageddon,"** where fighting intrudes on life but the values determining the struggle are enigmatic. . . . Before one can encompass war and its causes, one must be able to determine values or the truth of experience, and to Muldoon this seems to mean allowing oneself to feel the real mystery of experience. In part this is a debunking, a stripping down of illusion, particularly in poems concerning love where, as when Oisin gets off the enchanted steed in part II of **"Armageddon, Armageddon,"** mystery is destroyed. The destruction of mystery, a theme of so many poems in *Mules*, is not an end in itself: mystery is to have a reality equal to the most stripped down cynicism. . . . The balance of "one arm as long as the other" is what the poet craves, as he examines childhood, adolescent, and adult experiences to get at least two views of the same object and some sense of its reality. As a child matures, his adult friend seems to shrink in **"Cass and Me."** After a homosexual encounter in **"How to Play Championship Tennis,"** a young boy realizes that life, like tennis, is not always played to his rules. **"Cheesecake," "Ned Skinner,"** and **"Ma"** each contain experiences that cause a child to reevaluate the adults in his life as people whose lives have functions independent of him: his mother once posed as for "cheesecake," while his aunt once had a lover of whom she is ashamed.

The truth of mystery is struggled with in two romanticized deaths in **"Keen"** and **"Vaquero,"** while the hard eyed collier in **"Big Liz,"** unconcerned about a stripper's art, sees only the diamond in her navel. Instead of the bearded woman's breast-feeding of a child being the focus of wonder in **"The Bearded Woman, by Ribera,"** it is the bearded woman's husband; instead of a merman's plowing the ocean being a source of wonder in **"The Merman,"** a poem similar to many by James Dickey, the merman wonders at a man farming and his "difficulties" with the permanent earth. Tools like logic and language may not be enough to handle experience as the narrator of **"Boon"** finds when the girl who asks him riddles loves him without his finding the answers, and when in **"Largesse"** he discovers the fallacy of "things shaped by their names." He sees in **"Paris"** that "The world's less simple for being travelled" and that the fragmentary knowledge of his parents in **"The Mixed Marriage"** is dangerous.

This attempt to see, to understand, is necessary before peace or war can be understood as Muldoon suggests in ironically bringing America's Viet Nam experience to bear on Irish peace. "In each fresh, neutral place / Where our differences might have been settled / There were men sitting down to talk of peace / Who began with the shape of the table." Of the slaughter itself, Muldoon probably agrees with Vonnegut who says, in *Slaughterhouse-Five,* that "There is nothing intelligent to say about a massacre." Muldoon well answers his pamphleteer of the first poem as to why he does not deal with troubled Ulster in his poetry. His short lyrics, suggestions of sonnets, dramatic monologues, burlesques of ballads are psychological epiphanies whose parts fuse into single awarenesses. Some of the poems testify to the youth of the poet, particularly the seductions in **"Boon," "At Martha's Deli," "The Country Club,"** and the appropriately titled **"Bang,"** where love is minimized by the wit of men's room graffiti, but frequently poems like **"Mules"** show a maturity of thoughtful language that belie Muldoon's years. (pp. 149-51)

Craig Wallace Barrow, in a review of "Mules," in Éire-Ireland, Vol. XIII, No. 2, Summer, 1978, pp. 149-51.

SEAMUS HEANEY

[The essay from which this excerpt is taken was originally broadcast over Radio Telefís Eireann in 1978.]

Paul Muldoon's first book was aptly titled *New Weather:* it introduced us to a distinctive sensibility, a supple inward music, a poetry that insisted on its proper life as words before it conceded the claims of that other life we all live before and after words. *Mules* continues and develops this hermetic direction and is a strange, rich second collection, reminding one sometimes of the sophisticated repose of *poésie pure,* and sometimes bringing one down to earth in the simple piety of the local ballad. It is as if the poems spring from some mixed imaginative marriage, as if their genesis is mule-like, and indeed one excellent entry-point into the book is a poem called **'The Mixed Marriage'.** . . . [In this poem one hears the poet's] delicate tone, half-way between cajolement and disdain, and the deft transitions, half-way between the playful and the poignant. . . . Of course, the first thing [in the poem] is the melody, the play on the octosyllabic metronome, a music that by its deliberation and technical self-assurance belies the naif wording. There is a connoisseur's savouring of the dialect and of the arcane in farcy, Caravats, billhook and loy, ferrets and faction-fights, all of which invite us to indulge a version of Ulster pastoral. But that indulgence is just disallowed by Proust and the Latin Quarter, not to mention Castor and Pollux and *Gulliver's Travels.* It is as if the imagination is fathered by the local subculture on the mothering literate culture of the schools. Muldoon's is a sceptical, playful imagination, capable of allegory and parable, in poems like **'How to Play Championship Tennis'** and **'At Martha's Deli',** in love with riddles and hints and half-disclosures in poems like **'Cheesecake', 'Boon', 'The Country Club'** and **'Duffy's Circus',** but finally at its richest

when it dwells and broods over one suggestive image—**'The Merman',** for example—until that image slowly and richly begins a series of metamorphoses and the poem is finally and simply the process of the image's life-history. . . . [A poem called **'Centaurs'**] clearly shows this process in action. It is as if the centaur notion is the larva from which the butterfly gorgeousness of the poem's movement emerges naturally. . . . I think the wrong question here is 'What's it about?', the wrong quest the quest for the poem's relationship to the world outside it. Fundamentally, the poem displays the imagination's confidence and pleasure in re-ordering the facts of place and time, of history and myth. The milkman in the milkcart heading into a backstreet under the figure of William of Orange flourishes and blooms into voluptuous conceptions of Cortez and Saul of Tarsus. If we miss the opulence of the music, the overspill of the creative joy, we miss the poem. The life of the thing is in the language's potential for generating new meanings out of itself, and it is this sense of buoyancy, this delight in the trickery and lechery that words are capable of, that is the distinguishing mark of the volume as a whole.

I think this is where reviewers of Muldoon's earlier book missed the point when, after praising the technique, they asked what he had to say. What he has to say is constantly in disguise, and what is disguised is some conviction like this: the imagination is arbitrary and contrary, it delights in its own fictions and has a right to them; or we might quote Wallace Stevens: 'Poetry creates a fictitious existence on an exquisite plane.' In Muldoon, the plane varies from sequences like **'Armageddon, Armageddon',** from a parable like **'Lunch with Pancho Villa'** to a beautiful direct meditation like **'Paris'.**

The hermetic tendency has its drawbacks, however, and leads him into puzzles rather than poems—at least, that's my response to some work here such as **'The Big House'** and the **'Ducking Stool';** and when in different poems we find girls called Faith, Grace and Mercy, and a boy called Will, our patience with the mode gets near to breaking point. But it holds, finally, and gratefully, because most of the time, we know we can trust ourselves to Muldoon's good intentions. He is one of the very best. (pp. 211-13)

Seamus Heaney, "The Mixed Marriage: Paul Muldoon," in his Preoccupations: Selected Prose, 1968-1978, *Farrar, Straus, Giroux, Inc., 1980, pp. 211-13.*

ANDREW MOTION

Why Brownlee Left is Paul Muldoon's third book, and like its predecessors is written in a style which aspires to the condition of clear glass. There are no outbursts of recherché language, and no strong rhetorical gestures. Just plain phrases and conversational cadences. The result is to make his poetry look simple—child-like, even, at times. Children themselves make a significantly large number of appearances in his work, but even when not actually present, their wide-eyed straightforwardness is recreated. In **'October 1950',** for instance:

> Whatever it is, it all comes down to this:
> My father's cock
> Between my mother's thighs.
> Might he have forgotten to wind the clock?

For all its lack of ornament—Shandyan reference notwithstanding—this child-begetting poem suggests that Muldoon's simplicity isn't quite what it seems. Typically, we look straight through his unclouded language, and are made to concentrate on oddities and difficulties in the actual situation he describes. What is 'it', exactly? And if it does 'all' come down to 'My father's cock / Between my mother's thighs', is such an opinion reductive? Can it avoid being written off by the self-irony it generates? Throughout *Why Brownlee Left* Muldoon resists complexities of diction in order to cultivate them in other such—usually narrative—terms. And since the book contains a larger number of story-poems than *New Weather* or *Mules*, it is proportionately more absorbing.

There are, though, obvious dangers in this method, and Muldoon doesn't always escape them. The most serious are caused by a kind of excessive refinement, which suffocates narrative resonances at birth. The short poem **'Ireland'** is a case in point. . . . Here what is meant to be glancingly evocative merely sounds rather coyly 'significant'. But while a number of other poems (**'Bran'**, for example, or **'The Avenue'**) suppress their potential subtleties in a similar manner, Muldoon invariably manages to prevent his reserve from becoming evasion. At his best he often writes like a miniaturised Robert Frost, and since so many of his characters are poised on the edge of action, rather than being fully involved in it, his intriguingly suggestive language is entirely appropriate. Like Brownlee's horses, his lines are constantly 'Shifting their weight from foot to / Foot, and gazing into the future'.

The book's preoccupation with imminence is most memorably treated in the final long (10 page) poem **'Immram'**.

To start with, the narrator, who is told 'Your old man was an ass-hole. / That makes an ass-hole out of you', reflects that 'My grand-father hailed from New York State. / My grand-mother was part Cree. / This must be some new strain in my pedigree', and then spends the rest of the poem searching for his father. It is, in fact, a pilgrimage—and one in which the journey is just as important as the arrival. . . . The poem's most abiding fascinations are the shifts between fact and fiction, and clear sight and hallucination. The form is skilfully maintained throughout, and so is the tone. It's as if Raymond Chandler had recast a chunk of Coleridge's notebooks—and the result is much the best poem Muldoon has written. (pp. 21-2)

Andrew Motion, *"Some New Strain,"* in New Statesman, *Vol. 100, No. 2583, September 26, 1980, pp. 21-2.**

ALAN HOLLINGHURST

Fiction nowadays can scarcely afford to be unselfconscious, and Irish fiction has often been particularly canny about its own business, the artificiality as well as the serious compulsiveness of telling stories. Paul Muldoon opened his second book *Mules* three years ago with a poem which both established and then exploded a fiction, a process by which he could ask "where do I stand?" in relation to things "made up as I went along." Behind this merely theoretical question lie issues closer to life, to do with the chosen subject of the poet, whether it is to be a lyric one drawn from tradition ("About pigs and trees, stars and horses") or a more engaged and political one, "something a little nearer home." Either way, Muldoon suggests, an essential and impartial moral truth is beyond the reach of an art which is by its very nature personal and unpredictable. . . . His new collection [*Why Brownlee Left*] develops this interest in the story to a higher stage through a series of anecdotal poems and through the 300 line **"Immram"**, a logical but none the less amazing new departure. The key to the book

is given in **"October 1950"**. . . . [Life] is indeed *ondoyant et divers,* springing from the random moment of conception and refuting any philosophical attempts to organise or direct it. The irony of experience sabotages moral patterns and mislays the answers to questions. In pursuing an expression of this time-honoured irony Muldoon has written a book less tidy and more oblique than *Mules,* and which sometimes approaches the complacency of riddle, as in the poem **"Ireland."** Peter Porter has written of the "friendly tone" of Muldoon's work, but it is not a tone which gives one the warmth or security of friendliness. Behind his colloquial manner he remains distant and cryptic, and the greater the apparent directness the more cagey the commitment seems to be, the more reticent the voice of judgment. His continuing use of half-rhymes is itself a part of his avoidance of moral formality.

Many of the poems are unexplained parts of tales, bizarre and inconclusive narrative fragments which linger tantalisingly in the mind. One searches them out for a certain knowledge which, as he says in **"History"**, one does not have. . . . The story-teller, who is also the teller of tall stories and a showman and performer, capitalises on his vulnerability by exploring his memory, but it is "Not that distance makes anything clearer": most explanations, such as precisely Why Brownlee Left, are never vouchsafed by time: the riddle of the event, like the poem, is deliberately empty.

Muldoon is still fascinated by the mulish, the crossbred, a symbolism which stems from obvious dualities within Ireland itself, and which the poems extend on to English territory—Irish loam in English gardens, Irish navvies in Camden Town; the "sly quadroon" is a further instance (a quadroon being the offspring of a mulatto and a white). The linguistic vehicle for this is the pun which (like his continuing use of symbolic names, Wetherall, Golightly) both lightens the mood and renders the description more portentous. A medium in which punning short-cuts are made between the garrulously anecdotal and the seriously allegorical is broadly Irish and specifically Joycean; and **"Immram"** plays an extravagant (Chandleresque) narrative manner on the Joycean subject of a boy's search for his father. Muldoon's poetic personality, from his first book *New Weather* on, has been a cross of the coarse-grained and the aesthetical, and he makes something at once robustly humorous and calculatedly fine from his extended exploration of a purely personal fiction. It is a *tour-de-force* which leads nowhere, and can seem to gain its technical exhilaration from a recognition of its final pointlessness: the story is a compound of bravura and bravado and is performed above an inevitable and baffling vacuity. (pp. 80-1)

Alan Hollinghurst, *"Telling Tales,"* in Encounter, *Vol. LVI, Nos. 2 & 3, February-March, 1981, pp. 80-5.**

RODNEY PYBUS

Paul Muldoon's third collection [*Why Brownlee Left*] is as humane, ingenious and formally skilful as one would expect after *New Weather* and *Mules,* and just a mite disappointing. The poems here show (and sometimes show off) his quirky, off-beat talent for sudden revelatory flights from mundane contexts. At the close of **'Whim'** the man, making love to a woman in the Botanic Gardens, gets literally stuck into her. . . . Here again are many examples of childhood recollection and the anecdotal, and the complete inability to resist a crafty pun: 'There is such splendour in the grass / I might be the picture of happiness' ('**Promises, Promises**'). I don't get from many of these new poems much sense of Muldoon extending himself beyond, rather than refining the virtues of, his earlier work, where he found very early a distinctively wry and deceptively simple-sophisticated lyric voice. Yet there are many things to be ungrudgingly grateful for in this book, like the delicate ending of '**Cuba**' where a girl is in confession. . . . The longest poem '**Immram**' is a sly parodistic piece about the narrator's search for his father, a tour-de-force of intricately-wrought ten-line stanzas which work fruitfully for and against the slangy American diction and dramatised Private Eye stance. . . . This is Mitchum with rhyme, a re-make of Chandler in the 'land of cocaine', 'Everyone getting right up everyone else's nose'. It's an immensely entertaining and colourful development from a poem like '**Lunching with Pancho Villa**' in *Mules,* self-mocking as well as mocking the America that's filtered through Hollywood and the Hammett genre. But I wonder if there's not something fashionable about this breezy persiflage—an amusing version of the contemporary writing that parades its self-consciousness about its literary status? '**Immram**' apparently draws on an old tale (Gaelic saga? romance? fantasy?), 'Immram Mael Duin', but when he writes 'I am telling this exactly as it happened' I'm reminded of modern American tales with a hero called Pilgrim (and of Will, Grace and Mercy in earlier poems by Muldoon). His 'singleminded swervings' from the quotidian into fable, fantasy or mystifying ambiguities can distract one from his care for nuances and inflections of feeling and his often revealingly extra-ordinary imagination. (pp. 76-7)

Rodney Pybus, "Matters of Ireland: Recent Irish Poetry," in Stand, *Vol. 22, No. 3 (1981), pp. 72-8.**

JOHN KERRIGAN

Muldoon's *Quoof* begins and ends . . . with an epigraph from Rasmussen's *The Netsilik Eskimos*—telling how a female shaman made herself a penis of willow, a sledge out of her genitals and a dog from shit-stained snow—and a long last poem 'loosely based', according to the blurb, 'on the Trickster cycle of the Winnebago Indians'. . . . Muldoon relishes [the] inventive unpredictability [of Amerindian myths]. His dazzling long poem, '**The more a man has the more a man wants**', jumps like a firecracker, hectically mixing the Everyday with What Might Be, and crosscutting so extravagantly from the epic to the banal that the fiction finally seems governed by its own law, or lore, and questions about the 'intrinsic interest' of its 'subject-matter' sound solemn and irrelevant. Muldoon's trickster . . . Gallogly alias Golightly starts his poem in a Belfast bedroom amid 'a froth of bra and panties', makes off in a milk van and stolen Cortina, is peppered with shot somewhere near the border, stops to masturbate, murders a UDR man, eats a Beauty of Bath, and gets taken into Armagh jail by a snatch-squad of paras—while shadowing, through the story, an Apache named Jones (who may or may not be engaged in genealogical research), and, in a particularly perplexing branch of the fable, Alice B. Toklas, loosely conflated with Alice in Wonderland, munching a magic mushroom. It's a bewildering display of narrative invention, less meretricious on each rereading, and written with that combination of visual clarity and verbal panache which has become the hallmark of Paul Muldoon. . . .

The argot of *Quoof* is foppish and odd. Even more than *Mules* (1977) and the poet's last volume *Why Brownlee left* (1980), it cultivates the strange. 'Blewits', 'jissom', 'quim', 'glanders', 'I make / do with her umlaut', 'a radar-blip / of peyote'. Muldoon once called an effect of his 'whimful', and that seems right for *Quoof* at large, with its mischievous scribbling in the margins of English. As a nonceword, indeed, 'whimful' squares with 'quoof', the private family coinage which covers here an entire collection, a strategy of writing, almost a way of life. . . . (p. 23)

John Kerrigan, "The New Narrative," in London Review of Books, *February 16, 1984, pp. 22-3.**

JOHN MOLE

The obscurity in Paul Muldoon's work is . . . evasive, and often downright teasing. He's a sophisticated high-gloss technician, managing rhyme and stanza forms with dazzling accomplishment, but the greater the verbal clarity in his poems the more puzzling they seem to become. . . . *Quoof* (the family name for a hot-water bottle), is prefaced by an account of an Eskimo shaman, and begins and ends with poems which make reference to psilocybin. This sets the tone and the scene. Throughout the book Muldoon seems intent on taking anecdote and recollection as the starting points for exercises in pushing the actual through a series of transformations, breaking them up into hallucinatory fragments.

[For Muldoon action is anything but solid], though his shapely poems give an illusion of firmness. He'll often begin with a plain statement, something vivid and recognisable (even cunningly reassuring) and go on to develop it in a manner which confidently insists on its bearings even while readers may be losing theirs. Everything stays marvellously in focus, but what is happening? . . . [Muldoon's] fantastic imagination is not so much wool-gathering as mushroom (or cactus) gathering— "**Mushroom Gathering**" being, in fact, the title of the volume's first poem. It acts upon what he can see "out there" with his eyes open, and puts the pieces together in bizarre new formations. His reader is admitted to the sometimes whimsical, sometimes scary world of an artfully controlled *trip*. Along the way there are moments of tender lyricism and accessible humour but they keep loosening into a kaleidoscopic spin that lets nothing settle. This tiny poem, "**Mink**", is in small measure typical:

> A mink escaped from a mink farm
> in South Armagh
> is led to the grave of Robert Nairac
> by the fur-lined hood of his anorak.

Authoritative, neat as an epigram, provoking as a riddle, but with just a slight suspicion that the reader is being led by the sensitive tip of his nose. (pp. 49-50)

John Mole, "The Reflecting Glass," in Encounter, *Vol. LXII, No. 3, March, 1984, pp. 46-52.**

GEOFFREY STOKES

Faber published *New Weather* in 1973, when Muldoon was barely 21 years old, and his self-assured technical virtuosity was already startling. Yet for all the wit of the opening stanzas' self-effacing apology, the poem's claims were both grandiose and to some degree contradictory. I have, he announced in "**Wind and Trees**," a consciousness that is willy-nilly universal, but at the same time a special sort of vision that lets me see—and see through—metaphors. I reject violence (though it is both fascinating and beautiful), but it has given me the gift of prophecy. These are the boasts of a highly accomplished and *very* young man; time, it seemed, would inevitably administer a salutary spanking.

It hasn't. In *Quoof*, . . . the poet is as good as his word. In part, the new weather Muldoon foretold was a function of literary history. His was the first generation of Irish poets to come of age in a post-Yeatsian era; before Muldoon was out of his teens, pamphlets and full volumes by Seamus Heaney, Derek Mahon, and Michael Longly had broken the mold, creating a delicious freedom. . . .

[The] language of *Quoof,* though hardly high-falutin, is full of small, precise surprises. In **"Cherish the Ladies,"** the poet remembers his father filling the cows' drinking trough (". . . the water scurries along the hose / till it's curled / in the bath"), and offhanded personification gives a particular freshness to the familiar sight of an angled stream of water spiraling to rest in its container.

Yet it is not in such verbal felicities, profuse as they are, that Muldoon's genius resides, but in his visionary, frankly hallucinatory ability to bundle disparate chunks of time—imaginings as well as memories—into a continuous present. **"Gathering Mushrooms,"** which opens the book, begins with a memory of his father, a commercial grower of mushrooms in a small way, preparing a mushroom shed. The memory is filtered through a 15-years fresher memory of a psilocybin trip, which is itself interrupted by a thoroughly real dynamiting of a building. It

then segues through a snatch of ballad, back to the father's harvesting "till kingdom come," and forward, via a sly reference to John Allegro's theory about the early Christians' mushroom-eating habits, to a bad moment during the trip and finally on out of time entirely, into a perhaps remembered/perhaps invented hallucinogen-tinged elegy for that now dead mushroom gatherer. These last lines enclose not only the leaping of blasted buildings skyward, but a haunting reference to the prisoners "on the blanket" at Long Kesh.

If all this in five effortless, irregular sonnets sounds a little breathless, it's meant to; Muldoon is always multilayered, kaleidoscopic. Yet at the same time he is delicate. . . . Muldoon is shifting, allusive, and sometimes downright baffling, but he is never insistent. The poems are almost infinitely suggestive, but diffidently so. There is beauty and charm enough on the surface to satisfy the casual reader, but once these poems have made their way into our minds—which they do by means of those deceptively easy and musical surfaces—they open and open and open.

There are some strategic reasons for Muldoon's tact, however. Beneath his surfaces lurk beatings, bombings, shootings—the quotidian vigilante injustice of Northern Ireland. . . .

Geoffrey Stokes, "Bloody Beautiful," in VLS, *No. 24, March, 1984, p. 15.*

Shiva Naipaul

1945-

Trinidadian novelist and nonfiction writer.

Naipaul once described his life as "defined by three poles that don't meet." A Hindu of Indian descent, he was born and raised in the West Indies island nation of Trinidad and settled in England at the age of nineteen. The central concerns of his works are the social and political conditions in Third World countries. Naipaul portrays "a world where feeling has gone dead from despair and helplessness," according to Peter Levi. Problems of individual and cultural identity are recurrent themes in Naipaul's novels. Critics note many similarities between Shiva Naipaul's thematic concerns and attitudes and those of his brother, the novelist V. S. Naipaul.

Naipaul's first two novels, *Fireflies* (1970) and *The Chip-Chip Gatherers* (1973), are family sagas set in Trinidad, and each explores a society in transition. The old order is represented in *Fireflies* by the declining Khoja dynasty, while the new is represented in *The Chip-Chip Gatherers* by the Ramsarans, a poor family trying to break into the middle class. Naipaul ironically presents the failings of both elements of society, especially in the latter novel.

After the publication of *The Chip-Chip Gatherers*, Naipaul took a ten-year break from writing fiction, during which he traveled and wrote two nonfiction books. *North of South* (1978) is a combination travelogue and political essay focusing on race relations in Kenya, Tanzania, and Zambia. *Black and White* (1980), an interpretive study of the mass suicide of members of the Reverend Jim Jones's People's Temple in Guyana in 1978, explores the social and political conditions which promoted the tragic event.

Naipaul said in an interview that he regards his fiction and nonfiction as one body of work because his nonfiction research has yielded experiences and information that he has developed in his novels. His recent novel, *A Hot Country* (1983), is evidence of this, for it is set in the fictional, politically volatile country of Cuyama, a thinly disguised version of Guyana.

(See also *Contemporary Authors*, Vols. 110, 112.)

© Jerry Bauer

AUBERON WAUGH

[*Fireflies*] is a masterpiece. It's a long book . . . and a reviewer's first inclination, when confronted with a long book, is to see what he can safely skip. It must say something for Mr Naipaul's power that despite a firm determination to skip whole pages and even whole chapters at a time, I was unable to miss a page of his absorbing, inconsequential narrative.

The story . . . centres around the disintegration of one family in Trinidad's upper-class Indian community. As subjects go, this might not seem to be one which automatically commands a wide readership. Those who approach novel-reading as a vehicle for self-improvement might be prepared to accept some (passionately) involved, committed, compassionate, etc. treatise on the problems of Trinidad's Indians, or even a biting satire on Trinidad's upper class, but a poignant, uncommitted account of what it is to be a conservative, upper-class Trini-

dadian Hindu in our present deplorable age is more than most people are prepared to take even in World Conservation Year. I can only report that the book is a delight and a miracle of enjoyment. . . .

Mr Naipaul's own attitude to the society he describes is ambivalent. He satirises its absurdities with conventional rigour but he is also keenly alive to the tragedy of its destruction, and it is this quality which makes his book so exceptional. For an English reader, and most especially, perhaps, for an English conservative, the poignancy is doubly acute because of the extreme unfamiliarity of the society he describes. Various attempts have been made to demonstrate the tragedy of the old order changing in England, and these have met with varied degrees of success. . . .

Suffice to say that anyone who misses reading Shiva Naipaul's *Fireflies* will miss an entirely delightful experience. . . .

Auberon Waugh, "The Old Order Changeth Not,"
in The Spectator, *Vol. 225, No. 7427, October 31,*
1970, p. 526.

LINDA HESS

[Shiva Naipaul] writes with the ironist's detachment, expertly and unobtrusively observing those details that mark his characters' idiosyncrasies, tracing through them the warp and woof of a social fabric that becomes increasingly frayed. . . .

The world Naipaul paints [in *Fireflies* is] . . . drab, ugly, sad. But throughout the work he allows, almost absentmindedly and despite himself, gleams of humor, beauty, and spirit to shine through. We remember these, along with the vivid realizations of the violent and grotesque.

There are occasional clichés of language and implausibilities of character in *Fireflies*. These, however, are minor flaws. What bothers me more is a quality of style that—in common with Mrs. Lutchman's personality—is stable, thorough, emotionally limited. Not that it's boring: the details of dialogue and description are consistently sharp and well selected. But for a panoramic human comedy it seems to me to lack lightness. The pall of doom and decay hangs over nearly everything. Although Mr. and Mrs. Khoja are comic figures, behind his muddling and pomposity, behind her fussiness, the heavily stupid and grimly neurotic lurk so close that we seldom can laugh freely. Mrs. Lutchman is the only character who demonstrates a sense of humor, and she very rarely. The closest the others come is a sort of bitter sarcasm.

Readers who are primarily concerned with current experiments and theories in fiction will find Naipaul obviously out of date. There is no self-consciousness about the novelist's role, no playing back and forth between art and life, no surreal divagations or electronic adumbrations. *Fireflies* is a social novel, part of a solid tradition extending from Balzac to *Buddenbrooks*. The genre has by no means lost its appeal, although it is now more peripheral than it was a century ago.

Shiva Naipaul has written an ambitious, skillful, memorable first novel. My taste leads me to hope that he will move toward a lighter touch, a more personal and exploratory style, in his next.

Linda Hess, in a review of "Fireflies," in Saturday Review, *Vol. LIV, No. 12, March 20, 1971, p. 37.*

MICHAEL THORPE

The reader of *Fireflies,* a novel as alive with a keen (and more compassionate) awareness of the pathos and absurdity of Trinidad Indian life as V. S. Naipaul's early works, may doubt the sincerity of Shiva Naipaul's disillusion with his subject matter. Yet it *is* an amorphous society he depicts, fundamentally materialistic, bogus on its spiritual side, as unpromising to the sensitive artist as the English society of Dickens' time; but it falls short of that society, in Mr Naipaul's presentation, in lacking centres of moral growth. No such centre is provided by the Hindu Khoja family which, weakly propped by tradition, is shown crumbling in an insecure atmosphere of selfishness and opportunism. The jungle laws of competition regulate everyone's actions. Everyone's, that is, except Mr Naipaul's triumphant creation, the simple and simple-minded Mrs Lutchman. . . . [She] endures in the midst of decay, salvaging what she can in the name of a stability which is its own justification. . . . To have concentrated for over 400 pages upon so barren a life without forfeiting interest and sympathy is, especially when seen against the love agonies of our customary novelistic diet, a uniquely admirable achievement. It is sustained in a Wellsian manner in Part I by scenes of bitter-sweet comedy centring upon Ram's confrontations with photography, gardening and his Morris Minor, and throughout by dramatic set pieces involving the "clan", such as the Khoja "cattha"

. . . , the elder Mrs Khoja's dying (the death of the past) and an anachronistic Hindu "Christmas." These parts of the narrative convey, without authorial comment, a strong impression of the sterility and aimlessness of the society both Naipauls have despaired of. Yet it is to be hoped that Shiva Naipaul will not desert the Mrs Lutchmans; after her lumpish son Bhaskar has sailed for England and educational enlightenment, this moving, commonplace heroine is left in a memorable last paragraph longing "for nothing", soothed only by a breeze from the sickly canefields. She will go on needing Mr Naipaul's compassionate plea. (pp. 71-2)

Michael Thorpe, "Laws of Life," in Encounter, *Vol. XXXVIII, No. 6, June, 1972, pp. 71-2.*

RONALD BRYDEN

It would be polite but ridiculous to talk about Shiva Naipaul as if he had leapt, full-armed and *sui generis,* into a literary world miraculously swept of all footprints of his famous brother V. S. . . . The relationship between the two is fraternal in much the same sense as that between Chekhov and Gorky. Like Chekhov, the elder Naipaul works from a fastidious, ironic private sensibility to humane public conclusions: because people behave badly, the world needs changing. The younger, more sweeping and less fastidious, starts where his brother ends: because the world needs changing, people behave badly. Bred within the old imperial culture, V. S. Naipaul sees its failure as one of individual wills, brains, imaginations. For his brother, born in 1945, it is the culture that blights the brains and wills. Like Gorky, he's fascinated by the perverse energies of primitive capitalism, the ferocious battling for a better life which, re-channelled, could transform society. In its raw appetite, depressing to his brother, he finds back-handed hope. For its casualties, pitiful and exasperating to the elder Naipaul in their self-delusion, he has only pity.

An image for their striving gives [*The Chip-Chip Gatherers*] its title. Chip-Chip are tiny shellfish which bed themselves just below the tide-line of Trinidad's Atlantic beaches. . . . Only in an utterly impoverished society, Naipaul implies, could they be a delicacy.

That is how the people of the novel survive. Egbert Ramsaran, founder of the Ramsaran Transport Company, maintains his ramshackle lorries by lending money at high interest to his former neighbours in the Settlement, a straggling village lost in mud and sugar-cane. They console themselves with the idea that one of themselves has escaped to the great, affluent world, and the hope that his heir, Wilbert, may marry one of their daughters. But Wilbert knows he is as much a prisoner as they. His educated cousin Julian is ruthless enough to shed family and sweetheart for a scholarship to England. But Wilbert stays trapped in the cannibal web of kinship, feeding on the tiny, marooned lives which also feed on him.

Shiva Naipaul's broader certainties make his style less fastidious than his brother's—he's fond of Dickensian rotundities and character-labelling tags—but his construction is if anything more magisterial. He marshals disclosures like a chess master: perhaps his finest is the chapter in which Julian's sweetheart, who has never allowed herself to hope while hope remained, surrenders finally to fantasy as she goes off to spinsterhood and a clerical job in Port-of-Spain. Oddly, it's this moment, closer to Chekhov than to Gorky, which proclaims most clearly a talent comparable with his brother's, but wholly distinct from it.

Ronald Bryden, "Kinship," in The Listener, *Vol. 89, No. 2298, April 12, 1973, p. 489.*

MARTIN AMIS

In *The Pleasures of Exile* George Lamming scolded V. S. Naipaul, as he no doubt would his younger brother Shiva, for taking too soft a line on Trinidadian social conditions, for being smug when he ought to be angry, for writing 'castrated satire'.... What the Naipauls write is irony, not satire, and irony is by definition non-militant.... Caribbean social conditions have for them, *qua* novelists, an imaginative significance only.

It is true that a primitive society offers a Hobson's choice of styles to its authors: tantrumese, noble-savagery, or a combination of irony and pathos. But like all limitations this brings special liberties. Irony and pathos are essentially downward-looking viewpoints, so a society of grotesques, fools, snobs, show-offs, martinets and ingenues who think and talk in illiterate clichés has obvious perks for a writer with as delicate a touch as Shiva Naipaul.... Although Mr Naipaul must, so to speak, keep his distance, this doesn't cut off sympathy but creates an undertow of restrained emotion.... The compassion is there in the sheer quality of the writing and never has to become explicit....

[*The Chip-Chip Gatherers,* like *Fireflies*], is predominantly concerned with one question about Trinidadian life: what happens when a backward people starts to educate itself? The most imaginatively appealing answer is that the old 'atavistic' instincts are not transcended, merely adulterated: what used to express itself in abuse and beatings turns into inarticulate malice; worry becomes anxiety, nostalgia becomes regret, apathy becomes morbidity, vague aspiration becomes obsessive ambition. This, like so much else, can best be observed through child-parent relationships, and Mr Naipaul again requires a broad canvas and a 40-year period in which to examine it....

If the book isn't quite as successful as the startlingly mature *Fireflies,* it is because Mr Naipaul has started to deal with the problem of focus. He is concentrating on nuance rather than ambiance, shaving down his sentences, and holding his vast—perhaps Dickensian—comic talents carefully in check. But for a writer in his twenties these are further precocities, not constraints, and there can be little doubt that his next novels will establish him as one of the most accomplished, and most accessible, writers of his generation.

Martin Amis, "Educated Monsters," in New Statesman, *Vol. 85, No. 2196, April 20, 1973, p. 586.*

ROLAND OLIVER

In 1976 Shiva Naipaul spent 20 weeks in Kenya and Tanzania, concluding with a brief dash down the Great North Road to Zambia in the company of a party of trekking hippies. He does not seem to have been well prepared for his journey nor to have met anyone of much consequence while he was there. The story [told in *North of South*] is mostly one of chance conversations in aeroplanes, buses, taxis, customs posts and, above all, hotel bars. All this is told with a great deal of novelist's sparkle, a power of vivid description and of characterisation through reported dialogue, which will not endear Mr Naipaul to his many acquaintances when his book comes into their hands....

On the whole, Mr Naipaul's book is more informative about touts and tourists, pimps and prostitutes, than about the national and international politics of the East African countries. He makes it quite clear that he has no admiration for Uhuru, whether capitalist-style in Kenya or socialist-style in Tanzania, but the evidence for both is disappointingly thin. So far as Tanzania is concerned, one must be a little sympathetic about the real difficulties placed in the way of would-be observers and the extreme reluctance of ordinary people to hold any converse with strangers....

Kenya, however, is another matter. There is freedom of travel. There is, as Mr. Naipaul's stories show, considerable freedom of speech. He could, and should, have looked beneath the surface and examined the basis of the capitalist economy, the inter-tribal situation and the prospects for the future. Instead of this, all we get is a blisteringly callow analysis of the black-white alliance against the brown....

It would be only natural to expect that Mr Naipaul, himself a Trinidadian of Indian descent, should have a sharp and compassionate eye for the predicament of the Asian communities in East Africa. In fact it proves not particularly compassionate.... [*North of South* is] a witty but not very wise book.

Roland Oliver, "Ujamaa," in New Statesman, *Vol. 96, No. 2471, July 28, 1978, p. 124.*

JOHN DARNTON

"The African soul is a blank slate on which anything can be written, onto which any fantasy can be transposed," writes Shiva Naipaul halfway through his narrative of travels in East Africa. The quotation is out of context.... But the dictum—of Africa as a repository for the foreigner's fantasies—goes a long way toward explaining the peculiar deficiencies of his own book.

"North of South," which recounts Mr. Naipaul's peregrinations through Kenya, Tanzania and Zambia, is in the genre of travelogue *cum* essay. When the form succeeds, as it does, say, with a writer such as Paul Theroux, it is an effective device for larger statement. The voyager's day-to-day experiences are transformed into insights, theories, and finally, complete systems for generalization. When it fails or only partially succeeds, it degenerates into a string of observations, some interesting, some not so interesting, but on the whole leading nowhere.

The book is a collection of hapless encounters—with rapacious immigration officials, reckless taxi drivers, street hustlers, ideological robots and racist expatriates—strung together by the author's sardonic, often bilious observations. It is built on vignettes and cameo portraits....

These people undoubtedly do exist—we have to take Mr. Naipaul's word on that—but as representative types they are hardly the defining personalities in Africa today. One wonders how he failed to meet, or at least record, a single non-racist white or a single articulate, intelligent black. At times, he seems to go overboard, the novelist overpowering the journalist. (p. 14)

Elsewhere Mr. Naipaul's theories collapse from sheer intellectual weightiness.... He finds that the "obsessive concern with wildlife" in East Africa leads to the degradation of the more backward tribes, who become "mere adjuncts to the animals"—a point supported by the fact that bookstores carry glossy albums of the two side by side.

Nevertheless, **"North of South"** is superbly written, even in the evocation of the scenery that Mr. Naipaul finds uninspiring. Many of the points are well taken, if not altogether new—that independence has primarily benefited a black elite, that the continent craves the material goods of the West, that its ideologies and sometimes even its wars are rhetorical. But it is marred by a snideness of tone. One moment the author records with obvious scorn the pejorative asides of a colonial housewife, the next he incorporates and elaborates on them in his own private observations. The shift between defender and detractor is disconcerting: It blurs the author's own standing. Who is it, in the final analysis, that is relating all these tales of "native ineptitude" and why? It's a bit like pornography masquerading as a sex manual. (pp. 14, 24)

Mr. Naipaul's central thesis is that black-white relations in independent Africa today are rotten to the core. . . .

There is, of course, some truth to the construct. From the point of view of social integration, Kenya's multiracial society is a myth. Whites do enjoy inordinate privilege, many blacks aspire to European possessions if not life styles, and the Indians remain a group apart. . . . But to see in these remnants of the past the whole future, and in these individual truths the single overriding truth, is to ignore some contradictory evidence. . . .

The grotesque caricatures Mr. Naipaul reveals do exist—it would be remarkable if they did not—but there are many more subtle and perhaps more important trends at work. To see nothing in black Africa today but a continuation of the master-slave relationship betrays a myopic vision. Africa's ambiguities are good for fiction, not for journalism. The continent seems contradictory: Its scenery can be uplifting or oppressive, its land nurturing or unyielding, its people kind or brutal. What one sees depends to a certain extent on who one is. This is the "blank slate" that Mr. Naipaul found and that he filled with his own projections. (p. 24)

> John Darnton, "Black and White and Middleman,"
> in The New York Times Book Review, May 6, 1979,
> pp. 14, 24.

JACK BEATTY

An account of a journey through Kenya, Tanzania and Zambia, *North of South* is a remarkably bad-tempered book. Africa annoyed Shiva Naipaul. . . . Shiva Naipaul is a West Indian novelist now living in London; he has no warrant in Africa. He is on a moral holiday there. Testy as it is, *North of South* is a first-rate book—spirited, funny, written with economy and care—but it is not a great book like *India: A Wounded Civilization*, because Shiva Naipaul is not implicated in what he indicts. He went to Africa seeking precisely what he found: he includes a letter to his publisher which sketches out his ideological itinerary. So there is little in Africa that can shock him; and, though much angers him, nothing there can hurt him.

Nothing, that is, except the way black Africans feel toward people like himself, toward "Asians." (p. 38)

It is a paradox, a mystery; this popularity of the whites, this hatred of the inoffensive Asians, and, underneath his urbane bafflement, it makes Shiva Naipaul furious with the Africans. "Transitional states," he writes, "are full of pain, riddled with illusion." There is much pain in what he describes, but he shows very little sympathy for it; his forte is exposing the illusion. Here is his farewell to Africa: ". . . Nothing but lies."

"Nothing but"—it is the language of obsession, not that of observation. Africa is unproblematic to Naipaul. He needn't have gone there at all; he could have written his book straight from his prejudices. Those prejudices light up the plight of the marginal men, the Asian population in the new black nations, but they stand between the reader and Africa. This would not be a problem in a novel but in a work which claims to be transparent on reality it causes a loss of belief, it induces an indiscriminate skepticism, finally it makes the reader as churlish and ungenerous as Mr. Naipaul.

North of South presents a satirical view of a parody civilization, and this is ironic, because it reads like a parody of the travel books of Shiva Naipaul's more illustrious brother. So one must take Shiva's fulminations against the inauthenticity of the Africans with a dose of irony. Who is he, writing in a form borrowed from his brother, to talk about authenticity? I found myself asking. For here are the themes of V. S. Naipaul's books: authenticity, fantasy as an immobilizing force, the squalid racket of third-world politics. . . . Is it ungenerous of me to wonder aloud if some of the anger in Shiva Naipaul's narrative has its sources in his feelings not about Africa but about borrowing his brother's form, striking his brother's rhetorical stances, and using his brother's tropes and tones and even his brother's diction? Mrs. Naipaul may of course have produced two sons with very similar obsessions; in that very likely case there would be no question of parody, of unconscious imitation. And perhaps that is the least churlish way to leave the matter, as the problematic, conjectural thing that it is. (pp. 38-9)

> Jack Beatty, in a review of "North of South: An
> African Journey," in The New Republic, Vol. 180,
> No. 23, June 9, 1979, pp. 38-9.

PETER L. BERGER

Not only have there been many accounts of the macabre events [of the Jonestown Massacre] but the question of interpretation has continued to intrigue many commentators. . . . [With] so much data already on hand, it seems unlikely that any startling new facts will be uncovered and the question of interpretation becomes more pressing. [**"Journey to Nowhere: A New World Tragedy"**] stands out by its resolute attack on this question and its refusal to accept easy answers. Mr. Naipaul . . . is a sharp, sometimes pitiless observer. He is a masterful writer. And he was determined to gain an independent understanding of the Jonestown phenomenon. These qualities make for a book that no one interested in the matter can afford to ignore.

Mr. Naipaul's quest for an explanation took him both to California and to Guyana, to the beginning and end points of the movement, and **"Journey to Nowhere"** is an account of these travels as much as an interpretation of Jonestown. Travelogue and commentary keep on intersecting, but given the evidence of a fine mind working to understand a complex and shocking subject, one tends to get as interested in Mr. Naipaul as in what he is writing about so well. Whether one finds the constant intrusion of the author into so terrible a story a flaw or a benefit is a matter of taste; be this as it may, in Mr. Naipaul's case, the continual presence of the inquiring author makes the book lively and readable.

Other authors have interpreted Jonestown as an expression of America as a "sick society," or as yet another product of the anti-American madness that previously spawned Charles Manson and the Symbionese Liberation Army. The ecumenicity of Mr. Naipaul's antipathies protects him from the simplicities of either cliché. Mr. Naipaul's Guyana is a country beyond re- demption—hopelessly stagnant, corrupt and violent. He did not like California either, and, one gathers, this dislike extends to America as a whole. California is for him the perfect symbol of all the ills of Western civilization, a place without meaning or identity, and therefore vulnerable to any doctrine, however lunatic or murderous, which promises a semblance of either. The present reviewer has very little knowledge of Guyana (though, even thus ignorant, one finds it hard to believe that any country could be so bereft of hopeful features); he is in a position to dissent vigorously from Mr. Naipaul's vision of California, not to mention America. Curiously, though, such disagreement does not detract from Mr. Naipaul's essential interpretation of what took place at Jonestown and, before that, in Jones's American movement. (p. 8)

Mr. Naipaul's is a harsh perspective; it is also a very persuasive one. To be sure, a less idiosyncratic writer would have softened his interpretation, introduced more nuances, perhaps shown more compassion. One strength of the book is that Mr. Naipaul does none of these things, letting the reader make his own modifications if he is so inclined. . . .

There is one omission in **"Journey to Nowhere,"** though, that must be mentioned as a serious weakness: Except for some passages about the rather pathetic remnants of the Black Panth- ers in Oakland, Calif., Mr. Naipaul's account barely touches on the motives and the fate of Jones's black followers. . . . By no stretch of the imagination can they be seen as products of the "California syndrome." They were fascinated by Jones's putative gift of healing, seduced by his cynical use of traditional Protestant rhetoric and touched by his concern (which, for all one knows, may have been genuine at the beginning). It would have been important to enter into their story too, along with the stories of all those assorted gangsters, revolutionaries and deranged intellectuals. What is more, an examination of their story might have introduced the note of compassion that one misses in this book. (p. 20)

> Peter L. Berger, "Revolutionary Suicide," in The New York Times Book Review, *July 5, 1981, pp. 8, 20.*

PETER LEVI

[Shiva Naipaul's] novels have dealt with a world where feeling has gone dead from despair and helplessness. He draws with the utmost precision a picture of the backwoods of Trinidad, and a people obsessed with the earnest, lifelong struggle to climb into the lower middle class. (p. 25)

Fireflies was a heavily documentary family saga, rather flatly constructed, but at the same time it was an utterly original book; the impression its abundant detail made was unforget- table. If Shiva Naipaul seemed never quite to get inside his characters, that is because he thought there was straw inside them. They were without some indefinable essential part of man. He wrote like a sociologist, unstylishly, at great length and with academic coldness. Still, for whatever reasons, *Fi- reflies* was a runaway success. It was certainly a most promising first book although it reads now as if it were written with suppressed passion by a writer who was a quarter poet, forcing himself into social science, hardly by a novelist at all.

By the end of *The Chip-Chip Gatherers*, that reservation dis- solves. He still specialises in characters whose feelings have gone dead. Liberation, if it ever arrives, comes too late to

matter. . . . But the novelist's ear for dialogue, and the fluent, truthful movement of one scene into another, which differs from family saga as history does from chronicle, and the bril- liant spare delineation of certain scenes and characters, make this a novel in a new sense. *Fireflies* was more than promising in more than one direction. But *The Chip-Chip Gatherers* re- veals glimpses of a rapid and wonderful novelist.

Since then we have been starved. In 1973, Shiva Naipaul was 28; we have had no more novels from him. . . . But Shiva Naipaul's two documentary books, *North of South* (1978), a sharply sardonic travel book about Africa, and *Black and White* (1980), about Guyana and the mass suicide under Jim Jones, are so extremely good that if we have lost a novelist we have still gained a writer who is now much more than promising. (pp. 25-6)

And yet one has the sense with Shiva Naipaul, in *Black and White* particularly, that he is still feeling his way. . . . [He] deals swiftly and powerfully with many themes a novelist might use. His eye for detail, his wry observation of character and his ear for dialogue are as remarkable as ever. He is still able to plunge himself into the lower depths of a society as thor- oughly now as in the days of *Fireflies*. What he is doing is not quite *reportage;* as Pater said of the other arts striving towards the condition of music, all Shiva Naipaul's books tend towards a novel.

In *Black and White* he casts a beady eye on a number of extremist groups on the West Coast that lurk in the background of the Jim Jones movement. This is investigative journalism, the last infirmity of men of letters, who are often better at it than regular journalists. It is the closest they can come to action. Shiva Naipaul's eye is admirably bleak. He is still fascinated by those whose lives are a nonsense. 'They are redundant. They are good for nothing. They do not even evoke fellow feeling'. And yet he writes from the very strong position of a thoroughly prejudiced and scornful humanist with unlimited curiosity. What rules his writing now is a sense of determining structure, the curve of a story, the hammer-blow of an expla- nation. He has always produced significant details, like a man picking winkles out of shells, but he has become a more con- trolled writer as time has gone by. . . .

Shiva Naipaul's close relation with Trinidad has meant a burden of love-hate which he might be glad to forget. Yet the only oracles that Apollo offers to writers are Dig deeper, and Know thyself. (p. 26)

> Peter Levi, "Shiva Naipaul," in The Spectator, *Vol. 250, No. 8068, February 26, 1983, pp. 25-6.*

FRANCIS KING

In its implacable depiction of one of those anterooms to hell that liberated Third World countries seem doomed to become, [*A Hot Country*] is impressive; but it has an odd air of being no more than the first draft of another novel, far fuller of incidents and characters. Just as the flood of the colonisers' dreams of untold wealth soon dwindled to a trickle and was then lost in sand, so the flood of the narrative, so confident at first, also thins away. The last two pages are superb in their evocation of a world of void, darkness and unspecified hunger, in which people, robbed of their souls by their former con- querors and exploiters, now have only one genuine desire left to them: 'To wreak vengeance. To tear down. To burn. To loot. To insult. To kill.' But it is impossible not to feel disappointment with a writer capable of such passionate eloquence and yet lacking the stamina to create the epic that his book seems constantly to adumbrate.

Francis King, "Potent," in The Spectator, *Vol. 251, No. 8099, October 1, 1983, p. 22.*

DAVID D'ARCY

[*Love and Death in a Hot Country*], Naipaul's subtly crafted account of abandonment and degeneration in a thinly-veiled version of Guyana, focuses on two casualties of the new redemptive order, Dina and Aubrey St. Pierre, whose marriage is suffering its own parallel decline. Disgusted by the lavish promises of the electoral masquerade, the St. Pierres inhabit a political and psychological void between the vanishing past and the balloting's foregone conclusion. In divergent ways, their lives assume a frustration and incompleteness that obliquely but unmistakably reflects Cuyama's apparently hopeless course. (p. 20)

Naipaul's portrait of a nation coming apart before having a chance to take political or cultural shape is neither explosive or overtly dramatic. His is a vision of gradual decomposition, tautly revealed in personal histories, the rhythms of daily life and details of the landscape. . . .

Love and Death in a Hot Country draws much of its inspiration from the author's nightmarish trip to Guyana several years ago, recorded in *Journey to Nowhere* (1980), an extended report on the Jonestown massacre. Some revolutionary terminology and bits of conversation reappear exactly as they did in the earlier volume. Perhaps because Naipaul is dealing here with characters he created, though, the novel exhibits a tone of genuine sympathy for those condemned, through no fault of their own, to endure the whims of a brutal dictatorship modeled after the autocratic rule of black President Forbes Burnham. *Journey to Nowhere* all too often drifted into facile contempt for the Guyanese, portrayed as fatuous or irremediably ignorant. Nor did it have any patience for the credulous, manipulable Americans, whom the writer held responsible for the phenomenon of Jim Jones.

Naipaul observes in his documentary account that politics in Guyana had a racial basis: Lines were drawn according to deep and often violent hostilities dividing the black and Indian populations. Similar hatred underlies the novel's action, taking the form of an official ideology that infuses the black characters. Indeed, their venom approaches hysteria. The author, a native of Trinidad where blacks and Indians are roughly equal in number, would likely take issue with any notion of racially determined behavior. Nevertheless, he seems to be suggesting that racism in the developing world does not necessarily have its source in dealings between "imperialists" and newly independent peoples.

But most impressive is this book's success as fiction. Emerging from Naipaul's despairing view of "liberation" is his wondrous, near-poetic description, his acute sensitivity to the complicated interplay of public and private, and his uncanny skill at fashioning realistic people out of circumstances that lead many novelists into wild exaggerations. Moving closer to his distinguished brother's skepticism about human nature, Shiva Naipaul has given us starkness amid lushness, politics stillborn in an atmosphere of gloom. (p. 21)

David D'Arcy, "Lost in a Landscape of Neglect," in The New Leader, *Vol. LXVII, No. 9, May 28, 1984, pp. 20-1.*

John G(neisenau) Neihardt

1881-1973

American poet, novelist, biographer, critic, dramatist, auto-biographer, and short story writer.

Neihardt based much of his poetry and prose on the history of the American frontier of the nineteenth century and emphasized the spiritual and psychological import of the settling of the West. Although he is best known as the author of *Black Elk Speaks* (1932), the life story of a Sioux holy man, Neihardt devoted most of his career to the creation of his long five-part poem *A Cycle of the West* (1915-1941). Neihardt called this work an attempt to "preserve a mood of race courage" and to "remind men that they are finer than they think." This belief that all people are capable of overcoming the weaknesses of human nature was central to most of his work.

While *A Cycle of the West* occupied Neihardt for the majority of his writing years, his additional literary output was large and varied. *Divine Enchantment* (1900), his first major publication, is a long lyric poem revealing his interest in Hindu mysticism; *The River and I* (1910) is an autobiographical account of a trip down the Missouri River; *The Splendid Wayfaring* (1920) is a biography of Jedediah Smith; and *Poetic Values: Their Reality and Our Need of Them* (1925) is a critical account of Neihardt's poetics. In addition to these works, Neihardt also published collections of short stories, two plays, volumes of lyrics, including two collected works, *The Quest* (1919) and *Collected Poems* (1926), many novels, including his last major work, *When the Tree Flowered* (1952), and two volumes of autobiography written at the end of his life. Out of his long career Neihardt emerges as a man of considerable talent who nevertheless received minimal critical attention during his lifetime.

Born in Illinois and raised in Kansas and Nebraska, Neihardt devoted much of his life to the study of the history of the Old West from the perspectives of both the native Plains Indians and the white settlers. The pursuit of this interest and his work with the Office of Indian Affairs led to extended contact with Sioux Indians and his friendship with and biography of the Sioux shaman Black Elk.

In *Black Elk Speaks*, Black Elk describes his visions and his personal struggle to maintain his tribe's spiritual unity in the face of cultural obliteration. Although the story is told in the first person, the book was composed by Neihardt, who selected appropriate details and used simplified syntax and rhythmic repetition to convey Black Elk's sensitive insights. *Black Elk Speaks* has been widely studied "as anthropology, as sociology, as psychology, and as history," according to Sally McCluskey, and it gained international recognition when psychologist Carl Jung took an interest in its mystic and psychological significance.

The five parts of *A Cycle of the West* concern the period between 1822, the beginning of the Ashley-Henry fur trading expeditions, and 1890, the official closing of the frontier. Three of the five sections recount the heroic deeds of western trappers and settlers: *The Song of Hugh Glass* (1915), *The Song of Three Friends* (1919), and *The Song of Jed Smith* (1941). *The Song of the Indian Wars* (1925), considered by some critics to be the

Photograph by Ron Nieodemus. Courtesy of Hilda Petri

most important portion of the cycle, and *The Song of the Messiah* (1935) center on the conflicts between the Plains Indians and the white settlers. Throughout the poems, the characters overcome both physical and spiritual hardships, gradually bringing morality and civilization to a chaotic world.

Like much of Neihardt's work, *A Cycle of the West* blends classical literary techniques with historically accurate details and regional folklore. Some critics contend that the tightly structured rhyme and rhythm schemes, lofty language, and classical allusions conflict with the expansive scope and the western particulars of the work. Others, however, agree with Kenneth S. Rothwell that with the creation of *A Cycle of the West* Neihardt produced "a long American poem which celebrates the timeless themes of Creation, Warfare, Journey, and Settlement intensely, urgently, and transcendentally. . . ."

(See also *Contemporary Authors*, Vols. 13-14; *Contemporary Authors Permanent Series*, Vol. 1; and *Dictionary of Literary Biography*, Vol. 9.)

HARRIET MONROE

[*The Song of Three Friends*] has not hitherto been reviewed in *Poetry*, because it seemed unnecessary to repeat criticisms fully suggested, in February, 1916, in a notice of *The Song of Hugh*

Glass, the first poem published of its author's projected epic series, though the second in artistic order. But the recent P.S.A. award to this book, as one of the two best American books of verse of 1919 . . . seems to call for a more complete statement of our exceptions to the committee's verdict, our reasons for thinking this poem "fundamentally unsound as a work of art."

The reasons are essentially one—the discord between the story and the style. The poet's project—a series of narratives presenting that most romantic period of American history, the winning of the West by adventurous wanderers and traders—is an heroic adventure itself, and not more deliberate a literary plan, perhaps, than most epics. But having started, he lacked the native human spirit, the unconscious courage, of his heroes—he couldn't give himself wholeheartedly to his adventure, let his subject carry him, but must needs load it with all the rhetorical and legendary impedimenta of many races, many literatures. He set out carrying not only the "heroic couplet" of Pope, and all the archaisms of so-called "poetic" language, now quaintly rococo; but also all the approved lesser-classic traditions of epic form and style. These details of manner, when applied to a story of wild-western pioneers, effect a discordant incongruity, at times absurd. (pp. 94-5)

> Harriet Monroe, "A Laurelled Poem," in Poetry,
> Vol. XVII, No. 11, November, 1920, pp. 94-8.

FRANK LUTHER MOTT

In ["**The Song of the Indian Wars**"], the history of the Indian wars in the west during the decade following the Civil War is detailed in verse which is always competent and sometimes brilliant and powerful. The moods of the times—in the Indian village, in the soldiers' camp, and in the pioneer's cabin—are poignantly distinct; and the human note, as always in Neihardt's work, rises clear and plain. Here is the greatest Indian fighting, without a doubt, in American poetry, as well as veridic and memorable Indian oratory, rough and desperate heroism of troopers, and pictures of the plains in all seasons of the year. The story of the death of Crazy Horse, with which the poem ends, is a very effective narrative poem by itself.

The case of John G. Neihardt, doing a big task so well and with so much clear sighted idealism, gives one about as much pride in America and hope for American literature as anything else on the horizon. (p. 89)

> Frank Luther Mott, "The Devotion of John G. Nei-
> hardt," in The Bookman, London, Vol. LXII, No. 1,
> September, 1925, pp. 88-9.

BERENICE VAN SLYKE

I have certain quarrels on minor points [in *The Song of the Indian Wars*]: the use of *'twas, 'twere, alas, aye,* etc., for which this poet has been sorrowfully reproached before; the lack of feminine endings which, rhymed, would have given variety and animation; the very rare use of the trochee for the iamb in search for musical relief and emphasis; the lack of an occasional illegal dactylic foot for suppleness; the use of the French word *coup;* the heading of the first part, *The Sowing of the Dragon.* Rhyme indubitably holds back the story, the machinery of it is evident in lines not important in themselves completing the couplets. If only the author had fallen by sectional moments into blank verse he would have gained brevity, lost nothing of accuracy or music; and when at the Council with the white men, Red Cloud, Spotted Tail and Man-Afraid

spoke, I longed to hear the forceful rhythms of free verse carry their pungent words.

Why head a portion of this narrative, indigenous to our own soil, with a title taken from the Greek? Could not a symbol have been found, in what American tradition we have, equally expressive of the fertility of hatred, and more country-colorful, country-suggestive? (p. 329)

As unfailingly as one climax moved me, the opening of the following part wearied me, partly because of the fatal "picking up" necessary to the continuance of the same rhythm and rhyme-scheme, partly because the story involves a sequence of many men in series of events rather than a few carried through to the end; and here the question arises, whether in presenting heroic material, matter of history, the poet must stick to the order of facts or present the essential element of truth in a guise best adapted to the ear of eternity. *The Song of Hugh Glass* and *The Song of Three Friends* are both better constructed, more fused and unified, than the present book.

The concrete details are excellent, Mr. Neihardt's knowledge of the country of the "Sioux, Arapahoes, Cheyennes, Commanches, Kiowas and Crows" so exact that I looked for a map; his feeling for words has advanced a long way beyond the mere vehicles that they were in his early lyrics. . . . (p. 330)

[The value of *The Song of the Indian Wars*] lies in the long sweep, in the moving caravan of bloody episodes that crossed by Powder River, Little Horn and Fort Phil Kearney. The shouts of battle dwindle in the last to the lamenting "Hey—hey-hey!" of Indian defeat and sorrow, and down the vital stream of pride in conquest floats the dark leaf of shame. In spite of flaws, in spite of my acknowledged prejudices, my sometime wearying, this is a book of power and worth. Mr. Neihardt is a poet with steel in him; and in his cyclic effort, still unfinished, he owns the nerves and sinews of his undaunted scouts although the weapon of his verse is single. (p. 331)

> Berenice Van Slyke, "Neihardt's Epic," in Poetry,
> Vol. XXVII, No. VI, March, 1926, pp. 328-31.

HARRIET MONROE

Mr. Neihardt has always taken himself and his mission as a poet seriously, and worked with high ambition and a sense of responsibility. His *Collected Poems* represents a life-work loyally carried on against all the crushing distractions—domestic, worldly, financial—which impede and often conquer so many a fine vocation. His most important offering, filling nearly four hundred of these over six hundred pages, is a series of *Epics of the West,* in which he has given a poetic setting, in rhymed couplets, to dramatic and characteristic episodes of our pioneer history. Thus he has fulfilled, to an exceptional degree, the command of his muse; and, in doing so, he has endeavored patriotically to monumentalize certain fast-fading figures, to give heroic form to our conquerors of the wilderness. (pp. 99-100)

The more personal part of Mr. Neihardt's poetry was the work of his youth—the lyrics comprised in *A Bundle of Myrrh* and two or three other small volumes published from 1907 to 1912. This was a rather barren period in America, and those critics who admired the young poet gave him extravagant praise. Reading these books now, one realizes how many voices clearer, richer and more moving have been thrilling us since Mr. Neihardt startled his world. Surely that early over-praise did him an injury, for it encouraged an egoism always too eager, and never held in check by a sense of humor.

Reading these early books now, in the first third of the *Collected Poems,* one feels that perhaps lack of humor is the root of the trouble. . . . Ever so little of it would have saved this poet from the self-conscious attitudinizing one observes here, from his preoccupation with himself as the poet, the *vates,* and from strident and declamatory utterances in this character. . . . [When] he becomes conscious of another Being in his universe, the lady of his love is never individualized, is never a humble little human girl, but always that impossible She of man's invention, the Woman who never was on sea or land. . . . (pp. 100-01)

Youthful egoism is common enough, and not always impenetrable; but one would hardly expect Mr. Neihardt's later work to be influenced by the swift currents of "the new movement," which set in soon after the completion of the two series, *The Stranger at the Gate* and *The Poet's Town.* Indeed, one would not have wished him to be affected by its greater simplicity and directness if his style had been inherently original, unmistakably an indigenous growth of his own soul. We may pass over the two plays—*Agrippina* and *Eight Hundred Rubles*—as experimental essays in the well-worn sock-and-buskin mode, and consider briefly the three *Epics of the West.*

In narrative we find the poet at his best—more dramatic than in the plays, and less bombastic than in the lyrics. Sometimes he almost forgets himself and his poetizing in his story, and molds the heroic couplet into a swift and efficient instrument of his chosen style, so that the story moves along, for pages at a time, quite freely. Here he does a good job of the kind he set out to do, and hands on to the future some lively rhymed tales of pioneers and their Indian wars.

Thus one's quarrel, if there be any, is fundamental. In my opinion, there is, between Mr. Neihardt's subject and his method, an inherent inconsistency which necessarily artificializes the resulting work of art. It is, like Pope's Homer, "a pretty poem, but not"—our rough-and-tumble pioneer adventuring. Not only is the couplet too smooth an instrument, but the poet polishes it with a too poetic diction. (pp. 103-04)

Mr. Neihardt has given us some interesting chapters, as Longfellow did, for the juvenilia of our literature, and for this he deserves "much thanks." But the "epic of the West" is still to be written. Whether it ever will be adequately written—ah, that is quite another question. (p. 104)

> Harriet Monroe, "What of Mr. Neihardt?" in Poetry, Vol. XXX, No. 11, May, 1927, pp. 99-104.

WILLIAM ROSE BENÉT

["The Song of Hugh Glass," "The Song of Three Friends," and "The Song of the Indian Wars"] are Mr. Neihardt's most important work to date, and they partially compose a work to which he is devoting the twenty best years of his life. To judge by his handling of the episodes of the Ashley-Henry time and of the time of Custer he is eminently justified. He has given us vivid, heroic, authentic canvases. He has handled the flow of his couplets with power and beauty, he has evoked thrilling drama. His lyric period is past; but he was never a lyric poet of the first water, while he is nigh to be narrative poet of that kind. . . .

Neihardt is, above all things, a good teller of tales. That is indicated also by the book of his prose ["**Indian Tales and Others**"]. . . . It is uneven, but the best stories have considerable power. . . .

There is no doubt that Neihardt knows the Indian. His understanding of and sympathy with the Redskin go deep. . . . Never, I venture to say, has red Indian warfare been described so well. It is as if we were actually present at the epidodes. (p. 39)

> William Rose Benét, "A Homer of the West," in The Saturday Review of Literature, Vol. IV, No. 3, August 13, 1927, pp. 38-9.

LUCY LOCKWOOD HAZARD

The Splendid Wayfaring, as the subtitle informs us, is "the story of the exploits and adventures of Jedediah Smith and his comrades, the Ashley-Henry men, discoverers and explorers of the great central route from the Missouri River to the Pacific Ocean." Mr. Neihardt lists his sources, and a student familiar with the authorities realizes how accurately and intelligently he has followed them throughout his narrative; how he has clarified and vivified them by the careful selection and animated expression of the material; how important a service he has done in the recreation of history, in the rescuing from oblivion of one of those "forgotten brave men" whose hands, as Carlyle says, have made the world for us. Jedediah Smith, as he appears in *The Splendid Wayfaring* is one of the "immortal dead who live again" in the choir invisible of generous heroes.

There is more work to be done in this resurrection of heroes. Mr. Neihardt is admirably fitted to do it and it is to be hoped that he will do it. *The Splendid Wayfaring* (1920) the last of these three books on the frontier, has been followed by another installment of the "epic cycle": *The Song of the Indian Wars.* Evidently Mr. Neihardt instead of following the rich vein which he struck in *The Splendid Wayfaring* intends to follow the less profitable one which he explored in his first books, *The Song of Hugh Glass* and *The Song of Three Friends.*

As the titles of these books imply, they are written in verse while *The Splendid Wayfaring* is written in prose. They are as meretricious as *The Splendid Wayfaring* is meritorious. Mr. Neihardt makes an acceptable Carlyle but a feeble Masefield. Perhaps Mr. Neihardt is a better prose-writer than he is a poet; perhaps prose is the more appropriate medium of expression for the epic of the American frontier. Whatever the cause, certainly the germ stories of the two poems are more dramatic, more moving, more convincing, in the prose form in which they appear in *The Splendid Wayfaring* than they are in the expanded poetic versions. (pp. 127-28)

In the poem the story is expanded to one hundred and twenty-five pages. As a result, of course, the frontier is diluted with a good deal of Neihardt. Now Mr. Neihardt's poetry *per se* is neither better nor worse than that of many contemporary versifiers. But when a poet presumes to "approach that body of precious saga stuff which I have called the Western American Epos" (I use Mr. Neihardt's own words), and offer himself as the Homer of the Frontier, the reader has a right to expect that the "precious saga stuff" shall be treated in a style worthy of epic tradition. What has Mr. Neihardt contributed to the raw material?

In the first place, classical allusions. . . . Now classical allusions may find a place in a literary epic, such as the *Divina Commedia* or *Paradise Lost.* But they have no place in a folk epic such as the *Iliad* or *Beowulf* or (to use Mr. Neihardt's own modest climax) *The Song of Three Friends.*

Secondly, Mr. Neihardt has contributed painfully elaborated figures of speech. The metaphor with its direct audacious identification of the objects of comparison is a mode of expression well adapted to primitive tales; the simile with its detached, deliberate, intellectual parallelizings betrays immediately the sophisticated poet. Such similes abound in these "Songs." (pp. 129-30)

The third contribution: lavish descriptions, chiefly of nature. . . . Some of these descriptions have a lyric delicacy, others are forced and incongruous; the bulk of the description in proportion to the bulk of the action falsifies the impression of the whole.

The plot is smothered not only by descriptions but by reflections. Mr. Neihardt is true to epic tradition in his frequent introduction of gnomic passages. He begins with the conventional *ubi sunt*. . . . At each turn of the story he tucks in a platitude. . . . These philosophizings, unlike the "commonplaces" of the Greeks and the gnomes of the Anglo Saxons, represent external comments, intrusions of the author's own thought into an alien world. (pp. 130-32)

The essentially swift and primitive action of the episode is further clogged by detailed and subtle analyses of mental states. Mike [Fink's] passion for the Long Knife's daughter is sentimentalized into the dawning of a pure romance. The resultant jealousy, the fight, the fatal shooting of the whiskey cup—this catastrophe which Neihardt tells in nineteen lines of prose is dragged out over thirty-seven pages of verse, chiefly telling how Neihardt supposes Fink and Talbeau felt. Entirely of Neihardt's own invention is the closing scene on the fire-swept plain where Talbeau "plays God" and exacts a fearful retribution of one friend for the murder of the other. (p. 132)

It is not our purpose here to discuss the merits of the poem as a poem. Parts of it have dramatic power; parts are labored and artificial. It is our purpose to discuss Neihardt's use of frontier materials in the poem; and it is a use which on the whole is regrettable. . . . The trapper, as we meet him in frontier chronicles, is essentially crude, primitive, healthyminded, given to action rather than to thought or feeling. The trapper as Neihardt presents him in the Songs is credited with a refinement of feeling, a complexity of motives, a power of introspection which would have effectually incapacitated him for fighting Indians, cheating Mexicans, outwitting other trappers, exploring undiscovered country. Neihardt's trappers would serve as the heroes of romantic poetry or psychological fiction, but they are sorry heroes for an epic. (p. 133)

The last, the most elaborate, and the most significant portion of Mr. Neihardt's epic cycle of the West is *The Song of the Indian Wars,* published in 1925. This, in Mr. Neihardt's own words, "deals with the last great fight for the bison pastures of the Plains between the westering white men and the prairie tribes—the struggle for the right of way between the Missouri River and the Pacific Ocean." A large order—and it is hardly to be wondered at that the result is in places confused and sketchy. The confusion is augmented by Mr. Neihardt's inability or reluctance to decide which characters are to play the role of heroes and which of villains. He describes himself in the preface as a "Custer partizan" but his hero-worship fails to vitalize the section of the poem devoted to Custer's last stand. Custer remains throughout the action, elusive and nebulous. In the preface, also, Mr. Neihardt disclaims any intention of sentimentalizing his characters; yet his account of the assassination of "the last great Sioux" Crazy Horse and the

reduction of his people to "whining beggars in a feeding pen," reads much like the propagandist pathos of Helen Hunt Jackson's *A Century of Dishonor.* Confusion is inherent in the very nature of Mr. Neihardt's theme. Paradoxically enough, the effect of the book would be less blurred if the confusion were deliberately accentuated. Mr. Neihardt has always been stirred by the pulsating urge of the western migrations. He recognizes in the apparently unscrupulous, coldblooded pushing out of the Indian tribes an inevitable manifestation of this westering. . . . But this belief in the manifest destiny of Aryan stock to inherit the earth does not deaden Mr. Neihardt's sympathies to [the American Indians]. . . . (pp. 134-35)

One could wish that this divided sympathy had sharpened the clash of cultures which is the theme of *The Song of the Indian Wars.* But even though weakened by a seesawing between the opposing parties, and by a failure to establish with sufficient clarity the connection between episodes, though disproportioned by an elaborating of the trivial (as in the incident of little Hohay's imaginings) and a neglect of the obligatory (as in the incident of the death of Custer), even though marred by the sententious gnomes, the labored personifications, and the longwinded descriptions which characterize his other Songs, *The Song of the Indian Wars* marks a forward step in Mr. Neihardt's employment of frontier materials. He occasionally sketches situations with a few stark, powerful strokes, as in the description of the despairing wait of the wounded survivors of Beecher's Island. (pp. 135-36)

The most significant feature of *The Song of the Indian Wars* is its perhaps unconscious impersonality. No heroic character such as Leatherstocking or John Jacob Astor dominates Mr. Neihardt's most recent frontier, although many nameless heroes emerge, play their brief parts, and vanish. In spite of Mr. Neihardt's professed admiration for Custer, his evident sympathy with Crazy Horse, neither the General of the Gray Fox nor the brave of the Sioux stands out as a unifying figure of the narrative. Greater than Red Cloud, Roman Nose, or Crazy Horse, greater than Fetterman, Forsyth, or Custer, greater than that "Omniscience in a swivel chair" who "half a continent away" blandly bungles the handling of Indian affairs, is the relentless destiny which makes for the expansion of the Americans and the extermination of the Indians. . . . Is it too fanciful to see as the real hero-villain of Mr. Neihardt's frontier, the railroad, "the many-footed monster," fit symbol of a mechanistic civilization. (pp. 136-37)

Lucy Lockwood Hazard, "Hunter and Trapper: Heroes of the Fur Trade," in her The Frontier in American Literature, *Thomas Y. Crowell Company Publishers, 1927, pp. 94-146.**

W. E. BLACK

The nature of our concept of reality determines the nature of our actions because every ethical act is performed within a metaphysical framework. In his writings, John G. Neihardt has investigated this relation of attitude to action, of metaphysics to ethics; and especially two of his lengthy poems *The Divine Enchantment,* a poem of Hindu mysticism, and *The Song of the Messiah,* a poetic treatment of the Sioux ghost-dance religion, demonstrate his statement that "our conception of values, by which we live, must grow out of our genuine belief as to what is real." (p. 205)

The Divine Enchantment recounts the tale of the virgin Devanaguy who, according to ancient prophecies, would bear

Christna, the incarnation of Vishnu. The tyrant Kansa has imprisoned her to prevent this, yet Vishnu nonetheless "overshadows" and impregnates her. "During the term of her gestation, Devanaguy was transported by a continual ecstatic dream." It is the revelation of this dream which forms the central content of the poem. (p. 206)

The philosophical premises which underlie *The Divine Enchantment* and Neihardt's subsequent works are rooted in two Hindu triads. The first is composed of Brahman, Universal Being; of Atman, the ego of the individual consciousness; and Maya, illusion created not by our perception of the phenomenal world but by the concept of individuality which accepts only a partial, and hence faulty, view. To escape maya, it is necessary to transcend a partial view; it is necessary to attain Nirvana. The three stations leading to Nirvana form the second triad basic to our understanding of Neihardt's metaphysics.

The first station is Waking Consciousness, a state of awareness totally blinded by illusion. The second is the Dream-sleep, a partial loss of self; and the third is the Deep-sleep, the total loss of self. (pp. 206-07)

It is from illusion-ridden Waking Consciousness that Devanaguy is freed: it is from Waking Consciousness that Neihardt wishes to free his reader. . . . (p. 207)

In essence, both *The Divine Enchantment* and *The Song of the Messiah* are the sharing of a vision: the one from youth, the other, maturity. It is with a certain degree of self-consciousness that Neihardt interrupts the flow of *The Divine Enchantment* an Interlude composed of but four quatrains. Still they point ahead twenty-five years to Neihardt's lecture statement that

> The value of a poem is in proportion to the largeness of the mood that it is capable of creating in the properly sensitive recipient. The major inspiration of the poet is concerned with the conception of that mood and not with details of mechanism in the translation of the mood.

In the Interlude, concerned with how the vision may be shared, Neihardt dramatizes his grappling not only with form but with content—the elusive qualities contained in the expanded mood which he represents in the symbol of the lotus. . . . (p. 208)

[In *The Divine Enchantment,* Man's] creation is followed closely by his "most wordy flow" of debate on the subject of death, after-death, and religion. Neihardt, attacking the idols which illusion has established as "Gods on thy hills, and gods within thy glades / [Man's] rude conceptions, rudelier put in clay," insists on a view which will transcend the maya, the partial view, found even in religion. However, even Reason cannot overcome the maya of religion, and Man is left in a situation from which he cannot extricate himself.

To free mankind from maya, Vishnu the Preserver decides to father a messiah; but in order to prepare the way for his son, Vishnu first must bind the sun, then must sprinkle the world with lotus-seed. (Here, in Devanaguy's retrospective dream which supplies the narrative, as well as in the Interlude, the lotus is used to symbolize expanded consciousness.)

Thus having seen the cosmic events leading to her impregnation, Devanaguy is recalled to the present as discordant worldly contentions break into the rapture of her dream. Even as she wakes, Christna the Messiah is born; with him the lotus-dream spreads among mankind. (pp. 209-10)

Neihardt's conclusions arrived at in *The Divine Enchantment* are still basic to *The Song of the Messiah,* though twenty-one years separate the two works. The subject matter itself necessitated subtle changes in the presentation. The abstract account of the flatly-characterized Devanaguy is replaced by the richly-humanized story of the visions which, around 1890, gave substance to the ghost-dance religion of the Sioux Indians. The mystical experience is symbolized, not by the lotus, but the Blooming Tree. As the earlier work had paraphrased the Immaculate Conception, "in a letter to Henry Latham of Macmillan's, Neihardt described [*The Song of the Messiah*] as 'a retelling of the universal Christ story in an unfamiliar medium, with a new emphasis and, perhaps, with a significance not commonly derived from it'."

Most importantly, the revelation of *The Divine Enchantment* ("They saw that all is one") motivates the ethic in *Song of the Messiah.* It is the pantheistic element in their ecstatic visions which give the followers of the ghost-dance cult both their calmness and their eschatology. Dealing with the actions of these real people rather than with the motions of cosmic abstractions, Neihardt treats his material sympathetically, realizing that the actions of the Sioux stemmed from their conviction, and achieving an esthetically-satisfactory balance between metaphysics and ethics. (pp. 210-11)

Where in *The Divine Enchantment* the dream-vision had been centered on the cosmos itself awaking and forming, *Song of the Messiah* depicts the waking of the individual and his ultimate immersion into a pantheistic universe. . . .

However, the mystically-revealed ghost-dance religion cannot survive in a world blinded by illusion, a country whose maya is characterized by the figure of the Indian Agent. In keeping with the rest of the poem, this portrait, too, is drawn on the human level, the individual scale. . . . (p. 211)

Persecuted for their religion and forced to take refuge in the Sand Hills beyond the borders of their reservation, the followers of the ghost-dance religion are hunted down by the Army and shamefully massacred at Wounded Knee. The transcendent calm of the ethic, however, by which the Sioux meet their deaths reflects the transcendent nature of their metaphysical vision. . . .

In *The Divine Enchantment,* Neihardt, discovering the nature of the One, presents a basically Hindu metaphysic which, in his lectures on *Poetic Values,* he envelopes in a systematic philosophy outlining the need in his own country for expanded consciousness and tracing its ethical implications, especially for the artist. In *Song of the Messiah* the didactic traces have virtually vanished; Neihardt is able to eliminate the distinction between metaphysic and ethic. The abstraction, quietly but completely, has become the motive of the action. (p. 212)

> W. E. Black, "Ethic and Metaphysic: A Study of John G. Neihardt," in Western American Literature, Vol. II, No. 3, Fall, 1967, pp. 205-12.

KENNETH S. ROTHWELL

[The] heroic celebration of the conquest and settlement of the Trans-Mississippi West has remained a viable theme, ripe for the attention of America's would-be epicists. Such a narrative poem, when and if it were successfully composed, and then widely accepted by an American audience, might be called an "Astoriad." As Astoriad, it would be a verse sequel to Washington Irving's *Astoria* . . . , a history of John Jacob Astor's opening up of the West to the fur trade, his establishment of a trading post at Astoria on the Columbia river, and his triumphs as a capitalist. (pp. 53-4)

Of the perhaps two dozen poets who have attempts Astoriads, John G. Neihardt, poet laureate of Nebraska, once praised by William Rose Benét for his "vast panorama of the West," makes the first claim to attention. Not only is he epicist but he is also regionalist. If regionalism may be thought of as a preoccupation with the history and ecology of a particular geographical section, then Neihardt's *A Cycle of the West* serves as an outstanding example. (p. 54)

In an age when "spontaneity" has become the higher virtue, the qualities of industry and self-sacrifice displayed by Neihardt, who is neoclassical in training but romantic in practice, are almost impossible to explain or defend. Moreover the flaws in his work are flagrantly apparent, easy to pounce on, and they cannot readily be accounted for. Neihardt's virtues are much less apparent, entirely subtle, and they emerge in a reader's slow recognition that *Cycle* is another triumph of the human spirit over the chaotic, mindless powers of the universe. Neihardt endows his cosmos, his region, with an identity. (p. 55)

Uneven in style, no doubt the result of the lengthy incubation period, [the five "Songs" of *A Cycle of the West*] yet add up to a compelling account of the Old West, the frontier at a time when man's challenges were direct and physical. The earliest of the songs, **"Three Friends,"** tells of the legendary Mike Fink, here somewhat romanticized, and his friends, Will Carpenter and Frank Talbeau.... [Discussion] of plot, *mythos*, does little to evoke the flavor of Neihardt's poem, the poet's gift for apprehending a physical landscape.... The prairie as sea is a recurring motif in *Cycle* ..., while echoes of Odyssean journey, the physical quest, remain in Neihardt's fascination for the serpentine rivers that twist through the Plains: the Kaw, the Platte, the Sioux, the Missouri. The imagination of John G. Neihardt is essentially that of a pastoralist without illusions. The size of the land, the sky, the heat of the winds, the ferocity of the sun, the snarl of thunderheads, the smoke of prairie fires—these are the elements he knows first-hand, loves, and respects.

In *Cycle* the land itself becomes epic protagonist, or antagonist, as though puny man were relegated to mere deuteragonist. The second song, **"Hugh Glass,"** ostensibly looks into the ordeal of Hugh, a trapper with Ashley's party, but actually reverts to the theme of the land.... Less rich in texture than **"Three Friends,"** ["Hugh Glass"] descends to a style too plain, even indecorous and unceremonious, for epic. (pp. 55-6)

Neihardt's third tale, **"Jed Smith,"** a series of campfire stories, shows how the hero's expedition crossed the continental divide to find Salt Lake, and, after heroic struggles with the Indians, made its way into California.... In this song, Neihardt often achieves a balance between the rhetorical excess and defect of the first two sections. At his best he displays epic objectivity in finding an American voice to celebrate the Midwestern topography.... (p. 56)

The last two sections, **"Song of the Indian Wars"** and **"Song of the Messiah,"** record famous Indian battles, including the fight at Fort Kearney, the Fetterman massacre, the Wagon Box incident, the battles at Beecher's Island and Little Big Horn. Here is Neihardt's *Iliad* phase as the gorier intimacies of battle injury confront the reader, much as in the Homeric tale of Troy.... And the point of view shifts as the red man rather than the white man becomes the principal actor, a change in

perspective that allows Neihardt opportunity to display his considerable knowledge of Indian lore and customs. The growing disenchantment of the red man is increasingly shared by the poet, who would agree with Red Cloud's Council speech that the white man's "hearts are bad and all their words are lies." The last song, **"Messiah,"** shows the defeat of the Sioux at the Battle of Wounded Knee after the Indians had discovered signs and portents of a Messiah among their own kind. They had been motivated toward this delusion by "Black Robes" (Roman Catholic priests), who had told them of a man long ago who had died and been reborn.... *Cycle* here hovers on the edge of that ultimate tragedy of the frontier, the destruction of the red man to allow the white man fulfillment of his Manifest Destiny. To establish the new land, the new cosmos, the white man slaughters redskins much as St. George slew the dragon to signify the founding of the English nation. Neihardt's epic is a belated ritual accompaniment to an act that has scarred the soul of a nation.

A Cycle of the West emerges as an epic of the West, an Astoriad, whose thematic core is local color, regionalism, a profound, indeed mystical, sense of the land. Setting and atmosphere overwhelm character; *Cycle* is a triumph of verbal *opsis* over *ethos*, so to speak. Saturated in his region, Neihardt makes it believable.... Not that Neihardt's work has not posed problems for the critic. Undoubtedly his greatest flaw has been in the area of diction. Caught between a classicist's training and an aboriginal instinct for a region, Neihardt succeeded in being not entirely successful as either folk poet or literary epicist. He lacked Walt Whitman's gift for echoing but not aping the accidence of epic. He shows little or no awareness of that definitive trait of the modern poet, a passion for the renewal of language.... Neihardt has been rebuked by several critics, among whom the severest has been Lucy Hazard [see excerpt above]. But against the record of excess, of flawed language, undeniably there, must be balanced a transcendent achievement, an ultimate impact, of several hundred pages devoted to a love affair with a region. Despite the Victorianisms "'Twas" and "Alas," and so forth, which prejudice the modern reader, Neihardt, as previously suggested here, is also capable of terseness, a stoic decisiveness, which approximates what one expects of epic.... (pp. 56-8)

A major objection to thinking of *Cycle* as "epic" lies in the poem's multiplicity and diversity of plot, its failure to focus on a single hero engaged in a well-defined enterprise. This lack of narrational unity, though compensated for by the thematic concentration on the land, places Neihardt's poem more in the category of epic romance than romance epic. Only the poet's choice of a rough meter saves *Cycle* from being another metrical romance, those lengthy pseudo-Indian narratives of the class of Longfellow's *Hiawatha* and James Eastburn's *Yamoyden*.... During the thirty years of the poem's gestation, the poet apparently grew increasingly sympathetic with the plight of the Indian. The Indians of the first song, **"Three Friends,"** may sound like stereotypes ... but the Indians of **"Messiah"** are Christ-figures, crucified on the cross of the white man's rapacity.... While some have seen this shifting perspective as an artistic flaw, others may choose to regard it as a reflection of the poet's, as well as the nation's, growing sophistication. Homer never made it entirely plain either, as to whether the reader should admire Achilles or Hector, Greeks or Trojans. In these closing sections, Neihardt almost looks into the fire, almost sees America as Eden awaiting corruption. (p. 58)

Cycle is a step toward that elusive entity, a long American poem which celebrates the timeless themes of Creation, Warfare, Journey, and Settlement intensely, urgently, and transcendentally in a prosody that endows the American language with dignity and sobriety. (p. 59)

> Kenneth S. Rothwell, "In Search of a Western Epic: Neihardt, Sandburg, and Jaffe As Regionalists and 'Astoriadists'," in Kansas Quarterly, Vol. 2, No. 2, Spring, 1970, pp. 53-63.*

SALLY McCLUSKEY

[*The essay from which this excerpt is taken was read at the annual meeting of the Western Literature Association in October 1971.*]

Black Elk Speaks has been many things to many people, and has been studied at various times as anthropology, as sociology, as psychology, and as history. It has been cited as evidence of a religious revival and used as an ecological handbook. But no one, as far as I know, has written about *Black Elk Speaks* as literature, and while its protagonist, Black Elk, has become a sort of culture hero and underground prophet, the man who wrote Black Elk's story, John G. Neihardt, has received surprisingly little credit for the artistry with which the book is written. Neihardt's very faithfulness to Black Elk's spirit and his skill in expressing that spirit have, ironically, eclipsed the effort he spent in writing the book, and often Neihardt has been ignored by press and scholars as if he were merely the instrument Black Elk used to tell his story, and not the shaping intelligence and lyric voice of the book. (p. 231)

There are difficulties in discussing the book as literature, for it had a peculiar genesis and belongs to no clear-cut genre unless one accepts Robert Sayre's term "Indian autobiography": an Indian's life story written down by a white interviewer, editor or translator. *Black Elk Speaks* is not really an autobiography, for Black Elk could neither read nor write; indeed, because he could not speak English, he told his story to Neihardt through his son, Ben Black Elk, who acted as interpreter. Neihardt's daughter Enid took stenographic notes, and Neihardt used the transcript of these notes to write the book. The content is partly biography, partly history, partly anthropology, partly anecdote, but all told through Black Elk. . . . Dee Brown pronounced it the finest book in existence on the American Indian, and Oliver La Farge lauded it. Paul Engle wrote that it "seems as close as we can ever get to the authentic mind and life of the plains tribes."

But the book's power is in the persona of Black Elk and in the texture of the prose itself. His story progresses in seemingly artless fashion and at a leisurely pace, but on closer examination we can see that Neihardt, as editor, was careful to catch the details that made Black Elk human. One can pick up any "as told to" autobiography recounting the life of some celebrity and encounter literary personality and prose style flatter than the pages that contain them. But Black Elk emerges fully rounded, and so does the world he lived in. . . . His faith, his fears, his rage, and his humanity unite, making him a complex human being who walked real roads, saw real clouds, smelled real winds, and tasted real meat.

Neihardt's use of the first person, he said, was a literary device, for he had to fashion Black Elk's story from many days of talk, many reminicences recalled not necessarily in order. That Neihardt's conversations with Black Elk contained a good deal more information than Neihardt included in *Black Elk Speaks*

is indicated by the novel *When the Tree Flowered*, published some twenty years later, and showing a great knowledge of Sioux rite and ritual, much more rite and ritual than is included in *Black Elk Speaks*. It is my guess that he edited such information from *Black Elk Speaks* so that he could include more detail about Black Elk's life. (pp. 231-33)

It is not that Neihardt neglected religion in the book: Black Elk's faith is presented, but in clean outlines. (p. 233)

Similarly, the history the book recounts is told dramatically. . . . There is also plenty of action, as in Black Elk's account of the Battle of Little Big Horn, and humor as in the "High Horse's Courting" episode. And there is pathos, as when, after having fled to Canada, Black Elk and a few other braves go out into the bitter cold on a hunting party. (pp. 233-34)

It is this emotional range and the lyrical quality of the prose that give *Black Elk Speaks* its power, for it has no plot to speak of, and no suspense—we all know who won the Indian wars. It does not follow the standard form of an autobiography, for other old Indians speak in it besides Black Elk. Standing Bear, Iron Hawk, and Iron Thunder occasionally break into the narrative to tell what they saw. It does not even recount the whole life of Black Elk, but only the first twenty-seven years, and one eighth of the narrative is taken up by Black Elk's first power vision. It is a loose, free recollection, held together by the powerful persona of Black Elk, and the increasing conviction on the reader's part that it presents, in the story of one man, the tragedy of two nations, red and white.

It is the personality of Black Elk that dominates the book, and while his story is that of a mystic, and therefore strange, and of dramatic times, and therefore interesting, it is ultimately the *way* the story is told that endows it with greatness, and Black Elk's language which creates the power of *Black Elk Speaks*. (p. 234)

If the book touches a generation that never saw a buffalo, never saw an eagle flying free, and never knew anything of Indian life except what it saw on the screen, it is because John Neihardt was the kind of man he was, and a writer of sensitivity and discipline. The forces that defeated Black Elk and the Sioux are the same that many Americans revolt against today: technological rape of environment and soul, progress without humanity, values too materialistic, and individualism too sterile. John Neihardt had warned of such things before he ever met Black Elk, in his poetry, his novels, his criticism, and his book about the Missouri *The River and I;* for he knew that if men were too intent on getting, they would have little time for seeing and if they lost their sense of continuity with the earth and with their fellow men, all the shining power lines and roaring power plants and jingling money in the world could not fill the sense of that loss. (pp. 241-42)

> Sally McCluskey, "'Black Elk Speaks': And So Does John Neihardt," in Western American Literature, Vol. VI, No. 4, Winter, 1972, pp. 231-42.

PHILIP K. BOCK

An old Indian man sits alone in his snow-shrouded tipi, dreaming of the past and blowing meditatively on an eagle-bone whistle. A younger White man comes to visit him, bringing gifts and a sympathetic ear for the old man's tales of long ago. This situation, incidentally portraying the early fieldwork of many [American ethnographers] . . . has been skillfully used by poet-novelist John Neihardt [in *When the Tree Flowered*] to recreate the experience of the Oglala Sioux in the mid-nine-teenth century. The form admirably fits the content: the old man is speaking freely to an outsider, and tries to make clear things that an outsider would not understand; but his listener still occasionally misses the point, becomes impatient, or needs further explanation. There are tales of adventure and of ro-mance, of war parties and vision quests, of hunger and of ritual (the first-person description of the Sun Dance is superb). And if the poet is occasionally carried away with the symbolism of a prayer or an explanation, he always stays within an idiom that seems (at least to me) authentic.

The theme is old age—the place on the "black road" where "there is a cane," and where "the road becomes steeper before it ends." What age (which sees, though not with eyes) can teach to youth, and the obligations of youth to age—these problems are not irrelevant to contemporary society. American Indians had (and perhaps still have) solutions that are wiser than those of our professional gerontologists.

> *Philip K. Bock, in a review of "When the Tree Flow-ered: A Fictional Biography of Eagle Voice, a Sioux Indian," in* American Anthropologist, *Vol. 74, Nos. 1-2, 1972, p. 31.*

JERRY GALLAGHER

[*All Is but a Beginning*] is a masterpiece of autobiography.

The only regrettable aspect of the book is that it is simply the first installment covering Neihardt's first twenty years. We must be grateful for small favors, however, and hopeful that God will be generous enough to allow him enough time to complete what he has started.

It is not that Neihardt's first twenty years were all that unique. They were not. He makes them unique, however, using words with the skill and precision of a surgeon. His finely etched portraits of people, places, and events flow from cover to cover with a mastery that defies the reader to describe anything he set down better than he has done it. It simply can't be done. His portraits of his father, his fourth-grade teacher, and his boy friend, John Chaffee, are unforgettable. . . .

The most amazing aspect of the book is its extremely contem-porary feel. The events are from another century, yet has any-thing really changed? Are John Chaffee and John Neihardt on the road anything more than "Easy Riders" with a time warp? Are John Neihardt's experiences with his students anything more than "Room 222" in a one room schoolhouse? Not really. It is hard to believe that a man ninety years old could write with such vivid imagery.

> *Jerry Gallagher, in a review of "All Is but a Begin-ning," in* Best Sellers, *Vol. 32, No. 15, November 1, 1972, p. 357.*

LUCILE F. ALY

[*Black Elk Speaks*] is told in language that suggests Indian idiom, as in Neihardt's Omaha stories. Short sentences, simple syntax and connective words, Indian expressions ("Yellow metal" for "gold"; "four-leggeds" for "horses"; "horse-backs" for "horses and riders") created the impression of Indian speech so well that some critics mistakenly assumed Neihardt had simply typed up Enid's notes *verbatim*, a notion that irritated as much as it amused him. As in the *Cycle*, the simple surface structure is deceptive; much of the complexity

of the style comes from the use of apparently concrete state-ments that are actually abstract and enthymemic. . . . An in-teresting stylistic feature is Neihardt's frequent dependence on flattened adjectives like *good* and *bad* for a double effect: they suggest the limitations of the Sioux vocabulary, but more im-portant, they reflect by understatement the stoic endurance of the Indians. "The good days before the trouble began," for example, and "It was a very bad winter for us and we are all sad," are more than cliché; they are understated to imply the particulars of suffering from cold, hunger, and fear. Closing the story with Black Elk's prayer is dramatic; in the dignity and pathos of the old man, Neihardt epitomizes the tragedy of the Indian people. (p. 175)

> *Lucile F. Aly, in her* John G. Neihardt: A Critical Biography, *Rodopi, 1977, 307 p.*

JOHN T. FLANAGAN

Patterns and Coincidences is the second part of [John Nei-hardt's] autobiography. It is a slight book but not without its charm. In his modest introduction Neihardt denies that "the life story of an ordinary man is necessarily of sufficient interest to justify the telling." But he adds that almost any life has high spots which are worth sharing with the rest of humanity. As a consequence, he brings together without much coherence and with no obligation to preserve chronology some incidents, reminiscences, and visions of a long life. Some knowledge of earlier Neihardt books will help the reader to understand at least his choice of material, but the eighteen short chapters present a pleasant view of a sensitive and articulate man at the end of his career. (pp. 284-85)

Patterns and Coincidences is a low-keyed book with few dra-matic scenes and no heroes. But details of events in a remote past are skilfully recalled and the pages are deftly written. (p. 285)

> *John T. Flanagan, in a review of "Patterns and Coincidences, a Sequel to All Is but a Beginning," in* Western American Literature, *Vol. XIII, No. 3, Fall, 1978, pp. 284-85.*

LUCILE F. ALY

[Neihardt's] youthful lyrics show his attentiveness to poetic forms; testing meters and rhyme schemes, he experimented with free verse and chant forms of the Omahas, as well as rhythm and sound combinations. By the end of his lyric period he had rejected the influence of Whitman, abandoned free verse, and modified the super-sonics of Poe and Swinburne that affected him temporarily. In his matured poetic technique he shows most clearly the influence of F.W.H. Myers' theory that rhythm and sound, through the manipulations of vowel and consonant combinations, pause and stress, create an emo-tional overtone to reinforce the mood and sense of poetry by releasing a subconscious human response unbounded by cen-tury or geography. From his self-taught study of Greek Nei-hardt worked for compression of images in a disciplined econ-omy of expression fostered by the use of rhyme. He thought that the same poem, written in unrhymed verse and then in rhymed, would be shorter in the rhymed version. Only after long, arduous apprenticeship did he consider himself ready to undertake an epic. (pp. 314-15)

However closely Neihardt's abilities and preparation met the requirements of Goethe and Vida for an epic poet, whether he actually achieved the American epic—or *an* American epic—is an entirely different question entailing all the perils of prediction. Early critics like William Rose Benet [see excerpt above] and others, thought he had produced an enduring work; some unhesitatingly pronounced him the American Homer and assigned a permanent place in literature to the *Cycle.* The verdict was not unanimous; some critics, carping chiefly about points of style, conceded narrative power but renounced Homeric comparisons. Harriet Monroe, in particular, disapproved outspokenly when *The Song of Three Friends* won the American poetry prize in 1920 [see excerpt above], but Harriet Monroe's pronouncements about Neihardt after their quarrel in 1913 must be read with some reservations. Critics have concurred amazingly well on Neihardt's devotion to his task, his narrative and descriptive powers, and the authenticity of his settings; Arthur Murray Kay called him the kind of authority film producers must consult for information. Critics have, however, questioned the right of the *Cycle* to status as the American epic on grounds of flaws in style and structure. Kenneth Rothwell, for example, judged the *Cycle* only a "memorable document in the unfinished search for an American epic," although it succeeded "as well as any other American epic as being an Astoriad [see excerpt above]." Kay conceded a "genuine epic temper" and considered Neihardt above the "popular and household poets," but agreed with Harriet Monroe that it was not the epic of the West.

Such critics may be right—but they may also be wrong. Every age suffers its myopia, not to say prejudices, and our age may well be a third sophistic, a stylistic-structuralist sophistic—and Neihardt was exactly the kind of poet to activate the syndrome. He would not leave the West, as most writers did, and he kept himself aloof from literary coteries and publishing circles. His rural seclusion undoubtedly denied him the personal contacts that assist the building of a literary reputation. On the other hand, it enriched his sense of man in the natural world. . . . (pp. 315-16)

Critics may also be wrong, or at least partly wrong, about the style of the *Cycle.* Kay's denunciation of Neihardt's "enslavement to outmoded form and diction" has some justification, particularly in the early epics, where Neihardt too profusely employed contractions like *'tis, 'twas,* and *twixt,* interjections like *lo* and *hark* to presage emphasis, and such rhetorical questions as "What augury in orniscopic words / Did yon swart sibyls on the morning scrawl?" Words like *orniscopic, yon,* and *swart* distressed critics too, as did "inappropriate" allusions to classic myth or Rabelais. The meaning of the quoted line, however, is exact if the words are examined carefully. Awkward flaws almost disappeared in the later epics, and allusions of any sort should not unduly exasperate critics in an age dominated by Ezra Pound and T. S. Eliot. In Neihardt, such references as "comrades of Jason and his crew" to describe the Ashley-Henry men derive from his sense of human experience as timeless; he had absorbed from Bergson the theory of continuity in flow. Judgments on the *Cycle* too often seem to rest on superficial reading and misapplication of lyric standards. Blends of style, fused levels of language, rhetorical questions, and classical references are defended by various critics as necessary accoutrements of epic. Epics are not written for the short attention-span. (p. 317)

A Cycle of the West is not written in heroic couplets, as some critics assume. Neihardt had labored long over his verse form and selected pentameter as a line long enough for epic dignity and better suited to English cadences than the classical hexa-

meter; as he himself explained, he used the techniques of blank verse and added two-line rhyme, not couplets, because rhyme enriched the tone and forced a tighter precision. . . . As he worked with meter Neihardt manipulated pause and stress for flexibility and used his "sound mosaic" in vowel and consonant combinations to carry complex emotional overtones. . . . In many lines sound webbed to sense builds emotional tone, as in the description of the Beecher Island fight in *The Song of the Indian Wars.* . . . [His] lines are clearly not the work of a clumsy stylist, nor is Neihardt's ability to blend into his dignified epic style Indian idiom or trapper phrases, or the rich Irish brogue of Mike Fink. Neihardt's lines were written from his belief that poetry was meant to be heard, particularly epic poetry, based as it is on oral tradition.

If skeptical critics are wrong about their judgments of Neihardt, and *A Cycle of the West* is destined to stand in the future as an—or the—American epic, its durable qualities should be discoverable today, even though epics are likely to share the fate of a prophet in his own country. How well does the *Cycle* meet established criteria for an American epic?

To begin with, it tells a rousing story of heroes and heroic action—history in the making, for in concert if not individually, the fur-trade men and the Indians certainly affected the destiny of America. In seeking to "preserve a mood of race courage" and "remind men that they are finer than they think," Neihardt drew arresting pictures of brave men in action. . . . (pp. 317-19)

Neihardt's heroes, mostly drawn from real men, are given sufficient authenticity, but in details of character are adjusted to the needs of epic: Mike Fink, for example, is considerably deloused. Critics who faulted Neihardt for putting too elevated language into the mouths of his characters may be forgetting that epic heroes cannot be given the full-blooded portraits necessary for characters in novels. The epic hero must be generalized to embody universal human experience. (p. 319)

The *Cycle* meets the requirement of "spaciousness," both in setting and in theme. The *Songs* cover the area of the American West from the Missouri River to the Pacific in a panorama of formidable snowy mountains, tongue-swelling deserts, lush valleys with crystal streams or tumbling rivers and dangerous rapids. (p. 320)

Expansiveness of theme is clear in the *Songs,* but its full impact requires more than a single reading. The one great theme in literature, Neihardt said more than once, must be the relation of man to the cosmos and to other men. In the *Songs* he intended both a structural and a thematic progression, in time and space from the departure of the Ashley-Henry men in 1822 to the battle of Wounded Knee in 1890; from St. Louis, the point of embarkation, to the Pacific coast. This progression covers the opening of the West by the fur-trapper explorers, and in the last two *Songs* the displacement of Indian tribes by white men. (pp. 320-21)

The thematic progression, the real point of the *Cycle,* rests on Neihardt's belief that values operate on a vertical, not a horizontal, scale, and that men must respect each level of values without confusing the lower with the higher. *The Song of Three Friends* explores the values of physical courage, lowest on the scale but essential, for courage is necessary to all values. In this *Song* the heroes perpetrate tragedy because physical courage cannot solve problems that demand moral force. Fink is blinded by wounded pride, Carpenter by inarticulateness, Talbeau by anger. At the end, Talbeau's belated repentance, when he realizes that he has no right to play God by assuming Fink's punishment, prepares for the rise of value level in the next *Song*. **The Song of Hugh Glass** lifts the level to magnanimity as Hugh progresses from lust for vengeance to recognition of its dehumanizing force when he sees his face in a pool, and then begins to learn the way out of hate through forgiveness and love—the "miracle of being loved at all" and the "privilege of loving to the end." The lower values serve a purpose, for hate has saved Hugh's life by prodding him on. **The Song of Jed Smith** develops the value of spiritual faith, the security of man in a cosmos where all creatures and all nature are linked in a spiritual whole. (p. 321)

The last two *Songs* about the defeat of the Indians rise to the level of self-sacrifice for the good of the group in **The Song of the Indian Wars,** where brave men fight valiantly—men on both sides—and to the level of the Christian ethic in **The Song of the Messiah,** where Neihardt shows in Sitanka the victory of the spirit over physical defeat. (p. 322)

Like the Greek epics, the *Songs* are informed by a balanced, compassionate objectivity about the lot of mankind trying to survive against odds. The sense of universal experience runs through the epic in sharp pictorial scenes. . . . (pp. 322-23)

The real power of epics, according to Thomas Greene, comes from the movement through archetypal images or themes. In this respect the *Cycle* takes on stature in the interweaving of archetypal experiences of men. Immediately prominent is the theme of the integrated universe, the kinship of man and nature, chiefly textured in the metaphor and in the attention to birds and animals. (p. 323)

The archetype of man against a chancy world runs through the *Cycle,* often in choric prophesies or wry reminders of universal uncertainty—the "unseen player" that stacks the deck. . . . Other archetypes include the noble sacrifice and also the tragic waste of war, when white men and Indians exert all but superhuman energies and rise to heroic heights to destroy each other for essentially the same goals. Crazy Horse and Sitting Bull become archetypes of the conquered hero, meeting death courageously—summing up, as Crazy Horse does directly in his death chant, the tragedy of a defeated society.

The Messiah archetype appears in the final *Song,* interwoven with the cycle-of-sin pattern strong in **The Song of Three Friends** and **The Song of Hugh Glass**—temptation, fall, repentance, atonement, and redemption. The betrayal theme epitomizes human experience, for men are always betrayed by their expectations of life and of their fellows; they save themselves only by learning to love past imperfections. The Messiah theme parallels the quest for spiritual truth, the archetype that dominates the *Cycle.* (pp. 323-24)

The Song of Jed Smith, the last *Song* written, actually completes the theme by showing that men can live by the spiritual principle; Jed's life demonstrated the possibility. Other archetypal images might also be traced; for example, it is possible to see in the Hugh Glass story an archetype of the artist in an unsympathetic world. (p. 324)

> *Lucile F. Aly, "John G. Neihardt and the American Epic," in* Western American Literature, *Vol. XIII, No. 4, February, 1979, pp. 309-25.*

Seán O'Faoláin

1900-

(Born John Whelan) Irish short story writer, novelist, biographer, autobiographer, editor, nonfiction writer, journalist, dramatist, and translator.

O'Faoláin is considered a master of the short story. Although he has been one of Ireland's most outspoken reformers, his love for his country and admiration for its people are evident throughout his work. O'Faoláin depicts the Irish with compassion, humor, and irony. As he said in an interview with his daughter, author Julia O'Faolain: "Everything I write is [romantic]. But I know too that I have to put in—that my only hope of sanity and balance is to put in—irony. Irony is the one element that saves me from being soppy." O'Faoláin has, in both his fiction and his nonfiction, documented much of the history of twentieth-century Ireland, often basing his works on his own experiences as an active participant in important events.

Born in Cork, O'Faoláin was the son of parents who aspired to the British middle-class way of life. For many years O'Faoláin also followed this ambition until, as an impressionable adolescent, he witnessed the Easter Rebellion of 1916. Abhorring the brutality of the British, he soon found himself in sympathy with the proponents of an independent Ireland. He studied Gaelic, changed his name to the Gaelic variant, and joined the Irish Volunteers. His subsequent experiences in the Irish revolution of 1919-21 and as director of publicity for the Irish Republican Army during the Irish civil war led to a fervor of loyalty and patriotism. O'Faoláin was disillusioned and disappointed when the war ended with a humiliating defeat for the IRA.

While in his teens, O'Faoláin underwent another experience which affected his work. His home was located near the Opera House; many of the actors and actresses lodged with the Whelans. O'Faoláin was fascinated by what appeared to be the exotic life of the theater and, with stage passes from the lodgers, he often attended performances. In 1915, he saw an Abbey Theatre performance of Lennox Robinson's *The Patriot*. Until then, all the dramas he had seen were about English life. *The Patriot* depicted life in an Irish country town, and the realistic setting and characters touched O'Faoláin. As he wrote of Robinson's work: "It brought me strange and wonderful news—that writers could also write books and plays about the common everyday reality of Irish life." Although O'Faoláin's first works were romantic and exotic, he later began to write about "common everyday Irish life" and never abandoned that subject.

The first collection of O'Faoláin's stories, *Midsummer Night Madness and Other Stories* (1932), are highly romanticized accounts of the Irish war of independence and civil war. Although the censorship board in Dublin banned the book, O'Faoláin was elected to the Irish Academy of Letters, whose members included George Bernard Shaw and W. B. Yeats. In his later collection, *A Purse of Coppers* (1937), O'Faoláin tempered his romanticism somewhat; he later wrote: "I hope a certain adjustment and detachment shows itself in the stories...." O'Faoláin was indeed successful in this attempt, for critics often cite this book and the following collection, *Teresa and*

Photograph by Godfrey Graham

Other Stories (1947; published in the United States as *The Man Who Invented Sin and Other Stories*), as examples of O'Faoláin's "more mature" style—compressed, subtle, ironic, and subdued.

In 1940, O'Faoláin founded an Irish literary journal, *The Bell*. It was his belief that Ireland, now cut off from England, needed to establish its own culture and standards. In this periodical O'Faoláin included articles on fashion, theater, and other social and cultural topics, and he encouraged and assisted new writers in contributing to *The Bell*. Even though it was often sold under the counter, the journal became quite popular and O'Faoláin edited it until 1946.

The mixed reception of his books and of *The Bell* exemplify O'Faoláin's status in Ireland. He has faced constant derision and contempt while also finding a small number of sympathizers. As Julia O'Faolain has written: "Seconded by very few liberals, Sean pitted himself against an alliance of patriot prigs whose ideal society was to be protected from free speech or foreign ideas." In many areas of his life O'Faoláin has been dedicated to the creation and preservation of Irish culture. As evident in the recent publication of *The Collected Stories of Sean O'Faolain* (1983), his aims are the same in his works of fiction—subtle, compassionate depictions of the everyday concerns of Irish life.

(See also *CLC*, Vols. 1, 7, 14; *Contemporary Authors*, Vols. 61-64; *Contemporary Authors New Revision Series*, Vol. 12; and *Dictionary of Literary Biography*, Vol. 15.)

LEWIS JONES

Sean O'Faolain writes proper stories, and most of them meet his excellent criterion: 'As I see it, a Short Story, if it is a good story, is like a child's kite, a small wonder, a brief, bright moment.'

Many of them are about the cruelties and beauties of memory. He sees growing up as a painful realisation that the world is an illusion and suggests, paradoxically but sensibly, that our solace must be to embrace illusion, which 'saves us from having to admit that beauty and goodness exist here only for as long as we create and nourish them by the force of our dreams.' This Jesuitical twist is typical: the stories [in *The Collected Stories of Sean O'Faolain: Volume Two*] are about Ireland, bogs, pubs, IRA and all, and through them runs the skein of the Roman faith. There are stories about theological jokes, pilgrimage, humbug, miracles, atheism and conversion; like the kite they soar in the face of heaven and swoop to earth. Mr O'Faolain's prose is playful and vivid like the kite and can describe, with equal facility, the aching sensuality of asceticism or a woman looking out of a window: '. . . her eyes opened and narrowed like a fish's gills as if they were sucking something in from the blue sky outside.' (p. 21)

> Lewis Jones, "Short Stories," in The Spectator, *Vol. 248, No. 8007, January 2, 1982, pp. 21-2.**

DENIS DONOGHUE

It is good to have the second volume of Sean O'Faolain's short stories [*The Collected Stories of Sean O'Faolain: Vol. II*]. The first brought together seven stories from *Midsummer Night Madness* (1932), 14 from *A Purse of Coppers* (1937), and 13 from *Teresa, and Other Stories* (1947). Now the second has ten stories from *The Stories of Sean O'Faolain* (1958), 11 from *I remember! I remember!* (1961), and ten from *The Heat of the Sun* (1966). In the Preface he wrote for the Penguin *Stories of Sean O'Faolain* (1970) he said that 30 stories were all he had to show, or all he was content to show, for more than thirty years of storywriting. One thinks, he said, of George Sand turning out volume after volume while never once neglecting a love affair, never missing one puff of her hookah. Well, no matter, O'Faolain has done many other things and written many other books besides his collections of stories. He has been, he is still, a man of letters, a novelist, biographer, autobiographer, historian, critic. But his short stories have a special place in the affections of those who care for good writing.

I should declare an interest, or a prejudice. I much prefer his later stories to his earlier ones. Many of the earlier stories sound as if they were written not only to charm the birds out of the trees but to show that one Sean O'Faolain could charm them out of the trees. The reader is forced to believe that life in Ireland was simpler, more beautiful, nobler then than now, that the people were a nest of simple folk, richly expressive, articulate, eloquent, that the grass was greener, the rain softer, the mackerel-crowded seas more mackerel-crowded than any seas a man of my age can describe. It may be true. It may be true. You're born in Cork in 1900, you grow up with the new century and with a sense of an equally new Ireland. . . . Yet O'Faolain's early stories want you to feel that life in Ireland

was a romance, and sometimes an epiç. I have never been convinced. I'm an agnostic in these sentiments. I don't believe that O'Faolain's early luscious style represents his effort to be equal to the rich occasions he describes. I believe, rather, that the style came first, and demanded incidents, landscapes and sentiments fit for the style to live in. . . .

[His] early stories never say 'colour' if they can say 'hue', or 'morning' if they can say 'morn'. He started writing seriously in 1927, several years after *Prufrock* and *The Waste Land* and *Ulysses*, but his taste was still that of Palgrave's *Golden Treasury*. University College, Cork, Daniel Corkery's place, was probably slow to receive the good news from Eliot, Pound, Mann, Kafka, Valéry and Joyce. Yeats was inescapable, but there was nothing in Yeats to discourage a young writer from preferring 'hue' to 'colour'. O'Faolain, living among words, chose for company the words he thought were already poetry. Looking back in 1970, he thought the most romantic of all his words were the 'and' and 'but' which he used 'to carry on and expand the effect after the sense has been given'. The writer who luxuriates, he says, 'goes on with the echoes of his first image or idea'. His emotions and his thought 'dilate, the style dilates with them, and in the end he is trying to write a kind of verbal music to convey feelings that the mere sense of the words cannot give.'

Take, for instance, **'Fugue'**, which O'Faolain wrote in 1927: he thinks it his first successful story—in fact, 'a very lovely story'. And it is. 'I wish I felt like that now,' he said in 1970. Which I take to mean: I wish I were young again, with feelings that chimed with my exorbitant style. **'Fugue'** is about two young men on the run from the Black and Tans: one of them is killed, the other survives to tell the tale and turn it into lyric poetry. The story includes a lonely house, a woman, fear of dying, and landscape strikingly receptive to the hero's desire. It stays in the mind as a very lovely story, and so long as I'm not forced to believe it, I am content. . . .

The trouble is that O'Faolain, on his hero's behalf, is trying to make me feel more, and more tenderly, than anything the story compels me to feel. He is eking out the story, dilating it as with 'and' and 'but', in the desperate hope of leaping the gap between the lyrical reach of his style and any merely finite effect the story can have. That is: his style is in excess of any occasion he can remember or imagine for it. It remains a lovely story because we feel in it the void between the hero's feelings and anything the world might offer him to appease them. My trouble with the story is that I believe the endlessness of O'Faolain's desire, because it corresponds to the strain of his style, but I don't believe in his hero as anything but a function of the author. He is not, as we used to say, a real character.

The early stories have two problems, which often merge. There is the large, general problem of Romantic Ireland, not that it was dead and gone but that it wasn't. In the first years of the 20th century it was impossible for a young writer to see Ireland 'as in itself it really was': he saw it only through a veil of associations, ancient pieties, sagas not entirely forgotten. Corkery's 'hidden Ireland' had to be recalled, disclosed. Romantic Ireland called for heroic emotions or, in defeat, elegiac emotions: either way, styles extraordinarily high and grand. The particular version of this general problem, for O'Faolain as a short-story writer, was to imagine characters and situations large enough to contain not only the 'object' but the halo, the aura, that already surrounded it, the words that were already poetry, if only bad poetry. His early stories rarely succeed in finding such characters, such situations. So the narrative style has to force the characters to feel more than they could really feel, consistent with the probability the stories claim: the result is that there is always a remainder of sentiment which has to be added, as if between the words, to satisfy the demands of a rhetoric greedy as if by nature. O'Faolain's patriots, young warriors, priests, all those mothers, all their sons, are well enough, but not quite good enough for the rhetorical work they have to do.

These problems may explain why so many of O'Faolain's stories show their characters caught in the coils of memory. Most of his characters, especially in the early stories, live on their memories while they die otherwise. *I remember! I remember!* is the best of his titles, though not the best of his books, and it is all the better, all the richer, when you remember the way the old poem goes: 'I remember, I remember, the house where I was born, the little window where the sun came peeping in at morn.' Morn, yes. Indeed, O'Faolain's flair for memory, and the flare of his memories, were so vivid that he must often have been tempted to proust his way through the Ireland of his childhood and keep his art to that pleasure. But he hasn't yielded, as some of his colleagues yielded. There is a sense in which Frank O'Connor stayed, imaginatively , in the small towns of his boyhood, and let the new Ireland mind its own grubby business. Liam O'Flaherty, too, wrote as if his first experiences were definitive and could only be lost if pestered by later matters. Michael MacLaverty, a gifted and largely forgotten writer, nearly broke my heart with a beautiful book, *Lost Fields,* one of the first books that I recall caring for. But again, he stayed where he started: perhaps the experience of childhood and boyhood was too cherished to admit a rival or the fear of a lapse.

In these respects, O'Faolain has been strong where his colleagues have been timid. He has written well of the mandatory themes, childhood, mothers, first confession, priests, monks, young girls, but he has forced his art to pay attention to an Ireland which has often disappointed him as a citizen. The stories he has written since 1945 have cast an ironic but not a cold eye upon Dublin, its upper-middle-class life, its lawyers and doctors, the remnants of Ascendancy Ireland, their marriages, their mistresses. . . .

O'Faolain's imagination has kept up with the European Ireland: he has been writing of diplomats and their foreign affairs, of lawyers and their tiresome girlfriends, of Catholics good but mostly bad, of priests and bishops wise in a world they have not made and can't control, of emotions provoked by foreign cities (Turin, called Torino) and dragged back, excess baggage, to Dublin. (p. 18)

The most famous story in the second volume is **'Lovers of the Lake',** about two lovers, one of whom, the woman, suddenly decides to do the pilgrimage of fasting and pain at Lough Derg. The pilgrimage, which might have been ignored or set aside as a whim, an eccentricity, comes between them, and the affair is wrecked. It is an odd story, dangerously garrulous on occasion, but I have long admired the art of it. O'Faolain's lovers are either too young or too old, they never fully coincide with themselves or their time. They are always decent people, and the feelings they express and act upon are genuine, but they are never exactly the feelings the lovers need at the time. At another time, or in another country, the same feelings would answer beautifully, but in these stories there is a fated disjunction between the feelings and what the lovers need. They need different feelings—poorer or richer, it would not matter.

O'Faolain's attitude to his lovers is tender, rueful, sharp at times but only when a more extreme sharpness would be fair. His heart is kind, but not soft: no fool where emotions are in question, he is never taken in by the charm he allows his lovers to express. There are no really evil, wicked people in his stories: some are vain, pretentious, silly, but O'Faolain doesn't find satisfaction in observing malice. So, while he is often ironic toward his characters, and agile in detecting their follies, evil is not his theme. He is not, in fact, a satirist. 'I still have much too soft a corner for the old land,' he confessed in the Penguin Preface. It is true. In the years after the War, he was much occupied with public issues, the question of censorship, for an irritating instance, and he showed that he could write wounding prose when his ire was up. But that was in polemical vein. In his fiction, he is always ready to see the other side of the situation, and to feel the hidden motives. I mention, as if evidence were necessary, such stories as **'A Meeting', 'The Confessional', 'Unholy Living and Half Dying', 'Shades of the Prison House', 'The End of a Good Man', 'Passion', 'Childybaun', 'Lovers of the Lake'** and **'Charlie's Greek'.**

Thirty? Yes, I could name them, or as many, though they might not tally at every point with O'Faolain's choice. The differences would be slight. To write 30 successful stories, in an extremely competitive art . . . is a rare and exhilarating achievement. I salute a master. (p. 19)

Denis Donoghue, "Romantic Ireland," in London Review of Books, *February 4 to February 18, 1982, pp. 18-19.*

STEPHEN BANN

Collections of short stories as rich and copious as those of Sean O'Faolain are impossible to review in a short compass. But this third volume of the collected works [*Collected Stories, Volume III*], which includes stories published from 1971 onwards, has the advantage of concluding with a group of unpublished texts; these are not only individually enthralling, but suggest a general position on the range and possibilities of the short story.

If Maupassant stands for the short story in its classical form, there could scarcely be a more convincing sign of the opposite strategy than in the stories of Kipling. In place of the observance of unities, and the controlled progression to a *pointe* or punch-line, we have a deliberately wayward use of time and space, and an inclination to make of the mysterious oppositions and convergences of cultures one of the principal sources of subject matter. Sean O'Faolain's subtle and haunting **'One Fair Daughter and No More'**, among the unpublished texts, could indeed be described as Kiplingesque. Through the intermediacy of a neutral, official narrator, it sets up an imaginative parallelism between Italy and Northern Ireland, focused on the character of a young woman who is Italian by origin but has been adopted by Northern Irish parents. Through the light which it casts on terrorism in Italy and Ireland, and the parallel illumination of the violence of Latin love in the inappropriate context of Belfast, this story sets up a resonance which cannot easily be dispelled. The same is true of **'From Huesca with Love and Kisses'**, where the transplanted heroine is a cosmopolitan Jewish painter taking a working holiday in Western Ireland. Sean O'Faolain exploits to the full the vivid counterpoint set up by the clash of cultures. His Ireland is not an untarnished, uncontaminated domain of pure ethnicity, but the site of a play of conflicting allegiances. (p. 11)

Stephen Bann, "Mythic Elements," in London Review of Books, *December 30, 1982 to January 19, 1983, pp. 10-11.*

A. N. JEFFARES

[In *The Collected Stories of Sean O'Faolain, Vol. 3*] Sean O'Faolain proves himself yet again a master of narrative, a writer whose eyes select, whose ears record and whose insights illuminate and enrich our understanding, and stir our emotional sympathy while appealing to our intellectual understanding. O'Faolain is also an imaginative interpreter of the men, women, children and adolescents whom he invents and draws with such an apparent ease, so evocatively and so convincingly. Some of his stories remain in the memory; they compel us as we read them to envisage the characters in all their diversity, to give them voices, to dress and, at times, undress them. And with the gently increasing insistence of the author we come, through contemplating them, to an increased awareness of the complexities of life, of its mingled joys and frustrations, of the courage that informs its continuance. . . .

O'Faolain has a tolerance for his characters; he captures wisdom and allows some of his men and women to express it, as in **'Our Fearful Innocence'** and **'Brainsy'**. On other occasions his own appreciation of life irradiates his stories, however poignant a sense of loss it conveys, as in the bitter-sweet **'The Time of Their Lives'**. He understands both men and women; his priests are real, just as his sexually curious adolescents are. He is interested in the growth of maturity, the birth and formulation of ideas. He has achieved a style which allows him complete and varied freedom in narrating a story, in describing a place, or in revealing the inner thoughts and voicing the outer expression of some of them—in dialogue that can be aggressive, ruminative, jocose, mocking, moving, virtually inarticulate or diamond sharp. He can suggest the tone of a voice, the colour of eyes or hair, the shape of lips, the set of garments, the whole physical attitude of a character with economical ease.

> *A. N. Jeffares, in a review of "The Collected Stories of Sean O'Faolain, Vol. 3," in* British Book News, *March, 1983, p. 189.*

JULIA O'FAOLAIN

[In *The Collected Stories of Sean O'Faolain* there 90 stories] written between 1927 and 1982. None has been written or retouched. As [Sean] once explained: "You can rewrite while you are the same man. To rewrite years after is a form of forgery." Bravely, he resists the urge to forge and I, rereading him, am back in his head—or rather in the heads of a series of Seans, the youngest of whom I never knew. It is an odd but exhilarating experience because his best stories are as good as you'll find in anyone's canon—so good they spark off that glee which comes when art triumphs over intractable material: meaning, of course, life.

Life was very intractable indeed during the Irish Troubles and Sean, writing in 1927, was still stunned by its shifts. Unsurprisingly, he wavered beween mythifying and demystifying: an electric mix. His diction was romantic and relied, as he has since observed, "on a kind of verbal music to convey feelings that the mere sense of the words cannot give." It is an unfashionable mode now but, like Romantic Opera, can sweep you up—and it is good at holding metamorphic moments in its ken. Take the first story here. It is about the downfall of an autocratic landlord and manages to combine a *Cherry-Orchard*-like pathos with a cold-eyed view both of the old order's shortcomings and of the loutish insurgent who represents the new one. Elegy plus caricature convey an impression of completeness, and the whole is fused by a lyric exultation in the sodden beauty of the land. Here and there, meanwhile, a judiciously accurate word pinpoints the social context. I am thinking of the landlord leaping in pagan nakedness from his bathing place to terrify some children who are creeping past carrying their shoes and socks. In fright they drop them and later their fathers come "timidly" to look for them. The quiet adverb explains the roots of our botched revolution.

Disenchantment with *that* prevails in stories about the priggish Ireland of the '30s. It can crystallize in compassion or in farce so particularized as to remind one of Gogol. Extreme particularization is a way of avoiding realism: you focus so close that all you see is the tic or mania brought on by social pressure. Sean wrote few satires but those he did—like **"The Old Master"**—are savagely funny.

Later, his humor mellowed and so did his characters. In his middle and late stories these belong to Ireland's new, native upper middle class and have acquired cosmopolitan tastes which they often lack the nerve to indulge. Aging guerrilla fighters, they make love as furtively as they once made war, and their battlefields are purely private.

Critics have praised Sean for keeping up with a changing Ireland, and the Irish themselves are pleased to see their new sophistication reflected in his fiction—for now that the bulk of the population live in towns the old peasant image has ceased to fit. He, however, is not in the business of holding mirrors up to society. As he explained years ago, the short story is *too* short to do more than release the imagination, make characters "appear to appear" and, under the guise of simply telling a story, to "communicate personality." The personality in Sean's later work is rueful, mild, sensuous and indulgent, but also shrewd. Amplifying effects (with the help of landscape and religion), teasing, mocking, engineering reversals and re-reversals of expectancy, he can deal plausibly with the most nuanced and protean reality—and it is to the protean that he is most responsive. His best stories fizz with amusement at his characters' efforts to shirk the rigors of choice. . . . His lenient and lyric eye reminds me of Magritte's painting in which the eyeball is a cloud, and indeed clouds are Sean's favorite prop. Sometimes they are clouds of unknowing which help him to preserve ambiguities, but not always. Sometimes he will yoke airborne imagery to a ballast of realism or even to a deliberately ungainly word, as when he talks of "stars hooked" in the trees. This is from **"The Talking Trees"** (1971), a story about some small boys in the Ireland of his childhood who pay the local bad girl a pound to let them see her naked. Sordid? It could be but for Sean's technical bravura. Take that word "hooked." Its associations (pot hook, grappling hook, addiction) coupled with the distant allure of "stars" focus the contrasting impulses which propel the narrative: innocence and pruriency, anticipation and nostalgia. The story is almost too beautifully written. It needs the clumsy word to connect it to life as we know it. (pp. 5, 7)

My overall favorite is **"The Kitchen"** (1971) in which he grapples with a reality which, he tells us, gives him nightmares even now. These are about his mother whom in earlier stories he conjured away with humor and other therapeutic weapons. Here he confronts her empty-handed. Unflinchingly he lets truth home in so close that it seems there will be no time to bend it to artistic shape before the story explodes with the stressful messiness of life. Then, in the last two short paragraphs, like a skilled martial artist using the momentum of his opponent's attack, he defeats truth with truth. The irrational stubbornness which made his mother so maddening in old age comes from the same source as the nightmares in which, irrationally, he confronts her still. "It was all about the scratching mole. In her time, when she heard it she refused to listen, just as I do when, in my turn, I hear her velvet burrowing, softer than sand crumbling or snow tapping, and I know well whose whispering I had heard and what she had been saying to me." A dark image, but whether they deal with death or life, it is felt reality which powers the most haunting metaphors. (p. 7)

Julia O'Faolain, "The O'Faolain Tradition," in Book World—The Washington Post, October 9, 1983, pp. 5, 7.

BRUCE ALLEN

["The Collected Stories of Sean O'Faolain"] includes everything that appears in the eminent Irish writer's eight previously published collections, plus half a dozen "uncollected stories" dated 1892. Among these 90 "stories and tales" are several undeniable classics, and a few dozen effective entertainments. But, on balance, this is uneven work, unworthy of his publisher's claim that Sean O'Faolain is "one of the great storytellers since the death of Chekhov."

What he is is a remarkably skillful and sophisticated technician who can render a small private world in such evocative, echoing detail that its universal relevance is instantly suggested; a chronicler of local conflicts who's adept at presenting two sides of a contretemps. He's one of the masters of realistic dialogue, and he can bring a character to life in a quick, vivid paragraph.

Why, then, do I not feel O'Faolain qualifies as a great writer? The answer lies partly in his very virtuosity (his ability to create someone or something fascinating, and his habit of shifting impatiently to focus elsewhere), and partly in the distance and distastefulness I infer from his many portrayals of Ireland at war with England and itself. O'Faolain was a republican fighter during the Civil War, but his subsequent writings are far from a glorification of his country's rebellious history. He seems to connect Ireland's truculent separatist spirit with its people's material poverty and their virtual enslavement to obsolete political and religious ideas. It's as if Ireland is a ghost that haunts is own citizens, and Sean O'Faolain is so appalled by their superstitiousness and timidity he's unable to take them fully seriously.

This curious coolness is evident even in O'Faolain's best work, much of which appeared in his first two collections, "Midsummer Night Madness," (1932) and "A Purse of Coppers" (1937). These stories of revolutionary ardor and social disruption are often conveyed to us by a young (usually idealistic) listener-narrator, who's quick to imply judgments on the characters he thus observes. (p. 21)

Several of O'Faolain's thinnest glibbest stories picture ignorant or dishonest priests and nuns; a few are critical of Roman Catholic rigidity. "Teresa" is an engrossing story about a young girl's inconsistent wish to become a nun, and eventual rejection of the religious life; it's interesting because its title character is honest and complex, and because her vacillating devotion is attractively and movingly portrayed. "The Man

Who Invented Sin" describes the experiences of four young novices—two men and two women—on a boating party and then following the accusation that their innocent high spirits have skirted impropriety—a charge that has a lasting, cramping effect on their later lives. This celebrated story (probably its author's best) features one of O'Faolain's finest strokes—a vision of the elderly priest-accuser (as he walked away, "his elongated shadow waved behind him like a tail") as the devil.

Later works, from the 1950s and after, offer more general laments for the passing of the "old ways" ("The Silence of the Valley") and portrayals of people inhibited by the past; then some find they can't escape its grip ("The Fur Coat"), others long for lives different from the ones they've chosen ("A Touch of Autumn in the Air," "The Sugawn Chair.").

This autumnal mood is still dominant in O'Faolain's very recent work, of which not much need be said. The stories from "The Talking Trees" (1970) and "Foreign Affairs" (1976) bring their hidebound locals out of Ireland, into other countries, and into erotic involvements, handled with an increasing sexual explicitness that's far from O'Faolain's best manner. His narrative skills have remained undiminished, and he's never less than entertaining. But of the final two dozen or so stories in this collection, the only one I'd strongly recommend is "Hymeneal," the portrayal of an elderly couple in retirement that builds toward its protagonist's surprise understanding of the kind of person ("an irate man full of cold principle") he has always been.

It will not do, as I've indicated, to compare Sean O'Faolain with the short-story masters—certainly not with James Joyce (whose Olympian view of Ireland's cultural paralysis he shares and imitates), or Henry James (with whom he seems to beg comparison). Still, his best work will be remembered and should be properly valued. (pp. 21-2)

Bruce Allen, "Sean O'Faolain Collection: Evocative but Uneven," in The Christian Science Monitor, October 12, 1983, pp. 21-2.

DENIS DONOGHUE

In the foreword to a collection of his stories published in 1970, O'Faolain acknowledged that his early work was heavily poetical, "full of romantic words, such as dawn, dew, onwards, youth, world, adamant, and dusk"; full, too, of "those most romantic of all words, and and but, words that are part of the attempt to carry on and expand the effect after the sense has been given." His first problem was to find or imagine events splendid enough to appease his style, a style compounded not only of poems learned by heart but of a desire to find the heroic note fulfilled in daily practice. He had the words he loved but not always the occasions to justify them. So he imagined an Ireland continuous with the aftermath of 1916, a country of young men and the glory they longed for. . . . (p. 11)

[In] "Midsummer Night Madness and Other Stories" (1932) and "A Purse of Coppers" (1937), O'Faolain wrote with lilts that preceded the need of them. Even in memorable stories like "Fugue" and "A Broken World," the style is ready to be exorbitant compared to anything it is given to produce. The events come to the end of their tether, but the sentences can't bear to stop. Even in later stories, O'Faolain loves a verbal flourish. . . .

In September 1926, O'Faolain went to Harvard University for three years on a fellowship. These years had the effect of distancing him not from Ireland but from the clamorous rhetoric in its favor. . . . At Harvard, O'Faolain was trying to write fiction in a spirit continuous with what he divined of the European novel and short story. Stendhal was his chosen master, and he learned nearly all he needed to know of the short story from Maupassant and Chekhov. Not from Joyce, incidentally: he admired some of the stories in "Dubliners" but not the book as a whole. Presumably Joyce's pre-emptive irony was alien to O'Faolain. For a different tone of experience, he was already turning his mind toward Italy, a country he came close to adopting imaginatively as his own. For one consideration, Catholicism was Roman even more than it was Irish, though no Irish priest would have accepted the fact.

Within a few years after his return to Ireland, O'Faolain was yet again a changed man. He still loved Ireland but not the Ireland De Valera was governing. O'Faolain turned aside from his hero and wrote a severe book largely disowning him. The De Valera in power was not, O'Faolain maintained, the leader he had followed in the Civil War. Now he found Ireland a dispiriting place, meanspirited, repressive, parochial. For a while, he continued to write stories of priests and penitents, saints, lords and masters, but increasingly he found himself reaching out toward a larger imaginative space. . . .

It is clear from **"The Man Who Invented Sin"** and the collection in which it appears, **"Teresa and Other Stories,"** that by 1947 O'Faolain had accepted, with as much grace and humor as he could produce, that Ireland was now bent on new purposes: money and the determination to get on in the world. So long as De Valera remained in office, the new motives had to be deviously pursued. He was still the old De Valera in

certain respects. He wanted Ireland united, the wretched Border removed and the Irish language revived. O'Faolain didn't object to these aims but to the bigoted, narrow-minded atmosphere in which De Valera worked for them. . . .

O'Faolain's recent stories tell of the new Ireland and its discontents. He still has a soft heart for the country—haven't we all?—but he sees it now in a sharper style. He has made his most telling stories from the incongruity between old and new ways. The recent stories tell of bourgeois Ireland, new Dublin rather than old Cork; not priests and heroes but upper-class doctors with mistresses and laundered money, Catholicism in the sleek suburbs. O'Faolain has stayed the course, rueful but even yet not totally disenchanted.

Now we have a large volume of his short stories [**"The Collected Stories of Sean O'Faolain"**], choice work of more than 50 years in his favorite genre. He has written in many other forms—the novel, autobiography, biography, history, travel—but the short story might have been invented to gratify his talent. Such stories as **"Childybawn,"** **"The Silence of the Valley,"** **"Lovers of the Lake"** and—a favorite of mine—**"Charlie's Greek"** are the work of a true artist. It is splendid to know that O'Faolain, reading and writing now in Dun Laoghaire outside Dublin, is still observing the scene, making notes, putting up with Irish follies as if they were foibles rather than evidence of a settled disposition. "To me, now," he said a few years ago, "Ireland is worth my attention only when it is the world." But it is, Sean, it is. (p. 27)

Denis Donoghue, "Ireland and Its Disconents," in The New York Times Book Review, *October 30, 1983, pp. 11, 27.*

Sharon Olds
1942-

American poet and critic.

Olds is regarded as a promising poet on the basis of her first two volumes, *Satan Says* (1980) and *The Dead and the Living* (1984). She often writes about pain, anger, and violence with extreme emotional involvement, but she also depicts with gentle humor her experiences as a girl, a woman, and a mother. Despite the intensely personal nature of Olds's poetry, critics note her ability to evoke the universal. They also praise her handling of such contrasting topics as violence and love, death and life, and terror and humor.

(See also *Contemporary Authors*, Vol. 101.)

ROCHELLE RATNER

[*Satan Says* is] an emotionally young book: hate and love of parents, woman suddenly out on her own, the frightened wife and mother. Olds's experience can easily be shared: she focuses on simple, everyday occurrences and uses the poem to give them deeper meaning. There are a few first-book problems, such as an overuse of tough sexual words (which after a while seem thrown in for shock value), a self-consciousness about being a writer, too many similes, and a few images which verge on the superficial, but these are all things which can be outgrown easily.

Rochelle Ratner, in a review of "Satan Says," in Library Journal, *Vol. 107, No. 6, March 15, 1980, p. 728.*

SARA PLATH

Sharon Olds' poems [in *Satan Says*] are perpetually balanced at the edge of hyperbolic violence—a balance maintained between the deep psychological sources of her poems and the vivid, many-layered imagery in which they are expressed. . . . There are poems of extreme emotions, and though Olds occasionally becomes mired in her own tendency toward bombast, the many poems that achieve their proper mixture of reality and nightmare are simply stunning.

Sara Plath, in a review of "Satan Says," in Booklist, *Vol. 77, No. 1, September, 1980, p. 26.*

LISEL MUELLER

Sharon Olds's first book [*Satan Says*], which is uncompromisingly autobiographical, is divided into sections titled for the roles in which she experiences herself, "Daughter," "Woman," and "Mother." There is also a fourth section, called "Journeys," which implicitly connects the three roles. The poems are passionate and, especially in the "Daughter" group, explosive with pain and anger. She moves (and usually persuades) us by the very passion, even need, of her utterance. By the same token, she sometimes allows her rage to go out of control, using a voice so vehement, a language so hyperbolic, as to incur disbelief, at least in this reader. The line

between a language that can accommodate extremes of hurt and outrage, and a language that either distorts or fails to sustain its momentum, is especially thin in the first half of the book, which also contains some instances of uneasy metaphor. In **"Love Fossil,"** for example, the poet's father is compared with a "vegetarian" dinosaur: "massive, meaty, made of raw steak, / he nibbled and guzzled, his jaw dripping weeds and bourbon . . ." And in **"Monarchs"** she compares a lover's touch to that of the butterfly: "their wings the dark red of / your hands like butchers' hands . . ." Even if one accepts the comparison between the orange wings of a monarch butterfly and a man's hands, the match is annulled by the added simile. Monarch wings can't be like butchers' hands, by any stretch of the imagination.

Having got the carping over with, I want to point out that these problems are restricted to the first two sections and are even there intermittent. By far the greater number of her poems are believable and touching, and their intensity does not interfere with craftsmanship. Listening to Olds, we hear a proud, urgent, human voice. The divisions of the book—the theme-and-variations approach with its clustering of poems that overlap in tone and subject—accentuate its urgency. It's as though Olds wanted to mine one vein relentlessly and exhaustively before striking elsewhere. The "Daughter" section is an act of exorcism, a way of coming to grips with an unhappy, brutal childhood and the poet's love for a rejecting father. The "Mother" poems explore more fully than I've seen before the complex feelings of a young mother whose overwhelming desire is to protect and whose fear for her children is rooted in self-knowledge. "Journeys" stands somewhat apart from the rest of the book, partly because it is less concentrated thematically and partly because the language is purer and darker, pointing perhaps to Sharon Olds's next volume. (pp. 171-72)

Lisel Mueller, "Three Poets," in Poetry, Vol. CXXXVIII, No. 3, June, 1981, pp. 170-74.*

JOYCE PESEROFF

Sharon Olds survives the battling of an alcoholic father and a mother who ". . . took us and / hid us so he could not get at us / . . . so there were no more / tyings by the wrist to the chair, / no more denial of food" ("That Year"). Olds consistently sees her personal survival in terms of the primal, female relationships of Daughter, Mother and Lover. These are, in fact, three of the [four divisions of Satan Says], and the relationships quiver to life in poems bristling with comparison, metaphor and simile—mighty attempts by one woman to connect a disconnected world.

For instance, in ["Love Fossil"] from the section "Daughter" what is most striking is Olds' vigorous and fecund metaphorical imagination. . . . Father as dinosaur is a fit beginning for Olds' habit of describing the body as spirited, inhabited, and wild. . . . And in "First Night" (first poem in the section "Woman"): "The inhabitants of my body began to / get up . . ." as "Rivers changed course, / the language turned neatly about / and started to go the other way."

Throughout Satan Says the language often does "turn neatly about." In Olds' vocabulary ordinary objects, landscapes—even whole planets—are in constant motion. Using verbs which might seem, at first, almost grotesque, she manages to describe a violent, changing universe where "the sky rubs against itself / as if about to create a planet" ("Geography") and trees "looked as if they could do anything— / put down the other leg and walk away" ("The Opening"). Explanations such as, "When two plates of the earth scrape along each other / like a mother and daughter / it is called a fault" ("Quake Theory"), assign to that primal relationship the weight and gravity of the ground on which all of us stand.

As well as describing the dangers, Sharon Olds creates a standard of heroism for her survivors. In "The Language of the Brag" the accomplishments of a common woman—more heroic than "excellence in the knife-throw" or "the crossing of waterfalls"—demonstrate an "epic use" for her "excellent body". . . . (pp. 21-2)

Sea change is a motif in "Drowning," "Pilgrimage," "Encounter," and "Fishing Off Nova Scotia," as well as in the poems about pregnancy and birth. In a way, these poems describe a psychic world as turbulent, sensual, and strange as a world seen under water. In each poem there is a risk the speaker will not come up for air. In Satan Says, Sharon Olds convincingly, and with astonishing vigor, presents a world which, if not always hostile, is never clear about which face it will show her. (p. 22)

Joyce Peseroff in a review of "Satan Says," in The American Book Review, Vol. 4, No. 2, January-February, 1982, pp. 21-2.

PUBLISHERS WEEKLY

The deeply felt cycle of poems [in The Dead and the Living] concerns the universal experiences of death, both public and private, and life. . . . From executions in Iran to her own miscarriage, Olds writes about the loss of life with passion, yet control. Her language is direct, her imagery vivid, her subjects credible. There is a poem about her aging grandmother, still witty and full of life, another about her mean grandfather who drank, and her father who resembled him. In "Poems for the Living," Olds confesses her mother's fierce hatred of her husband and the influence of this on the children. In a gentler vein, she tells of her own children growing up, and the depth of a mother's love. This admirable volume is the poet's second collection of verse.

A review of "The Dead and the Living," in Publishers Weekly, Vol. 224, No. 20, November 11, 1983, p. 40.

HAROLD BEAVER

"The Dead and the Living" is a family album prefaced by snapshots of the century's agonies—images of executions, race riots and gory death from Tulsa, Okla., to Chile and from Rhodesia to Iran. O.K., we can take it. At this theatrical distance we are not touched to the core. . . .

Such horrors are thawed by the rhythm of words: They remain static conundrums to be puzzled out with a meditative gaze. Only when this photographic technique of intimate exposure is transferred to her family does Sharon Olds come into her own. It is the private scrutiny that shocks—the day of her mother's divorce, her first period, sex after childbirth, a 6-year-old boy's erection on the back seat of a car. Nothing is too personal, too intimate for such scrutiny.

The confidence of the best of these family portraits is astonishing. Only rarely does Miss Olds fall into cliché or sentimentality. Patterns are traced from grandfather to father to son—a family curse of "cruelty and oblivion" as relentless as that of the house of Atreus. Not that Miss Olds would make such gestures. She is consumed wholly by the present. . . . Confidences are made without a trace of embarrassment but with a hint of sacrificial pride. Each family, as it were, harbors its own little Dachau. (Here a macabre form of modern self-regard creeps in.) The poet might dream of a perfect father in place of the real one with "his bad breath, / his slumped posture of failure," but the female is as ugly as the male: "Finally I just gave up and became my father."

This identification evolved into the brilliant "Poem to My Husband From My Father's Daughter." . . .

Even her 6-year-old son is a killer. . . .

So the theme spills over from the public to the private and so to the children themselves. It corrodes the century. Yet Sharon Olds is no Sylvia Plath. Her "bad grandfather" who "wouldn't feed us" and her Hitler entering Paris are the stuff of very private, generous ruminations. They are not the cries of a soul in torment. What lingers is not horror, but laughter—her grandmother's cackling crack-corn laugh when taken on an outing from her nursing home or the poet's own amused celebration of her son's birthday party, which he and his friends transform into something between a bankers' conference and a war game. . . When the confessional drive is tamed to such life studies, it is not the agony we are likely to remember but the persistent comedy of human love.

Harold Beaver, "Snapshots and Artworks," in The New York Times Book Review, *March 18, 1984, p. 30.*

ELIZABETH GAFFNEY

[*The Dead and the Living*] explores the bonds of love and terror that hold a family together. This beautifully structured collection, the Lamont poetry selection for 1983, moves from public to private, from poems for the dead to poems for the living. Always, Sharon Olds's voice is a private one, even in the "public" poems. She insists on making us see the intimate details of public atrocities: the "pale spider-belly head" of a newborn dead in Rhodesia, the face of a starving girl in Russia, the "blazing white shirts" of white men in Tulsa race riots. Her images in this first section of poems are as unflinching and immediate as news photographs.

Sharon Olds takes risks. This is clear as we move into her "private" poems for the dead and the living. "My bad grandfather wouldn't feed us," begins a poem called **"The Eye."** "He turned the lights out when we tried to read." The effect of this sort of revelation is not to titillate or to unload old grievances, though at times I was taken aback by the poet's boldness. Olds accumulates many details of her family history, some shocking, and with these she weaves new patterns, startling images of recognition. (pp. 497-98)

Sharon Olds's poems for her own children are among the best in this volume. Here her tenderness and her unshrinking eye for detail work together to create new ways of seeing children's growth and vibrant sexuality. Olds is wry, inventive, full of humor and love in these poems. . . . In **"Exclusive,"** the poet watches her daughter at the beach, "memorizing" her "against the time when you will not be with me," and concludes: "Today I see it is there to be learned from you: to love what I do not own."

I admire Sharon Olds's courage in *The Dead and the Living*. Out of private revelations she makes poems of universal truth, of sex, death, fear, love. Her poems are sometimes jarring, unexpected, bold, but always loving and deeply rewarding. (p. 498)

Elizabeth Gaffney, in a review of "The Dead and the Living," in America, *Vol. 150, No. 24, June 23-30, 1984, pp. 497-98.*

Craig Raine

1944-

English poet, critic, and editor.

Raine is regarded as an important new poet who has brought a sense of vitality to English poetry of the late 1970s and early 1980s. His distinctive style emphasizes startling images and strange metaphors to make the familiar world seem fresh and newly discovered. Several of Raine's contemporaries, most notably Christopher Reid, share this technique of presenting images from an alien viewpoint. Critic and poet James Fenton used the term ''Martian School'' to describe this group of poets.

Raine first gained recognition for poems he contributed to such British periodicals as *The New Statesman* and he was known in England as a clever poet by the time his first book, *The Onion, Memory* (1978), appeared. In his second and third volumes, *A Martian Sends a Postcard Home* (1979) and *A Free Translation* (1982), Raine continued his playful use of language and metaphor. Some critics fault his work for not addressing human emotions or concerns, but most agree that his impact on English poetry has been enlivening and significant.

(See also *Contemporary Authors,* Vol. 108.)

DEREK MAHON

Only occasionally does a poet appear whose voice is instantly and uniquely recognisable, and Raine is such a poet. Pseudonymous and badly type-written, as for a competition, a poem by him would not long retain its pseudonymity. His peculiar and startling metaphors would give him away at once. Also his predilection for the present indicative tense. Thus:

> Surrounded by sausages, the butcher stands
> smoking a pencil like Isambard Kingdom Brunel.

Most things in [*The Onion, Memory*] happen like this, and while they can become tiresome, wearying you with their gratuitous cleverness, one must acknowledge the figurative sureness of touch, the surprise and pleasure Raine provides, not only at his best but almost as a matter of course.

Contemporary English poetry is full of people—living, loving, dying and being remembered. This is appropriate in a humanistic culture. Raine's poetry, too, is densely populated, but the object has a life of its own—not as a rule the anthropomorphic life attributed to it by certain French and American poets, although at one point he does say precisely this:

> Esse is percipi. Berkeley knew
> the gentle irony of objects, how
> they told amusing lies and drew laughter,
> if only we believed our eyes.

But something (a fear of pretension, a distrust of the numinous?) keeps him chary of an intellectual commitment to this line of thought, with the result that what might have been (might yet be, perhaps) metaphysical in the strict sense, remains merely playful. Some, including the poet himself no doubt, will take issue with that 'merely', but I offer the observation for what it's worth. This is, of course, a first volume;

and who, contemplating, say, the early work of Wallace Stevens, could have foreseen 'The Idea of Order at Key West'? Playful or not, an attentive interest in the things of this world is no bad way for a poet to begin. Perhaps it's the best way, even the only way. An accusation of mereness would be premature. But I'm reviewing *The Onion, Memory,* not his future work, so let me return to it, with its Nabokovian title.

Nabokov, in *The Real Life of Sebastian Knight,* speaks of 'that real sense of beauty which has far less to do with art than with the constant readiness to discern the halo round a frying pan'. Raine appears to have little interest in 'beauty', 'art' or halos, but his imagination is fired by the sight of a cheesewire ('a sun-dial selling by the hour'), a wall-phone ('the flex / is Jewish Orthodox'—I presume he means Hassidic), the 'Regency stripes' of a college lawn, a horse's mouth 'like a boxing glove', 'cabbage whites with caviar eyes', a spectacle case 'like a mussel'. These are the things for which this collection will be deservedly praised.

As for its human population, I'm not so sure. A poet like Douglas Dunn, who has already submitted objects to the Rainean treatment, and as arrestingly (television aerials like Chinese calligraphy, 'the music inside fruit'), has also written so well and with such insight about other people that nothing less will suffice. I fear that Raine, preoccupied with the quiddity of objects and the figurative *trouvaille,* doesn't really give a damn about the butcher, the baker and the candlestick maker: he prefers the company of the chop, the loaf and the candlestick. This wouldn't matter if he didn't sometimes seem a little heartless.

Thus, consider **'Home for the Elderly'**, where youth appears to mock at age, or **'Danse Macabre'**, where a man who has collapsed on the pavement is whimsically compared to a Blue Period Picasso. 'All day he wrings his hands, crying buckets', says Raine of a window cleaner; but this tells us nothing about the window cleaner, only about language. James Joyce, whom he clearly admires (two of the poems bear Joycean epigraphs), told us about both. . . .

Conventionally enough, the one moving poem in the book, and the most achieved, is the title poem, in which the poet revisits his ex-wife:

> Divorced, but friends again at last,
> we walk old ground together

They pass an amicable and inconsequential day while, outside, 'the trees are bending over backwards / to please the wind'. He slices onions; she does some sewing: 'It is the onion, memory, that makes me cry.' Here, at last, is the human face; and, as if to acknowledge the depth of his engagement, the object itself rises to the occasion.

> *Derek Mahon, "Have a Heart," in* New Statesman, *Vol. 95, No. 2466, June 23, 1978, p. 852.**

DEREK STANFORD

Aristotle once said that the capacity to mint new metaphors was the readiest test of a new poet. If we accept this rule-of-thumb as valid, Craig Raine commences with a full head start on most of his versifying coevals. To borrow from his own method, I might describe his first volume *The Onion, Memory* as a bee-hive, a wasps' nest, a tank of tropical fishes. All imply animation and colour, and all these have the power to irritate and sting the literal-minded reader or one with a conservative imagination.

One does not win the first and second prizes in the Cheltenham Festival for nothing; and there is no doubt that Mr. Raine has a feather-fine weathercock way of catching the nuances of similitude where another would discover only incongruity. With words as the instrument of observation, he is phenomenally quick on the draw; quick to spot an unlikely likeness and swift to convert it into something rather like a visual epigram. . . . This trigger-happy cleverness, however, reminds me—not directly, but status-wise—of the Scots poet Norman MacCaig (who has one over him in verbal music), and I wonder whether Mr. Raine's kind of talent is of the sort that might stay imprisoned in the strait-jacket of a virtuosity which he is forever renewing. No doubt, it is proof of his style's infectiousness that again I express my doubts in terms of his own figurative fashion when saying that he seems like a public entertainer who, in Trafalgar Square or on Margate sands, draws his crowd by binding his arms with knotted ropes which he then skilfully proceeds to undo, only to repeat the trick again and again. One thing must be allowed him: it is not a confidence trick but a real one; and only an exceptionally agile dealer in language could carry it through with such self-assurance.

What I have previously said may seem an ungracious niggling way of welcoming a new poet well worthy of critical salutation. (pp. 22-3)

> *Derek Stanford, "The Muse and Metaphors," in* Books and Bookmen, *Vol. 24, No. 1, October, 1978, pp. 22-3.**

ALAN BROWNJOHN

The Onion, Memory is about the drunkenness of things being transmutable: transmutable not into symbols (which is a comfort) but into other things which can be cajoled or laughed into seeming ridiculously like them. . . . The brilliance of Raine's invention does serve to prevent the poems becoming mere boxes of whimsical tricks, even where one sees that he might have gone on for as long as the available detail lasted out— he seems aware of the dangers in **"Professor Klaeber's Nasty Dream"**; and Craig Raine in a junk shop could be a nightmare indeed. But the whole procedure also precludes much chance of normal human concerns breaking in; whereas they always did with MacNeice, and one at least respects McCaig for pushing his fancies out to wider horizons.

The Onion, Memory contains no more than three or four poems where the poet himself manages to emerge from under his own pile of coloured balloons. These include the title-poem, and **"Epithalamion"**, arguably the best one in the book, where the lovers lying in a field—transmuted into a wedding party with "a thousand parsley parasols"—sense a destructiveness in their liaison. . . . There is something unsatisfactory about a poetry which obliges the reader first to puzzle out, and then to test, the appositeness of a hundred local effects. This can't be the way poetry should be read, and if a telling point *is* made through bizarre clusters of metaphorical devices, it is quite possible that it could be made without them. With so much enterprise about—and so much intelligent calculation—one waits eagerly for those dim shadows in the wings to come out and show themselves as poems which are moving as well as ferociously ingenious. (pp. 63-4)

> *Alan Brownjohn, "Heads, Tongues & Spirits," in* Encounter, *Vol. LI, No. 5, November, 1978, pp. 63-9.**

LAWRENCE SAIL

Craig Raine's first collection [*The Onion, Memory*] displays a formidable gift for metaphor and simile. Thus a barber 'flies electric shears fringed with steel / from a row where they sleep like bats', dogs 'grin like Yale keys', lizards asleep are 'perched pagodas with tiny triangular tiles'. Throughout the book comparisons come thick and fast (together with a liberal smattering of puns). Often they are remarkably apt and precise—chickens in a butcher's are 'stripped to their aertex vests'; a spectacles case 'lies on the counter like a mussel'—and they succeed best where they are not strained beyond their capacity, in poems like **"Meditation at Spring Hill"**, **"Memory"** and (beautifully observed) **"The Horse"**. But sometimes the sheer weight of detailed comparison threatens the original object of the poet's attention, and the images become arresting in a bad sense: feelings and attitudes, though present, are too often submerged. The division of the book into six sections, and of nearly half of the poems into couplets, tends to heighten the impression of dislocation. Likewise with the final long poem, *Anno Domini*—there are brilliant moments, but no very clear overall shape or purpose, for all the biblical references. The reader may wonder uneasily whether, in this book, the total is less than the sum of its parts—a poet accumulating power without quite knowing what to do with it. Mr. Raine seems to be aware of the problem, when he writes of '. . . metaphor, / God's poetry of boredom'. . . . Given his obvious acuteness, it would be good to see Mr. Raine moving closer to the centre, and in the process increasing the traffic along what he calls in one poem 'the branch-line of the heart'. (pp. 58-9)

Lawrence Sail, "Fruits of the Fall," in Poetry Review, *Vol. 68, No. 4, January, 1979, pp. 57-60.**

ANDREW MOTION

If Craig Raine didn't exist he'd have to be invented. After the Movement's ironical circumspection, and the agonised candour of confessional poets, his work represents a long-awaited return to exuberant imaginative playfulness. But fulfilling the prophecies of literary trend-spotters hasn't ensured him a universally warm welcome—like most original books his first collection, **The Onion, Memory,** sharply divided public opinion. In the year or so since its publication, however, there have been signs that several erstwhile opponents have become repentant advocates—sometimes so admiringly that Raine has been promoted from *enfant terrible* to Grand Young Man with unseemly haste. **A Martian Sends a Postcard Home** gives a chance to assess his claim to the new title, and because it follows hard on the heels of its predecessor, it does so at a point which would seem previous in almost any other poet's career. The advantage of this, obviously, is that it confirms the impression of abundance he has already given. The disadvantage is that it risks provoking the charge of repetitiveness or self-parody.

A few poems in the new book can be accused and found guilty. But feelings of *déjà vu* are usually infiltrated by pleasure at discovering Raine's energy and generosity undiminished. The innocent precision of his metaphors is astonishing—nowhere more so than in the title poem's description of a telephone:

> In homes, a haunted apparatus sleeps,
> that snores when you pick it up.
>
> If the ghost cries, they carry it
> to their lips and soothe it to sleep
>
> with sounds. And yet, they wake it up
> deliberately, by tickling with a finger.

This kind of perception is more than simply a means by which the ordinary becomes strange again. It's also Raine's method of realising and releasing emotion. Once, extraordinarily, he was accused of heartlessness; in fact, poem after poem registers a deep affection for what he sees. His way of looking is also a way of baring his heart.

Raine knows this only too well. But where he was prepared to keep quiet about it in **The Onion, Memory,** his recent poems suggest that he wants to tell us—as well as show us—how much he cares. The result is that we feel less inclined to believe him. **'Shallots'** and **'Down on the Funny Farm'** both threaten their own integrity by introducing chunks of self-analysis, and **'In the Mortuary'** contains another, related cause for anxiety. As so often elsewhere, he seeks to record his compassion by examining a physical detail, but exploits the strategy to a point at which technique commands more attention than content. . . . (p. 947)

This tendency for Raine's poems to be knowingly tender, and thereby have too palpable a design on us, is a disquieting

development. To some extent, no doubt, it's the product of containment within the peculiarities of his style: the longer he uses it, the more debilitatingly self-conscious he becomes. But he's aware, as well, of the need to overcome this danger—hence the significantly large number of narrative poems in the book. The stories and characters in **'Oberfeldwebel Beckstadt',** for instance, or **'In the Kalahari Desert',** are seized upon as the means of escaping his own tyrannical characteristics. The trouble is that try as he might, he can't keep himself at bay. Brilliant metaphors break up the sequential flow into a series of fragments, and masks slip to reveal the poet as we've always known him. Raine is not the first poet to cast a Martian eye on life, on death—it's his concentration on the procedure that makes him an innovator. (p. 948)

Andrew Motion, "Alien Eyes," in New Statesman, *Vol. 98, No. 2543, December 14, 1979, pp. 947-48.**

PETER PORTER

It's hard to decide where Craig Raine's originality lies. Every poet uses metaphor, and some do so more bizarrely than him. Yet, after only two books, it can be said, of him, as Wyndham Lewis wrote of Auden, that he 'is the new guy who's got into the landscape.' We are beginning to see things in a Martian way ('Martian' is James Fenton's adjective for the Rainian method).

This is a considerable achievement, since Raine bypasses avant-garde battles, while setting style too high among his priorities to be a documentary realist. **'A Martian Sends a Postcard Home'** is a better book than **'The Onion, Memory,'** because it is a concentration of his talent, and an intensification of his mannerisms. He hasn't set out on new paths after his initial success, but decided to tune a shining engine to perfection. To his detractors, the Raine mechanics are by Fabergé, to his admirers, by the Supermarine company. This new collection may seem to depart from his former practice by including several poems telling stories—**'In the Kalahari Desert,' 'In the Dark'**—but there were plenty of submerged narratives in his first book.

Raine's Martian describes life on earth from plausible clues which misinterpret everything. . . . Throughout these poems, the purpose of metaphor is not the illumination of the unfamiliar by the better-known, but the sophisticated discovery of parallels which raise us above the everyday by their striking distortions of emphasis. . . .

Those of us who retained strong doubts after Raine's first book appeared have been rebuked by his admirers for failing to appreciate how haunting his images of human feeling are. Certainly **'A Martian sends . . .'** touches our nerves and remains in our memories more than most books of poems do. For me, the test remains whether this triumph of style can escape from its own brilliantly contrived limits.

Peter Porter, "The World Upside Down," in The Observer, *January 6, 1980, p. 36.**

DAVID YOUNG

I was contemplating some interesting differences between two established British poets and two new ones, when I learned that I had stumbled into a School. We don't have those very often in poetry these days, but if my source, a newspaper mention, is correct, both Christopher Reid . . . and Craig Raine

. . . belong to the "Martian School" of poets, who presumably try to look at the world as though they had just arrived from another planet, seeing it new and making it new by powerful and unusual metaphors.

It isn't wise to take journalistic mentions of literary schools too seriously, but I can testify that I was mildly intrigued, before I had any notion of a connection between these two poets, by their joint effort to introduce some new vitality into British poetry. I had been looking at new books by two established poets, Ted Hughes . . . and George MacBeth . . . , and shaking my head in dismay. . . .

That's the context, anyway, in which I found myself intrigued by [Raine's volume *A Martian Sends a Postcard Home* and Reid's *Arcadia*]. Both books . . . are uneven, as though their authors were feeling their way into something new, but both have an air of freshness and discovery. These poets seem to locate the interest of poetry in its genius for metaphor and transformation, so that their work is less pretentious and more imaginative than that of Hughes and MacBeth. Raine, for example, holds himself to a strict program of going from one comparison to another, stepping-stone fashion. In Athens he finds "columns of corduroy, weatherworn / lions vague as Thurber dogs" and "pillars sleeping if off / or standing tipsily." These comparisons—to cloth, cartoons, drunks—are reductive and comical. "Mosquitoes," says Raine in the same poem, "drift with paraplegic legs." So they do, and what a strange kiss of particulars that turns out to be. Often the poems add up merely to clever fragments, and sometimes the comparisons ("a naughty wind has blown / the dress of each tulip / over its head") strike the reader as simply childlike, but in his best poems, as for instance **"Flying to Belfast, 1977,"** Craig Raine brings his talent for metaphor to bear on his material in an evocative and reverberating way. . . .

It hasn't happened yet, but if the exuberance of early Auden and Day Lewis and MacNeice were to creep back into British poetry, who wouldn't be grateful? These Martians may bear watching.

> *David Young, "Earthly Observers and Martian Chroniclers," in Book World—The Washington Post, September 7, 1980, p. 5.**

MICHAEL HULSE

With Cheltenham Festival and Poetry Society prizes and *New Statesman* Prudence Farmer Awards to his name, Craig Raine seems to have discovered the formula for the winning poem. His typical aha!-effects, the quick sharp thrusts of his couplets and the riddlemaker's precision of his images all suggest an abundance of that gift for ready metaphoric connection which Aristotle thought central to the poetic sensibility. And critical acclaim has not been lacking. (p. 13)

[Loose] couplets are Raine's preferred form; in *The Onion, Memory* twenty-five of the fifty-two poems are cast in them, and in *A Martian sends a Postcard Home* the proportion rises steeply, twenty of the twenty-four poems being in these irregular couplets. Elsewhere in *The Onion, Memory*—for example, in the title poem or **'On the perpetuum mobile'**—Raine deploys metrical patterns more closely based on iambs, and often allows rhyme, but in the couplet poems rhyme is usually banished (the occasional rhyme or off-rhyme in a poem like **'Kublaikansky'** is untypical) and the cadences are further removed from any iambic model. Out of this rejection of familiar poetic

disciplines grows a new approach to the notion of the couplet, which, in Raine's hands, becomes a vehicle of new firmness and flexibility. Characteristic of this vehicle are four stylistic features. First, we may note the use of the present tense as a norm whose effect is to impart to specificity of observation a sense of general relevance and validity. Second, the syntactic pattern in the couplet poems tends almost invariably toward short, simple sentences containing one finite verb. Third, where a further finite verb is introduced it is common for this verb to be linked by the conjunction 'and' and to be placed at the beginning of the line. This high incidence of lines beginning with 'and' produces a sense of thoughts added, as it were, as afterthoughts; frequently the conjunction yokes together disparate images, and in this way innocent syntax is transformed into the image-maker's linguistic hold-all. It is worth noting here that it is extremely rare to find adjectives linked by 'and' in Raine's poetry; for obvious reasons, the density of imagery well-nigh eliminates description. Fourth, it is characteristic of Raine's couplet line that it ends on a noun. Elementary in itself, this device, in conjunction with the others mentioned here, endows Raine's couplet line with a unity and rightness that are equivalent, in the overall scheme of his poetics, to the Augustan propriety of Pope's couplet line.

Outside his couplets, Raine can sound unfortunately derivative. The title poem of *The Onion, Memory* recalls both Eliot and W. D. Snodgrass, and in **'On the perpetuum mobile'** we find a tone unmistakably borrowed from the early Eliot. . . . The peculiar barrenness of this poem comes from its slavishly derivative use of the tone of Eliot's 1917 volume, and in particular the tone of the 'Portrait of a lady'. It is the strength of Raine's couplet poems that in them (and, it is true, occasionally elsewhere) he develops a manner and tone entirely his own.

This manner and tone, this style in which, for all its necessary limits, the poet is able to achieve triumphs, is always dictated by the overall scheme of Raine's poetics. When I use this phrase I mean to refer to his conception of the role played in poetic creation by images. Without question, poetry has always availed itself of metaphor and simile, but Raine's approach is different in so far as he elevates image-making to the supreme structural principle of his work. In **'The gardener'** Raine is clearly interested in the man at work primarily as a peg on which to hang images; the images *are* the poem, they represent its total structure, and without them the poem would not exist. We can rarely, if ever, say this of the use of imagery by any other poet in the language. (pp. 14-15)

When George Orwell wrote [in his essay "Politics and the English Language"] that 'The whole tendency of modern prose is away from concreteness' and maintained that 'A newly invented metaphor assisted thought by evoking a visual image' he was speaking of prose in terms which, as Pound and Raine would well have understood, apply equally well to poetry; we need only compare (for example) Pound's observation in the *ABC of Reading*: 'In Europe, if you ask a man to define anything, his definition always moves away from the simple things that he knows perfectly well, it recedes into an unknown region, that is a region of remoter and progressively remoter abstraction.' The notion that image-making is the clearest form of definition, and therefore the clearest means of communicating experience, is central to Craig Raine's aesthetic.

Other contexts for Raine's aesthetic suggest themselves, possibly the most persistent being one from outside the Anglo-Saxon tradition. From 1902 to about 1908 Rainer Maria Rilke worked according to a concept of 'Dinge', or things, which he developed fully during his acquaintance with the sculptor Rodin and expounded in his monograph on Rodin, as well as in letters. For Rilke, 'Dinge' held within them the absolute; it is as if all meaning and all relation to life in its relative phases could be perceived through a close enough contemplation of the thing in question. That thing might be anything, from the perceptible or conceptual world: Rilke's poems of this period take animals, birds, flowers, cathedrals, works of the visual arts, people, well-nigh anything as their centres—but *not* emotion, or experience immediately related to a persona. It was important to Rilke, as to the Imagists in their different way, to present his things simply and without discursive interpretation. (pp. 17-18)

Returning to Raine, we find that he too, like Rilke and like the Imagists, possesses an active, outward-looking curiosity which fastens on anything and everything as a possible subject for poetry. His poetry—as he puts it in 'An enquiry into two inches of ivory'—deals with

> Daily things. Objects
> in the museum of ordinary art.

It is interesting that his weaker poems—those in which, as I have already suggested, he adheres too faithfully to the forms of other men—are also those in which he comes closest to examining emotion, and experience related to a persona; his better work looks outward and attempts to embrace the full thisness of the world through exactness of definition. . . .

Raine's images recreate the object-subject, giving us, at their most effective, a Rilkean sense of penetration akin to symbolism. That Raine's things are *not* symbols is evident from the fact that there is nothing beyond themselves that they could represent; but they partake of the flavour of universal validity which we associate with symbols.

Occasionally Raine's images take on a slightly different function, in poems where his prime concern is not so much with essence as with narrative. **'In the dark',** arguably the finest poem in the second collection [*A Martian Sends a Postcard Home*] is an excellent example of this shift of function, the images in it serving as a sort of imagistic shorthand to represent areas of life which are familiar and do not need elaborate delineation. The poem is the story of a girl, her unwanted child, and the social pressures which inflict an inevitable tragedy. No one would claim the story is original; but Raine invests it with a 'ne'er so well expressed' felicity that conjures forth every essential element in the narrative in a handful of precisely-chosen words:

> God danced on his cross
> at the foot of her bed
>
> like Nijinsky having a heart attack . . .

The moral-religious pressures brought to bear in such a case have rarely been as succinctly expressed, and something too of the girl's own mental torment comes over in that image of a Christ crucified, represented in the traditional almost-S shape so close to squirming pain. Raine is surely right to suppose that such images speak for themselves and do not require 'overt moralizing'. The echoes and extremities of the image are clear and whole.

If we look again at **'The gardener'** we see, of course, that it lacks the large moral dimensions of **'In the dark'** and, existing as it does in a realm of sheer exuberance in the activity of image-making, represents a less serious artefact. As I have

already said, Raine uses his gardener as a useful peg on which to hang images. The difference could be compared to the difference between Rilke's poem about the panther, which makes a profound statement on the relationship of will to liberty, and his poem about flamingos, where the simple pleasure and accuracy of observation are the poem's sole justification. If **'The gardener'** is to be defended against those who, like Brownjohn, would see in it (and others of Raine's poems which resemble it) an abdication of seriousness of purpose, the defence must be the same as we would offer for Rilke's poem: that a poetic experience uncomplicated by moral perspectives is no less valid *qua* poetic experience simply because it is simpler. It offers a different pleasure and a different reward; it would be a wilful aesthetic that would therefore reject it out of hand.

In addition to this defence we can add that Raine occupies a position in British poetry in the final quarter of the century similar to that of the Imagists in the first, in so far as his aesthetic of image-making necessarily exposes him to objections such as that which Firkins aimed at the Imagists; and it is undeniably true that when the poetic process becomes merely a process of seeing the poems produced *can* have limitations of the kind Firkins, Fletcher and Hughes suggested. Thus the title poem of *A Martian sends a Postcard Home* is too flashy and glib, too self-consciously manufactures new vision. Poems on familiar moral issues can at times be less successful than **'In the dark',** too: **'In the mortuary'** is an easy poem in a vein long ago made familiar by Gottfried Benn's morgue poems, and the tale of **'Oberfeldwebel Beckstadt'** is an unfortunate string of clichés. *The Onion, Memory* is uneven too; in one poem Raine's talent can be an elevation and a revelation, in the next the rather pompous huffing and puffing of a superannuated wolf. To say this much is to say only that Raine's achievement so far is uneven, and this much can be said of any poet.

But, having placed his aesthetic in perspective, we are equipped to follow his success not only in one, but in two directions: in the production of poetry, and in the changing of the conditions in which poetry can be produced. For one thing already appears certain: that Raine's impact on British poetry must be assessed not only in terms of his own work but in terms of the effects it has on the prevailing climate of poetry. It may even be that his own work will fail to maintain the high standards he has set himself in his best poems in the two volumes to date, and to a certain extent that will cease to matter. If he has a truly robust talent he may well develop along the lines of Rilkean symbolism, or he may follow Pound's course towards fragmentation and juxtaposition, or he may find an alternative of his own—or he may cease to produce good poetry; speculation is foolish. But his impact on British letters in the brief span of time since his first two collections appeared, in 1978 and 1979 respectively, has been immense. The adjective 'Martian' is everywhere current whenever an unusual angle of looking at the world is under discussion, and, looking beyond Raine's Oxford stable-mate Christopher Reid, whose poetry shares many of the characteristics of Raine's, we can already detect the influence of Raine in poems by various hands in magazines, as well as in the first collection [*Looking into the Deep End*] by . . . David Sweetman. It was a commonplace in the second half of the 1970s that British poetry was becoming enervated and lifeless. If Raine has succeeded in injecting new vigour where it was needed his contribution will have been twofold, creative and corrective. (pp. 18-20)

Michael Hulse, "Alms for Every Beggared Sense: Craig Raine's Aesthetic in Context," in Critical Quarterly, *Vol. 23, No. 4, Winter, 1981, pp. 13-21.*

ROBERTA BERKE

[The] boldness, which distinguishes Raine from other young British poets, comes from his audacious use of images to make his poems vivid and multifaceted. "Rain is when the earth is television." His descriptions are precise but unfussy. Excessive details can make some of his poems rather static; yet, "In the end, the detail reaches out." These details enable him not only to extend his metaphors, but also to concentrate them. Because he can capture an object with a few details, he can move from idea to idea very quickly and conjure incongruities. This startles us and makes us look more closely: suddenly we realize that incongruities have concealed similarities. (p. 156)

Raine's poems are not surreal, nor are they the result of automatic writing. The everyday (with a few exceptions) is not transported to a personal dream-world. Most of the time, his poems' accuracy of observation keeps them anchored to reality. Yet often they have a very peculiar atmosphere, which the reader first senses in the fusion of the natural and the mechanical.... There are fewer risks of sentimentality if you write about people in the guise of objects, and one might call Raine's method the "ironizing" of both emotions and objects. And he does effectively vault over our cynical defenses, so that by the end of **"Down on the Funny Farm"** we feel sorry for what we thoughtlessly break every day—an egg.... (pp. 156-57)

Not only do objects assume human feelings; they also undergo the death that comes to all of us, and which we attempt to deny and disguise, as we do the crematorium: "this poetic diction, / this building at the edge of town, / its elaborate architectural periphrasis / to avoid calling a spade / a spade...." Often the focus shifts uneasily between the general and the particular, as in **"In the Mortuary."** Here a female cadaver lies without name or distinguishing marks, yet the poem reveals her body in vivid focus and "Somewhere else, not here, someone / knows her hair is parted wrongly / and cares about these cobwebs / in the corners of her body."

Raine's poems also flicker between being "funny" meaning odd and being "funny" meaning amusing. Frequently they have a playful tone, with whimsical puns and juxtapositions that at first may appear as carefree as the toys dropped by a toddler. Yet the jaunty surface of these poems is often a kind of nervous laughter concealing disturbing implications. (p. 157)

Now that Raine has accomplished a great deal in his first two books, he must wrestle against his own natural strength, the metaphor, to prevent it from becoming a mannerism. Raine's achievement is to give us a fresh and even naive gaze at our world, to make us recognize that we are all our own Martian invaders, even on our home planet. (p. 158)

Roberta Berke, " 'We Say, Today. This Day': New Poets," in her Bounds Out of Bounds: A Compass for Recent American and British Poetry, *Oxford University Press, New York, 1981, pp. 150-76.**

LAURENCE LERNER

Craig Raine has given us the very opposite to a *Collected Poems*—six poems [that make up the volume *A Free Translation*].... Because I consider him the most exciting new poet of the decade, the booklet is well worth absorbing and discussing. His talent for seeing the world anew by means of a precise image is as fine as ever: he watches a man rowing "knit / with clumsy oars, / While the waves / unravel their

length", and the circus giraffe "manipulates its jib / like an Anglepoise / awkwardly precise." In this group of poems he has settled to a fixed rhythmic pattern, three-line stanzas—or hardly stanzas, rather breath-groups—with no rhyme and no metrical regularity: an easy-going movement into which the poems fit comfortably. Perhaps too comfortably: one hopes he will begin to experiment in metre in a way that will match his experiments in metaphor.

Unsympathetic readers of Raine's poetry ask if his poems add up to anything more than a patchwork of descriptive *aperçus*. The answer, I am sure, is yes.... Like a true modernist, Raine does not tell us what the situation is, and when we are moving from one speaker to another. The argument for such a method is of course that what we lose is only the prose structure, which a poem is finer and more suggestive for breaking free of; but I find that the information withheld from us is sometimes crucial to the receiving of the poem. **"The Season in Scarborough 1923"** is a wonderful account of the life of the rich as seen by a servant, ending with the poet himself sitting "on the train / to literary London" thinking of her "the day she packed / suddenly homesick / for the real...." Now what is the relation between the poet and the servant? Is it a stranger he happens to know about, or someone he has made up to write a poem about her, or (for instance) his mother? I would like to know this, but I must admit I can see the case for not being told. A more clear-cut case of needing to know is provided by **"The Man who Invented Pain"**, which asks us to imagine how a firing squad in the morning turns the rest of the day into a kind of Sunday for the soldiers, and in this it succeeds brilliantly. But it is introduced with six stanzas about the "he" of the poem—presumably the man they shot—which come so tantalisingly close to telling his story that I feel simply teased at not knowing more. Perhaps Raine wishes to tease me. I can see it would be against the spirit of his poems to offer any but the necessary minimum of explanation; sometimes, for my taste, he drops below the minimum.

Laurence Lerner, in a review of "A Free Translation," in Encounter, *Vol. LVIII, No. 1, January, 1982, pp. 56-8.*

DICK DAVIS

Do our modern poets ever read Richard Hooker? There is a sentence deep in *Ecclesiastical Polity* that describes a great deal of new poetry with alarming precision: 'The mixture of those things by speech which by Nature are divided is the mother of all error.' Craig Raine has made his reputation as the arch-priest of such 'error' and his new chapbook [*A Free Translation*] has its fair share of giraffes as Anglepoise lamps and jelly-fish as Dali watches (Dali, the artist as rearranger of the familiar *par excellence*, comes twice in the book). But Mr. Raine seems already to be growing tired of such games—his first poem moves towards its emotional climax with the question 'What is real?' and in the most interesting of the six offered he compares himself to a housemaid 'suddenly homesick / for the real ...'. In the same way the last poem shows up the sad truths behind the tricks and pretences of a circus: these poems mark a welcome advance on his former work—he seems ready to replace its cute visual punning with a more interesting need to confront the realities that persist beneath the merely spectacular. (p. 22)

Dick Davis, "Missed Worlds," in The Listener, *Vol. 107, No. 2742, January 7, 1982, pp. 22-3.**

DANA GIOIA

At the moment the biggest news in British poetry is the "Martian" school, a group of young poets headed by Craig Raine and Christopher Reid.... This fashionable gang owes its extraterrestial sobriquet to James Fenton, who, when his friends Raine and Reid shared *The New Statesman*'s poetry prize, pointed out the unusual stylistic traits they had in common. Borrowing the central conceit from Raine's prize-winning **"A Martian Sends a Postcard Home,"** Fenton summarized their mission as an attempt to make the reader see the familiar world in an alien way, especially by using bizarre metaphors for everyday objects.

Book reviewers love nothing more than a new school of poetry. It gives some shape, however illusory, to the depressingly vague mass of contemporary verse that crosses their desks. Not surprisingly, therefore, no sooner had Raine and Reid been playfully nicknamed "Martians" than the term worked its way into general critical parlance. Reviewers fiercely debated the merits of the so-called "school," and for a while any poet who ventured a fancy metaphor was comfortably pigeonholed. The resulting publicity made Raine and Reid famous in the attention-starved world of poetry. Their books sold; their poems were anthologized; their imitators proliferated; and Raine, the undisputed leader of the group, emerged as the most influential poet of his generation—not only the E.T. of English poetry but its Audie Murphy as well, having won nearly every honor and award short of the Laureateship.

A skeptical reader might justifiably complain that there is nothing especially new in the "Martian" theory of poetry, their method being only the latest variation of the many *Entfremdung* techniques that have characterized modern literature. But poetic theory ultimately matters very little and practice very much. And in their practice Raine and Reid have created a tangibly new and different poetry, even if the differences are more of degree than of kind. How is this possible in a period when the average poem is bloated with imagery and metaphor? The "Martians'" metaphorical density and ingenuity of language is not in itself as new as their ability to use it to produce poems of suave and graceful transparency. Their best poems are ex-traordinarily rich without being cloying. Likewise if critics complain that the "Martian" aim of making the familiar world seem new is the traditional mission of poetic metaphor, this too is to be expected. All poetic schools earn their reputations by announcing old truths as new discoveries and claiming private patents on general techniques. (pp. 12-13)

If Raine's importance has been overrated by the media, it has also been underestimated by his critics. He is a remarkably inventive poet with a fine ear. The problem with his work—and indeed that of the whole "Martian school"—is not so much one of present performance but future development. The poetry is often bright, fresh, and entertaining; the question is, how long will it remain so? How long can the "Martian" style be exploited before it becomes tired and predictable? How long can metaphor alone command a reader's attention and hide the frequently mundane content of the poetry? As one critic mused, "Metaphor as a way of life. One wonders if it is quite enough."

Raine himself must sense these limitations, for his latest work, *A Free Translation,* shows him tentatively broadening his scope. While this small pamphlet may not mark a new stage in his career, it does reflect a difficult maturation. These six new poems all written in thin three-line stanzas are quieter and more somber than his early work. The sharp metaphors are still there but less densely, and they no longer serve as the driving forces of the poem. Most importantly, however, Raine now shows more personal involvement in his material, more humanity in his approach. As the *enfant terrible* has become a family man, he seems more keenly aware of the responsibilities people have toward one another. But while this humanity adds weight to Raine's poetry, he has not yet mastered it as distinctively as he has imagery and metaphor. *A Free Translation* is a curious book. It contains much wonderful writing but no whole poems as captivating as his best earlier work. Almost every line works well, and yet the poems as a whole are disappointing. They are not bad, just not good enough. (pp. 13-14)

Dana Gioia, "The Barrier of a Common Language: British Poetry in the Eighties," in The Hudson Review, *Vol. XXXVII, No. 1, Spring, 1984, pp. 6-20.**

Ishmael (Scott) Reed

1938-

(Has also written under pseudonym of Emmett Coleman) Black American novelist, poet, essayist, editor, and critic.

One of the leading satirists in contemporary black literature, Reed is best known for those novels in which he examines politics, religion, and technology as repressive forces. Although the central target of his work is Western civilization, Reed's primary concern in his writings is the establishment of an alternative black aesthetic. His new aesthetic, termed Neo-HooDoo, focuses on such ancient rites as conjuring, magic, and voodoo. Reed contends that by reclaiming these primordial rituals, black Americans and third world peoples will purge themselves of Western conditioning and will ultimately regain their freedom and mystic vision. Reed identifies this process as necromancy. In an interview, he stated that "people go into the past and get some metaphor from the past to explain the present or the future. Necromancers used to lie in the guts of the dead or in tombs to receive visions of the future. The black writer lies in the guts of old America, making readings about the future."

Reed's parodies of literary genres produce a combination of the ridiculous and the didactic. His first novel, *The Free-Lance Pallbearers* (1967), is structured as a nineteenth-century Gothic *Bildungsroman*. The young hero in the novel undergoes a chaotic search for self-awareness and purpose in a society obsessed with power. In *Yellow Back Radio Broke Down* (1969), Reed introduces his Neo-HooDoo concept. The novel is a spoof of the Western "dime" novel fused with allegory, contemporary urban culture, and history. Reed extends his Neo-HooDoo concept in *Mumbo Jumbo* (1972) and *The Last Days of Louisiana Red* (1974). Both novels are mysteries in which a voodoo detective, Papa LaBas, attempts to combat the spells and charms cast by the white establishment to anesthetize the artistic and political black communities. Houston A. Baker contended that *Mumbo Jumbo* offers "a conspiracy view of history, a critical handbook for the student of the black arts, and a guide for the contemporary black consciousness intent on the discovery of its origins and meaning." Other critics, however, proposed that Reed's attempt to promote Neo-HooDoo obstructed his creative process and feared that his work was becoming repetitious and rhetorical. In his novels *Flight To Canada* (1976) and *The Terrible Twos* (1982), Reed abandons Neo-HooDoo for zany farce, complete with the irony and hilarious dialogues that are trademarks of his earlier work.

Reed has also published several volumes of poetry and two collections of essays devoted to black culture. In addition, he founded a publishing company devoted to producing and distributing works of unknown ethnic artists.

(See also *CLC*, Vols. 2, 3, 5, 6, 13; *Contemporary Authors*, Vols. 21-24, rev. ed.; and *Dictionary of Literary Biography*, Vols. 2, 5, 33.)

EDMUND WHITE

Flight to Canada is, of all things, a comic exploration of slavery by the best black writer around. The novel is genuinely funny,

© *Thomas Victor 1984*

for Reed has not rendered faithfully the horrors of servitude but rather created a grotesque Civil War America out of scraps and snippets of the past, the present and the mythic. In the process he has put together a brilliant montage of scenes, potent with feeling and thought, designed to flash on the mind's eye with the brilliance of stained-glass windows in a dark interior. The book is memorable, original and wonderfully entertaining.

The main character, Raven Quickskill, is a slave who runs away from his master, Arthur Swille, hides out in Emancipation City and finally, after the war has ended, makes it over the border into Canada. Until his former owner is dead and buried, Quickskill must remain a fugitive, since Swille has resolved to capture him come what may. Throughout the tale the narration alternates between scenes back at the plantation in Virginia and scenes of Quickskill's precarious freedom. (p. 247)

The acrid merriment that boils under the Southern scenes thrills and disturbs us. How can we like these monsters? What moral sense can we make of a novel in which a fugitive slave ends up a whore and an Uncle Tom inherits a fortune (even if he has to forge his master's will to do so)? Reed's fantasia on the classic themes of black suffering is a virtuoso performance. His endless list of names for blacks (cocoas, sables, kinks, mahoganies, spooks, shines, sbleezers, smokes, picks) is as funny and intolerable as a minstrel show. What troubles me is that *Flight to Canada,* the best work of black fiction since *Invisible Man,* both invites and outrages moral interpretation.

I'm not saying that Reed is endorsing inhumanity simply by portraying it; his views are not to be confused with those of his characters. No, the sin and the glory of this book is far more subtle. What Reed has done is to assign to his vicious characters, and to them alone, his own creative vitality—the very same "mistake" Balzac made, the titan whose novels Reed's book brings to mind, not for its style but for its remarkable drive. As someone once pointed out, Balzac's characters were not representative of humanity in general because he made them all geniuses in his own image; Reed has done the same thing with his terrifying Mammy Barracuda.

Quibbles aside, *Flight to Canada* must be hailed as an irrepressibly funny and mordant meditation on the eternal present of slavery in America. The book, however, functions not only as a distorting mirror held up to the continuing history of servitude but also as the record of a single consciousness attempting to kill off the slave within—an heroic project that Chekhov once commended to us all. (pp. 248-49)

> Edmund White, "A Fantasia on Black Suffering," in The Nation, Vol. 223, No. 8, September 18, 1976, pp. 247-49.

JEROME CHARYN

["**Flight to Canada**"] is a demonized "Uncle Tom's Cabin," a book that reinvents the particulars of slavery in America with a comic rage. Reed has little use for statistical realities. He is a necromancer, a believer in the voodoos of art. Time becomes a modest, crazy fluid in Reed's head, allowing him to mingle events of the last 150 years, in order to work his magic. We have Abe Lincoln and the Late Show, slave catchers and "white-frosted Betty Crocker glossy cake," Jefferson Davis and Howard K. Smith. Every gentleman's carriage is equipped with "factory climate-control air conditioning, vinyl top, AM/FM stereo radio, full leather interior, power-lock doors, six-way power seat, power windows, white-wall wheels, door-edge guards, bumper impact strips, rear defroster and soft-ray glass."

It isn't simple fun, backdrops for a minstrel show. The author seems to be telling us that the cluttered paraphernalia of our past, present and future are interchangeable, abused extensions of ourselves, flat and unreal. They enslave us, turn us into pieces of property that smother our feelings, inhibit our rage. (p. 5)

The closest thing to a hero is an Uncle Tom, called "Uncle Robin" in the book. Explaining himself to "Massa Swille," Robin says, "I loves it here. . . . We gets whipped with a velvet whip, and there's free dental care." When his master dies, Uncle Robin inherits the entire estate, after "dabbling" with Arthur's will. "Yeah, they get down on me and Tom. But who's the fool? Nat Turner or us? . . . . Now Nat's dead and gone for these many years, and here I am master of a dead man's house."

The situations in the book remain fairly slick. The comedy often lugs along without a sense of terror. We aren't really moved by Quickskill and Uncle Robin. But it isn't Reed's intention to stick flesh on his characters. They are tropes, ideas that sing and dance for us as Reed plays out his sense of history. "**Flight to Canada**" is a clutch of circus acts that demonstrate paranoia, American-style. For the white man it is "nigger fever," a curious disease. (pp. 5, 12)

The black man isn't immune. He has his own "nigger fever," his own mad jump into the great North American maw. We are all confidence men, for Ishmael Reed. We are masks within masks, little kingfish in a murderous country.

"**Flight to Canada**" could have been a very thin book, an unsubtle catalogue of American disorders. But Reed has the wit, the style, and the intelligence to do much more than that. The book explodes. Reed's special grace is anger. His own sense of bewilderment deepens the comedy, forces us to consider the sad anatomy of his ideas. "**Flight to Canada**" is a hellish book with its own politics and a muscular, luminous prose. It should survive. (p. 12)

> Jerome Charyn, in a review of "Flight to Canada," in The New York Times Book Review, September 19, 1976, pp. 5, 12.

ROGER ROSENBLATT

Ishmael Reed's new novel, *Flight to Canada,* is high and wild comedy, sometimes funny, too often forced, acknowledging a painful life, but not deriving from it. . . . The time is the Civil War, but the jokes are contemporary—jokes about history, religion, education and politics, which are merely okay; and literary jokes which are better by inches. . . .

Reed's central literary joke is also his most sober point: the impossibility of escape (flight) from bondage except by way of oneself; and the attendant conception of North (Canada) as heaven. Writers of black fiction have been dealing with both ideas since the turn of the century, with Walter White's *Flight* in the '20s and Wright's crucial chapter ("Flight") of *Native Son,* and countless versions of "Exodus." In a state of slavery, ancient or modern, the problem is not whether to flee, but where. The so-called "great" migration North changed nothing in and after the long run. By the time Reed takes up the theme, it has become a running gag. . . .

The trouble with *Flight to Canada,* however, is that its laughter also rides only on words, and the words are not sufficient. If the book were funnier than it is, its seriousness would be more memorable. But too many of Reed's jokes are weak or old standup routines, and when you come to the end of his joy ride you haven't laughed enough to be moved by the change of direction. Comedy has to laugh at something other than itself to bring down the house. Or to build it up again.

> Roger Rosenblatt, "North Toward Home," in Book World—The Washington Post, November 14, 1976, p. L4.

NORMAN HARRIS

Central to understanding Ishmael Reed's fiction is an analysis of the ways in which he creates and uses literary folklore. It has for him dual purposes: it is practical and theoretical. Practically it serves to advance the plot, provide structure, defend and raise questions about the nature of society. Theoretically it has at its disposal a vast and largely untapped reservoir of African and Afro-American history, folklore and myth. The components of the practical and theoretical categories are intricately interwoven into a fiction which raises external questions of verisimilitude . . . that are largely absent in the literary folklore of Killens, Chesnutt, Hurston and Alice Walker. Reed labels this confluence of history's external realities and myths' internal or subjective realities "La Bas," a term deeply associated with HooDoo.

In Reed, then, literary folklore can be seen as a structured innovation. The structure relates largely to historical parallels. The history, however, is rewritten through a process that Reed calls necromancy: using the events in the race's past to comment on the present and prophesy about the future. Through necromancy Reed offers us alternative views of slavery, the Harlem Renaissance and the sixties. The innovative aspect is also a function of necromancy: it asserts alternative views of history. This aspect also has a political reality which emerges as a set of reactions to changes in the external world. At such times it attempts to restore order by invoking the old gods, heroes, and heroines and a novel worldview which is based on the old ways of HooDoo. His political literary folklore also seeks, however obliquely, to offer alternatives to existing reality. (p. 41)

As literary folklore, Neo-HooDoo and HooDoo differ radically. Neo-HooDoo is largely urban while HooDoo is rural. Consider, for example, the rural conjurers in Chesnutt's *Conjure Woman* and several of Alice Walker's short stories in *In Love And Trouble* and then contrast them to Papa Labas in *Mumbo Jumbo* and *The Last Days of Louisiana Red*. He is cultured and urbane. His customers arrive in chauffered limousines to "have their heads fitted." In the Chesnutt and Walker stories the conjurers' customers are slaves, or other destitute blacks, who go to the conjurer as more or less a last means of resort. In such cases the problems are specific and limited: a better master or the need to have one's lover returned. Thus HooDoo as literary folklore rarely transcends the resolution of a particular problem. The concern is primarily existential and the larger society, which in most cases is either slave or southern rural, is left unaffected. (pp. 41-2)

Neo-HooDoo takes on whole cultures and thus assumes an epic structure. Linear time is dismissed and replaced by a spatial time which can make ancient history current. Due to its engulfing approach the conjurers in the Neo-HooDoo religion are not, in contrast with the HooDoo conjurers in some Afro-American fiction, specific about their conjurations. Ed Yellings' "Solid Gumbo works" in *The Last Days of Louisiana Red* is loosely defined and amorphous. We only know that it functions to end the plague of "Louisiana Red." (p. 42)

Among the important themes in Reed's fiction are the conflict of blacks and whites, the function of the white critic, the impact of the white man and black woman on the black man, the "field nigger" as political opportunist and the importance of self-reliance. In each instance the literary folklore involved varies in focus and intensity. In delineating the black/white conflict the ancient African past serves as the basis for explanation while the Afro-American slave experience plays a similar role in explicating the theme of the "field nigger" as political opportunist. Similarly, the role of "LaBas" varies: it may be fundamental and precise in making the role of necromancy clear as in *Mumbo Jumbo;* or it may be less crucial and more nebulous as in *The Last Days of Louisiana Red*. The literary folklore, especially necromancy and LaBas, are therefore variable. An explication of the above themes will allow generalizations about the unique politics that influenced them.

In Reed the black/white conflict avoids the stance of a protest novel by being skillfully placed in a historical context which undermines traditional positions on the subject. This occurs most graphically in *Mumbo Jumbo* where in an extended, though truncated, world history, Black Herman relates the conflict between Set and Osiris and how it evolved into two opposing world views. Set, the killjoy "Atonist" (sun worshipper), is the prototype of a certain type western man: as a progenitor of the military-industrial complex, reason must forever remain separate from feeling. Osiris is the working sensualist who combines reason and feeling. As a jazz musician he travels around the world with his original "Roots" band, blaring out the infectious "Black Mud Sound" of the river Nile. While Osiris is away on a gig—this according to Black Herman—Set takes over and ushers in a kind of Puritanism which outlaws dancing and other sensual delights. When Osiris returns Set challenges him to perform his famous seed trick in which he, Osiris, is buried and then springs up like a new bud. If successful, Set says that he will gladly relinquish his Puritanical reign. Osiris accepts the challenge, is encased in a large vase and lowered into the Nile. He is to rise the following day at noon. He never makes it because Set sends his henchmen to remove the vase and to murder and dismember Osiris. Thoth, an Osiris devotee who is given credit for having established a "text" (the "LaBas" method) for the spiritual sensuality which characterizes the Osirian world view, demands an investigation. For his efforts he is run underground where he joins other clandestine Osirian worshippers.

Black Herman's history is considerable: little is left unaffected by the conflict between Set and Osiris. But for our purposes—viewing the black/white conflict in Reed's fiction—it is sufficient to note that Set's followers are primarily white while the Osirian followers are predominantly black. Racial origins are not sufficient, however, in determining to which group an individual might belong. Many blacks in Reed's world have taken the Atonist path—consciously or otherwise. Conversely, numbers of whites find the Osirian approach more to their liking. These, however, are primarily exceptions. Functionally, then, the white/black dichotomy is reflected in the Set/Osiris duality.

In *Mumbo Jumbo* it is the Atonist path that "'Jes Grew'" threatens to humble. "'Jes Grew'" is an infectious entity which animates its host, causing once sober individuals to feel "as if they could dance on a dime." Significantly, *Mumbo Jumbo* is set in the Jazz Age, the era of the Harlem Renaissance—a period when Afro-American cultural activity reached a zenith. In the Jazz Age of *Mumbo Jumbo* this activity, especially as it represented black potential, was symbolized by "'Jes Grew,'" a manifestation of the Osirian worldview. It ignored color, causing even whites to "shake that thang" and to feel "like the gut heart and lungs of Africa's interiors." Therefore the Atonist had to crush this ancient, recurring, though always nebulous plague. For it threatened "civilization as we know it." (pp. 42-4)

The Harlem of the twenties is a hotbed for practitioners of the Osirian worldview. It is a place that the Atonist finds intolerable—too much movement and passion for Set's task. Reed's necromancy places the Jazz Age squarely in the context of an ancient and epic struggle. (p. 44)

The Atonist path in *Mumbo Jumbo* is epitomized by Hinkle Von Vampton. . . . A resourceful white critic, Von Vampton will have no more "white negroes." This heathen thing called "'Jes Grew'" must be eradicated. His chosen method of eradication is, in a generic sense, what it is that "'Jes Grew'" is after: an institutionalized process, that fusion of the psychic and the real—"LaBas." Von Vampton starts a journal, the *Benign Monster,* in which he publishes certain Afro-American writers who follow the Atonist Path. These writers, the *Benign Monster*'s contributors, are intolerant of innovation. They are frozen in time like artifacts of Elizabethan England, dutifully churning out Shakespearean sonnets.

Anything suggestive of an Afro-American folk culture—part of the material which forms literary folklore—is, like "'Jes Grew," anathema. It lacks culture and is primitive: Papa LaBas, the book's hero, is stopped, along with Black Herman, at the door of a reception by an irate black hostess. She shouts, ". . . get out of here you men you gate crashers. I don't want no conjure men's detectives in this house you ain't society you ain't money you ain't no artist you don't have no degree." Such eloquence encapsulates the *Benign Monster*'s editorial policy. (pp. 44-5)

Minnie the Moocher is the Bitch in league with the white man in *The Last Days of Louisiana Red*. (p. 45)

Reed makes understanding Minnie and the Moochers [a parasitic political organization] possible in a broad sense by using the Afro-American slave experience as a reference point. The slave experience provided the occasion for white men and black women to form "unholy" alliances—the former as a kind of patient and the latter as a sex therapist. Together they work to keep the black man in his place. He is acceptable only when he is "on the corner sipping Ripple." Any black man who attempts action that is in his best interest is destroyed. Black men are effectively reduced to a monolith. . . . Minnie is merely a reincarnation of a century old type who functions with the white man to keep the black man in his place. Such is the necromancy; the sixties, or specific aspects of it (certain interracial groups which focus only on a supposed commonality of oppression: a mechanical materialist notion, almost Pavlovian in its predictability, ignores those who confronted and transcended these conditions), are to be understood in this context.

The slave experience also provides the context for the "field nigger." In Reed, this figure is not afforded romantic or sympathetic treatment. Street Yellings, another of Ed's offsprings gone bad, is the modern version of the "field nigger." His field, as his name asserts, is the street; there he is at his spontaneous best. Street is imprisoned for smashing the skull of one of his comrades. There he has his "conscious raised" and escapes to an "emerging African nation." In this nation Street has all the sensual delights imaginable—uppers and downers, endless orgies, and the latest movies. Street is the kind of "nigger" that white men and (black) women can love. They, the women, in fond remembrance of his skill, named a rape clinic after him. Maxwell Kasavubu [a white critic], attempting to lure Street back to the United States in order to head the Moocher organization, resorts to a pastoral tradition which transforms Street into a noble savage. (pp. 45-6)

Flight To Canada treats the phenomenon of the house slave more directly than other Reed novels. In highlighting the character traits of a successful house slave, one who has managed to inherit the plantation, Reed brings self-reliance and Neo-HooDoo together in a fashion that is unique in its thrust. Being aware of the dictum that "God helps those who help themselves," Uncle Robin and Aunt Judy deal with their oppression in two ways. They first do the necessary physical labor, albeit in a cunning fashion, and Uncle Robin then invokes one of the old gods. He says, "Well sometimes the god that's fast for them is slow or even indifferent to us, so we have to call on our gods who work for us." So, through hard work Uncle Robin and Aunt Judy buy their children's freedom and by

praying to the proper god, a HooDoo god, they are able to alter reality.

What is unique about Reed's combination of self-reliance and Neo-HooDoo is its functional duplicity, the getting the job done without broadcasting the intent or technique. In much black fiction a great deal of time is taken in exposing and depicting various injustices. In Reed these things are given; consequently, Reed can concentrate on his Neo-HooDoo informed necromancy. Therefore Reed's characters move with full knowledge: a practical knowledge of past injustices results in a self-reliant attitude which is united with an explanatory Neo-HooDoo. In Reed, then, self-reliance and Neo-HooDoo merge to create a kind of practical/super-natural Horatio Alger story. (p. 47)

The scope, intent and method of Reed's literary folklore are what separates him from other black writers with similar concerns. His channeling of millenium old tales and history into an enlightening contemporary context is unique. His intent is not a flag-waving affair which asserts that "my culture is better than yours" but rather an attempt to let flow the stifled information and accomplishments of third world (non-white) cultures. The method is a structured innovation: all is said but it is said in an unpredictable fashion. The structure relates to historical parallels and the unpredictability to Neo-HooDoo.

Despite what I call "the political uniqueness" of Reed's literary folklore, his writing is not heavy in a pedantic sense. It is inclusive, but its inclusiveness is presented in a manner that is exciting. The aesthetic approach of Neo-HooDoo is what allows Reed's writing to cover so much ground without being tired. (p. 49)

Norman Harris, "Politics As an Innovate Aspect of Literary Folklore: A Study of Ishmael Reed," in Obsidian: Black Literature in Review, *Vol. 5, Nos. 1 & 2, Spring & Summer, 1979, pp. 41-50.*

CHARLES W. SCRUGGS

It is a mistake to see any one black writer as representative of the "black experience" (whatever that is), and it is even a greater mistake to pin a label on a writer like Ishmael Reed. His name is appropriate—he is a genuine maverick. As a critic of American culture, he has taken on smug feminists, omniscient white scholars (who *know* Negro literature), and con men of all colors, creeds, and sexes. . . . As a writer (poet and novelist), Reed belongs to no "school" of Afro-American art, and he has managed to be maligned, with equal intensity, by white and black critics alike. . . . Although the satire in his novels is frequently outrageous (he delights in using the comic strip as a literary device), it can also be subtle—even sneaky. Reed is constantly reminding America of skeletons in her closet, and while his method is often that of the minstrel show, his message is sometimes a pie in the face when you are not looking.

[*Shrovetide in Old New Orleans*] is something different for Reed: a collection of essays, interviews, book reviews, self-appraisals and appraisals of others. Actually, *Shrovetide* is an *apologia pro vita sua* in the guise of a tossed salad. . . .

The best part of *Shrovetide* is the satire. Reed has a sharp eye for absurdity, be it of the white man's making or the black man's. (p. 275)

Reed also uses his mischievous laughter to make some serious observations about American society. The theme of *Shrovetide* can be seen in the title. In Christian lore, "Shrovetide" refers to the three days before Lent, the last day being Shrove Tuesday or "Mardi Gras" ("Fat Tuesday"). This day is one of merrymaking and thus provides the Christian explanation for the famous holiday held each year in New Orleans. Reed insists, however, that another religious spirit is responsible for the joyous anarchy which prevails on "Fat Tuesday": Voodoo (or vodoun, as it is sometimes called). According to Reed, voodoo is the survival of African religion in the New World; this religion (or religions) was transformed by the New World but it remained untouched by (and ran counter to) the dominant Judeo-Christian tradition. Voodoo embraces both the sacred and profane. . . . (p. 276)

Reed argues that as a writer he is "influenced by as many cultures as possible," but in *Shrovetide* he often juxtaposes life-giving voodoo with the life-denying Judeo-Christian tradition. He goes into this subject in some depth, and for this reason I would recommend *Shrovetide* to anyone about to pick up one of his novels. . . . In all of them, Reed sets up a dialectical opposition between Western civilization and the pagan world which it fears and despises. . . . Reed is most brilliant when he turns Western myth on its head, making heroes of the bad guys, and bad guys of the heroes. In *Yellow Back Radio,* the devil is a black cowboy in a white hat (Loop Garu) who squares off with the Pope (who talks like a used-car salesman). In *The Last Days of Louisiana Red,* selfish, willful Antigone tries to push Chorus off stage; the community is threatened by a monomaniac.

I like Reed's brand of looniness, but I run into a problem when I hear him defining his own satire. He calls his "so-called 'humor' . . . affirmative, positive," and goes on to give the impression in his introduction to *Shrovetide* that he is as tolerant and fun-loving as his hero Osiris. Yet on another occasion in *Shrovetide* he says that he is "just a muckraker at heart." Now which is it—muckraker or Osiris? He may be both, but I doubt it. Reed finds too many things wrong with America. His "humor" serves his fierce indignation; he is more Juvenal than Horace.

And this brings up another minor disagreement which I have with Ishmael Reed. For all his talk about being influenced by "many cultures," I find his "humor" distinctly Western, via Aristophanes, Rabelais, Swift, Pope, et al. When he actually visits Haiti, he seems as much a stranger there as I would be— yet I found his essay fun, enlightening and full of the satire I have come to expect from him. . . . My impression of Reed's interest in other cultures is that as a satirist he uses the values of these cultures as a means by which he can expose *our* moral turpitude. He may describe his satire as the "exorcism" of evil spirits, as though he were a voodoo houngan, but the whole tradition of satire in Western civilization is founded upon this very principle of "exorcism." When Reed wrote "D Hexorcism of Noxon D Awful" in the 1960s, he said that he was trying to put a "hex" on Richard Nixon because he thought that America would never impeach him. Jonathan Swift did exactly the same thing to Robert Walpole in *Gulliver's Travels.* Swift felt that England might never rid herself of this power-hungry prime minister, so Swift transfixed his image for all the world to see—and to laugh at. Satire *is* putting a hex on your enemy, and you don't have to go to other cultures to find an explanation for this truth. (pp. 276-77)

Charles W. Scruggs, in a review of "Shrovetide in Old New Orleans," in Arizona Quarterly, *Vol. 35, No. 3, Autumn, 1979, pp. 275-77.*

STANLEY CROUCH

The trouble with *The Terrible Twos* is that [Reed has] said it all before and said it much better. This time out, he's picked another genre to tear apart with his imposition of varied forms and combinations of perspective. Just as he used *Antigone* in *The Last Days of Louisiana Red* to create a brilliant satire that collapsed under the strain of its near-misogyny, and just as he used the western for *Yellow Back Radio Broke-Down,* the detective story for *Mumbo Jumbo,* the slave narrative and *Uncle Tom's Cabin* for *Flight to Canada,* Reed weaves Rastafarianism and a reverse of the Todd Clifton dummy sequence from *Invisible Man* together with Dickens's *A Christmas Carol* in *The Terrible Twos.* Again we get the self-obsessed harpies, the mission Indians, the black hero who takes over the white form (unlike Todd Clifton, Black Peter is not controlled by whites who speak through his mouth—he speaks through theirs), the dumb black street hustlers who get into a game too complicated for them to understand, the corruption of Christianity, the secret society of powerful white bosses, the argument that preliterate custom and belief are just as good as modern civilization (if not better) and the beleaguered black hero who has woman problems (Reed touches on the sexual provincialism of black women, which didn't begin to change until the late 1960s when they had to compete with liberated and liberal white women for the affections of black men, but he doesn't do anything with that proverbial hot potato).

I'm not saying that Reed should abandon his concerns, but I am saying that for all the literary appropriations in *The Terrible Twos,* it hasn't the level of invention that made his best work succeed. There is too much predictability, too much dependence on revelation through conversation and interior monologue. Most of the mysteries must be explained by the characters, and what we do discover through their narratives isn't very interesting. When the President, for instance, is taken into hell, what he sees are the ghosts of presidents and vice presidents past, and there follow heavy-handed scenes of contrition and retribution—Truman grieving over the atom bomb, Rockefeller chained to the corpses of the Attica victims, etc. When Santa Claus and the President get their chance to speak out against the commercialization of Christmas on the one hand and the manipulation of the country by industrialists on the other, the clichés resound. But since Reed considers this novel a surrealist variation on the social realist novel of economic complaint, maybe he thought he should pop the corn rather than serve it in hard kernels. There are some funny passages along the way, however. There is even an attempt to infuse his surreal puppet show with realistic relationships, especially on an erotic level, and this brings what freshness there is to the novel. It also suggests that Reed may soon examine the range of sexual and social attractions that a multiracial society makes so possible, especially since the passage from Europe to the Third World can sometimes take place within only a few city blocks. If that is what he intends for his sequels— *The Terrible Threes* and *The Terrible Fours*—then the world he has developed, one quilted with endless allusions, mythology, improvisation and concentric circles of time and culture, could give birth to the potential so basic to the social contract and to the diversity of this country—Ishmael Reed's All-American Novel. *The Terrible Twos,* unfortunately, is mostly a shadow of his former work, and a shadow that tells us little we don't already know. (pp. 618-19)

Stanley Crouch, "Kinships and Aginships," in The Nation, *Vol. 234, No. 20, May 22, 1982, pp. 617-19.*

IVAN GOLD

The notion that contemporary America—with its movie-star President, passion for military hardware, increasing polarization of haves and have-nots—is as politically mature as a 2-year-old child is socially adept, would seem a thin enough idea on which to peg a novel. But while Ishmael Reed's sixth book of fiction, **"The Terrible Twos,"** takes its title from this notion, and some paragraphs are devoted to developing it, this one theme does not begin to exhaust what the novel is about. Like **"Mumbo Jumbo"** (1972) this latest book is an idiosyncratic mix of political comment, legend, historical analysis, irony, left-handed storytelling, third-world consciousness, pure rage and—amazingly—hope and good will.

"The Terrible Twos" has two parts. The brief opening section, called "A Past Christmas," describes the global and national disarray prevailing around the time of Christmas, 1980, and it introduces some of the characters who will reappear a decade later in the fullness of their influence and/or decline. Part Two, "A Future Christmas," projects ahead to the awful days of December 1990, when the gap between the people called "vital" (those in power) and the people called "surplus" (everyone else) is virtually unbridgeable. The President of the United States is a former male model (clearly a step down the ladder). And Santa himself has been expropriated and syndicated—the result of "a decision handed down in a California court awarding exclusive rights to Santa Claus to Oswald Zumwalt's North Pole Development Corporation." (p. 9)

Lest the plot get away, Mr. Reed jerks the action to a stop from time to time to summarize developments. His own ventriloquial gifts are such that his stick-figure characters take on an eerie life. He can brilliantly parody almost anything: soap opera, newspaper headlines, political cant, the well-made novel. But while the reader is oohing and aahing and ducking for cover, the pyrotechnics sometimes obscure the author's own intent.

Yet some of the best efforts are obtained by two Dickensian excursions. In the first, St. Nick takes the feckless President, Dean Clift, on a trip to "the American hell," where they are greeted by . . . [Dwight Eisenhower] wearing "the jacket he made famous." . . . Harry Truman, who is also there, is described by Ike as the most tormented of the inhabitants: "That was no military act," Ike says of Hiroshima, "that was an insult to nature and to God." Then there is Nelson Rockefeller, the man Mr. Reed seems to love most to hate. He is described as being engaged in a *ménage à trois,* and therefore unable to answer the telephone, when the carnage at Attica occurs.

In his introduction to **"Shrovetide in Old New Orleans,"** his 1978 collection of essays, Mr. Reed (who is also a poet) wrote: "Many people have called my fiction muddled, crazy, incoherent, because I've attempted in fiction the techniques and forms painters, dancers, film makers, musicians in the West have taken for granted for at least fifty years, and the artists of many other cultures, for thousands of years. Maybe I should hang my fiction in a gallery, or play it on the piano."

Maybe he should; but it continues to come at us between covers, pleasantly packaged and modest in length, and apparently he'll "keep on keepin on" until he gets it right. (p. 21)

Ivan Gold, "The Spirit of Christmas Future," in The New York Times Book Review, *July 18, 1982, pp. 9, 21.*

ROBERT TOWERS

The Terrible Twos is the latest in the series of pop-art novels . . . which, with their bizarre inventions and liveliness of language, have won for Reed a small but vociferous following. The book takes its title from the well-known proclivities of toddlers, aged two, who, according to the novel's fake Santa Claus, set the standard of maturity for our great republic:

> "Two years old, that's what we are, emotionally—America, always wanting someone to hand us some ice cream, always complaining, Santa didn't bring me this and why didn't Santa bring me that. . . . Nobody can reason with us. Nobody can tell us anything. Millions of people are staggering about and passing out in the snow and we say that's tough. We say too bad to the children who don't have milk. I weep as I read these letters the poor children send to me at my temporary home in Alaska."

Expanding on this theme, Reed has put together an odd contraption made of many disparate parts—among them the Reagan administration, the Macy's Thanksgiving Day Parade, the hagiography of St. Nicholas, and Dickens's *A Christmas Carol.* . . .

We quickly meet a crowd of cartoon-like characters: a TV executive, Bob Krantz, who, as soon as Reagan's election was confirmed, ordered all the network's black employees to get rid of their corn-row hairstyles; Dean Clift, the top male model of the United States; a little black Rastafarian ventriloquist and his dummy; a dissatisfied wife named Vixen; and a bright young man, Oswald Zumwalt, who works in a department store and has the bright idea of replacing all the Santa Clauses in America with a single Santa who will have exclusive rights to the name. "Santa Claus is too dispersed as it is," says Zumwalt, whose monopolistic Santa will be made available only to those who can pay for his services. . . .

There is nothing subtle about Reed's satire. The ghosts of Eisenhower, Truman, and Nelson Rockefeller, whom President Clift encounters during his descent into the underworld, all perform much as they would in the pages of *Mad Magazine.* Occasionally Reed uses a bludgeon: Truman's ghost can't sleep for fear of dreaming of "Japanese faces, burnt, twisted, and peeling, with no eyeballs"; Rockefeller, damned for his role in the Attica uprising, is taunted on the manner of his death. But mostly the ridicule is as cheerful as it is broad. . . .

Reed must be tired of hearing from reviewers that he should take more responsibility for his inventions, that he needs to hold on to them longer and squeeze them harder before tossing them away. But such criticism is inescapable. While Reed's clowning is sufficiently entertaining as one turns the pages, it isn't, in the long run, clever enough, bitter enough, or (above all) funny enough to nourish the reader's imagination after the book is finished. (p. 35)

Robert Towers, "Good Men Are Hard to Find," in
The New York Review of Books, *Vol. XXIX, No. 13,
August 12, 1982, pp. 35-6.**

MICHAEL KRASNY

I find myself with a troublesome voice sounding off warnings
about what I should and should not say about Ishmael Reed's
new novel, *The Terrible Twos*. And I wonder to what extent
that voice is a phantom of white liberal guilt I thought I had
exorcised.

Exorcism is a good place to begin with Reed. He is the darling
of a number of new fiction critics who see him as the all-
purpose literary necromancer, the black shaman who conjures
vital new myths against the backdrop of the dead carcass of
white western aesthetics. This version of Reed as the juju man
incanting powerfully pyrotechnic amulets called "words" to
rouse us from our cultural decadence is itself a bit moribund.
Reed's powers—and I am speaking here of the literary rather
than the hierophantic—have been on the wane for quite some
time. Like Kurt Vonnegut, he began as a clever new voice of
satire and sanity and simply ran out of steam after too many
novels.

The new novel is a case in point. Which is not to say that there
is nothing in it to challenge our imaginations. But mostly it is
a hodgepodge of social satire that either falls flat or reads silly.
There is little in the book's narrative that is new or even funny,
and funny is at least what we had come to expect from Reed.
Even the compelling qualities of a good comic book, identifiable with earlier Reed fiction, are gone from *The Terrible
Twos,* a would-be spoof on an infantilized and merchandizing
American culture.

The Terrible Twos has all of the material in it for good satire.
Madison Avenue's selling of Santa Claus. America's complicity with Nazis. Reagan as Scrooge. Characters who suggest
the Reverend Jerry Falwell and Richard Viguerie. Somehow
it all adds up to a bunch of sketchy silliness with characters
so flat that, should we choose generously to see them as cartoon
animations, they still seem to have been run over by a steamroller. Reed is the steamroller. With too many targets, esoteric
facts such as the Kentucky Wild Turkey distilleries being protected by guard dogs get interspersed freely with a lot of diffuse
and mostly ineffectual satiric bits. . . .

The Terrible Twos is experimental but nonetheless weak fiction
from a novelist who has thrown some terrible, albeit justified
tantrums publicly, and who has been one of the most visible
and vocal fighters of the good fight of breaking down racial
barriers in the publishing and literary reviewing worlds. But
he has never been the heavyweight that some critics, perhaps
feeling themselves up against the wall of white liberal guilt,
have championed. An experimental black fiction writer like
Clarence Majors would lay Reed out cold. So would . . . writers
like Ernest Gaines and Al Young, neither of whom is as visible
or as vocal, and hence, as recognized as Reed. One thinks,
too, of a host of more gifted black writers who have been
virtually ignored by critics. . . . Both Alice Walker and Toni
Morrison, who, like Reed, have received a great deal of attention and spotlight, unfortunately in some instances more for
their being black women than for their obvious gifts, both could
easily whomp Reed.

Why then has Reed been singled out for so much extravagant
praise and attention? . . .

Reed's reputation emerged at a time when, to borrow from
Langston Hughes, blacks were in vogue. Since the '70s he has
turned out a slew of mediocre novels of which the most recent
is the most inferior and the most self-indulgent. What once
was celebrated in his fiction as the new black ethos with indigenous folk roots that spanned from Buffalo to Berkeley and
hearkened back to voodoo and Egyptology, has turned into, to
use Julius Lester's word on Reed, "sophomoric" lightweight
polemics. The early invective against the likes of Harry Sam
is gone. The cowboy has fallen out of the boat of Ra. . . .

Understand that Reed wrote initially with enough charm and
innovative use of language to deserve a good deal of the attention. His voice was inventive and fresh. He wrote essays
and began presses and promoted young writers and did prodigious research and read and lectured everywhere. But like
most other worlds of entertainment, which authorship most
certainly is these days, the exposure began to count for far
more than the quality. Reed became the black literary "celeb."
His symbolic role as the black Ishmael not getting his due, as
the West Coast writer not getting his due, began to dwarf his
declining talent. The white eastern literary establishment, which
he inveighed against so indignantly, went on praising him and
reviewing him even after his magic was gone. (p. 10)

[I] recall how outraged Reed felt at the success of Doctorow's
Ragtime which he believed was a direct rip-off of his work.
This was no case like Margaret Walker suing Alex Haley. It
was Reed seeing himself as the victim of white purloining going
all the way back to the slave era when blacks were prohibited
from owning patents. Reed has that personal sense of history
and he makes his readers and public acutely aware of it in
ways which make him personally seem the ongoing victim of
hostile literary apartheid. The white folks in this all too often
real scenario are ubiquitous, hovering, ready to steal every
single dance routine. But the equation hardly applies when, as
in the case of *The Terrible Twos,* the dancing has almost all
gone lame. (p. 14)

*Michael Krasny, "Pyrotechnic Amulets: 'The Ter-
rible Twos'," in* San Francisco Review of Books,
January-February, 1983, pp. 10, 14.

JEROME KLINKOWITZ

In *The Terrible Twos* Reed is supposedly outside of history; he
sets his story in 1990, when the President is a former male
model, the economy is worse than ever, and all that's left to
trickle down is Christmas, which a bunch of power-hungry
goons who run the country successfully buy and sell. *God Made
Alaska for the Indians,* on the other hand, assembles eight
essays and an afterword on environmentalists, Native Americans, literary politicians, prize fight promotions, male sexuality, race relations, the troubles in Ulster as seen by Irish-
Americans, and the problems of multicultural artists—all of
which deal directly with the demoralizing state of events since
1976. But with Reed in control there's no real difference in
subject or method, and the result is a penetrating vision which
by now surely ranks as the new decade's most insightful literary
critique of American morals and manners.

It's at this intersection that the battle over Reed's work is
fought: can the identity of history and imagination, just because
our age apparently confuses them, be a valid method for the
critique itself? For years Reed has been complaining about the
intellectual colonialism which judges American literature by
nineteenth century English and European standards—"all those

books in rusty trunks,'' as he puts it, which by contrast make his own writing seem ''muddled, crazy, and incoherent.'' In his attack on these old-order standards Reed does disrupt some emotionally-held ideals, but his genius is to base his method solidly within the multicultural American lower-middle class, which he claims is more ready to allow ''the techniques and forms painters, dancers, film makers, and musicians in the West have taken for granted for at least fifty years, and the artists of other cultures for thousands of years.'' Hence you'll find Reed talking about (and writing like) Cab Calloway, who since 1928 has never lacked a lowbrow audience, black or white, rather than the intellectually uptown musicians conventionally taken as models. . . .

Syncretism is one of the few formally-abstract words among Reed's critical vocabulary, and he feels it is the key to a true national American literature reflecting the uniquely multicultural art which has evolved here. ''Anglo'' culture, as he calls it, then becomes one element among many, and the only loss is that of a dominant intellectual academy sworn to upholding the beliefs of a long-dead order. Gabriel García Márquez says much the same about his own multicultural, coastal Caribbean background where, as opposed to the rigidly colonial Spanish culture of the highlands capital in Bogata, history and fiction were allowed to blend, making truth ''one more illusion, just one more version of many possible vantage points'' where ''people change their reality by changing their perception of it.'' Within this aesthetic, fact and imagination become one. And as our present age has been shaped by this union, so Reed creates a common method for writing novels and essays by using the best of it while warning of its dangers when abused.

Both *The Terrible Twos* and *God Made Alaska for the Indians* are filled with Reed's customary mischief and fun. In the novel President Dean Clift does things like helping sell merchandizing rights to Santa Claus and declaring Adolf Hitler a posthumous American citizen, but balks when his advisors plan nuclear war with Nigeria as a way of wiping out the economically ''surplus people'' on both sides. Meanwhile, back in the quotidian reality of *God Made Alaska,* Reed's research uncovers a ''late 19th century American movement called Teutonism'' in which a serious politician ''proposed a way of ridding the land of both the unwelcome black and Irish: 'Let an Irishman kill a Negro and get hanged for it.''' Both books are hilarious in their accounts of people being swallowed by their own cultural signs, but things get serious when Reed shows how dangerous a dead semiotics—a code of social behavior deriving from discredited cultural authority, such as monocultural white male dominance—can be. (p. 16)

In our time history and imagination are confused because there's been a king-hell conflict going on between two rival sign-making authorities, one authentic (the multicultural and nativistically American lower-middle class, which has invented jazz, blues, rock and roll, country swing, comic books, detective novels, fast food, and other items native to our shores) and the other a carry-over from a long-dead power (the European colonization, with its monocultural rhetoric and mono-logical dictates). What can Reed do in these circumstances: write a counter-history of the Western world, as Khachig Tölölyan says Thomas Pynchon has done, exposing ''the patriarchal and technological white West'' while rallying for ''the imposed-upon'' who've been ''inscribed with other peoples' meanings''? That's the negative side of his program, but our man Reed takes such positive joy in the real American culture which now and then wins a fight that Pynchon's solution seems fully unsatisfac-

tory—there's too much joy to miss, both in exposing the phonies and giving credit for the good stuff.

At times in the past Reed's stridency has cost him part of his audience, but the gentler fun of *Twos* and *Alaska* will definitely open some minds even as it closes some mouths. The egoless self-apparency of his method, based as it is on the common language and sentiment of most Americans away from the intellectual centers, virtually guarantees this; for when Reed simply ''sits back and takes it all in'' as the monocultural aristocrats hang themselves with their own devoluted chatter, how can you help but take his side? The emotional two-year-olds of his novel are their own worst enemies; there's no need for the author to turn the knife in them as he's been tempted to do in earlier novels. (pp. 16-17)

What Reed calls the Anglo establishment thrives on dead signs, cliches of a once-living culture which now misdirect and deplete our country's imaginative energy. Therefore his first job is to expose this state of affairs and then to bring our language and its signs back to life as self-apparent realities. *God Made Alaska for the Indians* does this for the history we've shared since 1976, and *The Terrible Twos* takes further license to push the argument through fiction. All systems are fictions, our times have taught us, and fictions in turn create functional realities. Reed likes to demonstrate how the folks in control manipulate us—that's the wickedly funny part. Where Ishmael Reed triumphs as a writer is when he seizes the oppressor's tools and forges his own reality: a perception of disparate forces brought together in a single complex vision which is clearly superior, based as it is on a broader range of seeing and expressing. . . .

[Reed] can pull together the many different and contradictory levels of our contemporary American ''truth'' and give us a persuasive account of how we live today. Reed the novelist and essayist is a careful semiotic researcher who, once he's done the hard work of running up and down the stairs for facts, gives language free play to project itself into previously unexplored corners of public experience, lighting up some truths which those afflicted with cultural tunnel vision might otherwise never see. (p. 17)

> Jerome Klinkowitz, ''Reed's Syncretic Words,'' in *The American Book Review, Vol. 5, No. 4, May-June, 1983, pp. 16-17.*

JERRY H. BRYANT

I like Ishmael Reed. There is so much of him. He is going on forty-six at the time I write, is still healthy and pugnacious, and has already incarnated himself in more forms than two normal men do in a lifetime. . . . Not everyone likes him as much as I do. Some call him too conservative. Some call him unreadable. Some call him silly and superficial. But he is so active and productive in so many fields of contemporary American art that he cannot be ignored. In the late sixties, when he was one of a couple dozen young black writers seeking an audience in that atmosphere of black revolutionary chic, he came on as a kind of enfant terrible. Yet, even at the time, before we knew better, his revolution didn't seem that much different from that of William Melvin Kelley, or Ronald Fair, or John O. Killens. Now it is clear that he was not created by a movement or a time. He has survived the ways of publishers who, perhaps for their own survival, will not print what they assume will not sell—and black literary anger has not sold for some time.

Reed is an artist of many talents with a clear and consistent world view and a vision of America that is both affectionate and critical. In the six books of prose fictional satire he has so far written, he pieces that vision together in a style that is sometimes lyrical and poetic, sometimes flat and unimaginative.

In his younger days, we might have called Reed an "experimental" writer. He worked hard to break free of traditional forms and create a fiction for his own ideas. (p. 195)

We are still too close to Reed to say whether he is a true original. If he is, he doesn't seem to have created a school; no one seems to be imitating him. But not many black American writers have cut their links with realism and naturalism so completely as Reed has done. He does not belong in the same historical line as Hemingway, Steinbeck, or Faulkner. His context is the American pop culture: the political cartoon, the routine of a stand-up comedian, the high jinks of Mad Comics. His vocabulary and allusions come from the cliches of TV, best-selling books, newspaper and magazine commercials, and movies. (p. 196)

Reed is not an exceptional stylist. He can be graceful and elegant, but much of his prose is flat and arhythmical. If he has models, one of them is the Nathanael West of *A Cool Million,* the crazy parody of the Horatio Alger success story, and *The Dream Life of Balso Snell,* the schmaltzy, surreal chronicle of Balso and the Trojan Horse. Another model is Charles Wright, one of the really authentic black experimentalists of the 1960s. In *The Wig* (1966), Wright presents a young black naif who swallows whole the American Dream. But in trying to convert his kinky black hair to the silken blond locks of the privileged Anglo-Saxon, he is destroyed. Reed's fictional satires have something of the same tone—a surface of sophomoric wisecracks and oversimplified comedy, beneath which lies the rage of a born moralist. Reed, however, is not interested in showing man's sin, but his ridiculousness.

He works principally through caricature: of types, movements, attitudes. He exaggerates and simplifies to reveal the absurdity of the world he describes, to suggest what America is "really" like when we strip away its rationalizing myths and self-justifying assumptions. Most satirists have the same aim—"to get us to see ourselves," as Sheldon Sacks says of Swift, "our institutions, our acts, from points of view which reveal to us the ridiculous inhumanity of our customs and the pathetic shoddiness of our ethical pretensions." The caricatures that Reed devises to get us to see this way develop into metaphors of wide scope and imaginative power. For example, in *The Free-Lance Pallbearers* (1967), Reed anticipates the quaint rumor that Lyndon Johnson liked to carry on presidential business while sitting on the toilet. With customary exaggeration, Reed afflicts one of his central characters with a spectacular case of diarrhea. Harry Sam is the "democratically elected dictator" of the country HARRY SAM. The commode that he uses so much is his cathedral, decorated with diamonds and carved with figures of griffins and gargoyles, like Notre Dame.

But when Reed pictures a head of state sitting on a toilet, he sees much more than a head of state sitting on a toilet. Harry Sam's diarrhea is a symbol of America's obsession with power. This is the power to consume as well as to produce. Some call it America's greatness and point to our standard of living as proof. Reed makes us see it as a case of diarrhea, emphasizing devouring, digesting, defecating. He suggests it is a disgusting sickness, reflecting a consumption and waste cycle unprecedented in history.

The consumption that Reed ridicules is not only of commodities but of people. Reed takes Swift several steps further, showing that the earlier satirist's "modest proposal" has been accepted and implemented. "SAM's eating your children," cries one of Reed's characters. The sewage of Sam's waste is what is left of HARRY SAM citizens (mostly black) after Sam has devoured their labor, their time, their personal lives, their souls. It is pumped into the "Black Bay," now so contaminated that no one can swim in it and remain alive. The pollution of America does not come simply from the literal waste of industrial effluvia, says Reed. It also comes from the institutional power process in which the privileged and the powerful dine off the powerless and discard what is left over. (pp. 196-97)

The Free-Lance Pallbearers has a nerve-jangling speed to it that is appropriate to the urban world it depicts, in which things happen with a dreamlike swiftness and illogic. There is a flavor of apocalypse about it, of a civilization speeding out of control to its destruction, and in so doing recapitulating the inevitable fate of similar civilizations. The desire for power affects everyone. Bukka Doopeyduk, a clownish protagonist right out of *A Cool Million* or *The Wig,* begins as a docile innocent who patriotically worships all of Harry Sam's myths about hard work and its rewards, about individual initiative, middle-class respectability, and blacks keeping their place. But like the proof of a theorem in geometry, Bukka's experience leads him inexorably to the reality behind the moral posturing of his country's leaders. He changes from an earnest young man who wants to do right into a power-hungry fascist who overthrows Sam and assumes control. Reed's target is not only those blacks who, from their middle-class security, suddenly discovered the profit in black revolution and became as totalitarian as the whites they attacked; it is also the nature of human ways. Bukka is himself replaced by "the next on the civil service list" in a triumph of impersonal bureaucracy. No one in the story has the last word. That remains for the laughing, godlike author, observing all from his perch outside the system, for he sees that all *systems* are alike, all with an equal potential for oppression and injustice.

There are no soft edges to *The Free-Lance Pallbearers.* No one escapes ridicule and exposure.... (pp. 197-98)

Maybe all this results from the fact that this first fictional satire is Reed's most political book. It is full of allusions to Richard Nixon and Lyndon Johnson, and the action itself involves government power and how one gets it and abuses it. In his next three books, Reed changes neither his satirical technique nor his picture of America as a country in which democracy is permanently under siege. He does, though, begin to develop a worldview based upon wider and wider reading—reading in American history, Egyptian mythology and religion, African and Caribbean magic and witchcraft, and black commentaries on blacks' experience in white America.

In the version of the modern experience that Reed constructs out of his reading, most of us have been victims of Western rationalism; that includes whites as well as blacks, and other people of color. Western rationalism has overthrown early man's practice of magic and worship of mystery, and consolidated its victory by associating the instinctual and spontaneous with everything that is evil. Through the Christian church and other organizations, it has killed off what is most vital in the healthy, living being—laughter, joy, singing, dancing. It has produced a dubious technology and created institutionalized creatures to serve it: "willess robots," children who are "docile" and "obedient," people who have been cut off from the sources of the natural power in themselves and their surroundings.

The point is to effect a return to those sources. In *Yellow Back Radio Broke-Down, Mumbo Jumbo* (1972), and *The Last Days of Louisiana Red* (1974), Reed works out his picture of modern times and the way we can escape the suffocation of the rationalism that is the foundation of the modern state and the society that serves it. The vehicle for our return is the Third World and the "colored" people that make it up, with their ties to prerationalist history, their alleged belief in the hidden powers of nature, and their respect for the mystery of the individual. The black person in particular is a special "carrier" of the ancient sensibility, the impulse to laugh and sing and admit the forces that support life.

The Afro-American artist is the most powerful liberator, for as Reed sees it, he is "similar to the Necromancer.... He is a conjuror who works JuJu upon his oppressors, a witch doctor who frees his fellow victims from the psychic attack launched by demons of the outer and inner world." The result of these psychic attacks is that the victim voluntarily represses his truest, pleasure-loving, spontaneous self. Thus he lives in a world characterized by "glumness, depression, surliness, cynicism, malice without artfulness." This describes the Western world, and its intellectuals admire only "heavy, serious works." A character in *Mumbo Jumbo* remarks that there is no "account or portrait of Christ laughing. Like the Marxists who secularized his doctrine, he is always stern, serious and as gloomy as a prison guard."

In Reed's view, the black artist establishes his integrity by refusing to abide by these "gray" rationalist forms. He must, we assume, deconstruct the old genres and replace them with newer and livelier forms.... When he does, he becomes a demon in the eyes of the white rationalist, undermining the latter's old gods. By invoking his natural sense of humor, the black artist becomes a satanic threat to the holy tradition of humorless Western thought. Reed proclaims the potential of all black artists to be demons, to practice voodoo and witchcraft, and with the magic of their words and images to challenge the old Western gods. (pp. 198-99)

We cannot score Reed for taking on a task beneath his talents or limiting the fish he wants to catch in his net. He goes after the entire Western tradition and anyone who submits to it.... I like a man who doesn't underestimate his importance, but doubt nags me, especially about Reed's claims of necromantic power and control of a hoodoo aesthetic. For one who has such harsh words for Western rationalism, and such contempt for English teachers who take a scholarly approach to Milton, he seems very Western to me. True, he laces his writing with words like "voudon" and "hougan" and "loa," but it looks to me as if he has gotten much of that vocabulary from his reading. He is, after all, better educated than your average voodoo witch doctor. His invocation of Caribbean hoodoo seems more anthropological than practical, and I see his allusions to magic and writing to be metaphorical. For example, in *Flight to Canada* (1976), Raven Quickskill says that "a man's story is his gris-gris." Surely this is only sophisticated analogy, as Keats's "La Belle Dame Sans Merci" is high rather than folk art. Indeed, while Reed urges replacement of rationalism with magic and intuition, his own style takes its strength directly from rationalism. His metaphors sway us not because they appeal to our passion or emotion but because they please our intellect. They are not in the slightest incantatory, and produce no altered states. We are delighted by the inventiveness with which Reed yokes together the unexpected, but it is an intellectual delight, similar to what generations of John Donne readers have felt when they are drawn into an effective metaphysical conceit.

As a white Western rationalist myself, I feel a little badly treated by Reed. It may be that Reed is attacking only one or two strains in the Western tradition. But it comes off as a blanket indictment, as if there were no mystery or emotion in the West, no St. Francis or St. Theresa, no mystical poetry. Reed employs the same techniques he accuses the Western rationalists of using, guilt by association. Reed labels as fraud any attempt by the Western mind to uncover some of the forces he celebrates. Only the properly initiated are authentic. Nor can I accept an unqualified rejection of rationalism. The truth that rises from the "possessed" can no more guarantee completeness than the truth that rises from rational observation and inference. If it is true that the Western mind has swung excessively toward rationalist scientific empiricism, we do no service to the species by swinging excessively to the other extreme.

But a satirist who writes with an ax rather than a scalpel will inevitably destroy a few innocent cells unintentionally. And that may be the case with Reed. He quotes Muhammad Ali for his own *raison d'écrire:* "Writing is fighting." He is fighting a system that measures up neither to its promises nor to his expectations of it. The focus of his anger is that system's refusal to acknowledge him and the culture he identifies with.... [Reed speaks] for all unrecognized but important cultural elements of America, but his real constituency is the black American male. That, for Reed, is the truly oppressed class in America, "the most exploited and feared class" in the country. He and his Afro-American brothers are under siege, alone, pariahs not only to the white males that dominate America but also to the black female who conspires with white males to suppress the black man's energy, and to the black males in other countries. From behind the barricades, Reed tries to protect what is his and force his country to expand its cultural tolerance and recognize what is already there.

In his fiction, Reed does not aim to create great characters or probe the human psyche. All he wants to do is rewrite history and change America. Stylistically, all his books sound alike. They are pastiches of real and invented people doing real and invented things. They are Mad Comics, Doonesbury, Monty Python, Max Schulman, Ornette Coleman, John Cage, the *Encyclopedia Britannica* all mixed up together within one frame of reference. And if his satires sound alike, they seldom fail to disclose a new dimension to America or to provoke us with a reading of history that reverses everything we have accepted as true. Reed may outrage us, but he makes us see in different ways. With a virtually unlimited reservoir of revealing metaphors, he seeks to shame us out of our complacency and hypocrisy. That is what a satirist should do, and Reed is one of the best satirists around. (pp. 200-02)

Jerry H. Bryant, "Old Gods and New Demons— Ishmael Reed and His Fiction," in The Review of Contemporary Fiction, *Vol. 4, No. 2, Summer, 1984, pp. 195-202.*

Tom Robbins

1936-

(Born Thomas Eugene Robbins) American novelist and short story writer.

Robbins writes wildly playful novels which express his view that "playfulness is a form of wisdom and not of frivolity." The tone of his novels is not a denial of the more sobering aspects of life but an advocacy of "joy in spite of everything." He communicates this message through the philosophies his characters present as well as through his elaborate writing style. Outrageous puns, nonsequiturs, oxymorons, and digressions on top of digressions characterize Robbins's narrative. His novels question not only literary conventions but also societal assumptions about the best way to assure human satisfaction. Robbins incorporates alternative ideas from such diverse sources as pantheism, Eastern mystical religions, and New Physics.

Robbins is often considered a literary descendant of such postmodern writers as Thomas Pynchon, John Barth, and Kurt Vonnegut. Like these authors, Robbins acknowledges the absurdity of modern life, rejects conformity in favor of individual expression, and uses elements of metafiction in his writing. He often speaks directly to the reader, commenting on the work in progress or appearing as a character in the novel. However, unlike his recent forebears—who often write black comedy and present a bleak prognosis for the modern world—Robbins's tone is optimistic and his humor usually lighthearted.

Another Roadside Attraction (1971) earned Robbins praise from most critics. However, the novel was not a popular success until the paperback edition was published in 1973, when it began to attract a cult following. Robbins's greater success in paperback is often attributed to the fact that his novels, which irreverently question and satirize those social conventions which fail to increase the level of joy in people's lives, are appreciated especially by the young and the unconventional. Robbins's second and third novels were brought out in paperback immediately and became bestsellers. Mitchell Ross dubbed Robbins "Prince of the Paperback Literati."

Another Roadside Attraction displays the characteristics typical of Robbins's fiction: an outrageous plot, unusual characters, and imaginative use of language. It is narrated by Marx Marvelous, an academic whom many critics identify as Robbins's alter-ego. Robbins's main concerns in the novel are to advocate the joyous acceptance of the mystery of the universe and to portray the romance between Marx and the heroine, along with Marx's journey towards self-awareness.

In *Even Cowgirls Get the Blues* (1976) Robbins focuses on an attractive heroine, Sissy Hankshaw, a woman with nine-inch thumbs who is an obsessive hitchhiker. Sissy moves between New York City, where she is a model, and South Dakota, where a cosmetic health farm has been taken over by a group of feminist cowgirls. As the narrative traces Sissy's travels, such themes as the human relationship with the universe and the importance of individual freedom are explored. Although some critics find Robbins's digressions and wordplay to be self-indulgent, *Even Cowgirls Get the Blues* was on the whole very well received.

Still Life with Woodpecker: A Sort of a Love Story (1980) is the least critically acclaimed of Robbins's first three novels. In contrast to the complicated plots of his earlier works, the story of *Still Life* is simple and, according to some critics, slow-moving and fable-like. In this tale of a modern environmentalist princess and her "metaphysical outlaw" lover, Robbins maintains that individual romantic and personal fulfillment are more important than social activism; he rejects dogma, believing that "good can be as banal as evil." Despite Robbins's efforts to communicate his message, some critics did not find *Still Life with Woodpecker* deeply meaningful. For example, Donald Hettinga argued that the novel "never becomes more than a clever package of words." Many critics, however, appreciate Robbins's creative use of language, as well as his celebration of the human spirit and his perpetuation of upbeat values.

In the recent *Jitterbug Perfume* (1984), a typical varied cast of characters traverse time and space in search of both the ultimate perfume and the secret of immortality.

(See also *CLC*, Vol. 9; *Contemporary Authors*, Vols. 81-84; and *Dictionary of Literary Biography Yearbook: 1980*.)

WILLIAM CLOONAN

In recent years we have seen wild enthusiasm, much discussion, and some handwringing for the likes of Kurt Vonnegut,

Richard Brautigan, and Thomas Pynchon. The latest discovery is Tom Robbins.

Several qualities distinguish the novels by these contemporary cult figures from those of authors such as [Henry] James. The most obvious characteristic is their enormous popularity, which entails equally large financial rewards. . . .

A second characteristic of these recent novels is a fascination with travel, but the sort of travel that precludes round-trip fares and forty-five-day limits. Concerns of time and cost do not matter, because neither the destination nor the purpose is always very clear. In Robbins's *Even Cowgirls Get the Blues,* the heroine, Sissy Hankshaw, "the world's greatest hitchhiker," freely admits that "it was the act of hitchhiking that formed the substance of her vision," and that she was never really going anywhere. Movement itself, rather than any specific place, is the goal, and Kerouac, rather than Kafka, is the guide. . . .

A third distinguishing quality of these popular cult novels is the appearance of the wise man who usually comes from the Far East or at least the Third World. Indian mystics, Oriental sages, and an occasional witch doctor behave as if they have cornered the market on Truth. . . . *Cowgirls* features the Chink who, depending upon the circumstances, is equally adept at displaying his philosophy or phallus before an enraptured audience.

Finally, what these writers have is the ability to express themselves in a wonderfully accessible English. Except for moments where one or another lapses into that form of verbal flatulence currently termed "lyricism," most employ an exciting, often very witty prose. . . .

If Tom Robbins's writings were nothing more than compendia of the qualities listed above, they would be fun to read, but not worth an extensive review. To a large extent, [*Another Roadside Attraction*] falls into this category. While the book has its humorous moments, it is finally nothing more than a collection of outrageous situations and boringly typical counterculture posturings. . . .

Cowgirls, however, is quite different. In this novel Robbins manages to parody many elements of the popular cult novel, while at the same time he makes an interesting commentary on both the American novel and the American way of life. (p. 5)

In *Cowgirls* Robbins is not primarily interested in one more debunking of intellectuals and the radical chic East Coast. He is concerned instead with teasing the commonly touted alternatives: counter-culture life-styles, the new gurus, and militant anybodies. . . .

An important moment in the novel occurs when the cowgirls switch their herd from cows to goats. In pastoral literature this change usually heralds a transition from fantasy to reality. Robbins appears to be waggishly playing with this tradition because, when goats replace cows, right-on feminism suddenly encounters the return of the repressed. . . .

It would be a mistake to assume that in *Cowgirls* Robbins is seriously attacking Women's Liberation or any other ideological commitment. Rather, he is exploiting the humor implicit in any militancy and thereby suggesting that however important a movement's goals, no writer can pass up the chance to make fun of a sacred cow. . . .

Just as the thumb is the "cornerstone of civilization," so Sissy Hankshaw is the cornerstone of *Cowgirls*. She means different things to different people, but for Tom Robbins author, who must occasionally but not always be distinguished from Dr. Tom Robbins, psychiatrist and closet flowerchild who shows up in the book, Sissy is most certainly all that is vital in America, i.e., the United States. Pretty as a picture, even better looking in motion, capable of giving a "fairytale" quality to life, part Indian, and somewhat flawed (remember the thumbs!), this is as much Robbins's vision of America as it is Sissy Hankshaw's. His celebration of her innocence, beauty, and occasional wisdom is a salute to a fabulous America where every event or person who buzzes by is just one more roadside attraction to be enjoyed and not pondered. The novel has an episodic structure, a series of set pieces (Sissy on the road, Sissy at the Countess', etc.) which function mostly to make us laugh while we marvel at the degree of zaniness human beings have been able to maintain in this somber century.

There is, alas, a sad edge to the laughter. What threatens Sissy and those she loves is what menaces America. [Sissy's husband] Julian started out as a full-blooded Mohawk who might have been a great artist and a fine lover, except for a type of education that pushes him toward European culture as an unassailable ideal and which fostered a subtle contempt for what might be unique in the American experience. The end result was a "brainy" watercolorist. Sissy narrowly escapes a similar fate. But she does lose a thumb. In order to please Julian she has one thumb amputated by a friendly European doctor who has gone mad, and, after an elaborate operation, she manages to grow a new, boringly common thumb in her womb. This is apparently for Robbins the great danger that threatens America: sacrificing what is special even if it is a little strange, for what is more normal. Happily, Sissy does not lose both thumbs and, at the novel's end, she is pregnant and destined to produce a large-thumbed progeny; yet, except for circumstances, she might have given away her birthright and not even gotten a decent borsch in return.

Something much less scary, but still quite interesting, is what Sissy represents to American letters. Throughout both of Robbins's novels the reader is made aware that he is not just writing an American novel, but writing *about* the American novel, and specifically about the failure of his contemporaries to fabricate the by now mystical "Great American Novel." In *Roadside,* a dead fascist monk pollutes one of Brautigan's trout streams, and in *Cowgirls* things get worse. Early on we learn that Kerouac had a tumble in the hay with Sissy, and although she admired his efforts, he could not quite make it. The Countess usually has pretty good instincts, but he keeps getting bad advice from a fellow named Truman who now lives on Long Island. The Barths, copywriters for a New York advertising agency, also have a go at Sissy, but their interest in sodomy gets them off on the wrong track. Julian might eat a bowl of Joyce Carol Oats every morning, but it does not seem to help. Delores del Ruby declares that "Violence is the dullard's Breakfast of Champions," and John Updike provides sustenance for overfed suburbanites. Dr. Tom Robbins, who might now also be the author, would like to bed Sissy, but so far he has not had much luck.

The author of *Cowgirls* could have two things in mind. Perhaps he believes that his talent has yet to grow to the point where he can do Sissy justice. My personal preference is, however, for another explanation. I think Robbins is saying that no artist will ever be able to control Sissy totally without violating what she is, and that for him America must be experienced in fragments since that is very much the nature of the country. The trick then is to catch the piece of Sissy-America that you can, and it should come as no surprise that her best lover was the Chink. During the war this Japanese-American was informed that he was not a ''real'' American (no such animal exists. By now, not even the Indians qualify.), but who proved capable of enjoying the woman who came his way without presuming either that he completely understood her or that she was his forever. Since the Chink's efforts with Sissy proved fecund, the next generation, the next subject for American writers, will be liberated, travel-loving, Chinese-looking Japanese-Southerners whose rednecks are as much a result of their Indian heritage as they are of their racist heritage and who know how to increase their sexual pleasure by the skillful manipulations of big thumbs. For Tom Robbins, America's greatness lies in her ability to unite contradictory forces and this is the principal source of joy and frustration for the American novelist.

Noel Coward, in a moment of feigned modesty, once described himself as possessing ''a talent to amuse.'' A wonderful compliment, indeed, and one that can easily be extended to Tom Robbins. *Cowgirls* is a particularly funny book and provides a great deal of pleasure. Yet it remains true that on second reading even *Cowgirls* falls a little flat. Like a number of his colleagues, Robbins depends to a large extent on a fast pace and lots of jokes so that the second time through, foreknowledge considerably lessens the impact.

Henry James sought to capture in his writings some sort of eternal verity about the human psyche. His aim was to do more than detail the unwholesome confrontation of the American with Europe; it seems to me that his genius resides less in his depiction of a particular social class at a particular historical moment, than in his description of the ways that human beings often live the best and worst moments of their lives in their minds. The purpose of Tom Robbins is otherwise. His focus is the milieu rather than the individual, and he wants to seize the transient instead of the eternal. This is why his characters are most often caricatures; yet it is the rush of events and not the artist's lack of skill which distorts the individuals he describes.

Milieu, especially in ultra-modern America, is never a permanent place. It changes with each new fad and counter-fad, with the latest whatever that comes hurtling down the road. Tom Robbins is a chronicler of the experience of transience; he can make the traveling circus stop for an instant and let us partake of a particular moment in time with all the disparate personalities, half-digested ideas, and residual myths which inform it. This is a noble service to the reader, but one fraught with danger for the writer. His books take on the very ephemeral qualities they describe, and once read and enjoyed they can easily be put aside. Nevertheless, Robbins is an undeniably talented artist whose fascination with America and natural gifts promise greater things to come. Only the future will tell us how much of Sissy Hankshaw Tom Robbins will finally get. (p. 6)

William Cloonan, *''Tom Robbins's Culture: The Brain Takes Its Lumps,''* in New Boston Review, *Vol. III, No. III, December, 1977, pp. 5-6.*

R. V. CASSILL

Old fashions of escape literature never die; they come back with new drapes, dyes and hemlines, and the cotton candy of yesteryear is now laced with cocaine to dull the ache in teeth rotted by sugar. Fairy tales that charm the young invite their elders to scan them as symptomatic fantasies of flight from the anxieties of the age. So there's something for everyone in [**''Still Life With Woodpecker''**], Tom Robbins's medley of antique fairy tales, Aquarian shibboleths and didactic Yippie formulas for living the good life across the rainbow from the reality principle. The speed of his ricocheting metaphors may well hustle you past the patent falsity of the moral that crowns his tale of a princess and her princely savior. . . .

[All the] whirligigs of plot spin out opportunities for the elaboration of the Woodpecker's thought, which is the chief sweetener in the whole concoction of metaphor and whimsy.

Choice—''the word no mirror can turn around''—is the supreme good in Woodpecker metaphysics. . . .

Poor Leigh-Cheri. One would like to tell her and all her sister princesses that the old Woodpecker has only got her out of the doll's house of faddish movements by inducting her into a doll's universe. For the noble faculty of choice is here presented as operative only between the ''Yum'' and the ''Yuk'' of existence. Such pitiable reductions from traditional hedonism are the ''alternate mantras'' with which the Yippie liberator has equipped the child-mind of his bride for her ultimate retreat from the banal laws that govern the pismire and the stars. If it's not a Yum, it's a Yuk, and children indoctrinated by television, the neo-Aesopian laugh machine, watch the world end not with a whimper but a ''Yuk!'' . . .

So much for where free choice can bring you if you buy the Woodpecker's whimsy ticket.

R. V. Cassill, ''Whimsy with Moral,'' in The New York Times Book Review, *September 28, 1980, p. 15.*

DONALD R. HETTINGA

In considering contemporary fiction, John Barth writes, ''My own analogy would be with good jazz or classical music: one finds much on successive listenings or on close examination of the score that one didn't catch the first time through; but the first time through should be so ravishing—and not just to specialists—that one delights in the replay.'' Tom Robbins's *Still Life With Woodpecker* does not fare well with this kind of test. As witty as the novel is in places, it never becomes more than a clever package of words.

Wrapped up in the package is, the subtitle tells us, ''A Sort of a Love Story.'' A pretty silly one, in fact: an exiled princess falls in love with a commoner who is also an outlaw. Her lover is captured and imprisoned. The princess remains faithful until she misinterprets a message from the outlaw as a rejection of her love. On the rebound, she gives her favor and her troth to an Arab prince who has been courting her. However, on the night before the wedding the princess discovers her outlaw lover escaped and waiting for her. They are discovered in mid-embrace. The confrontation initiates a period of trial in which the two lovers discover each other's true character. All that remains is the novel's catastrophe—not necessarily bad news, we should remember—before the princess and the outlaw ''live happily ever after.''

The sort of love story, then? A fairy tale, although *Still Life*, of course, is not simply that. It is also a novel for adults. . . . (p. 123)

Elements of social commentary and humor are added to the plot, but do not serve to alter the novel's essentially melodramatic character. Robbins's attempts at social commentary produce rather flat characters acting in predictable situations. Surveying these elements, we sense Robbins merely trying for effects. The outlaw hero is developed from the real-life character who in the Sixties blew up a chemistry building at the University of Wisconsin to protest the Vietnam War. The princess is a nostalgic devotée of the Sixties, fanatically searching for a cause, while sporting her "No Nukes" t-shirt and nursing a crush on Ralph Nader. The adults . . . well, as in all fairy tales, the adults in *Still Life* simply do not understand the younger generation. The servant of the princess, who takes a heady liking to cocaine, is the only exception.

The intention behind this collection of types is humorous social commentary, but the types are drawn too starkly to allow for very much humor or commentary. . . . The sum of these things is to couple passé comments on the Sixties and Seventies strangely with the hype of contemporary fads.

But are we taking a playful novel too seriously? Probably not. Robbins has said that he writes "to change people's lives." Literary playfulness is his *modus operandi;* he sees such playfulness as "a form of wisdom and not frivolity." Substantiating this is Robbins's moralizing in the final section of *Still Life*. . . . Robbins gives no hard and fast advice on how to preserve the mystery, but he does leave us a couple of guidelines: 1) "Everything is part of it," and 2) "It's never too late to have a happy childhood."

This essentially hedonistic philosophy is supported by the novel's formulaic structure. Whatever Robbins's intentions, *Still Life* is strictly entertaining. And the moral he draws is valid only in the world of the novel. We have no reason to believe Robbins's philosophy will work in the real world, for *Still Life* presents only a world of escape. (pp. 124-25)

> Donald R. Hettinga, "Tom Robbins's 'Still Life with Woodpecker'," in Chicago Review, Vol. 32, No. 2, Autumn, 1980, pp. 123-25.

SUE M. HALPERN

Emma Goldman would like Tom Robbins. Having amassed a youthful following with his earlier novels, *Even Cowgirls Get the Blues* and *Another Roadside Attraction,* Robbins uses his latest offering, *Still Life With Woodpecker,* to instruct his constituency on matters of free will and social responsibility. He is riotous yet resolute, not subtle, but shrewd.

Still Life With Woodpecker is a fable for and against the last quarter of the twentieth century. Nevertheless, Robbins relies on the elements used by classical fabulists. There is a beautiful princess, a loyal handmaiden, a barren attic, exile and court intrigue, many varieties of frogs and, most important, an anarchist prince. In this, it is a formula novel. (p. 415)

[It] is a fable. Before there can be a happy ending, there must be truth. Before there can be truth, there must be mystery and confusion. Somewhere in the ruins are a pack of Camels and a deserted romance.

If this sounds silly, it should. *Still Life With Woodpecker* is an imbroglio of outrageous details. Usually they are playful and funny; sometimes they are overdrawn. But as a farce, *Still Life With Woodpecker* is apocryphal, for Robbins's relentless attention to detail is subterfuge.

Like most fables, Robbins's story is told in service to his moral. Unlike most moralists, however, he is a latter-day libertarian disguised as a saint in Western wear. Through Bernard, Robbins echoes Bakunin when he says that "a bomb is a question, not an answer," and he rivals Goldman herself with his jurisprudence. . . . Robbins also rails against junk-food, sex, unions as big business, movement sycophants and totalitarianism. He exalts love which is truly free, and curses the dark of dullness.

The moral of the story is that which "throws a window open after the final door is closed." It is that which "puts the free in freedom and takes the obligation out of love." The moral is "CHOICE. To refuse to passively accept what we've been handed by nature or society, but to choose for ourselves." Certainly this is not novel, yet *Still Life With Woodpecker* states the case ingeniously. For a generation that knows more about mutual funds than mutual aid, Robbins may be apostolic. (pp. 415-16)

> Sue M. Halpern, "A Pox on Dullness," in The Nation, Vol. 231, No. 13, October 25, 1980, pp. 415-17.*

JEROME KLINKOWITZ

Can innovative fiction address the world and its problems, yet remain free of the limiting conventions of realism? Following the achievements of the avant-garde, can there still be fiction with feeling? A newly emergent group of writers in the late 1970s has defined itself in response to these problems. Best characterized as the authors of "bubble gum fiction" (as "bubble gum music" of the last decade was an answer to the abrasiveness and stridency of the period's heavier rock), William Kotzwinkle, Tom Robbins, Rob Swigart, and Gerald Rosen have tried to write a socially responsive fiction which does not sacrifice the aesthetic gains of the great sixties innovators. (p. 123)

The first underground classic of bubble gum fiction is Tom Robbins' *Another Roadside Attraction.* . . . Robbins, a former student of religion and practicing art critic, brings a wealth of philosophical interest to the writing of this novel. He feels that the excessive rationalization of Western culture since Descartes has severed man from his roots in nature. Organized religion has in like manner become more of a tool of logic and control than of spirit. Robbins' heroine, Amanda, would reconnect mankind with the benign chaos of the natural world, substituting magic for logic, style for substance, and poetry for the analytical measure of authority. But to show the reader how magical, suprarational connections work, to involve the reader in recomposing the world according to their wacky structures, Robbins describes each point of action with a mind-bending metaphor or simile, often run to considerable length. . . . [Some] examples are about language itself ("The 'but' that crouched like a sailor there in the doorway of his second sentence did not in any way tie his first remark to his second one. It was a 'but' more ornamental than conjunctional"). . . . At his best, Robbins gives the reader one metaphor, then asks cooperation in tying a second one to it, as in "It was a peekaboo summer. The sun was in and out like Mickey Rooney." . . . (pp. 124-25)

Robbins is a master of plain American speech, as simple as hot dogs, baseball, apple pies, and Chevrolet, and his greatest trick is to use its flat style to defuse the most sacred objects. The plot of his novel is most appealing precisely because of this subverting style, as when Amanda's friend bodysnatches the corpse of Christ for a roadside zoo. . . . (p. 125)

The point of *Another Roadside Attraction* is the reinvention (through perception) of reality, a revitalization of life which logic and authority have dulled beyond appreciation. But as a message, it is not simply preached or discussed. Instead, Robbins makes the actual reading of his novel an experience in the stylistic transformation he has in mind. A successful reading of his book makes the reader an initiate, for he or she has performed the same mental tricks, the same imaginative acrobatics, as have the fictional characters in Robbins' story.

Tom Robbins' second novel, *Even Cowgirls Get the Blues*, extends both technique and belief from the earlier book. Here the heroine is Sissy Hankshaw, whose physical deformity (giant thumbs) is transformed into a positive asset: hitchhiking. "Freedom of movement" becomes her credo, and Robbins' too (to expound upon it, he puts himself into the novel as a clinical psychiatrist). As Sissy uses her magic to travel great distances, so does Robbins carry the reader across great expanses of metaphorical connections, as in *Another Roadside Attraction*. But now Robbins makes his metaphors even more kinesthetic, so that every scene is put into motion; the book must be read with body English. (pp. 125-26)

Motion and change, by now familiar to the reader who has been practicing them in every sentence, are explained as recent developments in human evolution, spurred on as a relief from the oppressive limits of analytical reason. "By pushing it, goosing it along whenever possible," Robbins explains, "we may speed up the process, the process by which the need for playfulness and liberty becomes stronger than the need for comfort and security." . . . Repeating his message from the first novel, Robbins adds that "the vagrancies and violence of nature must be brought back into the foreground of social and political consciousness, that they have got to be embraced in any meaningful psychic renewal." The writing of his novels, and the new style of imagination they speak to (Robbins' following is almost entirely countercultural), indicate that such change may already be under way. (p. 126)

> Jerome Klinkowitz, "Avant-garde and After," in his The Practice of Fiction in America: Writers from Hawthorne to the Present, *The Iowa State University Press, 1980, pp. 114-28.**

MARK SIEGEL

The novels of Tom Robbins, *Another Roadside Attraction* (1971), *Even Cowgirls Get the Blues* (1976), and *Still Life with Woodpecker* (1980), are set mostly in Washington state and the Dakotas, yet at first glance seem to have little in common with the formula Western or with Western writing in general. However, a more than cursory reading of Robbins's novels shows that climactic showdowns and shootouts are present, conflicts between unambiguously good and bad guys are, at least temporarily, resolved, and heroes do ride off into the sunset. When the construction and themes of his work are examined, it becomes clear that Robbins has reworked in an unusual style many of the conflicts familiar to the genre.

By redefining and reorganizing the confrontation of the individual and society, he has been able to go beyond the dead-end of the formula Western to suggest new resolutions to these conflicts that traditionally have been embodied in most Western fiction. As is the case with many other Western writers, Robbins's romantic vision enhances and idealizes the American pioneering spirit. However, while Robbins clearly believes in the value of individualism and diversity, he also seems to

recognize the need for some kind of social structure, even if it may be radically different from anything we have now. Through this vision his characters work out the conflicts between their love of free, primitive, pantheistic lifestyles and the complex restrictions of a sophisticated, bureaucratic society. Robbins's characters often seek a physical frontier environment along out-of-the-way roads or in unpeopled mountains, but more importantly, they carry a new American frontier of the culture and spirit with them wherever they go. Robbins's "romantic" novels are some of the few sources we have today of positive, concrete suggestions for living in the modern world. (pp. 6-7)

[There are two] major paradoxes in Robbins's ideas. . . . One is the emphasis he places on individual fulfillment while he simultaneously castigates egotism. The second is his apparent devotion to Eastern philosophies in *Another Roadside Attraction*, although he warns against adopting Eastern religions in *Cowgirls*. Actually, the two issues are closely related, both stemming from Robbins's notion that any truly fulfilling way of life must evolve from the individual's recognition of his true, personal relationship to the world. Thus, although Americans can learn from Oriental philosophies much about liberation from the ego, Western man must nevertheless find a way of liberation that is natural to him in his own world. (p. 32)

The American novel has taken a long time to adjust itself to the concepts of relativity in both physics and metaphysics, essentially stumbling against the idea that if nothing is absolute, nothing is sacred or even valuable. Nihilism and existentialism are the two best known responses to this situation. The 1970s saw the rise of a new wave of novelists who decree with Tom Robbins: "I believe in everything; nothing is sacred / I believe in nothing; everything is sacred." . . . Here the "problem" of the relativity of values is circumvented by the adoption of a multiplicity of successive perspectives, some of which may be contradictory. Robbins seems to say that to believe in something is not to canonize it and remove it from the relative, changeable human realm. To "believe" in the value of something is to make it part of oneself, to embrace its contradictions, and thereby to know the value of the thing on a personal, relative level. (p. 33)

All things have value, but only because we invest them with sacredness in our otherwise profane world. The goal of Robbins's art is to alert us to the sacred, to get us to see things in a new, intense way—to get us to let go of our own limited perspectives by exciting us into a new awareness of the world.

The mysterious, hip, comic, and apparently discontinuous narrative voice that Robbins employs seems to mislead many readers who don't perceive the ultimate seriousness of his playfulness or the sense in magic. Robbins repeatedly insists on the urgency of restoring magic and poetry to our lives. Magic, he says [in *Cowgirls*], is "the seemingly unrealistic or supernatural" that "occurs through the *acting of one thing upon another through a secret link*." . . . A causal explanation exists, but once it is explained the relationship is no longer "magical," no longer "marvelous" and capable of exciting us to a new awareness. (p. 34)

Style is more important than content to Robbins, since the "contents" or events of our lives are most easily improved through alterations in our styles of life, which in turn are basically functions of our perspectives toward emotional or physical events. The "best" perspectives are those that allow us to enjoy our lives the most while allowing others to enjoy theirs. The generally accepted, sophisticated perspective that everything of value must be fully understood and categorized can cause a good deal of damage. . . . (pp. 34-5)

Robbins is not abdicating responsibility for struggling to alter the facts of our existence—he is merely alert to the possibility that we are often decreasing the quality of our lives by demanding unnatural things of nature. As quantum physics has shown us, nature promises only the probability of certain outcomes, never the predictability of the course of specific events. Contemporary science implies a universe that is not solvable by any single equation, but that reveals itself in onionskin layers of pattern, applicable in a variety of ways to a variety of situations and perspectives. We waste our time and limit our potentials by refusing to admit the existence of anything over which we do not have logical dominion. (p. 35)

Robbins shows that the outdated vision of such mechanistic physics is responsible for our dysfunctional, reactionary metaphysics. Our new morality ought to be based on the realization that individual behavior cannot be absolutely defined and contained by rigid social rules. What is "right" for human beings is polymorphous and changes from one situation to the next. Morality, then, is a matter of style, not merely events. (p. 36)

Robbins's novels do not deny the physical world nor suggest that we live outside of it. Rather they remind us of both the urgency with which we sometimes live life and the truth that art and life are both games to which we make up many of the rules. He does this by undercutting the traditional narrative "ego" of the novel with its own self-consciousness, by mixing and overlapping his metaphors to suggest their interchangeability, by personifying the earth, organic and inorganic objects, the novel itself, and the sentences within the novel. . . . His narrators frequently talk about the shortcomings of various narrative forms, but Robbins himself employs narrative formats that are standard except for his expressed self-consciousness of them. (pp. 37-8)

A good demonstration of Robbins's belief that many different approaches can be equally valid is **"The Purpose of the Moon."** His only published short story to date, it is an exercise in stylistic liberation that indicates how his form and thematic content are inextricably linked. **"The Purpose of the Moon"** is constructed from multiple considerations of the same imaginary situation: "Vincent Van Gogh cut off his ear and sent it to Marilyn Monroe." While this conjunction of essentially symbolic personalities initially may have occurred to Robbins simply because of the sounds of their names, the story is an examination of a basic human situation, indicated in the story's subtitle, "if love is a matter of giving, momma, why is it so hard?" Each of the nine permutations of this situation examines a possible reaction of Marilyn Monroe's to receiving Van Gogh's ear, each suggesting a different perspective on romantic action.

While each episode is very funny, the sublime emotional quality of Van Gogh's sacrifice somehow permeates all of them. Just as in Wallace Stevens's "Thirteen Ways of Looking at a Blackbird," no way is better than another, so no one vision of Van Gogh-Monroe is more "correct" or "real" than another. Each vision is an enrichment of our appreciation of the situation. Some of the situations are highly improbable; in one of the episodes, after sharing a package of Twinkies, Monroe sews the ear back on her "silly boy." These anomalies clearly indicate Robbins's addiction to diversity and his taste for flaunting unusual possibilities in our often close-minded society.

Robbins's novels suggest several Zen lessons: that objectivity is impossible, that we are all connected to all events; but that

self-conscious perspective is the key to improving the depth of our perceptions. Far from eschewing the personal, egocentric narrator for a sham objectivity, Robbins insists on the subjectivity of every narrator, since every narrator takes part in the history he is recreating. In *Another Roadside Attraction*, the narrator declaims at great length about the impurity of history . . . and insists on telling his historically important tale as a fragment in the life of Amanda, not because she is central to the history, but because he is in love with her. The narrator of *Even Cowgirls Get the Blues,* who calls himself Dr. Robbins, also falls in love with one of his heroines and builds his tale around her. However, Robbins has not cut himself loose from narrative form, but is telling stories of personal growth and enlightenment under the guise of symbolically related adventure stories. These narrators discover the meaning of meaning—that is, in the end, that they must create their own values based on personal fulfillment. (pp. 38-9)

Probably the most noticeable aspects of Robbins's writing style are his play with language (his abundant, often comic figures of speech, for instance) and the comic, self-conscious tone that pervades even the most dramatically serious moments of his work. For instance, the amputation of Sissy's thumb in *Cowgirls* is essentially ironic in tone. Robbins concentrates on conveying the symbolic importance of the scene rather than on manipulating the reader's emotion. By contrast, Thomas Pynchon's description of Esther's nose-job in *V.* is grotesque and frightening, as well as comic.

The difference between Robbins's brand of comedy and the styles of apparently similar contemporary novelists such as Pynchon and Joseph Heller is that the latter are writers of "black comedy." That is, their comedy tends to emphasize rather than alleviate the reader's horror at the terrible things that they describe. Robbins's vision is not "black." Unlike Pynchon and Heller, he is not concerned so much with making us re-experience the terrible condition of humanity and man's ultimate inability to do much about it. Rather, he is concerned with what we can do to make things better.

Robbins's style of comedy, although uncommon for a serious contemporary novelist, harkens back to the mainstream of comic tradition. Mainstream comedies, such as many of the great plays of Aristophanes and Shakespeare, most often begin with situations in which society is in chaos and the characters are in trouble. In the end, these comedies redress all wrongs, reintegrate any misfits into society, and suggest solutions to social problems.

Northrop Frye has suggested that black comedy is essentially one phase in a comic cycle which reflects a time when a culture's vision of itself is so bleak that no solutions seem probable. If this is true, Robbins may be signalling the upswing in the comic cycle to a more positive vision in which social changes must be fought for, but in which success is possible. While *Another Roadside Attraction* ends in tragedy and the dissolution of the bonds between the characters (some are dead, some go their separate ways), its final note is one of limited optimism; the narrator says that your reading this manuscript is a sign of hope and possibility. While the end of *Cowgirls* also sees the death of two characters and the dissolving of a number of other relationships created during the course of the novel, these relationships were described all along as being transitional steps toward fulfillment. Furthermore, the main character and the narrator are apparently joined in marriage, the classic comic affirmation that promises the unification and survival of society. (pp. 40-1)

Robbins's basic themes might be summarized in this way: Our current society does not seem to be fulfilling many of our emotional and psychological needs. Part of this problem arises from the fact that our culture and our social institutions in particular were developed to meet needs occasioned by conditions that have changed radically over the last thousand years. Christianity compounded our problems, because (1) it was a subversion of the Pantheism that is more natural to Western man and induced Western man to cut himself off from nature, and (2) it made the personal joy and mystery of existence subservient to rules and institutions. Because our social structures are no longer responsive to our environment, those structures ought to be changed.

On the individual, psychological level, our egos are also structures which do not always correspond to our entire selves as we really exist in relationship to the universe as a whole. If we are more self-conscious but less self-centered, we may find more fulfilling lifestyles by being better aware of why we really value what we value.

In short, we must break out of our old patterns and learn from experience what we really want. We must blaze new trails of experience fighting off the Indians of chaos and defying the over-rigid schoolmarms of traditional society, until we have cleared ourselves a new territory in the realm of human experience. Most of all, we must remember that attaining fulfillment is the work of life that is continuous and always, at some level, play. (pp. 41-2)

> Mark Siegel, in his *Tom Robbins, Boise State University*, 1980, 51 p.

FRANK McCONNELL

If Thomas Pynchon were a Muppet, he would write like Tom Robbins.

That may be, indeed, a large part of the problem in reading Robbins. He's so *cute*: his books are full of cute lines populated by unrelentingly cute people, even teeming with cute animals—frogs, chipmunks, and chihuahuas in *Still Life With Woodpecker*. No one ever gets hurt very badly . . . , and although the world is threatened by the same dark, soulless business cartels that threaten the worlds of Pynchon, Mailer, and our century, in Robbins it doesn't seem, finally, to matter. Love or something like it really does conquer all in his parables, with a mixture of stoned gaiety, positive thinking, and Sunday Supplement Taoism. (p. 153)

But these are harsh words for a writer who is, undoubtedly, *the* underground undergraduate enthusiasm of the seventies. . . . Furthermore, writers as reticent as Graham Greene and as reticent as Pynchon himself have expressed high praise for his work. And (dammit, let's be honest) Robbins *is*, as a storyteller, as engaging and as fun to read, as *cuddly*, as anybody currently working at the trade.

But should we trust a cuddly novelist? The last twenty or so years of American fiction have taught us that comedy, satire, the absurd are all powerful tools for mapping the shape of the apocalypse upon whose edge we tremble. But how can we handle a writer who is comic, satiric, absurdist—but not at all apocalyptic? Cheerful, even?

His novels, laced with deliberately dopey puns, goofy digressions, and half-mixed metaphors, are virtually plotless. But not quite. "Nothing is implied here," he writes in *Still Life*,

at the end of a digression on banyan trees, Thomas Jefferson, figs, and red hair. "Except the possibility that everything is connected." Users of pharmaceutical consciousness-raisers, from cannabis to distilled malt, will of course recognize that state of mind in which everything does seem magically connected—the "oh, wow!" state of happy and temporary satori. Robbins, however, does not simply echo "oh, wow": he writes books, and that makes all the difference. (pp. 153-54)

By now there is something almost too familiar about . . . [Robbins's] fare: refried Gnosticism, twice-baked existentialism, and parboiled science fiction have all but lost their tang for us, we have had it so often. But that is almost the point of Robbins's novels. A "second-generation post-modernist" (such are the absurdities spawned by literary-critical jargon), a man for whom Pynchon, Barth, Mailer, Vonnegut el al. are elder statesmen, Robbins seems determined, at whatever cost, to reassert the fact that writing and reading fiction is fun: and, even more daringly, that fun itself is—well, fun. . . .

I have said that the plots of his novels are all fairly uncomplicated: a heroine discovers an ancient wisdom that validates her own mystic sensibility and proceeds to save the world (or part of the world) with it. But that is a distortion. In each of his novels there is also an important subplot (para-plot? hyperplot?) in which the narrator himself, a definitively masculine and definitively confused writer, falls in love with his own heroine. In *Another Roadside Attraction* the implied and wished-for mating actually takes place; in *Even Cowgirls Get the Blues* it may or may not occur after the last sentence in the book; in *Still Life With Woodpecker* it can never occur, just because the writer of fiction has finally admitted that he *is* a writer of fiction, that there is no way through his electric typewriter (a minor character in the novel) to the wonderfully sexy heroine he and the typewriter invent.

But in that distance between the rationalizing, distraught novelist and his wonderfully liberated creations lies Robbins's real strength and real brilliance. His stories insist that everything is all right, that everything rightly perceived is beautiful, is part of the Tao (the path, the way, the great lump—all translations work). But his *storytellers* incarnate his, and our, difficulty in accepting such a simple, pacific, happy gospel. So that the real plot of a Robbins novel is very like the real plot of our learning to trust his fiction.

This accounts also for his most common, and most distinctive, stylistic trick: the animation of the inanimate. Buildings, appliances, molecules, sexual organs—*anything* in his fiction apparently can, and surely will, be described as if it were alive, conscious, and lovable. During the long central section of *Still Life*, the Princess, isolated from her lover, reinvents her love and incidentally reinvents the history of civilization by contemplating that most banal artifact of advertising technology, a Camel pack. "Leigh-Cheri had come to consider the smallest, deadest thing as if it had some life of its own. . . . Her grip lingered on doorknobs much longer than necessary."

Cute, we might think. But beneath the cuteness is a very high seriousness, indeed: so serious that it refuses to take itself seriously. Leigh-Cheri's love for doorknobs not only inverts what may well be the moment of birth, in fiction, of the existentialist sensibility—the moment in Sartre's *Nausea* where Roquentin discovers the horrifying *otherness* of the world by grasping a doorknob—it also reverses, precisely, the direction of avant-garde American fiction prior to Robbins. In the world of Thomas Pynchon's stunning, paranoid fables we are all in danger of being reduced to the state of inanimacy, of flesh-and-blood robots, by the dark cartels who control our destiny. And in the world of Tom Robbins's grownup fairy tales, the world itself is on the verge of becoming as alive, as happy, and as loonily free as we think we ourselves might be in our best moments. The difference is only a matter of perception. (p. 154)

> *Frank McConnell, "Should We Trust a Cuddly Novelist?" in* Commonweal, *Vol. CVIII, No. 5, March 13, 1981, pp. 153-55.*

ROBERT NADEAU

Although the fiction of Tom Robbins may not yet appear on the syllabi of many surveys of contemporary literature, his novels seem to have something like the same following among college students as the fiction of Barth or Pynchon did before they became fully legitimated as makers of elitist art. It is interesting from our point of view, however, that concepts from physics, which are for the most part implicit as structuring principles in the art of the more established novelists, are treated in the fiction of this relative newcomer as concerns that must be reckoned with openly. Robbins boldly assumes his reader's familiarity with the fundamental precepts of the new physics and proceeds to explore their metaphysical implications as if that were the inevitable consequence of confrontation with these new ideas. (p. 149)

Another unique aspect of Robbins's fiction relating to physics is the recognition that the unitary conception of being in the great religious philosophies of the East (Hinduism, Buddhism, Taoism) is far more compatible with discoveries made in the new physics than the dualistic Western model. As Fritjof Capra nicely demonstrates [in *The Tao of Physics*], . . . the Eastern emphasis upon the unity and interrelatedness of all things in a cosmos that is forever moving, alive, and organic is rather strikingly close to the understanding of the life process implied in the new physics. Although Robbins is aware of the correspondences and frequently takes note of them, he is clearly not advocating that the spiritually impoverished West take the first boat, metaphorically or otherwise, to the spiritually enlightened East. Even if such a dramatic restructuring of Western consciousness were desirable, it is not, as Robbins makes clear in [*Even Cowgirls Get the Blues*], a possibility. The backlog of inherited culture is simply too great, as Barth suggested in *Giles,* to effect such a transformation within any of our lifetimes. Robbins's intent rather is to hammer away relentlessly at those assumptions about self and world in Western cosmology which he feels are injurious to our emotional well-being and a threat to our continued survival as a species.

The narrator of *Another Roadside Attraction,* a whiz kid who once dreamed of "becoming a great theoretical physicist on the order of Werner Heisenberg or Einstein," describes in an admittedly "indeterminate" fashion the wonderfully bizarre happenings in the life of Amanda and John Paul Ziller and their zany partner in the greatest heist in any century—Plucky Purcell. (pp. 149-50)

The metaphysics endorsed by this wonderfully unique couple owes much to Eastern religious thought, but what is most striking is their continued reliance upon concepts from the new physics to illustrate the efficacy of this vision of the nature of being. . . . The notion from the new physics that all life processes are unified appears quite frequently in Amanda's mystic pronouncements. After concluding in a discussion with Marx

Marvelous that it is just as spiritually proper to eat animals as plants, Amanda offers the following explanation for this change in her philosophical position: "At the higher levels of consciousness all things are one anyway. There is no difference between animal, vegetable and mineral. Everything just blends together in energy and light." . . . (pp. 150-51)

For the quantum theorists the indeterminacy principle . . . implies that no static, abstract law or formula can predict to the nth degree the results of interactions on the micro level. There is, then, a mystery in natural process that is quite literally "behind *everything* in life" which will inevitably frustrate our desire to know or discover meaning in the absolute sense. Amanda has no difficulty with this realization because she recognizes that "not knowing" in the sense of being unable to predict the direction and force of physical change is the condition of our freedom. If we are simply one of the expressions of the energy that is all life, then that element of hazard in nature which makes all the happenings in the cosmos ultimately open-ended and hence free is also present in our own experience. (p. 152)

The strident criticism of the Roman Catholic Church occasioned by Plucky's theft of Christ's corpse from the lower-level catacombs at the Vatican should not be read simply as an ill-mannered attack on one of the greatest civilizing influences in the Western world. The Roman Catholic church is simply a convenient vehicle used by Robbins to point up those features of Western cosmology that delimit our freedom and engagement in a life process whose internal workings now appear to suggest that several major assumptions upon which that cosmology is based are false. . . . It is clearly Robbins's hope, and perhaps even belief, that the new cosmology and the new ethics advertised in the novel are already at work in this culture and displacing the old world order. As Marvelous puts it, we stand at the beginning of a "Golden Age." . . . (p. 153)

Robbins's second novel, *Even Cowgirls Get the Blues,* is also replete with references to concepts from the new physics, but the emphasis here appears to be on the potential impact of these concepts upon our understanding of the nature and function of time. We have assumed in the Judeo-Christian tradition not only, as Newton formalized it, that time is a separate dimension, but also that our experience in time is a linear, rational progression with beginning, middle, and end. Einstein's relativity theory in addition to proving that time cannot exist separately from space also demonstrated that perception of events in time is relative because it is dependent upon the position of the observer in relation to the observed event. Quantum theory invalidates the notion of linear, rational progression of events in time because of the quantum interconnectedness of all subatomic events and also because of the indeterminate nature of these processes. Outfitted by one of nature's chance mutations with incredibly oversized thumbs, Sissy's commitment to hitchhiking is justified as a mode of being-in-time by appealing to concepts from physics: "Einstein had observed motion and learned that space and time are relative; Sissy had committed herself to motion and learned that one could alter reality by one's perception of it." (p. 156)

The "clocks" constructed by the Clock People and the clock in the Chink's cave on Siwash Ridge overlooking the Rubber Rose Ranch, occasion an extended, rather formal philosophical discourse upon experience-in-time in light of what is now known in physics. Robbins's parody of the accepted view of time as a series of discontinuous units which divide up, contain, and measure experience, takes the form of the huge seven-foot-wide and thirteen-foot-tall hourglass in the clockworks. Approximately thirteen hours are required for the acorns to funnel through the waist of the device representing the twenty-six-hour day of the Clock People. Our own twenty-four-hour day may be a bit more commensurate with the diurnal revolutions of this planet moving about its sun, but the measure is, finally, simply an arbitrary convention like that of the Clock People. (pp. 156-57)

The Chink's clockworks . . . is designed to help him sustain an awareness of the randomness or indeterminacy of natural process that makes freedom a human possibility. Laws, as the ostensible narrator Dr. Robbins notes, "that pretend that reality is fixed and nature is definable are antilife." . . . It is our belief in the existence of such laws, nicely fostered by classical physics, which, the novel suggests, causes us to live within the narrow confines of received conceptions of the real and precludes an active, imaginative realization of life's enormous possibilities. (pp. 157-58)

The present state of Western civilization is obviously, as Robbins sees it, a product of the belief in a cosmology that assumes that man, existing on some higher plane of being, has a rightful dominion over all nature. . . . According to the cultural anthropologists, the ability of our prehistoric ancestors to manipulate the thumb in a manner that allowed for the facile use of tools, which resulted in a rapid increase in the size of the brain, eventually making it possible to use symbolic language systems, has culminated in the development of a technology that in the long term could make the planet unlivable and in the short term transform it beyond all recognition in a nuclear holocaust. Robbins highlights what he considers to be our profound stupidity at the close of the novel by suggesting that Sissy and Dr. Robbins will be protected from the effects of the nuclear disaster in their cave dwelling on Siwash Ridge and will become, like Adam and Eve, the "first parents" of generations of men outfitted with thumbs that make any elaborate use of tools an impossibility. In this garden there will be no God-parent and forbidden fruit, for the cosmology derived in part from the Chink and firmly implanted in the minds of these enlightened scientifically minded primitives, counsels full participation in a unified, holistic life process that is essentially indeterminate in character and hence not governed by any fixed, immutable laws.

We need not conclude, of course, that concepts from physics will occasion a commitment to the bizarre and essentially adolescent lifestyle of Robbins's major characters, but it is difficult not to take seriously his philosophical speculations upon their metaphysical import. When writers of popular fiction like Robbins borrow concepts that not so very long ago were merely the esoteric concerns of a small community of scientists and make them accessible to something like a mass audience, I suggest that it is time to begin contemplating the appearance in our culture of a revolution in thought of the first order. Academic humanists who have grown accustomed to thinking of physics, or of all science for that matter, as a dull, predictable and, in their own terms, essentially unimaginative pursuit that has very little to do with the "real" business of life, may very well be in for a shock. (pp. 159-60)

Robert Nadeau, "Tom Robbins," in his Readings from the New Book on Nature: Physics and Metaphysics in the Modern Novel, *University of Massachusetts Press, 1981, pp. 149-61.*

RUDY RUCKER

Jitterbug Perfume has a large and exotic cast of characters, all of whom are interested in immortality and/or perfume. There is Priscilla in Seattle, a "genius waitress" who spends her off hours trying to invent the ultimate perfume. In New Orleans, we have Madame Devalier and V'lu, sometime potion-merchants now in search for the same jasmine-based scent as Priscilla is. In Paris there are the LeFever brothers of LeFever Fragrances. . . . Back in Seattle, there is Wiggs Dannyboy, a Timothy Leary work-alike who's given up acid for immortality research. And most important of all, there are Alobar and Kudra, immortal lovers who trek from medieval Bohemia to present-day Paris by way of a Tibetan lamasery, the Bandaloop caves in India, Byzantine Constantinople, Pan's Greece, frontier America, and the after-world.

The Alobar and Kudra story is the living heart of this book; somehow these two seem to have solved the problem that exercised Robbins in his last book, *Still Life With Woodpecker:* "Who knows how to make love stay?" Alobar and Kudra stay in love century after century. (pp. 1, 9)

What do perfume and immortality have to do with each other? They are both related to memory. Marcel (!) LeFever makes the point that familiar smells seem to bring back memories more effectively than, say, photographs or tape-recordings. . . . [When] Kudra dematerializes and visits the afterworld, she learns that each soul brings along, as a kind of memory-aid, his or her favorite aroma: "a child's blanket, a backyard garden, a mother's kitchen, a horse, a factory, an artist's brush, an opium pipe." A nice feature of *Jitterbug Perfume* is that all the smells in it are pleasant.

Another nexus between perfume and immortality is sex: sexual attraction has a strong olfactory component, and orgasms give sensations of timelessness. The characters in this book make love a lot. Simple, commercial pornography has a surreal and transcendent quality that, in some ways, approaches good primitive art. But primitive art gentrifies easily into polystyrene masks and giant salad-spoons. By the time Wiggs gets Priscilla for the fourth or fifth time, I found myself thinking, "Who cares?". . . . Still, with regard to Robbins' fascination with sex, one might best echo Alobar's comment on Pan: "'I feel somehow that his lechery was secondary, although to what I cannot say.'"

The real joy in any Tom Robbins book is the mesmerizing flow of remarkable observations and fresh similes. . . . A chauvinistic Frenchman feels that English is "a language fit only for narrating animated cartoons and inciting crowds at sporting events"; but how can we believe him, when Robbins begins a scene in New Orleans with, "Louisiana in September was like an obscene phone call from nature. The air—moist, sultry, secretive, and far from fresh—felt as if it were being exhaled into one's face." . . .

Robbins' first two novels, *Another Roadside Attraction* and *Only Cowgirls Get The Blues,* were '60s novels—filled with mushrooms and visions, radicals and police. *Still Life With Woodpecker* is about the '70s viewed as aftermath of the '60s. How does *Jitterbug Perfume* fit in? Has Tom Robbins moved into the '80s?

Yes and no. Robbins is still very much his old Pan-worshipping self, yet his new book is lovingly plotted, with every conceivable loose end nailed down tight. Although the ideas are the same as ever, the form is contemporary, neo-realistic craftsmanship. Robbins toys with the 1980s' peculiar love/hate for the '60s through his invention of the character Wiggs Dannyboy: drug-guru, jailbird, immortality advocate. As if to push the Leary similarity into deliberate parody, Robbins often has Dannyboy talk in a corny Irish accent that set this reader's hair on end. . . .

But I've forgotten the *beets*! It would be hard to find any other book that even mentions beets, yet this intricate book, about perfume and immortality, has beets on nearly every page. Why? Go see for yourself; you'll have a good time. (p. 9)

> Rudy Rucker, "In Search of the Ultimate Love Potion," in Book World—The Washington Post, *November 25, 1984, pp. 1, 9.*

GARY BLONSTON

When Tom Robbins published **"Another Roadside Attraction"** in 1971 and then topped it with **"Even Cowgirls Get the Blues"** in 1976, it appeared a new madman-genius of fiction had been loosed from the American counterculture. But the counterculture grew up, and in 1981, when he put out the humdrum and commercial **"Still Life with Woodpecker,"** he sold some books, but phrases like "sold-out" and "burned-out" kept coming to mind.

Well, not true. The old Tom Robbins is back, and with his newest novel, **"Jitterbug Perfume,"** he proves he is fully as crazy as ever, as full of astonishing word play, unimaginable characters and swooshing flights of observation. **"Jitterbug"** is as funny and weird and wise and wide-ranging and bizarre as even the most jaded ex-Robbins fan could ask.

It is about beet pollen.

And a thousand-year-old man. And three succulent women, and one aging fat one. And Pan, and perfume, and Paris, and permanence, and perfidy. And sex.

Robbins writes about sex the way Roger Kahn writes about baseball, the way Calvin Trillin writes about food, the way Boswell wrote about Johnson, and none of his books lack a woman of such sexual pliance and aptitude that most people probably could live happy, fulfilled sex lives just savoring Robbins' leftover fantasies.

[**"Jitterbug Perfume"**] is generally about the value and enhancement of life and the creation of the ultimate scent. It isn't easy to explain Tom Robbins books.

It is easy to extoll them, though, and this one in particular takes the wild energy and fancy of his early books and combines them with a raft-in-a-rapids sort of control that, in comparison to his first work, makes **"Jitterbug Perfume"** at times seem downright disciplined. Without sacrificing any of his remarkable unravelings of imagination and his renegade comic philosophy, without diluting the wonderful madness at the heart of what he does, Robbins has produced an intricately fitted novel capable of neatly resolving the relations of beets and gods and immortalists and perfumists while having and giving a very good time.

> Gary Blonston, "A Welcome Return of the Old, Maniacal Tom Robbins," in Detroit Free Press, *December 5, 1984, p. 9C.*

JOHN HOUSE

Tom Robbins is Carlos Castaneda in motley, Leo Buscaglia in love beads. Like his earlier books, **"Jitterbug Perfume"** is not so much a novel as an inspirational fable, full of Hallmark sweetness, good examples and hope springing eternal. Its message is a simple one—"it is better to be small, colorful, sexy, careless, and peaceful, like the flowers, than large, conservative, repressed, fearful, and aggressive, like the thunder lizards." While the world has changed substantially since 1971, the year of Mr. Robbins's first novel, **"Another Roadside Attraction,"** his odd corner of it has remained intact, caught in the amber of 1960's romanticism. . . .

Mr. Robbins's style is unmistakable—oblique, florid, willing to sacrifice everything for an old joke or corny pun. . . . Here and there, like SMILE buttons pinned to the narrative, are wry digressions on plant life and arcane lore. The cast is always the same—the lumpy, stolid authorities; the wavering skeptic (usually played by the author); the seekers after truth, who, if pure of heart, are soon initiated into the higher mysteries; the outlaws, one male and one female (the goat god and the mother goddess), stamped with shining individuality and a salty holiness. There are homilies about balance and fullness and cautionary tales about succumbing to reason. The heroes are Thoreauvian idealists preaching sexual enlightenment. Reading Mr. Robbins, you could almost believe that not everyone went back to business school after Woodstock. . . .

"Jitterbug Perfume," Mr. Robbins's fourth book, is neither as haywire as [**"Still Life with Woodpecker"**] nor as imaginatively and engagingly loony as [**"Even Cowgirls Get the Blues"**]. The imagery is strained . . . and the pronouncements are suspect. . . . The primitive mysteries taste suspiciously modern—earth, air, fire and water become the components of a life-prolonging regimen and are interpreted as whole foods, yogic breathing, frequent sex and soaks in the hot tub. And though its central lesson is "Lighten up," it suffers from a kind of existential fatigue. As the author charts the ascendancy of "the gold-dust twins, Christianity and Commerce," over joyous, Pan-theistic paganism, a certain crankiness enters his voice; he seems unwillingly resigned to the idea that being here now will never be as exciting as having been there then. The 60's, he argues, were the years of "a collective spiritual awakening that flared brilliantly until the barbaric and mediocre impulses of the species drew tight once more the curtains of darkness."

At the heart of **"Jitterbug Perfume"** are odor, with its undying capacity to stir up longings and memories, and spiritual illumination, timeless and complete. Thrown together into Mr. Robbins's now familiar stew, they emerge as "floral consciousness," a concept only Timothy Leary could love. . . . Tom Robbins . . . has stopped showing signs of aging. In four books over 13 years, he has clung to the values and attitudes of a peculiar slice of American history, and the nostalgic kick that his work gives—that of "The Big Chill"—is wearing off. "As the afternoon progresses," he laments, "our shadows grow longer. At night, we *become* our shadows. That is as true today as then. In the old days, people were aware of it, that's all. In the old days, the whole would was religious and full of interest." Is it really all over?

> John House, "They Brake for Unicorns," in The New York Times Book Review, *December 9, 1984, p. 11.*

Louis (Aston Marantz) Simpson

1923-

Jamaican-born American poet, critic, editor, novelist, dramatist, and nonfiction writer.

Simpson is an important figure in post-World War II American poetry. While the nature of his poetry has changed during the course of his career, he has been consistently praised as an insightful and resourceful poet whose work is accessible to a wide audience. Simpson has adopted a number of different approaches toward his subject matter, which has focused on such topics as war, love, and American society. In all of his works, Simpson relies heavily on imagery to evoke emotion and suggest meaning.

Critics have distinguished three stages of development in Simpson's work. The poems collected in his first three published volumes—*The Arrivistes* (1949), *Good News of Death* (1955), and *A Dream of Governors* (1959)—are characterized by his use of conventional poetic forms and are communicated through a detached voice. For the most part, these volumes contain finely crafted lyrics written with careful attention to meter and rhyme. Some of these poems recount Simpson's experiences as a soldier in World War II and express antiwar sentiments, while others deal with love. The war poems are generally considered Simpson's most effective early work, particularly "Carentan O Carentan" from *The Arrivistes*.

At the End of the Open Road (1963) is regarded as a transitional work. With this volume, Simpson adopted a more personal and direct expression and he began writing poems in free verse. Much of Simpson's poetry composed during the 1960s reproves contemporary American culture and society. During this period, Simpson often used surreal imagery to express his feelings of alienation, a practice that probably reflects the influence of Simpson's friend and fellow poet, Robert Bly. Most critics were impressed with those poems in *At the End of the Open Road* which invoke Walt Whitman's idealistic view of American democracy and society. Simpson expresses a sense of loss and regret by contrasting the idyllic future prophesied by Whitman with the materialistic culture of modern, urbanized America. *At the End of the Open Road* was awarded the Pulitzer Prize for poetry.

In the 1970s, Simpson began to express empathy for America and its citizens. His poetry became plainer, unadorned, and almost prosaic, conveying meaning through fully developed images rather than through the surreal imagery of much of his verse of the 1960s. Many of these poems are lyric narratives that focus on the routine activities of modern Americans, especially ordinary, middle-class, suburban residents. Like Whitman and William Wordsworth, Simpson attempts to render such experiences in common, informal language. The volume *Caviare at the Funeral* (1981), which contains many poems written with this purpose, is viewed as one of Simpson's most important works. Some critics have compared his concerns and narrative approach to similar elements in the short stories of Anton Chekhov, whom Simpson has acknowledged as a strong influence. In *The Best Hour of the Night* (1983), Simpson continues to focus on the lives of ordinary Americans, finding significance in their everyday activities.

Photograph by Susan Demarest, reproduced by permission of Louis Simpson

People Live Here: Poems 1949-1983 (1983) offers a retrospective of Simpson's career and shows the continuing development and sustained achievement of Simpson's poetry. On the basis of this collection and *The Best Hour of the Night*, critics have reaffirmed that Simpson is among the finest contemporary American poets.

(See also *CLC*, Vols. 4, 7, 9; *Contemporary Authors*, Vols. 1-4, rev. ed.; *Contemporary Authors New Revision Series*, Vol. 1; and *Dictionary of Literary Biography*, Vol. 5.)

DAVE SMITH

In 1967, M. L. Rosenthal, in *The New Poets*, described a number of poets he found to have some tenuous connection with Robert Bly's *The Sixties* and said of them ". . . this group, which includes Robert Bly, Donald Hall, Louis Simpson, James Wright, and James Dickey, is seeking to affect the aims of American poetry. . . ." (p. 10)

More than two decades have passed since the first books of these poets appeared and though it is still unclear that any of their names will name the literary age to be described in anthologies years hence, no serious reader of poetry can be unaware that each has affected not only what American poetry is but also what it might be. If it is impossible to think of Bly,

Hall, Simpson, Wright, and Dickey as conspirators of one mind, it is nevertheless true that together they have created poetry of a surfaced, examined, and revitalized inner life, a life not merely of the mind, but of the personalized mind. They have been noisy, exuberant, truculent, testy, and necessary—like many children in a house too small. Of Rosenthal's appointed group, perhaps the quietest and least public and even least affective on younger poets has been Louis Simpson.

A practising Christian would surely remind me here that the least shall enter Heaven first and a good case for that could be made on Simpson's behalf. In the end it is not going to be noise or influence that matters, but the durable quality and scope of achieved art. No one of that grouping seems to have so steadily and honestly gone on creating a credible and sharable vision of life in this world, in these times, more than Simpson has. It is, of course, not necessary to reduce the value and accomplishment of another poet to praise Simpson. I have no wish to do that. I only say that the poetry of Louis Simpson seems to me extraordinarily beautiful and complex, that it demonstrates an engagement with the vissicitudes and antinomies of American life in the sixties and seventies that is equal to the best we have, and that it may even possess a greater, quieter power of staying because it is extremely accessible. Accessible, yes, but scarcely without the deep resonance and luminosity of an imaginative intelligence whose reach is inward and outward, vertical and horizontal at the same time. . . .

Louis Simpson's poetry is marked by its steady development in two directions. From the beginning he has wanted a synthetic vision, hence his attraction to Whitman, which would discover and fix the true nature of human existence and which, moreover, would reaffirm traditional and timeless values of the human as social and responsible creature who might, nevertheless, intuit some binding, beyond-human force. He has been, therefore, a consistently moral and ethical poet. Not, I insist quickly, a moralistic poet, one who writes a poetry whose bent bends our ears with a prefabricated polemic. He has not been a ferocious preacher in the manner of Bly, but he has been a kind of conscience in the way of Wright. And, like Wright, Simpson has always found himself equipped with an ironist voice, a disposition toward a poetry of steely intelligence which would play Mercutio to a poetry of Romantic and synthetic moaning in the dark bushes. It is this second strain in his poetry which accounts for his frequent humor, satire, social comment, good citizenry, and, ultimately, the evolution of his mature poetic style. Simpson has come far from that ideal music of the fifties—his language now, as Randall Jarrell would say, is clear enough even for cats and dogs; he has come to a certain unfashionable narrative base, to a poetry that unabashedly employs the devices of prose fiction. But not, it should be noted, to the fashionable prose-poem, for he appears to believe he can still detect a valuable difference between poetry and prose, a difference that is marked by the continued prominence of such tensions and ironies as are generated by the contending of mind and heart under equal pressure.

Louis Simpson has made a poetry out of ourselves who want mystical unity, harmony, and escape from the almost unendurable brutalities of the world; but he has also made it out of ourselves who are grinning realists, who know that escape from the difficulties of being human, especially in poetry—whose function is to help us be more human, serves the forces of brutalization and division. Simpson has never forgotten, moralist and artist as he is, that a poem must have an audience before it is a true poem, that such a poem is a bridge to

somewhere and someone. His poems, therefore, are always testing their own authority and reality—they are always having to prove their right to exist—for he has wanted what he has increasingly created, an art which speaks in plain language about subjects experienced in a social world of ordinary people. He says, "I have a sort of Wordsworthian vision: a picture of a very ordinary human being who is also highly intelligent and likes to read poetry; he is the one I write for. This man knows what a garage looks like, this man knows what a milk-bottle sounds like on the back porch in the morning." Simpson does not aspire to mass pablum, however, but to a total and authentic communication through art, a speaking that is both deeply personal and broadly human. . . .

More than his contemporaries, then, Simpson has searched for a poetry which would not be content with either a fabric of associational images and an esoteric mysticism nor a poetry of received ideas and rational discourse. Though his early work demonstrated the traditional, literate, and neatly cadenced character of late Modernism, there was also a strain of fresh diction which was not decorative figuring but muscular nomination. He moved away from the poem *bien fait,* closer to that diction which James Wright called the "poetry of a grown man." Increasingly he has employed rhythms and organizational units which parallel actual human speech, knowing it was this speech which would allow the resonance of both personal and mythic, or psychic if you will, depths. This direction has meant a reliance on image juxtaposition that has seemed to some critics to keep him in lock-step with Robert Bly, but he has never been truly illogical or surreal. While others have gravitated toward hermetic languages of utter personality, toward European modes of the fabular, toward anecdotal journalism, Simpson, like Wordsworth, has sought a dialect of the actually spoken. He has told stories in a parabolic speech of local roots. It is as if he had believed everything in the phenomenal world might speak if the right plain language would be wrestled to the purpose. The risk, and he has sometimes succumbed to it, has been a loss of tension, a flattened music, a prose. The gain has been that widened world of human experience which is not *merely* personal, which is never parlor gamesmanship or cosmic buffoonery, which is recognizably diverse, contradictory, mature, and immediate. He has come to a poetry that, as he says, "addresses itself to the human condition, a poetry of truth, not dreams . . . [that] depicts human actions and the way we live. . . . Not a mere relation of events, but a narrative of significant actions." (p. 11)

Dave Smith, "A Child of the World," in The American Poetry Review, Vol. 8, No. 1, January-February, 1979, pp. 10-15.

PETER STITT

The astonishing thing about *Caviare at the Funeral* is its radical presentation of American life. It has long seemed to me that Louis Simpson is among the most American of all American poets. Somehow the fact that he was born and raised in Jamaica and came to this country only in his eighteenth year has enabled him to see us, our land and our ways, with unusually clear vision.

His earlier work, especially in *At the End of the Open Road,* shows an understanding of America rarely seen. . . . In *Caviare at the Funeral* Simpson carries his insights several steps further in the creation of a poetry of everyday American life. I don't mean the life we see in most of our poetry, life as it is lived in the university classrooms and college towns, in the slick bars and elegant cafés, nor even on the unreal, atypical streets of New York. No, Simpson gives us something altogether more usual and unusual, the commonest life of all and the one least often found in our poetry—the suburban life of the average middle-class family.

The most remarkable poem in this regard, and one of the best poems in the book, is **"The Beaded Pear."** A family goes shopping—"Dad in Bermuda shorts, Mom her hair in curlers, / Jimmy, sixteen, and Darlene who is twelve, / are walking through the Smith Haven Mall."—and later we see them at home. . . . The most important question about a poem like this concerns its tone—are the lines satiric, sarcastic, destructive, hateful? They are not, however much we may be tempted to read them that way. Nor are they celebratory; rather, Simpson is concerned to describe, carefully, emphatically, the nature of American life.

Of course a distinction must be drawn between the sensibility (the relative level of understanding and intelligence) of the poet and that of the people he writes about. His insights are more acute than theirs, for he sees with a double sight—his stance as writer places him both within the action and apart from it; he is both participant and observer. . . . The difference is that most of the people Simpson writes about live only on the surface of things, whereas he, the poet, wishes to know that level at the same time as he penetrates beyond it. (pp. 183-84)

The quality of the writing in this book is very high. So close is Simpson's mature style to prose, excluding the obvious musical devices of poetry, that great pressure is placed on his use of voice, structure, and imagery. In all three areas, these poems are near models of perfection. . . . *Caviare at the Funeral* is a courageous book, in content as well as in form. Simpson is going against the tides of fashion in his attempt to reestablish the narrative line and a version of the common man at the heart of American poetry. What looks so average and everyday on the surface actually represents a radical originality; Simpson's discoveries are akin in importance to those of Wordsworth and Whitman, who also tried, in their differing ways, to bring the common life into poetry. (pp. 184-85)

Peter Stitt, "Purity and Impurity in Poetry," in The Georgia Review, *Vol. XXXV, No. 1, Spring, 1981, pp. 182-89.*

G. E. MURRAY

At a minimum, incisive poets may serve [their] era by suggesting some levels of personal good sense relative to certain senseless, impersonal realities. Further to the point, the right poet's eye can fire mysteries in both extreme and ordinary events. Such aspects of the art connect with the modern poet's secret goal to establish a private foothold of authority, what John Berryman called "imperial sway," or that which Wallace Stevens understood as "a sensible ecstasy." It would seem that this is the potential edge poetry makes available to any number of its most capable and intimate handlers.

Louis Simpson, of course, knows where and how this authoritative edge cuts. Indeed, just when it seems that Simpson has reached the comfortable height of his powers, as evidenced by six formidable earlier collections, including the Pulitzer Prize winning *At the End of the Open Road,* he penetrates forward with *Caviare at the Funeral.*

All of his best ruling qualities are displayed in this work: the introspective and observant eye, expressive detail, an easy mastery of line and stanza, the storyteller's craft and unassailable wisdom, a spirit of slightly cryptic conversation, his way of rendering anew the tactile world, usually in lamentable decline or disrepair. All this we have come to expect from Simpson.

But now there is more: this poet's ability to transmute elements of his poems into something even richer and more profound than before, to invest the poem with an unmistakable radiance that inspires the lines yet somehow remains outside them, like a nimbus around the head of a saint. One begins to suspect that he sanctions this effect, in part, through an extensive range of delivery systems—descriptive, lyrical, funny, somber, fantastic. So much of Simpson's maturity comes, ironically, from his ability to heed the challenges of experiment, to stay verbally energetic.

The longer storytelling poems remain his most compelling, in this instance particularly the title work, **"Chocolates," "The Man She Loved," "Sway," "Typhus,"** and **"Why Do You Write About Russia."** Sometimes it is as if Simpson is the most cunning of sleuths, able to reconstruct the far-fetched story of a life from "the contents of your purse . . . / among Kleenex, aspirin, / chewing gum wrapper, combs, et cetera." Then other times the story merely emerges from air, the narrator staring out the kitchen door on a hot, bug-ridden night.

There is humor here, too, but what to call it? Not black humor, and not white humor either. Poetic humor, then, in the most delicate of circumstances. And the wisdom of the humor comes from the association created between the body of the poem's stated experience and Simpson's imposition of a conclusion, his valued judgment at the end, which understands that the "words you thought were a joke, / And applied to someone else, / were real, and applied to you."

As usual, Simpson also examines the underbelly of American landscape, our urban shams and sorrows, especially in the excellent three-part movement **"The Beaded Pear."** But he confronts more than the bitter shortcomings inherent in our roadside junkyards, shopping malls and real estate agencies. American life—in its abundance and flux—is his projected subject. Since he does encompass so much, in unpredictable patterns, unconcerned with climaxes (the usual poetical devices are unnecessary here), the lines at last just move. Then the pointillist's dots of individual images begin to shape into surprisingly complex yet familiar configurations. Once onto this mode, one is forced to conclude that it's the real world that is arbitrary, while these poems seem inevitable.

Such is the final authority Simpson commands in this edition of thirty-four new titles, most of which provide conclusive evidence of remarkable advances in suppleness, clarity, balance, scope of feeling and thought amid the strangeness of contemporary passions. (pp. 155-56)

G. E. Murray, "Seven Poets," in The Hudson Review, *Vol. XXXIV, No. 1, Spring, 1981, pp. 155-60.*

ROBERT B. SHAW

Louis Simpson's poems in *Caviare at the Funeral* are typically narrative; they are also typically brief, none going beyond a few pages. The poet hasn't made things easy for himself. Telling stories in verse is a demanding procedure because many of the features we appreciate in prose fiction—a sense of events spawning events, of characters developing or disintegrating, days passing into days—are seemingly at odds with the compactness of poetry. It has been often observed that poems relax in style as they grow in length. I would have expected that in composing such brief narratives Simpson's aim would be to avoid this stylistic dilution. But the style of the poems is, if not diluted, systematically understated. There is an odd mingling of effects, offering within tightly drawn boundaries a language that lacks the heightening which many poets would attempt to bring to such pieces.

Because the style is so determinedly unobstrusive the reader's attention focuses on content. The results vary. **"New Lots"** wanders randomly in and out of decades in the lives of an immigrant family transplanted from Russia to New York. The poet seems more concerned with evoking atmosphere and recording period detail than with rendering character or significant incident. This and some of the other poems employ the gestures of narrative without having, apparently, much of a story to convey. I found myself wondering: Shouldn't our past, rather than our nostalgia for it, be the chief object of interest?

In **"Sway,"** a poem made up of memories of a summer friendship, far in the past, with a resort hotel waitress, the narrator recalls wryly his youthful ambition: "to write novels conveying the excitement / of life." The waitress herself, he tells us, went into an attempted novel.... It is not very exciting, as the speaker proceeds to admit with an admirable ingenuousness: "Then the trouble begins. I can never think of anything / to make the characters do." This is a blandly crafty apologia, in which the poet, by opting to beat the critic to the punch, exposes the most vulnerable aspect of his enterprise. I doubt whether any but a highly intelligent writer would be capable of imperiling a poem in this particular way, through such a sudden yet calculated eruption of self-consciousness.

Although I have found Simpson's aims and methods sometimes puzzling, I would not wish to say that the book is a bad one. There are examples in which the stance of the poet toward his material is not so much in question, and in such cases the poems are impressive. In **"Working Late,"** the poet's memories of his lawyer father and of his own childhood in the West Indies are clearly on target.... **"Caviare at the Funeral"** and **"Chocolates,"** based on Chekhov's life and writing, are poems which might have been mere versified anecdotes but which achieve a memorable tone, sad and probing, which approaches Chekhov's own. (If Simpson were as frequently effective in dealing with eventlessness as Chekhov, my objections to some of his longer poems would be gladly abandoned.) **"Typhus"** is a quietly harrowing piece which the content is easily strong enough to carry; the dry, unemphatic presentation here seems absolutely right. Rhetoric would have ruined this piece drawn from a woman's memories of an epidemic she survived and the harsh childhood in old Russia which she survived into. It would be ill-served by anything but full quotation. Celebrating the unconscious heroism of one survivor, it remains in the mind as an emblem of human endurance. For poems such as this Simpson's book is well worth having. (pp. 171-73)

Robert B. Shaw, "Quartet," in Poetry, *Vol. CXXXIX, No. 3, December, 1981, pp. 171-77.**

PETER BLAND

Louis Simpson once wrote that 'The Open Road goes to the used-car lot.' It doesn't any more. It goes to a suburban cul-de-sac where:

Most people are content
to make a decent living.
They take pride in their homes and raising a family.
The women attend meetings at the PTA ...
There aren't too many alternatives.

The prosaic nature of the language mirrors the life-style, as does its easy-going, good-natured tone of speech. Simpson's poems [in *Caviare at the Funeral*] are all 'up front'. He can talk about spiritual emptiness without being boring. He's never superior to his subject. It's a considerable and democratic art. If life is prosaic it still has to he understood. A couple stand by the freeway with their broken-down car. 'They look surprised, and ashamed / to be so helpless ... let down in the middle of the road!' ... The American Dream is beached by the roadside. Simpson's characters are like people in an Edward Hopper painting. They look up from their work-bench or office-desk to find themselves strangely exiled in the light and landscape that surrounds them. America is something 'other' than they thought and worked for. The gods killed at Wounded Knee now stare back above the sprinklers in Orange County. They are placated at the golf club and in the shopping mall, but still something is missing.... If America (like other Super Powers) is isolated in the world at large, then the individual American is also isolated within his own self-created world. Simpson has gradually moved from more general and symbolic statements about the American way of life ('**At the end of the Open Road 1963**') to a more detailed and disturbing—but essentially humane—analysis of everyday actualities....

[The sequence *The Beaded Pear* follows] an 'average' American suburban family through its day, using place-names, reported speech, narrative asides, and all manner of literary collage to re-create 'reality'. Simpson lets America speak for itself but, of course, the truest poetry *is* the most feigning, and the *impression* of reality so beautifully created is a considerable work of imagination, of skillfully *imposed* order. (p. 81)

Peter Bland, "Summer Cobwebs," in London Magazine, *Vol. 21, No. 11, February, 1982, pp. 79-81.**

PETER STITT

The simultaneous publication of these two books—*People Live Here: Selected Poems 1949-1983* and *The Best Hour of the Night*—offers the opportunity for both a retrospective view of the career of Louis Simpson and an assessment of his maturest and most characteristic work. *People Live Here,* which is based upon seven separate earlier volumes, makes clear that there are three major phases to be found in the body of Simpson's work, phases which are separated by major changes in style, subject matter, and approach.

The poems in Simpson's first three books—*The Arrivestes* (1949), *Good News of Death* (1955), and *A Dream of Governors* (1959)—are written in tight, traditional English lyric forms, forms that have the effect of dissociating the poet's sensibility from the very material he is attempting to write about. In many of these early efforts, Simpson sounds rather like the new metaphysical poets, who had their vogue in the 1940's and '50's. (p. 662)

It was after the publication of his third book that Simpson made the first major change in his work. To bring more of his own voice into his poetry, he abandoned traditional English forms and began to write in free verse.... Besides being more relaxed, the new style is more personal than the old, giving the reader a more direct impression of the sensibility that informs these poems. In fact, the feature which above all others gives unity to the poetry of Louis Simpson is his concern with the way this sensibility reacts to and interacts with the society that surrounds him.

We must not conclude from this, however, that Simpson is a confessional poet. Confessional poetry is personal because it takes for its subject matter the literal details of the poet's life and feelings, the truth of that life as lived in the real world; Simpson's poetry is personal because it emerges from and expresses a single, central, perceiving sensibility. Although the effect of this can be even more intimate than what the reader experiences in confessional poetry, it is achieved while the poet maintains a reticent posture with regard to the external details of his life. (p. 663)

At the same time that he was striving for a greater directness in his style, Simpson also effected a radical change in the subject matter of his poetry. Generally speaking, his early poems may be said to exist in the disembodied nowhere land of traditional lyric poetry. With the publication of his fourth volume, *At the End of the Open Road* (1963), Simpson turned emphatically to America for both his setting and his themes. . . . The sensibility which speaks and thinks in Simpson's poems is seriously alienated from America during the second phase of his work. America is seen as the country which not only had killed the Indians but was also participating, indefensibly, in an unjust war in Vietnam. The only recourse open to the sensitive individual was to retreat into a kind of protective isolation. . . . (pp. 663-64)

With the publication of *Adventures of the Letter I* (1971), Simpson's work began to develop away from the alienation expressed in phase two towards a stronger feeling of brotherly love. . . .

Simpson is coming to empathize more directly with his fellow "footsoldiers" and their ordinary "human suffering." No longer will his protagonist feel so "cut off in his affections from the people around him"; he will not hold the citizenry at large responsible for such atrocities as the American participation in Vietnam—that rap will be pinned on those who earn it, the "officer class" generally. The most important change in Simpson's work at this point in his career, then, is the increased sense of empathy those poems express for other people. The change in attitude—and in method of operation—on the part of the Simpson protagonist is made clear in a poem like **"The Mexican Woman,"** from *Caviare at the Funeral* [1981]. In the first section of this poem, the speaker is panhandled by an old man who claims to have been "in Mexico with Black Jack Pershing". . . . (p. 664)

The second section tells the reaction of the speaker to this chance encounter; "the old man's tale still haunts me," he begins:

> I know what it's like to serve
> in Mexico with Black Jack Pershing. . . .

Through the use of his imagination, the speaker is able to become the old man, to experience a portion of his life. The poem is curiously both objective and subjective; objective because of its interest in the life and concerns of a character other than the speaker, but subjective in that it is also the speaker's story, the story of his imagination.

In its use of a narrative structure and reliance on significant, telling details for action, character, and meaning, this poem resembles prose fiction. Simpson is the author of one novel,

Riverside Drive, published in 1962, and recently has talked about writing another. In fact—if such things can be judged by what the protagonist of his poems says—it would appear that as a young man Simpson may have aspired more to writing fiction than poetry. (pp. 664-65)

And yet, despite this ambition, despite his skill at manipulating narrative, detail, and imagery, Simpson did not become a good novelist. . . . The failure occurs in the area of plot—the individual scenes of *Riverside Drive* are pointed and affecting, excellent at conveying mood, but never add up to a cohesive overall statement. In short, Simpson's fiction embodies all the qualities that would be needed if one wished to write a narrative kind of lyric poetry—which is precisely the choice he ultimately made. (pp. 665-66)

Narrative is used in Simpson's best poems, then, not to channel action towards an exciting climax but to organize images and relatively minor incidents towards some revelation of personality and feeling. Because this poetry is more or less static in terms of external action, imagery is of considerable importance in the achievement of its effects. Simpson, in fact, considers himself a kind of latter-day Imagist poet. . . . In Simpson's use of imagery there is something of the idea behind Eliot's objective correlative: if the image is properly prepared for and invested with appropriate suggestions, it should call up in the reader the same emotions it evokes in the author or in the created character.

Most often, the feelings that are expressed in the poems of phase three are again those of the Simpson protagonist, the sensibility that has always been at the heart of his work. However, because of the greater degree of empathy that informs this phase, we find as well poems spoken by characters who are obviously different from this one; also, there are poems written from the third-person point of view, in which Simpson imagines from the outside and sympathetically presents the feelings of another. . . . Perhaps the most astonishing thing about Simpson's recent work is just how different the people he writes about are—not just from the sensibility that inhabits his work, but from the characters who appear in contemporary American poetry generally.

Most contemporary poets, of course, write primarily about their own personalities; Simpson is no exception to this rule. When we get beyond this level, what we commonly find are characters who are very much like the poets—sensitive, intelligent, well-educated, of refined taste in food, music, literature, what have you. When we go beyond the poet as character in the poems of Simpson's phase three, by contrast, what we find are the *ordinary* citizens of America—not college professors and orchestra conductors, not manual laborers and nuclear protesters, but middle-class burghers, people who shop in shopping centers rather than in boutiques, people who watch "Love Boat" rather than "Masterpiece Theatre," people who worry about their mortgages, their false teeth, their teen-age children when they don't come home on time. Simpson's goal is to write not about an unusual, privileged way of life, but about the life most people are living in this country today. (pp. 666-67)

"Quiet Desperation," which appears in *The Best Hour of the Night* [1983], is written from the third-person point of view and concerns a single day in the life of an unnamed citizen of suburbia. (p. 667)

"Quiet Desperation" establishes a common ground of ordinary human feelings where the guiding sensibility of Simpson's poems and his middle-class protagonist can meet to share what they have in common. There are many poems like this in this latest period, poems which express, on the part of that sensibility, an authentic degree of empathy for humankind generally. However, there are also many poems in this phase which express something that may seem contrary to this—the continuing recognition by the Simpson sensibility of a difference between himself and most other people. It is not the feelings themselves that make him different, nor their quality and depth; rather, it is the degree to which these feelings are speculated upon and understood. This realization does not lessen the empathy felt by the protagonist, but it does reinforce his sense of isolation, of an ultimate and irremediable aloneness. (p. 669)

The problem faced by the sensibility of Simpson's poems is that the society of which he is a part is so much more superficial in its interests than he is; it is committed to money, to the everyday problems of work, but ignores the depths of human emotion, the life of the soul. . . .

The alienation of Simpson's protagonist results precisely from his devotion to the things which are unseen by the middle class generally: a full range of genuine emotions, the life of the soul. (p. 671)

[Crucial] differences between the Simpson protagonist and the average middle-class citizen remain; it is the expression of these differences that makes some readers think the poems are satirical. The tone of these poems is an extremely delicate one— in part due to the understatement and restraint that is built into their form. Simpson is attempting to balance very different opinions of two nearly identical things—his empathy for the people and his contempt for the values by which they sometimes live their lives. (p. 672)

At the end of *The Best Hour of the Night,* Simpson has placed an ars poetica devoted to the plight of the poet who chooses to live and work in suburbia. Entitled **"The Unwritten Poem,"** it begins by asking where poetry is to be found; "Not in beautiful faces and distant scenery," he answers, but:

> In your life here, on this street
> where the houses from the outside
> are all alike, and so are the people.
> Inside, the furniture is dreadful—
> floc on the walls and huge color television.

However much he may dislike the details of this way of life, its tastelessness, the absence of emotion, the poet still must also love the people he writes about; as Pound said more than fifty years ago, a poetry which is simply satirical will inevitably corrode and die from the inside out. Simpson knows, however, that his feelings will never be reciprocated by the community: "To love and write unrequited / is the poet's fate." The poem ends with a vision of the soullessness of American life, as the poet watches the morning commuters "grasping briefcases" as they "pass beyond your gaze / and hurl themselves into the flames." They are like the dead souls of Eliot's "The Waste Land," seen crossing London Bridge every morning. Ultimately, it is the soullessness of American life that places the individual in Simpson's poems at odds with this society.

Though he has not often been recognized as such, Louis Simpson is certainly one of America's more original poets. Most of today's poets occupy a middle ground, writing with great sincerity about their own feelings, using the literary forms most in vogue. Originality is to be found in poets willing to question the received truths about their art. For some, this has led directly to an interest in the possibilities of craft, the possibilities

of pure imagination; the personal self is abandoned in favor of a world of make-believe, where anything the author can imagine can happen. Simpson's direction is different, but no less original. While he too abandons the egotistical self, he plunges not into a world of make-believe but into a relentlessly realistic world, a world most poets think is hopelessly prosaic. Even more remarkable is the high quality of the work produced from these raw materials—these poems are readable and aesthetically attractive, engaging both the intellect and the emotions with their imagistic density. Although Louis Simpson has been publishing poems for nearly forty years, his best work has come in the last ten. The simultaneous appearance of these two handsome volumes will go a long way towards solidifying his position among the best poets of today. (pp. 674-75)

Peter Stitt, *"Louis Simpson's Best Hour,"* in The Georgia Review, *Vol. XXXVII, No. 3, Fall, 1983, pp. 662-75.*

ALAN WILLIAMSON

Over the years, one has often been tempted to ask, "Will the real Louis Simpson please stand up?" For there have been several. There was the correct but amazingly precocious young Briton from Jamaica, the coeditor of **"New Poets of England and America,"** a few of whose poems are preserved in the opening sections of **"People Live Here."** There was the brief but shrill convert to the school of Robert Bly. There was the author of critical books like **"A Revolution in Taste,"** which seems to me all too English in its breezy mixture of gossip and snap judgments. Finally, there is the wonderful poet of the last 10 years, whose bare, unadorned poems of the common life remind me of Randall Jarrell.

That Mr. Simpson knows where his best work is to be found is indicated by both the title of **"People Live Here,"** a selection of poems written in the past 24 years, and its organization. He has arranged the poems chronologically within thematic sections, so each early poem, whether on war, Jewish life in Russia or modern lives, seems a kind of preliminary draft for a recent masterpiece, such as **"On the Ledge," "Typhus"** or **"Sway,"** placed at or near the end.

"I am the man, I suffered, I was there," Walt Whitman wrote. Mr. Simpson, who has given us a very lovable, if deconstructive, portrait of our national bard in the poem **"Walt Whitman at Bear Mountain,"** suffers and benefits from the same inability to distance himself from the pathos of other lives. . . .

[In] **"The Mexican Woman,"** the poet relives an old beggar's tales of war and infidelity. . . . Here "wise," the old beggar's word, expands marvelously to its full meaning, as if to participate in the pain and the victory of other lives were the essence of wisdom.

But wisdom has a less ecstatic dimension—the need to face up to hard moral facts and unresolvable contradictions in our lives. Mr. Simpson has been adamant about the place of such facts and contradictions in poetry and about the need to emphasize them by breaking rules at times. . . .

But Mr. Simpson did not arrive at this difficult, equalizing wisdom easily. The one group of displeasing poems in **"People Live Here"** is in a section called "A Discovery of America" that gathers together poems from the 1960's. In them Surrealism is used to distance and dehumanize Americans, particularly Californians: "The businessmen of San Francisco / . . . rise from the ooze of the ocean floor." The compassion is merely condescending, and the contrasting praise of traditional societies is peculiarly simple-minded, even allowing for the general simple-mindedness of modern poets on this subject:

> You were born to waste your life.
> You were born to this middleclass life
>
> As others before you
> Were born to walk in procession
> To the temple, singing.

Even Mr. Simpson's best previous book, **"Caviare at the Funeral,"** did not allow quite the same degree of humanity to his Long Island neighbors as to soldiers, prostitutes, immigrant Jews, sad young proletarian girls and sad, corrupt editors. He does extend his compassion to those neighbors in his new book, **"The Best Hour of the Night."** But what makes his suburbanites most sympathetic, one finds, is their discontent. They know dimly that something is lost when life ceases to be raw and cruel, although they also know that rawness can brutalize. On a fishing trip to Alaska, one Jim Bandy (Simpson's comic names can be wonderful) has a brush with the uncompromisingness of life. . . .

This poem says what most of Mr. Simpson's best poems seem to say—that, finally, no life is satisfactory but there is the paradoxically healing corollary that all lives are somehow the same life. Perhaps that is a kinder way of reading the unsuccessful early poem mentioned before—"You were born to this middleclass life." But the healing insight is expressed much more charmingly in **"Physical Universe,"** the first poem in **"The Best Hour of the Night."** As the poet is ranting late at night about metaphysics—"Or should we stick to the Bible?"—his wife mutters in her sleep, "Did you take out the garbage?" The poet "thought about it," and her words become an answer, the only possible answer:

> Like a *koan* . . . the kind of irrelevance
> a Zen master says to the disciple
> who is asking riddles of the universe.

> *Alan Williamson, "We're All in the Same Boat," in* The New York Times Book Review, *January 29, 1984, p. 26.*

RICHARD TILLINGHAST

Having been from the beginning an admirably "impure" poet (to borrow Czeslaw Milosz's sly term for Whitman, Shakespeare, Homer, Dante, et al., as opposed to those modern poets who aspire to an art of "pure" imagination), Simpson has taken on the challenge of trying to make sense of contemporary life, from his soldiering experiences in World War II to American historical myths and realities—wherein "The Open Road goes to the used-car lot." Increasingly, he writes about ordinary characters and their everyday experiences. Simpson stoutly refuses the pressure from "purists" to force poetry into a limited and marginal role. The title of his selected poems, *People Live Here,* is an indication of this writer's determination to engage his imagination with characterization and plot. For him, as for Matthew Arnold, poetry has been a "criticism of life." Simpson has consistently chosen a large canvas, and this selection displays thirty-four years of work that is various, compassionate, committed and often astonishingly beautiful. He is adept enough—and I would say, humane enough (I take the will to communicate as a gauge of an artist's humanity)—to be clear and readable. If the rhetorical intensity of his poems

slackens in the process, it should also be noted that their plainness of diction contributes to their directness.

Reading the more than 200 pages of *People Live Here,* one is struck both by the range of subject and treatment and by the unifying effect of Louis Simpson's voice and attitude on heterogeneous material. While capable of lyric rapture, the poet typically holds himself at some distance from his subjects and is by turns satirical, bemused, sorrowing, disdainful, sympathetic, wry. Yet to say that he *holds* himself at some distance is less accurate than to note that while sympathetic, Simpson seems by his very nature to be an outsider. . . . While he engages himself passionately with American life, at times it is as if the poet were an anthropologist from an alien culture observing American ways. (pp. 166-67)

The Best Hour of the Night reflects Simpson's increasing focus on life in the suburbs. "Suburbia" is a word that one rarely pronounces without sneering, but to dismiss or ignore it is to eliminate from consideration a significant slice of the American pie. As Robert Lowell put it, "History has to live with what was here." Someone who knew nothing of present-day America would get little idea of our life from most contemporary poetry. I often think of a student of mine some years ago who said, "I never feel completely at ease outside of Great Neck," and I can almost imagine her in a Simpson poem. His view of these briefcase-carriers, deal-strikers, Saturday-night poker players and village-meeting-goers combines detachment with a self-effacing sense of identification. . . .

In staking out fresh material for his poetry, it is not surprising that Louis Simpson should feel the necessity of creating new or at least hybrid forms. This he has done notably in **"The Previous Tenant,"** which is something like a short story in free verse. The form allows the writer to highlight certain details without being bound to the three-dimensional realism and continuity of traditional fiction. . . .

The speaker rents a cottage where the previous tenant has left some of his belongings, and through conversations with the landlord and others, pieces together the story of an affair his predecessor had that caused him all sorts of trouble including the divorce that necessitated his moving into the cottage in the first place. It's a fascinating, skillfully spun tale in which we learn all sorts of different things about the characters involved, the speaker, the little suburban town in which the story is set and, finally, about American values.

If you cling to the impression that poetry is by nature obscure, forbidding and otherworldly, buy one of these books by Louis Simpson. You may be the only passenger on the 5:51 reading it, but you will feel a shock of recognition at poems that dare to come to terms with this country we live in. . . . (p. 167)

> *Richard Tillinghast, "The Poet of the 5:51," in* The Nation, *Vol. 238, No. 5, February 11, 1984, pp. 166-67.*

ROBERT McDOWELL

Many years ago in my reading I was shopping for a good contemporary lyric poet. I had trouble finding what I was looking for until a friend recommended the poems of Louis Simpson. "The best we've got," he said. *People Live Here* includes more than 100 poems from the author's ten previous books and chapbooks, and from recent uncollected poems. Also included is an afterword by Simpson himself, **"The Sake of Words for Their Own Sake."**

This latter piece consists of a charming and honest description of Simpson's Jamaican childhood ("I am the other Jamaican, a child of the middle class, some of us white, some 'colored,' but all of us borrowing our manners and prejudices from the English"), his early inspiration to become a writer ("the stories my mother read to me"), his education and war experience, his political awakening and what he was reading at various times. Readers will be touched by the ease and good humor with which Simpson examines Simpson. An example of that humor occurs when he mentions his discovery of A. E. Housman: "... for a year or two [I] read his lyrics with the kind of sympathy that a young American now feels for rock."

The poems, too, should shake a lot of napping readers awake. The thematic continuity spanning the thirty-four years covered here is remarkable. Simpson has always focused on physical and spiritual love, reconciling the present with the past via the family, man's inhumanity to his fellow man, war, and spiritual poverty.

The book's first two sections display traditional, and beautiful, lyrics; Section Two contains poems inspired by his war years. These are some of the most powerful anti-war poems of our time. **"The Heroes"** is an example of this. . . . (p. 119)

Section Three chronicles the poet's relocation to America. A significant thread here is an ongoing debate with the spirit of Whitman. Having absorbed the latter, Simpson arrives with great expectations only to find himself striding, lonely, through a land "where malls are our churches."

"Modern Lives," the fourth section, is the most cantankerous and didactic expression of Simpson's social criticism. The poet settles into suburbia with its prefab specters and infidelities and bears a collective suffering.

Section Five explores his mother's (and his own) eastern European roots. Here is a fascinating contrast with Section Three, for Chekhov supplants Whitman as the narrator's aggressively remote foil.

"Armidale," the shortest section in the book, takes as its impetus an Australian journey, which inspires a number of weighty assertions concerning our misuse of nature, our misuse of ourselves.

The final section, "Recapitulations," recombines these various byways and offers a fitting coda.

Another offering, *The Best Hour of the Night,* proves that Louis Simpson's work and development, luckily for us, continues. Here the poet adds to his canon of poems about contemporary life by employing deft recombinations of, primarily, historical and mimetic impulses. In addition, he reminds us again that laughter can work in a poem and even be necessary. In **"Physical Universe"** a man comes downstairs at 5 A.M. and pours a cup of coffee. Finding his son's science text on the table, he begins to read. The text triggers a meditation on our civilization, on the fact that we find ourselves at-and-away-from home in it. The meditation comes full circle, back to the present day—"Tuesday, the day they pick up the garbage! / He leapt into action." This witty transition sets up the return to bed and one of the most tender moments I've seen in recent poetry. (pp. 119-20)

In ["The Previous Tenant"] the central character, sometimes detached, sometimes obsessed, pieces together the story of his predecessor. That fellow, a doctor, ruined his position by engaging in an ill-advised affair. Though he actually appears only once, in the poem's eighth section (to retrieve sullenly some of his belongings), we feel that we know him all too well by poem's end. And worse, we feel that we know the community's upstanding snobs who hounded him, too. Simpson's surgical social commentary is as devastating as ever. . . . Louis Simpson makes our collective fear beautiful, and helps us to believe that we can manage it. (p. 121)

    Robert McDowell, "Recombinative Poetry," in The
    Hudson Review, *Vol. XXXVII, No. 1, Spring, 1984,
    pp. 115-31.**

T. R. HUMMER

In a recent *Georgia Review* [see excerpt above], Peter Stitt writes that Louis Simpson's *People Live Here: Selected Poems 1949-1983* "makes clear that there are three major phases to be found in the body of Simpson's work, phases which are separated by major changes in style, subject matter, and approach." Simpson is certainly one of those poets (like James Wright, Robert Penn Warren, Robert Lowell, and Elizabeth Bishop, to name only a few other such writers of recent vintage) the study of whose entire body of work is particularly rewarding, partly because it exhibits drastic, unpredictable, and yet characteristic change. Anyone who is at all familiar with Simpson's poetry knows that there are two major shifts in his work that divide his canon into three stylistically different parts. . . . No one who has written on Simpson in the past few years has failed to notice the differences: the highly traditional and polished but often stilted early work; the far more interesting middle phase, which embodies so many of the teachings of Simpson's friend Robert Bly; and the less easily definable recent work, which is at once straightforward and aphoristic, narrative and parabolic, passionate and prosaic, mysterious and clear.

Evaluations differ, but the descriptions agree adequately. It is not my purpose to repeat them, as descriptions, any more than I have already done. Certain perhaps unanswerable questions interest me far more: what do these transitions *mean*? What do they mean to Simpson, and what do they mean to us? The generality of such questions is appalling, but it is necessary to take a stab at answering them here, because Louis Simpson seems to me perhaps the most representative poet among us—representative in that he so clearly embodies the issues with which every poet worth the name unavoidably grapples. The publication of his new selected poems *People Live Here* reveals how true this has been for Simpson in the long course of his career; the new work in *The Best Hour of the Night* demonstrates how true it continues to be.

Clearly I agree with Stitt that Simpson's work, viewed linearly, divides neatly into three distinct stylistic stages; however, I strongly disagree that *People Live Here* makes that division clear. On the contrary, Simpson has chosen to give new book an unchronological arrangement which seems calculated to obscure that often-remarked-on developmental unfolding. Simpson explains in a headnote to the book:

> This is not the usual chronological arrangement. . . . Instead I have selected poems from all my books and placed them in groups. . . . I believe that this arrangement shows the nature of my writing more clearly than has appeared up to now in separate books.

Simpson's final sentence invites us to a different kind of understanding of his body of work from the one a chronological reading yields, that linear change which Stitt, among others, is at pains to describe. Indeed, *People Live Here* seems particularly designed to undercut such description. "It follows," Simpson continues ingenuously in his headnote, "that poems in contrasting forms may stand side by side—an early poem in meter and rhyme next to a more recent poem written in free form." It also follows that, as far as Simpson is concerned, poems from one "phase" of his work can stand side by side with poems from another—not, perhaps, without tension, but certainly without contradiction—and that such a structuring should yield a different way of investigating the poems, one which is no longer concerned with the linear history of their composition, but now seeks to explain this representation (or perhaps I had better say this illusion of a representation) of the way the poems exist contemporaneously, side by side in the mind of the poet himself. (pp. 115-16)

Stitt's view is attractive, yielding as it does to discussion of Simpson's work in the context of the large movements of the poetry of this century: the poetry war which Pound championed, the famous "revolution in taste." And clearly that is pertinent. The problem with such an explanation is that, beyond a certain point, it loses Simpson in the pack. That line of approach only leads us to say that Simpson has done what everyone else has done, which is, to be fair, both true and untrue. The linear progression of Simpson's work bears it out; the power and unique quality of his work belies it.

The nonlinear structure of *People Live Here* suggests a more appealing angle of approach. First of all, we see right away that Simpson *has* no single "natural voice"; he has a multiplicity of voices. There is Simpson the dogface, sure enough; but there is also Simpson the "British" Jamaican, Simpson the New Yorker, Simpson the tourist, Simpson the Long Island suburbanite, Simpson the Russian Jew (!); there is Simpson the liberal, Simpson the conservative, Simpson the man on the street, Simpson the aesthete, Simpson the sophisticate, Simpson the *naïf*—the list could go on and on. At the same time, we see that every facet of Simpson's body of work reflects all the others. (p. 118)

People Live Here makes it clear not that Simpson's work is divisible into phases (though from one angle of view, of course, it is); this book makes it clear that Simpson wants us to see a different truth about his and any good poet's way of working: that there are never absolute divisions, and that no poet can ever afford to turn his back on any possibility, because just when he does, that which he has rejected or neglected will turn out to be precisely what is called for. . . . (p. 119)

It seems to me that Simpson has been working for his whole career to reach, more and more effectively, that silent, entrenched audience he first set out to address without embarrassment. As he has grown older, though, he has come to recognize that wars are not fought only on literal battlefields— that such wars (like arguments among critics) are impressive, but they are only the fringe skirmishes of the real war that goes on constantly in the human soul. . . . But the difference is not simply the result of a man's aesthetic desire to write a different kind of poem; it is a symptom of a vastly increased understanding and compassion. For Simpson, on the evidence of the text, to be conventional for the sake of convention is to be narrow, and to be narrow is to be unconscious, uncompas-

sionate, inhumane. Unconventionality for its own sake leads to the same result. Only those who have been genuinely outside what most of us usually think of as either "real life" or "the life of the mind," where convention applies no more than anticonvention, see clearly; even for them, "vision" is unreliable and transient. . . . (pp. 119-20)

The "revisionary" structure of *People Live Here* is a new use of what in another context looks like outdated material in the service of the struggle. What resonates throughout is a tension of voices, all existing, as the book presents them, in a single mind, or a single world, meeting on any edge of things where "real life" meets the life of the mind, and where both those worlds meet the unknown. The linear view of his work—which of course has its own kind of truth—depicts Simpson constantly turning his back on his past practice. Certainly there are things he has turned his back on; no doubt he will never write a poem quite like **"Carentan O Carentan"** again. But—as Simpson's structuring of *People Live Here* suggests—to try to leave the past behind completely would be to abandon the very thing that set him in motion in the first place: the impulse to speak to people, to real people in the real world, straight out, without embarrassment. Simpson's search has been for the means of doing that, and his great discovery seems to be that there *are* no particular means; there is only what the poet can scratch together at the moment, with his bare hands, out of the life of the language and out of a constantly altering sense of what possibilities poetry as a medium offers. There are, of course, dangers in this method, and sometimes Simpson fails in ways that more elegant and cagey writers would never allow themselves. There are times when he becomes Zennish without sufficient justification, and other times when the flatness that so often serves to further either amazement or irony seems only flat. But in the main, Simpson's greatest virtue is his willingness to chip away, with marvelous control, at the monolithic cultural notion—in the shadow of which he began his career, and on which he continues to keep a wary eye—of what a poem *is*. The answer, I suppose, that emerges from his work is that a poem is nothing in particular: it is something that works, something unpredictable.

Of course there is a linearity in the structure of this book, but it is a revised linearity. The seven sections of *People Live Here* present, in part, an unfolding awareness of humanity and of significant human relationships. The first section, "Songs and Lyrics," brings together a selection of relatively inward-turning lyrics. Section two, "The Fighting in Europe," contains most of the poems concerned directly with World War II, and begins to depict—despite the striking multiplicity of voices in the poems here, which range through all Simpson's linear phases—the forced social awareness which any serious consideration of war entails. The third section, "A Discovery of America," is a more stylistically uniform selection, which, as Alan Williamson has recently pointed out, "gathers together poems from the 1960s." Many of these poems reflect, more directly than any of Simpson's other work, the influence of Robert Bly, not only in their strategies and diction but also in their particular mode of social awareness. Williamson [see excerpt above] finds these poems "displeasing," and it is true that many of them are more overt in their moral intent than Simpson usually allows himself to be. America is often directly depicted, in the Bly mode, as a spiritual disaster area. However, this section also seems to me a necessary pole of Simpson's vision. "One does not want to hate society," Simpson has written, "but society being what it is, how can one stomach it?" Simpson's placement of these poems after the war poems suggests a justification for the views he presents in this third section: section two concerns culturally sanctioned death by violence; section three presents the perhaps too familiar (but not therefore untrue) spectacle of American spiritual death by automobile and electric can opener. And section four, "Modern Lives," is still another facet of the same phenomenon. Here American suburbanites and insurance salesmen try to resurrect themselves by acts of passion which are often self-destructive. . . . (pp. 121-22)

The next two sections, "Tales of Volhynia" and "Armidale," center on Russia and Australia respectively and seem designed, in this structuring, to place the previous sections in a new perspective, as tales of exotic and peculiarly beautiful places. It may seem odd to say, but Simpson is our most accomplished poet of the exotic, and if the America he so often depicts does not seem weird and wonderful and dangerous and depraved to those of us who are accustomed to it, it is only because we *are* accustomed. Seen side by side with the poems of Russia and Australia, the poems about America take their place in a larger vision of the beautifully and perilously strange. The final section, "Recapitulations," returns us to America, but with a new aura of mysteriousness verging on the metaphysical. This structure adds up, I think, to an ever-expanding primary awareness not simply of poetry as an aesthetic mode but of the nature of the audience, a definition and redefinition carried on in virtually every poem: humanity as embattled dogface, for whom Simpson wants to write "poems that would be, in their laconic and simple manner, tolerable to men who had seen a good deal of combat and had no illusions."

If *People Live Here,* with its important structural revision of Simpson's ongoing poetry war, allows us to see his past and present work in a tense and effective suspension, *The Best Hour of the Night* plays off (perhaps) the present and the future. (This assertion is risky, I realize, but the fact that the last poem of *People Live Here* is also the first poem of *The Best Hour* gives credence to the notion that Simpson at least wants us to consider continuities.) *The Best Hour* is distinctly like Simpson's last two books in its narrative structures, its use of the rhythms of prose, and its focus on the exotic potential of the "ordinary." But Simpson is far from formulaic here; in fact, *The Best Hour* seems to me his best book yet, dense and rich. It performs, again and again, miraculously well, the thing we demand and have every right to demand of poetry: Simpson wrestles with the world for the world's own sake, to discover within it the necessary articulation, the artifice adequate to convince us of its effective truth. What makes him what I have called a representative poet is the honesty with which he reveals the contours of that struggle with the indeterminate but recognizably human voice every poet fights to claim as his own and to name by its truest possible name: without embarrassment, poetry. (pp. 122-23)

T. R. Hummer, "Revising the Poetry Wars: Louis Simpson's Assault on the Poetic," in The Kenyon Review, *Vol. VI, No. 3, Summer, 1984, pp. 114-23.*

Gary (Sherman) Snyder

1930-

American poet, essayist, and translator.

Snyder's stature as both a counterculture figure and an innovative and important mainstream poet places him in an uncommon position in contemporary literature. Although only briefly involved with the San Francisco Beat movement of the 1950s, Snyder's influence on the Beats was nevertheless significant and he is often linked with them. However, unlike most Beat writers, Snyder has also received extensive serious scholarly attention. Whereas a rejection of literary traditions characterizes much Beat writing, Snyder's work is seen to embody the influence of such literary giants as Walt Whitman, Ezra Pound, and Ralph Waldo Emerson. He is the recipient of several literary honors and awards, including a Pulitzer Prize for his poetry collection *Turtle Island* (1974), and his reputation as a significant author, though not uncontested, is largely secure.

Snyder was raised on small farms, first in Washington and later in Oregon, and held jobs as a logger, seaman, fire lookout, and United States Forest Service trail crew worker. His interest in American Indian culture led him to acquire degrees in literature and anthropology at Reed College. Snyder began graduate work in linguistics at Indian University, and then transferred to University of California at Berkeley, where he pursued his interest in Asian thought and culture by studying Oriental languages. During this time, between 1953 and 1956, Snyder became involved with the Beat community; just as it began gaining national attention, however, he moved to Japan, where he became actively involved in Zen Buddhism. The influence of Eastern literature and philosophy and Snyder's application of Zen Buddhism to Western culture are perhaps the most distinguishing characteristics of his poetry.

Snyder's writing reveals an appreciation for the hard work of rural life and the closeness it affords with nature, an interest in the spiritual link between primitive cultures and nature, and a deep sense of involvement with humanity. As Thomas Parkinson notes in a discussion of *Myths & Texts* (1960), "Snyder wants to reach a prehuman reality, the wilderness and the cosmos in which man lives as an animal with animals in a happy ecology." Over the course of his career, Snyder has developed and refined his vision, creating a body of work marked by its clarity, depth, and rhythmic beauty. Like the Japanese poetry which he has studied and translated, Snyder's poems are built not on symbol or metaphor but on sharp, clear images created out of precise and immediate language.

Snyder's first collection of poetry, *Riprap* (1959), is largely based on his experiences as a manual laborer; the title itself is taken from a term which designates the laying of stones for a horse trail in the mountains. *Myths & Texts,* his next collection, is a long, highly allusive lyrical poem divided into three sections: "Logging," "Hunting," and "Burning." This work is often considered his most accomplished collection. Most critics contend that *Myths & Texts* far surpasses *Riprap* in literary merit: it is more tightly constructed, unified, and expansive, while also retaining the clarity and exactness of the shorter poems in *Riprap. The Back Country* (1967), divided into five

© Lüfti Özkök

sections—"The Far West," "The Far East," "Kali," "Back," and translations of work by the Japanese poet Miyazawa Kenji—reveals the influence of East and West on both the style and content of Snyder's poetry. His subsequent major collections—*Regarding Wave* (1969), *Turtle Island,* and the recent *Axe Handles* (1983)—continue to develop the themes and concerns introduced in the early collections. In addition, Snyder has continued to work on *Mountains and Rivers without End,* an ongoing lyrical series, begun in the 1950s, which explores internal and external landscapes.

He Who Hunted Birds in His Father's Village (1951), Snyder's recently republished senior thesis at Reed College, explores how the ancient "Swan Maiden" myth reflects and shapes the lives of the Haida Indians. This early work, revealing Snyder's interest in and his commitment to poetry, society, and the natural world, is seen to foreshadow the main concerns developed throughout his career. Snyder's other nonfiction works, most notably *Earth House Hold* (1969), *The Old Ways* (1979), and *The Real Work* (1980), are collections of essays which relate to his poetry thematically. Of central concern in both his essays and poems, as Scott McLean notes in his introduction to *The Real Work,* is Snyder's belief in "the complementary nature of inner and outer realities." Snyder views poetry as "'the seat of the soul'—the area where the inner world and the outer world touch. . . ."

(See also *CLC*, Vols. 1, 2, 5, 9; *Contemporary Authors*, Vols. 17-20, rev. ed.; and *Dictionary of Literary Biography*, Vols. 5, 16.)

CRUNK [PSEUDONYM OF JAMES WRIGHT]

I have three ideas about Snyder's work as a whole that I want to bring up. First, his is essentially a Western imagination. His poems are powerfully located—sown, rooted—in the landscape of the far Western states. He is a Western writer just as, for example, Delmore Schwartz, Anthony Hecht, and Howard Moss are Eastern writers.... These two sets of writers deal with different geographical landscapes but the distinction is deeper and subtler than that. They differ in what might be called the landscape of the imagination—which each in his way tries to discover and explore.

The Western writer feels a need to approach his characters and incidents with an imagination totally, if temporarily, freed from all concern with abstract ideas. The Eastern writer . . . does not. (p. 34)

One of the most interesting features of Gary Snyder's poetry is that in him we see this "western" imagination in a poet.

The point is worth examining further: it helps to identify Mr. Snyder's originality and it suggests a kind of American poetry that hasn't been very much explored—a kind of poetry which Mr. Snyder has been writing with freshness and dignity, which might be called a poetry of the Western imagination. The term itself doesn't matter much, except for the sake of convenience. It ought to suggest, however, certain features of poetry which are imaginative rather than rhetorical. In such poetry the forms of poems emerge from within the living growth of each particular poem and most definitely *not* in a set of conventions (such as the classical English iambic, with all its masterpieces of the past and its suffocating influence in the present). This new poetry is also marked by the presence of a powerful intelligence which does its thinking through the imagination itself, and not through repetition of the thoughts of established philosophical authorities or of classical myths which are degenerated through excessive or inaccurate use into obstructions rather than doorways to clear thought. Mr. Snyder does indeed embody certain myths in his poetry, but they are not classical myths, but "bear myths," and myths of the senses.

My second idea is that Mr. Snyder's poetry is very different from "Beat" poetry. Snyder has been associated primarily in magazines with the Black Mountain school and the Beats. . . . Snyder's poetry is, however, immediately distinct both in imagination and in style from Beat work. A certain gentleness and care for civilization in Snyder is utterly absent in Ginsberg or Orlovsky, who are in favor, as they say, of "cat vommit." Ginsberg and Orlovsky make strong efforts to coarsen themselves, whereas Snyder does the very opposite. The Beat writers are opposed to civilization of all kinds: Snyder is not. Snyder's work everywhere reveals the grave mind of a man who is highly civilized and who, moreover, makes no pretense of denying his own intelligence. (pp. 35-6)

My third idea is the reality of the oriental influence on Snyder. The influence of the orient on Snyder is interior: it is the desire to overcome vanity and ambition. . . . (p. 37)

The great poets of Japan and, especially, of China, are almost invariably men who pride themselves on being men who devote their entire selves to the life of contemplation and imagination.

In their poems they succeed in the struggle against vanity and the desire for power.

Another oriental influence concerns the method of construction of the poem. Chinese poems are formed out of images whose sensory force strikes the mind directly, not as an abstract substitute for an experience, but as an original experience in itself. . . .

[For example, Mr. Snyder's poem **"Water"**] contains no external reference to China or to Chinese poetry. Somebody once said that the prose of the young Ernest Hemingway resembled clean pebbles shining side by side at the bottom of a clear stream-channel; and that is the way Mr. Snyder has let the images of his poem arrange themselves into lines. There is no forcing of the imagination into external and conventional rhetorical patterns, such as have ruptured a good many poems during recent years in America. And yet Mr. Snyder's poem is not formless. It is exquisitely formed from the inside. It follows the clear rhythm of the poet's run down the hill in the hot sun, turns suddenly when he plunges his head in the cold water, and comes to a delightful close with the poet, his skin alive with the chill, gazing under the surface, face to face with a fish.

I began by noting Mr. Snyder's conscious debt to Chinese poets, and ended by admiring his ability to convey the astonishment of a fish. The two points suggest the importance of Mr. Snyder's study of Chinese. He has bypassed its biographical and historical externals, such as might be flaunted by someone who wanted to impress his readers, and has learned how to form his imagination into poems according to a tradition which is great and vital, and which is wholly distinct from the tradition of British poetry, very great in itself but somewhat inhibiting to American imaginative experience. (pp. 37-9)

But American poets, with a frequency that is dismal in proportion as it seems automatic—that is, conditioned—tend either to give up all hope of imaginative precision and delicacy altogether, as Ginsberg in his "Howl" or Freeman in his *Apollonian Poems,* or to regard all deviation from the iambic rhetoric of the British tradition as an absurdity when it fails or as a crime akin to parricide when it succeeds. Whitman patiently suggested the exploration of traditions beyond the British; but, as Hart Crane complained with terrible despair in one of his greatest letters, many people won't even read *Democratic Vistas.*

Perhaps the reading of such a work, endangering as it does the trite and completely false public image of Whitman which still persists in America despite the Beats' attempt to appropriate him, requires a courage which few men are willing to assume—a courage akin to Whitman's own. In any case, Gary Snyder has displayed a courage of similar kind, not in order to face Whitman's devastating and perhaps unsurpassed criticism of America's puritanical materialism; but in order to undertake one of the tasks of the imagination for which Whitman often felt poets in America should prove most capable: the exploration of living traditions which, shunning the British tradition, nonetheless display powers of poetry which equal and sometimes surpass that tradition; and to make this search for the purpose of claiming America itself—by which I mean literally our own lives and the people and places we live among day by day—for the imagination.

I have discussed the Chinese poets at some length . . . because they mean so much to Mr. Snyder, and because they reveal in their own work the possibility of a further growth in American poetry which has scarcely been considered. My final impression of Mr. Snyder himself, however, does not depend on his debt to this or that writer.

What matters most to me is that Snyder has been able to live his daily life with the full power of his imagination awake to all the details of that life. . . . (pp. 40-1)

Mr. Snyder has courage and an air of faithful patience. He keeps his voice low, not out of timidity but out of strength. (p. 42)

> *Crunk (pseudonym of James Wright), "The Work of Gary Snyder," in* The Sixties, *No. 6, Spring, 1962, pp. 25-42.*

BOB STEUDING

Snyder has recently mentioned that the direction of his future work after the completion of *Mountains and Rivers Without End* will be religious and philosophical. He has also stated that after that work has been completed, he may donate his books to the local library and retire to the anonymity of friends and family life in the mountains. This desire and such a life are, of course, in the true Oriental style. However, if Snyder ends his poetic career after this decade, it would even then be premature to make any final pronouncements. Although the figure of Gary Snyder as a man may still overshadow that of Snyder the poet, certain *tentative* statements can now be made. First of all, Snyder's reputation as a poet rests at present on *Myths & Texts,* his most complete work; on a few excellent poems from *Riprap, The Back Country,* and *Turtle Island;* on the cycle of poems in *Regarding Wave* . . . ; and especially on the more recent sections where Snyder's work reaches synthesis in his *magnum opus, Mountains and Rivers Without End.* In these poems, one finds directness and simplicity of statement, clarity and brilliance of mind, and profundity and depth of emotional range. In these instances, Snyder's is a poetry of incredible power and beauty. (pp. 163-64)

Myths & Texts (1960), many readers' favorite work, is, as yet, Snyder's most complete and most unified book. This is not a collection of poems organized around a catchy title, as to a certain extent are *Riprap* and *The Back Country,* no matter how perfect some of their individual poems. *Myths & Texts* coheres perfectly. . . . [All] three of its sections relate specifically to one another, and there is a definite progression and feeling of completion while reading this book. Like "The Waste Land," which influenced its composition, *Myths & Texts* makes an over-all comment on our society and will probably stand the test of time. Within this work are individual poems of startling beauty and insight, for example, "**Poem 2**" from "Logging," in which Snyder relates his own complicity in the destruction of the forests. (p. 164)

Of particular note in *The Back Country* (1968) is "**A Berry Feast,**" written to commemorate a summer spent with good friends in the woods of the Pacific Northwest. It is a saucy poem, filled with zest for life, written by Snyder while in a trickster-like mood. Also significant are the many simple songs of peace and happiness, such as "**Marin-an**" in which the poet listens to the people of middle America driving their cars to work. The "Kali" poems are also notable . . . for their frank exploration of the demonic potential in man and in the poet in particular. And the poems in "Far East," inspired by Snyder's travels and studies in Japan are particularly important as well as poignant. "**Six Years**" adeptly portrays the rhythm of the

poet's Zen studies. And "**Yase: September**" succinctly captures the essence of old Japan. . . . (p. 165)

Turtle Island (1974) . . . and *Regarding Wave* (1970) collect many poems which extend and complete themes and subjects treated in earlier works. For example, both books are concerned with social revolution and the search for alternate sources of energy. The cycle of poems from *Regarding Wave* concerning the birth of Snyder's first son, Kai, completes the poem "**Praise for Sick Women**" from *Riprap.* These four beautiful poems, describing the growth of Kai from conception until after birth move further into the mystical experience that is birth and life. . . . "**Song of the Taste**" from *Regarding Wave,* possibly Snyder's most perfect poem, finishes his development of the idea of eating, first described in the "Hunting" section of *Myths & Texts* and later in the many "food" poems in *The Back Country:* "**A Berry Feast**" and "**Oysters,**" for example. It seems that in "**Song of the Taste,**" in which the reader learns how he draws "on life of living," . . . Snyder has reached the farthest extension and expression possible of this experience. The effect of this poem on the reader is startling. (pp. 165-66)

And finally, in *Mountains and Rivers Without End,* Snyder's continuing work, published periodically in sections, the reader can also see the gradual creation of a book, a collection of long poems, which may last for the same reasons that Whitman's *Leaves of Grass* lasts. Of particular note in this growing work are the sections titled "Bubbs Creek Haircut," "The Market," "The Blue Sky," and "The Hump-Backed Flute Player." The earlier poems, "**Bubbs Creek Haircut**" and "**The Market,**" are clever and technically interesting: the poet takes liberties with the time sequence and describes exotic locales with a rapid and effective series of images. But it is in the last two sections mentioned in which this long work begins to achieve its potential. In "The Blue Sky" and "The Hump-Backed Flute Player" both Snyder's philosophic vision and incredibly adept technique coalesce. In these poems, Snyder has reached the pinnacle of his art, acting as poet-shaman, using language in its fullest magical properties—the poem as chant or mantra. Here, especially in "The Blue Sky," the poems not only describe healing, they actually heal. This is truly astonishing writing in which Snyder's poetry nearly transcends art. (p. 166)

Writing, in the main, within the Imagist tradition of Pound, Williams, and the Orient, Snyder's poetry is not solely Imagistic. The gradual development of his work from the crafted to the visionary poem, his interest in primitive oral poetry, and his recent allusions to Whitman, Duncan, and other mystical poets attest to this. Significantly influenced early in his career by the demands of Oriental nature poetry for precision, sharpness, and spontaneity, Snyder's movement into Imagism and later toward the "visionary" was assured when he began his study of Buddhism in college. Its influence on the mind of Gary Snyder is profound, and it is deepening as he matures. From the sometimes "easy" references of *Riprap* to the basis of his later more mature work, *Regarding Wave* and the later sections of *Mountains and Rivers Without End,* one finds this deepening of thought. However, since Buddhist theory is integral to these latter works, their richness and depth may be lost to those who do not have some knowledge of Buddhism. No poet in American literature has made Buddhist psychology so completely his own. Applied to the wilderness locale, found earlier in the work of Kenneth Rexroth, this Buddhist perception of oneness, creates a poetry of immediacy and startling originality.

No one can predict with accuracy how the work of this engaging poet . . . will be received in a future, different era. Will *Myths & Texts* be scrutinized by scholars fifty years from now as are Eliot's "The Waste Land" and Pound's *The Cantos?* Will *Riprap* and *The Back Country,* with their flavor of woodsmoke and snow-melt tea, be read and loved as they are now by a generation learning to travel in the wilderness? Will Snyder's *Mountains and Rivers Without End* be cherished as is Whitman's *Leaves of Grass* as a record of a spiritual journey? And will *Regarding Wave* and *Turtle Island,* pointing to the "power within," continue to energize, as does Blake's poetry, when no fossil fuel is left? No one can say; it is too early to tell.

Nonetheless, it seems that Snyder's works are secure, even if his reputation is, as yet, in flux. After the biographical comment has ceased and when his work is seen in perspective, the dominant voice of Gary Snyder as a poet will become evident. Essentially mystical, Snyder's pre-scientific and mythological perception, grounded in his studies of Buddhism and primitive consciousness, has created a new kind of poetry that is direct, concrete, non-Romantic, and ecological. More than as follower of Pound and Williams, or as a clever adaptor of Oriental poetic forms, Snyder's work will be remembered in its own right as the example of a new direction taken in American literature. (pp. 167-68)

Snyder's poetry truly influences one who reads him thoroughly to "see" in a startlingly new way. Presenting the vision of an integrated and unified world, this heroic poetic effort cannot but help to create a much needed change of consciousness. (p. 168)

> *Bob Steuding, in his* Gary Snyder, *Twayne Publishers, 1976, 189 p.*

EKBERT FAAS

["True insight"] to Snyder is "a love-making hovering between the void & the immense worlds of creation," . . . and poetry, as its subtlest medium of expression, walks "that edge between what can be said and that which cannot be said . . . [I]t's going out into emptiness and into the formless" while at the same time resting on "an absolute foundation of human experience and insight." . . . The "pure inspiration flow" bringing it forth is "not intellect and not—(as romantics and after have confusingly thought) fantasy-dream world or unconsciousness." On the contrary, true poetry "reflects all things and feeds all things but is of itself transparent." . . .

True to this theory, Snyder's poetry, like that of his Eastern peers, often radiates with an almost unearthly clarity and precision, whereby the sensual concreteness of every detail seems as if suffused with this transparence or awareness of the void. What seems so deceptively simple, is, in fact, a unique, by now widely imitated, yet probably inimitable achievement within Western poetry. Little gaps of silence frequently seem to separate one utterance from the next, and, like the brush strokes of calligraphic paintings, each phrase or remark, like the phenomenon or event it embodies, seems to rest within the energy of its own tension, autonomous, and yet related to all others in the hidden field of force, creating its "complexity far beneath the surface texture." . . . (p. 96)

[Just] as the Eastern poets he translated cover a wide range of modes and tones, from the mystical luminosity of Chinese Hanshan to the mythopoeic deep imagery or colloquial satire of Japanese Miyazawa Kenji, so [Snyder's] own work is by no means limited to the lyric mode of his **"Flowers for the Void"** . . . "going out into emptiness and into the formless which is the nature of pure joy." . . . Snyder often speaks with a funny, self-ironical, satirical or outspokenly didactic voice, while a work like *Myths & Texts* (1960), hailed by Robert Bly as "one of the two or three finest books of poetry" of its decade . . . , presents us with a subtly orchestrated structure, centered around specific symbols and myths that were inspired by "the happy collections Sapir, Boas, Swanton, and others made of American Indian folktales early in this century." . . . Julian Gitzen, in an extensive interpretation of the poem, has compared *Myths & Texts* with *The Waste Land,* though one may add that the "fragmental texture" which in Eliot's poem expresses anguished spiritual chaos in the face of nothingness ("These fragments I have shored against my ruins") serves Snyder as a positive means for apprehending reality in its pre-conceptual suchness (*tathātā*) and as a medium for his poetic "re-enactment of [the] timeless dance: here and now, co-creating forever, for no end but now." . . . (pp. 99-100)

Another major poetic mode, that of his long poem in progress entitled *Mountains and Rivers without End,* at first seems to invite comparison with the American epic tradition from *Leaves of Grass* to the *Maximus Poems.* Yet as Snyder explained in 1959, it in fact emulates further models of Eastern literature and art. Its "dramatic structure follows a certain type of *Nō* play," while its overall structure (which "threatens to be like its title") was conceived "after a Chinese sidewise scroll painting." . . . (p. 100)

It would be tantamount to splitting hairs to try to trace these various modes in terms of their successive evolution in the poet's life. Even in his beginnings, Snyder, unlike Robert Lowell or other poets of the "confessional" genre, for instance, displays none of the tormented, self-questioning, and often suicidal spiritual tendencies, so typical of post-Romantic poetry in the West. Instead, he seems to have evolved these several modes almost simultaneously and as from a common basis, and to have deepened, refined and elaborated them ever since. As Snyder points out himself, *Mountains and Rivers without End* (of which the first *Six Sections* were published in 1965) was begun as early as 1956, *Myths & Texts* (1960) "grew" between 1952 and 1956 . . . , while the poems of the more "lyric order" as he calls them . . . already dominate his first published collection of 1959 (*Riprap*). Even earlier, in his diary of the years 1952-3, Snyder had begun to formulate the basic premises of his philosophy and poetics: his experience of "*no identity*" and "the void," his epistemological "love-making hovering between the void & the immense worlds of creation," his concept of form as "ellipse, is emptiness," the subsequent experience of linguistic disintegration ("my language fades. Images of erosion") and the attempt to reconstitute language after the model of Chinese poetry cross-bred with the primordial potential of the Anglo-Saxon heritage. It was equally early in his career that Snyder assumed his clean-slate stance in favor of Primitive and Eastern mentality ("Let's be animals or buddhas" . . .) and against the Judaeo-Christian world view. . . . (p. 101)

To be sure, Snyder's early work shows traces of the confessional ("Bitter memory like vomit / Choked my throat") or romantically subjective mode, at times almost reminiscent of a poet like Matthew Arnold, stoically resigned to the cruelty of life, yet at the same time yearning for human compassion. . . . But far more forceful and ubiquitous is the impulse to negate all the "pointless wars of the heart" . . . and to come to terms with human suffering generally. Questioned about his attitude towards the confessional school of poets, Snyder replied: "I'm a Buddhist, which is to say you take suffering and impermanence for granted, as a base fact of the universe, and then proceed on from there." . . . Again, such an attitude is by no means new to Snyder and was in fact assumed even before the confessional poets made their first appearance in Anglo-American literature. As early as 1956, Snyder, age 26, concluded that there comes

> a time when the poet must choose: either to step deep in the stream of his people, history, tradition, folding and folding himself in wealth of persons and pasts; philosophy, humanity, to become richly foundationed and great and sane and ordered. Or, to step beyond the bound onto the way out, into horrors and angels, possible madness or silly Faustian doom, possible utter transcendence, possible enlightened return, possible ignominious wormish perishing. . . .

By his subsequent creativity, personal development and indefatigable involvement in ecological, social, cultural and purely human concerns, Snyder has left no doubt as to which of these two paths he has chosen as his own. (pp. 102-03)

> *Ekbert Faas, "Gary Snyder: Essay," in* Towards a New American Poetics: Essays & Interviews, *edited by Ekbert Faas, Black Sparrow Press, 1978, pp. 91-103.*

SCOTT McLEAN

[The essay from which this excerpt is taken was written as an introduction to The Real Work *in August 1979.]*

In 1969 Gary Snyder published a collection of journal excerpts, reviews, translations, and essays under the title *Earth House Hold.* (p. xi)

Thematically and structurally the interviews and talks gathered in [*The Real Work: Interviews and Talks, 1964-1979*] complement and extend the positions taken in *Earth House Hold.* A line can be traced in the earlier prose collection from Snyder's first statements on poetics in the **"Lookout's Journal"** to the essay "Suwa-no-se Island and the Banyan Ashram," celebrating a sense of community that has been lost all too long. A similar line can be followed in *The Real Work,* from Snyder's comments on the complementary nature of inner and outer realities explored in his poetry to the talk "Poetry, Community, & Climax." But whereas the relationship between poetry and community was only sketched out in the later essays of *Earth House Hold,* it becomes the focal point early in this collection, as poetry is seen more and more by Snyder to be a binding force in the fabric of community life.

Gary Snyder's poetry has continued a tradition first pursued in late eighteenth-century Romantic thought and carried on in American literature most notably by Thoreau: a belief that the "outer and inner life correspond" and that poetry is "the self-consciousness of the universe," the voice of the universe reflecting on itself and on the interdependence of outer and inner nature. Poetry as "the seat of the soul"—the area where the inner world and the outer world touch, where they "interpenetrate" each other.

But if Snyder's work follows this thread in European and American literature, the bases for his poetry lie elsewhere: in oral traditions of transmission, in Chinese and Japanese poetics, and in the ancient and worldwide sense of the Earth Goddess as inspirer of song.

Snyder's early work in *Riprap* was directed toward getting down to a flat surface reality, to break what William Carlos Williams called the "complicated ritualistic forms designed to separate the work from reality." This attention to phenomena in order to discover poetic form in that reality was sharpened by the meditative teachings of Japanese and Chinese poets leading to mind before language and in what is now more than twenty-five years of Zen practice, a discipline which takes one "to *anything* direct—rocks or bushes or people." . . . (pp. xi-xii)

In reaching that "absolute bottom transparency," Snyder's meditative poetry has taken two directions. One is toward a short lyric that pushes up against an edge of silence, an ellipsis where the silence defines the form and substance. In a number of these poems (**"Pine Tree Tops"** is a good example) the texts represent "arrested phenomena," and the poems become, as Donald Wesling says in a related context, "like the 'objects' of modern physics, . . . at once product and process." These poems are small "knots," "whorls in the grain," a bit of stored energy that draws the reader/listener at the end of the poem to follow out in his or her mind the pathways marked.

The second form Snyder's meditative poetry takes is the long poem that begins in the everyday world but then spirals up from that area, working on more mythological and archetypal levels. *Myths & Texts* (1960) has the movement of an elegy, going back and forth between the present and the past, as the poem follows various paths in history, in nature, in the world of work. . . . Pushed up hard against phenomena, in the smoky burn of the mind that leads up through an area described in the Hopi image of the smokehole that connects the worlds, Snyder's longer meditative poetry functions like a double mirror, showing "multiple reflections in multiple mirrors," in which you "see yourself going this way and you see yourself going that way." The poems in *Myths & Texts* and in sections of *Mountains and Rivers Without End* touch on the most basic, deeply felt mythological ground, and they do what myth has always done: they give us some access to the intense instance of our lives in the vast series of interrelationships established by the figures, events, and images of the myth.

All of Gary Snyder's study and work has been directed toward a poetry that would approach phenomena with a disciplined clarity and that would then use the "archaic" and "primitive" as models to once again see this poetry as woven through all parts of our lives. Thus it draws its substance and forms from the broadest range of a people's day-to-day lives, enmeshed in the facts of work, the real trembling in joy and grief, thankfulness for good crops, the health of a child, the warmth of the lover's touch. Further, Snyder seeks to recover a poetry that could sing and thus relate us to: magpie, beaver, a mountain range, binding us to all these other lives, seeing our spiritual lives as bound up in the rounds of nature.

Snyder's concerns are, as Luis Ellicott Yglesias recently noted, "archaic in the primal sense—a going into the deep past not to escape or to weep with loud lamentations, but to see whether with the help of the earth-lore that is 'all forgot' it might be possible to open life to a more livable future." In terms of any future we may have, Snyder's look toward the primitive may vouchsafe one of the only real alternative directions available. (pp. xii-xiii)

Taking up the oldest songs, extending them and sustaining them, is a part then of what Gary Snyder has called "the real work of modern man: to uncover the inner structure and actual boundaries of the mind." ...

What then of the interviews and talks collected [in *The Real Work*] in the context of Snyder's poetry? A lot of what follows is simply good, plain talk with a man who has a lively and very subtle mind and a wide range of experience and knowledge. But there is one important aspect of these texts that I'd like to follow out for a moment: the place of the interview in our literature. (p. xiv)

The interview . . . has opened a substantial range of possibilities for far-reaching discourse. In collecting a series of his own interviews, the poet Donald Hall noted that since World War II the interview had become "the dominant form by which poets made public their poetics." For Gary Snyder the interview has been much more—although, indeed, some of his most incisive statements on poetics are contained in the interviews that follow. For Snyder the interview has become an occasion to publicly tie together a complex series of interests and concerns and, within the context of the dialogue generated, follow new directions suggested. . . .

The rise of the literary interview has been dependent upon a concern with the individual writer's particular state of mind, a concern that marks the beginnings of modern literature. But if the interview benefits us in the attention it brings to an individual writer's practice, it also shares in the excesses of an extreme and quirky individualism. Interviews with writers often circle constantly about the individual writer's personal life. (p. xv)

I think there is a turn away from this overt personal concern, and that it can be seen in those dialogues where the poetic intelligence is led to make a series of genuinely new connections generated in the talking. The current popularity of the interview reflects, on its most intense level, an exploratory quality in modern American poetic theory and practice, what George Quasha has called the "dialogical" in modern poetics. In those instances where the interview is generated by this kind of participation, it not only provides an open area for critical discussion, it participates directly in a poetics of process, a poetry engaged, seeking to draw the listener/reader into the act of *poesis,* the active process of speaking and following out the discovery, transformation, and invention that poetry seeks.

Gary Snyder's interviews and talks belong to this line of exploratory dialogue. (p. xvi)

One final note then on a tradition that relates directly to the substance of this book. The question-and-answer (Japanese: *mondo*) and the recorded saying (Japanese: *goroku*) are Buddhist texts of what were originally orally transmitted teachings, talks given on a specific occasion or addressing a certain question, spoken freely, spontaneously. The teachings of these texts (the *Lin-chi-Lu* or *Record of Rinzai* is perhaps the single most important text for Snyder) inform Snyder's talk, but more than the content material of these texts it is perhaps the direction the dialogue often takes—turning the question back around to the one who asked—that bears on the interviews that follow. There is a web of interests and concerns that remains constant in these talks, but rather than viewing the texts as representing any final statement on those issues, I think Gary Snyder would like to see the process that initiated the questioning sustained, bringing many of the questions raised back to the individual reader's own life. (pp. xvi-xvii)

Scott McLean, in an introduction to The Real Work: Interviews & Talks, 1964-1979 *by Gary Snyder, edited by Wm. Scott McLean, New Directions, 1980, pp. xi-xvii.*

CHARLES ALTIERI

Gary Snyder is one of the very few poets since 1900 to command both a large popular appeal and considerable respect from his peers. The reason for the former is his articulation of a possible religious faith at a time when cultural alienation was pushing many people to experiment with various non-Western metaphysical systems. The reason for the latter is evident if one compares Snyder with other poets responding to the same quest for alternate religious doctrines. On the one hand there are poets like Cid Corman and Philip Whalen who directly translate Zen materials and forms into English, and on the other there are those like Allen Ginsberg or Jerome Rothenberg who achieve the intense and dramatic religious emotion the former lack, but only at the cost of a considerable sacrifice of secular intelligence. . . . Snyder differs from Corman and Whalen by exercising care to adapt his Eastern meditative habits to concrete dramatic experiences and to make his syntax reflect those habits of vision which justify and give resonance to his religious assertions. And unlike Ginsberg, Snyder tries to limit his affirmations to claims he can support or at least embody within the affective context and attitude created by his dramatic lyrics. When he goes bad, Snyder's work collapses into one or the other of the types I have mentioned, but he normally avoids them by basing his religious vision on dramatic techniques and situations that manifest their relevance to Western culture.

Snyder, in short, repeats the central strategies of Dante and Donne, conceiving his religious vision as a repetition in a finer tone of what the imagination in fact does and discloses when it constructs a set of metaphoric relationships attesting to some ideal unity not readily evident to the discursive logical mind. . . . By naturalizing the mind and placing it at once within and beyond natural process, Snyder can . . . easily accept the organic poem as testimony to an organically unified cosmos. . . . (pp. 131-32)

For the skeptic or half-believer, the real miracle is the skill with which Snyder uses the aesthetic devices of lyrical poetry to sustain his religious claims. His basic achievement is his power to make his readers reflect on the ontological core of the lyrical vision by calling attention to the way it can be things or processes themselves, and not merely the elements of a poem, which mutually create one another's significance and suggest a unifying power producing, sustaining, and giving meaning to these relationships. (p. 132)

[Snyder's] earliest lyrics make clear by their lack of full interrelationships how difficult it has been to achieve the easy, confident sense of interbirth in more recent poems. These early lyrics concentrate more on the moral task of achieving freedom from Western ways than on realizing the goal of a new religious vision. What freedom they achieve from the struggle to escape slavery to "culture" is expressed primarily in the form of naming particulars, not of discovering relationships. . . . [For example, some poems in *Riprap* dramatize] a sense of place and a sense of cosmos, but that cosmos is backdrop and not active agent. Similarly, the language is essentially nominal (Olson's hated push to the nominative) and neither active in itself nor alive with interrelationships. Snyder has escaped into the territories, but not yet mapped their ecology.

The opening poems in *The Back Country* provide the first maps. Interbirth here is not yet a cosmic dance, but one does see its genesis in Snyder's sense of the way particulars require one another if they are to be appreciated fully. The resultant mode of consciousness, in poems like **"A Walk,"** might best be described as an ecological one—bringing the ''vast 'jewelled net''' to ''conscious knowledge and practice.'' . . . (pp. 132-33)

[In **"A Walk,"** Snyder] builds from the fact that the organic poem is a kind of ecological system to make the poem illustrate moral qualities basic to an ecological perspective on experience. First of all, there is the tone that by its quiet casualness denies the traditional assumption (taken to extremes in confessional poetry) that lyric poetry is the expression of unique moments charged with extraordinary intensity. Second, the syntax of the poem supports its ecological intent, for as the speaker becomes more involved in his actions he forgoes any explicit references to himself as subject. The reader gets instead a series of verbs and almost dangling participles that tend to blend actor and action, man and world. Finally, the preponderance of concrete details has two effects. So much pointing asserts the referential power of language and denies the self-reflexive implications that accompany more metaphoric styles. It is not words but things that are being related to one another. And these concrete relations enable Snyder to communicate a non-Western frame of mind without references to occult philosophy or a series of abstractions. Ecology deals not with ideas, but with modes of action and with the unity of inter-relationships in nature, and its verification is the fullness of the environment it creates. In a poem that realizes Snyder's ecological perspective, myth and text no longer require separate statement; they are unified in one's quiet reverence at the depth of connection suggested by the poem. (pp. 134-35)

Much of Snyder's work manifests a movement like that of **"Burning the Small Dead,"** a movement out to an awareness of self in cosmos complemented by the perception of cosmos contained within the self. His volumes, for example, tend to expand their frame of awareness—from localized Western contexts and images of the individual in nature, through journeys to the East and exercises in Eastern philosophy, mythology, and meditation, to a synthesis in which these materials all are restored within a simple domestic context. Such a movement is evident in *Myths and Texts'* gradual union of logging, hunting (with its emphasis on Indian mythology), and burning (with an emphasis on Eastern thought) till a particular fire becomes text for an all-encompassing mythic vision of distances within and without (''the mountains are your mind.'') . . . *Earth House Hold* begins with Snyder as lonely wanderer in the American west, imaginatively explores several cultures, and concludes with a traditional communal celebration of a marriage between Western man and Eastern woman set in the context of all human time and embodying a relationship with the elements to be developed poetically in *The Regarding Wave.*

The unified volume exemplifies the metaphoric gathering of otherwise contingent elements and expands lyric states of awareness into a general style of life. Snyder's fullest dramatic achievement of these goals occurs in *The Back Country,* where the first part of the volume employs poems . . . in order to represent a state of innocence characterized by Snyder's self-sufficiency in the American wilderness. But a full religious vision must encounter other cultures and come to terms with a sense of loss and evil. Hence the second part of the volume takes Snyder to Japan and confronts him with his own root-lessness (the Robin poems) and, more important, with his dif-

ferences as an American from other men. . . . **"Six Years,"** the section's final poem, then moves toward resolving some of these tensions by dramatizing a rhythm of repetition and a gradual absorption of Snyder into his new environment and of the environment into him. The poem's last section compresses Snyder's six years in Japan into the rhythms of a year's seasonal movement and parallels that temporal order to the daily cycle of life in a Zen monastery. The joyful acceptance of discipline (the road to a deeper freedom than he had known in the territories) and the sharpness of detail, especially of the poem's final perception, then summarize what those six years have meant. ''A far bell coming closer'' literally promises the beginning of a new day exactly like the one recorded, but that coming closer has profound psychological reverberations as Snyder internalizes what this essence of Japanese life can offer him. . . . The entire six years can be focused in the quality of a moment's inner awareness. Time is recapitulated and extended as the capacity for action in concert with a new, more reflective environment.

In the third section, the fear is that cycles might not have any progression, that the Hindu vision of all as fleeting illusion bound to the wheel of Maya might be a true one (the section is titled for Kali, the Hindu goddess of destruction). India provides the landscape of evil previously only glimpsed—both in its religion and in the economic and social conditions of the people. . . . And this sterility in turn throws Snyder back upon the failed love that is the volume's emblem of the loss one must undergo to be saved. Now, however, that love evokes in Snyder images of his own psychic sterility as a creature too caught in words, self, and memory to love another. . . . (pp. 138-40)

Having broadened his experience and internalized what knowledge his travels could bring, Snyder in the fourth section can assume a cosmic perspective and a prophetic stance. The universe as illusion becomes the universe as cosmic play within which no loss or failure need be final. . . . The poet who passively witnesses social evil can now give political advice to both West and East. And the failed lover discovers another whom he can love and who embodies a ground or ''field for experiencing the universe as sacramental.'' . . . Particulars blend not only with one another but with the infinite energies beyond and ''below.'' . . . Even the words themselves (through the awkward device of . . . quotation marks) seek to burst out of their nominal functions to participate in those energies leaping forth to meet the poet's hand as it traces the line where love through desire generates form and gathers all the burning into a collective and expanding '''we.'''

The volume ends, though, with a less triumphant note; for too intense a conclusion would return the reader to the world of individual lyrics and the dialectic of intense presence emerging from a neutral or dead context and thrusting one back there when the visionary force is expanded. To push the lyrical consciousness into nature demands that one also adapt it to continuing process (another reason, perhaps, for a unified volume of lyrics). One must be left with a quiet joyful acceptance, at once open ended and returning the reader to the simplicity and style of the volume's opening poems—now with a cosmic perspective informing the image of eating (''loving what it feeds on''):

> First   Samish Bay.
>   then all morning, hunting oysters

A huge feed on white
wood State Park slab-plank bench-
                and table
                    at Birch Bay
                where we picked up rocks
        for presents.

And ate oysters, fried—raw—cookt in milk
        rolld in crumbs—
all we wanted.

                    ALL WE WANTED

& got back in our wagon,
drove away. . . .

Snyder is dealing here in concrete terms with the perennial philosophical and theological problem of reconciling the achievement of plenitude with an acceptance of change. Christianity tends to promise plenitude at the cost of renouncing flux, while Eastern religions often come to terms with flux by an ascetic rejection of all desire for plenitude (hence there can be no Eastern *Divine Comedy*). In this poem, however, Snyder's dialectical method shows how one can have both plenitude and change. In fact the two conditions are necessary if one is to appreciate either. Full satisfaction with the feast is possible only because the act can be enjoyed entirely on its own terms, as an absolute present unspoiled by desires to prolong or transcend it. The plenitude cannot be imprisoning, cannot "hook" the actors so that they become unwilling to move on. . . . At the same time, when the present is completely accepted, there is nothing to fear from change. The actors can move on without anxiety and open to future moments of fullness.

Snyder reinforces the affirmative dialectic here by picking up and reversing in the last line one of the symptoms of cultural malaise he had presented earlier in the volume. In [*The Back Country*'s] second poem, he records watching "thousands of cars / driving men to work." . . . Liberated now, he overcomes the passivity of Western man trapped by his possessions and the culture that supports them. He moves on, content and in control of his own destiny. To have all one wants is the American dream, and Snyder with his innocence, pragmatism, vitality, and perpetual wandering Eastward or into the wilderness belongs in the tradition of American romanticism. But the contrast created by the last line and, more important, the tone of the poem suggest a new way of realizing that dream. All one wants cannot be achieved by the way of self-transcendence, for every triumph depends on another failure and adds a new possibility of failure. Only when one learns to control the desire for plenitude by a sense of the simple necessities whose satisfaction constitutes one mode of that plenitude will one free the dream and the dreamer from the bitter disillusionment that often torments self-consciousness.

Snyder's next volume of lyrics, *The Regarding Wave,* follows thematically from the last section of *The Back Country*. The images of cosmic play and the sacramental body of the beloved woman, which embodied Snyder's enlarged perspective, are central to the new volume, but the more recent poems try to enact a vision Snyder only described or projected in *The Back Country*. Interbirth is no longer the controlled mutual dependency of specific events; rather it is universal intercourse or **"Communionism,"** . . . a dance of energy permeating, informing, and transforming all particular phenomena. There is no absence and no contingency. All particulars retain their identity and even find it reinforced through their functioning as dynamic parts of a single whole. **"The Way Is Not a Way"**

(or "away") but the continual presence of all ways within a single process. . . . (pp. 140-43)

Snyder is trying to create poetically not so much a system of references that will articulate "The Way" as an emotional consciousness of what it feels like to know oneself as a part of such a total system. To achieve his vision he enacts a style considerably different from that of *The Back Country,* and he creates a carefully unified volume not as dramatic context but rather as an exemplum of the dynamic intercourse of concrete and universal typified in his own sacramental roles as poet, husband, and father within a universe suffused with creative love. The stylistic shift is most readily described as the movement from an essentially dramatic, psychological style to a meditative, religious one. The specific interchanges between a mind localized in time and space and its environment give way to a sense of mind as recording, praising, and gathering energy while only slightly tied to a specific personal context. The goal is to put mind more directly into the impersonal processes of the world and still be true to its powers of encompassing those processes. (These generalizations will be reversed in the volume's climactic central section.) Thus instead of dramatic contexts there are numerous songs gathering various manifestations or "transformations" . . . of phenomena like seeds or clouds or taste. The mind is a point of focus, not an active agent locked in events. Moreover, attention to mind as a gatherer of being allows Snyder to stand partially outside the particular acts of mind within process and to see them as aspects of a deeper connecting principle. Behind individual acts of perception lie the experiences of the collective mind captured in language and myth and recoverable through etymology. Words are treasure-hoards, records of the mind's sense of the rhythms it shares with nature and of its own active participation in that interchange. . . . (p. 144)

Snyder's achievement is a considerable one. Judged simply in aesthetic terms, according to norms of precision, intelligence, imaginative play, and moments of deep resonance, he easily ranks among the best poets of his generation. Moreover, he manages to provide a fresh perspective on metaphysical themes, which he makes relevant and often compelling. Yet it is impossible for me, perhaps for most academics, to be completely satisfied with his work. One reason may be his ambition. He wants not only to provide poems but to offer a total vision of a new redeemed man at home with himself and celebrating his place in the cosmos, yet the field of experience in his poems is quite limited and it therefore renders problematic his claims to totality. One requires a more complex sense of human nature, of social reality, and of one's own self-conscious awareness of the gaps between desire and realization, faith and works, before accepting his authority as one offering more than moments of metaphysical insight. Moreover, Snyder's dramatized version of himself, especially before *The Regarding Wave,* gives readers a hero from the mythic American past who is closer to their fantasy lives than to their practical needs to give sense and significance to specific situations in society.

This last point, I think, gets to the heart of the matter. One cannot judge poets according to strict philosophical canons of truth and falsity. But especially when the poet himself claims the authority of a wisdom tradition, one must ask whether readers can seriously entertain in their imagination the hypothetical relevance of his values and his dramatic situations for their own basic concerns. This is not simply a question of intellectual resonance. It involves the very conditions for a really deep participation in and commitment to the poet's work.

I can achieve this with Snyder only by abstracting from his specific dramatic contexts and his social positions to concentrate exclusively on his treatment of epistemological and metaphysical themes and strategies. This clearly would not satisfy Snyder, and it does not satisfy me; nonetheless it does allow me to see him as considerably more than the poetic Marlboro man he is called by Robert Boyers. (pp. 149-50)

> Charles Altieri, *"Process As Plenitude: The Poetry of Gary Snyder and Robert Duncan,"* in his Enlarging the Temple: New Directions in American Poetry during the 1960s, *Bucknell University Press, 1979, pp. 128-69.**

THOMAS J. LYON

[*He Who Hunted Birds in His Father's Village*] is Gary Snyder's senior thesis done at Reed College, from which he was graduated in 1951 with a dual major in anthropology and English. It is, in a way, a model of all his subsequent work, because it attempts to lead through literature—in this case, a "Swan Maiden" myth among the Haida tribe—to the living roots of cultural practice and psychology. By itself, it is an impressive study, bringing the theories of Graves, Freud, Jung, Campbell, Eliot, and I. A. Richards, among others, to bear upon the Haida. What Snyder is trying to show is that this people was a rooted people, enmeshed in a complex, wild ecology in which animals were tremendously significant, and at the same time a regardful people, self-conscious and artistic to an extraordinarily high degree. (p. 61)

In 1951, Snyder had penetrated to the human meaning of a myth—perhaps helped or motivated by certain personal considerations, which he mentions at the close of his "Foreword." He had "lived into" another time and place, another cultural mind.

The "Foreword" is also interesting because, in almost throwaway fashion, Snyder presents the essence of his (and all) poetic practice.

> To go beyond and become what—a seagull on
> a reef? Why not. Our nature is no particular
> nature; look out across the beach at the gulls.
> For an empty moment while their soar and cry
> enters your heart like sunshaft through water,
> you are that, totally. We do this every day.

And so did the Haida. What is remarkable is that a "green would-be scholar in Oregon," as Snyder describes his twenty or twenty-one year old self, should have seen into that heart of the matter so clearly. (pp. 61-2)

> Thomas J. Lyon, in a review of *"He Who Hunted Birds in His Father's Village,"* in Western American Literature, *Vol. XV, No. 1, Spring, 1980, pp. 61-2.*

KEVIN ODERMAN

In an aside to one of his other remarks [in *The Real Work: Interviews and Talks, 1964-1979*], Gary Snyder implicitly criticizes the "stress on individual names" which characterizes the way we readers respond to our poets; he does so because he writes out of a tradition of self-effacement, and his yearnings are for a communal poetry rooted in place. But without a "name," poets aren't asked to do interviews, and without a big name such interviews are never collected into a book like Snyder's *The Real Work: Interviews & Talks, 1964-1979*. And,

I think, it takes a *very big* name on such a collection to find readers, and to convince readers to be open enough to engage ideas like Snyder's, which lead, paradoxically, to self-effacement and no names. (p. 113)

In his introduction, Scott McLean suggests a Buddhist model for the nature of this talk: "The question-and-answer (Japanese: *mondo*) and the recorded saying (Japanese: *goroku*) are Buddhist texts of what were originally orally transmitted teachings, talks given on a specific occasion or addressing a certain question, spoken freely, spontaneously" [see excerpt above]. While McLean, perhaps, only means to place the book in a tradition, his suggestion seems to me congratulatory and even a little misleading. For while there is a good deal of talk-about-Buddhism in the book (some of it, on the part of the questioners, extremely naive), there is little besides that to make us think of *mondo* and *goroku* rather than other books of interviews with authors. The explanation for this is to be found in the mode of Snyder's talk: it remains, with few exceptions, entirely within the confines of conventional logical discourse. This, of course, is not a fault, but for Zen, the Buddhism of most concern to Snyder, it is a little surprising. While listening to Snyder the realm of logical discourse seems to be a very large one, and there seems to be little danger of bumping into anything unspeakable. This is not true of the best interpreters of Zen for the West, not true of those to whom Snyder himself owes a great—and acknowledged—debt: D. T. Suzuki, R. H. Blyth, and Robert Aitken. In their work logical discourse is a box rather than a realm, and the constant recurrence to paradox points the way out.

Snyder's "real work," in this volume at least, is application. This is a "how to" book in many ways, and how to live day by day perhaps admits of less paradox and more exposition that we would like to think. In one interview, Snyder laughs when asked if he had ever considered himself a "hopeless idealist," and then answers that he has always thought himself very practical. I, for one, accept his judgment, without laughing. His practicality is everywhere in evidence in *The Real Work*, and it is what confers on the book its significance, its solidity. (pp. 113-14)

Snyder's knowledge is broad, and he is able to talk with authority on many topics. In the pages of *The Real Work* he talks extensively about the relation between poetry and community, the primitive, zazen, anthropology, biology, *and* poetics. He is very interesting in his discussions of regionalism, and the sense of rootedness, of Snyder's involvement in his own region—"the Nevada County west slope of the Sierra, drainage of the Yuba"—is of a quality to generate enthusiasm for one's own place. But Snyder is most interesting when he surprises, and for this reason I found his discourse on the relationship of the primitive's state of mind while hunting to the state of mind engendered by zazen one of the most fascinating in the book. What other contemporary poet could or would take up such a subject?

While *The Real Work* makes us believe in Snyder as a talker, there are a few passages that are about as pleasant to read as chewing sand. There are leftovers from Snyder's days as a Dharma Bum-like "nation-state bag," and unfortunate infiltrations from biology and anthropology. While St.-John Perse can make the language of science sing in a poem like *Oiseaux* or in his letters, there is nothing cantabile, indeed speakable, about Snyder's use of it: the earth has become a "biosphere," a translator is characterized as "a valuable switch in an energy exchange flow," there is a "biopoetic," a "biogeography," and so forth. So much life! No doubt we all sin verbatim, but Snyder's **"Turtle Island"** seems to me to be overpopulated by Buckminster Fullers. But these are blemishes only, *Real Work* is solid work. (pp. 114-15)

*Kevin Oderman, "The Talk of Nevada County, CA,"
in* The Denver Quarterly, *Vol. 15, No. 3, Fall, 1980,
pp. 113-15.*

THOMAS W. PEW, JR.

Gary Snyder comes to *The Real Work* having accomplished some very real work himself. . . .

The titles of these interviews hint at some of the directions his work has taken. From "Landscape of Consciousness" through "The Zen of Humanity" and "Tracking Down the Natural Man," on to "The Bioregional Ethic," these talks with Snyder form the author's first non-poetry collection since *Earth House Hold* (1969).

For those readers who are arriving at Snyder for the first time *The Real Work* is an ideal introduction; for readers familiar with his poetry and previous prose work it is a refreshing collection of his clear thinking and unique sense of our particular time and place.

Snyder, like a handful of other writers since Carl Jung, has discovered the similarities of myth, religion, and his own personal dream content as well as the product of his meditations and has fashioned that collective material into words that set off little explosions in our thought process and our own deeper memory. . . .

These talks tell us how Snyder has come to perform the details in a life that has had more variety than most. And they let us hear these details in a voice that is Snyder's own unique blend of East and West, Native American and rural White, blue collar and academic.

There is a quality of toughness in Snyder and his writing, a kind of conservatism that cuts across the loose meaning that word has come to carry in our society and gets down to the basics of work, family, and community.

Few poets writing today are more careful with words than Snyder. To hear him read his own poetry is almost like sitting at table with a great lover of good food. The words come out of his mouth as though each one has been thoroughly tasted, tested for quality, and spoken only when the speaker is finally satisfied that it is the best of its kind.

This sense of care comes through in these interviews; so does the sense of humor and the sense of fallibility. Snyder is so sure of the progress of his own ideas, that without these two latter qualities some of the ideas might be hard to take. But as they are presented here we always have that sense of a smile behind the seriousness. . . .

This book is fascinating reading. Each interview has at least one powerful mind-hit that keeps the echoes going for a long time. For those readers interested in an original approach to the rationale behind preserving Native American values as well as some of our own most basic European values, this book presents material that is not the usual fare of conservationists.

Besides, Snyder is as good a talker and storyteller as he is a poet.

*Thomas W. Pew, Jr., in a review of "The Real Work:
Interviews & Talks, 1964-1979," in* The American

West, *Vol. XVIII, No. 1, January-February, 1981,
p. 61.*

BERT ALMON

The tape recorder often gives us wordy ramblings of egocentric writers. Fortunately Gary Snyder is neither wordy nor egocentric, and the interviews and lectures collected in [*The Real Work: Interviews and Talks, 1964-1979*] show his usual wit and concision. He talks better than most people write. Anyone who wants to know how Snyder's thinking on social and literary issues has evolved since *Earth House Hold* in 1969 will find much to mull over. The six pieces collected in *The Old Ways* (1977) were an uneven batch, but these statements are consistently strong. (p. 55)

Much of the book is given over to social and political issues, but poetry is not ignored. The most illuminating remarks pertain to shamanism and poetry. Snyder has been attacked from a native American viewpoint in recent years for appropriating the persona of the shaman. His interview with Michael Helm sets the matter straight. Shamanism, Snyder points out, is a world-wide phenomenon, and its core is learning from the nonhuman, "not a teaching from an Indian medicine man, or a Buddhist master. The question of culture does not enter into it. It's a naked experience some people have out there in the woods." The crucial encounter in western American poetry, and often in the novel (thinking of Rudolfo Anaya and Frank Waters), is a spiritual encounter with the non-human. Snyder has written about the experience in his poetry and his prose has taught a generation where the documents of shamanism can be found. (pp. 55-6)

Snyder places himself at one point of a vast network of American intellectual life that embraces the cities and universities as well as the Allegheny Star Route in northern California. He doesn't speak as a solitary prophet although he does live in the hills. The scope of this network is shown by the sources of these interviews, which include academic journals, a health food magazine, poetry journals, counterculture newspapers— and there is an uncollected interview in a skiing magazine. Eclectic and esoteric as his interests may be, they are shared by a sizable community. (p. 56)

Bert Almon, in a review of "The Real Work: Interviews & Talks, 1964-1979," in Western American Literature, *Vol. XVI, No. 1, Spring, 1981, pp. 55-6.*

ROGER JONES

Of all poets who have published [books of interviews], Gary Snyder's interviews seem to be most organically harmonious with his poetic practice as a whole, for his work has a social purpose to it that makes his comments about all matters valuable. And besides, Snyder possesses a keen inelligence about a tremendous range of subjects. Accordingly, the fourteen interviews in *The Real Work* don't have the totally literary tang to them that an academic writer might create in such talks. They present, instead, a poet whose concerns go beyond his poetry into a wide active range of social and spiritual matters. It is interesting, in fact, that so few of Snyder's remarks have to do strictly with poetry or literature. Reading through this book, one realizes that poetry simply serves as the nucleus for Snyder's whole work. Similarly, it is clear that Snyder perceives the poet as a religious figure whose prime duty is shamanistic—acting as a medium for the songs and chants sung to him from the earth. (pp. 246-47)

In an interview with Paul Geneson of the *Ohio Review* (easily the best interview in the book), Snyder explains: "The real work is what we really do. And what our lives are. And if we can live the work we have to do, knowing that we are real, and it's real, and that the world is real, then it becomes right. And that's the *real work*: to make the world as real as it is, and to find ourselves as real as we are within it."

What keeps us from being "real" within the world, as Snyder makes clear here, is the maze, created by modern technological thought, of abstraction and subservience to our own tools. Accordingly, Snyder's own work seems to be the spiritual dialectic—smashing idealistic, romantic, or intellectual molds that draw the mind into abstraction, out of reality, and thus away from the spiritual realities inherent in Being itself. . . . In the past twenty years, as can be seen by the chronological sequence of these interviews, Snyder's poetic vision has crystallized because of his timely dedication to ecological and political sanity. As is stressed in many of the interviews, Snyder's view is that inner and outer realities are virtually identical, though artificially muddled by abstraction and modern diversion.

The most interesting remarks in the book, however, deal with poetry. . . . (p. 247)

Reading through Snyder's interviews, what is most striking is that Snyder is one of the century's *healthiest* writers. He perceives man as completely situated within the schemes of natural order, and sees as a necessity man's awareness that he is as real and as whole as the world. . . .

[Contrary] to critics who see his work as simply a modern version of the "noble savage," or "back-to-nature" philosophy, these interviews demonstrate that Snyder has taken such concepts one step farther, advocating peaceful stewardship, economy, responsibility with the world's resources, and, most importantly, sanity—all still within the capabilities of modern societies, and bound up in the perception of the world and its life-sources as a glorious whole. (p. 248)

> Roger Jones, "On Seeing the Universe Freshly," in Southwest Review, Vol. 67, No. 2, Spring, 1982, pp. 246-48.

MARY KINZIE

Most striking [about the work of Gary Snyder] is the fact that he avoids metaphor of the kind . . . [wherein] two realms of conjunction, frequently one physical and the other spiritual, mix on the surface in such a way that the depths beneath will beckon, until *any* surface glancingly has something of depth in it. Contrary to this principle of steady sympathetic evocation, Snyder gives us *only* the surface and expects us *not* to expect it to ripple down to the depths beneath:

> soaked drooping bamboo groves
> swaying heavy in the drizzle,
> and perfectly straight lines of rice plants
> glittering orderly mirrors of water,
> dark grove of straight young Sugi trees
> thick at the base of the hill. . . .

Even the title of this poem ["**Delicate Criss-Crossing Beetle Trails Left in the Sand**"] alerts us to the presence of a devoted nominalist, perhaps of an oriental persuasion—a suggestion

made by the details (beetle, bamboo, rice, rain) and corroborated by the implied disciplines of composure, composition, linearity, and crystalline geometric design ("glittering orderly mirrors of water"). But implication is only casual. The rich nominalism of this fine description is not perfected in the service of any larger pattern. There is no sure link between the smooth, wet, attractively rectilinear scene and any answering order in the psyche. Rather, the "heavy" description is uneasily floated in a medium of "light" conversational realism. This happens to be the Japanese village his wife Masa comes from, although even this fact seems to pull the poem away from rather than toward its center:

> Walking out on the beach, why I know this!
> rode down through these pines once
> with Anja and John
>
> And watch bugs in their own tiny dunes.
> from memory to memory,
> bed to bed and meal to meal,
> all on this road in the sand

Beds and meals are of equal weight with memories—in fact they are pretty much all the memory this poet of the present moment manifests. Whoever Anja and John may be, they belong with the troupe of chums named Steve and Mike and Wendell and Tanya and Ron and Bill and Cindy and Rod and Patty who move through Snyder's recitals with their earnest but illusory circumstantiality. These rural cherubim, who have shrugged off their surnames, are also an aspect of the author's new domestication, part of the cultural baggage taken on in an attempt, in middle age, to steal a little back from time, to settle down without compromising the basic orientation of the wanderer, the taster and tryer, the genial and honest vagabond of the spirit. . . .

Whatever is unpleasant in Snyder's work comes about from his refusal to distinguish the poetic from the nonpoetic in his writing. Many of the pieces in [*Axe Handles*] raise no resistance to the jargon of causes; Snyder does not try to render or place the clichés of ecological activism and California zen ("biome," "biomass," "ecosystem," "petrochemical complex," "joyful interpenetration"), which he has taken into himself as equably as he'd done earlier with the languages of primitive myth, monasticism, logging, and the merchant marine: he simply blurts the phrases out. His poem on breasts is at once offensive and hilarious (his is not a world for women, except in their function as squaws). . . . (p. 41)

Gary Snyder's refusal to monitor his style is matched by his inability to extend his thought, either in length or by extending his range to intellectual wit: he is simply not good at working out puzzles with logical mirrors. The title poem of *Axe Handles* is an awkward attempt to bring into the task of teaching his son a skill the deeper riddle of mind. The two are making a new handle for an axe-head in the same shape as the handle on the hatchet they must wield to carve the new one with. He says to his son, "'Look: We'll shape the handle / By checking the handle / Of the axe we cut with—' / And he sees." The son may indeed have seen, but the lines in which the claim is made are flat and unseeing. . . .

Like Pound, Snyder prefers the sort of maxim . . . that closes one off, that tends to repel participation and extension. Ideas become runic and dense. The process is one of inscrutable-making whose reverse side is the self-evident and commonplace. But at the same time, it is only fair to observe how close Snyder's verses, quoted earlier, about bamboo groves and glittering orderly mirrors of water come to matching [Howard] Nemerov's exquisite lines, both in precision of view, and in precision of feeling.

Snyder has a real knack for the seasonal, geographical haiku, brief, rapid, spontaneous, and striking in its reticence. On a trip to a large aborigine reservation in central Australia, the speaker of one such "haiku" blends/falls so effortlessly into the land and culture, it would appear he had no shedding of civilized traits to perform. As you read one of the best of the sequence called **"Uluru Wild Fig Song,"** notice how little the author's memory intrudes. He successfully resists any urge to compare what he sees and feels and tastes, now, with feasts and outings closer to home. . . . Such a poem can work only when mundane consciousness has been excluded and the actor in the piece is entirely but not effusively given over to the habits and emanations round about. It's crucial that the quality of his attention be both flexibly aimless and disciplined by nonverbal awareness. By withholding all responses but the obvious physical ones, feeling clean, getting full, hearing accurately, stepping on thistles, Snyder makes [problematic elements within the poem] factual rather than arbitrary. . . .

Thom Gunn has a perceptive essay in *The Occasions of Poetry* (1982) on Snyder's method of firing up the merely perceptual into a fully conscious and even celebratory poem. The means of transition is a careful retardation as the items of notice separate themselves out from the myriad-teeming visual field. Yet the poems move not from sleep to vision, or from dullness to sparkle; the descriptive poem at which Snyder is adept is an always open general field in which perceptions "overtake each other and accrete" by virtue of a sensibility already, and throughout his work, "imbedded in time." This may be the most American of all of Snyder's characteristics, to dig in rather than transcend, though of course the digging-in matters most when the experience is of more than polemical or procedural significance.

Gary Snyder's gift still shows in poems of coolly excited physical well-being, in his strange combination of country ease and monastic stubbornness, in restraint of ego that is like and unlike T. S. Eliot's doctrine of impersonality, because Snyder's impersonality does not bring with it the mannerisms of restraint, only the clarities of openness and humility. This poetry is the product of control that yet does not suppress or reject what is produced by energies and motives unlike its own. And this is the difference between real impersonality and Eliot's kind of decorum. Snyder's identity is not bound up with style. The logical and experiential upshot of this state of mind is that the poem dims while the experience grows. At its most logical (or most extreme) this attitude sidesteps art and subsides into a state of soul. At times, however, by no means consistently, the poem that dims out into life can present sounds, contours of phrase, and aptness of image and illustration that move and delight. (p. 42)

Mary Kinzie, "Pictures from Borges," in The American Poetry Review, Vol. 12, No. 6, November-December, 1983, pp. 40-6.*

CHARLES MOLESWORTH

[Hannah] Arendt's main point [in *The Human Condition,* her critical reassessment of the main tradition of European political philosophy,] is that the modern world is most hampered by its elevation of action over contemplation, with the concomitant devaluation of thought itself within the realm of action. To restore to political vision the awareness of the value and necessity of thought, not only as a form of activity but also as its most fully human form: this is Arendt's central project, and it is close to [Gary Snyder's] as well. From the objectivist poetics of *Riprap* and *Myths & Texts,* on to the personal doubt of *The Back Country,* and then through to the new senses of community and selfhood in *Earth House Hold* and *Turtle Island,* the curve of Snyder's career has been from the factlike density of perceptual intensity to the harmonious patternmaking of the immanently mythic imagination. Such a course of development has taken Snyder deeper and deeper into the workings of the political imagination as well.

At the same time, Snyder's artistic development has been equally deepened and yet balanced. I think that at his best Snyder is a moral visionary who is neither a scourge nor a satirist; that he has spoken as a prophet whose "tribe" is without definite national or cultural boundaries; and that he is a writer with deep allegiances to modernism who yet is not overridingly obsessed with verbal perfectionism for its own sake. In each of these balanced stances can be located his weaknesses as well as his strengths. Another way of stating this paradox at the heart of Snyder's work is to say that he wants more than most to overcome the alienation and isolation of the poet in the modern world, but the terms of his vision have, by their very extravagance, made him often seem a party of one. In this sense Snyder is a quintessential American artist, torn by an idealizing vision between opposing hungers for both a new sense of community and a new sense of radical individuality.

But rather than concentrate too much . . . on the tensions and contradictions in Snyder's work, I would like to [stress] . . . that he is above all a poet of celebration and ecstasy. As such, his vision must terminate with, or open out into, a utopian vista where the rightness of the political realm finally produces a world of plenitude. For me the best statement of Snyder's celebratory completion comes in one of the interviews in *The Real Work,* where he formulates an Archimedean point of his own. He has been talking about the limits of his own system of things, and how his stress on local awareness and regional consciousness may limit one's ability to respond to people who live in other places and with other cultural ties. Snyder's solution is to imagine the universal dimension of all human experience that is fully informed about its relation to both the earth and the world, a fullness "where all natures intersect." The healing he speaks of is the healing of the breach that physical and cultural separation might cause. What follows is a marvelous metaphoric interweaving of both human and natural fullness:

> This level of healing is a kind of poetic work that is forever "just begun." When we bring together our awareness of the worldwide network of folktale and myth imagery that has been the "classical tradition"—the lore-bearer— of everyone for ten thousand and more years, and the new (but always there) knowledge of the worldwide interdependence of natural systems, we have the biopoetic beginning of a new level of world poetry and myth. That's the beginning for this age, the age of knowing the planet as one ecosystem, our own little watershed, a community of people and beings, a place to sing and meditate, a place to pick berries, a place to be picked in.

The communities of creatures in forests, ponds, oceans, or grasslands seem to tend toward a condition called climax, ''virgin forest''—many species, old bones, lots of rotten leaves, complex energy pathways, woodpeckers living in snags, and conies harvesting tiny piles of grass. This condition has considerable stability and holds much energy in its web—energy that in simpler systems (a field of weeds just after a bulldozer) is lost back into the sky or down the drain. All of evolution may have been as much shaped by this pull toward climax as it has by simple competition between individuals or species. If human beings have any place in this scheme it might well have to do with their most striking characteristic—a large brain, and language. And a consciousness of a peculiarly self-conscious order. Our human awareness and eager poking, probing, and studying is our beginning contribution to planet-system energy-conserving; another level of climax!

One way to appreciate fully the deeply human richness of this vision of plenitude is to see it as a liminal utopia, poised between fullness and yet more growth. Another way to see it is as a modern apocalypse that features woodpeckers and berry-picking. Either way, assuming the real work always includes some formulation of an ideal world, I would offer this vision as sufficient proof that Snyder has built a place for the mind to stay and to imagine more far-reaching harmonies while preserving all the wealth of the past. This, of course, is the world of his books where he is willing and even eager to give us another world both more ideal and more real than our own. The rest of the work is ours. (pp. 126-28)

> *Charles Molesworth, in his* Gary Snyder's Vision: Poetry and the Real Work, *University of Missouri Press, 1983, 128 p.*

ROBERT PETERS

[*Axe Handles* is] Snyder's first book of poems in almost ten years. . . . How have the years treated Snyder? Pretty well, I'd say. Despite a few limp efforts (included are throwaway poems about Jerry Brown's visits to Snyder's yurt, nature and trivia, and Snyder's role on the California Arts Council), some of these poems rank with Snyder's best. There is a quieter, mellower tone throughout than we find in much of the earlier work; and he now writes of what he scrutinizes before him, without much reminiscing. It's as if the passing years have made the immediate experience more valuable than ever—a deeper delving in the earth itself as a means to awareness.

"Getting in the Wood" is vintage Snyder. His trademarks are all here: 1). the effortless, nonsentimental beginning. The phrases, shorn of their definite articles, are subtle ink-strokes on the page. They possess an odd, marvellous tactile quality. Here is the event of the poem: Snyder gathers wood-rounds which have lain aging on the forest-floor, and splits them with an iron wedge driven by a sledge-hammer. The poem opens as easily as a greeting, evoking a quick mix of smell, color, and the kineticism of spurting water. . . . (p. 180)

2). Argot from the trades, from the survival arts. These (''peened,'' ''wedge,'' ''axe,'' ''peavey,'' ''maul,'' etc) he employs with a zest like that of Gerard Manley Hopkins in his sonnets to Welsh laborers. . . . What Hopkins and Snyder say

. . . seems to be something like this: if you aren't meticulously observant of physical details, you miss important signs for spiritual growth. Details become symbols. In such namings Snyder fuses both his Zen Buddhism and his American pragmatism. Tu Fu and Thoreau.

3). The concentrated evocations of the senses: how the skin feels as sweat drips, the smell of ''crushed ants,'' the sounds of wood tumbling, the cantering sledge emitting the ring of ''high-pitched bells.'' Snyder is a poet of the synaesthetic effect; he is as often as esoteric, I feel, as Baudelaire or Swinburne charging poems with highly orchestrated dynamic sense-fusions. On one level, Snyder is a pure art-for-art's sake poet. And I love him for that.

4). The incredibly compact music created as Snyder joyously names tools, or details of flora and fauna. These moments create exciting verse music. (p. 181)

5). The celebration of human effort as intense energy spent towards both survival and spiritual growth (what I call the John Muir Syndrome: see Snyder's poem to Muir in *Rip-Rap*). (pp. 181-82)

In lesser hands, Snyder's triumphs over the physical worlds of forest and machine, rendered almost with eyelids peeled, might seem silly, a phony primitivism engendering a Grease-Can School of Poetry, or, as I have called it elsewhere, Ugh-Poetry. This verse Snyder himself avoids through his zestful music, which at times almost serves to make the meanings of his words superfluous. We must struggle against enjoying these pure effects too esoterically—we would miss the didactic intentions beneath nearly all that Snyder writes. Isn't such purity of effect, though, what most good poets aim for? an avoidance of sermonizing? a transcendence of raw materials? (p. 182)

Brilliant techniques in themselves do not, of course, constitute a whole poetry. Tone matters too, as does theme. The pragmatic, self-reliant voice so characteristic of Snyder never appears as a pushing or a bullying of the reader—in his best poems, he never overtly urges us to march, axes in hand, out to enroll in woods-survival courses, or to build our personal leantos, saunas, yurts, and field-kitchens. Like John Muir and Thoreau, his mentors, his experiments are his own (Thoreau never intended that anyone else live his experiment, to stake a claim at Walden Pond, plant beans, or eat woodchuck raw). Snyder's experiments in living are uniquely his. Yet, while he does not propagandize, the life he creates, evokes, and describes is so appealing that we also feel welcomed to join in, creating the ecosystem he envisions. He plants his own appleseeds. And his self-reliance is one of his most attractive strengths. His awe/respect for nature, for spirituality, for each human life, drops almost casually, at times with touches of humor and gentle ironies, often at his own expense. Those who choose to pick his apples may. Feel free, he seems to say. But you'll have to use your own ladders and pails, and your own hands, not his.

Another dimension is thematic. A lesser poet would be content merely to record their quests after the mythic omphaloses of the universe. Snyder's framework is far more ambitious; he is always a mere breath away from universals. There's a poignant continuity, he feels, in all human experience, from the remotest primitive ancestor to the squalling, puking infant emerging from the uterus at this very second. His efforts to create a self-sustaining ground-earth-house for his family echo the efforts of an ancient Oriental grubbing for his existence, physical and metaphysical. . . . Snyder's tenacity, his faith in his immediate time-locked experiences as their smoke flows towards the transcendental, his love for the earth (one ecosystem for all) provide inspiration for those of us lacking his gifts and his trenchancies. All this, of course, is quite other than the beauty of his writing; his themes and techniques are a rare fusion for these times. By imagining Nature as a "sweet old woman" who gathers her firewood (the Heraclitean fire?) in the moonlight, he celebrates his life and reassures us about our own. (pp. 183-84)

Robert Peters, in a review of "Axe Handles," in Sulfur 10, Vol. IV, No. 1, 1984, pp. 179-84.

THOMAS PARKINSON

Snyder is not interested in fad, fashion, or convention: he is interested in tradition, and he is concerned with constructing a valid culture from the debris that years of exploitation have scattered around the Pacific Basin.

RIPRAP is Snyder's first book. The title means "a cobble of stone laid on steep slick rock / to make a trail for horses in the mountains." In the last poem in the book he wrote of Poetry as a riprap on the slick rock of metaphysics, the reality of perceived surface that grants men staying power and a gripping point. . . . The body of the mind—this is the province of poetry, a riprap on the abstractions of the soul that keeps men in tune with carnal eloquence. Snyder's equation is one of proportions: poetry is to metaphysics as riprap is to slick rock. Things and thoughts are not then in opposition but in parallel. . . . The aim is not to achieve harmony with nature but to create an inner harmony that equals to the natural external harmony. There is not then an allegorical relation between man and natural reality but an analogical one: a man does not identify with a tree nor does he take the tree to be an emblem of his own psychic condition; he establishes within himself a condition that is equivalent to that of the tree, and there metaphysics rushes in. Only poetry can take us through such slippery territory, and after *RIPRAP* Snyder tries to find a guide in his *Myths & Texts. RIPRAP* was an engaging uneven first book of poems. It is still in print and deserves to be so, but it lacks unity of impact and style, however proper its intentions.

Myths & Texts is a different matter. Although some of the poems were printed as early as 1952 and Snyder gives its date of completion as 1956, it is a world away from the first book. It has a genuine informing principle and coherence of purposeful movement, and the line has a life that is particular to its subject. The first two sections of the book are on Logging and Hunting, what men do to the earth; the third on Fire, why they do it. In this book appear in complex form the issues that compel the verse at its base. Snyder wants to reach a prehuman reality, the wilderness and the cosmos in which man lives as an animal with animals in a happy ecology. This precivilized reality he finds embodied in Amerindian lore, especially of the Pacific Northwest and of California, and in Buddhist myth. He occupies the uneasy position of understanding this mode of perception and of acting, as logger and hunter, against its grain. This realization is the dramatic core of the book and holds it from sentimentality, granting it a kind of tension and prophetic force (evident in the pro-wobbly poems) that *RIPRAP* and much of his later work lacks. *Myths & Texts* is an elegy of involvement. . . . In these poems action and contemplation become identical states of being, and both states of secular grace. From this fusion wisdom emerges, and it is not useless but timed to the event. The result is a terrible sanity, a literal clairvoyance, an innate decorum. (pp. 50-1)

One of the touchstone lines for modern poetry is Pound's "Quick eyes gone under earth's lid." It holds its unity partly through the internal rhyme of the first and final word, partly through the unstrained conceit of random association between eyelid and coffin lid, and the earth as dead eye and graveyard. Mainly, though, it has no waste, no void spaces, none of the flab that English invites through the prepositional phrase designs of a noninflected language. Solid poetry in English manages compressions that keep up the stress, and relaxations from that motive have their justification in the larger poetic unit of poem or book. The temptation of composition in serial form, the method of *Myths & Texts,* is vindicating the relaxed line in the name of a higher motive, the world view of the poet, the personal relevance. Snyder doesn't fall back on such flimsy supports. Sometimes, straining to maintain the stress, he loses control: ". . . fighting flies fixed phone line." This is not only pointlessly elliptical but meaninglessly ambiguous and far too clogged. But in its excesses it demonstrates the basic prosodic motive, full use of consonant and vowel tone as organizing devices, reduction of connective words having merely grammatical function and no gravity. (p. 52)

I talk at such length of prosody because it is the main factor ignored in most recent discussion of poetry. . . . New criticism (old style) placed heavy weight on suggestion and symbolic reference; now as our poetry stresses drama and syntactic movement, vocality, it seems necessary to supplement the notion, and a pernicious one, that poetry functions through symbol mainly. Language functions symbolically and metaphorically, but poetry makes more precise and delimiting use of syntax through its prosodic measure. This is after all what Pound and Williams were agitated about: the dance of language. I don't want to hang everything on syntactic and metric effects and take a plunge into providing new mechanical vocabulary that will deaden poetic study from yet another perspective. What poets like Snyder, Duncan, and Creeley ask is that readers take the poem as indicator of physical weight. Until the day, not far off, when poems are related to taped performances as musical scores now are, the poem on the page is evidence of a voice and the poetic struggle is to note the movement of that voice so that it can be, as is music, followed. . . . (pp. 52-3)

[*Myths & Texts*] creates and denies one of the greatest of American experiences, that of a wild ecology. But it is not merely American; the human race really is on the way to destroying the planet, if not by some mad outrageous single explosion then by steady careless greedy attrition of all those qualities that have over the centuries kept men as sane as they have been. Curiously, although this has been the overriding historical fact of the past generation, only one extensive book of poetry has tried to tackle this problem as subject and come to some prophetic stance. Yet there is nothing pompous or portentous about *Myths & Texts;* it is genuinely contemplative. . . .

In 1965, Snyder published *Six Sections from Mountains and Rivers Without End,* part of a very long sequence of poems. The book has some fine matter in it, but much of it is taken up by poems that are not sufficiently concentrated, though they may serve a function in the whole sequence once completed. . . .

Snyder has spoken often of the importance of the rhythms of various kinds of work for his poetry, and his sense of experience is largely a sense of work, of measured force exerted on the world. . . . His world is a world of energy constantly reformulating itself, and most often a world of human energy, exploited, misdirected, and full of pathos—he can't take it for granted but sees at its base the wilderness and fundamental man, and the products generated through history. This is why **"The Market,"** full of dangers of sentimentality in tone, and mere cataloguing in technique, has an inner vigor that the hitchhiker poem lacks. This is not entirely a matter of mood but of conviction and of consequent drive. Technical considerations aside, poetry like all art comes out of courage, the capacity to keep going when reason breaks down. (p. 54)

Snyder's *The Back Country* [is] an inclusive collection, the longest and in many ways most representative book of Snyder's poetry. It includes poems written after the publication of *Myths & Texts* in 1960 and some earlier poems that did not fit the design of the three earlier collections. The book is carefully structured, with sections treating Far West, Far East, Kali (goddess of creation and destruction), Back (return) and translations of Miyazawa Kenji.... *The Back Country* has the advantage both of variety and secure control of the medium of poetry. If it lacks the unified impact of *Myths & Texts,* it covers even more ground. The point of view remains constant, the wilderness as repository of possibilities and reminder of psychological richnesses that cities, notably **"This Tokyo,"** pervert or destroy, the reality and importance of work, what a simpler age called the dignity of labor, while recognizing the horror of exploitation both of nature and of the working man.

Many of these poems are, like the hitch-hiking poem of *Mountains and Rivers,* the poems of a wandering man, wandering in his travels, wayfaring in his sexuality, solitary, exploratory, inconstant, seaman and bindlestiff, finding his true Penelope only in the world of poetry and thought. Like much of Snyder's work, these poems have the quality of a very good *Bildungsroman.* In fact, as narrative and description and characterization, they are far superior to the novels of the 1960s in this country. They are not tricked up, contrived, and in spite of their autobiographical content, they are not egotistical. They are articulations, not mere expressions. Their motivation is perhaps best expressed in essays written contemporaneously with the poetry: "Buddhism and the Coming Revolution," "Passage to More than India," and "Poetry and the Primitive," printed in *Earth House Hold....* The prose in *Earth House Hold,* parts of *Turtle Island, The Old Ways* and *The Real Work* should be read not only as partial explanation of the poetry but as the record of an evolving mind with extreme good sense in treating the problems of the world.

Regarding Wave is best thought of as two books. *Regarding Wave* is both the title of the book and the first thirty-five pages of text. It is a unified work of art with some of Snyder's best poems, for instance, **"Not Leaving the House."** ... Unlike some of the poems in the sections that succeed **"Regarding Wave,"** this poem shows Snyder in the grip of a major principle, so that he becomes the agent of a voice, that of common experience, and the personal and superficially exotic change to the general and present.

Snyder's ... recent books, *Turtle Island* (poetry with some essays, notably "Four Changes") and *The Old Ways* reiterate his chosen themes and methods. Some critics complain that Snyder does not develop or change in any major way. Why should he? He has chosen a substantial body of thought and experience to explore. Poets change not through fad and fashion but through a realization that their idiom no longer fits their experience. When that occurs, change is valid, but Snyder's wide and varied idiom is adequate to his intense and rich experience. (pp. 56-9)

[Snyder] is distinguished not only as poet but as prose expositor—he has a gift for quiet, untroubled, accurate observation with occasional leaps to genuine eloquence. He has taken to himself a subject matter, complex, vast, and permanently interesting, a subject so compelling that it is not unreasonable to assert that he has become a center for a new set of cultural possibilities. There are two kinds of trouble that readers experience with this impressive accomplishment.

The first is the Gary Snyder poem. I have already described this short, anecdotal, erotic, concrete poem set in the wilderness with Zen masters and Amerindian mythological creatures commenting on each other and on nature. There comes a time when tedium sets in, when the personal style seems to be carrying along for no particular reason except to carry along, keep busy in the act of writing. The poems then exist all at exactly the same level and seem to have interchangeable parts. Objects from one could be moved to another without loss or gain. The prosody retains the same tone. The surfaces are attractive and monotonous. Even though there are variations from high rhetoric to self-deprecating humor, the unanimity of the poems is restrictive. Too much goes along the surface, gliding. And often I get the impression that Snyder doesn't care about the art, that poetry for him is only one of a set of instruments in a spiritual quest, that the act of construction is not something that requires its own special resolutions. Like most writers with a coherent world view, he sometimes refuses to let his material be intractable; there is no sense of contention between subject and object, no dramatic struggle toward a new form. Then the poems do not seem *forms* but *shapes.*

I don't think this happens often or that it is a totally crippling defect.... The complaints here registered could have been made against Blake, Whitman, and Lawrence. The second complaint ... is that Snyder does not face the problems of modern life. In this view, the great bulk of Americans live in cities and in an age of anxiety verging on total panic. The wilderness exists only in a mythical past or in the lives of those privileged by money (for pack animals and guides) or skills based on specialized work in areas remote from normal experience. Hence Snyder's poetry doesn't answer to the tensions of modern life and depends on a life no longer accessible or even desirable for men. A mystique of the wilderness based on the humane naturalism of the highly limited Zen Buddhism sect and the primitive insights of American savages can't satisfy the existential *Angst* of modern man. Everything is too simple, too easy, too glib, a boy's book in verse, Huck Finn on the Skagit, Innocents in Japan. The poetry is archaic, not in the sense that all poetry is, but out of tune with life in the current era.

But the argument that a poet must speak to the problems of the bulk of the people seems to me to support rather than undermine Snyder's work. Properly understood, Snyder's poetry does *speak to* basic current problems, but it does not simply embody them. (pp. 59-60)

[Snyder] is calling upon the total resources of man's moral and religious being. There is no point in decrying this as primitivism; it is merely good sense, for the ability to hold history and wilderness in the mind at once may be the only way to make valid measures of human conduct. A larger and more humble vision of man and cosmos is our only hope, and the major work of any serious person. In that work, Snyder's verse and prose compose a set of new cultural possibilities that only ignorance and unbalance can ignore. (p. 61)

*Thomas Parkinson, "The Poetry of Gary Snyder,"
in* Sagetrieb, *Vol. 3, No. 1, Spring, 1984, pp. 46-61.*

PAUL BERMAN

[Gary Snyder] occasionally makes his ideas too obvious. His new collection, *Axe Handles,* ends with a painfully clear commitment to North American ecology: "I pledge allegiance to the soil / of Turtle Island, / one ecosystem / in diversity / under the sun / With joyful interpenetration for all." The new book hops along the ground instead of flying in the upper ether of Buddhist poetry. A good many poems are relatively disconnected I-do-this-I-do-that Zen diaries, which get wearisome. But in other moments, Snyder does remind us of his strengths: his strange tunefulness, as if he were strumming some kind of weird Japanese instrument, his ability to embrace the wild or the savage, as if he were a peasant in closer touch with real life than the rest of us.

Paul Berman, in a review of "Axe Handles," in The Village Voice, *Vol. XXIX, No. 18, May 1, 1984, p. 44.*

BRUCE BAWER

Gary Snyder's last book was his Pulitzer prize-winning *Turtle Island* (1974), whose title, as he explained in an introductory note, was "the old/new name for the continent, based on many creation myths [in which the earth is seen as resting on a turtle's back] of the people who have been living here for millennia, and reapplied by some of them to 'North America' in recent years." Like *Turtle Island, Axe Handles* is about North America, in particular about the underpopulated, still unspoiled regions of the American West which Snyder has made his home. (pp. 346-47)

The title of the present book signals Snyder's heightened interest in tradition, culture, and family. The title poem begins with Snyder helping his son Kai (who, with his other son Gen, plays an important part in this book) to make an axe handle. They carve the handle with Snyder's axe, and the poet remem-bers Pound's words: "'When making an axe handle / the pattern is not far off.'" The carving of the boy's axe handle with his father's axe comes to represent, for Snyder, the passing on of knowledge and skills from one generation to the next—which is, in fact, the dominant theme of the book. Snyder derives great strength and security from the recognition that his sons are his "gifts to the future / to remember us." Because of this strength and security, Snyder is more successful in *Axe Handles* than in most of his earlier works at avoiding the temptation to deal in the angry abstractions ("Freedom," "Nature," "the People") which filled *Turtle Island,* or to beat the drum for his Zen-Amerindian-Marxist philosophy. He reads like a man who has found tranquility: the form of his poems has grown more regular, the language more conventional, the tone more pensive, less self-conscious, and never hysterical or pretentiously nutty or shrill. He is still a man of convictions, but they are for the most part (the relatively blunt **"For/From Lew"** is an exception) communicated implicitly through simple, significant dramatic episodes. (p. 347)

Indeed, so tranquil is Snyder that even when he makes a point of noticing the various computer-age (or even industrial-age) phenomena which do intrude into his world from time to time, he perceives them not as symbols of evil (as was his practice in *Turtle Island*) but as exotic manifestations of his revered natural order. Snyder does, however, come upon a few phenomena which he has trouble fitting into the natural universe as he has come to understand it. One such phenomenon is a Strategic Air Command jet. Yet even this emblem of destruction does not incite his wrath toward the "Amerika" which he described in his previous book as a nation of "invaders" who stole Turtle Island from the Indians and "who wage war around the world." . . .

Quietly, gently, *Axe Handles* conveys a luminous, poignant vision of a life afforded joy and strength by recognition of the essential things which give it meaning. It is, to my tastes, Snyder's finest book. (p. 348)

Bruce Bawer, in a review of "Axe Handles," in Poetry, *Vol. CXLIV, No. 6, September, 1984, pp. 346-48.*

Gary Soto
1952-

American poet.

Considered one of the most talented Chicano poets, Soto is consistently praised for his gripping depictions of poverty and desolation, especially among Mexican-Americans. Although his work is frequently autobiographical in theme and locale—Soto's childhood in California's San Joaquin Valley included experience as a migrant laborer—the strength of his poetry rests on its ability to transcend the particulars of the situations he depicts. Reviewing Soto's first collection, *The Elements of San Joaquin* (1977), Jerry Bradley notes that the characters "rise above the meanness of their appearance, not as unscarred ideologues or saints or rhetoricians, but as human—frail and impoverished—whose heritage is simply and redemptively the earth."

Critics often cite in Soto's writing the influence of Philip Levine, an established American poet associated with the "Fresno School" of poets who characteristically employ short, enjambed lines, clear, unencumbered diction, and an elliptical accumulation of concrete images. While some critics fault his detached narrative style as lacking power and true poetic rhythm, many praise Soto's tight linguistic control and contend that his suggestive understatements successfully induce the reader's sympathy and involvement. Soto's second and third volumes, *The Tale of Sunlight* (1978) and *Where Sparrows Work Hard* (1981), have further contributed to his growing reputation as an important contemporary poet.

Photograph by Carolyn, reproduced by permission of University of Pittsburgh Press

PUBLISHERS WEEKLY

Soto's poems [in **"The Tale of Sunlight"**] are set in an abstract landscape of sun, wind, sky and river that seems alive to the emotional needs of his people. His poems are simple, idiomatic, rhythmic and notable for the strange interplay between images of desperation and transcendence. In a key lyric called **"The Shepherd,"** for example, a pickled three-legged chicken intrudes on the perfectly Apollonian picture of a boy descending from the hills with a harp swung over his shoulder. There's an ambivalence here between worldly and spiritual values that distinguishes the poetry from protest or apology—so the more you look between the lines, the more you see.

A review of "The Tale of Sunlight," in Publishers Weekly, *Vol. 214, No. 6, August 7, 1978, p. 78.*

JERRY BRADLEY

The biggest failure of many ethnic and minority-group writers is that their political viewpoints often turn them into moralizing zealots or righteous cultural revolutionaries. . . . Chicano poet Gary Soto, a former fieldhand in the San Joaquin Valley, manages to avoid such shortcomings in *The Elements of San Joaquin* and thereby establishes that he is considerably more than just a good ethnic writer; he is a good poet. (p. 73)

Soto's topics extend beyond the fields and farms into all aspects of migrant life in the valley—the charity hospitals, the barbershops, the streets and alleys—and he depicts them all in a lean, simple style. And although Soto is capable of mimicking the mannerisms of uneducated Chicanos in a straightforward, uncomplicated style, his verses are not unintellectual. His simplicity is merely a stylistic device, one appropriately suited to his seemingly primitive and occasionally bucolic subjects. Consequently his metaphors are drawn from poverty, work, and failure, but they are nonetheless evocative, enlightening, and haunting. . . . [Soto's] characters, much like his metaphors, are transcendent. Imaginatively they rise above the meanness of their appearance, not as unscarred ideologues or saints or rhetoricians, but as human—frail and impoverished—whose heritage is simply and redemptively the earth.

Jerry Bradley, in a review of "The Elements of San Joaquin," in Western American Literature, *Vol. XIV, No. 1, Spring, 1979, pp. 73-4.*

JASCHA KESSLER

I'm sure that one of the reasons we are always looking for a new poet is our expectation of some novelty, some word from a place we have not been before in our imagination. (p. 1)

[The poems of Gary Soto's *The Tale of Sunlight*] are not simply descriptions of the life of the poor Mexican-Americans on both sides of the border. They are far more ambitious than that, which is why I spoke of the poet as the imagination that integrates something new for us, something unknown. Not that poverty is unknown, but that this people's life in the cities of the Southwest, the fields and the factories in the U.S. and in Mexico, is not something the fantasy and the news of the media can ever offer, from the inside, from the experiences of a lifetime, as it were.

And Soto is a young poet who has quite a firm sense of how to use the language, and often brilliantly, because he wants to convey what he has heard, seen, touched and felt vividly, from the point of view of certain stereotypes in the villages and towns. The stereotype, used by the poet, becomes representative and typical, not something flat and banal. Prostitutes, drunks, barkeepers, and family figures, mothers, fathers and uncles, sisters and brothers, say, who stand for something in a still family-centered community. Being young and having seen much, Soto is both harsh and brutal, cynical, fatalistic and despairing . . . but he is also full of visions and dreams that he turns into bitter satire . . . the natural romanticism of passionate youth that is soured by the truth of poverty and misery and sheer tedious hopelessness.

The Tale of Sunlight is a very ambitious book, and it wants to present the poetic world of a young Chicano, largely a rural one in Soto's case, where natural images abound and play with force, rather than an urban one, where plants and birds and animals have no chance to enter the poems. Soto talks impersonally, which is very effective, by means of having a set of poems about a boy named Molina, and a set about one Manuel Zaragoza, who keeps a cantina. The technique through the book is largely the same, so we know it's Soto talking through others' eyes and senses, though the senses are far more intense than their characters would have available to them: they are the poet's, and we accept his truths because they are grounded solidly in the sensations of facts. I am myself not much impressed by his poetic technique, which is simply prose sentences in lines of 5 or less words standing vertically on the page, a second version of the poems of Philip Levine, whose lines are similarly without much technical meaning. Which is not to say that the intensity and precision of language of Soto's sentences and poems is altogether vitiated. No, merely that one reads closely to find the poetry in the vision and the fact, the presentations of persons and lives unknown to us in this way. And that poetry is there alright. (pp. 2-3)

> *Jascha Kessler, "Gary Soto: 'The Tale of Sunlight',' in a radio broadcast on KUSC-FM—Los Angeles, CA, May 16, 1979.*

PETER COOLEY

[*The Elements of San Joaquin*] is a younger man's book; it isn't patronizing to say so. The poems lay down before us a period in the speaker's life which is only recently finished, the 1950's of his childhood. But Soto's first book is no nostalgic venture into "Happy Days." Soto is a Chicano, and probably the most important voice among the young Chicano poets because his poetry comes to us through poems, not propaganda in drag. . . . (p. 304)

A former student of Philip Levine, Soto shows stylistic affinities with what has been called "The Fresno School": short lines, a denuded vocabulary, an enumeration of small objects seen not as symbols but presences which build the speaker's situation. The single line is not of great interest in itself; in fact, it may sound "anti-poetic" to some ears. Soto has learned

from Levine to enjamb a flat statement with another flat but raw one, exposing the soft underbelly—and the claws. (p. 305)

At times the poems talk to us by shifting from one foot to the other, as if in a hurry to be off somewhere; side by side, too, the enjambed lines may seem melodramatic or mannered. Worst of all, strong statements may assume a kind of equivalence. . . . Soto does not want to shut us out in protesting his condition and that of his brothers—one understands his need for a quiet insistence—but when the texture of a poem is reduced to the objects of everyday life and the poem sets image after image before us, a tremendous pressure is put on the poet to find exactly the appropriate correlative line after line. (pp. 305-06)

In most poems, though, Soto is convincing in giving us a situation which is some part of his lost world of San Joaquin. The speaker approaches his reconstruction with a genuine tenderness, the short lines suggesting tentative, halting evocations. . . . (p. 306)

Though both urban and rural, there is no great city/country topology at work in Soto's San Joaquin. The earth, in fact, is related in the title sequence to the enslavement of the speaker as a worker in the fields. This sequence implants us in the minute particulars of the worker's situation by drawing us down to the insects and plants which crawl and scratch the lines. It is a protest poem that succeeds by its gentle but willed negations, offering no salutary measures but merely insisting on our sympathy. . . . Gary Snyder's sheer pleasure in physical work which removes him from the life of industrial society seems tepid middle class revolt after reading Soto. (p. 307)

The more one reads *The Elements of San Joaquin* the sadder seems Soto's sense of absolute loss, of a world all but erased except for his poems' memorializing. He has avoided the sentimental and the strident, and his voice possesses the kind of unaffected honesty we experience only in conversations with friends.

As if himself feeling the reservations voiced above about *The Elements of San Joaquin,* Soto's new book attempts to answer them. Two-thirds of the poems focus on two characters, who live in separate worlds and never meet each other. Molina, the character of Part One, is a sort of Doppelgänger for the Soto-I speaker; Manual Zaragoza, who owns the last third of the book, is a cantina owner and sad clown. The middle third of *The Tale of Sunlight* contains poems which generally, through third- or second-person narration, avoid the stance of the naked-I speaker. Soto's abiding theme is still loss, but his new points of view open the lyric enclosure of his earlier poems to an imaginative expansiveness in which irony can sometimes sort out the images he hurries through his fingers.

The flat warp of the earlier poems' continuous enjambments is woven richer now with more cross-stitched rhyme. The rush of enjambments still comes at us, however; one would like to slow the loom when encountering a poem like ["**The Point**"]. . . . [In this poem] enjambing reduces all the lines to the same texture; one is tempted, as in most prose, to read for an extractable idea. (pp. 309-10)

Sometimes the cross-stitching is too tight [as in "**The Little Ones**"]:

> When fog
> Stands weed-high
> And sky

Is the color
Of old bed sheets,
Molina and I . . .

The "high"-"sky"-"I" rhymes in the right margin along with the "when"-"stands"-"and" of the left shut down the language, making it difficult to believe amorphous objects are being compared to the vertical dimension of weeds or the potentially dynamic "old bed sheets."

Soto's earlier difficulty in ending poems has been solved, however, in poem after poem by just the right choice of images. The small fabliaux of many of his character poems are complete in themselves in *The Tale of Sunlight* and furnish a pleasant contrast to the naked-I poems Soto continues to write. (p. 310)

Soto's tone is now so much his own and his control of it so strong in poems such as **"The Shepherd," "The Cellar,"** or the title poem that after reading the book I can hear my own Soto poems writing themselves in my head. To put it otherwise: it would be easy to create parodies of Soto's voice. And to say this is to show how much his voice belongs to him, not to any "school" at all. (p. 311)

> *Peter Cooley, "I Can Hear You Now," in* Parnassus:
> Poetry in Review, *Vol. 8, No. 1, Fall-Winter, 1979,*
> *pp. 297-311.**

VICKI ARMOUR-HILEMAN

Following the tradition he established in his two previous books, Gary Soto makes the subject of *Where Sparrows Work Hard* the Chicano experience and the setting California. . . . The people are Mexican factory workers, or others whose lives become emblems of the Mexican-American experience. Many of the poems are narrative and reminiscent of Philip Levine's, particularly in the use of colloquial diction and short, enjambed lines. Soto also shares with Levine a surrealistic bent and much subject matter. It is difficult to read Soto's **"Joey the Midget"** without thinking of Levine's "The Midget." . . .

There are at least three types of poems in *Where Sparrows Work Hard.* The first is pure narrative of the sort found in **"Mexicans Begin Jogging."** . . .

[This poem] is typical of the detached narration, the somewhat ironic perspective, the perfectly flat language of this brand of Soto's poetry. Soto seems to rely on the experience itself for interest, or on the implied subjects of prejudice and suffering. Yet in the closing lines, Soto backs away even from these:

> What could I do but yell *vivas*
> To baseball, milkshakes, and those
>   sociologists
> Who would clock me
> As I jog into the next century
> On the power of a great, silly grin.

Perhaps Soto hopes this "grin" will open the poem up, letting it suggest the speaker's detachment from, yet acceptance of, his situation. Instead it smacks of indecision. It is merely a way to get out of the poem without committing the speaker to a point of view.

The second type of poem (of which **"Joey the Midget"** is an example) flirts with transcendence. . . . (p. 154)

The real problem [with this type of poem] is not the inaccuracy of the images, but their elliptical movement. [In **"Walking With Jackie, Sitting With Dog"**] Soto takes small leaps from image to image, hoping we will follow him from sadness to oranges to the cryptically cheerful statement "no one need die." These ellipses are intended to make each image reverberate with possibilities, and the images themselves are supposed to build until the last one is transcendent, a glimpse beyond the quotidian and into the realm of life and death and meaningful truths. I don't object to the latter realm, but I do object to the suddenness of the movement.

The third type of poem is surrealistic and strikes a balance between the details of the dramatic situation and the larger problems they suggest. . . . [For example, in **"The Widow Perez,"**] the movement is not really elliptical; it's transformational. The images sprout from one another, one changing into the next. . . . The unexpected merging of images gives the poem its surrealistic qualities. . . .

The details . . . [are] so appropriate to the experience that they open the images out onto the world beyond the poem. Or perhaps "open" is wrong; they move more deeply into the human experience at the heart of the poem.

These surrealistic poems are most frequent in the third and last section of the book, and it is interesting to speculate whether the poems in sections one and two are earlier works. If so (and perhaps even if not) Soto seems to be working toward the third type of poem which is superior because of its humanness and the tangibility of the experience it presents.

Except for her last name, there is nothing particularly Chicano or Californian about the Widow Pérez. She is merely a widow, one of the many misfits and sufferers in Soto's poems. And when he writes about her, Soto becomes not an ethnic poet, but a poet who writes about human suffering and does so, particularly in these last poems, with a great deal of success. (p. 155)

> *Vicki Armour-Hileman, in a review of "Where Sparrows Work Hard," in* The Denver Quarterly, *Vol. 17, No. 2, Summer, 1982, pp. 154-55.*

CARLOS ZAMORA

In *Where Sparrows Work Hard,* the poet takes the reader on a journey of exploration through the subterranean, labyrinthine, infernal world of the human soul, where everything gives evidence of a cosmic devastation. It is not by chance that in the external world which is at once the setting of the poems and the symbolic analogue of that hell, one finds over and over again the images of ruination and perdition. . . .

This is a profoundly elegiac poetry, in which everything appears condemned to pass away without possibility of ever achieving fruition. The fated abortion of man's being appears illustrated in the repeated depictions of his finiteness: his smallness and fragility vis-a-vis the forces of violence which pervade an essentially hostile universe; his temporal limitation, sentenced as he is to old age and death; his intellectual deficiency, in light of his inability to understand the causes of his very great misfortune; his sheer impotency to convert the ought-to-be into reality.

Given this negation of what remains only a dreamed-of fullness of being, it is not surprising that in the poems man appears typically trivialized, thingified, reduced to the level of so many other objects of equal unimportance which clutter the world. Reified in this way, he is also shown as abandoned by god and his fellow man, as unnoticed when he walks by others, as unheard when he calls out, as faceless and nameless: a solitary wanderer amid the desolate landscape of earth.

Trapped in this terrifying world and unable to change it, man in the poems characteristically adopts an evasive behavior which takes many different forms: habitual drinking of alcohol and watching of television; reverie; fantasy; dreams; remembrances of the past, including of childhood; the longing for a reversion to still more ultimate, primeval origins: the sea; the journey; and even, in one case, suicide. In exceptional instances there does appear a flash of revolt, a defiant affirmation of the self. But the *non serviam* theme is not at all common in the poems. Neither is the stoicism which only a few characters display as a kind of irrepressible determination to go on, to endure. What one sees instead is what has been indicated: man as fugitive from a hellish world which he comes to perceive as unbearable and which he is convinced he cannot transform or "save." . . .

Undoubtedly some readers will find themselves objecting to this fatalistic conception of life. . . . Such readers could not deny that the poems do depict more than well enough the dehumanization of man in our time. For in their own way these are, without question, songs or dirges about oppression and against oppression, which the poet illuminates and dramatizes through a sometimes brilliant imagery and symbolism (in this insightful and strikingly vivid portraiture of the oppressed, if not of the oppressor, lies the very great value of the poems). But the suggestion contained in the volume that the degradation of man has root causes which are metaphysical rather than social, the intimation that what is described is an eternal condition of man and not a transitory situation which is changeable and surmountable, present problems to which, it goes without saying, each reader will have to address himself. . . .

However different readers decide these questions, I doubt that any will come away from this collection without feeling that they have been in the presence of an extraordinary poetic talent whose evolution continues to be marked by a ceaseless experimentation with poetic diction as the primary tool with which to probe more and more deeply into the flesh and bones concreteness of fallen man.

> Carlos Zamora, in a review of "Where Sparrows Work Hard," in The American Book Review, *Vol. 4, No. 5, July-August, 1982, p. 11.*

BRUCE-NOVOA

In Gary Soto's ***The Elements of San Joaquin*** (1977) the world struggles to survive disintegrating forces, from natural, to social, to human, that grind on in cyclic fashion. While one line of energy seems bent on reducing the elements to stasis and nothingness—entropy—another tries to structure the elements into combinations of living units. Even the writing of the text is a struggle between the word and a silence that would confirm human isolation and social chaos. Yet there is no reassuring idealism or even optimism in Soto. He reduces things to bare elements, speaks of them coldly, as if from a distance. Yet this is not the clarity of objectivity. The metaphor for his life-vision can be found in **"Field Poem."** From a bus for migrant farm workers, the persona looks back and sees the cotton field "From the smashed bus window." . . . Soto and his persona look back at what they know intimately as participants, victims, and their vision is fragmented, shattered, though still a related and framed whole. (p. 185)

Elements resembles T. S. Eliot's *The Waste Land*. Society is sterile, about to collapse, with God the Father and the father as god absent, leaving no absolute in their stead. The *axis mundi* has disappeared, though nature recalls its old presence. But order is a façade, a vain effort to hold back entropy, or, in colloquial terms appropriate to the book, to keep the bottom from falling out. Just behind or below the surface lie the sewers. From this situation the persona begins a pilgrimage to the source, a motif of regeneration; but, as in *The Waste Land,* the shrine is deserted. The trip, however, retains the capacity to order life; this is a poor substitute for the return to the sacred, but we live in an ersatz time. At this point the text itself becomes the possible substitute; and we confront, once again, the text as *axis mundi*—which is a question of reading.

Elements suggests a wasteland. Winds erode everything to dust, which, in turn, permeates whatever survives. Clouds cover the sky; gray predominates. Violence is ubiquitously imminent; life's underside threatens to collapse or explode. Soto accents this with offensive details, from several rapes and at least one murder in section 1, to a drowned baby in section 3. . . . When beauty or peace appears, negative elements arise to counterbalance or deny it, usually in the last lines. . . . This is not a pleasant land.

This vision is obviously that of the persona's limited experience, because the area described is also the milk-and-honey land of the American Dream—California. Soto implicitly contrasts the affluent paradise with the world of the migrant worker. The *axis mundi* connects heaven, earth, and hell; the last is Soto's choice of route back home. (pp. 186-87)

Hence his negative perspective. His garden of paradise was inexplicably shattered, and he came down . . . into hell, and has lived there ever since.

The search culminated, one wonders if this is all. Is the discovery of reasons for a negative view of life enough? It certainly does not satisfy us. We can look back on the work as a carefully structured path, as a poetic success in terms of craft; but the results are still unsatisfying. The chaotic world cannot be denied, the garden is devastated, but the journey itself can give structure to life—yes. This is the lesson of *The Waste Land* and essentially that of ***Elements,*** though the latter seems more negative in outlook. What of misogyny, ugliness, fear; do they become the affirmed elements of life? Do they define culture?

Yes; and we must live with Soto's vision, in spite of its horror. In social terms the condition of the lower economic class has not changed at all since the writing of ***Elements.*** Life is no less perilous. What the book achieves on this level is to force its presence upon a segment of society that usually ignores the reality the poems express. It rapes the reader; admittedly, the metaphor is poor, because in spite of the ugliness of many images and the violence of the constant undermining of particular hopes and beauty, the collection is more of a seduction than a rape. It convinces because of its well-wrought structure, the craft, the coherence of its totality—because of its overall beauty. Yet it also represents one more invasion of the U.S. literary establishment by Chicano culture; it forces the reader to travel a route not usually chosen by the literate public. This is a social as well as a literary achievement. (pp. 206-07)

> Bruce-Novoa, "Patricide and Resurrection: Gary Soto," in his Chicano Poetry: A Response to Chaos, *University of Texas Press, 1982, pp. 185-211.**

PATRICIA DE LA FUENTE

[*The essay from which this excerpt is taken was read, in a slightly different version, at the Louisiana Conference on Hispanic Languages and Literatures in Baton Rouge in February 1982.*]

One of the principal characteristics of Soto's poetry is the apocalyptic vision it reflects of the universe. Recurring images of loss, disintegration, decadence, demolition, solitude, terror and death create a desolate landscape in which the voice of the narrator is that of a passive, impotent observer. helplessly caught up in the inexorable destruction of human ties. Within this seemingly hopeless, profoundly grey world of Soto's poems, however, occasional affirmative images introduce muted, contrapuntal notes of something akin to hope.

In his first collection, ***The Elements of San Joaquín,*** for example, the presence of dust, both from the fields and from the mortal remains of the men who work them, and the action of the wind that sweeps everything before it and reduces all things to dust, are two of the most persistent images. Both dust and wind are elements of an environment that is both hostile and indifferent to human solitude and suffering. Soto often juxtaposes these two images in the same poem to suggest apocalyptic forces:

> The wind strokes
> The skulls and spines of cattle
> To white dust, to nothing . . . .

At first glance, this image [from **"Wind"**] appears to be totally negative since it depicts the slow, irreversible disintegration of the cattle skulls, and by extension those of mankind as well, into dust and then into nothingness. Faced with the terrifying indifference of the wind, which destroys everything—mountains, cattle, or the footprints of beetles, each individual existence becomes inconsequential, ephemeral, all traces of its presence obliterated as if it had never been. Upon closer examination, however, we discover an image that functions on multiple levels in this passage, one which is simultaneously harmonious and discordant. On one hand, the image "strokes" accentuates the terror and aggression implicit in the action of the wind because it denotes hitting or striking a blow. . . . On the other hand, "strokes" also . . . represents the diametrically opposite action of caressing, flattering, soothing. On another level, "strokes" also means the sound of a bell or clock ringing the hour, an image which inevitably recalls the passing of time, an action which brings with it the natural disintegration and wearing away of things, a universal law to which man has yet to discover an alternative. (pp. 35-6)

By reducing all the creation to dust: the mountains, reduced grain by grain to loose earth; the cattle, whose bones become white dust; the insects, birds and plants, whose tracks are obliterated by its action, and finally man, whose exhalations are dissipated in the air, the wind acquires the personification of an anti-generative, anti-mythic force. Parallel to this negative vision, however, a regenerative force coexists within the poem which mitigates the negative indifference of the wind. Without being diverted from its destructive course, the wind pushes beyond physical disintegration, beyond chaos, beyond nothingness, to initiate a new creative cycle of existence, within which, ironically, the same demolishing wind becomes a generative force:

> The wind picks up the breath of my armpits
> Like dust, swirls it
> Miles away
>
> And drops it
> On the ear of a rabid dog,
> And I take on another life. . . .

At this point it becomes evident that the ambiguity between the contradictory functions of the wind . . . constitutes the axis upon which the poem itself hinges since it establishes a dramatic tension between the disintegrative and regenerative forces operant within the poem.

The importance of this device of ambiguity in Soto's poetry becomes apparent in the consistency with which it is used to create precisely this impression of dramatic tension within the apocalyptic framework so characteristic of his artistic expression. Repeatedly one encounters similar images of disintegration and death mitigated by an ironically positive twist. . . . (p. 37)

[Soto] achieves his highest artistic brilliance and aesthetic subtlety in those poems, of which **"Wind"** is an excellent example, in which ambiguity becomes an expansive force not only by multiplying metaphorical and linguistic levels of meaning, but also by dilating the philosophical and dramatic dimensions of the fundamental theme of human existence. Such existence is revealed in Soto's poetry as a long and painful *via crucis,* a spiritual pilgrimage into a past peopled by spectres of privation, loneliness and death. Nevertheless, subtly but unequivocally, Soto manages to counterbalance this inhospitable existence by incorporating ambiguities that not only reduce the power of death to subjugate man definitively, but also substantially reduce the terror and finality of annihilation by implying a capacity in man to survive and overcome the limitations of his destiny. (p. 38)

Patricia de la Fuente, "Ambiguity in the Poetry of Gary Soto," in Revista Chicano-Riqueña, *Vol. XI, No. 2, Summer, 1983, pp. 34-9.*

Christina (Ellen) Stead

1902-1983

Australian novelist, short story writer, translator, and editor.

Stead's masterpiece, *The Man Who Loved Children* (1940), was neglected for twenty-five years until Randall Jarrell's laudatory afterword to the 1965 edition of the novel sparked interest in all of Stead's work. In his essay, Jarrell stated that "*The Man Who Loved Children* knows as few books have ever known—knows specifically, profoundly, exhaustively—what a family is" and that it "seems to me as plainly good as *War and Peace* and *Crime and Punishment* and *Remembrance of Things Past* are plainly great." Although Stead's reputation still rests largely on *The Man Who Loved Children*, most of her early works have been reissued in recent years, and current consensus maintains that Stead deserves to be regarded as a significant twentieth-century author.

Born and raised in Sydney, Australia, Stead also lived in England, Europe, and the United States. The wide variety of geographical and sociocultural milieus in which Stead set her novels reflects her extensive traveling. *The Salzburg Tales* (1934), a collection of short stories, was written after Stead attended a music festival in Austria. *House of All Nations* (1938) and *The Little Hotel* (1973) are both set in Europe. The former deals with high finance and the destructive avarice of the protagonists; the latter concerns a group of expatriates immediately after World War II, living in isolation and fearing the loss of their limited wealth. In *Cotters' England* (1966), Stead recreates England's dismal, industrialized north.

Stead is often compared to Charles Dickens and other nineteenth-century novelists for the density of realistic detail in her novels and for her commentary on social conditions and social relationships. However, despite its prominence in Stead's work, setting is secondary to characterization. She is noted for her keen power of observation and her precision in recording human nature. Without being judgmental, Stead explores the human psyche in its darker manifestations. Critics agree that through the characters of Sam, Henny, and Louisa Pollitt, family members portrayed in *The Man Who Loved Children,* Stead offers a view of family life which is at once horrifying and astonishingly realistic. One of Stead's major themes, personal and artistic fulfillment, finds its most dramatic realization in this novel as Stead shows how circumstance, environment, and heredity combine to shape the young artist.

(See also *CLC*, Vols. 2, 5, 8 and *Contemporary Authors,* Vols. 13-16, rev. ed., Vol. 109 [obituary].)

MICHAEL WILDING

Seven Poor Men of Sydney and *For Love Alone* can profitably be discussed together, not merely because they share an Australian setting, but because they have thematic concerns in common, and because the later book to some degree restates the themes of the earlier one, and offers a development from them. The Australian settings—mainly of Sydney—are emphasized in both, and sometimes seem a restriction when documentation becomes a substitute for creation. . . . Even for a

reader who knows Sydney, these passages hardly succeed; the need to create a mental map, to correlate names with street signs, dissipates the attention. To someone unfamiliar with the city, the details can only be boring. They are not at all evocative; they are supported by hardly any description or imaging. The streets and views may have been meaningful to Christina Stead, but nothing is communicated to the reader except a provincial lack of proportion, a lack of realization that places need to be created, not just names; the centre of one's own world is not the world's centre.

It is something of a paradox that the cosmopolitan expatriate—as she has tended to be viewed by Australian critics—should show what seems to be such provincialism. It cannot be explained as prentice work since the features appear not only in her first novel [*Seven Poor Men of Sydney*], but in *For Love Alone,* which was her fifth. [In his *Australian Literature,* Frederick] Macartney, noting that *Seven Poor Men* is her only novel set wholly in Australia, adds a rider—"though the references to the locale are overlaid by her intellectual grotesquerie." The "though" sounds disappointed—but rather than agreeing with such disappointment, we might argue that the "references to the locale" are successfully imagined only when they are so overlaid.

It is this grotesquerie that marks Christina Stead as so distinctive a writer. She uses the setting of Sydney in the depression, but makes of it far more than her social-realist contemporaries could. Certainly she is concerned with the social-realist aspects of poverty; the provincialism of the place-naming is perhaps an attempt to establish a "real" setting; and she deals with the social aspects of poverty, the economic factors determining it. But her picturing of the streets of depression transcends the merely limited socio-economic, historic reportage. She is brilliantly successful when, from the documentation of cartography, she reaches out to a phantasmagoria. . . . (pp. 20-2)

[At times, the grotesquerie leads] to allegorization and Gothicizing—a tendency always present in these novels, and running riot in the adolescent-like fantasy and whimsy of *The Salzburg Tales*. In the novels her control is firmer; even such shamelessly Poe-like Romantic touches as Kol Blount's hearing Michael's voice calling him in a dream as Michael is committing suicide, are carried off in *Seven Poor Men.*

The problem in the novels is not that of the grotesquerie becoming wildly Romantic, but of becoming boring, of becoming not macabre but dully descriptive. . . . (p. 23)

The less Christina Stead strives for realism, the more successful she often is, because her realistic mode drops too easily to mere listing (of place names or objects) or to an imaginative thinness. (p. 24)

There is a disjunction in *Seven Poor Men* ultimately between the overall theme and organization of the book (poverty), and the individual successful imaginative passages, between the Romantic and the low-life caricature. . . . [There] is not a strong enough structure of action, plot or image to make a total unity of the disparate elements of *Seven Poor Men*. And the disjunction leads to a sort of compartmentalization in treatment of characters. Winter, for instance, is limited because he is shown only in this socio-economic context; similarly the young theorist, Baruch Mendlessohn, is presented mainly as someone who gives long, and tedious, analyses of the social and political situation: whereas Michael and Catherine are given a much fuller characterization, yet hardly fitted into the socio-economic aspect of the novel.

And Christina Stead is much more successful with the bizarre or the Romantic than with the naturalistic; she fails with Winter and even with Mendlessohn. But the brilliance of the portrayal of Michael Bagenault is of a different order, there is a richness of psychological presentation, as well as of the macabre or grotesque. (pp. 24-5)

But his dizziness, his dreams "that he was suffocating or being attacked by bears, or being followed by gigantic funereal phantoms," . . . his speculations—all these that so brilliantly establish his personality, have little to do with the novel's central theme. (p. 25)

The organization of Christina Stead's novels is not conventional. Various critics have indicated the lack of plot in *Seven Poor Men;* but lack of plot does not necessarily imply lack of structure. The novel deals with the lives of seven poor men, all of whom are connected by friendship, work, or family; the connections, though, are shaky and other characters—such as Michael's sister, or the Folliotts, or Montagu the financier—are at least as important as some of the seven. What unity the novel has comes not from plot (there isn't one), nor from character relationship, but from the theme stated in the title—poverty. It is this, the varieties of poverty, its different effects, that provides the organization—so that the novel can be seen almost as a "meditation" on poverty. And the meditation is

not restricted to the economic manifestations—Chamberlain's printing works for instance; the way poverty determines and limits lives not merely economically, but also culturally, mentally and sexually is the book's concern. We can say that Michael is a born misfit, is created as a melancholic and irrational child; but poverty subdues him, too, plays on his character to lead him to his final destruction. The social-realist novel has tended too often to deal with the "normal" individual oppressed by his economic and social environment; Christina Stead extends the analysis to show the abnormal similarly, indeed worse, afflicted.

Seven Poor Men ends on a note of despair, as if poverty has defeated all the characters: Michael has committed suicide, Winter is sick and perhaps dying, Catherine is in a mental hospital, Chamberlain is ruined. There are notes of hope, but they are not strong ones. . . . No one achieves fulfilment.

For Love Alone, retreading the same ground, does offer a development from the same situation. Poverty is still an omnipresent force for the first three-fifths of the book, but it is now presented as not totally determining. There are other aspects of life that are influentially and motivationally important. There were in *Seven Poor Men,* too: the thematic frame would not contain some of the imaginative aspects of the novel such as the incest motif. *For Love Alone,* likewise organized by theme, has its theme stated in the title, too. Poverty now becomes a background for the exploration of love. It is a theme perhaps more suited to Christina Stead's abilities: her grotesqueries superbly established some aspects of the poverty she was describing, but her failure with the social and political aspects of the theme weakened *Seven Poor Men:* they were aspects that needed to be established for a theme of poverty. With love—and especially with an adolescent girls' imaginings about love—fantasy, nightmare, grotesquerie are a manner more fully appropriate, and a less adequate grasp of naturalism can be concealed.

For Love Alone may initially seem to be organized on plot—telling the story of Teresa Hawkins' life at home, her first love, her journey to England, her disillusion, despair and true love. But such an account would have to concede numerous excrescences and imbalances. The opening chapter, for instance, a superb portrayal of Tess's father, establishes him as vain and egotistic, demanding an audience from his family, narrating a monologue of his sensual successes. . . . Hawkins' blinding egotistic portrayal of his own egotism is a brilliant *tour de force.* Hawkins, though, is only a minor figure in the novel henceforth. His being established in the novel in such fullness here would be a structural flaw, if character and plot were the structural organizing elements. In a novel organized thematically around love-sex-sensuality, though, the establishment of this sort of attitude can be seen as basic to the structure of theme and tone. (pp. 26-8)

The creation of an external world of narrated event, of external causality (the social-realist axis, as it were) is only a minor purpose in these novels. More important is the meditation on the chosen theme, and the narration of the psychological life of the characters. Events are selected to establish not the outer world of external causality, but the causality and causal connections of psychological states. Returning to Hawkins's egotistic monologue, we can see how this, and nineteen years of it, should affect the sexual and emotional nature of Tess. . . . It is the psychological drama, psychological cause and effect, that concern Christina Stead.

The earlier claim that the organizing pattern of these novels is thematic, might now be augmented by the claim that it is "psychological" too. She is interested in character psychology, but she draws also from the symbolism of Freudian psychology, and the incidents of the casebook, for organizing images and events. (pp. 28-9)

For Love Alone is more successful than *Seven Poor Men* very much because its organizing theme is one more suitable to Christina Stead's talents. The grotesquerie is appropriate to Teresa's fantasies: the old man following her along the bush track with his penis hanging exposed is an incident both relevant to her preoccupations with love and sex, and homogeneous with the fantasies and daydreams that she has—though more explicit than those she allows herself. But it is not merely that the grotesque or macabre or fantastic is more appropriate—it is appropriate and successful for aspects of the poverty theme, too; more important, *For Love Alone* does not have the disjunction between theme and realization of the earlier novel. . . . The memorable episodes of *For Love Alone* are all part of the love-sex-marriage theme. And the social-naturalistic aspects, too, are generally more successful. . . . Poverty is still pervasive in *For Love Alone,* and this, and the same settings . . . emphasize the similarities with *Seven Poor Men.* But poverty is here not the supreme determinant, the totality of existence. Tess's brothers and sisters are dragged down by it, or by the hard work to avoid it. But Jonathan Crow, who teaches Tess in a night school, is a slum child who has struggled his way to and through the university to escape from the degradation and destruction of poverty. He seems someone who will escape, and Tess channels all her fantasies of love on to him, until when he leaves for England, she saves for three years in order to afford the fare to join him.

Christina Stead has attempted something very difficult with Crow: presenting him as the struggling young man for our sympathy, as someone who is not content, as is Tess's father, to lapse into poverty and apathy; having done this she risks suggesting Crow is not a first-rate mind, but essentially mediocre, distinguished mainly in application and hard work. . . . It is not until Tess has been in England for some time that she comes to a realization of Crow's worthlessness. He is, in fact, not someone freed from poverty by the intellect and study, but someone destroyed, like her family, like the figures in *Seven Poor Men,* by it. (pp. 30-1)

[Crow] is presented with a superb understanding. He is one of the finest pictures of someone who in trying to escape from the poverty of his background is destroyed unwittingly by himself. He nearly destroys Tess—but he is as much a victim himself.

Tess though is saved; Quick, the wealthy, cultured, literary, handsome American financier employs her, rescues her from her decision to die, and gives her love. Crow's part in this should not be ignored, though; if it had not been for him and his determination to escape from the Sydney slums, Tess would never have escaped from the world of the *Seven Poor Men.* Her dependence on and disillusion with Crow is a necessary part of her ultimate saving. (p. 32)

From the same world of the *Seven Poor Men* a solution has in this later novel developed. Poverty and its spiritual despair can be escaped; the escape—like Mendlessohn's ambiguous one—demands a flight; but the flight leads to a solution in *For Love Alone.* And the solution offered is one that avoids being sentimental—as Quick at first seemed to be—because it is not a solution offered as a simple, final answer. What Quick has given Tess is not an answer; instead he has given her the conditions requisite for finding her own answer. . . . While Teresa is saved from poverty and despair romantically, even unrealistically, the sentimentality of that is qualified and repudiated by the presentation of her new life as a new life to develop, one only just beginning, one posing new problems; they will need new decisions, new resolutions—or another fairy godmother. (p. 33)

> Michael Wilding, "Christina Stead's Australian Novels," in Southerly, Vol. 27, No. 1, 1967, pp. 20-33.

CHARLES THOMAS SAMUELS

[Christina Stead] appeals through the oddness of her characters and the relentless, uniquely resourceful dialogue through which she creates them. But the very amplitude of her portraits demands a significance she finds difficult to establish. The baby-talking egoist Sam Pollit [in *The Man Who Loved Children*] never comes to represent colonial condescension, though Stead hints at the connection, just as Nellie Cotter, in last year's *Dark Places of the Heart,* never quite distills the cant of England's welfare state. Since the novellas which make up [*The Puzzlehead Girl*] are both short and witty, they don't seem aimless; but, for the most part, they are scarcely more edifying than her novels.

"**The Dianas,**" for example, portrays a nervous, virgin tease, who is apparently an object of satire. Juggling dates like a busy executive, Lydia satisfies none of her admirers, preferring to give her attention to the love-crossed girlfriend [Tamara] she torments with unwanted solicitude. . . . Though Tamara ends a suicide, Lydia, who has littered Europe with wounded males, is back in America at the story's end, the bride of some special Acteon.

Lydia's machinations are amusing and her ultimate success through surrender is both ironic in itself and in contrast with Tamara's failure. But the implication that love conquers even so devious a maiden seems banal for such vivid eccentricity, while the hint that nice girls finish last is merely sarcastic. In its original magazine appearance, the story was called "**The Huntress**"; significant universality can't be achieved through a change in title.

In "**The Puzzleheaded Girl,**" universality is the obvious goal, but this story only indicates how Stead's characters resist definition. Honor Lawrence, who materializes one day at the Farmer's Utilities Corporation, is a mystery crying out to be interpreted. One of the firm's partners, Gus Debrett, thinks her innocent but tantalizing; as the story progresses, she feeds the latter impression by qualifying the former. (p. 30)

We are told that, like "the ghouls of Prague," Honor enters the forms of many women, yet Stead also insists that the girl is no fantasy figure; and, in any case, obscure realism can't be solved through intermittent allegory. Though some of the characters sport names like Honor's—Good, Zero, Magna—at least two—Debrett and Scott—resist hermeneutics. Finally, the puzzleheaded girl is too various for Stead's summation. She is also too fey; what begins by resembling "Bartleby, the Scrivener" veers fatally in the direction of "Breakfast at Tiffany's."

A third novella, "**The Rightangled Creek,**" is even more baffling. (pp. 30-1)

Though energetic and witty, all three stories have similar flaws. Dotty characters parade in such profusion that we sometimes see only a vaudeville lacking principles of inclusion more expressive than the impresario's taste and the curtain's fall. Aphorisms, excellent in themselves, becloud the plots which transpire in an atmosphere of demi-realism that is frequently disorienting and sometimes incredible. Typical obsessions—with sexual warfare and bogus ideology—are evident, but they never quite achieve the status of themes. Just as we are ready to write Stead off, however, she comes along with a novella, richly ironic and admirably developed, but similar in technique to her comparative failures.

"The Girl from the Beach" convincingly realizes that comedy of senescent lust versus lethal girlishness which unites the three best tales. Half of the story . . . depicts a Bulgarian crime-reporter, sentimental in his womanizing, theatrical in his nationalism, and ludicrous in the care of his fifty-year-old body that retains the muscle tone of a young man's. Stead has often done such charming phonies, but never with such *brio*. . . .

The second half introduces [Linda Hill], a young tease like Lydia and Honor Lawrence, but it makes of her a more representative, believable figure. . . . Crossing her path, George immediately succumbs. For him, mature women are "an army of aunts and mothers, midwives and charwomen"; Linda must become the fourth of his girl-wives. . . .

Though gayer and less adorned, Stead's story is an unsentimental, small-scaled *Lolita*.

Finally, Stead seems to exist between the extremes set by her critics. In an age when most novelists are shooting the form through a cannon, making up in technical display for loss of purpose and confidence, her mimetic zeal is invigorating despite its frequent pointlessness. Moreover, her attempts at articulating a theme are so lively and musical in themselves that one wants to test the possibility of a leitmotif throughout her work. (p. 31)

> *Charles Thomas Samuels, "The Puzzling Miss Stead,"* in The New Republic, *Vol. 157, No. 11, September 9, 1967, pp. 30-1.*

RODNEY PYBUS

The novellas [collected in **The Puzzleheaded Girl**] make an excellent introduction to Christina Stead. They are permeated by quirky spontaneity and a sense of threatening torment, a combination which one quickly learns is the distinctive note of her fiction. They reveal too her special gift for psychological exploration, and a passionate intensity. . . . More than most novelists writing today, she creates her own world: recognisably the everyday world, at least superficially, but occupied by the charged emotional relationships which stamp all her writing. These densely-textured, astringently observed, autonomous relationships strike one as compounded of almost too much hate and love, and with their radical insights they disturb many of our most comfortable prejudices and preconceptions. (p. 31)

Christina Stead is obviously interested, as Lawrence confessed he was not, in what her characters feel, in 'the old stable *ego* of the character'. At the same time, she is fascinated by that other ego which Lawrence referred to in his famous letter to Edward Garnett:

'another *ego,* according to whose action the individual is unrecognizable, and passes through, as it were, allotropic states which it needs a deeper sense than any we've been used to exercise, to discover are states of the same single radically unchanged element.'

In this seems to me to lie the success of Christina Stead's work, what makes her approach to the novel valid in the second half of the 20th century: she combines many of the virtues of the outmoded 19th century novel (Russian and French, rather than English), with the radical, uncomfortable insights of a sensibility as modern in its way as Lawrence's. I see no reason to expect Miss Stead to be modern in the sense in which Alain Robbe-Grillet or Susan Sontag might be said to be modern; she is after all part, I think a significant part, of that generation which links the 19th century with the post-war period.) The hallmark of [**Cotter's England, Seven Poor Men of Sydney, For Love Alone,** and **The Man Who Loved Children**] is what Dostoevski called the 'tragicofantastic element'; her recognition of it, and the tension between it and reality in the conventional sense, are what make her novels valuable. (p. 33)

> *Rodney Pybus, "The Light and the Dark: The Fiction of Christina Stead,"* in Stand, *Vol. 10, No. 1 (1968), pp. 30-7.*

DOROTHY GREEN

[In **The Man Who Loved Children**] Christina Stead has created what is extremely rare in modern literature: three archetypal characters who have a life of their own, independent of their author; characters like Dickens's Uriah Heep or Mr Micawber, who can be known to those who have never read the books in which they figure. This is particularly true of Sam Pollit, 'the man who loved children'. The ironical title defines him as the phrase 'humble as Uriah Heep' defines Heep. Figures who take on mythic proportions in a literature, who become part of its language, nearly always have a touch of caricature about them: they are always larger than life. Quite often they are not drawn in any depth at all—like the caricature, they acquire immortality with a few telling strokes. Sam Pollit however is drawn in great detail and in great depth, so that he becomes more, not less plausible as the book progresses. At first, it is almost impossible to believe in such a character at all; then it becomes clear that it is the seeming exaggerations which make the portrait convincing: the reader, like the children, becomes part of the illusionary world Sam constructs for his illusionary self. (p. 175)

. . . it makes sense to describe this work as an 'ecological novel'. It presents the observer with the spectacle of a struggle for survival in a habitat which is too small and too impoverished for the 'fighting fish' it contains. The dominant male survives in it, his mate succumbs, but his daughter, partly because of, partly in spite of her genetic inheritance from her father and her own mother, partly because of characteristics acquired from her step-mother, manages to fight her way out of this closed ecosystem and goes for a walk 'round the world' to find a new one in which she can flourish more easily. Horrifying as the book often is, there is no tone of grudging resentment in the narrative; behind it is the clear awareness that only this particular combination of circumstances, this extraordinary mixture of tragedy and buffoonery, could have led to the evolution of this particular species of artist. Louisa's temporary hatred for her father is the healthy hatred of an animal whose existence is threatened; it passes when the threat is removed and is an ingredient in the book, not the ground of it.

What saves Louisa's sanity, as the battle between Henrietta and Sam runs its course, is her contempt for those she is associated with, learned from Henny, and a belief in her own genius, an inheritance from Sam. We do not watch the battle, however, through Louisa's consciousness, nor indeed through the consciousness of any particular figure in the novel. Neither is it correct to speak of an omniscient narrator. It is as if we were standing beside an expert observer, watching with her the behaviour of these strange beings and listening to author-itative descriptions of what they are doing. The observer is perhaps the finished artist Nature intended Louisa to become, looking back at her early experience and confirming her ten-tative interpretations of what she was living through. It is not true to say, as Ron Geering has said, that comment is rare in the novel. There is a great deal of it, especially in the second half, after Sam's return from the Smithsonian Expedition to Malaya. The reader, like Louisa herself, learns gradually to contemplate and classify the Pollits from a distance, while participating in their lives at close quarters. . . . The commen-tary that accompanies the action from the early stages is not the usual kind of 'interior' psychological analysis the twentieth century novelist specialises in. What the author does is to marshal an overwhelming abundance of evidence in speech, action and indirect description of physical and mental behav-iour, which will lead the reader inevitably to the correct clas-sification of Sam. A psychologist might have deduced the ex-istence of an 'oral-erotic' type merely from watching Sam as he is presented, but the novelist does not start, as so many do nowadays, with a psychological abstraction and then proceed to clothe it in flesh. She begins, as all genuine artists do, from the flesh. (pp. 176-78)

What the novel does is to show what *one* particular family was like and what its peculiar combination of characteristics achieved that was of value to the race; and it does that supremely well. There are infinite varieties of families and it would be difficult to imagine a scientifically trained mind like Christina Stead's confusing a species with a phylum. The inexplicable union of Henrietta Collyer and Sam Pollit resulted in a family of a very unusual kind: the only bond between them is their carnality and this and their other characteristics are distributed among their children in surprising ways. Moreover, there is nothing particularly representative about Henrietta's antecedents, nor those of Louisa on her own mother's side. (p. 179)

The figures of Sam and Henny are so powerfully drawn, that of Louisa, the eldest child, their 'punching ball', so memorable and moving, that it is not surprising the book should be read simply as a horrifying account of marital incompatibility. But if it is justifiable to see each example of a family as a miniature eco-system, then the principal product of this one is a unique species of artist and the novel is an account of the extraordi-narily complex interactions needed to produce it. The book is also the record of the growth towards awareness of the members of the system: all the main characters, according to their age and capacity, move from incomprehension towards some sort of painful insight, except perhaps the little girl Evie, who remains perpetually dependent and bewildered. (p. 180)

The ten chapters of the book fall into three main sections which correspond roughly to three different stages in Louisa's growth to awareness. She is equated from the beginning with the 'night-rider', the horseman she seems to hear galloping through the dark, awake like herself when the rest of the world is asleep—

an image of the artist she aspires obscurely to become. She has no notion where her talents lie, and like so many gifted children who are ugly ducklings has vague dreams of becoming a famous actress, like Duse. Just past eleven, moving towards early puberty, she is beginning to sense that there may be two sides to the matrimonial debate which rages continually over her head. . . . (p. 181)

The main concern of the first section is to depict the Pollits in their home environment, a habitat which is really designed as a permanent playground for Sam. He rationalises his own re-quirements in terms of what is desirable for the children's growth, their growth as he plans it. His first playground, of which he is inordinately proud, is Tohoga House, the property of Henny's father [David Collyer], reputedly a millionaire, with a large family of spoilt children. (p. 182)

By the end of the first book, Sam is forever immortalised as the ultimate solipsist. (p. 192)

The second 'movement', which accelerates Louisa's progress towards freedom of opinion, begins about Chapter 5. It exposes the fragility of Sam's authority; he has not even imposed him-self strongly enough on his family to ensure that his instructions are carried out during his absence and the children write to him with great reluctance. His enforced association with adults, especially those who belong to a different race, an older civ-ilisation, makes it clear that his ideas have no meaning outside his own closed world. (p. 193)

The laying down of clues to action and character in this book is as complex and elaborate as the occurrence of links in a food-chain; they are buried in the same kind of circumstantial details that makes them so hard to discern in real life. Christina Stead's narrative method is trying to the patience of readers whose taste is conditioned to the laconic, or to the carefully refined and unified structures of a James or a Conrad; but it is the only possible method open to a novelist setting out to write a Natural History of the house of Pollit. (p. 198)

[The] section ends with the news, by telegram, of David Col-lyer's death. (p. 200)

The book now enters its final stage. The disappointment of Sam's hopes of being Collyer's heir, through Henny, the need to find a new house, scandal and trouble at the office and his suspension from the Department: the collapse of the outer world hastens the decay of his family relationships. The change is marked by the move from Tohoga House to the ramshackle home on the waterfront, Spa House. . . . (p. 201)

It is Louisa's going to High School that makes the first real breach in the enclosed system of Sam's playground. She is at last able to measure the family's intellect against others. Her adulation of her English teacher, Miss Aiden, accelerates and concentrates her random creativity and the Poet rises to meet the Scientist in a fruitful symbiosis. As well as an idol, she acquires a friend, Clare, and her father characteristically at-tempts to annex both. His attempt to invade Clare's mind, as well as her own, leads to Louisa's open rebellion. (p. 203)

Louisa was very clear about what she did not want: she did not want to be like Sam or Henny, or to have her self invaded before she could define her wants more precisely. This is why she is able to make more use of Henny's neglect than of Sam's educational programming. Henny rightly regards Sam's eternal busyness as play: 'What a world of things Sam had to have to keep him amused!' she comments. It is a comment on Western man in general: the never-ending competition of male-domi-

nated governments over nuclear weapons and supersonic aircraft is Sam's Sunday-Funday on a horrendous scale. However
unsatisfactory Henny's grasp of economics might seem, it is
closer to reality than Sam's, since it puts the feeding and clothing of children before the provision of useless toys. And it
needs to be said in Henny's defence and in defence of her
species that she has been conditioned to be dependent. The
Hennys of the world have been largely created by the Sams
who in turn have been created by the Hennys. Louisa insisted
on breaking out of this vicious circle, on her right and her
ability to create her own 'self': 'I am my own mother', she
says proudly. Hindsight, of course, reveals the young Louisa's
boast as an illusion: what the book demonstrates is how that
self is made by her heredity, her books, the natural environment, her brothers and sister, her immediate associates, her
teachers and acquaintances as well as by her own responses
and resistances to all of these influences. From both Henny
and Sam she derives sensuousness, her delight in carnality, in
the world; from Sam her will to survive ('You would keep
yourself alive', says Ernie to Sam during one of his eugenic
tirades). Both give her training in observation: Henny in imag-
inativeness, Sam in precision; Henny gives her mystery, Sam
gives her music; Henny gives her passion and wit, Sam gives
her a clownish humour. Their gifts indeed are rich and inextricably intertwined. For the kind of artist Louisa was to become, there could hardly have been a better training ground,
severe as it was. This is why there is no bitterness in this great
novel: only the loving detachment of the poet and the detached
concern of the biologist. It was far ahead of its time when it
was written; we have not overtaken it yet. (pp. 207-08)

> *Dorothy Green, "'The Man Who Loved Children':
> Storm in a Tea-Cup," in* The Australian Experience:
> Critical Essays on Australian Novels, *edited by W.
> S. Ransome, Australian National University 1974,
> pp. 174-208.*

JAMES ATLAS

The long-windedness that tends to spoil [Miss Stead's] novels
is nowhere evident in **"A Christina Stead Reader."** . . . [In]
this **"Reader,"** enforced brevity has served Miss Stead very
well. There is nothing from **"The Man Who Loved Children,"**
for whatever reason, but 11 of her other novels are represented
in chronological order, with succinct introductions by the editor
to fill in the plot. A few of the selections are so brief as to be
scarcely intelligible, even with these summaries; even so, to
read them through is to receive a distinct, perhaps enhanced
sense of her achievement.

Miss Stead's considerable powers of evocation were manifest
from the start, in **"Seven Poor Men of Sydney,"** set in her
native Australia. The grim world conjured up in that novel
would seem derivative of the London depicted in "Keep the
Aspidistra Flying" had it not prefigured Orwell's novel by a
year. . . . (pp. 9, 28)

In her later novels, Miss Stead has tended to concentrate on
middle-class women—many of them aspiring writers—who
feel themselves oppressed; **"The Beauties and Furies," "For
Love Alone"** and **"Miss Herbert"** feature strong-willed, independent women made wretched by insensitive husbands or
lovers, and determined to forge new lives. Yet however admirable or true, their resistance invariably seems willed. Unlike
so many American novelists, she manages to imbue her working-class characters with a reality largely absent in her liberated
heroines.

Miss Stead is sufficiently versatile to command several literary
styles. She can strike off a Lawrentian image of a ravaged
industrial landscape . . . ; produce a sustained burlesque . . . ;
infuse with pathos a vulnerable young man contemplating in
the mirror "that single leaf of flesh which had been given to
him to write his own history upon"; or re-create the haunted
atmosphere of a Gothic novel, as she does in **"The Rightangle
Creek: A Sort of Ghost Story."** . . .

Still, her proclivity for tendentious speeches can become tiresome, her plots laborious, her characters overwrought and
wooden. And the intensity of her prose often lapses into melodrama. . . .

The virtue of **"A Christina Stead Reader"** is that it displays
the variety of her achievement in a single volume. However
imposing the giant sprawl of Miss Stead's novels, one comes
away from this collection wondering if she might not have been
better served by that archaic literary form, the short story.
(p. 28)

> *James Atlas, "A Book of Parts," in* The New York
> Times Book Review, *February 4, 1979, pp. 9, 28.*

DAPHNE MERKIN

A Christina Stead Reader was presumably conceived with the
hope of whetting interest in the work of this prolific and largely
ignored writer. . . . Because she has written a lot . . . and, on
the face of it, about many different subjects, she would seem
to be the perfect candidate for publication in excerpted form.

The present volume is unmistakable evidence to the contrary:
Christina Stead will not be nibbled at. She is a writer on the
grand scale; she needs space—like D. H. Lawrence, whom she
resembles in other ways—and to curb her is to make her look
foolish. There is something *architectural* about Stead's prose
which only justifies itself from the longer view; one notices
rather quickly in these short takes that Stead is not really a
stylist. She throws adjectives around indiscriminately—"The
hideous low scarred yellow horny and barren headland . . ."—
and she is rarely graceful. She is, in fact, a remarkably *uncomfortable* writer because she sees clearly into the ways of
the world and she is mirthless about what she sees. . . . (pp. 36-7)

This collection spans over 40 years of Christina Stead's output
and includes selections from eight novels. Although she writes
about financial empires (*House of All Nations*), impoverished
fishing communities (*Seven Poor Men of Sydney*), and jaded
sophisticates (*The Beauties and the Furies*) with equal familiarity, Stead's theme resounds with grim consistency from behind the many shapes she gives it. Hers is an obsession with
human savagery, especially in its licit manifestations—"the
naked domestic drama and hate of parent and child"—which
are unavoidable because they are endemic to our race. "The
brutish spirit of solitude" hovers over all her characters, a
spirit they are able to dispatch, however temporarily, through
developed powers of will and imagination. . . . It is not so much
that the possibility of love is *absent* from her novels, as that
it appears with radically less conviction than more malignant
possibilities. . . .

Christina Stead is a major writer; her flaws stem directly from
her inability to be casual (again, like Lawrence) and the ruthless
honesty with which she perceives even frivolous pastimes. Her
work deserves a fuller reading than is provided by this *Reader,*
but it probably comes as no surprise to Stead herself that recognition of her worth has been so slow in coming. ". . . . [T]he

things that are tabu,'' she writes, ''are always accepted as part of society, like the dark of the moon.'' By refusing to pay attention to her we are refusing to pay attention to the dark side of ourselves. (p. 37)

> Daphne Merkin, in a review of ''A Christina Stead Reader,'' in The New Republic, Vol. 180, No. 8, February 24, 1979, pp. 36-7.

ELIZABETH PERKINS

The energy that informs the novels of Christina Stead is that which Dylan Thomas called ''the force that through the green fuse drives the flower'', that which centuries before Chaucer had called the vertú ''of which engendred is the flour''. Among the flowers so engendred in Christina Stead's novels are Letty Fox, the heroine of the detailed and compact novel, *Letty Fox: Her Luck* (1946), and Eleanor Herbert in *Miss Herbert (The Suburban Wife)* [1976]. . . . (p. 107)

One problem that concerns the reader when examining the women who flower, so handsome and so energetic, in these novels, is whether they grow self-organised from within, as their vigour and beauty and confidence demand, or whether they end stunted and distorted by the pressure of their surrounding social structures. Letty and Eleanor are beautiful, dynamic, educated and sexually active. Concerning their aims, their beauty and their intelligence they are perfectly articulate—some of the vitality of the novels derives from their ability to talk with apparent freedom, quite unaware that they are constantly lying and contradicting themselves. In fact the lies and contradictions give them a curious vitality.

What these women want is security, respectability and solid monogamy, and when marriage comes they wipe out the memory of their pre-marital sexual life as if it had never been. Letty Fox, born in New York in the twenties, and educated partly in Europe, and more liberally than Eleanor, tells fewer lies but struggles more ruthlessly to reach her goal.

Miss Herbert (The Suburban Wife) appears at first sight to be a plain unvarnished tale about an English woman. . . . (pp. 107-08)

Eleanor Brent is a beautiful woman, educated but insincere—a bad actress, Christina Stead has called her—and gaining little from her social environment other than a thorough training in mendacity. She actively co-operates in the social process of sedating her intellect, collaborating here with her genteel mother, a former Miss Herbert of some social standing, and ignoring the awkward adventurous thinking of her socialist father and brother. Even her beauty has a drugged and sluggish quality as though it sleeps under bourgeois sedation. After marriage her now somnolent sexual drive sometimes stirs into a sordid, covert activity.

Her husband Henry (born Heinrich) Charles is sedulous in conformity as she, but he suggests that they reinvigorate their sexual relationship with some of the love play she must have learned from her great variety of pre-marital lovers. Eleanor weeps, protests ignorance and little real experience. . . . This is not hypocrisy but a complicated psychological feat and an instinctive movement to preserve what she hopes is the security of the present. The characters in Stead's novels who perform these feats spend no energy fighting or denying the reality of their situation, but soundly assert a different reality, as Eleanor does here. Confronted by such psychic demolition forces, the facts disappear. (p. 108)

The ability to put aside one set of facts and create new ones, or to alter course without acknowledgement of the fact, has no morbid psychological repercussions on the characters who do it. And so no energy is lost in self-examination, in remorse or self-recrimination. The characters who most successfully and frequently convert the fact are those who best survive. It is this that accounts for Eleanor Herbert's survival, as it helps explain the vitality of Sam Pollit in *The Man Who Loved Children* (1940) and Nellie Cook in *Cotter's England* (1966). Not all the characters in Christina Stead's novels do this—those whom she has said are modelled partly on her husband William Blech—e.g. James Quick in *For Love Alone* (1944), Alphéndery in *House of all Nations* (1938), Eleanor's father, Lindsay Brent, and Letty's father, Solander Fox, either tell the truth or remain silent. Those who cannot convert reality to their needs, like Michael Baguenault in *Seven Poor Men of Sydney* (1934), or Philip Morgan in *Letty Fox: Her Luck,* commit suicide, while Catherine Baguenault leaves society temporarily at least to teach art and handicraft in an asylum.

The successful converters of reality may seem morally or socially degraded and tawdry to the reader, and two of them at least, Tom and Nellie Cook, drive a weaker character to death by their lies and distortions. Together, Tom and Nellie absolutely confuse reality for Caroline Wooller, who is thereby driven to suicide, and in *Letty Fox: Her Luck,* the relentless efforts of Dora Dunn to bend the clever, wayward Philip Morgan to her notion of domestic reality in no small way contributes to his suicide. But at the close of each book the changers of reality vigorously assert their self-satisfaction and moral integrity. They have done their best, as Eleanor says at the end of the novel. . . . As the reader sees it, Eleanor has broken every rule of the book in attempting to maintain the illusion that ''she had done all the most usual things possible, knowing that was a recipe for happiness.'' (pp. 109-10)

Eleanor's pettiness, evasions, disloyalties and spite originate in her fear of not achieving the average. She is terrified of radical ideas, and maintains a sly, vicious attack on her good friend Cope Pigsney because he wrote an early book ''under Communist influence.'' Her malice is the product of her fear that she will not measure down to the safety of the accepted.

Eleanor and Letty lack a spiritual dimension, but this does not account for their state. Their plight is not metaphysical but social. They want to shine, but they do not want to excel; they would like to be at the top in their little world but they do not want to be different from it or to extend it. Even when the world treats them cruelly, they refuse to criticize it.

Christina Stead is not an historian of the fall of the middle class: indeed, she may be showing precisely why the middle class is indestructible, but in these novels she observes the effort involved in conforming to middle class existence. Showing her fiance some photos of herself naked in various poses, Eleanor says ''We middle class girls have so many inhibitions: it takes years of struggle to become normal, healthy, hearty women.'' . . . But in the middle class as Eleanor conceives it, the goal of normal, healthy, hearty womanhood is the worst inhibition of all. The energy and cunning employed in not rising above the ideals of normality show as tragically wasteful in novels that are balanced between social satire and human compassion.

Eleanor's husband, Henry Charles, expresses one of the central beliefs by which these characters survive:

We are surrounded by those human strains that survived, by success. The law of survival insists that we survive. This is a great over-riding law. . . .

(pp. 111-12)

The originality and organic vitality of Christina Stead's novels deny this truncated Darwinism, this lore of the shoal. The central paradox of her work, implicit not only in each individual novel but also in the heterogeneity of the total opus, is the contradiction between the pseudo-originality of these characters and the truly creative idiosyncrasy of the style and form of her art.

Christina Stead's novels are generally accepted as dealing with the middle classes from the standpoint of a writer who happens also to be a socialist. Some critics regret that the novels are not better organised to show clearly the strengths and weaknesses of the social structure she is observing, they regret that she does not take more seriously what one critic has described as her role as an historian of the fall of the middle class. Others regret the lack of artistic shaping in her novels, and the incongruous mixture of social realism and imaginative lyricism that they feel threatens the unity of her stories. But most critics show that her lyricism and realism are perfectly compatible. Moreover in structure each of her novels is an organism, *self*-organised in the manner that Kant and Coleridge recognised as essential to an organic art, as opposed to an external structure organised mechanically. (p. 112)

Unlike Eleanor Herbert, Christina Stead as a writer dares to swim rivers. If she does not root out the fevers from the villages of the bourgeoisie, she does indicate that the effort of maintaining middle-class standards of average normality demands from women a tragic expenditure of creative energy. (p. 113)

> *Elizabeth Perkins, "Energy and Originality in Some Characters of Christina Stead," in* Journal of Commonwealth Literature, *Vol. XV, No. 1, August, 1980, pp. 107-13.*

BILL GREENWELL

[The title of *A Little Tea, A Little Chat* (1948)] is the euphemistic phrase employed by the central figure, Robert Grant, when tempting women to partake of bed without breakfast, which he does with effortless regularity throughout the novel. Grant is a shallow, soulless man, an amoral profiteer in wartime New York who holds court to a succession of dreary people while idly but constantly expounding his hypocritical ideals. . . .

The problem for the reader is sustaining interest in Stead's poisonous creation. Much as I appreciate the title's irony, the novel contains a great deal too much chat. Page after page consists almost entirely of Grant's monologues, diatribes, phoney wisdom, and it becomes both frustrating and exhausting to wade through it all. As an exercise in maintaining one man's relentless voice, as it travels monotonously down one's inner ear, it succeeds. As a novel, it is progressively less absorbing. By the final page, I was too clapped out to clap, and wearily suspicious of the wisdom of representing *A Little Tea* as a 'modern classic'.

But it took only two-and-a-half ticks to kick the match-sticks from my eyes once I'd entered, this time with foreboding, the world of *The People with the Dogs* (1952). The opening is spectacularly casual. An estate agent, Miss Waldmayer, is on the way to visit her client, Edward Massine, when she witnesses a murder. The stabbing she sees is of no consequence to her, to the plot, but it is a neatly nasty glimpse into the restless, rootless world of suburban New York which is the backdrop for the long opening section.

Once Miss Waldmeyer has introduced us to Edward, the leading player, she vanishes. . . . Edward's world, in town and later at a family retreat in the country, Whitehouse, is by turns a sad, whimsical, musical, emotional, scatty, magnetic and even magical place.

It's an astonishing novel, one which sprawls, ripples and explodes beneath the fingers. It might be tempting to ascribe its attractions, as against the self-defeating torpors of *A Little Tea,* to its cheerier outlook. Indeed, it is a kind of antidote to the earlier work. But the real difference is one of quality. *The People with the Dogs* is genius on the loose. It's practically the only novel I know which fully captures the conversational quirks of human beings: certainly the only one which lets its characters crack the daftest jokes.

The dogs—and cats—are as essential as the people. Oneida, Edward's aunt, replies, 'Like women! And like men!' to a suggestion that dogs are 'forgetful, cruel, selfish, cowardly, lazy, dirty, stupid'. But Stead is not using them simply as metaphorical mutts: the dogs, and the slavering affections of their owners, provide us with any number of perspectives on human behaviour. This is a novel of affecting, affectionate sensibility, and I can't recommend it enough.

> *Bill Greenwell, "A Touch of Class," in* New Statesman, *Vol. 102, No. 2631, August 21, 1981, pp. 21-2.**

LORNA SAGE

[Christina Stead's] *oeuvre* is unwieldy and anomalous. She packs her novels with weighty significance, and yet at the same time she is shockingly volatile, even flighty, apt to fly off at strange tangents, and rhapsodise.

'The Beauties and Furies' is no exception to this misrule. It's set firmly in Paris . . . and it concentrates seemingly soulfully on a runaway romance, but poetic licence takes over almost immediately. Student Oliver and adulteress Elvira—like Olivia and Viola in 'Twelfth Night'—are an ambiguous sexual cocktail, shaken up still further by the improbable addition of a voyeur-villain called Marpurgo, a character on loan from Jacobean tragedy. . . .

[Contemporary] reviewers found the book, as one of them said, 'distinctly queer.' Yet it's rooted in a prosaic and tough-minded diagnosis of the Depression, as a period in which the appetite for luxury and the need for security, sharpened by deprivation, took on a viciously obsessive quality. Stead—characteristically—has nothing against greed; it's unfulfilment, she thinks, that's the corrupting force that turns people into mythomaniacs.

The plot drives Elvira back to her sterile marriage, and launches Oliver on a career as a Don Juan, basically because love needs money. This sounds a banal conclusion, but in Stead's version it has a special force, since she's so aware of the ironic counterpoint between the wealth of imagination and the poverty of action. Her point is that in an unjust world art and life corrupt each other, and—being supremely an artist—she's naturally faintly hysterical about such a state of affairs.

Excess is thus the key note of her style, and her favourite device is the enormous, exorbitant list. . . . Her favourite metaphors for the writers' craft are drawn from weaving and embroidery, and her purple patches are so deliberately worked that the years have failed to fade them. Just the writer for hard times.

Lorna Sage, "Nothing Succeeds Like Excess," in The Observer, *July 25, 1982, p. 31.*

ANGELA CARTER

To open a book, any book, by Christina Stead and read a few pages is to be at once aware that one is in the presence of greatness. Yet this revelation is apt to precipitate a sense of confusion, of strangeness, even of acute anxiety, not only because Stead has a devastating capacity to flay the reader's sensibilities, but also because we have grown accustomed to the idea that we live in pygmy times. To discover that a writer of so sure and unmistakable a stature is still amongst us, and, more, produced some of her most remarkable work as recently as the Sixties and Seventies, is a chastening thing. Especially since those two relatively recent novels—*Cotters' England* (1966) and *Miss Herbert (the Suburban Wife)* (1976)—contain extremely important analyses of post-war Britain, address the subject of sexual politics at a profound level, and have been largely ignored in comparison with far lesser novels such as Doris Lessing's *The Golden Notebook*. To read Stead, now, is to be reminded of how little, recently, we have come to expect from fiction. Stead is of that category of fiction writer who restores to us the entire world, in its infinite complexity and inexorable bitterness, and never asks if the reader wishes to be so furiously enlightened and instructed, but takes it for granted that this is the function of fiction. She is a kind of witness and a kind of judge, merciless, cruel and magnificently unforgiving. . . .

[Randall] Jarrell thought that *The Man Who Loved Children* [1940] was by far Stead's best novel and believed its commercial and critical failure blighted her subsequent development [see *CLC*, Vol. 2]. . . . However, at least three of her other novels—I'd say *For Love Alone* (1945), *A Little Tea, A Little Chat* (1948) and *Cotters' England* (1945)—equal that extraordinary novel, and in some ways surpass it, while *Letty Fox: Her Luck* (1946), is, unusually for Stead, a fully-achieved comic novel of a most original kind. But none of her work is negligible.

However, it wasn't surprising that *The Man Who Loved Children* should acquire the romantic reputation of a unique masterpiece. . . . The single-minded intensity of its evocation of domestic terror gives it a greater artistic cohesion than Stead's subsequent work, which tends towards the random picaresque. And Stead permits herself a genuinely tragic resolution. The ravaged harridan, Henny, the focus of the novel, dies in a grand, fated gesture, an act of self-immolation that, so outrageous has been her previous suffering, is almost a conventional catharsis. One feels that all Henny's previous life has been a preparation for her sudden, violent departure from it and, although the novel appals, it also, artistically, satisfies, in a way familiar in art. Later, Stead would not let her readers off the hook of life so easily. She won't allow us the dubious consolations of pity and terror again. . . .

[Only one of Stead's] novels has a wholly Australian setting, and that the earliest, *Seven Poor Men of Sydney* (1934). Even here, she has already established her characteristic milieu as that of the rootless urban intelligentsia, a milieu as international as it is peculiar to our century. Teresa Hawkins in *For Love*

Alone is the only major Australian character in Stead's later fiction, and Teresa is the most striking of these birds of passage, who sometimes become mercenaries of an ideology, sometimes end up as flotsam and jetsam.

Stead is also one of the great articulators of family life. There is no contradiction here. Stead's families . . . are social units that have outlived the original functions of protection and mutual aid and grown to be seedbeds of pathology. These are families in a terminal state of malfunction, families you must flee to preserve your sanity, families it is criminal folly to perpetuate—and, on the whole, Stead's women eschew motherhood like the plague. (Stead's loathing of the rank futility of home and hearth is equalled, in literature, only by that expressed by the Marquis de Sade.) These are degenerated, cannibal families, in which the very sacrament of the family, the communal meal when all are gathered together, is a Barmecide feast at which some family member, wife or child, is on the emotional menu. . . . Once away from the nest, Stead's birds of passage tend to eat in the neutral environments of restaurants—as do the runaway lovers in *The Beauties and Furies*. When they do not, something is up.

These rancid, cancerous homes may provide a useful apprenticeship in the nature of tyranny (several times in *The Man Who Loved Children* Stead stresses that children have 'no rights' within the family): that is all. The only escape is a plunge into an exponential whirl of furnished rooms, cheap hotels, constant travelling, chance liaisons, the blessed indifference of strangers. Stead's families, in fact, produce those rootless, sceptical displaced persons she also describes, who have no country but a state of mind, and yet who might, due to their very displacement and disaffection, be able to make new beginnings. . . .

Stead's greatest moral quality as a novelist is her lack of pity. . . . [For] Stead, pity is otiose, a self-indulgent luxury that obscures the real nature of our relations with our kind. To disclose that real nature has always been her business. Essentially, she is engaged in the exposition of certain perceptions as to the nature of human society. She does this through the interplay of individuals both with one another and with the institutions that we created but which now seem to dominate us. Marriage; the family; money. . . .

It is possible to be a great novelist—that is, to render a veracious account of your times—and a bad writer—that is, an incompetent practitioner of applied linguistics. Like Theodore Dreiser. Conversely, good writers—for example, Borges—often prefer to construct alternative metaphysical universes based on the Word. If you read only the novels Stead wrote after *The Man Who Loved Children*, it would seem that she belonged to the Dreiser tendency. She patently does not subscribe to any metaphysics of the Word. The work of her maturity is a constant, agitated reflection upon our experience in *this* world. For her, language is not an end-in-itself in the current, post-Modernist or 'mannerist' mode, but a mere tool, and a tool she increasingly uses to hew her material more and more roughly. Nor does she see the act of storytelling as a self-reflexive act. Therefore, as a composer of narrative, she can be amazingly slipshod. She will even allow utterly careless lapses in continuity. People can change names, parentage, age, occupation from page to page, as though she corrected nothing. They can also slip through holes in the narrative and disappear. . . . All this would be unforgivable if, in Stead, narrative mattered, much. It does not. Her narrative is almost *tachiste*: she composes it like a blind man throwing paint against a wall. Her narratives shape themselves, as our lives seem to do.

Interestingly enough, however, she started her career as a very mannered writer indeed. *The Salzburg Tales* of 1934 is a massive collection of glittering, grotesque short fictions, parables and allegories not dissimilar to the *Seven Gothic Tales* that Isak Dinesen published in the same year. *The Salzburg Tales* are contrived with a lush, jewelled exquisiteness of technique that recurs in *The Beauties and Furies,* which first appeared in 1936. (p. 11)

In *House of All Nations* (1938), which comes after *The Beauties and Furies,* the puppy-fat is already beginning to fall away from the bare bones of Stead's mature style, and of her mature purpose, for this is a novel straightforwardly about the root of all evil: that is, banking. However, the complications of its plotting recall the Jacobean drama at its most involuted, so that it is quite difficult to tell exactly what is going on. In fact, the elaborately fugal plotting of *House of All Nations* is beginning to dissolve of its own accord, just because too much is going on, into the arbitrary flux of event that characterises Stead's later novels. And she is beginning to write, not like a craftsman, but like an honest worker.

At the time of *The Man Who Loved Children,* she relinquished all the capacity of the languge of her narrative to bewitch and seduce. But Sam Pollitt, the father almighty or Nobodaddy of that novel, uses a babbling, improvised, pseudo-language, a sort of Pollitt creole, full of cant words—'cawf' for coffee, 'munchtime', 'orfus'—with which to bemuse, delight and snare his brood. This is the soft, slippery, charming language of seduction itself. Louie invents an utterly opaque but grammatically impeccable language of her own and confronts him with a one-act play in it, acted by her siblings. . . . Louie's ugly language is vengeance. Stead does not go as far as Louie. Her later style is merely craggy, unaccommodating, a simple, functional, often unbeautiful means to an end, which can still astonish by its directness. . . .

Since she is technically an expressionist writer, in whose books madmen scream in deserted landscapes, a blue light turns a woman into the image of a vampire and a lesbian party takes on the insanely heightened melodrama of a drawing by George Grosz, the *effect* is the thing, not the language that achieves it. But there is more to it than that. The way she finally writes is almost as if she were showing you by demonstration that style itself is a lie in action, that language is an elaborate confidence trick designed to lull us into acceptance of the intolerable, just as Sam Pollitt uses it on his family, that words are systems of deceit. And that truth is not a quality inherent in any kind of discourse, but a way of looking at things: that truth is not an aspect of reality but a test of reality. So, more and more, Stead concentrates on dialogue, on language in use as camouflage or subterfuge—dialogue, or rather serial monologue, for Stead's characters rarely listen to one another sufficiently to enable them to conduct dialogues together, although they frequently enjoy rows of a polyphonic nature, in which it is not possible for anybody to hear anybody else. If the storytellers in *The Salzburg Tales* reveal their personalities through the gnomic and discrete fables they tell, Stead's later characters thunder out great arias and recitatives of self-deceit, self-justification, attempted manipulation, and it is up to the reader to compare what they say with what they do and draw his or her conclusions as to what is really going on. The monologue is Stead's forte, dramatic monologues comparable to those of Robert Browning.

In *Letty Fox: Her Luck* . . . she extends this form of the dramatic monologue to the length of an entire novel. It is an elaborate imitation autobiography almost in the manner of Defoe, a completely successful impersonation of an American woman, in which we are invited to extract bare facts from Letty's account of her own life. . . . Letty is as full of bad faith as Nellie Cotter but is saved by her unpretentiousness and by what Stead calls somewhere the 'inherent outlawry' in women. . . .

Others in Stead's gallery of monsters of existential bad faith— Sam Pollitt, Nellie Cotter, Robert Grant in *A Little Tea, A Little Chat*—are not treated so genially. They are killers. They precipitate suicide and madness in those who come close to them. Letty uses bad faith to bolster her faltering self-respect: these pernicious beings base their entire self-respect on bad faith. The mouths of these grotesque, nodding carnival heads are moving all the time as they rage, bluster, cajole, manipulate, provoke, enlightening us as to what bad faith does.

Stead's fictional method obviously presupposes a confidence in the importance of fiction as the exposition of the real structures on which our lives are based. It follows that she has gained a reputation as a writer of naturalism. . . . Stead is certainly not a writer of naturalism nor of social realism, and if her novels are read as novels about our lives, rather than about the circumstances that shape our lives, they are bound to disappoint, because the naturalist or high-bourgeois mode works within the convention that there exists such a thing as 'private life'. In these private lives, actions are informed by certain innate inner freedoms and, however stringent the pressures upon the individual, there is always a little margin of autonomy which could be called 'the self'. For Stead, however, 'private life' is itself a socially-determined fiction, the 'self' is a mere foetus of autonomy which may or may not prove viable, and 'inner freedom', far from being an innate quality, is a precariously-held intellectual position that may be achieved only at the cost of enormous struggle, often against the very grain of what we take to be human feeling. . . .

The hard edges and sharp spikes of Stead's work are rarely, if ever, softened by the notion that things might be, generally, other than they are. It is tempting to conclude that she does not think much of the human race, but it is rather that she is appalled by the human condition. It is illuminating that Teresa, in *For Love Alone,* says to herself, near the end of the novel: 'I only have to do what is supposed to be wrong and I have a happiness that is barely credible.' Teresa has freely chosen to be unfaithful to her beloved lover, to follow her own desire. To become free, she has exercised her will; to remain free, she follows her desires. Stead rarely states her subversive intent as explicitly as this, nor often suggests that the mind-forged manacles of the human condition are to be so easily confounded. But when Teresa meditates, 'It was easy to see how upsetting it would be if women began to love freely,' she is raising the question of female desire, of women's sexuality as action and as choice, of the assertion of sexuality as a right, and this question, to which she returns again and again in various ways, is at the core of Stead's work. (p. 12)

For Love Alone is an account of a woman's fight for the right to love in freedom. . . . This is a fight we see one woman, Teresa herself, win. . . . Stead then published *Letty Fox: Her Luck,* a crazy comedy about a girl who fights, and fights dirty, to get a ring on her finger. It is as if Stead were saying: 'There is Teresa, yes: but there is also Letty.' . . . Thesis and antithesis, as if the successive novels were parts of one long argument.

Stead's work always has this movement, always contains a movement forward and then a withdrawal to a different position. *A Little Tea, A Little Chat,* her New York novel of 1948, presents us with another kind of woman: the thoroughly venal Barbara Kent, who is depicted almost exclusively from the outside. She is a mystery, with a complicated but largely concealed past, and she does not say much. She is like a secret agent from the outlawry of women, on a mission to destroy. . . . The novel makes a seamless equation between sexual exploitation and economic exploitation. It thoroughly trashes all the social and economic relations of the USA. It etches in acid an impressive picture of New York as the city of the damned. It is also, as is all Stead, rich in humour of the blackest kind. It occurs to me that Stead has a good deal in common with Luis Buñuel, if it is possible to imagine a Buñuel within a lapsed Protestant tradition. A Calvinist Buñuel, whose belief in grace has survived belief in God.

However, this definitive account of a New York fit to be destroyed by fire from heaven is followed, in 1952, by *The People with the Dogs,* a description of a charming clan of New York intelligentsia who are modestly and unself-consciously virtuous and, although bonded by blood, are each other's best friends. Why is Stead playing happy families, all of a sudden? What, one wonders, is she trying to prove? Perhaps, that amongst the infinite contradictions of the USA, where anything is possible, even Utopia might be possible. . . . Stead seems to be saying that, given a small private income, beautiful people can lead beautiful lives, although the very circumstances which nourish their human kindness are those which succour the morally deformed profiteers and whores of *A Little Tea, A Little Chat.*

But there is something odd about *The People with the Dogs,* as if the dynamo of her energy, ill-supplied with the fuel of distaste, were flagging. She permits the Massines to be charming and even writes about them in a charming way, as if she herself has been moved by the beautiful promise of the Statue of Liberty, which always touches the heart no matter how often it is betrayed. There is nothing fraudulent about this novel, although, perhaps revealingly, it is exceedingly carelessly written. (pp. 12-13)

An internal logic of dialectical sequels connects all Stead's work in a single massive argument on the themes of sexual relations, economic relations and politics. . . . If I were to choose an introductory motto for the collected works of Christina Stead, it would be . . . from Blake, from *The Marriage of Heaven and Hell.* It would be: 'Without contraries is no progression. Attraction and repulsion, Reason and Energy, Love and Hate, are necessary to Human existence.' One might take this as a point to begin the exploration of this most undervalued of our contemporaries. (p. 13)

Angela Carter, *"Unhappy Families," in* London Review of Books, *September 16 to October 6, 1982, pp. 11-13.*

JOAN LIDOFF

At the heart of Christina Stead's fiction echoes the persistent moral issue: egotism. She sees everyone striving by subtle or overt manipulations to subordinate others to his or her own needs and desires, trying to take as much while giving as little as possible. In her 1940 masterpiece, *The Man Who Loved Children,* Stead criticizes this ongoing struggle between competing egotisms, not only in her characterization and analysis, but in the very form of her fiction. This novel takes as protagonist no single hero, but an entire family. The animating conflicts from which Stead has constructed her story are the

manifold tensions of family life. She shows each of her characters from his or her own point of view, but also as seen by the others. Creating all of her characters as they affect and are affected by each other, Stead achieves a multiple layering of distinct and fully developed perspectives. The world of the novel is an ironic suspension of the constantly colliding visions of the distinct personalities within the family, through which the family as a whole comes to life as a dynamic organism with its own personality and vitality. This interlayering of views is the objective correlative of Stead's moral stance against egotism. Through her imaginative generosity, she achieves in this novel what none of her characters do, a vision broader than the egotistical one, which admits the claim to life, space, and integrity of more than a single sensibility. (pp. 14-15)

One of Stead's special skills is to render with profuse particularity individual characters and dynamics so as to make clear their universal significance. . . . [This novel] penetrates the surfaces of personal sentiment and social pretense to expose an ongoing battle of domination, humiliation, and resistance that goes by the name of family love. Family relationships become psychological struggles in which female and male, young and old, the powerless and the powerful, are locked in relentless opposition. . . . And Stead shows with special brilliance the connection between the politics of the family and those of the larger world. In spite of this relentless analysis, however, Stead takes zestful delight in the very range of personal differences that such struggles seek to deny. With little of her characters' need to reduce the variety of experience to simple abstractions, she not only tolerates but enjoys multiplicity. The abundance of Stead's imagination is manifest in her exuberantly inventive imagery and in the vast range of human and natural detail she draws within her fiction's net. (p. 15)

Like an individual, a family establishes a self-image, a family myth, which allots each individual a characterization and a place within the working whole. The myth functions smoothly to the degree that each member accepts it and its commonly held explanation of the tenor of experience and of individual behavior. Significant deviation from its silently agreed-upon system of explanations and tacit rules upsets the finely integrated balance of family dynamics.

With ruthless persistence, Stead's narrative unmasks mechanics that the family mythology conceals, undercutting family fictions with unyielding revelations of the least graceful or generous of motives. Like fiction, the family myth lends coherence and meaning to experience; when it is shattered (before it gradually reforms), chaos ensues. Stead's special art, always, is to render this chaos in aesthetic form, to find a shape for shapelessness.

Stead captures the family organism in the process of change and growth. She does so by giving us a young heroine painfully probing, dissecting and discarding the family myth. Thirteen-year-old Louisa Pollitt starts to question her parents' versions of reality. She begins to develop an independent vision, which changes her perception of the family, and ours.

The real development in the novel is found in the multiple, changing visions and re-visions of the same core of family experience. The actual story of *The Man Who Loved Children* is rather melodramatic; more interested in the psychological exploration of character than in event, Stead is not an architect of well-built plots. She works, rather, . . . by compiling scenes of emotional and moral climax. *The Man Who Loved Children,* however, has a firmer structure than any of Stead's other novels, its unities lent by the family it describes. (pp. 17-18)

The power of vision and of language to shape vision is one of Stead's central subjects. Each of Stead's characters is determined by a different rhetoric, and each is extreme. While they are all acting on the same stage, the Pollits are reading scripts from different plays. Though both are characters of commanding imaginative and rhetorical power, Sam and Henny are so different that they scarcely speak the same language. Stead profoundly understands the way the primary gender division is a metaphor for the strife of otherness, the constant tension caused by the need to live with the existence of other wills and souls than our own. In Sam and Henny Pollit, Stead distinguishes a masculine and a feminine vision, at such irreconcilable poles that communication is almost impossible. (p. 19)

Setting her novel at the beginning of Louie's adolescence, Stead chooses a moment of crisis at which old family structures and mythologies are challenged. Louie's awakening sexuality evokes Henny's negative feelings about her own femininity, as well as her conflicts with her stepdaughter. Sex becomes an overt issue, and subtle shifts in the balance of power of the family configuration occur. Louie moves away from her strong attachment to her father and her acceptance of his point of view as absolute, into a new alliance with Henny (the coalition of the oppressed that unites the women of this novel). (p. 20)

The battle for control between Sam and Louie is fought in and over language, as Louie insists on the right to articulate her altered perceptions. The dramatic world views of Sam and Henny Pollit clash and collide to create a world for their children. As Louie's developing vision recasts the old family mythologies, it lends ironic perspective to the closed systems of her parents' thought and behavior. The tension of the conflict of Louie's vision with those from which it was derived generates the field of force of this novel, which frames all of these smaller visions in a wise if dark understanding.

To embody her own complex vision, Stead creates a style I call the Domestic Gothic, one which draws on a distinctive kind of grotesque imagery. Stead does what Louie wished to do: "invent an extensive language to express every shade of her ideas." "I never told any one what it is like at home . . . because no one would believe me!" cries thirteen-year-old Louisa; and indeed, the situations and conversations Stead reports, while not impossible, are extreme. The imagery and action of Stead's fiction are true not so much to ordinary behavior as to the workings of the inner life. Stead turns what Christopher Ricks describes as the "false . . . overblown, indiscriminately theatrical" rhetoric we use when "we speak to ourselves in the privacy of our skulls" into external speech that exceeds the cadences of normal conversation in order to expose fantasies ordinarily kept hidden and reveal the characters' personal ways of seeing.

Stead recasts words into new associations which, disjointed and dislocated, create painful new perceptions. While she never cedes her fiction to the forms of inner consciousness—like Joyce or Woolf or Kafka—she exploits the psychological fluidity of grotesque techniques. In her prose, unexpected analogies juxtapose the animate and the inanimate, animal and human, confounding the distinctions between them. Though people may be described in cockroach imagery, however, they do not become cockroaches, as they would in Kafka. Stead creates no logical or even psychological impossibilities; her

grotesque metaphors are used to give visible shape to her characters' distress. With realism more psychological than behavioral, Stead turns fantasies into fictional events and uses metaphor and dialogue to expose the emotional distortions of her characters' private realities. (pp. 21-2)

In Stead's distortions, paradoxically, is her story's realism. The family Stead recreates for us in *The Man Who Loved Children* is not quite like any we might see. It is closer to that internalized version of family experience that an individual reshapes to accord with his or her fears and desires, resentments, angers, and wishes. Stead and her characters create a world of language that penetrates by its very excesses to this psychological core of intensified experience.

While everything in Stead's fiction is intensified, stained with the violent colors of fantasy, the texture of her prose is nevertheless dense with naturalistic renderings of the material world and acute observations of the human. For all the extremity of language and feeling, the setting and materials of this novel are not surreal but ordinary. Though pervasively colored by the emotional and metaphorical excesses of gothic fiction, unlike the gothic, Stead's novel operates within the context of nineteenth-century realism. . . . Its settings and situations, characters and events, are realistic, or nearly so, its materials domestic commonplaces: housework, eating, playing, shopping, visiting. *The Man Who Loved Children* is rooted in a real time and place; its characters are neither stylized villains nor innocent victims, but complex figures with humanly mixed motivations. Stead's plotting and characterization, however, draw from the depths of the subterranean fantasy world that informs gothic fiction. Her grotesque imagery projects these violent fantasies onto the physical world, using ordinary domestic vehicles to release the emotional forces that seethe beneath ordinary events. This Domestic Gothic style with its capacity to encompass fantasy in the quotidian world, balances profound access to the turmoils of the inner life with equally acute observation of the natural and political world to express the comprehensive moral vision of the novel, one of depth and breadth of understanding greater than that of any of its characters. (pp. 22-3)

Of all the distinctive linguistic styles of this novel, the most interesting is that of Stead's framing narrative voice. In both style and spirit, Stead shares some of the charm and vitality of Charles Dickens. . . . (p. 53)

She has Dickens's comic eye for significant animating detail, and his ear for the exaggerated rhetoric with which they both define the idiosyncratic characters they delight in. *The Man Who Loved Children* is full of Dickens allusions. . . . But Dickens's direct influence is less striking than their similarities of vision and technique, most pronounced in the pervasive use each makes of the grotesque. Stead's Domestic Gothic style is devoted to the moral seriousness and specificity of observation of the quotidian, the concern with character and social relations of nineteenth-century realism. Simultaneously, like Dickens, she uses the grotesque to probe beneath the surfaces to capture, without entirley taming, the emotional field she finds in the depths of the human psyche. Writing in the immediate tradition of the nineteenth-century novel, Stead stands, however, on this side of Freud. She shuns the nostalgia frequently found in that genre, and the particular form in which it appears in Dickens, as dualism.

Stead's novel is colored by neither yearning for a lost golden past nor hopes for an idealized future. While both Stead and

Dickens perceive a world of oppressors and oppressed, built around the core of a child's feeling of helplessness in the face of adult power, Dickens mourns the destruction of an innocence Stead believes never existed; nor does Stead see in simplified black and white moral dimensions. There are in Stead no refuges in the past or future. The ideal of the middle-class family that, though remote, suggests for Dickens escape from exploitation at a cozy fireside is for Stead the crucible of strife. Dickens characters are "terrifyingly alone and unrelated." They meet in "sudden confrontations between persons whose ways of life have no habitual or logical continuity with each other." Dickens seems to imply their wistful solitariness and frequent silences might be dispelled by community. While Stead's characters collide rather than collaborate, in the Pollit family there is all too much "togetherness." Though their emotional interactions are nearly all conflicts, they are emotionally intertwined. Their intimacy is not satisfying, but they are intimate. The Pollits are inextricably connected by the habit of family life, and it does not do for them quite what Dickens hoped. (pp. 54-5)

Intrinsic to Stead's unsentimental stance is the absence of idealization in her fiction. She does not divide her characters into separate good and bad figures: Sam Pollit is both the tyrannical villain Mr. Murdstone, and Mr. Micawber, the loving, ineffectual father. In Stead's novel, there are no disciplined hearts capable of mature love, the ideal for which Dickens heroes strive. The Pollit children think adults "unreasonable, violent beings, the toys of their own monstrous tempers and egotisms." Yet, an overgrown child himself, Sam does love his children, in his way; and Henny, with all her vileness and violence, loves them too. What affection the Pollit children get comes not from separate idealized parental figures, but from these mixed characters themselves.

Stead is ruthlessly unsentimental. The restraint she exerts on feeling if not on form keeps her free from self-pity though often from pity as well. Dickens likes his good characters; he approved warmly of them and invites the reader's approval. Stead's sympathy is more tinged with distaste and controlled by ironic distance; it is expressed as acceptance rather than approval.

Like Dickens, Stead delves into fantasy to release energy both comic and aggressive, creative and destructive, and reveals the violence usually suppressed in everyday behavior. In *The Man Who Loved Children*, Stead's fantasy and realism, passionate language and tight ironic control reach their most productive equilibrium, and this, the best of her novels, stands at a height few other novelists achieve and she herself will never reach again. (pp. 55-6)

Joan Lidoff, in her Christina Stead, *Frederick Ungar Publishing Co., 1982, 255 p.*

J(ohn) I(nnes) M(ackintosh) Stewart

1906-

(Also writes under pseudonym of Michael Innes) English novelist, short story writer, critic, essayist, and biographer.

Stewart is best known as the prolific author of intricately plotted detective novels written under the pseudonym of Michael Innes. Through their academic settings and intellectual themes, these works reflect Stewart's status as a retired Oxford don. The main character in most of these novels is John Appleby, a gentleman-detective who solves his cases through a combination of skill and intuition. The series has followed Appleby from inspector to knighted chief of police and into retirement.

Stewart's fiction published under his own name has much in common with the John Appleby series, including scholarly settings and themes, humorous elements, and an interest in the world of art. However, rather than concentrating on art as their subject, as in the detective novels, these works deal with the artist's creative process and his role in society.

Critics admire Stewart's ability to be both suspenseful and insightful in all his fiction. Among the later John Appleby novels are *Sharks and Adders* (1982) and *Appleby and Honeybath* (1983); under his own name Stewart has recently published *The Bridge at Arta and Other Stories* (1982) and *A Villa in France* (1982).

(See also *CLC*, Vols. 7, 14 and *Contemporary Authors*, Vols. 85-88.)

Courtesy of Dodd, Mead & Company

MICHAEL INNES

John Appleby came into being during a sea voyage from Liverpool to Adelaide. Ocean travel was a leisured affair in those days, and the route by the Cape of Good Hope took six weeks to cover. By that time I had completed a novel called *Death at the President's Lodging* (*Seven Suspects* in the U.S.A.) in which a youngish inspector from Scotland Yard solves the mystery of the murder of Dr. Umpleby, the president of one of the constituent colleges of Oxford University. It is an immensely complicated murder, and Appleby is kept so busy getting it straight that he has very little leisure to exhibit himself to us in any point of character or origins. But these, in so far as they are apparent, derive, I am sure, from other people's detective stories. I was simply writing a yarn to beguile a somewhat tedious experience—and in a popular literary kind at that time allowable as an occasional diversion even to quite serious and even learned persons, including university professors. (p. 11)

Appleby arrives in Oxford in a "great yellow Bentley"—which suggests one sort of thriller writing, not of the most sophisticated sort. But "Appleby's personality seemed at first thin, part effaced by some long discipline of study, like a surgeon whose individuality has concentrated itself within the channels of a unique operative technique." This is altogether more highbrow, although again not exactly original. And Appleby goes on to show himself quite formidably educated, particularly in the way of classical literature. . . . This must be regarded as a

little out of the way in a London bobby lately off the beat. And there is no sign that Appleby is other than this; he is not the newfangled sort of policeman (if indeed such then existed) recruited from a university. Research in this volume will show that he is definitely not himself an Oxford man. (pp. 11-12)

What Appleby does possess in this early phase of his career is (I am inclined to think) a fairly notable power of orderly analysis. Had he been a professor himself, he would have made a capital expository lecturer. But I am far from claiming that he long retains this power; later on he is hazardously given to flashes of intuition, and to picking up clues on the strength of his mysteriously acquired familiarity with recondite artistic and literary matters. (p. 12)

What I am claiming here (the reader will readily perceive) is that Appleby is as much concerned to provide miscellaneous and unassuming "civilized" entertainment as he is to hunt down baddies wherever they may lurk. And I think this must be why he has proved fairly long-lived: and by this I mean primarily long-lived in his creator's imagination. In forty years I have never quite got tired of John Appleby as a pivot round which farce and mild comedy and parody and freakish fantasy revolve. (pp. 12-13)

[Appleby] is within a society remembered rather than observed—and remembered in terms of literary conventions which are themselves distancing themselves as his creator works. His is an expatriate's world. It is not a real world, controlled by actual and contemporary social pressures, any more than is, say, the world of P. G. Wodehouse.

But the sphere of Appleby's operations is conditioned by other and, as it were, more simply technical factors. Why does he move, in the main, through great houses and amid top people: what an Englishman might call the territory of *Who's Who*? It might be maintained that it is just because he likes it that way. We never learn quite where he comes from. . . . Eventually he makes a very convincing commissioner of Metropolitan Police, which is Britain's highest job in a police service. I'm not sure that he isn't more verisimilar in this role than he is as a keen young detective crawling about the floor looking for things. So one might aver that he finds his way into all those august dwellings because he fancies life that way.

But this isn't quite the fact of the matter. In serious English fiction, as distinct from a fiction of entertainment, the great house has long been a symbol—or rather a microcosm—of ordered society; of a complex, but on the whole harmonious, community. And indeed French, Russian, and American novelists have tended to see life that way; in the "English" novel the grandest houses of all have been invented by Henry James.

Something of this has rubbed off on the novel's poor relation, the detective story—the more readily, perhaps, because in England itself that sort of story was in its heyday rather an upper-class addiction.

But Appleby, like many of his fellow-sleuths in the genre, roams those great houses for a different and, as I have said, technical reason. The mansion, the country seat, the ducal palace, is really an extension of the sealed room, defining the spatial, the territorial boundaries of a problem. One can, of course, extract a similar effect out of a compact apartment or a semidetached villa. But these are rather cramping places to prowl in. And in detective stories detectives and their quarry alike must prowl. (pp. 13-15)

There is one other point that strikes me about him as I leaf through his chronicles. They *are* chronicles in the sense that time is flowing past in them at least in one regard. The social scene may be embalmed in that baronets abound in their libraries and butlers peer out of every pantry. But Appleby himself ages, and in some respects perhaps even matures. He ages along with his creator, and like his creator ends up as a retired man who still a little meddles with the concerns of his green unknowing youth. (p. 15)

> Michael Innes, "John Appleby," in The Great Detectives, *edited by Otto Penzler, Little, Brown and Company, 1978, pp. 9-15.*

CONNIE FLETCHER

The coast of Cornwall is the setting for [*The Ampersand Papers*], Sir John Appleby's return to crime investigation. The retired Scotland Yard inspector is admiring Treskinnick Castle when the external staircase to the tower collapses and Appleby witnesses an old man plunging to his death. . . . Appleby senses murder, and his investigation leads him to the core of family enmity and a fascinating literary puzzle involving correspondence between Ampersand's ancestor Adrian Digitt and Percy Bysshe Shelley.

> *Connie Fletcher, in a review of "The Ampersand Papers," in* Booklist, *Vol. 75, No. 16, April 15, 1979, p. 1274.*

NEWGATE CALLENDAR

[A] veteran writer who sees people clearly and with compassion is Michael Innes, and he brings Sir John Appleby back once again in **"The Ampersand Papers."** . . . Any Innes performance is sure to be urbane and amusing, and his latest book follows the pattern. There is plenty of background before Sir John appears (he is witness to the fatal accident), and the background includes a look at decaying British nobility. Mr. Innes has a lot of fun with the mental incapacities of a stuffy old lord, who in a way comes right out of P. G. Wodehouse.

There is also something about literary remains, a subject about which Mr. Innes knows a great deal. . . . But Michael Innes wears his learning lightly, and **"The Ampersand Papers,"** one of the lighter and less consequential in the Appleby series, is an utter delight.

> *Newgate Callendar, in a review of "The Ampersand Papers," in* The New York Times Book Review, *April 29, 1979, p. 22.*

A. N. WILSON

Opening a new volume by J.I.M. Stewart always provides one with the reassuring impression that art stopped short somewhere during the leisurely reign of George V. It is like coming off the busy squalor of Piccadilly and pushing back the door of some fusty old London club, where the leather armchairs and the thick Turkey carpets and the dull tick of the old clock seem to belie the existence of the modern world. . . . [*The Bridge at Arta and Other Stories*] is as polished and solid as an old mahogany table. . . .

Being one of the most accomplished authors of detective stories in our language, Mr Stewart has no difficulty in concocting improbable and exciting twists of plot whenever he picks up his pen. His delight in Henry James has never prompted him to imitate the Master's curiosity about the puzzling enigmas of human character. His medium is deft caricature, and the division between Michael Innes and J.I.M. Stewart, has, over the years, become so slight as to be inconsiderable. He does not provoke helpless laughter, like P. G. Wodehouse; something more of a chortle, a fruity, slightly donnish smirk is what his stories aim to produce. But like Wodehouse, the world he has created is entirely self-sufficient. The plots hang on lost art treasures, academic jiggery-pokery, macabre twists of fortune in colleges and country houses. And our pleasure in them is neither diminished nor increased by their complete lack of resemblance to anything which any of us would ever have called the real world. The snobbery, for example, of the Stewart world is totally innocent and fantastical. No one here speaks, in Anthony Powell's faintly creepy phrase of 'breaking new ground'. The hierarchy remains as untouchable as that which supports Lord Emsworth. The clever, good-looking plebs go on being plebs. However attractive they may be to males or females of the upper crust, they are happy, on the whole, to leave it that way.

> *A. N. Wilson, "Gentle Malice," in* The Spectator, *Vol. 247, No. 7999, October 31, 1981, p. 22.*

NEWGATE CALLENDAR

"Lord Mullion's Secret" is a throwback to the classic British mystery of the 1930's. Charles Honeybath of the Royal Academy, who has appeared in previous Innes books, is here engaged to paint a portrait of the lady of a castle.

Yes, a castle, inhabited by types beloved of British mystery writers of the past. There is a noble family, including a dotty old aunt. There are a disagreeable son, a rather mysterious young gardener of obviously superior breeding and two nice girls. There is a fake miniature substituted for a valuable Elizabethan one. In fact, the book has everything but sliding panels and secret rooms. And the prose matches. "You scoundrel, stop that instantly!" says Honeybath. Lovely.

> *Newgate Callendar, in a review of "Lord Mullion's Secret," in* The New York Times Book Review, *February 14, 1982, p. 22.*

BRYN CALESS

J.I.M. Stewart is well known as an academic, a prolific novelist, short-story writer and author of thrillers under the pen-name of Michael Innes. This time he has his short-fiction hat on, and has produced five stories and a novella (of some sixty pages) for [**The Bridge at Arta and Other Stories**]. . . . [All of the stories] exhibit that expertise in construction which is a Stewart hallmark. The first story, **'The Bridge at Arta',** is an ironic sketch of a widow meeting her first husband, whom she had divorced fifty years before. It affords Stewart the opportunity for wry reflections and juxtapositions, and although the characters are slight there is enough background interest to retain our attention. The same cannot be said of the long **'The Time Bomb'**, which takes ages to explode and does so only then like a damp squib. . . . The next story, **'The Little Duffer'**, about a boy wrongly accused of arson, is infinitely better since Stewart tries less hard to be clever and gives more time to developing the narrative. **'A Reading in Trollope'**, which concerns snobbery and family honour, would provide a pleasant diversion without the irritating academic overlay and too insistent irony. The final stories, **'The Chomsky File'** and **'The Real Thing'**, are competent, artificial exercises in applied irony.

Stewart is an able writer, but this collection suffers from several drawbacks. It is too much a performance, an elaborate orchestration of language without consideration of aim or purpose; the characters are too limited—academics or businessmen (and boring as well); and the plots are mere artifices for making philosophical excursions into the lofty. More muscle and less posturing would help the collection away from the banal, the quaint and the 'historical—literary'.

> *Bryn Caless, in a review of "The Bridge at Arta and Other Stories," in* British Book News, *May, 1982, p. 321.*

MARGHANITA LASKI

[With] Innes one can be confident of an elegant tale which, though easily putdownable without itchy suspense, is almost certain to be picked up again; and so it is with *Sheiks and Adders*, whose locale is a vulgar garden-party. But how, in such a phantasmagoria of improbability, even such a policeman (or ex-policeman) as Appleby may judge plausibility from reality is not to be known.

> *Marghanita Laski, "Feeling Like Death," in* The Listener, *Vol. 108, No. 2771, July 29, 1982, p. 27.**

HARRIETT GILBERT

[J.I.M. Stewart] has written, in *A Villa in France,* an eminently readable, amusing and vacuous novel. A pastiche on the styles and preoccupations of Trollope, Proust and—above all—Jane Austen, it has for its heroine a parson's daughter who, while a schoolgirl, refuses the hand of a dissolute, playwright neighbour; later to marry his tedious brother—an impoverished Catholic academic. Whether intentionally or otherwise, the plot pretty soon deteriorates into something closer to Mary Stewart than Austen—with mysterious wills, and strange young men lurking in foreign villas—while the disappointing denouement shows signs of authorial laziness, or boredom, or both. But then, as Stewart says in passing, when 'reviewed in batches by acrid women' what chance does a novel stand?

> *Harriett Gilbert, "Lunacies," in* New Statesman, *Vol. 104, No. 2695, November 12, 1982, p. 33.**

ANATOLE BROYARD

Michael Innes is one of those almost relentlessly-literary mystery writers who are "thick on the ground," as he would say, only in England. In **"Sheiks and Adders,"** his usual hero, Sir John Appleby, the retired head of the London police, is given to what might be called arch ratiocination. He goes to a local fete at Drool Court, for example, merely out of a curiosity to know why Cherry Chitfield's father "was being so intransigent over the detail of a particular piece of miming or charade." He is drawn to the fete "by a sense of a small mystery," which is surely the idlest speculation ever indulged in even by a retired English policeman.

Sir John is witty. He notices that when people dress up at a fancy dress ball, they do it literally, in the sense of upward mobility, choosing costumes of rather exalted rank. Mark Chitfield is an exception. He comes in rags as one of the Seven Deadly Sins, in order to "afford a juster representation of the human condition." For reasons buried in the plot of **"Sheiks and Adders,"** one of the guests is a real sheik pretending to be someone who is pretending to be a real sheik.

Mark is described by one of his peers as having "succumbed a little too much to education." A philologist points out that "the feminine of Führer means bus conductor." A party of Druids perform what is called "a perlustration of the house." A threatened Arab Emir refuses all sorts of security measures designed to protect him because they violate his sense of panache. There is a professor of advanced herpetology whose live specimens play an important part in the action, and a balloonist who also has his moment.

Though there is a murder in **"Sheiks and Adders,"** most of the shooting is at language, and this raises questions about the role of wit in mystery novels. Is wit an escape, or just another reminder that we must grin and bear the world? Will the punch line replace the punch in the jaw? Is wit fun to curl up with? Is it suspenseful?

One of the functions of the mystery novel is to let the reader regress in peace, and wit often interferes with that. It keeps teasing us to take on again the burden of our sophistication. Also, in witty mysteries, the joke begins to extend to the plot, which the reader then ceases to take seriously, so that the whole enterprise is likely to collapse into parody. Certainly the most popular mystery writers—such as Helen MacInnes and John Creasy—are deadly serious.

Anatole Broyard, "2 Civilized Mysteries," in The New York Times, December 11, 1982, p. 15.*

STEPHEN BANN

If a 19th-century paternity exists for [*A Villa in France*], it is surely in the mannered accomplishments of George Meredith, who is credited in passing with being the most recent novelist to be studied in the Oxford English School. *A Villa in France* has that beguiling property—so eminently characteristic of Meredith—of seeming to slide more or less uncontrollably between epochs. This is partly because the characters themselves seem to be based as much on well-known fictional prototypes as on anything specific to period and place: the Rev. Henry Rich is described on the first page as coming 'straight out of *Mansfield Park*', and it is a matter for debate whether he succeeds in emerging from that rarefied world. It is partly because Henry Rich's obsession with Time—which at one point he characterises as moving in our imaginations from left to right, like the reading of a book—spills over into the construction of the narrative. Events that might have been supposed to be important, like the deaths of two principal characters, are relegated to a dismissively subordinate position. . . .

The fact that J.I.M. Stewart is also the detective writer Michael Innes leads me to think that a clue may be lurking around these uncompromising demises. An innocent question is asked at the mid-way stage of the novel: 'Who wrote a novel called *The Amazing Marriage*?' Penelope Rich, the heroine, knows her Meredith, and can reply to the question, which has very little relevance to the issues being debated at the time. But the 'amazement' provoked by Fulke Ferneydale's death and legacy (the 'Villa in France' of the title) suggests that what we have in fact been following is an immensely protracted peripeteia, a plot which must be called devious even by Meredith's standards. Penelope must be placed in the deliberately contrived circumstances set up by Fulke Ferneydale's will, in order for her earlier, unsuccessful marriage to be nullified and superseded. When, like Homer's Penelope, she has been rescued from the attentions of the over-assiduous and dishonest suitor placed by Fulke to capture her, she can herself take the initiative in setting matters right. She proposes to, and is accepted by, her rescuer.

It really seems as if Dr Stewart has tried to write something which is as distant as possible from the design of a detective story. Instead of resolving the carefully distributed clues into a satisfactory solution, *A Villa in France* is full of random indications which both stress its literariness and resist incorporation into the plot. Penelope's eventual triumph is a triumph over plot, since the story of her seduction which Fulke has designed as his sadistic legacy is transformed into the story of her independent proposal of marriage. The feminist assertion (as in Meredith) implies a derangement of the customary strategies of narration. One is left with the puzzling conclusion that this . . . is a feminist book. (p. 11)

Stephen Bann, "Mythic Elements," in London Review of Books, December 30, 1982 to January 19, 1983, pp. 10-11.*

ROGER LEWIS

J.I.M. Stewart is a retired fellow of an Oxford college and *My Aunt Christina* is a book of short stories, each with an academic ring. Ostensibly tales of the unexpected, denouements can in fact be easily guessed. As a consolation the collection turns into an Eng. Lit. kit, with allusions made to other works. *The Aspern Papers* is behind Aunt Christina's secret trove and also **'The Doctor's Son'**, in which a vicar's annotations are found to be brilliant pieces of textual criticism. *The Picture of Dorian Gray* is the progenitor of Perley's pictures—by an artist who paints not what he sees but what will be seen. Michael Furey, the singer, is the name of the plaintive voice who sang to Gretta Conroy in Joyce's 'The Dead'.

Roger Lewis, "Left-Overs," in New Statesman, Vol. 105, No. 2722, May 20, 1983, p. 27.*

BOOKS AND BOOKMEN

If you recall all the epithets that have been used to describe Michael Innes' books in the past and repeat them [about *Appleby and Honeybath*], you will be pretty near the mark. A country house weekend, a body in a library, a most knowing butler and a houseful of rather eccentric guests would seem to be a recipe for a cliché-heavy whodunnit in the classic mould. Michael Innes does not exactly break the mould but he stands the clichés on their head with a flick of his whisk turns stodge into soufflé. As in *Sheiks and Adders* we can only marvel at what a long way a little style will make the old ingredients go. . . . Literature and art combine in the solution as they do in the book's composition. It is a slim volume but not one to gallop through, for its many pleasures of phrase, cameo, and characterization should be sampled slowly by the discerning palate.

A review of "Appleby and Honeybath," in Books and Bookmen, No. 333, June, 1983, p. 28.

ANATOLE BROYARD

Michael Innes, as experienced mystery readers know by now, is an Oxford don, and his suspense novels give us the kind of pleasures peculiar to Oxford dons. There is so much bel canto in them that the mystery assumes a secondary place, like the libretto of an opera. Yet, it could be maintained in his defense that wit, learning, civility and British eccentricity are all, in a sense, more mysterious than violence or crime.

In **"Appleby and Honeybath,"** there are "lurking miscreants" who "pernoctate," or remain in residence day and night, and detectives who ponder "velleities," which means impulses at the lowest level of volition. When Appleby, who has retired from his position of commissioner of metropolitan police, is drawn into a mystery during a weekend visit to a country house, his approach is naturally "teleological," or directed to the study of ultimate ends.

"Appleby and Honeybath" has the inestimable advantage of taking place in a British country house, and this gives Mr. Innes an opportunity to be amusing about architecture, landscaping, the class system, blood sports, the idea of the gentleman and other erudite questions. This particular country house contains lost drawings by Claude Lorrain and a never-published satire on the earlier tenants by none other than Alexander Pope, who, when he was turned out of the premises for rudeness, responded in savage heroic couplets. Honeybath, who is a portrait painter, provides what might be called a visual perspective on the problem of crime.

Mr. Innes gives his readers a lot of good talk, which is no small feat these days. . . . One character observes, "An incident in the briskly criminal way might liven us up." It is typical of Michael Innes that **"Appleby and Honeybath"** works the other way around. The characters liven up the crime, which is as it should be.

> *Anatole Broyard, in a review of "Appleby and Honeybath," in* The New York Times, *December 2, 1983, p. C25.*

ANNA SHAPIRO

The major ingredients in this staid little novel ["**An Open Prison**"] are: a proper English boys' public school; a boy whose father is sent to prison; an underclassman who is the grandson of the judge who sentenced the older boy's father; the father's prison break, and the subsequent running away of the two boys. . . . The story is narrated by Syson, the housemaster of the older boy, Robin, and from the outset clues pop up where there turns out to be no mystery. . . . As narrator, Syson comments on other people's remarks as being "oddly inconsequential," exactly what the accretion of clues turns out to be. His descriptions of characters are dully equivocal or weirdly at odds with his judgments of them; everybody's reactions seem to be either histrionically overstated or inappropriately muted. . . . Like so much else in the book, the digs seem to have no point unless it's all supposed to be a joke that Syson's incompetence as a housemaster is equaled by his ineptitude as a narrator. But reading a mystery that is more like a careful but meandering term paper is less like a joke to the reader than a joke on him.

> *Anna Shapiro, in a review of "An Open Prison," in* The New York Times Book Review, *July 29, 1984, p. 20.*

Julian (Gustave) Symons

1912-

English novelist, short story writer, poet, editor, historian, critic, biographer, and scriptwriter.

While Symons is well regarded as a poet, critic, and biographer, he is best known as the author of many highly praised crime novels. Unlike many authors of crime fiction, Symons is less concerned with presenting a baffling mystery than he is with exploring the state of society. From a skeptical and ironic perspective, Symons chronicles a world of decay, corruption, and alienation in which the distinction between lawbreaker and law keeper is often vague. Several of Symons's novels have Victorian or other historical settings, while others take place in the present. Critics claim that Symons's best fiction transcends the limitations of the mystery novel to stand as original and thought-provoking literature.

Symons first made his name in the 1930s as a poet, publishing two volumes of verse and editing a poetry journal. His reputation as a critic was also established before he published his first crime novel, and he has continued to write criticism, including books on Charles Dickens and Thomas Carlyle. Symons's interest in crime fiction has developed over his career. He initially viewed those works as secondary to his poetry and criticism but now sees them as an ideal forum for exploring the modern world. "If you want to show the violence that lives behind the bland faces most of us present to the world," he comments, "what better vehicle can you have than the crime novel?"

Symons's later publications reflect the diversity of his writings. *Bloody Murder* (1972) is a history of crime fiction built on the thesis that the plot-centered detective fiction of the 1920s and 1930s has given way to psychological crime novels that emphasize character and motivation. *The Tell-Tale Heart: The Life and Works of Edgar Allan Poe* (1978) is an unusual literary biography in that Symons refrains from conjecture as to the relationship between Poe's life and works. Two of Symons's recent fictional works reflect many of his recurrent thematic concerns. *The Tigers of Subtopia* (1983), a short story collection, features accounts of violence and cruelty in an apparently peaceful suburb, while *The Name of Annabel Lee* (1983) is a novel of failed love set against a backdrop of cultural decadence.

(See also *CLC*, Vols. 2, 14; *Contemporary Authors*, Vols. 49-52; and *Contemporary Authors New Revision Series*, Vol. 3.)

© *Thomas Victor 1984*

WILLIAM R. EVANS

Almost everyone likes a good mystery. Approximately one fourth of all fiction published in the United States and Great Britain falls into the category that includes crime fiction, detective stories, mysteries, thrillers, and spy novels. . . .

In his history of the genre [*Mortal Consequences*] Julian Symons traces its development from Poe's time to ours. All the major names are there, from Poe and his contemporaries— William Godwin, the first to delve into the psychological aspects of crime, and Eugene Vidocq, himself both criminal and detective—to such current authors as John Le Carré, Patricia Highsmith and Stanley Ellin. (p. 35)

The basic thesis of the book is that we have seen a change in the development of the mystery story from the intricate detective story with its emphasis on plot, which reached its peak in the Golden Age of the twenties and thirties, to the more psychological crime novel with its emphasis on character and motivation. Some writers are able to combine both elements effectively; Hammett is one example, and so is Julian Symons himself—his **"The Man Who Killed Himself"** contains a brilliant portrait of a fascinating murderer along with an extremely ingenious and suspenseful plot.

"Mortal Consequences" is probably the best book of its kind since Howard Haycraft's "Murder for Pleasure" which came out in 1941. It is too bad that there are so few books written about mysteries. One reason for this is that the genre is looked down on by most literary historians. Another is that most readers are too busy reading mysteries to think about them seriously. Julian Symons is an intelligent and perceptive man who has fallen into neither of these traps. (p. 36)

William R. Evans, in a review of "Mortal Consequences," in Best Sellers, *Vol. 32, No. 2, April 15, 1972, pp. 35-6.*

ROBERT HARRISON

If you have a passing interest in learning a bit about the detective story without having actually to read one, [*Mortal Consequences: A History From the Detective Story to the Crime Novel*] is just the book for you. Mr. Symons, with a good deal of critical insight and a pinch of condescension, tells us in his opening chapter what detective stories are ("part of the hybrid creature we call sensational literature") and why we read them (to exorcise "the guilt of the individual or the group through ritual and symbolic sacrifices"), then launches into a chronicle of the genre from the Godwin-Vidocq-Poe era to the present, gradually shedding enroute his academic regalia in favor of the fighting trunks of the professional reviewer cum literary critic.

When he analyzes, Mr. Symons is occasionally superb; when he opines, frequently silly. For instance, immediately after he has pointed out to us that the code of the Golden Age mystery writers dictated crimes should not be committed for reasons of state or on behalf of theoretical principles, we find him saying: "almost all of the British writers in the twenties and thirties, and most of the Americans, were unquestionably Right Wing. . . . It would have been unthinkable for them to create a Jewish detective, or a working-class one aggressively conscious of his origins. . . ." (pp. 384-85)

Despite occasional accesses of the how-can-you-stand-there-eating-that-cookie-while-little-children-starve syndrome (*viz.* "The Coles were both deeply involved in the Labour movement, and G.D.H. Cole was a famous figure within it, yet their books ignored the very existence of the social realities with which in life they were so much concerned"), the fact remains that Mr. Symons is quite literate and knowledgeable, and has a good nose for literary values. The mystery buff, with a bit of judicious skimming, will find the book useful in leading him to many choice and generally overlooked works in the field. I must emphasize the word "skimming," however, because often, to swell his essay to book length, Mr. Symons has committed the unpardonable sin of his profession: blowing the gaff. With malicious persistence he spoils stories for would-be readers, while telling those who have read them nothing they do not know already. . . . (p. 385)

> *Robert Harrison, in a review of "Mortal Consequences: A History from the Detective Story to the Crime Novel," in* The Georgia Review, *Vol. XXVI, No. 3, Fall, 1972, pp. 384-85.*

THE SPECTATOR

The Plot Against Roger Rider [is] by Julian Symons . . . , who is probably the foremost scholar of crime and thriller fiction now writing. Actually, there are two overlapping plots, one against Geoffrey Parradine, Rider's old friend, currently sleeping with Rider's wife; and one against Rider himself. There is a large cast of characters, and the action sweeps quickly from England to Spain and finally to Italy. disappearances and/or murders abound; there is a fetching Spanish detective who dreams of consuming bitter with his confréres of Scotland Yard and a pair of tiresome young lovers who, by pushing here and pulling there precipitate a solution to the eventual disappearance and death of Rider. It's an excellent, crackling read, but the structure is a little too academic; the cunning brain of the author of *Bloody Murder* is too busy with timetables rather than people; and the sociological orientations of that remarkable critique are too much in evidence, particularly in the case of

the young hero who can't make up his mind if he is queer or not. Good: but for Symons a bit disappointing.

> *A review of "The Plot against Roger Rider," in* The Spectator, *Vol. 231, No. 7572, August 11, 1973, p. 187.*

NEWGATE CALLENDAR

Leave it to Julian Symons. When he writes a mystery, you can be assured that this urbane stylist, this master of the traditional detective story, will have a puzzler that will keep your mind racing. And so it is with **"The Plot Against Roger Rider"**. . . . Even the title is comfortably traditional. But unlike such veterans as Agatha Christie, there is nothing old-fashioned about Symons. His dialogue is crisp and modern. He is capable of wry humor without becoming heavyhanded about it. And his characters have life in them.

In **"Roger Rider,"** Symons has cooked up a plot about the love-hate relationship of a domineering, successful man with one of his employees—and the relationships of those associated with him. All of this is done in virtuoso fashion, even if the pace is slow. Symons spends much time establishing those relationships. Not until he's at the half-way mark does catastrophe strike. There may be some slight murmurs about least likely suspects. But after it is all over, it can be seen that the author has played fair within the conventions. As he always does.

> *Newgate Callendar, in a review of "The Plot against Roger Rider," in* The New York Times Book Review, *December 9, 1973, p. 50.*

THE NEW YORKER

Mr. Symons is always an enjoyably sly and deceiving writer, and he has seldom been trickier than in [*The Plot Against Roger Rider*]. . . . It is not, however, among his better stories. He has seldom been so diffuse or so labored, and he has never been so tediously generous with unnecessary characters and unfinished subplots. It must also be said that although he gives us a plentitude of bloody murders, nothing much seems to happen.

> *A review of "The Plot against Roger Rider," in* The New Yorker, *Vol. XLIX, No. 42, December 10, 1973, p. 200.*

THE SPECTATOR

I have to say that Julian Symons's *Bloody Murder* . . . ("heartily recommended" in these columns by Kingsley Amis when it appeared in hardback; and, in spite of what I have to say, essential reading for all crime fans) is a pernicious and dangerous piece of work. In essence this book—sub-titled 'From the Detective Story to the Crime Novel: a history'—is a sustained and bitter, if unacknowledged, attack on the classical detective story, and on Dorothy Sayers in particular.

The fundamental fact is that Symons prefers the brooding, psychological, sociological modernism of Simenon and his followers to the puzzle story of the Golden Age of detective fiction; and to enforce this preference he tells all manner of fibs about the detective puzzles of the 'twenties and 'thirties—*viz.*, that their structure forbade characterisation, that their heroes and people were of purest cardboard, that the puzzle element itself forbade human interest. Hastily acknowledging Sayers's quality as a crime critic, Symons ignores the detailed passages in *Gaudy Night* in which Lord Peter and Harriet discuss just this problem, and triumphantly resolve it. Again, the high and beautiful comedy of the Ngaio Marsh novels is to all intents and purposes ignored, in favour of a friendly study of the appallingly cardboardish Agatha Christie.

Enough, or almost enough, said; but the ghosts of the Golden Age continue to rise up to reproach Julian Symons. . . .

Its basic proposition is that the detection element in a story—the puzzle element, to put it more precisely—tends to exclude the human; and that, therefore, the purer a detective story is the more bloodless it is, unless the author has an imagination sufficiently powerful to create a figure of myth—like Sherlock Holmes. Now, of course it is true that the detective element in a detective story, if over-pursued, will exclude the human, the literary and the cultural elements. But there is no need to over-pursue it. Emotions and human foibles can themselves be clues. . . . Moreover, the Symons exclusivity also eliminates from consideration the high comedy of the better Golden Age detective stories, as I have already mentioned in regard to Ngaio Marsh. In a brief but friendly disquisition, for example, he wholly misunderstands this facet of the early achievement of Michael Innes in such masterpieces as *Death At the President's Lodging* and *Hamlet Revenge!*; alas, he consigns Innes to the same discarded and reviled bracket of snobbish fun in which he has incarcerated Dorothy Sayers and Ngaio Marsh. . . . And I could go on on this theme of Symons's misunderstanding.

But I will not, for it is painful that a junior like myself should have so to rebuke a man the finesse of whose reviewing of crime fiction has been a delight and an instruction for a generation.

> *A review of "Bloody Murder," in* The Spectator, *Vol. 232, No. 7618, June 29, 1974, p. 805.*

DANIEL HOFFMANN

Julian Symons' **"The Tell-Tale Heart"** is a . . . dependable guide to Poe's life. This book makes no claim to original research but offers a brisk synopsis of extant biographical knowledge, leavened by an experienced novelist's insights. Mr. Symons handles well the tangled narrative of Poe's troubled life, sensibly telling this tale without pausing to analyze Poe's stories. Criticism is deferred to Mr. Symons' last 70 pages. . . .

Mr. Symons has mastered Poe's own milieu and renders well the social insecurity of the orphan raised among rich Virginians, his hard-scrabble life of drudging journalism, his fractious dealings with editors and minor writers. Mr. Symons properly emphasizes Poe's repeated and ever-blighted efforts to found his own literary review. (p. 15)

Mr. Symons cautions, "It would be idle to ask what reality lay beneath the masks he assumed. The reality was the sum of the parts he played." A more speculative reader of Poe may well wonder why such curiosity is idle, and whether Poe's reality is indeed the sum of his appearances.

But Mr. Symons is a common-sense empiricist with small patience for theories not grounded on the tangible and obvious. Himself a plotter of detective tales, he favors neatly plausible explanations of complex experiences. His book shows both the strengths and limitations of such a cast of mind explaining Poe,

whose own cast of mind included this one but in other respects was decidedly different from it.

Mr. Symons classifies two tendencies in Poe. Logical Poe is responsible for editing magazines, writing analytic criticism, devising puzzles and cryptograms, and creating tales of detection. Visionary Poe, on the other hand, sees poetry as a sacred mystery and is driven by the impulse to write stories "of a terror merging into horror and disgust." This bipartite separation, although reductive, appears convincing. Yet much of Poe's behavior, like his writing, was based on complex and mingled motives. In fact there are many more Poes than only two; but to deal with these other aspects of a writer, a critic must be willing to seek what lies behind the masks of his appearances. It would be well to ask why Poe was so obsessed with terror, horror and disgust as well as with sublunary visions and mechanistic puzzles and plots.

Mr. Symons' critical pages are perfunctory, without extended analyses of individual works. He derisively dismisses recent American criticism "as in varying degrees nonsensical . . . or trivial." Mr. Symons takes the work of such critics, myself among them, as attempts "to show widespread conscious symbolism in Poe"; such efforts result in "breathtaking absurdities," "gobbledegook," "theories spun entirely from the cloth of fantasy."

The truth is, Mr. Symons prefers his Poe unexamined—"The overt is to be preferred to the covert. . . . the literal reading is certainly the best"—because he agrees without demur to Poe's Romantic assumption that imprecision of meaning is required for the production of beauty or the illusion of terror. "Any attempt to clarify that vagueness runs the risk of damaging a story." In his own assumption that we must murder to dissect, Mr. Symons would seem to have confused an indestructible great work of fiction with a chicken.

In his no-nonsense scanting of the speculative interpretations of Richard Wilbur and others, Mr. Symons misrepresents their intentions. Few sensible critics maintain that all of Poe's symbolism is wholly conscious, nor does it need to be. Symbolism can be present in a tale—as Poe (calling it allegory in his review of Hawthorne) said it should—as "a profound undercurrent. . . . never to show itself unless *called* to the surface." Mr. Symons can tell us little about "The Fall of the House of Usher" or "Ligeia" because he balks at examining the profound undercurrents in such tales. (pp. 15, 36)

> *Daniel Hoffman, "Big with Baudelaire and Roger Corman," in* The New York Times Book Review, *July 9, 1978, pp. 15, 36.**

MEGAN MARSHALL

Julian Symons, himself a writer of detective stories, gives a straightforward, knowledgeable account of Poe's life in *The Tell Tale Heart*. This in itself is no mean feat: more than one biographer has turned the life into a florid gothic tale. But Symons is so wary of the maudlin and the melodramatic, so devoted to recording every event in its proper sequence, that he fails to uncover the full dimensions of his subject. The Poe Symons speaks of most often is the contented family man, the industrious journalist, the courteous southern gentleman. Of the darker side, like a good detective storyteller, he gives us all the evidence. But the mystery of Poe is not easily solved; a summary of the evidence is not enough to suggest a solution.

Consider the case of Poe's bizarre marriage to his 13-year-old cousin. What are we to make of this? Earlier biographers have suggested that Poe entered the marriage to save himself from a life of sexual activity he clearly feared. . . .

But Symons shies away from any such conjecture. He gives only two pages to this most central fact of Poe's adult life, beginning with the erroneous statement that, "the extraordinary nature of this marriage has been little commented on by Poe's biographers." . . . What was the emotional importance of the marriage? Symons does not say. . . .

Symons remains steadfastly superficial throughout his treatment of the life. Most often he is content to describe the ups and downs of Poe's life as "hard" periods, "happy" times, or "very strange" events. The very thought of applying principles of psychoanalysis to a life that almost begs for interpretation seems reprehensible to him; "the psychoanalytic approach" receives scarcely five pages at the end of his book, most of which are given over to refuting an outdated Freudian interpretation of the work. (p. 43)

There may be no real answers to the questions Poe's life raises. But when Symons reports an incident near the end of Poe's life, in which the poet was persuaded to attend church services at midnight only to "rush out when the passage, 'He was a man of sorrows and acquainted with grief' was spoken and repeated," we suddenly realize that Symons has altogether failed to introduce this character. Who was this Poe, and what were his sorrows? Having read Symons, we still don't know.

Symons is even more reluctant to plumb the depths of Poe's work. . . . [He] is content to state the obvious, labeling Poe's detective fiction "Logical," the horror stories "Visionary," and at best identifying combinations of "Logical" and "Visionary" writing in the poetry and criticism that make certain works "effective." As we have seen from his treatment of the life, struggle is not a subject Symons is competent or even willing to handle. . . .

Besides this disappointingly superficial reading of the work, Symons provides a few more pages debunking the two theories he knows about that attempt to reach further below the surface. First, he condemns all psychoanalytic interpretation of Poe's work on the basis of Marie Bonaparte's 1949 Freudian analysis. . . . Bonaparte's work would no doubt seem crude even to a fellow Freudian in the 1970s. Psychoanalytic interpretation has made such progress towards subtlety and sophistication since 1949. Symons's choice of Bonaparte's work as representative of the field is simply irresponsible.

Even more sophistical is Symons's rejection of symbolist interpretations of Poe. Symons mistakenly assumes that symbolist interpretations can only be made when the author has been proved to be "almost wholly conscious" of his use of symbols. Since Symons can find no explicit statement of symbolist intent in Poe's critical work, we must therefore stop looking for symbols in his poetry and fiction. I'm not sure what sort of criticism Symons has been reading lately, if any at all, . . . but certainly few symbolist critics today regard conscious intent on the part of an author as a prerequisite for discussing symbols that may emerge in a work. This last may in itself be worthy of attack—and if Symons had fought his battle on these grounds there might have been something worth reading here. . . .

Symons feels he must come up with some way of explaining the enduring fascination of Poe's work. And after 250 pages of anti-analytical writing on both life and work, Symons offers this frustrating conclusion: "It is impossible to ignore [Poe's] life in dealing with his art. . . ." The fascination we feel is with "the personality of Poe expressed through his art. The two are as nearly as possible identical." Why, then, has Symons separated his discussion of the work from the life? Why does he dismiss psychoanalytic interpretation of both the work and the life? Nowhere does he tell us *how* the personality is expressed through the art, nor even *what* personality is expressed. Symons fails to give his readers any feeling for Poe's genius as it was manifested during his life, nor any sense of the life as it is revealed in the art. This is the very least one expects from a biographer.

Edgar Allan Poe has been as little understood by his biographers as he was by those who knew him during his life. Unfortunately, Julian Symons's new biography does little to reverse that trend. *The Tell-Tale Heart* has pitifully little to tell. (p. 44)

> Megan Marshall, in a review of "The Tell-Tale Heart: The Life and Works of Edgar Allan Poe," in The New Republic, Vol. 179, Nos. 9 & 10, August 26–September 2, 1978, pp. 42-4.

BENNY GREEN

In going over ground likely to be familiar to the general reader, biographers often feel the need to buttress their presumption with a theory; if that theory can hint, no matter how vaguely, at some kind of 'reassessment', then all the better. The nervousness is understandable, but rarely can it have resulted in so eccentric a presentation of the material as in Symons's book on Edgar Allan Poe [*The Tell-Tale Heart*]. What we get is not so much a reassessment as a rearrangement, the manuscript being presented in two sections; first the life, then the works. Symons reasons that in few literary case histories has there been so marked a contrast between the bread-and-butter journalistic labours on the one hand, and the real creative achievement on the other, and that if we are to proceed in the conventional style, by taking a period of the life together with the works which appeared during it, we are likely to end up with a most misleading portrait; as Symons writes, it is the unconscious Poe who chiefly interests the twentieth century, but this was not the man his contemporaries saw.

I doubt the validity of the argument. . . . In any case, there is only ever one valid excuse for a biographer, and that is his ability to write well. This Symons does. I find his narrative as charming as his theory justifying it is specious. For those who know nothing of Poe apart from his development of the honourable trade of curdling the blood, much of the text will come as a surprise, especially an astonishing letter written by Poe in 1844, astonishing because it discusses such unUsheresque themes as umbrellas, veal cutlets and carpet slippers.

There are certain biographical themes which seem to suit Symons particularly well, and Poe is perhaps one of them. Where once emotions clashed furiously, where the echoes still resound of a certain controversy, Symons is a welcome guide, because of a certain worldliness which helps him disengage himself from the confusions and to understand at least some of the more contentious actions of his subject. . . . [So] sensible are many of Symons's remarks that they are in grave danger of being dismissed as platitudes when in fact they are nothing of the kind. I cite as one example among many his reflection that generally Poe's relationships with women were emotional, with men intellectual. He also confirms the theory first floated many years ago that Poe's life was a flight from the sham bestowed upon him by a foster-father who managed to bring himself to foster him but not to father him. The sting of not quite belonging left Poe with an overwrought conception of dignity, of aristocracy, of an élite which should order the world as it should be ordered. (p. 20)

If Symons's discussion of the writings very nearly disintegrates into a series of papers, they are at any rate well-written papers, closely reasoned, entertaining and enlightening, and most important of all, stimulating enough to send the reader running back to Poe himself. (p. 21)

Benny Green, "Incongruities," in The Spectator, *Vol. 241, No. 7845, November 11, 1978, pp. 20-1.*

PAUL GRAY

[Julian Symons] has been putting together intricately crafted and plotted novels for roughly four decades, earning along the way more respect from peers than public fame. . . . [Symons] is not so well known as [Eric Ambler, Graham Greene, and Daphne du Maurier], but like them he can invest a plot with significance beyond its conclusion. . . . Yet he may now be on the brink of solving the mystery of his comparative obscurity. At an age when most writers are, to put it gently, no longer productive, he is overseeing the publication of two new books on the same day. Taken together, they may prove a case to a wider array of jurors: Symons is far more than a maker of puzzles; he is a master of moral conundrums.

Exhibit No. 1 is *The Detling Secret,* a novel molded into the shape of the classic whodunit. The setting is England, the time the 1890s. Sir Arthur Detling is a crusty old Tory. . . . Among the burdens Sir Arthur must bear is his older daughter Dolly's determination to marry Bernard Ross, a Liberal M.P. with a mysterious past. . . .

While artfully setting up . . . comic relief and the mysteries to follow, Symons provides panoramic background. The question of Irish Home Rule charges the atmosphere. Prime Minister William Gladstone tries vainly to keep Parliament in session until it wears down and disposes of the Irish problem. . . . Symons also conducts a guided tour of London's *fin de siècle* bohemia, where the names conjured with include Whistler, Turner and Beardsley. Oscar Wilde drops in on a party and charms everyone he greets.

When the first body appears, the event is almost disappointing, since so many other interesting plots have been set in motion. Symons anticipates this problem and shows how everything must converge in the murder. Then he tops himself with a second, this one occurring within the time-honored no-exit confines of a British country house. When the killer is unmasked, Symons still has enough ingenuity in reserve to put some reverse English on the disposition of the discovery.

"I have come tonight to plead for romance in the world of crime, for the locked room murder . . ." Thus the hero of one of the eleven stories in *The Tigers of Subtopia* addresses a club of criminologists in London. As it happens, Oliver Glass is starring in a West End production of one of his own detective plays. He is simultaneously planning the perfect crime in real life: the murder of his wife, to be accomplished during a brief intermission. Everyone in the theater will believe he is confined onstage, awaiting the next curtain. A perfect crime does indeed take place, but Glass is not its architect.

Such a reversal is typical of the stories in this collection, which owe as much to the tradition of O. Henry as to that of Conan Doyle. First Symons reveals a talent for the irresistible opening sentence. . . . Once this pace has been established, Symons races through plot complications (the old revolver stored safely in a drawer, an incriminating letter to a spouse accidentally opened and read) toward conclusions that upset the best-laid plans.

Unlike *The Detling Secret,* these stories are set in the present, most often in snug English suburban neighborhoods that Symons infuses with malevolence. . . . In the world as Symons describes it, nothing seems more natural than that people who dwell in such places should go extravagantly bananas.

Two such vigorous books from a writer 70 years old pose a mystery: Where does Symons find the energy and inspiration? Since the achievement is not a crime, Symons does not try to solve it. As it has been doing for as long as most readers can remember, his work speaks for itself.

Paul Gray, "Crime and Craftsmanship," in Time, *Vol. 121, No. 7, February 14, 1983, p. 82.*

MARY CANTWELL

Julian Symons is mystery fiction's grand old man. Novelist, historian of the genre and student of true crime as well, he has brought all three passions together in his most recent novels: **"The Blackheath Poisonings," "Sweet Adelaide"** and now **"The Detling Secret."**

All three are set in Victorian England, a period and place that are to connoisseurs of crime what catnip is to a kitten. And with good reason. . . . Jack the Ripper excepted, it is the Victorian era's domestic murderers and their homely weapons (arsenic soaked from flypaper, ground glass in the gruel) that fascinate.

Mr. Symons' **"Sweet Adelaide"** was based on the case of Adelaide Bartlett, a Pimlico housewife who in 1896 was reluctantly acquitted of force-feeding chloroform to her husband. The members of the Detling family, though imaginary, seem equally based in reality. Surely more than one upper-class Victorian family consisted of a thickheaded baronet, a misleadingly wispy wife, a silly son, an older daughter with a social conscience and a younger one with a yen for life among the bohemians. (p. 12)

Mr. Symons' use of period detail is both scrupulous and economical: A lesser writer would have laid on the antimacassars. He journeys through a London slum as effortlessly as he visits a country house whose butler seems to have strayed from "Cold Comfort Farm." His exposition is flawless, his conclusion convincing. For Mr. Symons, as for certain of his peers, the Victorians have offered rich pickings.

The world of **"The Tigers of Subtopia: And Other Stories"** is today's, and there is no joy in it. Instead there are bad marriages, bad sex and bad intentions. A woman who as a child playfully pushed her sister off a stair does penance for a lifetime: Her sister is crippled and a guiltmonger. A man shocked by a young prostitute's solicitation stalks her, knife in pocket, after his late wife is revealed to have been an adulteress. To his mind, in killing the one he will be killing the other. A father witnessing the beating of the young punk who he thinks has hurt his son is horrified—and ecstatic. Cruelty breeds cruelty, a bed is as cold as a grave, all trust is misplaced.

Big themes, these, made small by their treatment: All are cast in the mystery-story mold. First comes the situation, then the twist and finally the surprise ending. Nobody does it better than Mr. Symons, which is why **"The Tigers of Subtopia"** will fully satisfy fans of the short mystery story. Fans of the short story, however, will be left hungry.

On the other hand, they probably wouldn't be reading **"The Tigers of Subtopia"** anyway. Mr. Symons, working well within the confines of mystery fiction, brings the genre to a high polish. His craftsmanship is impeccable, and so are his manners. There's not a story here that lasts a minute too long. And one of them, **"A Theme for Hyacinth,"** about an elderly man suckered into the murder of his young girlfriend's husband, is a killer. (p. 12, 42)

> *Mary Cantwell, 'Homicides, Victorian and Modern,'' in* The New York Times Book Review, *March 20, 1983, pp. 12, 42.*

MEREDITH TAX

Dudley Potter [the protagonist of *The Name of Annabel Lee*] is a bit of a nerd. . . . Dudley's soul lies dormant until a traveling avant-garde theater group involves him in audience participation, and he meets the blond and beautiful actress Annabel Lee. (Her mother had a thing for Poe.) But after a few months of passion, Annabel splits, leaving only a note; "End of the affair. Sorry I have to go." Has she really ceased to care? Dudley must know and goes in hot pursuit, without even a sabbatical. . . . Back in our own SoHo at "the House of Usher" (a sadomasochistic sex show with Annabel Lee as dominatrix), Dudley, who has shown no sign of deductive capacity so far, suddenly puts it all together. This reader stared in disbelief at the last page, thinking, "Only this and nothing more?" Julian Symons, a past master of the genre, can do better than this. The only things that seem to have caught his interest are his vivid and Juvenalian locations and background characters. Unfortunately, his social satire overshadows the perfunctory plot and zero of a hero, and all his Poe-tic references are not enough to make for suspense.

> *Meredith Tax, in a review of ''The Name of Annabel Lee,'' in* The New York Times Book Review, *January 29, 1984, p. 22.*

THE NEW YORKER

Mr. Symons has always given full measure. That is to say, he has never chosen to stand by ingenuity of plot alone; he also gives his attention to character, setting, and tone. In his new novel [*The Name of Annabel Lee*]—about a stiff British professor of English literature at a New England college who loses his habitual poise and balance in the arms of a transient English girl named Annabel Lee Fetherby—those qualities are present in abundance: in, unfortunately, an overabundance. The story is a good one—why Annabel Lee appeared and why she disappeared. But Mr. Symons has let his abundance run into irrelevancies—about the professor's former fiancée, now married to his father; about an old school friend and his trendy life and adulterous wife; about a dismal place of orgy called the House of Usher—and these, though not uninteresting, become annoying when they are discovered to have nothing to do with the problem of Annabel Lee.

> *A review of ''The Name of Annabel Lee,'' in* The New Yorker, *Vol. LX, No. 2, February 27, 1984, p. 136.*

Leon (Marcus) Uris

1924-

American novelist, dramatist, nonfiction writer, and script-writer.

Uris is best known for his popular novels based on events of contemporary history. These books, which are often panoramic in scope and include large casts of characters, are usually concerned with the events of World War II and its aftermath. Some critics have commented on the cinematic qualities of Uris's writing and, in fact, several of his books have been adapted for the screen. Foremost among these is *Exodus* (1958), Uris's work about the Jewish fight for independence and the resulting foundation of the state of Israel. *Exodus* was popular with critics and readers alike and became one of the best-selling novels ever published.

All of Uris's books combine fiction with extensive historical data. His first novel, *Battle Cry* (1953), is a realistic account of Marine Corps life during World War II. This work was an important departure from other war novels in its sympathetic treatment of the military. *The Angry Hills* (1955), another story about the Second World War, concerns the resistance to the Nazi occupation of Greece. *Mila 18* (1961) recreates the Jewish defense of the Warsaw ghetto during the German occupation of Poland. *Armageddon* (1964) tells of the rebuilding of Berlin. *Topaz* (1967), a complex spy story, is based on Soviet influence in the French government during the Cuban Missile Crisis of 1962. In *QB VII* (1970) Uris dramatizes a libel suit actually brought against him by a German doctor who claimed to have been maligned in *Exodus*. Ireland's troubled history from 1840 to 1916 is the focus of *Trinity* (1976). Uris's recent novel *The Haj* (1984) examines the Palestinian refugee situation in Israel as it existed until the late 1950s.

Critics dispute neither the popularity nor the readability of Uris's stories. They do, however, question the objectivity of his historical presentations and acknowledge technical flaws in his writing style. Uris has also been charged with creating stereotypical characters and unbelievable dialogue and with displaying propagandist intentions in his work. Sharon D. Downey and Richard A. Kallan have examined the methods Uris uses to develop his ideas and persuade his readers. They conclude that his work is an example of a growing trend in literature in which "documentary" novels and "literary" journalism blur the boundaries between fact and fiction.

(See also *CLC*, Vol. 7; *Contemporary Authors*, Vols. 1-4, rev. ed.; and *Contemporary Authors New Revision Series*, Vol. 1.)

MERLE MILLER

Leon Uris has done the nearly impossible. He has written a wonderfully different kind of war novel. . . . His **"Battle Cry"** is nearly as long as the other successful treatments of the Second World War; it has many of the same characters and now traditional Anglo-Saxon words, but Mr. Uris is not angry or bitter or brooding. He obviously loves the Marine Corps, even its officers. Thus, he may have started a whole new and healthy trend in American war literature.

Sam Huxley, Mr. Uris's officer as well as one of his heroes, is the fictional commander of the very real Sixth Regiment of the Second Marine Division, and he would have been an easy man to hate. He is hard, and he is harsh, and he discourages intimacy. . . . He is a Marine first and a human being second, and Mr. Uris has made him considerably larger than but also part of life.

Leon Uris knows that Huxley is the kind of man who wins wars. . . . (p. 16)

"Battle Cry" has faults. The women, a simple high school girl, a lovable prostitute, a New Zealand widow, an unattractive heiress, are too simple and too foolish. Marion is a caricature, and Gomez is tiresome. What's more, Mr. Uris's book would have been improved by considerable cutting. Almost 200 pages are devoted to the Stateside training. A third or half that many would have been enough.

But, at his best, which is most of the time, Mr. Uris is superb. That glorious and memorable country, New Zealand, comes completely alive, and the combat scenes are terrifyingly real.

Mr. Uris was obviously a good Marine; he's a good novelist, too. (pp. 16-17)

> Merle Miller, "The Backdrop Is Victory," in The Saturday Review, *New York, Vol. XXXVI, No. 17, April 25, 1953, pp. 16-17.*

GEORGE McMILLAN

The conventions of World War II fiction are hardening. Following them, the novelists assemble a group of self-conscious types meant to represent a cross-section of America's regional, racial and social problems. The war novelists continue to show us the types in civilian settings, emphasizing the social data. And then they shift the scenes, and the moral and social values, and take their types to war, to share a common experience. The treatment, by convention, is almost always realistic. If the result is not a novel, it has often turned out to be a social document. . . .

[Mr. Uris'] squad is a squad of Marines, and like almost every writer who comes upon that exotic branch of the service, Mr. Uris has tried to explain its mysteries. This has given his types a second function, and a far wider meaning.

If **"Battle Cry"** is not an original work of the imagination, it is probably, out of all World War II novels about Marines, the most intimate and accurate account of the way Marines were trained to fight and the way they did fight.

Mr. Uris is savvy about the Corps. He knows the mental anguish and the physical agony of boot camp, and he knows that a Marine's training never stops. He knows and describes how a Marine commander will order his men out for close drill the day after they have returned to a rest camp from a battlefield. Mr. Uris knows that, in the Corps, the tension of discipline is never relaxed. And he knows that, to a Marine, what he does is never quite so important as the way he is made to do it.

In Mr. Uris' most exciting chapter, his squad is not fighting a battle. They are on a hike, and not a particularly long hike. But they are speed-marching at a pace that tests first their physical and then their emotional endurance. To what purpose? Apparently to beat a record set by another battalion. But really each man is proving in his mind's eye—not himself, but whether he is a Marine. . . .

The final test, but not necessarily the most trying, is the battlefield itself. Mr. Uris' men first write their names in blood on a childish pact, and then on the beaches of Tarawa and Saipan. By then their civilian problems are hard to remember. And there they find an end, if not a solution to them all.

> *George McMillan, "Tension Never Eases," in* The New York Times Book Review, *April 26, 1953, p. 5.*

PAT FRANK

I don't know that ["**Battle Cry**"] does anything to advance American literature, but it makes the Marines understandable.

The first few hundred pages, to my mind the best part of the book, are perhaps the most explicit survey of the training of soldiers that I have ever read, anywhere.

"Battle Cry" takes a cross-section of young Americans, some good, one or two villainous or stupid, and tells how they are molded into a critical section of a fighting machine. . . . The men of whom Mr. Uris writes comprise the communications section. Some of the characterizations are excellent. . . .

It is unfortunate that **"Battle Cry"** should fall into the school of latrine fiction. The shocking words are true enough, but they intrude into the thought and flow of imagination and block the reader's comprehension of the story. . . .

However, Mr. Uris has recorded some magnificent battle scenes. He tells what really happens to men when they are hit, and what their thoughts are. . . .

Occasionally Mr. Uris is trapped by clichés; occasionally he lapses into the sentimental, but in this book are passages of great power. It is a book more honest, I believe, than "The Naked and the Dead." He knows his characters. There are no phoney generals, in the literary sense. He knows them all.

> *Pat Frank, "Tough Story of Transition from Hometown Boys to Men Trained to Kill," in* New York Herald Tribune Book Review, *May 3, 1953, p. 5.*

DAVID DEMPSEY

Send an American novelist to Europe, set the time during the German occupation, pick almost any country and make the girl a creature of the Underground and you are pretty certain to get a novel, else what's a writer for? Mr. Uris' Michael Morrison is such a person and **"The Angry Hills"** is his story—a "suspense" novel with plenty of briskly paced action meted out against a Grecian backdrop under the menacing overhang of war. . . .

As a slam-bang adventure novel, **"The Angry Hills"** is competently plotted and backed up by some vivid reportorial wartime details. As is the case with most novels of this type, the characters move too fast, and the story is a bit too skeletonized, for us to get more than a two-dimensional view. Also, Mr. Uris has a fondness for getting his hero out of trouble by calling frequently on the local gods of the machine. . . . (p. 32)

Readers who recall **"Battle Cry"** will be disappointed if they look for a repeat performance: slice-of-life jumbos with such explosive effect on best-seller lists as that love-song to the Marine Corps are few and far between in any publishing season. Yet, when one remembers the limitations of the novel of counterespionage, it is easy to accept **"The Angry Hills"** as a superior example of its genre. (p. 33)

> *David Dempsey, "Unwitting Go-Between," in* The New York Times Book Review, *October 16, 1955, pp. 32-3.*

TIME

Hmm. Bank balance down. Time to do another Big Novel. But what about? . . . Got it! Berlin and the airlift. It has flyers and wild blue yonders, and conflict with the Russkies, and a small band of far-seeing Army officers, and fräuleins, and bad Germans and maybe a few good ones this time, and . . .

Leon Uris' new novel [*Armageddon*] is the predictable end product of an interior monologue just like that. And it must be conceded that Uris, who once publicly pronounced himself "the most outstanding U.S. writer of today," has succeeded astonishingly in his aim: into this big bad book he has packed away every conceivable stock figure, from the nice Russian officer (Igor) trapped by the system, to the beautiful whore (Hilde) who reforms and then softens the hard heart of the dashing American pilot (Scott, what else?).

Uris put in about three years of research and writing to produce this book. It reads as if it were not written at all but dictated, Napoleon style, at top speed to at least two secretaries at once, and the resulting manuscript corrected with a glass in one hand, a cigar in the other, and no place to hold the blue pencil. Even the title is a piece of mindless sensationalism: Berlin was not a battle, let alone the last one.

Uris piles up countless petty errors of fact, even of grammar ("It's a good thing English has nothing to do with writing" is another Uris pronouncement). The airlift and the gutty Berliners deserve a better chronicler.

> *"Fresh Off the Assembly Line," in* Time, *Vol. 83, No. 24, June 12, 1964, p. 118.*

CADE WARE

Like Mr. Uris' other novels, *Armageddon* is a vast panorama of people, places, situations both fictional and quasi-historic, and romantic sentiment rather easy to come by. It ranges among locales as widely distant as Siberia and Hawaii and portrays such diverse characters as a Berlin lesbian, a martyred Kulak farmer, an American general much like Lucius Clay, a Madison Avenue adman, and Josef Stalin.

Each of these is as much a character in his own right as he is the illustration of a historical factor in Mr. Uris' argument that the Americans were really pretty swell about the whole Airlift business. So subtly does Mr. Uris arrange for nothing to happen that we really don't enjoy happening that the story of an extremely grim episode in European history turns out to be a surprisingly comfortable book.

Mr. Uris has a definite tale for what could be called the pre-movie novel. His research is detailed, his characters are believable without being overly complicated, his love scenes are intense and numerous though not soupy, and he throws dramatic moment after dramatic moment in a throbbing tempo to which only panoramic technicolor can do justice. If you've enjoyed these qualities in Mr. Uris's books before . . . , you'll enjoy reading *Armageddon*. Though, come to think of it, you may like the movie better.

> *Cade Ware, "The Good Guys Win," in* Book Week— The Sunday Herald Tribune, *June 14, 1964, p. 16.*

PAMELA MARSH

Leon Uris plunges heedlessly ahead, dabbling in half-truths to produce yet another example of the latest non-art form—the propaganda novel.

What he has done in **"Topaz"** is to take General de Gaulle at a time when his popularity is low in America, assign him an apocryphal but revealing name [Pierre La Croix], make his real identity crystal clear . . . , and then cast him as a prime villain in a routine spy tale by knitting history and cruel fiction tightly together.

The novel wanders confusingly between the United States, France, Spain, and Cuba with an anti-de Gaullist patriotic French agent as its hero. The date is usually 1962, the chief preoccupation, the Cuban missile crisis, until, thanks to the revelations of a Soviet defector, we are flashbacked to World War II to see how La Croix is manipulated by Soviet agents. And how cleverly Mr. Uris can manipulate history.

Few readers are expert enough to be 100 percent certain where Mr. Uris's imagination has taken over the record. For one of many instances, in history-according-to-Uris, Washington was in on the Franco-British plan to attack Suez and urged the aggressors to capture the canal within 72 hours. . . .

"Topaz," a mixture of history and mystery sensationalized with a scene of torture and one of rape, is high on the best-seller list.

> *Pamela Marsh, "You Can't Tell Fact from Fiction," in* The Christian Science Monitor, *November 16, 1967, p. 15.*

F. A. MACKLIN

Leon Uris' *Topaz* is an outlandish novel. In an attempt at reality, Uris has wed propaganda and political paranoia.

The basis of the novel is plot; there is little character or mood. The conversations, particularly those between André, the French secret service member, and his wife are unbelievable. . . .

The novel limps throughout its first two-thirds; in the final part, it works in torture and the sudden revelation of a surprise traitor, but there is little sustained conflict. The last third reads like a sketchy movie scenario. . . .

Although attempting a stern, straightshooting novel, Uris' effort is mostly laughable. In a precious gesture of self-aggrandizement, Uris has a character in the novel relate that the truth about Topaz has been given to a novelist who will relay it to the world.

Unfortunately, that novelist who has the truth couldn't possibly be the fanciful author of the present novel.

> *F. A. Macklin, in a review of "Topaz," in* America, *Vol. 118, No. 1, January 6, 1968, p. 17.*

CHRISTOPHER LEHMANN-HAUPT

However one reads it, **"QB VII"** induces tranquility, because a mind absorbed is a body at rest. The question is, How does Leon Uris do it? How does he manage to make so few demands on us in 500 pages? There is art to it. Mr. Uris explains part of the secret about a quarter of the way into **"QB VII"**— which, by the way, stands for Queen's Bench Courtroom Number Seven, and is, when it eventually gets down to business, a courtroom drama of sorts. Uris's hero is a writer, you see, and he knows a thing or two about writing novels. "And the key trick that few novelists know," Uris explains to us . . . is that "a novelist must know what his last chapter is going to say and one way or another work toward that last chapter." . . .

[It's] pretty clear that "the key trick" works all sorts of magic for Leon Uris.

For one thing, having his last chapter clearly in view keeps Mr. Uris's mind (and ours) off the problem of language, which can be distracting sometimes to a novelist who stops to think about it. Where writers who don't know how their novels are going to turn out sometimes start fiddling with the meanings of words, Mr. Uris is always satisfied with what first came to mind, as well as with what probably never got there at all. Thus, he is free to write that editors are of "legendary proportions" (the size of Polyphemus, one assumes he means); that "there were gray hairs in her head now. He had put them there with his own paint brush of misery"; that "his nostril was pelted with the odor of slabs of freshly pressed rubber, pepper, and sacks of bat dung collected from the caves by the ingenious Chinese and sold as fertilizer"; and so forth. . . .

For another thing, with his plot so carefully mapped out, Mr. Uris need never worry about his characters assuming independent life and taking his story away from him. And they never do; they are humbly obedient to his purpose throughout. Thus Adam Keino is a miserable drunkard tie-dying his wife's hair gray in one chapter, and a sobered-up, dedicated doctor being knighted by the Queen in the next. Thus Abraham Cady can make his prestigious switch from burnt-out Hollywood hack to "a Jew" who "wants to write about Jews."

Thus Mr. Uris has all the space in the world to tell us how much he disapproves of American taxi-drivers and experimental literature, the breakdown of middle-class values, the breakdown of the Chicago police, pollution and Judge Julius Hoffman. Fortunately, he does do us the favor of giving his characters different names, so we can tell them apart—except when they get bunched up in scenes together.

But best of all, by knowing the sins Mr. Uris keeps his story from degenerating into a real conflict. Oh, he tries to fool us for awhile there by pretending that the Polish doctor, Adam Kelno, had humanitarian reasons for removing the ovaries and testicles of Jewish inmates in the Jadwiga concentration camp. But we know, we somehow know, that when Abe Cady writes "The Holocaust" describing Dr. Kelno as a collaborator with the Nazis, and Dr. Kelno sues Cady for libel, and the case becomes the most important in English judicial history—we somehow know who's going to win. . . .

The trouble is: Knowing all along with Mr. Uris where "QB VII" is headed in its final chapter, what are we as readers supposed to do for entertainment in the meantime? That's what I was trying to explain when I said the book was so relaxing. You can do anything you like while reading it. In fact, you needn't even bother to read it at all.

> Christopher Lehmann-Haupt, "How to Write a Leon Uris," in The New York Times, December 2, 1970, p. 45.

MARTHA DUFFY

The Jews who have survived pogroms and genocide will doubtless weather this vulgar affront as well. Still, individual Jews who find themselves stuck in Leon Uris' paper detention camp must surely regard QB VII as a rather gratuitous endurance test.

Based on a libel suit that the author actually faced in England over a sentence in his third novel, *Exodus,* the book pits a Gentile Polish doctor, Adam Kelno, against a famous American Jewish novelist, Abe Cady. During World War II Dr. Kelno was forced to practice medicine in the infamous Jadwiga concentration camp. He sues Cady for libel because of a sentence that strayed into Cady's blockbuster novel, *The Holocaust,* which casually charges Kelno with performing "15,000 or more experimental operations without use of anesthesia." . . . After setting up these pasteboard people, Uris embarks on a lengthy trial scene in which the grisly camp testimony unfolds.

Many of QB VII's sins are standard for the genre. The prose is an illiterate shorthand. . . . The plot is interstitched with editorials, sermons and lessons in writing. . . .

Still Uris' fictional caveats—rung in through Abe's conversations with his British publisher—seem absurdly at odds with his own wretched writing performance this time out. According to Uris, what most writers apparently forget is basic storytelling—a skill he himself once practiced but has neglected in this heavily predictable tale. Then there is that literary creation

Author Abe himself, a *mensh* who makes Hemingway seem as mousy as Mann. . . .

Abe emerges, finally, as the shining avenger of Jewish wrongs, despite the fact that he is technically guilty of libel since the number of Kelno's crimes did not approach 15,000 and Abe, who cannot recall the doctor at all when charged, does not even know how that pesky sentence got into his book in the first place.

The result of Abe's fecklessness is a roundup of Kelno's victims, who must come to London to relive their tortures in court. . . . [Their testimony accounts] for pages and pages of excruciatingly detailed descriptions of sexual organs and agony. In reality it is the documentation of an atrocity, but in slapdash fiction it is only sadomasochism. Which is a popular theme in popular novels these days.

> Martha Duffy, "Bestseller Revisited," in Time, Vol. 97, No. 26, June 28, 1971, p. 80.

SHARON D. DOWNEY AND RICHARD A. KALLAN

After eight novels—*Battle Cry, The Angry Hills, Exodus, Mila 18, Armageddon, Topaz, QB VII,* and *Trinity*—Leon Uris continues to prompt conflicting assessments. Literary critics disparagingly dismiss his work as something less than "serious." . . . On the other hand, Uris has nurtured in the last thirty years a loyal American readership which renders almost every Uris novel a runaway bestseller. In short, Uris remains a reader's writer and a critic's nightmare.

The easy and conventional explanation for this discrepancy would be to acknowledge the sorry state of the audience and point to critics as having higher levels of taste. Admittedly, when judged by traditional literary canons, Uris *is* a poor writer. But that Uris's critics are at odds with his readers does not necessarily mean the latter have lower standards; it is equally plausible to assert they merely embrace *different* standards. . . . [While] surface appearances suggest that Uris's is a simple message packaged in a simple style, it unfolds, ironically, through complexity, necessitating a cognitive and affective sophistication by creating a reading experience wherein elements must be processed into a coherent reality. (p. 192)

Uris's work may best be understood if seen as representing a form which fuses fictional and external worlds, producing in effect a relationship between writer and reader—which we call *semi*-aesthetic detachment—wherein the demands of the former and the expectations of the latter deviate significantly from the "contract" underscoring traditional literature. The form may not be unique to Uris, but neither Uris nor the form has received much rhetorical attention. . . . [Literature such as Uris's] addresses an *immediate, specific, external* world concern and envisions its audience as capable of effecting change through an outwardly directed reader response. (pp. 192-93)

The plight of Jews is one major injustice Uris attempts to resolve. . . . Addressing what he calls "the great American public," Uris wrote four novels about the Jewish experience which portray past injustices and attempt to deter future ones: *Exodus,* a story about Israel's inceptional period and her fight for independence; *Mila 18,* a recreation of the Warsaw ghetto uprising; *Armageddon,* a chronicle of post World War II Germany and the Berlin Airlift; and *QB VII,* an account of sexual sterilization experiments performed on Jews at Auschwitz.

The dominant theme of these works is that the Jew must live in sovereignty. Throughout, Uris contends that Jewish survival rests on the establishment and maintenance of a sovereign state—the ultimate solution/deterrent to injustice against Jews. . . . In a sense, Uris reflects the Jewish hope from the time they were scattered 2,000 years ago: Israel must be reborn. (p. 194)

Once Jewish autonomy became a reality with the birth of Israel, the problem shifted to maintaining that sovereignty, a sovereignty seemingly forever in jeopardy. Uris, in fact, continually reminds the reader of the immediacy of the problem, noting that his novels recreate not past history, but "living" history, documenting persistent threats to Jewish homeland. *QB VII* character, author Abe Cady, echoes the philosophy matter-of-factly: "You learn to live with it [the Middle East uncertainty]. When I was writing *The Holocaust,* Shawcross [Cady's publisher] would get into a dither every time a new crisis came up, and he'd badger me for the manuscript. I told him, don't worry, whenever I finish the book, the Jews will still be in trouble."

Uris contends that the problem must be confronted by the West and, in particular, America because America's own moral and physical survival is linked to Israel's sovereignty. . . . America, Uris argues, is bound not only ideologically but emotionally and pragmatically to support Israel. *Armageddon*'s General Hanson underscores the obligation when he observes, "It is going to take time for our countrymen to realize that Americans can never go home again." As leading advocators of democracy, Americans share, according to Uris, in the responsibility for Israel's future. Foreign aid, especially in the form of weaponry, must be provided to guarantee Israel's military might. Concludes Uris, "Just keep the arms coming to Israel."

Uris's view of the novel as a situational and transitory tool by which to resolve specific injustices dramatically influences his rhetorical posture, consequently altering the implicit agreement between novelist and reader. (pp. 194-95)

Uris's works . . . differ from traditional literature both because of what they do and what they ask of the reader.

Uris precludes placing the reader wholly in another world because it would disserve his purpose. Less interested in the reader's intrapersonal growth *per se* than in the sovereignty of Israel, Uris aims at producing an external/public as opposed to internal/private reader response. Although, granted, self-reflection often precedes public action, Uris is primarily concerned with prescribing the latter and hence seeks to facilitate less an isolated, personal experience than a specific, external response similar for *all* readers. Virtually free of implication, subtlety, and ambiguity, Uris's writings require little in the way of "working" at meaning. Uris orchestrates linguistically "complete" speech acts with which readers may agree or disagree, but which permit only minimal variance of interpretation of the inherent characterizations. One is conscious not only of a narrator—as in traditional literature—but of Uris's *authorship,* his ever-dominating presence.

Uris's readers must weave between external personageship and ideal auditorship—asked to empathize with fictional characters in a primarily fictional setting, but not to the extent of becoming so aesthetically detached that external personage is obscured from its articulation to storyline. Uris suggests that fictional and external worlds are interrelated to the point that his fictional discourse cannot function independent of the external world—which is different from saying . . . that a fictional world experience may subsequently be externally generalized, as often

occurs with traditional literature. Uris's rhetoric mandates *semi*-aesthetic detachment: readers are required to slip into the role of ideal auditor to appreciate affectively Uris's story while continually slipping out of the role, back to external personage, to integrate fictional and external worlds. Without his readers seeing the interdependence of both worlds, Uris's purpose cannot be achieved. He hints at this when he observes that success usually comes only when words are coupled with violence, Israel's fight for sovereignty being a prime example:

> If you want attention, you only can do it through words sometimes. Of course, an article can stop the world cold, a book can stop the world cold. But in order to really achieve your goal, you've got to have violence. I could have written the most beautiful story about the Jews after World War II, but if there were no Israeli army or no Israel that novel wouldn't be worth a nickel, would it?

A novel can expose injustice, Uris believes, but correction requires external action. Ideally, he would have readers emphathize with Israel's quest for sovereignty, simultaneously remembering that in their external personages they possess the power, in the form of financial assistance, to help secure and maintain that sovereignty. Accepting a contract stipulating *semi*-aesthetic detachment, readers collaborate with Uris by calling into play the resources of their external world. (pp. 196-97)

Because his argument for Jewish sovereignty depends on the integrating of fictional and external worlds, Uris utilizes three devices which may be labeled, in order of ascending complexity, *transporters, exemplars,* and *stereotypes.*

The transporter is an external world reference which functions to remind readers of their external personages. It "transports" by momentarily moving one from Uris's fictional world back to one's immediate external world, thus guarding against total aesthetic detachment. The transporter stands apart from, although it has correspondence to, Uris's fictional world. Uris's use of bold historical narrative serves as an example. Accentuated by one sentence paragraphs, structural parallelism, and frequent exclamation, the passage [describing the horrors at Auschwitz] recalls the external world at perhaps its most shocking hour. . . . (pp. 197-98)

Uris's frequent use of Biblical references is another effective transporting device. . . . Moreover, when Uris quotes the Bible as predicting Israel's inevitable rebirth, and when those predictions appear to concur with specific events reported by Uris, the right of Israel's sovereignty must seem obvious, as, for instance, in *Exodus* where readers are told of how Arab troops have blockaded the old city of Jerusalem and how reinforcements and supplies cannot reach the besieged city because the main highway from Tel Aviv to Jerusalem cannot be traveled. However, David Ben Ami, a student of the Bible, suspects that a hidden road exists because the Bible says so. . . . The highway indeed is found, supplies replenished, and the siege of Jerusalem broken within days. Israel's sovereignty is temporarily secured.

More complex, the exemplar provides a model of ideal, external world behavior, and normally takes the form of an extended scene or episode featuring fictional and external worlds sharing a symbiotic relationship.

Uris's fictive depiction of Americans typifies his use of exemplars. Usually portrayed as heroes, American characters aid

Israel in times of crisis and play a major role in the achieving and maintaining of her sovereignty. In *Exodus,* for example, American reporter Mark Parker is asked to help outwit the British. Having devised a plan whereby three hundred volunteer refugee children threaten to commit suicide unless allowed to sail unmolested on the ''Exodus'' to Israel (then Palestine and under British protection), Jews seek Parker's help in writing and releasing the story to the press. When Parker's story reaches the public, it creates the world sympathy needed to guarantee the safe entry of the ''Exodus'' into Israel. Although others could have exposed the story, Parker is presented as the only source the public would believe. In a similar scenario, *Mila 18*'s Christopher de Monti is an American journalist allowed to remain in Warsaw after Poland's surrender to Germany because he works for a neutral Swiss news agency. Jews imprisoned in the Warsaw ghetto ask de Monti to tell of the extermination centers at Treblinka and Madjanek. A reluctant de Monti explains that his efforts to expose the atrocities against Spaniards years before passed unnoticed. Still, the ghetto Jews adamantly press de Monti, believing that only he can alter their situation. They realize that as a journalist de Monti is credible to the masses and that his professionalism will dictate that he write the truth. His conscience finally overwhelming him, de Monti acquiesces and breaks the story to the publics in America and England.

In these examples, Uris enables the notion of Jewish sovereignty to assume special, affective meaning by fictionalizing heroes whom the reader can admire and respect. . . . This weave of storytelling and historical chronicle allows Uris to forge a work of heightened excitement and intrigue having generalizable, external world immediacy and significance. Afforded the novel's license and control, Uris manufactures an American of romantic proportions who possesses—through Uris's inventional skills—qualities of strength, charm, and commitment, and whose ''good fight'' seems that much more justified because of Uris's fictive manipulations. Against this backdrop, Uris interjects both a skeletal history of the external realities to which his story corresponds and reminders of Israel's contemporary exigencies. When all of this is played out, the Americans portrayed emerge as models exemplifying how Uris's American readership should act.

Also provided are more specific models of how Jews should think and behave. Through the character of Alexander Brandel [in *Mila 18*] Uris exemplifies the ideal Jew as actively committed to freedom and capable, or at least accepting, of physical force as a defensive weapon. (p. 199)

Brandel's character reflects a lesson in Jewish intellectual history and a statement of contemporary public policy. Brandel's initial philosophy of nonviolence typified Jewish thought prior to and early on in the war, and most readers can be expected to recognize Brandel's minimal resistance as culturally characteristic of the period. Similarly, Brandel's rejection of outright pacifism has its historical counterpart in the growing militancy Jews experienced as the war progressed and afterwards. . . . As Uris argues, history demonstrates that without physical power the Jew cannot hope to survive. The Jew must become a fighter.

Similar to the exemplar but somewhat more structurally complex, Uris's use of stereotypes also represents a wedding of fictional and external worlds. The stereotype promotes *semi-aesthetic* detachment in that it is predicated on readers *suspending* themselves between both worlds. They are forced, on one hand, to recall the external world, given that any stereotype

survives apart from its fictional life and simply mirrors and/or embellishes external world preconceptions. . . . On the other hand, to accept Uris's stereotypes readers must distance themselves from external world sensibilities.

In presenting the Jew as a fighter, for instance, Uris refutes one stereotype by substituting another. ''The lowest writers on my totem pole,'' he notes, ''are those Jewish novelists who berate the Jewish people''; writers depicting ''caricatures of the Jewish people . . . the wily businessman, the brilliant doctor . . . the tortured son . . . the coward''; authors ''who spend their time damning their fathers, hating their mothers, wringing their hands and wondering why they were born.'' These portraits, Uris believes, are erroneous: ''We Jews are not what we have been portrayed to be.''

To evidence his claim that Jews ''have been fighters,'' Uris cites the work of the Warsaw ghetto fighters, Jews running sea blockades to reach Israel, and Israel's battle with surrounding Arab countries. Uris's characters are typically ''people who do not apologize either for being born Jews or (for) the right to live in human dignity.'' . . . Implicit in Uris's characterization of Jews is the idea they are worth battling for—worth saving—because *they* are willing to fight and accordingly risk their lives. The stereotype assures and motivates the Jew, and more significant, perhaps, provides the non-Jew with additional incentive to aid Israel.

The Jew is cast not just as a fighter, but one possessing strange mystical powers—a superhuman, capable of tasks seemingly impossible. In *Exodus,* Uris describes the Jews' chances for victory in their War for Independence as negligible: they are surrounded by enemies, can claim few allies, and possess virtually no military resources; yet they succeed. Uris explains the victory of the small, ill-armed Israeli fighting unit by suggesting an omnipotent presence at work. . . . (pp. 200-01)

Portraying the Jew as having mystical powers functions to eradicate negative Jewish stereotypes and imbue the quest for sovereignty with religious, metaphysical overtones. On one level, a mystical Jew represents a power of sorts which can be neither controlled nor predicted. Spiritually possessed and obviously devoid of cowardice, the Jew mandates respect, if not reverence. . . . On another level, the mystical powers of the Jew in connection with Jewish homeland suggest that irrespective of how readers may feel towards Jews, Jewish sovereignty must be taken seriously because it appears ''willed'' by God. Continually, Uris describes a watchful, omnipresent God, always siding with the Jews. (p. 201)

The credibility of Uris's stereotype of the Jew as a Herculean fighter grows out of Israel's fight for independence in 1948 and subsequent Israel-Arab skirmishes—in particular, The Six Day War of 1967. Uris's stereotypical characterization of the Jew reflects, with some distortion, what readers already know. Yet to empathize with Uris's stereotype, the reader must subordinate external world rationality and play the role of the all-believing ideal auditor, suppressing the knowledge that not *all* Jews are or were fighters and not all, if any, possess mystical powers. And too, the reader consciously must overlook Uris's major contradiction: If Jews have mystical powers and can perform extraordinary feats because God is on their side, why do they so desperately need American military and financial aid?

While a positive stereotype of the Jew serves to foster and enlist the Gentile's aid in securing Israel's sovereignty, so does Uris's negative stereotype of the Nazi. In a part factual, part fantastic, part conjectural explanation of Nazi atrocities, Uris describes the German as a pagan who rejects belief in one God. . . . (p. 202)

Granted, Uris's stereotype of the Nazi has some grounding in the chronicles of Nazi Germany, but it is extended by Uris to a point which denies external world plausibility. To think of Germans as barely domesticated, pagan animals requires considerable latitude in imagination; obviously, only by distancing external world personage can one accede to this portrayal. Exaggeration and dubious inference aside however, Uris, by linking anti-semitism to the Jews' religious beliefs, rhetorically places the Christian in the same league, because the one-God concept, the Bible, and the Ten Commandments are also foundations of Christian philosophy. Jew and Christian are wedded in common cause by virtue of having their religious tenets held in contempt by the Nazis.

Stereotypes—whether they be of Jews, Nazis, or otherwise—may encourage *semi*-aesthetic detachment by also keeping readers focused on the relationship of storyline to external world, allowing neither to be overshadowed by the kind of complex characterization which might elicit an internal/private reader response. Uris as such presents "social types rather than individual portraits," whose "main function is to carry along the plot that history has already written." Too, the stereotype *per se* can aid Uris's purpose by conditioning readers to think in simplistic terms. Fostering belief in a "grayless" world of clear-cut heroes and villains whose lines of demarcation never blur, Uris's stereotypes imply that nothing needs to be complex or uncertain. Not unreasonably, Uris's readers may begin to see the world similarly, and correspondingly dispose themselves to embrace Uris's facile contention that American aid to Israel can insure the latter's sovereignty and resolve all the intricacies of Israel-Arab conflict.

Although literary critics sharply attack Uris's reliance on stereotypes, those stereotypes, nevertheless, serve to support his case for Jewish sovereignty as well as render his audience cognitively receptive to the argument. Together with the transporter, which *reminds* readers of the external world, and the exemplar, which *fuses* external and fictional worlds, the stereotype helps implement Uris's purpose by *suspending* readers between both worlds and encouraging *semi*-aesthetic detachment.

If Uris's novels are seen as mutating the traditional contract between novelist and reader, the disparity in reader/critic evaluations may be given another explanation. Literary critics, it appears, perceive the combining of fictional and external worlds as producing a shoddy novel, at best deserving of another label: living history; quasi-history; documentary; "part novel, part journalism, and part history"; even nonfiction. However, the reader finds in Uris an entertaining yet credible message with direct and immediate, external world bearing. (pp. 202-03)

From another perspective, Uris's novels seem symptomatic of a growing condition where audiences care less about the rhetor's methods than with being presented and/or entertained with facile information. One finds today some "journalism" bearing considerable literary license while some "novels" seem little more than veneered external realities. Uris as well, albeit unconsciously, may influence how readers regard and process fictional and external worlds by tacitly promoting fuzzier boundaries between the two. Once such standards are relaxed, potential exists for the blending of ideal auditorship and ex-

ternal personage into a single persona which cares not to distinguish among varying realities. (p. 204)

Sharon D. Downey and Richard A. Kallan, " 'Semi'-Aesthetic Detachment: The Fusing of Fictional and External Worlds in the Situational Literature of Leon Uris," in Communication Monographs, *Vol. 49, No. 3, September, 1982, pp. 192-204.*

KIRKUS REVIEWS

"We Arabs are the worst. . . ." That is the theme of [*The Haj,* a] crude propaganda-novel . . . which traces the Palestinian-refugee problem up through 1956—blaming 100 percent of it on the British and the Arabs (Arab greed, decadence, laziness, backwardness, bestiality, etc.), putting the case into the mouths of a few relatively "good" Arabs. The title character is Ibrahim, who becomes the young chieftain of the Palestinian village Tabah in 1922. He feels affection for Gideon Asch, the noble Haganah leader who watches over the nearby kibbutz. . . . But, culture-bound and constantly threatened by rival Arab leaders, Ibrahim must reject Gideon's offers of aid and friendship. Meanwhile, Ibrahim's youngest son Ishmael—the off-and-on narrator—is growing up during WW II, only half-brainwashed into Koran-based hatred. . . . Then, in 1947, comes the Israeli/Arab warfare: Ben-Gurion vows that "under no circumstances will we force out a single Arab"; for tactical, power-ploy reasons, however, the *Arabs* force the Palestinian villagers to evacuate. . . . The Arabs spread false rumors of Jewish atrocities to cause mass flight; the women of Ibrahim's family are raped by rival Arab henchmen. And though the family survives, thanks to Gideon and a "very sympathetic" Irgun officer, their arrival in Arab territory on the West Bank is greeted by Arab disdain, neglect, cruelty. . . . They live in a cave, in refugee camps. . . . All UN attempts at bettering the refugee situation are ruined by "tribal avarice." And finally, "no longer able to combat or cope with the evils of our society," Ibrahim slips back into primitivism—hating Israel, killing his daughter for abandoning traditional ways—while young Ishmael ends up in despair, knowing that his "culture" is the villain . . . and that "the Arabs alone have the resources to dissolve their refugee problem, if they wanted to." Are there elements of truth in Uris' anti-Arab version of Palestinian history? Unquestionably. Here, however, presented in a blurred fact/fiction format, his arguments come across as grossly biased, untrustworthy, drenched in bigotry. Gratuitous scenes of Arab sex-and-violence are inserted to remind us that this is a "savage people"; generalizations about the Arab "nature" abound. . . . Furthermore, simply as storytelling, this is a sad comedown for veteran Uris: the narration is rudimentary, often clumsy; the dialogue is amateurish, riddled with anachronisms; flat little history-lessons are thrown in haphazardly; and there's no real characterization—just illustrations of the defects in Arab culture. In sum: a dreary, ugly lecture/novel—sure to attract an audience, but likely to embarrass all but the most unthinking Jewish readers.

A review of "The Haj," in Kirkus Reviews, *Vol. LII, No. 3, February 1, 1984, p. 113.*

EVAN HUNTER

Leon Uris's **"The Haj"** could have been a different and far better book. Returning to the scene of his huge 1958 best seller, **"Exodus,"** Mr. Uris attempts here to explore a Palestine in tumultuous upheaval between 1944 and 1956, hoping to shed light on what still remains a bewildering political and religious impasse. The illumination he provides, however, is so thoroughly dimmed by a severely biased viewpoint that the book loses all power as a work of fiction and all credibility as an objective study of that depressing and continuing deadlock.

The hero—if he can be called such—of the novel is Haj Ibrahim al Soukori al Wahhabi, *muktar* (or head) of the village of Tabah, close by the Shemetz Kibbutz on the road to Jerusalem. We come to know this man through an alternating dual narrative recited on the one hand in the first-person voice of his son, Ishmael, and on the other through an omniscient third-person voice that we can assume speaks for Mr. Uris himself. The stylistic device is clumsy at best, despite Ishmael's apology for it in the very first chapter. What is unforgivable, though, is the propaganda—there is no other word for it—that booms out from virtually every page of the book; it is insidious when Mr. Uris himself is speaking and despicable when it is framed in the thoughts and voices of his many Arab characters. . . .

According to Mr. Uris, Arabs in general and Palestinians in particular are lazy, cowardly, boastful, deceitful, untrustworthy, double-crossing, backbiting, lustful, undependable murderers, thieves and rapists. . . .

When a view is so biased, it becomes impossible to accept even what appears to be impeccable research on past events. History lessons in brief are inserted into the book at regular intervals lest we forget Mr. Uris's overriding theme. The Arabs are a hateful and hate-filled people and there is no chance they will ever change. It is no wonder that by the end of the novel, Haj Ibrahim explodes in an unspeakable act of violence that drives his son Ishmael mad.

One cannot deny a novelist his personal view; that would be akin to cutting out his tongue, something that, according to Mr. Uris, Arabs are adept at. But Anthony Burgess . . . said, "We do not demand of an author that he be an intellectual . . . but we have a right to intelligence, a knowledge of the human soul, a certain decency—quite apart from professional skill. Probably this imputation of decency is important: All the great novels have been about people trying to be kinder, more tolerant."

"The Haj" is not a great novel. It is not even a good one; Mr. Uris's head-on assault finally leaves the reader battered and numb. The effect might best be summed up by his own description of an Arab conference in Zurich: "Words hiss out like dueling rapiers, swish, clang. Moods of rage and disgust bounce off the lofty heights of the committee rooms and the intellect becomes dull and insulted."

> *Evan Hunter, "Palestine in Black and White," in* The New York Times Book Review, *April 22, 1984, p. 7.*

JANE STEWART SPITZER

Leon Uris's novels **"Exodus"** and **"Trinity"** moved me, captivated me, and kept me up late at night. I expected his latest, **"The Haj,"** to have the same effect, and I was very disappointed that it didn't.

The story failed to capture my interest until I was almost halfway through it, and I never got fully caught up in it. The writing is surprisingly poor; many of the characters never come

to life, and Uris continually hits the reader over the head with his prejudices against the Arab world and Islam. . . .

The opening chapters are confused, because Uris jumps around in time and switches viewpoints continually. Granted, in order for a reader to understand the historical events in which the characters are involved, he or she must know something of the history of Palestine. But Uris provides so much information I sometimes wondered if I was reading a novel or a history book—and then how much of the apparent history was really accurate and how much was fiction.

Uris paints a richly detailed portrait of Arab life and culture. However, this portrait is also completely unsympathetic to the Arab world in general and particularly to the Palestinian Arabs. In fact, **"The Haj"** reads like a treatise on the evils of Islam and the brutality of Arab culture. It conveys the distinct impression that there is no possibility for a peaceful solution in the Mideast.

The pessimism, combined with Uris's prejudices, saps the novel of its vitality and appeal. True, Uris displayed his views clearly in **"Exodus"** and in **"Trinity."** Yet, because of his sympathy for his subjects, these novels displayed more enthusiasm than bias, which contributed greatly to their readability. This is missing in the new novel.

"The Haj" also suffers from too little plot and too much talk—most of it in a stilted, awkward style that reads like a translation. It would seem that Uris attempted to capture the colorful, formal style of Arab rhetoric, but the result is unwieldy and boring.

> *Jane Stewart Spitzer, "'The Haj', Uris's Richly Detailed Palestinian Portrait, Lacks Vitality," in* The Christian Science Monitor, *May 2, 1984, p. 20.*

JERRY ADLER

"So before I was nine I had learned the basic canon of Arab life," says Ishmael, the young Palestinian boy who narrates about half of Leon Uris's new Zionist figburner [**"The Haj"**]. "It was me against my brother; me and my brother against our father; my family against my cousins and the clan . . ." and so forth, for most of the remaining 500-odd pages of this extended study in treachery, bigotry, obsequiousness, ignorance and sheer malevolence among the Arabs. . . . [All] of these vices come naturally to the Arabs in this book. They are Uris-Arabs, a species familiar to readers of Uris's early epic **"Exodus."** In intellect, the difference between a Uris-Arab and his camel is not great and in morality the camel wins by a furlong. . . .

The book begins in the 1920s, when the Jews first brought their absurd notions of sanitation, education and the rule of law to the surrounding valley, then proceeds through a series of battles in which the Arabs usually fall down and run when the Jews fire over their heads, and into a miserable exile in the refugee camps. Uris shows a glimmer of sympathy for the Palestinians' political plight, which he blames entirely on the other Arab states, but none whatsoever for their pigheaded rejection of the greatest blessing that can be bestowed on a backward race, Jews.

In all of this, one can discern the faint outlines of the book Uris evidently thought he was writing, about one man's struggle to throw off the burden of a thousand years and learn to live in peace with the infidels. . . . But a Uris-Arab is even less convincing when beset by self-doubt than when engaged in his normal pursuits of scratching, cursing and bragging. Uris is so totally out of sympathy with his Arabs that he scarcely troubles to put himself into their minds. Ishmael, the Haj and the minor character of Dr. Mudhil, an archeologist, are the only three Arabs out of the million or so in the book with a germ of sense, and all their insight seems to have done for them is to lift them part way out of ignorance and into shame. "We are a people living in hate, despair and darkness," Mudhil says at one point. "The Jews are our bridge out of darkness." **"Exodus"** said the same thing, but from the Zionist point of view. To put these sentiments into the mouths of Arabs results in a book that does not strike a single convincing note in a vast symphony of sound.

> *Jerry Adler, "The Unchosen People," in* News-week, *Vol. CIII, No. 21, May 21, 1984, p. 84.*

Wendy Wasserstein
1950-

American dramatist.

Wasserstein wrote her first off-Broadway play, *Uncommon Women and Others* (1977), while a student at Yale Drama School. Critics enjoyed this affectionate satire of a reunion of six Mt. Holyoke graduates; several commented that Wasserstein's wit and perceptiveness demonstrated a potential for future success in the theater. However, most agreed that she had not yet realized that potential with her second play, *Isn't It Romantic* (1981). Wasserstein based this play on a friendship between two women: Janie, a Jewish writer, and Harriet, a WASP business executive. In the course of the play, Janie questions her own personal and professional goals.

Although *Isn't It Romantic* wrestles with some serious contemporary issues, many critics thought that Wasserstein's heavy reliance on wisecracks and one-liners, while providing some genuinely humorous moments, detracted from these issues, and that the play as a whole was too episodic to allow for clear development of characters or ideas. Most agreed that Wasserstein remedied many of these problems in a later version of *Isn't It Romantic* produced in 1983. Critics found the second version of the play clearer than the first in its depiction of character motivation and growth, especially in the character of Janie. Wasserstein also presented a one-act play, *Tender Offer*, that same year.

EDMUND NEWTON

Wendy Wasserstein is apparently a young woman with a darting sense of the ridiculous, eyes which flicker mercilessly across a room and spy one absurd detail after another. She could easily have turned her play **"Uncommon Women and Others"** into an extended "Saturday Night Live" routine.

But she has put that Eastern school precocity in its place and created a group of characters who demand not only sympathy but affection. The laughs are there, many of them genuine thigh smackers, but Miss Wasserstein has shown triumphantly that she knows when to stop. . . .

There's more than a trace of nostalgia for the rarefied atmosphere of the old snob schools. For young women in their late 20s, confronting vaguely unsatisfying marriages and careers, the smack of young minds working off of each other has to be remembered fondly.

But the real triumph of **"Uncommon Women"** is that you leave the theater caring deeply about its characters.

> Edmund Newton, "Women One Can't Forget," in
> New York Evening Post, *November 22, 1977. Reprinted in* New York Theatre Critics' Reviews, *Vol. XXXVIII, No. 21, November 28-December 4, 1977, p. 140.*

RICHARD EDER

Wendy Wasserstein has satirical instincts and an eye and ear for the absurd, but she shows signs of harnessing these talents to a harder discipline.

Her play **"Uncommon Women and Others"** . . . is exuberant to the point of coltishness. Miss Wasserstein, who is young, uses her very large gift for being funny and acute with a young virtuosity that is often self-indulgent.

But there is more. Unexpectedly, just when her hilarity threatens to become gag-writing, she blunts it with compassion. She blunts her cleverness with what, if it is not yet remarkable wisdom, is a remarkable setting-out to look for it. She lets her characters—some of them, anyway—get away from her and begin to live and feel for themselves.

"Uncommon Women," is about women in a time of changing traps: new ones, set and hidden in the same current of feminine consciousness and liberation that is springing the old ones. Although the play deals with feminist ideas, it is not so much interested in the traps as in the women. It does not disassociate itself from the march but it concerns itself with blisters.

The women are a group of friends at Mount Holyoke, one of the Seven Sisters colleges. We see them in flashbacks that take off from a reunion they hold six years after graduation. Only a small part of the focus is upon the changes that have taken place since; the time has not been long enough for them to be very great. The main emphasis is upon the lacerations, hopes, despairs and confusions that the times inflict upon these students at a hatchery for "uncommon women," where walls have turned porous and let all the winds blow through. . . .

Susie . . . is a comic cartoon, very funny but hardly believable. So is her opposite, Carter, a genius freshman who sits catatonically on the floor practicing typing to the rhythm of the "Hallelujah" Chorus and plans to make a movie about Wittgenstein. . . .

These two caricatures mingle awkwardly with the more rounded and believable figures of the students who are the heart of the play. There is Kate, handsome, active, programmed for success as a future lawyer but terrified by it. There is Muffet, who is torn between being liberated and wanting to find her Prince. There is Rita, quirky, funny and appealing, with her detailed obsession with the sexual aspects of liberation and her determination to be a fantastic person by the time she is 30. And there is Holly, rich, overweight, full of longing and indecision.

A terror of choices and the future afflicts all of them, and Miss Wasserstein has made this anguish most movingly real, amid all the jokes and the knowing sophistication. . . .

If the characters, in their outlines, represent familiar alternatives and contradictions, Miss Wasserstein has made each of them most real. They do not stay within what they represent: In the reunion scene, set in the present, each has softened or shifted, and they will go on doing so. Miss Wasserstein's is an interim report and a convincing one.

> Richard Eder, *"Dramatic Wit and Wisdom Unite in 'Uncommon Women and Others',"* in The New York Times, *November 22, 1977, p. 48.*

VARIETY

"Isn't It Romantic," confirms and extends the promise shown by Wendy Wasserstein's first play, **"Uncommon Women and Others,"** a few seasons ago. The new comedy is a witty and involving exploration of a contemporary feminine dilemma, the conflict between personal independence and romantic fulfillment.

Wasserstein again shows keen humor and canny perception in her account of two well-educated friends, a chunky, wisecracking Jewish woman and her upperclass Wasp marketing exec pal, as they struggle against non-understanding parents, male condescension and their own romantic expectations in the bittersweet pursuit of happiness.

The Jewish heroine is the more fully developed of the two, and emerges as an endearing, funny, warm and principled contemporary woman. She's a convincing embodiment of the internal conflict of modern feminists who can't sacrifice independence and pride for love, even with a likable and sympathetic man.

Audiences will respond favorably to the character but may be disappointed at her climactic rebuff of the goodhearted young doctor who wants her to move in with him. But her action is obviously essential to the author's thesis.

The Harvard-educated businesswoman is also acutely drawn, and the device of complementary lead characters works well. But the latter character's affair with a snaky, egotistic office superior is tough to understand in view of the woman's obvious

intelligence. Her eventual decision to marry an offstage colleague comes too abruptly and suggests plot expediency.

Wasserstein is less successful with the characters of the Jewish girl's parents, who come over as affectionately written stereotypes. The friend's hardbitten business exec mother is another interesting and complex character.

A synopsis may suggest that the play is more message-oriented than it really is. It's stuffed with clever jokes of the hip New York variety and until the pace begins to lag toward the close, moves along at a brisk clip. Some of the scenes cover the same basic territory, and about 20 minutes could be shaved with no loss of impact. . . .

Wasserstein isn't yet a fully adept craftswoman, but she has a rare feeling for the feminine situation today and she writes with sunny wit. With the proper pruning, **"Romantic"** could be a good Broadway prospect.

> Humm., in a review of *"Isn't It Romantic,"* in Variety, *June 17, 1981, p. 84.*

EDITH OLIVER

Wendy Wasserstein's **"Isn't It Romantic"** . . . could, in a sense, be considered a sequel to her **"Uncommon Women and Others,"** of several years ago. **"Uncommon Women"** was a glorious comedy, with an undercurrent of satiric rage that held it taut. . . . **"Isn't It Romantic"** is about Janie Blumberg and her Gentile best friend and private-school and college classmate Harriet Cornwall, both of them aged twenty-eight and unmarried, and about their mothers, and about the men they see and sleep with and consider and discuss, and about the loving tie of best-friendship between women. . . . It is Janie, though, whose story is being told—a witty, original, overweight Jewish heroine whose life has come to a stop, and this time the undercurrent is of sadness, perplexity, and rootlessness. Janie simply cannot make a move without being pushed, and when at last the doctor she is in love with, sort of, tries to push her into sharing an apartment with him she puts her foot down and refuses, and she isn't sure why. Even though any play about low spirits is bound to be less springy than one about high spirits, or even anger, and even though this one seems at times as out of shape and as listless as its beguiling heroine, it is, episode by episode, very funny indeed. The source of the fun, of course, is Janie's (Wasserstein's) comic turn of mind, which is like no other on earth. The Jewish humor, for example, and the dropping of Yiddish words and phrases, which would seem to be an overworked vein by now, is as fresh and as funny as everything else.

> Edith Oliver, *"The Day before the Fifth of July,"* in The New Yorker, *Vol. LVII, No. 18, June 22, 1981, pp. 86-7.**

JOHN SIMON

With her previous *Uncommon Women and Others,* Wendy Wasserstein proved herself a playwright to watch and wait for; her current *Isn't It Romantic* throws the weight on the waiting rather than the watching, as the promise continues to be brighter than the delivery.

In *Uncommon Women,* Miss Wasserstein reminisced about herself and her college classmates, offering us enough uncommon and common women for a goodly cross section. Here . . . the cross section dwindles into a slice of life that, in turn, is mostly autobiography. That theme is apt to lead a young author down the garden path and straight into the flower beds of self-pity and sentimentality, which Miss W. avoids fairly successfully, but at the cost of landing in the shrubbery of prickly cuteness, a playful but all too defensive smart-aleckiness that tries to authenticate with ubiquitous thorns an absent rose. . . .

Miss Wasserstein has gathered a nosegay of droll vignettes— sweetly and pungently scented, often naughtily spiky, but in some cases also rather wilted. I doubt whether much fun can still be squeezed out of the amiable friendship-hostility (a platonic version of love-hate) between Gentile and Jew, epitomized by Harriet's mispronunciations of the Blumberg Yiddishisms—typical Cornwall humor. Another drawback is the limiting "sickness" of some of the best jokes, as when Harriet's "My mother identifies with Jean Harris" is topped by fat Janie's "I think her mistake was stopping with Hy; she should have done away with all of them!" (There follows a list of dieticians.) This barb can serve as an example of what I am not sure whether to call Yale Drama School or Christopher Durang humor, which consists of scrumptious, scattershot bitchiness that makes for a pointillism of pinpricks refusing to solidify into shapeliness.

One is amused and sometimes touched, but never shown what keeps Harriet wasting herself on the singularly callow Paul, or why Janie rejects the eminently endearing Marty. Miss W. is, clearly, better at parts than at wholes, more gag- than goal-oriented. But she has a lovely forte: the comic-wistful line, as when someone inquires about Janie's mother, who, being a compulsive dance-class taker, is termed by Janie a dancer, "What company is she with?" only to be told, "She's an independent." Or, again, when Janie remarks bittersweetly, "Marty, look: Everything with you is simpler than it has to be." This could be a vein of gold, and needs only proper engineering to be efficiently mined. . . .

Isn't It Romantic leaves us with too many not urgent enough questions, but its intermittent arid patches are relieved by an underlying puckish decency that, after every poisoned dart, blows another, smeared with antidote. We have every right to continue expecting more from this gifted writer.

      John Simon, "Failing the Wasserstein Test," in New York *Magazine, Vol. 14, No. 26, June 29, 1981, pp. 36-7.*

EDITH OLIVER

Wendy Wasserstein's **"Tender Offer"** is about a father who is so late picking up his little daughter at dancing school that he misses her recital. At the beginning, the child . . . is waiting alone, filling in time by improvising a dance to "Carolina in the Morning." She is furious, but we don't realize how furious until the father appears with some lame excuse about being detained at the office. Their conversation is stiff to begin with (and very funny, too), but when a silver trophy drops out from under the child's rolled-up dancing clothes the father begins to realize that what he has done to her is serious, and—two steps forward, one step back—a permanent reconciliation begins. Miss Wasserstein has used a trivial incident to trigger important emotions, and she doesn't falter for a moment.

      Edith Oliver, in a review of "Tender Offer," in The New Yorker, *Vol. LIX, No. 17, June 13, 1983, p. 98.*

MEL GUSSOW

In her new, improved version of **"Isn't It Romantic,"** Wendy Wasserstein has added a sweet humanity to her comic cautionary tale about a young woman's ascent to adulthood. When the play was first presented two years ago . . . it overflowed with amusing lines about such protean subjects as indulgent parents, rebellious offspring and food as a substitute for love. With careful rewriting, the playwright has turned the tables on her own play. . . . [It] is now a nouvelle cuisine comedy. . . .

Janie has the heart of a waif and sometimes the demeanor of a clown. Some of the character's jibes are still inner-directed, but the author has cut back on self-mockery and has even sacrificed a few of her funniest lines. She allows us to see the character as a trusting woman who wants "it all"—marriage, family, a job writing for the "large bird" on "Sesame Street," and loving parents who respect her distance. . . .

Breezy, fresh and unaffected, **"Isn't It Romantic"** skips to its mother-daughter showdown, becomes belatedly tearful, but is immediately redeemed by a touching conclusion in which everyone agrees that "It's just too painful not to grow up."

      Mel Gussow, "New 'Romantic' by Wendy Wasserstein," in The New York Times, *December 16, 1983, p. C3.*

EDITH OLIVER

[Wendy Wasserstein] is among the funniest and most inventive writers around, but the first version of **"Isn't It Romantic"** seemed to me "as out of shape and listless as its beguiling heroine." That has now changed. Miss Wasserstein has revised her script, and she and her director, Gerald Gutierrez, have given the play momentum and a sense of purpose; there is nothing listless here. . . . My first feeling was one of dismay that the play had lost its innocence, but eventually I realized that that was the whole point: it has indeed lost its innocence but in the doing has acquired muscle and form. Janie, for all her frustration and bewilderment, learns who she is and what she wants, and when she turns down the unsuitable doctor she knows exactly why. The statement "Life is negotiable" occurs several times in the text, but she is not about to negotiate. The troubling emotions that were an undercurrent the first time around have now been brought to the surface, and without any loss of humor. The action is still a matter of short episodes. . . . The conversations of Miss Wasserstein's Gentiles sound as authentic and bright as those of her Jews. Harriet's mother, in sharp contrast to Janie's parents, is the very model of detachment, and, when her daughter keeps pressing her for advice and counsel, replies, with some irritation, "What is this, 'Youth Wants to Know'?" That is just one, though, of many funny and telling episodes.

      Edith Oliver, in a review of "Isn't It Romantic," in The New Yorker, *Vol. LIX, No. 45, December 26, 1983, p. 68.*

BENEDICT NIGHTINGALE

A few weeks ago I was mildly deploring American dramatists' apparent inability to pull open the shutters and look out into the big world beyond the emotional hothouse within whose clammy confines they and their work would seem to have become terminally trapped. . . .

[The] arrival of Wendy Wasserstein's **"Isn't It Romantic"** at Playwrights Horizons convinces me that last month's diagnosis was too vague and general. True, the American theater seems more preoccupied than ever with personal relationships: but not all that many could honestly be dignified as fully adult ones. For quite a few playwrights, some of them very talented, the great contemporary problem appears to be whether, when, how and why to grow up at all.

Call this diaper drama, though the infants it involves are more likely to be 20 or 30 than two or three. The first essential ingredient is at least one parent capable of obsessing and preferably mesmerizing his or her progeny. . . .

Janie Blumberg, an aspiring writer so rumpled she wanly describes herself as "an extra for 'Potemkin'," has moved into her own tiny apartment; but that does not deter her doting father and voracious mother, who arrive to wake her up at 7 o'clock A.M. with importunate advice. . . . She has to hack herself free, and does so, not without difficulty and tears. Her mother, again arriving uninvited, is forced to shout "my daughter is a grown woman" outside Janie's front door: Only then is she allowed into the apartment for a big, climactic scene in which peace is rowdily negotiated.

Considering Janie is approaching 30, you might think this a less than remarkable victory; but I suspect Miss Wasserstein would not agree. At any rate, she spends much of the play tacitly comparing her heroine with her best friend Harriet Cornwall, a Wasp whose casual amours and burgeoning career in marketing both seem to proclaim the independence she enjoins on others. But she too has a formidable parent, a svelte tigress effortlessly in control of her particular piece of the business jungle; and, if I read Miss Wasserstein correctly, Harriet is fundamentally even more in thrall to this mother than Janie to her more obviously possessive one. She gets her promotion. She becomes engaged, after a few days' courtship, to a man who will doubtless prove as disposable as her own father turned out to be. "All right for a first husband" is her mother's offhand summing-up of the romance. The cub will turn into a spun-nylon copy of the tigress, or maybe just remain a cub.

Miss Wasserstein writes with warmth, verve, and a captivating wit; and if the jokes and repartee sometimes seem excessively feverish, it is because some of the characters are pretty feverish people, hectically using language to keep their more unmanageable feelings at bay. That is particularly so of Janie. . . . Again the play isn't lacking in the kind of intelligence that can make you suddenly appreciate the point of view of a mother, a lover, a friend you have been lured into seeing only from the stance of those trying to cope with him or her. Yet it is difficult to take these people and their feelings . . . quite as seriously as Miss Wasserstein seems to want. Perhaps the comic atmosphere is, in spite of everything, too strong, too infectious. Perhaps Miss Wasserstein's talent is more for ruefully recording the signs and symptoms of pain, less for entering and exploring it. Perhaps she makes too big a deal of what should, after all, be an every-day feat: growing up.

Or is this a smug view? Many psychiatrists, their couches overflowing with the paternally bruised and maternally maimed, would doubtless say so. A thousand non-professional voices— middle-aged daughters doomed to look after their fathers, wives

maddened by their husband's preoccupation with their mother-in-law—would promptly chorus their support. Neither life nor literature nor the theater is exactly lacking in instances of people who have found it difficult to sever what Sidney Howard, in his brilliantly observant study of manipulative mother and half-castrated son, called "The Silver Cord." (p. 2)

There would seem to be two main troubles with contemporary contributions to the genre. First, they tend to be narrow in scope. . . . Contemporary writers about parents and children make the odd gesture towards creating a context—professions are mentioned, jobs specified, and so on—but it is seldom seen as important or even relevant. The more they can isolate relationships within a social vacuum, the happier they would seem to be.

The second trouble with diaper drama these days is its proliferation. When there's too much about, the theater begins to look like a kindergarden and feel like an incubator for overgrown babies. There are, after all, other subjects than how to stand up to poppa, or how to stop momma pouring chicken soup down your throat when you're 30 years old. There are more exhilarating rallying cries than the one that comes at an important climax of **"Isn't It Romantic."** "It's just so painful not to grow up." There are other things for a heroine to do than battle her way to a long-overdue adulthood. In fact, there's a world out there to discover. (pp. 2-14)

Benedict Nightingale, "There Really Is a World beyond 'Diaper Drama'," in The New York Times, *January 1, 1984, pp. 2, 14.*

ELLIOTT SIRKIN

[*Isn't It Romantic* presents] a series of hard-driving skits, most of which conclude with some kind of punch line or shock—a new dramatic shape that probably issues from . . . [a childhood apprenticeship] in front of the TV screen. This gives *Isn't It Romantic* . . . a compelling stop-and-go movement. Unfortunately, . . . the prevailing emotional atmosphere is one of injured self-regard and subliminally rationalized prejudice. . . .

Isn't It Romantic, which is set in New York, has the kind of heroine the whole world thinks of as a New Yorker: Janie, a bright, plump, emotionally agitated young Jewish woman, who insults herself with sophisticated quips . . . and fights off a hopeless boyfriend whose family owns a chain of sit-down delis. If this ethnic waif seems less like a person than a tourist attraction, it's at least partly because she so resembles Rhoda on the old *Mary Tyler Moore Show.* . . .

[In] *Isn't It Romantic,* the cutting edge of . . . [Wasserstein's] swipes at the pretensions and eccentricities of young upper-middle-class New Yorkers feels a little blunted. If she's clever enough to name an overdressed, Don Juanish executive Paul Stuart, why doesn't she do a full-scale number on pretentious haberdashers, the way she once gave it to obnoxiously ladylike Seven Sisters girls? . . . [With] tightening and revising, the colloquial, wisecracking script might work as the libretto for a nice, old-fashioned musical along the lines of [Betty] Comden and Adolph Green's *On the Town.* But even in a musical, the crucial scene where Janie's parents try to buy her love with a mink coat would probably still be pushing things a bit.

What is disturbing about *Isn't It Romantic* is its ugly reverse bigotry, which grows uglier still for being unacknowledged and probably unconscious. Janie's great epiphany occurs when she realizes her idolized East Side girlfriend Harriet is going to marry a man she isn't crazy about. This act of supposedly coldblooded practicality throws both the heroine and the playwright into a tailspin of moral superiority. But Wasserstein's animus against Harriet goes deeper than mere priggish disapproval. What *Isn't It Romantic* really dramatizes is an old racial myth: Jews are warm and emotional, and WASPs, especially on Park Avenue or Wall Street, are cold fish.

Janie is a gentle freelance contributor to *Sesame Street;* Harriet is a corporate barracuda. Janie's mother is a middle-aged flower child; Harriet's is a hardboiled, bronzed tycoon. Love, evidently, is only a many-splendored thing if you're not a ritzy *goy*—a species *Isn't It Romantic* regards with a mixture of envy, resentment, disgust, and secret, worshipful fascination.

Elliott Sirkin, in a review of "Isn't It Romantic," in The Nation, *Vol. 238, No. 6, February 18, 1984, p. 202.*

Sloan Wilson

1920-

American novelist, short story writer, and autobiographer.

Wilson is the author of traditional novels of middle-class America. He is best known for his 1955 novel *The Man in the Gray Flannel Suit,* a work which portrays the struggles of the "average" businessman as he makes compromises in pursuit of the American dream of success. The novel became a best-seller and gave the American public a symbol for the big-city businessman with a suburban home and family. Wilson's main character, Tom Rath, is very aware of his conformity and the sacrifices he is making to achieve his goal. The novel touches upon the experiences of countless young men who faced the business world after World War II. As Herbert Gold has written, the novel "entered the collective soul of the middle class."

Wilson's other popular novel, *A Summer Place* (1958), deals with the *nouveau riche* who spend the summer months at Pine Island, off the coast of Maine. Through his portrayal of the complicated love affairs of two teenagers and their parents, Wilson shows the stereotypical problems of their class: alcoholism, infidelity, ennui. Yet his novel has a happy ending, a resolution some critics denounced as unrealistic and oversimplified.

The Man in the Gray Flannel Suit II (1983) is a sequel to Wilson's earlier success. It continues Tom Rath's story in 1963, when his boss is chosen to serve as chairman of a White House conference on mental health. As his assistant, Rath finds himself in Washington, heading towards a promising future. With the assassination of President Kennedy, however, the project is abandoned and Rath faces major career decisions. His personal life also becomes complicated. But again, everything is resolved neatly and Rath's life and new career look extremely hopeful.

According to Wilson, his books end happily because his own problems were miraculously resolved and he says many readers tell him his books mirror their lives. He maintains that he shows a broad picture of America, for, as he says: "America *is* business." *The Man in the Gray Flannel Suit* and *A Summer Place* were adapted to film in 1956 and 1959, respectively.

Wilson is currently serving as a consultant to Philip Crosby Associates, Management Consultants, in Winter Park, Florida. He is using his experience as the basis for a nonfiction work, *The New Executive.*

(See also *Contemporary Authors*, Vols. 1-4, rev. ed. and *Contemporary Authors New Revision Series*, Vol. 1.)

When you live within 180 feet of men twenty-four hours a day for two years, life gets pretty intimate. . . . The climax comes during a roaring sea typhoon, in which the author's clean and compact prose appears at its best.

For the most part, Mr. Wilson turns in a creditable performance. It is unfortunate that **"Voyage to Somewhere"** is the victim of bad timing: its author could hardly know that Thomas Heggen's "Mister Roberts" would reach the bookstalls first—or that that rowdy, incomparable tale of the naval supply service would make further commentary on that branch more or less superfluous.

Richard Match, *"Chocolate Bars to Leyte," in* The New York Times Book Review, *November 17, 1946, p. 42.*

RICHARD MATCH

"Voyage to Somewhere" is the story of Lieutenant Barton and his first command. Some time in May, 1944, Mr. Barton reported to a San Francisco yard to take over his new ship from the lady welders. . . . Lieutenant Barton and his green hands sailed the SV-126 safely to New Guinea and thereafter, for two years, shuttled her back and forth between steaming tropic islands. . . .

JOHN McNULTY

As calm and serene a garb as a man can wear is the standard gray flannel suit of commerce, a habiliment supposed to betoken solidity of character tastefully touched with quiet nonchalance. Calmness and serenity, however, frantically elude Tom Rath . . . [the title character of **"The Man in the Gray Flannel Suit"**], and his inward solidity of character peeps forth, in quite pat fashion, only at the end of the narrative.

Rath killed seventeen men as a paratrooper in action in World War II. In Rome, he spent an unblessed honeymoon with Maria, a lovely young lady-of-the-streets whom he picked up in a bar. . . .

Mr. Wilson succeeds in imparting the panicky quality of the lives of . . . [the] commuters in gray flannel. . . . The theme is that the dangers and worriments of New York-Connecticut life can be perhaps more difficult to overcome than the more dramatic perils of wartime combat.

This novel . . . is an interesting but spotty job. It is spotty because it is not easily believable in places. For example, Tom Rath gets a job as public relations officer for Ralph Hopkins, president of the United Broadcasting Company merely by walking into the offices in Radio City, applying for the position (not job), and filling out a brief autobiography. That doesn't seem the way in which such posts are handed out. . . .

Nevertheless, Mr. Wilson does picture the type of decent, post-war man who has a conscience and wonders if he should permit his conscience to rule him out of the big money he needs to provide a lush scale of living for a wife and children, or whether he should become a yes-man, a sort of Jeeves-With-A-Typewriter to a mogul and smother his conscience. Tom Rath keeps faith with the conscience yet he is on the way to the big money at the end, believe it or not.

> *John McNulty, "Tom Rath, Commuter," in* The New
> York Times Book Review, *July 17, 1955, p. 18.*

GERALD WEALES

The faceless figure on the dust jacket of Sloan Wilson's *The Man in the Gray Flannel Suit* is apparently supposed to imply Everyman. The title of the novel and the publicity that preceded its publication seem to insist that Tom Rath, the novel's hero, is universal, at least to the minimal extent that he represents the young veterans struggling suavely to make their mark in the world of Madison Avenue.

Briefly, the plot is this: Tom Rath, the assistant to the director of the Schanenhauser Foundation, is struggling to keep his wife and three children on seven thousand dollars a year . . . ; he resigns from the foundation to become special assistant to Ralph Hopkins, the head of the United Broadcasting Corporation, a position which he leaves after a bit of soul searching, a sacrifice that is rewarding both spiritually and materially.

These are the bare bones of the novel, and Wilson has covered them, not with flesh, but with a welter of incident, as commonplace as it is irrelevant. . . . The reader is also introduced to a host of casual characters, but the novelist is incapable of any characterization that goes beyond a few surface mannerisms and a little stock soliloquizing that is quite false. (p. 525)

At the end of the novel Rath is leaving his unrewarding job to step into a position specially created for him, one in which he will feel less like a prostitute. . . . He is easing his unruly conscience by financing the raising of the illegitimate child, with the moral support of dear Betsy, with whom he has a newer, warmer, purer relationship. What is the moral of the novel supposed to be anyway: the self-pitying shall inherit the earth? The sloppily happy ending with its emphasis on material rewards certainly implies no more than that, although Sloan Wilson probably imagined that there was a deal of moral fiber in this story of the faceless man who, as it turns out, is faceless,

not because he is Everyman, but because he is no man at all. (p. 526)

> *Gerald Weales, "Life on Madison Avenue," in* Com-
> monweal, *Vol. LXII, No. 21, August 26, 1955, pp.
> 525-26.*

LOUIS O. COXE

Without trying to be sociological or symbolical, Mr. Wilson has got more of the late 'forties and early 'fifties into [**"The Man in the Gray Flannel Suit"**] than any other writer I know of; he has captured something of the unease of the time, its neurotic worry and speed and pressure. Yet Mr. Wilson is never portentous nor grimly profound; he writes fiction, not a Ph.D. thesis, and he has wit. . . . The story concerns a not so very young couple and in particular the husband's attempt to keep alive his marriage, his own self, and his roots in the past. Mr. Lionel Trilling has somewhere said something to the effect that the novel is—must be—about money. Mr. Wilson's novel is about money; it is also about one of the important phenomena of our day, the dropping down in the social and economic scale of many formerly "aristocratic" members of society, the mad struggle to maintain and consolidate one's position in the face not only of terrible economic pressure but in the face, in the teeth, of one's own violent disinclination. All the pathos, absurdity, and humor of the struggle come out clearly in Mr. Wilson's picture of his nice young man on the run. If there is a certain glibness, perhaps, in the conclusion—if Mr. Wilson lets his couple off too easily—I am not sure that this is as grave a fault as may appear. . . . Much of what Tom Rath, our man in gray flannel, has to cope with is simply Life; we can find it being coped with in the pages of George Eliot or Balzac or Jane Austen in much the same way as here. Mr. Wilson has a grasp of reality, and the novelist's eye and ear.

> *Louis O. Coxe, in a review of "The Man in the Gray
> Flannel Suit," in* The Yale Review, *Vol. XLV, No. 1,
> September, 1955, p. 157.*

ARTHUR MIZENER

"A Summer Place" is much better written than **"The Man in the Gray Flannel Suit."** The trouble is that this craftsmanship serves a conception of life that will not stand examination. At its heart is a conviction that only the self-made man is a "builder." He builds society, of course, or at least "makes" money, but above all he builds the loving domestic community. In their big moments, Mr. Wilson's admirable people walk naked on beaches, feeling themselves washed of years of falseness. But most of the time they are too busy with domestic problems of a high-grade soap-opera kind for such indulgences.

On one side of them stand the aristocrats like Bart Hunter, who thinks no gentleman makes a point of winning or working and is a pessimist. On the other side stand the narrow-minded, hasty-minded, lower-middle-class people who love respectability, Airwick and spayed cats. All these characters are implausible; they are the oversimplified, fantasy images of what are, apparently, the dominant values of the present American middle class. Because Mr. Wilson describes them earnestly and thoroughly, they have their fascination, though it is a fascination different from the one Mr. Wilson intended, and not without its own kind of horror.

> *Arthur Mizener, "Builders and Breakers," in* The
> New York Times Book Review, *April 13, 1958, p. 5.*

TIME

[*A Summer Place*] keeps the reader in suspense at the end of every chapter—waiting for the soap commercial. Can Molly Jorgenson and Johnny Hunter, teen-age lovers and troubled children of divorce, find lasting happiness by racing the stork to the altar? Will Johnny's mother Sylvia desert her alcoholic husband, with his blueblood pedigree and red-ink bank balance, for an adulterous affair with Molly's self-made millionaire father? Is life a game of second chance or an inescapably heir-conditioned nightmare?

The answers to these and sundry other questions are offered in a fictional session of bland man's buff by Sloan Wilson, the man who did more for gray flannel suits than Brooks Brothers. . . .

Novelist Wilson is slick, readable and craftsmanlike. He has again chosen a highly American theme: the intensive pursuit of happiness. But he has recorded his findings without giving himself the satirical elbow room to comment on them. Author Wilson has chided gloomy fellow novelists who write "as if we were back in the Depression years," and his point is well taken. He himself is open to the opposite charge of a boom mentality about the human condition. The pithiest critique of this point of view came from F. Scott Fitzgerald during another boom: "The victor belongs to the spoils." (p. 105)

"Typewriter Tycoon," in Time, *Vol. LXXI, No. 15, April 14, 1958, pp. 105-06.*

WILLIAM JAMES SMITH

Off in a world not quite of its own there is a realm of literary endeavor known as "women's fiction." . . . Novels of this genre appear serially in one of the three or four big women's magazines and subsequently in book form. Sometimes, as in the case of *A Summer Place,* such a novel becomes a very successful book and earns the author a great deal of money. (p. 309)

Monetary considerations aside—and few women's fiction writers are so successful, or, frankly, as good, as Mr. Wilson—women's fiction has fairly consistent characteristics, none of which is necessarily sinful. This fiction must, first of all, be fairly "easy." Its aim is leisurely relaxation and it must not demand too much in the way of intelligence or patience. It should simulate a certain boldness of idea and at the same time incorporate all the current clichés. Here Mr. Wilson has succeeded admirably. He is quite seriously berated in some circles as a voice of the New Reaction because he portrayed a businessman sympathetically in *Gray Flannel.* He is, of course, an anthology of liberal aphorisms.

Story line is, by tradition, somewhat restricted in women's fiction. Like piped-in music the highest and lowest notes have been flattened out so as not to exacerbate sensitive nerves. (pp. 309-10)

A constant, almost an exclusive, theme of women's fiction is the Oak and the Willow motif. A Splendid Woman (all women are splendid except the heroine's foil, who is a Rich Bitch), is given a choice of two men as life's partner. One is an Oak and the other is a Willow. The story is how she ends up happily, after tribulation, with the Oak. In *A Summer Place* the heroine has made the terrible error of actually marrying the Willow, so you can imagine what she has to go through before she gets the Oak. . . .

This is all governed by fairly rigid conventions. The entrance of the Willow is always announced by the word "graceful." As soon as a man is described as having done something "gracefully" you know you have spotted your Willow. . . .

The Splendidness of the Woman is even more elaborately adumbrated. Though she is seldom more loftily placed than in the role of simple housewife she has true greatness in her. Without her the Oak is nothing. But, splendid though she may be, she has her Moment of Weakness, which is the hinge of the plot. In *The Man in the Gray Flannel Suit* the heroine's Moment of Weakness comes when she turns from her Oak in momentary doubt just when she has almost made a man of him. In *A Summer Place* the heroine's Moment of Weakness has occurred before the opening of the novel proper when she married the Willow. This may be one reason that the novel is not as good as the earlier one, judged either as women's fiction or in a less supercilious frame of reference. The total effect is relaxing, all right, but rather lugubriously so.

Oh, and another feature of women's fiction is that all the main characters come with their faces left blank so you can fill them in with the lineaments of your own favorite movie stars. (p. 310)

William James Smith, "Women's Fiction," in Commonweal, *Vol. LXVIII, No. 12, June 20, 1958, pp. 309-10.*

TIME

The latest 604-page redundancy by [Sloan Wilson, *A Sense of Values,*] may . . . serve a purpose: to stimulate total disenchantment with the disenchantment novel. . . .

Nathan Bond, Author Wilson's protagonist, runs true to formula. In most disenchantment novels, the hero is a non-hero who attends an Ivy League college (Nathan goes to Yale), where he is traumatically snubbed because he lacks good looks or money, the two top things, as F. Scott Fitzgerald put it. Lacking popularity, the non-hero decides to be different (Nathan wants to be an artist), but he invariably deserts his goal and runs rabbit-scared for life's lettuce (Nathan becomes a cartoonist and creates a Chaplinesque tramp called "Rollo the Magnificent").

But before the non-hero can be properly launched on his affluent career, otherwise known as the rat race, he must have a mate so that he can share his disenchantment. Early snapshots of his beloved are etched indelibly in the non-hero's mind, partly because he always lives his life flashbackwards. Nathan is forever recalling Amy arched against the sky on a diving board at poolside on her aunt's rambling estate. In disenchantment novels, these rambling estates are the toys of a gracious childhood soon to be whisked away by that legendary anti-Santa, the '29 crash. Nathan has his losses too—a father to cancer, a mother to an insane asylum. As Novelist Wilson handles them, these are life's little ironies.

Once Nathan's cartooning clicks, he and Amy move to Connecticut, where non-heroes almost always live. The couple has the standard non-heroic family, one boy, one girl. Nathan eventually makes $100,000 a year, above par for a non-hero, but the tax bite devours his bank balance. After a few years of this and nearly two decades of marriage, Nathan discovers, with the customary belated double take of the non-hero, that he does not know his wife, his children, or himself.

At this point the non-hero always has two anodynes for his despair: 1) alcohol, 2) another woman. Author Wilson generously allows Nathan to sample both.

This story may appeal to fans of vacuum keening. For others it will seem only a smooth and utterly mediocre version of an over-familiar American morality play.

> *"The Disenchanted Forest," in* Time, *Vol. LXXVI, No. 21, November 21, 1960, p. 115.*

THOMAS E. COONEY

"A Sense of Values" is another handling by Sloan Wilson of the theme of his earlier novel, **"The Man in the Gray Flannel Suit."** Once again he examines the conflict of ambition with marriage, but this time in a man who has been wildly successful in a corner of the world that Tom Rath in the earlier book partly rejected. Nathan Bond, an artist-poet *manqué* who finds he has a golden touch as a syndicated cartoonist, is a lot like Rath. . . .

Bond, unlike the temporizing Rath, sacrifices almost everything to his morbid drive for commercial success. . . .

Here, the conscientious reviewer has a problem. He reflects that he has read over 600 pages avidly, but at the end has not felt particularly satisfied. Why? Because **"A Sense of Values"** is a topical rather than a poetic novel. The topical novel absorbs the reader's interest with details of a life he knows well, or would like to daydream about. Historical novels and novels about such sub-cultures of the modern world as advertising, war and middle-class marriage tend to be topical. The poetic novel, on the other hand, may well have a topical background, but it transcends it with people and events that endure in memory because they are somehow tragic, symbolic, mythic. For all its topical evocation of the Nineteen Twenties, for example, "The Great Gatsby" is a poetic novel.

Thus, though Nathan Bond's crisis makes him a better man, and though he is a subtler and more mature character than Tom Rath, his own fears that there is nothing enduring in his life are ironically justified; he *is* ephemeral, because he is a topical, not a poetic, creation.

> *Thomas E. Cooney, "Perils of Fame," in* The New York Times Book Review, *November 27, 1960, p. 47.*

GEORGE STEINER

[Mr. Sloan Wilson] is an eminently proper writer with a shrewd eye to the feminine trade and Hollywood. But although his novel is in no way offensive, it is utterly hollow. In its narrative technique and vision, *A Sense of Values* suggests a kind of gigantic cliché, spun out over six hundred unruffled pages. The entire design is weary with previous use. . . . The scenario writer will be able to leave the text intact: "I realized that everything I had to say she already knew. Her hair smelled sweet. Her hands told me that she needed me." Fadeout, soft organ music flowing into the dawn. And everything in the long narrative has the same celluloid inevitability. On his first ship, Bond performs precisely the same gestures of grave incompetence and nascent triumph as are performed in *The Caine Mutiny* and *The Cruel Sea*. His remembrance of uneasy adultery is set down in the very cadence of Marquand and O'Hara, but without the mastery of either. (p. 423)

> *George Steiner, "Winter of Discontent," in* The Yale Review, *Vol. L, No. 3, March, 1961, pp. 422-26.**

THE TIMES LITERARY SUPPLEMENT

The sad thing about [*A Sense of Values*] is that Mr. Wilson, who has talent and at one stage seemed really to care about American society, now writes as if he were himself in the final grip of the exurbanite disease. . . .

As in so much American writing the style is flawless; but it is the sterile flawlessness of the *Saturday Evening Post*, so that one longs for an occasional lapse of taste or error in the custom-built plot in order to feel that either Mr. Wilson or at least his characters are human.

> *"Elegant Void," in* The Times Literary Supplement, *No. 3089, May 12, 1961, p. 297.*

MARTIN LEVIN

In the 1920's, all the best people hang out at the Paradise Point Inn, a restricted Lake George hostelry owned by a close-knit association of three families. And the best of this 50 year reprise [**"All the Best People"**] re-creates the folkways of upper-middle-class life around the Lake during the eras of boom and bust. Mr. Wilson concentrates on two clans, the Stauffers and the Campbells. . . .

As fortunes rise and wane, sailboat racing becomes a psychodrama for family hostilities, life at the hotel ambles on . . . , and the younger generation gropes innocently for its first love. When the younger Campbell son marries the Stauffer's younger daughter, the story loses its freshness and falls into a standard stereotype. Still, Mr. Wilson . . . has enough zest for the early days to give his novel a healthy momentum before it finally runs down.

> *Martin Levin, in a review of "All the Best People," in* The New York Times Book Review, *November 1, 1970, p. 49.*

HERBERT GOLD

[**"What Shall We Wear to This Party?"**, the] autobiography of the man who wrote **"The Man in the Gray Flannel Suit,"** seems to promise some unpromising confessions—self-hatred, divorce, alcoholism, middle-aged romantic yearnings, nostalgia about a faded WASP propriety, hapless vanity, Internal Revenue problems, an uneasy Harvard boy now lurking in the body of a grandfather. And, indeed, it delivers this load of splintered kindling. Yet this book, after eight novels, which led many readers to think Sloan Wilson had no surprises in him, is finally touching, charming, and revelatory in the best way—it tells what the author knows and also more than he knows. It is a near miss at summing up the experience of a generation, marred mostly by a hastily sentimental running down at the end, which is itself a symptom of the life his career has attempted to define. . . .

Whatever Sloan Wilson offers in his paltry last chapters, the book as a whole tells more, a more powerful instrument than the will of its harassed author. (p. 7)

Wilson begins by reminding us of how his war seemed "an authentic struggle between good and evil," and how he had to pass the tests of bravery and seasickness. After all this stalwartness, there was the scramble "to build the house which filled our dreams—or at least those of our wives—to join the country club. . . ." In Bicentennial America this sounds archaic, even to most of those who lived it, and yet this march to the sound of the same drummer was only yesterday. Time magazine writers wore the uniform and knew they were in the business of selling the opinions of Henry Luce. The world had its order, and, for those who knew the limits, there was a yacht in the pot at the end of the rainbow. "Girls, like loving cups, were trophies who always went to the victor of some strenuous event." A nice boy like Sloan went to Exeter and Harvard and hoped to end as a "winner" so that he could earn one of those loving cups.

The real relationship of such men is to other men, and Wilson is effective and moving about war, business, money, success. His eloquent matter-of-factness about armies seagoing among desolate ice floes is exactly right. His tender notice of the birth of his first daughter and of the final dying of his ancient mother, transcend the loving-cup standard, but most of his contacts with women echo the harassed and dreamy powerlessness of a driven class of men. (pp. 7-8)

"The Man in the Gray Flannel Suit" was a book which many of us snooted for its fuzzy neatness. The title seemed to make its point and to leave little left over to the novel itself. And yet it hit a nerve, it entered the collective soul of the middle class; if that's too clanging a statement, say simply that it gave a generation the mirror it craved for itself. . . .

It reflects a bygone period of American resurgence, a sort of internal Marshall Plan, which hid the real problems of American life—and of man's mortal destiny—under a convenient blanket of flannel. This reminiscence evokes the time of Sloan Wilson, Harvard boy turned writer, with some of the rueful best qualities of the decedent class. He was obedient even in sex—"the duty and pride of a man is to give pleasure to a woman in bed"—and this mournful Puritanism tells more about marriage in the 50's than most of the executive-suite books of the time and their honeyed episodes of executive sweets. . . .

The story's very familiarity is part of its value. In a shabby lobby he meets James T. Farrell, who offers him a wise saying about writers and women: "Women will go to you because of your intensity. They will leave you for the same reason." . . . Troubled by women, proudly obsessed by sex, Wilson gives clear evidence for his confusion; but it doesn't help to understand this homely ill. Rising to it would be better; growing from it would be best. But here too, his symptoms will make the men of his generation feel right at home, the children of F. Scott Fitzgerald out of J. P. Marquand, ever hopeful of perfect love and O.K. status.

The autobiographical form enables Sloan Wilson to unburden himself of a good deal of real wisdom unfortunately contradicted by his style during the self-consciously "wise" passages. In its way, this too is true to the confusions of morality and esthetics, elegance and doing it right, which distracted a class and a time. . . . The style is heavy—what could be called, with heavy reviewer's ambiguity, underwritten—and the book is too long, but the sincerity of its griefs makes it frequently touching; the life is felt, so that the journeyman style ultimately works better than it should, doing the real work of style—to say what the man means. The muzziness of some of the apologies, the sentimentality of the joyous second marriage (it may be true, but it doesn't convince) are often redeemed by sharpness of epithet and apposite incident. And the person who

comes through, in all his vanity and weakness, is finally an appealing one.

As epitaph to a type, the millions in their gray flannel suits, now peculiarly greened and denimed over, thanking gurus or lithium as they used to thank God and Fate and the Table of Organization, this book makes the wounded, inadvertent suggestion that the end of American youthfulness is not yet the end of everything. (p. 8)

> *Herbert Gold, "Epitaph to a Generation: What Shall We Wear to This Party?" in* The New York Times Book Review, *May 17, 1976, pp. 7-8.*

HOPE HALE DAVIS

It is a surprise to discover . . . unflinching honesty in Sloan Wilson's **What Shall We Wear to This Party? The Man in the Gray Flannel Suit Twenty Years Before & After.** . . . Wilson's book is virtually swamped in washes of the sentimentality that the author knows is a problem he has never been able to solve. Still, he does recognize his deficiencies, and it is a rare autobiography that puts pride second to truth. That sly, pathetic best foot nearly always slips forward. . . .

[Wilson] has written about what matters. **The Man in the Gray Flannel Suit,** for all its sentimentality, is based on a truth he saw early. Since then everyone, even President Ford, has learned to pay lip service to "the quality of life." But it was no cliché in 1955, when Wilson told the world the Madison Avenue-suburban rat race was not worth running. So many thousands welcomed the book, he fell prey to the very success he had seen as false. (p. 20)

> *Hope Hale Davis, "Excising the Hurt," in* The New Leader, *Vol. LIX, No. 22, November 8, 1976, pp. 19-20.**

KIRKUS REVIEWS

Can sincerity save a badly written book from being dreadful? Sometimes, but not always. [In *Small Town*], Wilson's obvious earnestness only intensifies the embarrassment of his most mawkish exploration of male menopause. Divorced photographer Ben Winslow comes back to his Vermont hometown from the empty singles life in California—and finds that his alienated teenage son Ebon has been taken in by a farmhouseful of obliging women. . . . Soon Ben is part of this extended family. . . . One wants to like this heart-on-sleeve novel, but the hopeless dialogue, toneless prose, and daytime-soap plotting make that a sad impossibility. (pp. 901-02)

> *A review of "Small Town," in* Kirkus Reviews, *Vol. XLVI, No. 16, August 15, 1978, pp. 901-02.*

MARC GRANETZ

The story [of **Small Town**] is a familiar one and Sloan Wilson . . . executes it with few surprises. Hewat, who drives a white Lincoln Continental, is the stock local businessman-politician; the Kellys are the stock Irish family down to their very names; the California to which Ben compares Livingston is the stock playground of rich, plastic, unhappy people; Ben and Rosie's battle against corrupt small town politics is as old as the upstate hills they love. For long stretches, moreover, the stories of Ben, Rosie, Ebon and Annie come so much to the fore that Livingston and its citizens are neglected, thus rendering **Small**

Town only mildly interesting as an exploration of the intricacies of small town living.

The language of the novel also leaves a lot to be desired. The modifiers are usually superfluous, the dialogue often fails to convey the intensity of the moment and is frequently so saccharine as positively to diminish intensity, the use of parentheses to separate thoughts from words in some conversations is a distracting device.... Still, despite the fact that they are given few eloquent words or thoughts, Wilson's major characters emerge as human beings of very definite proportions, dreams and troubles. Readers willing to look past stylistic inadequacies may find in *Small Town* a story of the search and fight of several memorable characters told by a highly compassionate man. (p. 42)

> *Marc Granetz, in a review of "Small Town," in* The New Republic, *Vol. 179, No. 18, October 28, 1978, pp. 40, 42.*

EILEEN KENNEDY

A literate soap opera, ["**Small Town**"] tells of middle-aged world-famous journalist, Ben Winslow, who wants to launder the gray years through a return to and possible renewal in his hometown. Life, like the laundry, never comes out sparkling-pure; but Ben, revolving in a continuous cycle of lechery and greed, a nefarious jealous brother, corrupt country-club and corporation politics, emerges clean. The powerful bleaching agent: *Love....*

["**Small Town**" is] clean (no smutty sex scenes) and, rare bird, a great love story of the over thirty. And it's dishonest. A cheap-dyed, slick distortion of reality: the apparent championing of traditional moral values doesn't hide the ring-around-the-collar. And the author's friends, puffing the work, titillate the potential reader by calling it "engrossing autobiography" and "personal history."

> *Eileen Kennedy, in a review of "Small Town," in* Best Sellers, *Vol. 38, No. 11, February, 1979, p. 343.*

MARC LEEPSON

In 1941, before the United States entered the war, the State Department called on the Coast Guard to patrol Greenland's coasts.... Before the war was over, the eight-ship American Greenland Patrol captured one German weather ship and sank another.

The Greenland Patrol is the focus of Sloan Wilson's novel, **"Ice Brothers."** ...

"**Ice Brothers**" is smoothly written and cleverly plotted. Wilson's fictional accounts of two sea and air battles seem plausible and realistic. Set against the frozen adventures of the crew of the converted trawler Arluk is the story of Wilson's hero, 22-year-old college drop-out Paul Schuman. Paul's adventures fighting the Germans are played out against his internal battles....

The Eskimos of Greenland are important characters as well. Wilson portrays them as innocent victims of German aggression, Danish colonialism, and American sailors' enthusiasm. It is the Eskimos who provide the book's title. "The Eskimos have a saying," a Danish official tells the Arluk's crew. "On the ice all men are brothers. It must be true, for these people

of the ice are the only human beings on earth who fight no wars." ...

Wilson's story-telling ability, his ear for dialogue, and his realistic portrayal of the icy environment of Greenland are the highlights of this book. The story rolls along smoothly as Wilson skillfully builds toward the climactic battle scene. The book is not in the same league with the best World War II novels, such as Joseph Heller's "Catch 22," Norman Mailer's "The Naked and the Dead," or James Jones's "The Thin Red Line." But "**Ice Brothers**" is nevertheless a crisply written, entertaining book.

> *Marc Leepson, "Patrolling Greenland Coasts," in* The Christian Science Monitor, *November 28, 1979, p. 24.*

PUBLISHERS WEEKLY

Following up on the success of "**Ice Brothers**," Sloan Wilson goes down to the sea again to launch a most commendable thriller ["**The Greatest Crime**"], a tale of drug-running gone awry. Meet Andy Anderson, a reformed alcoholic, a Harvard grad, an itinerant captain and a man in his late 50s who is deeply in love.... A $500-million shipment of cocaine can reach the U.S. from Columbia if assorted pros, from Andy to trigger men to benign government officials, all pull together.... Thus the voyage to Long Island becomes a cliffhanger: Can Andy and his cohorts abort the cruise? Will the Coast Guard arrive in time? Will backers retaliate? Like an orchestrator, Wilson succeeds in exploiting each of these disquieting notes right to the end.

> *A review of "The Greatest Crime," in* Publishers Weekly, *Vol. 218, No. 21, November 21, 1980, p. 47.*

BILL OTT

[*Pacific Interlude*] has some of the virtues and many of the vices of traditional war fiction. Examining the invasion of the Philippines from a perspective quite different from the usual hit-the-beaches fare, Wilson focuses on the dangerous lot of a Coast Guard gas tanker.... Unfortunately, the novel's genuinely exciting action sequences take a backseat to a cliché-ridden personal drama centering on the ship's captain, 25-year-old Sylvester Grant.... [Imagine] an earnest Van Johnson type as the hero and you've got the picture. Still, World War II buffs will be pleased with the action and willing to ignore most of the clichés.

> *Bill Ott, in a review of "Pacific Interlude," in* Booklist, *Vol. 79, No. 1, September 1, 1982, p. 31.*

JOHN CHAMBERLAIN

Back in the 1950's Sloan Wilson wrote a novel, "**The Man in the Gray Flannel Suit**," that caught the essence of what was then becoming known as the rat race. It was the story of a chronic worrier, Tom Rath, whose desire to be himself could not be reconciled with his ghostwriter's trade.... The novel had a happy conclusion. Tom inherited grandma's big house, and his wife, Betsy, forgave his wartime infidelity. But now, a quarter-century later, we learn in a sequel ["**The Man in the Gray Flannel Suit II**"] that the Raths' contentment was momentary. Tom Rath, as the new novel picks him up in his middle age, is just the same old worrier. He still loathes writing for other people, he still frets because his paycheck can't meet occasional extravagances. Moreover, his teen-age children present a whole new set of exasperations. His relationship with his wife is outwardly calm, but he is ready for a fling. The fling, with a good-humored woman who is not a worrier, makes the story. Sloan Wilson writes of dalliance with a sure touch. But, in pursuit of another happy ending, he contrives an unreal conclusion. It so happens that Tom and Betsy are each ready for divorce and each relieved to learn the other has been two-timing. The mutual rush to forgive and separate is hard for the reader to swallow. Could any divorce ever have gone so smoothly, shedding contentment on everyone involved? But if the novel as a whole is unconvincing, it has its idyllic moments. Readers will respond to the character of the woman who teaches Tom Rath not to worry.

> *John Chamberlain, in a review of "The Man in the Gray Flannel Suit II," in* The New York Times Book Review, *March 25, 1984, p. 20.*

(Arthur) Yvor Winters

1900-1968

(Also Ivor Winters) American critic, poet, short story writer, and editor.

Winters's prominence as a critic is based largely on his analyses of poetry. Although he was generally associated with the New Critics, whose critical methods adhered to close readings of a text, Winters was concerned with the functional relationship between content and form. He proposed that poetry should evoke a rational and moral observation of human experiences. Throughout his criticism, Winters expounded upon the importance of morality in literature. To the dismay of his professional colleagues, he often praised minor poets that met his criterion over more established writers. Because of Winters's insistence on absolute values and ethics in poetry, some critics found his doctrines rigid and dogmatic. However, his critical theories have been regarded highly for their clarity and force.

In *Primitivism and Decadence* (1937), Winters introduced the principles and concepts he was to follow throughout his career. He argued that rhythm and meter induce emotion in poetry and he believed that a poem's success lies in its ability to elicit strong moral impact through a balance of rhythm, emotion, and motivation. He extended his theories in *Maule's Curse* (1938), a study of obscurantism in the works of such nineteenth-century poets as Jones Very, Edgar Allen Poe, Emily Dickinson, and Ralph Waldo Emerson. In his best-known work, *In Defense of Reason* (1947), which combines *Primitivism and Decadence*, *Maule's Curse*, and *The Anatomy of Nonsense* (1943), Winters examines the roles of didacticism, hedonism, and romanticism in literature. The book provoked diverse reactions among critics, many of whom contended that Winters failed to attack the issues most pertinent to his theories. Some felt that his metrical analyses were too ambiguous for a full comprehension of the literary function of poetry. However, the book helped solidify Winters's reputation as a significant literary scholar.

Winters published several volumes of his own poetry that were well received. His early verse, like the poems of H. D. and Ezra Pound, is experimental and imagistic. Much of his early poetry contained naturalistic themes and subjects which reviewers found rich in emotional intensity and perceptual power. His later poems shifted away from free verse toward the classical tradition which he championed in his criticism. These poems concentrate on more philosophical subjects. Among Winters's important volumes of poetry are *The Immobile Wind* (1921), *The Magpie's Shadow* (1922), and *Collected Poems* (1952).

(See also *CLC*, Vols. 4, 8; *Contemporary Authors*, Vols. 11-12, Vols. 25-28, rev. ed. [obituary]; and *Contemporary Authors Permanent Series*, Vol. 1.)

Courtesy of Janet Lewis Winters

DELMORE SCHWARTZ

[*The essay from which this excerpt is taken was originally published in* The Southern Review, *Vol. 3, No. 3, 1938.*]

Mr. Yvor Winters has written [*Primitivism and Decadence*,] a book which every serious American writer, and indeed every-

one with the least pretense to serious interest in literature, ought to buy and ought to study. This is said by way of qualifying radically many of the difficulties which I wish to point out in his notions about the nature of poetry. And one ought also to say at the start that there are many remarkable insights in this book: Winters seems, for example, to have predicted, indirectly, Crane's death; he has managed, apparently by a deliberate effort, to extend his taste from such writing as Joyce's to such an opposite extreme as Churchill and Gay, and in doing so he has provided us with the means of extending our tastes in like manner; and he is, I think, the first American critic of the present century to concern himself explicitly with meter. . . . Winters is the first critic, I should think, who has attempted to show the *specific* ways in which meter, morality, structure, and meaning are related, and, in a way, identical.

It would seem ungrateful, then, in view of all this extremely valuable work, to turn about and say that in section after section, Mr. Winters indulges himself in excess and exaggeration, displays prejudices which are wholly arbitrary, and is guilty either of misconstruction or ignorance. But each of these charges can be clearly demonstrated. . . . [In] the most general terms, Winters' error is that of the reductive fallacy, which has many instances in the history of criticism: the critic, that is, decides to define Beauty (or aesthetic value, or worth, or whatever he calls it) and he decides that Beauty is unity in difference, or significant form, or the expression of the class struggle, or pleasure; and having decided this, he rules out all instances which do not conform to his definition or he attempts to reduce unlikely instances to the unique definition. The ruling definition for Winters is regularity of meter. This is a crude way of stating it; Winters has other criteria, which modify it; but I shall try to give a more adequate statement of this view later on.

Primitivism and Decadence divides itself into five parts, each of which reflects backward and forward upon the others; the subjects, in order, are: morality insofar as it is involved in poetry, structural methods of presenting the subject matter, poetic convention (a really illuminating discovery), ways of classifying types of poets, and finally, meter. All five refer to aspects of any given poem which are, ultimately, identical: the moral insight exhibited in a poem is, for example, the same thing as its firmness and lucidity of structure.... The range of his awareness is commensurate with the kind of meters he uses and the type of poet that he is and the way in which he presents his subject.

Beginning with the first and the most fundamental aspect of the poem with which Winters deals, one finds that the writing of a poem is a moral act because it is an attempt to order, control, and understand one's experiences. Each of the constituents of poetry is, in its very nature, an instrument of perception, so that poetry is "the last refinement of contemplation," "the richest and most perfect technique of contemplation."

Now the first difficulty is Mr. Winters' singular view of morality in general. Not only does he say that religion may be and philosophy can be a *preliminary* to poetry, but his whole view of what constitutes a moral act seems to be based upon a very narrow view of what the poet is involved in when he writes a poem. He thinks, for example, that social conditions and modern thought do not change the mode which moral responsibility will take and the mode which style and meter can take. Those who think these matters make the task of the modern poet different and more difficult suffer from "group hypochondria." This accusation when added to the different charges against various mdoern poets—Mr. Eliot's "spiritual limpness," for example—and when added to a good deal else which cannot be mentioned in a review, imply that Winters sees the poet operating in some kind of vacuum in which not only his act but the circumstances in which he acts depend upon his own choice.... [It] is worthwhile considering the moral preeminence which Winters gives to the act of writing a poem. He says that it is no substitute for action "in the face of a particular situation," but merely "a way of enriching one's awareness" and thus becoming more intelligent about the future; yet the emphasis betrays him: religion and philosophy are merely preliminary and the *richest* way of knowing is the act of writing a poem and the great poet has triumphed (in the terms of Mr. Richards' rhetoric) over life itself. (pp. 332-35)

[It] is worthwhile considering ... what seems to be the root of Winters' critical method. This is to be found, I think, mainly in the little book by I. A. Richards called *Science and Poetry,* and also in his *Principles of Literary Criticism* and certain pages on the "sincerity ritual" in *Practical Criticism.* The ideas of Richards are well-known and may be rapidly summed up. He thinks the poet is, in the poem, engaged in organizing his impulses—his appetencies and aversions: the good poem is the one in which a psychological balance or harmony—synaesthesis is Richards' term—has been achieved. And this view flows from the belief that nature has been "neutralized," that most of the values of the past have been unmasked and

repudiated, and that poetry alone is left to the human being as a means of integrating his life. Richards attacks Yeats, De la Mare and Lawrence as poets who refuse to face the modern situation, the neutrality and meaninglessness of nature, and who attempt to provide elaborate fictions to belie the truth. Winters duplicates this attack in some of his statements about Yeats and Crane. The difficulty here is that Winters has obviously changed his mind: he no longer accepts the crude naturalism of Richards—which Richards in *Coleridge on the Imagination* turns upside down into a kind of subjective idealism, and which was initially derived from doctrines which Lord Russell has long since abandoned—and Winters has taken upon himself beliefs and values of a neohumanist variety. One is permitted to change one's mind, but a certain thoroughness is preferable. Winters, however, still drags along Richards' psychological-moral notion of the substance of a poem. The mixture is indeed curious. Winters is perhaps as sensitive as anyone could be to the concrete poem, and he must know that a poem is not primarily a balance of appetencies and aversions, but an effort at perception and evaluation. But the former belief remains, transformed into the idea that the creative act itself, with all the absorption and effort it necessitates, makes the writing of the poem a moral act. One can only observe that the criminal may also exhibit a like devotion and concentration. (pp. 335-36)

Mr. Winters makes a good many of his judgments on the basis of the metrical character of a poem. From the meter of the poem he infers the spiritual or moral character of the poem.

There is, to begin with, the statement that "the limp versification of Mr. Eliot is inseparable from the spiritual limpness that one feels behind the poems." What spiritual limpness is, one can only guess, and even limp versification is a term which is fairly vague; the statement is made, moreover, rather tentatively ("one feels"). Still it will serve as an example of Mr. Winters' method. (p. 337)

Mr. Winters exhibits prejudice and a lack of tact and exactness in judging the meters of Eliot, although elsewhere in the book, in writing of "The Subway," by Allen Tate, he has provided a brilliant elucidation of the relationship of meter and feeling, meter and attitude, meter and meaning. If you abstract the meter of the poem from its statements and base your judgment upon the meter alone, then you conclude that Mr. Eliot is spiritually limp, or that Bridges is spiritually stiff, frivolous, and superficial. But there is a different situation in the concrete poem. One does not start with the meter, nor with the explicit statements, but with both, taken together. Their relationship is one of reciprocal modification; each "characterizes" the other, and they cannot be separated, a fact upon which Winters himself insists. This fact is often forgotten. One is offered examples of sublime verse and nonsense rhymes with the same vowels or in the same meter, in order to show that meter is not expressive. This is the error correlative to that of Winters. (p. 338)

But there is a good deal more than a metrical basis for Winters' dislike of Eliot's poetry, which recently, he says, has been a kind of "psychic impressionism, a formless curiosity concerning queer feelings related to odds and ends of more or less profound thought." Here again Winters' beliefs are intruded upon his literary judgment. Ultimately Winters would have to say that he just does not like Mr. Eliot's religion. Winters thinks that such poems as "Ash Wednesday," "Animula," and "Journey of the Magi" ... are the products of psychic impressionism and a formless curiosity only because of his own beliefs, which, so far as they are available, seem to relate mainly to a conception of nature as full of sensuous temptation, which must be resisted—and perhaps also to a view of rationality and consciousness as the supreme goods. One would scarcely wish to deny the importance of these concerns, but the point at issue is the way in which they distort his literary judgments. As a literary critic, Winters is justified in judging the *representation* of a belief, not the belief itself. This does not imply a purely formal approach to literature because the representation in question is a matter of understanding and evaluation as well as the use of language. It is difficult in literary criticism to avoid moral, political, and even theological judgments, not to speak of the tendency to praise our friends' poems, but one can with effort separate literary judgment from all these and thus avoid confusion. (pp. 338-39)

Mr. Winters' next subject is structural methods of presenting the subject matter and we are presented with what is, for the most part, an extremely valuable analysis of different forms, repetitive, narrative, and logical; pseudo-reference, of which seven varieties are elucidated; qualitative progression; alternation of method; double mood. Some of these structures, Mr. Winters claims, are better than others, and it would be foolish to deny it. But they are used as weapons in the continuous polemic which Winters is carrying on throughout the book against Laforgue, Eliot, Crane, Pound, and others; and in his application of these structures, Mr. Winters seems to force himself to misconstrue specific quotations. (p. 340)

[The] crux of our objection turns out to be the same as when Winters' morality was in question. He is using his own views of God, freedom, and immortality when he attacks a passage of Crane in "The Bridge" by saying, "What myths have we in mind here? None. Or none unless it be the myth of Pocahontas, which, as we have seen is irreducible to any idea." Winters has other objections to this passage also. The point involved here, however, is the exclusion of Crane's beliefs because Winters cannot accept them. If it were mainly a matter of not being able to find the poet's assertions *in* his actual words, the canon which R. P. Blackmur uses so ably, then the objection would be just. But this is not the objection and Winters a little later accepts the "reference to a purely private symbolic value," which is what this is. If, however, we begin to reject the poetry based upon beliefs which are different from our own . . . , then Winters knows very well that few great poets will be left to us. (p. 342)

There are according to Mr. Winters four different systems of measuring rhythm in a poem, the quantitative, the syllabic, the accentual, and the accentual-syllabic. The first two, except for Bridges' experiments, have almost no relevance to verse in English. Winters is mainly interested in showing how free verse can be analyzed out into accentual verse, and how accentual-syllabic verse is superior to it. The analysis of both types of verse will probably be very useful to poets, and the whole theory of meter is elucidated with both lucidity and subtlety. (p. 345)

To generalize crudely, what Winters wants in any meter is strict regularity, so that every divergence from regularity can be used to express or imitate the feelings or perceptions which are being referred to by the words. Now the requirement of a norm, strict regularity, cannot be denied. But from this, Winters' argument makes two rapid jumps. The best norm, it is claimed then, is the accentual-syllablic one just mentioned. And then the nature of this norm is generalized from the practice (but certainly not the theory) of Bridges, T. Sturge Moore, Pope, and Dryden. What would happen, however, if Winters

looked for the norm in *The Winter's Tale,* or *Samson Agonistes*? What, furthermore, would happen if Winters examined the free verse in the English Bible? In passing, Mr. Winters refers to the meters of *Samson Agonistes* as in part a failure, in part a *tour de force,* but he mentions neither the *Psalms* nor Shakesperean blank verse. If these types of writing were examined, it would be clear that several norms are possible, and each type of subject matter would imply a special modification of existing meters. (p. 346)

At times Winters writes of the use of the accentual-syllabic norm in a way so extreme that the use which Winters most emphasizes seems a fiction. It is as if the poet deliberately ticked off deviations from the norm on suitable occasions. Perhaps some poets do. But it is obvious that taken in metrical abstraction such deviations are more or less limited in number, unequal to the variety of perception, and insufficiently precise. One may substitute a trochee for an iamb at the beginning of a line in order to have a perceptive variation for anger: "Scoundrel!"—or the same substitution to express affection: "Darling!" The substitution as merely metrical is largely indeterminate.

But if we take meter and meaning together, as I suggested above, the way in which meter is expressive becomes a much more complicated matter than the deviation from a metrical norm. In the great sonnets of Milton, as Mr. Winters must be perfectly aware, the expressive effect of firmness of character and indomitable spirit is gained by the latinity of the diction as it conflicts with the meter, with the sonnet form, and with the normal sentence order of English. This results in certain metrical variations, but none equal to the expressive effect: the primary means of expressiveness is Milton's diction. And in general one must suppose that the meter plays a passive, although essential, role in the poem. It provides a kind of substratum whose evenness and regularity are, so to speak, cut into by the modulations of style and diction and meaning. The fusion of style and meter, meaning and meter, provides the expressiveness of the poem, and carries its tone and attitude. The deviations from the norm are for the most part minor aspects or consequences of this fusion. And it seems to me that one can say that the style *is* the poem. The quality of the style is the verbal and aural realization of the poet's sensibility. The style is, in fact, the poet's values, focused upon his perceptions and revealed in all their purity. No poet can escape from this style, although he may change his meters. The poem apart from its style is not a poem but something which belongs to psychology or biography or politics or history. Meter is a necessary element in style, but it is far from being the only one.

One concludes, then, by supposing that the nature of structure and meter is not as simple, not as exclusive as Mr. Winters has made it out to be; nor are their *specific* modes established for future experience and future writing (although the *principles* involved are so established: such a principle as Mr. Blackmur uses, that the poem be *contained* in the words, or such another one as Mr. Winters makes us more aware of, that there be a norm of regularity in the rhythm). One must be grateful, too, for the extension of taste to such poets as Churchill, Gay, Rochester, and T. Sturge Moore. If there is no meaning, on the one hand, in making this extension of taste, for the purposes of convincing others or oneself, negative to the extent that T. S. Eliot becomes a bad poet, on the other hand Mr. Winters' judgments are sometimes illuminating even when his reasons are unacceptable. The defects in Pound and MacLeish, for example, are not a mere willful departure from accentual-syllabic verse, nor merely a deliberate blindness to experience. Pound can see only surfaces and his favorite periods in history, and MacLeish can get no further, at any time, than a catalogue of objects and a reverie, but the reasons for this, whatever they may be, are not simple, as we see more clearly in the instance of Crane, a poet in search of objects of devotion in an age when there were no devotional objects. If, then, we permit religion and philosophy and the society in which we live to be somewhat more than preliminary to the act of writing poetry, perhaps "the clear understanding of motive, and a just evaluation of feeling," which Mr. Winters asks for on his last page, will be less difficult and rare. This much, however, is certain: when good poetry is written, Mr. Winters will recognize it (although he may later change his mind because of some peconception), and meanwhile he will be writing his own extremely fine verse. (pp. 348-50)

> Delmore Schwartz, "On Critics: 'Primitivism and Decadence' by Yvor Winters" (1938), in his Selected Essays of Delmore Schwartz, edited by Donald A. Dike & David H. Zucker, The University of Chicago Press, 1970, pp. 332-50.

RANDALL JARRELL

Maule's Curse, which is supposed to relate "the history of ideas (a history of ideas that, neglecting both science and philosophy, is almost wholly theology) to the history of literary forms," is interesting and plausible; but some of the parts of the argument are unproved, one or two unprovable—for instance, the vital point that the doctrine of predestination necessarily leads to religious apathy—and a disproportionate importance is given to causes that were certainly partial. Many or most of the good writers of the Nineteenth Century were similarly cut off from the religion of their predecessors. Mr. Winters might just as well have named his book *Copernicus' Curse* (or Galileo's, or Darwin's, or a hundred others'): for it is the development of the sciences (along with a good many minor causes) that has produced the changes in the world that seem to Mr. Winters so unqualifiedly evil. His indictment of the Puritans boils down to this: their mistaken dogmas led to religious apathy, thence to moral confusion; their continued emphasis on a harshly inadequate morality permanently soured their dispositions, and left them with an exaggerated moral sense after the morality which had produced and directed it had disappeared. The first point hardly seems of paramount importance, since the correct dogmas, throughout Europe and America, led to an equal apathy and confusion; the second point anybody who has known a New Englander admits already.

Still, Mr. Winters' approach has helped produce the extraordinary criticism that makes up most of *Maule's Curse;* it is, all in all, illuminating; but I am afraid it lights Mr. Winters even more piercingly than it does American literature. The abstractions Mr. Winters has chosen—which are, roughly, the traditional Catholic ones—will seem to many of the inhabitants of this planet "inadequate or irrelevant to experience"; he too is a victim of his characteristic American dilemma. His readers will find in Mr. Winters an absolute moral dogmatism, an aesthetic that reduces art to morals, and a metaphysic conscious of hardly any problems except those of determinism. If Emerson's universe is one of amiable but unconscious imbeciles, Mr. Winters' is that of a *crèche.* . . . (pp. 212-13)

Whitehead is supposed to have said of Russell: "Bertie thinks me muddle-headed and I think Bertie simple-minded." Now Mr. Winters is simple-minded, in this sense, to an astonishing degree; to him there are few questions unanswered, and none unanswerable. If ours is not the most rational of all possible worlds (for even Mr. Winters sometimes entertains the doubt), that does not excuse any confusion about it on our part; we *have* absolutely valid standards, both adequate and relevant, by which the universe can be understood and evaluated; if we are unfortunate or foolish enough to disregard these, we must take the consequences—which are disastrous. He writes as if the last three hundred years had occurred, but not to him: I know no one of comparable merit so wholly uncorrupted by "science," in any sense of the word. To him, fine art is correct moral judgment, highly formed and entirely unambiguous. . . . (p. 213)

It is the rigorous application of inadequate and inflexible standards which produces occasional judgments that a tactful admirer might characterize as trembling on the brink of absurdity. (p. 214)

But these are the lapses of a critic whose thoroughness, clarity, and real penetration are almost unequalled today; *Maule's Curse* is the best book on American literature I ever read, and I make so great a point of its author's vices only because his virtues are apparent and indeed overwhelming. He puts into exact and lucid shape judgments informed by an unusual sensitivity, a rigorous intelligence, and a dismayingly thorough knowledge. He reads each writer as if he had never been read before; he is a critical instrument completely uninfluenced by any fear of ridicule or consideration of expediency. We know precisely what he thinks and his reasons for thinking so. Most of his essays are intended to be definitive—a surprising number are. He is valuable both in widening taste (his own likings are unusual, and no one is better at championing neglected merit) and in correcting it (his attacks on the real excesses of modern literature are devastating). If I said just how good the essays on Melville and James are, I should seem extravagant; that on Poe (which leaves him looking like a china shop after a visit of the Marx brothers) is not far behind; Dickinson and Hawthorne are handled with intelligence and love, Cooper with a large and tremendously detailed surplus of the latter. Mr. Winters demolishes his old butt, Emerson, with automatic ease, and a gaze averted to Very. (pp. 214-15)

> Randall Jarrell, "The Morality of Mr. Winters," in The Kenyon Review, *Vol. I, No. 2, Spring, 1939, pp. 211-15.*

JOHN CROWE RANSOM

[*The essay from which this excerpt is taken originally appeared in* The Southern Review, *Summer 1940.*]

The critic who is best at pouncing upon the structure of a poem is Mr. Yvor Winters. There may be guardians of the honor of poetry who are grimmer; that would be because they are more literal, less imaginative, than he is. . . . Winters is not hostile to the modern poets as such, and in fact he works with them chiefly, and as lovingly as his conscience allows. He is not their most severe critic, yet he is a severe critic. In citing him as the ablest logical critic, I do not mean necessarily, and it would not follow, that he is blind to what I have called the texture of poetry; but his conscious theory does not know how to take hold of texture; and his distinction is his skill in analyzing structure. (pp. 211-12)

Winters is a poet, and in his writings about poetry he gives a proper impression of intimacy, so that he is anything but the illiterate moralist breaking into literary criticism. But he is an unusual case; if it were not for declared apostates on the order of Chaucer and Father Hopkins who recant from their literary careers and want their books burnt in honor of their conversion to some conflicting interest, I should think he is almost the most extreme case of his kind. Spontaneously on many occasions, and *ex cathedra* when he rehearses his careful theory of criticism, he subordinates the poetic interest to the moral; or he denies the poetic interest. Other critics may have done this, but less valiantly, and with discreet avoidance of a tone of finality. (pp. 212-13)

Winters believes that ethical interest is the only poetic interest. (If there is a poem without visible ethical content, as a merely descriptive poem for example, I believe he thinks it negligible and off the real line of poetry.) Now I suppose he would not disparage the integrity of a science like mathematics, or physics, by saying that it offers discourse whose intention is some sort of moral perfectionism. It is motivated by an interest in mathematics, or in physics. But if mathematics is for mathematical interest, why is not poetry for poetic interest? . . . Winters is obliged to think that mathematics is for mathematical interest—or so I suppose he thinks—but that poetry, in order that there may be an interest, must be for ethical interest. And why ethical? Looking round among the stereotyped sorts of interest, he discovers, very likely, that ethical interest is as frequent in poetry as any other one.

But these are generalities, a matter of big claims and counterclaims. Reading Winters, we shall come to the precise place where the poem is laid out before us, and we can see if his moral preoccupations really belong to the poet and determine the poetry. I am saying in advance that his moralism is a new moralism in poetic theory, because it is the first which has been sincere, with the complete courage of conviction.

There is nothing cheap about the form of Winters' moralism. Ours seems to be the day of the loosening of moral authority, and, on the other hand, and as if by way of compensation or natural provision, the day of the rise of many distinguished moralists to give a content and a ground to moral principle. None is abler than Winters. We must rule out at once the notion that he is guilty of that commonplace moralism which gets into literary criticism as it is practiced popularly: the external and episodical moralism, which would not seduce even a second-rate critic. Winters would never wish to Bowdlerize his literature, like the public censor, on the ground of some literal content that is objectionable, and regardless of what the poet is doing with it. That would be too shabby, and would quite remove him as a formative influence upon the new criticism. But there are subtler studies, and even philosophical studies, to be pursued respecting the moral ideals professed by the poets; they sometimes receive the rating of "ideological" studies. These excellent studies define the scholar nevertheless, if they monopolize him, as consenting to an absurd abbreviation of his critical career; they stop him on the threshold of criticism. Winters often has allowed himself to be stopped there. (pp. 213-15)

[The section on Allen Tate's poem "The Subway" in *Primitivism and Decadence*] is one of the most amazing passages in literary criticism. Its purport is so strange that we cannot at once grasp what is being said. I believe, first, that Winters deceives himself through his phrase, "total intention," at the beginning. The total intention of the poem is something, but not an in-

tention known to the poet at the moment when he begins to work up his logical content into a poem. Total intention is the total meaning of the finished poem, which differs from the original logical content by having acquired a detail which is immaterial to this content, being everywhere specific, or local, or particular, and at any rate unpredictable. And what, precisely, is the poet's intention at the beginning? It is to write a poem, and that is, since he has written poems before, to turn his logical content loose to shift for itself in the world of fortuitous experience; to get out of the world of pure logical content. It is a disrespect to the logic, if you are tremendously interested in the logic. If the given logical content is a moral one, it is a disrespect to morality, if you are devoted to that. It is a disrespect to morality in the degree that it is a respect to something called "poetic" experience. Poetic experience is only to be had by disrespecting whatever kind of logical content we start with. Mathematicians do not care to offer that disrespect to their own logical content, and do not turn it over to poetic composition. Poetic composition would compound their mathematical content with content that is not mathematical at all. And poetic composition will compound an ethical content with what is not ethical at all; so that if Mr. Winters is entrusting his morality to poetry he is not a man of greater moral scruple but of less. (pp. 224-25)

Winters has turned Mr. Allen Tate's poetic moment into a priggish but incredible moral experience. The madness was a real danger for Mr. Tate, says Winters in effect; it is a real danger for people with certain ideas who go to metropolitan areas and ride in subways. Mr. Tate was intelligent enough to forestall his peril by writing it up in a poem. But I think it more likely that Mr. Tate, who is strong-minded, had already forestalled it, and put it behind him, when he came to write the poem. Or we may even suppose that he had yielded, and had his little moment of madness, or blankness, and recovered, before the poetic activity set in. . . . Compare now with Mr. Tate's little guilt the greater guilt of Baudelaire, who yielded to metropolitan temptation of another kind, and lived to write poetry about it. Apparently, from Winters' account, Baudelaire could not pass off his temptation, when it presented itself in its practical form as an evil that ought to be avoided, by turning it into technical poems. Winters admires Baudelaire as the author of poems the best of which are probably "superior to any French verse of the nineteenth century" with the exception of two poems by Corbière. Baudelaire sinned and fell; but he was "morally intelligent among whatever sins he may have committed," and afterwards "wrote better poetry because of them." . . . I have no doubt that Baudelaire evaluated his experience of evil. I honor Winters for not being so tender-minded as to shy off from Baudelaire's poetry because its flowers are "flowers of evil." I wish he could say that the logical materials are evil, but that poetic flowers grow out of them; and drop the business of the "moral evaluation" and the "spiritual control." Aesthetic experience is beyond good and evil, in a plain temporal sense. Baudelaire is beyond good and evil at the stage when he is writing the poetry; he is not practically moved by them. . . . But the Baudelaire passage in Winters comes considerably after the passage on Tate, and in a later chapter; he has evidently not convinced himself, by the Tate passage, that a poem is a moral technique for resisting temptation. (pp. 226-28).

But I am dissatisfied with my haggling here; and presently a thought occurs which is exciting, and makes much of my comment appear to have missed the point; it makes Winters appear as himself a sort of hero who has advanced much further than we had understood. He writes in opposition to certain mystical poets (citing Hart Crane and Yeats) who evade the ethical issue by escaping from this world's experience and celebrating lyrically some perfectly vague and other-worldly experience. . . . At this language, we recall the passage about tragic drama; and if we have read him widely we recall other passages too. And suddenly we are startled by a new possibility: that Winters may be playing with a special and even exotic ethical principle of his own. This principle would be that of a man far from being the ordinary hard-headed moralist, and it would be Saintliness, or religious Resignation; for Saintliness, after some painful experience of this world's claims in the light of its actual rewards, is used to putting the claims by. More likely, it would be some kind of Stoicism, its secular counterpart. This is certainly not shocking enough to alienate us immediately. I for one am not unsympathetic with the attitude, and have moments when I seem to understand it, and I should expect sensitive persons to come to it increasingly if the world continues to go from bad to worse, and presently seems to arrive at worst. But that is hardly here or there, for our present purpose. For the critic, considering the possibilities of Winters' argument, the question is, whether this would be merely an ethical principle, or a literary principle as well. I think it might be the latter: a principle definitive of the whole function of poetry, asserting that poems are now the official or approved forms of our actions. I am struck by the fact that the moral evaluations Winters obtains from the poems are so negative in their effect; the poems seem to evaluate experiences by just imagining them, by having them vicariously, so that it becomes unnecessary for the poets and the readers to have them actually. Poetry becomes the survey of experience, reporting it in such a way as to indispose us to it. There is no law against this. It is a kind of moral decadence, disillusioned, yet keeping up a show of activity, and playing the game without putting real stakes into it.

By this view Winters achieves at once a strangeness, and therefore an irregular fascination for us, which is comparable with that of Eliot's personality. The trouble is that too much poetry simply is nothing of the kind in question; and there are too many moments when we will simply have nothing of the kind; and it is not quite possible to think of Mr. Winters as being so anemic. Winters cannot ordinarily be identified with decadence, unless we figure that he manages to evade his most explicit professions. But he ought not to permit us to be troubled by these confused interpretations of him.

The moralism sprouts everywhere in Winters' writings; in every single essay, if I am not mistaken, and on most pages. It has curious forms. For the critic the moralities are the tares, not the corn. But if we can pull them up we are generally left with something very superior: structural analysis. No other critic has as much, and has what he has so definitively.

There are two essays which seem to me better than any writings in the language on their subjects: the one on the meaning-structures employed by the modernist poets, and the one on metrical structures generally.

The first is entitled, "The Experimental School in American Poetry." . . . The sub-title is: "An Analytical Survey of Its Structural Methods, Exclusive of Meter." I saw it in earlier form in *The American Caravan* of 1929, if I am not mistaken, and marked it down as the most incisive criticism of the sort I had seen. In the present stage it is impure; the critic is interrupted by the moralist. But it will do, until we get something better; it is the best we have. (pp. 232-35)

The general effect of the essay is damaging, and the damage is done to the poetry of what Winters has called the Experimental Generation. . . . What Winters impeaches is their structural confusion, for they have plenty of subject-matter; see his chapter-title. He is the enemy of confusion; better, he is the enemy of technical poetic confusion, of the irresponsibility of craftsmen. And there we come also to the matter of metrical confusion, where he is just as valiant, and much more unimpeachable. (pp. 253-54)

With regard to the meters, Winters is a great formalist. This would mean that he adheres to some such doctrine as this: If metrical effects are wanted, they have to be secured within the meters; and the looser the meters the less the metrical effects. To secure metrical effects Winters is prepared to value every syllable of the line. He is entirely right; on its metrical side at any rate poetry is a craft whose effects are perfectly rational. And his view of the function of the formal meters is complete. The function is a double one; partly indirect, and partly direct. (pp. 259-60)

[The essay "The Influence of Meter on Poetic Composition"] is the most intelligent examination of free verse that has been offered; and still better, there is in it, along with much general metrical theory, Winters' plain understanding that the local "variation," or as we might say the local musical phrase, is nothing at all unless it is a variation within a definitive scheme—this last being of course the regular metrical pattern. It is the most important principle of metrical theory.

Of course free verse has been more and more becoming for the critic a dead issue. . . . But nothing could be more patient and more guarded than Winters' exposition of what scheme there is: not fixed as compared with the standard meters, but fixed as compared with prose. The name would be accurate: it is free, but it is verse. He analyzes many specimens for us. (pp. 261-62)

But when I come to the point of submitting a poem in free verse with Winters' marks of scansion upon it, I draw back my hand. The study is too difficult, and I spare my reader; especially as something much less than life and death seems at stake. Apparently free verse demands from the reader the most painful attention; first to the two grades of accent, the heavy and the light, which are found in each foot; then to the incessant variations in the precise placing of these accents from foot to foot, and in the number of the unaccented accompanying syllables. There is nothing easy about free verse as Winters construes it. It is hard to read the poem after he has marked it, it is still harder to find the scansion unassisted. (pp. 263-64)

We have found in Winters a great muddle of critical principles and moralities, but I hope I have indicated consistently that it is not more of a muddle than is the state of most bodies of serious criticism. I have tried to take the critical principles out clean from the muddle—they are principles more valuable than usual—and put them together into what seems peculiarly the desideratum of Winters' critical writings: a structural theory of poetry. (p. 267)

John Crowe Ransom, "Yvor Winters: The Logical Critic," in his The New Criticism, *1941. Reprint by Greenwood Press, 1979, pp. 211-78.*

R. P. BLACKMUR

[*The essay from which this excerpt is taken was originally published in* Poetry, *November 1940.*]

What is most valuable about Yvor Winters as a critic is just what is most valuable about him as a poet: his power of controlled discernment of matters usually only observed fragmentarily, by the way, willy-nilly, with the merely roving eye. His observations carry the impact of a sensibility which not only observed but modified the fact at hand; and we feel the impact as weight, as momentum, as authority. The weight is of focussed knowledge, the momentum that of a mind which has chosen—by an ethic of the imagination—its direction, and the authority is the authority of tone: the tone of conviction that cannot be gainsaid without being undone. The weight and momentum, as we feel them, give our sense of value—of the reality and exigence of what is said. The tone of authority, however, variously emphasises, impedes, or irritates—for it appears in the guise of explicit assertions of fact and affords the reader sensations—our sense of the validity of the judgments it is meant to buttress. This is another way of saying that Mr. Winters does not apparently find enough authority within his sensibility—in the very tone of experience itself—and is compelled to resort to constructions of the mind outside the data of experience, either because they ought to be given or because they are consonant with the emotion of what has been given. When it happens that these constructions are not disparate from those of his audience, they are successful, though not thereby valid in themselves; and emphasise the point of what he actually brings to view. When, on the other hand, the constructions are seen conspicuously to be imported, the audience tends to feel, for the most part with injustice, that their invalidity vitiates the whole operative force of the sensibility. Men everywhere are unwilling to trust, to confide, either in the work their own minds do or in that which they see actually performed by the minds of others, though that is all they have in either case finally to depend on. They are driven rather to accept or dismiss, to foster or destroy, the little work actually done in terms of work not done at all, but merely imputed. At least, this is so of every imaginative field; of religion, of politics, of philosophy, and of literary criticism.

Mr. Winters is one of these men, but only conspicuously so because his set of intellectual constructions are not superficially in keeping with those abroad in our time, and only dangerously so because his constructions occasionally permit him to issue in judgments which would be untenable without them. His elevation of Jones Very above Emerson, Bridges and Sturge Moore above Yeats, Williams above Pound and Eliot, and Edith Wharton above Henry James, taken together with the applications of his construction of the fallacy of expressive form, furnish examples both of what is dangerous and what is conspicuous. They make an artificial barrier—himself he might call it the framework—which obscures but does not touch the work he has actually performed. (pp. 167-68)

Mr. Winters' background point of view, and the same faculty of controlled discernment of illuminating fact, which produced the valuable aspects of his essays on modern poetry, are also responsible for the seven studies in American obscurantism which he calls *Maule's Curse*: the curse that required of Hawthorne, Cooper, Melville, Dickinson, Poe, Emerson and Very, Henry James, and the culture which they express, that they drink or shed their own blood: the curse of inadequacy, on the expressive level, of life lived. It seems to me that every fact and almost all the interpretive or explanatory observations brought forward in these studies are both pertinent and useful. No one who reads the section on Poe will be content to accept him indifferently thereafter, and no one who reads the quotations from Cooper will rink dismissing him indifferently, though I

doubt that in either case many readers will share Mr. Winters' extremes of opinion. Similarly, the remarks on James will well limit appreciation, as those on Melville will deepen it of those writers. The essays on Hawthorne and on Dickinson seem to me to achieve more, though they intended no more, than the others, possibly because of a greater native sympathy in the critic; they may be taken as tolerably complete versions of their subjects, but without any effect of substitution—the reader is driven back, guided and controlled with the sympathy of right preparation, to experience what is offered and to miss only what is not there. The essay on Jones Very and Emerson, by contrast, at least to me, is at its critical point an act of substitution: the substitution of a superficial attack upon Emerson (an attack, I mean, which strikes nowhere near the centre of Emerson, his extraordinary and fertile sensibility, but only upon the incoherence of its periphery) in order to elevate the absolutism, the rigid mysticism, of Jones Very: a substitution performed in lieu of critical observation in the interests of Mr. Winters' own intellectual predilections. It is good to have Jones Very; and there is no harm in Mr. Winters employing his prejudice in the discovery; but it is a very dangerous kind of criticism which judges one writer advantageously by applying *merely* prejudice, as appears here, to another writer. The danger is the vitiation of the very standards the prejudice is meant to support.

A closer illustration may be seen in the comparison of James and Mrs. Wharton to the disadvantage of James; closer, because no sooner does Mr. Winters make his comparison than he comes, with justice, to deny that after all, Mrs. Wharton's orderly competence—my summary of what Mr. Winters attributes to her—is anywhere equal to "the vast crowd of unforgettable human beings whom" James created. Here Mr. Winters was compelled by his experience of it to return—despite its diffuseness, its mad concentration upon detail, its confusion at crucial points of morals with manners, its lapses from the advantage of plot—to what James actually everywhere exposed, an inviolable and inexhaustible sensibility. That return is the obligation of the critic as it is the necessity, for survival, of the writer. The point about Mr. Winters is that he returns often enough so that we can afford to dismiss him where he does not: we lose little to gain much.

What we lose, if I may reverse the language of religion, we tend to find in a different, less annoying, more appropriate place. For example, in this nexus, if we apply the weight of Mrs. Wharton to the mass of Henry James and see just where it bears—see just how Mr. Winters did actually apply it—it modifies without diminishing our sense of the mass of James. We know better what *James* is; which is the object of criticism. Something similar is true of the relation between Very and Emerson, Moore and Yeats, Bridges or Mrs. Daryush and Eliot or Pound. It is only by a kind of mechanical inadvertence almost universal in intellectual operations that Mr. Winters himself would have us see more; or, to use a more familiar (though hiddenly more complex) term, it is only a difference in the *operation* of taste that comes between us. Which explains the justice of Mr. Winters' charge that Poe had no taste to operate, and that Emily Dickinson could not control the operation of hers.

To make these observations is not, I think, to injure the frame of Mr. Winters' thought; certainly it does not vitiate the moral insight upon which the frame rests; it merely reduces thought taken as principle back to the condition of thought taken as value, as discrimination, as an order, among other orders, of discernment, which is the condition or level where it is most useful in the reading or composition of literature, or for that matter, of religion or philosophy or politics. Here we come to the point of expedience where we began. Without the expedience of his principles—the logic of his taste—and without the exaggerations and irrelevances to which they led him, Mr. Winters could probably have gotten nowhere with the aspects of American poetry and fiction which absorbed his instinctive attention. It may even have been his principles which let him see what he sees. For his subject was confusion, confusion of mode, subject, source, and flux; and the best, or at any rate the quickest way to clarify a confusion is by imposing, as you think, an order upon it which you have derived elsewhere, whether from the general orthodoxy or from your special heresy of the orthodox—your version of the superrational. (pp. 171-74)

It is my contention that Mr. Winters knows all this is practice, and that if you will permit yourself to know what he knows you will be able both to ignore and to profit by the mere provisional form of his argument. It is the sensibility, in the end, that absorbs, and manifests like light, the notion of order. (p. 175)

R. P. Blackmur, "A Note on Yvor Winters," in his The Expense of Greatness, *1940. Reprint by Peter Smith, 1958, pp. 167-75.*

ROBERT DANIEL

As the title [of *The Anatomy of Nonsense*] is somewhat too cumbrous for convenience, perhaps we should use a short form of it, in the manner of the newspaper *Variety*. Two possibilities present themselves, and depend on the part of the book we are describing. *Anatomy* first of all defines a poem: a statement about an experience, real or imagined, in which the poet tries to understand the feelings that the experience gives rise to. Writing a poem is thus an act of moral judgment upon the feelings in question. . . . To make possible the judgment, the poet first organizes the experience so as to exclude all but the relevant feeling. Here the meter helps. Bearing in mind that "the emotional content of words is generated by our experience with the conceptual content," the critic tries to decide whether or not the poet has motivated the feeling—that is, understood it.

Anatomy then applies this definition to Adams and Stevens, and compares it with the critical definitions of Eliot and Ransom. Adams' confusion and bewilderment constituted a mere "literary mannerism." Stevens' poetry has declined. (This study does not reach *Notes Toward a Supreme Fiction*.) Eliot wrongly defended his chaotic form: as a poet, was describing not chaos but his understanding of the chaos. Ransom's doctrine of irrelevance, which, as in his remarks on Lady Macbeth's speech, "When Duncan is asleep . . . ," insists on the irrelevance of images that are plainly relevant, tends to make poetry contemptible. (pp. 603-04)

These and other illuminating things are *Anatomy*—but, alas, *Nonsense* must have its say too. Let us consider, besides those already mentioned, two of the things it says, both concerned with the modern world. *Anatomy* thinks the present is pretty bad; *Nonsense* thinks the past in all respects worse, and the Adams-Eliot admiration for thirteenth-century unity a mere Romantic longing for Never-never Land. The Church was then the product of a small class; social conditions were frightful; war, as devastating as today. The last reads strangely just now, while Rome and Berlin are being sacked. The difference came

in the democratization of war, or universal conscription, under Napoleon, at the beginning of the Industrial Era. And does Winters not know Lewis Mumford's studies of the medieval slum in *The Culture of Cities*? Briggs's *Architect in History* tells how cathedrals were built, and how the entire community used their naves. Neither Adams nor Eliot would deny material progress. Why does *Nonsense* make no spiritual comparisons? Of course there were horrors then (Chaucer is cited as proof), but how can we say "worse"? Pain is relative to the expectations of the man feeling it. The serenity, if not gaiety in Chaucer and other medieval writers contrasts oddly with the gloom that shrouds nearly all literature since 1800—

> and we others pine
> And wish the long unhappy dream would end.

Then what profits it a man. . . .? Winters thinks the Adams-Eliot view "can do nothing but paralyze human effort." The facts are otherwise: in the flame of his desire for an un-modern unity, Eliot forged his *Four Quartets*. Doubtless *Nonsense* sees little merit in that.

But Winters has his modern unifying force to oppose to the medieval Church: the American university. In it the student of literature who takes his profession seriously finds an institution where he may "quicken it and make it important." Winters resents the attacks of the *Kenyon* and *Southern Reviews* on the English Departments, and misrepresents them as having "picked a quarrel with the philologists and textual critics." . . . Above all other literary sins Winters deplores critical relativism; he honors the universities because they embody the belief in absolute truth. Has he not read *The Idiom of Poetry*, by Professor Pottle of Yale, which appeared soon after the attacks in the *Reviews* and, if believed, cuts the ground from under them? This almost persuasive argument *against* trying to reach absolute truth in literary judgment is representative, I believe, of the relativism with which universities are riddled.

It must be obvious by now that *The Anatomy of Nonsense* is provocative; it is also one of the most readable books of criticism that have appeared. Winters writes often with an acid wit, and there is a dramatic interest in watching him quote Ransom's attack on him, and rebut it. He is also a wide-ranging critic. Fond of tracing modern ideas back to the ooze, he can refer easily and more or less accurately to medieval philosophy and English history, as well as to the literatures of many lands. If only he were not jealous of anyone's condemning modern times except Winters. . . . (pp. 604-06)

Robert Daniel, "The Discontent of Our Winters," in The Sewanee Review, *Vol. LI, No. 4, Autumn, 1943, pp. 602-06.*

CLEANTH BROOKS

[Yvor Winters] is not amiable, not charming, obviously very earnest, and willing to split a hair to any distinguishable degree of fineness. Moreover, he exhibits all the rancor of a man who has pondered a matter long and carefully, and knows that he is right. He is perhaps our most logically rigorous critic; he is certainly one of the most intelligent; and he is undoubtedly the most cantankerous. (p. 283)

[*The Anatomy of Nonsense*] breaks up into five sections. The first treats Henry Adams under the damning subtitle, "The Creation of Confusion." It is a useful and able essay. Adams has, in my opinion, much to answer for, though the subtitle overstates the case. Winters is not interested in the whole story, and Henry Adams may well look elsewhere for his full due. But the negative job needed to be done, and Winters has done it thoroughly.

The second section interprets Wallace Stevens—as a hedonist. His progress of poetry since the publication of *Harmonium* is seen as a course of steady disintegration; the later poems, as a falling away from the early and fine "Sunday Morning." (pp. 283-84)

It is curious to see how Winters arrives at this conclusion. My own views of the nature and function of metrics are not too far from Winters' own. Moreover, I think I see what Winters means by the "imitative fallacy," and am in accord with his reprehension of it: a poet cannot excuse his own incoherence by claiming that he is describing incoherence. Yet, with full agreement on these points I simply cannot accept the judgment that the meter of *The Waste Land* "is a broken blank verse interspersed with bad free verse and rimed doggerel." Perhaps it is too simple to say that Winters applies good principles badly; that charge is too easy to make against any critic with whom one disagrees. But I think that this can definitely be said: there are a number of critics whose basic principles are not very dissimilar from those with which Winters, with an admirable straightforwardness, prefaces his book, whose principles in application yield radically different conclusions from those of Winters. It does very little good to agree on a theory of the relations of color if one person is continually turning up with green where others see red, or blue, where they see yellow. Winters' defect would seem to be organic, not functional.

Yet there is a sense in which Winters does seem constantly to write with an obtuseness for which he is morally responsible. He simply will not exert that effort of imaginative comprehension which he possesses (his analyses of certain poems prove that he does possess it) in trying to understand what another critic is saying. It is this rigidity—this insistence that every critic should speak by the card—this unwillingness to go at least part of the way in translating another critic's language into his own, that renders so much of Winters' work essentially negative in its value. I suppose that one should be grateful for the presence in modern criticism of a powerful corrective force like Winters who is always on the alert to pick up the critic who is inconsistent—alive to every *non sequitur,* censorious of every fuzzy term. Yet, the value would be greater if Winters gave the impression of correcting after an effort to understand. (pp. 284-85)

The truth of the matter is that Winters is something of a stoic. . . . As a stoic, he is thoroughly touchy on the subject of free will, and man's need to maintain his dignity. He is suspicious, therefore, of any concessions which the poet may seem to make to his environment. There must be no suspicion of giving in to the age, no "spiritual limpness" in the rhythms of the poem. The "form" of the poem must confront the chaos of the world of flux; the judgment on that world be unequivocal; the author know precisely what he is doing, and act with firmness and decision.

The most interesting part of the book is the fourth section which is really a reply to Ransom's critique of Winters in *The New Criticism*. . . . The basic contention has to do with the nature of poetic unity. Winters finds that principle—the governing principle of any successful poem—in an act of moral judgment. (pp. 285-86)

I confess that it is somewhat amusing to see the biter bit: Winters has hardly observed the obvious precautions in dealing with his opponents' terms. And Ransom's essay on Winters [see excerpt above] was characterized by critical sympathy and even ingratiation as he tried to find a common ground on which he and Winters might stand.

As to the merits of the controversy: I sympathize with Winters' attempts to center the poem in "a unique act of judgment," but even if such a judgment is moral, I think that Winters might distinguish more carefully between it and other "acts of moral judgment." Even a careful reader can scarcely be blamed for crediting Winters with an illegitimate moral bias in view of the fact that Winters in practise does seem biased in favor of poems which make their evaluations overtly and misses so many which do not.

I think, therefore, that Ransom's reprehension of Winters' narrowness is, on the whole, fair. Yet it should be said that Winters, in his answer to Ransom, searches some of the weaknesses in Ransom's position. (p. 286)

Winters rejects Ransom's invitation to give up the expressive functions of meter and metaphor. On these points, Winters' position lies rather close to that of critics like Richards and Empson. His principal point of theoretic difference with theirs resides in the special emphasis which he gives to the matter of the "rational content" of a poem. It is an overemphasis, I believe, and one which can be traced back to his curious statement that "The concept represented by the word, motivates the feeling which the word communicates." Therefore, he goes on to argue, "The relationship, in the poem, between rational statement and feeling, is thus seen to be that of motive to emotion." But *is* this the relationship?

Winters quotes the lines

> So wore night; the East was gray,
> White the broad-faced hemlock flowers,

and comments as follows: "The verb *wore* means literally that the night passed, but it carries with it connotations of exhaustion and attrition which belong to the condition of the protagonist; and grayness is a color which we associate with such a condition. If we change the phrase to read: 'Thus night passed,' we shall have the same rational meaning, and a meter quite as respectable, but no trace of the power of the line: the connotation of *wore* will be lost, and the connotation of *gray* will remain in a state of ineffective potentiality." Quite! An excellent account of power of the lines. But the word *wore* does not mean *literally* "that the night passed": it means *literally* that the night *wore: passed* is a thin abstraction of this. Furthermore, "So wore the night" and "Thus night passed" can be said to have the same *rational meaning* only if we mean by "rational meaning" a loose paraphrase. And can a loose paraphrase be the "motive to emotion?"—or are we not to equate "rational statement" and "rational meaning?" The real *motive* power, the horse, has been put squarely behind the cart in this account. And the reversal matters, and matters intensely, for the horse is, in this case, Pegasus himself. (pp. 287-88)

> Cleanth Brooks, "Cantankerous and Other Critics,"
> *in* The Kenyon Review, *Vol. VI, No. 2, Spring, 1944,*
> *pp. 282-88.**

RANDALL JARRELL

["**In Defense of Reason**"] is a particularly good book to buy; one can put it between Empson's "Some Versions of Pastoral" and Eliot's "Selected Essays," and feel for them the mixture of awe, affection and disagreement that one always feels for a first-rate critical book. But the proportion of disagreement, often of incredulous and despairing disagreement, is extraordinarily high as one reads Winters: there is no critic of comparable eminence who has made so many fantastic judgments.

Winters is what Kierkegaard said *he* was—a corrective; and Winters' case for the rational, extensive, prosaic virtues that the age disliked, his case against the modernist, intensive, essentially romantic vices that it swallowed whole, have in his later criticism become a case for any academic rationalistic vices, a case against any complicated dramatic virtues. Winters' tone has long ago become that of the leader of a small religious cult, that of the one sane man in a universe of lunatics; his habitual driven-to-distraction rages against the reprobates who have evidenced their lunacy by disagreeing with him go side by side with a startled, giant admiration for the elect who in a rational moment have become his followers.

His arguments often remind one of Tolstoy's: he takes a few facts, disregards the existence of the rest, and reasons simply, clearly, and convincingly to a partial and extravagant conclusion. All his vices are cumulative: in a book like Winters' last one, **"Edwin Arlington Robinson,"** one walks among the ruins of criticism.

But these are the ruins—temporary, one hopes—of an extraordinary critical talent, of someone who, at his best, is one of the finest of all critics of poetry. A note like this cannot be much more than a hand pointing dumbly to Winters' virtues; but it is a pleasure to testify to all the pleasure and insight one has gained from them, to acknowledge what a genuinely educational influence he has been to everybody except his disciples (to them he has been mesmeric).

Essentially he is an evaluative, analytical critic, concerned first of all with the intrinsic, objective methods of the work of art, with the quality and qualities of a particular work of art; his criticism is only secondarily interested in how these were arrived at, in the biographical, political and economic, genetic aspects of works of art. But these are the regular interests of *our* critical life; consequently, many critics dismiss Winters, a few join him, as they would join the Party or the Church, and a few more accept him as something different, partially wrong, and valuable. . . .

When Winters' taste is at its best one feels that he is an immediate contact with the reality of the poem, that his criticism has reached a level at which praise and objection are alike superfluous; but much of the time, in whole desolate areas, his taste can be depended upon to be valueless, since in them it is purely dogmatic and theoretical, proceeding not from his experience but from his standards. . . .

Winters' greatest theoretical mistake is this: he takes the act of criticism, assumes that the values involved are moral, that the act is an act of moral judgment, and then assumes that this process of judgment is itself the act of creation by which any work of art is produced. His practical misvaluations, at their most extraordinary, rival the Himalayas; perhaps their most forbidding peak is the judgment which pronounces Edith Wharton's "The Age of Innocence" the "finest single flower of the Jamesian art," and finds its prose "certainly superior to the prose of James."

But Winters' clear, independent and serious talent has produced criticism that no cultivated person can afford to leave unread. His essential insights can be found in their purest form in

"Primitivism and Decadence," but there are perceptions that match those scattered through his later essays on Hawthorne, Melville, Poe, Dickinson, James and Henry Adams.

> *Randall Jarrell, "Corrective for Critics," in* The New York Times Book Review, *August 24, 1947, p. 14.*

WILLIAM BARRETT

[In a] general sense Yvor Winters is one of the philosophical critics, and his work may be taken to illustrate both the difficulties and the dangers of the critical search for order. Now . . . [with *In Defense of Reason*] we have his three books within one cover, the occasion seems at last to have arrived for something like a summation of what we owe him. I do not pretend to anything so ambitious; what I have to offer are only some preparatory notes toward such an eventual and complete analysis, which we hope will soon assign Winters his just place.

Since he describes himself as a "moralistic critic" (a term he admits needs considerable definition), the questions I have to ask fall naturally under three headings: (1) the moral theory that is advanced or implied in support of his judgments; (2) the literary or aesthetic theory that derives from the moral premises; and (3) the actual work of taste itself, the perception brought to bear upon particular works and particular authors. (p. 533)

Just what Winters's positive moral theory is, is not easy to say. We know that he is an "absolutist" rather than a "relativist," but these particular terms are likely to play the trick, under dialectical pressure, of converting into one another, so that they do not by themselves take us very far. Perhaps his morality is best defined negatively, by its rejection of hedonism. But it is not always clear that Winters means one thing by this term: sometimes when he says hedonism, I think he should be saying naturalism. . . . (p. 534)

I do not know that hedonism can be formulated to embrace successfully all the moral data of experience; on the other hand, I do not know that there is any successful refutation of the *principle* of hedonism. Winters is not a Christian—he remarks somewhere that he is probably constitutionally incapable of Christian faith—and so we immediately inquire on what positive ground he is asking us to forsake pleasure, the opportunities for which are usually pitifully small for most of us in this brief duration of our life, with its frustrations and failures, against the continuous imminence of death. Certainly, the anti-hedonist is asking a good deal of our poor flesh. Hedonism at least offers us a principle that we can rationally accept: it tells us pleasures are to be rejected only for the sake of other superior and greater pleasures. Christianity does not deny this principle: it admonishes us to sacrifice certain pleasures in this life for the prospect of an eternal happiness, which will exceed in quantity and quality anything we have known here. (pp. 534-35)

But the point to be emphasized here is one made years ago by Eliot against Irving Babbitt: that in the absence of a positive religion we cannot expect the individual to check his desires in the name of an abstraction called morality. . . . Winters is very much under the sway of Babbitt—I think more even than he acknowledges—but it is doubtful that he has carried his morality very much further than Babbitt . . . toward some final basis. In the Foreword to the present collection Winters indicates, as a new development in his thought, that he has now arrived at the stage of theism. If this be taken to support his morality now, we might ask (I hope not invidiously) what has been supporting Winters' moral severity during the period of his critical activity over the previous fifteen years. But even now the question remains. A merely abstract or philosophical theism, unaccompanied by a positive religion, does not seem to me sufficient to insure the kind of morality that Winters wants. We need immortality as well as God, the concrete tie to the Deity provided by a positive religion, if we are to bear the sacrifices of an anti-hedonist morality. (pp. 535-36)

It might be captious to raise a good many of these questions if Winters did not leave us so often in doubt of his philosophic sophistication. At several points he makes the modest confession of the amateur, but as likely as not in the very same breath with some very dogmatic philosophical pronouncement. (pp. 536-37)

But perhaps all these questions about the positive moral theory, whatever it be, on which Winters rests are subordinate to a more fundamental problem—the meaning itself that is to be attached to the term "moralistic critic." . . . Among modern critics Winters is very severely moral in tone, and yet his severity upon art and artists looks quite gentle alongside of Plato's. Plato's theory is not always taken seriously; people assume it is something of a caricature, an extreme version of the limitations that are to be put upon art. But in reading Winters I cannot keep from feeling that in going as far as he does, but stopping short of Plato, he has not pushed his theory far enough, and so I am all the more inclined to take Plato seriously. (p. 538)

What, in short, I really suspect in Winters is a kind of inverted romanticism: in seeking to extract so much morality from literature, he seems to me to be giving it much more autonomy and significance than it deserves or than is consonant with his other attitudes; and precisely at this point the example of Plato becomes very relevant. (p. 540)

Of general aesthetic theory Winters has very little . . . ; what there is turns chiefly around the idea that a poem is essentially a moral evaluation of experience, conveyed through all the details and variations of rhythm, versification, and literary form. But he does have a good deal of *specifically literary* theorizing and deduction—concerning the types and structures of literary form—the sum of which constitutes largely an attack on modernism and experimentalism in literature.

Winters does not mean, he says he does not mean, that the poem must have an explicit moral tag—the moral evaluation may express itself through nothing more than the poet's control of the details of form. This raises the question: Does the control of his form show that the poet has or has not the correct moral evaluation of his subject? The moral evaluation, if it is there, must come as an explicit statement, or statements, about, or related to, the subject of the poem. This is what Winters must really mean, and he says so in several places, but on the other hand I think he does deal sometimes with the question—and this would hold too of certain poems of which he approves—with merely the first meaning in mind. But quite apart from any ambiguity of this usage, there is the more basic question as to what extent we demand that the poet be conscious at all of his evaluations. The notion of an unconscious evaluation—invoked to save the theory—seems to me a contradiction; in this case we should have to use some other word beside "evaluation." (pp. 540-41)

Winters's view brings us back to the old and recurring question of the relation between the beliefs and the value of poetry. For if the poet's moral evaluation is known to be wrong, it should, on Winters' theory, seriously invalidate the poetry; and yet we read with great pleasure many poems with whose express or implied beliefs we are not at all in agreement. . . . I suspect that Winters' insistence upon the moral in poetry may come from the unconscious desire to make literature more than it is, to extract from it something that has to be learned elsewhere.

It is obvious that my argument above has moved in agreement with Ransom against Winters. . . . The terms in which we must look at the phenomenon of artistic expression have moved far beyond Kant, and the notions of beauty as disinterested, and of the imagination as disinterested contemplation, do not tell us anything about the welter of interests, needs, and impulses from which the work has sprung and which it administers to in turn in the reader. Literary composition, if it has any vitality, takes place at the deepest levels of personality, and one hardly understands it if one remains at the formal surface only. This point . . . would hold just as well, though with some necessary qualifications, against Winters. (pp. 542-43)

Winters' literary theory—a principal part of which is the attack upon experimentalism in modern authors—can hardly be examined apart from the concrete judgments of taste about particular authors. And perhaps here we come to the center, the really significant core, of his criticism.

At any rate, this is the part of his criticism that is likely to leave some of us with the most powerful impression—alas, of startling idiosyncrasy. It is not only that, departing from an aesthetic principle of fixed form, Winters condemns experimentalism more or less wholesale, but that even where experimentalism is not particularly at issue, he turns his back on the great body of modern literature. Eliot and Joyce are continuously assaulted; the poetry of Yeats is neglected; figures like Proust, Mann, Gide, Rilke—to whom the age seems so much to belong—do not come in for mention. In place of these figures we are accustomed to think of as major, Winters introduces a very different, and highly personal order of valuation, singling out Robert Bridges, Elizabeth Daryush, and a number of lyric poets. (pp. 543-44)

Winters places an extraordinary emphasis upon the lyric poem, probably because this is the kind of literature he himself is concerned with creating; such emphasis may be unavoidable in the critic, but we might also ask that it be hedged about by the restraints of catholicity. Within the limits of his principal interest nobody can deny the delicacy and perceptiveness of Winters' taste. He has a knack for singling out individual poems that have either gone unnoticed by other readers or hardly received their just approbation. Sometimes he rides this knack too hard, as if he were zealously awarding prize ribbons at a fair. To single out the best pieces of a poet is a useful critical job, but one can expend so much energy upon it that one is prevented from seeing that the meaning of a writer is the life that circulates through the whole body of his writing. (p. 544)

In dealing with the question of experiment in literature Winters is haunted by the desire of some kind of rigorous deduction of literary form. But the descriptions of literary form must always be *post rem*, as we are reminded by Aristotle's *Poetics*. . . . Winters probably suffers most as a critic from a lack of this historical sense.

This makes him unable to see the historical necessity, and value, of experiment at certain periods. The history of literature is both the history of the medium and the history of individual men responding to their times. Some types of experiment may be simply to see how far the medium will stretch in a given direction, and other writers are not expected to follow the experimentalist as a new and binding norm. So with Joyce, and with Mallarmé too, whom Winters also abuses. And after the shock has worn off, the novelty of the experiment may bulk less to us than the traditional resources of literature which are affirmed: if you read certain poems of Mallarmé alongside, say, an ode of Horace, the experiments of the former may begin to look much more traditional in direction. . . . (pp. 546-47)

This lack of the historical sense shows itself most strikingly perhaps in Winters' summary decapitation of Henry Adams. He ridicules, and I think rightly, Adams' representation of the superior unity and virtues of the 13th Century, but seems not to see that he himself is tarred by much the same brush when he patronizes so condescendingly the mind and achievements of the acknowledged figures of our own age. And after so much petty nagging at him, Winters really misses the profound sense that Adams had for the disorder of our century. Does the history of the world since Adams' death give one any reason to rebuke him for an overemphasis upon chaos and disaster? What kind of a world does Winters think he is living in? No doubt, some of the points he makes against the *Education* are sound: Adams is often trivial and quibbling in his handling of ideas. But to rest with this is to fail to see the *Education* for the very serious, and at the same time ironic, *tour de force* that it is: Adams' quibbles with Darwinism, physics, and various ideologies, are not so much instances of *thinking* as they are artistic details in his portrait of uncertainty. This uncertainty is still with us, the universe has not ceased to be problematical, and history has become a worse nightmare than Adams dreamed. Winters may be more fortunate than most of us in having found a prestidigitator's hat from which to draw his superior certainties, but perhaps this is possible for him only because he is not living in the modern world at all. (p. 548)

But the world in which [the patient suffering from pernicious anemia] exists, and what is happening now to American culture, Winters treats as only minor obstacles to the writer's freedom. Any view that ties the literary work down to its time and place he labels as "determinism"—a bad word he brandishes at us almost as much as "hedonism." What limitations are to be put upon human freedom is an intricate and difficult subject, and Winters does not explore it; certainly the writer's would seem a very limited freedom: he cannot will to produce what he wants, since this would require that he already possess it; in the most elementary psychological sense he has to take what comes, exercising his freedom only as self-rejection, refusal, and the laborious preparation for future strokes of luck. These limitations are confirmed by the works of the past, as to which the more deeply we enter the more deeply we can embed in their time. Here again the enemy is Eliot, and chiefly for his remark:

> At the moment when one writes, one is what one is, and the damage of a lifetime, and of having been born into an unsettled society, cannot be repaired at the moment of composition.

I wonder if Winters thinks his own work evades the intent of this sentence. The irony is that his criticism could have been produced only in America and nowhere else in the world; it is as distinct a product of American life, though in the opposite direction, as any number of items of our popular culture. In its wrongheadedness, idiosyncrasies, rancorous eccentricities, and provincialism, it takes its place in the long line of that

pathetic and peculiarly American phenomenon: the wandering off of superior gifts into private byways. (pp. 550-51)

William Barrett, "Temptations of St. Yvor," in The Kenyon Review, *Vol. IX, No. 4, Autumn, 1947, pp. 532-51.*

DON STANFORD

It should be remembered . . . that Winters is a poet as well as a critic. His critical theories derive from his experience in writing poetry; his application of these theories to specific poems is marked by a perceptual sensitivity and understanding that can come only from a poet. Basic to all the essays in [*The Function of Criticism*] is his general theory of poetry—that a poem, the result of an act of contemplation, is a statement about human experience, that this statement should be rationally apprehensible and should communicate emotion appropriate to the rational apprehension of the subject. Closely linked with this theory is his analysis of the fallacy of imitative form— the "procedure by which the poet surrenders the form of his statement to the formlessness of his subject matter", and his distinction between prose and verse—"verse is metric or measured language", the rhythm of which is more effectively expressive of emotion than prose.

The first, longest, and most impressive essay in the book, *Problems for the Modern Critic of Literature* might have been entitled The Battle of the Genres. The lyric (or short poem) takes on all major contenders and wins. . . . [For Winters, the short poem is] *the only literary form in which the mature and civilized poet can at all times employ the best poetry of which he is capable on subject matter of major importance.* And as an illustration of what a modern civilized poet can do in this best of all forms, Winters concludes his essay with a brilliant analysis and explication of Valéry's great poem *Ebauche d'un Serpent.* (pp. 393-94)

The second essay, *The Audible Reading of Poetry,* is a plea for the formal or impersonal method of reading poems as opposed to "dramatic" rendition. It contains a fine analysis of English metrics which should be required reading for every young poet learning his technique. If this essay together with the remarks on meter in the article on Hopkins were more widely understood, the examples of shoddy prosody which fill the standard anthologies of contemporary poetry might be eliminated and the teachers of modern poetry courses . . . might be less frequently embarrassed in attempting to defend their subject before their colleagues.

Winters has much to say about the major faults and the minor virtues of Hopkins and Frost. Hopkins is severely criticized for his prosodic innovations which more often than not lead to unmotivated emotionalism and violence. His theory of inscape is defined as one more example of the romantic expression of the beautiful soul, and his Jesuit admirers are castigated for being closer to Emerson (in their defense of Hopkins) than to Aquinas. Frost is condemned for his relativism, his surrender to impulse, and for his petulant village anarchism. A few beautifully written but minor poems about the transience of the lovely frailties of nature are salvaged from the general wreckage. (pp. 394-95)

It has been almost fifty years since the so-called new poetry movement got under way. When the hurly-burly is done, Winters' criticism (and some of his poems) will remain as solid accomplishment. Those young poets who wish to be ahead of their time are urged to give *The Function of Criticism* their most serious consideration. (p. 395)

Don Stanford, "Mr. Winters' Recent Criticism," in Poetry, *Vol. XCI, No. 6, March, 1958, pp. 393-95.*

DENIS DONOGHUE

It is my understanding that the figure the story makes is crucial in the definition of Mr. Winters's work; what it marks is not merely one theme among many. Mr. Winters is concerned, unless I have misunderstood him, with life on the brink of darkness, where fear and terror come unsolicited and the available forms of order, to be good enough for the need, must be, in their own way, implacable. The forms of order which persuade, delight, and beguile are not enough: they are no good, it seems, when darkness insists. If much of Mr. Winters's work is dour and sullen, the reason is that this is the only kind of order he is prepared to invoke, darkness being what it is. It is hardly necessary to say that in his critical work the hated darkness takes the form of error, the stupidity of powerful men, the conspiracy against intelligence.

But this is to anticipate. It is interesting to see how often in *Forms of Discovery* Mr. Winters moves toward poems which share, in one way or another, the experience of invasion. . . .

There is a corresponding poetic theory, first outlined in *Primitivism and Decadence,* repeated in *The Function of Criticism* and now in [*Forms of Discovery*]. Language is essentially "conceptual or denotative." Words acquire "connotations of feeling," since human experience is not purely conceptual. The good poet makes a statement about a human experience, real or imagined, and makes it "in such a way as to employ both concept and connotation as efficiently as possible." But concept is master. The poem is "what one should say": the happiest condition is one in which the poet speaks with certitude and finality. It seems clear that this account of language is related to Mr. Winters's distrust of process, the flow of experience. The fluidity of process is alien to him: it is too indeterminate, too dangerous. Wilderness and the heat of the day are inescapable, but it is foolish to conspire with them. Poems are written in the cool of the evening, the invasion sustained, survived. (p. 22)

[In Winters's] work the experience itself often seems a necessary evil, tolerable only in the degree to which it has been mastered, held at bay. No experience is valued while it is happening. This accounts for Mr. Winters's insensitivity to the dramatic mode of life: he seems terrified of things while they are taking place. The sooner Act V comes, the better. If form is understood as finality, there is no welcome for the provisional experience, even when it is vivid. In Mr. Winters's aesthetic to say something is dramatic or dynamic is not to praise it; it is to mark a mode of being which comes as danger, a threat to poise, an invasion. Good poems are retrospective: after a storm of feeling, since storms will come, the mind labors to recover itself, to command the wilderness. . . . In the nature of the case, good poems are likely to be short, not because a poet's breath is short, but because process is not to be entertained. The psychological doctrine of Association is a menace because it invites a movement from one image to another along lines which are casual, contingent, therefore irrational. According to Mr. Winters, this denial of the purposive nature of the mind is the main source of the bad poetry which disfigures the eighteenth and nineteenth centuries, Gray, Collins, Wordsworth, Tennyson. Among the human resources, sensory perception is suspect, unless it is tied to the wheels of a conceptual chariot. The best literary forms are those which maintain, against flux and process, the finality of their own nature, their self-possession. The best vision is hindsight. We look before and after, but after is to be preferred: historians are more useful than prophets.

Forms of Discovery is not a history of English literature; it is a collection of chapters in the history of the short poem. In *The Function of Criticism* Mr. Winters argued that the short poem is, after all, the best form; better than the novel, the epic, the drama, because it is more stringent, more economical. Better also, I think he implies, because it is self-contained, restrictive, ascetic. So we are not to expect in this book an acknowledgment of *The Dunciad, Emma,* or *King Lear.* (p. 23)

It is difficult to be just to the book. Many paragraphs are painful to read, and would be tolerable only in an autobiography. I am sure that Mr. Winters has often felt the pain of being right while multitudes were wrong: over the past forty years, I am ready to believe, he has sustained injury and contempt from men who were not fit to tie his shoelaces. Now celebrated, he recalls every insult. Many injuries, bitterly remembered, are committed to the waste blanks in a footnote, a parenthesis. It is impossible to play Solomon to these occasions, beyond saying that it is a pity to see a man of Mr. Winters's stature so constantly exasperated. . . . I shall give Mr. Winters, I am afraid, further cause of impatience. I am sorry, for instance, that he abuses Thomas H. Johnson, the Editor of Emily Dickinson's poems, for what is at worst an error of judgment in the treatment of doubtful signs.

Mr. Winters's own record is not impeccable: one page of the chapter on Mr. Cunningham contains five errors, makes a complete mess of a quoted poem and a mess only less complete of a passage in prose, changes "projection" to "perfection," "unrippled" to "rippled," writes "rippled" again where the poet wrote "willowed." . . . In the eighteenth and nineteenth centuries, Mr. Winters says, "there is very little minor poetry which is readable today." I am forced to wonder whether he has not, on that score, dispensed himself from the labor of reading it at all. (pp. 23-4)

I want to say this quickly and be done with complaint. Mr. Winters is a major critic, one of the few critics who make a difference. In an age of bewilderment he has fought for intelligence, mind, the rational imagination. This must be acknowledged, even if we think that he has seen the mind only in one of its manifestations. But the new books lacks magnanimity. In Mr. Winters's finest work, in *Maule's Curse* notably, we are reminded of Samuel Johnson. There is in both critics a remarkably keen sense of the values (or some of the values) upon which poetry and criticism depend. There is no limit, we feel, to their concern, their gravity, their care; no point at which they are prepared to yield. We seem to have moved from Johnson to F. R. Leavis, a great critic too, but a writer to whom magnanimity comes hard. The best work of Johnson, Leavis, and Winters seems to me to occupy the same universe of concern and perception, but their risk is that concern, abused by the easy world, turns to petulance and then to venom. It is possible to say of Mr. Winters, for instance, that he is a crank; or, more accurately, that he has become a crank. But it is then necessary to consider the forces which have driven him into that corner. Critics who avoid this predicament are not therefore better critics or better men; more frequently, they are merely those whom Fate has disdained to wound. But while we feel in Mr. Winters's book the black ox of adversity, we also suspect, in certain pages, that he is engaging in what Johnson called "the habitual cultivation of the powers of dislike." (pp. 23-4)

Denis Donoghue, "The Black Ox," in The New York Review of Books, *Vol. X, No. 4, February 29, 1968, pp. 22-4.*

W. W. ROBSON

I cannot admire [*Forms of Discovery*]. It does not seem to me, as a whole, either sound literary history or sound criticism. Clearly Winters is not a writer like W. P. Ker, who tries to give as thorough and impartial an account of his subject as he can, given the inevitable limitations of his knowledge, taste, and capacity. He writes as an advocate, in causes in which he feels justice has not yet been done. And this is a perfectly legitimate way to write. . . . But the critical advocate does best when he takes us, his readers, by the hand, and shows us the evidence on which we can form our own opinion. He always remembers that critical argument can at most be persuasive, never demonstrative. In these respects Winters seems to me often to fail.

Then there is much in Winters's critical theory which I find unsatisfactory, and which I think has led him into wrong or blinkered judgments. I cannot see that the issue of 'absolutism' versus 'relativism' is worth all the fuss Winters makes about it. Presumably the absolutist does not claim to be actually in possession of absolute truths—at any rate, Winters does not. But in that case all he can do is what any other critic does: give reasons for his views, make plain what his judgments apply to, and allow them (in Plato's phrase) to run the gauntlet of argument; always bearing in mind that the criteria he employs, and his mode of arguing, are themselves open to further discussion. And if he succeeds in convincing a number of people who are interested in the subject, open-minded, and as unlike himself as possible, he may reasonably conclude that there is something in his views. The only way in which Winters seems to me to satisfy these requirements is his praiseworthy habit of specifying the poems on which his judgments are based. He says that he was rebuked for this by Austin Warren; but I agree with Winters against Warren that a critic should always do it. As for the critical approach Winters recommends, I think it wrong to judge a literary work according to whether it meets antecedent specifications (even if he had stated them). And the proposal that a critic should compare the work in front of him with some ideal, non-existent work I think quite misguided. Nor do I think Winters actually does this when he is at his best as a critic: like most critics, he compares and analyses existent poems. As to his general standards of judgment, they seem to be very narrow, and to attach far too much importance to a poet's explicit moral valuations. While the conventional wisdom may also be unsatisfactory, with its cant about 'dramatization' or 'tension' or 'the distancing of an attitude' &c., at least it recognizes, as Winters does not, the presence in most poems of a dramatic or fictional element. At the same time I think he has performed a service to literature in calling attention to poems of grave, reflective generalization, which the conventional wisdom of our day tends to overlook. There may be geese among his swans, but he has found fine poems, both old and new, which had not been noticed. . . . I think he also performed a service in questioning the conventional valuation of Shakespeare's sonnets, Donne, Hopkins, and Yeats, though I disagree with much that he says in those discussions. His dismissals of Wordsworth and Eliot, however, seems to me

quite inadequately based; he hardly bothers to conceal a hostility too strong for argument. It might be urged on Winters's behalf that these poets have been so extravagantly extolled by other critics that a little iconoclasm will do no harm. But that is not a becoming attitude in one who purports to write 'in defence of reason'.

Winters's conception of a great poet, as one who has written a great poem, seems to me also inadequate. . . . Surely the definition of a great poet should include some reference to an *oeuvre,* or to the need for range and variety? The definition Winters favours seems in part tactically motivated: he wishes to play down 'the cult of personality', to emphasize the poem rather than the poet. This seems to me in itself laudable. And with Winters's general anti-romanticism I have some sympathy. I share his dislike for modern irrationalism and emotionalism. . . . But I am unconvinced by Winters's account of its origins. I cannot believe that Shaftesbury, or even Emerson, are so important. . . . And I also feel misgivings about the tone of voice in which Winters proclaims his conviction that his 'absolutism' is the only alternative to the madness of the romantics. A rationalism more confessedly fallibilist would surely be more appropriate, just as a more effective tone might be that of a balanced, classical critic.

Even when Winters expresses his conservatism so temperately, it seems to allow too little for men's capacity to adapt themselves to change. He constantly appeals to 'human experience'. But human experience changes, and one of the things which change it is experimental art—something that Winters, after his early free verse phase, unvaryingly condemns. Yet history shows that much experiment is eventually accepted as normal, and indeed becomes part of the conventionality which the next experimental artist has to challenge. I agree with Winters that in a time like ours, so full of confusion about what is or is not good, a critic should strive for a comprehensive philosophy of life, of which his literary opinions are the partial expression. What I regret is, not that he has a philosophy, but that his philosophy seems so rigid—and so censorious. In this respect I prefer the implied philosophy of the 'New' critics, though I agree with Winters in rejecting their formalism, and in wanting to connect literature directly with life and society. (pp. 197-99)

The most attractive aspect of Winters's criticism is its style. He can write on subjects like the function of the university, as a symbol for the disinterested search for truth, with a moving dignity which rebukes the shallowness and corruption of our times. And he is surely a master of incisiveness and wit. Just as I suspect that he was a better prose-writer than poet, so I sometimes wonder if he may not be eventually judged a better critic of prose than of verse. At any rate, he seems to me to have written especially well on some American prose-writers— on Henry James, for example, in *Maule's Curse.* But he himself seems to have wished to stand or fall as a critic of poetry. To judge his achievement, we can only do what he asks us to do: read the poems on which he based his standards, decide if he was right to do so, and then see if he has applied them relevantly and consistently to other poems. I must admit that so far I myself am unconvinced. But I would be willing to accept the application to Winters of what C. B. Tinker says of Samuel Johnson: his opinions 'pique our pride, make us review the evidence, restate the case, and criticize the critic. They certainly do not terminate the discussion, but initiate a critical inquiry in us, the readers.' (p. 200)

W. W. Robson, "The Literary Criticism of Yvor Winters," in The Cambridge Quarterly, *Vol. VI, No. 2, 1973, pp. 189-200.*

W. W. ROBSON

[*Yvor Winters: Uncollected Essays and Reviews*] contains about forty essays and reviews by Yvor Winters which he did not republish in book form. . . . I found the collection disappointing. For one thing, Winters's *forte* seems to have been the full-dress discussion of an author (such as his treatment of Henry James in **Maule's Curse**). He did not have T. S. Eliot's gift for making a memorable essay out of an occasional review. The good formulations in this book are all to be found, better stated, elsewhere in his writings. Nor did he have Eliot's extraordinary power of quotation. But above all his particular judgments are again and again quite unconvincing. . . . Distinguished critics have, of course, sometimes made very odd judgments. . . . But aberrations simply abound in Winters's pages. (p. 169)

The main thrust of [Winters's] polemic is directed against the romantic theory, which he sees as still the dominant one in our time. This theory holds that literature is mainly or even purely an emotional experience. Behind it lies the conviction that man is naturally good; if he will rely upon his impulses, he will achieve the good life. When Pantheism is added, as it often is, he will achieve a kind of mystical union with the Divinity. Literature thus becomes self-expression, which is good in itself. Many romantics are also determinists. . . . Hedonists too are often determinists, because determinism is hostile to the intellect.

Winters, unfortunately, calls his own position 'absolutist'—unfortunately, because some have been led to suppose that he believes himself to be in possession of absolute truths. But he did not believe that he personally had free access to these absolutes and that his own judgments were final. What he *did* believe was that such absolutes exist and that it is the duty of every man and of every society to endeavour as far as may be to approximate to them. (pp. 173-74)

Winters was well aware of the difficulties in the 'absolutist' position. He confronted them more squarely than any other modern 'evaluative' critic I know, apart from those who, like Eliot, were content to assign final authority to the Church. This Winters was unable to do. . . . (p. 175)

To give literary application to this 'classical' position Winters worked out a theory of poetry, which he set forth in formulations that recur frequently in his criticism, with only slight variants. A poem is a statement in words about a human experience. The poet makes his statement in such a way as to employ concept and connotation as efficiently as possible. (By 'concept' Winters means something like the literal sense of a word or phrase; and by 'connotation' its suggestive overtones.) The poem is good in so far as it makes a defensible rational statement about a given human experience (the experience need not be real but must be in some sense possible) and at the same time communicates the emotion which ought to be motivated by the rational understanding of that experience. . . . Poetry has also rhythmic and formal aspects (Winters does not approve of the common use of the term 'poetry' to refer to some kinds of writing which are not in verse). Rhythm communicates emotion, and as part of the poem it qualifies the emotion. The form of a poem can be seen both as its rational structure, the orderly arrangement and progression of its thought, and as a broader, less easily measurable rhythm than the rhythm of the line; in this sense, form might be called the rhythmical progression of the poem.

Winters's fundamental theses are clearly vulnerable as they stand, and they have attracted much adverse comment. . . . But they should, I think, be treated with a charitableness which Winters himself does not always extend to other critics, when he castigates their looseness of expression. They should not be pressed too hard as *definitions* of poetry (to define a poem as 'a statement in words' is obviously unsatisfactory). What he achieves is not a definition but a reorientation of the reader's point of view, away from the romantic and post-romantic notions of our day towards something like the position of Matthew Arnold in the 1853 Preface, or of Sidney in the *Apology,* where Sidney speaks of 'peyzing each sillable of each worde by just proportion according to the dignitee of the subject'. But Winters has the advantage over earlier writers, in reinstating 'the dignity of the subject', of his familiarity with French Symbolist and post-Symbolist developments, in which 'the subject' becomes a very subtle matter. He was no archaizer, but a man very much alive to the literary problems of his own time.

Winters's particular judgments on poems and poets may seem narrow, cranky, and ill-founded. I confess that many of them seem so to me. And they must be taken into account when we are assessing the value of his theory. But his critical reputation should not stand or fall by his extravagant praise of dull English poets of the sixteenth century, or dull American poets of the twentieth. The proper claim for him should rest first of all on his passionate seriousness, sincerity and dignity; and then on the courage and incisiveness with which he confronted the impasse of all modern criticism which purports to be judicial. Few readers of Winters are going to be satisfied in the future with facile talk about 'imitative form', or 'the stylistic advances of Eliot and Pound', or the thoughtless assumption that 'colloquial language' is a guarantee of poetic value. But the claim for him can best be defended by appeal to the best parts of his full-length books. To dwell too much on the Winters of these *Uncollected Essays and Reviews* would be to fix him in memory as a fire-breathing dragon whose hoard, whatever it is, is not gold. (pp. 176-77)

W. W. Robson, "Yvor Winters: Counter-Romantic," in Essays in Criticism, *Vol. XXV, No. 1, January, 1975, pp. 169-77.*

GROSVENOR POWELL

[*The essay from which the following excerpt is taken was originally published in a slightly different form as "Two Essays: 'Quantity and the Meters of Yvor Winters' and 'Being, Poetry, and Yvor Winters' Criticism',"* in The Denver Quarterly, *Autumn 1975.*]

It is easy to ridicule a man who, like Yvor Winters, argues that poetry is a moral evaluation of experience and that poetry should use the full resources of the language. It is particularly easy in this century, since romantics seem, by and large, to have forgotten the religious origins of their position. . . .

Winters' crucial stance, despite all of its apparent unfashionableness and antiromanticism, was actually the romantic position that a poem is the result of a religious act, that it is an organic whole, and that reading it is a fusion of one's consciousness with the universe of the poem. The difference between Winters and virtually everyone else interested in poetry nowadays is that he acted on these principles while the majority of critics and poets merely affirm them. Whenever Winters encountered a similar degree of seriousness in another writer, he showed his admiration even when he disapproved of the other's position. (p. 3)

As a critic, Yvor Winters applied the logical and dogmatic method appropriate to theology to the analysis of literary content and form. At first consideration, this might seem an illegitimate procedure, but it has, in fact, proved highly successful. Regarding poetry as a technique of contemplation and as a means of extending and reintegrating the human spirit, Winters was able to evaluate modern literature both from within and without. Before he became a literary critic with a reputation for reactionary positions, Winters had been an Imagist poet, heavily influenced by Ezra Pound, William Carlos Williams, Wallace Stevens, and the French Symbolists. By approaching modern literature with an analytical procedure derived from scholasticism, Winters could see and evaluate his own early position and modern literature generally from a refreshingly unclouded perspective. He could perceive not only the virtues of romantic literature but also its limitations; and he could define the new areas of experience created in our time through literature, as well as those areas of experience that have disappeared from modern consciousness because our literary techniques are incapable of realizing them. What Winters saw most clearly was that modern poetic technique limits the total possibilities of human experience even though it treats certain limited aspects of that experience in a hyperintensive way. Winters wanted to preserve the virtues of the best modern poetry while reintroducing those areas of experience that could no longer be expressed within the conventions of twentieth-century poetry. That was his program. (p. 9)

Winters is generally classified as a formalist, and he is perhaps best known as the critic who defined and evaluated the various formal structures that occur in twentieth-century experimental poetry—the critic who saw most experimental structures as instances of either pseudoreference or qualitative progression. (pp. 14-15)

Winters' analysis of the structures that occur in twentieth-century poetry appears in his first book, *Primitivism and Decadence* (1937). The book struck reviewers as intolerant and insensitive, and it established Winters as a negative critic. In fact, however, the book was an effort to accomplish the necessary task of understanding that had to precede any evaluation of the real accomplishments of twentieth-century poetry—precision of diction and intense realization of sensory detail. But this negative approach is not Winters' unique contribution to literary criticism. (p. 15)

The great accomplishment of Winters' criticism lies in his definition through example and illustration of what is missing in modern poetry. Naturally enough, this positive work of reconstruction could not be undertaken until it had been shown that something was indeed missing. Unfortunately, Winters' most ambitious study of the great tradition in English and American poetry, of the best that the present offers and of the hope for the future, was not published until the year before his death. By this time, his reputation for unsympathetic attitudes was so firmly established that the book has been largely ignored. Nevertheless, *Forms of Discovery* (1967) is one of the most significant studies of poetry published in our century. (p. 16)

In *Forms of Discovery*, Winters proceeds as he had in the past. He defines fullness of being as it is or is not realized in particular poems; although, as I have said, the emphasis here is on achievement rather than on deprivation. The book is most useful as the definition and, in part, the creation of two major traditions in English verse. . . . One can define the first by saying that it is essentially the plain tradition of the sixteenth

and seventeenth centuries and is, in the main, a reaction against the better-known rhetorical or Petrarchan tradition; and that the second is a postromantic or, as Winters names it, a post-Symbolist tradition.

But Winters was suspicious of identifying poems with schools or traditions. He felt that this process accounts for much of the impressionistic criticism of our time and for the search for identifying idiosyncracies rather than for naked excellence regardless of idiosyncracies. In his mind, the true history of poetry is the history of the great poems. (pp. 16-17)

[It] is in the commentaries and analyses that Winters teaches us how to read poetry. His analyses of the great poems are extended and do not lend themselves to quotation out of context. But after reading them, one has some sense of what Winters means when he speaks of a great poem as the realization of the full potentialities of language in the service of an important theme. And one can see why he should be so sensitive to, and impatient with, any unrealized potentialities in the language of the poem.

The second great period of English verse—the greater of the two, in Winters' opinion—follows on and takes advantage of a long period in which the rational mind had been more or less suppressed; and it profits from the virtues that, paradoxically, resulted from the suppression. The antirational stance of the romantics produced at least one positive result: it led to the vivid realization of sensory detail. (p. 18)

Grosvenor Powell, in his Language As Being in the Poetry of Yvor Winters, *Louisiana State University Press, 1980, 172 p.*

ELIZABETH ISAACS

"Yvor Winters: poet, professor, critic . . ." This original sequence still holds when one turns from critical theory to actual practice in the development of Winters' double career. One need always remember that he developed his particular theories of criticism as a result of certain necessary practices in the creation of his poetry. His first published works were all poems, and his later critical canon is the direct result of his practical poetic experiments. . . .

It is ironic that he has been more widely acclaimed as critic than as poet since his controversial critical career was actually always secondary for him. He hoped people would read his poetry first and thereby better understand his criticism, since that was the order of its genesis; but few ever did. . . . It is a fact that his poetry was consistently read through the years only by other poets who understood how much might be learned here: Marianne Moore, Allen Tate, Robert Lowell, Louise Bogan, John Crowe Ransom, John Ciardi, Donald Justice, Thomas Gunn, J. V. Cunningham. (p. 65)

Before the poetry of Winters can be properly examined, it is necessary to review his own conception of the nature and function of poetry. "I believe that a poem is a statement in words about a human experience. In each work there is a content which is rationally apprehensible and each work endeavours to communicate the emotion which is appropriate to the rational apprehension of the subject. The work is thus a judgment, rational and emotional, of the experience—that is, a complete moral judgment in so far as the work is successful. . . . We regard as greatest those works which deal with experiences which affect human life most profoundly and whose execution is most successful." In every poem Winters ever wrote he literally stood trial for such a judgment, and he expected all serious poets to submit themselves in their work as he did. He could take the slightest subject . . . and develop it into a full-scale, universalized theme with carefully-wrought images and emotionally-controlled tones.

He sought for his own poetry that style which he was eventually to call "Post-Symbolist"—intellectual, plain, pure, precise, yet highly charged with emotional tension; he acknowledges that few readers will be able to comprehend it fully. After abandoning his early Symbolist-Imagist poetry of the thirties, he analyzed his later style as having been influenced by a disparate group including Wallace Stevens, Emily Dickinson, Robert Bridges, T. Sturge Moore, Lecomte de Lisle, Baudelaire, and Valery. He saw himself in a "counter-romantic" mode of writing and sought a final style that could use "abstract words in descriptive context."

For these demands he chose the medium of the short lyric poem—"the most essentially poetic, the most powerful, the most sensitive." This form left no room for the dangerous habit of reverie or associationalism. It could never allow the poetic mind to be casual or contingent, thereby denying its purposive nature in which he believed so completely. Rather, it cultivated the mind's better qualities: its stringent, economical, self-contained, restrictive, ascetic, orderly processes. Poetry from such a mind and spirit would reach its greatest heights, he thought, when its sensory perceptions and its philosophical themes were combined—not as ornamental background or metaphysical abstraction, but in simultaneous visual and intellectual synthesis. His ideal Post-Symbolism combined carefully controlled association with this new image "in which sense perception and concept were simultaneous, in which phrases contain certain image and idea together." These were the requirements for the ideal poems that he sought in his own creative practice. The final marks of the true artist were, for him, constant care and correction for reasoned control.

So Winters in his mature years set himself to the immense task of changing his style and developing it as inspired by the masters of the sixteenth century lyric. (pp. 70-1)

When one examines Winters' poetry to identify its various themes, there is one striking impression. Most of them are involved in one way or another with "moral" attitudes. His themes always reflect his seriousness of purpose, his assurance that he does know right from wrong, and his absolutist *dicta*. The "moral" quality of his art dictates his choice of poetic themes. He believed that the poet's chief end morally was to exercise judgment so that he could maintain a balance between his understanding of his experiences and his emotional responses to them—avoiding both the primitive and the decadent pitfalls. His system of absolutes centered around a half-dozen themes that recur from his earliest poetry to his latest. In a progressive sequence, half of these concern his own personal experiences and develop in the early poetry first; the other half evolve from them into universals and are more evident in the later poetry. They are all sufficiently interrelated to show the steady growth in this poetic and philosophical mind from groping adolescence to resigned maturity. One of his favorite definitions of poetry—"a spiritual exercise leading toward intelligence"—would make an excellent title for the sequential development of his six main themes. They exemplify the spiritual autobiography which his poetry collections comprise:

1) Perception of *the artist's identity* in the Universe

2) His *appraisal of forces* of truth, wisdom, and justice against evil, ignorance, and injustice

3) His humanistic *relationship of man to nature:* his artifacts versus Nature's laws

4) His *development of stoic strength*

5) His *spiritual search for the ultimate mystery*

6) His *desire for timelessness*

(p. 73)

Throughout the entire Winters canon, a survey of his six themes shows the first to be his apprehension of the artist's self-identity, his perceptions as a "feeling" person. There is good reason to claim much of this early poetry as autobiographical; *The Brink of Darkness* showed to what lengths this self-awareness might be disastrously carried as the young artist's personality seemed to be gradually invaded by the powers of darkness. His earliest Imagist poetry is full of a young poet's absorption of sense impressions and perceptions for their own sakes; later he begins to worry about their effects, emotional and psychological. He is titillated by the sheer physical ecstasy of "hawk's eyes," "the immobile wind," "the pale mountains," "goats' hooves," "desert sands,"; and the early poetry builds on this "awareness" theme as it is related to its Imagist forms. One of the most beautiful of these simple poems is **"Song"** in which the form and images reflect the utter simplicity of the theme of artistic sensitivity. But even as early as the second poem in the first book there is the menacing **"One Ran Before,"** where the theme involves more than mere physical image. . . . The foreboding silence of this early poem and the "darkness" of the early short story are similar, audibly and visually, in the development of this theme; as the senses rise to higher and higher pitch, the mind is driven to contemplate a possible hysteria which might surrender to the invasion of unreason unless checked. Instantaneous perceptions of the artist's sudden or arrested movement against the universe's implacable background provide tense images for this theme. . . . In his later work, Winters was more complex in images and forms, but this same theme remains: the artist's highly attuned sensibilities confront the universe in time and space with a certain hysteria lest it either be lost to him or absorb him completely. The tightly reined later poetry shows the artist finally in control of both theme and form (see **"The Vigil"** and **"The Proof"**) but with the same old haunting fear of the Imagists' juxtaposition of irrational, disparate associations. The theme suggests the artist caught up in the constant Heraclitean flux of his physical world: glorying in his super powers of perception; reeling in the terror of his romantic seriousness, but clutching firmly for balance to a classical control of his art form. (pp. 74-5)

One of his best mature poems, **"Sir Gawain and the Green Knight,"** tells of the artist-hero's successful war within himself against such sensuality and epitomizes his spiritual salvation after having confronted nature and experience without evasion or submission. If Winters seems to some critics to have dwelt overlong on the control of such temptation, it is only because he recognized its great attraction for aesthetes like himself. The reader of his *Collected Poems* always gets the feeling that he was never able to omit completely this constant theme of the awareness of the artist's own private hallucinatory perceptions. It runs like a dark "remembrance of things past" from first to last as the most personal undercurrent in all of his writing. His sharp apprehension of the physical always seems to end in profound disenchantment. Two of his best, **"The Longe Nightes When Every Creature . . ."** and **"Sonnet"** at the end of *The Proof,* show him in complete control of this theme. His dedicatory poems to Melville and Emily Dickinson evidence his intense kinship with earlier writers using this same theme.

Winters' second theme concerns the artist's awareness of his position in the mundane world around him. This involves his appraisal of the forces of truth, justice, and wisdom as they battle in the here-and-now against evil, injustice, and ignorance. And since this is Winters at his most realistic level, it sometimes results in what critics have scoffed at as merely "occasional" poetry. But when one analyzes the total performance, it is obvious that any "occasion" merely serves the poet as touchstone for a full-scale treatment of man's inhumanity. . . . There is no impersonal occasionalism about such poems as **"Postcard to a Social Muse."** Its ponderous title bespeaks the high irony of the situation in which a naïve critic had engaged in an inexact search for wisdom and thus enraged this erudite poet by her shallow claims. Similarly, **"On the Death of Senator James Walsh"** expresses in formal sonnet cadence the tribute owed by *all* men to those . . . "whose purpose and remorseless sight pursued corruption for its evil ways." Another long-titled poem, **"To a Woman on Her Defense of Her Brother . . . ,"** rails against the "villainy of pride in scholarship" and in "cold impartial hate" debates a case in which Winters himself historically engaged. He uses his cool power here to appraise evil and to seek compassionate justice. **"To a Military Rifle"** condenses the futile problem of war into a fine, lean poem; **"The Prince"** laments the irony of a political establishment that breeds corruption from power. The most personal of many poems on this theme is his **"Hymn to Dispel Hatred at Midnight"** in which he seeks to exorcise his own heart's evil thoughts. . . . There is a tragic force about this poetry as he refuses to abandon the world, but attempts always to subject it to "a lasting proof." He resents each break or defilement of the moral order by general chaos or specific evil, and his poetry predicts doom for our civilization if these continue to pile inexorably on one another. So "occasional" verse becomes universal poetry; and "A Prince" of wisdom and good heart must be found to save us from our fatal drift toward self-destruction. (pp. 76-7)

The third theme—man's humanistic relationships in nature—begins to move away from personal references but not completely deny them. Rather it contrasts the human condition with the vast imponderables of the natural world. It shows the frail human highlighted against the backdrop of nature's vast panorama, contrasts his puny artifacts with nature's laws, and is sometimes reminiscent of the nineteenth century's pathetic fallacy in its longing for nature's kinship. But this poetry often abandons that romantic longing for a thematic irony that is akin to Hardy or Dickinson. This man sees himself in perspective against the flat immensity of cosmic forces and examines his own small niche maintained by scientific technology. . . . His theme reflects the dignity of man's reason, his commitment to his preservation in spite of his limitations. A poem may take off from any single person, place, or thing; but it will always return to the one great ironic cosmic fact of man's boundaries. Such a Winters poem will usually be a combination of perception first and meditation second, with a highly sharpened focus as the one is juxtaposed against the other. In **"Quod Tegit Omnia"** one finds the cosmic background given first—"Earth darkens . . . ;" then ". . . the mind, stored with mag-

nificence, proceeds into the mystery of Time." An early poem in *Fire Sequence* entitled **"The Bitter Moon"** opens with traditional Imagist background and ends with the narrator swearing wistfully, yet recognizing his own futility. . . . In the poetry of his later mode he sets the same theme—**"Before Disaster," "By the Road to the Air Base," "At the San Francisco Airport"**—where the small artifacts of man take on limited significance as great relativistic ironies are developed. His sharp apprehension of man-made, physical things against the mysterious screen of eternity etches the mind of the reader in such poems as **"The Streets"** ("I met God in the streetcar but I could not pray to him . . .") and **"Rows of Cold Trees."** . . . (pp. 77-8)

The next theme develops naturally in the sequence toward some search for salvation and reconciliation with maturity. In several poems Winters examines the possibilities of a religious experience—even a Christian experience. He wrote as an absolutist in his late criticism that he felt such an experience was impossible for any thinking man in the modern world; yet a good deal of the poetry hints at an active religious hope. In one of his wilder (and worst) poems, he shrieks "Belief is blind!" His sense of the mystery of the universe runs throughout all of the poems: from the early perceptual ones (such as the hedonistic **"Song of Advent"**) to the sophisticated metaphysical ones of the *Collected Poems* (**"To the Holy Spirit," "A Fragment,"** and **"A Song in Passing"**). These last three indicate his stern compulsion for a religious experience. . . . They seem to represent some sort of milestone in his spiritual development. And yet its source seems to elude him. . . . It is obvious that he was attracted by the ultimate mystery of the Christian experience, but as an avowed rationalist he could go no farther than the profound knowledge that the mystery exists; and he is never sure that it exists for *him*. In **"To the Holy Spirit,"** he achieves a kind of reconciliation with the mystery and accepts his own ignorance of it; he finally dismisses the pain and anxiety of his search. . . . (p. 81)

In the absence of traditional religion, he sought timelessness and perpetuity for his artistic productions—whether in his garden or his poems. His perceptive earliest poems had concerned the timeless present as opposed to the fleeting past; his later poetry repeats this theme as it reaches for the future timelessness that he desired. The theme is often revealed through the use of particular images: the association of stone with the nonliving and wood with the living runs throughout many of his poems. As the one is compressed into the other by time, so is timelessness achieved as this poetry is compressed. In **"Hill Burial,"** for instance, such finality is given to the imagery of the last lines. In some of the early poems of *Fire Sequence* the sheer quality of incantation compresses this theme into a reiterated order. **"Quod Tegit Omnia"** shows the only true timelessness or renewal to be found in the individual artist's transforming new experiences. If his identity is to be preserved at all, it must be in his art. Hence the poet becomes more alive and "timeless" as his perceptions are more uniquely his own. If Winters were any sort of theist at all, his god would probably be a poet, and a rational one. (p. 82)

Choice of poetic subject matter for Winters might be any interesting thing that was significant enough to evoke the moral concepts that his critical theory demanded. According to this theory, the poet makes a judgment—final and unique—that the subject of his poem will be a strong enough vehicle to carry the more important theme—"the concept"; and it will be a "moral" poem if all the chosen elements are technically able to produce the proper emotion. This leaves the poet a wide latitude for choice of subject matter, but restricts his use of it stringently. (p. 83)

For Winters, the subject—however simple or esoteric—should carry a new perception, not only of the exterior universe, but of human experience as well. It should, in his words, "add to what we have already seen." And the fact that he so often took commonplace subjects "already seen" is evidence that he asked the sensitive reader to take a *second* look with him at all the important metaphysical perceptions of the artist. He was often accused by superficial critics of using banal, every-day subjects that were beneath the level of his highly abstract themes. This very juxtaposition was often a careful part of Winters' deliberate technique to force the philosophical reader to see the macrocosm around the microcosm. He discussed this technique in his essay entitled "Poetry, Morality, and Criticism." . . . (pp. 83-4)

The subject matter of Winters' early poetry was suffused with an imagistic ecstasy as the young poet examined every single cause for his own perceptual reactions. The subjects of the first three volumes come mainly from the poet's physical environment; their content was actually a description of feelings and reflections attendant upon a scene, an animal, a plant, a seasonal change, a shift of light. By the time *The Journey* was published in 1933, he had abandoned these acute perceptual moments with their attendant nervous tensions and begun to concentrate on more earthly subjects of a broader appeal. While much of this earlier poetry was apt to use geographical, historical, or seasonal materials, his mature poetry concentrated on more mundane subjects (family relationships, friends, hobbies, events in his professional life, colleagues, students). The *Collected Poems* shows him by the end of his career using cosmic, philosophical subjects. This sequence parallels the development of his themes; however it should be noted that these divisions are based only on tendencies, and that a variety of all types actually occurs in all three periods in his career.

Winters' use of geography and history as subject matter varies widely from the early perceptual poems, such as **"Aspen's Song"** or **"Jose's Country,"** to the later fully orchestrated **"Winter Evening"** or **"Summer Moon."** Early in life he developed into an amateur biologist and was widely read in esoteric fields of this subject. No item of the natural world was too small to escape his use in poetry. Some of the most beautiful examples of the early free verse in *The Immobile Wind* . . . used desert and mountain animals as subjects for the one-line nature poems. (pp. 84-5)

Perhaps the most important category of his subjects is that which is religious or aesthetic in temper. The stated subject itself may be, as in the early poetry, a well-known place or artifact, but the actual subject is its poignance for the poet that sends him off into a religious perception of higher relevance. Such specific content turns later to abstract subjects: from **"Hill Burial"** to an individual's death, from **"The Invaders"** to an individual's solitude, from **"The Empty Hills"** to his fears. Finally in the most mature poetry, this same sort of transformation becomes the subject of **"To the Holy Spirit"** and **"Time and the Garden."** These subjects ultimately symbolize the tension between mortality and immortality, and they represent the peak of his virtuosity. (p. 87)

["Form"] is what makes "great" poetry for Winters. His main themes and subjects all evolve eventually from one concept: his confrontation with confusion. His horror of instability of

all sorts—from the purely personal, through the mundane and social, to the cosmic—is the total and constant preoccupation of this man. His biography as "poet-teacher-critic" is dominated by it; his one short story reveals it; and all of his poetry reflects it. He turned gratefully at midpoint in his poetic career to the security and discipline of form in "good verses," and he developed his particular "morality" around it. He chose to clarify confusion by imposing an order on it; that order was form.

The major primary source for the critical development of this theory comes from his fifth essay in *Primitivism and Decadence,* entitled "The Influence of Meter on Poetic Convention." Here he states his basic premise: "The morality of poetry is inextricably involved in its form and is related to the norm of feeling." If the poet makes a wise choice (or is happily intuitive) with a "form" which can best control the theme and evoke the proper emotional feeling toward the subject, then the poem is aesthetically "moral." It is then under the control of the poet's reason. By "form" Winters means primarily verse pattern, meter, and rhythm, though he does include in his theoretical remarks some random comments regarding rhyme and syntax.

His own shift from his early style of free verse to his later formal verse was made because of what he conceived to be the paradoxical fact of *greater* freedom in traditionally patterned verse. . . . When Winters first rebelled against the Pound-Eliot associational school of free verse in *Primitivism and Decadence,* he condemned experimentalism for its incompleteness, its confusion, its ultimate emptiness: a poetry without either proper subject or form, no matter how hallowed its theme. He called for a reiteration of objective substance and the proper forms to preserve it: in other words, he wrote "in defense of reason." (pp. 88-9)

Winters' scrupulous dedication to all aspects of "form" seems to stem from his philosophical desire to set his poetic world in rational order, however fragmented may be the rest of it. He felt himself living in an age "in which the insistence of the contemporary has obscured the vision of the permanent." He saw other poets of his age writing formlessly with over-emotional, irregular, rhymeless regularity. He diagnosed their problems as symptomatic of the great artistic malaise that came from social and moral decay. (p. 104)

An analysis of Winters' use of image shows an historical development in his management of its varying levels: image, metaphor, symbol. The imagery in his first book is defined mainly in terms of the landscape of the Southwest, to which he had gone for physical cure. The young poet's images here are recorded with a sense of hallucination; he seems unable to get beyond his own private perceptions, and he fears them as he savors them in a kind of youthful romanticism. In the first poem, **"Two Songs of Advent,"** he records two precise images, one visual and one audible, then warns his readers: "Listen! Listen! for I enter now your thought." All through this volume he seems to wonder whether or not his perceptions are more than his own; and in **"The Morning,"** his exquisite, painful, solitary identity is contained in the image of the directionless insect, with no meaning beyond its beauty. . . . (p. 106)

Winters' philosophical theory and artistic practice of imagery are best defined by an actual classification of his favorite images. These fall into three categories and seem naturally related to the classifications of his themes and subjects. Together they all reveal the personality behind the poetry. His images come first from the world of nature, of which he was a close observer with highly attuned senses. An ever-abiding interest in science—from botany, through protozoology, to physics—shows in his careful descriptions. The second category includes images that come from the human, mundane world around him: everyday things such as doors, lamps, newspapers, automobiles, houses. Finally, the third category has to do with the visionary imagery of the spirit: those recurring hallucinations that were always returning to him in a certain form. These seem to hold more than merely sensual quality for him, and they are the main source of the metaphysical and philosophical poetry of his later years, though predictable from certain early poems. (pp. 111-12)

[However, his] use of imagery from the everyday world . . . are used for more than mere local color. Always there is the added human dimension involved in juxtaposition to the image. The poem that uses newspapers also involves the newsboy—as ''muezzin''; the puppets become their puppeteers; the narrator who observes the portrait on the wall finds himself reflected back in its image; and the compassionate observer finds his own loneliness increased by the drab, austere exterior of the miners' shacks or the farmers' houses. . . . In one poem he identifies his title character—''Bill''—with accurate profanity and coarseness; in another he describes ''A Miner'' with ''granite strength''; and he obviously patterns **''The Schoolmaster in Spring''** on himself. . . . (pp. 114-15)

In many poems the physical images of the mundane world are elevated to symbols. In **''To a Military Rifle,''** the gun, which is minutely described in all of its physical characteristics, becomes by the end of the poem the symbol of all modern warfare. In **''Before Disaster,''** the contemporary auto becomes the lethal symbol of contemporary civilization. In **''On a Portrait of a Scholar,''** the physical aspects of the single painting eventually become the symbol of all mankind's ephemeral transition from flesh to spirit. (p. 115)

Winters' practice of diction [as defined in *In Defense of Reason*] shows his choice of language for ''what one should say'' to be in keeping with the doctrines of his sixteenth century masters and yet highly contemporary. It is an ''open'' diction in the modern mode, using the everyday patterns of speech of our time (''muscles,'' ''sediment,'' ''traffic,'' ''mineral,'' etc.). It is unmannered and unidiosyncratic except for a few archaic abbreviations and contractions in his early writings before he was sure of his rhythms. When appropriate, he varies the diction to the subject and its time. His directives in **''To a Young Writer,''** for instance, are couched in the plain language he would have his pupil use in today's businesslike, no-nonsense world (''arrears,'' ''discreet,'' ''knowledge,'' ''discern,'' ''dispel'' etc.). On the other hand, the poem **''Anacreontic''** is full of old words that give a sense of the ancient tradition of dignified classicism from which the substance and the form of the poem comes. (''Tuscan,'' ''Grecian,'' ''swathed,'' ''august,'' etc.) In both cases the diction has been chosen ''morally'' to fit content and form with appropriate language.

Choice of diction is also directly related to tone and may well be its determining factor. Although Winters' poems generally use contemporary language, they do not partake of any particularly contemporary idiom or jargon. Their diction is neither innovationist nor tricky; neither is it dated. Generally it has a rather formal tone as befits its high seriousness, but it is never anachronistic. Often it is a direct blunt ''masculine'' diction uniquely suited to the movement of its plain speech style. In Winters' mature poetry, he works as hard at achieving just the

right rational word in this terse, nonfigurative language as he had worked for the exact, colorful imagist word in his earlier verse. (pp. 124-25)

After his emotional experimental early verse (whose tone was mainly terror and uncertainty), his poetry began to take on the tone of authority as it adopted formal patterns. He achieved this mood in a variety of ways: declarative statements, short, cryptic lines, tight stanza patterns, periodic sentences, formal diction, rhetorical questions and climactic exclamations, close rhymes (such as those of the heroic couplet), etc. All of these devices added to the image of the ''single physical whole''; and all were set off by the ''tone'' of pure reason in concept or ''motive,'' so that the total effect was one of dignified verse, *ex cathedra*. His defense of reason in these later poems was not always successful, though he strove for rationality constantly; sometimes the prevailing temper seems to be a strong stoniness, a bitter stoicism, a resigned endurance that is not actually reasonable at all; but it *is* authoritative. Critics whom he has antagonized have called it ''priggish, and pedagogical''; others, who admire it, go so far as to call it ''mystic.'' Whatever the term, Winters *knew* he knew. But when he was absolutism, he wrote some of his most successful poetry out of the stoicism to which he turned in his despair. Having passed beyond foreboding, he turned to authority for endurance.

This tone of authority often put off his critics and readers, and Winters was well aware of their resentment. He seems to have intended this tone to emphasize the validity of his judgments, but it frequently impeded or irritated his audience instead. Taken in large doses, it may well grow wearing; but in the individual poem, it most often succeeds in evoking respectful attention from the reader who is attracted by the highly intellectual theme. It is the quality of his tone that establishes his esoteric coterie of readers who would not be interested in lesser matter taken less seriously. (pp. 132-33)

It is a fact that this one element of tone, more than any other, has earned for Winters his most negative criticism. To some he has seemed dogmatic, bigoted, and sullen in his pronouncements. And yet what he actually says is that we know we *cannot* know. Though a shy man personally, he felt impelled to a public stance of bravado. He is a sort of contemporary Socrates without the grace of the Greek. Yet he speaks with such knowledgeability and authority that the message is often confused by those who mistake tone for them. If no solution is offered to our mortal problems save endurance, at least this is proposed vigorously and with conviction. . . . (p. 134)

What can be said in final assessment of Winters' poetic practice? It is natural—even tautological—that it follows the tenets of his criticism because his criticism was literally developed as a result of his practice. His final ''style'' was ultimately determined after years of experimentation with free verse, Imagism, supercharged perception, emotional and psychological orgy. When he finally selected ''everything I wish to keep,'' he printed mainly the poems that were characterized by a deliberate leanness of line, a careful neatness with studied sharpness of expression, and a formal epigrammatic tone of authority. It is a poetry that has been guided by a rigorous and isolated critical intelligence, in almost direct opposition to the patterns of his contemporaries. From his earliest one-line poems to his most complex formal sonnets, he has sought to arrest both intuition and sensory perception in one stroke; then to make the idea and its physical realization coincide with a ''moral'' accuracy of judgment which makes for truly metaphysical poetry.

Allen Tate first wrote that Winters had as few mistakes to live down as any living poet, but it is true that there are some. It would seem that most of them stem from his effort to be too purely reasonable and too firmly controlled. It is true that this taut technique gave him a firm sense of order and direction, but it has also limited his freedom of movement, for all his sense of variation. Sometimes the poems are *too* full of abstraction, tiring in their pontifical tone and diction; but these are all faults of the lesser poems, and since even they are full of high gravity, his faults, as such, merely point up the serious, courageous intelligence behind them. As a matter of fact, many of the poems wrestle with this absolutist tendency, and sometimes the didactic treatment robs the meaning of the symbol . . . or taints the imagery . . . to unfortunate distortion.

When one looks on the positive side of the Winters achievement, one finds that rare species—a poet who works by limitation rather than by expansion. He does not reach out through deliberate symbolic echoes or ironic parallels of associational techniques. His references are crystal-clear and refined for one particular citation only; hence the meaning of each poem is precise, restricted, and technically controlled. He is in no sense a sterile formalist yearning for the past though he adopts classical forms. His is a completely contemporary conservative poetry whose conservatism is so original and radical that his poems are still not reprinted in any great quantity in anthologies. Some of his best poetry is that which comes out of the world of formal occasions, in touch with the tragic circumstances of our public times as they reveal the personal terrors of our private psyches. This poetry reveals a fine fusion between the personal and the universal. (pp. 136-37)

This is, after all, a poetry of self-preservation: the preservation of the poet's identity by the very act of writing. . . . His main theme is always the predominant mystery of existence, particularly his own. It is his "style" to be preoccupied with his own unique relation to the universe and to seek his rational position in it. As such he is completely contemporary. In *Maule's Curse,* Winters wrote: "Poetry is truth and something more. It is the completeness of the poetic experience which makes it valuable." Praised by such brothers in the priesthood of poetry as Allen Tate, Robert Lowell, J. V. Cunningham, and Donald Justice Winters—who always prized poets over critics or scholars—could be justly proud of his poetic accomplishment. (pp. 137-38)

> *Elizabeth Isaacs, in her* An Introduction to the Poetry of Yvor Winters, *Swallow Press, 1981, 216 p.*

Appendix

The following is a listing of all sources used in Volume 32 of *Contemporary Literary Criticism*. Included in this list are all copyright and reprint rights and acknowledgments for those essays for which permission was obtained. Every effort has been made to trace copyright, but if omissions have been made, please let us know.

THE EXCERPTS IN CLC, VOLUME 32, WERE REPRINTED FROM THE FOLLOWING PERIODICALS:

America, v. 150, June 23-30, 1984 for a review of "The Dead and the Living" by Elizabeth Gaffney. © 1984. All rights reserved. Reprinted with permission of the author./ v. 111, October 17, 1964; v. 118, January 6, 1968; v. 137, October, 1977. © 1964, 1968, 1977. All rights reserved. All reprinted with permission of America Press, Inc., 106 West 56th Street, New York, NY 10019.

American Anthropologist, v. 74, 1972 for a review of "When the Tree Flowered: A Fictional Biography of Eagle Voice, A Sioux Indian" by Philip K. Bock. Copyright 1972 by the American Anthropological Association. Reprinted by permission of the American Anthropological Association and the author.

The American Book Review, v. 4, January-February, 1982; v. 4, July-August, 1982; v. 5, May-June, 1983. © 1982, 1983 by *The American Book Review.* All reprinted by permission.

American Literature, v. 54, March, 1982. Copyright © 1982 Duke University Press, Durham, NC. Reprinted by permission.

The American Poetry Review, v. 12, November-December, 1983 for "Pictures from Borges" by Mary Kinzie; v. 13, January-February, 1984 for "The French Connection" by Marjorie Perloff. Copyright © 1983, 1984 by World Poetry, Inc. Both reprinted by permission of the respective authors.

The American West, v. XVIII, January-February, 1981. Copyright © 1981 by the American West Publishing Company, Tucson, Arizona. Reprinted by permission.

Arizona Quarterly, v. 35, No. 3, Autumn, 1979 for a review of "Shrovetide in Old New Orleans" by Charles W. Scruggs. Copyright © 1979 by Arizona Board of Regents. Reprinted by permission of the publisher and the author.

The Atlantic Monthly, v. 251, March, 1983 for "A Warrior's Legacy" by Robert Sherrill; v. 252, September, 1983 for "Assaulting Realism" by Robert Towers. Both reprinted by permission of the respective authors./ v. 193, June, 1954; v. 240, September, 1977. Copyright © 1954, 1977 by The Atlantic Monthly Company. Both reprinted with permission.

Best Sellers, v. 29, November 1, 1969; v. 32, April 15, 1972; v. 32, November 1, 1972. Copyright 1969, 1972, by the University of Scranton. All reprinted by permission./ v. 38, August, 1978; v. 38, February, 1970; v. 43, March, 1984. Copyright © 1978, 1979, 1984 Helen Dwight Reid Educational Foundation. All reprinted by permission.

Booklist, v. 73, September 1, 1976; v. 75, April 15, 1979; v. 77, September, 1980; September 1, 1982; v. 80, September 15, 1983. Copyright © 1976, 1979, 1980, 1982, 1983 by the American Library Association. All reprinted by permission.

Allen, Michael S. From *We Are Called Human: The Poetry of Richard Hugo*. University of Arkansas Press, 1982. Copyright © 1982 by Board of Trustees of the University of Arkansas, The University of Arkansas Press, Fayetteville, Arkansas 72701. All rights reserved. Reprinted by permission.

Altieri, Charles. From *Enlarging the Temple: New Directions in American Poetry during the 1960s*. Bucknell University Press, 1979. © 1979 by Associated University Presses, Inc. Reprinted by permission.

Aly, Lucile F. From *John G. Neihardt: A Critical Biography*. Rodopi, 1977. © 1977 by Lucile Folse Aly. All rights reserved. Reprinted by permission of the author.

Andersen, Richard. From *Robert Coover*. Twayne, 1981. Copyright 1981 by Twayne Publishers. Reprinted with the permission of Twayne Publishers, a division of G. K. Hall & Co., Boston.

Berke, Roberta. From *Bounds Out of Bounds: A Compass for Recent American and British Poetry*. Oxford University Press, New York, 1981. Copyright © 1981 by Roberta Berke. Reprinted by permission of Oxford University Press, Inc.

Blackmur, R. P. From *The Expense of Greatness*. Arrow Editions, 1940. Copyright, 1940, by R. P. Blackmur. Reprinted by permission of the Estate of R. P. Blackmur.

Bradbury, Malcolm. From ''Putting in the Person: Character and Abstraction in Current Writing and Painting,'' in *The Contemporary English Novel*, Stratford-Upon-Avon Studies, No. 18. Edited by Malcolm Bradbury and David Palmer. Arnold, 1979. © Edward Arnold (Publishers) Ltd. 1979. All rights reserved. Reprinted by permission.

Bruce-Novoa. From *Chicano Poetry: A Response to Chaos*. University of Texas Press, 1982. Copyright © 1982 by the University of Texas Press. All rights reserved. Reprinted by permission of the publisher and the author.

Brushwood, John S. From *Mexico in Its Novel: A Nation's Search for Identity*. University of Texas Press, 1966. Copyright © 1966 by John S. Brushwood. All rights reserved. Reprinted by permission of the publisher and the author.

Costello, Bonnie. From ''The Impersonal and the Interrogative in the Poetry of Elizabeth Bishop,'' in *Elizabeth Bishop and Her Art*. Edited by Lloyd Schwartz and Sybil P. Estess. University of Michigan Press, 1983. Copyright © by The University of Michigan 1983. All rights reserved. Reprinted by permission.

Craig, Patricia, and Mary Cadogan. From *The Lady Investigates: Women Detectives and Spies in Fiction*. Gollancz, 1981. © 1981 by Patricia Craig and Mary Cadogan. Reprinted by permission of the respective authors. In Canada by Victor Gollancz Ltd, London.

Del Rey, Lester. From ''Introduction: The Three Careers of John W. Campbell,'' in *The Best of John W. Campbell*. By John W. Campbell, edited by Lester del Rey. Ballantine Books, 1976. Copyright © 1976 by Lester del Rey. Reprinted by permission of Ballantine Books, a Division of Random House, Inc.

Doležel, Lubomír. From *Narrative Modes in Czech Literature*. University of Toronto Press, 1973. © University of Toronto Press 1973. Reprinted by permission.

Eshleman, Clayton, and Annette Smith. From an introduction to *The Collected Poetry*. By Aimé Césaire, translated by Clayton Eshleman and Annette Smith. University of California Press, 1983. Copyright © 1983 by The Regents of the University of California. Reprinted by permission of the University of California Press.

Faas, Ekbert. From ''Gary Snyder: Essay,'' in *Towards a New American Poetics: Essays & Interviews*. Edited by Ekbert Faas. Black Sparrow Press, 1978. Copyright © 1978 by Ekbert Faas. All rights reserved. Reprinted by permission.

Freeman, E. From *The Theatre of Albert Camus: A Critical Study*. Methuen, 1971. © 1971 E. Freeman. Reprinted by permission of Methuen & Co. Ltd.

Green, Dorothy. From '' 'The Man Who Loved Children': Storm in a Tea-Cup,'' in *The Australian Experience: Critical Essays on Australian Novels*. Australian National University Press. Canberra, 1974. Edited by W. S. Ramson. © 1974 by W. S. Ramson and Dorothy Green. Reprinted by permission.

Green, Martin. From ''Transatlantic Communications: Malcolm Bradbury's 'Stepping Westward','' in *Old Lines, New Forces: Essays on the Contemporary British Novel, 1960-1970*. Edited by Robert K. Morris. Fairleigh Dickinson University Press, 1976. © 1976 by Associated University Presses, Inc. Reprinted by permission.

Hazard, Lucy Lockwood. From *The Frontier in American Literature*. Thomas Y. Crowell Co., Inc., 1927.

Heaney, Seamus. From *Preoccupations: Selected Prose, 1968-1978*. Farrar, Straus and Giroux, 1980. Faber and Faber, 1980. Copyright © 1980 by Seamus Heaney. Reprinted by permission of Farrar, Straus and Giroux, Inc. In Canada by Faber and Faber Ltd.

Henderson, Katherine Usher. From *Joan Didion*. Ungar, 1981. Copyright © 1981 by Frederick Ungar Publishing Co., Inc. Reprinted by permission.

Hoffmann, Charles W. From "The Search for Self, Inner Freedom, and Relatedness in the Novels of Max Frisch," in *The Contemporary Novel in German: A Symposium*. Edited by Robert A. Heitner. University of Texas Press, 1967. Copyright © 1967 by the University of Texas Press. All rights reserved. Reprinted by permission of the publisher and the author.

Hollington, Michael. From *Günter Grass: The Writer in a Pluralist Society*. Marion Boyars, 1980. © Michael Hollington 1980. All rights reserved. Reprinted by permission.

Innes, Michael. From "John Appleby," in *The Great Detectives*. Edited by Otto Penzler. Little, Brown, 1978. Copyright © 1978 by Otto Penzler. All rights reserved. Reprinted by permission of Little, Brown and Company.

Isaacs, Elizabeth. From *An Introduction to the Poetry of Yvor Winters*. Swallow Press, 1981. © 1981 by Elizabeth Isaacs. All rights reserved. Reprinted by permission of Ohio University Press, Athens.

King, P. R. From *Nine Contemporary Poets: A Critical Introduction*. Methuen, 1979. © 1979 P. R. King. All rights reserved. Reprinted by permission of Methuen & Co. Ltd.

Klinkowitz, Jerome. From *The Practice of Fiction in America: Writers from Hawthorne to the Present*. Iowa State University Press, 1980. © 1980 by Iowa State University Press, Ames, Iowa. All rights reserved. Reprinted by permission.

Knight, Damon. From *In Search of Wonder: Essays on Modern Science Fiction*. Revised edition. Advent, 1967. Copyright ©, 1956, 1967, by Damon Knight. All rights reserved. Reprinted by courtesy of Advent:Publishers, Inc. and the author.

Lidoff, Joan. From *Christina Stead*. Ungar, 1982. Copyright © 1982 by Frederick Ungar Publishing Co., Inc. Reprinted by permission.

Mac Adam, Alfred J. From *Modern Latin American Narratives: The Dreams of Reason*. University of Chicago Press, 1977. © 1977 by the University of Chicago. All rights reserved. Reprinted by permission of The University of Chicago Press and the author.

McCaffery, Larry. From *The Metafictional Muse: The Works of Robert Coover, Donald Barthelme, and William H. Gass*. University of Pittsburgh Press, 1982. Copyright © 1982, University of Pittsburgh Press. All rights reserved. Reprinted by permission of the University of Pittsburgh Press.

McLean, Scott. From an introduction to *The Real Work: Interviews & Talks, 1964-1979*. By Gary Snyder, edited by Wm. Scott McLean. New Directions, 1980. Copyright © 1980 by Wm. Scott McLean. All rights reserved. Reprinted by permission of Scott McLean.

McMurray, George R. From *José Donoso*. Twayne, 1979. Copyright 1979 by Twayne Publishers. Reprinted with the permission of Twayne Publishers, a division of G. K. Hall & Co., Boston.

Molesworth, Charles. From *Gary Snyder's Vision: Poetry and the Real Work*. University of Missouri Press, 1983. Copyright © 1983 by The Curators of the University of Missouri. All rights reserved. Reprinted by permission of the University of Missouri Press.

Moskowitz, Sam. From *Explorers of the Infinite: Shapers of Science Fiction*. World Publishing Co., 1963. Copyright © 1963, 1959, 1958, 1957 by Sam Moskowitz. Copyright © 1960 by Ziff-Davis Publishing Co. Reprinted by permission of the author.

Moskowitz, Sam. From *Seekers of Tomorrow: Masters of Science Fiction*. World Publishing Co., 1966. Copyright © 1966, 1964, 1963, 1962, 1961 by Sam Moskowitz. Reprinted by permission of the author.

Nadeau, Robert. From *Readings from the New Book on Nature: Physics and Metaphysics in the Modern Novel*. University of Massachusetts Press, 1981. Copyright © 1981 by The University of Massachusetts Press. All rights reserved. Reprinted by permission.

Nigro, Kirsten F. From "From 'Criollismo' to the Grotesque: Approaches to José Donoso," in *Tradition and Renewal: Essays on Twentieth-Century Latin American Literature and Culture*. Edited by Merlin H. Forster. University of Illinois Press, 1975. © 1975 by the Board of Trustees of the University of Illinois. Reprinted by permission of the publisher and the author.

Powell, Grosvenor. From *Language As Being in the Poetry of Yvor Winters*. Louisiana State University Press, 1980. Copyright © 1980 by Louisiana State University Press. All rights reserved. Reprinted by permission of Louisiana State University Press.

Rawlins, Jack P. From "Confronting the Alien: Fantasy and Anti Fantasy in Science Fiction Film and Literature," in *Bridges to Fantasy: Essays from the Eaton Conference on Science Fiction and Fantasy Literature*. George E. Slusser, Eric S. Rabkin, Robert Scholes, eds. Southern Illinois University Press, 1982. Copyright © 1982 by Southern Illinois University Press. All rights reserved. Reprinted by permission of Southern Illinois University Press.

Cumulative Index to Authors

This index lists all author entries in the Gale Literary Criticism Series and includes cross-references to other Gale sources. References in the index are identified as follows:

AITN: *Authors in the News*, Volumes 1-2
CAAS: *Contemporary Authors Autobiography Series*, Volume 1
CA: *Contemporary Authors* (original series), Volumes 1-113
CANR: *Contemporary Authors New Revision Series*, Volumes 1-13
CAP: *Contemporary Authors Permanent Series*, Volumes 1-2
CA-R: *Contemporary Authors* (revised editions), Volumes 1-44
CLC: *Contemporary Literary Criticism*, Volumes 1-32
CLR: *Children's Literature Review*, Volumes 1-7
DLB: *Dictionary of Literary Biography*, Volumes 1-35
DLB-DS: *Dictionary of Literary Biography Documentary Series*, Volumes 1-8
DLB-Y: *Dictionary of Literary Biography Yearbook*, Volumes 1980-1983
LC: *Literature Criticism from 1400 to 1800*, Volume 1
NCLC: *Nineteenth-Century Literature Criticism*, Volumes 1-7
SATA: *Something about the Author*, Volumes 1-37
TCLC: *Twentieth-Century Literary Criticism*, Volumes 1-15
YABC: *Yesterday's Authors of Books for Children*, Volumes 1-2

Author Index

Author Index

Author Index

Author Index

Author Index

Author Index

Author Index

Cumulative Index to Critics

Aalfs, Janet
Jane Rule **27**:422

Aaron, Daniel
Claude Brown **30**:38
Thornton Wilder **15**:575

Aaron, Jonathan
Tadeusz Różewicz **23**:363

Aaron, Jules
Michael Cristofer **28**:96
Jack Heifner **11**:264

Abbey, Edward
Robert M. Pirsig **6**:421

Abbott, James H.
Juan Benet **28**:21

Abbott, John Lawrence
Isaac Bashevis Singer **9**:487
Sylvia Townsend Warner **7**:512

Abeel, Erica
Pamela Hansford Johnson **7**:185

Abel, Elizabeth
Jean Rhys **14**:448

Abel, Lionel
Samuel Beckett **2**:45
Jack Gelber **6**:196
Jean Genet **2**:157
Yoram Kaniuk **19**:238

Abernethy, Peter L.
Thomas Pynchon **3**:410

Abicht, Ludo
Jan de Hartog **19**:133

Ableman, Paul
Brian Aldiss **14**:14
Beryl Bainbridge **22**:45
Jurek Becker **19**:36
William Boyd **28**:39
William S. Burroughs **22**:85
J. M. Coetzee **23**:125
Len Deighton **22**:116
William Golding **17**:179
Mary Gordon **13**:250
Mervyn Jones **10**:295
Michael Moorcock **27**:351
Piers Paul Read **25**:377
Mary Renault **17**:402
Anatoli Rybakov **23**:373
Andrew Sinclair **14**:489
Scott Sommer **25**:424
D. M. Thomas **22**:419
Gore Vidal **22**:438

Abley, Mark
Margaret Atwood **25**:65
Clark Blaise **29**:76
Harry Crews **23**:136
John le Carré **28**:226
William Mitchell **25**:327
Brian Moore **32**:312
Michael Ondaatje **29**:341, 342
Agnès Varda **16**:560
Miriam Waddington **28**:440

Abraham, Willie E.
William Melvin Kelley **22**:249

Abrahams, Cecil A.
Bessie Head **25**:236

Abrahams, William
Elizabeth Bowen **6**:95
Hortense Calisher **2**:97
Herbert Gold **4**:193

Joyce Carol Oates **2**:315
Harold Pinter **9**:418
V. S. Pritchett **5**:352

Abrahamson, Dick
Fran Arrick **30**:19
Sue Ellen Bridgers **26**:92
John Knowles **26**:265
Norma Fox Mazer **26**:294

Abrams, M. H.
M. H. Abrams **24**:18
Northrop Frye **24**:209

Abramson, Doris E.
Alice Childress **12**:105

Abramson, Jane
Peter Dickinson **12**:172
Christie Harris **12**:268
S. E. Hinton **30**:205
Rosemary Wells **12**:638

Achebe, Chinua
Amos Tutuola **29**:435

Acheson, James
William Golding **17**:177

Acken, Edgar L.
Ernest K. Gann **23**:163

Ackerman, Diane
John Berryman **25**:97

Ackroyd, Peter
Brian Aldiss **5**:16
Martin Amis **4**:19
Miguel Ángel Asturias **8**:27
Louis Auchincloss **6**:15
W. H. Auden **9**:56
Beryl Bainbridge **8**:36
James Baldwin **5**:43

John Barth **5**:51
Donald Barthelme **3**:44
Samuel Beckett **4**:52
John Berryman **3**:72
Richard Brautigan **5**:72
Charles Bukowski **5**:80
Anthony Burgess **5**:87
William S. Burroughs **5**:92
Italo Calvino **5**:100; **8**:132
Richard Condon **6**:115
Roald Dahl **6**:122
Ed Dorn **10**:155
Margaret Drabble **8**:183
Douglas Dunn **6**:148
Eva Figes **31**:163, 165
Bruce Jay Friedman **5**:127
John Gardner **7**:116
Günter Grass **4**:207
MacDonald Harris **9**:261
Joseph Heller **5**:179
Mark Helprin **10**:261
Russell C. Hoban **7**:160
Elizabeth Jane Howard **7**:164
B. S. Johnson **6**:264
Pamela Hansford Johnson **7**:184
G. Josipovici **6**:270
Thomas Keneally **10**:298
Jack Kerouac **5**:215
Francis King **8**:321
Jerzy Kosinski **10**:308
Doris Lessing **6**:300
Alison Lurie **4**:305
Thomas McGuane **7**:212
Stanley Middleton **7**:220
Michael Moorcock **5**:294; **27**:350
Penelope Mortimer **5**:298
Iris Murdoch **4**:368
Vladimir Nabokov **6**:358

Critic Index

Critic Index

Critic Index

Critic Index

Critic Index

Critic Index

Critic Index

Critic Index

Critic Index

Critic Index

Critic Index

Critic Index

Critic Index

Critic Index

Critic Index

Critic Index

Critic Index

Critic Index

Critic Index

Critic Index

Critic Index

Critic Index

Critic Index

Critic Index

Critic Index

Critic Index

Critic Index

Critic Index

Critic Index

Critic Index

Critic Index

Critic Index

Critic Index

Critic Index

Critic Index

Critic Index

Critic Index

Critic Index

Critic Index

Critic Index

Critic Index

Critic Index